Born in London in 1936 and resident in London, Sir Martin Gilbert was educated at Highgate School and Magdalen College, Oxford. An outstanding historian of the twentieth century, he became the official biographer of Sir Winston Churchill in 1968 and has written to great acclaim on many aspects of both world wars. Visit his website at www.martingilbert.com.

*By Martin Gilbert*

THE CHURCHILL BIOGRAPHY
Volume III: The Challenge of War 1914–1916
Document Volume III: (in two parts)
Volume IV: The Stricken World 1917–1922
Document Volume IV: (in two parts)
Volume V: 1922–1939
Document Volume V: The Exchequer Years 1922–1929
Document Volume V: The Wilderness Years 1929–1935
Volume VI: Finest Hour 1939–1941
Churchill War Papers I: At the Admiralty September 1939–May 1940
Churchill War Papers II: Never Surrender May–December 1940
Churchill War Papers III: 1941: The Ever-Widening War
Volume VII: Road to Victory 1941–1945
Volume VIII: Never Despair 1945–1965

OTHER BOOKS
The Appeaser (with Richard Gott)
The European Powers 1900–1945
The Roots of Appeasement
Atlas of the Holocaust
Sir Horace Rumbold: Portrait of a Diplomat
Jerusalem: Rebirth of a City
Jerusalem in the Twentieth Century
Exile and Return: The Struggle for Jewish Statehood
Israel: A History
Auschwitz and the Allies
The Jews of Hope: The Plight of Soviet Jewry Today
Shcharansky: Hero of Our Time
The Holocaust: The Jewish Tragedy
The Boys: Triumph over Adversity
The Second World War
The Day the War Ended
In Search of Churchill
Churchill: A Photographic Portrait
Churchill: A Life
Empires in Conflict: A History of the Twentieth Century 1900–1933
Descent into Barbarism: A History of the Twentieth Century 1934–1951
Challenge to Civilisation: A History of the Twentieth Century 1952–1999
Never Again: A History of the Holocaust
The Jews in the Twentieth Century
Letters to Aunt Fori: The 5,000-Year History of the Jewish People
and Their Faith
The Righteous: The Unsung Heroes of the Holocaust
The First World War
Churchill and America
Churchill and the Jews
Atlas of the First World War
Atlas of the Second World War

# THE SECOND WORLD WAR

*A Complete History*

## Martin Gilbert

PHOENIX

A PHOENIX PAPERBACK

First published in Great Britain in 1989
by Weidenfeld & Nicolson
This paperback edition published in 2009
by Phoenix,
an imprint of Orion Books Ltd,
Orion House, 5 Upper St Martin's Lane,
London WC2H 9EA

An Hachette UK company

3 5 7 9 10 8 6 4

A CIP catalogue record for this book
is available from the British Library.

ISBN 978-0-7538-2676-8

Printed and bound in Great Britain
by Clays Ltd, StIves plc

The Orion Publishing Group's policy is to use papers
that are natural, renewable and recyclable products and
made from wood grown in sustainable forests. The logging
and manufacturing processes are expected to conform to
the environmental regulations of the country of origin.

www.orionbooks.co.uk

to
Hugo

# Contents

| | | |
|---|---|---|
| List of Maps | | ix |
| List of Photographs | | xii |
| Acknowledgements | | xvi |
| 1 | The German invasion of Poland, September 1939 | 1 |
| 2 | Poland defeated, October 1939 | 15 |
| 3 | Finland defiant, November 1939 | 31 |
| 4 | The Scandinavian cockpit, winter 1939–1940 | 44 |
| 5 | The German attack in the West, May 1940 | 61 |
| 6 | Dunkirk, May 1940 | 75 |
| 7 | The battle for France, June 1940 | 85 |
| 8 | France's agony, Britain's resolve, June–July 1940 | 103 |
| 9 | The battle for Britain, August–September 1940 | 117 |
| 10 | 'The war is won!' (Hitler), October 1940 | 126 |
| 11 | The 'new order of tyranny' (Roosevelt), winter 1940–1941 | 138 |
| 12 | The widening war, January–March 1941 | 153 |
| 13 | The German conquest of Yugoslavia and Greece, April 1941 | 165 |
| 14 | The fall of Crete; war in Africa, April–May 1941 | 177 |
| 15 | The German invasion of Russia, June 1941 | 198 |
| 16 | Terror in the East, July–August 1941 | 212 |
| 17 | Towards Leningrad, Moscow and Kiev, September 1941 | 222 |
| 18 | Russia at bay, September–October 1941 | 237 |
| 19 | 'Deciding the fate of Europe' (Hitler), November 1941 | 249 |
| 20 | The limits of German conquest, December 1941 | 259 |
| 21 | Japan strikes, December 1941 | 272 |

CONTENTS

22 'We are no longer alone' (Churchill), New Year 1942                286

23 Global war, February–April 1942                                    301

24 The spread of resistance and terror, summer 1942                   321

25 Axis triumphs, July 1942                                           336

26 Guadalcanal, Dieppe, El Alamein, August–September 1942             350

27 Stalingrad and 'Torch', September–October 1942                     365

28 The turn of the tide for the Allies, winter 1942                   381

29 Casablanca: blueprint for victory, January 1943                    390

30 The German armies in danger, February 1943                         402

31 'Drive the enemy into the sea' (Montgomery), spring 1943           417

32 'The first crack in the Axis' (Roosevelt), summer 1943             434

33 Germany and Japan in retreat, autumn 1943                          458

34 'Bleeding to death in the East' (Goebbels), winter 1943            471

35 Anzio, Cassino, Kwajalein, January–February 1944                   485

36 Bombing, deportation, and mass murder, February–March              503
   1944

37 Resistance, sabotage and deception, spring 1944                    521

38 D-Day, June 1944                                                   534

39 Germany encircled, July 1944                                       548

40 The battles for Poland and France, summer 1944                     561

41 The bitter-sweet path of liberation, autumn 1944                   572

42 Into Germany; towards the Philippines, September 1944              589

43 Fighting for every mile, October–November 1944                     603

44 Flying bombs, suicide pilots, death marches, January 1945          626

45 Berlin, Manila, Dresden, Tokyo, February–March 1945                637

46 The Axis in disarray; the Allies in conflict, March–April 1945     654

47 The deaths of Roosevelt, Mussolini and Hitler, April 1945          662

48 The end of the war in Europe, May 1945                             682

49 Germany in defeat, Japan unbowed, May–July 1945                    692

50 Alamogordo, Potsdam, Hiroshima, July–August 1945                   704

51 The defeat of Japan, August 1945                                   715

52 Retribution and Remembrance, 1945–1952                             720

53 'Unfinished business', 1953–1989                                   737

   Bibliography                                                       749

   Regional Maps                                                      765

   Index                                                              787

# Maps

*Maps in the text*

|   |   |   |
|---|---|---|
| 1 | The German invasion of Poland, September 1939 | 3 |
| 2 | Poland partitioned, October 1939 | 17 |
| 3 | Greater Germany, November 1939 | 21 |
| 4 | The Russo-Finnish war, November 1939–March 1940 | 33 |
| 5 | Scandinavia, spring 1940 | 41 |
| 6 | The German invasion of western Europe, May 1940 | 63 |
| 7 | Dunkirk, May–June 1940 | 71 |
| 8 | The battle for France, June 1940 | 87 |
| 9 | The fall of France, June 1940 | 95 |
| 10 | Europe from Norway to Egypt, summer 1940 | 113 |
| 11 | The battle of Britain and the 'Blitz', August–September 1940 | 119 |
| 12 | The Italian invasion of Greece, October 1940 | 135 |
| 13 | Yugoslavia and Greece, April 1941 | 171 |
| 14 | The evacuation of Attica, April 1941 | 176 |
| 15 | Crete, May 1941 | 183 |
| 16 | Germany and the Middle East, June 1941 | 189 |
| 17 | Germany and Russia on the eve of war | 193 |
| 18 | The Volga-Archangel line and the Berlin-Tiflis axis | 195 |
| 19 | The widening war, June 1941 | 200 |
| 20 | The German invasion of Russia, 22 June 1941 | 202 |
| 21 | The Eastern Front, August 1941 | 215 |
| 22 | The siege of Leningrad, October 1941–January 1944 | 229 |
| 23 | The Eastern Front, September and October 1941 | 231 |
| 24 | The battle for Moscow, winter 1941 | 252 |
| 25 | Pearl Harbour, December 1941 | 264 |
| 26 | The Eastern Front, December 1941 | 269 |
| 27 | The Japanese Empire and the coming of war, December 1941 | 273 |
| 28 | The first death camp, murder sites, and the Eastern Front, December 1941 | 274 |

29  The South China Sea, December 1941                                     277
30  The Eastern Front, March 1942                                          289
31  The Bataan Peninsula, January–May 1942                                 294
32  Soviet partisans, 1942                                                 309
33  Death camps, deportations, air raids and reprisals, 1942              311
34  The Eastern Front, May 1942                                            313
35  The German offensive, July–November 1942                              342
36  Terror in the East, July 1942                                          344
37  Stalingrad besieged, September–November 1942                          356
38  Behind the lines in the East, winter 1942–1943                         362
39  The Soviet reconquest of the Caucasus and the Don, winter 1942–       382
    1943
40  The battle for Tunisia, January–May 1943                               403
41  The German retreats, February–August 1943                             411
42  From Tunis to Sicily, May–July 1943                                    437
43  The Battle for the Kursk Salient, July 1943                            442
44  The Eastern Front and the Red Army advance, July–August 1943          454
45  Some execution sites of Soviet prisoners-of-war, Poles and Jews,      483
    1943
46  The Eastern Front, winter 1943–1944                                    487
47  The Italian Front, 1943–1944                                           491
48  The Normandy and South of France deception plans                      493
49  'Big Week' air raids, 20–26 February 1944                             501
50  Burma, 1944                                                            507
51  France, 1 February–5 June 1944                                         518
52  Slave-labour camps in Eastern Silesia, 1944                           524
53  The Normandy landings, 6 June 1944                                     535
54  The Red Army offensive, June–August 1944                              545
55  The Warsaw uprising, July–October 1944                                563
56  The battle in France, June–September 1944                             569
57  Europe at war, September 1944                                          575
58  The oil campaign, August 1944, oil targets                           577
59  The Eastern Front, September–December 1944                            579
60  The Slovak uprising, August–October 1944                             583
61  The battle for north-west Europe, September 1944                      586
62  The Eastern Pacific, October 1944–March 1945                         605
63  The Western and Italian Fronts, October 1944                         607
64  The Eastern Front, October 1944                                       609
65  The German counter-offensive in the Ardennes, December 1944          619
66  Crossing the Rhine, March 1945                                        647
67  The landings on Okinawa, 1 to 23 April 1945                          656
68  From the Rhine to the Elbe, April 1945                                665
69  The battle for Berlin, March–April 1945                               671
70  Berlin besieged, April 1945                                           675
71  Europe from war to peace, May 1945                                    685
72  The fall of Okinawa, 30 April–21 June 1945                           698

73 Post-war Europe      706
74 The seven bombing missions of 5–6 August 1945      713

## REGIONAL MAPS

*After page 765*

1 Germany
2 The Ruhr
3 Germany from the Elbe to the Oder
4 Eastern Germany, East Prussia, Poland and the Baltic States
5 Western Russia
6 France
7 Holland
8 Great Britain
9 The Thames Valley
10 London
11 Northern Italy
12 Austria, Slovakia, Hungary and Yugoslavia
13 The Mediterranean
14 The Egyptian–Libyan border
15 The Dodecanese Islands
16 Southern Yugoslavia, Bulgaria, Greece and Crete
17 Scandinavia and the Baltic
18 The Arctic Convoys
19 The Atlantic Ocean
20 East Africa and the Middle East
21 The Indian Ocean
22 Burma, Indo-China and China
23 The Philippines and the Dutch East Indies
24 Japan
25 The United States
26 The Eastern Seaboard of the United States
27 The Pacific Ocean
28 New Guinea and the Solomon Islands

# Photographs

SECTION ONE, *between pages 206 and 207.*

1  The German invasion of Poland, 1 September 1939
2  German troops on their way by train to the Polish front
3  German soldiers enter the Polish town of Gdynia
4  Polish prisoners-of-war, captured by the Germans in September 1939
5  Hitler reviewing his troops in Warsaw, 5 October 1939
6  The German occupation forces in Poland
7  The Russo–Finnish war; a church ablaze in Helsinki
8  The Russo–Finnish war; Finnish soldiers leave their trench
9  The German pocket-battleship *Graf Spee* destroyed
10  German troops celebrate Christmas 1939
11  The Siegfried Line, 14 January 1940
12  British leaflets, stacked for dropping over Germany
13  German troops enter Norway, 9 April 1940
14  British spitfire pilots, 20 April 1940
15  Allied ships ablaze in Narvik harbour
16  German parachute troops land in a Dutch field, May 1940
17  German parachute troops in Holland prepare to advance
18  Rotterdam in flames, 14 May 1940
19  German troops ride through a Belgian town
20  German troops in Holland
21  London: British troops await a German parachute landing
22  Dunkirk: British troops await evacuation
23  French soldiers and sailors being rescued from the sea
24  British and French soldiers going into captivity
25  The Franco–German armistice negotiations, 20 June 1940
26  Hitler in Paris with German soldiers, 23 June 1940
27  Hitler at the Eiffel Tower
28  German soldiers practise for the invasion of Britain
29  German fighter pilots waiting to be sent against Britain
30  A German fighter shot down over southern England, August 1940

31 The Battle of Britain; vapour trails above London
32 A London Underground station receives a direct hit
33 Hitler during the Yugoslav campaign
34 Crete; British warships attacked by German aircraft
35 British prisoners-of-war in Crete, May 1941
36 A British war grave in Crete
37 Two German war graves in Crete
38 The German battleship *Bismarck* in action, 27 May 1941
39 A German Enigma machine
40 The German invasion of Russia, 22 June 1941
41 German troops and Russian prisoners-of-war
42 The Russian city of Smolensk on the eve of its capture
43 Battle-weary German troops on the Eastern Front
44 A British fighter pilot and his 'V for Victory' crest
45 A Yugoslav victim of Nazi terror
46 The Western Desert; the grave of an Australian soldier
47 The Western Desert; British troops surrender
48 German troops in western Russia
49 Russian dead in Leningrad
50 Soviet troops prepare for the defence of Moscow
51 Russian women volunteers prepare for the defence of Moscow
52 Pearl Harbour, 7 December 1941
53 American battleships ablaze at Pearl Harbour, 7 December 1941
54 Pearl Harbour; an American bomber destroyed on the ground
55 Burying the dead at Pearl Harbour
56 Pearl Harbour; a memorial stone to an unknown American soldier
57 German soldiers pull back from Moscow, 7 December 1941
58 The Japanese air attack on Hong Kong, 11 December 1941
59 Hong Kong surrenders, 25 December 1941
60 Japanese troops celebrate victory in Malaya, 31 January 1942
61 Japanese troops invade Burma, 31 January 1942

SECTION TWO, *between pages 526 and 527.*

62 A British naval gun at Singapore fires a practice volley
63 British soldiers in Singapore marching into captivity
64 Hitler meets wounded soldiers in Berlin
65 American soldiers taken captive in Bataan, April 1942
66 Prague; the car in which SS General Heydrich was ambushed
67 The execution of four Jews in German-occupied Poland
68 Japanese soldiers occupy the American Aleutian island of Attu
69 British soldiers surrender at Tobruk, June 1942
70 Jewish women being deported to 'the East'
71 Soviet soldiers in German captivity, July 1942
72 German troops and Canadian dead at Dieppe, August 1942
73 British troops advance in the Western Desert, November 1942

74 The Eastern Front; the Russian mud and a German motorcyclist
75 German wounded being evacuated from Stalingrad
76 The swastika flies over Stalingrad University
77 The swastika decorates two German war graves
78 Soviet units link up on the Leningrad front, January 1943
79 The German V1 rocket
80 A German secret teleprinter
81 Italian troops retreating on the Eastern Front
82 Italian war dead on the Eastern Front
83 Admiral Yamamoto and his staff
84 The wreckage of Admiral Yamamoto's bomber, April 1943
85 American bombers drop incendiary bombs on Kiel
86 The crew of a British bomber about to set off
87 The British 'bouncing' bomb on a test drop
88 The effect of the 'bouncing' bomb, May 1943
89 American warships in the Aleutian Islands, August 1943
90 American Marines on Tarawa, November 1943
91 Roosevelt, Churchill and Stalin at the Teheran Conference
92 British soldiers, captured by the Germans on the Island of Kos
93 American troops go ashore at Anzio, January 1944
94 American dead at Anzio
95 Hitler greets the German woman aviator, Hanna Reitsch
96 Soviet forces renew their offensive, March 1944
97 Churchill and Eisenhower visit American troops in England
98 Rommel inspecting the low-tide defences along the Channel Coast
99 Soviet forces land on the Kerch Peninsula, April 1944
100 The Italian village of Cassino, May 1944
101 German war graves at Cassino
102 The 'Mulberry Harbour' used for the Normandy Landings, June 1944
103 A German flying bomb falls on central London
104 The American heavy cruiser *Indianapolis*
105 Hitler immediately after the attempt on his life, 20 July 1944
106 Carl Goedeler on trial in Berlin
107 Judge Freisler addressing one of the accused
108 Ulrich von Hassell on trial
109 Julius Leber on trial
110 Hitler visits one of those injured in the bomb blast
111 An American Private guards six hundred German soldiers
112 A British air reconnaissance photograph, taken above Auschwitz
113 Hungarian Jews arriving at Auschwitz
114 German soldiers in the Ardennes offensive, December 1944
115 Three German infiltrators, captured and executed in the Ardennes
116 Bodies of American soldiers, massacred near Malmédy
117 An American pontoon bridge across the Rhine, March 1945
118 Japanese–Americans, serving in the American army in Italy
119 An American aircraft carrier damaged by another American warship

120 Hitler says farewell to young soldiers, 20 April 1945
121 American soldiers in Munich, 29 April 1945
122 The Hammer and Sickle raised on the Reichstag, 30 April 1945
123 The three German signatories of unconditional surrender, 7 May 1945
124 Hiroshima
125 A former British prisoner-of-war after the Japanese surrender
126 The Japanese surrender on board the *Missouri*, 2 September 1945
127 General MacArthur adds his signature to the instrument of surrender
128 Marshal Goering on trial at Nuremberg, 1946
129 General Tojo on trial at Tokyo, 1947
130 The skeleton of a crewman of an American bomber, discovered in 1958

# Acknowledgements

In the preparation of this book, I have been helped by many people, who have provided me with historical material and answered my various queries, or who have guided me towards documentary and printed sources. For help on several points of historical detail, I am grateful to Oliver Everett, The Librarian, Royal Archives, and Pamela Clark, Deputy Registrar. Over many years, I have been particularly helped by Dr Christopher Dowling, Keeper of the Department of Museum Services, Imperial War Museum, London, and, on all matters concerning Signals Intelligence, as well as many aspects of military, naval and air history, by Edward Thomas, whose willingness to guide my steps has been much appreciated.

On a wide range of historical matters I have also received considerable help from Winston G. Ramsey, founder and editor of *After the Battle* magazine, and a pioneer in revisiting and exploring historical episodes both large and small in all the war zones.

For the answers to a wide range of questions concerning the United States, I am indebted to Larry Arnn, President, the Claremont Institute for the Study of Statesmanship and Political Philosophy, and to his colleagues Steven Lenzer and Daniel C. Palm.

In response to my enquiries for material and information, I must thank Rupert Allason (Nigel West); Ralph Amelan, Jerusalem Post Archives, Jerusalem; F. Bartlett Watt; Mikhail Beizer; Jeremy Carver; Alan Clark; Reuven Dafni, Vice-Chairman, Yad Vashem, Jerusalem; Kingston Derry; Barbara Distel, KZ-Gedenkstätte Dachau, Museum, Archive, Library; John Doble; Professor John Erickson, Defence Studies, University of Edinburgh; Professor M. R. D. Foot; Birthe N. Fraser, Royal Danish Embassy, London; Nechama Gal, Yad Vashem, Jerusalem; Professor Yoav Gelber, University of Haifa; Katherine Hafner; Peter Halban; Lizzie Haugbyrd, Royal Danish Embassy, London; Dr Cameron Hazlehurst; Dr Hugo Hungerbühler, City Archivist, Zürich; Barbara Jones, Lloyd's Register of Shipping; Alexander Kitroeff, Centre for Byzantine and Modern Greek Studies, Queen College, City University of New York; Serge Klarsfeld; George Klein, Holocaust Memorial Commission, New York; Igor Kotler; Dr Shmuel Krakowski, Yad Vashem, Jerusalem; Anita Lasker-Wallfisch; Wim van Leer; Norman Longmate; Lorraine Macknight, Curator, Australian War Memorial, Canberra; H. V. S. Manral, The High Commission of India, London; Mrs M. Milosavljević, Embassy of the Socialist Federal Republic of Yugoslavia, London; Kenneth Murphy, Archivist, the *Guardian*; G. W. Peters, Ambassade de France, London; Heidi Potter, Japan Information Centre, Embassy of Japan, London; David Pryce-Jones; Giorgio Guglielmino, Consolato Gener-

## ACKNOWLEDGEMENTS

ale d'Italia, London; F. de Rochemont, Netherlands State Institute for War Documentation, Amsterdam; Mikhail Salman; Eileen Schlesinger; Monsignor C. Sepe, Secretariat of State, Vatican; Michael Sherbourne; Professor Shoji, War Archives Office, Tokyo; Major H. Støvern, Royal Norwegian Embassy, London; Mrs C Laken, Royal Netherlands Embassy, London; Jean Ring; Lieutenant Colonel George Sunderland, Royal Army Medical College, London; W. Tobies, Embassy of the Federal Republic of Germany; A. Vanhaecke, Sous-Archiviste, Service des Archives, Le Havre; Kurt Vonnegut.

In the final stages of my work, further historical material was provided by P. Berninger, Der Magistrat der Stadt Darmstadt, Stadtarchiv; Jack Bresler; Sir William Deakin; Georgette Elgey, Le Conseiller Technique, Présidence de la Republique, Paris; Roy Farran; John E. Franklin, Executive Director, The Fulbright Commission; Herman Friedhoff; Terje H. Holm, Norwegian Defence Museum, Oslo; Igor Kotler; Trevor Martin; Frances Penfold, Commonwealth War Graves Commission; Michael D. Piccola; Gordon Ramsey, Assistant Editor, *After The Battle*; Dr C. M. Schulten, Head of the Army Historical Section, Royal Netherlands Army Staff, The Hague; Thomas L. Sherlock, Historian, Department of the Army; Arlington National Cemetery, Arlington, Virginia; Dr Shmuel Spector; Professor Thanos Veremis, Department of Political Science and Public Administration, University of Athens; and Paul Woodman, Royal Geographical Society.

While selecting the illustrations, I was helped in my quest by Graham Mason, of the Robert Hunt Picture Library, and Milica Timotic, of the Hulton-Deutsch Collection. I am also grateful to the following photographic archives and photographic copyright holders, for access to, and permission to use, the photographs in their collections:

*After The Battle* Magazine: photographs number 19, 26, 27, 33, 34, 36, 37, 39, 56, 58, 62, 66, 80, 83, 84, 87, 88, 93, 111, 117, 118, 121, 123, 130;

Associated Press Ltd: photographs number 66, 92;

Bruce Adams: photograph number 84;

Bundesarchiv: photographs number 98, 106, 107, 108, 109, 110;

Defence Department Photo (Marine Corps): photograph number 68;

Foto-Studio Euler Werl: photograph number 88;

Hulton-Deutsch Collection: photographs number 1, 3, 6, 9, 10, 11, 12, 13, 14, 15, 21, 22, 31, 42, 44, 50, 86, 102;

Illustrated Copyright: photograph number 125;

Imperial War Museum: photographs number 25, 29, 45, 46, 48, 49, 59, 72, 73, 90, 91, 97, 98, 100, 101, 114, 115, 124, 127;

International Magazine Service, Stockholm: photograph number 38;

Keystone Photo: photograph number 121;

National Archives, Washington DC: photographs number 52, 53, 54, 55, 89, 103, 126, 128;

Novosti Press Agency, Moscow: photographs number 51, 78;

Pan-Asia Photo News: photograph number 129;

Portsmouth & Sunderland Newspapers Ltd: photograph number 30;

Robert Hunt Library: photographs number 4, 5, 7, 8, 16, 17, 18, 20, 23, 24, 28, 29, 32, 35, 38, 40, 41, 43, 45, 47, 48, 49, 51, 57, 60, 61, 63, 64, 65, 68, 69, 71, 74, 75, 76, 77, 78, 79, 81, 82, 84, 85, 89, 92, 95, 96, 98, 99, 101, 103, 104, 105, 106, 107, 108, 109, 110, 114, 115, 116, 118, 119, 120, 122, 129;

Sado, Brussels: photographs number 71, 118;

Science Museum, London: photographs number 39, 80;

Signal Corps Photo: photographs number 123 (Lieutenant Moore), 128 (Technical Sergeant Sievers);

U.S. Air Force Photo: number 85;

U.S. Army Photograph: photographs number 94, 116, 117;

Yad Vashem, Jerusalem: photographs number 2, 67, 70, 112, 113;

Zenarro: photograph number 82.

For help in sorting the many thousands of folio sheets of material, I am grateful to Jessica Wyman. Tim Aspden has transformed my map drafts into maps of the highest quality. The typing of the manuscript of this book, as of my previous manuscripts for more than a decade, was done by Sue Rampton. All correspondence and extra typing was undertaken by Kay Thomson. The copyediting was under the expert eye of Peter James. While preparing the index, I was helped by Carmi Wurtman, Oren Harman, Ephraim Maisel and my son David.

In preparation for the second edition, I am particularly grateful to Adam O'Riordan for his scrutiny of the text, as well as to all those who also sent me notes of errors. For this help, I should like to thank George Clare, D. S. Goodbrand, George Howard, Hugh Humphrey, A. C. H. Irvine, David Littman, Zvi Loker, D. M. Neale, Colonel Geoffrey Powell, Arthur Farrand Radley, Captain A. B. Sainsbury, Alan L. Shaw, Otto Sigg, P. F. Smith, Sir Alexander Waddell, Andrew Wigmore and A. J. Williamson. For subsequent notes of errors, I am grateful to Ray Bailey, Elihu Bergman, Warren Duke, Kevin McCabe, Richard Smock, L. A. Smith, Tormod Torp, Christopher Niebuhr, Richard Cardosi and Admiral of the Fleet Lord Lewin.

For the ninth printing (2000) I was able to make factual corrections as suggested by several of those who wrote to me in the decade since the book was first published. I am grateful in this regard to C. J. Amsterdam, John Calder, Richard Cardosi, Edward Cuneo, Blaine M. Gordon, James Harris, William O. Hays, Gary A. Nelson, Christopher Niebuhr, Vispi Petigara, Jo Reilly, Collin Sells, Kathy Sinclair, and Hugh Toye.

At every stage since the book's inception I have been encouraged by my publisher, David Roberts, and by Ben Helfgott, a survivor of the Holocaust, who gave me the benefit of his considerable knowledge and wisdom.

As with each of my previous books, it is to my wife Susie that I owe both the meticulous scrutiny of the text, and the determination to see fulfilled my aim of a single-volume history of the Second World War which would cover the many different regions of conflict, and the suffering, heroism and achievement of soldiers and civilians alike.

Merton College,
Oxford
22 February 1991

# 1

# The German invasion of Poland

SEPTEMBER 1939

The Second World War was among the most destructive conflicts in human history; more than forty-six million soldiers and civilians perished, many in circumstances of prolonged and horrifying cruelty. During the 2,174 days of war between the German attack on Poland in September 1939 and the surrender of Japan in August 1945, by far the largest number of those killed, whether in battle or behind the lines, were unknown by name or face except to those few who knew or loved them; yet in many cases, perhaps also numbering in the millions, even those who might in later years have remembered a victim were themselves wiped out. Not only forty-six million lives, but the vibrant life and livelihood which they had inherited, and might have left to their descendants, were blotted out: a heritage of work and joy, of struggle and creativity, of learning, hopes and happiness, which no one would ever inherit or pass on.

Inevitably, because they were the war's principal sufferers, it is the millions of victims who fill so many of these pages. Many of them can be, and are, named; it is they, and the unnamed men, women and children whose tragedy is the bitter legacy of the war. There is courage, too, in these pages; the courage of soldiers, sailors and airmen, the courage of partisans and resistance fighters, and the courage of those who, starving, naked and without strength or weapons, were sent to their deaths.

Who was the first victim of a war that was to claim more than forty-six million victims? He was an unknown prisoner in one of Adolf Hitler's concentration camps, most probably a common criminal. In an attempt to make Germany seem the innocent victim of Polish aggression, he had been dressed in a Polish uniform, taken to the German frontier town of Gleiwitz, and shot on the evening of 31 August 1939 by the Gestapo in a bizarre faked 'Polish attack' on the local radio station. On the following morning, as German troops began their advance into Poland, Hitler gave, as one of his reasons for the invasion, 'the attack by regular Polish troops on the Gleiwitz transmitter'.

In honour of the ss Chief who had helped to devise the Gleiwitz deception, it had been given the code name Operation Himmler. On that same evening of August 31, the Soviet Union, Germany's ally of less than a week, had finally

been victorious in its battle with the Japanese on the Soviet–Mongolian borderlands, as Soviet forces, commanded by General Zhukov, destroyed the last
resistance of the Sixth Japanese Army at Khalkhin Gol. As one war ended,
another began, known to history as the Second World War.

The German advance into Poland on 1 September 1939 was not a repeat of
the tactics of the First World War of 1914–18. Then, infantrymen, advancing
towards each other until caught in a line of trenches, had mounted a series of
attacks against a well dug-in enemy. Hitler's method was that of 'Blitzkrieg' –
lightning war. First, and without warning, air attacks destroyed much of the
defender's air force while it was still on the ground. Second, bombers struck at
the defender's road and rail communications, assembly points and munitions
dumps, and at civilian centres, causing confusion and panic. Third, dive-
bombers sought out columns of marching men and bombed them without
respite, while at the same time aircraft machine-gunned civilian refugees as they
sought to flee from the approaching soldiers, causing chaos on the roads, and
further impeding the forward movement of the defending forces.

Even as the Blitzkrieg came out of the sky, it also came on land; first in wave
after wave of motorized infantry, light tanks and motor-drawn artillery, pushing
as far ahead as possible. Then heavy tanks were to drive deep into the countryside, bypassing cities and fortified points. Then, after so much damage had been
done and so much territory traversed, the infantry, the foot soldiers of every
war, but strongly supported by artillery, were to occupy the area already
penetrated, to deal with whatever resistance remained, and to link up with the
mechanized units of the initial strike.

Twenty-four hours after the German attack on Poland, an official Polish
Government communiqué reported that 130 Poles, of whom twelve were soldiers, had been killed in air raids on Warsaw, Gdynia, and several other towns.
'Two German bombers were shot down, and the four occupants arrested after
a miraculous escape,' the communiqué noted, 'when forty-one German aircraft
in formation appeared over eastern Warsaw on Friday afternoon. People
watched a thrilling aerial battle over the heart of the city. Several houses
caught fire, and the hospital for Jewish defective children was bombed and
wrecked.'

On the morning of September 2, German aircraft bombed the railway station
at the town of Kolo. At the station stood a train of civilian refugees being
evacuated from the border towns of Jarocin and Krotoszyn; 111 of them were
killed.

Hitler's aim in invading Poland was not only to regain the territories lost in
1918. He also intended to impose German rule on Poland. To this end, he had
ordered three ss Death's Head regiments to follow behind the infantry advance,
and to conduct what were called 'police and security' measures behind the
German lines. Theodor Eicke, the commander of these three Death's Head
regiments, explained what these measures were to his assembled officers at one
of their bases, Sachsenhausen concentration camp, on that first day of war. In
protecting Hitler's Reich, Eicke explained, the ss would have to 'incarcerate or
annihilate' every enemy of Nazism, a task that would challenge even the

The German invasion of Poland, September 1939

© Martin Gilbert 1989

'absolute and inflexible severity' which the Death's Head regiments had learned in the concentration camps.

These words, so full of foreboding, were soon translated into action; within a week of the German invasion of Poland, almost 24,000 officers and men of the Death's Head regiment were ready to embark on their task. On the side of one of the railway carriages taking German soldiers eastward, someone had written in white paint: 'We're off to Poland to thrash the Jews.' Not only Jews, but Poles, were to be the victims of this war behind the war. Two days after Eicke had given his instructions to the Death's Head regiments, Heinrich Himmler informed SS General Udo von Woyrsch that he was to carry out the 'radical suppression of the incipient Polish insurrection in the newly occupied parts of Upper Silesia'. The word 'radical' was a euphemism for 'ruthless'.

Whole villages were burned to the ground. At Truskolasy, on September 3, fifty-five Polish peasants were rounded up and shot, a child of two among them. At Wieruszow, twenty Jews were ordered to assemble in the market place, among them Israel Lewi, a man of sixty-four. When his daughter, Liebe Lewi, ran up to her father, a German told her to open her mouth for 'impudence'. He then fired a bullet into it. Liebe Lewi fell down dead. The twenty Jews were then executed.

In the weeks that followed, such atrocities became commonplace, widespread and on an unprecedented scale. While soldiers fought in battle, civilians were being massacred behind the lines.

On the afternoon of September 3, German bombers attacked the undefended Polish town of Sulejow, where a peacetime population of 6,500 Poles and Polish Jews were swelled by a further 3,000 refugees. Within moments, the centre of the town was ablaze. As thousands hurried for safety towards the nearby woods, German planes, flying low, opened fire with their machine guns. 'As we were running to the woods', one young boy, Ben Helfgott, recalled, 'people were falling, people were on fire. That night the sky was red from the burning town'.

On 3 September, Britain and France both declared war on Germany. 'The immediate aim of the German High Command', Hitler told his commanders, 'remains the rapid and victorious conclusion of operations against Poland.' At nine o'clock that evening, however, a German submarine, the U-30, commanded by Julius Lemp, torpedoed the British passenger liner *Athenia*, which it had mistaken for an armed ship. The *Athenia*, which was bound for Montreal from Liverpool, had sailed before Britain's declaration of war, with 1,103 passengers on board. Of the 112 passengers who lost their lives that night, twenty-eight were citizens of the United States. But the American President, Franklin Roosevelt, was emphatic when he broadcast to the American people on September 3: 'Let no man or woman thoughtlessly or falsely talk of America sending its armies to European fields. At this moment there is being prepared a proclamation of American neutrality.'

Confident of a swift victory, on the evening of September 3, Hitler left Berlin on board his special train, *Amerika*, in which he was to live for the next two weeks amid the scenes and congratulations of his first military triumph. The British Government, meanwhile, had put into operation its 'Western Air Plan

14', the dropping of anti-Nazi propaganda leaflets over Germany. On the night of September 3, thirteen tons of leaflets were flown, in ten aircraft, across the North Sea and across the German frontier, to be dropped on the Ruhr; six million sheets of paper, in which the Germans were told: 'Your rulers have condemned you to the massacres, miseries and privations of a war they cannot ever hope to win'.

Britain's first bombing raid over Germany took place on September 4, as German troops continued to advance into Poland behind a screen of superior air power. That day, ten Blenheim bombers attacked German ships and naval installations at Wilhelmshaven. No serious damage was done to the ships, but five of the bombers were shot down by German anti-aircraft fire. Among the British dead was Pilot Officer H. B. Lightoller, whose father had been the senior British officer to survive the sinking of the *Titanic* before the First World War.

In Britain, morale was boosted by the news of this raid on German warships. 'We could even see some washing hanging on the line,' the Flight Lieutenant who had led the attack told British radio listeners. 'When we flew on the top of the battleship,' he added, 'we could see the crews running fast to their stations. We dropped our bombs. The second pilot, flying behind, saw two hit.' Both the Flight Lieutenant and the reconnaissance pilot were awarded the Distinguished Flying Cross.

The British pilots were under orders not to endanger German civilian life. At that point in the war, such orders seemed not only moral, but capable of being carried out. The German commanders had given no such orders. 'Brutal guerrilla war had broken out everywhere,' the German Quartermaster General, Eduard Wagner, wrote on September 4, 'and we are ruthlessly stamping it out. We won't be reasoned with. We have already sent out emergency courts, and they are in continual session. The harder we strike, the quicker there will be peace again.' That striking came both on land and from the air. At Bydgoszcz, on 4 September, more than a thousand Poles were murdered, including several dozen boy scouts aged between twelve and sixteen. They had been lined up against a wall in the market place – and shot. Entering Piotrkow on September 5, the Germans set fire to dozens of Jewish homes, then shot dead those Jews who managed to run from the burning buildings. Entering a building which had escaped the flames, soldiers took out six Jews and ordered them to run; five were shot down, the sixth, Reb Bunem Lebel, died later of his wounds.

Many towns were on fire in Poland that week; thousands of Poles perished in the flames, or were shot down as they fled. Two wars raged simultaneously; one on the battle front of armed men, and the other in towns and villages far behind the front line. At sea, also, a war had begun, the course of which was to be savage and all-encompassing. That 5 September, German submarines sank five unarmed merchant ships, four British and one French. The British had not been slow to respond; HMS *Ajax*, in action that day, sank two German merchant ships 'in accordance with the rules of warfare', as Britain's First Lord of the Admiralty, Winston Churchill, informed his War Cabinet colleagues. The merchant ships had failed to stop when ordered to do so.

Each day saw the rules of war ignored and flouted by the Germans, as they advanced deeper and deeper into Poland. On September 6, in the fields outside the Polish village of Mrocza, the Germans shot nineteen Polish officers who had already surrendered, after fighting tenaciously against a German tank unit. Other Polish prisoners-of-war were locked into a railwayman's hut which was then set on fire. They were burned to death. Henceforth, prisoners-of-war were not to know if the accepted rules of war, as laid down by successive Geneva Conventions, were to apply to them: the rules whereby the Nazis acted were completely at variance with those which had evolved over the previous century.

For the Jews, it seemed that extremes of horror were to be perpetrated by this conqueror who boasted that the Jews would be his main victim. Speaking in Berlin seven months before the outbreak of war, Hitler had declared that, if war broke out, 'The result will not be the Bolshevization of the earth, and thus the victory of Jewry, but the annihilation of the Jewish race in Europe.' Six days of war had already shown that the murder of Jews was to be an integral part of German conquest. In a gesture of defiance, Dr Chaim Weizmann, the elder statesman of the Zionist movement, wrote to the British Prime Minister, Neville Chamberlain, to declare that the Jews would fight on the side of the democracies against Nazi Germany; his letter was published in *The Times* on September 6. That day, Hitler was driven by car from his special train to the battlefield at Tuchola, where a Polish corps was surrounded. While he observed the scene of battle, a message reached him that German forces had entered the southern Polish city of Cracow.

The war was one week old; Cracow, a city of more than 250,000 inhabitants, was under German control. On the following day, September 7, the ss chief Reinhard Heydrich told the commanders of Eicke's special ss task forces, which were about to follow behind the advancing soldiers: 'The Polish ruling class is to be put out of harm's way as far as possible. The lower classes that remain will not get special schools, but will be kept down in one way or another.' Eicke himself directed the work of these ss units from Hitler's headquarters train, and it was on the train on September 7 that Hitler told his Army Commander-in-Chief, General von Brauchitsch, that the Army was 'to abstain from interfering' in these ss operations. Those operations were relentless. On the day after Hitler's talk with Brauchitsch, an ss battalion executed thirty-three Polish civilians in the village of Ksiazki; such executions were soon to become a daily occurrence.

Hitler's entourage quickly learned what he had in mind. On September 9 Colonel Eduard Wagner discussed the future of Poland with Hitler's Army Chief of Staff, General Halder. 'It is the Führer's and Goering's intention', Wagner wrote in his diary, 'to destroy and exterminate the Polish nation. More than that cannot even be hinted at in writing.'

Britain and France saw little scope for military action to assist Poland in any substantial way. On September 7, French military units crossed the German frontier at three points near Saarlouis, Saarbrücken and Zweibrücken. But no serious clash of arms took place. The Western Front was quiet. In London, a specially created Land Forces Committee of the War Cabinet discussed the scale of Britain's future military effort. At its first meeting, on September 7, Churchill, the new First Lord of the Admiralty, proposed the creation of an army of twenty divisions by March 1940. 'We must take our place in the Line', he said, 'if we are to hold the Alliance together and win the War.' In its report on the following day, the Land Forces Committee set out, as the basis for Britain's military planning, that the war would last 'for at least three years'. The first twenty divisions should be established within the next twelve months, a further thirty-five divisions by the end of 1941. Meanwhile, the main thrust of Britain's war effort would of necessity be defensive: September 7 saw the inauguration of the first two convoys of merchant ships, escorted by destroyers, one from the Thames estuary, through the English Channel and into the Atlantic, one from Liverpool into the Atlantic.

That day, near the western Polish industrial city of Lodz, the last of the Polish defenders were still seeking to bar the German advance. Their adversaries, ss fighting troops, noted how, that afternoon, at Pabianice, 'the Poles launched yet another counter-attack. They stormed over the bodies of their fallen comrades. They did not come forward with their heads down like men in heavy rain – and most attacking infantry come on like that – but they advanced with their heads held high like swimmers breasting the waves. They did not falter'.

It was not lack of courage, but massively superior German artillery power, which, by nightfall, forced these defenders to surrender. Pabianice was lost. The road to Lodz was open.

Inside Germany, those who had opposed the pre-war excesses of Nazism were equally critical of the attack on Poland. But the threat of imprisonment in a concentration camp was a powerful deterrent to public criticism. Before the war, thousands of Germans had fled from tyranny. Once war began, escape became virtually impossible, as Greater Germany's frontiers were sealed and mounting restrictions imposed on movement and communications. The six months that had passed since the German occupation of Bohemia and Moravia in March 1939 had enabled the Gestapo system to be extended throughout the annexed regions. Two once-independent European capitals, Vienna and Prague, both suffered ruthless Nazi control, with all criticism punished and all independence of spirit crushed. The outbreak of war saw no slackening in the arrest of opponents of the regime; on September 9, Gestapo records show that 630 Czech political prisoners were brought by train from Bohemia to the concentration camp at Dachau, just north of Munich. Few of them were to survive the harsh conditions of work and the brutal treatment.

The speed of the German advance in Poland now trapped soldiers and civilians. In the Poznan sector, nineteen Polish divisions – virtually the same number of troops which Britain wished to have ready for action in March 1940 – were surrounded; in the ensuing battle on the River Bzura, 170,000 Polish soldiers were taken prisoner.

Behind the lines, the atrocities continued. At Bedzin, on September 8, several hundred Jews were driven into a synagogue, which was then set on fire. Two hundred of the Jews burned to death. On the following day the Germans cynically charged Poles with the crime, took a number of hostages, and executed thirty of the hostages in one of the main public squares. On September 10

General Halder noted in his diary that a group of ss men, having ordered fifty Jews to work all day repairing a bridge, had then pushed them into a synagogue and shot them. 'We are now issuing fierce orders which I have drafted today myself,' Colonel Wagner wrote in his diary on September 11. 'Nothing like the death sentence! There's no other way in the occupied territories!'

One eye-witness to this killing of civilians was Admiral Canaris, head of the Secret Intelligence Service of the German Armed Forces. On September 10 he had travelled to the front line to watch the German Army in action. Wherever he went, his Intelligence officers told him of 'an orgy of massacre'. Polish civilians, they reported, having been forced to dig mass graves, were then lined up at the edge of the graves and mown down with machine gun fire. On September 12, Canaris went to Hitler's headquarters train, then at Ilnau in Upper Silesia, to protest. He first saw General Wilhelm Keitel, Chief of the Armed Forces High Command. 'I have information', Canaris told Keitel, 'that mass executions are being planned in Poland, and that members of the Polish nobility and the Roman Catholic bishops and priests have been singled out for extermination.'

Keitel urged Canaris to take the matter no further. 'If I were you', he said, 'I would not get mixed up in this business. This "thing" has been decided upon by the Führer himself.' Keitel added that, from that moment on, every German Army command in Poland would have a civilian chief alongside its military head. This civilian would be in charge of what Keitel called the 'racial extermination' programme. A few moments later Canaris saw Hitler, but said nothing. Shaken by all that he had learned, he returned to Berlin, his allegiance to Hitler much weakened. One of those who had been opposed to Hitler since 1933, Carl Goerdeler, formerly Mayor of Leipzig, told a fellow opponent of Nazism that Canaris had returned from Poland 'entirely broken' by Germany's 'brutal conduct' of the war.

What Keitel had referred to as the programme of 'racial extermination' was given another name by those who carried it out. On September 13, the day after Canaris's visit to Hitler's train, one of the ss Death's Head divisions, the Brandenburg Division, began what it called 'cleansing and security measures'. These included, according to its own report, the arrest and shooting of large numbers of 'suspicious elements, plunderers, Jews and Poles', many of whom were killed 'while trying to escape'. Within two weeks, the Brandenburg Division had left a trail of murder in more than thirteen Polish towns and villages.

The focus of the battle now turned to Warsaw, against which German bombers had been striking with considerable ferocity. Indeed, one of the points of protest raised by Canaris with Keitel had been the 'devastation' of the Polish capital. On September 14 the bombing was particularly severe. For Warsaw's 393,000 Jews, one third of the city's inhabitants, it was a holy and usually happy day in their calendar, the Jewish New Year. 'Just as the synagogues were filled,' a Polish eye-witness noted in his diary, 'Nalewki, the Jewish quarter of Warsaw, was attacked from the air. The result of this bombing was bloody.' That day, German forces entered the southern Polish city of Przemysl, on the River San, where 17,000 citizens, one third of the total population, were Jews. Forty-three of the leading Jewish citizens were at once arrested, savagely beaten and then shot, among them Asscher Gitter, whose son, like so many sons of Polish Jews, had emigrated to the United States, hoping that one day his father would join him. That day in the town of Sieradz, five Jews and two Poles were shot; in Czestochowa, the German civil administration ordered all Jewish industrial and commercial property to be handed over to 'Aryans', irrespective of whether its owner had fled the city or remained; in Piotrkow, a decree was issued forbidding Jews to be in the streets after five o'clock in the afternoon; the twenty-seven year old Getzel Frenkel, returning to his home five minutes after five, was shot dead for this breach of the decree.

The Polish Army, fighting tenaciously, was in retreat, its routes to eastern Poland bombed without respite. East of Przemysl, on September 14, a Polish officer recalled how, after his infantry division had retreated across the River San, German aircraft 'raided us at frequent intervals. There was no shelter anywhere; nothing, on every side, but the accursed plain. The soldiers rushed off the road, trying to take cover in the furrows, but the horses were in a worse plight. After one of the raids we counted thirty-five dead horses.' That eastward march, the officer wrote, 'was not like the march of an army; it was more like the march of some Biblical people, driven onward by the wrath of Heaven, and dissolving in the wilderness.' On the following morning, at Jaroslaw, Hitler himself watched while German forces crossed the River San in close pursuit.

Hitler's generals, with the Polish Army in disarray, proposed that Warsaw, now surrounded, should be starved into submission. But Hitler rejected the notion of a long, or even a short, siege. The Polish capital was, he insisted, a fortress; it should be bombed and bombarded into submission.

The Polish Army, struggling to escape the German military thrust and air attacks, had hopes of regrouping in the country's eastern regions, and in particular around Lvov, the principal city of Eastern Galicia. But in the early hours of September 17 these hopes were dashed. Unknown to the Poles, unknown even to Hitler's own generals, a secret clause in the Nazi–Soviet non-aggression Pact of 23 August 1939, created a demarcation line across Poland, east of which the Soviet Union could take control. That September 17, the Soviet Foreign Minister, Vyacheslav Molotov, in a statement issued in Moscow, declared that the Polish Government had ceased to exist. As a result, he said, Soviet troops had been ordered to occupy eastern Poland. The Poles, so desperately engaged in seeking to defend themselves from the German onslaught, had no means of effective resistance.

Two Soviet Army groups now moved up towards the demarcation line. A hundred miles before they reached it, they met German troops who, at considerable cost, had fought their way into Poland's eastern regions. Those Germans withdrew, handing over to Russians the Polish soldiers whom they had taken prisoner. In Lvov, it was a Soviet general who ordered the Polish troops to lay down their arms. They did so, whereupon they were surrounded by the Red Army and marched off into captivity. Thousands of other Poles were captured by the advancing Russian forces. Other Poles surrendered to the Russians, rather than risk falling into German hands. In Warsaw, the battle continued, with heavy loss of Polish civilian life as the bombs fell without respite. That night, in the Atlantic Ocean, the British suffered their first naval disaster; the loss of 518 sailors on board the aircraft carrier *Courageous*, torpedoed off the south-west coast of Ireland by the German submarine, U-29, commanded by Lieutenant Schuhart. The head of the German Submarine service, Admiral Dönitz, wrote in his diary of 'a glorious success'. For Churchill, as First Lord of the Admiralty, it was a dire reminder of the perils of the war at sea, for he had already seen, during the First World War, how nearly the German submarines had choked Britain's food and raw-material lifeline.

In Britain, the fate of Poland distressed those who had seen the two Western allies unable to take any serious counter-initiative. 'Poor devils!' one Englishman wrote to a friend in America on September 18, 'they are magnificent fighters, and I think we all here have an uneasy feeling that, since they are our allies, we ought – at whatever cost – to have made such smashing attacks on the Western Front as to divert the Germans. I imagine that why we have not done so is that neither we nor France have enough machines yet in hand'.

The Germans were confident that no British or French move would impede their imminent victory. On September 18, British radio listeners heard for the first time the nasal tones of William Joyce, quickly nicknamed 'Lord Haw-Haw', broadcasting to his fellow countrymen from Berlin to tell them that the war was lost – less than a month after he had renewed his British passport. Just north of Berlin, at Sachsenhausen concentration camp, on September 18, Lothar Erdman, a distinguished German journalist and pre-1933 trade unionist, having courageously protested about the ill-treatment of his fellow prisoners, was savagely kicked and beaten, suffering severe internal injuries, from which he died.

In Warsaw, the defenders refused to accept the logic of German power. A Polish doctor, joining a group in search of medicines on September 18, found some in the cellar of a medical store which was already under German artillery bombardment. Also in the cellar was a German spy, a man who had lived in Poland for the past twelve years. He was caught with a miniature wireless transmitter, sending messages to the German siege headquarters. 'After brief formalities,' the doctor noted, 'he was despatched "with greetings to Hindenburg".'

By September 19 Warsaw had been under artillery bombardment for ten consecutive days. So many thousands of Poles had already been killed by air as well as by artillery bombardment that the public parks were having to be used for burials. Tenaciously, the Polish forces struggled to hold the city's perimeter. Several German tanks were immobilized when they penetrated too swiftly into the suburbs. German troops, advancing too far, were captured. But the bombardment was relentless. 'This morning', one police officer noted in his diary on September 19, 'a German bomber dropped a bomb which hit a house, not far from my headquarters, which I had converted into a temporary prison for about ninety Germans captured during last night's fighting. Twenty-seven of them were killed.'

While Warsaw bled under bombardment, the first British troops, an army corps, landed in France. But no action was envisaged for it. The Western Front remained firmly on the defensive; quiet and passive. Meanwhile, north of Warsaw, Hitler made a triumphal entry into the Free City of Danzig, which had been detached from Germany at the insistence of the victorious powers at the end of the First World War. The crowd which greeted him were hysterical with joy. 'It was like this everywhere,' Hitler's chief Army adjutant, Rudolf Schmundt, explained to a recent recruit to the Führer's staff, 'in the Rhineland, in Vienna, in the Sudeten territories, and in Memel. Do you still doubt the mission of the Führer?'

Addressing the citizens of Danzig on September 19, Hitler spoke of 'Almighty God, who has now given our arms his blessing'. He also spoke mysteriously, and for Britain and France ominously, when he warned: 'The moment might very quickly come for us to use a weapon with which we ourselves could not be attacked'.

From Danzig, Hitler moved to a hotel at the holiday resort town of Zoppot. There, to a group which included his personal physician, Dr Karl Brandt, the head of his Party Office, Philipp Bouler, and the Chief Medical Officer of the Reich, Dr Leonardo Conti, he set out his plans for the killing of the insane inside Germany itself. The purity of the German blood had to be maintained. Dr Conti doubted whether, medically speaking, there was any scientific basis for suggesting that any eugenic advantages could be produced through euthanasia. But the only serious discussion was about the quickest and least painful method of killing. Backdating his order to September 1, Hitler then gave Bouler and Brandt 'full responsibility to enlarge the powers of certain specified doctors so that they can grant those who are by all human standards incurably ill a merciful death, after the most critical assessment possible of their medical condition'.

The operational centre of the euthanasia programme was to be a suburban house in Berlin, No. 4 Tiergartenstrasse. It was this address which gave its name to the organization itself, known henceforth as 'T.4'. Its head was the thirty-seven year old Werner Heyde, Professor of Neurology and Psychiatry at the University of Würzburg, who had joined the Nazi Party at its moment of political triumph in 1933. Henceforth, the mental asylums were to be combed for those who could be given 'a merciful death'. In the words of one Nazi euthanasia expert, Dr Pfannmüller, 'The idea is unbearable to me that the best, the flower of our youth, must lose its life at the front, in order that feebleminded and asocial elements can have a secure existence in the asylum.'

From the first days of Operation T4, particular attention was paid to young children, and especially to newborn babies. At Görden near Brandenburg, a state paediatric institution established a Special Psychiatric Youth Department to which children were sent from all over Germany, and killed. One of its aims, a doctor who worked there later recalled, was 'to put newborns to sleep as soon as possible', in order specifically to prevent 'closer bonds between mothers and their children'.

The euthanasia programme had begun. At Görden, and at six other institutions throughout Germany, those Germans judged insane were put to death. During the first two years of the war, tens of thousands were to perish in this way, the victims of perverted medical science.

In Poland, the Special Task Force troops of the ss had continued the killing of Jews in more and more towns as they came under German control. On September 20 the Operations Section of the German Fourteenth Army reported that the troops were becoming uneasy 'because of the largely illegal measures' taken in the Army's area by the task force commanded by General von Woyrsch. The fighting soldiers were particularly angered that the ss men under von Woyrsch's command, instead of fighting at the front, 'should be demonstrating their courage against defenceless civilians'. Field Marshal von Rundstedt immediately announced that von Woyrsch's ss Task Force would no longer be tolerated in the war zone, and that the anti-Jewish measures already under way in the Katowice area should cease.

The crisis which had arisen between the professional, fighting soldiers and their ss counterparts could not be resolved. But far more ambitious plans were now being prepared. On September 21, Reinhard Heydrich summoned the commanders of all ss units in Poland to an emergency conference in Berlin. Those commanders who could not be present were sent a secret note of the discussion. The 'ultimate aim' of German policy to the Jews must, he said, be kept 'strictly secret' and would take 'a prolonged period of time'. Meanwhile, and as a prerequisite of this 'ultimate aim', Polish Jews were henceforth to be concentrated in a number of large cities. Jews living outside these cities, and in particular all Jews living in western Poland, were to be deported to those cities. Western Poland must be 'cleared completely of Jews'. All farmland belonging to Jews should be taken from them and 'entrusted to the care' of local Germans, or even of Polish peasants. Once deported to the cities, the Jews would be confined to one particular quarter, forbidden to enter the rest of the city. In each city a council of Jewish elders was to be charged with ensuring that German orders about the movement of Jews were carried out on time. In case of 'sabotage of such instructions', these Jewish Councils were to be theatened with 'the severest measures'.

Heydrich's plan to recreate in the twentieth century the medieval concept of the ghetto was intended merely as a first 'stage' toward what he and his ss colleagues called 'the final solution of the Jewish question'. This plan led to no halt, however, in the Special Task Force killings which had already provoked German Army protests; on September 22, the day after Heydrich's conference, the ss Brandenburg Division arrived in Wloclawek, where it began what it called a 'Jewish action' lasting four days. Jewish shops were looted, the city's synagogues blown up, dozens of leading Jews rounded up and shot. Even as this 'action' was in progress, Eicke instructed the Division's commander to send two of his battalions to Bydgoszcz to conduct a further 'action' against Polish intellectuals and municipal leaders. As a result of this instruction, eight hundred Poles were shot on September 23 and September 24, less than three weeks after the first mass random killings in the city.

The first day of the renewed killings of Poles in Bydgoszcz was also the holiest day in the Jewish calendar, the Day of Atonement. To show their contempt for Jews and Poles alike, the German occupation authorities in Piotrkow ordered several thousand Polish prisoners-of-war, among them many Polish Jews, into the synagogue, and, forbidding them access to lavatories, forced then to relieve themselves in the synagogue itself. They were then given prayer shawls, the curtains from the Holy Ark, and the exquisitely embroidered ornamental covers of the Scrolls of the Law, and ordered to clean up the excrement with these sacred objects.

On the day of the perpetration of this disgusting, puerile order, another order, sent from Berlin to all German warships, led to an intensification of the war at sea. It was an Admiralty decree that any British or French merchant ship making use of its radio once it had been stopped by a U-boat should be either sunk or taken in prize.

German and Soviet troops now faced each other along the Polish demarcation line agreed upon by Ribbentrop and Molotov a month earlier. Only in the city of Warsaw, in the town of Modlin just north of the Vistula, and on the Hel peninsula near Danzig, were the Poles still refusing to surrender. 'The merciless bombardment continues,' a Polish officer in Warsaw noted in his diary on September 25. 'So far German threats have not materialized. The people of Warsaw are proud that they did not allow themselves to be frightened.' They were also on the verge of starvation. 'I saw a characteristic scene in the street today,' the officer added. 'A horse was struck by a shell and collapsed. When I returned an hour later only the skeleton was left. The meat had been carved off by the people living near by.'

On September 25 the Germans launched Operation Coast, an air attack on Warsaw by four hundred bombers, dive-bombers and ground-attack aircraft, supported by thirty tri-motor transport planes. It was these latter which, dropping a total of seventy-two tons of incendiary bombs on the Polish capital, caused particularly widespread fires, havoc and human destruction. A Polish officer's wife, Jadwiga Sosnkowska, who later escaped to the West, remembered, a year later, 'that dreadful night', when she was trying to help in one of the city's hospitals. 'On the table at which I was assisting, tragedy following tragedy. At one time the victim was a girl of sixteen. She had a glorious mop of golden hair, her face was delicate as a flower, and her lovely sapphire-blue eyes were full of tears. Both her legs, up to the knees, were a mass of bleeding pulp, in which it was impossible to distinguish bone from flesh; both had to be amputated above the knee. Before the surgeon began I bent over this innocent child to kiss her pallid brow, to lay my helpless hand on her golden head. She died quietly in the course of the morning, like a flower plucked by merciless hand'.

That same night, Jadwiga Sosnkowska recalled, 'on the same deal table, there died under the knife of the surgeon a young expectant mother, nineteen years of age, whose intestines were torn by the blast of a bomb. She was only a few days before childbirth. We never knew who her husband and her family were, and she was buried, a woman unknown, in the common grave with the fallen soldiers.'

The citizens of Warsaw were at the end of endurance. Even the determination of 140,000 soldiers could not sustain them much longer. Wild rumours began to circulate, the last resort of those who were desperate. It was said by some that a Polish general was on his way from the East at the head of Soviet troops. Others claimed that they had seen Soviet aeroplanes, marked with the hammer and sickle, in actual combat with German aircraft over the city. In reality, Soviet aircraft are marked, not with the hammer and sickle, but with five-pointed red stars. Such a detail was irrelevant however, as rumours of rescue spread.

Not rescue, but a renewed German military assault, was imminent. On the morning of September 26 General von Brauchitsch ordered the German Eighth Army to attack. That evening, the Polish garrison commander asked for a truce, but von Brauchitsch refused. He would accept only a complete surrender. The city fought on. That day, in Berlin, at a conference held in the strictest secrecy, German scientists discussed how to harness energy from nuclear fission. It was clear to them that a substantial explosive power was possible. A 'uranium burner' would have to be made. Considerable quantities of heavy water would have to be distilled, at considerable expense. Excited at the prospect of a weapon of decisive power, the German War Office agreed to sponsor the necessary, and complex experiments. Whatever funds were needed would be made available.

At two o'clock on the afternoon of September 27, Warsaw surrendered; 140,000 Polish soldiers, more than 36,000 of them wounded, were taken into captivity. For the next three days, the Germans made no effort to enter the city. 'They are afraid', a Polish officer wrote in his diary, 'to march their soldiers into a city which has no light and no water and is filled with the sick and the wounded and the dead.'

Hundreds of wounded Polish soldiers and civilians died who might have been saved, had medical help been offered to them. But this was not the German plan or method; by the day of Warsaw's surrender, Heydrich was able to report, with evident satisfaction: 'of the Polish upper classes in the occupied territories only a maxiumum of three per cent is still present'. Once more, words were used to mask realities: 'present' meant 'alive'. Many thousands, probably more than ten thousand, Polish teachers, doctors, priests, landowners, businessmen and local officials had been rounded up and killed. The very names of some of the places where they had been held, tortured and killed were to become synonymous with torture and death: Stutthof near Danzig, Smukala camp near Bydgoszcz, the Torun grease factory, Fort VII in Poznan, and Soldau camp in East Prussia. In one Church diocese in western Poland, two-thirds of the 690 priests had been arrested, of whom 214 had been shot. Poland had become the first victim of a new barbarism of war within war; the unequal struggle between military victors and civilian captives.

# 2

## Poland defeated

OCTOBER 1939

In London and Paris there was shock at the fall of Warsaw, deep sympathy with the fate of the Poles, amazement at the speed of the German advance, anger at the Soviet connivance in the partition of a State which a month earlier had been independent, a certain shame at not having helped, or been able to help Poland to resist the onslaught, and, above all, fear that the practitioners of 'lightning war' might turn their weapons and their tactics against the West. This fear was heightened in Britain by the suspicion that German agents must have skilfully infiltrated into many areas of British life, to report back to Germany on military preparations and to carry out acts of sabotage against British war production.

Unknown to the British public, however, all but a handful of these German agents had been arrested on the outbreak of war; a secret, unsung triumph for British Intelligence. This loss was also unknown to the Germans. Nor was it their only defeat in the clandestine world of espionage. For on 28 September 1939, the day after Warsaw's surrender, German Intelligence fell into a bizarre trap. That day a Welshman, Arthur Owens, whom German Intelligence believed to be one of its own agents, crossed from Britain to Holland, to make contact with his German superiors, while in fact working for Britain. His British Intelligence masters gave Owens the code name 'Snow'. He was able to persuade the Germans that he had set up a considerable network of German agents in Wales. Now he asked for both instructions and money. He was given both, and returned that same evening to Britain. Thus began the system known to its British operators as the 'Double Cross' system, or 'xx' in the coded style of wartime espionage. It was to deceive the Germans entirely; two weeks later Owens crossed back to Holland with another alleged recruit for the German Intelligence network. This was Gwilym Williams, a retired Police inspector from Swansea, hitherto active in the Welsh Nationalist movement. The Germans were again successfully deceived. They not only gave Williams, whom they designated agent A-3551, a series of sabotage tasks which they were later tricked into believing that he had carried out, but also gave him the address of one of the very few genuine German agents in Britain who had not been located by British Intelligence. This was agent A-3725, who was now himself to join the

Double Cross system as 'Charlie'. By the end of the year this spurious spy ring was sending almost daily radio messages to German Intelligence in Hamburg, recruiting further fictitious agents, and preparing a sham sabotage scheme, Plan Guy Fawkes, to poison the reservoirs in Wales which provided water for Britain's aircraft and munitions factories in the industrial Midlands.

While Arthur Owens was on his Double Cross mission to Holland, the German Foreign Minister, Joachim von Ribbentrop, was on his way to Moscow. There, during two days of negotiations, he accepted for Germany the whole of Poland west of the River Vistula – an area including most of Poland's populated regions and industry – while accepting Soviet rule over eastern Poland and – this was an unexpected Soviet demand – Lithuania. The treaty embodying this new partition of Poland was signed at five in the morning of September 29. It was called, without reference to the Polish and Lithuanian States which had thereby disappeared, the German–Soviet Boundary and Friendship Treaty. Stalin himself drew the new border line on a map, and signed it. In return for including Lvov, with the nearby oilwells of Drohobycz, on the Soviet side of the line, he promised to provide Germany with 300,000 tons of oil a year.

In the finer points of map making, Stalin agreed to withdraw from the line of the River Vistula to that of the River Bug. This meant that German troops, who having reached the Bug had withdrawn to the Vistula to allow the Red Army to occupy the region, now returned once more to the Bug. Twenty-two million Poles were now under German rule. On September 29, as Ribbentrop returned to Berlin, the Soviet Union signed a Treaty of Mutual Assistance with the small Baltic State of Estonia, giving the Russians the right to occupy Estonia's naval bases at Narva, Baltiski, Haapsalu and Pärnü. Six days later, a similar treaty was signed with Latvia, and eleven days later with Lithuania. Stalin was not going to leave a vacuum between the Soviet frontiers established in the years after the First World War, when Bolshevism was weak, and the now triumphant Nazi juggernaut whose eastern border had moved well inside what once had been the imperial frontiers of the Russian Tsar. Nor, quite naturally, was Hitler content to set up an undefended eastern border for his Thousand Year Reich. In a top secret Directive No. 5 on September 30, he gave instructions that his Polish borderlands 'will be constantly strengthened and built up as a line of military security towards the East' and that 'the garrisons necessary for this purpose will eventually be moved forward beyond the political frontier of the Reich'.

This same directive of September 30 also increased the scale of German activity in the West. The 'war at sea', Hitler decreed, was to be carried on 'against France just as against England'. Troopships and merchant ships 'definitely established as being hostile' could henceforth be attacked without warning. This also applied to ships sailing without lights in British coastal waters. In addition, merchant ships which used their wireless after they had been stopped would be fired on. The sinking of such merchantmen, the German Naval Staff noted that day, 'must be justified in the war diary as due to possible confusion with a warship or auxiliary cruiser'.

The sinking of British merchant ships was taking place on a widening scale.

Poland partitioned, October 1939

On the day of Hitler's directive, the German pocket battleship *Admiral Graf Spee*, sank the British merchant ship *Clement*, raising the Allied losses in merchant shipping to a total of 185,000 tons in less than a month.

In Paris, on September 30, a Polish General, Wladyslaw Sikorski, set up a Polish Government-in-Exile. As he did so, the city of Warsaw still awaited, as it had done for the past three days, the arrival of the German Army. 'There were so many corpses lying still unburied,' Jadwiga Sosnkowska recalled, 'there was no food, and there were no medical supplies. These were sorrowful days, but they will live for ever in my memory as days of the greatest solidarity and brotherly compassion of the whole community.' Nor was it only a question of good deeds; 'an ocean of kindness' she added, 'welled from human hearts, eager to save, to help, to console. The walls of the city had fallen, but the people of Warsaw remained erect, with unbowed heads.'

On October 1 the German Army prepared to occupy Warsaw. Before doing so, it demanded twelve hostages – ten Christians and two Jews – who would be responsible with their lives for any disturbances that might occur while the Army was marching in. On entering the city, the Germans set up field kitchens and began to distribute free soup and bread to the starving population. Thousands flocked to the kitchens. At once, German film operators set up their cameras and filmed the evidence of how German troops were bringing sustenance to the hungry Poles. The film completed, the field kitchens disappeared with the cameramen.

That day, the last Polish soldiers still in action, on the Hel peninsula, were forced to surrender. Three Polish destroyers and three submarines succeeded in escaping the German naval blockade, and made their way to British ports. The Eastern war was over; 694,000 Polish soldiers had been captured by the Germans, 217,000 were in Russian hands. More than 60,000 Polish soldiers had been killed in action, as had as many as 25,000 Polish civilians in three weeks of aerial and artillery bombardment, especially on Warsaw. The Germans, forced despite their tactic of 'lightning war' to fight a tenacious enemy, had lost 14,000 men.

On the night of 1 October, British bombers flew over Berlin itself. They dropped, not bombs, but leaflets, telling the German public that whereas they were forced to go to war 'with hunger rations', their leaders had secreted vast sums of money overseas. Even Himmler, the leaflet declared, 'who watches like a lynx that no German takes more than ten marks across the frontier has himself smuggled abroad a sum of 527,500'. After one month of war, ninety-seven million leaflets had been printed, of which thirty-one million had already been dropped. A joke popular at that time told of an airman who was rebuked for dropping a whole bundle of leaflets still tied up in its brick-like packet: 'Good God, you might have killed someone!' Public scepticism about the efficacy of the leaflets led to many of them – thirty-nine million in all – being pulped instead of being dropped. This, said its critics, was not real war, but 'confetti war'. It went on nevertheless.

In German-occupied Poland, it was a cruel war that continued, despite Poland's defeat. On October 4, in Berlin, Hitler signed a secret amnesty, releasing from detention those ss men who had been arrested by the Army authorities on charges of brutality against the civilian population. On the following day he flew to Warsaw, where he took the salute at a victory parade. Returning to the airfield, he told the foreign journalists there: 'Take a good look around Warsaw. That is how I can deal with any European city.'

Photographs of Warsaw's bomb damage were reproduced in newspapers throughout the world, nor did the question of whether such destruction would also be visited on London and Paris go unasked. It was indeed Hitler himself who, speaking in Berlin on October 6, declared: 'Why should this war in the West be fought? For the restoration of Poland? The Poland of the Versailles Treaty will never rise again.' Yet, other than Poland, what reason was there for war. All important problems could be resolved at the conference table.

Hitler's suggestion of negotiations was addressed to Britain and France; Poland would be excluded. In the East, terror, and terror alone, was the order of the day. On October 8, two days after Hitler's soothing words in Berlin, a group of more than twenty Poles in the town of Swiecie was taken by an ss detachment to the Jewish cemetery. Among the Poles were several children between the ages of two and eight. All were shot. Watching the execution were about 150 German soldiers. Three of them protested to their medical officer. He at once wrote, in outrage, direct to Hitler. Not long afterwards, Hitler received a further protest about such executions from General Blaskowitz. Hitler was shown the report by his Army adjutant, Captain Gerhard Engel. 'He took note of it calmly enough at first', Engel noted, 'but then began another long tirade of abuse at the "childish ideas" prevalent in the army's leadership; you cannot fight wars with the methods of the Salvation Army.'

On October 8 Hitler signed a decree annexing the Polish frontier regions to Silesia and East Prussia, and creating out of Polish territory three enlarged districts of the German Reich, 'Greater East Prussia', 'Danzig West Prussia' and 'Posen'. Four days later the remaining area of German-occupied Poland, including Warsaw, was constituted a General Government, with its capital in Cracow. Warsaw was to be relegated from a capital city to a provincial town. The Governor-General chosen by Hitler was the Nazi Party's legal adviser, Dr Hans Frank. His tasks included the 'restoration' of public order. Frank's own description of his task was more explicit. 'Poland shall be treated like a colony,' he wrote, 'the Poles will become the slaves of the Greater German Empire'.

On October 9, in Berlin, Hitler received a Swedish businessman, Birger Dahlerus, who had been flying between London and Berlin, through Sweden, with a proposal, emanating originally from Goering, for a negotiated settlement between Britain and Germany. On October 5, in London, Dahlerus had seen the British Foreign Secretary, Lord Halifax; on October 9, in Berlin, he reported to Hitler that Britain was insisting upon the restoration of Polish statehood, the immediate destruction of all weapons of aggression, and a plebiscite inside Germany on certain aspects of Hitler's foreign policy. On the following day, 10 October, Dahlerus saw Hitler again, twice, before being asked to convey the German terms to Britain: the territorial aspects were Germany's right to fortify her new frontier with Russia, and the return to Germany of her pre First World

War colonies or 'suitable substitute territories'. Between his two meetings with Dahlerus, Hitler issued a new directive to General Keitel, the Chief of Staff of the German armed forces, and to his Army, Navy and Air Force commanders. This directive set out Operation Yellow, the code name for an offensive against France and Britain.

Hitler's directive of October 9 gave precise details of an offensive, to be carried out 'in greatest possible strength', through Luxemburg, Belgium and Holland. The purpose of this northern advance into France was to defeat 'as much as possible' of the French Army, and 'at the same time to win as much territory as possible in Holland, Belgium and Northern France, to serve as a base for the successful prosecution of the air and sea war against England'. It would also create a 'wide protective area' for the economically vital Ruhr.

'War against England'; the words were chilling in their implications of impending conflict. Chilling in a different way were the census forms sent out that day from Philipp Bouler, the head of Hitler's Party Office, to all hospitals and doctors, asking them, ostensibly for statistical purposes, to list all patients who were senile, criminally insane or of non-German blood. Meeting in secret, three assessors would then decide whether the patient should live or die. The Head of Hitler's Chancellery, Hans Lammers, had wanted the procedure codified as part of German law. This, Hitler had refused. It was not only in the euthanasia institutes in Germany that the killing of mental patients now began. In occupied Poland, at Piasnica, not far from Danzig, several thousand so-called 'defectives' were killed by the end of the year. As well as Poles and Jews, twelve hundred Germans perished at Piasnica; they had been sent there from psychiatric institutions inside Germany.

On the morning of October 10, Hitler received seven of his most senior military commanders at the Chancellery, the very building from which the euthanasia census forms had been sent the previous day. To the commanders he spoke of the reasons for a war in the West, reading out to them a memorandum which he had written, in which he gave as Germany's war aim 'the destruction of the power and ability of the Western powers ever again to oppose the state consolidation and further developments of the German people in Europe'.

It was his treaty with Russia, Hitler explained, which made it possible to attack Britain and France, for it ensured that such a war would be a war on a single front. But time was not on Germany's side. 'By no treaty or pact', Hitler warned, 'can a lasting neutrality with Soviet Russia be ensured with certainty.' What was now needed was 'a prompt demonstration of German strength'. Plans must be made at once. The attack could not begin 'too early'. It was to take place 'in all circumstances, if at all possible, this autumn'.

Fifteen days had passed since German scientists, meeting in Berlin, had informed the military authorities of the possibility of using nuclear fission to create a bomb of massive destructive power. Meanwhile, in the United States, an American economist, a friend of Albert Einstein, had been seeking a private meeting with Roosevelt. The meeting took place on October 11. The economist, Alexander Sachs, brought with him a letter from Einstein, the contents of which he explained to the President. Atomic energy would enable a man to 'blow up

Greater Germany, November 1939

his neighbour' on a scale hitherto unimagined, and unimaginable.

'This requires action' was Roosevelt's comment. Ten days later, an advisory committee on uranium held its first meeting in Washington. America was now actively in search of the new force. Einstein, who, as a Jew, had been forced to flee from Germany in 1933, had shown the way forward for the development of a revolutionary weapon of war. But more than five years were to pass before that weapon could be developed. Meanwhile, the destructive power of the existing weapons continued to be felt. On the evening of October 13 a German submarine, U-47, commanded by Günther Prien, penetrated the British naval defences at Scapa Flow and, in the early hours of October 14, with three torpedoes, sank the battleship *Royal Oak* as she lay at anchor; 833 sailors were drowned.

Two days after the sinking of the *Royal Oak*, two German bombers flew, unescorted, over the east coast of Scotland. Both were shot down by fighters. Three of the eight crewmen were drowned. It was the first time that British fighter pilots had destroyed enemy aircraft over home territory. A month later, over France, a young New Zealander, Flying Officer E. J. Kain, shot down a

German bomber from the then record height for air combat of 27,000 feet. But such successes could not offset the tragedy of the *Royal Oak*.

In Poland, there was no abatement in the German pursuit of its goals; on October 16 all Poles were ordered to leave the port and city of Gdynia. There were similar mass expulsions from towns throughout the area annexed by Germany. The Poles who were expelled had to find homes elsewhere in war damaged Poland, in regions already suffering from severe shortages of food. Yet they could take with them only such goods as they could pack into suitcases or bundles. Their homes, the bulk of their possessions, and for most their very means of subsistence, had to be left behind. Executions, too, continued, often to the accompaniment of physical and mental tortures of a perverted kind. On October 17 the seventy-year-old Father Pawlowski, the parish priest of Chocz, was arrested by the Gestapo and charged with illegal possession of arms. A search of his home revealed two cartridge cases, all that remained of his pre-war love of partridge shooting. Pawlowski was then beaten up so badly that his face was lacerated beyond recognition. He was then taken to the nearby town of Kalisz, to an execution post set up in the main square. There, the Gestapo forced local Jews to bind him to the execution post, to unbind him after he had been shot, to kiss his feet, and to bury him in the Jewish cemetery.

That same day, October 17, a decree of the Ministerial Council for the Defence of the Reich gave the ss field divisions judicial independence from the German Army. Henceforth, ss soldiers would no longer be tried by German Army courts martial, but by their own ss superiors. Also on October 17, the Army lost its administrative control in Poland; at a conference in the Chancellery at which Heinrich Himmler and General Keitel were both present, Hitler announced that the government of Poland was now in the hands of Hans Frank for the General Government region, Albert Forster for Danzig–West Prussia and Artur Greiser for Posen. It was to be the task of these senior members of the Nazi Party to prevent any future emergence of a Polish leadership. Poland must become so poor that the Poles would want to work in Germany. Within ten years, Greater Danzig–West Prussia and Posen must both be transformed into 'pure and Germanic provinces in full bloom'.

That evening, General Keitel spoke of these plans to an Army colonel who had arrived at the Chancellery. 'The methods to be employed', Keitel commented, 'will be irreconcilable with all our existing principles'. Such principles were everywhere being set aside. On October 18, Hitler's Directive No. 7 for the Conduct of the War, sent to Keitel on October 18, authorized German submarine attacks on passenger ships 'in convoy, or proceeding without lights'.

A massive forced movement of peoples had now begun in the East. In the eastern areas of Poland occupied by Russia, Germans whose ancestors had settled there two centuries earlier were sent, bewildered, across the new Soviet–German frontier into western Poland. Jews whose ancestors had settled in the Czecho-slovak – now German – city of Moravska Ostrava equally long ago were put into railway coaches under ss guard and deported to the General Government, where they were dumped east of Lublin in a special 'Jewish reservation', soon to be joined by Jews deported from the Baltic ports and from Vienna, and even with Jews who had been seized at the Hamburg docks, waiting to board ship for the United States. Other Jews, especially those living in Chelm, Pultusk and Ostrow, fled eastward from German-occupied Poland, across the River Bug to the Soviet side. There, to their bewilderment, they met Polish Jews fleeing westward, desperate to escape the perils of Communist rule, and hoping that, as had been true in the First World War, German rule might prove less burdensome.

With the Soviet Union suddenly predominant in the Baltic States, German Balts, who could trace their Baltic ancestry back many hundreds of years, found themselves the somewhat amazed beneficiaries of the new found Soviet–German co-operation; they too were now unexpectedly on the move, the first German Balts reaching Danzig from Estonia on October 20. Two days later, the Germans began to deport Poles from Poznan, the largest city of western Poland, with a population of more than a quarter of a million Poles. The decade of preparing the 'pure and Germanic provinces' had begun.

The world awaited Hitler's next move, not knowing if he would strike again. Some saw in his offer of peace on October 6 a hopeful sign. Others were alarmed by one passage in it, in which Hitler declared: 'Destiny will decide. One thing is certain, in the course of world history there have never been two victors, but very often only vanquished.' In a secret speech to senior Nazi Party officials on October 21, Hitler assured his followers that, once he had forced Britain and France to their knees, he would turn his attention back to the East, 'and show who was the master there'. The Russian soldiers, he said, were badly trained and poorly equipped. Once he had dealt with the East, 'he would set about restoring Germany to how she used to be'.

Already, in occupied Poland, the New Order was being established. On October 25, in the first official gazette of the General Government, Hans Frank announced that henceforth all Jewish males between the ages of fourteen and sixty would be 'obliged to work' at Government-controlled labour projects. Some would go each day in work brigades to tasks near the cities. Other would be taken to special labour camps set up alongside distant projects. By the end of the year, twenty-eight such labour camps had been set up in the Lublin region, twenty-one in the Kielce region, fourteen near Warsaw, twelve near Cracow and ten near Rzeszow. Conditions in these camps were terribly harsh. Yet the pittance paid to those who worked in them provided a means of survival for many Jews who, expelled from the towns and villages in which they had lived and worked all their lives, now had no other means of subsistence.

Typical of the New Order in Poland was a notice posted in the streets of Torun on October 27 by the head of the local State Police. Its ten points set out instructions for the Polish citizens whose 'brazen behaviour' would have to change. All Poles must 'leave the pavement free' for Germans. 'The street belongs to the conquerors, not to the conquered.' In shops and at the market place, representatives of the German authorities, and local ethnic Germans, must be served first. 'The conquered come only after them.' Male Polish nationals must raise their hats to the 'important personalities of State, Party and armed forces'. Poles are forbidden to use the 'Heil Hitler!' greeting. 'Whoever annoys or speaks to German women and girls will receive exemplary punishment. Polish females who speak to or annoy German nationals will be sent to brothels.'

The seriousness of these regulations was made clear in a final paragraph. 'Poles who have failed to understand that they are the conquered and we are conquerors,' it read, 'and who act against the above regulations, expose themselves to the most severe punishment'.

The Poles were now a subject people. But, for the Nazi ideology, it was not enough to conquer. A new race had to be created, based upon the spurious notion of 'Aryan' ethnic superiority. On October 28 Himmler issued a special 'Procreation Order' to the SS whereby it would become 'the sublime task of German women and girls of good blood, acting not frivolously but from a profound moral seriousness, to become mothers to children of soldiers setting off to battle'. To make sure that the creation of a race of 'supermen' was undertaken on a systematic basis, Himmler established special human stud farms, known as *Lebensborn*, where young girls, selected for their allegedly perfect 'Nordic' traits, could procreate with SS men. Their offspring would be taken care of in maternity homes, where they would receive special benefits.

The breeding of the 'master' race and the destruction of the 'inferior race' went on side by side. For many German Army officers, however, the treatment of the 'inferior' race had taken unacceptable forms. General Blaskowitz, in the protest at such treatment which he sent to Hitler's Chancellery, described an incident in the Polish town of Turek on October 30, when a number of Jews 'were herded into the synagogues and there were made to crawl along the pews singing, while being continuously beaten with whips by SS men. They were then forced to take down their trousers so that they could be beaten on the bare buttocks. One Jew, who had fouled his trousers in fear, was compelled to smear his excrement over the faces of other Jews'.

What the future of these Jews was to be, no one knew. Hitler's Minister of Propaganda, Josef Goebbels, visiting Lodz on November 2, wrote, of the city's 200,000 Jews: 'It is indescribable. They are no longer people, but beasts. There is therefore not a humanitarian, but a surgical task. Here one must make a radical incision. Otherwise Europe will be ruined by the Jewish sickness.' 'Behind all the enemies of Germany's ascendancy', a Berlin magazine declared that day, 'stand those who demand our encirclement – the oldest enemies of the German people and of all healthy, rising nations – the Jews.'

A week after this article, and the visit of Goebbels to Lodz, the Germans began the expulsion of all 40,000 Jews who lived in those regions of Poland which were now annexed to Germany. Most families were forced to leave their homes overnight, abandoning their property, their shops and businesses, and all their possessions save those which could be put on a cart or packed into a suitcase. All those deported were sent into the General Government.

On November 3, it was the fate of ninety-six Polish schoolteachers in the town of Rypin to be summoned to the Gestapo, arrested, and shot, some in their school building, others in nearby woods.

* * *

On October 28 a German bomber on a naval reconnaissance mission was shot down over Scotland, near the village of Humbie. It was the first German aircraft of the war to be brought down on British soil. Two of its crew, Gottlieb Kowalke and Bruno Reimann, were killed, and the other two crew members, the captain, Rolf Niehoff, and the pilot, Kurt Lehmkühl, captured. They were both to spend the next six years as prisoners-of-war, first in Britain and then in Canada.

In the West, preparations mounted to meet a possible German attack. On October 27 a distinguished Canadian soldier, Brigadier H. D. G. Crerar, had arrived in Britain to establish the nucleus of a Canadian military headquarters in London. On November 3, in Washington, at President Roosevelt's urging, Congress repealed that provision in the Neutrality Act which, since 1937, had forbidden both the shipment of American arms to belligerent countries and the granting of economic credits to belligerent countries which wished to buy arms in the United States. Both these barriers to British and French arms purchases were now swept away, and an Anglo-French Purchasing Board set up in Washington. The head of the Board was a British-born Canadian industrialist, Arthur Purvis, who at the outbreak of the First World War, aged twenty-four, had been sent from Britain to the United States to buy up all available stocks of acetone, the scarcity of which was then seriously impeding the British manufacture of explosives. The return of Purvis to America marked an important stage in the Anglo-French search for the arms and munitions with which to confront any German military onslaught.

On November 5, two days after the arms embargo was repealed in Washington, Hitler, having violently abused General von Brauchitsch for the 'defeatist' spirit of the German Army High Command, set November 12 as the date for the attack on France, Belgium and Holland. Two days later, however, Hitler issued a postponement. The points which von Brauchitsch had made at the Chancellery, and which had so outraged him, could not be denied. The Army was unready. The wet winter weather impeded the advance of the tanks and limited the hours of daylight during which the German Air Force could fly. Most important, the Air Force needed five consecutive days of good weather to destroy the French Air Force, a crucial element in the success of 'lightning war'. But the meteorological report on November 7 was too negative for safety.

Ironically, Britain and France had learned of the November 12 date from two separate sources. The first source was General Oster, second in command on Admiral Canaris's Intelligence staff, who on November 7 passed on the date to Colonel Jacobus Sas, the Dutch Military Attache in Berlin. The second source was Paul Thümmel, also a member of Canaris's military Intelligence agency, who, as agent A-54, passed on the same date and details to Western Intelligence through the Czechoslovak Government-in-exile in London. Since 1936, Thümmel had been sending details of German military intentions to Czechoslovak Intelligence. No other military machine had such high placed spies in its midst – in its very nerve centre.

Hitler could easily set aside the date for war, and was to do so several times. But the German New Order in Poland brooked no postponement. On November

5, the day of Hitler's decision to attack in the West, all 167 Polish professors and lecturers at Cracow University were seized by the Gestapo and sent to Sachsenhausen concentration camp, north of Berlin. There, seventeen of them died from the torture to which they were subjected. Those who died included Professor Ignatius Chrzanowski, the foremost historian of Polish literature, Professor Michael Siedlecki, a leading zoologist and former Rector of the University of Vilna, and Professor Stanislas Estreicher, Professor of Western European Jurisprudence, who had earlier refused a German offer to become President of a puppet Polish Protectorate. All three were in their mid-seventies.

Hitler, his attack on the West postponed, travelled on November 8 from Berlin to Munich, to celebrate the sixteenth anniversary of his beer-hall *Putsch*, the moment in 1923 when he had led his followers on an abortive march to seize power in the Bavarian capital. His speech on this particular anniversary was a denunciation of Britain for its 'jealousy and hatred' of Germany. Under Nazi rule, Hitler declared, Germany had achieved more in six years than Britain had achieved in centuries.

Hitler left the beer hall earlier than scheduled, in order to be back in Berlin for a discussion with his generals about the new date for the Western offensive. Eight minutes after he had left, a bomb exploded inside the pillar just behind where he had been speaking. Seven people were killed and more than sixty injured. Hitler was already on the train to Berlin when the news of the explosion reached him. 'Now I am completely content', he remarked. 'The fact that I left the beer hall earlier than usual is corroboration of Providence's intention to let me reach my goal.'

The would-be assassin was caught that same evening at Konstanz, trying to cross the German border into Switzerland. His name was Johann Georg Elser, a thirty-six-year old watchmaker, who had recently been discharged from Dachau concentration camp, near Munich, where he had been held as a Communist sympathizer. Now he was sent to Sachsenhausen as 'Hitler's special prisoner'.

At Munich's Roman Catholic cathedral, Cardinal Michael von Faulhaber, the Archbishop of Munich, celebrated Hitler's 'miraculous escape' from assassination with a solemn mass. There was a more prosaic miracle which Hitler himself could celebrate on November 9, shortly after his return to Berlin – the kidnapping, by ss agents, of two British Intelligence agents in the Netherlands, lured over the Dutch–German border at Venlo. The kidnap plan had been led by the twenty-eight-year-old Alfred Naujocks, who had earlier led the faked 'Polish attack' on Gleiwitz radio station on the eve of the German–Polish war. The aim of the Venlo incident, apart from learning as much as possible of the techniques and plans of British Intelligence, was to give the Germans a pretext for invading Holland, on the grounds that the Dutch, in allowing two British agents to operate on their soil, had abandoned their neutrality.

Hitler appreciated the value of this spectacular kidnap, awarding one of its organizers, Helmut Knochen, the Iron Cross, First and Second Class. Knochen, an expert on the German refugee Press in France, Belgium and Holland, held a doctorate in English literature from Göttingen University. The two British agents, Captain Best and Major Stevens, were imprisoned, first in Sachsenhausen and then in Dachau. A Dutch Intelligence officer, Lieutenant Dirk Klop, who had gone to the border with them, was shot and captured; he died of his wounds later that day, in Düsseldorf.

In Buchenwald concentration camp, November 9 saw the execution of twenty-one Jews who had been forced to work in the stone quarries there. The youngest, Walter Abusch, was only seventeen years old; the oldest, Theodor Kriesshaber, was fifty-five.

November 11 was Polish Independence Day. Two days earlier, in Lodz, the Germans had seized a number of Jews on the street and ordered them to break down the monument to the Polish hero, Kosciuszko. The Jews were old; the monument was strong; even rifle butts could not accelerate their work. The monument was therefore blown up with dynamite. On Polish Independence Day itself, the Germans celebrated by marching past the rubble. That same day, once such a day of rejoicing for the Poles, the Germans took 350 Poles from a labour camp near Gdynia to a prison yard in the town of Wejherowo. There, they were ordered to dig a series of deep pits. Divided into groups, the first was taken to the edge of the pit and shot, the others being forced to watch. As each group was brought to the edge of the pit and shot, they cried out: 'Long live Poland!'

Throughout German-occupied Poland, such atrocities were becoming commonplace. On November 8, in the resort spa of Ciechocinek, a group of fifty Polish officers, now prisoners-of-war, had been led through the streets of the town with their hands above their heads. All were subsequently shot. In Warsaw, on November 9, a thousand Polish intellectuals – writers, journalists, artists – had been arrested.

The expulsion of Poles and Jews from the German-annexed areas was proceeding with considerable speed, amid hardship for those expelled. In all, 120,000 Poles, most of them peasants, were expelled from the Posen district, now known as the Warthegau, 35,000 from Greater Danzig–West Prussia and 15,000 from East Upper Silesia. 'I have been appointed by the Führer', Albert Forster declared at Bydgoszcz on November 27, 'as a trustee of the German cause in this country, with the express order to Germanize it afresh. It will therefore be my task to do everything possible to remove every manifestation of Polonism within the next few years, no matter what the kind.'

For the Jews who were expelled from these annexed regions, one area of relocation was the Lublin district. There, on November 9, Odilo Globocnik was appointed ss and Police Leader; a well-known virulent anti-Semite, he had in the years before the war, as Deputy District Leader of the Nazi Party in Austria, helped pave the way for Hitler's annexation, and Nazi control.

In the General Government, measures were now being taken which surpassed in severity, and indeed in savagery, the random beatings and killings of the six pre-war years of Nazi 'struggle'. On November 15, in Lodz, the main synagogue was set on fire; on German orders the local Polish fire brigades were called out to prevent the flames spreading to the adjoining buildings. In Warsaw, on November 16, a German wall poster curtly announced the execution that day of fifteen Poles, one of them a Jew. In Lublin, Odilo Globocnik's new headquarters, the books from the town's Jewish Religious Academy were taken to the market place and burned. 'It was a matter of special pride', a German eye-witness later reported, 'to destroy the Talmudic Academy, which was known as the greatest in Poland.' The fire lasted twenty-four hours. 'The Lublin Jews', the German recalled, 'assembled around and wept bitterly, almost silencing us with their cries. We summoned the military band, and with joyful shouts the soldiers drowned out the sounds of the Jewish cries.'

'Truly we are cattle in the eyes of the Nazis,' the Warsaw educationalist Chaim Kaplan noted in his diary on 18 November. 'When they supervise Jewish workers they hold a whip in their hands. All are beaten unmercifully.' On November 19 Hitler himself was informed by Himmler, as Himmler's notes record, of the 'shooting of 380 Jews at Ostrow'.

Measures were now begun throughout the General Government to isolate the Jews from the Poles. Among those who had earlier been expelled from the areas of Poland annexed by Germany were the Jews of the small town of Sierpc. When they reached Warsaw with their pathetic bundles, it was seen that, as well as the indignities of expulsion, they had been subjected to a peculiar humiliation while still in Sierpc; each of them had been forced to sew a yellow patch on his or her coat lapel, and to mark the patch with the word 'Jew'. On November 17, in Warsaw, Chaim Kaplan had noted how, when his fellow Warsaw Jews saw the badge, 'their faces were filled with shame'. Kaplan, however, advised a counter-measure, adding, next to the word Jew, the words 'my pride'. When he suggested this to one of the Jews from Sierpc, however, 'the Jew answered, as one who knows, that the conqueror calls such things "sabotage" and condemns the guilty one to death'.

On November 23, Hans Frank announced, from Cracow, that all Jews and Jewesses over the age of ten throughout the General Government must wear a four-inch armband in white, 'marked with the star of Zion on the right sleeve of their inner and outer clothing'. In Warsaw, the star must be blue. 'Transgressors', Frank warned, would be imprisoned. Far worse punishments were already being enacted, however, against the Jews of Warsaw. On the day before Frank's announcement, fifty-three Jews, the inhabitants of No. 9 Nalewki Street, had been executed as a reprisal for the death of a Polish policeman, killed by a Jew who lived at the same address. The Germans had offered to ransom the fifty-three, but when representatives of the Warsaw Jewish Council brought the money to the Gestapo, and handed it over, they were then told that the imprisoned Jews had already been shot. The money was not returned.

The execution of the fifty-three Jews of No. 9 Nalewki Street was the first mass killing of Jews in Warsaw. 'It threw the Jewish population into panic,' one Jew later recalled. Among those killed in this reprisal action was the forty-five-year-old Samuel Zamkowy, one of Warsaw's leading gynaecologists.

Some individuals in the German Army were shocked by what was being done; on November 23, the day after the Nalewki Street executions, General Petzel, the German military commander in the Warthegau, wrote a report, which General Blaskowitz sent on to Hitler, in which he said that in almost 'all major localities' the ss and Gestapo 'carry out public shootings'. More than that, Petzel added: 'Selection is entirely arbitrary and the conduct of the executions in many cases disgusting.'

On November 25, two officials in the Racial Political Office in Berlin, Eberhard Wetzel and Gerhard Hecht, sent the Nazi leaders, including Himmler, their suggestions for the future of the Poles. 'Medical care from our side', they wrote, 'must be limited to the prevention of the spreading of epidemics to Reich territory.' All measures that served to 'limit' the Polish birth rate must be 'tolerated or promoted'. As for the Jews, 'We are indifferent to the hygienic fate of the Jews.' As with the Poles, 'their propagation must be curtailed in every possible way'.

In his plans to force Britain and France to submit, Hitler had launched a weapon intended to revolutionize naval warfare. It was a magnetic mine, detonated by the magnetism of any iron-hulled ship which passed over it. On November 14, in London, Churchill informed the British War Cabinet of this new device, which had begun to wreak havoc on British and French merchant shipping. A German submarine had already laid a line of magnetic mines at a vital point for British seaborne traffic, opposite the entrance to the Thames estuary. A British minelayer, HMS *Adventure*, had struck a mine and been badly damaged. Twelve sailors had been killed.

British naval experts worked around the clock to try to find a means of countering what Churchill called, in the secrecy of the War Cabinet, 'a grave menace which might well be Hitler's "Secret weapon" '. Hitler himself was now deep in his plans for an all out war in the West; on November 15 he discussed these plans with General Rommel, whose military skills had been shown in the Polish campaign. 'The Führer's mind is absolutely made up,' Rommel noted. 'The assassination attempt in Munich has only made his resolution stronger. It is a marvel to witness all this.'

Five days after his discussion with Rommel, Hitler issued a new directive to his senior Army, Navy and Air force commanders, setting out details of the attacks to be mounted against Belgium and Holland. 'Where no resistance is offered', he wrote with reference to Holland, 'the invasion will assume the character of peaceful occupation.' The Navy would undertake the blockade of the Dutch and Belgian coasts.

Meanwhile, the German Navy continued to wreak havoc off the east coast of Britain, dropping magnetic mines into place by aeroplane. These mines sank merchant shipping indiscriminately; on November 19, of five merchant ships sunk, two had been British, one French, one Swedish and one Italian. On November 20 a minesweeper, the *Mastiff*, was itself blown up by a magnetic mine during a sweep. But on November 22 there was a turn in fortune for Britain's sea lifeline; a magnetic mine, dropped by air, had fallen on the mudflats near Shoeburyness, and was nestling on the mud, intact. Recovered the next night, it was dismantled, and its secret discovered. On November 23, work began at the Admiralty to find an antidote.

Hitler knew nothing of the recovery of the magnetic mine. That same day, November 23, he spoke to his generals of the coming attack on Belgium, Holland and France. Britain would not have to be invaded, however, as she 'could be forced to her knees by the U-boat and the mine'.

Hitler's speech was a confident assertion of imminent victory in the West, if the opportunity were taken quickly. 'For the first time in history we have only to fight on one front. The other is at present open. But nobody can be certain how long it will remain so.' His own life, Hitler continued, was of no importance; 'I have led the German people to great achievements, even if we are now an object of hatred in the outside world.' He had decided to live his life so that he could fall 'unashamed' if he had to die. 'I shall stand or fall in this struggle,' he ended. 'I shall never survive the defeat of my people.'

These were stern words. 'The Führer spoke very bluntly,' Rommel wrote on the following day. 'But that seems quite necessary, too, because the more I speak with my comrades, the fewer I find with their heart and conviction in what they are doing.'

At sea, Hitler's confidence continued to seem well placed. On November 24, the day after his speech to his generals, the German battle cruiser *Scharnhorst* sank the British armed merchant cruiser *Rawalpindi* after a fourteen-minute bombardment. In all, 270 British officers and men were drowned; there were only 38 survivors, 27 of whom were picked up by the Germans.

On November 28, as a reprisal for the mining of British coastal waters, the British Government instituted a naval blockade in the North Sea of all German export shipments. On the following day, in his Directive No. 9, Hitler issued further war instructions which began: 'In our fight against the Western Powers, England has shown herself to be the animator of the fighting spirit of the enemy, and the leading enemy power. The defeat of England is essential to final victory'. The 'most effective' means of securing this defeat was 'to cripple the English economy at decisive points'. Once the German Army had defeated the Anglo-French armies in the field, and was 'holding a sector of the coast' opposite England, the paramount task of the German Navy and Air Force would be to 'carry the war' to English industry. This was to be done by naval blockade, mining of the seas, and aerial bombardment of industrial centres and ports.

Minelaying activities off British shores were already on a considerable scale. Now the number of German air reconnaissance flights over Britain were increased. In London, the War Cabinet asked the principal interpretation body of German intentions, the Joint Intelligence Committee, what all these activities meant. On November 30 the committee replied that it was impossible to do more than guess at their significance.

# 3

# Finland defiant

NOVEMBER 1939

On the morning of 30 November 1939 the Red Army launched a massive military assault across the Soviet–Finnish border. To those in Western Europe who had already been at war for nearly three months, it seemed certain that Finland would quickly succumb; twenty-six Soviet divisions, totalling about 465,000 men, had thrown themselves against nine Finnish divisions, totalling 130,000 men. At the same moment, a thousand Soviet aircraft went into action against 150 Finnish aircraft, none of them modern. So confident was the Soviet High Command of a rapid victory that many of its troops wore summer uniforms, despite the imminent onset of winter.

As Hitler's Air Force had earlier bombed Warsaw, so Stalin's Air Force bombed Helsinki. On that first day of war, as a result of a Soviet air raid, sixty-one Finns were killed in the capital. The hospitals were overwhelmed with casualties. 'One dying woman,' a New Zealand born journalist, Geoffrey Cox, later wrote, 'was brought in clutching a dead baby in her arms. One girl, Dolores Sundberg, twelve years old, had both her legs smashed to ragged stumps, and died on the operating table.'

This air raid, and the photographs of it which were reproduced throughout Finland for many weeks to come, convinced the Finns of the need to resist. 'On every front I was to visit later,' Geoffrey Cox recalled, 'man after man spoke angrily of this afternoon of November 30. I saw newspapers and photographs of the burning streets of Helsinki in peasants' homes and workers' flats all over the country. Not a little of the steel strength of Finnish morale in this war was due to the raid on Helsinki.'

On December 2 the Soviet news agency Tass announced the establishment of a People's Government of Finland. But on the frontiers, Finnish resistance was formidable. Small units of Finnish soldiers were able to move rapidly by bicycle and on skis along narrow forest paths. Finnish defenders threw bottles filled with petrol, with lighted rags in their necks, into the turrets of Soviet tanks: this simple but devastatingly effective incendiary grenade was quickly dubbed the 'Molotov cocktail'.

Momentarily, the Russian assault on Finland captured the main headlines of the world's press. In Britain, France and the United States, even in Germany, there was admiration for a small country striving to withstand so massive an attack. But behind the diversion of attention caused by this new war, the cruelties initiated by the old war and the tightening of the Nazi grip continued unabated. By the first week of December, every Polish inmate of the Stralsund mental hospital had been taken to Stutthof camp near Danzig, and shot. Their bodies were then buried by Polish prisoners, who were themselves shot once their gruesome task had been completed. On the new German–Soviet border, at Chelm, in the General Government, patients in the local asylum were lined up and shot by ss troops; those patients who managed to run off were chased through the asylum grounds, hunted down and killed.

Those who supervised these killings were not soldiers, but doctors. On December 2, following complaints to the Reich Ministry of Justice that two ss surgeons, Dr Karl Genzken and Dr Edwin Jung, had conducted successful experiments at Sachsenhausen for sterilizing professional criminals, the head of the concentration camp system, Richard Glueks, pointed out, in a letter to ss General Wolff, the chief of Himmler's personal staff, first that the medical experiments were justified in view of the dangerous nature of the criminals involved, and second that neither doctor could be questioned by the Ministry of Justice, because both had been transferred to the Death's Head Division and were at that very moment serving 'at the front'. It was of course a front on which all fighting had ceased more than two months earlier. Dr Genzken was soon to leave eastern Poland to take up a post in the Medical Inspectorate of the Waffen ss, the medical service of which he was later to become the head.

The work of the ss in Poland was discussed on December 5, in Berlin, by Hitler and Goebbels, who had just returned from Poland. 'I tell him about my trip', Goebbels wrote in his diary. 'He listens to everything very carefully and shares my opinion on the Jewish and Polish question. We must liquidate the Jewish danger. But it will return in a few generations. There is no panacea for it. The Polish aristocracy deserves to be destroyed. It has no links with the people, which it regards as existing purely for its own convenience.' Hans Frank, who had travelled to Berlin with Goebbels, was present during this meeting. 'He has an enormous amount to do,' Goebbels noted, 'and is framing a series of new plans.' Two days later, Hitler issued a new decree, entitled 'Night and Fog', authorizing the seizure of 'persons endangering German security'. Those seized were not to be executed immediately, but were to 'vanish without a trace into the night and fog'. In the concentration camp lists, the German initials 'NN' – *Nacht und Nebel* – against an inmate's name were to signify – execution.

The new policy did not bring an end, however, to the public executions, which were intended to terrify and to deter. On December 8 thirty-one Poles were shot in Warsaw, six of them Jews. It was alleged that they had been involved in 'acts of sabotage'. 'There is no strength left to cry,' Chaim Kaplan wrote in his diary, 'steady and continued weeping finally leads to silence. At first there is screaming; then wailing; and at last a bottomless sigh that does not even leave an echo.'

*             *             *

The Russo-Finnish War, November 1939–March 1940

In Finland, the Red Army continued its advances along an 800–mile front from the Arctic Ocean to the Gulf of Finland. In the far north, the Arctic port of Petsamo was overrun, but at Nautsi, at the Norwegian end of the Arctic highway, the Soviet forces were halted. They were also halted at Kuhmo and Ilomantsi. Three Soviet naval assaults, launched across the Gulf of Finland against the three southern Finnish port cities of Turku, Hango and Porvoo, were repulsed.

In Britain and France, the struggle of Finland to stave off the Soviet attack had aroused strong sympathy. On December 7 the British Prime Minister, Neville Chamberlain, announced that thirty fighter aircraft were being sold to Finland. Four days later, in Geneva, the League of Nations began an emergency debate, which ended with the expulsion of the Soviet Union from the League, and a plea that all possible aid should be given to the Finns. Edouard Daladier, the French Prime Minister, later listed the military aid which France had sent: 145 planes, 496 heavy guns, 5,000 machine guns, 200,000 hand grenades, 400,000 rifles and 20,000,000 rounds of ammunition. British, French and Italians volunteers offered their services to fight, and travelled to Helsinki, where they were welcomed with enthusiasm by the Finns.

On December 12, Finnish troops east of the town of Suomussalmi were in action against a far larger Soviet assault force. Lacking artillery or anti-tank weapons, the Finns were able nevertheless to hold the line for five days, in temperatures that had fallen far below zero. Soviet reinforcements under General Vinogradov, caught along a narrow earth road hemmed in by dense trees, were attacked in fierce hand to hand fighting, by Finnish troops determined not to yield. On other sectors of the front as well, the Red Army tanks were unable to make progress against Finnish mines and Molotov cocktails; Finnish soldiers even used logs to wrench tracks off tanks.

Watching the course of the Finnish battle with admiration for the fight being put up by the Finns, Hitler was busy preparing for his own Western battle. On December 12 he ordered a substantial increase, almost double, in German artillery ammunition, as well as the mass manufacture of naval mines. He had already ordered a substantial increase in submarine construction. But the war at sea did not always go in his favour; in the South Atlantic on December 13, the German pocket battleship *Graf Spee*, having sunk three British merchant ships in five days, was tracked down by three British cruisers, *Achilles*, *Ajax* and *Exeter* and, having been hit more than fifty times, sought sanctuary in Uruguayan territorial waters. Four days later, she was scuttled by her captain, Hans Langsdorff. Two days later, Langsdorff shot himself in a hotel room in Montevideo.

The British public, still puzzled that it had not been possible to save Poland, and sceptical of the efficacy of the 'confetti war' – the total number of propaganda leaflets now printed had risen to 118,500,000 – rejoiced at a naval victory. In German-occupied Poland, however, the scourge of tyranny grew ever more severe. On December 11 all Jews living within the borders of the General Government became liable to two years' forced labour, with a possible extension 'if its educational purpose is not fulfilled'. The tasks were supervised harshly: clearing swamps, paving roads and building fortifications along the new Soviet border. On December 14, when 1,500 Jews were deported from Poznan into the General Government, they were told that they could bring with them as much luggage as they wished. That evening the luggage was loaded into special goods wagons on their train. Just before the train was about to leave, the goods wagons were uncoupled. The Jews were deported with only the clothes they were wearing.

What the fate of the Jews in the General Government would be, no one knew, not even the Germans. 'We cannot shoot 2,500,000 Jews,' Hans Frank wrote in his diary on December 19, 'neither can we poison them. We shall have to take steps, however, designed to extirpate them in some way – and this will be done.'

The war at sea continued; on December 17 five passenger liners, converted into troopships, and escorted by a battle-cruiser, a battleship and an aircraft-carrier, arrived safely in Britain from across the Atlantic. On board were 7,500 men, Canadians, all volunteers in the war against Germany. Two days after their arrival, the German Navy launched the 7,860 ton armed cruiser *Atlantis*, converted from a freighter. For the next three and a half months she was to be prepared for a dramatic mission. The ship was to contain a special compartment, capable of holding ninety-two magnetic mines. Also being prepared was a camouflaged armament of six six-inch guns and two anti-aircraft guns. The *Atlantis* was to be given the task of sinking or capturing Allied merchant shipping. To help her do so, she would also carry various national flags to fly as a deceptive friendly greeting whenever she came across a merchantman; these flags included the British, Dutch and Norwegian.

The *Atlantis* was to prove a successful raider, one of Germany's deadliest. But the 'secret weapon' of the magnetic mine was about to lose its terror. On December 19 the British Admiralty was able to report to the War Cabinet that a system had been devised, whereby individual ships could be demagnetized by means of a coil wrapped around the ship. Once demagnetized, the ship's resistance to the magnetic mine was greatly increased. In order to keep this success secret from the Germans, Churchill gave instructions that whenever a ship was sunk by an ordinary mine, 'it will be well to state that they are sunk by magnetic mines whenever this possibility exists'. And to President Roosevelt, Churchill telegraphed with understandable relief: 'We think we have got hold of its tail.'

December 22 was Stalin's sixtieth birthday. Among the telegrams of greeting which he received was one from Hitler. Two days later, Hitler left Berlin for Munich. There, in conversation with Else Brückmann, a friend of twenty years, he spoke of how he would force Britain to her knees over the next eight months by using magnetic mines. Travelling to the Western Front, he was able, opposite the French village of Spicheren, to cross over the frontier at a point where the Germans had pushed the French back during a brief skirmish in September.

As Hitler toured his military units in the West, joining in their Christmas celebrations, his rule in the East was marked by yet another lurch into barbarism. In the small Polish town of Wawer, across the River Vistula from Warsaw, two German soldiers had been killed by two Polish common criminals seeking to evade arrest. Two hours later, 170 men and boys were rounded up in Wawer and in the neighbouring village of Anin. One woman was forced by the Germans to chose which of her menfolk should be taken – her father, her brother or her son. All 170 of those seized were taken to a nearby railway tunnel, where they had to stand for several hours with their hands above their heads. They were then taken out in groups of ten and shot. The last ten were reprieved; they had to dig the graves of those who had been murdered. Among the dead was a twelve-year-old boy, Stefanek Dankowski, and two American citizens, whose American passports were of no avail to them, a man named Szczgiel and his sixteen-year-old son.

While Hitler's police and Gestapo consolidated their cruel grip on Poland, Stalin's Army was facing a weaker enemy that nevertheless would not give up its resistance. The Finns not only were trying to hold the line, but were also trying to drive the Russians out of Finland altogether. The day of the Wawer massacre near Warsaw was also the day of a Finnish counter-attack at Suomussalmi which, after four days, in temperatures of thirty-five degrees centigrade below zero, drove the Soviet 163rd Division and General Vinogradov's 54th Division back across the Soviet frontier. More than 1,500 Russian troops were buried by the Finns. But 25,000 more lay dead under the snow, either killed in action, or dying, wounded, in the frozen air. General Vinogradov was later executed for his failure.

For the Finnish troops on other sectors of the front, the victory at Suomussalmi was a powerful boost to their morale. Colonel Hjalmar Siilasvuo, who had commanded the Finnish defenders, was promoted general and sent sixty miles further south, in pursuit of another Russian division, pinned down in the woods at Kuhmo. After the war, he was to write, of the defenders of Suomussalmi: 'They showed the road of glory to the people, which was full of hardship, but the only way.'

Returning to Berlin, Hitler was confronted with a letter, sent from Switzerland on December 28, from Fritz Thyssen, the industrialist who had so strongly supported him between 1932 and 1935. Thyssen had protested in 1937 about the persecution of Christianity in Germany and in 1938 about the persecution of the Jews. 'Now', he wrote, 'you have concluded a pact with Communism. Your Propaganda Ministry even dares to state that the good Germans who voted for you, the professed opponents of Communism, are, in essence, identical with those beastly anarchists who have plunged Russia into tragedy and who were described by you yourself as "bloodstained common criminals".'

The quotation was from Hitler's book, *Mein Kampf*, first published in 1925. But Hitler had no intention of breaking his pact with Stalin, until, at least, he had brought Britain to her knees. Nor did he intend to moderate in any way his attitude to the Jews. 'The Jewish–capitalistic world', he declared on December 30, in a New Year's message to the German people, 'will not survive the twentieth century.' For the Jews in German-occupied Poland, this did not seem an idle prophecy. During the first week of January 1940, as many as seventy Jews were dying of starvation each day in Warsaw alone. On January 2, in an attempt to conceal the scale of these deaths, the General Government forbade the posting of obituary notices.

Strict curfews were enforced throughout the General Government. In Warsaw, Jews had to be in their houses by eight at night. Those who were not, even if they had a special pass, could be shot. For Poles, the beginning of January saw yet another tragedy on the scale of the Wawer shootings of mid-December. At one of the Warsaw stations, sealed cattle trucks arrived. In them, thirteen days earlier, had been locked 2,000 Polish prisoners-of-war being sent back from a camp in East Prussia. When the trucks were unlocked, 211 of the soldiers were found frozen to death. The survivors were emaciated; several more died within hours of their arrival. Others had been driven insane by their thirteen day ordeal. That same week, on January 7, at Plaszow station just outside Cracow, in a cattle truck which arrived from the Warthegau, carrying Poles expelled from that German-annexed province, twenty-eight bodies were found. At Debica station, eighty miles further east, thirty children were found frozen to death in a single truck.

Hitler's war was about to spread from East to West, with the planned invasion of Britain, Operation Yellow, waiting only for a clear spell of good weather to be set in train. Preparations for Britain's defeat continued without respite. On January 3, German naval Intelligence had received a report from one of its agents in the United States, Marie Koedel, reporting on those American military supplies purchased by Britain which were being loaded at Hamilton dock in Brooklyn, on the ships being loaded, and on their sailing schedules. Marie Koedel was even able to enlist the services of a British sailor who had jumped ship, Duncan Scott-Ford; later he was uncovered, captured, brought back to Britain, tried and hanged. But the information he sent back, as that of Mary Koedel, added to the German understanding of British shipping operations. A considerable amount of German information also came, not from any individual spy, but from a careful reading of the uninhibited American press.

Along the Norwegian coast, German merchant ships were flouting Norwegian neutrality to bring Swedish iron-ore, vital for the German war effort, from the railhead at Narvik to the German North Sea ports. On January 6 the British Foreign Secretary, Lord Halifax, warned the Norwegian Government of Britain's intention to lay mines in Norwegian waters in order to force these German ships out to sea, where they could be attacked. The warning was noted, but the mines were not laid, and the German ore ships continued on their way unmolested. Two days later, uncertain how long its Atlantic lifeline could be kept open, the British Government extended food rationing, hitherto limited to meat, to butter and sugar. But a sense of confidence, or at least of lack of danger, permeated Britain; that same day, January 8, saw the return to their homes in London of the last of 316,192 children, almost half of those who had been evacuated to the countryside on the outbreak of war.

One man who did fear a German attack on Britain was the Italian dictator,

Benito Mussolini. On January 8 the Italian Ambassador in Berlin handed Hitler a letter from Mussolini, asking if it was really worthwhile 'to risk all – including the regime – and to sacrifice the flower of German generations, in order to hasten the fall of a fruit which must of necessity fall and be harvested by us, who represent the new forces of Europe'. The 'big democracies', Mussolini added, 'carry within themselves the seeds of their decadence'.

Hitler made no reply. Mussolini made no further protest. Two days later, on the afternoon of January 10, at a meeting with his commanders-in-chief, Hitler set January 17 as the date for the attack on the West. Saturation bombing of French airfields would begin on January 14. Two million German soldiers were in position along the borders with Holland, Belgium, Luxemburg and France. Ten to twelve days of clear weather were forecast. Operation Yellow could go ahead. But on the following day Hitler was told of a possible setback to his plans; a light German Air Force plane had strayed across the Belgian frontier and crash-landed near the Belgian town of Mechelen-sur-Meuse. One of its passengers, Major Helmut Reinberger, had with him in his briefcase the operation plans for the airborne attack on Belgium. While burning the plans, the Major was seized by Belgian soldiers. 'It is things like this that can lose us the war!' was Hitler's frank comment on learning of the crash landing. That afternoon, however, he confirmed that the invasion of the West was to proceed as planned on January 17.

One immediate effect of the crash of Major Reinberger was an order, issued by Hitler on January 11, to be put up in every military headquarters, that 'No one – no agency, no officer – is permitted to learn more about a matter that is to be kept secret that he absolutely needs to know for official purposes.' Not any breach of security, but the possibility of fog, led, on the afternoon of January 13, to Hitler ordering a three day postponement of the offensive, to January 20. But that same evening it became clear in Berlin that both the Dutch and Belgian armies had begun to mobilize their troops on the border. Also on the evening of January 13, Colonel Hans Oster, the deputy chief of the German Secret Service, passed on details of the imminent assault to the Dutch Military Attaché in Berlin, Major Sas, who in turn passed them on to his Belgian colleague, Colonel Goethals, who sent them by coded message to Brussels. As German Intelligence was reading the Belgian codes, this particular leak must have become known in Berlin on the morning of January 14. Even so, it would seem to have been the worsening weather, rather than any fear of an alerted resistance, that finally persuaded Hitler, on the afternoon of January 16, just before the postponed air strikes would have had to begin, to postpone the offensive yet again. 'If we cannot count on at least eight days of fine and clear weather,' Hitler informed his staff, 'then we will call it off until the spring.'

War in the West had been postponed yet again; in Finland, Soviet strategists had embarked upon a new method, heavy air bombardment of road and rail junctions, Army depots and docks, in the hope of being able to launch an effective military strike later in the month. On January 14 alone, thirty-five different towns and villages were bombed. Aid from the West, promised in the first days of December, was now beginning to reach the Finns in significant quantities. Volunteers, too, were starting to arrive. Despite a strong Soviet protest, on January 13 the Swedish Government agreed to a British request to allow volunteers to pass through Sweden, provided they travelled unarmed, without uniforms and without being on active service with the Allied armies.

The British Government waited uneasily for some intimation of when the German blow in the West might fall. Hitherto, it was from last-minute tips from men like Colonel Oster, or the chance of mislaid documents such as those of Major Reinberger, that dates and details might become known. But, during January, a remarkable Intelligence success was, in due course, to transform British Intelligence-gathering, and Britain's war-making capacity. During that month British cryptographers began to read, with some frequency, messages sent by the most secret system of German communication, the Enigma machine.

This crucial development of the war was not a British effort alone; for many months French cryptographers had been equally active in what was essentially a joint Anglo–French effort against the clock. Both the British and the French were indebted to pioneering work done for more than a decade by Polish mathematicians. It was above all a Pole, Marian Rejewski, helped by material obtained by a French secret agent, Asché, who made the crucial breakthrough in Poland before the war. On 16 August 1939, two weeks before the outbreak of war, Polish Intelligence handed its British counterparts the latest model of a rebuilt Enigma machine.

The breakthrough of January 1940 was one of method; it had no immediate benefit for the Allied cause. The cypher which had been broken, after prodigious effort, was a German Army Enigma key used on October 28, more than two and a half months earlier. It was to take nearly nine months before the first of several Enigma keys, the one used by the German Air Force, was to be broken regularly, and at times almost simultaneously with the despatch of the message from Berlin to the field commanders. Nevertheless, the success of mid-January, for all its limitations, was one which was in due course to have a profound influence on the conduct of the war.

There was nothing secret about the German terror in the East. Details of most atrocities were smuggled to the West within days. Neutral diplomats in Berlin were well informed. Public wall posters throughout Poland openly publicized the executions.

Mass executions had become the method both of seeking to cow the Polish population and of destroying those Germans who were considered unworthy of life. On January 9, the Chief of the ss and Police of Greater Danzig–West Prussia, Dr Hildebrandt, informed Himmler that the two units of stormtroopers at his disposal had carried out 'the elimination of about 4,000 incurable patients from Polish mental hospitals', as well as a further 2,000 German mental patients at a mental hospital in Pomerania.

Reprisals, publicly announced, were also a feature of the new terror. On January 18, following the capture of Andrzej Kott, the leader of a clandestine youth association in Warsaw – a young man whose family had converted from Judaism to Catholicism long before – the Gestapo arrested 255 Jews at random, took them to the Palmiry woods outside Warsaw, and shot them. Four days later, as the death toll of Polish civilians since the outbreak of war was estimated at 15,000, the Pope broadcast from the Vatican: 'The horror and inexcusable excesses committed on a helpless and a homeless people have been established by the unimpeachable testimony of eye-witnesses'.

Germany Army officers were among those eye-witnesses: on the day of the Pope's broadcast, Major General Friedrich Mieth, Chief of Staff of the German First Army, told his assembled officers: 'The ss has carried out mass executions without proper trials,' executions which had 'besmirched' the honour of the German Army. Hitler was informed of Mieth's speech, and Mieth was dismissed.

On January 25, from his headquarters in Cracow, Hans Frank issued an order for the remodelling of the Polish economy within the General Government 'for the immediate reinforcement of the military power of the Reich'. Poland was henceforth to provide Germany with the wood, the raw materials, the chemicals and even the manpower that she needed. One item of Frank's order authorized 'Preparations and transportation into the Reich of not fewer than one million male and female agricultural and industrial workers, including approximately 750,000 agricultural workers, at least fifty per cent of whom must be women – in order to safeguard agricultural production in the Reich and supply the deficiency of industrial labour in the Reich.'

Thus the slave labour system, already applied to Jews, was extended to Poles, just as it already applied to Czechs. 'A hundred thousand Czech workmen', Churchill told a public audience in Manchester on January 27, 'had been led off into slavery to be toiled to death in Germany.' But what was happening to the Czechs, Churchill added, 'pales in comparison with the atrocities which, as I speak here this afternoon, are being perpetrated upon the Poles'. From the 'shameful records' of the Germans' mass executions in Poland, Churchill declared, 'we may judge what our fate would be if we fell into their clutches. But from them also we may draw the force and inspiration to carry us forward on our journey and not to pause or rest till liberation is achieved and justice is done.'

On January 30, three days after Churchill's speech, Reinhard Heydrich established in Berlin a new government department, IV-D-4, whose task was to complete the deportation plans of Jews from the annexed regions of western Poland, and to handle all future deportation of Jews from wherever they were to be brought, and to whatever destination.

On January 29, confronted by continued Finnish military resistance, the Soviet Government began secret negotiations in Sweden, based upon a willingness to abandon the 'People's Government of Finland', made up of Communist nominees, and to talk instead with the existing Government of Risto Ryti. From that moment it was clear that some form of compromise could be reached; that the war, savage though it still was at the front, was now a war, not about the introduction of Communism into Finland, but about borders and fortresses; an attempt to satisfy the Soviet desire for a longer coastline on the Gulf of Finland for the protection of Leningrad, as well as some measure of control at the

Scandinavia, 1940

entrance to the Gulf, and a greater measure of Soviet territorial control in Karelia.

The way was now clear for peace. Two days later, it was announced in Helsinki that 377 Finnish civilians had been killed in Soviet air raids since the beginning of the war two months earlier.

Despite the opening of secret talks, the Russo-Finnish war continued. On February 1, under the command of General Timoshenko, the Red Army launched a large-scale offensive against the principal Finnish defences, the Mannerheim Line. But despite a combination of simultaneous tank, infantry and air attack, the line still held; by February 3 it was clear that the Soviet Union would not be able to secure an early victory. Two days later, on February 5, the British and French Prime Ministers, meeting in Paris as the Supreme War Council, agreed to intervene militarily in Finland, and to send an expeditionary force of at least three divisions. 'Finland', said Neville Chamberlain, 'must not be allowed to disappear off the map.' It was also agreed in principle that the Allies should take control of the Swedish iron ore fields at Gällivare. If this were done by landing a force at Narvik, which could then cross Sweden to Finland, as part of the British help to Finland, this would offer the preferred prospect, as Chamberlain expressed it, 'of killing two birds with one stone'. In fact, a decision was reached to effect the initial help to Finland by a landing at three Norwegian ports, Stavanger, Bergen and Trondheim, an operation to be carried out by Force 'Stratford', and to begin on March 20. Only by beginning then, Chamberlain explained to the War Cabinet on February 7, would Britain and France 'be sure of forestalling the Germans'.

Whether such help would come in time was cast into jeopardy three days later, when Soviet forces attacked the Mannerheim Line in such strength that the line was breached. But by a supreme effort of martial vigour, within forty-eight hours the Finns had fallen back in good order to a second defensive line, which held. It was not to be a very long respite, however. On February 13, a further Soviet attack led to a half mile long break in the second line. The Finnish troops thrown into the breach, from Finland's crack regiment, the Tavast Light Horse, were almost completely wiped out. Wave after wave of Soviet troops now exploited the gap; this was the tactic devised by the Soviet Minister of Defence, Marshal Voroshilov, of the 'crescendo offensive'. In a communiqué issued on the evening of February 13, the Finnish High Command admitted to the loss of 'a few of our most advanced positions'. Geoffrey Cox, the British journalist who had been with the Finnish Army since early December, later recalled: 'It was the first of the bulletins of gradual defeat which were to come steadily, day after day, till the end of the war.'

Numbers had proved decisive. By February 16 the Finnish troops were exhausted. Their reserves had been used up. No serious counter-attack was any longer possible. The Red Army still had men to spare.

The day of gloom in Finland was a day of satisfaction in Britain; for on February 16, in Jösing Fjord, just south of Egersund, sailors from a British destroyer, the *Cossack,* violating Norwegian neutrality, boarded a German supply ship sheltering in Norwegian waters, before making a dash through the Skagerrak to the Baltic. The German ship was the *Altmark*; locked below her hatches were 299 British sailors and merchant seamen who had been taken prisoner in the South Atlantic. There was a short fight, four German sailors were killed, and the British prisoners-of-war were released.

As a reward for this exploit, the Captain of the *Cossack*, Philip Vian, was awarded the Distinguished Service Order. German propagandists denounced the British violation of Norwegian neutrality. But Hitler took the view that history judged only between successes or failure; nobody asked the victor if he had been in the right or in the wrong. The British Government, in answer to a formal protest from Norway about the violation of its territorial waters, replied that Norway itself had violated international law by allowing its waters to be used by the Germans to transport British prisoners to Germany.

The greatest violation of international law that February was not, however, taking place in a Norwegian fjord. On February 2, in Poland, General Ulex, the German Commander-in-Chief of the Frontier Sector South, had written in protest to his senior officer, General Blaskowitz: 'The recent increase in the use of violence by the police shows an almost incredible lack of human and moral qualities; the word "brutish" is almost justified.' General Ulex continued: 'The only solution I can see to this revolting situation which sullies the honour of the entire German people, is that all police formations together with all their senior commanders, should be dismissed in a body and their units disbanded.'

Blaskowitz now drew up a list of ss crimes, citing in detail thirty-three incidents of the murder and rape of Poles and Jews, and the looting of Polish and Jewish property. As to the German Army officers and men under his command, their attitude to the ss and German police, Blaskowitz noted on February 6, 'alternates between abhorrence and hatred. Every soldier feels disgusted and repelled by these crimes committed in Poland by nationals of the Reich and representatives of our State.'

Angered by these accusations, on February 13 Hans Frank travelled to Berlin to ask Hitler to dismiss Blaskowitz. Two days later, Blaskowitz reiterated his charges in a letter to General von Brauchitsch. His protest was to no avail; incidents such as those of which he had complained continued on a daily basis, against individuals, and against those dragooned into forced labour gangs. 'The humiliations and tortures inflicted upon the Jewish workmen', the *Manchester Guardian* reported on February 18, 'who are compelled by their Nazi overseers to dance and sing and undress during their work, and are even forced to belabour each other with blows, show no signs of abating.'

Not only Polish Jews, but all Poles, were to be subjected to the harshest cruelty. On February 21, Richard Gluecks, head of the German Concentration Camp Inspectorate, informed Himmler that he had found a suitable site for a new 'quarantine' camp, in which Poles could be held, and punished, and put to work, for any acts of rebellion or disobedience. The site was, a former Austro Hungarian cavalry barracks, a series of imposing, well-built brick buildings, on the outskirts of the Polish town of Oswiecim, now, having been annexed to the German Reich, known once more by its German name, Auschwitz.

It was not intended to use Auschwitz as a place of incarceration for Jews; its sole initial purpose was as a punishment camp for Poles. Work began at once to convert the barracks to a camp, and to find, from the existing German concentration camps, suitable personnel to administer and supervise a regime which was intended from the outset to be of the utmost severity.

# 4

# The Scandinavian cockpit

Hitler intended to conquer Britain, or at least to bring Britain to her knees, before turning his armies against Russia. Stalin intended to protect Soviet neutrality for as long as possible. In August 1939 he had made his pact with Hitler; this had not only spared him involvement in the German–Polish war in defence of Poland, but had given him a substantial swathe of Polish territory. Following the German defeat of Poland, Stalin had still further protected himself against a possible German attack by asserting Soviet predominance over, and acquiring military bases in, Lithuania, Latvia and Estonia, thus making sure that the Baltic Sea would not be used against him, at least not as easily as it might have been without control of the Baltic States. At the end of November he had sought to establish a Communist government in Finland; this had failed. Now he strove to conquer at least a defensive belt of territory from Finland.

Did Stalin foresee a German onslaught on the Soviet Union? On 15 November 1939 he had approved a decision of the Red Army's Chief Military Council to reduce by more than one third the strength of the permanent border Fortified Areas. Six days later, he himself had been present at a session of the council which decided to disband all the Soviet tank corps as soon as possible, in deference to the views of General Kulik, that cavalry still had a major part to play in war. Undoubtedly there were decisions which weakened the Soviet defence capacity. At the same time, he tried to drive as hard a bargain as possible with Hitler; by a commercial agreement signed in Moscow on 11 February, 1940, the Soviet Union, in return for oil and agricultural products, was to receive manufactured goods, arms and the blueprints of the most recent developments in naval armaments, as well as prototypes of the most recent aircraft, anti-aircraft artillery, bombs and tanks.

Hitler accepted Stalin's demands. He was determined to do everything necess-ary to keep the Soviet Union neutral while Germany attacked in the West. Even the blueprints of Germany's most modern battleship, the *Bismarck*, were handed over. Hitler was still confident that he could in due course conquer Russia, but he was equally certain that he could not win in the West unless he could be guaranteed a one-front war. Yet even in the West there were dangers. One, of which he knew nothing, was the sinking by a minesweeper, HMS *Gleaner*, on February 12 of a German submarine, U-33. From the submarine, once she settled at thirty fathoms, were recovered three Enigma rotors. This marked one more step forward in the slow breaking of Germany's most secret wartime communications system. Unfortunately for Britain, and luckily for Hitler, the three naval Enigma keys could not be broken. But they did give the British Government's cryptanalysts at Bletchley Park, north-west of London, an important insight into German operating procedures. The three cypher keys recovered from the submarine were given the code names 'Dolphin', 'Pike' and 'Oyster', and strenuous efforts were put in train to break them. 'Dolphin', which was used by all German surface vessels, was briefly broken, giving Britain a short, temporary advantage.

For his skill in sinking the submarine, and in recovering its precious Enigma rotors, the Captain of the *Gleaner*, Lieutenant-Commander Hugh Price, was decorated with the Distinguished Service Order.

While British Intelligence continued to try to develop methods of decrypting more of the most secret German messages, which they could as yet read only irregularly, Soviet Intelligence was able to keep a close watch on the vulnerable Soviet frontier with Japan. All Stalin's calculations about when and how to act in the West, if he were to act at all, had to take into account the substantial Soviet frontier with Japanese-occupied Manchuria. Japan's strength and intentions were an integral part of the Soviet policy equation.

Soviet Intelligence was fortunate that a German journalist in Tokyo, Richard Sorge, who was a Soviet agent, had close contacts inside the German Embassy. Indeed, the Embassy staff, and even the Ambassador, frequently called on Sorge for his views and comments; in September 1939 the Embassy had appointed him editor of their daily news bulletin. On February 16 Sorge was able to send Moscow a detailed account of the Japanese output of munitions, aircraft and trucks, together with a report on the factories which made them, and on the iron and steel production of Japan. Using the code name 'Ramsay', Sorge enabled Stalin to gauge the danger threatened on his most distant, but no less vulnerable flank.

It was from German Intelligence's reading of British naval signals that Hitler learned of a threat to Germany very close to home; the Anglo-French plan to land a military force at Stavanger, Bergen and Trondheim, as decided upon by Britain and France on February 5. At German Army Headquarters at Zossen, near Berlin, a special unit under Hitler's personal supervision, headed by a naval captain, Theodor Krancke, worked to organize a counter-move. The plan which the unit evolved was to land German troops at seven points: not only Stavanger, Bergen, Trondheim and Narvik, but also Arendal, Kristiansand and Oslo, the Norwegian capital. On February 21 Hitler appointed General Nikolaus von Falkenhorst to command the invasion; working with Captain Krancke's unit, von Falkenhorst widened the plan to include the invasion of Denmark, in order to secure the lines of communication between Germany and Norway.

A new war was in the offing; British and German naval, air and Army personnel were in training. British troops who had been preparing to go to

France were told that there was a new destination with new conditions, including ice and snow. Their training was to be adapted accordingly. On the evening of February 24, Pilot Officer Reginald Whitmarsh, aged twenty, took off from Croydon aerodrome in a Blenheim bomber on his first practice solo night flight. He crashed on take-off, hitting a house at the edge of the aerodrome. Whitmarsh was killed. So too, in the house, were a mother, Doris Bridge, and her five-year-old daughter Jill. Commenting on the accident, the coroner said that Whitmarsh had died 'no less gallantly and bravely' than if he had been in battle.

British pilots were in the air on February 25, at the start of an intensive, six-day mission over Berlin, Bremen, Kiel, Lübeck, Cologne and Hamburg. This was the largest leaflet-dropping campaign of the war. The leaflets, known in the Air Ministry as 'white bombs', were intended to warn of the evils of Nazism; in Poland no such warnings were needed. An eye-witness report sent from Katowice on February 27, and reaching the West, where it was immediately publicized by the Polish Government in exile in Paris, told of 'mass executions' of Poles near the city's municipal park: 'Among the victims were priests. Their eyes were bandaged with pocket handkerchiefs. After the volley had been fired, these same handkerchiefs, bloodstained though they might be, were used to bandage the eyes of others of the condemned. One of the priests was not killed and began to rise. He was then despatched by blows from gun-butts'.

The military purposes of Germany were not served by such executions; at the end of February, in an attempt to make full and effective use of the mass of manpower now at Germany's disposal, it was decided in Berlin to find someone who would supervise and centralize the direction of labour, including that of the conquered Czechs and Poles, in munitions factories throughout the Reich. The man chosen for this task was Dr Fritz Todt; the system which he was to set up, known as the Todt Organization, was soon to become the largest single employer of labour in Germany, sending men and women to industrial regions throughout the Reich where munitions bottlenecks or deficiencies needed to be put right. At the same time, Todt ensured that the arms industry made the most economical use possible of raw materials and metals which were in short supply.

Allied organization was proving less effective. Even Britain's Force 'Stratford', the promised military expedition to Finland due to start on March 20, would, the Finnish Minister to London told Lord Halifax on March 1, come 'too late' to help Finland. That same day, the British Chiefs of Staff warned that, as a military operation, the expeditionary force would not work; even 'mild' opposition from Sweden, as now seemed likely, would make it impossible for the Franco-British force to reach Finland in time to be of help, or even to reach the iron ore fields at Gällivare en route, 'before a German force could get there'. On March 4 'Stratford' was abandoned. One member of the British War Cabinet was much relieved; Churchill was convinced that British involvement in the Russo-Finnish war 'could not be regarded as a profitable diversion, since German forces were not engaged'. Any despatch even of further aircraft to Finland, he warned his War Cabinet colleagues, would 'weaken ourselves against Germany.'

German plans to occupy Norway and Denmark were taken a stage nearer to completion on March 1, when Hitler issued a detailed directive, 'Weser-exercise', in the first paragraph of which he explained that this new operation of war 'would anticipate English action against Scandinavia and the Baltic, would secure our supplies of iron ore from Sweden, and would provide the Navy and Air Force with expanded bases for operations against England'. Weakness in German numbers, Hitler added, 'will be made good by skilful action and surprise in execution'. The campaign was to have 'the character of a peaceful occupation, designed to protect by force of arms the neutrality of the northern countries', but any Norwegian or Danish resistance would be 'broken by all means available'.

The Norwegian campaign, Hitler concluded, would be the 'most daring and most important undertaking in the history of warfare'.

On March 4 Soviet forces launched a massive attack on the Finnish city of Viipuri. The ice, which had hindered their earlier attacks because it was too thin, was now thick and hard, enabling them to attack across the water, bypassing the Mannerheim Line. One Soviet column crossed thirty-four miles of ice, attacking the Finnish coastline between Helsinki and Viipuri, in the rear of the city's defenders. Soviet artillery set up its positions offshore, bombarding the Viipuri defence lines from the ice. These renewed bombardments continued throughout the night, as did Soviet bomber attacks from the air. Then, on the morning of March 5, the Soviet Government announced that it was 'once more' prepared to negotiate peace with Finland. The Finnish Government, unable to resist the renewed military onslaught, accepted. Shortly after midday on March 7, the Finnish Prime Minister, Risto Ryti, arrived in Moscow by air. He had come to talk peace; but around Viipuri the battle continued. On March 9, while Ryti was still in Moscow, a communiqué issued in Helsinki admitted that the second Finnish defence line had now been turned. 'In these last bitter days of fighting', Geoffrey Cox recalled, 'the battle was more intense than at any time in the whole war.'

As the Russo-Finnish peace talks continued in Moscow, German preparations for the invasion of Norway continued. Anglo-French plans to go to Finland's help having been abandoned, there was, from March 4, no British or French operation of war in prospect. 'Those who understand the political and military situation', Chaim Kaplan noted in his diary in Warsaw on March 7, 'are going about like mourners. There is no ground for hope that the decisive action will come this spring, and lack of a decision means that our terrible distress will last a long time.' On March 8, in Cracow, a Polish workman who was overheard by a member of the Gestapo humming the tune of the national anthem, 'Poland Has Not Yet Perished' was shot dead in the street.

The inability of Britain to take any initiative was highlighted on March 8, when the British Chiefs of Staff revealed, in a secret report, that of the 352 anti-aircraft guns intended for the British Expeditionary Force in France, only 152 had arrived. Of the forty-eight light anti-aircraft guns needed by the British Advanced Air Striking Force in France for its protection against a possible German counter-attack, not one had arrived. For the defence of Britain itself, the planned armaments had simply not become available; of 1,860 anti-aircraft guns considered the minimum needed for the Air Defence of Great Britain, no more than 108 were in place. These had been, of necessity, concentrated around naval bases and radar stations, leaving aircraft industries 'and other vital points unprotected against the very form of attack which is likely to fall upon them'.

Britain's own air activity was still confined to dropping leaflets. When leaflet raids were made on the Ruhr between March 5 and March 7, one of the pilots reported that 'the glow of the blast-furnaces was easily seen'. On March 9, leaflets were dropped over Prague. That same day, an irate Englishman, H. Harwood, wrote to the magazine *Time and Tide*: 'Finland is in extremis, Poland's death-rattle echoes through Europe. In both cases lack of air power has been the decisive factor. There are doubtless many good reasons why we have been powerless to help, but is that a reason for adding mockery to impotence? If petrol and pilots are not to be lightly risked even for vital objects, what is the excuse for sending machines 1,400 miles across enemy country to drop leaflets?'

A decision was about to be made by the British War Cabinet to embark upon Britain's first military operation of the war. It did so at the very moment when President Roosevelt's Under-Secretary of State, Sumner Welles, was visiting Rome, Berlin, Paris and London, in search of a formula to bring the war to an end before it widened. Welles had spoken to Hitler in Berlin; on March 10 he reached London. But before Welles could put his peace proposals to Neville Chamberlain, the War Cabinet, over which Chamberlain presided, decided to send a British military force to the Norwegian port of Narvik, seizing a million and a half tons of iron ore waiting there for shipping to Germany, and preparing to move across the Swedish frontier to seize the iron ore fields at Gällivare. In addition to this Narvik operation, which was given the code name 'Wilfred', British forces would land at three other Norwegian ports, Trondheim, Stavanger and Bergen, in order to forestall any German counter-attack.

Later that day, when Sumner Welles explained his peace plan to Chamberlain and Halifax, stressing to them that it would involve the progressive disarmament of the belligerents, the British Ministers replied that 'we could not trust Hitler; that even with a considerable measure of disarmament, Germany could easily overrun a weak country, e.g. Roumania'. Britain might agree, the ministers said, to give 'a formal undertaking to the United States not to attack Germany', but must be free to fulfil 'obligations of assistance to a third party which might be a victim of German aggression'.

On the day after this declaration of principle, the British War Cabinet gave formal authority to the military landing at Narvik. Once news had been received of a successful landing there, a second force would land at Trondheim. Further forces would be held in readiness for Stavanger and Bergen. It was also decided, at this meeting on March 12, that no communication should be made to the Norwegian Government 'as to our intention to land a force at Narvik' until the ships had actually arrived at the port.

Britain's decision to take this military initiative, and thereby, it was hoped, to deprive the Germans of their essential supplies of iron ore, was followed a day later by the signature in Moscow of a Russo-Finnish treaty. One war in Scandinavia had ended. Another, it seemed, was about to begin. But as soon as news of the Russo-Finnish Treaty reached London, the British War Cabinet reconsidered its decision and, on the morning of March 14, decided to abandon the Narvik plan altogether. Churchill protested vigorously, but in vain. The only effect of such an action, Lord Halifax warned his War Cabinet colleagues, 'would be to drive the Norwegians and the Swedes into the arms of the Germans'. Operation Wilfred was dead.

Finland paid a heavy price for peace, ceding to Russia large tracts of territory along the Baltic coast and in the north, and leasing the Hango peninsula to Russia for thirty years. More than 27,000 Finnish soldiers had been killed. According to Molotov, the Russo-Finnish war had left 58,000 Russians dead.

For three and a half months, Soviet troops had been tested in a savage conflict; despite their losses, they had given notice of skill, tenacity and courage. Despite initial setbacks, they had taken full advantage of the rigours of winter. Above all, with their considerable numerical advantage in population, they had been able to call upon substantial reserves of manpower, far greater than those of their adversary. Frequently repulsed, they had always renewed the attack. 'One more of the wars of history was over,' wrote Geoffrey Cox, sitting that March 13 in a small Finnish café as the news of the end of the hostilities was broadcast. 'Outside, the station clock, lit up for the first time since November 29, glowed against the sky, a twentieth-century sign that peace had come.'

For the people of Poland, there was no peace, and no prospect of peace. Even as Soviet and Finnish guns fell silent at the eastern end of the Baltic, from the port of Stettin and the former border town of Schneidemühl, north-east of Berlin, German Jews were being deported in sealed freight cars into the Lublin district. These deportations were completed on March 12. In a fourteen hour march on foot from Lublin eastward, through snow and biting winds, 72 of the 1,200 deportees from Stettin died of exposure.

On the night of March 15, two British bombers flew across the North Sea, Denmark and the Baltic to Warsaw, dropping between six and seven million leaflets on the former Polish capital. Both bombers, having flown so far and used up so much fuel, intended to return across Germany to airbases in France. One landed mistakenly in Germany itself, but, watched by astonished peasants, managed to take off again and reach France safely on the morning of March 16. That day, the Germans were more aggressively active, fifteen German bombers attacking the British fleet anchorage at Scapa Flow, when the heavy cruiser Norfolk was hit by a bomb, and three officers killed. One bomb, falling on land, killed a civilian who was standing at the door of his cottage watching the raid. 'There was considerable feeling in the country', Churchill told the War Cabinet two days later, 'that while the Germans used bombs we only dropped leaflets.'

A reprisal raid was at last prepared, and on March 19 fifty British bombers flew across the North Sea to drop their bombs on the German aeroplane base at Hornum, on the island of Sylt. Forty-one of the attacking planes claimed to have found their targets, but a British fighter reconnaissance flight later confirmed German assertions that no damage had been done. One British navigator, whose enthusiasm exceeded his navigational skills, led his pilot to the wrong island, the wrong sea and the wrong country, the bombs being dropped on the Danish island of Bornholm, in the Baltic Sea. Fortunately for Anglo-Danish relations, no damage was done.

Within Germany, a small group of diplomats, churchmen and soldiers had revived the discussions, originally begun at the time of Hitler's threatened invasion of Czechoslovakia in 1938, for a means to step back from the brink of an all-out war with Britain. On March 16 one of these diplomats, Ulrich von Hassell, encouraged to do so by the former mayor of Leipzig, Carl Goerdeler, discussed possible peace moves with two senior members of the German armed forces. One of these was General Ludwig Beck, the other, Colonel Oster. It appeared Pope Pius XII had expressed interest in some sort of negotiations, involving the 'decentralization' of Germany and a 'plebiscite' in Austria, provided that those who initiated them were also prepared to support 'a change in the régime and an avowal of Christian morality'.

Nothing came of these talks; the anguish of the sincere but small opposition group was in stark contrast to the unrelenting work of military preparation and the consolidation of Nazi rule throughout Greater Germany. On March 17, the day after Ulrich von Hassell's clandestine talk, Dr Fritz Todt was formally appointed Reich Minister for Weapons and Munitions, heralding a new era of industrial efficiency and the exploitation of captive labour.

On March 18, Hitler met Mussolini at the Brenner Pass, on the border between Greater Germany and Italy. The Italian dictator was anxious to secure a three- or four-month postponement of Germany's Western offensive. Hitler declined to change his plans. Once France had been defeated, he said, Britain would come to terms. In France, there was emerging a new mood of defiance.

Two days after Hitler's meeting with Mussolini, Daladier's Government fell, and Paul Reynaud became Prime Minister of France. He at once proposed reviving the Anglo-French plan for action in Norwegian territorial waters, arguing, in a secret memorandum for the British War Cabinet, that the expected German retaliation after such an action would give Britain and France an opportunity to take control of the Swedish iron ore fields. Reynaud went even further; Britain and France, he said, should cut off Germany's oil supply from Russia by bombing the Soviet oilfields in the Caucasus.

Reynaud's proposal to activate the Narvik–Gällivare operation was welcomed by the British Chiefs of Staff who, on March 26, told the War Cabinet that they were in the process of considering the question 'of stopping the iron ore trade from Gällivare by certain naval operations'. These operations, they explained, would involve 'infringing both Norwegian and Swedish territorial waters'. On the following afternoon their efforts were given a sudden urgency, when a report reached the Director of Intelligence at the Air Ministry in London that, according to Swedish Intelligence sources, the Germans were 'concentrating aircraft and shipping for operations which Swedish intelligence consider might consist of seizure of Norwegian aerodromes and ports'.

All was set for a revival of the Anglo-French plan of action against Narvik.

On March 28, Paul Reynaud flew to London for a meeting of the Supreme War Council.

Neville Chamberlain, despite his previous hesitations about these plans, was in combative mood. In order to 'maintain the courage and determination of their peoples', he said, 'and also in order to impress neutrals, the Allies should take active measures'. His first proposal was to float naval mines down the River Rhine 'immediately'. His second proposal was to take 'all possible steps' to prevent Germany obtaining iron ore from Sweden. It would be a 'comparatively simple naval operation', Chamberlain explained, 'to block the route, at any particular moment, with a minefield. This would force the ore ships into the open sea, where they would be seized by a British naval squadron'. Chamberlain also proposed, as Reynaud had done, an attack on the Soviet oilfields at Baku in the Caucasus, in order to deny to Germany 'supplies of oil of which she was very much in need'.

All three proposals for action were finally agreed, as was a timetable for them. Aerial reconnaissance of Baku was to begin on March 30. Naval mines were to be dropped by parachute into the Rhine on April 4, though this decision was later postponed. Minefields were to be laid in Norwegian territorial waters on April 5. Furthermore, if Germany invaded Belgium, British and French troops would move through Belgium to the German frontier 'without waiting for a formal invitation to do so'.

These decisions were of course secret. But in a public communiqué issued that day it was announced that the British and French Governments had agreed that 'they will neither negotiate nor conclude an armistice or treaty of peace except by mutual agreement'.

The war at sea had continued since September 1939 with serious losses to Allied merchant shipping. On March 31 the German commerce raider *Atlantis* was ready to set sail on a marauding voyage which would see her sink twenty-two merchant ships, 145,697 tons in all. By the day of her sailing, 733,803 tons of Allied shipping had already been sunk in the waters around Great Britain by German submarines, a further 281,154 tons by mines, and 36,189 tons by German air attack. This substantial tonnage had been sunk for the total loss of only eighteen German submarines. In Berlin, the hopes of the opposition circle of which Ulrich von Hassell was part now looked to a senior member of the German General Staff, General Halder, to join them. On April 2, Hassell spoke to Carl Goerdeler, who had made contact with Halder. The result was not at all encouraging, however; Halder had refused to consider any action 'for the time being'. England and France, he said, 'had declared war on us, and one had to see it through'.

The German opposition to Hitler pinned its hopes on the unwillingness of generals and colonels to go to war with Britain – a war, they were convinced, that Germany could not win. But the tyranny which lay at the root of Nazism had already cowed the will to resist. Nor was it a tyranny that ever rested. On April 2, the day on which von Hassell learned of the abortive approach to General Halder, a distinguished German Social Democrat, Ernst Heilmann, was nearing death in Buchenwald concentration camp. Of Jewish parentage, Heilmann had been a deputy in the German Reichstag from 1928 to 1933. Arrested in 1933, he had been confined since then in several concentration camps, including Dachau. Continually subjected to harsh treatment, on one occasion he was attacked by bloodhounds that mangled his arms and hands. On April 3, he died in Buchenwald. The camp medical report, part of the meticulous bureaucracy of totalitarianism, called his death 'a clear case of weakness and old age'. He was fifty-nine years old.

On April 2 Hitler gave the order that the invasion of Norway was to begin in five days' time. As had happened the previous November, one of the first to pass on information to the West of the date of the offensive was Colonel Oster who, on the afternoon of April 3, told the Dutch Military Attaché, Colonel Jacobus Sas, of what had been decided. Sas passed on the information to both the Danish and Norwegian Naval Attachés. The Dane at once passed back the information to Copenhagen. But Oslo was not told; the Norwegian Attaché, Sas later learned, was sympathetic to the German interest.

In the early hours of April 3, the first three German supply ships, camouflaged as colliers, left the German shore of the Baltic for Narvik, a thousand miles to the north. The coal was real; underneath it, however, were hidden large quantities of artillery and ammunition. Two thousand troops had already embarked on ten destroyers, ready to sail north when the order was given. Further troops were under orders to be landed at Trondheim and Stavanger, Kristiansand, Bergen and Oslo. The German plan had kept its scale and purpose.

The British plan, now reduced to a mine-laying operation off the Norwegian coast, scheduled to begin on April 5, was about to be carried out without the knowledge that a far larger German operation was in prospect; in fact, although the British did not yet know it, the German landings would come four days later. British Intelligence reports from Norway and Sweden did however indicate, on the morning of April 3, that 'substantial numbers' of German troops were already on board ship in Stettin and Swinemünde harbours, with a further 'strong force of troops' ready to embark at Rostock.

Despite these indications, Neville Chamberlain declared, in a public speech on April 5, that 'Hitler has missed the bus'. That day, a special British naval force left Scapa Flow, on its way to mine Norwegian waters. It was divided into two sections, one to lay mines off northern and the other off southern Norway. By ill-chance, the date of April 5 laid down by the Supreme War Council for mining Norwegian waters had been taken as the date on which the naval force was to sail from Britain, not the date on which it was to lay its mines. Throughout April 6 the two British forces steamed eastward across the North Sea, at the beginning of a three-day passage. That night, when the British ships were still forty-eight hours from Norwegian territorial waters, a reconnaissance aircraft of British Bomber Command reported 'intense shipping activity and brilliantly lit wharves' at the German port of Eckernförde, near Kiel. A little while later, at twenty-five minutes to midnight, another British reconnaissance aircraft sighted a large German ship, 'possibly a battle-cruiser', steaming twenty miles north of Heligoland.

Far from the North Sea, in a darkness which was not to be pierced even by the most secret of Intelligence reports, an event was taking place which was to leave its mark on the demonology of the war. Beginning on April 5, and continuing for nearly six weeks, small groups of Polish officers who had surrendered to the Red Army in September 1939, and had been held since then in prisoner-of-war camps in Russia, were taken under Soviet Secret Police escort from their camp in the village of Kozelsk in the direction of the nearby city of Smolensk. In all, 5,000 Poles set off on this journey, leaving Kozelsk in groups of between sixty and three hundred. Not one of them was to reach Smolensk. Instead, still dressed in military uniform, their hands in most instances tied behind their backs, they were taken to a small wooded area near the village of Katyn, and shot in the back of the neck. It was to be three years before their bodies were discovered. The bodies of a further 10,000 Polish officers, likewise captured in September 1939 by Soviet forces, and held in captivity in Russia, have never been discovered.

On Sunday April 7, while the two British minelaying forces were on their last day's journey across the North Sea, ready to mine Norwegian territorial waters, German warships left their Baltic harbours and headed northward, carrying below decks an army of troops for the landing on Norwegian soil. When the first news of this reached the Admiralty in London it was not believed. A Danish Intelligence report, based in all probability on what Colonel Oster had told Colonel Sas, who had passed it on to his Danish colleague in Berlin, stated that Hitler had ordered 'the unostentatious movement of one division in ten ships to land at Narvik', with simultaneous occupation of Denmark. The date given for the arrival at Narvik was April 8. 'All these reports', the British Admiralty Intelligence Division concluded, 'are of doubtful value and may well be only a further move in the war of nerves.'

When, a few hours later, news of the actual German seaborne troop movements reached London, the British naval force which was to have laid the southern minefield was ordered to turn back. Had it not done so, it would have run straight into the German warships. The northern force continued on its way.

On April 8, having reached Norwegian territorial waters, the British northern minelaying force began to lay its mines. As it did so, the German invasion fleet continued to sail unmolested towards its various objectives. In the early hours of April 9, German warships were off Trondheim, Bergen and Stavanger; at dawn, four more German warships were reported entering Oslo Fjord. At Narvik, as correctly reported by the downplayed Danish Intelligence report, ten German destroyers landed two thousand German troops. The local Norwegian commander was a supporter of Vidkun Quisling, Norway's former Foreign Minister and leading fascist sympathiser; he ordered the garrison to allow the Germans to land unopposed. This news, when it reached the War Cabinet in

London, caused particular dismay; the original British plans to land at Narvik, later laid aside, had envisaged a landing on March 20, nearly three weeks earlier.

At Bergen, Kristiansand and Trondheim, as well as at Narvik, German troops came ashore during the early hours of April 9. They also occupied Copenhagen. The Danish King, Christian x, knowing that his Army was in no condition to resist, ordered an immediate ceasefire, but the Commander-in-Chief of the Danish forces, General Pryor, refused to pass on the order, hoping that armed resistance could continue. At 6.45 that morning, however, the King's adjutant passed the order on. Denmark now followed Poland, to become Hitler's second military conquest.

Later that morning, the German Minister in Oslo handed the Norwegian Government a note demanding the surrender of Norway to a German administration. 'In event of refusal, all resistance will be crushed.' The demand was refused. Two hours later, as German parachute troops landed, the Norwegian Government evacuated its capital transferring it to Hamar, seventy miles to the north.

That afternoon, Reynaud flew to London with his Foreign Minister, Edouard Daladier, for a meeting of the Supreme War Council. It was agreed that 'strong forces' should be sent to Norway. Their destination would be 'ports on the Norwegian seaboard'. It was also agreed to ask the Belgian Government to invite British and French forces into Belgium. But the Belgians refused to agree; they intended, they said, 'to keep a policy of absolute neutrality'.

Late that afternoon, Reynaud and Daladier returned to Paris. From Oslo, General von Falkenhorst telegraphed to Hitler: 'Norway and Denmark occupied as instructed.' Hitler was overjoyed, telling Alfred Rosenberg: 'Now Quisling can set up his Government in Oslo.' Quisling did so, becoming Prime Minister of the country that he so wished to lead according to the fascist code. All did not go well, however, for the new Norway, or for the invading forces. On April 10, to Hitler's intense anger, five British destroyers entered the harbour at Narvik and sank two of the ten German destroyers. But one of the British destroyers was sunk, one beached, and the commander of the attack, Captain Warburton-Lee, was killed.

Norwegian forces, loyal to the King, and refusing to accept the Quisling Government's submission to German rule, regrouped as best they could and prepared to fight; thousands of young Norwegians joined the units which took up positions along the narrow, winding mountain roads, still covered in their winter cloak of snow. One such volunteer was Eiliv Hauge, a clerk; he first saw action on April 11, as a column of German buses filled with troops wound its way inland towards his unit's position. The Norwegians had blocked the road with tree-trunks. As the Germans began to leave the buses, the Norwegians opened fire. Within minutes, Hauge later recalled, four buses were ablaze. Dead and wounded Germans lay in the road. White flags of truce were waved – in vain. 'Coming shamefully of age', as the historian of this episode has written, 'Hauge and his comrades fired on these, too, until two hundred Germans lay silent in the snow.'

There was a strange contrast between this Norwegian unit in action for the first time, and the British units stationed in France. 'There's nothing doing on the Western Front,' Ronald Cartland, an officer and a Member of Parliament, wrote home on April 12. 'We've settled in again to a comparatively peaceful war existence. The "Season" is with us. I give "smart" lunch parties and dine out twice a week with other Batteries!'

In London it was decided by the War Cabinet that April 12 to land a military force at Narvik, to dislodge the Germans, make touch with the Norwegian troops in the neighbourhood, and cross, with War Cabinet sanction still to be given, into Sweden, to destroy the iron ore installations at Gällivare, the objective of the earlier, abandoned scheme. On the following day, before any such landing could take place, British warships, in a second action at Narvik, sank the eight remaining German destroyers. That same day, British troops landed at two more Norwegian ports: Åndalsnes, to the south of Trondheim, and Namsos to the north. Hitler, alarmed at this adverse turn of events, ordered the evacuation of Narvik.

For the British, the weather in Norway was proving as much a hardship as for the Germans. The British troops at Namsos reported on April 15 that the town was under four feet of snow, with no cover from possible air attack. A British force of six hundred, due to cross the North Sea and land at Ålesund, had been held up throughout April 15 by gales off the coast of Scotland. In the Narvik area, where British troops were now ashore at Harstad, Salangen and Bogen, deep snow, and a night-time temperature of zero fahrenheit, had created the added danger of frostbite and amputations. At Namsos, German gunfire made it impossible for the British military commander, General Carton de Wiart, to disembark from the flying boat which had brought him from Britain. Off Narvik, the destroyer *Kimberley* had suffered casualties from German machine gun fire from the shore. On April 16, a plan, approved by the War Cabinet, to seize the forts at Trondheim, using a thousand of the Canadian troops then in Britain, had to be postponed for at least six days, after the Chiefs of Staff had reported that the assault as planned would be 'costly in execution'. There were signs, one of Neville Chamberlain's Private Secretaries wrote in his diary that night, that the Norwegians 'will lose heart unless quickly assured of substantial support'.

A clash of armies had begun along the whole length of the Norwegian coastline. On April 17, eight days after his troops had landed at so many points in apparent triumph, Hitler sent out the order: 'Hold on as long as possible.' More than 13,000 British troops were now ashore north of Narvik and north and south of Trondheim. French troops, units of the French Foreign Legion, and Polish naval units seeing action for the second time in nine months, participated in all the zones of operation. Against them, the German Air Force turned its dive-bombing aircraft which had struck with such devastating effect against troop concentrations and movement during the 'lightning war' in Poland. The German High Command also had a precious advantage in the Norwegian fighting, as a result of being able to read more than thirty per cent of the British naval signals in the North Sea and Norwegian area; this led to many ships being found and attacked which might otherwise have proceeded unmolested.

Britain, too, was not without an Intelligence window on German military and air operations. Beginning on April 15, the Government Cypher and Signals School at Bletchley Park had broken the relatively uncomplicated Enigma key which had been introduced for use by the German Air Force and Army during the Norwegian campaign. The number of messages sent through Enigma, and therefore read at Bletchley, was voluminous. Most of them were now decrypted within a few hours, and some within an hour, of their transmission by the German stations. Not only air and Army matters, but also such naval matters as concerned the other two services, were being decrypted each day from 15 April. A mass of information, not only on the state of the German organization and supplies, but also on their intentions, was decrypted at Bletchley.

The Intelligence authorities were completely unprepared, however, to make use of what Churchill was later to call the 'golden eggs'. Neither Bletchley itself, conclude the historians of British Intelligence, nor the Government departments concerned, 'were equipped to handle the decrypts efficiently'. No secure means had yet been prepared for transmitting the precious information to the commanders in the field, or even of explaining to them the nature of its unique insight into enemy actions and plans.

The breaking of the Norway Enigma Key, a triumph of cryptography, thus had no influence on the course of the Norwegian campaign. With the ending of the campaign, its use by the Germans was to be discontinued. Nor was a similar opportunity to read the German messages so swiftly and so completely to arise until almost another month had passed. In the Intelligence war, Germany, not Britain, had been the victors in Norway.

The land war was also going badly for Britain; for several days beginning on April 17, the War Cabinet's plan to land a force at Narvik was strenuously opposed by the British military commander at Harstad, General Mackesy. 'There is not one officer or man under my command,' Mackesy telegraphed to London on April 21, 'who will not feel shame for himself and his country if thousands of Norwegian men, women and children in Narvik are subject to the bombardment proposed.' Mackesy's opposition was decisive. The plan to seize Narvik was abandoned. With it was also abandoned the plan, already postponed earlier, to seize Trondheim, using a substantial part of the forces which would have driven the Germans from Narvik. Hitler, so despondent on April 12, was now, after scarcely a week, elated; on his fifty-first birthday, April 20, he had ordered the establishment of a new s s regiment, Norland, in which Norwegians and Danes would serve alongside Germans. 'Who knows', General Rommel wrote in a private letter on April 21, 'whether any other German exists with such a genius for military leadership and such a matching mastery of political leadership too!'

Hitler's political acumen was seen on April 24, when he appointed a German Nazi Party official, Josef Terboven, to take over effective control of Norway from Vidkun Quisling. After only fifteen days, the man whose name was to come to represent betrayal of one's country was pushed from his brief pinnacle of power.

In Poland, torture and killing had continued without abatement. On April

14, 220 Poles, including many women and children, had been seized in several villages and hamlets near Serokomla; all were shot. At Stutthof, on the evening of April 23, during the first hours of the Jewish festival of Passover, when Jews celebrate their liberation from bondage in ancient Egypt, all Jews in the camp were ordered to run, drop to the ground, stand up and run again, without respite. Anyone who was too slow in obeying the order was beaten to death by the overseer with his rifle butt. A Polish prisoner at Stutthof, in reporting this episode of mock celebration, also told of how the ss had harnessed a Jewish sculptor to a cart filled with sand. They had then forced him to run with the cart, while flogging him with a lash. When he collapsed in pain and exhaustion, they tipped the cart over him, burying him under the sand. He managed to crawl out, whereupon, amid much glee, they doused him in water, and then hanged him. But the rope was too thin, and broke. They then brought a young Jewess who was pregnant and, with scornful laughter, hanged them both on a single rope.

The killing of Jews had become a matter of laughter and mockery; the persecution of Poles was also terrible. On April 29 a thirty-nine-year-old ss man, Rudolf Hoess, arrived in the newly established camp at Auschwitz with five other ss men. Calculating the future size of the camp, and the nature of the punishments and hard labour to be instituted against their Polish prisoners, they ordered thirty German convicted criminals, to be sent from Sachsenhausen concentration camp in order to serve as barrack chiefs in the new camp.

On May 1 the German authorities in Poland ordered the establishment of a 'closed' ghetto in the industrial city of Lodz. More than 160,000 Jews lived in the city; now they were not to be allowed out of a limited, overcrowded area. Of the 31,721 apartments in the ghetto area allocated to them, most with a single room, only 725 had running water. On May 1, German police were ordered to shoot without warning any Jew who might approach the barbed-wire fence which now surrounded the area.

A few Germans were so disturbed by such developments that they protested to their superiors. At the end of April, the President of the Berlin police, Count Wolf Heinrich von Helldorf, once one of Hitler's most enthusiastic and prominent supporters, heard from his deputy, Canstein, details of his recent visit to Cracow. On May 1, Count Helldorf went to see Colonel Oster, to tell him of Canstein's impressions. He had found the local ss chief in Cracow in a state 'bordering on hysteria' because neither he nor his men felt capable of carrying out their orders unless they made themselves drunk first. No one who performed tasks such as they did, Helldorf told Oster, could come back and live a normal life.

Oster than asked Helldorf about morale in Berlin, to which the Police President replied that only thirty-five to forty per cent of the population of the capital were in favour of the war.

During the last three days of April 1940, British and French troops prepared to withdraw from their precarious Norwegian footholds. On April 29 the Norwegian military commander, General Ruge, whose troops had fought a series of rearguard actions in the south, warned the British General withdrawing from Åndalsnes that unless the Norwegians could hope for 'further Allied intervention' he would advise the Norwegian Government to begin peace negotiations. In reply, the British General was authorized by the War Cabinet in London to say that although the Allied forces in central Norway were withdrawing, those north of Namsos would be reinforced, 'as a preliminary to counter-attack southwards'. On the day on which this reply was transmitted to the Norwegians, German troops which had set off from Oslo and Trondheim on 10 April linked forces. 'That is more than a battle won', was Hitler's comment, 'it is an entire campaign!'

Hitler no longer had to worry about any last minute shifts and changes in Allied plans in northern Norway; on April 30 he ordered the German Army to be ready to launch Operation Yellow against the West within twenty four hours of any day from May 5.

The British, not knowing exactly where the blow would fall, withdrew almost a whole division from France on May 2, fearing that a German landing on British soil might be a part of Hitler's military plan. Any Enigma messages from Berlin to the senior German commanders, which might have revealed all, could not be decrypted. The Norway Enigma triumph, so unexpected as to be without the means of exploitation, was not to be repeated over France or the Channel in time to influence the British retreat to the coast.

Off Namsos, the Royal Navy, arriving to evacuate the troops ashore, found the town itself ablaze. The first ship to reach the quayside was the destroyer *Kelly*, commanded by Lord Louis Mountbatten, a great grandson of Queen Victoria. The *Kelly* took off 229 French troops, ferried them to a waiting transport, and returned to evacuate more. From the air, the Germans, aware of all British naval movement as a result of reading and decoding the messages passing from ship to ship, bombed the evacuating force continuously. A French destroyer, the *Bison*, was hit and blew up. The British destroyer *Afridi*, hurrying to rescue the survivors, was herself hit, and eventually capsized. The *Kelly*, more fortunate, shot down at least one of the German dive-bombers. 'What a party', was Mountbatten's comment, 'but what luck it was no worse'.

As German troops prepared to open hostilities in the West, the last act of the northern drama was being played out. On May 4 a Polish destroyer, the *Grom*, was hit by German bombs near Narvik, and broken in two; fifty-six Polish sailors were killed. While British warships steamed to the rescue, German machine gunners opened fire from the shore at the wounded men floundering about in the water. It was the old British battleship *Resolution* which rescued the men. Once they were aboard, its band struck up the Polish hymn, 'While Yet We Live, Poland Shall Not Perish!' One of the Poles who had been rescued later recalled: 'Our eyes were wet, but our hearts were throbbing with a new sense of power, with the promise of life.'

As had happened the previous November, bad weather forced a series of short postponements to Operation Yellow, though only until May 8. Also as in November, news of the planned attack, as well as details of each of the postponements, was passed on by Colonel Oster to the Dutch Military Attaché in Berlin, Colonel Sas. Among those who opposed the attack in the West was General Beck; he, with Colonel Oster's support, instructed a Catholic lawyer, Dr Joseph Müller, to travel to Rome, ostensibly on a secret service mission, in order to warn the Vatican, and through the Vatican the Allies, of Hitler's intentions.

With the agreement of the Pope, the information brought by Dr Müller was sent by coded radio message to the papal nuncios in both Brussels and The Hague. These messages were heard by the German radio monitoring services, and decoded. Canaris was at once ordered to investigate the leak, of which he himself was the true source. With what has been described as 'a stroke of genius equalled only by its wit', Canaris ordered Dr Müller, who had just returned from Rome, to return there to investigate how the news of the invasion date could have leaked out. Hitler, unaware that his own Intelligence chief was betraying him, went ahead with his plans. Even prior warning could not help to mitigate the effect of the overwhelming superiority of the blow which he had devised. It was on May 7 that Hitler was shown two decoded telegrams which the Belgian Ambassador to the Vatican had just sent to Brussels. He was not deflected from his course. Nor did he need to be; on May 8 a British Intelligence summary, prepared by the War Office in London, stated that there was 'still no sign' that an invasion of Belgium or France was imminent, though some action was to be expected 'in the immediate future'. Germany's dispositions, the report warned, would enable her to move against Holland 'at any moment with a minimum of notice'.

Off the Dutch coast, German minelayers were at work, laying the mines with which to deter any British naval effort in support of Holland. On May 9 the destroyer *Kelly*, having been withdrawn from Norway, was among the British warships searching for the minelayers. Attacked by a German submarine, she was crippled, but survived. Twenty-seven of her crew were killed. Her captain, Lord Louis Mountbatten, brought her back across the North Sea, to sail and fight again.

Early on the morning of May 9, following favourable weather reports, Hitler set May 10 as the day of his Western offensive. Every indication was favourable to this expansion of the war. In London, two days earlier, the Air Ministry had informed the War Cabinet that, at the estimated scale for active air operations over France, Britain's reserves of petrol and aviation fuel 'would only last some ten to eleven weeks'. Throughout May 9, Hitler's senior commanders studied a mass of valuable Intelligence, partly from British Army documents captured in Norway, which provided them with details of the British order of battle in France. Further details came from the coded radio messages passing between the French Ministry of War in Paris and the French military forces along the border. From these messages, picked up by radio and quickly decoded, the German High Command was able to learn the dispositions and qualities of the Allied forces that would be against them: their size, unit by unit; their plan of campaign to advance to the River Dyle when the German attack began, and the knowledge that the French had no plans to launch an effective counter-attack against the flank of the main German line of advance.

On the afternoon of Måy 9, Hitler left Berlin. To maintain strict security, it was intimated even to his staff that he was on his way to Oslo. That evening, when his special train reached Hanover, the code word 'Danzig' was sent out to the commanders in the field: the attack on Holland, Belgium and France was to go ahead. Hitler's train continued westward. Shortly before dawn on May 10, having crossed the Rhine, it reached Euskirchen, a small German town less than thirty miles from the Belgian frontier. An hour later, an ambitious, hazardous and daring offensive was under way.

# 5

# The German attack in the West

MAY 1940

As dawn broke on the morning of 10 May 1940, the German forces advanced into Belgium and Holland; 136 German divisions, facing half that number of Allied troops. For the British and French, as a result of the earlier Belgian insistence on strict neutrality, the first Allied advance had to be across the French border and through Belgium to the line of the River Dyle. As the Allies moved forward, 2,500 German aircraft attacked the airfields of Belgium, Holland, France and Luxemburg, destroying many aircraft on the ground. Commanded by General Kurt Student, 16,000 German airborne troops, the spearhead of the German attack on Holland, parachuted into Rotterdam, Leiden and The Hague. A hundred German troops, landing silently in gliders as dawn broke, had seized the Belgian bridges across the Albert Canal.

Dominating the Albert Canal defences was the Belgian fortress of Eben-Emael. For six months an elite group of German parachutists had trained for its capture. Fifty-five of them landed at the fort at the very moment of the opening of the German offensive, but throughout May 10 the Belgian defenders, protected by massive gun emplacements, held out against considerable explosive charges and firepower.

In London, at seven o'clock that morning, an appeal for help was received from both the Dutch and Belgian governments. The British Government at once gave orders for mines to be dropped into the River Rhine, a decision made more than a month earlier, but, on account of the sudden Norwegian crisis, never implemented. An hour later it was learned in London that German aircraft had dropped mines into the Scheldt; German troops had crossed into Luxemburg; the French city of Nancy had been bombed, and sixteen civilians killed.

That morning, the British Government authorized Operation XD, to demolish the Dutch and Belgian port installations at the mouth of the Scheldt, in the event of a German thrust that far. Shortly after four o'clock that afternoon Hitler learned that the 4th German Panzer Division had crossed the River Meuse. Half an hour later, in London, Neville Chamberlain announced to his War Cabinet that, with the new emergency, a coalition government was essential, bringing the Labour and Liberal opposition parties into the war-making circle. But the Labour Party leaders had refused to serve under his leadership; for them, he was the man principally responsible for Britain's lack of preparedness, even though they themselves had voted against conscription in April 1939.

With the Labour Party unwilling to serve under his leadership, Chamberlain had little option but to resign. He was succeeded as Prime Minister by Winston Churchill, the principal critic of his pre-war policies, and a man whom the Labour leaders believed would have the will and ability to direct the war with energy and zeal. A new government was formed, in which members of all the political parties had a place; Churchill becoming Minister of Defence as well as Prime Minister, with additional authority as the head of a special Defence Committee, consisting of himself and the Chiefs of Staff, the task of which was to make the day by day, and if necessary hour by hour, strategic decisions.

Ronald Cartland, one of several Conservative MPs then serving on the Western Front, was delighted by the news from London. 'Winston – our hope – he may yet save civilisation,' was his comment in a letter home. Cartland's own unit had moved that day into Belgium. 'Crowds of evacuees,' he wrote. 'I'm sorry for the Belgians, second time in twenty-five years, but they're very brave and resolute.'

In spite of bravery, the superior German firepower was overwhelming; shortly before midday on May 11 the Belgian defenders of Fort Eben-Emael surrendered. Twenty-three of the seven hundred defenders had been killed. Of the fifty-five German attackers, six were dead. Hitler, who had literally hugged himself with joy on learning of the fort's capture, personally decorated all the surviving attackers with the Iron Cross. The first Iron Cross of the campaign, however, was awarded to an SS officer, Captain Krass, of the Leibstandarte regiment, who, on the morning of May 11, crossed the Ijssel river in Holland with a small patrol, penetrated forty miles into Dutch territory, and brought back a hundred Dutch soldiers whom he and his little force had captured during their incursion.

At the Dutch town of Doorn, the former German Kaiser had lived in exile since 1919, when the Dutch Government had refused to extradite him to Britain to be tried as a war criminal. Now, as one of the first acts of the Churchill Government, the ex-Kaiser was asked if he would like to come to Britain, to escape the Nazis. He declined; and, a few hours later, Doorn was overrun.

For the Allies, the news of German successes came not only from Holland and Belgium; on the morning of May 11 it was learned in London that the Allied base at Harstad, north of Narvik, was being severely bombed by German aircraft, while at the same time German troops, taking advantage of the Nazi-Soviet Pact, were being moved by rail from Leningrad to Murmansk, as part of a possible pincer attack into northern Norway. Churchill's instinct, on this, his first full day as Prime Minister, was to move the troops at Harstad southward to Mosjöen, where a small British garrison was still holding out; but the Chiefs of Staff argued that, in view of the 'life and death struggle on the Western Front', there were insufficient troops to hold either Mosjöen or Bodö – like Narvik, north of the Arctic Circle – which Churchill also hoped to reinforce. As was to happen throughout the war, when Churchill's suggestions were strongly opposed by his Chiefs of Staff, those plans were abandoned. The British Prime Minister,

The German invasion of Western Europe, May 1940

unlike Hitler, had no power to overrule his principal strategical advisers. He was able, however, to support their recommendations with considerable vigour, and to insist upon their rapid implementation; on his first day as Prime Minister, British forces occupied the Danish dependency of Iceland, an important strategic base, and one which had to be denied to the Germans, now that they were rulers of Denmark. Now the need was to develop Iceland's naval and air bases and facilities as quickly as possible.

On the Western Front, the German commanders had vied with each other during May 11 on how far they could advance. 'Everything wonderful so far,' General Rommel, commanding the 7th Panzer Division, wrote to his wife that day, and he added: 'Am way ahead of my neighbours'. On May 12, in Holland, after a march of a hundred miles, the German Eighteenth Army linked up with the paratroops who had been dropped two days earlier. That evening, the British War Cabinet were told that seventy-six British aircraft had been lost in the two days of fighting.

On May 13 Rommel's troops, advancing through Belgium, crossed the Meuse at Dinant. That same day, further south, General Guderian's troops pushed through the Forest of the Ardennes and crossed the Meuse near Sedan, the first substantial German crossing of the French border. At five o'clock that morning King George VI, asleep at Buckingham Palace, was woken by a police sergeant to be told that the Dutch Queen, Wilhelmina, wished to speak to him. 'I did not believe him,' the King wrote in his diary, 'but went to the telephone and it was her. She begged me to send aircraft for the defence of Holland. I passed this message on to everyone concerned and went back to bed.' The King commented: 'It is not often that one is rung up at that hour, and especially by a Queen. But in these days anything may happen, and far worse things too.'

Queen Wilhelmina, warned that she might be kidnapped by the Germans and used as a hostage, left The Hague for Rotterdam, where she embarked on a British destroyer, the *Hereward*. Her aim was to join those of her armed forces still resisting in Zeeland. Heavy German bombardments made it impossible, however, for her to land; she therefore crossed the North Sea to Harwich, determined to make one further appeal for British air support. Once at Harwich, however, it was made clear to her that the situation in Holland was hopeless. That evening she was met by King George VI at Liverpool Street station in London. 'I had not met her before,' the King noted in his diary. 'She told me that when she left The Hague she had no intention of leaving Holland, but force of circumstances had made her come here. She was naturally very upset.'

That afternoon, Churchill told the members of his new Government: 'I have nothing to offer but blood, toil, tears and sweat.' He repeated those words a few hours later in the House of Commons, telling the Members of Parliament: 'You ask, what is our policy? I will say. It is to wage war, by sea, land and air, with all our might and with all the strength that God can give us; to wage war against a monstrous tyranny, never surpassed in the dark, lamentable catalogue of human crime. That is our policy.'

As to what Britain's aim might be, Churchill was equally emphatic. 'It is victory, victory at all costs, victory in spite of all terror, victory however long and hard the road may be; for without victory there is no survival.'

That evening, in the War Cabinet, Churchill learned that whereas the Air Staff estimated that sixty fighter squadrons were needed for the 'adequate defence' of Britain, only thirty-nine were available. The areas of Allied initiative were few and scattered. That night, several hundred aerial mines were dropped in the Rhine, disrupting German barge traffic near Karlsruhe and Mainz. For this enterprise, two Distinguished Service Crosses, and seventeen Distinguished Service Medals, were awarded. In Norway, even further from the decisive battle, French forces commanded by General Béthouart landed near the tiny fishing village of Bjerkvik, thirty miles from Narvik by road. 'I hope you will get Narvik cleared up as soon as possible,' Churchill telegraphed on May 14 to the British commander, Lord Cork, 'and then work southwards with increasing force.' It was a forlorn hope; yet after the French Foreign Legion, on May 15, had captured Bjerkvik, taking seventy prisoners, it was a hope that Churchill refused to abandon.

On the morning of May 14, confronted by a stronger Dutch defence than he had envisaged, Hitler included in a directive of that day an order to break Dutch resistance. 'This resistance must be broken quickly,' the order read. German aircraft were at once diverted from the Belgian frontier 'to facilitate the rapid conquest of Fortress Holland'. Their target was the bridges over the River Maas at Rotterdam. Many bombs, missing their target, fell on the city centre; 814 Dutch civilians were killed. Rumour, and Allied propaganda, quickly multiplied the figure to 25,000, even 30,000. The reality was harsh enough. The rumour gave added terror to the lives of those in France and Belgium who were as yet unbombed.

At midday, grave news reached the Allied commanders. Near Sedan, the Germans had greatly enlarged the bridgehead established earlier by Guderian. It now became possible that, with substantial British and French forces pinned down in Belgium, the Germans would be able to use this bridgehead as a base for operations to sweep behind the Allied armies, pushing through the Ardennes in a broad semi-circle to the Channel ports. This was indeed Hitler's plan. 'The progress of the offensive to date', he noted in his Directive No. 11, issued that day, 'shows that the enemy has failed to appreciate in time the basic idea of our operations.'

Seriously alarmed, the French High Command asked the British for the maximum of air support in the Sedan sector. This was promptly given. In all, seventy-one British bombers were sent to the southern sector. Attacking the German pontoon bridges and troop columns in successive waves, they were savagely mauled both by the German fighters and by anti-aircraft defences on the ground. By nightfall, forty of the seventy-one British planes had been lost. One of those shot down, Flight Lieutenant Parkinson, managed to make his way to the French front line, but was shot at and severely wounded. Later, escaping from France, he served once more as a pilot; later, on an operation dropping supplies to the French Resistance, he was again shot down. This time, he was killed.

The failure of the British bomber offensive to halt the German advance through Sedan was matched by a failure of the French troops to hold the line. Hitler's sweep behind the Allied lines had begun; within a month it was to have cut off the British Expeditionary Force from the main battle, and left Paris vulnerable to a swift advance. The British and French had still, on May 14, to extricate themselves from Norway. That day the British base at Harstad was attacked with incendiary bombs and two Allied ships destroyed. A third ship, the Polish liner Chrobry, was taking a battalion of the Irish Guards, four hundred troops in all, south to Bodö, when it was attacked; the twenty soldiers killed included the Commanding Officer, and every senior officer in the battalion.

There was a glimmer of good news for the Allies on May 14, when Arthur Purvis, head of the Anglo-French purchasing mission in Washington, reported that, of a hundred fighter planes then being built in the United States, Britain would be allowed to purchase eighty-one; of 524 further aircraft on order, 324 would be ready for delivery 'within two or three months'.

The diversion of so many aircraft to Britain represented, Purvis explained, 'real sacrifices by United States Services, as many squadrons on account of this will not be able to get their complement of modern planes'. This decision, vital for Britain at least in the long term, Purvis attributed to the 'goodwill' both of Roosevelt and of his Secretary of the Treasury Henry Morgenthau, who had gone so far as to give an 'emphatic assurance' that the new orders being placed by the United States Army Air Force, as part of its own expansion programme, would not be allowed to interfere with Britain's existing orders.

These benefits to come were not only long term, but secret. On May 14 the full focus of Allied fears was on Holland and the Ardennes. In Holland, the airborne forces of General Student had entered Rotterdam and were negotiating the city's surrender. Student himself, before concluding the negotiations, watched while his men began disarming a large party of Dutch troops. ss troops, arriving at that moment and seeing so many armed Dutch soldiers, opened fire. Student himself was shot in the head. But for the skill of a Dutch surgeon who operated on him that night, he would almost certainly have died.

The French had by now begun to panic. Shortly after seven o'clock on the morning of May 15, Paul Reynaud telephoned Winston Churchill to say that a French counter-attack on the German forces which had broken through at Sedan had failed, that 'the road to Paris was open' and that 'the battle was lost'. Reynaud went on to talk of 'giving up the struggle'. Churchill did his best to calm the French Prime Minister. He must not be misled, he said, by 'panic-stricken' messages. But Churchill was under no illusions about the gravity of the situation. 'The small countries', he telegraphed to Roosevelt on May 15, 'are simply smashed up, one by one, like matchwood.' As for Britain, Churchill added, 'We expect to be attacked here ourselves, both from the air and by parachute and air-borne troops in the near future, and are getting ready for them.'

Churchill's confidence was also seen in the mood of the British troops in France. Ronald Cartland, writing to his mother on May 15, shortly before his unit withdrew from the line of the Scheldt, was in fighting, if sombre, mood: 'We shall win in the end, but there's horror and tribulation ahead of all of us. We can't avoid it.' To the south, where Rommel had crossed the Meuse, French tanks at the village of Denée engaged in a desperate attempt to halt the German thrust. As tank after tank was disabled, the Germans kept up a relentless barrage of fire. The commander of one company, Captain Gilbert, was killed by machine gun fire with most of his crew, when getting out of his blazing tank. By nightfall, sixty-five French tanks had been destroyed, and twenty-four Frenchmen killed. They had given their lives at a high price, destroying at least thirty of Rommel's panzers. One of the French company commanders, Captain Jacques Lehoux, killed when his tank blew up, was posthumously made a Chevalier of the Légion d'Honneur. His principal adversary in the battle, Major Friedrich Filzinger, was awarded the Knight's Cross; it was given to him by Hitler personally three weeks later.

On the evening of May 15, British troops were still landing at the Dutch port of Ijmuiden, in a last minute attempt to bolster Dutch resistance. As they landed, six buses reached the port from Amsterdam. On them were two hundred Jews, mostly children, being brought to the port by a Dutch woman, Geertruida Wijsmuller. Many of her charges were German–Jewish children who had managed to reach Holland before the war. Now they were on the move yet again. 'At seven o'clock we sailed,' one of the boys, Harry Jacobi, later recalled. 'Far away from the shore we looked back and saw a huge column of black smoke from the oil storage tanks that had been set on fire to prevent the Germans having them. At 9 p.m. news came through, picked up by the ship's radio. The Dutch had capitulated.' The children found safety in Britain.

Hitler was now the ruler of yet another European State. In Holland, Harry Jacobi's grandparents, for whom there had been no place on the crowded coaches, were to be among his tens of thousands of Dutch Jewish victims. That night, for the first time since the German Army had struck in the West five days earlier, British bombers attacked German industrial targets in the Ruhr. In all, seventy-eight bombers set off. All returned safely, although sixteen had failed to locate their targets. Twenty-four found oil targets, some of which were seen by the crews burning fiercely as they turned for home.

Unable to breach American neutrality by shipping aircraft to Britain uncrated and ready to fly, Roosevelt himself proposed, on the night of May 15, a way round a surviving provision in the Neutrality Act. This was to fly the aircraft to the American side of the Canadian border, 'push' them across the border, then fly them on to Newfoundland, where they could be put on board ship. 'We already know', Purvis reported to London, 'this method is legal and feasible.'

Throughout May 16 the German advance continued, with Rommel penetrating fifty miles into French territory, towards Cambrai, and Guderian reaching a point sixty miles east of Sedan. That day General Gamelin ordered French forces to leave Belgium. Churchill, on his way to Paris, gave orders for Operation XD to be carried out at once. At Antwerp, as part of this demolition scheme, two British officers, Lieutenant Cadzow and Lieutenant Wells, drained off 150,000 tons of fuel into the Scheldt.

Reaching Paris that afternoon, Churchill urged an Allied military stand on the line Antwerp–Namur. 'We have lost Namur' was Reynaud's comment. The French, led by Gamelin, then pressed for six extra British fighter squadrons to be sent to France, in addition to the four already there, and a further four to which the War Cabinet had agreed, that morning, in London. But Churchill pointed out that Britain's own air defences were already in jeopardy; she had only thirty-nine squadrons for her own defence, four of which had now been allocated to work in France. But the urgency of the French request caused Churchill to put it, by telegram, to his War Cabinet. 'It would not be good historically,' Churchill warned, 'if their requests were denied and their ruin resulted.' In addition, one must not underrate 'the increasing difficulties' of the German advance 'if strongly counter-attacked'.

That night, the War Cabinet agreed that three further British squadrons, based in Britain, would 'work in France from dawn till noon', after which a second three squadrons would replace them 'for the afternoon'. This would at least save them from the danger of being attacked on the ground at French airfields.

In Paris, fears of an imminent German breakthrough led to panic. Bundles of official documents, thrown from the windows of the French Foreign Ministry, were set alight on the ministry lawn. But it was not towards Paris that Guderian's panzers were advancing. Instead, they turned north-west, and by noon on May 17 had reached the River Oise, at Origny, less than ten miles east of St Quentin. Attacking them, but unable to halt them, were the tanks of the French 4th Armoured Division, commanded by one of the pioneers of armoured warfare, Colonel de Gaulle. In recognition of his bravery that day he was promoted to the rank of brigadier-general.

On every sector of the front the Germans were succeeding beyond their hopes. On May 17 troops of General von Reichenau's Sixth Army entered Brussels, the fifth capital to be occupied by German troops in nine months. Falling back from Brussels towards the Channel coast, the British 3rd Division, commanded by General Bernard Montgomery, took up its position on the line of the River Dendre. Only at Hitler's headquarters did there seem to be a moment of doubt. 'A very disagreeable day!' General Halder noted in his diary. 'The Führer is excessively nervous. He mistrusts his own success; he's afraid to take risks; he'd really like us to stop now.'

Hitler's nervousness was misplaced. On May 18 his panzer commanders continued their advance at the same swift pace as before, Rommel reaching Cambrai and Guderian occupying St Quentin. One of France's senior commanders, General Giraud, entering Le Cateau with the remnants of the French Ninth Army, was captured by the Germans – unknown to Giraud, German troops had reached the town a few hours earlier. During the day, Belgium's principal port, Antwerp, fell to the Germans. 'I do not need to tell you about the gravity of what has happened,' Churchill telegraphed to Roosevelt. 'We are determined to persevere to the very end, whatever the result of the great battle raging in France may be. We must expect in any case to be attacked here on the Dutch model before very long and we hope to give a good account of ourselves.'

The 'Dutch model' was the use of parachute troops to seize the vital points. It was to protect Britain against the 'large number' of German troops that might be landed from transport aircraft 'preceded by parachutists' that Churchill and the Chiefs of Staff considered the possibility, on May 18, of bringing British troops from as far away as Palestine, and even India, by the fastest possible naval convoy.

In Paris, fearful of subversion, the new Minister of the Interior, Georges Mandel, began on May 18 a massive round-up of suspicious persons. 'Numerous arrests have been made in the street,' a Canadian businessman recalled at the end of the month. 'Traffic is strictly controlled. Policemen, bayonets fixed, stop passers-by and ask for identification.'

As the battle for France continued, British morale was boosted by the belief that the bombing raids over the Ruhr, begun on May 15, and continued for the next three nights, had been effective. But when the American journalist, William Shirer, drove on May 19 through the Ruhr he could see 'very little damage'. As for the population, on whose morale the raids were said by the British Broadcasting Corporation to have had 'a deadly effect', Shirer found them, 'especially the womenfolk, standing on the bridges over the main roads cheering the troops setting off for Belgium and France'. The only sign of the Royal Air Force's presence which Shirer noted that day was near Hanover, where he saw a large British bomber 'lying smashed in a field a hundred yards off the Autobahn'.

That day, in France, the ss Death's Head Division saw action for the first time, when it was ordered to go to the assistance of Rommel's 7th Panzer Division near Cambrai. Their adversaries were French Moroccan troops, whose defence of several small villages was tenacious. The ss troops fought with an equal fury, killing two hundred Moroccans for the loss of only sixteen ss men. That night Churchill broadcast to the British people, his first broadcast as Prime Minister. 'This', he said, 'is one of the most awe-striking periods in the long history of France and Britain. It is also beyond doubt the most sublime.' The British and French peoples, side by side, 'have advanced to rescue not only Europe but mankind from the foulest and most soul destroying tyranny which has ever darkened and stained the pages of history'. Behind the armies and fleets of Britain and France there gathered 'a group of shattered States and bludgeoned races: the Czechs, the Poles, the Norwegians, the Danes, the Dutch, the Belgians — upon all of whom the long night of barbarism will descend, unbroken even by a star of hope, unless we conquer, as conquer we must; as conquer we shall'.

How Britain and France could conquer was, at that moment, quite unclear. It was they, not Germany, that seemed about to succumb. That morning, as the German thrust threatened to drive a wedge between the British and French forces north and south of the River Somme, Churchill ordered the British Admiralty to assemble 'a large number of vessels' in readiness to cross over 'to ports and inlets on the French coast'. It was now clear, he told the Admiralty, that plans must be made at once, in case it became necessary 'to withdraw the British Expeditionary Force from France'. Plans were also made, that day, for 'mobile columns' to reinforce airport guards in case of German parachute landings in Britain. Even London was now felt to be a possible target of such landings; on May 20 Churchill approved a scheme of Bren gun posts and barbed wire road blocks to protect the Government offices in Whitehall, and 10 Downing Street itself, from a German attempt to seize the centre of the capital.

That night, German armoured columns, reaching Amiens, pushed on towards Abbeville, cutting off the British Expeditionary Force from the main French Army, and from its own bases and supplies in Western France. Hundreds of thousands of British, French and Belgian soldiers were now trapped, with their backs to the sea. Hitler was elated. General Jodl, who was present, noted that Hitler 'Talks in words of appreciation of the German Army and its leadership. Busies himself with the peace treaty which shall express the theme, return of territory robbed over the last four hundred years from the German people. ....'

Hitler would 'repay' the French for the peace terms imposed upon Germany in 1918 by conducting his own peace negotiations at the same spot in the forest of Compiègne. As for the British, 'The British can have their peace as soon as they return our colonies to us.'

Hitler, in his elation, was already musing about peace terms. But west of Compiègne, the bloody business of war went on; that evening, near Beauvais, two German airmen were shot down in an area over which German planes had been machine-gunning French and Belgian refugees as they sought to flee southwards. Both airmen were unarmed. As they stood by the roadside, surrounded by a crowd of civilians, a French soldier went up to them, drew his pistol and shot one of the Germans in the head, killing him instantly. The dead airman was the twenty-three year old Sergeant Wilhelm Ross; he was buried by the roadside, one of 1,597 Germans 'killed in action' that week in western France. Another German soldier who died on May 20, as a result of injuries sustained in battle, was Prince Wilhelm of Hohenzollern, the grandson of the ex-Kaiser, and heir to the German Imperial throne. The ex-Kaiser himself, in exile in Holland since 1918, having refused an offer from Churchill to come to Britain on 10 May, remained in Holland, his place of exile at Doorn being first overrun and then guarded by the successors to those very armies which he had launched against France and Belgium in 1914.

On May 21, German troops reached Le Crotoy, a small seaside resort on the Channel coast, at the mouth of the River Somme. With their arrival at Le Crotoy, the Allied armies in France were cut in half. The way was now open for Hitler's forces to drive the British back to the North Sea coast, and to destroy them. This very danger led, that day, to a British counter-attack at Arras by fifty-eight tanks under General Martel which caused near panic to Rommel's 7th Panzer Division. Eighty-nine of Rommel's men were killed, four times the losses he had suffered during the breakthrough into France. The ss Death's Head Division, sent once more to Rommel's support, knocked out twenty-two tanks, but lost thirty-nine men. Only the arrival of German dive bombers averted further losses.

For the first time in eleven days of battle, German troops had been forced back; nor was it troops alone, but the prized panzers, on whom so much depended. Hitler, concerned lest the panzers should be mauled still further, and fearing that the British would fight in France to the last man, ordered a halt to the advance against the Channel ports.

In the East, the war against the mentally ill took a new turn on May 21, when a so-called 'Special Unit' was sent to Soldau, in East Prussia, to kill more than 1,500 mental patients who had been transferred there from hospitals throughout East Prussia. The killings were completed in eighteen days; when they were over, the Special Unit reported back to Berlin that the mental patients had been 'successfully evacuated'.

On the Western Front, the British and French now planned a counter attack, to link up their forces across the German spearhead, with General Weygand, whose plan it was, promising to attack the Germans from the south. That night, in Britain, the head of the British Union of Fascists, Sir Oswald Mosley, and

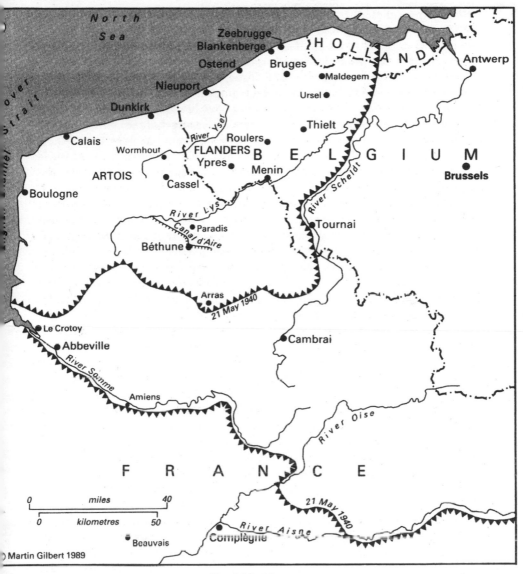

Dunkirk, May 1940

thirty-five other leading members, were arrested, to be joined in prison within
a week by 346 of their followers.

May 22 marked an important, and indeed dramatic stage in Britain's ability
to read some of the most secret German wireless communications, for on that
day the decrypters at Bletchley Park broke the German Enigma key most
frequently used by the German Air Force. Henceforth British Intelligence was
able to read, each day, every German Air Force message sent from headquarters
to the field, and from the field to headquarters. Among the most important of
these were messages sent by the German Air Force liaison officers with the

German Army; these messages provided many pointers to the position and intentions of the German field formations, as they turned towards the sea.

The 'flood of operational intelligence', the official historians of British Intelligence have written, was 'decrypted, translated, amended and interpreted' at the rate of a thousand messages a day. These were then sent by teleprinter or courier to Whitehall. At the same time, beginning on May 24, the most important items were passed direct from Bletchley to the headquarters of the British Expeditionary Force, and to Air headquarters. To ensure that the Germans never learned that their most secret method of communication had been breached, a special cypher was used, sent by a special signals link, through a Secret Intelligence Service mobile unit which assisted the commanders-in-chief in the interpretation of the material, and advised on how it could be exploited.

The breaking of the Enigma provided the British commanders, then at their most stretched, with a valuable window on to German Air Force activities and intentions, and on many of the activities and intentions of the German Army. It took some time, however, for those at Bletchley to master the many problems. 'Apart from their sheer bulk,' the historians of Enigma tell us, 'the texts teemed with obscurities – abbreviations from units and equipment, map and grid references, geographical and personal code names, pro-formas, Service jargon and other arcane references,' not to speak of the difficulties sometimes created by poor interception or by textual corruption as a result of the messages having been sent in the heat of battle. A particular difficulty during the early days of decryption that May was that the German Air Force headquarters, in its instructions, and the German commanders in the field, in their replies, made frequent reference to points on a British General Staff map series, scale 1:50,000, which had long ago been withdrawn from use in the British Army. Unable to obtain a set of these maps, the cryptographers at Bletchley were forced to reconstruct them from the German references to them, a laborious process. Despite these difficulties, information was yielded which could have been invaluable had the British Army not been in headlong retreat.

The British forces falling back to the sea were spared an immediate German onslaught, not as a result of any Intelligence coup, but because the Germans, having split the Allied armies, treated the troops in Flanders as a secondary target compared with the French troops falling back towards Paris. Nor were the Germans aware of just how many men were trapped towards the coast; German estimates on May 23 were of only 100,000, a quarter of the real figure. In addition, the General upon whom the main responsibility for the attack would lie, Ewald von Kleist, had seen almost fifteen per cent of his transport put out of action in the previous two weeks of fighting; he therefore welcomed the pause which Hitler had ordered. Nor did it seem possible that the British forces would be able to be evacuated by sea. Goering had assured Hitler that the German Air Force could prevent that. There was therefore no urgency in attacking in force the men who, on May 21, had shown themselves capable of so spirited and costly a counter-attack. On May 23, therefore, at six in the evening, General von Rundstedt, on his own initiative, issued orders to the German Fourth Army to 'halt tomorrow'.

Knowing nothing of Rundstedt's order, the British Army still waited for the planned French counter-attack from the south. At ten o'clock that night Churchill went to see the King at Buckingham Palace. 'He told me', the King wrote in his diary, 'that if the French plan made out by Weygand did not come off, he would have to order the BEF back to England. This operation would mean the loss of all guns, tanks, ammunition and all stores in France'. 'After ten days,' Ronald Cartland wrote to his mother from the British Expeditionary Force on May 23, 'we're back now in the same place from where we started. It's a rum war!'

'On the go all day of course,' General Rommel wrote to his wife on May 24. 'But by my estimate the war will be won in a fortnight.' Hitler, visiting von Rundstedt's headquarters that day, predicted that the war would be over in six weeks. Then the way would be free for an agreement with Britain. Hitler and Rundstedt then discussed the fate of the British troops trapped on the Channel coast. The two men were agreed that air attack could be used against the besieged perimeter. But Rundstedt went on to propose that his tanks should halt once they reached the canal below Dunkirk, so that his armoured forces could be saved for operations against the French. Hitler agreed. Shortly after midday, a second 'halt' order was issued to the Fourth Army in Hitler's name. For the time being, all attacks in the Dunkirk perimeter were to be 'discontinued'.

One effect of the second 'halt' order was that the SS Death's Head Division, in order to strengthen the line near Béthune, had to make a small withdrawal across the Canal d'Aire. The British, noting the German move, began an intense artillery barrage, during which forty-two SS men were killed.

When, late that evening, General Halder sent Rundstedt permission to attack Dunkirk, Rundstedt refused, telling Halder: 'the mechanized groups must first be allowed to pull themselves together'. 'Contrary to expectations,' Hitler's Army adjutant noted a few days later, 'the Führer left the decision largely to Rundstedt.' But it was only a decision to halt for a short while, to regather strength and to await reinforcements. The German aim was still a military victory. 'The next object of our operations', Hitler stated in his Directive No. 13 on May 24, 'is to annihilate the French, English and Belgian forces which are surrounded in Artois and Flanders, by a concentric attack by our northern flank and by the swift seizure of the Channel coast in this area.'

While the German Army paused, the British evacuation began. On May 24 a thousand men were embarked from Boulogne. Two hundred more, however, could not be got away before German troops entered the port on the following morning. Above the sea, off Dunkirk, the air attack which Hitler had authorized began at once; on May 24 a French ship, the *Chacal*, was sunk. Off Calais, where the British garrison was cut off even from the Dunkirk perimeter, the destroyer *Wessex* was likewise sunk, and the Polish destroyer *Bzura* badly damaged, while bombarding German positions on the coast.

The British Government now began plans to evacuate the British troops from Dunkirk. To the east of the Dunkirk peninsula, however, the Germans had managed to drive a wedge between the British and Belgian forces holding the line between Menin and Ypres. 'Soldiers!', King Leopold of the Belgians exhorted his troops on May 25, 'The great battle which we expected has begun. It will be hard. We will wage it with all our power and supreme energy.' The battle was taking place, the King added, 'on the same ground upon which we victoriously faced the invader in 1914'.

The Belgian soldiers, responding to the King's appeal, continued to resist, but their counter-attacks, aimed at closing the gap, though mounted with considerable vigour, were repelled. Fortunately for the British, a German staff car, captured on May 25, contained a document giving precise details of the German plans to exploit the gap. As a result of this timely Intelligence, the British Commander-in-Chief, Lord Gort, was able to order into the gap two divisions which were preparing to attack elsewhere. These were, in fact, the very divisions which were to have pushed southward, out of the German trap, as the British part of the Weygand plan. Only by abandoning the possibly false hope of a breakthrough to the south could the perimeter be held whereby a sea evacuation was possible. That day, in pursuance of Hitler's discussion with General von Rundstedt, the German Air Force threw all its available aircraft into an attack on the port installations of Zeebrugge, Blankenberge, Ostend, Nieuport and Dunkirk. Not realizing that Dunkirk was to be the main embarkation port, Goering directed the heaviest bombing against Ostend.

Despite Hitler's 'halt' order, on May 25 a small combat unit of the ss Death's Head Division, led by Captain Harrer, crossed the Canal d'Aire near Béthune, over which they had withdrawn on the previous day. Spotting a British motorcyclist speeding in their direction, one of the ss men opened fire, knocking the soldier off his machine. The ss men then approached him; he was lying in a ditch, wounded in the shoulder. Pulling him to his feet, the ss men tried, unsuccessfully, to converse with him. Captain Harrer then asked him, in halting English, if he spoke French. When the British soldier did not reply, Harrer drew his pistol and shot him through the head at point-blank range.

# 6

# Dunkirk

MAY 1940

It was on 26 May 1940 that Hitler realized he had made a grievous error in approving the 'halt' order of May 24. Hitherto, he had not appreciated that the British Expeditionary Force was preparing for evacuation. That morning, however, German air reconnaissance planes reported that there were thirteen warships and nine troop transports in Dunkirk harbour. 'It is probable', German Army Intelligence concluded, 'that the embarkation of the British Expeditionary Force has begun.' At half past one that afternoon, Hitler sent for his Army commander-in-chief, and agreed, General Jodl noted, 'to a forward thrust from the west by armoured groups and infantry divisions in the direction Tournai–Cassel–Dunkirk'. The order went out by telephone from Hitler's headquarters at half past three that afternoon. Three and a half hours later, at seven o'clock in the evening, a radio signal sent from the Admiralty in London to Vice-Admiral Bertram Ramsay at Dover instructed the Admiral: 'Operation Dynamo is to commence.'

'Dynamo' was the code name chosen for the evacuation from Dunkirk of as many soldiers as possible. On May 26 it was expected that 45,000 men could be taken off in the two days which were seen as the maximum that would be available. As Hitler and von Rundstedt had agreed, the German Air Force struck with all its strength to make the evacuation impossible. But the pilots of Fighter Command, Britons, Canadians and Poles among them, were equally determined to keep the skies above the beaches clear enough to evacuate the maximum number of troops. In the nine days of evacuation, 176 German aircraft were shot down over the beaches, for a loss of 106 British aircraft. The battle in the sky had helped to avert disaster.

Also contributing to the success of the evacuation were the British troops fighting rearguard actions around the whole Dunkirk perimeter, as well as those who were besieged in Calais. Commanded by Brigadier Nicholson, the British troops in Calais were engaging the German troops in a fierce struggle. Ships had arrived at Calais to take them off. But shortly before midnight on May 26 Nicholson received a telegram from the War Office in London: 'Evacuation will not (repeat not) take place, and craft required for above purposes are to return to Dover.' Every hour that the Calais garrison continued to exist, the message declared, was of the 'greatest help' to the British Expeditionary Force.

On the night of May 26, President Roosevelt broadcast an appeal for the American Red Cross. 'Tonight', he said, 'over the once peaceful roads of Belgium and France, millions are now moving, running from their homes to escape bombs and shells and machine gunning, without shelter, and almost wholly without food. They stumble on, knowing not where the end of the road will be.' A few hours after Roosevelt had spoken, the Belgian Army committed its last reserves, scarcely three regiments, to the battle. But even their tenacity in combat could not close, or even narrow, the gap between the British and Belgian forces; between Roulers and Thielt, five miles of the front line were undefended; further north, in a gap between Maldegem and Ursel, the road to Bruges lay open. 'The ring of fire tightens round us', General Michiels wrote in his journal on May 27. 'Thousands of refugees, mixed with the local population, fly through a narrow strip of territory exposed in its entirety to shell fire and aerial bombardment. Our last means of resistance is broken under the weight of a crushing superiority; we can no longer expect any support, or any other solution but total destruction'.

At the southern edge of the Dunkirk perimeter, fifty miles from the port itself, there was savage fighting on May 27 between units of the ss Death's Head Division, and British troops. In a farmhouse near the village of Paradis, ninety-nine men of the Royal Norfolk Regiment held up an ss company until their ammunition was exhausted. Their commanding officer, Major Lisle Ryder, made a final appeal for artillery support, but was told that none was available. Within the cowshed to which they had retreated, it was agreed, by a show of hands, that they should surrender. A white towel was tied to a rifle, and the men filed out, only to be met by a spate of machine gun fire. Five minutes later they again tried to surrender; this time the Germans stood up shouting in triumph and waving their rifles. An English-speaking officer ordered the Englishmen across a small road into the adjacent field, where they were told to kneel. Then, five at a time, they were ordered to their feet, to be searched, and a pile was made of their gas masks, steel helmets and cigarettes. Any soldiers who refused to co-operate were struck with rifle butts.

The prisoners were then marched to the road, where they had to wait for a while as German soldiers drove past, moving westward; then they were ordered into a field, along one side of which was a long brick barn, in front of which was a shallow pit. Two machine guns had been set up, facing the barn. As the head of the columns of prisoners were marched into the pit, and drew level with the far end of the barn, the order was shouted out: 'Fire!'

As soon as the shooting stopped, the German soldiers were ordered to fix bayonets and to move forward. They did so, bayoneting to death those who were only wounded, while others were killed with pistol shots. Then a whistle was blown, and the German soldiers climbed out of the pit. Ninety-seven British soldiers were dead. Incredibly, two had survived: Private Albert Pooley and Private William O'Callagan, who lay among the bodies.

That night, in heavy rain, Pooley and O'Callagan were able to crawl away.

After being sheltered for some days by a French farmer's wife, Madame Duquenne-Créton, who did her best to tend their wounds, they gave themselves up to the Germans and were made prisoners-of-war yet again. Pooley had been so severely wounded, in the leg, that he was later repatriated to England, via the Sudan, in an exchange of badly wounded men in April 1943. His story was met with considerable scepticism; only after the war, when O'Callaghan returned to Britain, was the savagery of the episode made clear; so much so that their joint testimony was instrumental in having the officer who had given the order to fire, ss Captain Fritz Knochlein, tried by a British military tribunal in Hamburg, condemned to death, and hanged.

On May 27 Operation Dynamo was under way, the Dunkirk beaches crowded with troops waiting for boats to take them off. Above Dunkirk that day, fifty German aircraft were destroyed, for the loss of fourteen British planes. But the German air attacks were on such a scale that many of the troops cursed the Royal Air Force for not doing more to protect them. Among the hundreds of craft which came from all the ports and seaside resorts of southern Britain that day was *Mona's Isle,* a former pleasure steamer which was already in commissioned service as an armed boarding vessel. Bombed as she reached the open sea, forty of those being evacuated on her were killed.

That day, in a measure designed to make a German parachute landing in Britain more difficult, orders were given for fields in eastern England to be ploughed, and suitable obstacles scattered on other possible landing grounds. At the same time, British bombers, taking a new initiative, flew over the Ruhr to aim their bombs at the German oil-producing plant at Gelsenkirchen. At eleven o'clock that night, even as the bombers were flying over the North Sea, news reached the British Expeditionary Force that, the Belgian front having broken under ceaseless German aerial and artillery bombardment, the King of the Belgians was asking for an armistice. He had indeed sent an emissary through the German lines at five o'clock that afternoon. The emissary had returned five hours later, to say that the Germans were demanding unconditional surrender. After consulting with his Army Staff, the King accepted. At four in the morning of May 28, the ceasefire came into effect. Belgium had resisted, bravely, for eighteen days.

In Paris, the Belgian Government, already in exile, repudiated the King's action. But the Belgian Army no longer existed; it had been broken to pieces in the field. In the House of Commons, Churchill warned that it was not the time to attempt to 'pass judgment' on King Leopold's action. 'Whatever our feelings may be upon the facts so far as they are known to us,' he said, 'we must remember that the sense of brotherhood between the many peoples who have fallen into the power of the aggressor and those who still confront him will play its part in better days than those through which we are passing.'

Churchill went on to speak of the situation of the British troops withdrawing from Dunkirk. It was, he said, 'extremely grave'. The surrender of the Belgian Army 'adds appreciably to their grievous peril'. The troops, meanwhile, were fighting 'with the utmost discipline and tenacity'. Nevertheless, the House of

Commons should prepare itself for 'hard and heavy tidings'. Nothing which might happen at Dunkirk, Churchill declared, 'can in any way relieve us of our duty to defend the world cause to which we have vowed ourselves; nor should it destroy our confidence in our power to make our way, as on former occasions in our history, through disaster and through grief to the ultimate defeat of our enemies'.

During the previous twenty-four hours, 14,000 men had been brought back safely from Dunkirk to Dover. Even as their evacuation proceeded, Allied troops in northern Norway were still advancing; during the early hours of May 28 the long-awaited but now virtually ignored entry into Narvik took place. During the final battle for the port, a hundred and fifty British, French, Norwegian and Polish soldiers were killed. Unknown to those who entered Narvik, the British War Cabinet had already authorized Operation Alphabet, the evacuation of Narvik once it had been captured. Authorization had been given four days earlier, on May 24, with the withdrawal date set at no later than June 8. That same War Cabinet had authorized the evacuation of Bodö by May 31. All that was to remain of the whole Norwegian enterprise was one final naval operation, proposed by Churchill on May 24 and given the code name 'Paul', for the laying of mines in the approaches to the Swedish port of Luleå, to deny the German iron ore ships an easy passage across the Baltic now that the ice had melted. 'This Operation Paul is indispensable,' Churchill told his principal military adviser, General Ismay, ten days later, and he added: 'Make sure we do not find ourselves prevented by any neutrality argument.'

During May 28, a further 25,000 British troops were brought safely back from Dunkirk. Among the rescue vessels was a holiday resort paddle steamer, the *Brighton Belle*; in collision with a wreck, she was one of four ships to be sunk that day. Still holding the dwindling perimeter, British troops even managed for a while to cut off the ss commander, Sepp Dietrich, from his men; he was forced to spend much of May 28 hiding in a ditch. At the village of Wormhout, only seventeen miles from Dunkirk, forty-five men of the Royal Warwickshire Regiment were stubbornly resisting the efforts of ss Leibstandarte Regiment in its advance. Finally, their ammunition gone, they, like the soldiers at Paradis on the previous day, surrendered. One of them, Private Alfred Toombs, later recalled how, after their surrender, a soldier of his regiment, Private Gould, who had been wounded in the fighting, was shot dead by one of the ss guards 'as he lay on the ground'. Another wounded man 'was shot as he lay on the road'. The remaining prisoners-of-war, disarmed, were taken to a field, where they were joined by forty other men captured that day, all but one of whom were wounded. They were then taken to a large barn. ss soldiers then mounted guard.

'I could see', Private Toombs recalled, 'that they had collar badges which resembled forked lightning.'

One of the guards called four men out of the barn and shot them. The senior-ranking prisoner-of-war, Captain Allen, at once left the barn to protest. He too was shot. The prisoners-of-war were then ordered into the back of the barn. Two of the German guards then threw in grenades, whereupon other guards, at the front, side and rear of the barn, opened fire with machine guns. At that moment, Private Toombs managed to run out; others who did so with him were shot down. Toombs, and four others, survived. But forty-five of their fellow prisoners-of-war had been killed.

Later that day, also at Wormhout, a further thirty-five British prisoners-of-war were murdered after they had been captured. The ss officer who ordered the Wormhout killings was Captain Wilhelm Mohnke. Asked for 'disposal instructions' about the prisoners, he had replied, according to the recollection of Carl Kummert, an ss corporal, that 'they were to be shot'.

Many of the ss soldiers who participated in the massacres at Paradis and Wormhout had already seen action the previous September in the Polish campaign. They knew of the type of actions which could be carried out behind a mask of secrecy, and with the approval of their superiors. On May 28, the day of the Wormhout killings, Himmler had put the final touches to a document, earlier approved by Hitler, for a massive reduction in the population of the conquered East. The document envisaged that the population of what had once been Poland, with its diverse groups, should be 'broken up into the largest possible number of parts and fragments'. Then the 'racially valuable elements' would be 'extracted from this hotch-potch', leaving the residue to 'wither away'. If these measures were to be carried out consistently, Himmler wrote, then over the course of the next ten years the population of the General Government 'will necessarily be reduced to a remnant of substandardized human beings'; it would then consist of a 'leaderless labour force' capable of furnishing Germany with a yearly supply of casual labourers. Children who were 'racially valuable' would be carried off to Germany and 'Germanized'; the 'remainder' would be deliberately made to vegetate, each person given a primary school education sufficient only to learn 'how to count up to a maximum of five hundred, how to write his name, that it is God's command that he should be obedient to Germans, honourable, industrious and brave'.

On May 28 Himmler noted that Hitler himself directed that only a 'limited number' of copies of this document should be made, 'that it was not to be reproduced and that it was to be treated as top secret'. Those senior ss commanders to whom it could be shown were to be brought the document by hand. The officer bringing it would then wait while it was read, demand a written acknowledgment from the reader, and return with it.

At Dunkirk, the evacuation continued throughout May 29. In the early hours, the destroyer *Grafton* was attacked by two German motor torpedo boats while picking up survivors from another ship; thirty-five officers on board were killed. Later that day, when HMS *Waverley*, a paddle steamer previously converted into a minesweeper, with six hundred soldiers on board, was attacked on her return journey by twelve German dive bombers, it too proved an unequal battle. The single anti-aircraft gun on board was augmented by the massed rifle fire of the soldiers; but after half an hour of persistent air attack, *Waverley* disappeared beneath the waves. More than three hundred of the troops on board were drowned. 'In these dark days,' Churchill wrote to all Government Ministers and senior civil servants that day, 'the Prime Minister would be grateful if all his colleagues in the Government, as well as high officials, would maintain a high morale in their circles; not minimizing the gravity of events, but showing confidence in our ability and inflexible resolve to continue the war till we have broken the will of the enemy to bring all Europe under his domination'.

During May 29, a total of 47,310 men were evacuated from Dunkirk. Hitler, meeting that day with his Army Group commanders at Cambrai, informed them that he had decided to 'deploy the armoured forces immediately for a southward offensive to settle matters with the French'. 'Perhaps France will give up her now hopeless struggle,' General Rommel wrote to his wife. 'If she doesn't, we'll smash her to the last corner.'

For the British Army, the Dunkirk saga was almost at an end. After four days of evacuation, the Germans were drawing closer, and the German air strikes becoming more intense. Up to the early hours of May 30, as many as 80,000 men had been evacuated, but conditions on the beaches, Churchill told the War Cabinet that morning, were 'difficult'. At two o'clock that afternoon Churchill instructed Lord Gort that once his fighting force in the Dunkirk perimeter was reduced to the equivalent of three divisions, he should hand over his command and return to England. Gort's successor would be ordered to carry on the defence of the perimeter but, Churchill added, 'when in his judgement no further organized resistance is possible, and no further proportionate damage can be inflicted upon the enemy, he is authorized, in consultation with the senior French commander, to capitulate formally to avoid useless slaughter'.

'To capitulate formally ....' These were ominous words. Less than three weeks had passed since Gort's army had been moving forward through Belgium, to shut the door on the German advance across the Belgian border. Now, as an historian of the Dunkirk evacuation has written, that door 'had slammed back upon France and splintered'. Among the defenders of the Dunkirk perimeter who were killed on May 30 was Ronald Cartland, a Member of Parliament. 'The way of life for which he fought', Winston Churchill wrote six months later, 'will certainly prevail and persist because of the striving and sacrifices of such men as he.'

At Dunkirk, French ships had joined with British in the work of rescue. On May 30 the French destroyer *Bourrasque,* striking a mine while on her way back to Dover, sank; approximately 150 of the men whom she had just rescued from the beaches were drowned. A little later, the British destroyer *Wakefield* was attacked by German dive bombers and sank. That morning, however, despite the air bombardment, 4,000 men were evacuated in a single hour. On Churchill's specific instructions, French and British troops were being evacuated side by side. On May 31, the total figure of British and French troops evacuated during that one day was 68,104.

Despite the Belgian surrender, many Belgian fishing vessels had also joined the armada of little ships; on 31 May the *Lydie Suzanne* brought 105 men back to Dover, the *Zwaluw*, 58; the *Cor Jésu*, 274; the *Jonge Jan*, 270; and the *A5*, 234.

On May 31, in Paris, at a meeting of the Supreme War Council, Paul Reynaud begged Churchill to send more troops to France, to join the French forces still holding the line of the River Somme. 'There were now no forces left that could be sent at once,' Churchill replied. 'Something had to be kept in the United Kingdom to deal with a possible invasion by sea or air.' Even Britain's defence against invasion was in danger as a result of the battle in France. Of the thirty-nine squadrons originally regarded as the minimum needed for the air defence of Great Britain, ten had been sent to France; 'there was now very little of these ten squadrons left'. As for troops, there were only three divisions left in Britain itself; even these were not fully equipped. The fourteen further divisions undergoing training were equipped only with rifles, 'and therefore totally unfit for modern warfare'. Yet two British divisions were already in western France, able to join in the defence of Paris, and a further force of 14,000 Australian troops was due to reach Britain on June 12; although not yet fully trained or equipped, they were men 'of the highest quality'.

Determined to persuade the French not to give in, Churchill then spoke of his conviction that Britain and France 'had only to carry on the fight to conquer'. Even if one of them was struck down, the other must not abandon the struggle. 'The British Government were prepared to wage war from the New World if, through some disaster, England herself was laid waste.' It must be realized, Churchill said, that if Germany defeated either Ally, or both, 'she would give no quarter; they would be reduced to the status of vassals or slaves for ever.'

In his talks with the French leaders on May 31, Churchill stressed the willingness of the United States 'to give us powerful aid'. Even if they would not enter the war, they had been 'roused' by recent events. The French should therefore order steel and other essentials from America 'in vast quantities'. Even if Britain and France could not pay for those supplies, 'America would nevertheless continue to deliver'. On the previous day, in Washington, Arthur Purvis had purchased a vast armoury: five hundred mortars, five hundred field guns, 'some thousands' of anti-aircraft guns, 10,000 machine guns, 25,000 automatic rifles, 500,000 Lee Enfield rifles, and 100 million rounds of machine gun and rifle ammunition. On May 31, shortly after Churchill's return to London, Purvis was able to report yet another success: General Marshall, the Chief of Staff of the United States Army, had been 'prepared to stretch a point' in the United States neutrality legislation and, by declaring substantial quantities of United States munitions to be 'surplus', make them available to Britain. Purvis had also secured a 'priority' position for Britain for the purchase of 15,000 tons of the new explosive, trinitrotoluol, TNT.

Among those whom Churchill met in Paris was Marshal Pétain, the 'hero of Verdun' during the First World War, and a symbol then of French determination to resist Germany, whatever the cost. But when another of the Frenchmen present, Roland de Margerie, spoke of fighting it out in French North Africa if France were to be overrun, the look on Pétain's face, Churchill later recalled, was 'detached and sombre, giving me the feeling that he would face a separate peace'.

That night General Gort left Dunkirk and returned to England, leaving General Alexander to supervise the final phase of the evacuation. Only 20,000 British and 60,000 French troops were still waiting to be embarked. During 1 June, however, several German units had pressed near enough to Dunkirk to be able to bombard the beaches with their artillery. In the air, German dive-bombers intensified their attack; in a few hours, three British and one French destroyer were sunk, together with two troop transports, a minesweeper and a gunboat. That day, however, despite the air and land bombardments, 64,229 men were taken off.

One of the craft that brought men back from Dunkirk on June 1 was the yacht *Sundowner*, owned and piloted by a retired Naval Commander, C. H. Lightoller, the senior surviving officer of the *Titanic*, whose younger son had been one of the first pilots to be killed in action the previous September. Lightoller later recalled how, before the war, his son had 'at different times given me a whole lot of useful information about attack, defence and evasive tactics (at which he was apparently particularly good) and I attribute, in great measure, our success in getting across without a single casualty to his unwitting help'. Commander Lightoller, together with his elder son and a Sea Scout, had brought back 130 men.

For Britain, the urgent question as the Dunkirk evacuation drew to its close was whether the Germans would launch an immediate invasion of Britain, possibly within days. The British Army was at its weakest, with its two best divisions now ready to move into action from their bases in western France. The number of Royal Air Force squadrons available had been reduced to less than the minimum believed necessary to resist an invader. The public's anxiety of not knowing whether Hitler would turn immediately on Britain was not however shared by the twenty or so men who were directing British policy.

For the past nine days, since May 22, British Military Intelligence had been able, as a result of the efforts of hundreds of codebreakers decrypting the German Air Force Enigma at Bletchley, to read the most secret German Air Force directives within a few days, and sometimes within hours, of their being issued to the German Air Force commanders in France. This not only gave local operational details, but, as Military Intelligence reported on June 1, made it clear that the German priority was the defeat of France. Before France fell, an invasion of Britain was unlikely; there were simply no plans or preparations for it. Had such preparations existed, the Enigma decrypts would have revealed them. But not a single Enigma message referred to any move of aircraft needed for Hitler to follow up the Dunkirk success by an assault across the Channel.

Churchill's determination, that June 1, was reflected in a message which he sent to the Director of the National Gallery, who had suggested sending the Gallery's most valuable paintings to Canada. 'No', Churchill wrote. 'Bury them in caves and cellars. None must go. We are going to beat them.' Hitler, at

Brussels that day, told his senior generals that he had earlier halted his armoured divisions outside Dunkirk because he 'could not afford' to waste military effort. 'I was anxious', he said, 'lest the enemy launch an offensive from the Somme and wipe out the Army's weak armoured force, perhaps even going as far as Dunkirk.'

As British Intelligence had surmised, all Hitler's military effort was now to be centered upon the drive south of the Somme, to Paris. To help the French meet this threat, Churchill had promised Reynaud that as many as possible of the 16,000 British, French and Polish troops about to be evacuated from Narvik would be sent, after regrouping in Scotland, direct to the Somme–Aisne front. In order to expedite this, Churchill had agreed to bring forward the Narvik evacuation by six days, to June 2. On the following day, basing themselves upon the Enigma decrypts, which revealed no immediate German plans for invasion, the British Chiefs of Staff agreed that reinforcements should be sent to France, despite the fact that Britain was, as they expressed it, 'dangerously exposed to the risk of decisive air attack and/or invasion'.

At midnight on 2 June the last 3,000 British and French troops had been evacuated from Dunkirk, bringing the total to 338,226 men in seven days. This was almost exactly three times the number of men evacuated from the Gallipoli Peninsula at the end of 1915. In all, 222 naval vessels and 665 civilian craft had ferried between Dunkirk and the British coast. Six destroyers and twenty-four smaller naval vessels had been lost. Thirty-eight British destroyers, never built to carry a mass of men, had brought away 91,624. Minesweepers had brought back 30,942. Thirty Dutch motor vessels had carried 20,284. French destroyers had lifted 7,623. Hundreds of merchant vessels, troop transports and sloops had brought back tens of thousands more. But in many ways the most remarkable feat of all was performed by the little ships: trawlers, coasters, tug boats, open boats, ship's lifeboats, fishing vessels, river cruisers, paddle steamers, and more than six hundred small pleasure craft, which between them brought off more than 80,000 men, in groups from several hundred to half a dozen.

The success of these ships was no less effective an act of war than a naval victory. Also, above the skies of Dunkirk, the Royal Air Force won what was certainly the first substantial victory of the Allied air; on several of the eleven days between May 25 and June 5, as many as three German planes had been destroyed for every British plane shot down, an augury of air battles yet to come. There was, however, a depressing side to these successes; 34,000 British soldiers had been taken prisoner-of-war in and around Dunkirk.

The last 3,000 troops having been evacuated, as well as 71 heavy guns and 595 vehicles, General Alexander, together with the Senior Naval Officer at Dunkirk, Captain Tennant, toured the harbour and shore line in a fast motor boat to make sure that not a single soldier remained to be taken off. Satisfied that this was indeed so, they then returned to the quayside, and embarked for Britain. Hitler, at Charleville that day, spoke to his generals of his admiration for Britain's rule in India. 'He points out', one general wrote in his diary, 'that without a navy the equal of Britain's we could not hold on to her colonies for long. Thus we can easily find a basis for a peace agreement with Britain. France, on the other hand, must be stamped into the ground; she must pay the bill.'

Hitler's thoughts were already turned toward the East. 'Now that Britain will presumably be willing to make peace,' he told General von Rundstedt at Charleville, 'I will begin the final settlement of scores with Bolshevism.'

# 7

# The battle for France

JUNE 1940

With his forces in the Dunkirk perimeter about to be liberated to join the move south, Hitler began the most ambitious step of the war so far, to achieve what the Kaiser had failed to achieve during four unremitting years of battle between 1914 and 1918, the capture of Paris. 'Ordered to the Führer today', General Rommel wrote to his wife on 2 June 1940. 'We're all in splendid form'.

On June 3 the German Air Force bombed Paris. In all, 254 people were killed, 195 of them civilians, the rest soldiers. Among the civilian dead were many schoolchildren who had taken refuge in a truck which had received a direct hit. It was only under threat of severe penalties that Georges Mandel, the Minister of the Interior, was able to prevent a flight of public officials from the capital. In Berlin, Admiral Fricke, Chief of the Operations Department of the German Navy, circulated a memorandum on post-war strategy. All the peoples in the German-occupied countries in the West – Norway, Denmark, Holland, Belgium and France – should be made 'politically, economically and militarily fully dependent on Germany'. As for France, she should be so militarily and economically destroyed, and her population so reduced, that she could never rise again to encourage the smaller states.

German confidence was easy to understand. But on June 3 the British War Cabinet was told that the Norwegian King, Haakon, although preparing to leave Norway for exile in England, 'believed that the Allies would win in the end'.

On June 4 the British took stock of their ability to combat an invasion force, should France fall and the full German strength be turned, at last, across the English Channel. There were only five hundred heavy guns on British soil, some of them museum pieces. On June 4 the War Cabinet learned that, between May 19 and 1 June, 453 aircraft of all types had been produced; in that same period, 436 had been lost. Thirty-nine Spitfires had been produced and seventy-five lost. The number of aircraft actually serviceable on June 2 was 504. If the Germans were to mount an air attack on Britain, the head of Fighter Command, Sir Hugh Dowding, had told the War Cabinet on June 2, 'he could not guarantee air superiority for more than forty-eight hours'. Dowding, incidentally, was not one of those who, at that time, knew of the Enigma decrypts which made it clear that an invasion would not take place at least until after France's defeat.

Nevertheless, the British had been forced to leave a vast armament behind in the Dunkirk perimeter: 475 tanks and 38,000 vehicles; 12,000 motorcycles; 8,000 field telephones and 1,855 field wireless sets; 400 anti-tank guns, 1,000 heavy guns, 8,000 bren guns and 90,000 rifles, together with a staggering 7,000 tons of ammunition. There were now less than 600,000 rifles and 12,000 bren guns in Britain. The losses would take between three and six months to make good.

On the afternoon of June 4, Churchill spoke in the House of Commons, telling Members of Parliament, who were elated by the Dunkirk evacuation but understandably fearful for the future: 'Even though large tracts of Europe and many old and famous States have fallen or may fall into the grip of the Gestapo and all the odious apparatus of Nazi rule, we shall not flag or fail. We shall go on to the end. We shall fight in France, we shall fight on the seas and oceans, we shall fight with growing confidence and growing strength in the air, we shall defend our island, whatever the cost may be'.

Addressing himself to the millions of Britons who did not see how Britain could resist a German invasion, Churchill declared: 'We shall fight on the beaches, we shall fight on the landing grounds, we shall fight in the fields and in the streets, we shall fight in the hills; we shall never surrender, and even if, which I do not for a moment believe, this island or a large part of it were subjugated and starving, then our Empire beyond the seas, armed and guarded by the British Fleet, would carry on the struggle, until, in God's good time, the New World, with all its power and might, steps forth to the rescue and the liberation of the Old'.

Churchill's words gave courage to his fellow countrymen; in their hours of doubt and anxiety he had told them 'we shall never surrender'. Those who heard him speak felt themselves stronger, able to face the future with a sense of national unity and pride. 'We shall fight in France ...'; these five words were not a vague promise but an immediate reality; 224,318 British troops had been evacuated from Dunkirk, but 136,000 still remained in Western France, ready to be thrown into the battle. Yet more were on their way from Norway; the first 4,500 Allied troops had been successfully evacuated from Narvik on the night of June 3. There were also 200,000 Polish soldiers in France, the remnants of the Polish Army which had confronted the Germans nine months earlier in Poland, and who had managed to escape through Roumania.

On the evening of June 4, Hitler, having moved his headquarters to a village on Belgian soil, Brûly-de-Pesche, near the border with France, ordered 143 German divisions to advance along a 140-mile front. Facing them were sixty-five French divisions. At four in the morning of June 5 the battle was begun. As German forces now opened their southward attack with a fierce aerial and artillery bombardment along the line of the Somme and the Aisne, General Weygand issued an appeal to the French troops who would have to meet the onslaught. 'Let the thought of our country's sufferings inspire in you the firm resolve to resist,' it read. 'The fate of the nation and the future of our children depend on your determination.' That day, searching for the ablest of the soldiers to help direct the battle, Paul Reynaud appointed the recently promoted General de Gaulle to be Under-Secretary of State for War.

British troops were also in action on June 5, holding the line on the French right flank, between Abbeville and the sea. These troops, 'though they fought with dogged tenacity', noted the British Official History, were forced back and then virtually overwhelmed as a result of their mounting casualties, dwindling ammunition, and 'the superior numbers of the enemy'. Such, despite innumerable heroic actions, was the fate of the whole Allied line.

That day, over the front line north of Chantilly, one of Germany's most successful fighter pilots, Werner Molders, was forced to bail out of his burning Messerschmitt. Parachuting to earth, he found that he was on the German side of the front. Returning at once to action, he was to end the year with sixty-eight French and British 'kills' to his credit, becoming the first German pilot to receive the coveted Knight's Cross with each of its three enhancements, Oak Leaves, Swords and, most rarely awarded of all, Diamonds.

In London, now that the Enigma decrypts had been accurately understood, and with imminent invasion no longer a possibility, Churchill decided to make available to Reynaud for the battle in France two squadrons of fighters and four

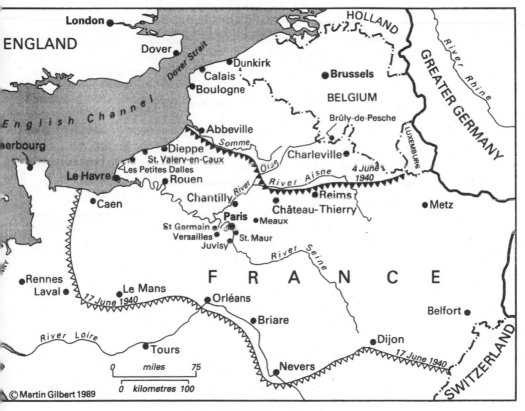

The battle for France, June 1940

squadrons of bombers. Churchill also agreed to Reynaud's request for more British troops to be sent to France; the 52nd Division would begin its southward crossing of the Channel on the following day. Churchill also wanted immediate action against the German forces already holding parts of the Channel coast, asking his military experts to prepare enterprises 'with specially trained troops of the hunter class, who can develop a reign of terror down these coasts', even landing tanks ashore in France which could 'do a deep raid inland, cutting a vital communication, and then crawl back, leaving a trail of German corpses behind them'.

The 'best' German troops, Churchill argued, would be attacking Paris, leaving the 'ordinary German troops of the line' along the Channel coast between the Somme and Dunkirk. The lives of these troops, he wrote, 'must be made an intense torment'.

On June 6 the Germans broke through the French defences at several points. The scent of a total German victory was in the air. 'After the war,' Goebbels wrote in triumph in his diary that day, 'we shall deal quickly with the Jews.' On the following day, King Haakon of Norway and his Government embarked at Tromsö on board the British cruiser *Devonshire*, bound for London. Before he left, the king broadcast to the Norwegian people, informing them that all military operations were at an end; the 6th Division had been forced to capitulate, and the Chief of Defence, General Otto Ruge, had been taken prisoner. 'When the orders became known,' Colonel Munthe-Kaas later wrote, 'it was as though the units had been paralysed. Profound grief and anger filled men's minds. Some wept. All the fighting, all the tough endurance, all the victorious combats had been of no avail.' 'All our hopes had collapsed,' one young Norwegian soldier later recalled, 'and the people felt that they had been deserted by their leaders and their Allies.'

Elsewhere, those Allies were engaged in yet another struggle, similarly outnumbered. In order to try to hamper British air support for France, on June 5, and again on June 6, the Germans had sent about a hundred bombers over Britain. But the British Government, encouraged to do so by Churchill, substantially increased its air support to France on June 6, and again on June 7, contributing on the 6th a total of 144 fighters to the air battle over France, the equivalent of twelve squadrons, and carrying out that day more than a hundred bomber sorties on targets indicated by the French High Command. Two additional fighter squadrons would be sent to France on June 8, as well as twenty-four complete barrage balloon outfits, together with their crews, for the defence of Paris.

As the Germans advanced, so their elation increased. 'As we drove along the main Dieppe–Paris road,' Rommel recalled on June 7, 'we passed a German tankman bringing in a French tractor with a tank trailing behind it. The young soldier's face was radiant, full of joy at his success.' Rommel himself was also in buoyant mood. 'Prisoners and booty for that day', he wrote, 'were tremendous and mounting hourly. Our losses were insignificant.' But on June 8, alarmed by the 'extremely strong resistance' being offered by the French north of Paris, Hitler issued his Directive No. 14, effectively halting the advance in the Château-

Thierry–Metz–Belfort triangle, and switching to the Paris front the troops which he had hoped to use to overrun eastern France.

In Norway, on June 8, the British evacuation of Narvik had reached its completion. During the last British naval efforts, the aircraft carrier *Glorious* and two destroyers, *Ardent* and *Acasta*, were sunk, and 1,515 officers and men were drowned. Only forty-three survived; forty from *Glorious*, two from *Ardent* and one, Able Seaman Carter, from *Acasta*. But with the successful evacuation that day of the last of the 25,000 troops who had been ashore, a sense of relief was mingled with the sense of loss.

Going down with the *Glorious* were the aircraft of two complete squadrons, with all but two of their pilots. That same day, June 8, Paul Reynaud pleaded with Churchill to send two or even three more squadrons to France, to join the five British squadrons already stationed there. But when the War Cabinet met that afternoon, they learned that two of those five squadrons, in action that very day, had lost ten of their eighteen aircraft. Churchill now tried to weigh up Reynaud's request. 'We could regard the present battle as decisive for France and ourselves,' he said, 'and throw in the whole of our fighter resources in an attempt to save the situation, and bring about victory. If we failed, we should then have to surrender.' Alternatively, Churchill told his War Cabinet colleagues, 'we should recognize that whereas the present land battle was of great importance, it would not be decisive one way or the other for Great Britain. If it were lost, and France was forced to submit, we could continue the struggle with good hopes of ultimate victory, provided we ensured that our fighter defences in this country were not impaired; but if we cast away our defence the war would be lost, even if the front in France were stabilized, since Germany would be free to turn her air force against this country, and would have us at her mercy'.

The issue was no longer one of balancing home and continental needs or forces; it was now a question of survival. 'One thing was certain,' Churchill told his colleagues, 'if this country were defeated, the war would be lost for France no less than for ourselves, whereas provided we were strong ourselves, we could win the war, and, in so doing, restore France to her position.'

The War Cabinet were unanimous in accepting the logic of Churchill's argument. No more fighters would be sent to France. And on the following day, June 9, as German troops swept towards Rouen, more than 11,000 British and French troops were assembled at the Channel port of Le Havre, to be evacuated to Britain. Other French troops, cut off entirely from the main body of the French Army, fell back on St Valery-en-Caux. There, on June 10, the British 51st Division, under General Fortune, was fighting a desperate action against far larger German forces. The French commander, General Ihler, urged Fortune to join him in the surrender of their respective armies, but Fortune refused to do so. At one moment, as British troops of the Gordon Highlanders were about to open fire on German tanks advancing towards them, French troops carrying white flags of surrender marched directly across the Highlanders' front, making it impossible for them to open fire.

Throughout June 10 the evacuations by sea continued, from Le Havre, from Cherbourg and from St Valery-en-Caux itself. Further east, the French had been driven back across the Seine, and were retreating amid much disorder towards the Loire. Reynaud suggested that day that there should be a final stand in Brittany; he was supported in this idea by de Gaulle. But Weygand had come to the conclusion that defeat was imminent, and wanted his forces to surrender.

That afternoon, as if to indicate how close France must be to defeat, Mussolini declared war not only on France, but on Britain. Commented Hitler: 'First they were too cowardly to take part. Now they are in a hurry so that they can share in the spoils.'

In London, all Italians between the ages of sixteen and seventy who had lived in England for less than twenty years were rounded up and interned, 4,100 in all, among them many managers, chefs and waiters from the principal London hotels and restaurants. In Washington, Roosevelt broadcast to the American people: 'On this tenth day of June 1940, the hand that held the dagger has struck it into the back of its neighbour.' Roosevelt also made a pledge to both France and Britain: 'We will extend', he said, 'to the opponents of force, the material resources of this nation. We will not slow down or detour. Signs and signals call for speed: full speed ahead.'

Alas for Britain and France, it was the Germans who were the only ones going full speed ahead. 'The sight of the sea with the cliffs on either side', wrote Rommel of his arrival on June 10 at Les Petites Dalles, on the Channel coast, 'thrilled and stirred every man of us; also the thought that we had reached the coast of France. We climbed out of our vehicles and walked down the shingle beach to the water's edge until the water lapped over our boots.'

For the British, evacuation had once again come to dominate their naval activity. On June 10, Lieutenant-Commander Peter Scott, son of the Arctic explorer Robert Falcon Scott, who had died in his attempt to reach the South Pole in 1912, brought the destroyer HMS *Broke* into St Valery-en-Caux to take off as many of the men of the 51st Division as he could. Going ashore, with only three quarters of an hour before he would have to lift anchor, he was able to assemble 120 soldiers, 95 of them wounded, and embark them safely.

The declarations of war by Italy opened up vast new war zones. In East Africa, Italy was sovereign in Eritrea, and ruler by conquest of Ethiopia. Britain was Italy's African neighbour in both British Somaliland and British East Africa. In North Africa, Italy was sovereign in Libya, its border with Egypt less than 450 miles from the Suez Canal, Britain's vital imperial waterway. On June 11, as if to show that their declaration of war on Britain was in earnest, the Italian Air Force bombed Port Sudan and Aden. Also during June 11, the Italian Air Force carried out eight separate raids on the British island of Malta, in the Mediterranean.

The British and French governments, alerted by their Intelligence services more than a week earlier as to Italy's likely declaration of war, had made plans on June 3 to bomb military targets in Italy as soon as war had broken out. On the night of June 11, from their bases in England, British bombers flew across France to bomb their targets in Genoa and Turin. From British East Africa, a small bombing raid was also carried out on Italian military installation in

Eritrea. The war had come to Africa. It had also come to the Pacific Ocean. Within forty-eight hours of Italy's declaration of war, not only on Britain and France, but on their Empires, the Australian armed merchant cruiser *Manoora*, steaming near the island of Nauru, sighted and gave chase to an Italian merchant vessel, the *Romolo*. The *Romolo*, unable to defend herself, and unwilling to surrender, scuttled herself instead.

Not Africa, however, nor the Pacific, but France, was the fulcrum of war on June 11, as German forces occupied Reims, and the French Government left Paris, heading southward towards the Loire. That afternoon, Churchill flew across the Channel to try to find out for himself what France intended to do; he found the Government at Briare, on the River Loire. There, he learned from General Georges of the enormous scale of French losses since the renewed German offensive had begun on June 5. Of the 103 Allied divisions in the line, 35 had been lost in their entirety. Other divisions had been reduced 'to two battalions and a few guns'. The existing line, such as it was, 'was held by nothing more than a light screen of weak and weary divisions, with no reserves behind them'.

Churchill urged the French to make Paris a fortress, to fight in every street. A great city, he said, if stubbornly defended, 'absorbed immense armies'. At this, a British eye-witness noted, 'the French perceptibly froze'. To make Paris 'a city of ruins', replied Marshal Pétain, 'will not affect the issue'. The French troops, said Reynaud, 'were worn out through lack of sleep and shattered by the action of the enemy bombers. There was no hope of relief anywhere.'

Once more, Reynaud appealed for extra British air support. But once more Churchill reiterated that none was available. To send more fighter squadrons to France, where between six and eight British squadrons were already taking part each day in the battle over France, might, Churchill said, 'destroy the last hope the Allies had of breaking the back of Germany's might'. Although the collapse of France opened up 'the most distressing picture', Churchill added, 'yet he felt certain that even then Germany could at last be brought to her knees'.

Despite a brief discussion of a plan to hold Brittany, which a number of French generals, including de Gaulle, were prepared to examine, it was clear that the resources for a successful military resistance were almost totally used up. Churchill now spoke of the day when France would herself be under German occupation, telling Reynaud and his colleagues: 'It is possible that the Nazis may dominate Europe, but it will be a Europe in revolt, and in the end it is certain that a regime whose victories are in the main due to its machines will one day collapse. Machines will beat machines.'

This long-term prospect could give no comfort to the French. That night, as Churchill prepared to go to bed at Briare, Marshal Pétain informed Reynaud 'that it would be necessary to seek an armistice'.

'Machines will beat machines': Churchill's words were not mere wishful thinking. That same night, as he slept in France, the first American military supplies for Britain and France were being loaded on board ship at the United States Army docks at Raritan, New Jersey. Six hundred railway freight cars had brought their precious cargoes to the dockside; these were the supplies authorized by Roosevelt ten days earlier, including 900 field guns and 80,000 machine guns. There were also half a million rifles, manufactured in 1917 and 1918, and stored since then in grease, together with 250 rounds of ammunition each. In London, before leaving for France, Churchill had approved a munitions programme whereby five hundred to six hundred heavy tanks would be ready for action by the end of March 1941.

That same June 11, far from the débâcle in France, the Norwegian army was finally demobilized and, having been disarmed, its soldiers returned to their homes. Some, determined to join the Allies, managed to leave Norway on the last of the British warships to sail westward back across the North Sea, or across the border to Sweden. One of them, Theodor Broch, Mayor of ill-fated Narvik, has recalled: 'It was a harsh land we had had, but never had it been so delightful, so desirable as now. Our leading men had already been driven abroad. Our ships had sunk or sailed away. All along the border were young men like myself. Thousands more would follow. We had to leave to learn the one craft we had neglected. We had built good homes in the mountains, but we had neglected to fence them properly.' Broch added: 'Now strangers had taken over our land. They would loot it and pluck it clean before we returned. But the country itself they could not spoil. The sea and the fjords and the mountains – to these we alone could give life. We were coming back. The mountains would wait for us.'

The morning of June 12 saw yet another setback for the Allied cause; at St Valery-en-Caux, on the Channel coast, 46,000 French and British troops under General Ihler, including the 8,000 British troops under General Fortune, surrendered to Rommel. German artillery, firing directly on to the beaches, had prevented more than 3,321 British and French troops from being evacuated by sea; there was to be no second Dunkirk. 'No less than twelve generals were brought in as prisoners,' Rommel later wrote, 'among them four divisional commanders'. A German Air Force lieutenant, who until an hour earlier had been a prisoner-of-war, was put in charge of guarding the captured generals and their staffs. 'He was visibly delighted,' Rommel wrote, 'by the change of role.'

That evening, General Weygand telephoned to the French Military Governor of Paris, General Hering, ordering him to declare Paris an open city. The French capital would not, as Churchill had wished, become the scene of fighting. No tanks, no barricades, no snipers would challenge the German troops when they arrived. The Germans agreed to accept this arrangement only if the French would cease all military activity along a wide belt of suburban towns. General Hering agreed. Through St Germain, through Versailles, through Juvisy, through St Maur, and through Meaux, the Germans would march unchallenged.

Seventy years had passed since the first German siege of Paris during the Franco-Prussian War, when the French capital had sent out messages and supplies by hot-air balloon. More than twenty-five years had passed since the Kaiser's armies had swept forward as far as Meaux, but had failed, during four subsequent years of war, to reach Paris, despite advancing as far as Château-Thierry in June 1918. Now, for the third time in seventy years, Paris was in danger.

*       *       *

Britain did not intend to abandon France to her fate. As Churchill had earlier promised Reynaud, extra British troops had been ordered to France, including men evacuated from Narvik, and Canadian troops already based in Britain. On June 12, the commander-designate of these forces, General Brooke, arrived in France. Churchill, himself still at Briare, was able to inform Reynaud on June 12 that these reinforcements were already being deployed around Le Mans. At the same time, a hundred British bombers, from their bases in Britain, were attacking the German lines of communication according to targets specifically designated by the French. In addition, fifty British fighters and seventy British bombers were still operating from bases in France against the advancing German forces.

That afternoon, Churchill flew back to England. Beneath him, from 8,000 feet, he saw the port of Le Havre burning. It too was under German attack. That night it was Le Havre's turn to be the scene of yet another evacuation; by the early hours of June 13, 2,222 British troops had been taken back safely to England, while a further 8,837 had been taken around the French coast to Cherbourg, where they prepared to return to action side by side with the French troops on the Loire. But would the French be fighting for much longer? On his return to London, Churchill had told his War Cabinet that at Briare the French Ministers 'had been studiously polite and dignified, but it was clear that France was near the end of organized resistance'.

In a last minute effort to stiffen French resolve, Churchill returned to France on June 13. The French Government was then at Tours. It was now 'too late', Reynaud said, to organize a redoubt in Brittany. There was now no hope of 'any early victory'. France had given 'her best, her youth, her lifeblood; she can do no more'. She was entitled to enter into a separate peace with Germany.

Churchill urged Reynaud to explore one more avenue of hope, a direct appeal to Roosevelt 'in the strongest terms' for American participation. 'A firm promise from America', Churchill said, would introduce 'a tremendous new factor' for France. Reynaud agreed to try, and in a telegram to Roosevelt urged the United States to 'throw the weight of American power in the scales, in order to save France, the advance guard of democracy'. In his telegram, Reynaud asked Roosevelt 'to declare war if you can, but in any event to send us every form of help short of an expeditionary force'. If this were done, then, with 'America's full help, Britain and France would be able 'to march on to victory'.

That same day, Hitler granted an exclusive interview to the Hearst Press correspondent, Karl von Wiegand, to whom he stressed Germany's total lack of territorial designs in North or South America.

Reynaud's determination to continue the fight, if Roosevelt's reply were favourable, was not shared by his Cabinet colleagues. After Churchill had returned to Britain, Weygand repeated his call for an armistice. Other Ministers, led by Mandel, wanted to move the Government to French North Africa, and to carry on the fight from there. Later that day, as German troops drew even closer to Paris, the Government moved further south, to Bordeaux. There, they received Roosevelt's reply. The American Government, it said, was doing 'everything in its power to make available to the Allied Governments the material they so urgently require, and our efforts to do still more are being redoubled'.

This message was clearly not a declaration of war; but at least its publication might encourage the French to carry on the fight. Roosevelt was agreeable to having the message published. But the Secretary of State, Cordell Hull, was opposed. The British Government did its best to persuade Hull to change his mind. 'It seemed to us', Lord Halifax telegraphed to Bordeaux, to the British Ambassador to France on the morning of June 14, 'that it would have been impossible for the President to send such a message unless he meant it to be published, and it seemed very near to the definite step of a declaration of war.'

Churchill was still hopeful that the American response would persuade the French to fight on. Were France to continue to resist, he telegraphed to Reynaud late on 13 June, an American declaration of war 'must inevitably follow', and with it a 'sovereign opportunity of bringing about the world-wide oceanic and economic coalition which must be fatal to Nazi domination'.

No such coalition was yet in prospect. On June 14 it was other forces who were gathering their strength. That day the Soviet Union delivered an ultimatum to the Lithuanian Government to allow Soviet forces to occupy their country. Lithuania complied. Two days later, Latvia and Estonia suffered a similar fate. Meanwhile, Roosevelt confirmed that his telegram to Reynaud could not be published. His message reached London at dawn on June 14. The United States, noted one of Churchill's Private Secretaries, 'has been caught napping militarily and industrially. She may be really useful to us in a year but we are living from hour to hour.'

At the very moment Roosevelt's depressing negative reached London, German troops were entering Paris. By half-past six on the morning of 14 June German military vehicles had reached the Place de la Concorde, and a German command post had been established in the Hôtel Crillon. Two million Parisians had already fled the city. The 700,000 who remained woke up to the sound of German loudspeakers announcing that there would be a curfew that evening starting at eight o'clock. That morning, a huge swastika flag was hung beneath the Arc de Triomphe, and promptly at 9.45, led by a military band, German soldiers of General von Kluge's Fourth Army marched down the Champs Élysées, in deliberate imitation of the French victory march of November 1918.

An hour and a quarter later, at eleven o'clock, the Prefect of the Paris Police, Roger Langeron, was summoned to the German Commandant and ordered to hand over the police files on all those who were politically active. To the Commandant's anger, Langeron explained that these files had already been removed from Paris.

The German celebrations continued. So too did the establishment of the Gestapo system; espionage, informers, arrests and terror. That morning, the first twenty Gestapo functionaries arrived in Paris, headed by the thirty-year-old ss Colonel, Helmut Knochen, who had earlier made a name for himself during the successful kidnapping of Major Stevens and Captain Best at the Dutch frontier the previous November.

The fall of France, June 1940

At that moment of German triumph, a British officer, the Earl of Suffolk, together with his secretary Miss Morden and his chauffeur Fred Hards, were in France on a special mission at the request of the British Government. Their task was to find and bring back to Britain £2½ million of French industrial diamonds essential for the making of machine tools, as well as specific rare machine tools essential for the manufacture of armaments. They had also been asked to bring back to Britain the heavy water which had been manufactured in France by a group of nuclear scientists; and also to offer the scientists a safe haven in Britain.

The Earl of Suffolk's mission was successful. On June 14, two scientists, Hans von Halban and Lew Kowarski, who had earlier moved south from Clermont Ferrand, were at Bordeaux with twenty-six cans – the world's supply – of heavy water, an essential factor in the uranium research needed for the construction of an atomic bomb. At Bordeaux, the Earl, his chauffeur, his secretary, the scientists, the heavy water, the industrial diamonds and the machine tools were taken on board a collier, the *Broompark*, which was waiting for them. As they sailed for England, the ship next to them was sunk by a magnetic mine; four days later they reached the safety of Falmouth.

Others were unable to flee. That June 14, as the Germans marched through Paris in triumph, the fifty-six-year-old Austrian-born Ernst Weiss committed suicide in his Paris apartment. A novelist, a former medical officer in the Austro-Hungarian Army in the First World War, a pupil of Freud and a friend of Kafka, he was also a Jew. In March 1938, when Hitler annexed Austria, Weiss had fled from Vienna to Prague. In March 1939, when German forces entered Czechoslovakia, he had fled Prague for Paris. Now he felt that there was no more hope. A thousand miles to the east, the Germans had begun the deportation of 728 Poles, held until then in prison in Tarnow, to the new concentration camp at Auschwitz. Some had been imprisoned because they had tried to escape from the General Government southwards into Slovakia. Others had been imprisoned because they were leaders of their local communities, priests and schoolteachers. Three of these deportees were Jews, two lawyers and the director of the local Hebrew school; none of the Jews, and only 134 of the Poles were to survive the torments of the camp. As the passenger train in which they were being taken to Auschwitz passed through Cracow station, the deportees heard an excited train announcer trumpet over the loudspeaker system the fall of Paris.

As the citizens of Paris watched their German conquerors, the citizens of Rennes, in western France, were surprised to see Canadian troops hurrying through their town. They had disembarked that morning at Brest, and were intent on moving up to the front as quickly as possible. 'Everywhere the people cheer us,' one of their officers noted. 'Our lads are puffed up like a load of dynamite.' Continuing their journey by train, by nightfall they had reached Laval. As they bedded down for the night, they could see the long line of cars and carts loaded with bedding parked beside the road, or heading west towards the coast.

On June 15 German troops took Verdun, the fortress which in 1916 had withstood every German onslaught, and for whose tenacious defence Marshal Pétain had won such acclaim. In western France, the Canadian troops who had moved forward as far as Laval on 14 June, began preparations to go into action against the Germans, who were then less than twenty miles away. But on the morning of June 15 they were ordered to take the train to St Malo, on the coast, where, at five o'clock that evening they boarded a British ship, the steamship *Biarritz*, bound for Southampton. Their only losses: six men who had gone missing during their journey to Laval and back.

On June 15, in Bordeaux, Reynaud told the British Ambassador that, if America did not agree to come into the war 'at a very early date', France would be unable to continue to fight, even from French North Africa. As soon as he received Reynaud's message, Churchill telegraphed to Roosevelt to reinforce Reynaud's plea for an American declaration of war. 'When I speak of the United States entering the war', Churchill explained, 'I am, of course, not thinking in terms of an expeditionary force, which I know is out of the question. What I have in mind is the tremendous moral effect that such an American decision could produce, not merely on France, but also in all the democratic countries in the world, and, in the opposite sense, on the German and Italian peoples'.

This telegram was sent from London to Washington at 10.45 on the evening of June 15. It was no more effective than those which had preceded it. Roosevelt had no intention of entering the war, no matter how the matter was phrased or disguised. Nor did the facts on the ground give any confidence that France could maintain the battle for much longer. Paris was lost. Verdun was lost. On June 15, of 261 British fighters sent to France in the past ten days, 75 had been shot down or destroyed on the ground by German bombers. A further 120 were unserviceable or lacked the fuel to fly back to Britain; they were burned on the French airfields on June 15 to prevent them from being captured by the Germans. Sixty-six were flown back to Britain. In ten days, the Royal Air Force had lost a quarter of its fighter strength.

On June 16 the Germans entered Dijon. As the French Cabinet met in Bordeaux to discuss the new crisis, a German Army Group, hitherto quiescent, crossed the Rhine at Colmar. At the Cabinet meeting, Pétain, as Deputy Prime Minister, called for an immediate armistice, and threatened to resign if his colleagues refused. Reynaud, in despair, asked Britain to release France from its agreement not to make a separate peace. The British Government had no choice but to agree. It did so, giving as its condition that the French Fleet 'immediately sails for British ports'. No such promise was made. As a last resort, the British Government offered France an 'Anglo-French Union' which would continue to make war even if France were overrun. The two countries, joined as one, could not then be defeated unless Britain also went down. Reynaud favoured this plan. His colleagues were not enthusiastic. Thereupon Reynaud resigned.

That evening, Marshal Pétain formed a new government. Its first act, at eleven o'clock that night, was to ask the Germans for an armistice. In the late morning of June 18, at his headquarters at Brûly-de-Pesche, Hitler learned of the French Government's request. In delight, he jerked up his knee in a jump of joy, a single, ecstatic movement which was caught by his official cameraman, Walter Frentz, but which John Grierson, a documentary producer then serving in the Canadian Army was to 'loop' — that is, to repeat in a series of frames — so as to give the impression that Hitler was dancing.

Negotiations for an armistice began almost at once; nevertheless, Hitler took the precaution to order his troops to continue their advance in the west, to take Cherbourg and Brest, and to take Strasbourg, the city which Germany had conquered in 1871 and France regained in 1918.

Hitler's principal concern, as the negotiations for an armistice continued throughout June 17, was that the French might still be tempted by Britain, or pushed by the severity of his own peace terms, to carry on the war in North Africa. To avert this danger, he was prepared to contemplate the survival of France as a sovereign power; in this way the legitimate Government of France would continue to be sovereign over the French colonies overseas, which otherwise might go over to a North African based government, or be seized by Britain. To ensure that a sovereign French Government would have a semblance of reality, he would have to leave it with a part of France unoccupied, under the direct rule of a French Prime Minister and Cabinet. This he was prepared to do, even though Paris would remain within the German occupied zone.

At midday on June 17, Pétain broadcast to the French people, to inform them that negotiations for an armistice were in progress. 'Thank God, now we're on our own' was the comment of Tubby Mermagen, commander of a British fighter squadron. 'He expressed the feelings of us all,' one of Mermagen's Flight Commanders, Douglas Bader, later recalled. That afternoon, Churchill broadcast to the British people: 'Whatever has happened in France', he said, 'makes no difference to our actions and purpose. We shall do our best to be worthy of this high honour. We shall defend our Island home, and with the British Empire we shall fight on unconquerable until the curse of Hitler is lifted from the brows of mankind. We are sure that in the end all will come right.'

That night, British bombers struck at the German oil installations at Leuna, south of Leipzig, in the heart of Germany.

Throughout June 17, British troops were being evacuated from France; Operation Ariel, as the new evacuations were called, was almost on the scale of Dunkirk's Operation Dynamo, though without its risk of an imminent assault from the land. From Cherbourg, 30,630 men were taken off; from St Malo 21,474 Canadians; from Brest, 32,584 soldiers and airmen were rescued; from St Nazaire and Nantes, 57,235; from La Pallice, 2,303 Britons and Poles, and, from a dozen ports on the southern half of the Atlantic coast of France, 19,000 troops, most of them Poles. In the eight days between June 16 and 24, all 163,225 had been taken off to safety. One boat load, however, was not so fortunate; on June 17 the passenger liner *Lancastria* took five thousand soldiers and civilians on board at St Nazaire. As she left the port, heading for England, a German bomber struck, and the ship was sunk. Nearly three thousand of those on board were drowned.

Churchill, on being given details of the disaster, forbade immediate publication of the news, fearing its effect on public morale. 'I had intended to release the news a few days later,' he was to recall after the war, 'but events crowded upon us so black and so quickly, that I forgot to lift the ban, and it was some time before the knowledge of this horror became public.' It was only six weeks later, after the facts were publicized in the United States, that the British Government released the news.

The British, Polish, Canadian and French troops who left France in Operation Ariel had reason to believe that their return to Britain would be followed quickly enough by a German invasion of the now vulnerable island. But Hitler had as yet no such plan. 'With regard to the landing in Britain,' German naval headquarters were informed on June 17 by the High Command, 'the Führer has not yet expressed any such intention, being well aware of the difficulties involved in such an operation. Up to now, therefore, the High Command of the armed forces has not carried out any preparatory work.'

That night, as on the previous night, British bombers set off for targets in Germany, their task being to strike at 'aircraft factories, factories making aluminium, oil-producing plants and communications' throughout the Ruhr. But the confidence and determination which such raids showed could not mask the grave reality in France, where, in the five weeks since May 10, a total of 959 aircraft had been destroyed, and 1,192 pilots and aircrew shot down.

At noon on June 18 Hitler met Mussolini at Munich. To Mussolini's surprise, Hitler made 'many reservations', as the Italian Foreign Minister, Count Ciano, noted in his diary, 'on the desirability of demolishing the British Empire, which he considers, even today, to be an important factor in world equilibrium'. Despite Mussolini's objections, Hitler then supported the proposals put forward by Ribbentrop, but in fact Hitler's own, for lenient peace terms for France. 'Hitler is now the gambler who has made the big scoop,' Ciano wrote, 'and would like to get up from the table, risking nothing more.'

Hitler was confident that the French will to resist was broken. At Bordeaux, the French Foreign Minister, Paul Baudouin, and the Minister of Marine, Admiral Darlan, both assured the British Ambassador that the French Fleet would be sailed to safety or scuttled rather than be allowed to fall into enemy hands. These brave words masked a lack of ability to carry them out. Equally brave, and apparently equally empty except in courage, were the words broadcast from London at six o'clock that evening by General de Gaulle. The French Government, he said, 'alleging the defeat of our armies', had entered into negotiations with the Germans with a view to bringing about an end to the hostilities. 'But has the last word been said? Must we abandon all hope? Is our defeat final? – No!'

De Gaulle went on to assure his listeners 'that the cause of France is not lost. The very factors that brought about our defeat may one day lead us to victory. For France is not alone! She is not alone! Behind her is a vast Empire, and she can make common cause with the British Empire, which commands the seas and is continuing the struggle'. Like Britain, de Gaulle added, France could also 'draw unreservedly on the immense industrial resources of the United States'. The outcome of the struggle, de Gaulle asserted, had not been decided by the Battle of France. 'This is a world war.' Mistakes had been made, but the fact remained 'that there still exists in the world everything we need to crush our enemies some day. Today we are crushed by the sheer weight of the mechanized forces hurled against us, but we can still look to a future in which even greater mechanized forces will bring us victory. Therein lies the destiny of the world.'

With this forceful echoing of Churchill's words at Briare on June 11 – 'Machines will beat machines' – de Gaulle went on to call upon all French officers 'who are at present on British soil or may be in the future, with or without their arms', as well as on all French engineers and skilled workmen, 'to get in touch with me. Whatever happens, the flame of French resistance must not and shall not die.'

A forty-nine-year-old Brigadier-General in exile was challenging the authority of a Marshal of France. His words were heard by many with respectful incredulity. Today they are inscribed on a plaque attached to the wall of the building in which he spoke them.

Throughout June 18, German forces continued their advance across France, intent upon creating a zone of occupation, not by negotiations, but by military force; by nightfall they had occupied Cherbourg. 'There were some bad moments for us,' Rommel wrote to his wife, 'and the enemy was at first between twenty and forty times our superior in numbers. On top of that they had twenty to thirty-five forts ready for action, and many single batteries. However, by buckling-to quickly, we succeed in carrying out the Führer's special order to take Cherbourg quickly.' Other German commanders were equally successful. Also, on June 18, Vannes, Rennes, Briare, Le Mans, Nevers and Colmar were occupied.

That same day, as a trumpet call of defiance, British bombers struck at military targets in Hamburg and Bremen.

On June 19 the British began the evacuation of the Channel Islands, so close to France that they must inevitably fall to Germany once France fell. In all, 22,656 British citizens were taken off in five days. Also on June 19, as German forces entered Nantes and Brest, and approached St Nazaire, a French naval officer, Captain Ronarch, succeeded in sailing the battleship *Jean Bart* out of the dry dock at St Nazaire, where she was being fitted out for action, and sailing her to Casablanca, in French Morocco. That day, on the battlefield, it was thirty troops from French Morocco who suffered from the savagery of an SS unit, then in action between Dijon and Lyon; in clearing out a rearguard position, the SS refused to take any prisoners, regarding the Moroccans as racially inferior, and killing even those who offered to surrender.

On June 20 a French delegation, consisting of a diplomat, an Army general, an Air Force general, and an admiral travelled to Rethondes, in the forest of Compiègne, to conduct the armistice negotiations with the Germans. That same day, Hitler told Admiral Raeder that one benefit of the defeat of France would be that Germany could send all her Jews, and all the Jews of Poland, to the French island of Madagascar, in the Indian Ocean.

As the negotiators at Rethondes continued their talks on the morning of June 21, the last German troops reached their point of furthest advance. From Rennes, Rommel wrote to his wife: 'The war has now gradually turned into a lightning tour of France. In a few days it will be over for good. The people here are relieved that it is all passing off so quietly.' Things were not so quiet near the village of Villefranche, south of Nevers, where a platoon of the SS Death's Head Division, in action against both French and Moroccan troops, took twenty-five white French prisoners, but no Moroccans. That day's fighting, stated the division's communiqué, had yielded 'twenty-five French prisoners and forty-four dead Negroes'.

Far from the battlefield, in a sun-drenched clearing in the forest of Compiègne,

21 June saw the final humiliation of the French Government. Hitler had chosen to present its plenipotentiaries with the armistice terms in the same railway coach in which the Germans had signed the surrender at the end of the First World War, and which since then had been a proud French exhibit to the victory over Germany. Until being brought to Compiègne, from Bordeaux, the French negotiators had had no inkling of where the negotiations were to be held. Now, at half past three on the afternoon of June 21, they found themselves confronted, in the railway coach itself, by a triumphant, silent Hitler, as General Keitel read out to them the preamble to the German armistice terms. After ten minutes, Hitler left; Keitel then told the four Frenchmen that there could be no discussion, only compliance. Three-fifths of the territory of European France would be under German occupation. A French Government would be set up in the unoccupied zone, and would be responsible for the administration of the French colonial empire. The French Fleet would not be allowed to pass out of French control. All 1,538,000 French prisoners-of-war would remain under German control.

Hitler having left the scene of France's triumph in 1918 and its humiliation now, the French negotiators continued to argue; as they did so, several members of the former Reynaud Government who had hoped to continue resistance in North Africa, including Georges Mandel, were on their way by sea to Casablanca. That same day, coming by ship from France, the President and Ministers of the Polish Government-in-exile, which had been set up in Paris after the defeat of Poland, reached Southampton; as a gesture of support, King George VI went to Paddington station in London to greet them in their new city of exile.

The armistice negotiations at Compiègne continued throughout June 22. That day, the Italian Army, advancing along the French Riviera, occupied Menton. At six o'clock that evening, General Keitel, vexed at the delays upon which the French negotiators at Compiègne were still insisting, told them: 'If we cannot reach agreement within an hour, negotiations will be broken off, and the delegation will be conducted back to the French lines.' The negotiators then telephoned to the French Government at Bordeaux for instructions. They were instructed to sign. At ten minutes before seven, the armistice was signed. A sixth nation had succumbed to Germany in less than nine months.

Those French ex-Ministers who had hoped to maintain a sovereign France in North Africa were told of the signature of the armistice while still on board ship on their way along the Atlantic coast to Casablanca. From the North Sea shore, the German commerce raider *Pinguin* sailed on June 22 for 'Siberia', the code name for a point in the Indian Ocean between Mauritius and Australia where she and three fellow commerce raiders could meet their supply ships for food, ammunition and fuel, while sinking British merchant ships.

Hitler, the master of Poland, Norway, Denmark, Holland, Belgium and now France, had not forgotten his determination to bring Britain to her knees. But in Churchill he had an adversary who was equally determined. 'His Majesty's Government believe', Churchill declared that night, 'that whatever happens they will be able to carry the war wherever it may lead, on the seas, in the air, and upon land, to a successful conclusion.'

Britain was trying to make clear that she intended to fight on; the very newspaper which on June 23 carried the headline 'French Sign Armistice' on its front page had, as its back page banner headline: 'RAF Bomb Berlin, Sink Ships, and Set Oil Store on Fire'. That night, the first of a special volunteer group of British 'Striking Companies' carried out a series of hit-and-run raids on the French coast between Calais and Boulogne. They were unopposed, and returned safely.

At 3.30 on the morning of June 23 Hitler left his headquarters at Brûly-de-Pesche and flew to Le Bourget aerodrome outside Paris. It was to be his first and only visit to the French capital. Reaching the city at a quarter to six, he was driven quickly to the most notable sites, including the Opera, the architecture of which he had admired from afar as a student, and Napoleon's Tomb. 'That', he said to his entourage after leaving the tomb, 'was the greatest and finest moment of my life.' He then gave orders that the remains of Napoleon's son, the Duc de Reichstadt, which rested in Vienna, should be transferred to Paris to lie next to his father. 'I am grateful to fate', Hitler told one of those with him, 'to have seen this town whose aura has always preoccupied me.'

During his tour of Paris, Hitler ordered the destruction of two First World War monuments, the statue of General Mangin, one of the victors of 1918, and the memorial to Edith Cavell, the British nurse shot in Brussels by a German firing squad in 1915. His order was carried out. Leaving Paris at half past eight that morning, he returned to the airport, ordered his pilot to circle several times over the city, and flew back to his headquarters. 'It was the dream of my life to be permitted to see Paris,' he told his architect friend Albert Speer. 'I cannot say how happy I am to have that dream fulfilled today.'

Sixteen months later, recalling his visit to Paris, Hitler told General von Kluge: 'The first newspaper-seller who recognized me stood there and gaped.' The man had been selling copies of Le Matin. Seeing cars approach, he had rushed forward to the prospective customers, seeking to thrust the newspaper in their hands and calling out all the while, 'Le Matin! Le Matin!' Suddenly, seeing who was in the car, he beat a quick retreat.

Back at Brûly-de-Pesche, Hitler asked Albert Speer to draw up a decree 'ordering full-scale resumption of work' on the proposed new public buildings and monuments which Speer had designed for Berlin, with Hitler's guidance. All building work had stopped on the outbreak of war in September 1939. Now it must begin again. 'Wasn't Paris beautiful?' Hitler said to Speer, 'But Berlin must be made far more beautiful. In the past I often considered whether I would not have to destroy Paris. But when we are finished in Berlin, Paris will only be a shadow. So why should we destroy it?'

The new Berlin was to be ready in 1950. This 'accomplishment', Hitler told Speer, would be 'the greatest step in the preservation of our history'.

# 8

# France's agony, Britain's resolve

JUNE-JULY 1940

On 24 June 1940 the first ship carrying German- and Italian-born internees left Britain for Canada. Churchill and his Government were determined to have no possible fifth column in their midst. Many of those sent across the Atlantic were Jewish refugees from Nazism who had found haven in Britain. But the urgency of the hour did not give time to sort out the harmless from the potentially dangerous. Further south on the same ocean, the French ex-Ministers reached Casablanca on June 24, only to find that the Governor-General of Morocco, General Noguès, who a week earlier had appealed for a continuation of the war from North Africa, had already accepted the armistice. In London, General de Gaulle called for the establishment of a French National Committee to rally all Frenchmen who wished to continue to fight; it seemed a voice in the wilderness.

The future for Britain appeared bleak, even to Churchill at this time. 'I shall myself never enter into any peace negotiations with Hitler,' he told the Canadian Prime Minister Mackenzie King, on June 24, 'but obviously I cannot bind a future Government, which, if we were deserted by the United States and beaten down here, might very easily be a kind of Quisling affair ready to accept German overlordship and protection.'

In Holland, on June 24, the German Governor-General, Seyss-Inquart, pro-rogued Parliament; eleven days later he was to make it a criminal offence to listen to British radio broadcasts. In the wake of such a total German victory such orders seemed natural, irresistible. When, in the early hours of June 25, the Franco-German armistice formally came into force, the cost of unsuccessful war had become brutally clear: 92,000 French soldiers had been killed, 7,500 Belgian soldiers and 2,900 Dutch soldiers. The British, fearful now of invasion, had lost 3,500 men. The Germans, now masters of Europe from the North Cape to the Pyrenees, and from the Atlantic Ocean to the River Bug, had lost 45,000 men in this, their third victorious campaign in less than ten months. 'At last the armistice is in force,' Rommel wrote to his wife on 25 June. 'We're now less than two hundred miles from the Spanish frontier and hope to go straight on there so as to get the whole Atlantic coast in our hands. How wonderful it's all been.'

Throughout France's time of agony, the United States had preserved a tenacious neutrality. On June 26 the Government of Turkey, anxious not to be drawn into any widening conflict, announced its 'non-belligerency'. The Soviet Union, ever mindful of its territorial losses after the First World War, and of Hitler's power of lightning action now, demanded from Roumania the cession of the province of Bessarabia and of the region of northern Bukovina. Hitler, anxious neither to stir up nor to alarm his Soviet ally, urged the Roumanian Government to agree to the Soviet demands. On the following day, the Roumanians complied.

Hitler had remained at his headquarters at Brûly-de-Pesche throughout June 25. Once more, it was the architectural future of the Reich that was on his mind. 'Berlin must be reconstructed as soon as possible,' he wrote that day, 'so as to reflect the grandeur of the capital of a strong Reich in keeping with the greatness of our victory.' The same applied, he wrote, to the reconstruction of Munich, Linz and Hamburg, and of the Party Halls in Nuremberg. All Reich officials, local government officials and Nazi Party officials must help the General Building Inspector for Berlin 'in the implementation of his task'.

Leaving Brûly-de-Pesche on June 26, Hitler visited the Western Front of his First World War service, taking with him two of his former comrades-in-arms. Together, they found the house in which they had been billeted behind the lines. At one moment in the tour, Hitler climbed up an overgrown slope in search of a concrete step behind which he remembered having taken cover in those distant days. It was still there. But driving through Lille, he experienced an unpleasant incident, which he was to recall sixteen months later in conversation with General von Kluge. 'I still have before me', Hitler said, 'the mental picture of that woman in Lille who saw me from her window and exclaimed: "The Devil!"'

That 'Devil's' work was never done. On June 26, while Hitler was revisiting old haunts, his police and Gestapo were shooting down Polish writers, politicians and civic leaders in the Palmiry forest execution site. Among those killed that day was Mieczyslaw Niedzialkowski, the leader of the Polish Socialists, editor of the Socialist newspaper *Robotnik* and a member of the Polish Parliament.

In German-occupied France, on June 27, the Germans set up two radio stations, one at Brest and one at Cherbourg, to send out radio beams along which their bombers could be directed to targets in Britain. The Germans used their most secret communications system, the Enigma, to transmit the instructions setting up those two stations; as a result, the British learned of the stations that same day. There was also a continuing sense of relief in Britain that she was alone. 'Personally', King George VI wrote to his mother, Queen Mary, on June 27, 'I feel happier now that we have no allies to be polite to and to pamper.'

From Italy came news on the following day that Marshal Italo Balbo, the Governor of Libya, and a renowned aviator, had been killed in the air above Tobruk; returning from a reconnaissance flight, on the border with Egypt, his aeroplane was shot down by mistake by Italian anti-aircraft fire.

On June 28 the Enigma messages alerted British Intelligence to the fact that most of the German long-range bombers, their work above France completed, would end their refitting by July 8. A bomber offensive on Britain was thus an imminent possibility. On June 30 German troops landed on British soil: the Channel Islands of Jersey and Guernsey, off the French coast. They were unopposed. That same day, in distant Bessarabia, Soviet airborne forces landed near the Danube port of Izmail. They too were unopposed.

The Germans, masters of so much territory, did not delay in planning how best to exploit it. On June 30, Hitler issued instructions to the German military authorities in Paris 'to take into custody all objects of art, whether state-owned, or in private Jewish hands'. This was not, he explained, an expropriation, 'but a transfer to our safekeeping, as a security for eventual peace negotiations'. Not only were the museums ransacked, but also the main Jewish private collections, and the stock of the principal Jewish art dealers.

Stock of a different kind was discussed that day by Hitler, when he was shown by Himmler a further plan for settling the German-annexed areas of Poland with 'strong German stock'. What Himmler proposed was for one-eighth of the Polish population of these areas to be transferred to Germany as 'racially acceptable stock', while the other seven-eighths would be expelled into the General Government. German soldiers and ss men, after two and four years' service respectively, would be sent to the annexed areas to work the land for eight years, then marry and take over a farm or estate. Poles from the General Government would provide the labour force. Poles who had sexual relations with their masters would be sentenced to death, or given long prison sentences. 'The Führer said that every point I made was right,' Himmler noted.

On the day after this conversation, it was announced in Berlin, by the Ministry of the Interior, that at the psychiatric instititute at Görden, 'under the direction of specialists, all therapeutic possibilities will be administered according to the latest knowledge'. Behind this bland formality, the killing of children judged mentally defective was instituted without delay, according to the 'T.4' euthanasia programme. Death usually occurred within twenty-four hours of the child's arrival at Görden. Under a rule laid down by Dr Viktor Brack, the head of the euthanasia department of Hitler's Chancellery, the actual killing had to be done by a doctor.

Some killings were carried out by injections, four to six patients at a time; but, increasingly, gas was used, and the patients led in groups of eighteen to twenty to false 'shower' rooms, where they sat on benches while the gas was inserted along the water pipes. Dr Irmfried Eberl, head of the euthanasia department at Brandenburg, had perfected this technique of gassing; both Dr Brack and Hitler's personal physician, Dr Brandt, expressed themselves satisfied by it. Those who were to be gassed had to be certified according to certain criteria: mental deficiency, schizophrenia, long hospitalization or total inca-pacity to work. German Jews who were patients in mental homes did not have to meet these criteria. Even before the Ministry of the Interior announcement, the first gassings of Jews had taken place at Brandenburg, when two hundred Jews, men, women and children, had been brought in six buses from a Berlin mental institution.

While Hitler and Himmler discussed racial purity, and their staff took steps, as they believed, to secure it, the British Government continued to prepare for the German air bombardment which it believed to be inevitable, if not imminent. On June 30 the merchant ship *Cameronia* left New York for Glasgow with sixteen American aircraft on board, destined for Britain. On the following day, as a sign of British determination to take the war against Hitler back to Europe, Cabinet Ministers and officials examined a proposal to establish an organization to control all sabotage, subversive activities and black propaganda in enemy, enemy-controlled and neutral countries. Thus was born the Special Operations Executive, known by its initials SOE; Churchill was to give it a motto and an aim when he told its first political head, the Minister of Economic Warfare, Hugh Dalton: 'Set Europe ablaze!'

On July 2, Marshal Pétain moved his Government from Bordeaux, where it had been formed in the last moments of the French retreat, to Vichy, designated the capital of the 'Unoccupied Zone'. Among Pétain's Ministers was Admiral Darlan who, as head of the Navy under Reynaud, had been determined not to allow the French Fleet to fall under German control, but who, as Minister of Marine in the Government which had signed the armistice, seemed equally determined not to break the armistice terms by sailing that same Fleet to neutral or British waters. Afraid that the French Fleet would be taken over by the Germans and used as part of a German invasion fleet, the British Government launched Operation Catapult, the despatch of a British naval force from Gibraltar, to the French naval base of Mers-el-Kebir, at Oran, to persuade the French naval commander there to sail his ships away from German reach, or to scuttle them.

Before there could be a naval confrontation off Oran, disaster struck for some of the civilian internees whom Britain was shipping across the Atlantic to Canada; their ship, the *Arandora Star*, formerly a Blue Star luxury liner, was torpedoed off the coast of Ireland with the loss of 714 lives. Most of those drowned were Italian and German nationals. The Germans included several Jewish refugees who were still technically enemy aliens, and more than a hundred German merchant seamen who had earlier been captured at sea. Also drowned were thirty-seven guards and four crewmen, as well as a former German spy, No. 3528 in the German Intelligence listing. His brother, code named 'Charlie', formerly spy No. 3725, had earlier agreed to work for the British. No. 3528, having proved less co-operative than his brother, had been assessed as a category A alien, interned, and then sent across the Atlantic. A Canadian destroyer rescued the remaining 868 passengers. Churchill, reading a report of the sinking which detailed several rescue efforts, wrote: 'The case of the brave German who is said to have saved so many raises the question of his special treatment, by parole or otherwise.' Unfortunately, there was no evidence of his identity.

The U-boat commander whose torpedoes sank the *Arandora Star* was Günther Prien, who had earlier sunk the *Royal Oak*. But, despite Prien's success, the internee ships continued to cross the Atlantic. On July 2 it was the turn of another liner, the *Ettrick*, to set off for Canada. It arrived safely. On board was a twenty-nine-year-old refugee German physicist, Klaus Fuchs, who was to return to Britain within six months to continue his work on the secrets of atomic physics; later he was to betray those secrets to the Soviet Union, to whose cause, even while on board the *Ettrick*, he was committed.

On July 2 Hitler ordered his Army, Navy and Air Force to prepare detailed plans for the invasion of Britain. He set no date, but stated that a landing was possible 'provided that air superiority can be attained and certain other necessary conditions fulfilled'. Air superiority could not be taken for granted; each week saw an increase in the flow of munitions from the United States to Britain. On July 3, the *Britannic* sailed from New York to Britain, with more than ten million rounds of rifle ammunition, 50,000 rifles and a hundred field guns in its cargo holds, followed six days later by the *Western Prince*. Both crossed unmolested. Nor was British Intelligence unaware of the gist of Hitler's intention; on July 3 the British Chiefs of Staff concluded that it was probable that an invasion attempt would be preceded by a major air battle.

Not a German action, however, but a British one, dominated that first week of July; for it was on July 3 that Britain put into force Operation Catapult, the plan to seize, or at least to neutralize, all French warships wherever they might be, and to prevent them being taken over by Germany. The largest single concentration of such warships was at Mers-el-Kebir; some had fled there from ports in continental France to escape seizure by the Germans. The British gave the ships at Mers-el-Kebir four choices: to sail to British harbours 'and fight with us', to sail them into a British port and hand them over to British crews, to demilitarize them, or to scuttle them in such a way that the Germans could not use them. The French refused. Britain then gave a fifth choice, to sail them to the French West Indies, where they would either be disarmed, or handed over to the United States until the end of the war. Again, the French refused, whereupon the British naval forces encircling Mers-el-Kebir opened fire. The bombardment lasted for five minutes. When it was over, more than 1,250 French sailors, Britain's allies a mere two weeks earlier, had been killed.

During that five minute bombardment, the French lost the modern battle cruiser *Dunkerque* and the old battleships *Provence* and *Bretagne*. But a second battle cruiser, the *Strasbourg*, the aircraft carrier *Commandant Testa*, and five destroyers, managed to raise steam, pass the encircling force, and cross the Mediterranean to Toulon.

Also on July 3, all French ships in British ports were boarded and captured without a shot being fired, except on board the submarine *Surcouf* where, due to a misunderstanding, a French and a British sailor were shot and killed.

The deaths at Mers-el-Kebir caused considerable bitterness in France. As to the judgment of Britain's action, Churchill told the House of Commons on July 4: 'I leave it with confidence to Parliament. I leave it also to the nation, and I leave it to the United States. I leave it to the world and to history.' It was Britain's action at Oran, Churchill was told six months later by an American emissary, that had convinced Roosevelt that Britain had the will to continue the fight, even if she were alone.

On July 5, two days after the sinkings at Mers-el-Kebir, Marshal Pétain's Government at Vichy broke off diplomatic relations with Britain. In south-eastern Europe, Roumania, stripped by Russia of the eastern province of Bessarabia, opted to join the German–Italian Axis. In the Far East, Japan had asked Pétain's Goverment for military, naval and air bases in French Indo-China; then, while negotiations were still in progress, occupied strategic points along the coast. In reaction to this, on 5 July the United States Congress passed the Export Control Act, forbidding the export of aircraft parts, minerals and chemicals to Japan without a licence. This was followed three weeks later by the establishment of a licence system for the exports of aviation fuel, lubricants, iron and scrap steel to Japan. The very existence of Vichy territory in the Far East opened up the spectre of a Pacific war; a war in a region where two European states, France and Holland, both overrun by Germany, had substantial and now virtually indefensible colonial territories coveted by Japan, and where German commerce raiders had begun the systematic sinking of British merchant ships.

The British Government, whose imperial responsibilities included Burma, Malaya and Hong Kong, had now to consider a demand by Japan to close the main overland supply route of arms for China, the Burma road. On July 6 the British Ambassador to Japan was instructed to resist the demand, on the ground that it was discriminatory against China. He replied, however, that if the road was not closed, there was a real danger of a Japanese attack. The road was closed, but, as a result of British insistence, only for three months. Nevertheless, this act of appeasement testified to Britain's inability to take on a third enemy.

There was encouraging news, however, for the inner circle of British policy makers, when on July 6 it became clear, following a scrutiny of the German Air Force's Enigma messages, that the German first-line bomber strength was not as great as had been believed. Air Intelligence had earlier estimated that the Germans could launch 2,500 bombers against Britain, with a daily bomb delivery capacity of 4,800 tons. The Enigma revealed that the true figure was 1,250 bombers, with a daily capacity of 1,800 tons of bombs.

Two days after learning that the German bomber strength had been exaggerated, Churchill set down his thoughts on how the war would develop. If Hitler were to be 'repulsed here or not try invasion, he will recoil eastward, and we have nothing to stop him. But there is one thing that will bring him back and bring him down, and that is an absolutely devastating, exterminating attack by very heavy bombers from this country upon the Nazi homeland.'

That homeland itself was in the midst of a period of rejoicing. On July 6, Hitler returned to Berlin for the first time since the opening of the war in the West nearly two months earlier. A million swastika flags had been distributed free to the vast crowds which turned out to cheer him. All the States against whom his armies had marched on May 10 had surrendered. Britain alone remained unconquered, but apparently defenceless. Even as Hitler's cavalcade made its triumphal drive through Berlin, German bombers were beginning their daylight raids over Britain; on July 6, high-explosive bombs, dropped at Aldershot, killed three soldiers of the Royal Canadian Ordnance Corps.

There was shock in Britain at the vulnerability of a peaceful public, even of soldiers who could be killed far from the battlefield. But there was also a battlefield far from Britain which was beginning to impinge upon British public awareness; that July 6, as a result of successful aerial photographic reconnaissance, British carrier-based aircraft attacked Italian naval targets in the Libyan port of Tobruk. On the following day, the French Admiral in command of the French naval vessels then in the Egyptian port of Alexandria, agreed to neutralize his ships as Britain requested; there was to be no second Mers-el-Kebir in the Mediterranean. At the Atlantic ports of Casablanca and Dakar, however, the French naval authorities remained loyal to Vichy. As a result, British motor torpedo boats and torpedo-carrying aircraft attacked the battleship *Richelieu* and *Jean Bart*, putting them out of action for several months.

War on land had given way almost entirely to war at sea. On July 9, British and Italian naval forces clashed off the toe of Italy. Flying from the aircraft carrier *Eagle*, British aircraft dominated the skies above the action, which ended when the Italian flagship, the battleship *Giulio Cesare*, was badly damaged by the British flagship, the *Warspite*, and had to seek refuge in Messina harbour. Also on July 9, the German commerce raider *Komet* sailed northwards from Germany and, helped by Soviet icebreakers, completed the long and arduous North-East passage to debouch through the Bering Strait into the northern Pacific; she was to sink six merchant ships before returning to Germany.

Briefly, Hitler contented himself with other concerns than war. It was on July 9, at his mountain retreat of Obersalzberg, near Berchtesgaden, that he did a series of pencil sketches for a new opera house at Linz, as part of his plan to transform this provincial town in which he had lived as a young man into a major city. But on the very day that he was musing and sketching, a German protestant Pastor, Paul-Gerhard Braune, the administrator of a medical institution in Berlin, was writing him a letter, protesting against the euthanasia programme. That programme, Braune wrote, constituted a 'large-scale plan to exterminate thousands of human beings'; the killings 'gravely undermine the moral foundations of the whole nation'; they were 'simply unworthy' of institutions dedicated to healing. The killings, Braune added, had already been extended to people who were 'lucid and responsible'. They endangered 'the ethics of the people as a whole'. And he went on to ask: 'Whom if not the helpless should the law protect?'

Braune was informed by the head of Hitler's Chancellery, Hans Lammers, that the euthanasia programme could not be stopped. A month later he was arrested. The arrest warrant, signed by Heydrich, charged him with having 'sabotaged measures of the régime in an irresponsible manner'. Held for ten weeks in the Gestapo prison in Berlin, he was released on condition that he would undertake no further actions against the policies of the Government or the Party.

On July 10 a formation of 120 German bombers and fighters attacked a British shipping convoy in the English Channel. At the same time, a further seventy German aircraft bombed dockyard installations in South Wales. The British had only six hundred serviceable fighter planes to oppose these raiders; urgent measures were needed to raise this figure to what was felt to be a minimum for safety, at least a thousand. Even the public were asked to contribute to the new priority for aircraft production by sending whatever aluminium it could find to the Ministry of Aircraft Production, which declared on July 10: 'We will turn your pots and pans into Spitfires and Hurricanes, Blenheims and Wellingtons. Everyone who has pots and pans, kettles, vacuum cleaners, hat pegs, coat hangers, shoe trees, bathroom fittings and household ornaments, cigarette boxes, or any other articles made wholly or in part of aluminium, should hand them over at once ...'.

In an attempt to maintain British morale, and to discomfort the Germans, on July 14 a further raid by the special Striking Companies of British commandos was launched against the Channel Island of Guernsey, where 469 Germans were stationed. Code named Operation Ambassador, it carried out a few demolitions, but one of the commandos was drowned and two taken prisoner of war. 'Let there be no more silly fiascos like those perpetrated at Guernsey' was Churchill's comment.

That July 14, Bastille Day in France, was for Frenchmen a time of national mourning and grave reflection. In London, General de Gaulle and other leaders of his new Free French movement laid wreaths at the Cenotaph and pledged to fight on until France was liberated. 'A year ago, in Paris,' Churchill broadcast to Britain and to France, 'I watched the stately parade down the Champs Élysées of the French Army and the French Empire. Who can foresee what the course of other years can bring?' There were 'vast numbers', Churchill said, not only in Britain but in every land, 'who will render faithful service in this war, but those names will never be known, those deeds will never be recorded. This is a War of the Unknown Warrior, but let all strive, without failing in faith or in duty, and the dark curse of Hitler will be lifted from our age.'

Two days after Churchill's speech, Hitler issued Directive No. 16, 'on preparations for a landing operation against England', code name 'Sea Lion'. An air offensive was to begin on August 5, with its main objective to make it impossible for the Royal Air Force 'to deliver any significant attack against the German crossing'. As to that crossing itself, Hitler gave no date, though he asked for 'preparations' to be completed by mid-August.

Air attacks were now a frequent feature of British life, and danger. In the first seventeen days of July, 194 British civilians were killed. On July 19, three days after his 'Sea Lion' directive, Hitler made a speech in Berlin in which he outlined his 'peace offer' to Britain. 'If the struggle continues', he warned, 'it can only end in annihilation for one of us. Mr Churchill thinks it will be Germany. I know it will be Britain,' and he went on to declare: 'I am not the vanquished begging for mercy. I speak as a victor. I can see no reason why this war must go on. We should like to avert the sacrifices that claim millions.' It was possible, Hitler added, 'that Mr Churchill will once again brush aside this statement of mine by saying that it is merely born of fear and doubts of victory. In this case I shall have relieved my conscience of the things to come.'

Not only Churchill, but also Roosevelt, dismissed Hitler's offer. There was

The German invasion of Poland, 1 September 1939; view from a German bomber of a Polish position on fire after being hit.

German troops on their way by train to the Polish front. The slogan on their railway carriage reads: 'We're off to Poland to thrash the Jews' (*see page 4*).

German soldiers enter the Polish town of Gdynia, on the Baltic coast, September 1939.

Polish prisoners-of-war, captured by the Germans in September 1939.

Hitler reviewing his troops in Warsaw, 5 October 1939 (*see page 19*).

The German occupation forces in Poland, October 1939, including horse-drawn artillery.

The Russo-Finnish war; a
church ablaze in Helsinki, after
a Russian air raid, 30 November
1939 (*see page 31*).

The Russo-Finnish war; Finnish
soldiers leave their trench as a
Russian shell explodes nearby.

The war at sea; the German pocket-battleship *Graf Spee* scuttles herself after being severely damaged by British naval gunfire, 17 December 1939 (*see page 34*).

The 'Phoney War'; German troops celebrate Christmas in a dug-out on the Western Front, 25 December 1939.

The Siegfried Line, 14 January 1940; General von Brauchitsch, Commander-in-Chief of the German Army, on a tour of inspection.

March 1940; at a bomber station in Britain, packets of leaflets are stacked up, for dropping over Germany. In this publicity photograph, one of the airmen holds a bundle of leaflets on the special chute down which it would be sent once the aircraft was over its 'target'.

Oslo, 9 April 1940; German troops enter Norway (*see page 53*).

British Spitfire crews scramble for their aircraft; this photograph was published in *Picture Post* on 20 April 1940.

Narvik; Allied ships ablaze in the harbour, as the Germans complete their conquest of Norway.

only one way to deal with a totalitarian country, Roosevelt declared later that same day, 'by resistance, not appeasement'. Also on July 19, Roosevelt signed the Two-Ocean Navy Expansion Act, authorizing a substantial increase in American naval strength in both the Pacific and the Atlantic. With 358 warships already in service, and 130 being built, the Act provided for a further seven battleships, eighteen aircraft-carriers, twenty-seven cruisers, forty-two sub-marines and 115 destroyers.

Although only Britain was now at war with Germany, a sense of global conflict pervaded the nations of the Western world; the closing of the Burma Road and the Two-Ocean Navy Expansion Act were clear signs of this. So also, on July 21, was the Soviet Union's formal annexation of the three Baltic States, Estonia, Latvia and Lithuania. This action by Stalin was more timely than he knew, for it was on that very day that Hitler summoned his military commanders to Obersalzberg and told them of his intention to invade the Soviet Union.

Hitler's words were not mere musing; on the following day he instructed General Halder to begin the detailed planning, and a special staff, headed by General Erich Marcks, was set up to prepare a working plan, to be ready for submission to Hitler two weeks later. To those whom he had summoned to Obersalzberg, Hitler also spoke of the invasion of Britain, but he did so with a noticeable lack of enthusiasm, telling them that without air superiority there could be no landings; yet unless the first wave of landings could be completed by mid-September, worsening weather would make it impossible for the German Air Force to provide adequate air cover. 'If preparations cannot be completed with certainty by the beginning of September,' Hitler warned, 'it is necessary to consider other plans.'

It was certain that Britain did not intend to give up the struggle. 'We never wanted the war,' the British Foreign Secretary, Lord Halifax, declared on 22 July, in answer to Hitler's 'peace proposal' of three days earlier, 'certainly no one here wants the war to go on for a day longer than is necessary. But we shall not stop fighting till freedom for ourselves and others is secure.' That day in Tokyo, a new government came to power, headed by Prince Fumimaro Konoye. It began at once to put increased pressure on Vichy France to cede military bases in French Indo-China. The new Government warned that it did not rule out the use of force to achieve its aim. That aim, it declared nine days later, was 'the setting up of a New Order in greater East Asia'.

The moralities of Prince Konoye's New Order, like that of Hitler's Thousand Year Reich, were those of a 'master race' for whom the end always justified the means. That end was supremacy, discipline and unanimity; the means were as brutal as circumstances dictated. When therefore, on July 24, a German motor torpedo boat sighted an unarmed French merchant steamer, the *Meknès*, sailing from Southampton at night with 1,179 repatriated French naval personnel on board, her French ensign spotlighted by a searchlight, her sides illuminated, her portholes lit up, it nevertheless attacked. When the Captain of the *Meknès* brought his ship to a standstill, signalled by a siren to that effect, and flashed her name and nationality by Morse, the only answer was a torpedo. The *Meknès* sank; 383 French sailors drowned.

In Britain, it was not only de Gaulle who had set up the standard of defiance. On July 23 a Czechoslovak Provisional Government had been formed in Britain. Two days later, Churchill authorized the Polish forces then in Britain, 14,000 in all, to be given American rifles direct as they arrived from the United States. Other forces then under military training in Britain were 4,000 Czechs, 3,000 anti-Nazi Germans, 2,000 Frenchmen, 1,000 Dutchmen, 1,000 Norwegians and 500 Belgians. But Britain's principal need remained aircraft. On July 25 Churchill learned of the signature in Washington on the previous day of an agreement whereby American aircraft would be allocated according to British as well as American needs; indeed, of the 33,000 aircraft being manufactured in the United States, 19,092 would be kept for the American Army Air Force, and 14,375 delivered to Britain. Similar ratios were being worked out for all American rifles, tanks, field guns, anti-tank guns and their ammunition. These agreements would cover Britain's needs as calculated up to the end of 1941.

For the peoples of German-occupied Poland, there was no abatement of tyranny. Two thousand Jews, sent from the town of Radom to the German–Soviet border to dig anti-tank ditches, died within a few months as a result of the harsh treatment. On July 26, in the stone quarries of Mauthausen concentration camp, near Linz, Dr Edmund Bursche, former Dean of the Faculty of Protestant Theology at the University of Warsaw, died from the relentless work and beatings. He was seventy-nine years old.

The deaths of the Jews from Radom, as of Profesor Bursche, were kept secret; but other aspects of the German New Order were widely publicized. In a published review of the German sterilization laws, Ernst Rudin, Professor of Psychiatry at the University of Munich, and a pioneer of the Nazi 'racial science', praised Hitler's political leadership for having had the courage to break 'the terror of the inferior kind of people' by means of 'racial-hygienic measures'.

It was easy to impose racial policy on conquered lands. It was proving less easy to extend the areas of conquest. On July 29 German Naval Headquarters informed Hitler that a landing on the British coast would not be possible until the second half of September, and that even then the German Navy would not be able to support it against any sustained British counter-attack from the sea. 'It is impossible', wrote Admiral Schniewind, the Navy's Chief of Staff, 'to accept responsibility for any such operation during the current year.'

It was not only towards a Western offensive that the German professional military men were hesitant. It was also on July 29 that general Jodl informed the chief of the planning section of the German Army Staff, Colonel Walther Warlimont, of Hitler's plan to attack Russia 'as soon as possible'. Jodl mentioned May 1941 as the likely date. Warlimont and others in his planning section protested that this was the very two-front war that had led to Germany's defeat in 1918. But Jodl gave them an answer which allowed no counter-argument. 'Gentlemen,' he said, 'it is not a question for discussion but a decision of the Führer!'

Europe from Norway to Egypt, summer 1940

On July 21, a total of fifteen ships set sail from American ports with arms and equipment for Britain. As they proceeded on their slow journey eastward, Hitler called the High Command, Navy and Army chiefs to Obersalzberg, to discuss invasion. Admiral Raeder, the Commander-in-Chief of the Navy, who had flown from Berlin, first suggested a postponement of 'Sea Lion' from September 13 until at least September 19; but then expressed his preference for a much more distant date, May 1941. In May 1941, Raeder pointed out, Germany would have two new battleships, the *Tirpitz* and the *Bismarck*, to augment her existing two battleships. There would also be many more smaller warships by then.

Hitler could not easily dispute Admiral Raeder's arguments. Yet he put up a show of determination. The invasion would take place on September 15, he said, provided that a week-long bombing attack on southern England could do substantial damage to the Royal Navy, the Royal Air Force and essential harbours. 'Otherwise,' he conceded, 'it is postponed until May 1941.'

Admiral Raeder flew back to Berlin. General von Brauchitsch and General Halder, who had flown from General Staff headquarters at Fontainebleau, remained with their chief. To them, Hitler spoke of his plans to invade Russia. Even the future of Britain fitted into these plans. If Russia was 'smashed', Hitler told his two Generals, 'England's last hope is extinguished, and Germany will be master of Europe and the Balkans.'

Hitler went on to explain to Halder and von Brauchitsch that the invasion of Russia could take place in the spring of 1941. 'The sooner we smash Russia the better,' Hitler said, and he added: 'The operation only makes sense if we smash the State to its core in one blow. Mere conquest of land areas will not suffice.' A total of 120 German divisions, out of the 180 planned to be in existence by then, would launch a triple attack, the first against Kiev, the second through the Baltic States to Moscow, and, once these two had linked up, a third operation would advance against the Baku oilfields.

On July 31, while Hitler briefed his senior officers on the planned invasion of Russia, the British took a small but important step to secure their Mediterranean lifeline, launching Operation Hurry, whereby the aircraft carrier *Argus*, having steamed from Gibraltar to a point off Sardinia, released twelve fighter planes to fly the two hundred miles to Malta, the British island already under persistent Italian air attack. The operation was almost entirely successful, marred only by the shooting down of one of the twelve fighter pilots, Lieutenant Keeble, killed in a dogfight over Malta's Grand Harbour. His Italian adversary was also killed. Over Germany, over Britain, over France until the armistice, and over the Mediterranean, during the two months of June and July 1940, 526 British pilots had been killed in action.

Hitler now issued Directive No. 17, 'for the conduct of air and sea warfare against England'. Following up what he had told Admiral Raeder, he stated that a successful German air offensive was a prerequisite of a seaborne landing. Dated August 1, the directive called for an 'intensification of the air war' on or after August 5. This was to be 'The Day of the Eagle'. British Intelligence knew the code-name but not what it stood for. The attacks were to be directed 'primarily against flying units, their ground installations and their supply organizations, but also against the aircraft industry, including that manufacturing anti-aircraft equipment'. That day, while a German pilot reported to Goering that the British Spitfires which he had encountered over England were fully as good as the German fighter planes, Goering replied: 'If that is so, I will have to send my Air Inspector General before the firing squad.' The Air Inspector General, the First World War flying ace Ernst Udet, who was present, smiled politely; but he was unable to forget the insult.

A less effective insult was hurled by radio on August 2, by William Joyce, now known derisively to his British listeners, on account of his accent, as Lord Haw-Haw. 'The glorious Royal Air Force', Joyce broadcast that evening over Radio Bremen, 'was too busy dropping bombs on fields and graveyards in Germany to have any time available for the Battle of France.'

The British were in no mood to be abused, or wooed. When, on August 2, King Gustav of Sweden secretly offered his services to both Hitler and King George VI in order to set up contacts with a view to a negotiated peace, George VI noted in his diary: 'Until Germany is prepared to live peaceably with her neighbours in Europe, she will always be a menace. We have got to get rid of her aggressive spirit, her engines of war, and the people who have been taught to use them.'

On August 3, a large contingent of Canadian troops arrived in Britain. Among them were several United States citizens, who had volunteered for service. On the following day, a further draft of Australian troops arrived. Two days later, it was a contingent of pilots and aircrew from Southern Rhodesia. None of this boded well for Hitler's invasion plans, if indeed he still believed his Air Force could really create the necessary conditions for a landing which would be unopposed from the air. On August 5 the German air offensive against British air targets was postponed because of bad weather. That day, Hitler was presented with a plan that was clearly much closer to his instinct and ambition, the plan which he had asked General Erich Marcks to draw up, for the invasion of Russia.

The plan presented by General Marcks envisaged an eventual German advance to the line Archangel–Gorky–Rostov.[1] In all 147 divisions would attack, with Leningrad, Moscow and Kiev–Rostov as the first objectives; 44 divisions would be held in reserve. Surprise and speed were to be the key to victory, which General Marcks envisaged would be secured between nine and seventeen weeks after the attack had begun.

On August 8, three days after receiving the Marcks plan, Hitler appointed Colonel Warlimont to prepare the deployment areas in East Prussia and German-occupied Poland for the coming offensive; above all, nothing must be done to arouse Stalin's suspicions. Let him be led to believe that these troops were being moved east to get them out of range of Britain's bombers.

Even before the start of the German air onslaught envisaged in Hitler's directive of August 1, aerial dogfights over Britain were a daily occurrence, as

[1] See map on page 195.

were British bombing raids on German industrial targets, particularly in the Ruhr. On August 8 a Polish pilot-officer was one of those killed on an operational flight. 'Poor fellow,' another Polish pilot wrote, 'he will never see Poland again. He will be missing from his Flight when one day, by God's mercy, it lands again on the Deblin airfield. Well, he was not the first to go, and he won't be the last.'

On August 9, three hundred German aircraft flew over South-East England and the Channel coast. Their targets were the radar stations at Portland Bill and Weymouth. In battle with British fighters sent to intercept them, eighteen German aircraft were shot down. On August 11, and again on August 12, there were further attacks on radar targets. These were the final preliminaries for the main assault; on August 13, with Britain's radar defences still essentially intact, the German Air Force launched 'The Day of the Eagle', a day on which wave after wave of German aircraft, 1,485 in all, flew in search of the air stations and aircraft factories which had now to be destroyed, and to be destroyed quickly, if invasion were to follow.

# 9

# The battle for Britain

AUGUST–SEPTEMBER 1940

The Day of the Eagle, 13 August 1940, launched Germany's fourth campaign in less than a year. But unlike the three previous attacks, on Poland, Scandinavia, and France and the Low Countries, this one was an air attack without any ground-based activity at all. From the outset, the Germans were surprised by the skill of the British pilots who opposed them. Of the 1,485 German aircraft which crossed the English Channel that day, forty-five were shot down, for the loss of only thirteen British fighters. Almost all the German aircrew were killed or captured where they parachuted or crash-landed; only seven British pilots were killed, the rest crash-landing or parachuting to safety on British soil. On the second day, poor weather limited the number of the attacking aircraft to 500. Even so, seventy-five, an even larger number than on the previous day, were brought down, for thirty-four British planes lost. The same pattern was repeated on the third day, with seventy German losses as against twenty-seven British. In three days of air combat, the Germans had lost 190 machines. But in the first ten days of the German attacks, a hundred British aircraft had been destroyed on the ground.

As the Battle of Britain was being fought in the skies above southern England, those at the centre of British policy learned exactly what that battle was about; for on August 14, following a careful scrutiny of the German Air Force Enigma messages, the Inter-Service Combined Intelligence Committee gave as its considered opinion that no final decision about invasion had been, or would be, taken by the German authorities 'pending the result of the present struggle for air superiority'.

Good news also reached the beleaguered island on August 14 from across the Atlantic, when Roosevelt agreed to give Britain fifty American destroyers, in exchange for the use by the American fleet of British bases in the Caribbean and western Atlantic. Ironically, August 14 was also the day on which General Halder recorded in his diary that the German Army was looking for a site in East Prussia which could serve as Hitler's headquarters during the invasion of Russia.

If August 14 was a day of relief for Britain, the following day, August 15, marked the day on which the German Air Force put its strength and tactics to the crucial test. If that day's attack could succeed, then it might still be possible to mount an invasion before the autumn storms. In all, 520 German bombers and 1,270 fighters crossed the Channel between 11.30 in the morning and 6.30 in the evening.

Seventy-five German aircraft were shot down on August 15, for a British loss of thirty-four. It was a rate of loss which could not be long sustained. But, on August 16, an equally severe raid was similarly mauled, even though it succeeded in destroying forty-seven British aircraft on the ground at Brize Norton and thirteen at airfields elsewhere in southern England. General Ismay, watching the battle as it was being plotted in the Operations Room of No. 11 Group Fighter Command, later recalled: 'There had been heavy fighting throughout the afternoon; and at one moment every single squadron in the group was engaged; there was nothing in reserve, and the map table showed new waves of attackers crossing the coast. I felt sick with fear.'

On August 16, the Inter-Service Combined Intelligence Committee repeated its assessment, drawn from the German Air Force Enigma, that there would be no invasion of Britain without a clear-cut air victory beforehand. German radio had already won such a victory: 'We are informed by Lord Haw-Haw', a Canadian officer wrote in his diary on August 16, 'that south east England is in ruins and the morale of our people completely shot. Well there are a lot of large holes in many fields and some buildings have been destroyed. But there are German bombers and fighters strewn all across the countryside from Maidstone to Guildford. As for our morale – it's going up – and up – and up!'

That day, further west above Southampton, a fighter pilot, Flight Lieutenant James Nicolson, patrolling over Southampton in a Hurricane, was attacked by four German fighters. His own fighter was hit, and Nicolson himself wounded by canon shell. With flames reaching his cockpit, he was about to abandon his aircraft when he saw a German Messerschmidt fighter. This he attacked and shot down, although as a result of staying for four minutes longer in his burning aircraft he sustained serious burns to his face, neck and legs. For this action, Nicolson was awarded the Victoria Cross, the only fighter pilot to receive this highest award for valour during the Battle of Britain, and indeed throughout the entire war. Today, a plaque marks the spot near which the badly burned Nicolson landed by parachute.

On August 17 the Germans were forced to reduce the level of their attack; some of their fighters, the Stukas, had proved too vulnerable and were withdrawn. That night, British bombers flew over the Channel and the North Sea in the opposite direction to the daytime raiders, striking yet again at oil plants and munitions factories. That day, a secret tally was made of all British losses since the first day of the war: 8,266 sailors had been killed, 4,400 soldiers and, from German air attack, 729 civilians. The number of pilots and aircrew killed or missing was 3,851.

On the pilots who remained, there fell on August 18 the burden of one further German effort to break Britain's air defences. But German losses were again formidable, seventy-one aircraft shot down, as against twenty-seven British

The battle of Britain and the 'Blitz', August–September 1940

losses. That evening, as one of Britain's air aces, Douglas Bader, later wrote: 'Goering withdrew to rest his pilots, lick his wounds and count the cost: losses to the tune of 367 aircraft destroyed.'

On August 19 there was no German air attack on Britain. 'They are making a big mistake', Churchill told one of his Secretariat that night, 'in giving us a respite.' On the following day, in the House of Commons, Churchill spoke of how the gratitude 'of every home in our island, in our Empire, and indeed throughout the world, except in the abodes of the guilty, goes out to the British airmen who, undaunted by odds, unwearied in their constant challenge and mortal danger, are turning the tide of war by their prowess and by their devotion'. Churchill went on to say, of those airmen: 'Never in the field of human conflict was so much owed by so many to so few.'

In the five days of intense air attack between August 13 and 18, Hitler had failed to fulfil his one condition of invasion, the breaking of Britain's air power. Churchill now warned that British bombers would continue to strike at German military industries and communications, as well as at the German air bases and storage depots used to launch air attacks on Britain, and would strike 'upon an ever-increasing scale until the end of the war, and may in another year attain dimensions hitherto undreamed of'. The bombing of Germany, Churchill declared, was the 'most certain', if not the shortest, 'of all the roads to victory'.

Churchill did not know that Hitler had already prepared the groundwork for an attack on Russia. He knew however that such an attack was likely, and wanted Hitler to know that Britain would not stand idly by. 'Even if Nazi legions stood triumphant on the Black Sea,' he said in his speech of August 20, 'or indeed the Caspian, even if Hitler were at the gates of India, it would profit him nothing if at the same time the entire economic and scientific apparatus of German war power lay shattered and pulverized at home.'

Taking advantage of Britain's preoccupation with the German air onslaught, on August 19 Italian forces occupied Berbera, the capital of British Somaliland. On August 20, Italian bombers raided Gibraltar. But these were mere pinpricks, quite eclipsed in importance in the third week of August, when an American mission of three senior Staff officers reached London, to co-ordinate Anglo-American policy at the highest level. These three officers, Admiral Ghormley, Brigadier-General Strong and General Emmons were immediately able to contradict the recent report by the American Ambassador in London, Joseph P. Kennedy, to Roosevelt, of 'the devastating effect of German air attacks on England's ports, fields, and armaments industry'.

Under the guise of being a relatively low grade mission to discuss the standardization of arms, the three Americans constituted in fact the first Staff Conversations between Britain and the United States, the one a belligerent, the other neutral, but both united in a common and ever closer purpose. Not only were British and American military, naval and air matters becoming more closely interwoven, but in the sphere of Intelligence there was a growing realization of the need to share what was known. As if to confirm Churchill's remark of August 20 about the Nazis 'standing triumphant on the Black Sea', on August 22 Paul Thümmel, the German Intelligence officer who was Britain's agent A-54, reported that he had learned from an officer of the German General Staff that the German Intelligence branch responsible for the Russian area had been expanding since June, that German counter-Intelligence activities against Russia were also to be increased, and that the German counter-Intelligence organization in Roumania had been reinforced by specialists on the southern Ukraine, the Crimea and the Caucasus.

The possibility of a German invasion of Russia could not deflect from the urgency of the hour; on August 23 the German Air Force launched its fourth massive bombing attack since The Day of the Eagle, striking at British aircraft factories and oil storage tanks. One flight of bombers, about twelve in all, flying off course, dropped its bombs on London. Nine civilians were killed. On the following day, in a British experiment designed to halt any German invasion force before it could come ashore, petrol, poured through twelve pipes at the rate of twelve tons an hour, was set on fire, creating a wall of flame on beach and sea, through which no invader could possibly pass. To boost British morale, considerable publicity was given to the experiment; but those who conducted it were aware that, whenever the wind changed, the billows of thick black smoke blew back on the beach, blinding and choking the potential defenders.

On the evening of August 25, British bombers struck at German armament factories in the north of Berlin; some of the planes, confused by the low ceiling of cloud, and inadvertently flying off course as the German bombers had done two nights earlier over London, dropped their bombs on the centre of the city. 'The concentration of anti-aircraft fire', William Shirer noted in his diary, 'was the greatest I've ever witnessed. It provided a magnificent, a terrible sight. And it was strangely ineffective. Not a plane was brought down; not one was even picked up by the searchlights, which flashed back and forth frantically across the skies throughout the night.'

No German civilians were killed that night; but leaflets dropped by the bombers warned those few Berliners who could find them that 'the war which Hitler started will go on, and it will last as long as Hitler does'.

On August 26 a further German air raid was launched against British aerodromes throughout southern England; but, for the first time, all but one of the German formations were forced back by successful British fighter interception. On the following day, those in Britain who were reading the German Air Force Enigma messages were able to conclude, with confidence, that 'On the success of this operation will depend the decision as to the invasion.' Not merely the date of the invasion, but whether or not the Germans would invade at all, was now at issue.

On the night of August 28, during a further British air raid over Berlin, likewise intended to seek out only military targets, ten German civilians were killed. On the road towards Tempelhof airport, William Shirer noted in his diary, 'two hundred-pound bombs landed in the street, tore off the leg of an air-raid warden standing at the entrance to his house, and killed four men and two women, who, unwisely, were watching the fireworks from a doorway'.

The German Air Force was determined not to give up its attempt to destroy British air power. On August 30 there was a renewed attack, by eight hundred German aircraft, against the nine British fighter operational command centres in southern England. Over Biggin Hill, one of the principal aerodromes attacked, seventeen German aircraft were shot down, for the loss of only a single British plane, whose pilot, parachuting down, survived and returned to the battle. That night, as if to ensure that there would be no let-up in the pressure, German bombers dropped incendiary bombs on London. Crossing the same Channel coast in the other direction, British bombers again struck at military targets in Berlin. 'The British gave us a good strafing last night,' William Shirer noted in his diary, 'and even German officials admitted that the damage was greater than ever before. A German friend dropped in to tell me the great Siemens works had been hit.'

By the end of August, the air battle for Britain had been in progress for two and a half weeks, the focus of intense public concern in Britain, and of enthusiastic hopes in Germany. But a more distant danger was ever present in the minds of the British War Cabinet, the vulnerability of the British forces in Egypt. For more than a month, they had faced a hostile Italian army in Libya which might at any moment take the offensive. In order to build up British strength in Egypt, even at some risk to the land defence of Britain, on August 30 the British Navy began Operation Hats, sending the battleship *Valiant*, the aircraft carrier *Illustrious* and several other warships the whole length of the Mediterranean, from Gibraltar to Alexandria, with aircraft, guns and ammunition. Their six day voyage passed without interference from Italian air or naval forces.

On August 31 the German air offensive against British fighter operational bases was renewed; three aerodromes were attacked, and thirty-nine German aircraft shot down. On the following two days there were further raids on Biggin Hill. There was also a further night bomber raid over London on September 2; it coincided with the news that 1,075 civilians had been killed during August in bombing raids over Britain. Better news that day was the signature of the Anglo-American Destroyers–Bases agreement; four days later the first six American destroyers were handed over to the British at Halifax, Nova Scotia.

On September 3, the first anniversary of Britain's declaration of war against Germany, four German spies – one German and three Dutchmen – were landed by boat on the southern coast of Britain. Their tasks were to report on coastal defences, and on Army and Air force strengths and movements. All four were caught within hours of coming ashore; they were brought to trial in November, and three of them hanged in December. The fourth man, one of the Dutchmen, was kept in prison for the duration of the war; after the war he was imprisoned in Holland.

On September 4, in a speech in Berlin, Hitler told an audience primarily of German women nurses and social workers: 'When they declare they will increase their attacks on our cities, then we will raze their cities to the ground,' and he added: 'The hour will come when one of us will break, and it will not be National Socialist Germany.' William Shirer, who heard Hitler speak, wrote in his diary: 'Though grim and dripping with hate most of the evening, Hitler had his humorous, jaunty moments.' His listeners had found it 'very funny' when Hitler told them: 'In England they're filled with curiosity and keep asking, "Why doesn't he come?" Be calm. Be calm. He's coming! He's coming!'

Under interrogation, the four German spies who had landed in Britain on September 3 confirmed their status as an advance guard for the invasion, which, they said, could be expected at any moment. On September 5, the British Photographic Reconnaissance recorded an increase in the number of barges at Ostend. On September 6, German bombing raids on port installations along the south coast of Britain led to the issuing of the 'Yellow' invasion alarm: 'Probable attack within three days'. Unknown to the British, these indications were all either meaningless or deliberate deceptions; in fact, September 6 was the day on which additional German divisions began their movement to the German-annexed regions of Poland, and to the Soviet border, where thirty-five divisions, six of them armoured divisions, were now assembled. Equally unknown to the British, September 9 also saw Admiral Raeder ask Hitler about the invasion timetable. 'Decision of the Führer to land in England', Raeder told his senior subordinates, 'is by no means yet firm, since the Führer has the conviction that the submission of England will be achieved even without landing.' Hitler had 'no thought of executing the landing', Raeder added, 'if the risk of the operation is too high'.

To secure the 'submission of England' without a landing, and having struck for more than three weeks at Britain's fighter bases and command posts, Hitler now ordered German bomber raids on London. Goering, confident of an aerial masterstroke, went to the Pas de Calais in his train, *Asia*, to take personal command of the operations.

Shortly before four o'clock on September 7, three hundred German bombers, escorted by six hundred fighters, arrived in two waves, their target, the London docks. That very afternoon, British Intelligence tried to work out the meaning of the apparent large-scale movement of barges to forward bases in the Channel, of the cancellation of all German Army leave on the following day, and of the interrogation reports of the four spies caught four days earlier, whose task, it now seemed, was to report the movement of all British reserve formations in the quadrilateral Oxford–Ipswich–London–Reading. It suddenly seemed that invasion itself might be imminent. This deduction was given to the Chiefs of Staff at half past five.

As the Chiefs of Staff discussed this ominous prospect, German bombers continued their massive bombardment, their onslaught challenged by the whole remaining British fighter force. 'Air battles high overhead all afternoon,' a Canadian officer, Tony Foster, noted in his diary. 'At one time I counted twenty-four parachutes descending.'

That afternoon and evening, 337 tons of bombs were dropped on London. The docks were the principal target, but many bombs fell on the residential areas around them; 448 Londoners were killed. The bombers, seeking the docks, dropped their bombs on some of the poorest and most overcrowded streets of London, their slum buildings and tenement houses more vulnerable than most to the pounding blast of bombs and the ensuing fires. Not all the deaths were caused by bombs; one British fighter, shot down while itself shooting down a German bomber, crashed on to a family air raid shelter after its pilot had bailed out. All three people inside the shelter were killed instantly.

At precisely 8.07 that evening, as the air bombardment was at its height, the code word 'Cromwell' was sent to military units throughout Britain. The code was clear: the German invasion of Britain was about to begin.

Throughout the land, church bells rang out, as a further prearranged signal that invasion was imminent. All home defence forces were to be brought to a state of 'immediate action'. 'Everyone confined to barracks,' Tony Foster wrote in his diary that night. 'The invasion is expected tomorrow. We're ready to move at an hour's notice'.

On the morning of September 8 the German invasion was expected from hour to hour. But no invasion was scheduled or in prospect. All depended upon the outcome of the new air battle, the direct bombardment of the capital. Yet the German Air Force, having failed to eliminate Britain's fighter power in the three weeks following The Day of the Eagle, now suffered considerably from the ability of the British fighters to challenge each wave of incoming bombers and their fighter escorts. On September 8, as two hundred German bombers attacked London's electricity power stations and railway lines, eighty-eight German aircraft were shot down, for British losses of twenty-one. That afternoon, Churchill was taken to an air raid shelter in the East End of London where forty people had been killed on the previous night. 'It was good of you to come, Winnie,' the survivors called out to him as they crowded round. 'We thought you'd come. We can take it. Give it 'em back.'

Polish, Czech and Canadian fighter pilots were as eager as their British counterparts to strike the enemy out of the skies. On September 8, when four hundred German aircraft crossed the British coast, they were met by more than two hundred British fighters; in the ensuing air battle, twenty-eight German aircraft were shot down, for nineteen British fighters lost. But, for the Londoners whose homes were being bombed, there was increasing fear at what the outcome would be. 'In dockside areas,' a Home Intelligence Report noted on September 9, 'the population is showing visible signs of its nerve cracking from constant ordeals.' That day, King George VI was told of the distress in the East End. He immediately set off to visit the scenes of devastation, assuring the bombed-out victims of two nights of terror that all of their countrymen were with them in sympathy.

The London 'Blitz', as it had become known, continued on September 10. 'Increased tension everywhere,' a further Home Intelligence report declared, 'and when the siren goes people run madly for shelter with white faces.' At midday, the War Cabinet were told that the bombing of the previous two nights had been 'quite indiscriminate'. It was at once agreed that, as an act of retaliation, British bombers over Germany should be instructed 'not to return home with their bombs if they failed to locate the targets which they were detailed to attack'. The bombs should be dropped anywhere. That night British bombers raided Berlin in force; one bomb fell on Josef Goebbels' garden.

On September 11, in yet a further switch from his Western to his Eastern ambitions, Hitler decided to send German Army and Air Force missions to Roumania. Their task was to organize the protection of Roumania's oilwells and oil installations at Ploesti, and to prepare Roumania's facilities for use in future operations against Russia. Five days earlier, in Bucharest, King Carol had abdicated in favour of his son, handing over effective power to Marshal Antonescu, whose pro-German leanings were well known, and whose desire to regain the eastern province of Bessarabia could only be fulfilled in alliance with Germany.

*           *           *

Not only the London docks, but docks in Liverpool, Swansea and Bristol, were among the German targets on the night of 12 September. One bomber, on its return flight, crashed on to a house in Newport. As the house caught fire, a fourteen-year-old Jewish girl, Myrtle Phillips, was trapped in the flames. Her seventeen-year-old brother Malcolm rushed back into the flames to bring her out. Both of them perished. Their father, a convinced pacifist, visited the German pilot, who alone of a crew of four had survived the crash, in the local hospital, to assure him that the tragic deaths of his children was not his fault, but part of the many horrific injustices of war.

On September 13 the Italians crossed their Libyan border into Egypt, occupying Sollum. Britain was now endangered on two fronts. But on September 14, Hitler explained to his commanders that the preconditions for an invasion of Britain were 'not yet on hand'. Nevertheless, the bombing of London would continue. 'If eight million inhabitants go crazy,' Hitler commented, 'that can lead to catastrophe. If we get good weather and can neutralize the enemy's Air Force, then even a small-scale invasion can work wonders'.

It was not the British Air Force, however, but the German, which was being 'neutralized'. On September 12, Churchill had declared: 'There is no doubt that Herr Hitler is using up his fighter force at a very high rate, and that if he goes on for many more weeks he will wear down and ruin the vital part of the Air Force.' Three days later, on September 15, the German Air Force launched a massive attack, by 230 bombers and 700 fighters, against London, Southampton, Bristol, Cardiff, Liverpool and Manchester. Of the attacking force, fifty-six were shot down, for British losses of only twenty-three.

One of the German planes crashed into the forecourt of Victoria railway station in London. Its pilot, Robert Zehbe, baled out over Kennington. Badly wounded, he was set upon by irate civilians, but was rescued by the authorities. Later, he died of his injuries.

Even though 1,419 British civilians had been killed during the second week of August – 1,286 of them in London – the attrition in the skies of which Churchill had warned was turning Hitler's Western plans into a nightmare. On the following day, as part of the British plan to destroy as many invasion barges as possible, Polish pilots attacked the docks at Boulogne. 'Our boys dived like mad,' a Polish pilot officer wrote in his diary, 'tearing Basin No. 6 to bits, together with dozens of boats prepared for the invasion.'

On September 17 Hitler postponed the invasion of Britain 'until further notice', telling his naval adjutant, Lieutenant Karl von Puttkammer: 'We have conquered France at the cost of 30,000 men. During one night of crossing the Channel we could lose many times that – and success is not certain.' The Blitz would go on. But Hitler's battle for Britain had to all intents and purposes been lost. The British would continue to suffer. But they would not succumb. The roar of German panzers, the screech of German dive-bombers, the march of German soldiers – all of which had brought the horrors of conquest and the curse of occupation to Poland, Denmark, Norway, Holland, Belgium, Luxemburg and France – would not be heard in Britain, not at least in 1940.

# 10

# 'The war is won!' (Hitler)

OCTOBER 1940

Hitler's failure to weaken Britain sufficiently in the air to make invasion possible ended neither the conflict between Britain and Germany, nor its savagery. On 17 September 1940, the day of Hitler's true defeat in the skies, 77 British children, and a further 217 adults, were drowned when the ship taking them to Canada, the *City of Benares*, was torpedoed in mid-Atlantic. One of the children on board, the eleven-year-old Colin Ryder-Richardson, tried to rescue his nurse from drowning. 'I just couldn't release her when she died,' he later recalled, 'and others had to help me to get her out of my arms.' The young boy later received the King's Award for Bravery, never before awarded to one so young. The courage of several members of the crew and civilian escorts was also recognized; among them Assistant Stewart George Purvis, who rescued four children from drowning, and one of the children's escorts, Mary Cornish, who, with forty-six adults and six children, was adrift for eight days in an open boat before being rescued.

In the war of spies, the Germans were doing badly. On September 19 their Welsh agent, Arthur Owens, who had in fact been working for the British since the outbreak of war a year earlier, began to transmit a series of reports recommending targets for German bombers. These messages had been prepared for him by British Air Ministry Intelligence. That same day the Germans parachuted in another agent, Wulf Schmidt. Arrested, interrogated, persuaded to change masters, and given the code name 'Tate', Schmidt was sending back his first message as a double agent within two weeks. So successful did the Germans consider Schmidt's espionage, and his work as 'pay master' for their other spies – all, also, turned – that he was eventually to be awarded the Iron Cross, First Class.

There were many sources of honour; on September 21, a Canadian officer, Lieutenant J. M. S. Patton, who had had no training in bomb disposal, removed an unexploded bomb which had fallen on to a factory in Surrey. He was awarded the George Cross. His fellow Canadian, Captain D. W. Cunnington, who helped him roll the bomb on to a sledge and take it away, was awarded the George

Medal. In the forty days which had passed since The Day of the Eagle, 15,000 tons of bombs had been dropped on Britain.

Britain and France were about to launch their first offensive; on September, 23 British and French forces combined to carry out Operation Menace, the seizure, meant to take place without a struggle, of the Vichy-controlled port of Dakar, as a preliminary to winning over French West Africa to the Free French cause. To the surprise of the attacking forces, the Vichy authorities not only refused to transfer their loyalty to de Gaulle, but opened fire on the British ships. The garrison at Dakar had one formidable weapon at its disposal, the battleship *Richelieu*, which opened fire with its fifteen-inch guns, never before fired in combat. After two British warships, the cruiser *Cumberland* and the old battleship *Resolution*, had been hit, the action was called off. To have persisted with the landing, Churchill told Roosevelt, 'would have tied us to an undue commitment, when you think of what we have on our hands already'.

During the week ending September 26, as the Blitz had continued despite heavy German air losses, more than 1,500 British civilians had been killed, 1,300 of them in London; by the end of September, the civilian death toll for the month had climbed to 6,954.

Inside German-occupied Europe, the hardships of the population had known no abatement, and life was marked by almost daily incidents of terror. On September 19, several hundred Poles had been arrested in Warsaw and sent to forced labour, and almost certain death, some to the stone quarries of Mauthausen, others to the punishment cells of Auschwitz. On September 20, an SS officer, Philip Schmitt, had received his first fifteen Belgian prisoners at a new punishment camp, Fort Breendonk, in one of the southern suburbs of Antwerp. On September 22, in Poznan, capital of the German-annexed region of western Poland, Gauleiter Artur Greiser informed all German officials under his authority: 'It is necessary that relations with the Poles should be ruthlessly restricted to the necessities created by service and economic regards.' Any Germans having relations with a Pole other than those arising from the Pole's work 'will be placed under protective arrest'. Polish women who have sex with a member of the German community 'may be sent to a brothel'. 'We know', William Shirer wrote in his diary that day in Berlin, 'that Himmler hanged, without trial, at least one Pole for having had sexual relations with a German woman'.

The produce of Polish farms was first and foremost at the disposal of the Germans. When Polish farmers refused to hand over their contribution, the punishments were drastic. On September 30 a printed wall poster in Sochaczew informed the local inhabitants that 'The miller Niedzinski has acted against the regulations for ensuring food supplies to the General Government, so his mill at Kuklowka near Radziejowice has been burned down.'

The isolation of Jews was also spreading, not only in Poland but elsewhere in Europe. Anti-Jewish measures had been introduced in Roumania on August 10. On August 27 Marshal Pétain's Government had abrogated a pre-war French decree which forbade all incitements to race hatred. In Luxemburg, on September 5, the occupation authorities had introduced the German Nuremberg Laws of

1935, turning the Jews into second class citizens, and had seized all 355 Jewish-owned businesses in the Duchy. In Germany itself, the night of September 24 marked the first showing of a film, *Jud Süss*, in the production of which Goebbels had taken a close interest. The film, by deliberately and crudely distorting an historical episode, portrayed the Jews as doubly dangerous: first there were the physically repulsive 'ghetto' Jews, with their grotesque 'Semitic' accents, who could easily be recognized as such; then there were the far more dangerous, sophisticated 'Court' Jews, of whom Jew Süss was one, for whom no infamy was too great if it served them in their quest for money and power.

Suffused with hatred, this Nazi version of an historical story was shown in cinemas throughout Germany and occupied Europe, as well as at special sessions for the Hitler Youth. On September 30, Himmler personally ordered all s s men and the police to see it during the course of the winter. Even the world of film and entertainment had been dragooned to serve the cause of race hatred.

One element of the Nazi policy of terror and murder was economic; the homes, the businesses, the property and even the personal belongings of the victims could all be turned to profit. On September 23, in his capacity as head of the s s, Himmler signed a decree ordering that 'all teeth, gold fillings and bridgework should be taken out of the mouths of camp inmates'. The carrying out of the order, known as Operation Tooth, was the responsibility of s s Lieutenant-Colonel Hermann Pook. On arrival at a concentration camp, inmates were examined for dental gold. If any was found, a small tattoo was made on the left upper arm, for quick and easy identification in due course in the camp morgue. At the same time, a form was filled in giving the location of the tooth, and its estimated yield in gold. Several million such forms were captured by the Allies after the war.

The gold collected in Operation Tooth was delivered to the Reichsbank and credited to the Economic and Administrative Main Office of the s s, which also employed slave labour in stone and earth quarries, saw mills, and textile factories and throughout German-occupied Europe.

The British were now bombing Berlin almost every night. On September 24, William Shirer noted that the previous night's raid had hit 'some important factories in the north of the city, one big gas works' and two large railway yards. Dr Goebbels, dining at the Adlon Hotel with the Spanish Foreign Minister and a host of dignitaries, had to finish the dinner in the hotel's air raid shelter. On September 25 the raid was even heavier and longer, five hours of bombing. 'The British ought to do this every night,' Shirer wrote. 'No matter if not much is destroyed. The damage last night was not great. But the psychological effect was tremendous.'

While their own capital city was being bombarded, the Germans were tightening their grip on their recent conquests. On September 25 the German ruler of Norway, Josef Terboven, after abusing those Norwegians with whom he had been negotiating to set up a Council of State, removed the existing Administrative Council from office and installed a new Government in Oslo consisting of Nazi sympathizers. Almost immediately, a 'Norwegian Front' was created, to serve as a broad-based underground focus of resistance. 'The first feeling', one Norwegian has written, 'of resentment, grief and bitterness over the dishonourable negotiations, gave place to a liberating sense of relief. We breathed purer air because the situation had at last been clarified: resistance was the only way to go, however long and difficult that way might be.'

In the Far East, a further widening of the division between the confronting powers took place in the last week of September. On September 25 the United States announced a further loan to China; it would continue to support General Chiang Kai-shek in his struggle against Japan. On the following day, the United States extended the licence system for goods exported to Japan, to include all grades of iron and steel scrap. On September 27, Germany, Italy and Japan concluded a tripartite pact, extending the Rome–Berlin Axis to the Far East, lauding the creation of a New Order in Europe and Asia, and pledging each of the parties to help the others if any of them were attacked by a power not involved in the war in Europe: that is, by the United States. On October 8, Britain reopened the Burma Road for supplies to China.

On September 27 Jews in the occupied zone of France were ordered to carry specially marked identity cards and, if shopkeepers, to put a yellow and black poster in their window announcing 'Jewish business'. On the following day, the works of 842 authors were withdrawn from all French bookshops, including works by Jewish writers and émigrés and French patriots. At the end of the month, the twenty-seven-year-old Theodor Dannecker reached Paris. His task was to set up a special Jewish section of the Berlin Main Security Office, reporting back directly to his superior there, Adolf Eichmann. Jews were now forced to register in alphabetical order at French police stations, where they had to give details of their domicile, nationality and profession. Henri Bergson, who was to die of old age a few months later, filled in his form: 'Academic. Philosopher. Nobel Prize winner. Jew.'

On September 30, three German agents, two men and a woman, landed by boat off the coast of Scotland, near the tiny fishing village of Buckie. All three were caught within forty-eight hours, and brought to trial. The two men, Karl Drugge and Robert Petter, were hanged. But elsewhere, the autumn and winter of 1940 were a time of considerable German success. In October, twelve German submarines, operating in 'wolf packs' from the occupied zone along the French Atlantic coast, and no longer having to run the gauntlet of the North Sea and the Channel, sank thirty-two Allied merchant ships. Later they were to call this period the 'fat year'.

On October 1, the German Army embarked upon Operation Otto, a comprehensive programme of construction and improvement on all roads and railways leading to the Soviet border. On the western bank of the River Bug, an 'Otto Line' was built, using Polish and Jewish forced labour. Not only were Jews brought to work on the line from several Polish cities, including Warsaw, Radom and Czestochowa, but also from cities throughout Slovakia. One camp set up as a base for work on the Otto Line was at Belzec, a Polish village on the eastern border of Greater Germany.

In October 1940, in the occupied countries of Europe, Alfred Rosenberg established a special task force to transport valuable cultural objects to Germany. More than five thousand paintings, including works by Rembrandt, Rubens, Goya, Gainsborough and Fragonard, were removed from museums and private homes, as were thousands of porcelain objects, bronzes, old coins, icons and seventeenth- and eighteenth-century furniture. At Frankfurt, Rosenberg set up the Institute for the Investigation of the Jewish Question, declaring in his opening speech: 'Germany will regard the Jewish Question as solved only after the last Jew has left the Greater German living space.' Meanwhile, 'ownerless Jewish property' could be taken at will, from hundreds of Jewish homes and shops in France, Belgium and Holland.

On October 3, the 150,000 Jews of Warsaw who lived throughout the capital were ordered to move to the predominantly Jewish district of the city, which was to be walled in, forcing more than 400,000 Jews to live in the already crowded space where 250,000 had lived before. Those Jews who had to move to this specially created 'ghetto' could take with them only what they could carry, or load on handcarts. The rest of their possessions, the heavy furniture, home furnishings, stoves, ovens, shop furnishings, stock, had all to be abandoned. More than 100,000 Poles, living in the area now designated a 'ghetto', had likewise to move, and to abandon all their possessions except those which they could carry with them.

'Black melancholy reigned in our courtyard,' the historian Emanuel Ringelblum, who lived in the Jewish quarter of Warsaw, wrote in his diary when details of the move to the ghetto were made public. 'The mistress of the house' – a Polish Catholic woman – 'had been living there some thirty-seven years, and now has to leave her furniture behind. Thousands of Christian businesses are going to be ruined.' On the following day, Jews from the suburb of Praga, across the river from Warsaw, were expelled from their homes and ordered into the new ghetto. 'Today was a terrifying day,' Ringelblum wrote, 'the sight of Jews moving their old rags and bedding made a horrible impression. Though forbidden to remove their furniture, some Jews did it.'

'The war is won!' Hitler told Mussolini when they met at the Brenner Pass on October 4. 'The rest is only a question of time.' The British people were under 'an inhuman strain'; only the hope of American and Russian aid kept them in the war. However, in spite of this boast, on the following day, unable to bear a loss of fighter aircraft, which had totalled 433 since The Day of the Eagle on August 13, Hitler ordered an end to daylight raids on Britain. October 5 saw the first of the German raids which came only at night. Hundreds of thousands of Londoners took to sleeping, for safety, in the deep stations and tunnels of the Underground; one tunnel, a mile long, between Bethnal Green and Liverpool Street station, provided shelter for 4,000 people. Hundreds of thousands of children again left London, to live in the countryside; by mid-October the number of child evacuees had reached 489,000.

On October 7, German troops entered Roumania; one more step towards Hitler's goal of an unbroken eastern front against Russia. Five days later, he issued orders to abandon Operation Sea Lion altogether, except as a deception operation to divert the Russians' attention from the preparations being made for war against them.

For the British prisoners-of-war in France, there now began a search for some means of escape. On October 10 a young subaltern, Jimmy Langley, captured at Dunkirk with severe arm and head wounds, and with his shattered left arm amputated and still suppurating, escaped from a hospital at Lille. A French family living a mile from the hospital sheltered him, giving him clothes and a night's shelter. A few weeks later he was at Marseille, in Vichy France, and on his way back to Britain.

Langley was soon to play a leading part in guiding, from London, the dangerous work of escape, evasion and return to Britain of many hundreds of prisoners-of-war and airmen. This work went further than rescue; each returning soldier, sailor or airman brought back precious fragments of knowledge and Intelligence about the German Army, Navy and Air Force, and about civilian life in Germany and the occupied lands.

For those airmen who were shot down in aerial combat over Britain, and who had been badly burned in combat, a special burns unit at East Grinstead, headed by the New Zealand-born plastic surgeon, Archibald McIndoe, became their lifeline, as they embarked upon the slow, painful and disfiguring process of recovery, a process which, but for the dedication and skill of McIndoe and his team, would have been impossible. In five and a half years, 4,500 airmen were to be treated at East Grinstead, of whom two hundred needed a total reconstruction of face and hands.

On October 12, President Roosevelt spoke in Dayton, Ohio. 'Our course is clear,' he said. 'Our decision is made. We will continue to pile up our defence and our armaments. We will continue to help those who resist aggression, and who now hold the aggressors far from our shores.' At Lashio, in Burma, with the Burma Road now reopened for the despatch of supplies to China, five thousand Chinese labourers had on the previous day been loading twenty million dollars of high octane fuel, aircraft wings, rifle barrels and raw cotton on to two thousand American-built trucks. Although Roosevelt said nothing about this in his speech, it was clear that China was not to be abandoned.

Speaking of the Blitz, Roosevelt told his listeners: 'The men and women of Britain have shown how free people defend what they know to be right. Their heroic defence will be recorded for all time. It will be perpetual proof that democracy, when put to the test, can show the stuff of which it is made.' Hitler thought otherwise: 'Let the British announce what they will,' he told a visiting Italian Minister on October 14, 'the situation in London must be horrific.' That lunchtime, in London, a theatre company which had opened the previous day, but whose changing rooms had been bombed during the night, changed on stage for its second performance. Its repertoire was an hour-long selection of scenes from Shakespeare. 'Shakespeare beats Hitler' was the headline next morning in the Daily Express.

Hitler was not impressed by such bravado. In his talk with his Italian visitor on October 14 he said: 'Let's wait and see what London looks like two or three months from now. If I cannot invade them, at least I can destroy the whole of their industry!' On the following night, the most intense bombing raid of the war thus far struck Londoners a ferocious blow. Nine hundred fires were started. Dozens of shelters were hit. A bomb above Balham underground station broke through to the platform below; of the six hundred people in the shelter, sixty-four were killed – buried alive under the mound of ballast and sludge which poured on to the Underground platform. From eight in the evening until five in the morning the bombs rained down. By morning, four hundred Londoners had been killed.

On the following night, October 16, British bombers struck at the German naval bases at Kiel. That day, the British Cabinet had decided that, if bad weather made it impossible to bomb specific targets, the bombers should drop their bombs on large cities such as Berlin. It was also agreed that the public should not be told of the new policy, in case people were upset that Britain's one offensive weapon, precision bombing, was revealed to be far less effective than they had imagined.

In the United States, October 16 marked the first registration day under the Selective Training Act. On that one day, more than sixteen million Americans registered. 'We are mobilizing our citizenship,' Roosevelt declared in a radio address, 'for we are calling on men and women and property and money to join in making our defence effective.'

An unexpected example of the effectiveness of American defence came on the day Roosevelt spoke, with the arrest in Boston of George Armstrong, a British merchant seaman who had deserted his ship in Boston, gone to New York, made contact with the German Consulate-General, and then returned to Boston to collect information about the Atlantic convoys. Caught before he could do any damage, in due course he was deported to Britain, where he became the first Briton of the war to be tried for spying. He was found guilty and hanged.

Armstrong's would-be activities highlighted the perils of the Atlantic crossing for merchant seamen. On the day after his arrest, six German submarines, hunting in a 'wolf pack', attacked a convoy of thirty-five ships bringing war supplies from Canada to Britain. Code named SC – for Slow Convoy – 7, it had sailed from Sydney, Nova Scotia. Twenty of its ships were sunk. A day later, the same six submarines attacked a second convoy, HX – coming from Halifax – 79. Of its forty-nine ships, twelve were sunk. In two days, 152,000 tons of shipping had been destroyed. Among the submarine commanders whose torpedoes had done such devastating work was Günther Prien, who had sunk the *Royal Oak*, and Heinrich Bleichrode, whose torpedoes had sunk the *City of Benares* almost exactly a month earlier. On October 21, as the victorious submarines returned to their base at Lorient, on the Atlantic coast of France, German bombers made their two hundredth air raid on the port of Liverpool, one of Britain's main gateways to the Atlantic.

It was from Liverpool that the passenger liner *Empress of Britain* set sail for Canada in the third week of October. Attacked from the air when 150 miles off the coast of Ireland, fifty of her crew and passengers were killed. The rest were taken off safely, and the liner towed back towards Britain. But during the journey she was torpedoed by a German submarine and sunk.

Not every German submarine could carry out its raids unchallenged; four days after the SC 7 and HX 79 sinkings, a German submarine, U-32, was forced to the surface by depth-charges. Its commander, Hans Jenisch, was the first of the German submarine aces to be captured. He and his crew were interrogated. 'The prisoners were all fanatical Nazis,' the British interrogator noted in his report, 'and hated the British intensely, which had not been so evident in previous cases. They are advocates of unrestricted warfare, and are prepared to condone all aggressive violence, cruelty, breaches of treaties and other crimes as being necessary to the rise of the German race to the control of Europe.'

German successes during 1940, the interrogator added, 'appear to have established Hitler in their minds, not merely as a God, but as their only God'.

In German-occupied Europe, the bonds of tyranny were continually tightening. On October 20, Artur Greiser told his officials in the eastern German province of the Warthegau: 'The Pole can only be a serving element,' and he reiterated his call 'to firmness: be hard, and again hard'. Two days later, from the western German provinces of Baden, the Saar and the Palatinate, more than five thousand German Jews were sent by train across France to internment camps in the French Pyrenees. All the property of the deported Jews, their homes, businesses and belongings, was seized by the Germans in the towns and villages from which they were expelled, and in which their ancestors had lived for many centuries. The largest of the camps to which they were sent was at Gurs. 'From this camp Gurs', a German pastor, Heinrich Grüber, later recalled, 'we had – in Berlin – very bad news, even worse news than reached us from Poland. They did not have any medicaments or any sanitary arrangements whatsoever.'

Pastor Grüber protested. For this courageous act, he was arrested and sent as a prisoner to Sachsenhausen concentration camp.

As news of the deportations, the camps and the persecution reached Britain, there was a determination not to weaken under the continuing German air bombardment, which in the week ending October 16 had killed 1,567 people, 1,388 of them in London. On October 21 Churchill broadcast to the French people: 'We seek to beat the life and soul out of Hitler and Hitlerism. That alone, that all the time. That to the end. We do not covet anything from any nation except their respect.' Churchill ended his broadcast with words – which a Frenchman who heard them described as drops of blood in a transfusion: 'Good night, then: sleep to gather strength for the morning. For the morning will come. Brightly will it shine on the brave and true, kindly on all who suffer for the cause, glorious upon the tombs of heroes. Thus will shine the dawn.'

In the third week of October, Hitler left Germany for France in his special train, *Amerika*. On October 22 he met Pierre Laval, Deputy Prime Minister of Vichy France, at Montoire, in the German-occupied zone. Hitler was anxious that Laval should agree to a more active Vichy policy against Britain, whose defeat, Hitler said, was inevitable. Laval assured him that he desired the defeat of the country which had sullied France's honour at Mers-el-Kebir and Dakar. On the following day, Hitler continued southward by train to the French border at Hendaye, where he met the Spanish leader, General Franco. But despite Hitler's urgings, Franco refused to enter an alliance with Germany, or, as Hitler pressed him, to allow German troops through Spain to attack the British at Gibraltar. That attack, Hitler told Franco, could take place on January 10. After it, he would give Gibraltar to Spain. But Franco was not to be wooed; after nine hours of discussion, he still refused to cast in his lot with Germany. 'I would rather have three or four teeth extracted', Hitler told Mussolini, 'than go through that again.'

Franco returned to Madrid, and Hitler to Montoire, furious that Franco had refused to join the Axis, and had denied him the means of striking at Gibraltar. At Montoire, Hitler now met Marshal Pétain, on whom he likewise pressed the need for closer collaboration between Vichy France and Germany, 'in the most effective possible way to fight Britain in the future'. Pétain, like Franco, was evasive. Unlike Franco, he appeared to Hitler a more dignified figure, receiving praise as a man 'who only wants the best for his own country'. But even though it might have secured the return to France of more than a million and a half French prisoners-of-war, Pétain refused to agree to enter the war against Britain, and evaded Hitler's request that Vichy France should take steps to drive de Gaulle and the Free French forces from their bases in French Equatorial Africa.

It was from French Equatorial Africa that, on October 27, de Gaulle announced the setting up, for the Free French movement, of the Empire Defence Council. All French possessions still loyal to Vichy were invited to join it. In a powerful appeal to Frenchmen everywhere, de Gaulle declared: 'I call to war, that is to say to combat or to sacrifice, àll the men and all the women of the French territories which have rallied to me.' In 'close union' with France's Allies, that part of 'the national patrimony' which was in the hands of the Free French would be defended, while elsewhere the task would be 'to attack the enemy wherever it shall be possible, to mobilize all our military, economic and moral resources, to maintain public order, and to make justice reign'.

Churchill was much impressed by this Brazzaville Declaration, as it became known. It was bound, he wrote to his Foreign Minister, Anthony Eden, a few days later, 'to have a great effect on the minds of Frenchmen on account both of its scope and its logic. It shows de Gaulle in a light very different from that of an ordinary military man.' Were the Vichy Government to bomb Gibraltar, Churchill assured de Gaulle two weeks later, or to take other aggressive action, 'we shall bomb Vichy, and pursue the Vichy Government wherever it chooses to go'.

Not Pétain's France, however, but Mussolini's Italy, was on the eve of military action.

On 28 October 1940, Italian forces in Albania, their conquest of Albania a year and a half old, invaded Greece. In less than fourteen months, nine countries had been invaded without warning: Poland, Finland, Denmark, Norway, Holland, Belgium, Luxemburg, France and now Greece. Yet again, soldiers and civilians were to be subjected to air bombardment. Yet again, those in combat and those in hiding were to suffer equally the devastation and sorrow of war.

The news that Italy had invaded Greece reached Hitler in his train, *Amerika*,

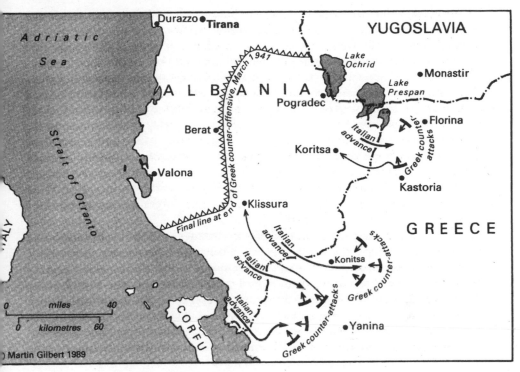

The Italian invasion of Greece, October 1940

as he was on his way from Munich to Florence, where Mussolini greeted him in German with the words, 'Führer, we are on the march!' Hitler was furious, regarding the attack on Greece as a major strategic error. To have continued the advance into Egypt, seizing the British naval base at Alexandria, or to take Crete, in the Mediterranean, would, Hitler believed, have made far more sense. But now Italy was embroiled in a mountainous country, against a tenacious enemy, while leaving her Libyan flank exposed to a British counter-attack.

One country apparently still determined not to be embroiled in direct military action in Europe was the United States. On October 30, two days after the Italian invasion of Greece, Roosevelt, then on a re-election campaign tour, told an audience in Boston: 'I have said this before, but I shall say it again and again and again: Your boys are not going to be sent into any foreign wars.'

Those 'foreign wars' were twofold, with a distant third in prospect; in Greece, the third day of the Italian attack saw Mussolini's forces already unable to advance as far as they had intended, and forced, as a result of bad weather conditions, to give up the plan to land on the island of Corfu. In Britain, October 1940 had seen 6,334 civilians killed, of whom 643 were children under sixteen; and in the East of Europe, so Churchill told his senior military commanders on October 31, the Germans 'would inevitably turn their eyes to the Caspian and the prize of the Baku oilfields'.

Churchill's forecast was not a fanciful one; on the day that he made it, the

German ruler of the Warthegau, Artur Greiser, was lunching with Hitler and Martin Bormann at the Chancellery in Berlin. Greiser was upset that the eyes of the German people were now turned west instead of east. The spaces that Germany needed for expansion and settlement could only be obtained from the East. 'The Führer agreed that this opinion was a correct one,' Bormann noted.

British Intelligence, based partly on Enigma, confirmed what Churchill had forecast and Greiser wished. On October 31, British Military Intelligence reported that a vast programme of motorization was being undertaken in the German Army, that there had been a steady movement of German divisions from western Europe to Poland, and that there were now seventy German divisions in eastern and south-eastern Europe. The number of mechanized divisions was also increasing; these would be fully trained by the spring. What Military Intelligence did not know was whether these forces were intended for operations in Russia or in the Middle East.

Four days before Italy's invasion of Greece, Britain and the United States had concluded a secret agreement which gave the British Government considerable confidence in its long-term ability to turn the tide of invasion against Germany during 1942. Under this agreement, signed on October 24, the United States Administration agreed 'to equip fully and maintain' ten additional British divisions, using American weapons then under production, and equipping the divisions in time for the 'campaign of 1942'. The United States also promised to 'ensure priority' for the material needed to maintain these divisions in the field. 'This is splendid', was Churchill's comment when he heard the news. He was also told, on October 26, that the current British request for military supplies to be purchased from the United States included seventy-eight million rounds of rifle ammunition, seventy-eight million cartridges suitable for the Thompson machine gun, more than two and a half million tons of explosives, and 250 aircraft engines. In urging Roosevelt to approve these orders, and to expedite them, Churchill telegraphed on October 27: 'The World Cause is in your hands.'

Britain's plans to take the land war to Germany in 1942 were a sign of her leaders', and of her people's determination not to accept the German mastery of Europe. But the fury of the German air attacks was unabated. On October 28, more than 450 German aircraft attacked strategic targets throughout southern England. Twenty-eight were shot down, for the loss of only seven British fighters, but the damage which they did was considerable. In London, fifty people were killed while sheltering under a railway arch at Croydon, and eighteen in a church crypt at Southwark. On November 1, determined to carry the war to both enemy capitals, British bombers struck at military targets in Berlin and Rome. But Churchill was not yet content, writing to the Chief of the Air Staff: 'The discharge of bombs on Germany is pitifully small.'

Britain now sent what aid she could to Greece, including a squadron of fifteen aircraft which had been stationed in Egypt to defend Alexandria and the Suez Canal against an attack by the Italians, whose troops were now entrenched sixty miles inside the Egyptian frontiers, at Sidi Barrani. 'If Greece was overwhelmed,' Churchill warned his War Cabinet on 4 November, 'it would be said that in spite of our guarantees we had allowed one more small ally to be swallowed up.'

Britain's guarantee to Greece had been given in April 1939. There was almost no military equipment, however, that could be spared. Some British troops, some anti-aircraft guns and a coastal defence battery were on their way. But it was to be by Greece's own exertions that the Italian invasion was brought to a halt. On November 4, a week after the Italian attack had begun, Greek forces, counter-attacking, began to drive the Italians back towards their starting points.

On November 3, for the first night since September 7, there was no German air raid over London. The German Air Force was reaching a point of exhaustion. In the previous three months, 2,433 German aircraft had been shot down over Britain, and more than six thousand German airmen killed. These losses were particularly unacceptable in view of Hitler's determination to move against Russia.

'Everything', Hitler told General Halder on November 4, 'must be done so that we are ready for the final showdown'. There were those in the German High Command who wanted to use the Dardanelles and the Bosphorus – the Straits – as a means of opening the way, through Turkey, to Syria, which was under Vichy control. 'We can only go to the Straits', Hitler told Halder, 'when Russia is defeated.'

# 11

# The 'new order of tyranny' (Roosevelt)

WINTER 1940–1941

On 5 November 1940, Franklin D. Roosevelt was re-elected President of the United States. 'It is a resounding slap for Hitler and Ribbentrop and the whole Nazi regime,' William Shirer wrote in his Berlin diary. That regime was nevertheless determined, while the United States remained neutral and her warships passive, to cut off Britain's transatlantic lifeline. On the very day of Roosevelt's re-election, a convoy of thirty-seven ships, HX 84, sailing from Halifax, Nova Scotia to Britain, was attacked in mid-Atlantic by the German pocket battleship *Admiral von Scheer*.

Escorting the convoy was a converted Australian passenger liner, the *Jervis Bay,* now an armed merchant cruiser. Ordering the convoy to scatter, her Captain, Edward Stephen Fogarty Fegen, took on the unequal contest, determined to delay the German attack on the convoy. Fegen, an Irishman from Tipperary, who had served in the Royal Navy throughout the First World War, continued to direct the fight even after most of his left arm had been torn off by a large fragment of a German shell. Later in the action he was killed. After twenty-five minutes the *Jervis Bay* went down; 189 of her officers and men were drowned. The commander of the *Admiral von Scheer,* Captain Krancke, made no attempt to rescue the sixty-five survivors who clung to the wreckage. Later that night, Sven Olander, the master of the Swedish merchant ship *Stureholm,* returned to pick them up, at great risk to his own vessel. As a result of Captain Fegen's order to the convoy to scatter, only five merchantmen in the convoy were caught by Krancke and sunk. For the next five months, he was to restrict his destructive efforts to unescorted merchantmen, sinking a further eleven. Captain Fegen was awarded the Victoria Cross, 'for valour in challenging hopeless odds and giving his life to save the many ships it was his duty to protect'.

For the people of Britain, each convoy disaster at sea seemed to threaten the possibility of a German invasion of Britain itself. In fact, however, Hitler's orders to bring all invasion preparations to an end were being carried out, and on November 6 a German Air Force Enigma message was sent from the headquarters of the German Sixteenth Army, giving instructions that a part of the apparatus used for equipping invasion barges in Belgium and northern France 'should be returned to store', leaving behind only sufficient apparatus for 'exercises'.

This message was simultaneously picked up by its intended German recipients and by British Signals Intelligence. A translation of the British interception was sent to the thirty-one people 'in the know' early in the evening of November 6. They could now be certain that Hitler's military plans could not include the invasion of Britain for a long time to come.

There was further good news for those at the centre of British policy on the following day, November 7, when, a mere forty-eight hours after Roosevelt's re-election as President, the head of the British Purchasing Mission in Washington, Arthur Purvis, discussed with Roosevelt himself the armaments needed by Britain if she were to be able to put a fifty-five division army into action by the middle of 1942. An army on such a scale would be impossible without substantial American help; Roosevelt, now the confident victor of the Presidential election, told Purvis that 'his rule of thumb' was to make available to the United Kingdom arms and munitions 'on a fifty–fifty basis'. He would also help Britain to meet the depredations of German submarine warfare by reconditioning, for Britain, seventy 'war boats' which had been kept in store since the end of the First World War, and building, again for Britain, three hundred new merchant vessels. To enable Britain to afford these purchases, Roosevelt said that the United States would bear the cost of building the ships; she would then 'rent' them to Britain, a system, he said, which might be extended to cover other arms purchases.

To build and to rent; from this concept, proposed by Roosevelt to Purvis on November 7, was born the solution which enabled Britain to obtain arms from America even after her credit, and her gold reserves, had been exhausted: Lend–Lease. With the knowledge that Roosevelt himself was not only responsive but also inventive in regard to Britain's needs, the British Government could pursue the war with a confidence far greater than if Britain had been truly 'alone'.

On November 7, British bombers struck at the Krupp armament factories at Essen. That same day, Operation Coat saw five British warships, headed by the battleship *Barham*, leave Gibraltar for a voyage the whole length of the Mediterranean to Egypt, to reinforce the naval forces there. They made the journey unmolested. On November 8, Hitler had to bring forward by an hour his speech in Munich on the anniversary of his 1923 attempt to seize power in Bavaria, to avoid the speech being interrupted by British bombers. On the following evening, one of the British pilots who had flown over Munich that night broadcast over the BBC: 'It was so light that we could see houses and streets quite clearly. It was a bomb-aimer's dream of a perfect night. Altogether we stooged about for twenty minutes checking up on our target.' That target was a railway yard. 'All the way down,' the pilot added, 'I could see those big, black locomotive sheds coming up in front of us. And the front gunner was shooting out searchlights, which I thought was a pretty good effort. ...'

On the Greek–Italian front, the Italian divisional commander of the Julia Division had picked up that night a BBC broadcast announcing that the Italian Alpine Division, which was in fact next to his in the Line, 'will be crushed by three Greek divisions'. He at once ordered his own division back towards the Italian frontier. Two days later, on November 11, twenty-four British torpedo bombers, flying from the aircraft carrier *Illustrious* in the Ionian Sea, 170 miles off the Italian coast, carried out Operation Judgement, striking with their aerial torpedoes at the Italian fleet, then at anchor in the port of Taranto. The Italian battleship *Duilio* was sunk, and two other battleships, as well as two cruisers, badly damaged.

That night, four Italian merchant ships were sunk by British warships in the Straits of Otranto. Over Britain, thirteen Italian bombers were among the twenty-five aircraft shot down during the day. 'The Italians fell very quickly out of the sky,' King George VI noted in his diary. 'I will not try to be vindictive, but this news has pleased me.'

Unknown to the King, November 11 was also a day of bad omen for the British, when, in the Indian Ocean, the steamer *Automedon* was attacked by the German raider *Atlantis*. Twenty-eight shells were fired at the bridge. Not only were the Captain of the *Automedon* and many of his officers and crew killed in the encounter, but a bag, carefully sealed, and weighted so as to be thrown overboard in case of danger, was found intact on the steamer's bridge when the Germans boarded her. Inside were a number of secret documents, including a copy of the British Merchant Navy code book valid from January 1, and a Chiefs of Staff appreciation that, in the event of war with Japan, it would be impossible to hold Hong Kong, Malaya or Singapore. Rushed to the German Embassy in Japan, the Chiefs of Staff appreciation was then radioed back in code to Berlin, where it was handed over to the Japanese Naval Attaché. The *Automedon* bag was an important success for German Intelligence, and a sign to Japan of the vulnerability of the British in South-East Asia.

Not only the secrets of the *Automedon,* but the British naval victory at Taranto, gave comfort, and inspiration, to Japan. The successful use of aerial torpedoes was noted at once in Tokyo, where Admiral Isoroku Yamamoto, Commander-in-Chief of the Japanese Combined Fleet, saw a means of eliminating America's power at sea, by striking at Pearl Harbour, at a fleet at anchor, as Britain had done. This was Operation Z. From the day after Taranto, its planning was given priority above all other naval projects. One American, too, took note of the part played by aerial torpedoes in the Taranto victory. 'The success of the British aerial attack against ships at anchor', wrote the Secretary of the Navy, Frank Knox, 'suggests that precautionary measures be taken immediately to protect Pearl Harbour against surprise attack in the event that war should break out between the United States and Japan.' The 'greatest danger', Knox added, 'will come from aerial torpedoing'.

At Dachau concentration camp north of Munich, in the Bavarian heartland, November 11 saw the first official mass execution. The victims were fifty-five Polish intellectuals, who had been deported earlier from Cracow to Germany. In Paris, on the morning of November 11, individual Frenchmen laid wreaths at the Tomb of the Unknown Soldier, and groups of Parisians gathered in the streets to remember the dead of both wars. By the afternoon, the Germans had begun to disperse the demonstrators, and 123 arrests were made, among them ninety schoolchildren. In the scuffles, four people were hurt. 'Presently', Churchill had told the people of France in his broadcast three weeks earlier, 'you will be able to weight the arm that strikes for you, and you ought to do so.' That time had not yet come. Two days later however, in Central Africa, Free French forces entered Libreville; within forty-eight hours, the whole of Gabon had been wrested by de Gaulle from Vichy.

Hitler had already decided that the invasion of Britain was a virtual impossibility. On November 12, in Directive No. 18, he proposed, for the consideration of his commanders, Operation Felix, to bring Spain into the war on Germany's side. 'Felix' envisaged, first and principally, the seizure of Gibraltar, then the use of the Spanish Canary Islands, the Portuguese island of Madeira and parts of Spanish Morocco, in order to 'drive the English from the western Mediterranean'. As to Russia, the new directive stated, 'all preparations for the East for which verbal orders have already been given will be continued', and further directives would follow 'on this subject, as soon as the basic operational plan of the Army has been submitted to me and approved'.

This clear indication that an invasion of Russia remained Hitler's goal coincided with the visit to Berlin of the Soviet Foreign Minister, Vyacheslav Molotov. In a talk with Hitler on November 12, Molotov wanted to know what Russia's part would be in the New Order of Germany, Italy and Japan, as created by the Tripartite Pact, and where matters stood in the Balkans and Roumania, with regard to Russia's interests. Hitler had no answer, telling Molotov that they must break off their discussion, 'Otherwise we shall be caught by the air raid warning.'

On November 13, Molotov continued his talks with Ribbentrop, who proposed that the Soviet Union become a partner in the Tripartite Pact. Molotov was dubious of Soviet adherence to the Axis, referring to Italy's setbacks in Greece and at Taranto, and telling Ribbentrop he thought that 'the Germans were assuming that the war against England has already been won'. Ribbentrop's discomfiture was increased when British bombers came over Berlin yet again, and they had to break off a celebratory dinner in the Soviet Embassy, and to continue their talks in Ribbentrop's own air-raid shelter at home. Rubbing salt in the wound, Molotov said that 'he did not regret the air raid alarm', as it had provided the occasion for an 'exhaustive' discussion. When Ribbentrop insisted that Britain was beaten, and her Empire therefore up for partition among the Axis powers, whom Russia ought therefore to join, Molotov remarked acerbicly: 'If that is so, why are we sitting in this air-raid shelter? And whose bombs are those that are falling so close that their explosions are heard even here?'

It was something else, however, that Molotov said to Ribbentrop in the shelter, which convinced Hitler that he would only be put further and further in difficulties by Soviet ambitions if the Molotov–Ribbentrop Pact of August 1939 were to remain the basis of German policy; at one point in their underground discussion Molotov went so far as to tell Ribbentrop that Russia could never entirely give up its interest in the western approaches to the Baltic: the waters of the Kattegat and Skagerrak, between Denmark, Norway and Sweden, once under Danish, but under German control since May.

Hitler was indignant; but his own plans to move against Russia had proceeded without interruption. On November 13, when Goering warned that the German Air Force might not have the strength to destroy Russia's industrial power, Hitler told him that the long term needs of the war against Britain meant that German control of the Caucasian oilfields was essential. The war against Russia could be won in a few months. Goering should prepare his air forces to begin it on May 1.

British Intelligence was aware of these plans. By November 13 it had learned that Germany planned to motorize one third of all her divisions, making a total of seventy armoured and motorized divisions, and that she was also increasing her paratroop and motorized divisions. It was already known that there were plans to increase the number of German divisions in Roumania to eighteen, far more than were needed to train the Roumanian Army or protect the Roumanian oilfields at Ploesti.

British Intelligence was not alone in seeing Hitler's preparations to move against Russia; on November 18 Richard Sorge, Stalin's German spy in Tokyo with close contacts in the German Embassy there, sent his first messages to Moscow reporting on German preparations for an eastern front.

Hitler had been much angered by Britain's 'pretty good effort' in bombing Munich on his festive anniversary on November 8. On November 14, as five hundred German bombers set off once more across the North Sea, they were told that neither Hitler nor Goering was 'willing to let an attack on the capital of the Nazi movement go unpunished'.

The bombers' target was Coventry. Their raid was so successful that twenty-seven vital war factories were hit, and production halted for many months. But in the course of the bombardment, a firestorm was started, which burned out much of the city centre. In all, 60,000 out of 75,000 buildings were destroyed or badly damaged, and 568 men, women and children killed. More than four hundred of those killed were too badly burned to be identified; they were buried in a communal grave.

For more than a square mile, Coventry's city centre was in ruins, giving a new verb to the German language, 'Koventrieren', to 'Coventrate', that is, to annihilate, or to raze to the ground. At the Air Ministry in London, Air Marshal Harris, who was eventually to be made the head of Bomber Command, later observed that the German raid on Coventry had taught the British the 'principle' of starting 'so many fires at the same time' that no fire-fighting services could get them under control. Meanwhile, the German air raids continued nightly; in the following week, as a result of bombing raids on the Coventry scale, 484 civilians were killed in London and 228 in Birmingham: the total number of British civilians killed that November was 4,588. Four days after the Coventry raid itself, thirty-one soldiers were killed at Theydon Bois, north of London by a German parachute mine, a weapon which, floating to the ground on the wind, could make no pretence of being directed upon a specific target.

The British response to these raids was swift. On November 16, two days after Coventry, during a raid on Hamburg, where cloud and severe icing made an accurate attack on military targets impossible, the bombs were dropped nevertheless, and 233 German civilians killed.

For the Italians, the Greek campaign had proved a fiasco. On November 15, Greek forces broke through the Italian line, taking many prisoners. At Menton, the French town just beyond the Italian border, posters appeared with the words: 'This is French territory. Greeks, do not advance further!' To assist the Greeks yet further, British air and artillery reinforcements were on their way, including twenty fighter aircraft and twenty-four field guns. On November 18, at Obersalzberg, Hitler expressed to Count Ciano his anger at the failure of the Greek campaign. If, as a result of Italy being at war with Greece, the British were to acquire an airbase in Athens, they would be able, Hitler warned, to bomb the Roumanian oil wells and installations at Ploesti. To prevent such an outcome, it would be necessary for Germany to intervene; but this she could not do before mid-March.

The Italians had succeeded only in turning Greece into a power at war; one, in addition, that was allied with Britain. In his talk with Ciano, and that same day with the Spanish Foreign Minister, Serano Suner, Hitler stressed the urgent need to close the Mediterranean, isolating the British in Egypt and Malta, and preventing them from using the Mediterranean as a base from which to attack Italy itself. To do this, Spain would have to attack Gibraltar, and close the Straits of Gibraltar.

On November 19, Suner told Hitler that Spain would need 400,000 tons of grain before it could declare war on Britain. Hitler understood that this demand was merely a tactic to delay, and in the end to avoid any commitment. Meanwhile, the British had kept up their bombing raids on a regular schedule, bombing industrial targets in Hamburg on November 15, and the Skoda armaments works at Pilsen, in Czechoslovakia, four days later, and striking, from Egypt, at Italian bases in Libya, including Benghazi, on November 21. On the following day, Greek forces, still advancing, reached Koritsa, fifteen miles inside the Albanian border, capturing 2,000 Italian troops, 135 artillery pieces and 600 machine guns, thus securing a far greater armament than Britain had been able to provide.

The Greek President, General Metaxas, exhilarated by the crossing of the Albanian border, told his people: 'We fight, not only for our own existence, but also for the other Balkan peoples and Albania's liberation as well.' By his invasion of Greece, now so ignominiously repulsed, Mussolini had dealt the Axis its first blow. But the signs elsewhere were still of an Axis triumph; on November 23, Roumania signed the Tripartite Pact. That night, German bombers made a heavy night attack on the British port of Southampton.

On November 24, Slovakia joined the Tripartite Pact. That night, over Britain, German bombers struck at the city of Bristol, while, from Libya, Italian bombers raided the British naval base at Alexandria. On November 25, however, despite the appearance of a large Italian naval force, three fast British merchantmen sailed without loss from Gibraltar, in Operation Collar, bringing essential war supplies to Malta and Alexandria. This was the first time that British merchant ships, as opposed to warships, had successfully traversed what Mussolini had boastfully described as the 'Italian lake'. Two days later, as the merchantmen approached their destinations, British warships damaged an Italian cruiser and two destroyers in action off Sardinia.

In German-occupied Europe, the German authorities worked without respite that November to impose their will. In the Warsaw ghetto, Emanuel Ringelblum wrote in his diary: 'Today, November 19, a Christian, who had thrown a sack of bread over the wall, was shot dead.' In Holland, on November 27, after protests by teachers and students at Delft University against new anti-Jewish laws, the Germans closed the university and forbade the students to enrol elsewhere. From Berlin on November 28 the Ministry of Propaganda sent a memorandum to Otto Abetz, the German Ambassador in Paris: 'The result of our victorious struggle should be to smash French predominance in cultural propaganda, in Europe, and in the world.' Any support given to French culture would be a 'crime' against the German nation. Also in Berlin that day, a second anti-Semitic film, *The Eternal Jew*, received its first showing. Purporting to explain the destructive part played by the Jews in world history, the film juxtaposed scenes of Jews and rats; the Jews, it explained, like rats, were carriers of disease, 'money-mad bits of filth devoid of all higher values – corrupters of the world'.

Such was the Nazi ideology; on the day of the film's première, the chief Nazi ideologue, Alfred Rosenberg, setting up his task force for the pillaging of French art, chose as its headquarters the house of a Jew who had managed to escape abroad, and took over four large warehouses, including a Jewish-owned department store, in which to hold the stolen works.

For the captive Poles, a daily revenge was being exacted over the skies of Britain, as Polish pilots flew with the Royal Air Force against the continuing German bombing offensive. On November 28, one of those pilots, Sergeant Zigmund Klein, crashed into the Channel and was never seen again. 'It appears that we have lost a very gallant pilot and ally,' the British record noted.

In the Atlantic, a pack of four German submarines sank eleven merchant ships and an armed merchant cruiser on December 1. That month, in the Pacific, two German commerce raiders sank five Australian merchant ships, and shelled the phosphate plant at Nauru Island. But Hitler's mind was now set on Russia; at a four-hour conference with his commanders on December 5, he spoke in some detail of the plan and direction of the attack, stressing the importance of capturing Leningrad and Stalingrad, the 'Bolshevik breeding grounds', rather than Moscow, which Field Marshal von Brauchitsch argued was the central point both of Soviet communications and of munitions manufacture. 'Moscow is not all that important,' Hitler insisted. Only after Leningrad had been captured should his armies turn against Moscow. 'Hegemony over Europe', Hitler added, 'will be decided in battle against Russia.' It was the defeat of the Soviet Union which would help to bring Britain to her knees.

Whatever the strategy, all those at the conference were clear on one thing: the Russians would be defeated easily. 'The Red Army is leaderless,' General Halder told the gathering. The Russian soldier was 'mindless'. The Red Army was as inferior in weapons as the French Army had been. The lack of modern Russian field batteries gave the German panzer a free hand. The Russians had nothing but 'badly armoured' units to oppose the German armour. The German Army would split the Russian forces into separate pieces, thereupon 'strangling' them by encirclement.

'Leaderless', 'mindless', 'strangling'; these were confident words that December 5. The Russians had been relegated to the ranks of an inferior and hopeless people, whose Army mirrored their inadequacies. On the day after this conference, General Jodl instructed his deputy, General Warlimont, to prepare a detailed draft plan for the invasion of Russia; known initially as Operation Fritz, Hitler quickly changed its name to Barbarossa.

The Holy Roman Emperor, Frederick Barbarossa – Red Beard – had marched eastward with his Army in AD 1190 to conquer the Holy Land from the infidel. His descendants were already resorting to methods as vicious as any which Frederick had used 750 years earlier, before the veneer of Christian civilization had subdued, or at least momentarily suppressed, the baser instincts of mankind. 'There have been cases', Chaim Kaplan wrote in his diary in Warsaw on December 6, 'when courageous Jews were shot in full view of their entire family, and the murderers were not held responsible, because the excuse was that the "filthy Jew" cursed the Führer and it was their duty to avenge his honour.' Four days later, also in Warsaw, Emanuel Ringelblum wrote in his diary of how, on December 9, a German soldier 'sprang out of a passing automobile and hit a boy on the head with an iron bar. The boy died.'

Since September 13, Italian forces had been on Egyptian soil, occupying a band of desert coastline from Sollum to Sidi Barrani, and constituting a potential threat to Alexandria and the Suez Canal.

Working in Cairo, the British Army's cryptographers had broken the cyphers used by all Italian military formations down to brigade level for both their tactical communications and their Intelligence work. By the first week of December, it was known to the British commanders exactly where the Italian forces were strong and where they were weak. Based on this Intelligence, plans were made to strike at the Italian positions on 9 December. On the night of December 7, a special patrol by an armoured car unit verified details of a gap in a particular Italian minefield.

On December 9 the British offensive began. Two British divisions, totalling 36,000 men, a half of them Indian troops, attacked seven Italian divisions. The 75,000 Italians were overwhelmed, for the loss of less than a hundred British and Indian dead. The Italian Army, after its first serious engagement in the Western Desert, was in retreat.

This serious setback for the Italians in the eastern Mediterranean was followed within hours by a serious setback for the Germans at the western end. For on December 10, after General Franco had refused for the second time an appeal from Hitler to allow German troops to cross Spain and seize Gibraltar, Hitler was forced to issue a Directive cancelling Operation Felix. Franco's refusal was made particularly galling because the Spanish leader had added to his refusal an agreement to enter the war against England 'when England was ready to collapse'. Hitler now outlined plans to avert a further setback by including in his Directive No. 19 of 10 December – Operation Attila – the eventual occupation of Vichy France, in order to control the French naval base at Toulon and the French airfields on the Mediterranean. The war, which six months earlier had seemed confined to northern Europe, had now spread, entirely as a result of Italy's unsuccessful initiatives, to the Mediterranean.

That December, the war of bombers reached a new intensity, with British bombers flying eastwards and German bombers flying westward almost every night, their missions identical; to destroy each other's war-making capacity and will. On December 7, British bombers had struck at the German industrial city of Düsseldorf. On December 12, the Germans had bombed the British steel town of Sheffield. That day, the British War Cabinet, still sharing the popular indignation at the destruction of Coventry, as well as the secret knowledge of the German use of mines dropped indiscriminately by parachute, authorized 'the maximum possible destruction in a selected town'. The town chosen was Mannheim. Four days later Mannheim was bombed, but with far less than Coventry's devastation, and only twenty-three civilians were killed. Ironically, the day of the bombing of Mannheim was also the day on which a secret British Government report advised that Bomber Command give primacy in future to German oil targets; a directive to this effect was to be issued on 13 January 1941.

The cruelty of the bombing was matched on both sides of the North Sea by the courage of those who had to help its victims. On December 13, in the course of trying to make safe an unexploded bomb at Manor Park in East London, two bomb disposal experts, Captain M. F. Blaney and Lieutenant James, were blown up. The explosion was so great that it also killed a staff sergeant, a lance-corporal, five sappers and a superintendent of police, who were watching the bomb disposal operations from across the road. For his courage, Captain Blaney was posthumously awarded the George Cross.

On December 13, determined both to pursue his plans against Russia and not to have them undermined by Italian failures in the Mediterranean, Hitler issued Directive No. 20, ordering a further reinforcement of his troops in Roumania in order to be able to occupy northern Greece. This was Operation Marita, part of which, as outlined by Hitler that day, included the seizure of British bases in the Greek islands. At the conclusion of Operation Marita, Hitler informed his commanders, 'the forces engaged will be withdrawn for new employment'.

That 'new employment' was Operation Barbarossa, the invasion of Russia. In Russia, on 16 December, Marshal Voroshilov gave orders for the preparation of the land defence of the naval base of Sevastopol. Hitler's preparations, however, were on a far more extensive scale. On December 18, in Directive No. 21 to his senior military commanders, he instructed them to make preparations 'to crush Soviet Russia in a quick campaign'. These preparations were to be started at once, and to be completed by 15 May 1941. Both Finland and Roumania could be expected to fight alongside the Germans. 'It is of decisive importance, however,' Hitler warned, 'that the intention to attack does not become discernible.'

In his directive of December 18, Hitler set out in eleven pages of detailed description the parts which his Army, Air Force and Navy were to take, the lines of attack and the sequence of objectives, first Leningrad, then Kiev, then Moscow. The 'final objective', he explained, was to 'erect a barrier against Asiatic Russia' on the geographic line 'Volga–Archangel'.

For Hitler and the Nazis, the word 'Asiatic' was synonymous with 'barbarian'. Yet inside Germany there were many people, doctors and priests among them, who had begun to characterize Germany's own euthanasia programme as barbaric. Some written protests had reached Hitler; others had been circulated clandestinely. Vexed, Heinrich Himmler told Dr Brack and Dr Bouler on December 19: 'If Operation T4 had been entrusted to the ss, things would have happened differently. When the Führer entrusts us with a job, we know how to deal with it correctly, without causing useless uproar among the people.'

This 'useless uproar' was soon to force Hitler to abandon the euthanasia programme, though not before as many as 50,000 'defectives', including several thousand children, had been put to death. But Himmler and his ss men were to get another 'job' to do before half a year had passed.

In North Africa, British forces reached the Libyan border on December 17. 'Your first objective now', Churchill telegraphed to their Commander-in-Chief, 'must be to maul the Italian Army and rip them off the African shore to the utmost extent.' In Norway, on December 21, all members of the Supreme Court, including the Chief Justice, resigned rather than continue to administer German-dictated justice. On December 23, in Paris, the Germans executed a civil engineer, Jacques Bonsergent, who had been caught up inadvertently in the demonstration of November 11, and had been jostled by German soldiers who had arrested him. He had been in Paris for the wedding of a friend.

On the day of Bonsergent's execution, Hitler was in France, visiting military units on the Channel coast. His train, *Amerika*, was at Boulogne that day; it had to be shunted into a tunnel when British bombers began bombing German military installations nearby. Two nights earlier, British bombers had struck at Berlin, leaving forty-five civilians dead. 'So considerable losses, after all,' Goebbels commented in his diary on December 24.

In Warsaw, throughout the week before Christmas, several hundred telegrams had arrived in Polish homes, reporting the deaths of husbands, fathers or sons who had earlier been taken off to concentration camps. The majority of these deaths were at the punishment camp in Auschwitz.

In the sphere of Intelligence, several things had become known at the end of December which were not at all welcome to their recipients. On December 28, British Bomber Command learned that its repeated bombings of German oil installations at Gelsenkirchen had not been at all effective, despite no fewer than twenty-eight raids over seven months. That same day, from Tokyo, the Soviet spy Richard Sorge reported to Moscow that a new German reserve army of forty divisions was being formed in Leipzig. On December 30, British Intelligence, mostly from its readings of the German Air Force Enigma messages, accurately calculated the scale of the German build-up in Roumania, and also in Bulgaria, in preparation for the attack on Greece. Another source, an informant said to have 'proved reliable in the past', gave the beginning of March as the date for the German onslaught.

On December 29, President Roosevelt broadcast to the American people: 'The people of Europe who are defending themselves', he said, 'do not ask us to do their fighting. They ask us for the implements of war, the planes, the tanks, the guns, the freighters, which will enable them to fight for their liberty and for our security.' Roosevelt added: 'We must be the great arsenal of democracy.' That night, in Britain, the Germans dropped incendiary bombs on the City of London on an unprecedented scale, creating a swathe of fire on both banks of the River Thames. Many famous buildings, including the Guildhall, and eight Wren churches, were destroyed or severely damaged. Vigilant fire-fighters were able to save St Paul's Cathedral from being engulfed in the flames, but an exceptionally low tide made fire fighting even more difficult than it would otherwise have been. It was a raid which brought the total British civilian deaths that December alone to 3,793.

The new year of 1941 began with a considerable British attack against the Italian strongpoint of Bardia, on the Libyan frontier. British and Australian soldiers began their advance on January 1, assisted by a considerable naval bombardment. Among the bombarding ships was the battleship *Valiant,* on board which was a nineteen-year-old Midshipman, Prince Philip of Greece, son of Prince Andrew of Greece, later to become Duke of Edinburgh. 'The whole operation was a very spectacular affair,' he wrote in his log. On January 5 the fortress of Bardia fell, and with it 35,949 Italian prisoners. Retreating westward, the Italian commander, General Bergonzoli, managed to reach Tobruk with a few thousand men.

While preparing to drive the Italians even further westward, the British also continued with the despatch of reinforcements to Greece. *Valiant,* with Prince Philip of Greece on board, was among the ships which escorted British troops to the island of Crete. Encouraged by Britain's victory, and help, on 4 January the Greek Army had renewed its advance into Albania, pitting its own thirteen divisions against sixteen Italian divisions, and driving the Italians back across the border towards Klissura. Two days later, the British launched Operation Excess, sending three merchant ships, with an escort of five warships, from Gibraltar to Athens, laden with military supplies. The merchant ships were to reach Greece safely.

As the British ships set off through the Mediterranean on January 6, with their precious war cargo, President Roosevelt spoke in Washington of the 'four essential human freedoms' upon which a future world ought to be founded:

freedom of speech and expression, freedom to worship God, freedom from want and freedom from fear, which, he said, 'translated into world terms, means a world-wide reduction of armaments to such a point and in such a thorough fashion that no nation will be in a position to commit an act of physical aggression against any neighbour, anywhere in the world'.

This kind of world, Roosevelt added, was 'the very antithesis of the so-called New Order of tyranny which the dictators seek to create with the crash of the bomb'. In London, one such bomb fell that week on the Bank Underground station, killing 111 of those who had sought refuge in the apparent safety of its deep tunnels. In the Mediterranean, German bombers, based in Sicily, struck on 10 January at a convoy on its way from Gibraltar to Malta. Two merchant ships were sunk, and the aircraft carrier *Illustrious* badly damaged. The cruiser *Southampton* was so crippled that the British were forced to sink her themselves; during the German bombing attack, eighty of her crew had been killed. This was the first German air action in the Mediterranean, and boded ill for the British, at the very moment of Italy's severe discomfiture.

On January 7, the British and Australian forces now on Italian soil in Libya had begun their onward march towards Tobruk. On the following day, also on Italian soil, in Albania, the Greeks attacked the Italian garrison at Klissura, which was captured on January 10, the day on which the Lend–Lease Bill was introduced into the American Congress.

The Greek and British successes led Hitler, on January 11, to issue his Directive No. 22, in which he finally recognized that he must come to Mussolini's help, or face grave problems from the south. 'Tripolitania must be held', he wrote, 'and the danger of a collapse on the Albanian front must be eliminated.' German troops would therefore be sent to Tripoli, while German aircraft 'will continue to operate from Sicily', attacking British naval forces and sea communications. German troops would also be made ready to move into Albania, in order to enable the Italian Army 'to go over to the offensive at a later date'.

Hitler's new directive brought Britain and Germany into direct conflict in the Mediterranean. Coming only a day after the German bombing of the *Illustrious*, it was followed a day later by a British air raid, by aircraft from Malta, on German airbases in Sicily. In an attempt to strengthen his position in these hitherto Italian dominated regions of the Balkans, on January 13 Hitler invited King Boris of Bulgaria to Berlin, insisting that Bulgaria join the Axis, open her borders to German troops for their attack on Greece, and take an active part in military operations alongside the Germans. Like General Franco before him, however, King Boris declined.

That same day, January 13, in conference with his commanders in Moscow, Stalin spoke of the possibility of a two-front war, with Japan in the West and Germany in the East. It was for this, he said, that Russia must prepare. The future war would be one of rapid manoeuvre. Infantry units should therefore be decreased in size and increased in mobility. The war when it came would be a mass war; it was essential to maintain an overall superiority of at least two to one over a potential enemy, if a breakthrough were to be possible. For this, it would be necessary to create fast-moving motorized units, equipped with automatic weapons. Such units would need exceptional organization of their supply sources and a great reserve of materials which 'must flow to the front from all parts of our country'. Food stocks, too, should be prepared on a substantial scale. The Tsarist Government's decision to stockpile rusks, for example, was, he said, a 'wise decision', and he went on to explain to his generals: 'A sip of tea and a rusk, and you've got a hot meal'.

On the day of Stalin's talk to his commanders, setting out the tasks that would face them in the event of war, one of Stalin's most successful spies, Leopold Trepper, set up his offices in Paris, under the cover of a textile import–export house. Trepper, a Jew who had been born in the Polish provinces of the Tsarist Empire, gathered around him a small band of largely Jewish Communists, including Hillel Katz, also Polish-born, who had earlier been expelled by the British from Palestine because of his Communist activities. In the course of his 'import–export' work, Trepper befriended Ludwig Kainz, an engineer employed by Organization Todt. It was from Kainz that Trepper learned of German preparations along the German–Soviet borderland, and arranged for this information to be passed back, by radio to Moscow, as and when he received it.

The American Ambassador to Britain, Joseph Kennedy, had, in the last months of 1940, been sending reports to Washington in which he stressed the possibility of Britain's defeat, and the damaging impact of the Blitz not only on buildings but on morale. In an attempt to discover whether Britain really could remain at war, and would not merely receive American-manufactured weapons in order later to surrender them to the Germans, Roosevelt had sent a personal emissary, Harry Hopkins, to Britain. 'The people here are amazing, from Churchill down,' Hopkins wrote to Roosevelt on January 14, 'and if courage alone can win, the results are inevitable. But they need our help desperately, and I am sure you will permit nothing to stand in the way.'

In this letter, Hopkins reported Churchill's warning that the German bombers in the Mediterranean 'make the Fleet's operation more difficult'; two days later, more than seventy German dive bombers, taking off from their bases in Sicily, attacked Malta's Grand Harbour of Valetta in an attempt to sink the aircraft-carrier *Illustrious*. In the course of the attack, considerable damage was done to the port. In addition, two hundred public and private buildings in Valetta were destroyed, and more than fifty civilians killed. In this, the first of a series of raids which the Maltese nicknamed the '*Illustrious* Blitz', ten of the German attacking aircraft were shot down. But the German onslaught was not at an end; two days later, in a surprise German raid on the airfield at Luqa by eighty-five dive bombers, six British bombers were destroyed on the ground, and the airfield itself made unserviceable. Through all this, however, the *Illustrious* suffered only minor additional damage, and was able, before the end of the month, to leave the perils of Malta for the safety of Egypt.

The Battle of Britain had lasted for less than two months. The Battle of Malta was to last for more than two years. Under continual bombardment from the air, the people of Malta referred to their ordeal as the second siege, the first having taken place nearly four hundred years earlier, in 1565.

On January 17, as news of the first day of the Battle of Malta reached Britain, Harry Hopkins was the guest of honour at a banquet in Glasgow. 'I suppose you want to know', he said to Churchill that evening, 'what I am going to say to President Roosevelt on my return.' Churchill did indeed want to know. The answer was a quotation from the Book of Ruth: 'Whither thou goest, I will go; and where thou lodgest, I will lodge; thy people shall be my people, and thy God my God.' Then, very quietly, Hopkins added: 'Even to the end'.

That winter, in German-occupied Europe, the bonds of tyranny continued to tighten. On January 10 all Dutch Jews were required to register – a simple, orderly, bureaucratic act, which nevertheless boded ill. On January 13, in the German city of Brandenburg, the local newspaper had announced sentences of between fifteen and eighteen months in prison for three German women who had given food and cigarettes to Polish prisoners-of-war.

On 20 January, the German Security Service compiled a series of reports on the reception inside Germany of the film *The Eternal Jew*. According to the report from Munich, 'there was immediately relief and enthusiastic applause at the point in the film where the Führer appears and in his speech announces that a new war can only bring about the final annihilation of Jewry'. For many people, the Security Service stated, 'The repulsive nature of the material and in particular the ritual slaughter scenes are repeatedly cited in conversation as the main reason for not seeing the film.' According to reports from western Germany, and from Breslau, people had often been observed 'leaving the cinema in disgust' in the middle of the performance, with statements like 'We've seen *Jud Süss* and we've had enough of Jewish filth.'

In Paris, on January 21, the Gestapo arrested Roger Langeron, the former Prefect of Police whom the Germans had made Police Chief in the first days of the occupation, seven months earlier. Now he was to serve them no more; his patriotism had prevailed over German blandishments and threats. That same day, in the Roumanian capital, Bucharest, the anti-Jewish hatred of the Iron Guard legionnaires led to the hunting down of Jews in the streets. Thousands of Jews were caught and savagely beaten; 120 were killed. Many of those murdered were taken to cattle slaughterhouses and killed, as one report had it, 'according to the Jews' own ritual practices in slaughtering animals'. These were the very 'practices' which had been shown and pilloried in *The Eternal Jew*.

In Norway, helped by Norwegian informers, the Germans had arrested members of a resistance group centred upon the town of Haugesund; in February ten of the young men involved were imprisoned 'for life', only escaping the death penalty after four of them had undertaken to work at the dismantling of unexploded bombs. In Paris, on February 11 Rudolf Hilferding, a leading German Social Democrat between the wars, and twice Minister of Finance in the Weimar Republic, died in prison from injuries brutally inflicted by the Gestapo. Both as a Socialist and as a Jew, he had fled from Germany to Denmark in 1933, and then to Switzerland, finally settling in southern France in 1938;

constantly warning, as in 1934 in the Prague Programme of his exiled party, of the dangers which the rulers of Nazi Germany posed for the world. Now he had become yet another of their victims. The Vichy French police, having promised him immunity, had then brought him to the border of the occupied zone and handed him over to the Gestapo.

In the sealed and guarded ghettos throughout Poland, the Germans had imposed such severe restrictions on food supplies that hundreds of Jews died every month of starvation. In Warsaw, in January 1941, the death toll that month from hunger had reached two thousand. The February toll was just as high. 'Almost daily', Emanuel Ringelblum wrote in his diary on February 28, 'people are falling dead or unconscious in the middle of the street. It no longer makes so direct an impression.'

The power of the German occupation authorities to tyrannize through hunger, fear and terror was unlimited. In his diary, Ringelblum also recorded the case of a deportation of Jews into Warsaw. During a halt in the journey, a German guard threw a three-year-old child into the snow. 'Its mother jumped off the wagon and tried to save the child. The guard threatened her with a revolver. The mother insisted that life was worthless for her without her child. Then the Germans threatened to shoot all the Jews in the wagon. The mother arrived in Warsaw, and here went out of her mind.'

After five hundred days of war, that woman's madness testified to the triumph, not only of armies, but of evil.

# 12

# The widening war

## JANUARY–MARCH 1941

On 19 January 1941 another war front was opened, with the launching of a British attack against the Italians in Eritrea, Somaliland and Ethiopia. The day of the attack was chosen because British Intelligence had read and decoded the secret Italian instructions to withdraw that week from Kassala, a town inside the Anglo-Egyptian Sudan which had been occupied by the Italians in the summer of 1940.

For five months the British force, numbering in all 30,000 men, advanced in three converging directions, towards the Ethiopian capital of Addis Ababa. Throughout this campaign, from its first day, every secret Italian military instruction was read by British avid eavesdroppers. Every secret operational order sent to, or from, the Italian Viceroy, relating to the daily military moves and problems of the Italian Army, was picked up as it was issued, and used to foil whatever plan had been made, or to exploit whatever weakness had been revealed.

On the first day of the British offensive in East Africa, it was a chastened Mussolini who arrived at Obersalzberg as Hitler's guest. On Mussolini's second day at Obersalzberg, British forces entered Kassala. That same day, in Cyrenaica, Australian forces launched their attack on Tobruk, which had already been cut off by the British 7th Armoured Division. Hitler at once agreed, as he had already stated in his Directive to his commanders, that he would send a German force to Tripoli. The troops he chose were those of the 15th Armoured Division, under Rommel. It was none too soon, for on January 22 the British and Australian forces surrounding Tobruk finally entered the port, taking twenty-five thousand Italian soldiers prisoner.

These were encouraging days for Britain. On January 23, in Operation Rubble, five Norwegian merchant ships broke out of the Swedish harbour of Gothenburg, passed the Skaggerak, linked up with a British naval force and, despite several heavy German air attacks, reached Scapa Flow without loss. But in the war at sea the Germans had two formidable weapons, the battle-cruisers *Gneisenau* and *Scharnhorst*. On January 23 they too crossed the North Sea, narrowly missing the British naval force escorting Operation Rubble home, and, reaching the Atlantic, began a career of attacks which resulted in the sinking of twenty-two merchant ships.

The vulnerability of ships, and of port installations, was stressed on 24 January, in connection not with the Atlantic but with the Pacific. For on that day the United States Secretary of the Navy, Frank Knox, wrote to his opposite number at the War Department to point out that 'if war eventuates with Japan, it is believed easily possible that hostilities would be initiated by a surprise attack upon the Fleet or the Naval Base at Pearl Harbour', with, Knox warned, 'inherent possibilities of a major disaster'.

On January 24, it was the Germans who rejoiced, when one of their fighter pilots, Franz von Werra, who had crashed over southern England in June 1940, and been taken prisoner, turned up in New York to a considerable fanfare of publicity. Two weeks earlier he had been one of more than a thousand German prisoners-of-war who had left Britain on board the *Duchess of York,* for prisoner-of-war camps in Canada. Of eight escapees from the train that was taking the prisoners-of-war across Canada, von Werra was the only successful one. While he was in New York, Hitler awarded him the Knight's Cross of the Iron Cross for an earlier, and as yet unconfirmed, flying exploit. For three months Canada sought von Werra's extradition from the United States; then, while the legal wrangles continued, it was announced that he had returned to Germany, through Mexico, Panama, Brazil and Spain.

On January 27, while von Werra's escape was still the talk of the town in New York, a secret gathering of senior British and American officers met in Washington, authorized by Churchill and Roosevelt to determine 'the best methods by which the armed forces of the United States and the British Commonwealth, with its present Allies, could defeat Germany and the Powers allied with her, should the United States be compelled to resort to war'. These American–British Conversations, given the code name 'ABC', went so far as to envisage an eventual 'unity of field command in cases of strategic or tactical joint operations'.

One area of joint operations did not have to wait until the United States entered the war. Even as the Washington talks continued, and as a direct result of them, six Americans, including Major Abraham Sinkov and Captain Leo Rosten from the Signals Intelligence Service, were crossing the Atlantic with a precious cargo: a 'Purple' machine, the Japanese equivalent of the German Enigma. On this machine the Americans, and now the British, could read a series of the most secret Japanese diplomatic, consular, naval and merchant shipping messages. As with the Enigma messages, those received on the Purple machine were decrypted at Bletchley. Two further codebreaking successes were achieved at Bletchley that winter within the Enigma system, first the breaking of the hand cypher of the German Secret Service – the Abwehr – and then of the Enigma key used by the German Railways for their own most secret military transport communications.

The Germans had no equivalent success to match the Anglo-American codebreaking triumphs of the Enigma and Purple machines. It was from the far less comprehensive world of local and tactical signals interception, and from individual agents, that they gained much of their secret information. On January 28 the German-born Waldemar Othmer, who had lived in America since the age of ten, sent German Intelligence the details of American shipping sales to Britain. As Agent A.2018, Othmer reported regularly and in detail on American naval preparations on the eastern seaboard of the United States.

The bombing of Britain had continued during January, when 1,500 civilians had been killed. But there was no sense of despair. On January 30, Roosevelt's emissary, Henry Hopkins, lunched with King George VI and Queen Elizabeth at Buckingham Palace. At the beginning of the lunch an air-raid warning had sounded, but the lunch had continued uninterrupted. When it reached the coffee and port, however, a bell rang, and the King said: 'That means we have got to go to the air raid shelter.' There in the shelter the conversation continued, the Queen telling Hopkins that 'the one thing that counted was the morale and determination of the great mass of the British people'.

'There is definitely a much more cheerful spirit than there was a year ago — don't you think?' Churchill's Principal Private Secretary, Eric Seal, had written to his wife on January 25. 'We really do feel we are getting on with the war, and that we haven't done so badly since France fell out.'

On January 27, in Eritrea, the 4th Indian Division entered the town of Agordat. Two days later, in the Western Desert, Italian troops evacuated Derna. 'I am convinced', Hitler declared in a speech in Berlin on January 30, 'that 1941 will be the crucial year of the great New Order in Europe.' For Germany's espionage efforts, however, there was a further, though smaller setback on the following day, when a would-be German spy, Josef Jakobs, parachuted into Britain with a wireless transmitter, broke his leg so badly on landing that he had to fire a pistol shot in order to attract attention. He was at once arrested. Because of his broken leg, Jakobs had to sit in a chair for his execution by an army firing squad six months later.

Hitler's generals were confident of success in their design against Russia. On February 2 the German War Council discussed a report by General Halder, estimating that some 211 Soviet divisions and formations would face 190 German and Axis units. This, Halder said, gave the Soviet Union a substantial numerical superiority, but not the technical or strategic advantage needed to avert defeat. In discussing these factors with Hitler on February 3, both Halder and von Brauchitsch found themselves confronted by the Führer's scepticism about the Russian manpower. Soviet rule was so hated, Hitler argued, particularly by the younger Russians, that Russia itself would crumble under the weight of the first victorious German attack.

Hitler also dismissed General Halder's concern, in regard to Russian tank superiority, that, despite the obsolete design of many of the tanks, 'surprises cannot be ruled out altogether'. Hitler was convinced that the Soviet tanks were too thinly armoured to pose a serious threat. Nor did he accept General Halder's further concern in regard to Russia's vast manpower reserves and munitions potential.

Confidence was Hitler's order of the day, based on his contempt for the inferior nature of the Slav. Operation Barbarossa was to go ahead with the transfer of further German forces from the western to the eastern border in mid-March.

In North Africa, Mussolini's forces continued to be pushed back westwards; on February 5, as they suffered enormous losses after a British attack at Beda Fomm, Hitler wrote to Mussolini expressing his dissatisfaction at the course of the campaign, and offering to send yet more troops, provided what remained of the Italian Army put up a stronger resistance, and did not retreat to Tripoli. But the retreat continued, as British and Australian forces gave the Italians no moment of respite. On February 6, Australian troops entered Benghazi, destroying eighty tanks and capturing seven generals, including General Bergonzoli.

For Hitler, the Italian retreat in North Africa, as well as the failure of the Italian campaign in Greece, created the first spectre of danger, the loss of the southern flank of the Axis. On the day of Benghazi's fall, he told Rommel, who had gone to see him in Berlin, that all German mechanized units in Libya would be under his command. His task was to hold Tripolitania, and thus prevent the British from breaking through to Tunisia. 'My head reels to think of all that can go wrong,' Rommel wrote that night. 'It will be months before things take effect!'

Also on February 6, Hitler issued his Directive No. 23, calling for an acceleration of operations against the British war economy. It was by an ever greater increase in the sinking of merchant shipping, he wrote, that Germany 'can bring about the collapse of British resistance in the foreseeable future'. At the same time, continued air attacks on armaments factories 'must lead to a considerable fall in production'. But, Hitler warned, the 'least effect of all' of Germany's operation against England so far 'has been upon the morale and will to resist of the English people'.

It was at sea that Hitler now wanted the war to be concentrated and intensified. 'The sinking of merchantmen is more important than attacks on enemy warships,' he wrote. By reducing Britain's available tonnage 'not only will the blockade, which is decisive to the war, be intensified, but enemy operations in Europe and Africa will be impeded'.

To impede those operations was clearly not going to be easy; on February 7 the Italian forces at Beda Fomm surrendered to the British. A total of 20,000 Italian soldiers, 200 artillery pieces and 120 tanks were captured, for the loss of nine British soldiers killed. On the following day, in Washington, the House of Representatives passed the Lend–Lease Bill by 260 votes to 165. It still had to be passed by the Senate, and approved by the President, but a major hurdle had been surmounted. 'It seems now to be certain', Churchill declared in a broadcast on February 9, 'that the Government and people of the United States intend to supply us with all that is necessary for victory.' It was not the two million men whom America sent across the ocean 'in the last war' that Britain now needed, 'gallant' though the armies were that America was again creating, but weapons and ammunition. 'Give us the tools,' Churchill declared 'and we will finish the job.'

The Lend–Lease Bill was still not law. But Hitler's directive against British merchant shipping was already being put into effect, and the danger was immediately apparent. 'Herr Hitler will do his utmost', Churchill had warned in his speech of February 9, 'to prey upon our shipping and to reduce the volume of American supplies entering these islands. Having conquered France and Norway, his clutching fingers reach out on both sides of us, into the ocean.' That day, even as Churchill spoke, a British homeward-bound convoy from Gibraltar, HG 53, lost two of its ships to a single German submarine, and six to aircraft which the U-boat commander, Captain Oerhn, summoned to the unequal battle. On the following day, Oerhn sank another merchantman. Later that month, in two further attacks on convoys in which German submarine 'packs' and air forces combined, nine merchant ships, and then twelve, were sunk.

On February 10 the British launched their first airborne attack of the war, Operation Colossus, dropping thirty-eight paratroops against a railway viaduct at Trignano, near Potenza in southern Italy. Although the paratroops reached the viaduct, the damage they did was soon repaired, and they themselves were captured. This setback was minor, however, compared with the ominous news which was given to the Defence Committee in London on February 11, by the Director of Military Intelligence, that the number of German forces then in Roumania, twenty-three divisions, with twelve more arriving in the near future, made it almost certain that Germany intended to secure the capitulation of Greece, not by diplomacy but by war. On learning this, the Defence Committee instructed the British Commander-in-Chief in the Middle East to give priority to preparations for British military aid to Greece, over and above his continuing advance towards Tripoli. The defence of an Ally was to take precedence over the defeat of a foe; but it was an Ally whose defeat would bring the German Army and Air Force to within striking distance of Palestine, Egypt and the Suez Canal.

On February 12, Rommel arrived in Tripoli to stiffen the Italian resistance. Since the opening of the British offensive three months earlier, 20,000 Italians had been killed or wounded, and 130,000 taken prisoner. They had also lost 850 guns and 400 tanks. The British and Australian losses, by comparison, were very small, 500 dead and 1,400 wounded. There was now to be a pause; on the day of Rommel's arrival in North Africa, as a result of the switching of British resources to Greece, only a single squadron of fighters remained available to the British in Cyrenaica.

For more than a month, the situation in the Western Desert had remained static. It was the struggle in Greece that would determine Germany's future in the Mediterranean. But on February 14, Hitler failed to persuade the Yugoslav Prime Minister, Dragisa Cvetković, to join the Axis. In Rome, two days earlier, Mussolini had been equally unsuccessful in persuading General Franco to reconsider his neutral stance.

The German failure to enlist Yugoslav help against Greece was a serious one; on February 14, the day of Hitler's unsuccessful confrontation with the Yugoslav Prime Minister, Roosevelt sent personal messages of support both to the Turkish President, Ismet Inönü, and to Prince Paul, the Prince Regent of Yugoslavia. Roosevelt's messages were sent because an American officer, Colonel Donovan, after a tour of the Balkans and Middle East, had informed Washington that

Greece offered a field of operations in which Britain could defeat the German armies, but only on condition that Turkey and Yugoslavia, and also if possible Bulgaria, were to co-operate with the Anglo-Greek forces.

On February 16, the Nazis celebrated the fiftieth birthday of Hans Günther, the leading ideologist of Nazi racial policy. That day, Günther was awarded the Goethe Medal, and his work praised by Alfred Rosenberg as being of the 'utmost importance' for the safeguarding and developing of the Nazi philosophy. It was Günther who, in his book on the ethnology of the German people, first published in 1929, had described those whom he called the 'non-European' Jews as being among the 'fomentors of disintegration' of Nordic culture.

On the day after Günther's birthday, the results of his teachings were seen, though only by a few, at Fort Breendonk, in Belgium. There, an elderly German Jew, suffering from asthma, was unable, on his second day in the camp, to continue to push his wheelbarrow, and, against the regulations, stopped to take a rest. Seized by the German Commandant of his barrack, he was locked up, and by nightfall was dead. Six days later, in Holland, when strikes broke out among the workers of Amsterdam in protest against the round-up of nearly four hundred Jews, the head of the ss in Holland, Hanns Albin Rauter, ordered ss troops and German police to open fire on the strikers; eleven were killed. The Jews, 389 in all, were deported to Buchenwald. There, twenty-five died from the brutal treatment, or were shot; two months later, the rest were sent to the stone quarries of the Mauthausen camp; by the autumn, there were no survivors.

Poles as well as Polish Jews suffered cruelly as the Nazi grip tightened; on 22 February, it was announced that a Polish woman, Pelagia Bernatowicz, had been sentenced to death in the town of Grudziadz for listening to a Polish radio broadcast from London.

In the Soviet Union, the senior generals were pressing for a swifter pace of preparation. On 18 February, General D. G. Pavlov, the commander of the Western Military District, sent a telegram to Stalin, Molotov and Marshal Timoshenko, asking for considerable allocations for road-building. 'I believe', Pavlov warned, 'that the western theatre of operations must be organized during 1941 by all means. Therefore it is utterly impossible to drag out the construction over several years.' In reply to Pavlov's request, Stalin stated that, although his demands were 'legitimate', nevertheless 'we are not in a position to meet them'. A week later, on February 25, the new Chief of Staff of the Soviet forces, General Zhukov, issued a secret directive naming Germany as the probable enemy, and instructing the frontier regions to make 'appropriate preparations'. On the following day, the Soviet Baltic Fleet received its directive of assignments in the event of war with Germany. Minefields were to play a prominent part in the defensive plan; unfortunately for the plan's rapid implementation, there was a grave shortage of mines as well as a lack of sufficient minesweepers to deal with German counter-measures.

The Moscow staff discussions of February 25 and 26 had indicated the scale of the defensive measures needed, and the difficulties in pursuing them. At

Zhukov's urging, it was decided to organize twenty new mechanized army corps, and to create many more aviation regiments, equipped with new machines, and with the necessary support and servicing facilities. As Pavlov had earlier been told, however, in regard to road-building, so in regard to Army and Air Force expansion, and naval preparations, the problem was a considerable shortage of materials of all types. Nor, for the Soviet Air Force, did adequate ground facilities yet exist; of more than a thousand airfields, only two hundred were operationally serviceable.

There was now no doubt in Moscow of the danger. German reconnaissance flights over the Baltic had become an almost daily occurrence. Hitler told the Soviets that this was a deception measure, designed to lull the British into thinking that Britain was not in fact the next on the list for invasion. But the Soviet state security services had already obtained information, possibly from Sorge or Trepper, that the German attack on Britain had been postponed indefinitely – until the end of the war against Russia.

With the Western Desert quiet, and preparations for the war against Russia proceeding behind a mask of secrecy, it was in the Atlantic that the main German war effort was taking place. On 22 February, 650 miles off Newfoundland, Vice-Admiral Lütjens, Commander-in-Chief of the German Fleet, sailing in the *Gneisenau,* and accompanied by the *Scharnhorst,* found himself in sight of a group of Allied merchant ships which, because of a shortage of escort vessels, was sailing unescorted. Five of them were sunk. Admiral Lütjens then set sail back across the Atlantic, to the Cape Verde Islands and the coast of Africa.

Part of the success of the German attacks on Allied convoys arose from the work of German spies in the ports and dockyards of the Atlantic seaboard. The information which these spies gathered was sent back to Germany through the German Naval Attaché in Washington, a member of the Embassy which was a constant reminder in the American capital that Germany and the United States still maintained diplomatic relations, more than thirteen months after Hitler's invasion of Poland. One such message from the Naval Attaché informed Berlin of 'convoy rendezvous February 25, two hundred sea miles east of Cape Sable; thirteen cargo boats, four tankers, 100,000 tons aeroplane parts, machine parts, motor lorries, munitions, chemicals; probably the number of the convoy is HX 114'.

By one of the ironies of wartime espionage, this particular message, sent across the Atlantic by secret radio signal, was picked up and decoded both in Berlin – by those for whom it was intended – and at Bletchley, enabling the British Admiralty to take successful evasive action. Old fashioned espionage had been defeated by Signals Intelligence, the agent by the eavesdropper.

As a result of a report from Greece by the British Foreign Secretary, Anthony Eden, the British Chiefs of Staff advised the despatch to Greece of a British Expeditionary Force of 100,000 men. This decision was endorsed by Churchill and his War Cabinet. Its aim was to establish a 'Balkan front', hopefully of Greece, Yugoslavia and Roumania, to prevent a German march southwards, and to enable British bombers to strike more effectively at Germany's principal supply of oil, the Roumanian oil installations and refineries at Ploesti. On February 28, in a decisive forward step towards invading Greece from the east, German Army engineers threw three bridges across the Danube, from the Roumanian to the Bulgarian shore. On the following day, March 1, the first German Army units entered Bulgaria. That same day, in Vienna, Hitler watched while King Boris of Bulgaria signed his country's allegiance to the Axis.

While King Boris was in Vienna, accepting German troops on his soil, and the probability of joining a German attack on Greece, the American Ambassador to Moscow was instructed to seek an interview with Molotov, in order to give him, 'orally and confidentially', the following message: 'The Government of the United States, while endeavouring to estimate the developing world situation, have come into the possession of information, which it regards as authentic, clearly indicating that it is the intention of Germany to attack the Soviet Union.'

Before the Ambassador could deliver this message, it was passed on in Washington by the Under-Secretary of State, Sumner Welles, to the Soviet Ambassador, Umanskii. Unknown to either the Americans or the Russians, on March 3 Hitler discussed with General Jodl the nature of a future administration of the German-occupied regions of Russia. The 'Jewish–Bolshevik intelligentsia', Jodl noted, 'must be eliminated'.

It was to be more than three and a half months before this plan of mass murder could be put into effect. But the spirit that animated it had already been at work for a year and a half, and knew no rest. On March 3, the very day of Hitler's discussion with Jodl, a German Jew who had earlier sought refuge in Holland, Ernst Cahn, was executed by a German firing squad in Amsterdam, for accidently dousing a group of German soldiers with a small protective spray which he had installed in his cafe. No one had been hurt by the spray. But Cahn had to be 'punished'. He was the first person to be shot by a firing squad in Holland since the German occupation the previous May. Two days later, a Dutch Communist, Leen Schijvenschuurer, who had been caught distributing leaflets calling for a second strike, was arrested. Within twenty-four hours, he too had been shot.

That week, a special decree was issued to all senior German military commanders. Known as the 'Commissar Decree', and signed by Hitler, it declared in blunt terms: 'The war against Russia cannot be fought in knightly fashion. The struggle is one of ideologies and racial differences, and will have to be waged with unprecedented, unmerciful and unrelenting hardness.'

Hitler's new decree went on to explain: 'The Commissars hold views directly opposed to those of National Socialism. Hence these commissars must be eliminated. Any German soldier who breaks international law will be pardoned. Russia did not take part in the Hague Convention, and therefore has no rights under it'.

Coming direct from Hitler, this Commissar Decree was sufficient to lead to the brutal deaths of hundreds of thousands of innocent people, without right of appeal for its victims, and without remorse on the part of the perpetrators.

*       *       *

On March 4 the British launched Operation Claymore, a naval raid against the Lofoten Islands, just off the Norwegian coast and inside the Arctic Circle. To the British public, the operation was a daring episode which boosted morale; a German armed trawler, the *Krebs,* was damaged, fourteen German sailors were killed, twenty-five German combatants were captured, and Germany's local oil stocks destroyed. The aim of the operation had not been to sink ships, however, but to capture a German Enigma machine used by the Navy, whose code keys had been proving virtually impossible to break.

One such Enigma machine was on board the *Krebs*; its commander, Lieutenant Hans Küpfinger, had managed to throw his machine overboard before he was killed. He had insufficient time, however, to destroy other elements of the Enigma message procedure, including his coding documents, so that after three weeks' intensive work at Bletchley, it became possible for British Intelligence to read all German naval traffic in home waters for the last week of April and much of May, with only a relatively short delay of between three and seven days.

The Norwegians were to suffer for the Lofoten Islands raid, Josef Terboven setting up at once, as Goebbels wrote in his diary five days later, 'a punitive court of the harshest kind'. The farms of 'saboteurs' were to be burned, and hostages taken. 'This fellow Terboven is all right,' Goebbels added. 'One does not need to pussyfoot with him; he knows himself what he must do.'

On March 5, the British launched their second expedition in two days; this was Operation Lustre, the ferrying of British forces to Greece, despite Italian air attacks launched from airbases in Rhodes and the Dodecanese Islands. Every three days a convoy left Egypt; altogether, twenty-five ships were sunk, all but seven of them in Piraeus and Volos, after the troops had disembarked. A total of 60,364 men were carried across the eastern Mediterranean; four divisions in all, two of them armoured. Even as these troops arrived, Hitler's plans to invade Greece were nearly ready; he was confident that any British reinforcements could be overwhelmed and pushed aside. It was the Russian campaign on which his energies were focused. But the secrecy which he had enjoined on his senior commanders could not be maintained. Unknown to Hitler, on March 5, from Tokyo, Richard Sorge was able to send his masters in Moscow the microfilm of a telegram from Ribbentrop to the German Ambassador to Japan, giving the likely date of the German attack on Russia as mid-June.

Ironically, although the date sent by Sorge proved in the end to be the correct one, it was at the time only a skilful guess by Ribbentrop; the actual date was not to be finalized for more than two weeks.

In Holland, on March 6, the Germans sentenced eighteen members of the Dutch resistance to death; they were executed seven days later. On their way to the place of execution in the sand dunes, they sang, alternating psalms with the Dutch national anthem. To show the Dutch people that they were not forgotten, British aircraft dropped more than four thousand tons of Dutch tea from Batavia, in two ounce bags. Each bag bore the message: 'Greetings from the Free Netherlands Indies. Keep a good heart. Holland will rise again.'

In Poland, after the murder by Polish patriots on March 7 of a Warsaw actor, Igo Sym, who had declared himself to be an ethnic German, the Germans seized 160 hostages. When those who had killed Sym did not give themselves up, seventeen of the hostages were shot, among them two former teachers at Warsaw University, Professor Kopec, a biologist, who was executed with his son, and Professor Zakrzewski, an eminent historian.

Also in Poland, or in what had been Poland until September 1939, death was now the punishment even for singing the Polish anthem. On March 14 the local German newspaper in Poznan reported that two Poles had been sentenced to death for this 'crime'; they were Edward Lembicz, a thirty-six-year-old saddler, and Jan Mikolajczyk, a twenty-five-year-old carter.

Official looting, too, had continued throughout German-occupied Europe, at times on a substantial scale. In February and March 1941, Goering visited Paris four times; during the course of his visits he removed fifty-three works of art from private Jewish collections, including one painting each by Goya, Rembrandt, Teniers, Rubens, Boucher and Frans Hals. When a local German official objected that this was illegal, Goering replied: 'The highest jurist in the State is me'.

In the war at sea, March 7 saw the sinking of the German submarine U-47, and the death, together with his whole crew, of its commander, Günther Prien, whose exploit in sinking the *Royal Oak* had been one of the first German successes of the war. But Prien's death was eclipsed in significance for Britain on the following night by the passage through the United States Senate of the Lend–Lease Bill, by sixty votes to thirty-one. Under the Bill, both Britain and Greece were to get immediate military aid. It was, said Roosevelt six days later, 'The end of compromise with tyranny'.

In Greece itself, troop reinforcements were rushed to the Albanian front on March 9, as the Italians launched an offensive aimed, at least, at driving the Greeks out of Albania; but after five days of battle the Italian thrust was halted.

Not so fortunate as the Greeks were the British; heavy German air attacks had been renewed over London, and several other cities, and several thousand more civilians killed. The war at sea had also continued to take its toll; on March 15, Admiral Lütjens' warships, the *Scharnhorst* and the *Gneisenau,* began a two-day chase of merchant ships, in which sixteen were sunk.

The Atlantic sinkings gravely threatened Britain's ability to survive. But the counter-measures were continuous. Not only were Günther Prien and his U-47 sunk that month, but three more U-boats were destroyed. Two of Germany's leading submarine commanders, 'aces' in the destruction of merchant shipping, were also victims of a vigilant British naval response that March, Captain Joachim Schepke being drowned and Captain Otto Kretschmer captured.

Another British initiative that March was on a small scale, but of significance for the future. On the evening of March 15, the Special Operations Executive, SOE, flew five French soldiers from Britain to France, where, with two containers of small arms and a specially designed road block, they parachuted at midnight near Vannes. Code-named Operation Savannah, their task was to blow up a bus in which German Air Force pilots were known to travel to Vannes airport. In fact, German pilots no longer travelled by bus, but by car in twos and threes, so the commandos could not carry out their mission. Those who wished to return to Britain were taken off three weeks later by submarine.

Although Operation Savannah had failed in its aim, it had achieved one considerable success; it had shown, as the official historian of SOE in France has written, 'that subversive agents could be dropped into occupied France quite unobtrusively, move about inside it with reasonable ease, be welcomed by a decent French population, and – given time, bravery, trouble, and luck – be extricated'.

The leader of Operation Savannah, Georges Bergé, brought back to England much important information about living conditions in German-occupied France, including details of curfew rules, ration cards and identity papers, which were to be of great value to the agents who were soon to follow in his footsteps.

On March 17, as part of his preparations to invade Russia, Hitler moved the armoured units of Army Group South to Cracow. This move was known to the British through their reading of the Enigma messages. That same day, when German aircraft appeared over the Soviet Baltic port of Libava, the Soviet Naval Commander, Admiral Kuznetsov, gave orders for them to be fired on. But Stalin personally ordered Kuznetsov to revoke the order, and, when a German reconnaissance plane made a forced landing just outside Libava harbour, its pilot was rescued, given a dinner, his plane towed in and refuelled, and he was waved back on his way to Germany. Stalin wanted no provocation. Commanders of the border regions were specifically instructed not to fire on German planes that crossed the frontier. Caution was to be Stalin's watchword. He had every reason to be alarmed; on March 20, three days after the forced landing of the German plane at Libava, Ambassador Umanskii was told by Sumner Welles in Washington of a series of messages, passed on by the Greek Government, and emanating from Swedish diplomatic missions in Berlin, Bucharest and Helsinki, of definite German intentions to attack the Soviet Union.

All that remained unknown to Stalin was the precise date of the German invasion. But, even here, the Chief of the Intelligence Division of the Soviet General Staff, General Golikov, submitted on March 20 a report with an accurate description of the three-pronged German plan of attack, and the names of its commanders, ending with the comment: 'The tentative date for beginning the attack on the USSR is May 20'. In his conclusion however, Golikov stated: 'Rumours and documents that war against the USSR is inevitable this spring should be regarded as misinformation coming from the English or perhaps even the German Intelligence service.'

Golikov's interpretation was wrong. Substantial German troop movements were taking place from the central region of Germany to southern Poland. Nor was it only Hitler who was making plans to extend the war; on March 22 a Japanese agent in Hawaii, Nagai Kita, was instructed by Tokyo to obtain

Intelligence about United States Fleet movements in and out of Pearl Harbour. He was to get this information, he was told, 'even by bribing informants'. Kita's instructions were intercepted by American Signals Intelligence, and read. But they did not cause alarm.

# 13

# The German conquest of Yugoslavia and Greece

APRIL 1941

As German forces completed their forward movements in Bulgaria, on the eastern border of Greece, and King Boris of Bulgaria finally committed himself to the Axis, the situation for Greece had become one of imminent danger. On 18 March 1941 it was judged by British Intelligence that Paul, the Prince Regent of Yugoslavia, had, like King Boris, committed himself to the Germans, thereby also exposing the northern border of Greece to a German onslaught. British diplomats in Yugoslavia were authorized to do their utmost to secure the overthrow of the pro-German Government, even if this meant giving support to subversive measures.

On March 20, Prince Paul asked his Cabinet if they would agree to Hitler's demand, that Yugoslavia join the Axis, and allow the free passage of German troops through Yugoslavia to Greece. Four Ministers resigned rather than accept these terms. On March 25, however, in Vienna, the Yugoslav Prime Minister, Cvetković, signed Yugoslavia's adherence to the Tripartite Pact. Watched not only by Hitler, but by the Japanese Ambassador in Berlin, General Oshima, Yugoslavia became a member of the ever widening Axis.

The news of Yugoslavia's commitment to Germany coincided with two further blows to the Allied cause. On March 25 six Italian motor torpedo boats, commanded by Lieutenant Luigi Faggioni, entered Suda Bay in Crete, where a British naval convoy had brought troop reinforcements and arms. There, they so severely damaged the British cruiser *York* that she had to be beached. At the same time, Rommel, who in a surprise forward move had retaken the Western Desert fort of El Agheila from British troops, decided, contrary to his instructions and against Italian protests, to develop a full-scale offensive. The British forces facing him were depleted in men, munitions and aircraft because of the priority being given to helping Greece. 'I have to hold the troops back to prevent them bolting forward,' Rommel wrote to his wife on March 26. 'They've taken another new position, twenty miles farther east. There'll be some worried faces among our Italian friends.'

Those 'Italian friends' had other causes for alarm as well. On March 27, after twelve days of bitter fighting, their forces in Eritrea were driven from Keren. At the same time, their principal naval forces were steaming off Cape Matapan, the southernmost point of Greece, unaware that a formidable British force, alerted by the regular British reading of Italy's most secret coded radio signals, was steaming towards them. In the ensuing battle, fought first off Matapan and then off the island of Gaudo, south of Crete, the Italians lost five out of eight cruisers and three out of thirteen destroyers. About 2,400 Italian sailors were drowned. The cost to Britain was two naval aircraft. Among those in the battle was a Royal Navy Midshipman, Prince Philip, the son of Prince Andrew of Greece; for his work in directing the searchlights of the *Valiant* on two of the Italian cruisers, he was mentioned in despatches.

The Battle of Matapan eliminated the Italian Navy as a force in the struggle which had just begun in the Adriatic, Ionian and Aegean Seas. Throughout 26 March there had been mass demonstrations in many of the cities and towns of Yugoslavia, against the signing of the Tripartite Pact – the trade unions, the peasants, the Church, and the Army making common cause. In the early hours of the following morning, March 27, the Cvetković Government was overthrown, and the Prince Regent replaced by the heir to the throne, the seventeen-year-old King Peter. The new Government, headed by the Yugoslav Air Force commander, General Dusan Simović, at once withdrew from the Tripartite Pact. Within forty-eight hours of having secured his northern route to Greece, Hitler had lost it. Angrily, he told his military commanders that he was determined 'to smash Yugoslavia militarily and as a State'. The attack must begin as soon as possible. 'Politically', Hitler explained, 'it is especially important that the blow against Yugoslavia be carried out with merciless harshness and that the military destruction be done in Blitzkreig style.'

Once more, 'lightning war' was to destroy one enemy, and frighten another. Turkey would also be persuaded by such an example to maintain her neutrality. Later that morning, in a fifteen-minute interview, Hitler offered the Hungarian Minister the Bačka province of Yugoslavia in return for Hungarian help. 'You can believe me', he said, 'that I am not pretending, for I am not saying more than I can be answerable for.' To the Bulgarian Minister in a five-minute interview, he offered the Yugoslav province of Macedonia, as well as Greek Macedonia, which was to have been Yugoslavia's reward for joining the Axis. 'The storm', Hitler told the Bulgarian Minister, 'will burst over Yugoslavia with a rapidity that will dumbfound those gentlemen!'

During March 27, six hundred German aircraft were flown to airfields in Roumania and Bulgaria from German airfields along the whole of the Channel Coast, as well as from Sicily and from Libya. With their arrival, the total German air strength ready to strike at either Yugoslavia or Greece had reached a thousand. Belgrade, the Yugoslav capital, was particularly vulnerable. That evening, Hitler signed his war Directive No. 25. Yugoslavia and Greece would be attacked simultaneously. The invasion of Russia must be postponed from May to June.

Yugoslavia now faced the full weight of Hitler's fury. Even if she were to make 'initial professions of loyalty', Hitler wrote in his directive, she 'must be regarded as an enemy and beaten down as quickly as possible'. Meanwhile, internal tensions were to be encouraged by giving political assurances to the Croats. As to the start of the attack, as soon as sufficient aircraft were in place, and the weather allowed, 'the ground installations of the Yugoslav Air Force and the city of Belgrade will be destroyed from the air by continual night and day attack'.

The meaning of such an attack could not be in doubt; on March 28 it was announced that 28,859 British civilians had been killed in the previous seven months of air bombardment, and a further 40,166 seriously injured. In March 1941 alone, 4,259 civilians had been killed, among them 598 children under sixteen. At sea, the German submarine sinkings had also continued. 'The strain at sea on our naval resources', Churchill telegraphed to Harry Hopkins on March 28, 'is too great for us to provide adequate hunting groups, and this leads to a continuance of heavy disastrous losses inflicted on our immense traffic and convoys. We simply have not got enough escorts to go round, and fight at the same time.'

The German submarine sinkings of merchant ships was a daily worry for the British people and their leaders; but for the long-term outcome of the war, the last week of March saw two secret developments of profound significance for the Western Allies. On March 27 the American–British Staff Conversations in Washington reached agreement on Joint Basic War Plan Number One between Britain and the United States, a plan which envisaged 'war against the Axis Powers'. Comprehensive in its scope, the War Plan set out in detail what the dispositions of the land, sea and air forces of Britain and the United States would be, from the moment that America might enter the war. Also known as Defence Plan No. 1, it envisaged first the defeat of Germany in Europe, to be followed, should Japan become a belligerent, by the defeat of Japan in Asia.

Of equal relevance, as it was to prove, to the eventual defeat of Japan, was another secret development that week. On March 28, a group of Western scientists discovered a new element, the properties of which showed it to be an essential component of nuclear fission, and the evolution of an atomic bomb. In 1789 a newly discovered element had been named uranium, after the planet Uranus. The new element of 1941 was to be named after the planet Pluto, which had itself been discovered only eleven years earlier – it was to be called plutonium.

On March 30, in Berlin, Hitler spoke to two hundred of his senior commanders and their staff. The invasion of Russia, he said, would take place on June 22. 'We have the chance to smash Russia while our own back is free. That chance will not return so soon. I would be betraying the future of the German people if I did not seize it now!' Hitler then gave his commanders an explanation of his Commissar Decree. In the East, cruelty would be 'kindness for the future'. All Russian commissars, identified by the red stars enclosed in a golden hammer and sickle on their sleeves, were criminals, and must be liquidated. 'It is not our job to see that these criminals survive.'

Sensing the shock of many of the officers present, Hitler told them: 'I know that the necessity of making war in such a manner is beyond the comprehension of you generals, but I cannot and will not change my orders, and I insist that they be carried out with unquestioning and unconditional obedience.'

There had been no need to browbeat subordinates in carrying out orders in the concentration camps; at the end of March it was learned in the West, through the Polish Government-in-exile, that more than three thousand Poles had been murdered in Auschwitz, or had died there from exposure and cold, in the previous ten months.

On March 30, in the Western Desert, Rommel now advanced across Cyrenaica, from which the British had so recently driven the Italians. Further east, in Iraq, an anti-British general, Rashid Ali, seized power on April 2, cutting off the oil pipeline to the Mediterranean. Hitler, elated at this blow to Britain's position in the Middle East, ordered Vichy arms from Syria to be sent to Baghdad, and German military experts to be flown out to help Rashid Ali maintain his power.

Only in the war in East Africa, where Britain was total master of the Italian secret radio communications, did the British forces continue to make unbroken progress; on April 3, the day after Rashid Ali's seizure of power in Baghdad, five Italian destroyers on their way from Massawa to Port Sudan were attacked by a squadron of torpedo-carrying aircraft. Four were sunk.

Since March 26, in Russia, under Order No. 008130, the Western Special Military District had been under instructions to institute a 'state of readiness', to be maintained until June 15. Urgent instructions were also sent to the Baltic, Western and Kiev Military District commanders to strengthen their frontier fortifications. In a massive effort to make up for past neglect, 58,000 men began work on fortifications in the Baltic district, 35,000 in the Western district and 43,000 in the Kiev district. The work was impeded, however, by a shortage of concrete, timber and cable; and, in what was meant to be a continuous defence line, there were several gaps of between five and fifty miles. One gap, particularly serious, was in the Grodno 'fortified district'. Plans were being drawn up to make the gap less dangerous by building two 'support points', but these had not been completed by the third week of June.

Also at the end of March, at the persistent urgings of Timoshenko and Zhukov, Stalin agreed to call up 500,000 men to the border military districts, to augment the infantry divisions there; a few days later he agreed to the despatch of a further 300,000 men to the fortified districts, among them specialists in artillery, engineering, signals, air defences and Air Force logistics. Their training, and the implementation of a defensive strategy, was planned to begin in March and be completed by October. Yet time was clearly running out: in the first week of April, from Tokyo, Richard Sorge sent a radio message to Moscow in which he stated, citing his most senior German contact in Tokyo: 'According to the German Ambassador, the German General Staff has completed all its preparations for war. In Himmler's circles and those of the General Staff there is a powerful trend to initiate war against the Soviet Union.' This time, Sorge gave no date.

Himmler was in fact training his SS troops for combat with an intensity not seen before even in SS military circles. Between January and April, ten SS men had been accidentally killed in combat training, and sixteen wounded. They were expecting to be used next in the planned occupation of Vichy France, Operation Attila, but this Hitler had postponed. On April 3 Himmler summoned the ss military commanders to Berlin, and told them to prepare for action in Greece. At the same time, uninterrupted by the Balkan imbroglio, the Special Task Forces continued preparation for their work in Russia. On the day after Himmler's talk to the ss commanders who would be fighting alongside the German Army in Greece, that same Army agreed to give the Special Task Forces virtually unrestricted activity behind the lines, and they were specifically authorized 'to take executive measures affecting the civilian population'. These 'executive measures' were to be mass murder.

On April 3, Rommel's combined German and Italian Army forced the British to evacuate Benghazi. 'We've already reached our first objective', Rommel wrote to his wife, 'which we weren't supposed to get to until the end of May. The British are falling over each other to get away.' That day, in Hungary, the Prime Minister, Count Pal Teleki, committed suicide, feeling that the decision of the Hungarian Regent, Admiral Horthy, to join with Germany in the invasion of Greece, forfeited Hungary's honour. In his War Directive No. 26, Hitler, also on April 3, confirmed that Hungary was ready to take part, not only in occupying the Yugoslav province of the Bačka, but also in 'further operations for the destruction of the enemy'. Bulgaria would 'get back' Macedonia. Roumania would limit her efforts 'to guarding the frontiers with Yugoslavia and Russia'. The Italians would also move against Yugoslavia, but this would only be once the German attack 'begins to be effective'.

On April 4, as the German forces made their final preparations for their Balkan offensive, Rommel's troops entered Benghazi, from which the British had already withdrawn. That same day, in mid-Atlantic, a German commerce raider the *Thor*, disguised as a merchant ship, sank the British armed merchant cruiser *Voltaire*. In the first six months of 1941, these German decoy ships were to sink thirty-eight merchantmen, while the warship raiders, such as the *Pinguin*, sank a further thirty-seven.

At Sachsenhausen concentration camp, German doctors were continuing their experiments in euthanasia and death by gassing, using concentration camp prisoners for their experiments. 'Our work here', one doctor, Fritz Mennecke, wrote to his wife, 'Is very, very interesting.' He was collecting material for 'large quantities of new experiments'.

On April 5, in North Africa, despite Italian hesitations, Rommel ordered his Army to continue its eastward march. 'Off at four this morning,' he wrote to his wife that day, and he added: 'Things are happening in Africa. Let's hope the great stroke we've now launched is successful.' In Italian East Africa, the final humiliation came that day, when the Italian Viceroy of Ethiopia, the Duke of Aosta, ordered the evacuation of the capital, Addis Ababa. In Moscow, Stalin spent much of the evening of April 5 with the Yugoslav Minister in Moscow, Gavrilović, promising that, if Yugoslavia were attacked, the Soviet Union would adopt an attitude of goodwill, 'based on friendly relations'. 'And if the Germans, displeased, turn against you?' Gavrilović asked. 'Let them come!' was Stalin's confident reply.

Even as Stalin spoke, the German Air Force launched Operation Castigo, the bombing of Belgrade. The first bombs fell at five o'clock on the morning of April 6. The battle for Yugoslavia had begun.

Swiftly, and with savage brutality, Yugoslavia was struck, and overrun. In the bombing of Belgrade, the principal purpose of which was to create confusion through terror, 17,000 civilians were killed: the largest number of civilian deaths by bombing in a single day in twenty months of war. As had happened in Warsaw in September 1939, and in Rotterdam in May 1940, so in Belgrade in April 1941, a virtually defenceless civilian population, unprepared for the onslaught, and in this instance swelled by many Yugoslavs from other towns and villages who had come to their capital to celebrate Palm Sunday, was subjected to a day of aerial slaughter. Simultaneously, all Yugoslavia's airfields were bombed, and most of its six hundred aircraft destroyed on the ground.

Several German armies were on the move on April 6; one, advancing from Austria and Hungary, drove on Belgrade; another, advancing from Bulgaria, drove on Niš, Skoplje and Monastir; another, also advancing from Bulgaria, drove into Greece, striking at the port city of Salonica. That same day, the German Air Force bombed the Greek port of Piraeus. Six Allied ships with military cargoes were sunk before the port itself was devastated when a British merchant ship, the *Clan Fraser*, hit by German bombs, blew up with two hundred tons of explosives on board. In the massive explosion, ten other ships were sunk.

The Italians, eager to revenge the humiliation of their failed invasion of Greece, prepared yet again to advance from Albania; they also awaited the orders to march from Istria, in the north, and from the Italian enclave at Zara, against the Dalmatian coast of Yugoslavia. The Hungarians, too, were poised to strike. Twenty-eight Yugoslav divisions faced more than fifty Axis divisions; the Axis divisions had far greater armoured forces, and overwhelming air superiority. That night, hoping to delay German railway movement from Bulgaria to the front, six British bombers, flying from bases in Greece, bombed the railway yards in Sofia, the Bulgarian capital. But any gains from the raid were seriously offset by the sinking that day in the eastern Mediterranean of the *Northern Prince*, a British merchant ship bringing the Greek Army badly needed raw materials for the manufacture of explosives.

As Yugoslavia faced defeat and disintegration, with Italy among those who would share the territorial spoils, the Italian armies in Eritrea were finally and totally defeated, with the surrender of Massawa. Of the thirteen thousand defenders, more than three thousand had been killed. In North Africa, however, the German and Italian forces under Rommel's command were completing the reconquest of Cyrenaica. 'After a long desert march,' Rommel wrote to his wife on April 10, 'I reached the sea the evening before last. It's wonderful to have pulled this off against the British.' Less than a year had passed since Rommel had last reached the sea in triumph – at Les Petites Dalles on the Channel coast.

Stalin, watching as German forces entered the southern Yugoslav city of Niš

Yugoslavia and Greece, April 1941

and advanced towards Belgrade, approved a Soviet General Staff directive
on April 8 to the Western and Kiev Special Military Districts, ordering the
maintenance and completion of the frontier Fortified Areas. The necessary
improvements were to begin by May 1.

That night, April 8, German bombers struck again at the British aircraft
factories around Coventry. Considerable damage was done to three factories.
That same night, in Greece, German forces occupied Salonica, and on the
following day the Greek commander of the region, General Bakopoulos, was
ordered by the Greek Supreme Commander to surrender his 70,000 soldiers. At

Hitler's Chancellery in Berlin, the German diplomat Walther Hewel noted a 'magnificent mood'.

April 9 marked the first anniversary of the German invasion of Norway. In Oslo, there were silent demonstrations in streets, schools and workplaces. Over Berlin, as a reprisal for the bombing of Belgrade, British bombers dropped explosive and incendiary bombs on the city centre, destroying several public buildings. Hitler had to spend part of the night in his air raid shelter.

In Britain, the shock of the simultaneous German invasion of Yugoslavia and Greece was met with defiance. On April 9, Churchill told the House of Commons that once the Battle of the Atlantic had been won, and Britain had received 'the constant flow of American supplies which is being prepared for us', then however far Hitler might go, 'or whatever new millions, or scores of millions, he may lap in misery, he may be sure that, armed with the sword of retributive justice, we shall be on his track'.

It was on April 9, in the northern sector of the Greek frontier, that a British Army patrol crossed the frontier with Yugoslavia, near Monastir. There, it found groups of Yugoslav soldiers drifting across the frontier into Greece. The patrol returned to report that all Yugoslav resistance in the south was over. Snow falling in the mountains, and rain in the valleys, made any effective air reconnaissance impossible.

On April 10, the British Expeditionary Force in Greece began to withdraw from the Salonica front. In northern Yugoslavia, Zagreb fell to the German Army, giving the Croat nationalist leader Ante Pavelić the opportunity to declare Croatia a separate State. In North Africa, the Australian forces in Tobruk, together with their British artillery support, numbering 24,000 men in all, were cut off from their retreating comrades in arms, and besieged. That day, Goebbels found Hitler 'beaming with joy'. But two events that day were an omen, hardly glimpsed in Berlin, of things yet to come. In the Atlantic, in the first hostile gesture by the United States against Germany since war in Europe had begun, the American destroyer *Niblack* dropped depth charges against a German submarine responsible for sinking a Dutch freighter. And in Moscow a decree was issued creating a separate logistical service for the Red Air Force, setting up airbase areas and ground service battalions. Special fighter corps were also formed, to strengthen the air defences of Moscow and Leningrad. Belatedly, slowly, with a desperate lack of resources, the Soviet Union was awakening to the danger.

Hitler, with victory over Yugoslavia now certain, travelled from Berlin to the tiny village of Mönichkirchen in southern Austria, to be as near as possible to his troops while still remaining on German soil. For two weeks, living in his train *Amerika*, he followed the course of the Balkan campaign. Among those who visited him on the train was Franz von Werra, who had finally returned to Germany after his escape that January while he had been a prisoner-of-war in Canada.

With Yugoslavia in travail, both Italy and Hungary advanced on April 11 for their part of the spoil, the Italians entering the Slovene capital of Ljubljana and the Hungarians advancing on the principal Bačka town of Novi Sad. The Italians also chose April 11 to advance across the Albanian border into Greece, occupying the same regions from which they had earlier been driven with such ignominy. On the following day, as other Italian units began their advance along the Dalmatian coast, occupying the island of Uljan, German motorized units reached the outskirts of Belgrade.

Once more, a moment of German triumph was paralleled elsewhere by a little noticed move of great significance for the future of the war – the occupation of the Danish colony of Greenland by United States forces. This was one more step towards the American policy of support for Britain in the Atlantic, by means of shared bases and extended zones of naval patrol. That same day, Roosevelt told Churchill that the United States would extend her security zone and patrol areas in the Atlantic as far east as the 25th meridian.

Even so, Britain's position at sea was grave; in the three days up to April 10, 31,000 tons of Allied merchant shipping had been sunk at sea. German bombing had also reached a renewed intensity; on April 12 Churchill was in Bristol where, together with the new American Ambassador, Gilbert Winant, he visited the city centre, shattered by a raid the night before. Yet British morale was not being broken. 'People were still being dug out,' General Ismay later recalled, in a letter to Churchill, 'but there was no sign of faltering anywhere. Only efficiency and resolution. At one of the rest centres at which you called, there was a poor woman who had lost all her belongings sobbing her heart out. But as you entered, she took her handkerchief from her eyes and waved it madly shouting "Hooray, hooray".'

That April 12, in Greece, Australian troops had been among those surrendering to the superior firepower of the Germans, as they advanced on the Aliakhmon Line. In Yugoslavia, April 13 saw the occupation of Belgrade, the eighth European capital to be conquered by German arms in a year and a half. According to one account, the first Yugoslav civilian to be shot in cold blood in the capital that day was a Jewish tailor who, as the German troops marched by, spat at them and shouted: 'You will all perish.'

In Moscow, on the day of the fall of Belgrade, in an attempt to ensure that he was not stabbed in the back, Stalin signed a Soviet–Japanese Neutrality Pact, valid for five years. It was an agreement which gave both sides advantages. Stalin was now free to concentrate on meeting a German threat from the West. Japan could focus her attention on South East Asia and the Pacific. At the Kazan railway station in Moscow, Stalin made a rare public appearance to say goodbye to the Japanese Foreign Minister, Yosuke Matsuoka, remarking: 'We are both Asiatics.' But he also sought out the German Ambassador on the station platform, telling him: 'We must remain friends and you must now do everything to that end.' Then, turning to an officer whom he had never seen before, the acting German Military Attaché, Colonel Krebs, and after checking to make sure that Krebs was in fact a German, Stalin called out for all to hear: 'We shall remain friends with you – in any event!'

On April 14, the day after this scene in Moscow, Stalin approved a directive, issued by the Soviet General Staff, for the artillery emplacements in the Fortified Areas to be 'immediately mounted in combat emplacements'; and for the

Military Districts in which they were situated to be put 'in combat readiness'. Even where the full equipment needed by the gun emplacements was not available, it was still 'absolutely necessary' to mount the armoured doors, and to provide 'proper care and maintenance' of whatever armaments had been installed. In all, 2,300 major artillery emplacements were to come under the new directive; but such were the shortages of materials that less than a thousand were in fact completed or equipped by the third week of June.

In the Hungarian-occupied areas of northern Yugoslavia, April 14 marked the first day of an extension of the terror against civilians in the new area of conquest; for on that day Hungarian armed detachments seized five hundred Jews and Serbs, and shot or bayoneted them to death.

As the German armies now broke through more and more strongpoints along the Aliakhmon Line, and some Greek soldiers, demoralized by the imminent disaster, fired on their own officers, Hitler was continuing uninterrupted with his Eastern plans. On April 15 a German aircraft, forced down near Rovno, almost a hundred miles inside the Soviet frontier, was found by the Soviets to be carrying a camera, exposed film and a detailed topographical map of the Soviet frontier region.

All Europe was now caught up in one aspect or another of war. On April 16, as the Greek Commander-in-Chief, Marshal Papagos, contemplated surrender, and pressed the British to withdraw their forces from Greece altogether 'in order to save Greece from devastation', London experienced one of the most severe and indiscriminate bombing attacks of the war, a retaliation for Britain's deliberate raid on the centre of Berlin a week earlier. In all, 2,300 people were killed. Among them were more than forty Canadian soldiers, sailors and airmen on leave in the capital. In an air battle over southern England, as fighters sought to shoot down the German raiders, two Polish pilots lost their lives, Pilot Officer Mieczyslaw Waskiewicz and Pilot Officer Boguslaw Mierzwa.

On April 17 the Yugoslav Government signed the act of surrender in Belgrade. A total of 6,000 Yugoslav officers and 335,000 men had been taken prisoner. Once more, overwhelming military superiority, in numbers, firepower and air support, had proved too much even for the most determined defenders. On the following day, in Greece, the Germans broke through the last defences on the Aliakhmon Line, held by Allied troops from New Zealand. In despair, not only at the German military advance, but at the growing signs of defeatism and even treachery in Greek Government circles, the Greek Prime Minister, Alexander Koryzis, after having been refused permission by the Greek King to resign, kissed the King's hand and returned to his home, where he shot himself.

That day, two men whose armies had not yet been in combat, chose different ways to reflect on the rapid Greek collapse. In Moscow, Stalin approved a further directive of the Soviet General Staff, substantially increasing the number of troops assigned to defend the Soviet frontier. At Mönichkirchen, Hitler, on his train, discussed with his architect Albert Speer the building deadlines for the completion of the proposed new Government buildings in the centre of Berlin.

It was also on April 18 that a British brigade landed at Basra, on the Persian

Holland, 10 May 1940: German parachute troops land in a Dutch field.

Holland, 10 May 1940: German parachute troops prepare to advance.

Holland, 14 May 1940: Rotterdam in flames after a German bombing attack (*see page 65*).

Belgium, 15 May 1940: German troops ride through a Belgian town on the road to Brussels.

Holland, 16 May 1940: German troops on the bank of the river Maas, at Maastricht.

London, 18 May 1940: preparing to meet a German parachute landing (*see page 69*).

Dunkirk, 27 May 1940: British troops await evacuation.

*Left*
Dunkirk, 30 May 1940: French soldiers and sailors being rescued from the sea by a British ship.

*Opposite*
Dunkirk, 3 June 1940: British and French soldiers taken prisoner by the Germans, going into captivity.

The forest of Compiègne, 20 June 1940: French delegates being led to the armistice negotiations (*see page 100*).

Hitler in Paris, 23 June 1940: with German soldiers at Le Bourget airfield (*see page 102*).

Hitler in Paris, at the Eiffel
Tower, 23 June 1940.

German soldiers practising for
the invasion of Britain, July
1940.

German fighter pilots at an airfield in France, waiting to be sent against Britain, August 1940.

A German bomber shot down over southern England, August 1940.

Gulf, to challenge the pro-German Government which General Rashid Ali had set up in Baghdad. Two weeks later, 9,000 Iraqi troops attacked the British force of 2,250. The British successfully resisted the attack.

In Greece, on April 19, British troops moved back to the ports of southern Greece, chief among them Nauplia, Kalamata and Monemvasia, to prepare to embark for Crete, their evacuation made possible by the determined defence of Thermopylae by British, Australian and New Zealand units. In North Africa, a strong British commando force which landed at Bardia that day in an attempt to relieve the soldiers besieged in Tobruk was driven off. Learning from the Germans' Enigma messages that Rommel was to be reinforced by a German armoured division, on April 21 Churchill and his Chiefs of Staff agreed to send tank reinforcements from Britain to Egypt. This was Operation Tiger, a bold move, and a risky one, as the threat of a German invasion of England had not entirely receded.

On April 20, Hitler's fifty-second birthday, a German soldier, Corporal Rohland, was shot and fatally wounded at a Métro station in Paris. As a reprisal, the German Governor of the Greater Paris district, Otto von Stuelpnagel, an Army officer who had been a supporter of Hitler since before 1933, ordered the execution of twenty-two civilian hostages. Their deaths were announced in special red posters displayed throughout the capital.

On April 23 the Greek Army surrendered to the German and Italian invaders. Several thousand Greek soldiers had been killed, and more than nine hundred British, Australian and New Zealand troops. That day, in a scene repeated all over Greece, a Greek artillery major was ordered to surrender his battery. This particular major, however, had a heightened sense of the tragedy which had overtaken his country. As the official Greek Army report explained: 'Artillery Major Versis, when ordered by the Germans to surrender his battery, assembled the guns, and after saluting them, shot himself, while his gunners were singing the National Anthem.'

The evacuation of British, Australian, New Zealand and Polish troops from Greece, Operation Demon, began on April 24 and continued for six days. In all, 50,732 men were evacuated, from eight small ports. Most of them were taken under strong naval escort to Crete. There was no time, however, to bring away their heavy weapons, trucks or aircraft. As the evacuation began, German parachute troops occupied the islands of Lemnos, Thasos and Samothrace, while Bulgaria, eager to annex the coastline of Thrace, invaded broken Greece from the north.

Despite the capitulation of both Yugoslavia and Greece, Hitler was still on board his train at Mönichkirchen. Visited there on April 24 by the Hungarian Regent, Admiral Horthy, he listened to Horthy's warning that the invasion of Britain was fraught with a thousand dangers. 'But if Russia's inexhaustible riches are once in German hands, you can hold out for all eternity.' Unknown to Horthy, April 24 saw the first day of the move of a German Air Force unit

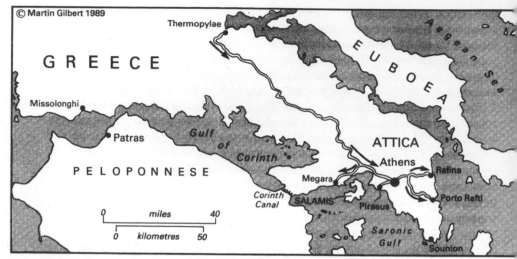

The evacuation of Attica, April 1941

from the English Channel to Poland. This move was known to the British as a result of their reading of the German Air Force Enigma.

On April 25 the British, Australian and New Zealand troops who had been defending Thermopylae in order to make the evacuation possible, were themselves forced back to the ports of Megara, west of Athens, and Rafina and Porto Rafti, east of the capital, where they too embarked. That day, with Greece at his feet, Hitler issued Directive No. 28, Operation Mercury, the invasion of Crete.

# 14

# The fall of Crete; war in Africa

APRIL–MAY 1941

In Moscow, Stalin was doing his utmost during April 1941 to accelerate Soviet readiness. In the third week of April, the British Military Attaché to Budapest, travelling by train to Moscow, had passed seven troop trains on the railway line between Lvov and Kiev, 'of which four were conveying tanks and mechanized equipment, and three, troops'. This report, radioed to London by the British Military Attaché in Moscow, was intercepted by the Germans, and shown to Hitler on April 25. That day, Stalin telephoned the Russian–Jewish novelist, Ilya Ehrenburg, to say that his novel about the fall of Paris in June 1940, an event which Ehrenburg had witnessed, could now be published. He, Stalin, would help to get it passed by the censorship, which in the heyday of the Nazi–Soviet Pact, had rejected it as anti-German. 'We'll work together on this,' was Stalin's comment. Ehrenburg realized at once that Stalin's telephone call could mean only one thing; Stalin was preparing for war with Germany. On the following day the Soviet leader was to order General Zhukov to set up five mobile artillery anti-tank brigades and an airborne corps, and to do so by June 1. One Soviet rifle corps command would also be arriving from the Soviet Far East by May 25.

April 25 saw Rommel preparing to advance still further in North Africa. 'The battle for Egypt and the Canal is now on in earnest,' he wrote to his wife that day, 'and our tough opponent is fighting back with all he's got.' Also on April 25 – for Britain, and especially for Australia, the day of the first Gallipoli landings in 1915 – an armed British merchantman, the *Fidelity*, put ashore on the Mediterranean coast of France, at the Étang du Canet, a Pole, Czeslaw Bitner and a Maltese civil engineer, Edward Rizzo – codenamed 'Aromatic' – who would work inside German-occupied France. Also coming ashore that night was a Belgian doctor, Albert-Marie Guérisse, who, under the name and rank of Lieutenant-Commander Patrick O'Leary, was later to operate an escape route for Allied prisoners-of-war, known to those who used it as the 'Pat Line', along which more than six hundred escapees were to move to safety, not only Allied aircrew and soldiers, but many Frenchmen and Belgians who wished to leave occupied Europe in order to fight in their respective forces overseas.

On April 26 Hitler left Mönichkirchen for a tour of the newly annexed regions of northern Yugoslavia, and their principal town, Maribor, renamed Marburg. That evening he travelled back to the Austrian town of Graz. 'The Führer is very happy,' Walther Hewel wrote in his diary, 'a fanatical reception.' That night, off Greece, the seven hundred survivors of a dive-bombed troop transport were dive-bombed again on the two destroyers which had rescued them, and 650 were killed. On the following day, as German troops entered Athens, the scale of the losses in the battle for Greece became clear. The Greeks had lost 15,700 men killed; the Italians, 13,755; the British Expeditionary Force, 3,712, and the Germans, 2,232; a total death toll in action of more than 35,000. Later that evening, it was learned in Berlin that Rommel's forces had crossed into Egypt, capturing Sollum, while in the Atlantic yet more British merchant ships, and also a cruiser, had been sunk. 'Bad days for London,' Goebbels wrote in his diary. 'Let us have more of them! We shall soon bring John Bull to his knees.'

Another of John Bull's enemies struck on April 28, when Rashid Ali, who had seized power in Baghdad on April 2, sealed off the British airbase and cantonment at Habbaniya, trapping 2,200 fighting men and 9,000 civilians. The forces at Habbaniya had no artillery and, on the base, eighty-two obsolete or training aircraft. 'Situation grave', the base commander reported on the following day. 'Ambassador under impression Iraqi attitude is not bluff and may mean definite promise Axis support.'

In Berlin, Ribbentrop had been urging Hitler to send aircraft and troops to Iraq. But Hitler, intent upon the destruction of the British forces in Crete, now wanted no diversion of his military resources. In a speech to nine thousand officer cadets on April 29, he declared: 'If you ask me, "Führer, how long will the war last?" I can only say, "As long as it takes to emerge victorious! Whatever may come!"' The word 'capitulation', Hitler added, was one which, as a National Socialist during the struggle for power, 'I never knew.' There was one word he would never know as leader of the German people and as Supreme Commander; that was also 'capitulation'.

Military superiority was on the side of the Axis, but luck was on the side of the Allies. When, on April 29, the German Minister in Washington, Hans Thomsen, telegraphed to say that an 'absolutely reliable source' had revealed to him that the Americans had broken Japan's most secret method of communications, the coded 'Magic' radio messages sent by Japanese ambassadors throughout the world, including Berlin, neither the Germans, nor the Japanese when alerted to the 'alleged leak', could believe that such a sophisticated and well-guarded Signals Intelligence code in fact could ever be broken.

German submarine successes in the Atlantic were now substantial and continuous. In April, the tonnage of Allied merchant shipping sunk had reached 394,107; a further 187,054 tons had been sunk in Greek ports during the evacuation. On April 30, in the Atlantic, the *Nerissa*, a troop transport, was torpedoed, and seventy-three Canadian soldiers drowned. These were the only Canadian soldiers ever lost at sea while en route from Canada to Britain. That night, a German air raid on Plymouth brought the civilian deaths that April from bombing to 6,065. 'Hard times,' Churchill wrote to a colleague on his return from visiting the scene of the devastation in Plymouth, 'but the end will repay!'

While preparing to meet a German attack, Stalin did everything possible not to provoke Germany. During April his deliveries of raw materials to Germany reached their highest since the signing of the Nazi–Soviet Pact in August 1939: 208,000 tons of grain, 90,000 tons of fuel oil, 8,300 tons of cotton, 6,340 tons of copper, tin, nickel and other metals, and 4,000 tons of rubber. The rubber had been bought by Russia overseas, imported through her Far Eastern ports, and then transported to Germany by express train on the Trans-Siberian Railway. On May 1, at the May Day parade in Moscow, Stalin put the recently appointed Soviet Ambassador to Berlin, Vladimir Dekanozov, in the place of honour near him on the platform above Lenin's tomb. That same day, the Soviet General Staff information bulletin, sent to the commanders of the Special Military Districts along the frontier, stated without prevarication: 'In the course of all March and April along the Western Front, from the central regions of Germany, the German command has carried out an accelerated transfer of troops to the borders of the Soviet Union.' Such concentrations were particularly visible in the Memel region, south of the Soviet Union's most westerly naval base at Libava. The distance between the two ports was a mere sixty miles.

On May 2, as if to emphasize the imminence of danger, Richard Sorge informed his Soviet masters from Tokyo that Hitler was 'resolved to begin war and destroy the USSR in order to utilize the European part of the Soviet Union as a raw-material and a grain base'. Sorge now reported: 'The decision regarding the start of the war will be taken by Hitler in May.'

Hitler's own confidence was reiterated in a speech in Berlin on May 4. 'In this Jewish-capitalist age,' he declared, 'the National Socialist state stands out as a solid monument to common sense. It will survive for a thousand years.' That day, in the Warsaw ghetto, as on every day that spring, more than seventy Jews died of starvation. In the smaller, yet equally isolated ghetto of Lodz, thirty Jews died that day; between January and June 1941, the combined death toll from starvation in both ghettos was more than 18,000.

On May 5 the Roumanian dictator, Marshal Antonescu, informed the Germans not only of the movement of Soviet troops westward from Siberia, and the concentration of Soviet forces around Kiev and Odessa, but also that the factories around Moscow 'have been ordered to transfer their equipment into the country's interior'.

German preparations for the invasion of the Soviet Union, and Soviet counter-measures were no longer being disguised. So obvious were German troop movements along the River Bug near Lvov that in the first week of May the commander of the frontier guards had asked Moscow for permission to evacuate the families of his men. Permission had been refused, and the commander rebuked for 'panic'. Stalin himself was determined not to appear to panic; in an address on May 5 to the graduates of the Soviet Military Academies, he spoke of his confidence that the Red Army, Navy and Air Force were well enough organized and equipped to fight successfully against 'the most modern army'. At the same time, in the version of the speech circulated by British Air Intelligence nine days later, Stalin warned that Germany had embarked on an attempt to seize the whole of Europe, and that Russia must be ready for any emergency.

'The war is expected to start after the spring planting,' Stalin was told by one of his own Intelligence staff that same day, May 5. Russia's only respite was to be a German attack on Crete; also on May 5, the Enigma messages decoded in Britain confirmed that Crete was Hitler's immediate goal.

British forces, with a substantial New Zealand contingent, and a New Zealand commander, General Freyberg, prepared as rapidly as they could to defend Crete against the Germans. Other news that day brought Britain a certain relief. On May 5 the Emperor of Abyssinia, Haile Selassie, entered his capital, Addis Ababa, five years to the day since the Italians had conquered it. Also that day, Major P. A. Cohen, who had been among several hundred British soldiers trapped in Greece, reached Crete by caïque, bringing with him 120 Australian troops who had avoided falling into German hands after Greece's surrender.

As some men escaped from German-occupied Europe, others entered it; also on May 5, in greatest secrecy, twenty miles north of the town of Châteauroux, in Vichy France, a Frenchman working for British Special Operations, Georges Begué, parachuted successfully into the Unoccupied Zone of France, to set up a clandestine radio transmission at Châteauroux. Four days later, Pierre de Vomécourt was parachuted nearby, as the first group leader in France for the Special Operations Executive: his two brothers, who lived in France, became the first members of his group. Georges Bégue, known as George Noble, and later as 'George One', provided the group's radio contact with London.

While Malta continued to be bombarded by German and Italian aircraft, on May 6 a second Operation Tiger saw a convoy of thirteen fast British merchant ships pass Gibraltar on their way to Egypt, eastward across the Mediterranean. Seven of the merchantmen took supplies and fuel oil to Malta, arriving without incident. In the cargo holds of the other five ships were 295 tanks and 50 fighter aircraft, urgently needed to reinforce the British troops in Egypt. During the voyage, one of the merchantmen was sunk. The remaining four, with 238 tanks and 43 fighters, reached Egypt safely.

The British had another success on May 8, when the German commerce raider *Pinguin*, having sunk twenty-eight merchant ships in ten months, was herself sunk in the Pacific by the British cruiser *Cornwall*. That same day the German submarine U-110 was captured in the Atlantic; its Commander was Julius Lemp, who had sunk the passenger liner *Athenia* in the first days of the war. On board his submarine the British found important cypher material which was greatly to expand Britain's ability to read the German naval Enigma. While being towed towards Iceland, the submarine sank; its crew, including Lemp, were drowned. In the previous week, they had sunk nine Allied merchant ships.

On May 6, Stalin took over Molotov's position as Soviet Premier. The German Ambassador in Moscow, von Schulenburg, in a despatch to Berlin, stressed the 'extraordinary importance' of this act, which was based, he said, 'on the magnitude and rapidity of German military successes in Yugoslavia and Greece, and the realization that this made necessary a departure from the former diplomacy of the Soviet Government, that had led to an estrangement with Germany'. Stalin moved, however, to build not bridges with Germany, but to build more and effective barriers against her, ordering several reserve forces from the Urals and the River Volga to the vicinity of the River Dnieper, the western Dvina and the border areas.

On May 9, the German Air Force messages sent through the Enigma machine revealed to British Intelligence that the German troops now massing on the Soviet border would all have reached their positions by May 20. On May 10, well on time, the German Army completed Operation Otto, the development, begun on 1 October 1940, for improved rail and road facilities leading through Central and Eastern Europe to the Soviet border.

In an effort to deceive Stalin into believing that Britain, not Russia, was the real object of his invasion plans, and that German troops were only moving east to escape British bombing reprisals, Hitler now embarked upon a renewed bomber offensive against Britain. Every night during the first two weeks of May, British cities and docks were pounded from the air. Once on the night of May 8, British radio counter-measures succeeded in bending the signal beam along which German bombers flew to their targets, and 235 high explosive bombs, intended for an aircraft engine factory at Derby, were dropped on empty fields more than twenty miles away. In a bombing raid on Clydeside, however, fifty-seven civilians were killed, and, in the Liverpool docks, thirteen merchant ships were bombed and sunk in seven nights of bombing. 'I feel that we are fighting for life, and survive from day to day and hour to hour,' Churchill told the House of Commons on May 7, 'but believe me, Herr Hitler has his problems too.'

That night, in a German bombing raid on Humberside, twenty-three German aircraft were shot down by British fighters and anti-aircraft fire. But Hitler's problems that week were not to be measured in terms of aircraft lost, for on May 10, like a bolt from the blue, the Deputy Leader of the Nazi Party, Rudolf Hess, Hitler's colleague and confidant for nearly twenty years, flew across the North Sea in a dramatic and risky solo dash, and parachuted into Britain, landing near the village of Eaglesham, in Scotland.

Hess claimed that he had come to make peace between Britain and Germany. He revealed nothing about Hitler's plans to invade the Soviet Union. Indeed, under interrogation he insisted that there was 'no foundation for the rumours now being spread that Hitler is contemplating an early attack on Russia'. The official Nazi announcement declared that Hess was suffering from 'a mental disorder'. This was also the view of those who interrogated him in Britain. That night, May 10, in another German air raid, London was again struck, and the Houses of Parliament badly damaged; the debating chamber of the House of Commons was completely destroyed. On the following morning, a third of the streets in central London were found to be impassable; 1,436 civilians had been killed, more than in any other single raid on Britain.

The air raid on May 10 marked the last raid of the 'Spring' Blitz of 1941.

Londoners were apprehensive that morning, as they had not been since the previous December. They could not know that Hitler now had other work for his bombers to do. The time for deception was over; the time for action had almost come.

Since April 17, Yugoslavia had ceased to exist as an independent State; in German-occupied Serbia, Italian-occupied Dalmatia, Bulgarian-occupied Macedonia, the Hungarian-occupied Banat, and the newly independent Croatia, the bonds of tyranny and persecution had begun. Serbs and Jews were the principal victims, also democrats and liberals; for all of them, forced labour in concentration camps, and random killings, became the daily dangers of life under occupation. On May 7, fleeing southwards from the Croat capital of Zagreb, a forty-nine-year-old Communist, a veteran of the Spanish Civil War, set up in Belgrade the nucleus of a Communist revolt. Known to Stalin as 'Valter', his real name was Josip Broz, and his alias in occupied and partitioned Yugoslavia, Tito.

Four days after Tito left Zagreb for Belgrade, a former officer in the Yugoslav Army, Colonal Draža Mihailović, established himself as a focus of revolt on the plateau of Ravna Gora, in Western Serbia.

The forces of Mihailović, like those of Tito, were to fight against the Germans and eventually make much of Serbia and Bosnia ungovernable. But Mihailović was also a bitter opponent of Communist aspirations, collaborated with the Italians, and tried to preserve his forces by avoiding conflict with the Germans, so much so that after two years the British were to switch their military support from the Četniks to the Communists.

In the second week of May, Hitler sent two bombers to Iraq to help Rashid Ali maintain his revolt against Britain. On May 12, a German Air Force officer, Major Axel von Blomberg, reached Baghdad to act as a liaison officer with Rashid Ali. Arriving over the Iraqi capital in the middle of a dogfight between British and Iraqi fighters, von Blomberg was shot dead by a stray British bullet.

On May 12, the Japanese Ambassador in Baghdad sent a report to Tokyo to say that Rashid Ali's resistance could continue for no more than three to eight days. If, however, British forces were to advance from Palestine as well as from Basra, the Ambassador believed that the Iraqi Army would collapse even sooner, and abandon Baghdad. This message, picked up by British Intelligence and at once decrypted, was sent by Churchill to the Commander-in-Chief, Middle East. On May 13 another special force, consisting of Arab troops from the Arab Legion and the Transjordan Frontier Force, crossed the Transjordanian frontier into Iraq. 'Will the Arab Legion fight?', General Wilson, commanding in Palestine, asked the Legion's commander, Major Glubb. 'The Arab Legion will fight anybody,' Glubb replied. Five days later, an advance column of Glubb's troops, having crossed three hundred miles of desert, reached Habbaniya. But a squadron of the Transjordanian Frontier Force did mutiny on the way,

Crete, May 1941

claiming that they had 'no quarrel with the Iraqis' and that the British 'made others fight for them'.

For many months, the death toll in Britain from German bombing had been reduced by the dedicated and dangerous work of special Unexploded Bomb Disposal Squads. The death toll among these squads was high. One such squad was made up of the Earl of Suffolk – who in June 1940 had brought the heavy water and the nuclear scientists from France – his secretary Miss Morden and his chauffeur Fred Hards; they were known in the bomb disposal world as the Holy Trinity. On May 12, at Erith in Kent, they were trying to defuse their thirty-fifth bomb when it exploded, and they were blown to pieces. The Earl was awarded a posthumous George Cross.

In Europe, the German plans for action against Russian Communists, and other civilians, reached a decisive point on May 12, when a German Army briefing agenda stated that high-ranking political officials and leaders 'must be eliminated'. General Jodl noted in the margin of this briefing: 'We can count on future reprisals against German pilots. Therefore, we shall do best to organize the whole action as if it were an act of reprisal.'

In Poznan, in German-annexed Poland, the local newspaper announced on May 14 that three Poles, Stanislaw Weclas, Leon Pawlowski and Stanislaw Wencel, had been sentenced to death for an alleged anti-German conspiracy. 'Everyone who believes in resistance', the report declared, 'will be destroyed.'

On May 14 the Germans began the massive air bombardment of Malta. Not aware that the British knew from the Enigma intercepts that Crete was their true invasion target, they sought to give the impression that it was Malta that was about to be attacked. The bombardment was ferocious; sixty-two German and fifteen Italian aircraft were shot down, but the British lost sixty fighters, half of them destroyed on the ground, losses that could not easily be replaced.

On May 15, nine days after learning from the Enigma intercepts that Rommel's forces on the Egyptian border were exhausted, and needed time for rest and reorganization, the British launched Operation Brevity, against the forward German positions, forcing a withdrawal from the Halfaya Pass. Rommel, however, by an extraordinary exertion, counter-attacked in strength two weeks later. The British, aware from Enigma of the exact size and direction of Rommel's advance, withdrew, avoiding an unnecessary clash of arms.

It was on May 15 that Hitler ordered the start of the aerial bombardment of Crete, in preparation for the invasion five days later. That day, Richard Sorge, in Tokyo, sent his Soviet masters in Moscow a radio message giving them the date of the German invasion of Russia – between June 20 and 22. That same week, Soviet reinforcements both from the North Caucasus and from the Soviet Far East were ordered to take up positions in the West, between Kraslava and Kremenchug. So urgent was their westward transfer judged to be that they were moved without arms or equipment.

The needs of German pilots on the Eastern Front were the reason given by Dr Sigmund Rascher, a German Air Force staff surgeon, in a letter to Himmler on May 15, asking permission to use concentration camp inmates from Dachau for experiments in atmospheric tests. These tests, Dr Rascher explained, were needed in order to find out the limits of the oxygen needs of German pilots, and their possible endurance to atmospheric pressure. Rascher also wrote of his 'considerable regret that no experiments on human beings have so far been possible for us because the experiments are very dangerous and cannot attract volunteers'. Two or three 'professional criminals' from Dachau would, he said, suffice. Himmler approved of this request.

On May 19, following the destruction of twenty-nine of the thirty-five British fighters on Crete, the six remaining fighters were transferred to Egypt. It was felt that there was no point in sacrificing them, in view of Germany's overwhelming air superiority. On the following morning, May 20, at 5.30 a.m., a violent German air attack was launched again against the two main airfields, at Maleme and Heraklion; an hour and a half later, in a second air attack, both airfields were completely immobilized. Then, as the second wave of bombers returned to Greece, the first wave of German airborne forces, commanded by General Kurt Student, were flown to the island in 493 transport planes. Only seven of the planes were shot down by anti-aircraft fire.

In the first day's battle, the forces defending Crete, 32,000 British, Australian and New Zealand troops, and 10,000 Greeks, succeeded, despite a second paratroop landing in the afternoon, in holding the airfields at Maleme and Heraklion. Two convoys of German troops, sent by sea from Piraeus and Salonica, many of them in fishing boats, were badly mauled by British naval forces, the second of the convoys being forced to turn back. By nightfall, it looked as if the invasion had failed. Indeed, of the three German regimental commanders of the airborne landings, Lieutenant-General Süssman was killed when his glider crashed and Major-General Meindl was seriously wounded.

During the night, however, the Germans succeeded in capturing Maleme airfield, enabling them to fly in reinforcements of men and weapons on the afternoon of May 21; in a final, unsuccessful attempt to recapture the airfield, a New Zealander, Second Lieutenant Charles Upham was awarded the Victoria Cross. Two other Victoria Crosses were awarded on Crete: one was won by a New Zealand sergeant, Clive Hulme, who having received news that his brother had been killed in the battle, single-handed killed thirty-three Germans; the other Victoria Cross was won by a British sailor, Petty Officer Alfred Sephton. Although previously wounded by machine gun fire as his ship, the *Coventry*, sought to rescue the hospital ship *Aba* from a ferocious dive-bombing attack, Sephton continued to direct his ship's anti-aircraft fire until the attacking aircraft were driven off. Lieutenant Upham was later to win a second Victoria Cross in the Western Desert, the only British or Commonwealth serviceman to be awarded it twice in the Second World War.

Neither the bravery of individuals, nor the tenacious courage of the troops as a whole, could successfully resist the overwhelming air and eventually land power of the German forces. On May 22, German dive-bombers sank the cruisers *Fiji* and *Gloucester*, and four destroyers. Several of the survivors of the *Gloucester* had been machine-gunned from the air while clinging to wreckage. The ship's captain, Henry Aubrey Rowley, was among the 725 dead. Four weeks later, his body was washed ashore near Mersa Matruh. Commented Admiral Cunningham: 'It was a long way to come home.'

Among the warships damaged but not sunk on May 22 was the battleship *Valiant*, with Midshipman Prince Philip of Greece on board; on one occasion, as he recorded in his log, she was attacked by fourteen dive-bombers. The ship was hit, however, by only two small bombs. Prince Philip's uncle, Captain Lord Louis Mountbatten, was less fortunate; on May 23 his destroyer, *Kelly*, was attacked by twenty-four dive-bombers, and sunk; 130 of her crew were killed. Although still on the bridge when his ship turned over, Mountbatten was able to swim clear, whereupon he proceeded to take charge of the rescue operation.

On May 23, as the battle continued both on land and at sea, the Germans were able to reinforce their men on Crete with mountain troops. It seemed, especially in Berlin, that all was lost for Britain, not only on Crete, but throughout the eastern Mediterranean, should Hitler choose to follow up his success. But on May 23, with his battle for Crete still being fought, Hitler issued his Directive No. 30, in which he made it clear that the decision whether or not to launch an offensive to 'break the British position' between the Mediterranean and the Persian Gulf, or on the Suez Canal, 'will be decided only after "Barbarossa"'.

Even as the battle for Crete reached its final forty-eight hours, the British had a naval disaster in the distant Atlantic. On May 18 the battleship *Bismarck*, commanded by Admiral Lütjens, and the heavy cruiser *Prinz Eugen* had sailed into the North Atlantic. Six days later, on May 24, the *Bismarck* sank the British battle-cruiser *Hood*, only three of whose crew of 1,500 survived. That same day, guided by intercepted Italian radio messages, a British submarine sank the

Italian liner *Conte Rosso*, with 1,500 Italian troops on board; it was on its way to reinforce the Italian troops in Libya.

On Crete, the British defenders continued throughout May 25 to resist the German advance, counter-attacking at Galatos with no fewer than twenty-five bayonet charges. That day, King George of the Hellenes, who had been evacuated from Athens to Crete, was evacuated again, with his Ministers, to Egypt. On May 27, near Pirgos, Australian and New Zealand troops succeeded, for a while, in driving the Germans back. But it was clear that the battle for Crete was lost. Several units were now without ammunition. During the day, General Freyberg drew up plans to evacuate the island; the evacuation began that same evening.

Even as the bad news from Crete reached Britain, news of a naval success raised morale; for on May 27 the German battleship *Bismarck* was attacked in the Atlantic by a ring of British warships; damaged and burning, she was unable any longer to fight or to escape. Admiral Lütjens gave orders for his ship, the pride of the German navy, to be scuttled. A hundred men were picked up by two British warships, *Dorsetshire* and *Maori*, but a German submarine alarm caused both captains to abandon their rescue work and move away at full speed. Hundreds of German sailors, desperately trying to cling to the side of their would-be rescue vessels, were cut to pieces by the churning propellers.

In all, 2,300 German sailors were drowned; Lütjens went down with his ship. 'She had put up a most gallant fight against impossible odds,' the British naval commander, Admiral Tovey, wrote in his official report of the action, 'worthy of the old days of the Imperial German Navy. It is unfortunate that "for political reasons" this fact cannot be made public.' The news of the loss of the *Bismarck* was received in Berlin with disbelief. 'Mood very dejected,' Walther Hewel wrote in his diary. 'Führer melancholy beyond words.'

Hitler had further cause to be melancholy on May 27, when Roosevelt, in one of his radio 'Fireside Chats', announced that United States naval ports 'are helping now to ensure the delivery of needed supplies to Britain', and that 'all additional measures' necessary for the delivery of these goods would be taken. 'The delivery of needed supplies to Britain is imperative,' Roosevelt declared. 'This can be done. It must be done. It will be done,' and he added, in words which were to inspire all the Western combatants and subject peoples: 'The only thing we have to fear is fear itself.'

In a telegram of appreciation to Roosevelt, King George VI declared that the President's announcement 'has given us great encouragement, and will I know stimulate us all to still greater efforts till the victory for freedom is finally won'.

'. . . is finally won'; on Crete, the embarkation of British troops began on the following night, May 28, and was to continue until the night of June 1. As the British left from the small south-eastern ports of Sphakia, Paleohora and Plakias, the Italians landed 2,700 men at Sitia, on the eastern end of the island.

As the evacuation continued, German dive bombers sank the anti-aircraft cruiser *Calcutta* and damaged several other warships. When the flagship *Orion* was dive-bombed on May 29, she had 1,090 passengers on board; 262 of them were killed.

In five nights, 17,000 men were taken off Crete, most of them from open beaches during the few short hours of darkness. Five thousand men, separated from their units and scattered about the island, had to be left behind. The Germans had lost 1,990 men killed in action. The British and Commonwealth forces, 1,742. A further 2,265 British and Commonwealth sailors had been killed at sea.

On May 27, as the British troops on Crete had begun to prepare the evacuation, Rommel captured the Halfaya Pass. His troops, having taken 3,000 prisoners and 123 guns, now stood where earlier the Italians had stood, at the gateway to Egypt. That same day, at Bir Hakeim, in the Libyan desert, a French Foreign Legion force, together with Free French soldiers who included among their numbers Bretons, Tahitians, Algerians, Moroccans, Lebanese, Cambodians, Mauritians and men from Madagascar and Chad, who had been besieged for more than a week, were attacked by Italian troops. Their attackers were driven off. 'We were told we could crush you in fifteen minutes,' the captured Italian commander of the attack, Colonel Prestissimo, told his captors. The French were understandably confident, all the more so when, in the following days, in the desert around Bir Hakeim, a young French captain, Pierre Messmer, held up fifteen German tanks which had hoped to succeed where the Italian troops had failed.

Messmer was later to become Prime Minister in post-war France. The 'glittering courage' of the defenders of Bir Hakeim, as one historian has called it, was to be remembered and honoured in France for many years to come. But after fifteen days the siege was ended by a mass breakout back to the British lines, and one more desert outpost came under Rommel's control. In the breakout, seventy-two French soldiers were killed, but 2,500 reached safety.

The British were now back in Egypt, their gains in Libya lost, and the defence of the Suez Canal once more a matter of urgency. Fortunately for them, the withdrawal from Libya coincided with the surrender of Rashid Ali in Iraq. Neither Germany nor Italy had been prepared to send more aircraft; on May 28 the British had learned from coded Italian radio messages that no further Italian air support would arrive, because of shortage of fuel. Two days later, on May 30, the Mayor of Baghdad and the army officers loyal to Rashid Ali, who were still holding out in the capital, asked for an armistice. The British triumph, however, was somewhat marred three days later, when supporters of Rashid Ali rampaged through the Jewish quarter of Baghdad, looting shops and houses, and killing their inhabitants; when the rampage was over, more than 150 Jews had been killed.

The last eleven days of May had seen the kaleidoscope of war in all its complexity: a defeat for Britain on Crete; a disaster for Germany at sea; a victory for Germany in the Western Desert, the collapse of a pro-Axis revolt in Iraq, and the murder of Jews. In German-occupied Europe, those same eleven days had also seen several manifestations of the darkest side of Nazism. Beginning on May 20, steps had been taken in both German-occupied France and Belgium to halt the emigration of Jews to neutral Portugal, and from there to the United

States. Such emigration, though difficult, had enabled several thousand Jews to leave German-controlled territory during the previous twelve months. Now Walter Schellenberg, acting for Heydrich, sent a circular to all the departments of the German Security Police, and to all German consulates, informing them that Jewish emigration was henceforth forbidden, 'in view of the undoubtedly imminent final solution of the Jewish question'. What this 'final solution' might be, Schellenberg did not explain; but it was clear that it did not envisage the departure of Jews to safe or neutral lands.

A clearer picture of the 'Final Solution' had been given by Himmler, in late May, to 120 Special Task Force leaders, meeting at the Frontier Police School at Pretzsch, on the River Elbe. These officers had been chosen to command three thousand armed men who would follow in the wake of the German armies as they advanced across Russia. The task in hand, Himmler explained, was to train 'for their annihilation campaign against the racial enemy'. On June 1, at a further briefing by Heydrich, the task force commanders were told that the 'eastern Jews' were the 'intellectual reservoir of Bolshevism' and, 'in the Führer's view', were to be liquidated.

From every corner of German-occupied Europe, troops were now being moved to the East. On June 3, the ss Death's Head Division left Bordeaux, travelling for four days and nights across France and Germany, to Marienwerder in East Prussia. In all, between January and June 1941, 17,000 trains had conveyed German troops towards the borders of Russia: on average more than a hundred trains a day.

As Hitler prepared to invade Russia, another German who had embarked upon a war in the East died in exile in Holland; the former Kaiser, Wilhelm II. In May 1940, after having turned down Churchill's offer of refuge in England, he had declined Hitler's offer to return to Germany as a private citizen, to live on one of his former royal estates in Prussia. Wilhelm's war with his cousin, the Russian Tsar, had led to the destruction of both their empires. Hitler, with his own invasion of Russia now little more than two weeks away, was confident that in the renewed clash of the German and Russian forces, it was Russia that would now be destroyed.

On June 6, two days after the death of the Kaiser, Hitler instructed General von Brauchitsch to issue the Commissar Decree to all commanders. Two days later, the first units of a German infantry division landed in Finland, whose leader, General Mannerheim had agreed to participate in the new conflict. On June 11, in a discussion with the Roumanian leader, Marshal Antonescu, Hitler said that while he was not asking for Roumanian assistance he 'merely expected of Roumania that in her own interest she do everything to facilitate a successful conclusion of this conflict'. Antonescu, who, unlike the Hungarians, Italians and Bulgarians, had gained nothing from the German conquest of Greece, accepted with alacrity this invitation to regain the lost province of Bessarabia, and to gain new territory, in the East.

At two o'clock on the morning of June 8, British and Free French forces entered Syria and the Lebanon. This was Operation Exporter, the plan to overthrow

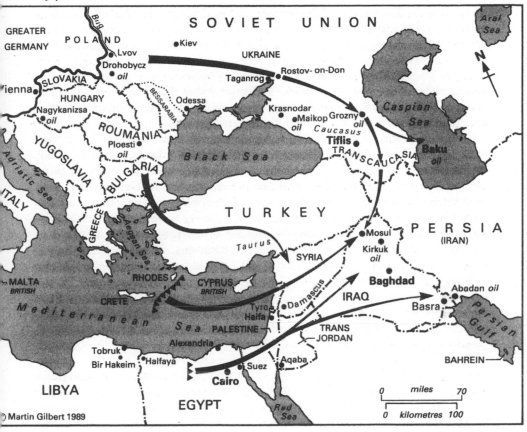

Germany and the Middle East, the German plan of 11 June 1941

the French garrisons loyal to Vichy France, and to raise the Free French flag over Beirut and Damascus. The 45,000 defenders of the garrisons, commanded by General Dentz, put up a strong resistance, which was to last for more than five weeks. Among those wounded in the first days was a Palestinian Jewish volunteer, the twenty-six-year-old Moshe Dayan, who lost an eye. During the decisive first three weeks of the battle, 18,000 Australian, 9,000 British, 5,000 Free French and 2,000 Indian troops took part in the advance, as well as several hundred Palestinian Jews. On July 9, British troops entered the Lebanese port city of Tyre.

The German invasion of Russia was less than two weeks away; on June 9 General Halder visited the German Fourth Army to discuss special measures for 'surprise attack' – artillery, smoke-screens, rapid movement and the evacuation of Polish civilians from the operational zone. On June 10 – the 751st anniversary of the drowning of the Emperor Frederick Barbarossa in 1190, the day on which, according to legend, the dead Frederick began to await his countrymen's call to lead them back to glory – the Germans put into effect Operation Warzburg, a ten day programme of minelaying in the Baltic, designed to prevent the Russian Baltic Fleet from escaping through the Kattegat into the North Sea. On the following day, June 11, in Directive No 32, Hitler laid down his plans for the German Army, Navy and Air Force 'After the destruction of the Soviet armed forces'.

Hitler's plans were wide-ranging. Operation Isabella would secure the Atlantic coastline of Spain and Portugal. The British would be driven from Gibraltar, with or without Spanish help. Strong pressure would be exerted on both Turkey and Iran to make direct or indirect use of them 'in the struggle against England'. The British would be driven from Palestine and the Suez Canal by 'converging attacks' launched from Libya through Egypt, and from Bulgaria through Turkey. Meanwhile, 'it is important that Tobruk should be eliminated'; the attack on the besieged fortress should be planned for November. If the 'collapse of the Soviet Union' had created the 'necessary conditions', preparations would also be made for the despatch of a German expeditionary force from Transcaucasia against Iraq. By using the Arabs, the position of the British in the Middle East would, Hitler added, 'be rendered more precarious, in the event of major German operations, if more British forces are tied down at the right moment by civil commotion or revolt'.

Quite apart from these Middle Eastern and Mediterranean operations, there was, Hitler wrote, another objective to be borne in mind: 'the "Siege of England" must be resumed with the utmost intensity by the Navy and Air Force after the conclusion of the campaign in the East'.

This directive made it clear how much depended upon Germany's victory over Russia. That night, as if to mock at these sentiments, British bombers struck at industrial targets in the Ruhr, the Rhineland and the German North Sea ports, and continued to do so for twenty consecutive nights. In France, British Special Operations agents continued their work in setting up escape lines for prisoners of war, and in making contact with Frenchmen who did not wish to remain passive under the German occupation. 'We shall aid and stir the people of every conquered country to resistance and revolt,' Churchill told the British people in a broadcast on June 12. 'We shall break up or derange every effort which Hitler makes to systematize and consolidate his subjugation. He will find no peace, no rest, no halting place, no parley.'

On June 14, as Hitler and his commanders made their final plans for the invasion of Russia, now only eight days away, Roosevelt took another step in the direction of substantial help for Britain, freezing all German and Italian economic assets in the United States. He also accepted Churchill's request for the United States to take over the defence of Iceland, which Britain had been occupying since the defeat of Denmark in April 1940. Substantial American arms were also on their way to the British forces in Egypt, in seventy-four merchant ships, thirty of which were flying the American flag. Among their cargoes were two hundred American tanks from United States Army production.

Two days after Churchill's broadcast, one of the heroes of the high summer of 1940, John Mungo Park, a Spitfire pilot, was killed in action over France. Nor was it only towards those States already under German rule that Britain directed her support. On June 13, in a serious attempt to show the Soviet Union that she would not be left to fight Hitler alone, Churchill offered to send Stalin a British military mission in the event of a German attack. It would seem, however, that Stalin considered this offer a provocation, part of a British scheme to precipitate him into the war against Germany. His reaction was similarly suspicious when Churchill sent him details about the German divisions concentrating on the Soviet frontier; these details had once again been culled from the Germans' own top secret Enigma messages. It was also on June 13 that Admiral Kuznetsov, the Soviet Navy Commissar, visiting Stalin in the Kremlin, failed to arouse his concern about recent German naval movements, or to elicit from him a request to prepare the Soviet naval forces for action.

Among the most secret messages decrypted by British Intelligence at Bletchley on June 14 were German orders sent in connection with the arrival of a 'Chief War Correspondent' at Kirkenes, in northern Norway, near the border with Russia. At the Kremlin that day, Timoshenko and Zhukov found Stalin apparently little concerned by the German military build up. When they pointed out that according to Soviet Intelligence reports the German divisions now on the border were 'manned and armed at wartime strength', Stalin's comment was: 'You can't believe everything Intelligence says.' During this meeting, the discussion was interrupted by a telephone call to Stalin from the Communist Party boss in the Ukraine, Nikita Khrushchev. 'Stalin picked up the phone,' Zhukov later recalled. 'We gathered from his replies that the call concerned agriculture. "Fine," Stalin said, and smiled. Evidently, Khrushchev had reported in glowing terms about the good prospects of a bumper crop.'

'We left the Kremlin', Zhukov added, 'with a heavy heart.' For the heads of German Intelligence, however, it was the continuous Soviet troop movements that were ominous; Russian troops brought westward into European Russia in the previous month had raised the Soviet strength to 150 rifle divisions, 7 armoured divisions, and 38 armoured brigades.

That day, June 14, in East Prussia, the commanding officer of the SS Death's Head Division, General Eicke, informed his commanders of the content of Hitler's Commissar Decree. The war with Russia, Eicke explained, must be fought as an ideological war, a life-and-death struggle between National Socialism and 'Jewish Bolshevism'. Political commissars attached to Red Army units were 'to be killed immediately after their capture or surrender, regardless of the circumstances'. The Division must be 'fanatical and merciless'. Russia had not signed the Geneva Convention, and therefore 'could not be expected to wage war in a civilized fashion'. The men in the Death's Head Division would therefore be expected to fight 'without mercy or pity'. The war in the East was a struggle 'upon which the fate of the German people depended'.

Hitler's fanaticism had now been communicated to the men who would have to put it into practice. That same day, in a final briefing for his senior commanders, Hitler warned that the Russian forces outnumbered the Germans, but that German leadership, equipment and experience were superior. At the same time, he warned them not to underestimate the Red Army. He also, echoing his Directive of three days earlier, told them: 'The main enemy is still Britain. Britain will fight on as long as the fight has any purpose....'

On June 15, the British forces in Egypt launched Operation Battleaxe, an attempt to drive Rommel back through Libya, and possibly even to relieve Tobruk. 'I naturally attach the very greatest importance to the venture,' Churchill telegraphed to Roosevelt on the eve of the attack. But the operation was seriously handicapped by its inferior equipment, and after an initial advance could make no real headway against Rommel's tanks and armoured cars. British Intelligence had judged the time and scale of Rommel's counter-attack correctly: the British forces simply did not have the strength to meet it. During four days of battle, 122 British troops were killed and a hundred British tanks lost.

On the day that Operation Battleaxe was launched from Egypt, all German commanders in the East, as ordered on the previous day, completed their preparations to launch the attack. They now awaited only one of two code words: 'Altona' – postponement or cancellation, or 'Dortmund' – proceed. That same day, the Soviet commander in Kiev, General Kirponos, convinced that war was imminent, sent Stalin by messenger a personal letter, asking for permission to evacuate 300,000 Soviet civilians from the frontier region along the River Bug, and to set up anti-tank barriers. Stalin replied, as he had to similar requests that week: 'This would be a provocative act. Do not move.'

In Germany's Army Group Centre, on June 15, a list of bombing targets was issued, each of which was to be destroyed in the opening hours of the assault: among them were the Red Army's communications posts and signals centres set up in the former eastern regions of Poland, at Kobryn, Volkovysk, Lida, and Baranowicze, as well as those east of the former Russo-Polish frontier, at Slutsk, Minsk, Mogilev, Orsha and Smolensk.

In Berlin, on June 15, fantastic rumours spread, 'that an understanding with Russia is imminent', as the diplomat Ulrich von Hassell noted in his diary, and that 'Stalin is coming here, etc.' But in London, Churchill's daily reading of the Germans' own Enigma radio messages made it clear that a German invasion of Russia was only a matter of days. 'From every source at my disposal, including some most trustworthy,' he telegraphed to Roosevelt on June 15, 'it looks as if a vast German onslaught on Russia is imminent. Not only are the main German armies deployed from Finland to Roumania, but the final arrivals of air and armoured forces are being completed.' Should this new war break out, Churchill added, 'we shall of course give all encouragement, and any help we can spare, to the Russians following the principle that Hitler is the foe we have to beat'.

In an appeal which he broadcast to the American people on the following night, June 16, Churchill tried to give expression to his sense of urgency, and of foreboding. 'Every month that passes', he warned, 'adds to the length and to the perils of the journey that will have to be made. United we stand, divided we fall. Divided, the dark ages return. United, we can save and guide the world.'

In the United States, two days after Churchill's broadcast, Roosevelt received Colonel William J. Donovan, whom he appointed Co-ordinator of Information, with the duty to collect and analyse all information bearing on national security, to 'correlate such information and data', and to make it available to the President. Donovan was also entrusted with the conduct of special questions and subversive propaganda.

Germany and Russia on the eve of war

On the day of Churchill's broadcast, the last German warship in the Soviet waters of the Black Sea had sailed away. Of the twenty German engineers still working in Leningrad in May, the last one had already gone by June 15. Those signs of an impending German onslaught were seen by Soviet naval observers, and reported to the commander of the Soviet Baltic Fleet, Admiral Tributs. On June 17, in tightest secrecy, all German military, naval and air commanders received the coded radio message, 'Warzburg': the attack on Russia was to begin at three in the morning of Sunday June 22. On the following day at noon, Soviet Frontier troops in Bialystok were put on alert.

The German leaders and ideologues were confident of victory; on June 18, Alfred Rosenberg completed his plans for the breaking-up of the Caucasus mountain region of the Soviet Union into a series of five separate German-administered 'General Commissariats' in Georgia, Azerbaidjan, North Caucasus, Krasnodar and Ordzhonikidze, and two 'Main Commissariats' for Armenia and the Kalmyk area. By such means, Rosenberg believed, Germany would control a Berlin–Tiflis axis friendly to Germany, and a permanent barrier to any future resurgence of Russian power.

In preparation for the imminent struggle, on June 19 the ss issued special regulations, establishing a welfare fund for the care of orphans and widows of ss men killed in action. But did the Red Army appreciate that an onslaught was imminent? On June 19 the Soviet Minister of Defence, Marshal Timoshenko, ordered the camouflaging of forward airfields, military units and installations, many of which were still plainly visible both from the ground and from the air. That same evening, in a telephone call from Leningrad to Moscow, Admiral Tributs, after reporting on the final departure on June 16 of the last German warship in Soviet waters, obtained permission from Admiral Kuznetsov, the Minister of the Navy, to bring the Baltic Fleet up to 'Readiness No. 2', the fuelling of all Soviet warships and putting their crews on alert. Also in Leningrad, however, June 19 saw the departure of the Secretary of the Regional Party Committee, Andrei Zhdanov, the Soviet Party boss in the city, and a member of Stalin's Military Council, for his summer holiday at the resort of Sochi, on the Black Sea. As Zhdanov left for his holiday, Admiral Kuznetsov also put the Soviet Black Sea Fleet on 'Readiness No. 2'.

In the Middle East, the early hours of June 21 saw the surrender of the Vichy forces in Damascus to the combined British and Free French expedition. Hitler had now lost any chance of an easy descent on Palestine and the Suez Canal. That same night, on the East Prussian–Lithuanian frontier, near Buraki, a group of German soldiers on reconnaissance mission tried to cross into the Soviet lines. Three were killed and two were captured. At 2.40 that morning, the Chief of Staff of the Western Special Military District, General Klimovskikh, radioed to Moscow from his headquarters at Panevezys, that 'German aircraft with loaded bomb racks' had violated the frontier on the previous day, west of Kovno, and, even more ominously, according to the report of one of his Army commanders, that the wire barricades along the frontier on the Augustow and Siena roads, though in position during the day, 'are removed towards evening'. General Klimovskikh added: 'From the woods, sounds of engines.'

At four in the morning, a submarine commander in the Red Navy, Captain Marinenko, reported sighting a convoy of thirty-two German troop transports at the entrance to the Gulf of Finland. Admiral Tributs was duly informed, and was alarmed. Ten hours later, at two o'clock that afternoon, Stalin himself telephoned from the Kremlin to the commander of the Moscow District, General Tiulenev, to tell him that 'the situation is uneasy', and instructing him to 'bring the troops of Moscow's anti-aircraft defence to seventy-five per cent of combat readiness'. A similar instruction was telephoned shortly afterwards to Nikita Khrushchev in Kiev. Once more, it was Stalin himself on the line.

On the afternoon of June 21, Hitler wrote to Mussolini that he had made 'the hardest decision of my life'.

Shortly after nine o'clock that evening, the Chief of Staff of the Kiev Military District, General Purkayev, telephoned to Marshal Zhukov in Moscow, to inform him that a German sergeant-major 'had come to our frontier guards and said that German troops were moving to jumping-off areas and that the attack would begin in the morning of June 22'. The deserter was Alfred Liskof, who had given himself up at the Ukrainian border town of Vladimir-Volynsk.

The Volga–Archangel line and the Berlin–Tiflis axis

Zhukov telephoned at once to Stalin, who summoned him and Timoshenko to the Kremlin. 'The German generals may have sent this turncoat to provoke a conflict,' Stalin told them. 'No,' replied Timoshenko, 'we think he is telling the truth.' 'What are we to do?', Stalin asked, to which Timoshenko replied: 'A directive must immediately be given to alert all troops in the border districts.'

Stalin still hesitated. 'It's too early', he replied, 'to issue such a directive – perhaps the question can be settled peacefully.' He did agree, however, to a directive to all Military Councils in the frontier districts warning them that 'a sudden German attack is possible'. Stalin added, however, that the Soviet troops must not be 'incited by any provocative action' by the Germans. The directive, as signed that night by Timoshenko and Zhukov, ordered the firing posts in the Fortified Areas to be 'secretly manned' in the early hours of June 22; for all aircraft to be dispersed 'before dawn' on June 22 among field aerodromes 'and carefully camouflaged'; for 'all units' to be put on the alert; and for preparations to be made 'for blacking out cities and other targets'.

By thirty minutes after midnight, in the earliest hour of June 22, Zhukov informed Stalin that this directive had been transmitted to all the frontier districts. Even as its transmission had begun, Hitler, in an after dinner conversation with Albert Speer and Admiral Raeder, spoke of his plans for the creation of a German naval base on the Norwegian coast near Trondheim. It was to be Germany's largest dockyard. Alongside it would be built a city for a quarter of a million Germans. The city would be incorporated into Greater Germany. Hitler then put on a gramophone record, and played his two guests a few bars from Liszt's *Les Préludes*. 'You'll hear that often in the near future,' he said, 'because it is going to be our victory fanfare for the Russian campaign.' His plans for the monumental buildings of Berlin, Linz and other cities, Hitler told them, were now to be sealed 'in blood', by a new war. Russia would be the source even of architectural advantage. 'We'll be getting our granite and marble from there,' he explained, 'in any quantities we want.'

Shortly after midnight, in that first hour of June 22, as the warning directive was on its way from Moscow to the frontier forces, the Berlin–Moscow Express crossed the railway bridge over the River Bug and steamed into the Soviet border city of Brest-Litovsk. A little later, two trains, coming from Kobryn, crossed the River Bug in the other direction. One was the regular Moscow–Berlin Express. The other, which followed immediately behind it, was a freight train carrying Soviet grain to the storehouses of Germany.

Life was proceeding as usual. From a point on the frontier further south, a German corps commander informed his superiors that the Soviet town opposite him was visibly unperturbed. 'Sokal is not blacked out,' he reported. 'The Russians are manning their posts which are fully illuminated. Apparently they suspect nothing.' At Novgorod-Volynsk the Soviet General, Konstantin Rokossovsky was the guest of honour at a concert at his headquarters. Receiving the Moscow Directive, he ordered his commanders to go to their units only 'after the concert'. In the Officers' House in Kiev, General Pavlov, commander of the Western Military District, was watching a Ukrainian comedy. Informed that 'things on the frontier were looking alarming', he chose to see the end of the play.

Not a concert, or a play, but a ball, was in full swing that Saturday night at the Soviet border town of Siemiatycze, attended, as had become usual for some weeks past, by the German border patrol from the other side, and by many Jews. At four o'clock in the morning, the ball was still in progress. Minute succeeded minute in raucous song and swirling dance. 'Suddenly', the historian of Siemiatycze has recorded, 'bombs began to fall. The electricity in the hall was cut off. Panic-stricken and stumbling over each other in the darkness, everyone ran home.'

As the German forces stood on the Soviet frontier in the early hours of June 22, ready to invade, 2,500,000 Soviet soldiers in the Western defence districts faced an estimated 3,200,000 Germans. A further 2,200,000 Soviet soldiers were in reserve, defending the cities of Moscow and Leningrad, and the industrial regions of the Donetz basin and the Urals. The numbers, however, were deceptive; only thirty per cent of the Soviet troops had automatic weapons. Only twenty per cent of the Soviet aircraft and nine per cent of their tanks were of the modern types.

The master of eight European capitals – Warsaw, Copenhagen, Oslo, The Hague, Brussels, Paris, Belgrade and Athens – ruler of Europe from the Arctic coldness of the North Cape to the warm island beaches of Crete, his armies unbeaten even further south, on the frontier of Egypt, Hitler had now set his sights and his armies on Moscow. But although the day was to come when the tall spires of the Kremlin were to be visible through the binoculars of his front line commanders, Moscow was never to be his, and the march to Moscow, Napoleon's downfall in 1812, was to lead, through suffering and destruction, to the end of all Hitler's plans, and, within four years, to the downfall of his Reich.

# 15

# The German invasion of Russia

JUNE 1941

It was fifteen minutes after four o'clock on the morning of 22 June 1941. At that moment, the German invasion of the Soviet Union began. In its first hours, German bombers struck at sixty-six Soviet aerodromes, destroying many of their aircraft on the ground. At the same time, five selected Soviet cities were subjected to aerial bombardment: Kovno, Minsk, Rovno, Odessa and Sevastopol. Yet more bombers struck at Libava, one of the principal Soviet naval bases in the Baltic. Then, as Soviet citizens woke up to the screech of bombs, the German Army began its advance along a 930-mile front.

June 21 was the shortest night of the year. It was also one year to the day since the French surrender at Compiègne. On that same day, 129 years earlier, Napoleon had crossed the River Neman in his own search for a victory in Moscow. At seven o'clock that morning, a proclamation by Hitler was read over the radio by Goebbels. 'Weighed down with heavy cares,' Hitler declared, 'condemned to months of silence, I can at last speak freely – German people! At this moment a march is taking place that, for its extent, compares with the greatest the world has ever seen. I have decided again today to place the fate and future of the Reich and our people in the hands of our soldiers. May God aid us, especially in this fight'.

Fifteen minutes after Hitler's proclamation was broadcast from Berlin, and with Stalin's approval, Zhukov issued a directive authorizing Soviet troops to 'attack the enemy and destroy him' wherever the frontier had been crossed. But Soviet troops were ordered not to cross the frontier into Germany. Air strikes would be mounted against German positions, including Königsberg and Memel, but none to a depth greater than 150 kilometres behind the lines. Molotov was to broadcast at noon.

Was Stalin hoping to negotiate some kind of settlement or ceasefire? 'Russians have asked Japan', General Halder noted in his diary,' to act as intermediaries in the political and economic relations between Russia and Germany, and are in constant radio contact with the German Foreign Office.' 'Only when it became clear that it was impossible to halt the enemy offensive by diplomatic action', one Soviet historian, Karasev, has written, 'was the Government announcement

198

about the attack of Germany, and the start of war for the Soviet Union, made at noon'.

The Russians could not halt the forward march of the German armies. That day, south of Kovno, a crucial bridge at Alytus was captured intact, and the Neman river line turned without a battle. Some Russian units, Halder noted in his diary that day, 'were captured quite unawares in their barracks, aircraft stood on the aerodromes secured by tarpaulin, and forward units, attacked by our troops, asked their Command what they should do'. At nine fifteen that night, Timoshenko issued his third directive in less than twenty-four hours, ordering all Soviet frontier forces to take the offensive, and to advance to a depth of between fifty and seventy-five miles inside the German border.

The tide of war could no longer be turned by a directive. By nightfall on June 22, the Germans had forced open a gap just north of Grodno between the Soviet North-Western front under Voroshilov, and the Western Front under Timoshenko. But not all observers took the German onslaught tragically. When news of the German attack on Russia had been broadcast over the German loudspeakers in Warsaw at four o'clock that afternoon, the Jews in the ghetto, as one of them, Alexander Donat, later recalled, were trying 'unsuccessfully' to hide their smiles. 'With Russia on our side,' they felt, 'victory was certain and the end for Hitler was near.'

The confidence of the Jews who were trapped, and starving, in Warsaw had a curious echo in the mood in Berlin. 'We must win, and quickly,' Goebbels wrote in his diary on June 23. 'The public mood is one of slight depression. The nation wants peace, though not at the price of defeat, but every new theatre of operations brings worry and concern.'

Hitler, leaving Berlin that day for a new headquarters, the Wolf's Lair, near Rastenburg in East Prussia, told General Jodl: 'We have only to kick in the door and the whole rotten structure will come crashing down'. But even Hitler's confidence was not unqualified. 'At the beginning of each campaign,' he told one of his staff later that day, 'one pushes a door into a dark, unseen room. One can never know what is hiding inside.'

By noon on June 22, the German Air Force had destroyed more than a thousand Soviet aircraft on the ground or in combat: a quarter of Russia's whole air strength. That day, both Italy and Roumania declared war on the Soviet Union.

By nightfall on June 22, the Germans had overrun the Fortress Area towns of Kobryn and Pruzhany. On the following day, in Moscow, an Evacuation Council was set up, with Alexei Kosygin as one of its three members, to organize the dismantling, removal and reassembly of more than 1,500 armament factories and industrial plants in Western Russia and the Ukraine, to safety in the East. Beyond the Urals, far from any probable or even possible battle zone, in distant cities such as Sverdlovsk, Kurgan and Chelyabinsk, in Siberia, and in Kazakhstan, the Soviet Union, in its very moment of shock and weakness, was rebuilding the basis of a massive war potential.

Within the first few days of the German assault, it was clear that it was not only to be a war of armies. When, in the bunkers around the frontier village of

The widening war, June 1941

Slochy, on the border, a German Army unit finally overran the Russian defenders, it then burned down the village and murdered all hundred of its inhabitants. On June 25, General Lemelsen, commanding the 47th Panzer Corps, protested to his subordinate officers about what he called the 'senseless shootings of both prisoners-of-war and civilians' which had taken place. His protest was ignored.

Lemelsen renewed his protest five days later, declaring in a further order that, in spite of his earlier instructions, 'still more shootings of prisoners-of-war and deserters have been observed, conducted in an irresponsible, senseless and criminal manner. This is murder! The German Army is waging war against Bolshevism, not against the Russian peoples.' Yet General Lemelsen went on to endorse Hitler's order that all those identified as political commissars and partisans 'should be taken aside and shot'. Only by this means, he explained, could the Russian people be liberated 'from the oppression of a Jewish and criminal group'.

On the field of battle, the last week of June saw continual Soviet setbacks. On June 25 two generals, Khatskilevich and Nikitin, were killed in action. Several strategic towns were also lost that day, including the railway junctions of Baranowicze and Lida in the north, and Dubno in the centre. Goebbels however was cautious. 'I am refraining from publishing big maps of Russia,' he noted that day in his diary. 'The huge areas involved may frighten the public.'

From the first days of the German advance, Jews were as usual singled out for particular and systematic destruction. When, on June 25, German forces entered Lutsk, and found in the hospital there a Jewish doctor, Benjamin From, operating on a Christian woman, they at once ordered him to stop the operation. He refused, whereupon they dragged him from the hospital, took him to his home, and killed him with his entire family.

On the morning of June 26, German forces reached the city of Dvinsk, seizing both the road and rail bridges across the River Dvina. This was a remarkable success, similar to the seizure of Fort Eben-Emael in Belgium little more than a year earlier. The German Army was now 185 miles inside the Soviet border. Later that day, Finland declared war on the Soviet Union, while in Verona, Mussolini reviewed an Italian division that was about to leave Italy in order to fight alongside the Germans inside Russia. That night, having flown back to Moscow from the South-Western Army's headquarters at Tarnopol, Zhukov obtained Stalin's approval to set up an emergency defence system on the line Drissa–Polotsk–Vitebsk–Orsha–Mogilev–Mozyr, together with an even more easterly line on the axis Selizharovo–Smolensk–Roslavl–Gomel. A glance at the map[1] shows how far both Zhukov and Stalin realized that their forces must in due course fall back. 'Where the enemy could be stopped,' Zhukov later recalled, 'what should be the advantageous line for the counter-offensive, and what forces could be mustered, we did not know.' That day, also in Moscow, Lavrenti Beria, the People's Commissar of the Bureau of Internal Affairs – the NKVD – ordered all his regional NKVD organizations in western Russia to form special home defence units, known as Destruction Battalions, to guard important installations behind the lines, to prevent sabotage, and to counter any German parachute landings. These battalions, one to two hundred strong, were made up mostly of men too old, too young or not physically fit enough to join the ranks of the Red Army.

On June 27 all civilian building work in Leningrad was brought to a halt, and 30,000 building workers and their equipment transferred out of the city, in the direction of Luga, to dig anti-tank ditches and to build reinforced fire-points from concrete blocks. That day, Marshal Mannerheim appealed to the people of Finland to play their part in the 'holy war' against Russia. It was proving a far from easy war, however, even for the ss Death's Head Division, which was astonished on June 27 by a succession of Russian

[1] See page 202.

The German invasion of Russia, 22 June 1941

counter-attacks, first with tanks and then, when the tanks had been knocked out, on foot. There was also fear among the ss troops at the many groups of Soviet soldiers who, isolated far behind the front line, consistently fought to the death rather than surrender. Orders were given that such stragglers should be dealt with ruthlessly. These orders were obeyed; after the first few encounters, those met with were usually shot even if they had not yet offered any resistance.

Not only Soviet stragglers, but organized Soviet partisans, were soon to make their appearance behind the German lines. On June 27, Nikita Khrushchev gave instructions for small partisan detachments of between ten and twenty men to be organized in Kamenets-Podolsk. More than 140 small groups were also set up by the local Communist Party authorities in the Lvov, Tarnopol, Stanislawow, Czernowitz and Rovno regions, about two thousand men in all. Once organized, they were slipped through the German lines into enemy-occupied territory.

It was on June 27 that Hungary declared war on the Soviet Union, followed a day later by Albania. Russia was now at war with five states – Germany, Finland, Roumania, Hungary and Albania. On June 27, at Bletchley, British cryptographers broke the Enigma key being used by the German Army on the Eastern Front. Known as 'Vulture', it provided daily readings of German military orders. On the following day, Churchill gave instructions that Stalin was to be given this precious Intelligence, provided its source could remain a secret. An officer in British Military Intelligence, Cecil Barclay, who knew of the work at Bletchley, and who was then serving in the British Embassy in Moscow, was instructed to pass on warnings of German moves and intentions to the head of Soviet Military Intelligence.

Despite being well informed of the German moves against them, Stalin and his commanders did not have the resources to counter these moves, or to resist the savagery with which they were conducted. On June 27 two German panzer groups, linking forces east of Minsk, turned against the 300,000 Russian troops caught in the trap, 50,000 of them in Minsk itself. In the ensuing battle, tens of thousands were killed. Almost all the rest were taken prisoner. Their fate was to be terrible: beaten, starved, denied medical attention, refused adequate shelter, shot down if they stumbled during endless forced marches, few of them were still alive a year later.

That day, June 27, in the village of Nieswiez, a young Jew, Shalom Cholawski watched horrified as a German soldier began punching a Soviet prisoner. 'The prisoner,' he later recalled, 'a short fellow with dull Mongolian features, did not know why the German had singled him out or what he was raving about. He stood there, not resisting the blows. Suddenly, he lifted his hand, and with a terrific sweep, slapped his attacker powerfully and squarely on the cheek. Blood trickled down the German's face. For a moment they stared at each other, one man seething with anger, the other calm. Several Germans brusquely shoved the man to a place behind the fence. A volley of shots echoed in the air.'

*            *            *

In an effort to counter the effect on Russian morale of the rapid German advance, on June 28 posters were put up in Leningrad, showing a photograph of the German deserter, Alfred Liskof, with the caption: 'A mood of depression rules among German soldiers'. But the advance of those German soldiers, and their growing number of allies, was continuous. On June 28 German troops advancing from Norway and Finnish troops coming from Finland attacked the Russians in Karelia. That same day, on the Minsk front, the advancing German units were already one third of the way from the German border to Moscow, in only one week of war.

The Red Army was not however without resources, or at least without courage and ingenuity. On June 29 the ss Death's Head Division was caught unawares by the appearance of Soviet fighter planes which, strafing the ss positions, killed ten men. General Halder, studying reports from the whole battlefield, noted in his diary: 'Information from the Front confirms that the Russians are generally fighting to the last man.' In the Grodno area, he was told by General Ott, the Russians were showing 'stiff resistance'. In the Lvov area 'the enemy is slowly retreating, putting up a tough fight for the last line'. Here, Halder added, 'for the first time, mass destruction of bridges by the enemy can be observed'. The Russian soldier, the Nazi Party newspaper *Völkischer Beobachter* reported on June 29, 'surpasses our adversary in the West in his contempt for death. Endurance and fatalism make him hold out until he is blown up with his trench, or falls in hand-to-hand fighting'.

It was on June 29 that a general directive was issued from Moscow. Before the Red Army withdrew from a town, the directive made clear, rolling stock and other moveable items, even food, must be removed, 'leaving the enemy not a single locomotive, not a truck, not a loaf of bread, not a litre of fuel'. Cattle must be driven to the rear; and any food or fuel which could not be removed 'must, without any exceptions, be destroyed'. Such was the scorched-earth policy; the directive also laid down the rules for partisan activities behind the lines, the task of the partisans being defined as 'blowing up bridges, railway tracks, destroying enemy telephone and telegraph communications, blowing up enemy ammunition dumps'. That same day, the Leningrad authorities began a week-long evacuation of 212,209 children, mostly to Yaroslavl, on the Volga.

On June 29, as German forces drove through what had once been the eastern provinces of Poland, the first Prime Minister of Poland, the pianist Paderewski, died in the United States, at the age of eighty. President Roosevelt at once offered Arlington Cemetery as his coffin's resting place 'until Poland is free'. Paderewski's lead-sealed casket, inside a cedarwood box, mounted on wheels for its journey back to Poland, is still at Arlington forty-seven years later.

On the night of June 29, the city of Lvov, capital of Eastern Galicia, fell to the Germans in what one historian has called 'a nightmare of carnage and chaos', beginning with a massacre of three thousand Ukrainian political prisoners by the NKVD. Hardly had the Russian troops withdrawn, some having to break out of an encircled city, when Ukrainian nationalists began slaughtering Jews in the streets. Further south, in the Roumanian city of Jassy, Roumanian soldiers went on the rampage, killing at least 250 Jews; a further 1,194 died after being sealed in a train and sent southward for eight days.

These were not the first Jews to be murdered in the latest onslaught. Three days earlier, within forty-eight hours of German troops entering Kovno, local Lithuanians had turned on some of the city's 35,000 Jewish inhabitants, killing more than a thousand.

On June 30, in the Borisov region, on the east bank of the Beresina river, the thirty-six-year-old Soviet general, Jakov Kreiser, a Jew, commanding a motorized infantry division, halted an attack of Guderian's tanks for two days. As he did so, Soviet reinforcements were being hurried forward to the Drissa–Mozyr line. Later, in recognition of his achievement, Kreiser was awarded the coveted Hero of the Soviet Union. To the south of Borisov, however, after capturing the town of Bobruisk, German forces established a bridgehead across the Beresina.

Each Soviet city, each town, each village, was to honour its heroes and its victims of those first weeks of war. Leningrad, for example, remembers to this day its first writer to fall in action, Lev Kantorovich, the member of a border detachment, killed on June 30. Even as Russians were being killed in action, the Commissar Decree was leading to hundreds of deaths each day in cold blood. It was on 30 June that the twenty-one-year-old SS officer cadet, Peter Neumann was told by his lieutenant to shoot two commissars whom his unit had just captured in a small village outside Lvov. When Neumann hesitated, the task was handed over to SS Lance-Corporal Libesis, 'a cheerful Tyrolean peasant', Neumann later recalled, 'who had twice won the Iron Cross in battle', and Libesis, 'quietly, casually, as if he had all the time in the world, approached the commissars'. 'You are a People's Commissar?' he asked, in simple Russian. 'Yes. Why?' they replied. Libesis then took his pistol from his holster, 'aimed at each shaven head in turn, and shot them both dead.'

The cohorts and collaborators of the Germans did their own killing. It was not only Ukrainians and Lithuanians who had begun to kill Jews; in Norway, Josef Terboven ordered the round-up of all Jews in Tromsö and the northern provinces. They were deported to Germany. Other Jews, arrested in Trondheim, were shot. From Holland, on 30 June, another three hundred young Jews were rounded up and deported to the stone quarries of Mauthausen. 'They followed the same stony path,' one Dutch witness of their deportation later recalled. 'Nobody survived.'

On June 30, the Australians lost their first warship to be destroyed by enemy action, the *Waterhen*, struck by German dive bombers off Sidi Barrani while on its way with supplies to besieged Tobruk. Not only was the ship's company saved by a British destroyer, but the Australian loss was quickly revenged, when a Royal Australian Navy cruiser, the *Sydney*, sank the Italian cruiser *Bartolomeo Colleoni*.

As the German Army continued its relentless thrust into western Russia on June

30, General Kirponos ordered a Soviet withdrawal from the Lvov salient to a new defensive line, Korosten–Novgorod–Shepetovka–Starokonstantinov–Proskurov. This line was reached by July 9, while behind it reinforcements were brought up.

Despite heavy Soviet losses, the Soviet front line had not disintegrated. In the far north, on July 1, the Germans launched two further military operations, Silver Fox, against the Soviet Arctic port of Murmansk, and Salmon Trap, against the railway line between Kandalaksha and Belomorsk. At the same time, the Finnish Army advanced eastward from central Finland. Hurrying reinforcements northwards, the Russians were able to hold their northern lifeline: the German troops had not been trained in forest warfare, and the Russian resistance, as in western Russia, surprised their adversaries by its tenacity.

It was in western Russia, on July 1, that a Russian counter-attack east of Slonim penetrated the German encirclement of two severely mauled Russian tank brigades, enabling the remnants to escape.

On the night of July 1, a train made up of twenty-two goods wagons and two passenger cars left Leningrad for the east; on board, under the vigilant eye of the art scholar Vladimir Levinson-Lessing, were some of the finest treasures of the Hermitage: Rembrandt's *Holy Family* and the *Return of the Prodigal*, two Madonnas by Leonardo da Vinci and two by Raphael, as well as paintings by Titian, Giorgione, Rubens, Murillo, Van Dyck, Velasquez and El Greco. Also on the train was a marble Venus acquired by Peter the Great, Rastrelli's sculpture of Peter, the museum's *Pallas Athena*, and its superb collection of diamonds, precious stones, crown jewels and ancient artefacts of gold.

Nearer to the front, at Mogilev, July 1 saw two Soviet Marshals, Voroshilov and Shaposhnikov, briefing those who were to stay behind as the Germans advanced, and set up partisan groups. 'Blow up bridges,' they were told, 'destroy single trucks with enemy officers and soldiers. Use any opportunity to slow up the movement of enemy reserves to the Front. Blow up enemy trains full of troops, equipment or weapons. Blow up his bases and dumps.'

On July 1, the Germans entered Riga. In Berlin, Ribbentrop urged the Japanese to enter the war at once, and to strike at the Soviet Union in the Far East. The Japanese refused to do so, the news of their refusal, and of their decision to push instead into French Indo-China, being radioed from Tokyo to Moscow by Richard Sorge on July 6. As a result of this Intelligence, Soviet troops from the Far East could continue to reinforce the armies battling in the West. Reinforcements were urgently needed; on July 2 the Roumanian Army, having watched the German forces advancing for eleven days, had attacked in the south, striking in the direction of the Ukrainian city of Vinnitsa.

This new onslaught made even more urgent the evacuation of factories from southern Russia. On July 2 it was decided to move the armoured-plate mill at Mariupol to the Ural city of Magnitogorsk. On the following day, the State Defence Committee in Moscow ordered the transfer eastward of twenty-six further armaments factories from throughout western Russia, including Moscow, Leningrad and Tula. From Kiev and Kharkov too, individual plants and essential machinery were ordered eastward.

On July 3, Stalin broadcast, for the first time since the invasion twelve days before, to the Russian people. 'A grave threat hangs over our country,' he warned, and he went on to tell his listeners: 'Military tribunals will pass summary judgement on any who fail in our defence, whether through panic or treachery, regardless of their position or their rank.'

Stalin's speech contained a powerful appeal, not to Communism but to patriotism. He addressed his listeners, in his opening words, not only as 'comrades' and 'citizens', but also as 'brothers and sisters' and 'my friends'. In one passage, he appealed for the formation of partisan units behind the lines 'to foment guerrilla warfare everywhere, to blow up bridges and roads, damage telephone and telegraph lines, set fire to forests, stores, transports'. The enemy, 'and all his accomplices,' must be 'hounded and annihilated at every step'.

The Germans failed to appreciate the storm which such an injunction was to raise against them. 'It is no exaggeration to say', wrote General Halder in his diary on July 3, 'that the campaign against Russia has been won in fourteen days.' Behind the lines, the cruelty was beginning to exceed all previous cruelty in this or any other war. On July 4 one of Himmler's Special Task Forces recorded the murder of 463 Jews in Kovno; two days later a further 2,514 were killed. In Tarnopol, within forty-eight hours of the German occupation, six hundred Jews had been killed, and in Zborow a further six hundred. In Vilna, fifty-four Jews were shot on July 4 and a further ninety-three on the following day.

On July 5, the part played in these massacres by Lithuanians was raised at Hitler's headquarters in East Prussia by a German Army officer. In Kovno, according to a report by the Special Task Forces, 2,500 Jews had been killed by the Lithuanians before the Germans had even occupied the city. German soldiers, Hitler's adjutant Colonel Schmundt, replied, were not to interfere in these 'political questions'; what was happening to the Jews was part of 'a necessary mopping up operation'. Hitler himself was confident of victory; that day, to his private staff, he spoke of making the 'beauties of the Crimea' accessible by autobahn from Germany: 'for us Germans, that will be our Riviera'. Croatia too, he said, would be 'a tourists' paradise for us'. In Russia, it was enough 'for the present' for the Urals to be the new Eastern frontier. 'What matters,' Hitler explained, 'is that Bolshevism must be exterminated. In case of necessity, we shall renew our advance wherever a new centre of resistance is formed.' Moscow, he added, 'as the centre of the doctrine, must disappear from the earth's surface, as soon as its riches have been brought to shelter'.

Those who were determined to prevent such an outcome to the war redoubled their efforts that July. From London, plans were made to send military and medical aid to the Soviet Union on a substantial scale, even diverting American aid – then on its way to Britain – from British to Soviet ports. In the air, the attacks on Germany continued, despite a considerable improvement in the German air defences. In a bombing raid on Bremen on July 4, five out of the twelve attacking aircraft had been shot down. For his bravery in persevering with the raid, and in bringing the survivors home, the leader of the raid, the Australian pilot Hughie Edwards, was awarded the Victoria Cross. More than a thousand miles to the south, on July 5 the Yugoslav Communist partisan, Tito, issued an appeal to his fellow Yugoslavs. 'Now is the time,' he declared, 'the hour has struck to rise like one man in the battle against the invaders and hirelings'. On the following day, Tito sent a Montenegrin student, Milovan Djilas, to his native province, to organize resistance against the German occupation forces. Tito told Djilas: 'Shoot anyone if he wavers or shows any lack of courage or discipline!'

On July 7, at the Serbian village of Bela Crkva, the first armed clash took place between a small Communist detachment and the German police. Two policemen were killed.

Plans for resistance went forward, slowly, in many lands; but the German advance into Russia struck fear into all the captive peoples. On July 6, on the Leningrad front, German troops reached Tartu, less than two hundred miles from the former Imperial capital. But in the German High Command it was the repeated ability of the Russians to counter-attack that was causing alarm. 'Everyone' at headquarters, Halder noted in his diary, 'is vying for the honour of telling the most hair-raising tales about the strength of the Russian forces.' On July 6, two German divisions had been driven back from Zhlobin. A panzer attempt to breach Stalin's first defence line at Rogachev, had been repulsed. There was evidence of Soviet reinforcements being brought up in force to Orel and Bryansk.

Early in July, British Intelligence learned from the German Army's Enigma messages that the Germans were reading certain Russian Air Force codes in the Leningrad area, as well as decrypting Russian naval messages in the Baltic. This information was passed on to the British Military Mission in Moscow on July 7, with the request that the Russians be alerted to this gap in their security. That day, in the Atlantic, the United States launched Operation Indigo, the landing of a Marine brigade in Iceland. To the American people, Roosevelt justified the operation in terms of the need to defend the Western hemisphere; but for Britain's transatlantic shipping it was an important contribution to seaborne traffic nearer home. Roosevelt himself, four days later, on a map torn out of the *National Geographical Magazine*, marked the new eastward extension of American patrols in the Atlantic; those patrols now came to within four hundred miles of the northern coast of Scotland.

American support was enabling Britain to extend her own support for Russia. On July 7, the day on which the American Marines landed on Iceland, Churchill wrote to Stalin to say that Britain would do 'everything to help you that time, geography, and our growing resources allow'. British bombing raids on Germany, Churchill explained, which had recently been intensified, would go on: 'Thus we hope to force Hitler to bring back some of his air power to the West and gradually take some of the strain off you.' On the day of this telegram to Stalin, Churchill instructed the Chief of the British Air Staff to use Britain's air resources for the 'devastation of the German cities' in an effort to draw German aircraft back from the Russian front.

On July 8, German forces entered Pskov, a mere 180 miles from Leningrad.

That same day, in pursuance of his stern words of five days earlier, Stalin removed General Korbokov from his command; accused of 'permitting the destruction of his army by the Germans', Korbokov was shot. On the day of the capture of Pskov, at Hitler's East Prussian headquarters at Rastenburg, General Halder noted in his diary: 'Führer is firmly determined to level Moscow and Leningrad to the ground, and to dispose fully of their population, which otherwise we shall have to feed during the winter.'

Hitler seemed to have cause for his confident bellicose assertions; on July 9 he learned that 287,704 Soviet soldiers had been taken prisoner, and 2,585 Soviet tanks destroyed, in the salient west of Minsk, where 'mopping up' operations came to an end that day. But, in every area overrun by German troops, partisan units were formed; some, like one set up by Colonel Nichiporovich, were created out of the remnants of fighting units which had been almost totally destroyed. Further north, as the Red Army withdrew along the road between Pskov and Luga, one partisan commander, Dudin by name, having spent ten days collecting 123 rifles and two light machine guns from Soviet units pulling back, 'went over', as he reported, 'to the position of a partisan detachment, taking refuge with the population in the woods'. On July 9, Dudin carried out his first action behind the lines; within two months he had destroyed more than twenty German lorries, and killed 120 Germans, 'not counting those accounted for by the Red Army on the basis of information we gave'.

Information was a key to survival; on July 9 a group of British cryptanalysts broke the Enigma key used by the German Army to direct its ground–air operations on the Eastern Front. But good Intelligence could seldom make up for a serious lack of weapons. On July 10, when the first division of volunteers left Leningrad for the ever encroaching front line, there were not enough rifles to go round. While each man had been given hand grenades and Molotov cocktails, many without rifles carried picks, shovels, axes and even hunting knives instead. That same day, at Korosten, a massive Soviet counter-attack in defence of Kiev was checked, and then driven back. 'He is infinitely confident of victory,' Walther Hewel wrote of Hitler, after seeing him at Rastenburg on July 10. 'The tasks confronting him today are as nothing, he says, compared with those in the years of struggle, particularly since ours is the biggest and finest army in the world.'

Hitler also spoke to Hewel on July 10 about the Jews. 'It is I', he said, 'who have discovered the Jews as the bacillus and ferment that causes all decay in society. And what I have proved is this – that nations can survive without Jews; that the economy, culture, art and so on, can exist without Jews and in fact better. That is the cruellest blow I have dealt the Jews.'

Crueller blows were, in fact, being dealt against the Jews daily, as German forces occupied areas with large Jewish populations, totalling more than a million Jews. On July 7, it was reported eleven days later from Berlin, 1,150 Jews had been shot in Dvinsk, 'without ceremony, and interred in previously prepared graves'. In Lvov, 7,000 Jews had been 'rounded up and shot'. In Dobromil, 132 Jews had been killed. In Lutsk, three hundred Jews had been shot on June 30 and a further 1,160 on July 2. At Tarnopol, 180 Jews were killed. At Zolochew 'the number of the Jews liquidated may run to about 300–500'.

Such reports, marked 'top secret', were compiled every few days; merely to print them in full would be a book itself, as large as this one. Not only Jews, but former Soviet officials and local dignitaries were executed in large numbers in every town and village overrun by the German Army. Soviet prisoners-of-war also continued to be the victims of deliberate barbarity from the first moments of their captivity; on 10 July information reached Berlin of the terrible conditions in the newly opened prisoner-of-war camp of Maly Trostenets, just outside Minsk, where hundreds of Soviet soldiers in captivity were dying every day from disease, starvation and the brutality of their guards.

The Red Army was determined to fight for every mile of the road to Moscow. 'The enemy Command is acting ably,' General Halder wrote in his diary on July 11. 'The enemy is putting up a fierce and fanatical fight.' On the following day, Britain and the Soviet Union signed a pact pledging 'mutual assistance' against Germany. Neither side would make a separate peace. At the same time, the British bombing raids on Germany, of which Churchill had written to Stalin a week earlier, began with a renewed intensity on July 14 when Hanover was bombed, followed, during the next nine days, by two more raids on Hanover, two on Hamburg, two on Frankfurt and Mannheim, and one on Berlin itself. 'In the last few weeks alone', Churchill declared in a broadcast on July 14, 'we have thrown upon Germany about half the tonnage of bombs thrown by the Germans upon our cities during the whole course of the war. But this is only a beginning ...'.

On the day of Churchill's speech, British Military Intelligence sent a top secret message to the British Military Mission in Moscow, to pass on at once to the Russians details, culled from the German Enigma messages, of the dispositions and order of battle of the German forces. Two days later, at Churchill's specific request, the Military Mission in Moscow was sent an appreciation of German intentions in both the Smolensk and Gomel areas, together with the news, once again taken from the Germans' own most secret instructions, that the German Air Force had been ordered to prevent Russian withdrawals by attacks on the railways leading to the rear.

The ability of the Russians to withdraw their troops was distressing to the German High Command, which had hoped to see those troops destroyed in battle. But Hitler's confidence was undimmed. On July 14, in a supplementary to his earlier Directive No. 32, he set out a plan for eventual reductions in German military, naval and air strength. Hitler began with the words: 'Our military mastery of the European continent after the overthrow of Russia ...'.

That day, at Orsha, a Soviet artillery officer, Captain Flerov, used a new multiple rocket launcher in action for the first time; this was the Katyusha, which could fire 320 rockets in twenty-five seconds. It was to wreak considerable havoc on the German forces in the months to come. But Nazi tyranny was still triumphant; on July 14, Martin Gauger, a German civil servant who had refused to take the oath of allegiance to Hitler in 1933, and had fled to Holland in 1940 by swimming across the Rhine, only a few hours before German troops entered Holland, died in Buchenwald. That same day, in the Galician town of Drohobycz, ss Sergeant Felix Landau, one of the instigators in 1934 of the murder of the Austrian Chancellor, Dr Dolfuss, described in his diary the moments before a massacre of Jews in a nearby wood: 'We order the prisoners to dig their graves. Only two of them are crying, the others show courage. What can they all be thinking? I believe each still has the hope of not being shot. I don't feel the slightest stir of pity. That's how it is, and has got to be.'

# 16

# Terror in the East

JULY–AUGUST 1941

On 15 July 1941, a German spy, Juan Pujol Garcia, sent his first letter from Britain to his German masters. Garcia was the chief of a network of spies whom he himself had recruited. They included a Dutch airline steward, a censor in the Ministry of Information, a typist in the Cabinet office, an American soldier based in London and a Welsh fascist. All were non-existent, as was Garcia himself: known to the Germans as 'Arabel', Garcia was in fact the British double-agent 'Garbo', sending a series of totally spurious reports back to Germany, using recruits who were a figment of his imagination.

The success of 'Garbo' in deceiving the Germans about British military preparations and intentions was considerable. On the day of his first letter back to Germany, another secret, and in the end far more fateful, communication took place; for on the day of Garcia's double-cross, a British Government Committee, reporting in the strictest secrecy, concluded that 'the scheme for a uranium bomb is practicable and likely to lead to decisive results in the war'. It recommended that work on this bomb should continue 'on the highest priority and on the increasing scale necessary to obtain the weapon in the shortest possible time.'

The urgency of the Anglo-American search for an atomic bomb arose from the Allied belief that the Germans were also working on a similar project, which could lead to the destruction of whole cities in Britain.

In mid-July 1941, however, it was Russia which seemed on the verge of destruction. On July 16, the day after the British 'uranium bomb' report, German forces began the encirclement of the Soviet city of Smolensk, halfway between Minsk and Moscow, and at the centre of the second of the defensive lines established a mere three weeks earlier. At his headquarters, Hitler was jubilant. 'In principle,' he told an inner circle of confidants, including General Keitel and Alfred Rosenberg, 'we must now face the task of cutting up our cake according to our needs in order to be able: first, to dominate it; second, to administer it; third to exploit it.' Never again must there be 'any military power West of the Urals, even if we have to fight a hundred years' war to prevent it'. As to criticisms of the killing that was proceeding behind the German lines, here Hitler was equally positive. 'The Russians', he said, 'have now given an order to wage partisan warfare behind our front. This guerrilla activity has some advantage for us; it enables us to exterminate everyone who opposes us.' That day, a German Army order, issued from Army headquarters, associated the regular Army with the new ruthlessness. 'The necessary rapid pacification of the country', the order read, 'can be attained only if every threat on the part of the hostile civil population is ruthlessly taken care of. All pity and softness are evidence of weakness and constitute a danger.' Everything must be done to promote 'the spreading of that measure of terror which alone is suited to deprive the population of the will to resist'.

On July 17, Hitler gave Himmler full authority for 'police security in the newly occupied territories'. The killing of Jews was now a daily occurrence, reported as a matter of routine by the Special Task Forces, as they moved forward steadily from town to town and village to village. 'Operational Situation Reports, USSR', as the killing squad statistical reports were called, were compiled regularly in Berlin and sent to as many as sixty German Government departments and officials. Report No. 26, dated July 18, gave the total number of Jews already 'liquidated' inside the former Lithuanian border by a Task Force based on Tilsit as 3,302. At Pskov, eighty Jews had been killed. On July 17, seven hundred Jews had been taken out of Vilna to the nearby holiday resort of Ponar; they had all been shot. On July 18, fifty-three Jews had been shot at Mariampolé.

The killing squads operated against Russians as well as against Jews. Three days after the Mariampolé executions of July 18, a group of forty-five Jews were forced to dig a pit, and were then roped together and thrown into the pit alive. The ss then ordered thirty White Russians to cover the live Jews with earth. The White Russians refused. The ss then opened fire with machine guns on Jews and White Russians alike: all seventy-five were killed.

Behind the lines, the Special Task Forces murdered unarmed and frightened civilians without interruption, but at the front the German Army was finding itself confronted by much stiffer resistance than it had been led to expect. British Intelligence learned from the German Army's own Enigma messages that this was so; that the Germans were disturbed by the scale of their own casualties, planned to slow down the advance, and could no longer provide adequate air protection either to the Panzer formations at the front or to strategic positions at the rear. On July 17, Churchill specifically requested that this information should be sent to Stalin.

News also reached Britain, through German top secret police messages likewise sent through the Enigma machine, of the mass murder, first reported and read on July 18, of 'Jews', 'Jewish plunderers', 'Jewish Bolshevists' and 'Russian soldiers'.

Hitler was now as worried as his commanders by the Russian ability to retreat and regroup. 'The aim of the next operations', he wrote in his Directive No. 33 on July 19, 'must be to prevent any further sizeable enemy forces from withdrawing into the depths of Russia, and wiping them out.' Admiral Canaris, returning from Hitler's headquarters, was reported by one of his staff as saying on 20 July that the mood at Rastenburg was 'very jittery, as it is increasingly evident that the Russian campaign is not "going by the book"'. The signs were multiplying, Canaris added, 'that this war will not bring about the expected internal collapse, so much as the invigoration, of Bolshevism'. That same day, July 20, Stalin ordered that all Red Army units 'should be purged of unreliable elements'.

The Russian people did not depend on purges to maintain the will to fight, and to survive. On July 20, a day before Hitler visited Northern Army Group headquarters and demanded that Leningrad be 'finished off speedily', a second trainload of treasures from the Hermitage was sent to safety, to the Ural city of Sverdlovsk. That day, from the Polotsk–Vitebsk area, less than a month earlier Russia's first line of defence, now behind the lines, a German infantry division assigned to comb the Polotsk–Vitebsk–Nevel triangle, described the area as a 'partisan region', and reported that the roads were being mined every day.

July 20 was also the day on which the first British naval vessel, a minelayer, crossed the North Sea on its way to the Soviet Arctic port of Archangel with military supplies. Three days later, a substantial British naval force of two aircraft carriers, two cruisers and six destroyers left Scapa Flow to carry out attacks, at Stalin's request, on German ships taking war supplies between the Norwegian port of Kirkenes, and Petsamo, the Finnish-controlled base for operations against the Murmansk region. These British warships were to be the first of a series of naval forces sent to help Russia, or to bring help to Russia, through Arctic waters, beyond the North Cape, in what the Soviet Ambassador to London, Ivan Maisky, was later to call 'a northern saga of heroism, bravery and endurance'.

On July 21 the Germans launched their first air raid on Moscow; watching the city's anti-aircraft defences in action, the Western journalist Alexander Werth noted 'a fantastic piece of fireworks – tracer bullets, and flares, and flaming onions, and all sorts of rockets, white and green and red; and the din was terrific; never saw anything like it in London'. There was a second raid on the following night.

At the Soviet–German border, the garrison of Brest-Litovsk, surrounded and isolated hundreds of miles in the rear, had held out for thirty days against German bombers and artillery. On July 23, after a pounding by a new German mortar, 'Karl', which fired a projectile weighing over two tons, the garrison surrendered. The courage of the defenders was cause for pride to those Russians struggling to hold the line so much further east, or to maintain the fight behind the lines. It was indeed the partisan war which caught the Germans by surprise. On July 23, in a supplement to his Directive No. 33, Hitler stressed that the commanders of all areas behind the front were 'to be held responsible together with the troops at their disposal, for quiet conditions in their areas'. They would 'contrive to maintain order', Hitler added, 'not by requesting reinforcements, but by employing suitably draconian methods'.

How 'draconian' these methods could be was clear from an SS report which listed the executions carried out in the Lithuanian town of Kedainiai on July 23

SWEDEN

FINLAND

*Gulf of Finland*

Baltic Sea

Lake Ladoga

Lake Onega

Tallinn
Kingisepp
Gatchina
Leningrad
Mga
Chudovo
Luga

*Lake Peipus*

Pskov

*Lake Ilmen*

Leningrad - Moscow

Riga

Velikiye Luki

Nevel

Rzhev

Roskiskis

Kedainiai

Polotsk

Moscow

Tilsit
Kovno
Mariampolé
Ponar
Vilna
Vitebsk
Vyazma

Marienburg
Rastenburg

Smolensk

*Hitler's journey 4-6 August 1941*

Borisov
Orsha
Yelnya

Stawiski

GREATER

WHITE RUSSIA

Minsk

S  O  V  I  E  T      U  N  I  O  N

1 September 1941

GERMANY

Bryansk

Brest-Litovsk

River Vistula

River Bug

*Hitler and Mussolini's journey 28 August 1941*

Lvov

Shepetovka

Zhitomir
Kiev

Berdichev

Drohobycz

Proskurov

U  K  R  A  I  N  E

Kharkov

DONETZ REGION

River Donetz

Chorostkow

Vinnitsa

1 September 1941

Kremenchug

Kamenets-Podolok

Uman

HUNGARY

ROUMANIA

BESSARABIA

Dnepropetrovsk

Zaporozhe

Kishinev

Nikolayev

Dnieper

Odessa

Black Sea

Sea of Azov

CRIMEA

Kerch

Partisan region

Moscow defence line, 29 July 1941

Hitler and Mussolini's journey by rail, 26 August 1941

0    miles    150
0    kilometres    200

© Martin Gilbert 1989

The Eastern Front, August 1941

as 'eighty-three Jews, twelve Jewesses, fourteen Russian Communists, fifteen Lithuanian Communists, one Russian Commissar'.

It was on July 23 that a new British film was shown to the press, two days before its public release. Called *Target for Tonight*, it centred on a bombing raid over Germany. The impact of the film was immediate. Produced by Harry Watt, and with a real pilot, Squadron Leader Pickard, at the controls, it provided a boost to British morale. The phrase 'Target for Tonight' became a national catchword on radio and the stage.

On July 24, British Bomber Command launched Operation Sunrise, against the German battle-cruisers *Scharnhorst* and *Gneisenau*, and on the heavy cruiser *Prinz Eugen*, then at Brest and La Pallice. The raid was a failure; seventeen aircraft were lost, for negligible damage to the ships. That day, in the Far East, following the decision taken in Tokyo on July not to move against Russia but through South-East Asia instead, 125,000 Japanese troops moved into Indo-China. Five days later they had occupied Cam Ranh naval base, only eight hundred miles from the Philippine capital of Manila and from the British base at Singapore. The Vichy authorities had said they would allow in 40,000 Japanese troops. But they had no means of insisting that this bargain was kept. Two days later, on July 26, as a gesture of disapproval and retaliation, Roosevelt seized all Japanese assets in the United States; this was followed by similar action by the British Empire and the Dutch East Indies, cutting off Japan, at a stroke, from three-quarters of her overseas trade and ninety per cent of her oil imports. Japan's own oil resources could last for three years at the very most. At the same time, the Panama Canal was closed to Japanese shipping, and General Douglas MacArthur took over command of American forces in the Far East, and of the Philippines force, now facing the Japanese in French Indo-China across the South China Sea. As he did so, Japanese forces entered Saigon, once more with the Vichy authorities' reluctant agreement.

On July 26, in the Mediterranean, Italian motor torpedo boats brought special piloted torpedoes – known to the Italians as 'pigs', and to the British as 'chariots' – into Malta's Grand Harbour. Before the men on these 'pigs' could find their targets, they were seen and attacked; fifteen of them were killed and the rest taken prisoner. Not all deaths that day were in action. On the Russian front, NKVD troops rounded up a thousand deserters from a single regiment; forty-five were shot, seven of them in front of the assembled regiment. That same day, in Lvov, Ukrainians began a three day orgy of killing against the Jews of the city; at least two thousand Jews were murdered in those three days.

Elsewhere in the conquered areas of Russia, the German plans for the Jews were changing. After the initial slaughter of thousands, ghettos were being set up in which those who had survived the massacres were to be confined. On July 27 the new Reich Commissar for the Baltic States and White Russia, Hinrich Lohse, was told that the inmates of the ghettos under his authority were to receive 'only the amount of food that the rest of the population could spare, and in no case more than was sufficient to sustain life'. These minimal food rations were to continue 'until such time as the more intensive measures for the "Final Solution" can be put into effect'.

In Vilna, even after the ghetto had been established, the killings continued, at the nearby resort of Ponar, the very name of which had already joined that dreaded vocabulary of places associated with brutality and killing: Sachsenhausen, Buchenwald, Mauthausen and many more, a growing number. On July 27 a Polish journalist, W. Sakowicz, who lived at Ponar, and was himself to be killed during the last days of German rule in Vilna, wrote in his diary: 'Shooting is carried on nearly every day. Will it go on for ever? The executioners have begun selling the clothes of the killed. Other garments are crammed into sacks in a barn at the highway, and taken to town.' Between two and three hundred people, Sakowicz added, 'are being driven up here nearly every day. And nobody ever returns....'

In Belgrade, after four bomb attacks on German military vehicles, the Germans acted swiftly to prevent further acts of resistance. No one had been killed in the four attacks. But on July 27 the Germans rounded up 1,200 Jews, brought them to a camp just outside the city, divided them into their professions, and declared every tenth person a 'hostage'. The 120 hostages were then taken away and shot.

It was only on July 27 that the Germans completed their encirclement of Smolensk, cutting the Russian lines of communication to Vyazma, and taking more than 100,000 Russian prisoners. That day, a Soviet order sentencing nine Soviet senior officers to death was read out to all officers and men. Those sentenced included Generals Pavlov, Klimovskikh and Korobkov. Also shot, but in secret, was General Pyadyshev, who had organized the Luga defence line for Leningrad.

On July 27, German bombers returned to Moscow for the fifth consecutive night. 'The Kremlin is a heap of smouldering ruins,' Goebbels declared. In fact, a single bomb had fallen just outside the Kremlin, making a deep crater.

On July 28 the Red Army was forced to abandon Kingisepp, less than seventy miles from Leningrad. To build defence works, 30,000 Leningrad citizens were taken with spades, picks and shovels under the slogan 'At Kingisepp – to the trenches'. Nearly 100,000 were sent to the area around Gatchina, known since the Revolution as Krasnogvardeisk. At the same time, plans were made to meet the German occupation with partisan activity; on July 28, the Soviet authorities in Vyazma issued 'Assignment No. 1', the creation of a partisan unit of 350 men who would deliberately be left behind when the Red Army retreated. Its task would be to destroy German food, fuel and supply dumps, to destroy the Smolensk–Vyazma and Vyazma–Bryansk railway lines, and to derail trains; to prevent the use of Vyazma airport by the Germans by destroying planes and fuel; to kill 'higher and lower level German war staffs', to capture 'high German officers'; to hand over to the Red Army any documents containing 'valuable information about the enemy'; and to set up two or three 'diversionist groups' to perform 'special tasks'.

On July 28, the day on which this Vyazma plan was laid down, and the would-be partisans received their instructions, Himmler issued orders authorizing ss military units that were fighting alongside regular German Army units to take 'cleansing actions' against villagers who 'consisted of racial inferiors' or who were suspected of helping partisans. In cases of help to partisans, anyone under suspicion was to be executed immediately, and the village then 'burned to the ground'.

In the town of Drohobycz, two weeks after the first massacre of Jews, ss Sergeant Felix Landau wrote in his diary: 'In a side turning we notice some Jewish corpses covered with sand. We look at each other in surprise. One living Jew rises up from among the corpses. We despatch him with a few shots. Eight hundred Jews have been herded together; they are to be shot tomorrow.'

The enormity of the crimes, and the vastness of the areas now occupied by Germany, had created unease among a small group of senior German officers, who feared that the grandiose hopes of victory were likely to be dashed by eventual stalemate and even defeat. 'No one has ever succeeded in defeating and conquering Russia,' Admiral Canaris had remarked in the presence of Lieutenant Fabian von Schlabrendorff, an officer on the staff of Major-General Henning von Tresckow, and the General's relative by marriage. It was Tresckow who, at the end of July 1941, while at Army Group Centre, tried to win the support of Field Marshal von Kluge for an attempt to arrest Hitler and depose him. But von Kluge, though Hitler had once dismissed him from his command in 1938, would not be drawn.

On July 29 a new Soviet defence line was created, between Rzhev and Vyazma, guarding Moscow. That day, in Moscow, Harry Hopkins spoke to Stalin about the American aid that was on its way: two hundred American fighter planes were being sent by ship to Archangel, and, Hopkins explained, 'an outstanding expert in the operation of these planes', Lieutenant Alison, was already in Moscow.

The despatch of aid to Russia by sea was only made feasible because, by the end of July, all German submarine instructions were being read by the British cryptographers at Bletchley 'continuously and with little or no delay'; that month the number of Allied merchant ships sunk, which had been more than ninety in May, fell to below thirty, because it was now possible to route Atlantic convoys around German submarine concentrations. A month earlier, a secret message system similar to the Enigma, the key to the Italian Navy's high grade cypher machine, c38m, had also been broken, giving the British details of the sailings of all Italian troop and supply ships from Italy to North Africa.

The setbacks to the Italians were eventually to draw Germany more and more deeply into the Western Desert struggle; but at the end of July 1941 it was Germany's triumph in the East which was predominant. By July 30, noted a senior German Staff Officer, General von Waldau, the Germans in Russia had taken 799,910 prisoners, and destroyed or captured 12,025 tanks. At the same time, the carrying out the Commissar Decree, and also the killing of Jews, had continued without respite, the killers following the German armies as they advanced more and more deeply into the Ukraine. On July 30, Himmler's

Special Task Forces compiled their fortieth Operation Situation Report USSR. In Zhitomir, 180 'Communists and Jews' had been shot, in Proskurov, 146 Jews; in Vinnitsa, 146; in Berdichev, 148; in Shepetovka, 17; in Chorostkow, 30. The report added: 'In this last place, 110 Jews were slain by the local population.' At Ponàr, outside Vilna, the Polish journalist Sakowicz wrote in his diary that day: 'About 150 persons shot. Most of them were elderly people. The executioners complained of being very tired of their "work", of having aching shoulders from shooting. That is the reason for not finishing the wounded off, so that they are buried half alive.'

In his Directive No. 34, issued from Rastenburg on 30 July, Hitler ordered that the Soviet troops fighting north-west of Kiev 'must be brought to battle west of the Dnieper and annihilated'. In this same directive, however, he urged caution and retrenchment elsewhere, in an attempt to focus his military efforts more effectively. Army Group Centre was 'to go over to the defensive'. Armoured units were to be withdrawn from the front line 'for quick rehabilitiation'. On the Finnish front, only such forces were to be left 'as are necessary for defence and to give the impression of further offensive operations'.

On July 31, in the Bessarabian city of Kishinev, the first 'five-figure' civilian massacre of the war came to its end; after fourteen days of uninterrupted slaughter, ten thousand Jews had been murdered. That same day, from Berlin, Field Marshal Goering sent Reinhard Heydrich a letter, 'on the Führer's instructions', ordering him to 'make all necessary preparations as regards organization and actual concrete preparations for a general solution of the Jewish problem within German sphere of influence in Europe'.

Behind this verbose and convoluted sentence lay a blueprint for mass annihilation.

'Hitler's greatest weakness', Stalin told Harry Hopkins on July 31, at their second meeting in the Kremlin, 'was found in the vast numbers of oppressed peoples who hated Hitler and the immoral ways of his Government.' These people, Stalin added, 'and countless other millions in nations still unconquered, could receive the kind of encouragement and moral strength they needed to resist Hitler only from one source, and that was the United States'.

In Auschwitz concentration camp, at the end of July, a Pole escaped from a labour detail. As a reprisal, ten men in his block of six hundred were chosen at random, to be locked in a cell and starved to death. After the selection, a Polish Catholic priest, Father Maximilian Kolbe, who was also a prisoner, approached the camp Commandant and asked to take the place of one of those who had been selected. 'I am alone in the world,' Kolbe said. 'That man, Francis Gajowniczek, has a family to live for.' 'Accepted', said the Commandant, and turned away. Father Kolbe was the last to die. Thirty years later, at a ceremony of beatification for Kolbe, the man whose place he took, Francis Gajowniczek, attended, together with Gajowniczek's wife.

In the week of Father Kolbe's act of courage, a German Army officer, Major

Rosler, was alerted in his barracks at Zhitomir by a 'wild fusillade' of rifle fire. Looking for its source, he climbed an embankment, from which he looked down upon 'a picture of such barbaric horror that the effect upon anyone coming upon it unawares was both shattering and repellant'. Major Rosler was looking down into a pit filled with the bodies of dead and dying Jews. At the edge of the pit were German soldiers, some in bathing shorts because it was such a hot day. Local civilians were watching the scene with curiosity; a number had brought their wives and children to watch the spectacle. In the pit, Rosler recalled, 'lay, among others, an old man with a white beard clutching a cane in his left hand. Since this man, judging by his sporadic breathing, showed signs of life, I ordered one of the policemen to kill him. He smilingly replied: "I have already shot him seven times in the stomach. He can die on his own now." '

Five months after witnessing this scene, Rosler protested about it to his superiors. 'I cannot begin to conceive', he wrote, 'the legal decisions on whose basis these executions were carried out. Everything that is happening here seems to be absolutely incompatible with our views on education and morality.'

On August 1, in Minsk, Himmler himself witnessed an execution. He had the 'bad luck' on that occasion, his senior liaison officer, SS General Karl Wolff later recalled, 'that from one or other of the people who had been shot in the head, he got a splash of brains on his coat, and I think it also splashed into his face, and he went very green and pale; he wasn't actually sick but he was heaving and turned round and swayed and then I had to jump forward and hold him steady and then I led him away from the grave'.

Following this episode, Himmler told those doing the shooting that they must be 'hard and firm'. But he also asked the head of the German Criminal Police, Arthur Nebe, who held the rank of general in the SS, and who, since June 22, had been in charge of Special Task Force B, operating in White Russia, to find some new method of mass killing. After the war, an amateur film was found in Nebe's former Berlin apartment, showing a gas chamber worked by the exhaust gas of a lorry.

A new policy on mass killing was about to emerge. At Auschwitz that August, the deputy camp Commandant, SS Captain Karl Fritsch, conducted experiments in killing by gas, using a commercial pesticide, prussic acid, marketed under the German trade name of 'Zyklon-B'. The victims on whom he chose to experiment were Russian prisoners-of-war.

In its frequently used commercial form, Zyklon B had a special irritant added, so that those who used it against insects would be warned by its noxious smell to stay well clear of it. Now the irritant was removed, so as not to create alarm or panic among those against whom it was being used; and a special label on each tin warned those who operated the gas chambers that these particular tins were 'without irritant'.

On August 2, the Red Army, which had been in almost continuous retreat for fifty days, began a twenty-eight-day tank battle to drive the Germans back from the Yelnya salient; although, in October, the Russians in Yelnya were to be encircled and destroyed, their success in August, the first victory of the Red

Army over the Germans, was a powerful boost to Russian morale. Visiting Army Group Centre at Borisov on August 4, Hitler told two of his senior commanders, Field Marshal von Bock and General Guderian: 'Had I known they had as many tanks as that, I'd have thought twice before invading.'

On August 6, Hitler flew from Borisov to Berdichev, to visit the headquarters of Army Group South. With him was Walther Hewel, who noted in his diary: 'Ruined monastery church. Opened coffins, execution, ghastly town. Many Jews, ancient cottages, fertile soil. Very hot.' Hitler flew back to his headquarters at Rastenburg. On the following day, the German police commander in the central sector, von dem Bach Zelewski, reported to SS headquarters in Berlin that his units had carried out 30,000 executions since their arrival in Russia. The SS Cavalry Brigade also sent in a report to Berlin that day, to say that it had carried out 7,819 'executions' to date in the Minsk area. To ensure maximum secrecy, both reports were sent by the most secure radio cypher system available, the Enigma. As a result, both were read by British Intelligence. Hitler too must have read these reports; five days earlier the Gestapo chief, Heinrich Müller, had written from Berlin to the commanders of the four Special Task Forces, including SS Geberal Nebe of Task Force B, that 'the Führer is to be kept informed continually from here about the work of the Special Task Forces in the East'.

The work of these task forces was continuous and comprehensive. Operational Situation Report No. 43, compiled in Berlin on August 5, spoke of measures in twenty-nine towns 'and other small places' in which the units had 'rendered harmless' people in the following categories: 'Bolshevik Party officials, NKVD agents, active Jewish intelligentsia, criminals, looters, partisans etc.'. The partisans could not, however, be so easily rooted out. From Vitebsk, on August 8, the local German authorities reported that the Soviet partisans in the region operated in such small groups, or even as individuals, that they 'could not be eliminated' by regular military or police operations.

# 17

# Towards Leningrad, Moscow and Kiev

## SEPTEMBER 1941

On 8 August 1941, as Russian troops and civilians fled from the Black Sea port of Odessa, orders arrived from Moscow: 'The situation on the land front notwithstanding, Odessa is not to be surrendered.' Three days later, as Churchill and Roosevelt met, for the first time as leaders, off Newfoundland, the Soviet Air Force carried out its first air raid on Berlin. Hitler now suspended the attack on Moscow and 'concluded' the operation against Leningrad.

On August 12, in a supplement to his Directive No. 34, Hitler set as the immediate German objectives the occupation of the Crimea, of the industrial region of Kharkov and of the coalfields of the Donetz basin. Once the Crimea was occupied, an attack across the Kerch Straits, in the direction of Batum, 'will be considered'. It was 'urgently necessary', Hitler added, 'that enemy airfields from which attacks on Berlin are evidently being made should be destroyed'.

On board ship, at Placentia Bay, Newfoundland, Churchill and Roosevelt agreed, after hearing Hopkins's account of his meetings with Stalin, to give immediate aid to Russia 'on a gigantic scale'. Churchill also drafted a statement, which Roosevelt agreed to issue under his own name, that any 'further encroachment' by Japan in the south-west Pacific 'would produce a situation in which the United States Government would be compelled to take counter-measures, even though these might lead to war between the United States and Japan'.

During their discussions, Churchill and Roosevelt agreed to issue a public document, the Atlantic Charter, setting out a joint Anglo-American commitment to a post-war world in which there would be 'no aggrandizement, territorial or other', as a result of the war, and no territorial changes 'that do not accord with the freely expressed wishes of the people concerned'. In a section directed at those who were under German, Italian or Japanese occupation, the Atlantic Charter pledged that Britain and the United States 'wish to see sovereign rights and self-government restored to those who have been forcibly deprived of them'.

These words of encouragement were made public on August 12. On the following day, in Paris, fighting broke out between demonstrators and the French and German police. Seven days later, two of the demonstrators were executed: Henry Gaultherot and Szmul Tyszelman. Both were Communists. Tyszelman was also a Jew.

In order to give aid to Russia, Churchill and Roosevelt had authorized, while on board ship in Placentia Bay, the immediate despatch of an Anglo-American Military Mission to Moscow, to discuss Soviet needs in relation to American production. Arthur Purvis, who had done so much in the United States to acquire war supplies for Britain a year earlier, was to be a leading member of the Mission. He was killed, however, when the aeroplane bringing him to Placentia Bay from Britain crashed on take off.

In spite of the death of Purvis, the importance of the Mission was underlined by the senior status of its two chiefs, Lord Beaverbrook for Britain and Averell Harriman for the United States. Both were masters of the questions of production and supply; it was Beaverbrook who, in the summer of 1940, as Minister of Aircraft Production, had ensured that the maximum possible number of fighter planes had been manufactured in the quickest possible time. For as long as the Russian front 'remained in being', Churchill explained to his War Cabinet on his return to London, 'we might have to make some sacrifices' as far as British supplies from the United States were concerned. He had 'thought it right', he said, to give Roosevelt a warning 'that he would not answer for the consequences if Russia was compelled to sue for peace and, say, by the spring of next year, hope died in Britain that the United States were coming into the war'.

On August 12, while Churchill was still with Roosevelt off Newfoundland, two squadrons of British fighters, forty aircraft in all, commanded by a New Zealander, Wing Commander Ramsbottom-Isherwood, left Britain on HMS *Argus* for Murmansk and Archangel. Even before the British fighters reached Murmansk, two British submarines, *Tigris* and *Trident*, had managed to make their way to the Soviet naval base at Polyarnoe, near Murmansk. There, they at once began operations against German troop transports and coastal shipping off the northern Norwegian and Finnish coastlines.

In the conquered regions of Russia, the terrorising of the population continued. On August 13, as Dr Moses Brauns, a Jewish doctor in Kovno, later recalled, three hungry Jews bought a few pounds of potatoes from a Lithuanian peasant on a street just outside the ghetto. The Germans punished this desperate purchase by rounding up twenty-eight Jews at random, and shooting them. On the following day, August 15, at Roskiskis, near the former Lithuanian–Latvian border, a two-day orgy of killing began, in which 3,200 Jews were shot, together, as the Special Task Force reported, with 'five Lithuanian Communists, 1 Pole, 1 partisan'. In Stawiski, near the former German–Soviet border, six hundred Jews were shot that day. Also on August 15, in Minsk, Hinrich Lohse issued a decree for the whole of German-occupied Russia, ordering every Jew to wear two yellow badges – one on the chest, one on the back – not to walk on the pavements, not to use public transport, not to visit parks, playgrounds, theatres, cinemas, libraries or museums; and to receive in the ghetto only food which was 'surplus' to local needs. All able-bodied Jews were to join labour gangs and to work at tasks laid down by the occupation authorities, such as road-building, bridge-building and repairing bomb damage.

On the day of Lohse's decree, casting the Jews of German-occupied Russia into a net of restrictions and isolation, Richard Sorge was able to send a radio message from Tokyo to Moscow, reporting that the Japanese Government had confirmed its unwillingness to enter the war against Russia. A war against Russia 'before the winter season', so it had been decided, 'would exert an excessive strain on the Japanese economy'. It was a welcome confirmation; that day, more than a hundred German bombers struck at Chudovo railway station, on the Leningrad–Moscow railway line.

On August 18 the Russians evacuated the Black Sea port of Nikolayev. At Hitler's headquarters, von Brauchitsch proposed a resumption of the attack on Moscow. He was overruled. The main German thrust, Hitler insisted, must be to the Crimea, the southern Russian industrial areas, and the Caucasus. In the north, the pressure on Leningrad must be intensified. Moscow could wait. But, Hitler told Goebbels that same day, he hoped to be 'beyond' Moscow by the time winter set in.

Goebbels had come to Rastenburg to raise two specific matters. The first was the growing protest inside Germany against the euthanasia programme. On August 3, in Münster, the Bishop, Count Clemens von Galen, had denounced the euthanasia killings from his pulpit. Public unease inside Germany was growing. Bowing to this unease, Hitler ordered the euthanasia programme to be brought to an end: the order was issued to Dr Brack on August 24.

It was indeed a 'job' of Himmler's that was the second matter raised by Goebbels on August 18. When the German soldier came back to Germany after the war, he urged, 'he must not find any Jews here waiting for him'. There were 76,000 Jews in Berlin. Hitler agreed, as Goebbels noted in his diary, 'that as soon as the first transport possibilities arise, the Berlin Jews will be deported from Berlin to the East. There they will be taken in hand under a somewhat harsher climate.'

Hitler now reminisced about his 'prophecy' of January 1939, that if the Jews 'once more succeeded in provoking a world war', it would end with the destruction of Jewry. Hitler was convinced, Goebbels noted in his diary, that his prophecy 'is coming true'. Goebbels added: 'It is coming true these weeks and months with a dread certainty that is almost uncanny. In the East, the Jews will have to square accounts. . . .'

On the day of this discussion at Rastenburg, some of these 'accounts' were indeed being 'squared'. In Kovno, a mere 120 miles from Rastenburg, a Lithuanian working for the German authorities in the city, had ordered 534 Jewish writers, intellectuals, professors, teachers and students to report at the ghetto gate for 'work in the city archives'. Many volunteered for what appeared to be a not too onerous task, perhaps even an interesting one. Among the volunteers was Robert Stenda, who before the war had been leader of the orchestra at the Kovno Opera House. 'They saw the promise of money and better food', one young Kovno Jew, Stenda's friend Joseph Kagan, later recalled, 'and perhaps better conditions for their families'. The Jews set off. 'The relatives waited that evening for their return,' Kagan wrote. 'They waited through the next day, and the next. The pick of the ghetto's young men did not return.' All had been taken on the day of the selection to one of the old forts that surrounded the city, and shot.

East of Kovno, the battles continued; that August 18, a young German Army officer, Lieutenant Kurt Waldheim, who had seen continuous action at the front for almost two weeks, was among those who received the Cavalry Assault Badge, in recognition of his valour. 'For the good of the German people,' Hitler told his visitors at Rastenburg on August 19, 'we must wish for a war every fifteen or twenty years. An army whose sole purpose is to preserve peace leads only to playing at soldiers – look at Sweden and Switzerland.'

Determined to plan the style of his victory, on August 20 Hitler instructed Albert Speer that, in the monumental centre of the new Berlin, thirty captured Soviet heavy artillery pieces would be placed between the remodelled south station and the yet to be erected triumphal arch. Any 'extra large' Soviet tanks that were captured would be reserved for setting up in front of the important public buildings. Both the artillery pieces and the tanks would be placed on granite pedestals.

That night, the first German armoured units reached Gatchina, only twenty-five miles from Leningrad. On the following day they captured Chudovo, cutting the railway line between Leningrad and Moscow. Even as the siege of Leningrad began, the Australian troops besieged in Tobruk for the past four months, having lost 832 men killed, sailed away from the city and back to Egypt, to be replaced by British troops. After the soldiers' sufferings in Greece and Crete, their commanders, and the politicians on the other side of the globe, were insistent that they should be pulled out; around Tobruk, 7,000 had been taken prisoner.

On August 20, Italian troops on the Dalmatian coast of Yugoslavia occupied the town of Gospic and the island of Pag. In both places they found evidence of the mass murder of Serbs and Jews by the local Ustachi fascists. On Pag, 791 corpses were exhumed, of which 293 were women and 91 were children. In the camp at Jadovno, twelve miles from Gospic, at least 3,500 Jews and Serbs had been murdered since mid-July, some beaten to death while at forced labour, and others shot.

In the early hours of August 21, in the former Yugoslav city of Sabac, Jews and Serbs were massacred in the streets as a reprisal against an attack on a German patrol. Other Jews were then rounded up and ordered to hang the corpses from lamp-posts. 'How can one hang a dead person,' Mara Jovanovic asked, recalling that terrible morning, 'and who will summon the courage to do it? A noose was put around one victim's neck, while the rest of the rope lay in the blood. People hurry by, their heads bent. . . .' On the next day the Jews were ordered to cut the bodies down, and take them away in rubbish trucks. 'There was not a soul who did not mourn', Mara Jovanovic recalled, 'not only for the dead in the lorries but also for the living behind the lorries.'

Also on August 21, in Paris, a twenty-two year old Communist, Pierre Georges, who was later to adopt the code name 'Fabien', shot and killed a young German officer-cadet in a Métro station. It was the first violent act against a German in Paris since the occupation more than a year earlier. More than a hundred and fifty Frenchmen were rounded up and shot as a reprisal.

That August, British Signals Intelligence had several successes, including glimpses of German rule in the East. One particular success in the global sphere was to intercept the text of a radio message from the Japanese Ambassador in Berlin, reporting on a conversation with Hitler, in which Hitler had assured him that 'in the event of a collision between Japan and the United States, Germany would at once open hostilities with the United States'. A decrypt of this telegram was immediately sent to Roosevelt. Another Intelligence success was the intercepting of German police messages sent from the East by Enigma on seventeen separate occasions, beginning on August 23 and continuing for eight days, setting out details of the shooting of Jews in groups numbering from 61 to 4,200; 'whole districts are being exterminated', Churchill revealed, in a broadcast to the British people on August 25. 'Scores of thousands, literally scores of thousands, of executions in cold blood are being perpetrated by the German police-troops upon the Russian patriots who defend their native soil. Since the Mongol invasions of Europe in the sixteenth century, there has never been methodical, merciless butchery on such a scale, or approaching such a scale'.

Churchill could make no specific reference to the Jews; had he done so, it would have indicated to the Germans that British Intelligence was receiving their most secret messages. But he did make it clear that the Germans were carrying out what he called 'the most frightful cruelties', telling his listeners: 'We are in the presence of a crime without a name.'

On August 25, British and Indian forces launched Operation Countenance, the occupation of the southern oilfield region of Iran, while Soviet troops entered Iran from the north. That same day, the British and Soviet ambassadors in Teheran, acting in unison, presented an ultimatum to the Iranian Government, requiring them to accept the 'protection' of the two Allies. Three days later, after protesting against this Anglo-Soviet 'aggression', the Shah, Reza Pahlavi, abdicated in favour of his son. In another Anglo-Soviet enterprise on August 25, Operation Gauntlet, British, Canadian and Norwegian commando units landed on the Norwegian island of Spitzbergen, in the Arctic Ocean. There, they destroyed coal stores, mining machinery and oil reserves, to prevent them being used by the Germans, and evacuated two thousand Russian civilians, who were then taken southward to Archangel on board the *Empress of Canada*. Also evacuated from Spitzbergen were fifty French officers who, having been captured by the Germans in France in May 1940 and taken to a prisoner-of-war camp in East Prussia, had then escaped to Russia, hoping to join the Free French forces. Instead, the Russians had interned them on Spitzbergen. Now they were free to fight again.

On August 26 the German forces in the Ukraine captured the industrial city of Dnepropetrovsk. Much of its industry, however, had earlier been evacuated to the Urals, leaving only empty buildings. That same day, Hitler was host to

Mussolini, showing him the battlefield of Brest-Litovsk, the citadel of which had been reduced to rubble by his mortar 'Fritz'. That day, near Velikiye Luki, the Russians launched a counter-attack, but were halted within twenty-four hours.

In Moscow, on August 27, the Russians published the casualty figures for the twenty-four German air raids on the capital since the German bombing had started on July 27; in all, 750 Muscovites had been killed. That night, in Leningrad, the poetess Vera Inber recalled over the radio the words of Alexander Herzen, the nineteenth-century writer, that 'tales of the burning of Moscow, of the Battle of Borodino, of the Berezina Battle, of the fall of Paris, were the fairy stories of my childhood, my *Iliad* and my *Odyssey*'. In these present days, Vera Inber told her listeners, Russia was creating for future generations new *Odysseys*, new *Iliads*. That night, the Russians began the evacuation of 23,000 soldiers and civilians by sea from the Baltic port of Tallinn. In this Baltic 'Dunkirk', Admiral Tributs commanded an evacuation fleet of 190 ships which had to traverse 150 miles of water between two coasts occupied by the Germans. Of his twenty-nine large troop transports, twenty-five were sunk, and more than five thousand soldiers and civilians drowned. The heroism of the sailors entered into legend; of the thirty-five crew members on one troop transport, the *Kazakh-stan*, only seven survived; each one was awarded the Order of the Red Banner. Their commanding officer, however, Captain Vyacheslav Kaliteyev, who was said to have left his ship at a crucial moment, without reason, was later accused of desertion under fire and cowardice. He was executed by firing squad.

As the Tallinn evacuation continued throughout August 28, in the Ukraine, the Russians destroyed the Zaporozhe dam on the Dnieper river to prevent its hydro-electric power being used by the Germans. That day, Hitler and Mussolini flew over that part of the Ukraine which was already conquered, to Field Marshal von Rundstedt's headquarters at Uman. Two hundred miles west of Uman, twenty-three thousand Jews were being murdered at Kamenets Podolsk. They had been deported from Hungary by the Hungarian Government. The German civil authorities in the region had demanded that the Jews be taken back, as they 'could not cope' with them. The Hungarian Government had refused. It was then that an ss General, Franz Jaeckeln, had assured the German civil administration that he would 'complete the liquidation of those Jews by September 1'. Marched to a series of bomb craters outside the city, and ordered to undress, the Jews were then mown down by machine gun fire. Many of them, gravely wounded, died under the weight of the bodies that fell on top of them, or were 'finished off' with pistol shots. By August 29, the task was done, two days in advance of Jaeckeln's promised date. Operational Situation Report No. 80 gave the precise figures of those shot as 23,600 'in three days'.

The death toll in the East was on an unprecedented scale; ten thousand Soviet evacuees had been drowned off Tallinn, and twenty-three thousand Hungarian Jews murdered at Kamenets Podolsk, in the same three day period. But these were far from the only deaths in those few August days. During those same three days, several thousand German soldiers, and several thousand Russian soldiers, had been killed in action on the battlefield. A list of all those killed may never be compiled. Yet in their meticulous records the Germans ensured that a clear pattern of the killing would at least be transmitted to the authorities in Berlin, to be filed. At Kedainiai, in Lithuania, the Special Task Force assigned to Lithuania noted its particular killing statistics on August 28 as '710 Jewish men, 767 Jewish women, 599 Jewish children': a further 2,076 victims of an unequal war which was being fought far behind the battlefield. Nor had the cancellation of the euthanasia programme brought any end to the killing by gas; on August 28 Dr Horst Schumann, the director of the euthanasia centre at Grafeneck, near Stuttgart, visited Auschwitz, where he participated in the selection of 575 prisoners, most of them Soviet prisoners-of-war, who were then sent to the medical experimental centre at Sonnenstein, near Dresden. None of them survived.

On the day of Dr Schumann's visit to Auschwitz, Pastor Bernard Lichtenburg, Provost of St Hedwig's Roman Catholic Cathedral in Berlin, unaware that the openly approved euthanasia programme was being stopped that very day, wrote a letter of protest to the Chief Physician of the Reich, Dr Leonardo Conti. 'I, as a human being, a Christian, a priest and a German,' wrote Lichtenburg, 'demand of you, the Chief Physician of the Reich, that you answer for the crimes that have been perpetrated at your bidding and with your consent, and which will call forth the vengeance of the Lord on the heads of the German people.' Lichtenburg was arrested, and sentenced to two years in prison. He died while being transferred, still a prisoner, to Dachau concentration camp. In the course of the euthanasia 'action', carried out under the code name 'T4', more than 80,000 mental patients and 10,000 concentration-camp prisoners had been gassed between September 1939 and August 1941; an average of nearly four thousand a month, or more than a hundred a day.

On August 29, Finnish forces, advancing towards Leningrad from the north, recaptured Terioki, which they had been forced to cede to the Soviet Union at the beginning of 1940. On reaching Terioki, however, they advanced no further. Despite German pressure, the Finnish Government had decided not to advance in the Leningrad region beyond the pre-1939 frontier. East of Leningrad, however, Finnish units were advancing towards the shore of Lake Onega, threatening to cut Russian communications between the Baltic and the White Sea. On the following day, August 30, German forces occupied the village of Mga, cutting off the last and most easterly railway link between Leningrad and the rest of Russia. But they were driven out of the village on the following day.

The Russians used every possible armament with which to defend Leningrad. On 30 August the naval guns of the Neva squadron had gone into action against the German positions at Gatchina. On the following day, more than 340 shells were fired. Many naval guns were taken from their ships and mounted on land. Even the gun batteries of the forty-year-old cruiser *Aurora*, which had fired blanks on the Winter Palace in November 1917, frightening the remnants of the Provisional Government into surrendering to the Bolsheviks, were dismounted, and placed in position on the Pulkovo heights.

In German-occupied Vilna, August 31 saw a German 'action' against the Jews

The Siege of Leningrad, October 1941–January 1944

of the city. One eye witness, Aba Kovner, saw two soldiers dragging a woman away by the hair. As they did so, a bundle fell from her arms. It was her baby boy. One of the soldiers bent down, 'took the infant, raised him into the air, grasped him by the leg. The woman crawled on the earth, took hold of his boot and pleaded for mercy. But the soldier took the boy and hit him with his head against the wall, once, twice, smashed him against the wall.'

That night, according to the precise German records of the 'action', 2,019

Jewish women, 864 men and 817 children were taken out of the city on trucks to the pits at Ponar, where they were shot. The Operational Situation Report compiled in Berlin called it 'special treatment'.

On September 1, the Germans recaptured Mga. Leningrad was now entirely cut off by rail from the rest of Russia. Throughout the previous month, a massive factory-evacuation scheme had been put into operation; the equipment of ninety-two factories had been taken out by rail, on a total of 282 trains, the two largest heavy tank works being relocated 1,200 miles to the east, at Chelyabinsk and Sverdlovsk. On September 3, two days after the recapture of Mga, Field Marshal Keitel assured the commander of the forces attacking Leningrad, Field Marshal von Leeb, that Hitler had no objection either to the shelling of the city or to its bombardment from the air.

Two years had passed since the German invasion of Poland in 1939. In the East, seventy days had passed since the German invasion of the Soviet Union. The victorious German war machine destroyed whatever it wished to destroy: Polish intellectuals, Soviet prisoners-of-war, Yugoslav partisans, French resistance fighters, each felt the full force of superior power. The Jews, scattered among many nations, were singled out for torture, murder and abuse. In Germany, September 1 marked the day on which all the remaining Jews of Germany, including the 76,000 in Berlin, were ordered to wear a yellow of Star of David on their clothing. Two days later, there was yet another experiment to find the most effective method of mass murder, without the publicly visible horrors and – for the executioners – often demoralizing methods of the pit executions. Six hundred Soviet prisoners-of-war and three hundred Jews were brought to Auschwitz, and gassed with prussic acid. This experiment, like the one which had preceded it, was judged a success.

On September 4, the United States destroyer *Greer* was attacked by a German submarine off Iceland. The submarine had wrongly attributed to the *Greer* the depth charges which had been dropped against it by a British aircraft. The *Greer* reached Iceland safely. 'From now on,' declared President Roosevelt, 'if German or Italian vessels of war enter these waters, they do so at their own peril.' With Roosevelt's words, an undeclared state of war existed between the United States and Germany in the North Atlantic. Ironically, two days after the attack on the *Greer*, a United States merchant ship, the *Steel Seafarer*, on her way to Egypt, was sunk by a German aircraft in the Red Sea, 220 miles south of Suez.

On the Eastern Front, Soviet forces recaptured Yelnya on September 6, their first major counter-attack since the Soviet–German war had begun two and a half months earlier. For the Moscow front, it was a considerable relief. Hitler now abandoned the Crimea–Caucasus strategy which he had laid down so emphatically on August 12, declaring in Directive No. 35, issued from Rastenburg, that conditions were now favourable for a 'decisive' operation on the central front. The new assault, on Moscow, was to be given the code name 'Typhoon'.

On September 8, while Operation Typhoon was still in its planning stage, German forces captured Schlüsselburg, on Lake Ladoga. At the same time, the

SWEDEN

FINLAND

Helsinki

Hango

*Gulf of Finland*

*Baltic Sea*

Lake Ladoga

Lake Onega

Tallinn

ESTONIA

Volkhov

Leningrad

Tikhvin

Tartu

*Lake Peipus*

*Lake Ilmen*

Pskov

Lushno

Kalinin

Libava

Riga

Zagare

Siauliai

Dvinsk

Rzhev

Zagorsk

Borodino

Moscow

Rastenburg

GERMANY

Kovno

Mozhaisk

Vilna

Vitebsk

Vyazma

Ryazan

Eisiskes

Smolensk

Yelnya

Kaluga

Shilovo

Butrimonys

Borisov

Shklov

Gorky

Minsk

Mogilev

Mstislavl

Maly Trostenets

Kletsk

Slutsk

GREATER

S O V I E T     U N I O N

Krasnaya Gora

Bryansk

Orel

Ovruch

Kursk

Rovno

Korosten

Nezhin

Radomyshl

Kiev

Belgorod

Berdichev

Fastov

Staraya Sinyava

Khmelnik

Lubny

Kharkov

Pilva

Vinnitsa

Poltava

Umane

Kremenchug

*River Donetz*

Kramatorsk

Dnepropetrovsk

Krivoi Rog

Stalino

Rostov-on-Don

HUNGARY

ROUMANIA

Taganrog

Mariupol

Nikolayev

Berdyansk

*River Don*

Odessa

Kherson

Perekop

*Sea of Azov*

*Black Sea*

CRIMEA

Kerch

*Caucasus*

Sevastopol

Yalta

1 October 1941

15 October 1941

2 September 1941

0    miles    150

0    kilometres    200

© Martin Gilbert 1989

The Eastern Front, September and October 1941

Finns cut the Leningrad–Murmansk railway at Lodeinoye Polye: Leningrad was besieged. That same day, German bombers dropped more than six thousand incendiary bombs on the city, destroying hundreds of tons of meat, flour, sugar, lard and butter in the four acre Badayev warehouse.

Far to the south-east, on September 8, on the River Volga, the eastward deportation began of all 600,000 ethnic Germans who had lived in the Volga region for two centuries. With the German forces already poised to enter Kiev, Stalin feared possible sabotage and subversion, and took the draconian steps of deporting a whole people. Henceforth, a hundred towns and villages along the Volga, from Marxstadt to Strassburg, were to be empty of their German-speaking inhabitants.

On September 9, the Soviet commander of the South-Western Front, Marshal Budyenny, asked Stalin's permission to abandon Kiev. Stalin refused. That day, in the North Atlantic, a German submarine 'wolf pack' of as many as sixteen U-boats attacked a convoy of sixty-five merchant ships being escorted to Britain by Canadian corvettes from Sydney, Cape Breton. In the ensuing battle, fifteen of the merchantmen were sunk, but not before one of the German attackers, U-501, was forced to the surface by depth charges from two further Canadian corvettes, *Chambly* and *Moosejaw*, both of which had been on a training voyage when news of the action reached them. Shortly after this success, *Chambly* was bombed by German aircraft; she too was sunk.

As the convoy proceeded, it was attacked again, but without loss, one of its attackers, U-207, being sunk.

On September 9, British cryptologists at Bletchley decrypted the German orders for Operation Typhoon, the planned attack on Moscow. That same day, Field Marshal von Leeb launched his attack on Leningrad. As the Germans drew closer to the city's suburbs, the naval guns of the cruiser *Maxim Gorky*, the battleship *October Revolution* and the battleship *Marat* sent a massive barrage of shells on to the German forward positions. An SS division, which had participated in May in the German parachute landing on Crete, was ordered to cross the River Neva north-west of Mga, and to attack Leningrad from the north. Lacking sufficient pontoons, it was unable to do so.

On September 10, as the German forces of Army Group North pressed in upon Leningrad, and those of Army Group Centre put the final touches to their plans for a two-pronged attack towards Moscow, Hitler ordered yet another change of priority: before attacking Moscow, his commanders must complete the encirclement of the Russian forces still holding out, tenaciously, in the central Ukraine. The new order, issued on September 10, was not so easily fulfilled; Russian troops fought tenaciously for two weeks to keep open the trap which was closing around them east of Kiev, between Nezhin and Lubny. By September 16 the trap had closed, and 600,000 Russian soldiers captured. The Germans then renewed their march on Moscow; but the two weeks lost were two weeks which brought nearer the danger which was now being spoken of openly at German headquarters – the encroaching winter. 'We are heading for a winter campaign. The real trial of this war has begun', General von Waldau had written in his diary on September 9, one day before the change of plan, but he added: 'My belief in final victory remains.'

On September 10, the day of his order to switch priority from Moscow to the Ukraine, Hitler took the Hungarian Regent, Admiral Horthy, to the East Prussian town of Marienburg. 'We don't have your Jewish problem,' Hitler told the Hungarian leader. What he did not tell him was the specific fate of the Jews under German rule. On the following day, the Operational Situation Report No. 80 of the Special Task Forces noted that, in the town of Korosten, 238 Jews 'who were rounded up and driven to a special building by the Ukrainian militia, were shot'. In nearby Fastov, 'all the Jewish inhabitants' between the ages of twelve and sixty were shot, 'making a total of 262 heads', bringing the 'total executions' of that particular Special Task Force during August to '7,152 persons'.

'We don't have your Jewish problem': while Hitler was telling Admiral Horthy this, on September 10, one of Hitler's overseas rulers, Josef Terboven, was proclaiming a state of emergency in Oslo. The mass arrest of trade union leaders began at once. Newspaper editors and journalists were dismissed. That evening Oslo radio announced that the labour unions' legal adviser, Viggo Hansteen, and the principal shop steward at a railway carriage works, Rolf Wickström, had been sentenced to death by court martial, and already executed. That same day, in the Slovak capital of Bratislava, the Slovak Government, following Germany's lead, issued a Codex Judaicum, removing the legal rights of Slovakia's 135,000 Jews.

Also on the night of September 10, German bombers again raided Leningrad. The city's creamery was hit, destroying tons of butter. The principal shipyard was badly damaged, and eighty fires started. By morning, more than two hundred of Leningrad's citizens were dead. Not only ordinary bombs, but delayed-action bombs dropped by parachute, had added to the city's torment.

On September 11, Marshal Budyenny again appealed to Stalin to to be allowed to begin 'a general withdrawal' from Kiev. His appeal was also signed by the senior Party official in the city, Nikita Khrushchev. Within hours, Budyenny was dismissed. Telephoning to General Kirponos in Kiev, Stalin told his commanders: 'Cease, after all, searching for new lines to retreat to, and search for ways to resist, and only resist.'

Stalin and his generals were struggling to find some means of holding on to what remained of western Russia, more than a third of which was now in German hands. In the United States, Major Albert C. Wedemeyer, who had been the American soldier–student at the German Staff College in Berlin from 1936 to 1938, estimated, on September 11, that Germany would have occupied all of Russia west of the 'general line: White Sea, Moscow, Volga River (all inclusive) by 1 July 1942, and that militarily Russia will be substantially impotent subsequent to that date'.

On September 12, the first snow flurries fell on the Russian front. But no snow settled. That same day, with his Moscow offensive, Operation Typhoon, calling out for the maximum possible armoured reinforcements, Hitler ordered a halt to the advance into Leningrad. Instead, the city was to be starved into submission. Five German tank divisions, two motorized divisions and much of the air support of von Leeb's army, were to leave the Leningrad front within a week. Von Leeb protested. The thirty Soviet divisions trapped in the city were on the brink of destruction. The German tank crews nearest the city could see the golden spires of the Admiralty building.

Hitler refused to change his decision. East of Kiev, his troops under von Kleist and Guderian had successfully trapped fifty Russian divisions in an enormous pocket. First Kiev, and then Moscow, were the prizes he now sought. This change of plan was passed on to Stalin by his 'Red Orchestra' agents in Paris, headed by Leopold Trepper. The Soviet High Command could therefore adjust its defensive plans to meet the reinforced thrusts.

The day on which Hitler ordered the transfer of his armoured forces from the Leningrad to the Moscow front, a briefing was held in his headquarters at Rastenburg which began: 'High-ranking political figures and leaders are to be eliminated.' The 'struggle against Bolshevism', Field Marshal Keitel explained to his commanders that day, 'demands ruthless and energetic measures, above all against the Jews, the main carriers of Bolshevism'. That same day, September 12, the British eavesdroppers at Bletchley decrypted a German Police Regiment message that it had 'disposed' of 1,255 Jews near Ovruch 'according to the usage of war'.

It was on September 12 that the British Royal Air Force Wing was first in action in Northern Russia. That day from its base at Vianga, seventeen miles north-east of Murmansk, it shot down three German aircraft for the loss of one of its own. For their activities in Russia at so desperate a time, the unit's commander, Wing Commander H. N. G. Ramsbottom-Isherwood, and three of his airmen, were each awarded the Order of Lenin, the only members of the Allied forces to be honoured in this way.

The defence of Leningrad was now being directed by Marshal Zhukov, who, on September 14, ordered a counter-attack on the German positions at Schlüsselburg. When the local commander, General Shcherbakov, replied that 'it simply could not be done', he was removed from his command, together with his political commissar, Chukhov. Learning of desertions in the Slutsk–Kolpino section of the siege line, Stalin himself ordered the 'merciless destruction' of those who were serving as 'helpers' of the Germans. Order No. 0098 informed the defenders of Leningrad of executions carried out as a result of Stalin's order. Two more outposts of the city were to fall on September 16, the town of Pushkin, and the city's tramcar terminus at Alexandrovka; but the defence perimeter held. No German troops were to march along the city's boulevards.

With the imminent halt of the German advance on Leningrad, the city's airport north of the Neva, to which Zhukov had flown on September 11, remained under Soviet control. Beginning on September 13, and ending two and a half months later, a total of six thousand tons of high-priority freight was flown in: 1,660 tons of arms and munitions and 4,325 tons of food. Hitler's confidence in victory over Russia was, however, undiminished; on September 15 the German diplomat, Baron Ernst von Weizsäcker, noted in his diary, of his leader's mood: 'An autobahn is being planned to the Crimean peninsula. There is speculation as to the probable manner of Stalin's departure. If he withdraws into Asia, he might even be granted a peace treaty.' It was at this very time, in mid-September, Albert Speer later recalled, that Hitler ordered 'considerable increases' in the purchase of granite from Sweden, Norway and Finland, for the monumental buildings planned for Berlin and Nuremberg.

In Paris, the most westerly capital under Hitler's rule, September 16 saw the execution of ten hostages, most of them Jews, in a reprisal for attacks by members of the French Resistance on German trucks and buildings. That same day, the German Ambassador to Paris, Otto Abetz, was at Rastenburg, where Hitler told him of his plans for the East. Leningrad would be razed to the ground; it was the 'poisonous nest' from which, for so long, Asiatic venom had 'spewed forth'. The Asiatics and the Bolsheviks must be hounded out of Europe, bringing an end to 'two hundred and fifty years of Asiatic pestilence'. The Urals would become the new frontier; Russia west of the Urals would be Germany's 'India'. The iron-ore fields at Krivoi Rog alone would provide Germany with a million tons of ore a month. From this economically self-sufficient New Order, Hitler assured Abetz, France would have its share; but must first agree to take part in the defeat of Britain.

Inside that New Order, a young German Army officer, Lieutenant Erwin Bingel, was at Uman on September 16. There, as he recalled four years later, he saw SS troops and Ukrainian militiamen murder several hundred Jews. The Jews were taken to a site outside the town, lined up in rows, forced to undress, and mowed down with machine gun fire. 'Even women carrying children a fortnight to three weeks old, sucking at their breasts', Bingel recalled, 'were not spared this horrible ordeal. Nor were mothers spared the sight of their children being gripped by their little legs and put to death with one stroke of the pistol butt or club, thereafter to be thrown on the heap of human bodies in the ditch....'

Two of Lieutenant Bingel's men suffered a 'complete nervous breakdown' as a result of what they saw. Two others were sentenced to a year each in a military prison for having taken 'snapshots' of the action. The two Operational Situation Reports that week, No. 86 of September 17 and No. 88 of September 19 – No. 87 has never been found  gave the statistics of the unceasing slaughter: these were, in part, 229 Jews killed in Khmelnik, six hundred in Vinnitsa; 105 in Krivoi Rog, together with 39 Communist officials; 511 in Pilva and Staraya Sinyava; fifty in Tartu, together with 455 local Communists; 1,107 Jewish adults and 561 'juveniles', the latter killed by Ukrainian militia, in Radomysl; 627 Jewish men and 875 'Jewesses over twelve years' in Berdichev; and 544 'insane persons' taken from the lunatic asylum in Dvinsk 'with the assistance of the Latvian self-defence unit'. Ten of the inmates, judged 'partially cured', were sterilized and then discharged. 'After this action,' the Report concluded, 'the asylum no longer exists.'

On September 16, as Hitler spoke with such confidence at Rastenburg, a transatlantic convoy, HX 150, set sail from Halifax, Nova Scotia. It was the first convoy to be escorted by American warships. On September 17, in northern Russia, the British Royal Air Force Wing was in action for the second time. That same day, the last assault by von Leeb on Leningrad failed to break through the city's defences; that day, he had finally to begin the despatch of his tank forces to the Moscow front. 'There will be a continuing drain on our forces before Leningrad,' a worried General Halder noted in his diary on September 18, 'where the enemy has concentrated large forces and great quantities of material, and the situation will remain tight until such a time when hunger takes effect as our ally'.

Hitler was still in optimistic mood on September 17, telling his guests at Rastenburg of the future demise of Russia. The Crimea would provide Germany with its citrus fruits, cotton and rubber: 'We'll supply grain to all in Europe who need it.' The Russians would be denied education: 'We'll find among them the human material that's indispensable for tilling the soil.' The German settlers and rulers in Russia would have to constitute among themselves 'a closed society, like a fortress. The least of our stable-lads must be superior to any native.'

German forces were now on the very outskirts of Kiev, the Soviet Union's third largest city after Moscow and Leningrad. On September 16, following four days of urgent appeals from General Kirponos to Stalin that it would soon be too late to pull back his troops from the city and its surroundings, Marshal Timoshenko had authorized the withdrawal from Kiev. It was another forty-eight hours, however, before Stalin confirmed the order. On September 18, as the belated withdrawal began, General Kirponos's thousand-strong command column was ambushed and encircled. Hit by mine splinters in the head and chest, Kirponos died in less than two minutes. His armies fought bravely to escape the trap. Although 15,000 did succeed in breaking out, as many as half a million were taken prisoner. For the Red Army, it was a grave and massive loss of fighting strength. But the Germans were not without cause for concern of their own; that week it was announced from Berlin that 86,000 German soldiers had been killed since the invasion of Russia had begun three months earlier.

There was further cause for concern in German military circles that September, as Tito's forces gathered strength inside German-occupied Yugoslavia. In the early hours of September 17, a British submarine, operating from Malta, landed a British agent, Colonel D. T. Hudson, on the Dalmatian coast, near Petrovac. He at once made contact both with Tito, and with the Cetnik leader, Mihailović.

A week after Hudson reached Yugoslavia, Tito's partisans, 70,000 men in all, but with few weapons and little ammunition, captured the town of Uzice, with its rifle factory producing four hundred rifles a day. They were to hold the town for two months. Resistance in Yugoslavia, as in Russia, had begun to harass and tie down considerable numbers of German troops.

# 18

# Russia at bay

SEPTEMBER–OCTOBER 1941

On 19 September 1941, German forces entered Kiev. That day, Leningrad suffered its worst air and artillery bombardment of the war, with 276 German bombers breaking through the city's anti-aircraft defences. More than a thousand citizens were killed, including many who, already wounded, were in one of the city's hospitals when it was hit. Two days later, on September 21, 180 bombers struck at Leningrad's principal defensive island, Kronstadt, seriously damaging the naval dockyard.

From London, with Churchill's authority, British Intelligence sent Stalin a series of warnings between September 20 and 25, based upon the reading of the most secret German Vulture messages being sent to and from the Eastern Front, giving details of German intentions and movements on the Moscow front. These details included information on the location and strength of German air and ground concentrations in the Smolensk area. For Britain herself, however, the end of the second week of September brought bad news at sea. On September 20, a convoy of merchant ships bound for Gibraltar lost five of its twenty-seven ships when German submarines struck. Morale was briefly raised when a German aircraft, flying over the convoy and radioing U-boat commanders of the location of the merchantmen, was shot down by one of the escort vessels. One of the merchant ships, however, the *Walmer Castle*, leaving the convoy to rescue survivors of two of the torpedoed ships, was bombed from the air, and sunk. Then, on September 21, the German submarines disappeared; they had found another target, a convoy on its way to Britain from Sierra Leone. In three nights, nine of its twenty-seven ships were sunk.

On the Eastern front, SS units fought alongside the regular German Army formations. Sometimes their brutality was particularly in evidence, as on September 23, when, near Krasnaya Gora, in reprisal for the killing of three SS sentries, the inhabitants of a whole village were lined up and machine-gunned. Sometimes it was the fearlessness of an SS man that was seen, as on September 24, at Lushno, when an SS corporal, Fritz Christen, after every soldier in his battery had been killed, remained at his gun, knocking out thirteen Soviet tanks.

The first Death's Head soldier to be awarded the Iron Cross First Class with the coveted Knight's Cross, Christen was later flown to Rastenburg to be decorated personally by Hitler.

In the Far East, the Japanese were making plans to start their war with the United States by means of a daring raid on the American naval base at Pearl Harbour, in mid-Pacific. On September 24 the Japanese Consul in Hawaii, Nagai Kita, was instructed to divide Pearl Harbour into five zones, and to report back to Japan on the precise number of warships moored in each zone. American Signals Intelligence in Hawaii intercepted this message, but, having no decrypting facilities, had to send it back to Washington by Pan Am Clipper. There was only one flight a week; but the weekly flight on September 26 was cancelled because of bad weather. The intercept was therefore sent by sea, reaching Washington on October 6. Shortage of decrypting staff, and the fact that the message was not in the very highest grade of codes, led to a further three days' delay; but even then, with the message finally decrypted, it was not considered to be more than a routine espionage assignment, typical of those in a dozen other places, such as similar orders which were being decrypted from Japanese agents in Manila, Panama and Seattle.

Stalin, meanwhile, continued to be informed of the contents of the Enigma messages in which the Germans were transmitting their most secret military positions and plans. The only other Russian to be told was the Chief of the General Staff, Marshal Shaposhnikov. Whenever the Russians asked for the source of the messages, Cecil Barclay, the special liaison officer with the British Military Mission, was instructed to maintain the utter secrecy of the intercepts by saying that the information came from an officer in the German War Office.

On September 25, the German forces launched their southern attack. Hitler intended this attack to precede the imminent assault on Moscow, for which German armoured units were even then reassembling after their transfer from the Leningrad front. But this twin drive towards Kharkov and the Crimea, which Hitler had expected to be swiftly accomplished, was to be checked and frustrated by a strong Soviet defence. A new and powerful Russian tank, the T-34, had begun to dominate the battlefield. It was on September 26 that the ss Death's Head Division was first forced to send into action special 'Tank Annihilation Squads' to attack the T-34, against which its hitherto devastating anti-tank guns had proved ineffective. These squads consisted of two officers and ten men who, carrying explosives, mines, grenades and bombs in satchels, had to go forward on foot towards any individual Russian tank that had penetrated through the German defensive line, and to destroy or disable the tank as quickly as possible with their hand-held explosives.

On September 26, an ss Captain, Max Seela, demonstrated what could be done when he destroyed the first of seven Russian tanks which had broken through to the German position. Seela crawled up to the tank on his own, placing two satchels of explosives against the turret, and detonating them with a grenade. He then led his squad forward to destroy the six remaining Soviet tanks. As their crews struggled to escape from their burning vehicles, they were shot down one by one and killed.

Not only in battle, but far behind the lines, cruelty continued to be a daily feature of the war in the East. That September 26, when a Lithuanian policeman patrolling a street in the Kovno ghetto thought that he heard a shot being fired, 1,800 Jews living in the street – men, women and children – were rounded up, loaded on to lorries, driven to one of the pre-First World War forts on the outskirts of the city, and killed. On the following day, on no provocation at all, 3,446 Jews in the Lithuanian town of Eisiskes, including more than eight hundred children, were taken to specially dug pits in the Jewish cemetery, and shot down by machine-gun fire.

The scale of the Special Task Force killings now exceeded anything previously recorded: by the end of September, in a two-day massacre, 33,771 Jews had been murdered in the ravine at Babi Yar, on the outskirts of Kiev, and a further 35,782 'Jews and Communists', according to the same Operational Situation Report – No. 101 of October 2 – in the Black Sea cities of Nikolayev and Kherson. There were German complaints, also, that their work of mass murder was being obstructed. On September 28, at Kremenchug, the Russian mayor, Vershovsky, ordered the baptism of several hundred Jews with a view to protecting them from the slaughter. He was arrested and shot.

On September 27, German forces captured Perekop, cutting off the Crimea from the rest of southern Russia. That day, in the Baltimore Naval Yard, the United States launched a 10,000 ton merchant ship, the *Patrick Henry*, the first of what were to be many thousand of standardized, mass produced vessels, known as 'Liberty ships', and overcoming by their sheer numbers and rapid construction the loss inflicted upon Britain by the incessant German submarine attacks. With many of the parts prefabricated before the final assembly, one such ship, the *Robert E. Peary*, was constructed in the extraordinary record time of four days.

On September 28, the first British convoy of war supplies to Russia, Convoy PQ 1, left Iceland for Archangel. Two days later, Churchill announced in the House of Commons that the whole British tank production of the week just ended was to be sent to Russia. Large quantities of aluminium, rubber and copper, as earlier requested by Stalin, had already been despatched. On October 2, as German forces prepared to launch Operation Typhoon against Moscow, Churchill read the German secret messages giving details of the assault. 'Are you warning the Russians of the developing concentrations?' he asked the head of the Secret Intelligence Service, and he added: 'Show me the last five messages you have sent. . . .'

In Moscow, the Anglo-American Mission headed by Lord Beaverbrook and Averell Harriman was finding out what Russia required, and doing its utmost to meet Stalin's requests. It was the Americans, for example, who were able to satisfy his appeal for four hundred tons of barbed wire a month. On September 30, Lord Beaverbrook agreed to send Russia the whole of Britain's share of her forthcoming supplies from the United States: 1,800 fighter aircraft, 2,250 tanks, 500 anti-tank guns, 23,000 tommy guns, 25,000 tons of copper, 27,000 tons of rubber and 250,000 soldiers' greatcoats.

The extent of Britain's material pledge to Russia was formidable, covering every facet of the naval, air and land war. The Russians were to receive, in nine monthly deliveries, a total of 1,800 British Hurricanes and Spitfires, 900 American fighters and 900 American bombers. For the Soviet Navy, 150 sets of Asdic submarine detection sets were to be supplied, as well as 1,500 naval guns, 3,000 anti-aircraft machine guns and eight destroyers 'before the end of 1941'. For the Red Army, the list of immediate requirements to be provided was staggering, eating into both Britain's and America's essential war needs, and including one thousand tanks a month together with 'a proper complement of accessories and spare parts', three hundred anti-aircraft guns a month, three hundred anti-tank guns a month, and two thousand armoured cars a month, together with their anti-tank guns.

Other Soviet needs which the British and American Governments promised to supply included 4,000 tons of aluminium a month, substantial quantities of copper, tin, lead, brass, nickel and cobalt, 13,000 tons monthly of steel bars for shells, as well as industrial diamonds, machine tools, rubber, wool, jute and lead. For the soldiers of the Red Army, Britain was to provide three million pairs of army boots immediately, followed by 400,000 pairs a month, the Americans sending in addition, also monthly, 200,000 pairs of army shoes. More than a million metres of army cloth were to be supplied each month.

Other Anglo-American committees in Moscow had agreed to supply 20,000 tons a month of petroleum products, including lubricating oil for aviation engines, shipping to enable the transport of cargoes of up to half a million tons a month for food, oil and war material imports, and medical supplies on a vast and comprehensive scale, including more than ten million surgical needles and half a million pairs of surgical gloves.

Other medical supplies sent to Russia included 20,000 amputation knives, 15,000 amputation saws, one hundred portable x-ray sets, four thousand kilogrammes of local anaesthetics, more than a million doses of the recently discovered antibiotics – including M & B 693 – sedatives, heart and brain stimulants, 800,000 forceps – including forceps for bone operations – instruments for brain and eye operations, and a million metres of oilcloth for covering wounds.

Not only Churchill, but his wife Clementine, sought to provide Russia with the military material and medical help needed to resist the renewed German attack; that September Clementine Churchill launched an Aid to Russia Appeal which had an enormous response, especially among British factory workers, where it 'touched', as one civil servant later recalled, 'the feeling of popular sympathy for the Russians in their gallant resistance'. Within a month, the appeal had raised enough money to send to Russia, without delay, fifty-three emergency operating outfits, thirty blood-transfusion sets, 70,000 surgical needles, half a ton – one million doses – of the painkiller phenacetin, and seven tons of absorbent cotton-wool for bandages.

Even as these supplies were being sent to Russia, the eastward move of Russian resources, as far out of reach of the German armies as possible, was approaching its conclusion; by the last week of September, 1,360 heavy industrial plants in western Russia had been successfully transferred to the Urals, western Siberia, the Volga, Kazakhstan and Central Asia. At the same time as this mass of essential war machinery was moving eastwards, on an estimated million and a half railway wagons, the railways were also moving two and a half million soldiers in the other direction, westwards, to the front line. It was a formidable achievement. On September 29, the Soviet Government ordered the evacuation to beyond the Urals of Russia's largest heavy-machine works, at Kramatorsk, south east of Kharkov. Despite continuous German aerial bombardment, the evacuation was ready to begin five days later.

Also on September 29, in Leningrad, plans were drawn up to establish priorities for partisan activity throughout the Leningrad region, including the sabotaging of the siege-gun batteries, and night raids on German barracks and airstrips. On the following day, however, there was another blow to Leningrad's chance of early relief, when Finnish troops broke through to the Soviet positions at Petrozavodsk, on Lake Onega.

As British and American scientists worked towards the development of an atomic bomb, one of their number, Klaus Fuchs, who had come to Britain from Germany as a refugee in 1933, and was a dedicated Communist, began passing the secrets of Tube Alloys – the British and American code name for the project – to his Soviet Embassy contact in London, Simon Davidovich Kremer, a member of the staff of the Military Attaché. Later that year, Fuchs' contact was a German–Jewish refugee, Ruth Kuczynski, code name 'Sonya', whose husband was in the Royal Air Force.

On October 3 the result of the British researches was communicated officially to Professor Conant in the United States, and six days later through him to Roosevelt – and no doubt, through Fuchs, to Stalin. It seemed that the explosive core of an atomic bomb, weighing no more than twenty-five pounds, might explode with a force equivalent to 1,800 tons of TNT. An enormous expenditure was needed, however, to bring the bomb into existence.

As Fuchs worked to alert Russia to Western progress on the atomic bomb, the Germans launched Operation Typhoon, the attack on Moscow. 'Today', Hitler declared in a communiqué broadcast on October 2, 'begins the last, great, decisive battle of the war.' Germany was shortly to have 'the three greatest industrial districts of the Bolsheviks' completely in her hands. 'At last we have created the prerequisites for the final, tremendous blow which, before the onset of winter, will lead to the destruction of the enemy.'

Nearly two thousand tanks advanced that day against the Russian Army. Far behind the lines, October 2 saw the machine gunning, at Zagare, of '633 men, 1,017 women, 496 children', all of them Jews, 150 of whom had been shot down while trying to resist being forced out of the town, and of a further 976 Jews at Butrimonys, where the German Special Task Force had also organized a 'spectacle', placing benches at the execution site so that the local Lithuanians could have a 'good view'.

For ten days the German Army drove forward on the road to Moscow. As the Germans approached each day closer to the capital, Russian peasants set fire to their already harvested crops, drove away their livestock, and blew up the main buildings in their villages. This was the pre-arranged and self-inflicted scorched-earth policy; the Germans were to be denied all but a blackened terrain.

In Paris, on October 2, the ss chief, Helmut Knochen, ordered the destruction of seven synagogues. Six of them were dynamited that night; the seventh, where the fuse had failed, was blown up on the following day 'for safety reasons'.

On the Eastern Front, the Germans seemed finally to have broken their adversary. On October 3, Orel was captured, so quickly that there was no time for the Russians to destroy its remaining factories. Hitler, returning by train to Berlin for a single afternoon, told an enormous crowd in the Sportpalast: 'Forty-eight hours ago there began new operations of gigantic dimensions. They will lead to the destruction of the enemy in the East. The enemy has already been routed and will never regain his strength.'

Hitler was back in Rastenburg on October 4. On that day, in Kovno, less than a hundred and twenty miles away, all the patients, doctors and nurses in the ghetto hospital, as well as the orphans in the adjacent Jewish orphanage, were locked in the building, which was then set on fire. Anyone who managed to break out was shot. Three days later, at Rovno, the mass murder began of more than seventeen thousand Jews.

With the Russian armies driven back to Vyazma and Bryansk in the centre, and forced out of Dnepropetrovsk in the south, the mood of the German generals was jubilant. 'Now the operation is rolling towards Moscow,' the Army's Quartermaster General, Eduard Wagner, wrote privately on October 5. 'Our impression is that the final great collapse is immediately ahead, and that tonight the Kremlin is packing its bags.' As to Hitler's military judgement, Wagner added, 'This time he is intervening – and one can say decisively – in the operation, and so far he has been right every time. The major victory in the south is his work alone.'

On October 6, in the southern sector, German forces entered Berdyansk, taking more than 100,000 Russian prisoners-of-war. That day, further north, the second snow flurries of winter fell. On October 7, snow flurries fell at Hitler's Rastenburg headquarters.

On October 4, and again on October 6, Stalin had learned, direct from Churchill, of the schedule of convoys being sent to Archangel. On October 12, twenty heavy tanks and 193 fighter aircraft would arrive. These would be followed on October 19 by a hundred fighters, 140 heavy tanks, two hundred bren-gun carriers, two hundred anti-tank rifles and fifty heavy guns. On October 22 a third convoy would arrive, with two hundred fighters and two hundred heavy tanks. Each convoy would take seventeen days on its journey around the North Cape, braving Arctic storms and German air strikes.

On October 8, in southern Russia, Mariupol fell to the German advance; Hitler's troops had reached the Sea of Azov. 'In a military sense,' Hitler's Press Chief, Otto Dietrich, told foreign journalists in Berlin on the following day, 'Soviet Russia has been vanquished.' But Soviet resistance had not been broken, nor had the T-34 tanks been overcome. And over the BBC's Foreign Service a German voice murmured after every seventh tick of the ticking clock: 'Every seven seconds a German dies in Russia. Is it your husband? Is it your son? Is it your brother?'

On October 10, Stalin brought General Zhukov back from Leningrad, where the first deaths from starvation had begun to occur, to take command of a newly formed Western Front, and to halt the German advance on Moscow. Zhukov's political adviser in his new task was Nikolai Bulganin. That afternoon, in his Rastenburg headquarters, Hitler told those who were with him: 'The law of existence prescribes uninterrupted killing, so that the better may live.' This was not mere thinking aloud; that same day, October 10, Marshal Walther von Reichenau, commander of the German Sixth Army, issued a directive in which he declared: 'The most essential aim of the campaign against the Jewish-Bolshevist system is the complete crushing of its means of power, and the extermination of Asiatic influences in the European region.' This, von Reichenau went on to explain, 'poses tasks for the troops that go beyond the one-sided routine of conventional soldiering'; the German soldier 'must have full understanding for the necessity of a severe but just atonement on Jewish sub-humanity'.

The spirit of Reichenau's directive was widely emulated; on October 12, in the Yugoslav town of Zasavica, several hundred Jews and Gypsies were murdered; the Gypsies, like the Jews, having now become a part of 'sub-humanity'. In its Operational Situation Report No. 120, dated October 21, the Special Task Force operating in Serbia reported 'for example' – as they phrased it – 2,200 Serbians and Jews shot as a reprisal for an attack on a train near Topola, when twenty-two German soldiers lost their lives, and a further 1,738 inhabitants, 'and nineteen Communist women' executed at Kraljevo. Further south, in Greece, two villages near the Strumen estuary, which were 'proved' to have given support for Greek partisans, were burned down, and 'all the male inhabitants (202) were shot'.

The first part of October was also covered in Operation Situation Report USSR No. 124, compiled in Berlin on October 25. Among the October executions which it recorded were 627 Jews 'liquidated' in Shklov, as well as 812 'racially and mentally inferior elements', and three thousand Jews, murdered in the Vitebsk ghetto.

The fate of those Russian soldiers who were captured by the Germans was horrifying; between the middle of August and the middle of October 1941, 18,000 Russian prisoners-of-war had been murdered in Sachsenhausen concentration camp alone; an average of three hundred a day. One of those who helped organize this mass murder was SS General Eicke, who had earlier been wounded on the Eastern Front.

On October 12 Russian troops were forced to abandon Bryansk and Vyazma. Eight Russian armies had been trapped and destroyed, and 648,196 men taken prisoner. That day, the Germans seized Kaluga, a hundred miles south-west of Moscow. 'Wonderful news from Russia,' General Rommel wrote to his wife from the Western Desert on October 12. 'After the conclusion of the great battles,' he forecast, 'we can expect the advance east to go fast and thus remove all possibility of the enemy creating any significant new forces.' Two days later, ninety miles north-west of Moscow, the town of Kalinin fell to the Germans. That day, the first German offensive against Soviet partisans, Operation Karlsbad, was launched between Minsk and Smolensk, where partisans had threatened to cut this essential supply route to the front.

It was not only the first anti-partisan operation that troubled the Germans on October 14; that same day, as the first snowflakes fell on Leningrad, the temperature throughout the central battle zone fell to below zero. 'Weather prediction is not a science that can be learned mechanically,' Hitler told his entourage at Rastenburg that evening. On the following day, October 15, one of the regimental diaries of the SS Death's Head Division recorded the first substantial snowfall, ten inches of snow.

Throughout the Eastern Front, a mixture of melting snow flurries and heavy rain had created a thick, glutinous mud, which slowed down and could even halt the advance of the German tanks; it was a mud which the Soviet T-34 tanks, with their wider tread, were better designed to overcome.

From Odessa, on October 15, the Soviet military authorities began the final evacuation of troops and equipment. Earlier, 86,000 men had embarked; now, in one night, thirty transports sailed from the port with 35,000 men, setting course for Sevastopol. More than a thousand lorries and four hundred guns had been taken off earlier, also 20,000 tons of ammunition, in 192 sailings. It had been a bloodless Tallinn; a third Dunkirk.

Also on October 15, all Soviet Government offices, and all diplomatic missions, in Moscow were told to prepare for evacuation. They were to be moved eastwards, to the Volga city of Kuibyshev. On the approaches to Moscow, fifty-six bridges were mined, ready to be blown up before the Germans could cross them. Inside Moscow itself, sixteen more bridges were mined, to be blown up 'at the first sight of the enemy'.

Even as Hitler saw Moscow within his grasp, his subordinates were ordering the deportation of 20,000 Jews and 5,000 Gypsies from the cities of Germany to the ghetto of Lodz, already a scene of desperate hunger and deprivation, in which as many as a hundred people had died of starvation in the previous month. In the Warsaw ghetto, where the daily death toll was twice that of Lodz, on October 15 the Germans imposed 'punishment by death' on all Jews who left the ghetto without permission, and also, as a warning of equal severity to the Poles, on any person 'who deliberately offers a hiding place to such Jews'.

The threats of tyranny were dire; but the Germans were becoming careless in their challenges. When a transatlantic convoy from Sydney, Cape Breton, was attacked by German submarines on October 16, and five American destroyers from bases in Iceland came to its aid, one of the submarines fired its torpedoes at one of the destroyers, the *Kearney*, which was badly damaged; eleven American sailors were killed.

'Hitler's torpedo was directed at every American,' Roosevelt told the American people in his Navy Day address eleven days later. But he was still not prepared to declare war on Germany. October 16, the day of the torpedoing of the *Kearney*, was also the day on which, in Tokyo, the Government of Prince

Konoye was forced to resign, giving way to an administration led by General Hideki Tojo, his Minister of War. For those who wanted to challenge the United States on the battlefield, Tojo was the ideal choice as Prime Minister. For Stalin, however, the Japanese threat was over; in the first week of October, he had learned from Richard Sorge in Tokyo that the Japanese Government had definitely decided that there would be no Japanese attack on the Soviet frontiers before the spring of 1942 at the earliest. Stalin had immediately ordered further troops, now totalling half of the divisional strength of the Far Eastern command, to rush to the defence of Moscow. In all, more than eight divisions were moved westward, together with a thousand tanks and a thousand aircraft. One of the first transferred divisions was ordered into action at Borodino in front of Mozhaisk, as soon as it could be hurried westward through Moscow, even though only half of its regiments had been assembled.

In the two weeks following Stalin's decision of October 15 to evacuate Moscow's government institutions and armaments factories, two hundred trains left the capital for the Volga and Ural regions; so too did 80,000 trucks, which evacuated the essential equipment of nearly five hundred factories. One factory, which manufactured infantry weapons, needed twelve trains.

There were other trains moving east on October 16, not from Moscow, but from several cities in Germany; on them were Jews being deported to the Lodz ghetto. One of the trains, with 512 Jews, came from Luxemburg. Five, with five thousand Jews in all, came from Vienna. Five, with a similar number of deportees, were from Prague, and four trains, with 4,187 Jews, came from Berlin. Four other trains came from Cologne, Frankfurt, Hamburg and Düsseldorf. The deportees were henceforth to share the fate of the Jews of Lodz.

For the Germans, the weather on the Russian front had become the dominant concern. On October 16, a pilot arriving at Hitler's Rastenburg headquarters reported that six inches of snow were covering the whole countryside. 'Our wildest dreams have been washed out by rain and snow,' General Hoffman von Waldau, Deputy Chief of Staff of the German Air Force, noted in his diary. 'Everything is bogged down in a bottomless quagmire. The temperature drops to 11°, a foot of snow falls, and then it rains on top of the snow.'

On the evening of October 17, Hitler did not seem too perturbed about the weather. Rzhev, Belgorod, Stalino and Taganrog – less than three hundred miles from the Volga – had all fallen to his armies in the previous forty-eight hours. In the south, General von Manstein had broken into the Crimea. That evening at Rastenburg Hitler told his guests, including Dr Todt, of his plans for motor roads to the Crimea and the Caucasus. 'These roads', he said, 'will be studded along their whole length with German towns, and around these towns our colonists will settle' – not only Germans, but Scandinavians, and even people from 'Western countries and America'. As for the local inhabitants, 'we'll have to screen them carefully. The Jew, that destroyer, we shall drive out.'

Even as Hitler spoke in the privacy of his headquarters, the 'top secret' Operation Situation Report USSR No. 117 was being compiled in Berlin, giving details of how, in the Nikolayev region, the districts occupied by the Special Task Force 'were cleansed of Jews', 4,091 Jews and forty-six Communists being executed in the first two weeks of October, 'bringing the total to 40,699'. Nor were Jews under German rule in Western Europe to be allowed, as a few had been, to seek a legal way out through neutral Portugal. On October 18, Himmler telephoned Reinhard Heydrich, who had just been appointed Protector of Bohemia and Moravia, and told him: 'No emigration by Jews to overseas.'

It was not only against Jews, but also against partisans, that the Special Task Forces were now in action every day. The Operation Situation Report USSR No. 116, sent from Berlin on October 17, had given details of partisan activity, and the efforts to combat it, in the Gatchina region near Leningrad. In an effort to combat acts of sabotage 'ten people had to be shot in Slutsk'. On October 18, between Smolensk and Vyazma, the one effective east-west highway on the road to Moscow was booby-trapped with high-explosive shells; when detonated by remote control, they caused craters in the road thirty feet wide and eight feet deep.

Closer to Moscow, Mozhaisk was ablaze, while both Maloyaroslavets and Tarusa were occupied, exposing a new threat to Moscow from the south.

In Moscow itself, workers had begun to form labour detachments, to dig anti-tank ditches around the capital. 'We were taken some kilometres out of Moscow', one of them, Olga Sapozhnikova, later wrote. 'There was a very large crowd of us, and we were told to dig trenches. We were all very calm, but dazed, and couldn't take it. On the very first day we were machine-gunned by a Fritz who swooped right down on us. Eleven of the girls were killed, and four wounded.'

The anti-tank ditch dug by Olga Sapozhnikova and her workmates was between Moscow and Kuntsevo. Another, four miles long, was at Naro-Fominsk.

It was on October 18 that, in Tokyo, the Japanese authorities arrested Richard Sorge. An extraordinary saga of successful espionage from the very centre of German diplomatic activity in Tokyo was at an end, three days after Sorge had been able finally to set Stalin's mind at rest about Russia's vulnerability to attack in the Far East. Also arrested were thirty-five members of the ring which Sorge had set up, including his four principal confidants, two of them Japanese.

Stalin's Far Eastern spy had proved his devotion to Soviet Communism and to the survival of Russia. On October 19, from Moscow itself, Stalin proclaimed a state of siege, and issued an Order of the Day: 'Moscow will be defended to the last.' In Leningrad, in a gesture of defiance to the German efforts to force the city to surrender, Professor Iosif Orbeli, Director of the Hermitage, obtained permission for half a dozen of the city's leading orientalists to be released for a few hours from the front line, to celebrate the eight hundredth anniversary of Nizami, the national poet of Azerbaidjan.

By October 20, a half million Russian men and women had been mobilized in Moscow to dig a total of five thousand miles of trenches and anti-tank ditches around the city. At the same time, 185 miles of barbed wire were laid out. The Germans were now only sixty-five miles from the Soviet capital. They had already occupied 600,000 square miles of Russian territory, with a population of sixty-five million. They had captured more than three million Soviet soldiers. 'A nightmare picture', Field Marshal von Bock wrote in his diary on October 20, 'of tens of thousands of Russian prisoners-of-war, marching with hardly any guards towards Smolensk. Half dead from exhaustion, these pitiful souls trudge on.' 'The columns of Russian prisoners moving on the roads', Colonel Lahousen, an assistant to Admiral Canaris, noted that same day, 'look like half-witted herds of animals.' General von Reichenau's Sixth Army, Lahousen added, 'has ordered that all prisoners who break down are to be shot. Regrettably this is done at the roadside, even in the villages, so that the local population are eye-witnesses of these incidents.'

In London, learning that evening that the German armies were within sixty-five miles of Moscow, Churchill and his Chiefs of Staff at once agreed that British tanks then being shipped to Russia should be furnished with three months' worth of spare parts, 'whatever sacrifice this might entail'.

On October 21, on the Russian front, the 2,500 technicians of the Kramatorsk heavy-machine works south-west of Kharkov were ready to follow their evacuated factory to the east, after three weeks of incredible efforts to dismantle its machinery and pack it on trains for its journey to safety. As the evacuation task was completed, German troops were only seven miles away. The technicians, unable to find a train, walked twenty miles eastward to the nearest railway station that was still functioning.

In Yugoslavia, the Germans carried out three massacres on October 21. At Kragujevac, 2,300 men and boys were killed, including whole classes of schoolboys. At Kraljevo, seven thousand were killed, and in the Macva region, six thousand men, women and children.

In France, on October 21, the Germans shot fifty hostages at Nantes, as a reprisal for the assassination on the previous day of the German military commander of the region, Lieutenant-Colonel Hötz.

In his conversations at Rastenburg at noon that day, Hitler's mind was still obsessed with the Jews. 'By exterminating this pest,' he told his confidants, 'we shall do humanity a service of which our soldiers can have no idea.'

Well aware of their service to 'humanity', German Army units joined with the Special Task Forces, as well as with Roumanian soldiers, in carrying out to the letter General von Reichenau's directive of October 10 for 'the extermination of Asiatic influences in the European region'. In Odessa, within twenty-four hours of Hitler's noonday comment, the mass murder began of 25,000 Jews, half of whom were locked into four vast warehouses; three of which were then set on fire. Those who were not killed by the flames, and who sought to escape through holes in the roof, or through the windows, were met with a hail of hand grenades and machine gun fire. Many women went mad, throwing their children out of the windows. The fourth warehouse, filled entirely with men, was then destroyed by artillery fire.

On the evening of October 21 Hitler's private talk was entirely of the architectural future of Berlin. 'Nothing will be too good', he said, 'for the beautification of Berlin. When one enters the Reich Chancellery, one should have the feeling that one is visiting the master of the world. One will arrive there along wide avenues containing the Triumphal Arch, the Pantheon of the Army, the Square of the People – things to take your breath away!' The new Berlin, Hitler explained, would be built in granite: 'Granite will ensure that our monuments last for ever.'

# 19

# 'Deciding the fate of Europe' (Hitler)

## NOVEMBER 1941

On 22 October 1941 air defence exercises were carried out through Japan, and Tokyo had its first practice black-out. That same day, an unarmed Japanese reconnaissance aircraft flew from an airbase in Indo-China to the Malayan Peninsula; in his report, the pilot advised that the British airfields of Khota Baru and Alor Star should be the prime objects of the invasion. Plans had also gone ahead to attack Pearl Harbour; a message sent on September 24 from Tokyo to Nagai Kita, instructing him to report on the location of American aircraft carriers at the base, was decrypted in Washington on October 9, but did not ring any alarm bells.

On October 24, German forces entered Kharkov, the second largest city in the Ukraine. That day, in Vilna, 885 children were among the 3,700 Jews hunted down in the streets of the ghetto and taken to nearby Ponar, to be shot. Hundreds, hiding in cellars to try to escape the round-up, were dragged out into the street and killed on the spot.

'From the rostrum of the Reichstag', Hitler told his visitors at Rastenburg that evening, 'I prophesied to Jewry that, in the event of war proving inevitable, the Jew would disappear from Europe.' Hitler added: 'That race of criminals has on its conscience the two million dead of the first World War, and now already hundreds of thousands more. Let nobody tell me that all the same we can't park them in the marshy parts of Russia! Who's worrying about our troops? It's not a bad idea, by the way, that public rumour attributes to us a plan to exterminate the Jews. Terror is a salutary thing.'

On the day of Hitler's recollection and reflection at Rastenburg, a civil servant in Berlin, Adolf Eichmann, who had hitherto been in charge of Jewish emigration, approved a proposal put forward a week earlier by Hinrich Lohse. This proposal was that the Jews who were now being deported by train to Riga from Berlin, Vienna and other cities in the Reich, and from Luxemburg, should, after reaching Riga, be killed by mobile gas vans. The decision to use gas vans to kill Jews was elaborated that same day, October 25, by Judge Alfred Wetzel. The Judge was the adviser on Jewish affairs in the Ministry for the Occupied Eastern Territories. He noted that Dr Victor Brack, the member of Hitler's

Chancellery whose euthanasia programme was now suspended, had already 'co-ordinated the supply of instruments and apparatus for killing people through poison gas'. In order to 'collaborate in the installation of the necessary buildings and gas plants', Wetzel explained, Dr Brack was willing to send his own chemist, Dr Kallmeyer, to Riga. The aim, explained Judge Wetzel, was to avoid 'incidents such as those that took place during the shootings of Jews in Vilna', when the executions 'were undertaken openly'. The 'new procedures', he explained, 'assure that such incidents will no longer be possible'.

Henceforth, a scheme to kill Jews out of sight of the local population, and without exposing Regular Army soldiers or Special Task Force units to the need to shoot down women and children in cold blood, and then shoot again those who had merely been wounded by the first salvoes, was increasingly put into effect. Experimental gassings were carried out in the western Polish town of Kalisz for four days, beginning on October 27. A total of 290 Jews were taken on that day by van from an old people's home, on the pretext that they were to be transferred to a similar home in another town. The inside of the van had been linked up to the exhaust pipe. As the van drove slowly and carefully out of Kalisz, to a wood just beyond the outskirts of the town, all those inside it were suffocated and killed.

When the final journey was completed, and all 290 Jews were dead, the surviving Jews of Kalisz were presented with a bill for the cost of the 'transport'.

The combination of inefficiency and the uneasiness of some German troops meant that it was time for the new method of mass murder to be put into operation. Even as the Kalisz gas van was making its journey from the town to the forest, two letters which indicated the disgusting nature of the Special Task Force killings reached Berlin. The first was a letter from a German Catholic girl, Margarete Sommer, who wrote on October 27 to Cardinal Bertram of a massacre that day in Kovno, in which not only eight thousand local Jews, but a thousand Jews brought by train from Germany, had been murdered at the Ninth Fort, one of the nineteenth century defence works on the outskirts of the city. Of those killed, according to the report of the Special Task Force carrying out the killings, 4,273 were children. 'The Jews must undress,' Sommer wrote, ' – it could have been eighteen degrees below freezing – then climb into "graves" previously dug by Russian prisoners-of-war. They were then shot with a machine gun; then grenades were tossed in. Without checking to see if all were dead, the task force ordered the graves filled in.'

The second protest at the method of mass murder, was from the German Civil Commissioner of the Territory of Slutsk, Dr Carl, who reported to his superiors in Berlin, first by telephone and then by letter, the statements of German troops in Slutsk during a round-up on October 27. Jews and White Russians had been 'beaten with clubs and rifle butts' in the streets; rings were pulled off fingers 'in the most brutal manner'; and in different streets 'the corpses of Jews who had been shot' were 'piled high'. The action, Dr Carl added, 'bordered already on sadism', the town itself being 'a picture of horror'.

The recipient of Dr Carl's letter, Wilhelm Kube, the Commissar General of White Russia, sent it on to Berlin, to the Reich Minister for the Occupied

Eastern Territories, Alfred Rosenberg. 'Peace and order cannot be maintained in White Russia with methods of that sort', Kube wrote. 'To have buried alive seriously wounded people, who then worked their way out of their graves again, is', he asserted, 'such extreme beastliness that this incident as such must be reported to the Führer and the Reich Marshal.'

The evolving plans for murder by gas would ensure that most future killings would be done behind a mask of secrecy, by methods which far fewer people would have to see, and in circumstances which would reduce to a minimum the chance of discovery. In anticipation of the new method, individual Jews with foreign passports were now refused permission to emigrate, even within regions under German influence. In refusing an application from a Jewish woman, Lily Satzkis, to move from Nazi Germany to Vichy France, Adolf Eichmann noted on October 28: 'In view of the approaching final solution of the European Jewry problem, one has to prevent the immigration of Jews into the unoccupied area of France'.

A third protest was made on the very day of Eichmann's letter, at General von Bock's headquarters at Smolensk. As Colonel Lahousen wrote in his diary, the question was raised, at a conference with the General's Intelligence officer, about the shooting of Jews at Borisov, von Bock's former headquarters. 'Seven thousand Jews had been liquidated there', Lahousen noted, '"in the manner of tinned sardines". The scenes that had resulted were indescribable' – often even the killers 'could not go on, and had to keep going by heavy consumption of alcohol'.

On October 25, deep snow fell on the Moscow front. On the following day, in Minsk, the Germans staged the first public hanging, intended to deter partisan activity. Three partisans were executed, Kirill Trus, Volodya Shcherbatseyvich and Maria Bruskina.A seventeen-year-old Jewish girl, Maria Bruskina had been working as a nurse in a field hospital for Russian officers and who had been taken prisoner in the battle for Minsk. Her 'crime' was to have smuggled into the hospital forged identity papers and clothes, enabling several prisoners-of-war to escape.

North-west of Moscow, on October 28, the Germans reached Volokolamsk, seventy-five miles from the capital. On the following day, near Borodino, the first Soviet troops rushed westward from the Far East were in action. Yet still the Germans were confident of victory: 'We're convinced we'll shortly finish off Moscow', was General Wagner's comment on October 29. There was certainly no danger of intervention from the United States. On that same day, in the Atlantic, the American destroyer *Reuben James*, which was escorting convoy HX 156 from Halifax, Nova Scotia, was torpedoed by a German submarine and sunk; 115 of her crew, including all her officers, were drowned.

For the second time in two weeks, Roosevelt took no action. He was determined not to be drawn into the war. But he was equally determined to help those who were at war with Germany. On October 30, the day after the sinking of the *Reuben James*, he telegraphed to Stalin that he had given his Presidential approval to one billion dollars of Lend–Lease aid for Russia, with no interest

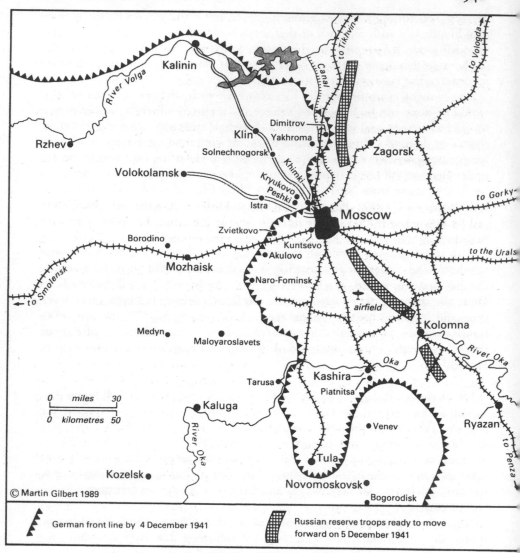

The battle for Moscow, winter 1941

to be charged, and with repayment not having to begin until five years after the war.

On October 31 the German Air Force carried out forty-five separate bombing attacks over Moscow. From Leningrad, the Russians completed the evacuation by air of 17,614 armament factory workers and 8,590 wounded Red Army, Navy and Air Force officers. Behind the German lines, on that last day of October, two hundred Jews were shot at Kletsk for having tried to obtain food from non-Jews living outside the ghetto. That same day, from the occupied Baltic States, in Report from the Occupied Eastern Territories No. 6, ss General von dem

Bach Zelewski reported proudly to Berlin: 'Today, there are no more Jews in Estonia.'

In southern Russia, the Special Task Forces were also confident that their work was thorough; on October 31, at Poltava, the executions began, over a six day period, of 740 people, listed in Operational Situation Report USSR No. 143, as ' – 3 political officials, 1 saboteur, 137 Jews, 599 mentally ill persons'. A further two hundred inmates of the Poltava Lunatic Asylum, who had been judged 'curable', were sent to work in an agricultural implement factory. After the executions, the asylum itself had been turned into a German field hospital, and the 'underwear, clothing and household articles' of the former inmates placed at the field hospital's disposal.

On October 30, Admiral Canaris had visited Hitler at Rastenburg. When Hitler asked him what the weather had been like at the front, he answered in one word: 'Bad!' On 1 November, snow stayed on the ground all day at Rastenburg. Hitler was undeterred. 'If Russia goes under in the war,' he told his guests on November 2, 'Europe will stretch eastwards to the limits of Germanic colonization. In the Eastern territories, I shall replace Slav geographical titles by German names. The Crimea, for example, might be called Gothenland.' On November 3, in a further measure of Germanization, Kiev's Cathedral of the Dormition was blown up.

On November 3, east of Leningrad, the German Army cut the railway line to Vologda and moved towards Tikhvin, a centre for the flying in of supplies to Leningrad. That same day, in Tokyo, the Combined Fleet Top-Secret Order No. 1 was issued to all relevant commanders: Pearl Harbour was to be attacked in thirty-four days' time. There were to be simultaneous attacks on the British in Malaya and on the Dutch in the Dutch East Indies, and a further attack on the Americans in the Philippines.

It was on November 4, a day after this final Japanese decision, that General MacArthur, commander of the American and Philippine forces, received a letter from General Marshall in Washington, reporting on the attitude of the United States Congress. 'They are going to give us everything we asked for,' MacArthur's Chief of Staff exclaimed, delighted. But a careful reading of Marshall's letter showed that the tanks, guns and soldiers MacArthur had asked for, while approved in principle, would not be fully in place until April 1942.

On November 4 the Soviet gunboat *Konstruktor*, crossing Lake Ladoga from Osinovets to Novaya Ladoga with refugees, most of them women and children, was hit by a German dive bomber; 170 refugees and 34 crew members were killed. On November 6, the twenty-fourth anniversary of the Bolshevik revolution, Stalin addressed a rally of Moscow Party workers, held underground, in the ornamental marble hall of the Mayakovsky Metro station. The Germans were 'men with the morals of beasts', he said. 'If they want a war of extermination, they shall have one.'

*        *        *

On November 6, two days after General MacArthur had received General Marshall's letter, promising reinforcements to the Philippines, Japanese warplanes, flying from their aircraft carriers, carried out a two hundred mile practice run on a Japanese equivalent of Pearl Harbour, Kagoshima Bay. The attack methods which they followed were those which they would use on the day itself.

On November 7, Stalin was in Red Square where, from the top of Lenin's mausoleum, he took the salute at a review of his troops, and, in his speech, urged them to do their utmost to defend 'holy Russia'. From Red Square, the soldiers marched up Gorky Street, and then on to the front. The ground had frozen in the night, giving the German tanks a chance to move forward, free from the cloying, seeping, all-pervading mud, which had been such an obstacle to their advance during the last two weeks of October.

As Stalin saw his soldiers leave Red Square for the front line after their march-past on November 7, Roosevelt officially extended the Lend-Lease Act to cover the Soviet Union, which had already been the recipient of considerable quantities of American weapons, and of British weapons which had been manufactured in the United States. For their part, the British had renewed their heavy air raids on Germany; in the raids of November 7, on Berlin, Cologne and Mannheim, thirty-seven out of the four hundred attacking planes were lost, due to exceptionally bad weather conditions.

For several days, over Leningrad, German bombers had dropped, not bombs, but leaflets, telling the inhabitants to beware of November 7. 'Go to the baths,' the leaflets advised. 'Put on your white dresses. Eat the funeral dishes. Lie down in your coffins and prepare for death. On November 7 the skies will be blue – blue with the explosion of German bombs.'

As British bombs had fallen on Berlin, so German bombs also fell on Leningrad that November 7, while behind the German lines, in the White Russian city of Minsk, twelve thousand Jews were slaughtered in pits just outside the city. Three days later, a train with a thousand Jews from Hamburg arrived in Minsk. 'They felt themselves', an eye witness later recalled, 'as pioneers who were brought to settle the East.' Almost none of them was to survive the massacres of future months, any more than the six thousand Jews who were sent after them later that November, from Frankfurt, Bremen and the Rhineland.

'However long the war may last,' Hitler told the annual beer hall celebration in Munich on November 8, 'the last battalion in the field will be a German one', and he added, on a note of triumph: 'We are deciding the fate of Europe for the next thousand years.' On the following day, in the Mediterranean, two Italo-German convoys, bringing fuel for the German Air Force and a large consignment of motor transport for Rommel's Army in North Africa, was attacked by a British naval squadron of two cruisers, a submarine and two destroyers. All ten Axis supply ships were sunk. Their cargoes, their date of departure, the strength of their escort and their route across the Mediterranean had all been revealed by Britain's now regular and unimpeded eavesdropping on Italy's most secret naval radio messages.

In Russia, Leningrad's eastern supply town of Tikhvin fell to the Germans on November 8. The encirclement of Leningrad was complete. On the following day, in the Crimea, German forces occupied Yalta. In Yugoslavia, General Mihailović and his Četnik forces, instead of attacking the Germans, had revealed, on November 9, their intention to destroy Tito and his Communist partisans. The Germans had gained an unexpected and an unwitting ally.

One success of the war against the Axis came on November 9, in Britain, when two German agents, both Norwegians, code named 'Jack' and 'OK', who had landed in Scotland from Norway seven months earlier, and had at once agreed to work for Britain, 'organized' an act of sabotage in a Ministry of Food warehouse at Wealdstone, just outside London. 'Fire Bomb in Food Depot', one British newspaper reported. 'Incendiarism Suspected at Foodstore' declared another. For Colonel Lahousen, it was a triumph for the sabotage efforts of 'Jack' and 'OK'. For the British it was proof that their double-cross system continued to work, thanks on this occasion to the men they knew as 'Mutt' and 'Jeff'.

That night, November 9, in Leningrad, the Radio Symphony Orchestra, conducted by Karl Eliasberg, performed Beethoven's Ninth Symphony at the city's Philharmonic Hall. The concert was broadcast live to London. 'Two parts of the symphony were played without interruption,' Eliasberg later recalled. 'When the third began, we heard the wail of the sirens and almost immediately the impact of bombs falling nearby, and the thunder of anti-aircraft guns. The building shook. To that accompaniment the orchestra played the symphony to the end. The announcer signed off and wished our listeners in Great Britain goodnight.'

On November 12, the temperature on the Moscow front fell to twelve degrees centigrade below zero. Many German soldiers found frostbite an unexpected and crippling enemy. Hitler, in Berlin, was still talking about the aftermath of victory over Russia. 'We shall give the natives all they need: plenty to eat, and rot-gut spirits. If they don't work, they'll go to a camp, and they'll be deprived of alcohol.' From oranges to cotton, Hitler added, 'we can grow anything in that country'.

Hitler had reason to be in a good mood that week; at sea, on November 13, a German submarine, U-81, commanded by Lieutenant Guggenberger, torpedoed the British aircraft-carrier *Ark Royal* off Gibraltar. She sank on the following day. But November 13 saw an event which balanced the blow of the loss of the *Ark Royal*, for on that day, by what one historian has called the 'chillingly narrow' margin of 212 to 194, the United States Congress amended the Neutrality Act, not only to allow all American merchant ships to be armed, but to permit them passage to the war zones. 'This is a very great help to us', King George VI noted in his diary two days later, 'though it appears the President had to send a special message to Congress to have it passed.'

Every few days, from Berlin, thirty and at times even more German officials were sent the Operational Situation Reports USSR. Report No. 133, sent out on November 14, went in all to sixty people. In it were details of some of the October massacres of Jews: nine hundred in Mstislavl; 2,200 in Gorky, north-east of Mogilev; 3,726 'of both sexes and all ages' in Mogilev itself. 'None has suffered more cruelly than the Jew', Churchill wrote that November 14 in a letter to the London *Jewish Chronicle* on its centenary, 'the unspeakable evils wrought on the bodies and spirits of men by Hitler and his vile regime'.

Churchill was aware of at least a percentage of the killings in the East from his reading of the decrypts of more than seventeen intercepted German police messages, as well as his regular scrutiny of a weekly secret summary of all such intercepted messages. In his letter to the *Jewish Chronicle* he added: 'The Jew bore the brunt of the Nazis' first onslaught upon the citadels of freedom and human dignity. He has borne, and continues to bear, a burden that might have seemed to be beyond endurance. He has not allowed it to break his spirit: he has never lost the will to resist'.

The Operational Situation Reports USSR detailed more than a hundred examples of Jewish resistance that autumn and winter. They also gave details of Jewish participation in partisan activity. The report of November 14, for example, spoke of the arrest and execution of fifty-five partisans in Mogilev, of whom twenty-two were Jews 'who worked with fanatical zeal to strengthen the organization further'. Also in Mogilev, the report noted, six Jews and one Jewess – Fania Leikina – 'were liquidated for refusing to wear the Jewish badge and for spreading inflammatory propaganda against Germany'.

Those who carried out these executions and liquidations, whether in the field or in the concentration camps, were not eligible for the Iron Cross. But their commanders wanted them to be rewarded. It seemed that the War Labour Cross was a suitable award. On November 14 the camp Commandant at Gross-Rosen concentration camp, in Silesia, asked what 'reasons' should be listed for the granting of the Cross. Should it be 'execution i.e. special action', or something more 'routine'? Six days later he received his reply from the acting inspector of the concentration camps, SS Lieutenant-Colonel Liebehenschel. Under 'reasons', he advised, the Commandant should 'enter "completion of vital war assignments"'. Liebehenschel added: 'The word "execution" should under no circumstances be mentioned.'

One of those most closely involved in these executions, Hinrich Lohse, the Reich Commissar for the Baltic States and White Russia, had taken independent action early in November, when, at Libava, he had ordered the killings in progress there to cease. Asked by his superiors to explain why he had called a halt to them, he replied on November 15 that 'the manner in which they were performed could not be justified'. Not moral, but economic reasons, were his complaint: the destruction of much manpower that could be of use to the war economy. Was it intended, Lohse asked, that Jews were to be killed 'irrespective of age, sex or economic factors'? In reply, he was informed from Berlin, by Alfred Rosenberg's Ministry of the Eastern Territories, that the demands of the economy 'should be ignored'.

Other extreme attitudes of Nazism were seen that month, when, on November 15, Himmler issued a decree, in Hitler's name, that henceforth any SS or police officer 'engaging in indecent behaviour with another man or allowing himself to be abused by him for indecent purposes will be condemned to death and executed'.

On the battlefront, November 15 saw a complaint by ss General Eicke, now returned from Sachsenhausen to his Death's Head Division, that within the division's ranks many of the ethnic Germans – those of German language and culture who lived in areas outside the Germany of 1938 – were wounding themselves in order not to have to serve any longer. Incidents of cowardice were common among them, Eicke wrote. But the pressures of battle were impinging even upon German nationals; since entering Russia four-and-a-half months earlier, his division had suffered 8,993 casualties, half its initial strength. On the following day, November 16, exceptionally severe wintry conditions were reported from the entire Eastern Front; in the Moscow region, Russian ski troops went into action for the first time.

The German forces were near the limit of their capacity; a German Air Force message, sent by Enigma on November 16, and read at Bletchley by the British decrypters, was a complaint from an Air Force liaison officer with the German troops in the Kursk section, to the effect that no German fighters had been seen for two weeks. On the following day, Ernst Udet, the First World War fighter pilot ace who since 1939 had been Director-General of Equipment for the German Air Force, committed suicide, in part because of the German Air Force failures on the Eastern Front.

One of those at Udet's funeral was his fellow fighter ace, Werner Molders, who came back to the funeral from the Crimea, where he was directing air operations. On his way back to the Crimea in fog and rain, he crash-landed at Breslau and was killed.

Even in the crisis of battle, the Nazi leaders could not rid themselves of their obsession with the imminent Final Solution. On November 16, Goebbels wrote in the magazine *Das Reich*: 'The Jews wanted the war, and now they have it'. But, he added, 'the prophecy which the Führer made in the German Reichstag on 30 January 1939 is also coming true, that should international finance Jewry succeed in plunging the nations into a world war once again, the result would not be the Bolshevization of the world and thus the victory of Jewry, but the annihilation of the Jewish race in Europe. We are in the midst of that process and thereby a fate fulfils itself for Jewry which is hard but which is more than deserved. Compassion or regret are entirely out of place here'.

On November 17, Himmler telephoned Heydrich, in Prague, to discuss with him the 'elimination of the Jews'. These were the words used in Himmler's own note of the conversation. That same day, eight Warsaw Jews were executed for trying to leave the ghetto in search of food. One, a girl not quite eighteen years old, asked a few moments before she was shot that her family be told that she had been sent to a concentration camp, and would not be seeing them for some time. Another girl 'cried out to God', the diarist Chaim Kaplan noted, 'imploring Him to accept her as the expiatory sacrifice for her people, and to let her be the final victim'.

Another Warsaw ghetto diarist, Emanuel Ringelblum, noted that during the execution of the eight Jews, a few ss officers had stood by, watching the scene, 'calmly smoking cigarettes and behaving cynically throughout the execution'.

# 20

## The limits of German conquest

DECEMBER 1941

On the Eastern Front, the German position, so impressive on the map, was worsening daily on the ground. By mid-November 1941 it had become so cold that sentries who accidentally fell asleep at their post were found frozen to death in the morning. The Russians were better trained to survive in extreme cold. They were also defending their heartland and their capital. On November 17, near Volokolamsk, a private soldier, Efim Diskin, the sole survivor of his anti-tank battery, and himself severely wounded, destroyed five German tanks with his solitary gun. He was later awarded the medal, Hero of the Soviet Union.

The Russians were not only fighting with a tenacity which surprised their German opponents, but they were also being steadily reinforced. On 18 November, the German troops attacking Venev were themselves attacked by a Siberian division and armoured brigade, both newly arrived from the Far East with a full complement of T-34 tanks. So cold was it that the German automatic weapons would only fire single shots. As the Siberian troops advanced, in their white camouflage uniforms, 'the panic', a German Army report later noted, 'reached as far back' as Bogorodisk: 'This was the first time that such a thing had occurred during the Russian campaign, and it was a warning that the combat ability of our infantry was at an end, and that they should no longer be expected to perform difficult tasks.'

On this very day, in North Africa, British and Commonwealth forces launched Operation Crusader. Determined to take some action to draw German pressure away from the Eastern Front, and having been alerted by the Germans' own Enigma messages to the weakness and dispositions of Rommel's forces, on November 18, British, Australian, New Zealand and other Commonwealth troops attacked the German line. After an initially successful defence by Rommel, the line was outflanked, forcing Rommel to withdraw to El Agheila, the point from which he had begun his attack on Egypt eight months earlier. In the Far East, however, there was a naval setback for the Commonwealth forces, when the German ocean raider *Komoran*, a converted cargo ship, sank the Australian light cruiser *Sydney* off the coast of Australia. All 645 officers and men aboard the *Sydney* were drowned. The *Komoran* also sank, but most of her crew were saved.

The Russians now began to prepare for a major offensive, to save Moscow. They were able, with great skill, to hide entirely from German reconnaissance and Intelligence eyes the forward movement of their reserves. The 'enemy', noted General Halder in his diary on November 18, 'had nothing left in the rear, and his predicament probably is even worse than ours'. Those, however, whose 'predicament' was worse even than that of the fighting soldiers in the wintry fields of Russia or the sand blown hills of Libya, were the Red Army men, numbering as many as three million, perhaps even more, who had been taken prisoner by the Germans in the previous five months. The fate of seven thousand of these Russian prisoners-of-war was noted on November 18 by the commander of a German artillery regiment who saw them in their camp. The windows of the building in which they were being held, he wrote, 'are several metres high and wide, and are without covering. There are no doors in the building. The prisoners who are thus kept practically in the open air are freezing to death by the hundreds daily – in addition to those who die continuously because of exhaustion'.

On November 20 the Germans captured Rostov-on-Don, less than two hundred miles from the western foothills of the Caucasus. That day, in an Order of the Day issued to all his troops, General von Manstein declared: 'The Jews are the mediators between the enemy in our rear and the still fighting remnants of the Red Army and the Red leaders'. The German soldier in the East, in fighting the Bolsheviks, was 'the bearer of a ruthless ideology'; he must therefore 'have understanding of the necessity of a severe but just revenge on sub-human Jewry'.

Nine days after von Manstein issued this order, 4,500 Jews were murdered in the Crimean port of Kerch. Two weeks later, 14,300 Jews were murdered in Sevastopol. These killings were witnessed by hundreds of bystanders, and reported on in detail in the Operational Situation Reports USSR, with their distribution to between thirty and sixty senior officials and civil servants. Far more secret were the gassing experiments, which were now nearing their operational stage. 'I spoke with Dr Heyde on the phone,' one of the 'euthanasia' experts at Buchenwald concentration camp, Dr Fritz Mennecke, wrote to his wife on November 20, 'and told him I could handle it all by myself, so no one else came today to help.' As to the 'composition of the patients', Mennecke added, 'I would not like to write anything here in this letter.'


On November 21, Albert Speer asked Hitler for thirty thousand Soviet prisoners-of-war, to help with the building of Berlin's new monumental buildings. Hitler agreed. The building, he said, could begin before the war was over. Among the projects, of which Speer showed Hitler miniature models that day, were a Great Hall for the Chancellery and an Office for Goering. Hitler also drew for Speer, in ink on lined paper, the design for a Monument of Liberation to be built at Linz, on the Danube, near Hitler's own birthplace. The monument, an imposing arch, was to be the centrepiece of a stadium holding thousands of spectators.

The siege of Leningrad, with its growing starvation, continued. On November 22, a column of sixty trucks, commanded by Major Porchunov, set off from Kobona and, following the tracks made by horses and sledges on the previous day, crossed the frozen waters of Lake Ladoga to Kokkorevo, with thirty-three tons of flour for the besieged city. One of the drivers, Ivan Maximov, later recalled how: 'I was with that column. A dark and windy night shrouded the lake. There was no snow yet and the black-lined field of ice looked for all the world like open water. I must admit that an icy fear gripped my heart. My hands shook, no doubt from strain and also from weakness — we had been eating a rusk a day for four days ... but our column was fresh from Leningrad and we had seen people starving to death. Salvation was there on the western shore. And we knew we had to get there at any cost'.

One truck, and its driver, were lost in the crossing, falling through the ice and disappearing under the freezing waters. Six more crossings were made in the next seven days, bringing eight hundred tons of flour to the city, as well as fuel oil. But, in those same seven days, forty more trucks had gone to the bottom. Along the road to the lakeside, German shelling also took its toll, as did the snow drifts; in three days, 350 trucks were abandoned in drifts near Novaya Ladoga. In all, 3,500 trucks were available, though at any one time more than a thousand were out of service, awaiting repairs. Nevertheless, a lifeline, albeit precarious, had been opened. It could not, however, do much to reduce the daily deaths from starvation; during November, as many as four hundred people were dying every day from starvation.

In German-occupied Warsaw, starvation in the ghetto was also a daily occurrence, to which as many as two hundred Jews succumbed daily. 'In the street', noted Mary Berg in her diary on November 22, 'frozen human corpses are an increasingly frequent sight.' Sometimes, Mary Berg added, a mother 'cuddles a child frozen to death, and tries to warm the inanimate little body. Sometimes a child huddles against his mother, thinking that she is asleep and trying to awaken her, while, in fact, she is dead.'

The Japanese Government now hid its preparations behind a flurry of negotiations in both Washington and London. 'I am not very hopeful,' Churchill telegraphed to Roosevelt on November 20, 'and we must all be prepared for real trouble, possibly soon.' Two days later, behind an unpenetrated veil of secrecy, and as the American negotiators continued in Washington to discuss the latest Japanese document with their British, Australian and Dutch counterparts, the Japanese put into effect Operation z, the assembly of the Japanese First Air Fleet in Tankan Bay in the Kurile Islands. It was an impressive, if unseen force: six aircraft carriers, a light cruiser and nine destroyers, supported by two battleships, two heavy cruisers, and three submarines for reconaissance.

As Japanese naval forces gathered in the northern Pacific, across the globe, in the South Atlantic, November 22 also saw the final day in the career of the German commerce raider *Atlantis*. The most effective German raider of the war, with more than 140,000 tons of Allied merchant shipping to its 'credit', it was caught by the British cruiser *Devonshire* while refuelling a German submarine, and sunk.

On the Moscow front, German forces advanced on November 23 to within thirty miles of the capital, reaching the village of Istra, a centre of Russian Orthodox pilgrimage known to the faithful as New Jerusalem. On the following day, the towns of Klin and Solnechnogorsk fell to a German assault, bringing German troops astride the main highway from Moscow to the north.

In the Far East, a sense of impending danger had begun to pervade the Anglo-American counsels; Canadian troops were on their way to Hong Kong, and, on November 24, the authorities in Washington informed all Pacific commanders that there was a possibility of a 'surprise aggressive movement in any direction, including an attack on the Philippines or Guam'. No mention was made of Pearl Harbour.

To reverse the tide of defeat in North Africa, the Germans despatched two ships, the *Maritza* and the *Procida*, to Benghazi, with fuel of decisive importance for the German Air Force. News that the ships were on their way was sent by a top secret Enigma signal, which, on November 24, was decrypted at Bletchley. Churchill himself urged action on the basis of the decrypt. Within twenty-four hours, both ships were sunk. A further Enigma message, decrypted on November 29, revealed that, as a result of the sinking of the two ships, the fuel supplies for the air forces supporting Rommel were in 'real danger'. The British Commander-in-Chief, General Auchinleck, at once exhorted his troops, in an Order of the Day issued on November 25: 'Attack and pursue. All out everywhere.' Churchill telegraphed that same day to Auchinleck: 'A close grip upon the enemy by all units will choke the life out of him.'

As the British forces struggled to take advantage of their Intelligence knowledge of Rommel's weakness, Hitler ordered several German submarines to the Mediterranean to redress the British successes against Rommel's supply shipping. On November 25, one of these submarines, U-331, commanded by Lieutenant von Tiesenhausen, sank the British battleship *Barham* off Sollum; 868 men were drowned. Two days later, the Australian sloop *Parramatta* was torpedoed off Tobruk, and 138 men were drowned.

In Berlin, there was a celebration on November 25, the fifth anniversary of the drafting of the Anti-Comintern Pact. A considerable array of States were now committed to the overthrow of Communist Russia: Germany, Italy, Hungary, Spain, Bulgaria, Croatia, Denmark, Finland, Roumania and Slovakia.

On November 25, the Russian defenders south of the capital were pushed back through Venev to the village of Piatnitsa, only four miles from the River Oka bridge at Kashira. To the north of Moscow, advance German units crossed the Volga–Moscow canal at Yakhroma and Dimitrov, threatening the capital with encirclement. After the fall of the village of Peshki, east of Istra, and a further Soviet retreat to Kryukovo, the Soviet commanding officer, General Rokossovsky, was given the order: 'Kryukovo is the final point of withdrawal.

There can be no further falling back. There is nowhere to fall back to.'

If Stalin was worried, so was Hitler; on November 25 his adjutant, Major Engel, noted after a long evening discussion: 'The Führer explains his great anxiety about the Russian winter and weather conditions, says we started one month too late. The ideal solution would have been the surrender of Leningrad, the capture of the south, and then if need be a pincer round Moscow from south and north, following through in the centre'. Engel added: 'Time is his greatest nightmare now'.

In Germany itself, the experiments in killing by gas continued; on November 25, at Buchenwald concentration camp, Dr Fritz Mennecke received, as he wrote to his wife, 'our second batch of 1,200 Jews', but, he explained to her, 'they did not have to be "examined".' No medical examination was needed, only the taking out of their files, to note down their imminent departure. The 1,200 Jews were then sent to a clinic at Bernburg, a hundred miles away, and gassed. A further 1,500 Jews, citizens of Berlin, Munich and Frankfurt, had been deported from Germany a few days earlier to Kovno. They had been told that they were being sent to a work camp. But instead, after being locked in underground cellars at the Ninth Fort for three days, without food or drink, freezing amid ice-covered walls and icy winds, on November 25 they were led, frozen and starving, to the pits that had been prepared for them, and ordered to undress. In their suitcases were found printed announcements urging them to prepare for a 'difficult' winter. 'They did not want to undress,' a Kovno Jew, Dr Aharon Peretz, was later told, 'and they struggled against the Germans.' But it was a hopeless, unequal struggle, and they were all shot, the Special Task Force recording with its usual precision the day's death toll: '1,159 Jews, 1,600 Jewesses, 175 Jewish children'. Four days later, it was '693 Jewish men, 1,155 Jewesses, 152 Jewish children', described as 'settlers from Vienna and Breslau', who were taken to the Ninth Fort and shot; a total death toll in the two 'actions' of nearly six thousand people.

On November 25, from Washington, Admiral Stark informed Admiral Kimmel that neither Roosevelt nor Cordell Hull would be surprised if the Japanese were to launch a surprise attack. An attack on the Philippines would be 'the most embarrassing'. Stark thought that the Japanese would probably attack the Burma Road.

Admiral Kimmel, in command at the mid-Pacific base at Oahu, of which Pearl Harbour was a part, was at that very moment in discussions with General Short about sending warships away from Pearl Harbour, in order to reinforce Wake Island and Midway island. 'Could the Army help out the Navy?' Kimmel asked Short. But it seemed that the army had no anti-aircraft artillery to spare.

American Intelligence knew, from an intercepted Japanese diplomatic message, that the rulers of Japan had set November 25 as their deadline for the working of diplomacy, and for an agreed end to the American economic sanctions against them. If no solution was agreed by then, the intercepted message read, 'things will automatically begin to happen'. What those 'things' were was not explained, but on November 25 Japanese troop transports were

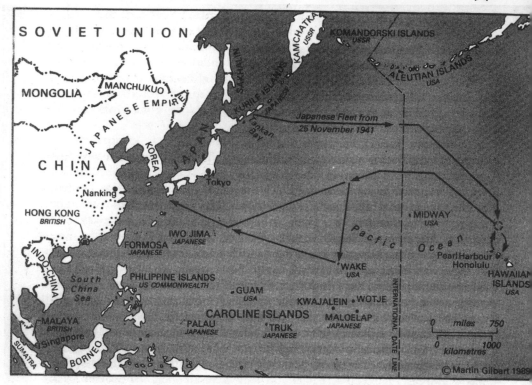

Pearl Harbour, December 1941

sighted off Formosa, heading towards Malaya. On November 26, unobserved by the Americans, the Japanese First Air Fleet sailed from the Kurile Islands, towards the International Dateline, maintaining complete radio silence.

As Japanese warships made what was in fact their way towards Pearl Harbour, the United States gave the Japanese negotiators in Washington the American terms for a settlement: Japan must give up the territory she occupied in both China and Indo-China, must end recognition of the Chinese 'puppet' Government at Nanking, and must withdraw from the Axis.

On November 27, Roosevelt and his advisers decided that Japan was now bent on war. 'Hostile action possible at any moment,' the War Department in Washington telegraphed to General MacArthur in the Philippines. 'If hostilities cannot be avoided,' the telegram continued, 'United States desires that Japan commit the first overt act.' That same day, Admiral Stark, chief of naval operations in the United States Supreme Command, sent to all the commanders of the American Asian and Pacific fleets a 'warning of state of war'.

On the Moscow front, Soviet forces were at last able, on November 27, to halt the German advance and, at certain points, to push the Germans back two or three miles. 'Prisoners taken', Zhukov was able to report that day to Stalin. Soviet partisan operations were also continuous. On the night of November 27, a unit of the SS Death's Head Division was attacked in its billets south of Lake Ilmen by a partisan band, which burned the SS vehicles and buildings, killing four Germans, seriously wounding twelve, and disappearing, leaving a burning camp behind them.

'New forces have made their appearance in the direction of the Oka river,' General Halder noted that November 27. North-west of Moscow, also, 'the enemy is apparently moving new forces'. These Soviet reinforcements were not large units, Halder added, 'but they arrived in endless succession and caused delay after delay for our exhausted troops'.

On November 28, the Germans were forced to give up Rostov-on-Don, their first serious setback on the Eastern Front. Between Dimitrov and Zagorsk, twelve Soviet ski battalions were assembling in reserve, opposite the Germans who now held the whole Moscow–Kalinin road. Southeast of Moscow, despite the German bombing of railway lines, the Soviet Tenth Army was likewise being brought forward, on November 28 from Shilovo to Ryazan. 'The enemy movements to Ryazan from the south are continuing,' General Halder noted in his diary on the following day.

In Berlin, Hitler learned on November 28 that the German siege of Tobruk had been broken, and that Rommel was in retreat. That same day, he received the Mufti of Jerusalem, Haj Amin el-Husseini, who told him that 'the Arab world was firmly convinced of a German victory, by virtue not only of the large Army, brave soldiers and brilliant military strategists at Germany's disposal, but also because Allah could never grant victory to an unjust cause'. In reply, Hitler reminded the Mufti that 'Germany had declared an uncompromising war on the Jews.' Such a commitment, he said 'naturally entailed a stiff opposition to the Jewish homeland in Palestine'. Germany was 'determined', Hitler added, 'to challenge the European nations one by one into a settlement of the Jewish question and, when the time came, Germany would turn to the non-European peoples with the same call'.

After gaining 'the southern exit of the Caucasus', Hitler told the Mufti, he would offer the Arab world 'his personal assurance that the hour of liberation had struck'. Thereafter, he explained, 'Germany's only remaining objective in the region would be limited to the annihilation of the Jews living under British protection in Arab lands.'

The German march to the Caucasus was, temporarily at least, halted. Following the loss of Rostov-on-Don, the Germans were forced to evacuate Taganrog on November 29. That day, in the village of Petrishchevo behind the Moscow front, as part of their attempt to halt the growing number of partisan attacks, the Germans hanged an eighteen-year-old Soviet girl, Zoia Kosmodemianskaya. 'She set fire to houses', read the placard around her neck as she was led to execution. Her own last words, as she was led to the scaffold, were to one of the German soldiers accompanying her: 'You can't hang all 190 million of us.'

Hitler's difficulties were now considerable. On November 29, Dr Todt, returning to Berlin from the Russian front, told him bluntly: 'Given the arms and industrial supremacy of the Anglo-Saxon powers, we can no longer militarily win this war.' That day, in southern Russia, the Germans were forced, after attacks by the Red Army which included repeated assaults over German mine-fields and into machine gun positions, to withdraw behind the River Mius. Reinforcements were hurried south from the German reserves in Kharkov; reserves that could not now be used against Moscow. 'Further cowardly retreats are forbidden', Hitler telegraphed to Field Marshal von Kleist.

Whatever the problems confronting the German troops in Russia, the killing of Jews continued. On November 29, a thousand German Jews, who had been deported from Berlin two days earlier, reached Riga. They were kept in the locked wagons all night, and then, at 8.15 on the morning of November 30, the survivors of the journey were taken into the nearby Rumbuli forest, and shot. Later that day, at 1.30 p.m., Himmler telephoned to Heydrich from Hitler's headquarters at Rastenburg, to which Hitler had just returned to say that there should be 'no liquidation' of this convoy. But it was too late; Heydrich replied that all the Jews on the convoy had been shot that morning.

Nineteen more trains were to reach Riga with German Jews during the next month. These Jews were taken not to Rumbuli, but to the Riga ghetto, where they were put to forced labour for the Germans. Place in the ghetto had already been found for them by the despatch, to Rumbuli earlier on the morning of 30 November, amid scenes of the utmost cruelty and terror, of nine thousand of Riga's Jews; all were killed during 'a shooting action', as it was described in Operation Situation Report USSR No. 151. A further 2,600 Riga Jews were murdered at Rumbuli a few days later.

Old, sick and frail Jews who could not manage to march the five miles from the Riga ghetto to the Rumbuli forest were shot down as they stumbled, fell, or sat exhausted on the ground; one such victim was the eighty-one-year-old doyen of Jewish historians, Simon Dubnov. According to one account, his last words as he lay dying were an injunction to his fellow Jews: 'Write and record!'

It was also on 30 November, the day of the 'shooting action' in Riga, that the first Jewish deportees, a thousand women, children and old people from Prague, reached a new German concentration camp at Theresienstadt, thirty-five miles north of Prague. There in the huts and barracks of an eighteenth century fortress, uprooted from their homes, penniless, deprived of all but their most personal belongings, overcrowded and ill-fed, they were to be joined during the coming weeks by almost all the remaining Jews of Vienna, Berlin and a dozen other German and former Czechoslovak cities. None was to be murdered while at Theresienstadt; but thirty-two thousand were to die there of hunger and disease.


In Leningrad, during the month of November, eleven thousand citizens had died of starvation, and 522 had been killed during the daily German shelling of the city. With the German occupation of Mga and Schlüsselburg secure, the only way by which supplies could reach the city was by truck over the ice of Lake Ladoga. On December 1, the siege of Leningrad entered its ninety-second day. That day Vera Inber saw a sight she had not seen before, a corpse on a child's sledge. Instead of being placed in a coffin, the body had been tightly wrapped in a sheet. That December, the deaths from starvation in the city rose from four hundred to more than fifteen hundred every day.

The statistics of death are numbing; on December 1, at Buchenwald, Dr Fritz Mennecke noted that although he had to begin work half an hour late in filling in the forms which sent Jews to Bernburg, and to their death by gassing, 'a record was broken. I managed to complete 230 forms, so that now a total of 1,192 are complete.' That same day, ss Colonel Karl Jaeger reported to Berlin that his Special Task Force had 'reached the goal of solving the Jewish problem in Lithuania'. Colonel Jaeger's 'goal' was far in excess of Dr Mennecke's 'record'. In all, Jaeger reported, his Special Task Force units had killed 229,052 Jews in Latvia and Lithuania since June, and a further thousand in Estonia. The only 'remaining' Jews, he explained, were those in the ghettos of Vilna, Kovno and Siauliai, employed in various German factories and at other labouring tasks.

That night, in conversation with Walther Hewel, Hitler declared: 'Probably many Jews are not aware of the destructive power they represent. Now, he who destroys life is himself risking death. That's the secret of what is happening to the Jews.'

On December 1, the Germans made two desperate bids to break through the Moscow defences. One was at Zvietkovo, west of the capital and the other towards Kolomna, from the south. But the Soviet defensive ring held, and a relentless German tank assault at Naro-Fominsk was driven back. As December 2 dawned, many German soldiers, unable to face a second day of fire and ice, screamed that they could not go on. There was also now a new rearward Soviet defence line, behind which, as the Moscow front line soldiers held on tenaciously, fifty-nine rifle divisions and seventeen cavalry divisions were grouping for a massive counter-attack, in a vast arc from Vytegra on Lake Onega to Astrakhan on the Caspian Sea, passing through the Volga cities of Kostroma, Gorky and Saratov.

As Soviet reinforcements gathered, the Germans were unaware even of their existence. 'Overall impression', General Halder noted on 2 December, 'enemy defence has reached its peak. No more reinforcements available.' That day, in a blinding snowstorm, which reduced visibility to fifty feet and even less, a German reconnaissance battalion pushed its way forward through Khimki, just beyond the northern suburbs of Moscow, and only twelve miles from the Kremlin. But Russian workers, hastily armed, were rushed northward from the city, and drove the German unit out.

Throughout the day, six miles south of the Moscow-Mozhaisk highway, German tanks had tried to break through towards Moscow at the village of Akulovo, when, briefly, German troops were within sight of the tall spires of the Kremlin. But twenty-four hours later, they were driven from Akulovo. The Russian defence of Moscow could not be broken.

In the south, the Germans had been forced to retreat to Mariupol. But in the Crimea they not only consolidated their positions, but murdered Jews and Soviet prisoners-of-war indiscriminately, meticulously recording the total Jewish death toll as 17,645, as well as 2,504 local Krimchak Jews who could trace their

Russian origins back more than a thousand years. In addition to the Jews, this same Operational Situation Report USSR No. 150 listed '824 Gypsies and 212 Communists and partisans', all shot; and went on, without explaining the higher figure: 'Altogether 75,881 persons have been executed.' The number of captured Soviet soldiers executed in those days was not specifically recorded.

On December 1, as Japanese troop transports crossed the South China Sea from Formosa, the British declared a state of emergency in Malaya. On the following day, the Japanese First Air Fleet, still sailing eastward across the Pacific, received the coded order which established that Pearl Harbour was now its target. That same day, December 2, a telegram was sent from Tokyo to the Japanese Consulate in Hawaii, asking if there were any barrage balloons over Pearl Harbour, and if torpedo nets were in use there. To those in Washington who decoded this telegram, it seemed a routine Intelligence enquiry.

On the day of this Tokyo request for information about the defences of Pearl Harbour, a British battleship, the *Prince of Wales*, arrived in Singapore, together with the cruiser *Repulse* and four destroyers. A third major warship, the aircraft carrier *Indomitable*, whose aircraft, a squadron of nine new Hurricane fighters, would have provided air cover for the battleship and its cohorts, was not however with them; it had run aground in the West Indies, and needed twenty-five days before repairs could be completed.

By an incredible coincidence, the British ships which had just reached Singapore had been given the code name Force z. The move of the Japanese First Air Fleet towards Pearl Harbour was Operation z.

On December 3, Japanese Intelligence received a report from Consul-General Kita in Hawaii about the American warships then at anchor at Pearl Harbour, including the battleships *Oklahoma* and *Nevada*, and the aircraft carrier *Enterprise*. Reaching a point 1,300 miles north-west of Hawaii, the Japanese First Air Fleet turned south-east, steaming towards its unsuspecting target.

Between November 16 and 4 December, 85,000 Germans had been killed on the Moscow front, the same number of troops as had died on the whole Eastern Front between mid-June and mid-November. But Hitler's order not to withdraw was obeyed; and with the arrival of a hundred fresh Russian divisions, a further 30,000 German soldiers were killed south of Moscow, where the Tula salient threatened the capital from the south. Despite these enormous losses, the German line held; Hitler, cheated of a swift march into Moscow, could still see on the map a German line full of menace to the Russian capital.

On December 3, the Russians were finally forced to evacuate their garrison at Hango, the Finnish naval base which they had occupied early in 1940, and which had been under Finnish siege since June 29. Not only was Hango lost but, south of Moscow, in yet another effort to break through to the capital, the Germans launched an attack on December 4 between Tula and Venev. That night, however, the temperature dropped to an incredible thirty-five degrees centigrade below zero, and in the morning their tanks would not start nor their guns fire, while frostbite brought agony to thousands of German soldiers, whose

The Eastern Front, December 1941

boots were not designed, as were the Russian boots, for such extremes of cold.

The Germans had hoped to defeat Russia before the onset of winter. For this reason, they were not equipped for winter fighting. Nor could a last-minute order to commandeer women's fur coats throughout Germany be effective in time to avert the terrifying effect of extreme cold during those first few days of December.

Meanwhile, three Russian reserve armies, fresh from the rear and undetected by German Intelligence, prepared to launch an offensive. Thrusting forward with superior tanks, driven by a desire to free their capital from the threat of conquest, better equipped for the biting cold, at three o'clock on the morning of December 5, shielded by a ferocious blizzard against which the Germans could hardly stand, and with snow lying more than a yard thick, the Russian soldiers began to drive the Germans back. In all, eighty-eight Russian divisions were in action that day, against sixty-seven German divisions, along a five-hundred-mile front from Kalinin in the north to Yelets in the south.

Counter-attacking from the north, Soviet forces crossed the frozen Volga near Kalinin. Further south, crossing the Moscow canal from the east, they drove the Germans from Yakhroma, liberating the railway line from Moscow to the north.

Despite Hitler's order that his armies should hold on at all costs, on December 5 they were driven back slowly, painfully, but inexorably, two miles, five miles and – north of Moscow, where the threat had been closest – eleven miles from the Russian capital. That day, Britain declared war on Hitler's three partners in the war against Russia – Finland, Hungary and Roumania. Simultaneously, with Britain's declaration of war, Australia, New Zealand, South Africa and Canada did likewise.

The spectre of a German failure to capture Moscow was no deterrent to the relentless imposition of tyranny behind the lines. On December 4, a decree had been published in Berlin which stated that Poles and Jews in the eastern territories who sabotaged or disobeyed, or incited others to disobey, 'any orders or decrees passed by the German authorities' would be punished by death. On the following day Himmler signed a letter for the creation, from concentration-camp inmates, of a reserve of five thousand skilled stonemasons and ten thousand bricklayers, 'before peace is concluded'. 'These workers are needed', Himmler explained, 'since the Führer has already ordered that the Deutsche Erd und Steinwerke company, as an undertaking of the ss, shall deliver at least 100,000 cubic metres of granite a year, more than was ever produced by all the quarries in the old Reich'.

Such plans were of no help to the German tank crews now being bombarded that week in the East by the full force of the unexpected Soviet offensive. Not only did German soldiers have to light fires in pits under their tanks for as much as four hours, in order to thaw out their engines sufficiently to bring them into action, but, in conflict with the Soviet T-34 tanks, the German anti-tank shells were useless.

On the morning of Saturday 6 December, a newly formed Government sub-committee met in Washington. Given the code name 'S-1', its task was to establish, within the following six months, if an atomic bomb could be produced in the United States and, if so, when and at what cost. Shortly after midday, in the Navy's Cryptographic Department, also in Washington, a member of the

The Battle of Britain: vapour trails of the battle in the sky above London, 6 September 1940.

The London Blitz: Balham Underground Station receives a direct hit from a German bomb, 5 October 1940 (see page 132).

Hitler at Mönichkirchen during the Yugoslav campaign, greeting officers who had been assigned to his Headquarters Battalion. In the background, his train *Amerika*.

Crete; British warships attacked by German aircraft in Suda Bay, May 1941.

British prisoners-of-war on Crete, May 1941. They were to remain in captivity, first on Crete and then in Germany, for four years.

A British war grave on Crete;
Lieutenant Simson was killed
on 20 May 1941.
Two German war graves on
Crete; Theo Klier and Wilhelm
Eiting were both killed on 22
May 1941.

The German battleship *Bismarck* in action against the *Hood*, 24 May 1941 (*see page 185*).

A German Enigma machine, on which the most secret German military communications, including front-line orders, were sent. These cypher messages were intercepted at British listening posts and then sent to Bletchley Park, near London, where they were broken, and their contents passed to Britain's war leaders and commanders in the field. It was an Enigma message which had indicated that the *Bismarck* was making for Brest.

The German invasion of Russia, 22 June 1941; German troops advancing.

German troops move forward along a road in Russia, as Russian prisoners-of-war pass them in the other direction.

Russia, July 1941; the city of Smolensk in ruins, as German troops prepare to enter it.

Summer 1941; battle-weary German troops rest at the side of a tank.

July 1941; a British fighter pilot
has notched up twenty-six
enemy planes shot down. Flight
Lieutenant Eric Stanley-Lock
has also painted a 'V for
Victory' crest on his plane.

In German-occupied
Yugoslavia, a Yugoslav victim of
Nazi terror is left hanging in one
of the main streets of Belgrade,
as a deterrent to acts of defiance.

staff, Mrs Dorothy Edgers, translated a secret diplomatic message, sent from Tokyo four days earlier to Consul-General Kita in Honolulu, by the 'Magic' code which the Americans had long ago broken, telling Kita that, from that time on, he must send regular reports of all ship movements, berthing positions and torpedo netting at Pearl Harbour. Fully alarmed, Mrs Edgers began translating other intercepts, all of which were in similar vein. Then, at three o'clock that afternoon, she presented her translation to the Chief of the Translation Department, Lieutenant Commander Alvin Kramer. After a few minor points of criticism of her translations, Kramer told her: 'We'll get back to this on Monday'.

'Monday' was December 8. By the time it came, no further studying was needed. On Sunday, December 7, Japanese forces struck, in ruthless succession, at Malaya, Pearl Harbour, the Philippines and Hong Kong, all within seven hours. The road to global war had been traversed.

# 21

# Japan strikes

## DECEMBER 1941

At five minutes before eight o'clock on the morning of Sunday, 7 December 1941, Hawaii time, 366 Japanese bombers and fighters struck at the American warships lying at their moorings at Pearl Harbour. Four of the American battleships were blown up, or sank where they lay at anchor. Four further battleships were damaged and eleven other warships sunk or disabled.

As well as striking at the American warships, the Japanese attackers struck at Pearl Harbour's airfields; 188 American aircraft were destroyed on the ground. As the Japanese planes flew back to the aircraft carriers of their First Air fleet, 2,330 Americans were dead or dying, 1,177 of them killed on the battleship *Arizona*. When Roosevelt informed Churchill, in secret, of the full extent of the casualties, explaining that these were 'considerably more than that given to the Press', Churchill's comment was: 'What a holocaust!'

The Japanese had lost twenty-nine aircraft and five midget submarines in the attack; sixty-four of their men were dead, and one, Ensign Kazua Sakamaki, whose midget submarine had run aground on the island, was taken prisoner; the first Japanese prisoner of the Second World War. As the scale of the American losses became known, the shock in the United States was considerable; of the nine American battleships capable of offensive or defensive action in the Pacific earlier that morning, only two remained able to enter combat. Japan's ten battleships were masters of the Pacific.

There had been many acts of heroism, however, among the surprised American defenders; at Kaneohe naval base, Chief Aviation Ordnanceman John Finn had been lying in bed when the Japanese attack began. Hurrying to the airbase, he managed to set up a machine gun near one of the hangars and, under heavy Japanese fire, began to fire back. 'Although painfully wounded many times', his Medal of Honour citation records, 'he continued to man his gun and to return the enemy's fire vigorously, and with telling effect throughout the enemy strafing and bombing attacks, and with complete disregard for his own personal safety.'

The attack on Pearl Harbour coincided with the planned attacks on three other American Pacific islands, Guam, Wake and Midway, each of which was bombed or shelled that day, and its airfields damaged. That same morning,

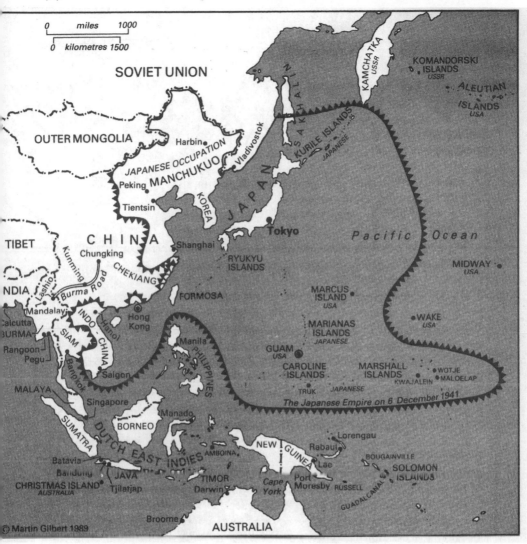

The Japanese Empire and the coming of war, December 1941

across the South China Sea, the Japanese Second Fleet escorted a convoy of troop transports bringing 24,000 troops from Indo-China to the Malayan Peninsula. At the same time, at Singapore, Japanese air attacks led to the death of sixty-one civilians, while at Hong Kong, Japanese war planes destroyed all but one of the eight British aircraft lined up on the tarmac of Kai Tak airport.

It was towards midnight on December 7, Central European time, that Hitler, at his headquarters at Rastenburg, in East Prussia, learned of the Japanese attack on Pearl Harbour. 'Now it is impossible for us to lose the war,' he told

The first death camp, murder sites, and the Eastern Front, December 1941

Walther Hewel, and he went on to explain: 'We now have an ally who has never been vanquished in three thousand years'. Earlier that day, Hitler had accepted the need to pull back from his now untenable front line positions in Russia. On the Leningrad front, the Russians had launched a massive assault on Tikhvin, while, in front of Moscow, German forces began their slow withdrawal to a line Kursk–Orel–Medyn–Rzhev, hoping to hold it by a series of defended strongpoints. The battle for Moscow was over.

At the very moment Hitler was rejoicing at Japan's entry into the war, and accepting that Moscow could not, for the time being at least, be his, another area of the Nazi plan was being put into effect. On that same European night of December 7, Pearl Harbour's disastrous morning, the long planned gassings of the Final Solution began to be put into effect, when seven hundred Jews from the small Polish town of Kolo, situated two hundred miles south-west of Rastenburg, were taken in trucks to the nearby village of Chelmno. There, on the following morning, eighty of the Jews were transferred to a special van, which set off towards a small clearing inside the nearby woods. By the time the journey was over, the eighty Jews were dead, gassed by exhaust fumes which had been channelled back into the van. The bodies were then thrown out into a specially dug pit, and the van returned to the village. After eight or nine journeys, all seven hundred Jews had been killed.

Henceforth, day after day, Jews from all the surrounding towns and villages were to be brought to Chelmno and killed. Told that they were being taken to 'the East' for agricultural labour, or to work in factories, up to a thousand Jews a day were taken to their deaths. When sick or old Jews were put into the van, the Germans in charge of the operation would advise the driver 'to drive carefully and slowly'. No one ever survived that journey; in all, it was to consume 360,000 lives, and to eliminate Jewish life altogether from more than two hundred communities. The whole plan was carried out by deception; without the need for publicly visible mass killings, at a place which was located in a remote woodland in German-occupied Poland, far from prying eyes and protests. A new method of mass murder had been devised; Chelmno had become its first, but was not to be its last, location.

On the morning of December 8, the scale of Japan's aggression became clear. The American fleet at Pearl Harbour had been all but eliminated. Japanese troops were ashore in Malaya. In the Philippines, a Japanese air attack on the island of Luzon had resulted in 86 of the 160 American aircraft on the island being destroyed, at a cost of only seven Japanese fighters shot down. There was also a successful Japanese landing on the small northern island of Batan. On the China coast, Japanese troops seized the American garrisons at Shanghai and Tientsin; at Shanghai the American gunboat *Wake*, after an attempted scuttling, surrendered. 'Yesterday', Roosevelt declared in a war message to Congress, 'December 7, 1941 – a date which will live in infamy – the United States of America was suddenly and deliberately attacked by naval and air forces of the Empire of Japan.' Roosevelt added: 'No matter how long it may take us to overcome this premeditated invasion, the American people in their righteous might will win through to absolute victory.'

From Rastenburg, on December 8, Hitler issued his Directive No. 39: the German forces in Russia were 'to abandon immediately all major offensive operations and to go over to the defensive'. The same day, it was made clear at the highest level that wherever German troops had to withdraw, all villages and all buildings in the area to be evacuated were to be destroyed. 'In the interests of the military operations,' Field Marshal Keitel informed Army Group North by telephone on December 8, 'there is to be no respect whatever for the population's situation.' This, he explained, was an instruction from Hitler himself.

For the Russians, December 8 saw two successes: the wresting of Tikhvin from German control, easing, if only slightly, the supply situation for Leningrad, and the production of the first twenty-five T-34 tanks from the Kharkov Tanks Works, now relocated in the Urals. It was less than ten weeks since the last group of factory engineers had left Kharkov for the East.

Behind the German lines in Russia, Soviet partisans maintained their pressure on German supply lines, forcing the Germans to take troops out of the front line in order to launch special military operations against them. In German-occupied France, the British continued to send in agents, both Englishmen and Frenchmen, to help organize resistance, and to maintain the escape lines into Spain for Allied pilots and prisoners-of-war. On December 8, however, a deserter from the British Army at the time of Dunkirk, Sergeant Harold Cole, helped the Germans to break one of the principal Allied escape lines. As a result of Cole's treachery, fifty of those who had helped maintain the line were arrested and shot.

On December 8, with Japanese troops already ashore in northern Malaya, Winston Churchill informed the Japanese Government 'that a state of war exists between our two countries'. The only two confronting nations not now at war were Germany and the United States. Amid the turmoil of the new Pacific war, the bitter confrontation in Russia, and the continuing war in North Africa, these two nations still maintained diplomatic relations. Roosevelt, so Hitler was told on his return to Berlin on December 9, would do all he could to avoid war with Germany, to avoid exposing the United States to a war in two oceans. That same day, however, the German Navy was told that it could begin operations against American ships, even within the Pan-American Security Zone.

For the United States, every avenue of activity against Japan had to be explored as a matter of urgency. During December 8, a United States Army Air Force captain, Claire L. Chennault, who had been an adviser to the Chinese Government since July 1937, flew his three squadrons, then based near Mandalay in Burma, across the mountains to the Chinese city of Kunming. Promoted that day to the rank of colonel, Chennault was to provide a visible and highly able United States presence in the defence of China against further Japanese inroads.

The Japanese conquests were formidable; during December 9 Japanese troops occupied Bangkok, the capital of Thailand, and made two further landings on the Malay Peninsula, at the Thai coastal towns of Singora and Patani. In mid-Pacific, their troops landed at Tarawa and Makin islands, in the Gilbert Islands group.

In the Warsaw ghetto, news of the war between the United States and Japan had brought considerable excitement. 'Most people believe that the war will not last long,' Mary Berg noted in her diary on December 9, 'and that the Allies' victory is certain.' America's entry into the war, she added, 'has inspired the hundreds of thousands of dejected Jews in the ghetto with a new breath of hope'.

For the Allies, that 'hope' was in fact still remote. On December 10, eighty-four Japanese torpedo-carrying aircraft spotted by chance and then sank the British battleship *Prince of Wales* and her sister ship, the *Repulse*. In all, 840 officers and men were drowned; 1,285 survivors were picked up from the sea. The two warships, Malaya's only serious naval defence, had been on their way to Kuantan, as decided upon by their commander at the last moment, following a false report that a Japanese naval force had begun to put troops ashore.

After three days of war, the Japanese were effective masters of both the South China Sea and the Pacific Ocean. In their attack on the two British warships, only four of the eighty-four Japanese aircraft had been shot down. That same day, fifteen hundred miles away, in the Philippines, two thousand Japanese troops landed at Aparri and Gonzaga, on the northern tip of Luzon, while a further two thousand landed at Vigan, on the western coast.

In Germany, yet another step in the spread of mass murder took place on December 10, a mere three days after Pearl Harbour. It was an order, issued by Himmler, that medical boards should visit all concentration camps to 'sort out' those who were unfit for work, ill, 'or psychopaths'. All those selected by this order – the sick did not have to be examined, their documents would suffice to

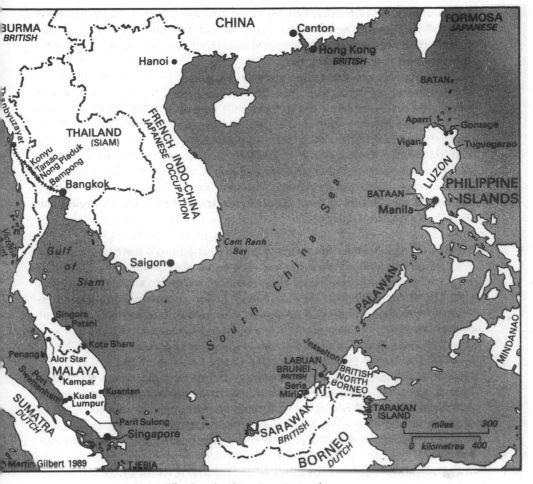

The South China Sea, December 1941

identify them – were to be taken to the nearest centre at which there was a carbon-monoxide gas chamber, and killed. Eleven German doctors, headed by two professors of medicine, Heyde and Nitsche, supervised the carrying out of this order; in all, several tens of thousands of concentration-camp inmates were murdered as a result of it.

On December 11, Germany declared war on the United States. It was perhaps the greatest error, and certainly the single most decisive act, of the Second World War. The United States, still neutral in Europe, had just been drawn into a struggle in the Pacific against enormous odds. The Atlantic, and the struggle on the continent of Europe, was half a globe away. Hitler, by his declaration of war, brought the United States back to Europe as a belligerent; first America's warships, then her warplanes, and finally her armies, would, whatever their

277

Pacific duties, ensure the overthrow of Hitler and his system. 'The accession of the United States', Churchill telegraphed on the following day to Anthony Eden – then on his way to Russia – 'makes amends for all, and with time and patience will give certain victory'.

In the Pacific, the Americans were showing that they had the resources and the willpower to strike back. On Wake Island, where twenty-three men had been killed on December 7 and a further twenty-one on December 8 by Japanese bombers, the Japanese fleet that arrived to seize the island on December 11 was met with such an effective initial defence that two Japanese destroyers, the *Hayate* and the *Kisaragi*, were sunk, with the loss of 5,350 soldiers and sailors on board. Three Japanese bombers were also shot down during the attack.

Resistance on Wake continued for sixteen days, the small force of 524 American servicemen and 1,216 civilian construction workers, offering the Japanese a tenacious defence.

By December 11, Soviet forces had recaptured four hundred towns and villages in a period of less than six days, including Istra, on the Moscow–Volokolamsk highway; and driven the Germans back from the Moscow–Volga canal; it was the Red Army's most successful day thus far in the counter-offensive. 'In Hitler's launching of the Nazi campaign on Russia', Churchill told the House of Commons that day, 'we can already see, after less than six months of fighting, that he has made one of the outstanding blunders of history.'

In the Far East, the Japanese, at the moment of their triumph, had come up against a first foretaste of the American ability to resist, not only on Wake Island, but also on Guam, where 5,400 Japanese troops attacked the 430 American Marines and sailors on the island. Although outnumbered by more than ten to one, the Americans on Guam held off the attackers for nine hours, before being forced to surrender; seventeen Americans and one Japanese had been killed.

In the battle for Malaya, six hundred civilians were killed on December 12 in a Japanese air raid at Penang, on the western side of the Peninsula. Further up the Peninsula, the British evacuated Victoria Point, the Burmese town nearest to the Thai border. On the following day, Japanese forces entered the northern Malayan town of Alor Star; there, in a conversation with Major Iwaichi Fujiwara of the Japanese Imperial General Staff, a Sikh prisoner-of-war, Major Mohan Singh, agreed to set up a special unit for Indians, Burmese and Thais who did not want the British or the French to return. The slogan which the Japanese suggested for the unit was 'Asia for the Asiatics'. Within a few weeks, Major Singh had agreed to lead an Indian National Army to fight against the British.

On December 14, as Japanese troops advanced southward in the Philippines, capturing Tuguegarao, American bombers attacked the troop transports. One such bomber, piloted by Captain Hewitt T. Wheless, was forced by partial engine failure to fall behind his flight. He decided, nevertheless, to continue on the mission. Reaching the target, and already left far behind by the other bombers, Wheless's plane was attacked by eighteen Japanese fighters. He managed to drop his bombs, then turned back to his base; but on the return flight he was pursued by the eighteen fighters for seventy-five miles. In the running battle, in which his radio operator was killed and one of his two gunners crippled, eleven of the Japanese fighters were shot down. Wheless was awarded the Distinguished Service Cross. He was, said Roosevelt later, 'a modest young man proud of his crew for one of the toughest fights a bomber has yet experienced'.

In German occupied Poland, the sealed van at Chelmno had made its short journeys to the woods each day since December 7. On December 10 more than a thousand Jews, from six small villages just to the west of the death camp, had been taken to Chelmno from a collection point in the village of Kowale Panskie, held overnight in the church at Chelmno, and then gassed. Four days later, it was the 975 Jews from the village of Dabie who were taken on that short but final journey. In Warsaw, on December 14, Emanuel Ringelblum recorded how, at a Jewish funeral, a German policeman 'suddenly, without warning, began shooting at the funeral procession'. Two of the mourners fell dead on the spot. 'Jews have no peace,' Ringelblum wrote, 'even when accompanying their dead to eternal rest'. On the following day, in Paris, forty Polish Jews were shot by the Gestapo for acts of resistance. Among those killed were four Jews who had been born in Warsaw.

With the gassings at Chelmno having been proved effective, swift and secret, Heydrich called a conference in Berlin to discuss the 'future' of Europe's Jews. The date set for the conference was early January. 'Do you imagine they're going to be housed in neat estates in the Baltic Provinces!', Hans Frank, ruler of the General Government, asked his senior officials on December 16, and he added: 'We were told in Berlin: why all this bother? We've got no use for them either in the Ostland or in the Eastern Territories. Liquidate them yourselves!'

Frank himself had no objection at all to this particular 'future' for the Jews of Poland. 'I ask nothing of the Jews,' he told his officials, 'except that they should disappear.' What was needed, he said, were 'steps which, one way or another, will lead to extermination, in conjunction with the large-scale measures under discussion in the Reich'.

What those 'large-scale measures' might be, the January conference would reveal.

On December 15 the Red Army drove the German forces out of Klin. On the Leningrad front, Field Marshal von Leeb asked permission for Army Group North to make a general withdrawal. Hitler refused to agree; that evening, as he left Berlin for Rastenburg on board his special train, *Amerika*, he drafted his first 'halt' order for the Russian front. 'Any large-scale retreat by major sections of the Army in midwinter,' he warned, 'given only limited mobility, insufficient winter equipment, and no prepared positions in the rear, must inevitably have the gravest consequences.'

On December 16, the Russians recaptured Kalinin. In North Africa, Rommel began his withdrawal west of Tobruk; during a week of fighting, he had lost 38,000 soldiers killed, as against 18,000 British dead. In the Far East, Japanese forces landed at Miri in Sarawak, and at Seria in Brunei: not only territory, but oil, was within their grasp.

At Hong Kong, after a week of air bombardment, Japanese envoys crossed the harbour under safe passage with a message to the British Governor, Sir Mark Young, that, as resistance was futile, the only choice for the garrison was surrender. The envoys were sent back. 'The Governor and Commander-in-Chief of Hong Kong', Sir Mark himself replied, 'declines absolutely to enter into negotiations for the surrender of Hong Kong, and takes this opportunity of notifying Lieutenant-General Sakai and Vice-Admiral Masaichi Nimi that he is not prepared to receive any further communications from them on the subject.'

On the following day, December 18, under cover of a heavy artillery barrage, Japanese troops landed on Hong Kong island. 'The Japanese are occupying all the islands, one after the other,' Hitler told Himmler that evening at Rastenburg, and he added: 'They will get hold of Australia too. The white race will disappear from those regions.'

In preparing to land on Hong Kong, the Japanese commander of the first wave of troops, Colonel Tanaka, had told his regiment that they were to take no prisoners. His order was obeyed. Having overrun a volunteer anti-aircraft battery in the first phase of the landing, the Japanese soldiers roped together all twenty survivors of the action and then bayoneted them to death. At a Royal Army Medical Corps dressing station, the staff and wounded soldiers offered no resistance when the Japanese arrived. They were led up a hillside, where Japanese soldiers shot and bayoneted to death eight Canadians, four Royal Army Medical Corps soldiers and three St John Ambulance Brigade men.

Some Canadian troops taken prisoner in Hong Kong were among a group whose lives had been saved by the action of Company Sergeant-Major J. R. Osborn, a veteran of the First World War. Seeing a Japanese grenade falling in the midst of his colleagues, and not having enough time to toss it away, Osborn shouted a warning and threw himself on it as it exploded. By his self-sacrifice, at least six other soldiers were saved. After the war, when returning prisoners-of-war told of Osborn's action, he was awarded a posthumous Victoria Cross.

On December 19, over China, Colonel Chennault sent his aircraft to intercept ten Japanese warplanes which were on a bombing raid from Hanoi and Kunming. It was the first combat mission of Chennault's 'Flying Tigers', as they were known. Nine out of the ten Japanese aircraft were shot down.

In the Mediterranean, the British suffered a setback that day, when Italian manned-torpedoes, known to the British as 'Chariots', penetrated Alexandria harbour and badly damaged two battleships, *Queen Elizabeth* and *Valiant*. This one attack gave the Italians temporary naval precedence in heavy warships.

Hitler's declaration of war on the United States had, as yet, led to no direct military confrontation between the two powers. But following the German declaration of war, Roumania and Bulgaria also declared war on the United States.

Behind the German lines in Russia, the Special Task Forces had continued their mass executions. Operational Situation Report USSR No. 148, sent from Berlin on December 19, recorded among several dozen separate mass executions 5,281 Jews shot in Bobruisk; 1,013 Jews and Jewesses in Parichi who had 'shown a hostile attitude to the Germans and had close connections with the partisans'; and 835 Jews 'of both sexes' in Rudnya 'because they lent extensive help to the partisans, spread disruptive propaganda, partly refused to work, and did not wear their Jewish badges'. In Vitebsk, the Germans had decided upon the 'evacuation' of the ghetto which they had earlier set up there. 'During this process,' Report No. 148 noted, 'a total of 4,090 Jews of both sexes were shot.' This Report also gave details of the shooting of sixteen 'mentally ill Jewish and Russian children' in Shumyachi. 'In fact', the report explained, 'the children were lying for weeks in their own excrement. All had severe eczema. The German chief military physician from the hospital in Shumyachi, who was called in for consultation, declared that the children's home and its inmates were an epidemic centre of the first degree, sufficient reason for their shooting.'

On December 20 the Japanese landed on the Philippine island of Mindanao, which they at once began to turn into a vast fortified base. On the Russian front, on December 20, Volokolamsk was wrested from the Germans; at the roadside the Russian troops found a gallows from which were still hanging the frozen corpses of eight members of the Moscow Young Communist League. They had been caught and executed six weeks earlier while on a mission behind the lines to establish contact with the partisans. All were posthumously awarded the Order of Lenin.

As his troops continued to retreat, Hitler told General Halder: 'The will to hold out must be brought home to every unit!' This was easier to say than to achieve; according to Soviet figures, 55,000 German soldiers had been killed in the battle for Moscow, now so decisively ended. But the cruelty of the campaign continued to be in evidence everywhere. On December 21, near Minsk, several thousand Soviet prisoners-of-war were frozen to death during a march across open fields. In Vilna, several hundred Soviet prisoners of war, most of them half naked, many of them without even boots, were forced to clear snow from the railway lines. A Jewish woman, taking pity on their plight, offered one of the Russians a piece of bread. This was noticed by one of the German guards, who at once shot dead both the Russian and the Jewess.

In Western Europe and the Mediterranean, it was the naval war which saw the main action in mid-December. In the Atlantic, in the course of a six-day and six-night battle, during which nine German submarines attacked convoy HG 76, on its way from Gibraltar to Britain, four of the attackers had been sunk or forced to scuttle, including the reigning German ace commander, Captain Endrass, in command of U-567, which was lost without trace.

Only one of the thirty-two Allied merchant ships had been sunk. 'After this failure,' Admiral Dönitz later wrote, 'and in view of the unsatisfactory results of the preceding two months, my Staff was inclined to voice the opinion that we were no longer in a position successfully to combat the convoy system.'

It was not only the convoy system with which the Germans were now confronted in their Western war. On December 22, in Washington, at the first of a series of meetings which were to continue into January, Churchill and Roosevelt agreed to set up a combined Anglo-American General Staff, to co-ordinate their strategies against both Germany and Japan, and to prepare for an eventual joint Anglo-American invasion of German-held Europe. Even with the immediate military situation against them, this unity of command and desire to take offensive action was to be a decisive factor in the evolution of a joint war policy. Meanwhile, setbacks had to be borne; on December 23 the Japanese returned to Wake Island with a force of two thousand marines, supported by aircraft from two aircraft carriers. In a fierce battle, 820 of the Japanese were killed. The Americans lost 120 men, before being overwhelmed. An American naval relief force, sent from battered Pearl Harbour, was still 425 miles from Wake Island when the Japanese landed. That same day, a further 10,000 Japanese troops landed on Luzon.

In Hong Kong, the defenders were still holding out on Christmas Eve; that day a further fifty-three British and Canadian soldiers were roped together after being captured, and then shot or bayoneted to death. On Christmas Day, the wounded Canadians of a platoon which had surrendered were also murdered, as were two doctors and seven nurses – four of them Chinese – who had been attending wounded soldiers at the St Stephen's College Emergency Hospital. The wounded, more than fifty in all, were then killed in their beds.

On the evening of December 24, General MacArthur had left Manila for the fortified island of Corregidor. Manila, in an attempt to save its inhabitants from being caught in a battlefield, was declared an open city. The Japanese continued, however, to bomb it. That night, fifty-four Japanese bombers and twenty-four fighters raided air installations in the Burmese capital, Rangoon, destroying many Allied aircraft on the ground. Even while the bombing and strafing was in progress, Chennault's 'Flying Tigers', which were also at the airfield, managed to take off safely, and to shoot down six of the Japanese planes for the loss of two of their own.

In the German-occupied Baltic States, December 24 marked the day of a new order, issued by the German civilian governor, Hinrich Lohse, that gypsies were 'a double danger'. They were carriers of disease, 'especially typhus', and they were 'unreliable elements who cannot be put to useful work'. They also harmed the German cause by passing on 'hostile' news reports. 'I therefore determine', Lohse added, 'that they should be treated in the same way as Jews.'

Soviet prisoners-of-war were also being murdered that winter on an horrific scale. At a prisoner-of-war camp set up by the Germans at Hola, in Poland, 100,000 Soviet soldiers were herded together in an open field and given no food. Desperately, they dug holes in which to try to get shelter from the wind and snow, and ate grass and roots to keep alive. Any nearby villagers who were caught by the Germans throwing food into the field were shot. By the end of December, the prisoners-of-war were dead. A further 7,000 were murdered in nearby Biala Podlaska.

On December 25, Hong Kong surrendered, the first British possession to fall under the emblem of the Rising Sun; 11,000 British soldiers were taken prisoner.

On Christmas Day in Leningrad, 3,700 people died of starvation. The recapture of Tikhvin had meant, however, that more supplies would now get through, by rail to the eastern shore of Lake Ladoga, and then across the ice to the city. On the following day, on the Moscow front, the Germans evacuated Kaluga, while in the south, three thousand Russian troops were put ashore during the night of December 25 on the Kerch Peninsula, to establish a new Crimean front, and to relieve the pressure on Sevastopol, which was still holding out against a German siege. Six days later, in a further series of landings in the Crimea, forty thousand Russian soldiers were put ashore at Feodosiya.

Crossing the North Sea on December 27, the British launched Operation Archery, a commando raid on the German naval base at Malöy, in western Norway. Five German merchantmen, with a total displacement of 16,000 tons, were sunk. Hitler, angered by the range and unexpectedness of the attack, began to talk of turning the whole North Sea, Channel and Atlantic coastlines under his control into an impregnable fortress: 'Fortress Europe'. Not knowing where an Allied attack might come, and faced now with the inevitability of eventual American participation in it, Hitler ordered the construction of coastal fortification from the border of Norway and Finland, above the Arctic Circle, to the border between France and Spain in the Bay of Biscay.

There was another change of German plans on December 27; Dr Todt, in conversation that day with Albert Speer, insisted that communication and transportation conditions in Russia, from which he had just returned, were so difficult, and the 'discouragement and despair' among the German soldiers so great, that grandiose architectural building plans would have to be suspended, in terms of priority use of skilled manpower, until the roads of the Ukraine could be put in order. Staff and workmen who were still 'frivolously engaged', as Speer later wrote, in working on road construction in Germany would have to be sent to Russia to repair and build the roads there, without which neither supplies nor men could move forward. Todt told Speer he had seen 'stalled hospital trains in which the wounded had frozen to death, and had witnessed the misery of the troops in villages and hamlets cut off by snow and cold'.

Speer would do his best to help Todt in the task of Eastern road-building. But he noted that Todt was convinced 'that we were both physically incapable of enduring such hardships, and psychologically doomed to destruction in Russia'. Hitler, however, when Todt saw him at Rastenburg two days later, was speaking confidently of his estimate of 'the employable Russian labour' at two and a half million people. With such a force, Hitler told Todt, 'we'll succeed in producing the machine tools we need'.

Throughout German occupied Europe, the faith of the captive peoples in Germany's eventual defeat was bolstered up by British radio messages of encouragement, by the news that Hitler was now at war with the United States, and by the continual despatch of men to join resistance groups behind the lines. On December 28, the British carried out Operation Anthropoid, parachuting two Czechs, Jan Kubis and Josef Gabcik, near Pilsen. Their task was to get in touch with the Czech underground movement, and to plan whatever acts of resistance might be possible.

In the Far East, on December 30, Japanese aircraft attacked the fortified island of Corregidor, to which MacArthur and the United States Philippines headquarters had been transferred four days earlier. On the following day, the last day of the year, American and Filipino troops completed the evacuation of Manila. In northern and central Malaya, despite a brave effort by Indian troops to hold up the Japanese at Kampar, on the western side of the Peninsula, and at Kuantan, on the eastern side, the British had already abandoned to the overwhelming force of Japan the most part of a vast territory which produced thirty-eight per cent of the world's rubber, and fifty-eight per cent of the world's tin.

As 1941 came to an end, Hitler told his circle of friends and confidants at Rastenburg: 'Let's hope 1942 brings me as much good fortune as 1941,' and in his New Year message to the German people, he declared: 'He who fights for the life of a nation, for her daily bread and her future, will win; but he who, in this war, with his Jewish hate, seeks to destroy whole nations, will fail.'

Churchill was in Ottawa on December 31, during a break in his Washington talks. Asked at a press conference about Yugoslavia, he said: 'They are fighting with the greatest vigour and on quite a large scale, and we don't hear very much of what is going on there. It is all very terrible. Guerrilla warfare and the most frightful atrocities by the Germans and Italians, and every kind of torture.' Churchill added, of the fighting behind the German lines in Yugoslavia: 'The people manage to keep the flag of freedom flying.'

In the Soviet Union, the struggle for survival had reached a crucial stage; December 31 saw the recapture of yet another town in the Moscow sector, Kozelsk, which lay to the west of the Medyn-Orel defensive line established by the Germans three and a half weeks earlier. On the Kerch Peninsula, the Russian landings of two days earlier at Feodosiya had secured a strong foothold, in temperatures so cold – minus twenty degrees centigrade – that, as one historian has written, 'the immobile wounded inexorably died as stiffened blocks of ice'. But the Feodosiya landings were a blow to the Germans, who were forced to break off their operations against Sevastopol to halt the new Russian thrust.

In just over seven months of fighting in Russia, as many as 200,000 German soldiers had been killed in action, or had died of their wounds; in the extreme cold, even a relatively minor wound and bleeding could lead to severe shock, and death. In one day alone, at the end of December, as a result of frostbite, more than fourteen thousand German soldiers had been forced to submit to amputation. Not all of them survived the operation. A further sixty-two thousand frostbite cases were classified as 'moderate': not involving amputation, but resulting in a total incapacity to return to action.

Through Arctic waters, British supplies for Russia had continued to arrive at Archangel where, after their hazardous journey, they were hurried southward by rail to Moscow, the railway line itself remaining well behind the German front line. In all, 750 tanks, 800 fighter aircraft, 1,400 vehicles and 100,000 tons of stores reached Archangel from Britain by the end of the year. Small in terms of what was needed, these supplies were not only useful in themselves, but an earnest of what was to come, and a pledge of continuing support.

The reality of war was of daily and desperate suffering. In Leningrad, where three to four thousand people were dying each day of starvation, despite an increase in a worker's daily bread ration from eight to ten-and-a-half ounces, the scenes reflected the true face of what was now a global war.

'Death would overtake people in all kinds of circumstances,' a city official later recalled. 'While they were on the streets, they would fall down and never rise again; or in their houses, where they would fall asleep and never awake; in factories, where they would collapse while doing a job of work. There was no transport, and the dead body would usually be put on a hand-sleigh drawn by two or three members of the dead man's family; often, wholly exhausted during the long trek to the cemetery, they would abandon the body halfway, leaving the authorities to deal with it'. In Leningrad, however, as everywhere in war torn Europe and Asia, these 'authorities' were themselves powerless to control suffering, disease, or even the burial of the dead. That winter, a Leningrader on his way by car to the Piskarevsky cemetery, on the north-eastern outskirts of the city, noted down his impressions of the journey. 'Coming out of town,' he wrote, 'where there were small one-storey houses, I saw gardens and orchards, and then an extraordinary formless heap. I came nearer. There were on both sides of the road such enormous piles of bodies that two cars could not pass. A car could go only on one side, and was unable to turn around.'

Hundreds of people, pulling the corpse of a loved one or a neighbour on a sledge, had hardly the strength to dump it on the ground. 'Not infrequently,' one historian has recorded, 'those who pulled the sledge fell beside the corpse, themselves dead – without a sound, without a groan, without a cry.' 'To take someone who has died to the cemetery', a Leningrad writer, Luknitsky, noted in his diary on December 29, 'is an affair so laborious that it exhausts the last vestiges of strength in the survivors; and the living, fulfilling their duty to the dead, are brought to the brink of death themselves.'

# 22

# 'We are no longer alone' (Churchill)

NEW YEAR 1942

The New Year of 1942 opened inauspiciously for the Allies. In the Kerch peninsula, German forces pushed back the Russian parachutists who had landed on this eastern extremity of the Crimea. In the Philippines, American and Filipino troops were being pushed back into the Bataan peninsula. In Malaya, Japanese forces, continuing their southern advance, occupied Kuantan. In Germany, 1942 was triumphantly declared the 'Year of Service in the East and on the Land'; a total of 18,000 Hitler Youth leaders from Germany serving in Poland and the western Ukraine. They were sent to form a nucleus of a future Germanic settlement in the East. During the year, several hundred young Dutch, Norwegian, Danish and Flemish volunteers were to join them: these 'Eastern Volunteers of Germanic Youth' were likewise to be a nucleus of the New Order. It was a New Order typically marked, on 1 January 1942, by the final disappearance of the Zagreb synagogue, pride of the Croat capital's 12,000 Jews, which had been demolished stone by stone over a period of four months.

There were also several acts of defiance that January 1. The most public was a declaration, issued by Churchill and Roosevelt in Washington, and signed by twenty-six nations, requiring the signatories to employ their full resources against the Axis, and not to make peace separately. Calling themselves the 'United Nations', and headed by Britain, the United States and the Soviet Union, these twenty-six nations declared that the aim of their struggle and their unity was 'to ensure life, liberty, independence and religious freedom, and to preserve the rights of man and justice'. In the Vilna ghetto, 150 young Jews gathered that January 1, not to mourn the 60,000 murdered Jews of their city, but, on behalf of the 20,000 who were still alive behind the guardhouses and the barbed wire, to declare: 'Hitler plans to destroy all the Jews of Europe, and the Jews of Lithuania have been chosen as the first in line. We will not be led like sheep to the slaughter!'

In German-occupied Europe, it was only slowly that even the smallest of steps could be taken to challenge German power. One such step was taken that January 1 when the former Mayor of the French city of Chartres, Jean Moulin, who had escaped four months earlier to Britain, was parachuted back into

France. His task was to try to unify the various and disparate Resistance groups, and to set a course of co-ordinated action. Known as 'Max', Moulin brought with him on his mission, hidden in the false bottom of a matchbox, a warm personal message from General de Gaulle to the Resistance leaders.

On New Year's Day 1942, in the Far East, Japanese forces already ashore on Borneo attacked the island of Labuan. It was a day he would not easily forget, the British Resident, Hugh Humphrey, later wrote, 'for I was repeatedly hit by a Japanese officer with his sword (in its scabbard) and exhibited for twenty-four hours to the public in an improvised cage on the grounds that, before the Japanese arrived, I had sabotaged the war effort of the Imperial Japanese Forces by destroying the stocks of aviation fuel on the island. ...' Humphrey was to remain a prisoner of the Japanese until the end of the war.

At Bletchley, where 1,500 British scholars and academics were now decrypting and analysing the German Enigma messages, the first day of January brought a remarkable success, the breaking of four separate Enigma keys: 'Pink', used by the German Air Force command for messages of the highest secrecy, and 'Gadfly', 'Hornet' and 'Wasp', used by three of the German air corps. On the following day, 2 January, a fifth key was broken; known at Bletchley as 'Kite', it carried the German Army's most secret supply messages from Berlin to the Eastern Front.

It was on the Eastern Front, on January 2, that Hitler issued an order forbidding his Ninth Army, which had just evacuated Kalinin, to make any further withdrawals. Not 'one inch of ground' was to be given up. But the Red Army was not to be deterred in its repeated attacks by any such instructions to its enemy; that same day, the Thirty-ninth Russian Army broke through the German front line north-west of Rzhev. Such victories were helped by the growing Russian efforts behind the lines. 'Repeatedly', the Second Panzer Army reported on January 2, 'it has been observed that the enemy is accurately informed about the soft spots in our front and frequently picks the boundaries between our corps and divisions as points of attack.' Russian civilians, the report added, were crossing between the lines, and passing back information. 'The movement of the inhabitants between the fronts', this report concluded, 'must, therefore, be prevented by all possible means.'

In Washington, Roosevelt and Churchill presided jointly on January 2 over a meeting, the main decision of which was in due course to overshadow all tactical manoeuvres: a staggering increase in the American arms programme. Instead of the target of 12,750 operational aircraft laid down by their Staffs a mere three weeks earlier, 45,000 were to be built by the end of 1943. Instead of 15,450 tanks, 45,000 were to be built; instead of 262,000 machine guns, half a million. All other weapons of war were to be increased in quantity by an average of seventy per cent.

Such plans held a long term threat for the Axis powers; but in January 1942 it was not clear that the Allied powers would have any such long term. On January 2, Japanese forces entered the Philippine capital of Manila. On January

3, General Marshall was advised by the American Army planners that there were insufficient forces to send a relief expedition to the embattled Philippines. On January 4, Japanese aircraft struck at Rabaul, a strategic base in the Bismarck Archipelago, guarded by 1,400 British troops.

In German-occupied Europe, there was a courageous protest on January 5 by the Dutch Council of Churches, against what they described as the 'complete lawlessness' of the German treatment of the Jews; but, despite the protest, round-ups for forced labour and expulsion from several towns and villages into Amsterdam continued. January 5 also saw the escape from the German prisoner-of-war camp at Colditz of two Allied officers, the Englishman Airey Neave and the Dutchman Tony Luteyn; both reached the safety of Swiss soil within the next few days. Reaching Gibraltar from Britain on January 5, an Englishman, Donald Darling, code name 'Sunday', organized a secret overland communication route to France, enabling escaped Allied prisoners-of-war to travel from Marseilles to Barcelona, then on to Gibraltar or Lisbon. 'Sunday' was substantially helped in this by 'Monday', a former British diplomat in Berlin, Michael Creswell, who based in Spain, would when necessary cross the Pyrenees into France to co-ordinate the escape lines.

In German-occupied France, resistance was fitful but growing. On January 7 a French policeman guarding a German Army garage was shot dead. Many Frenchmen feared that such acts of defiance were futile, provoking reprisals and a harsher occupation. But for those who carried out such acts, the will to strike, and to be seen to strike, was strong, overriding caution and fear.

On January 7, in Yugoslavia, the Germans launched their second anti-partisan offensive, driving Tito's forces from Olovo, to which they had been driven less than six weeks earlier, to Foca, fifty miles to the south. But although forced to flee southward, and suffering heavy losses, the partisans retained their determination to fight on.

On the Eastern Front, January 7 saw the launching of a Soviet counter-offensive north of Novgorod. Much of the fighting took place across a frozen swamp. Thousands of German soldiers were unable to fight because of frostbite. Amputations, and even double amputations, were frequent. Because of a severe shortage of blankets, wounded men froze to death even in field hospitals; each night the temperature fell to minus forty degrees centigrade. After five days of battle, the German commander, Field Marshal von Leeb, asked permission to pull back from the exposed pocket at Demyansk. Hitler refused, and 100,000 German soldiers were soon surrounded. Von Leeb resigned; nor was he to take any further active part in the war.

As the Red Army pressed the Germans back mile by mile, the Japanese were sweeping all before them in massive thrusts. On January 10, in Malaya, the British were forced to abandon Port Swettenham and Kuala Lumpur. In the Philippines, Bataan was under sustained Japanese attack, preceded by an air drop of leaflets calling upon the defenders to surrender. On Dutch Borneo, substantial Japanese forces, supported by two heavy cruisers and eight destroyers, landed on Tarakan; the island, with its oilfields, was under complete

SWEDEN

FINLAND

*Lake Onega*

*Lake Ladoga*

*Gulf of Finland*

Leningrad • Tikhvin

*Baltic Sea*

Riga

Novgorod

*Lake Ilmen*

Staraya Russa
Demyansk

Kholm

Königsberg

Kovno

Loknya
Velikiye Luki

Kalinin

Rzhev
Petrishchevo

Rastenburg
GREATER

Vilna

Kublichi  Ushachi
Ilja

Velizh

Mozhaisk

Moscow

Mlawa
Sierpc

Rakov  Minsk

Vitebsk
Rudnya

Vyazma

Dorogobuzh
Yelnya

Medyn

Warsaw

Baranowicze

Cherven

Smolensk

Kaluga

Sukhnichi
Kozelsk

7 December 1941

Hola

Osipovichi

Shumyachi

Bobruisk
Parichi

GERMANY

Brest-Litovsk

Klintsy

Orel

Lvov

Kiev

SOVIET UNION

*River Dnieper*

Kursk

Kharkov

HUNGARY

Uman

Igren

Izyum

1 March 1942

Balta

Dnepropetrovsk

Vasilkovka

Krivoi Rog

Berezovka

Nikolayev

Odessa

Kherson

*Sea of Azov*

*Black Sea*

Dzhankoi
CRIMEA
Simferopol

Kerch

ROUMANIA

Sevastopol

Feodosiya

Novorossiisk

0        *miles*        200
0      *kilometres*     300

© Martin Gilbert 1989

The Eastern Front, March 1942

Japanese control within twenty-four hours. Also captured on January 11, by Japanese naval parachutists, was the Dutch Celebes city of Manado, an essential airbase for the onward southern assault.

Swiftly, and with ruthless cruelties towards its prisoners, the Japanese Army, supported by powerful warships, moved from island to island. An Allied soldier who surrendered might be made a prisoner-of-war. He might equally be held captive for a few hours, and then, in defiance of all known rules of war, be bayoneted to death. Ruthlessness, coming so suddenly to South-East Asia, had already been commonplace against Russian prisoners-of-war on the Eastern Front for half a year. On January 12, in Kiev, the executions began, over a twelve day period, of what the Operational Situation Report USSR No. 173 described as '104 political officials, 75 saboteurs and looters, and about 8,000 Jews'. In Kovno, five thousand Jews, brought earlier by train to the former Lithuanian capital from Germany and Austria, were taken on January 12 to the Ninth Fort and shot. In Odessa, the deportations began that day of 19,582 Jews, most of them women, children and old people, to concentration camps near Balta. They were sent to the camps in cattle trucks. Those who died in the trains, as dozens did, were taken off at the station of Berezovka, their corpses put in heaps, petrol poured over them, and the bodies burned before the eyes of their families. Eye-witnesses later recalled that among those burned on the pyres were several who were not yet dead. Within the next year and a half, more than fifteen thousand of the deportees were to die, most of them the victims of starvation, severe cold, untreated disease or repeated mass executions in which hundreds would be shot at a time.

On January 12 there was also an extension of the war at sea, when the British merchant ship *Cyclops* was torpedoed off the eastern seaboard of the United States. She had been steaming independently and unescorted along the regular coastal route. Her sinking marked the start of Operation Drum Roll, a new, and for the Allies a disastrous, phase of the war at sea. The American East Coast towns were all well lit; the coastal resorts illuminated. Taking advantage of this, the German submarine commanders lay on the bottom by day, then surfaced at dusk to pick off their targets silhouetted against the lights of the coastal towns. War had come to the United States; but it was offshore, and thus remote to the majority of the population.

By the end of the month, forty-six Allied merchant ships had been sunk off the American coast, a total of 196,243 tons of ships and supplies.

Details of the killings in German-occupied Poland and western Russia had begun to reach, and to horrify, the Allied governments, including those in exile from the very lands in which the tyranny was at its most intense. On January 13 the representatives of nine occupied countries, meeting in London, signed a declaration that all those guilty of 'war crimes' would be punished after the war. Among the signatories were General Sikorski for Poland and General de Gaulle for France. Among their 'principal war aims', they declared, was 'the punishment, through the channels of organized justice, of those guilty of, or responsible for, these crimes, whether they have ordered them, perpetrated them, or participated in them'.

No day passed without the perpetration of crimes against defenceless civilians; on January 14, the day after the London Declaration, in the White Russian village of Ushachi, 807 Jews were driven to the edge of a pit and shot. Even as several dozen of them lay mortally wounded and in agony, amid the blood and corpses, peasants who had witnessed the execution clambered down into the pit to pull what gold they could from the teeth of the dead and dying. That same day, a further 925 Jews were murdered in the nearby village of Kublichi; again, local peasants searched the corpses for gold.

Hitler's thoughts that week were not on Russia alone: 'I must do something for Königsberg,' he told his guests on January 15. 'I shall build a museum in which we shall assemble all we've found in Russia. I'll also build a magnificent opera house and library.' He would also build a 'new, Germanic museum' in Nuremberg, and a new city at Trondheim, on the coast of Norway.

On January 15 the Japanese reached the northernmost mountains of the Bataan Peninsula. 'Help is on the way from the United States,' General MacArthur assured the men now battling for survival. 'Thousands of troops', he told them, 'and hundreds of planes are being despatched.' But no such reinforcements were on their way; nor, with Manila Bay under Japanese blockade, would they have been able to secure an easy access, even assuming that they could have crossed the Pacific without crippling loss. The only American troops travelling to a new war zone that day were the four thousand members of General Russell P. Hartle's 34th Division, who, having just crossed the Atlantic, became the first United States servicemen to arrive in Britain. At that very moment, Churchill was returning by flying boat from the United States to Britain; at dawn on January 17, when the flying boat deviated slightly from its course, it came to within five or six minutes' flying time of the German anti-aircraft batteries at Brest, in German-occupied France. The error was corrected; but, in turning sharply northward, the flying boat seemed to the radar watchers in Britain to be a 'hostile bomber' coming from Brest. Six aircraft were sent up with orders to shoot down the intruder. Fortunately, as Churchill later reflected, 'they failed in their mission'.

Less fortunate on January 17 was the British destroyer *Matabele*; on escort duty with a Murmansk convoy, she was torpedoed and sunk, with the loss of 247 officers and men.

On the Eastern Front, the Red Army now embarked upon a new and decisive tactic; beginning on January 18, and continuing for six days, a total of 1,643 Soviet parachute troops were dropped behind the German lines south-east and south-west of Vyazma. Linking up with partisan units, they began to harass and disrupt the German lines of communication and supply, forcing substantial numbers of German troops to be diverted to anti-partisan activity. On January 20, in the central sector of the front, Soviet troops recaptured the German positions at Mozhaisk, thereby further protecting Moscow from the danger of a direct assault. That same day, as far back as the railway line between Minsk and Baranowicze, the Germans reported Soviet partisan attacks on German railway guards.

It was on January 20, in the Berlin suburb of Wannsee, that senior German officials met to discuss the final and complete destruction of as many of Europe's Jews as possible. Among the Germans present, summoned there by Heydrich, was the newly appointed State Secretary in the Reich Ministry of Justice, Roland Freisler, and a leading Nazi member of the German Foreign Ministry, Martin Luther, whose task was to persuade the governments of Europe to co-operate in what was called, deceptively, 'the Final Solution of the Jewish Question'. The aim, Heydrich explained, was that all eleven million Jews in Europe should 'fall away'. To find them, Europe would be 'combed from West to East'. The representative of the General Government, Dr Joseph Bouhler, had 'only one favour to ask', that the 'Jewish question' in the General Government 'be solved as rapidly as possible'. Another participant, Wilhelm Stuckart, who had helped to draw up the 1935 Nuremberg Laws, turning Jews into second class citizens and outcasts, proposed 'compulsory sterilization' of all 'non-Aryans' and the forcible dissolution of all 'mixed' marriages between Jews and non-Jews. But it was the work of the gas vans at Chelmno which was to be the model; since the second week of December more than a thousand Jews a day, and many Gypsies, had been taken from their homes and villages in western Poland, packed into the vans and killed during the drive from Chelmno church to the nearby wood. In the months following the Wannsee Conference, similar gassing vans, and gas chambers using diesel fumes, were to be set up at three further camps – Belzec, Sobibor and Treblinka. Although remote, each camp was on a railway line; it was to be by rail that almost all the deportees were brought and killed. Only a handful, needed for menial work in the camps, were kept alive. There was no 'selection' of able-bodied men and women who might work in factories or farms; all who arrived – men and boys, women and girls, children, the old, the sick and the able-bodied – were murdered.

Death by gassing and by systematic killing was the 'Final', as opposed to any other, 'Solution', whether emigration or forced labour, or death by mass shooting. To ensure that the Final Solution worked smoothly, that the deportations were orderly and systematic, and that adequate deceptions worked throughout, Heydrich chose a senior officer, Adolf Eichmann, to carry out the Wannsee decisions. When the conference was over, Eichmann later recalled, 'we all sat together like comrades. Not to talk shop, but to rest after long hours of effort'.

It was on January 20, the day of the Wannsee Conference, that a young Jew, Jakub Grojanowski, having escaped from the labour gang at Chelmno which was being forced to bury the bodies when they were thrown out of the gas vans, reached the nearby village of Grabow. Seeking out the local Rabbi, Grojanowski told him: 'Rabbi, don't think I'm crazed and have lost my reason. I am a Jew from the nether world. They are killing the whole nation of Israel. I myself have buried a whole town of Jews, my parents, brothers, and the entire family.'

For the Western Allies, the news from all the war fronts was grim at the start of the third week of January. At Singapore, five British Hurricanes were shot down on January 21 by the Japanese Zero naval fighter aircraft. In North Africa, Rommel took the offensive on January 21, driving the British back across the desert halfway from Benghazi to Tobruk. 'Our opponents are getting out as though they'd been stung,' Rommel wrote to his wife on the following day. In the Philippines, MacArthur now ordered a withdrawal down the Bataan Peninsula, from the Mauban–Abucay line to behind the Pilar–Bagac road. That same night, however, the Japanese launched a series of amphibious landings south of Bagac. In Malaya, Japanese bombers struck at Singapore, causing heavy loss of life and considerable damage. Australian troops, trapped by a Japanese roadblock at Parit Sulong, tried to break through swamp and jungle to reach the British lines. Before setting off, they left their wounded at the roadside 'lying huddled round trees, smoking calmly, unafraid'. Captured by the Japanese, the wounded men were taken to a nearby hut, where they were bayoneted to death, or shot. At Rabaul, in New Guinea, six thousand Japanese troops attacked an Australian garrison of a thousand; once again, most of the Australians were killed after they had been taken prisoner.

On January 23, Japanese troops prepared to land at Kieta on the Solomon Islands, at Balikpapan in Borneo, and at Kendari in the Celebes; a vast geographic span.

In German-occupied Europe, a pattern of war and resistance was emerging. On January 23, at Novi Sad on the Danube, Hungarian soldiers drove 550 Jews and 292 Serbs on to the ice of the river, which the soldiers then shelled until the ice broke up and the Jews and Serbs were drowned. That day, in Vilna, a group of young Jews met to set up a sabotage group against German military installations in the region. Asked one of them: 'Where can we get the first pistol?' By morning, another of the group later recalled, 'We tenderly fondled the sanctified steel of our first pistol'.

Hitler's plan did not envisage Jewish resistance or survival. On January 23, three days after the Wannsee Conference had given administrative backing to the Final Solution, Hitler told his entourage, in Himmler's presence: 'One must act radically. When one pulls out a tooth, one does it with a single tug, and the pain quickly goes away. The Jew must clear out of Europe.' If the Jews were to 'break their pipes' on the journey, Hitler commented, 'I can't do anything about it. But, if they refuse to go voluntarily, I see no other solution but extermination'.

Lest his listeners were shocked by the word 'extermination', Hitler added, in words which could brook no misunderstanding: 'Why should I look at a Jew through other eyes than if he were a prisoner-of-war?'

The Russian soldier knew that, for him, captivity would mean death. He was also aware of the daily murder of Soviet civilians in all the occupied regions. He fought with tenacity to drive the invader back, and to avoid capture. On January 23 Kholm was retaken from the Germans, and Rzhev all but encircled. Further south, Russian troops were poised to break through the German defences

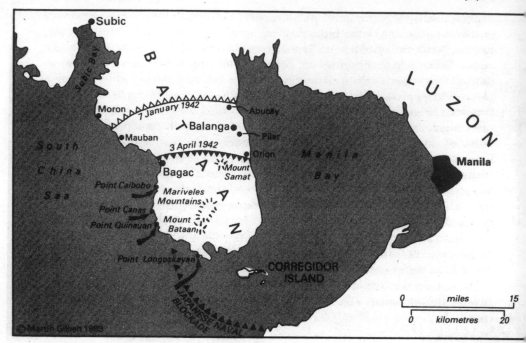

The Bataan Peninsula, January–May 1942

near Izyum, in an attempt to isolate the German troops in Kharkov by a southward thrust.

In Borneo, the Japanese invasion forces, about to land at Balikpapan, suddenly found their troop transports under sustained attack by four American destroyers and a group of submarines. Four of the sixteen Japanese transports were sunk, for no loss. It was America's first naval victory, but it could not halt the occupation of Balikpapan. That same day, January 24, Japanese troops already on northern Bataan, in the Philippines, landed at Point Longoskayan, south of the whole American defence line. To Washington, General MacArthur signalled that 'all manoeuvring possibilities' were now over, and he added: 'I intend to fight it out to complete destruction.' For the soldiers, such heroic words masked a fearful prospect, one which they encapsulated in the pithy style of fighting men:

> 'We're the battling bastards of Bataan:
> No mama, no papa, no Uncle Sam,
> No aunts, no uncles, no nephews, no nieces,
> No rifles, no planes, or artillery pieces,
> And nobody gives a damn.'

On January 25, American and Filipino troops continued their southward retirement, reaching their objective, the Pilar–Bagac road, on the following day. But the Japanese would give them no respite, and within twenty four hours were closing up to continue the attack. Dense jungle made defensive preparations difficult, though Mount Samat, and the Mariveles mountains behind it, rising to 4,700 feet, provided good observation points. Time, however, was against the defenders, as the Japanese bombarded them from the air and, by skilful use of landing barges, by-passed the American defence line by sending troops from Subic Bay and Moron, to Point Caibobo, south of Bagac. The Americans were not, however, without resources or tenacity, and the landing force suffered considerable losses when attacked by an American PT – fast patrol – boat. Two more Japanese landings further south, at Point Canas and Point Quinauan, were successfully contained, so much so that the Japanese gave up their hopes of a rapid conquest of Bataan, and, between Bagac and Orion, had to pull back slightly to a more defensive line of their own, while at the same time calling for reinforcements from Manila, and asking Tokyo to send yet more troops from beyond the Philippines as a matter of urgency.

In New Guinea, on January 25, Japanese troops landed at Lae. Meanwhile, American troops had continued to cross the Atlantic for participation, in due course, in the war in Europe. On January 26, accompanied by a strong protest from the Irish Prime Minister, Eamon de Valera, the first American troops landed in Ulster. It was to be two and a half years before these troops reached Europe; meanwhile, Europe's torment was unabated. On January 26, in German-occupied Yugoslavia, several hundred Jewish women and children were sent on foot, in the snow, from Ruma to Zemun. 'The white death reaped,' one eye witness later recalled. 'Children were freezing in the arms of their mothers, who tried to warm them in their embrace. Mothers buried the frozen children quickly in the snow, hoping that others would bury them properly when spring arrived. The wife of Kurt Hilkovec lost her three children on the way. The youngest, born in Sabac, froze in her arms'. The destination of this march of horror was a concentration camp at Sajmiste; there, almost all the survivors of the march were killed in May.

On the second day of the Zemun death march, Hitler was again sounding off to his guests about the Jews. 'The Jews must pack up, disappear from Europe,' he insisted. 'Let them go to Russia. Where the Jews are concerned, I'm devoid of all sense of pity. They'll always be the ferment that moves people against one another'. Hitler added: 'They'll also have to clear out of Switzerland and Sweden. It's where they're to be found in small numbers that they're most dangerous. Put five thousand Jews in Sweden – soon they'll be holding all the posts there.' It was 'clearly' not enough to expel Jews from Germany. 'We cannot allow them to retain bases of withdrawal at our doors. We want to be out of danger of all kinds of infiltration.' That same day, General Eisenhower criticized in his diary the American policy of 'giving our stuff in driblets all over the world, with no theatre getting enough', and he gave as his own view 'that we must win in Europe'.

Europe knew no respite; on January 28, in the Crimean city of Feodosiya, thirty-six Russian partisans were captured and killed. In Dzhankoi, 141 'suspicious people', as the Gestapo described them, were arrested; 'seventy-six have already been shot after having been interrogated', the report explained nine days later.

In the Far East, Japanese troops landed on January 28 on Russel Island, east of New Guinea. The threat to Australia was becoming a real one. In North Africa, Rommel's forces occupied Benghazi on January 29. The threat to Egypt had been renewed. But the ebb and flow of war was evident with every day; on January 29, on Bataan, American and Filipino troops succeeded in destroying the Japanese bridgehead on Point Longoskayan. On the Eastern Front, Russian forces inflicted heavy losses on the Germans south-west of Kaluga, retaking Sukhinichi. That same day, Britain and the Soviet Union signed a Treaty of Alliance with Iran; British and Russian troops would remain in Iran until six months after the end of the war. The 'Persian corridor', under Anglo-Soviet control, would become the principal route for war supplies from the West to Russia. For his part, the Shah of Iran undertook 'not to adopt in his relations with foreign countries an attitude which is inconsistent with the alliance'.

On January 30 Hitler celebrated the ninth anniversary of his coming to power in Germany. Speaking to a vast and enthusiastic crowd in the Sports Palace in Berlin, he declared: 'The war will not end as the Jews imagine it will, namely with the uprooting of the Aryans, but the result of this war will be the complete annihilation of the Jews.' The hour would come, Hitler warned, 'when the most evil universal enemy of all time will be finished, at least for a thousand years'. On the following day, Operation Situation Report USSR No. 170, sent from Berlin to more than sixty recipients, noted under the heading 'Top Secret' that in the previous six days, in the Crimea, '3,601 people were shot: 3,286 of these were Jews, 152 Communists and NKVD agents, 84 partisans, and 79 looters, saboteurs, and asocial elements. In all, to date 85,201.'

The statistics of death in the Second World War will never be complete. That same January 31, it was noted in Leningrad that more than 200,000 citizens had died of starvation and cold since the siege had begun nearly five months earlier.

For Leningrad, an avenue of hope now lay, across the ice of Lake Ladoga. Although during snow storms the journey could take seven hours, the journey time had been reduced to two and a half hours, even two; in the three months after January 22, when the shorter route first became possible, a total of 554,186 people were taken out to safety, among them 35,713 wounded soldiers. Among the Axis troops facing the Russians in Leningrad that winter were nearly a thousand Dutchmen, members of a Dutch Volunteer Legion. They were to serve on the front for more than a year, complete with their own Dutch Red Cross until, and a special propaganda company of fifty photographers and press cameramen.

Behind the lines, on the Eastern Front, Soviet partisans were active in disrupting German movement; on January 31 a German report noted that in the Yelnya–Dorogobuzh area 'the partisan movement is gaining the upper hand'.

Not only were ambushes and attacks a daily occurrence, but a partisan field hospital was said to have been set up near Yelnya.

On the last day of January 1942, the last British troops withdrew from the Malayan mainland to the island of Singapore, where British, Australian, Indian, Canadian and Malayan troops now awaited the Japanese assault. Shelling began at once. On Bataan, as at Singapore, a siege had begun in which superior Japanese numbers and firepower were ill omens. But 2,800 miles east of Bataan, in mid-Pacific, American aircraft carriers engaged in their first offensive action of the war, launching air strikes on the Japanese Marshall Island bases of Kwajalein, Wotje and Maloelap. During the action, the carrier *Enterprise* was damaged, but not sunk, by a Japanese torpedo bomber.

On Dutch Timor, as Australian troops surrendered, a group of several hundred Australian commandos took to the jungle, where they continued to harass the Japanese for eleven months, before being taken off to safety; in those eleven months, they killed 1,500 Japanese, for the loss of 40 of their own number. It was those Australians who surrendered whose fate was terrible; ten Australian soldiers, captured on February 1 at Sowacoad, on Amboina island, were bayoneted to death. This was done, the Japanese commander explained, because the prisoners 'were likely to become a drag' upon the movement of the Japanese forces in their march to join the other Japanese troops on the island. But elsewhere on the island, equal savagery was enacted; when the principal port of Amboina was overrun, and its small garrison of 809 Australian defenders surrendered, 426 of them were bayoneted to death by their Japanese captors, or died of torture or starvation as prisoners-of-war. On February 4, a further thirty Australian prisoners-of-war were taken to Sowacoad and bayoneted to death, or decapitated. 'They were taken one by one to the spot where they were to die,' their executioner, Lieutenant Nakagawa, later recalled, 'and made to kneel down with a bandage over their eyes.' Nakagawa's men then 'stepped out of the ranks, one by one as his turn came, to behead a prisoner-of-war with a sword or stab him through the breast with a bayonet'.

On February 5, a further thirty Australian and Dutch prisoners-of-war were similarly killed. Near Rabaul, a hundred and fifty Australian prisoners-of-war had been massacred on the previous day. Asia was competing with Europe in terror; on February 1, in German-occupied Russia, the last surviving thirty-eight Jews and Gypsies in Loknya had been murdered, followed three days later by all the hundred Jews in Rakov, near Minsk.

On February 1, British Intelligence suffered its most serious setback of the war. The German Submarine Command, as part of an internal security drive, altered its Enigma machine in such a way that it was to prove unreadable for the rest of the year. Suddenly, the bright light of knowledge which shone on German submarine movements in the Atlantic and Mediterranean was extinguished. At the same time, British cyphers carrying most of the Allied communications about the North Atlantic convoys were broken by German Naval Intelligence. In the signals war, the naval advantage swung suddenly and decisively away from Britain. But two more of Germany's Enigma cyphers were broken that February, 'GGG', the German Secret Service messages between Berlin and stations in the Gibraltar area, and 'Orange II', the messages between Berlin and the ss formations fighting as an integral part of the German Army on the Eastern Front.

For those ss combat troops, as for all German units facing the Russians, or behind the Russian lines, February 1942 saw a considerable increase in partisan activity. 'Since we have no continuous forward line,' a German Army report noted on February 1, 'traffic of every kind from the Soviet side and back again is possible, and extensive use is being made of such crossings. New partisan bands have infiltrated. Russian parachutists are being dropped and are taking over leadership.' In February 1942 the Second Leningrad Partisan Brigade received by parachute drop a Boston printing press, on which it was able to print its own paper, the *People's Avenger*.

Vengeance itself had become an almost daily event in the East. 'We prepared an ambush in the village of Bereski,' the eighteen-year-old Vyacheslav Balakin noted in his partisan diary on February 4. 'We shot down three Germans in cold blood. I wounded one. One was captured alive. I captured a cigarette lighter, a gold ring, a fountain pen, two pipes, tobacco, a comb. Morale is "Gut".'

Five days later, Balakin's partisan group 'shot a traitor'. Later that day, Balakin wrote: 'I went to do the same to his wife. We are sorry that she leaves three children behind. But war is war!!! Towards traitors, any humane consideration is misplaced.' In the evening, a German 'punitive expedition' reached Balakin's region. His group escaped, but two Russian peasants were killed.

Near Kiev, Operational Situation Report USSR no. 164 noted on February 4, sixty Russians were shot, several of them partisans. Five days later, the Germans launched Operation Malaria against Soviet partisans operating in the Osipovichi area. In the rear areas, German units which had to combat partisan activity had their own wry jingle:

> 'Russians in front,
> Russians behind,
> And in between
> There's shooting.'

Another region of increasing partisan activity against the Germans was Yugoslavia; on February 5 a British mission, Operation Disclaim, was parachuted near Sarajevo to link up with recently dislodged partisan forces. But the balance of massacre remained with the Germans; in the southern Russian city of Dnepropetrovsk, for example, in the four weeks up to February 6, an Operational Situation Report USSR, compiled in Berlin, noted that '17 habitual criminals, 103 Communist officials, 16 partisans and about 350 Jews were shot by order of the Summary Court'. In addition, four hundred inmates of the Igren mental hospital were 'disposed of': a total of 1,206 people.

From Lithuania, the head of the Gestapo, SS Colonel Karl Jaeger, reported to Berlin that, in the previous seven months, his special units had killed 138,272 Jews, of whom 34,464 were children. They had also killed, according to Jaeger's precise statistics, 1,064 Russian Communists, 56 Soviet Partisans, 44 Poles, 28 Russian prisoners-of-war, five Gypsies and one Armenian. Murders took place every day; driven on February 6 from their homes in the Polish town of Sierpc, five hundred Jews were shot down and killed during a march to the nearby town of Mlawa. That February, in Warsaw, 4,618 Jews died of starvation. From the village of Sompolno, a thousand Jews were taken to Chelmno and gassed.

These gassings were seen by certain fanatical Nazis as being able to serve a 'scientific' purpose. On February 9 the German anthropologist and surgeon, Auguste Hirt, head of the Anatomy Institute which had just been set up at the University of Strasbourg, wrote to Heinrich Himmler: 'By procuring the skulls of the Jewish–Bolshevist Commissars, who represent the prototype of the repulsive but characteristic subhuman, one has the chance to obtain palpable scientific data. The best practical method is to turn over alive all such individuals. Following induced death of the Jew, the head, which should not be damaged, should be separated from the body and sent in a hermetically sealed tin can filled with preservative fluid'.

Himmler gave Hirt the authority he needed. Henceforth, Hirt used the skulls of more than a hundred murdered Jews to pursue his medical–scientific work. More than a year later, Adolf Eichmann was informed that a total of 115 people had been killed for their skeletons: seventy-nine Jews, thirty Jewesses, four Russians from Central Asia and two Poles.

In an attempt to centralize and accelerate the German war effort, on February 6 the Minister for Armaments and War Production, Fritz Todt, took the chair in Berlin at the first meeting of a committee to co-ordinate all ministries involved in armaments design, manufacture and distribution. On the following day he flew to Rastenburg, to tell Hitler what had been decided; a fifty-five per cent increase in German arms production. On February 8 Todt left Rastenburg to fly back to Berlin. His plane crashed on take-off, and he was killed. Hitler was much shaken by the death of the man who had served him, and Germany, so well; whose Todt Organization utilized hundreds of thousands of slave labourers. That week, Todt was succeeded by Hitler's architect, the thirty-six-year-old Albert Speer. He too showed no scruples in exploiting the labour of Frenchmen, Dutchmen, Danes, Belgians, Poles and a dozen other captive peoples. In Todt's memory, the battery of naval guns, inaugurated by Grand Admirals Raeder and Dönitz on the Channel coast at Haringzelles on February 10, and protected by massive concrete towers, was given the name 'Battery Todt'.

In North Africa, the German army had continued to drive the British back towards Egypt: 'We have got Cyrenaica back', Rommel wrote to his wife on February 4. 'It went like greased lightning.' In the Far East, the Japanese struck at a troop convoy bringing Indian soldiers to Singapore; the slowest ship in the convoy, the *Empress of Asia*, was sunk. Most of the troops on board were rescued, but nearly all their weapons and equipment lost. That day, Japanese heavy guns opened fire on Singapore's defences. The city, declared General Percival on February 7, would resist to the last man.

On February 8, five thousand Japanese troops crossed the Johore Straits from Malaya, to land on Singapore Island. For seven days the British defenders fought against a numerically superior, and better armed, enemy. Leaflets dropped over the city on February 11, calling for its surrender, were studiously ignored. As the garrison in Singapore continued its stubborn defence, the Germans carried out Operation Cerebus, sending the battle cruisers *Scharnhorst* and *Gneisenau*, and the heavy cruiser *Prinz Eugen*, from the port of Brest through the English Channel into the North Sea. The British public was cast down by this spirited 'Channel Dash', as it became known, and by the loss of ten of the old-fashioned naval torpedo aircraft sent to intercept the warships. But in the inner circles of war policy there was immediate relief when the Enigma messages revealed that during the dash both *Gneisenau* and *Scharnhorst* had been damaged by mines laid with foreknowledge of the ships' route. This foreknowlege had itself been gained from Enigma. 'This will keep them out of mischief for at least six months,' Churchill told Roosevelt, 'during which both our Navies will receive important accessions of strength.'

Not Allied strength however, but weakness, now made up the daily diet of war news. On February 13 the Japanese destroyed Singapore's principal defence, its massive fifteen-inch coastal guns and, in south-eastern Borneo, occupied the port of Bandjarmasin. On February 14, Japanese parachutists landed at Palembang in Sumatra. On the following day, Singapore surrendered; 32,000 Indian, 16,000 British and 14,000 Australian soldiers being taken prisoner. More than half of them were to die while prisoners-of-war.

The fall of Singapore – the 'Gibraltar of the East' – was a serious blow to Britain's ability to resist Japan, and also a severe blow to British morale. 'Here is the moment', Churchill told the British people in a broadcast on February 15, 'to display the calm and poise, combined with grim determination, which not so long ago brought us out of the very jaws of death.' The 'only real danger', Churchill warned, would be 'a weakening in our purpose and therefore in our unity – that is the mortal crime'. Whoever was guilty of such a crime, or of bringing it about in others, 'it were better for him that a millstone were hanged about his neck and he were cast into the sea'.

Churchill urged his listeners not to despair. 'We must remember', he said, 'that we are no longer alone. We are in the midst of a great company. Three-quarters of the human race are now moving with us. The whole future of mankind may depend upon our action and upon our conduct.' So far, Churchill added, 'we have not failed. We shall not fail now. Let us move forward steadfastly together into the storm and through the storm.'

# Chapter 23

# Global war

SPRING 1942

On 14 February 1942, the day before the Japanese capture of Singapore, Hitler was in Berlin, for Dr Todt's funeral. That day, in a private conversation with Dr Goebbels, it was upon the surviving Jews of Europe that his thoughts were set. 'The Führer once more expressed his determination to clean up the Jews in Europe pitilessly,' Goebbels noted in his diary. 'There must be no squeamish sentimentalism about it.' The Jews had 'deserved the catastrophe that has now overtaken them. Their destruction will go hand in hand with the destruction of our enemies. We must hasten this process with cold ruthlessness.' In the Crimean city of Simferopol, that 'ruthlessness' had resulted, according to Operational Situation Report USSR No. 170, in the murder of ten thousand Jews between January 9 and February 15.

On February 15, while still in Berlin, Hitler exhorted that year's graduate officers of the SS to 'stem the Red tide and save civilization'. Beginning on February 16, and continuing for twelve days, further round-ups in the Crimea led to the execution, officially reported from Berlin, of 1,515 people, '729 of them Jews, 271 Communists, 74 partisans, 421 Gypsies and asocial elements, and saboteurs'.

In the Far East, horrifying slaughters had also begun. On February 16, on the coast of Malaya, sixty-five Australian Army nurses, and twenty-five English soldiers, surrendered to the Japanese. The soldiers were taken to the beach, bayoneted and shot; only two survived. The nursing sisters were ordered to march into the sea; once in the water, they were fired on by Japanese machine gunners. Only one nurse, Sister Vivien Bullwinkel, survived. Two days later, on Singapore Island, the first group of five thousand Chinese civilians, most of them prominent members of the island's Chinese community, was rounded up. After two weeks, all had been killed. Many, their hands tied behind their back, had been decapitated.

On February 16, five of the largest German submarines, each of a thousand tons, were sent across the Atlantic to the Caribbean. Their instructions were to attack Allied merchant ships off the coast of America, from Trinidad to New York. Once more, the darkened hulls of their victims were silhouetted against the bright lights of the still blackout-free coastal towns of the Atlantic seaboard, reducing the skills of naval attack to little more than those of target practice.

On the Eastern Front, the Red Army struggled to push back the German line near Rzhev, launching a new offensive on February 17. As well as a frontal assault, 7,373 soldiers were dropped by parachute behind the German lines; because of fog, more than a quarter fell directly on to the German positions and were taken prisoner. The German forces, despite heavy losses, and a temperature which fell to minus fifty-two degrees centigrade, held on to their line. One s s regiment came out of the battle with only thirty-five of its original two thousand men.

To 'make way' for the wounded German soldiers evacuated from the Eastern Front, Germany's remaining mental asylums were being 'cleared' of their patients. The method used was euthanasia: death by gassing or by lethal injection. On February 19 the British Government received a report to this effect from Sweden, sent by a leading Swedish expert on euthanasia who had just returned from a visit to Germany. He told of one asylum 'where 1,200 people had been removed by poison'.

On February 19, in the Far East, Japanese bombers struck at the Australian port of Darwin. All seventeen ships in Darwin harbour were sunk, including the American destroyer *Peary*. In the air battle above the port, twenty-two Australian and American warplanes were shot down, for the loss of only five Japanese aircraft. The Allied death toll was 240. In retaliation for the raid, American carrier-borne aircraft struck at Wake and Marcus Islands.

On Amboina Island, Lieutenant Nakagawa ordered the execution of a further 120 Australian prisoners-of-war on February 20. All were made to kneel down with their eyes bandaged, and were then killed either with sword or bayonet. 'The whole affair took from 6 p.m. to 9.30 p.m.,' Nakagawa later recalled. 'Most of the corpses were buried in one hole but because the hole turned out not to be big enough to accommodate all the bodies, an adjacent dug-out was also used as a grave.'

On February 20, President Quezon of the Philippines was taken off Luzon in an American submarine. On the following day, President Roosevelt ordered General MacArthur to leave the Philippines and transfer his headquarters to Australia. On February 23 the Allied Headquarters Staff on Java was evacuated to Australia; that day, six American bombers struck at the Japanese occupation forces in Rabaul, New Britain, the second American air raid on Japanese-held territory. 'We Americans have been compelled to yield ground,' Roosevelt declared on February 23, 'but we will regain it. We and other United Nations are committed to the destruction of the militarism of Japan and Germany. We are daily increasing our strength. Soon we, and not our enemies, will have the offensive; and we, not they, will win the final battles; and we, not they, will make the final peace.'

The Allies, despite the daily setbacks in the Far East, strove to take the initiative wherever possible. On February 23, off the coast of Norway, a British submarine, the *Trident*, torpedoed the German heavy cruiser *Prinz Eugen*, less than two weeks after its successful 'Channel Dash' from Brest. Although the warship was not sunk, fifty men were killed; not only crewmen, but also workers of the Todt Organization being transported to forced labour. On the Eastern Front, the activities of Soviet partisan units continued to disturb the German High Command. 'The area east of the Dnieper', a panzer division officer had reported on February 20, 'is infested with well-armed partisans under unified command. The roads are heavily mined. The whole male population is being recruited and is trained in special training areas. It would appear' – the report continued – 'that the partisans are constantly reinforced by airborne troops'. The 'top secret' German Operational Situation Report USSR of February 23 confirmed this picture. East of Minsk, it noted, was a partisan camp numbering between four hundred and five hundred men. Their weapons included heavy machine guns and anti-tank guns. In another village east of Minsk, where about 150 partisans were based, 'partisans arranged a dance'. In the Cherven region there were a further five partisan camps. 'The partisans have strict orders not to start any action,' the report noted, 'only to attack and destroy German search parties.'

Soviet partisans had also established a wide zone of operations behind the German lines east of Smolensk; in an area more than seventy-five miles long from east to west, and almost fifty miles deep, they worked with airborne and regular troops to disrupt German troop movements both eastward and on the north-south axis: a formidable obstacle to the maintenance of the German line, and German morale.

In the northern sector of the front, after a ten day battle, on February 24 Russian forces surrounded and cut off a German Army corps south-east of Staraya Russa. But as the situation in the Far East worsened, the news of Russian victories, so important on the Eastern Front, had a hollow ring for the Western Allies. On February 24, Churchill wrote despondently to King George VI: 'Burma, Ceylon, Calcutta and Madras in India, and part of Australia, may fall into enemy hands.' On the following day, the British Commander-in-Chief of the forces in the Far East, General Wavell, withdrew from Java, and on February 26 the American flying boat support ship *Langley* was sunk by Japanese air action, and all of her thirty-two aircraft lost. It was small consolation that, on the same day, the first of the Japanese warships used in the attack on Pearl Harbour was itself sunk – the submarine I-23.

On February 27, in the Java Sea, an Allied naval task force, commanded by a Dutch Admiral, Karel Doorman, sought to intercept a Japanese invasion fleet which was on its way to Java. In a seven-hour battle, Doorman's flagship, the light cruiser *De Ruyter*, was sunk and the admiral was drowned. Also sunk during the battle were the Dutch light cruiser *Java* and two British destroyers, *Electra* and *Jupiter*. Only one Japanese troop transport was sunk, and no Japanese warships. The American heavy cruiser *Houston* and the Australian cruiser *Perth* both escaped from the battle zone, but they were chased and sunk on the following night.

On the *Perth* alone, 352 sailors were drowned; of the survivors rescued by Japanese ships, 105 died while prisoners-of-war. On March 1, three more Allied warships, the British cruiser *Exeter*, one of the victors of the Battle of the River

Plate in December 1939, the British destroyer *Encounter*, and the American destroyer *Pope*, were sunk. So too, on March 4, was the British destroyer *Stronghold* and the Australian sloop *Yarra*; 138 of her sailors were drowned. The Japanese, now masters of the Java Sea, prepared for the conquest of Java itself.

On February 27, as the naval battle raged in the Java Sea, the British carried out Operation Biting across the English Channel. Its objective, to be achieved by parachute troops, was to seize key components of German radar equipment at the Bruneval radar station near Le Havre. The raid was a success: not only was the radar equipment captured, but also two German prisoners, one of them a radar operator. Two paratroopers were killed, and six Germans. For the British, the raid was a boost to morale, and proof of the prowess of their airborne troops. But still it was the Far East that dominated the news, and seemed to threaten disaster. 'I cannot help feeling depressed at the future outlook,' King George VI wrote in his diary on February 28. 'Anything can happen, and it will be wonderful if we can be lucky anywhere.' That day, Japanese troops landed on Java, while, from his headquarters in Berlin, the Indian nationalist and Bengali leader, Subhas Chandra Bose, broadcast on India's wish for freedom, and his consequent readiness to co-operate with Germany. Dr Goebbels noted in his diary: 'In London there is boundless wrath about the appeal of Bose, whose present abode is fortunately not known. At the last moment I prevented the Foreign Office from revealing it prematurely.'

Java could not be saved; on February 28 the carrier *Sea Witch* brought twenty-seven crated aircraft to Tjilatjap, but it was too late to assemble the planes, which the Dutch, to prevent them falling into Japanese hands, dumped in the harbour. In the Atlantic, the German submarine offensive, Operation Drum Roll, had scored an even greater success by the end of February than in the previous month, sinking sixty-five Allied merchant ships off the eastern seaboard of the United States. In Leningrad, still effectively besieged, more than 100,000 people had died that February of starvation.

On March 1, Field Marshal Fedor von Bock, the recently appointed commander of Army Group South, informed Hitler that despite their huge losses in battle, the Russians might still be able, not only to draw on enough reserve troops to counter the German spring offensive, but also to create new armies east of Moscow. General Halder disagreed. He did however give an estimate, on March 1, of the substantial German losses in battle thus far on the Eastern Front: in the eight months since June 1941, 202,257 German soldiers had been killed, 725,642 wounded, and 112,617 incapacitated by frostbite. A further 400,000 had been taken prisoner.

German losses in battle, though averaging two thousand a day, were nevertheless far lower than the daily murder of civilians by Germans. On March 2 at least five thousand Jews were taken from the ghetto in Minsk and murdered. From Krosniewice, in German-annexed Poland, nine hundred Jews were taken that same day to Chelmno, and killed in gas vans; on the following day a further 3,200 Jews from the nearby town of Zychlin were gassed. Further east, in White Russia, three thousand Jews were taken out of the ghetto at Baranowicze on

March 4, and killed; a total destruction of more than twelve thousand people in forty-eight hours. In an anti-partisan sweep that month, Operation Marsh Fever, its commander, General Jaeckeln, was able to report to Berlin at the successful conclusion of the sweep: '389 partisans killed, 1,274 persons shot on suspicion, 8,350 Jews liquidated'.

Jews were also used in medical experiments. In March, Dr Rascher conducted what he called a 'terminal experiment' on a 'thirty-seven-year-old Jew in good condition'. This man was put alive in a chamber in which Dr Rascher simulated altitude, gradually reaching twelve kilometres. The suffering and death of the Jew was meticulously noted, as first he began to perspire, then develop cramp, then become breathless, then become unconscious, and finally die.

This case, Dr Rascher informed Himmler, was 'the first one of this type ever observed on man'. The 'above-described actions', Rascher went on to explain, 'will merit particular scientific interest because they were recorded until the very last moment by an electrocardiogram'.

Dr Rascher conducted two hundred such experiments. It is believed that about eighty of those on whom he experimented died. In his twenty-four page report to Himmler, setting out his conclusions, Dr Rascher stated with assurance that flying without pressure suits and oxygen was 'impossible' above twelve kilometres.

On March 1, an Australian soldier, Colin F. Brien, was among more than fifty soldiers who, having been captured by the Japanese, was led to a freshly dug, shallow grave. 'I was told to sit down,' he later recalled, 'with my knees, legs, and feet projecting onto the grave. My hands were tied behind my back. A small towel was tied over my eyes and then – my shirt was unbuttoned and pulled back over my back, exposing the lower part of my neck. My head was bent forward, and after a few second I felt a heavy dull blow sensation on the back of my neck. I realized I was still alive, but pretended to be dead and fell over on my right side; after that, I lost consciousness.'

Brien survived. After he had fled, but been recaptured, the amazed Japanese put him first into hospital and then into a prisoner-of-war camp, where, as an historian of this episode has written, 'he survived the war as a novelty'. Brien was later to testify to this mass execution at the Tokyo War Crimes Trials.

On March 3, nine Japanese fighters raided the Western Australian town of Broome. In a fifteen minute attack on the flying-boat base being used to ferry soldiers and refugees from Java, twenty-three Australian, American, Dutch and British aircraft were destroyed, and about seventy people killed, many of them refugees from Java who had just arrived in Broome. One American bomber, managing to take off as the raid began, was shot down some way out to sea. Of the thirty-three men on board, only one survived.

Off Java, twenty-five Japanese warships attacked three British ships which had left Batavia on March 3 taking refugees towards Australia. All three ships were sunk. Twenty-six survivors scrambled on to two lifeboats. The Japanese ships steamed by them, not to shoot, but to stand solemnly to attention in their honour, saluting the brave, and then to steam away. The twenty-six remained at sea, running out of food and water. Rain water, and the raw flesh of three seabirds, were their only sustenance. On reaching the coast of Java, only eighteen were still alive. A further six died trying to get ashore in a heavy sea. The twelve survivors were taken prisoners-of-war.

On the night of March 3, in France, more than two hundred British bombers struck at the Renault vehicle works at Billancourt. Of the French workforce of three thousand, only five were killed. When, however, some of the bombs fell off target, hitting nearby houses, five hundred Frenchmen were killed, including many whole families. The Germans hoped to exploit these deaths to their advantage, but a French informer in German pay reported, disparagingly, to the military authorities: 'In general, if the pulse of public opinion is taken, indignation is not widespread enough.' On the following day a German guard was shot dead in a Paris street. Twenty French Communists were at once shot in reprisal. 'That's the method I proposed,' Dr Goebbels noted in his diary, and he added: 'If rigorously applied it will lead to visible results.'

In the Crimean town of Feodosiya, beginning on March 5, three anti-partisan sweeps within three weeks led to the killing of more than two thousand people, of whom, according to Operational Situation Report No. 184, '678 were Jews, 359 Communist officials, 153 partisans, and 810 asocial elements, Gypsies, mentally ill, and saboteurs'.

The German killing squads had no respite. On March 6, at Klintsy, thirty Gypsies and 270 Jews were brought by truck to a ditch outside the town, ordered to undress, and shot. 'The situation is now ripe for a final settlement of the Jewish question,' Dr Goebbels noted in his diary on the following day. 'Later generations will no longer have either the will-power or the instinctive alertness. That is why we are doing good work in proceeding radically and consistently. The task we are assuming today', Goebbels added, 'will be an advantage and a boon to our descendants.'

There were, however, still a handful of people who protested at the persecution of the Jews. On March 7, in Zagreb, Archbishop Stepinac wrote to the Croatian Minister of the Interior about rumours 'of impending mass arrests of Jews who are to be sent to concentration camps.' If such rumours were true, Stepinać wrote, 'I take the liberty to appeal to you to prevent, by virtue of your authority, an unlawful attack on citizens who are not personally guilty of anything.' The Archbishop's appeal was in vain.

On March 5, the Dutch announced the evacuation of Batavia; Java could no longer be held against the sustained Japanese attack. That day, in Burma, Japanese forces entered Pegu, a mere forty miles from the capital, Rangoon. On the following day, after Indian troops failed to reopen the Rangoon–Pegu road, General Alexander – who had been the last man to leave the Dunkirk beachhead in June 1940 – ordered the evacuation of Rangoon. On March 7, Rangoon was evacuated. That day, in Java, the Dutch surrendered; 100,000 Dutch, British, Australian and American troops were taken prisoner. Their travails had only just begun.

In all, 8,500 Dutch soldiers were to die in captivity, nearly a quarter of those who were taken prisoner. A further 10,500 Dutch civilian internees were to perish, out of 80,000 interned. Many soldiers and civilians died while hiding on remote islands, hoping for rescue, or building boats in which to seek possible succour on other islands On March 7, on Tjebia Island – known as a 'fever island' – off Sumatra, the first of nineteen Englishmen who had reached the island after escaping by boat from Singapore, died of disease and exposure. He was Commander Frampton, a member of the naval staff at Singapore. Three days later, another member of the group, the former Air Officer Commanding Far East, Air Vice-Marshal C. W. Pulford, died. So too, before the stranded soldiers, sailors and airmen were able to make their vessel seaworthy, did the former commander of the Singapore naval base, Rear Admiral E. J. Spooner. Those who did later get away were captured by a Japanese submarine and taken prisoner.

The Japanese forces now turned towards New Guinea, occupying Lae and Salamaua on March 8. Two days later they landed in Buka, one of the Solomon Islands. On March 11, with Luzon Island almost entirely under Japanese control, General MacArthur left by motor torpedo boat for Mindanao, the first stage of the journey being through a minefield. After thirty-five hours he reached Mindanao, a journey of 560 miles through Japanese controlled waters. Then, from Mindanao, leaving the Philippines behind him, he flew on to Australia, telling the reporters who met him at an airfield just south of Darwin: 'I came through, and I shall return'.

On March 7, the German battleship *Tirpitz* sailed from Trondheim with three destroyers. She failed, however, to reach the Arctic convoy, which was her target, while the British Home Fleet also failed initially to intercept her. Three days later, after Enigma fixed the ship's location, aircraft from the *Victorious* attacked her, but unsuccessfully. The mere existence of the *Tirpitz* in Arctic waters was to cause continual and grave alarm to the convoys to Russia. She had the power to attack any convoy and to sink all its ships. There was no way of taking for granted that she could be sunk, even when identified and located.

On March 12, ten Soviet parachutists landed near Birzai, in Lithuania. They were seen, chased and shot, and all their equipment, including a radio transmitter, was seized. But such setbacks did nothing to deter the despatch of further partisan units behind the German lines.

On March 13, the German war against the Jews took yet another evil turn. Hitherto, there was only one camp, Chelmno, to which Jews were deported with the sole aim of killing them the moment they arrived. Now a second such camp was ready, at Belzec, on the eastern edge of the General Government. The first six thousand Jews deported there, from the southern Polish town of Mielec, had been told that they were needed for agricultural work further east. But their destination was death. They were followed three days later by 1,600 Jews from Lublin. By the end of the year, Jews from more than two hundred communities throughout the Lublin region, and East and West Galicia, had been driven from their homes, deported by rail to Belzec, and killed there; a total of 360,000 victims. Also gassed at Belzec, as the death camp memorial stone records, were 1,500 Poles, deported to the camp 'for helping Jews'.

Even as the first of what were to be several trains a day took Jews to Belzec, the German Enigma messages revealed to the British a build up of German rail traffic, as well as airfield construction, in the Ukraine, especially south of Kharkov. On March 14 the War Cabinet's Joint Intelligence Committee concluded that the next major German offensive would be against the Russian southern front. Further Enigma messages showed that it was being fixed for May 15. Churchill, knowing the Russian disappointment that no Anglo-American landing in northern Europe was possible that summer, offered Stalin a massive British bomber offensive against German industrial targets, with the aim, Churchill explained on March 14 to the Chiefs of Staff representative in Washington, of 'taking the weight off Russia by the heaviest air offensive against Germany which can be produced, having regard to other calls on our air power'.

That British offensive had effectively begun on the night of March 8, with a raid by 211 bombers against Essen. Despite special marker flares and initial incendiary drops, little damage had been done. A few nights later, the whole force attacked the wrong town, Hamborn, eight miles from Essen, after a bomber which had been hit had jettisoned its direction-indicating incendiaries. On another occasion, decoy fires at Rheinburg, twenty miles from Essen, had lured most of the crews away from the real target. These setbacks did not however weaken Bomber Command's determination to bomb accurately and effectively. Hitler's pledge, on March 15, in a speech in Berlin, that Russia would be 'annihilatingly defeated' in the coming summer, only strengthened Churchill's resolve to give Russia the maximum support from the air, support for which Stalin, who was not always forthcoming, gave acknowledgement and thanks.

Stalin's armies did not intend to wait for Hitler's attack, nor were the Soviet forces behind the German lines relaxing their efforts in any way. 'The activity of the partisans has increased notably in recent weeks,' Goebbels noted in his diary on March 16. 'They are conducting a well-organized guerrilla war.' To combat partisan activity, a special air detachment had been set up two days earlier in Bobruisk, to bomb partisan camps and seek out from the air the movement of partisan units. This air detachment was to be made ready for action as part of Operation Munich, an anti-partisan sweep planned to begin in the third week of March. Further behind the lines, in Kovno, twenty-four Jews who were found outside the ghetto on March 17 trying to buy food from local Lithuanians were shot by the Gestapo. That same day, in Ilja, north of Minsk, nine hundred Jews were rounded up and shot, despite a courageous attempt at collective resistance.

Operation Munich was launched on March 19. Supported by the newly created air detachment, German troops struck at partisan bases throughout the Yelnya–Dorogobuzh area. In a further sweep, near Bobruisk, code-named Operation Bamberg, Russian villages were set on fire and their inhabitants killed in raids which, though punitive in the extreme, and killing 3,500 villagers, served only to intensify the hatred of the occupier, and to intensify the determination

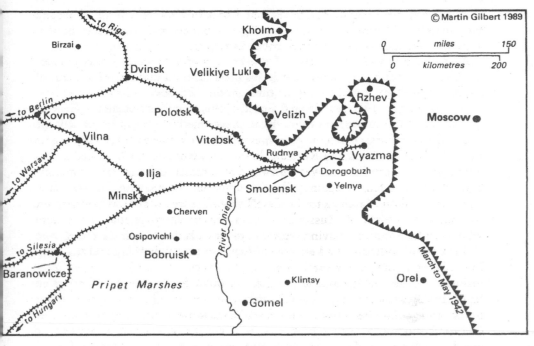

© Martin Gilbert 1989

Soviet partisans, 1942

to help the partisans, who almost invariably escaped the net to fight again, and to return. However ferociously the Germans struck, the partisans fought back, reinforced by parachute drops of arms and men. 'There are indications', the Third Panzer Army reported later in March, 'that the partisan movement in the region of Velikiye Luki, Vitebsk, Rudnya, Velizh is now being organized on a large scale. The fighting strength of the partisans hitherto active is being bolstered by individual units of regular troops' – men trained in the use of heavy weapons, artillery and anti-tank guns. A similar accretion of Soviet partisan strength was reported near Polotsk.

The first day of Operation Munich, March 19, was also the day of a German Army directive issued to all occupation troops in Serbia and Croatia, insisting that wherever Yugoslav partisan activity had taken place, the houses, and even the villages, suspected of having been used by the partisans were to be destroyed. 'Removal of the population to concentration camps can also be useful,' the directive added. If it was not possible to 'apprehend or seize' the partisans themselves, 'reprisal measures of a general nature may be in order, for example the shooting of male inhabitants of nearby localities'. This shooting was to be done, the directive explained, 'according to a specific ratio, for example, a hundred Serbs for one German killed, fifty Serbs for one German wounded'.

Similar acts and ratios of reprisals took place throughout the areas under German occupation. On March 20, in the Polish town of Zgierz, a hundred

Poles were taken from a nearby labour camp to be shot; all six thousand inhabitants of Zgierz and its surrounding villages being driven to the market place and forced to watch the execution. That same day, at Rastenburg, Hitler spoke to his guest, Dr Goebbels, of the Jews. 'Here the Führer is as uncompromising as ever,' Goebbels noted in his diary. 'The Jews must be got out of Europe, if necessary by applying the most brutal methods.'

On March 21, Hitler authorized Fritz Sauckel, his Plenipotentiary General for Labour Mobilization, to obtain, by whatever methods might be needed, the labour force required to push the German war economy into its highest possible productive capacity. Labourers could be brought from all the occupied lands; even seized, if necessary, from the streets. Yet from Eastern Galicia, for the rest of the year, Jews continued to be deported, not to forced labour, but to Belzec and to their deaths, including a thousand from Tarnopol on March 25 and six thousand from Stanislawow six days later. From Germany, too, Jews were sent to Belzec, and to their immediate destruction; on March 24 there were deportations to Belzec of 42 Jews from Jülich, 320 from Würzburg and 224 from Fürth. None of these deportees survived.

Under the Labour Decree of March 31, however, a different concept of deportation was about to be put into effect: the selection of deportees into those 'fit' to work and those 'unfit'. Whereas at Chelmno and Belzec, and shortly at Treblinka and Sobibor, all deportees were to continue to be killed, irrespective of whether they were 'fit' to work or not, at a new camp, Birkenau, attached to the existing concentration camp of Auschwitz, a 'selection' was to take place of all arrivals. The able-bodied, both men and women, were to be sent to the barracks of Birkenau as a labour force, cruelly treated, but set to work in factories and farms. The old, the sick and all the children were sent, within hours, to the specially constructed gas chambers, and killed by gas.

The first deportation of Jews to Auschwitz took place on March 26, when 999 Jewish women from Slovakia reached the camp, and were sent to the barracks. They were followed on March 27 by a deportation of Jews from France, a so-called 'special' train which left Paris with 1,112 deportees. One of the French deportees, Georges Rieff, managed to jump from the train before it reached the German border, and escaped. Of the rest, more than half were gassed not long after their arrival. Those 'selected' to work were fortunate, but only in the short term; only twenty-one of them were still alive five months later.

All over Europe, Jews were being rounded up for deportation, held in camps, and then sent by train to Auschwitz. The conditions in these holding camps were themselves cruel and demoralizing, weakening the physical strength and undermining the will. At Westerbork in Holland, at Malines in Belgium, at Drancy on the outskirts of Paris, isolation, hunger and constant indignities were the lot of tens of thousands of men, women and children uprooted from their homes at a moment's notice, and suddenly deprived of all but the most pathetic of personal possessions. In southern France, the holding camps were if anything more unpleasant and debilitating than those further north. At Gurs, Noé and Récébédou in the Pyrenees, at Rivesaltes near the Mediterranean coast, and at

Death camps, deportations, air raids and reprisals, 1942

Les Milles in Provence, the daily rigours of life were a grim prelude to the uncertainties of deportation and its evil outcome; in these four camps alone, 1,864 people, lacking even the rudiments of medical help or spiritual hope, died before deportation.

That March, the deportations to Belzec were being discussed in Berlin. 'Beginning with Lublin,' Dr Goebbels noted in his diary on 27 March, 'the Jews under the General Government are now being evacuated eastward. The procedure is pretty barbaric and is not to be described here more definitely. Not much will remain of the Jews. About sixty per cent of them will have to be liquidated; only about forty per cent can be used for forced labour.' Odilo Globocnik, the former Gauleiter of Vienna, who was carrying out the measure, was doing it, Goebbels noted, 'with considerable circumspection and in a way that does not attract too much attention'. Goebbels' diary entry continued: 'Though the judgement now being visited upon the Jews is barbaric, they fully deserve it. The prophecy which the Führer made about them for having brought on a new world war is beginning to come true in a most terrible manner. One must not be sentimental in these matters. If we did not fight the Jews, they

311

would destroy us. It's a life-and-death struggle between the Aryan race and the Jewish bacillus.'

'No other government,' Goebbels reflected with pride, 'and no other régime, would have the strength for such a global solution as this.'

On March 23, Japanese forces occupied the Andaman Islands in the Bay of Bengal, this former British penal colony having been earlier evacuated by its British and Gurkha garrison. In the Mediterranean, a British attempt to reinforce Malta met with disaster that day, when Italian naval forces sank four merchant ships bringing oil fuel to the beleaguered island; of the 26,000 tons of petrol carried by the convoy, only 5,000 tons were salvaged. It had been possible to send up only five British fighters to counter an attack by two hundred aircraft; later, when forty-seven Spitfires reached Malta as reinforcements, thirty of them were destroyed during a German air assault.

In the early hours of March 28, British naval and commando forces carried out Operation Chariot, an attack on the German dry-dock at St Nazaire. As this was the only dock on the Atlantic coast capable of repairing Germany's one surviving modern battleship, the *Tirpitz*, its destruction would seriously hinder the use of the *Tirpitz* as a commerce raider in the Atlantic. In the attack, the dock was seriously damaged, and four hundred Germans killed, many of them in their own cross-fire. Of the 611 British commandos taking part in the raid, 205 were killed, and most of the others taken prisoner; 185 British sailors were also killed. Four Victoria Crosses, two of them posthumous, were won in the action, which disabled the dry dock for the rest of the war. In the panic when the raid began, the Germans had fired on the French civilian workers at the dock, killing three hundred; a total death toll that March 28 of more than a thousand soldiers, sailors and civilians.

Even as the commando raid on St Nazaire was in progress, Hitler, at Rastenburg, was informing his military commanders of their tasks for the summer campaign against Russia, Operation Blue. First, the city of Voronezh, on the Don, would be captured, then Stalingrad, on the Volga. Further south, the Caucasus mountains were to be reached by early September. After the defeat of the Russian armies, an East Wall would be built along the Volga, behind which the remnants of Russia's armies would remain, to be attacked whenever they threatened to become too strong.

Also on March 28, in an attempt to tie down as many Russian troops as possible in the Far East during the coming offensive, Joachim von Ribbentrop pressed the Japanese Ambassador in Berlin, Count Oshima, to secure a Japanese attack on Russia simultaneously with Germany's 'crushing blow'. The German General Staff, in order to encourage such a Japanese attack, would send their Japanese opposite numbers a specific proposal for a Japanese attack against Vladivostok and on to Lake Baikal.

Such was Ribbentrop's proposal to Japan on March 28. But the Japanese took no action.

Over western Europe, British air forces were particularly active on March 28, a day which saw the first parachute drop of supplies to the British agents in

German plans for summer 1942

Russian gains February-April 1942

German front line 8 May 1942

Gulf of Finland

Lake Ladoga

Lake Peipus

Lake Ilmen

Leningrad

Tikhvin

Pskov

Dno

Demyansk

Polotsk

Vitebsk

Lepel

Smolensk

Orsha

Borisov

Dorogobuzh

Vyazma

Moscow

Minsk

Mogilev

WHITE RUSSIA

Roslavl

Kletnya

Bryansk

Orel

Klintsy

S O V I E T        U N I O N

Kursk

Voronezh

Zhitomir

Kiev

River Volga

Vinnitsa

River Dnieper

Kharkov

Poltava

River Don

UKRAINE

Izyum

River Donetz

Stalingrad

Volga

miles 150

kilometres 200

Rostov

Black Sea

Sea of Azov

CRIMEA

Kerch

NORTH CAUCASUS

Feodosiya

Sevastopol

Caucasus

© Martin Gilbert 1989

The Eastern Front, May 1942

France. The drop, at Blyes, was successful. That night, 234 British bombers left their bases in Britain to strike at the German Baltic port of Lübeck. 'The main object of the attack,' the head of Bomber Command, Sir Arthur Harris, later recalled, 'was to learn to what extent a first wave of aircraft could guide a second wave to the aiming-point by starting a conflagration; I ordered a half-an-hour interval between the two waves in order to allow the fires to get a good hold.' Harris added, by way of explanation of the choice of Lübeck as a target that night: 'Lübeck was not a vital target, but it seemed to me better to destroy an industrial town of moderate importance than to toil to destroy a large industrial city'. In addition, Harris wrote, 'I wanted my crews to be well "blooded" as they say in fox-hunting, to have a taste of success for a change.'

Two thousand of Lübeck's buildings were totally destroyed that night, and 312 German civilians killed. Of the 191 bombers which reached the city, twelve were shot down. Fifteen thousand Germans had lost their homes. 'This Sunday has been thoroughly spoiled', Goebbels noted in his diary, 'by an exceptionally heavy air raid by the Royal Air Force on Lübeck'. Eighty per cent of the medieval city, he added, 'must be considered lost'.

Even as Goebbels contemplated the destruction of Lübeck, the British faced a setback in the despatch of war supplies to Russia; on the morning of March 29, four Allied ships, scattered from their destroyer escort by a ferocious storm, were attacked and sunk. In the ensuing battles between the escort – including two Russian destroyers – and the German submarines, the cold was so intense that sea-spray, sweeping over the ships, froze solid on the gun-mountings. Nevertheless, two German submarines were sunk.

The month of March had seen the greatest Allied losses in the war at sea; 273 merchant ships had been sunk, including ninety-five in the North Atlantic and ninety-eight in the Far East, with a total of 834,184 tons. Also in the Far East, on March 31 the Japanese reached their most southerly point of conquest, the Australian territory of Christmas Island, south of Java, whose garrison of a hundred British troops surrendered that day. But although the island was a valuable source of phosphate, it was so small and rocky as to be unsuitable for the construction of an airstrip; the Japanese therefore evacuated it four days later.

On 1 April 1942, nineteen merchant ships, Convoy PQ 13, set sail from Iceland for Russia; five were sunk, and their principal escort, the cruiser *Trinidad*, crippled by German torpedoes. Also on April 1, Operation Performance saw the attempted breakout of ten Norwegian merchant ships from the Swedish port of Gothenburg; five of the merchant ships were sunk by the Germans before they could get clear of the Skagerrak, one was too severely damaged to continue, and two turned back; only two reached Britain safely.

That day also saw the Japanese launch Operation C, using five aircraft-carriers which had taken part in the attack on Pearl Harbor, to cross the Indian Ocean, refuel at Addu Atoll in the Maldive Islands, and bomb Colombo, the capital of Ceylon, four days later, sinking two British cruisers, *Dorsetshire* and *Cornwall*, the armed merchant cruiser *Hector* and the destroyer *Tenedos*; more than five hundred men were drowned. A further three hundred men died when the aircraft carrier *Hermes* and the destroyer *Vampire* were bombed and sunk at Trincomalee. During this same raid, twenty-three merchant ships were sunk in the Bay of Bengal, with a total of 112,000 tons lost. During the raids on Colombo and Trincomalee, thirty-six Japanese aircraft had been shot down; but the raid caused alarm in Calcutta, and seemed to herald yet further and spectacular Japanese advances.

On April 13 Japanese bombers struck at the Burmese city of Mandalay; two thousand people were killed and much of the city set on fire. That same day Japanese troops began a massive assault on the American troops still holding out in the Bataan Peninsula. From his headquarters in Australia, General MacArthur ordered a counter-attack. But his men on Bataan were wracked by malaria and dysentery, hunger, and a severe shortage of munitions.

The Japanese ability to strike at will was evident on April 6, when Japanese bombs fell on two towns in the Madras Presidency, Coconada and Vizagapatam, on the coast of India, while, more than four and a half thousand miles to the east, Japanese troops landed at Lorengau in the Admiralty Islands, less than eight hundred miles from Cape York in Australia.

In Hitler's Europe, tyranny spread its tentacles further with every day. On April 3, in Germany itself, the deportation of 129 Jews from Augsburg to Belzec marked the final destruction of a community which had been a centre of Jewish settlement and culture for more than seven hundred years. That same day, 1,200 Jews from the Eastern Galician town of Tlumacz were deported to Belzec, followed on April 4 by 1,500 Jews from the neighbouring town of Horodenka.

At his East Prussian headquarters at Rastenburg, Hitler agreed with Himmler, at a dinner-time talk on April 5, that 'Germanic' children from the occupied lands could be taken away from their parents and brought up in special Nazi schools. 'If we want to prevent Germanic blood from being absorbed by the ruling class of the country we dominate', Himmler explained, 'and which subsequently might turn against us, we shall have gradually to subject all the precious Germanic elements to the influence of this instruction.'

Himmler envisaged, as he explained to Hitler, that Dutch, Flemish and French children of 'Germanic' origin would all come within the sphere of the special schools. But opposition to Nazi ideology continued, courageously. On the very day that Himmler set out his 'Germanic' school scheme to Hitler at Rastenburg, the vast majority of Norway's Lutheran clergy, meeting in German-occupied Oslo, issued a declaration emphasizing the sovereignty of God above all ideologies; the declaration was read from pulpits throughout Norway, and 654 of Norway's 699 ministers of religion resigned from their positions as civil servants, while continuing to do their work as clergymen. In Germany, on April 7, the Protestant theologian Karl Friedrich Stellbrink was arrested, together with three Catholic priests, for daring to criticize Nazi rule; seven months later all four churchmen were executed.

In a further attempt to prevent German aircraft being sent to the Eastern Front, the British embarked, on April 8, on a series of sweeps along the Channel coast against German air and military installations. Many German air units were tied down by this method, although the Royal Air Force lost 259 aircraft, for 58 German fighters shot down. Nevertheless, as a result of this deliberate diversion, the Germans were forced to impose flying restrictions on their aircraft in Russia.

On April 8, as Japanese forces intensified their attack on the Americans and Filipinos trapped on Bataan, two thousand of the defenders managed to cross to Corregidor. The remaining 76,000, of whom 12,000 were Americans, surrendered to the Japanese on April 9. They were at once marched the sixty-five miles from Balanga northward, in conditions of such terrible brutality and privation that more than six hundred Americans, and at least five thousand Filipinos, perished in what later became known as the 'March of Death'. Many of those who died were clubbed or bayoneted to death when, too weak to walk further, they stumbled and fell. Others were ordered out of the ranks, beaten, tortured and killed. A further sixteen thousand Filipinos, and at least a thousand Americans, died of starvation, disease and brutality during their first few weeks in prisoner-of-war camps.

On the island fortress of Corregidor, General Wainwright continued to hold out, with 13,000 men under his command, despite a sustained and severe artillery bombardment. In India, the leader of the Congress Party, Jawaharlal Nehru, reacted with alarm to Japanese claims that their advance was one of liberation, even, in due course, for India. 'It distresses me', Nehru declared on April 12, 'that any Indian should talk of the Japanese liberating India.' That day, as the March of Death continued across Bataan, Japanese soldiers set upon nearly four hundred of their Filipino prisoners, hacking them to death with their swords.

As Australians watched with alarm the Japanese advances throughout the Far East and Pacific, Australian troops were in action in the Western Desert, defending Tobruk against a German siege. On April 13 the Germans launched an attack on the fortress, infiltrating between two Australian posts, and striking at a vital strongpoint. There, among the defenders, Corporal Jack Edmondson, a twenty-seven-year-old Australian farmer, although badly wounded in the stomach and neck, helped drive the Germans out. Shortly afterwards he died of his wounds. Posthumously, he was awarded Australia's first Victoria Cross of the war.

It was on April 14, in London, that the Combined Commanders Group set up by the British and American Chiefs of Staff finally concluded that no Allied action to help Russia was possible in Europe in 1942, apart from small raids. One such raid, albeit on the very smallest of scales, had taken place three days earlier, when two British commandos paddled a canoe into Bordeaux harbour, blowing up a German tanker. Larger raids were planned. But even a much modified European second front was not to take place in 1942. Meanwhile, the grave pressure on Russia continued. In Leningrad, April 15 marked the 248th day of the siege. On that day, the trams were run again, for the first time in many months. A German prisoner-of-war, Corporal Falkenhorst, later told his

captors that he had lost his faith in Hitler when he heard the sound of the tram
bells that morning. But the month of April also saw 102,497 deaths from
starvation in Leningrad, the highest death rate for any month of the siege,
though the burials by which the figure was calculated included a few thousand
bodies which had lain frozen in the streets throughout the last winter months.

On April 7, a third death camp began its work, when, south-east of Warsaw,
from the medieval town of Zamosc, 2,500 Jews were rounded up and sent by
train to an 'unknown destination'. That destination was in fact a camp just
outside the village of Sobibor, which had been chosen as the site of a third death
camp, on the pattern of Chelmno and Belzec. All who were brought to Sobibor
were to be gassed within hours, except for a few hundred set aside for forced
labour. From the 2,500 Jews of Zamosc, only one, Moshe Shklarek, was chosen
to work. The others were all gassed. By the end of the year, more than a quarter
of a million Jews had been brought to Sobibor and murdered, most of them
from central Poland, but some from as far west as Holland, more than eight
hundred miles away.

The killings at Sobibor were kept a close secret. Even the already deceptive
terminology was being tightened up. On April 10 Himmler's personal secretary
had informed the Inspector of Statistics of the Reich that henceforth 'no mention
should be made of the "special treatment of the Jews". It must be called
"transportation of the Jews towards the Russian East".'

No such secrecy masked the efforts of the Western Allies; on April 17, twelve
British bombers flew a daring, low-level daylight raid against the diesel-engine
works at Augsburg. Seven of the bombers were shot down. But the raid, flown
deep into Germany at a height of only five hundred feet, caught the British
public's imagination; the leader of the raid, John Dering Nettleton, a South
African, was awarded the Victoria Cross. Just over a year later he was killed in
action during a night bombing raid on Turin.

That same day, April 17, also saw the escape from German captivity of
General Henri Giraud; captured in June 1940, he escaped from the maximum
security castle prison at Königstein in Saxony by lowering himself down the
castle wall, jumping on board a moving train, and reaching the French border.
For the French population, now approaching their third year under German
occupation, Giraud's escape was a fantastic boost for morale, so much so that
Himmler ordered the Gestapo to 'find Giraud and assassinate him'; but the
General finally escaped from France on a British submarine, to reach North
Africa and safety; for his courageous escape he was awarded the Médaille
Militaire. Hitler, for some weeks after Giraud's escape, was, Goebbels reported,
'in a black rage'.

The Americans also had a success to celebrate in that third week of April,
though they were not to be told of it until the second week in May. On April
18, in strictest secrecy, sixteen American bombers, commanded by Lieutenant-
Colonel James H. Doolittle, launched a raid against the Japanese mainland.
Taking off from the American aircraft-carrier *Hornet*, the Doolittle raiders flew
823 miles across the Pacific, to bomb oil and naval installations in Tokyo, Kobe,
Yokohama, Nagoya and Yokosuka. At Yokosuka, the aircraft-carrier *Ryuho*

was hit while in dry dock. Unable to fly back over such a great distance, the American bombers flew on to China.

One bomber crash-landed on Soviet soil, near Vladivostock; its crew was interned. Two other bombers crash-landed on Japanese controlled territory; of their eight crew members, captured by the Japanese, three were executed. Angered by the raid, which showed that the heart of the Empire of the Rising Sun was not invulnerable, the Japanese occupied the Chinese province of Chekiang, intending thereby to prevent further overlying missions.

April 18, so successful a day for the Americans, saw the destruction in German-occupied Russia, of a Soviet partisan force in Dorogobuzh; its commander, Colonel Yefremov, having been severely wounded in the back, unable to help his men and unwilling to be taken prisoner, put a pistol to his temple. 'Boys,' he said, 'this is the end for me, but you go on fighting.' Then he shot himself; his men, fighting on, though almost beaten, never gave up. Some, reaching the nearby front line, returned in due course to harry the Germans behind the lines.

In the Atlantic, April 21 saw the first day of the sailing of the first of several German submarine tankers, boats with no offensive capabilities, but laden with stores, spare parts, and seven hundred tons of diesel fuel each, six hundred tons of which were available for the refuelling of fourteen combat submarines. Helped by this independent source of fuel supply far from their French coastal bases, thirty-two German submarines operated off the East Coast of the United States, and in the Gulf of Mexico and Caribbean Sea, sinking Allied merchant ships as they sailed northward to join the Atlantic convoys.

Behind Japanese lines, Allied prisoners-of-war were being confronted with a savagery of which they had no previous experience, or intimation. On April 22, at a prisoner-of-war camp at Bandung, an Australian medical officer, Colonel Edward Dunlop, recorded in his diary the fate of three Dutch prisoners-of-war who had been caught while trying to escape: 'Tied to poles and bayoneted to death like pigs before their comrades.' On being asked if they had a final request, Dunlop added, 'first man asked for eye bandage to be removed and said firmly "Long live the Queen" which all then said in turn'. A Dutch officer who fainted on witnessing the scene was 'severely rebuked' by a Japanese officer 'for his unmanliness'.

On April 20, the British and Americans launched a combined Operation, Calendar, to deliver forty-seven fighters to Malta. They were brought into the Mediterranean on the American carrier *Wasp*, then flown seven hundred miles to Malta. But once in Malta, before they could be put into sheltered revetments, or even refuelled, all but ten of them were destroyed in a German air raid. Mussolini now pressed the Germans to carry out Operation C3, the occupation of Malta, but Hitler, on the eve of his second major Russian offensive, refused.

While preparing for a second attempt to reinforce Malta by air, the British carried out a second small raid on the French coast on April 22. This was Operation Abercrombie, sending fifty British and fifty Canadian troops across the English Channel to land at the beach at Hardelot, as training for a more substantial raid planned for August. 'For the Canadians, unfortunately,' one of their military historians has written, 'this little enterprise was just another fiasco. The naval craft which carried them, failed to put them ashore, and while they came under German fire, they took no actual part in the operation.' A more distant, and highly secret, British operation was being planned that week, after the 'Tube Alloys' Technical Committee, responsible for atomic bomb research and Intelligence, recommended that an attempt should be made to stop the German production of heavy water in Norway. This heavy water was an essential component of the manufacture of the atomic bomb; as a result of 'recent experiments', the committee reported, it seemed that plutonium could be used in such a bomb, and that 'it would best be prepared in systems using heavy water'.

Special Operations Executive now had a new task, to plan the destruction of the German heavy water plant at Vermork. As it set about making its plans, the war of high-explosive and incendiary bombs intensified. On April 23, in retaliation for the British bombing raid on Lübeck, forty-five German bombers struck at Exeter. The raid having failed, sixty bombers came over again on the following night. Also on the night of April 24, a hundred and fifty German bombers attacked Bath. As they did so, British bombers, flying in the opposite direction, struck at Rostock, on the Baltic. But it was the German raids, all on medieval city centres, known therefore as 'Baedeker Raids', which caused the greatest damage to morale; in Bath, four hundred civilians had been killed. On April 27 Norwich was the target, and on April 28 both Norwich and York, where the fifteenth century Guildhall was destroyed. During the first five days of these 'Baedeker Raids', 938 British civilians were killed. The government departments concerned, Churchill told his War Cabinet on April 27, when the raids were at their height, 'should do all they could to ensure that disproportionate publicity was not given to these raids. Our attacks on Germany were inflicting much greater damage; and it was important to avoid giving the impression that the Germans were making full reprisal.' German Air Force losses on the raids were in fact too heavy for the Germans to continue them much longer; particularly harmful to Germany's air power were the losses in instructional crews brought in from the Reserve Training Units to help lead the raids.

Hitler, returning from Rastenburg to Berlin on April 26, was particularly angered by the raid on Rostock, where seventy per cent of the houses in the old city centre had been destroyed and the Heinkel aircraft works badly damaged. Discussing the bombing of Rostock and the reprisal raids with Goebbels, he told his Minister of Propaganda on April 27 that he would 'repeat these raids night after night until the English were sick and tired of terror attacks'. Goebbels noted: 'He shares my opinion absolutely that cultural centres, health resorts and civilian centres must be attacked now. There is no other way of bringing the English to their senses. They belong to a class of human beings with whom you can talk only after you have first knocked out their teeth.'

Churchill's fears in the last week of April were not for Britain, but for Malta. On April 24 he asked Roosevelt to authorize the American aircraft carrier *Wasp* to make a second dash with air reinforcements. 'Without this aid', Churchill warned, 'I fear Malta will be pounded to bits.' Its defence, however, was in Churchill's view 'wearing out the enemy's Air Force and effectively aiding Russia'. It was about Russia that Hitler spoke, on April 26, when he addressed the Reichstag in Berlin. The Russian winter of 1941 had been exceptionally severe, he said, the worst for 140 years, with temperatures as low as minus fifty degrees centigrade; but with the coming of spring he foresaw 'great victories' for the German forces.

Hitler's speech contained more than promises; it was dominated by an appeal for 'obedience to only one idea, namely the fight for victory'. In stern words, full of threat, Hitler warned his listeners: 'Let nobody now preach about his well-earned rights. Let each man clearly understand, from now on there are only duties.'

# 24

# The spread of resistance and terror

SUMMER 1942

On 27 April 1942 British bombers again struck at Rostock, on the Baltic. 'Seven-tenths of the city have been wiped out,' Goebbels noted in his diary. 'More than 100,000 people had to be evacuated'. There had in fact, Goebbels added, been 'panic' in the city. The American air raid on Tokyo was also the subject of much talk and speculation; it had not yet been admitted to by the United States. 'It is even reported from Japan', Roosevelt told the American people in his fireside chat on April 28, 'that somebody has dropped bombs on Tokyo and on other principal centres of Japanese war industries. If this be true,' Roosevelt added, 'it is the first time in history that Japan has suffered such indignities.'

It was not indignities, however, but successes, that came to the Japanese war machine as April drew to its close. On April 29, Japanese forces seized Lashio, the terminus of the Burma Road, through which Amerian and British supplies were being sent to China. On April 27, as the Japanese grip on Burma intensified, General Stilwell had sought permission, now that his position inside China was untenable, to withdraw to India, taking with him the 100,000 Chinese troops under his command; Washington authorized his withdrawal on April 30. Four days later, the British were forced to abandon the port of Akyab on the Bay of Bengal, less than a hundred miles from the border of India.

In German-occupied Europe, resistance was everywhere apparent, but ruth-lessly suppressed. In the Norwegian fishing port of Taelvag, two Germans and one Norwegian were killed when a resistance group was caught by surprise; in reprisal, every house and all the fishing boats of the village were destroyed, and all twenty-six men between the ages of sixteen and sixty-five sent to con-centration camps in Germany, where most of them died. At the same time, the Germans shot eighteen young Norwegians who had been arrested at Ålesund two months earlier, while trying to escape by boat to England. 'I hope these executions will have their effect in changing the attitude of the Norwegian population,' Goebbels wrote in his diary on May 5. 'If they don't want to learn to love us, they must at least fear us.'

In Greece, in May 1942, the Germans launched Operation Olympus against Greek partisans; but the peasants, themselves so often the victims of reprisals, provided food, hiding places and escape routes. On May 1, in German-occupied Russia, Soviet partisans in one region put up forty-five Red Flags, to which mines were attached to blow up anyone trying to pull them down. Elsewhere, May Day festivities were arranged with the local population, with village dancing and the singing of patriotic songs. There were also widespread anti-German demonstrations in France. But the daily terror was unremitting. On May 1 the German ruler of the Warthegau, Arthur Greiser, wrote to Himmler from Poznan to propose that Poles with tuberculosis should be sent to Chelmno for 'special treatment'. That same May, more than nineteen thousand Jews were gassed at Chelmno, as well as more than six thousand at Auschwitz, five thousand at Belzec and thirty-six thousand at Sobibor. That same month, in German-occupied Russia, five thousand Jews in Dubno, judged 'non-productive' for the German war effort, were taken outside the town and killed in a hail of rifle and machine-gun fire; elsewhere in German-occupied Russia, thirty thousand Jews were murdered that month in fields and ditches, a total Jewish death toll in a single month in excess of 130,000.

For the Western Allies, particularly as there was not to be any invasion of Europe in 1942, the justice of the Allied cause was something which seemed to need reiteration; on May 2 the United States War Department set up a special Photo Signal Detachment, in which seven Hollywood scriptwriters prepared a series of films, under the general title 'Why We Fight', to explain the origins and development of the war. The first of these films, *Prelude to War*, directed by Frank Capra, was only ready for release, however, a year after the detachment was set up.

On May 2, alerted by their daily reading of the most secret Japanese cyphers, United States naval forces intercepted a Japanese fleet escorting two invasion forces across the Coral Sea, one aiming for Tulagi in the Solomon Islands, the other for Port Moresby, on the southern coast of New Guinea, less than five hundred miles from Australia. For four days, a series of battles were fought, mostly from the decks of aircraft carriers, in which seventy Japanese and sixty-six American warplanes were shot down; almost equal losses in what was the first 'air–naval' battle in history: not a single shot was fired by the ships against each other, the battle being entirely fought by aircraft from the aircraft carriers of the two fleets, plane against plane and plane against ship. During the battle, the American fleet aircraft carrier *Lexington* was so badly damaged by aerial attack that she had to be sunk; of her crew, 216 had been killed by Japanese bombs and aerial torpedoes. The Japanese lost the light aircraft carrier *Shoho*. If ships lost were the measure, it was a Japanese victory. Japan, however, was forced as a result of her losses in the air battle, particularly of highly trained and experienced pilots, to call a halt to her southward expansion.

Among the heroes of the Battle of the Coral Sea was a United States Navy lieutenant, John James Powers. Four months later, Roosevelt was to speak during a radio broadcast of how, on the third day of the battle, Powers said to his fellow pilots: 'Remember, the folks back home are counting on us. I am going to get a hit if I have to lay it on their flight deck.' Dropping from eight thousand feet, Powers released his bomb less than two hundred feet from the deck of a carrier; his plane was destroyed by the explosion of his own bomb. 'I have received a recommendation from the Secretary of the Navy', Roosevelt said, 'that Lieutenant James Powers of New York City, missing in action, be awarded the Medal of Honour. I hereby and now make this award.'

On May 5, as the Battle of the Coral Sea entered its third day, Japanese forces landed on Corregidor in the Philippines. The landing had been long expected, and had been preceded by artillery bombardments of exceptional ferocity, culminating in 16,000 shells in the twenty-four hours before the landing. On the morning of May 6, after General Wainwright was told that nearly eight hundred of his men had already been killed, he broadcast a message of surrender to the Japanese, then radioed his decision to Roosevelt in Washington and MacArthur in Australia. The Japanese, in their initial amphibious assault on the island fortress, had lost 1,200 men. In Manila, the Japanese were seeking Filipino leaders to serve under them. The Chief Justice of the Philippines, José Abad Santos, refused to do so. He was executed on May 7.

More than five thousand miles to the west of the Philippines, May 7 saw the climax of Operation Ironclad, a British landing at the Madagascan port of Diego Suarez, an operation aimed at denying the Japanese a base from which to dominate the Indian Ocean. The troops of Vichy France, driven from the port, still resisted, however, any further British advance across the island, and plans had to be made to renew the operation in the autumn.

No day now passed without some military, naval or air initiative by one or other of the combatants. On May 4, in Yugoslavia, the Germans and Italians had launched Operation Trio, their third offensive in six months against Tito's partisans. One German division, three Italian divisions and several Croat units combed the countryside and villages, searching for partisans and seizing hostages. At Pljevlja, the Italians killed thirty-two hostages; more were killed three days later at Cajnice. Driven from their base at Foca, the partisans moved more than two hundred miles northward, to Bihac.

In German-occupied Russia, the first week of May saw the capture and torture of Isai Kazinets, who for many months had organized partisan activity, both sabotage and reconnaissance, in the Minsk area, and who had also made contact with the Jewish underground in the Minsk ghetto. Kazinets, himself a Jew, though brutally tortured, betrayed nobody. He was hanged on May 7. Twenty-three years later he was posthumously created Hero of the Soviet Union.

The Germans now embarked upon the preliminary phase of their Russian summer offensive, launching on May 8, in the Crimea, an assault on the Kerch Peninsula and on the besieged port city of Sevastopol. Dive-bomber attacks on the Kerch Peninsula devastated the defenders; 170,000 Russian soldiers were taken prisoner. But Sevastopol held out for more than a month. For the collective courage of its defenders, it received the title of Hero City. Also besieged, the island of Malta was the beneficiary on May 9 of a second attempt to provide its defenders with adequate air support. This was Operation Bowery, in which two aircraft carriers, the British *Eagle* and the American *Wasp*, brought sixty-two fighters to within seven hundred miles of the island. All reached Malta safely and were then refuelled so quickly as to be ready to take off again within only thirty-five minutes of landing; six of them were refuelled and airborne within nine minutes. That day there were nine German and Italian air raids against Malta, each one successfully intercepted. The safe arrival of the sixty-two fighters proved to be the turning point in Malta's struggle for air supremacy above the island. Morale in Malta received a further boost that week when the fast British minelayer *Welshman* managed to cross the Mediterranean from Gibraltar with 340 tons of supplies.

The night of May 9 also saw a British success in the clandestine war of sabotage, when three French agents, who had been parachuted into France three days earlier, blew up the main transmitter of Radio Paris, located near Melun, putting it out of action for two weeks.

Beginning on May 10, and continuing for two days each week until the end of the year, a new death camp came into operation in German-occupied Russia. It was located just outside Minsk, near the village of Maly Trostenets, where Russian prisoners-of-war and Jews had been forced to build barracks for six hundred slave labourers and their German and Ukrainian guards. To Maly Trostenets were brought by train tens of thousands of Jews from Germany, Austria and Czechoslovakia. From the train station they were driven towards the village in large vans. These vans were mobile gas chambers; when the vans reached the camp all those inside them were dead. The corpses were taken out, as at Chelmno, by a special prisoners' unit, which threw them into deep pits.

The existence of Maly Trostenets was kept a close secret. Although tens of thousands of Jews were brought there from Western Europe and killed, even the name of the camp was unknown to those who, in the Allied capitals, tried to monitor the fate of Hitler's victims.

War-weariness had led to a plethora of hopes and rumours throughout the warring globe. In the Warsaw ghetto it had been rumoured on May 8 that the Red Army had retaken Smolensk and Kharkov, that 43,000 Germans had been killed on Lake Ilmen south of Leningrad, that Mussolini had been deposed, and that Roosevelt had given the German people until May 15 to surrender. On May 11, in a prisoner-of-war camp at Bandung, the Australian, British and Dutch prisoners-of-war discussed the 'news', which Colonel Dunlop described as 'an extraordinary mixture and mostly tripe', that Hungary, Roumania and Bulgaria had each surrendered to the Russians, that the Germans had marched out of Holland, and that Anthony Eden had made a speech 'giving an ultimatum to Germany to surrender completely'. One item of real news, made public in America on May 10, was the 'Doolittle Raid' on Tokyo. On the following day, the aircrew which had crash-landed at Vladivostok and been interned by the Russians managed to make their escape from a village in the Urals to the Persian border; once inside Persia, a British consul guided them to the Indian border city of Quetta.

'We're all hoping that we'll be able to bring the war to an end this year,'

General Rommel wrote confidently to his wife from the Western Desert on May 12, and he added: 'It will soon have lasted three full years.' That day, on the Eastern Front, the Red Army launched a surprise attack on the German forces south of Kharkov, forcing the Germans to postpone their own plans for an offensive later in May. At his headquarters at Rastenburg, Hitler's thoughts, like Rommel's, were on the post-war world of victory and peace: that day, musing on the future of his empire, Hitler drew the floor plan of a new art gallery for Linz, and sketched out the rough plans of a mansion to be built on a hill above the Danube, with grand entrance hall, pavilion terrace and, upstream from the main house, a special 'architecture garden'.

On May 13, Russian troops were forced to withdraw from the Kerch Peninsula. South of Kharkov, however, they continued to advance. In Leningrad, the deaths from starvation, while not as many as in April, were still in their thousands every day. It was on May 13 that Tanya Savicheva, a young girl who had been in the city throughout the siege, noted in her child's address book, under the letter M: 'Mummy May 13 at 7.30 morning 1942. The Savichevs are dead. All dead. Only Tanya remains.' Earlier alphabetical pages showed 'Zhenya, died Dec 28', 'Granny, died Jan 25', 'Leka, died March 17', 'Uncle Vasya, died April 13' and 'Uncle Lyosha, May 10'.

Evacuated to Gorky, on the Volga, Tanya herself died of chronic dysentery in the summer of 1943.

On May 14, German torpedo bombers sank the cruiser *Trinidad* west of Bear Island, as it escorted Allied merchant ships on the summer route of the Russian convoy run from Iceland to Archangel. Eighty sailors were killed, twenty of whom were injured men who had been taken off the cruiser *Edinburgh*, when she had been hit on the same run two weeks earlier. But more than a hundred merchant ships managed to reach Murmansk that month, with their war cargoes for the Russian front. It was on May 17 that the Germans launched their second offensive of 1942 on that front, striking at the westward bulge in the Russian lines at Izyum, south-east of Kharkov; the Germans captured Izyum on the following day, clearing a major obstacle to the principal offensive towards Stalingrad, and capturing 214,000 Soviet soldiers and 1,200 tanks.

In Berlin, anti-Nazi posters had begun to appear in the streets that May, and several of the exhibits in an anti-Soviet exhibition had been set on fire. Twenty-seven people were arrested for these acts of defiance. All of them were Jews, led by Herbert Baum, a German Communist. Among the group were two sisters, Alice and Hella Hirsch, aged nineteen and twenty-two respectively, and Baum's sister, Marianne. All but two of those arrested were executed or perished. Also sentenced to death on May 18, at Wandsworth Prison, London, was a citizen of Gibraltar, José Key, arrested on the Rock two and a half months earlier for having passed on to the Germans information about the movement of Allied ships and aircraft.

As the Japanese advanced deeper and deeper into Burma, the British Commander-in-Chief, General Alexander, ordered his troops across the border into India, to the region of Imphal. The Chinese forces in Burma, led by General

Chiang Kai-shek, fell back to the road between Myitkyina and Fort Herz; they were also soon to cross into India, to the Ledo region. Inside China, an Australian surgeon, Lieutenant-Colonel Lindsay Ride, who had recently escaped from Japanese captivity, was formally appointed on May 16 to be the representative of British Military Intelligence's escape organization, MI9. Colonel Ride not only helped to organize the return to India of prisoners-of-war who managed to escape from Japanese captivity, but also provided medical help for tens of thousands of Chinese in an area where the Chinese Army had no medical service at all. From his base at Kweilin, Ride also issued twice-daily weather reports, which were of inestimable help to the Allied air forces operating over China, just as, from German-occupied Poland, the Polish underground Home Army sent twice-daily weather reports to Britain, to assist British bombing operations over Germany.

The German discomfiture in Europe was continuous; on May 19 British bombers raided Mannheim. That same day, as the German Army continued its counter-offensive on the Eastern Front against the Red Army, Soviet partisans, as Goebbels noted in his diary, 'blasted the railway tracks in the central front between Bryansk and Roslavl at five points – a further proof of their extremely discomfiting activity'. South of that region, Goebbels added, Hungarian troops were fighting 'under great difficulties', and he went on to explain: 'They must now capture one village after another and pacify it, a thing that has not proved exactly a constructive process. For when the Hungarians report that they have "pacified" a village, this usually means that not a single inhabitant is left. In consequence, we can hardly get any agricultural work done in such regions'.

Further behind the lines, 'pacification' had also been brutal. On May 21, 4,300 Jews were deported from the town of Chelm to the death camp at Sobibor, less than twenty-five miles away. On arrival, all were gassed. Also on May 21, more than two thousand Jews were taken from their homes in the Volhynian town of Korzec, and murdered in the fields near by. That same day, the German industrial firm of IG Farben set up a factory at Monowitz, just outside Auschwitz, for the manufacture of synthetic oil and rubber; the principal source of labour for the factory was to be Jews deported to Auschwitz, separated from their families, and sent, not to the gas chambers, but to the barracks. There, tattooed with an indelible number on their forearm, they became the slaves of German industry. Hundreds of thousands of them worked at Monowitz; tens of thousands died in conditions of unremitting toil, minimum sustenance and the sadistic brutality of their guards.

On many occasions, Jews were deported to an 'unknown destination' which was never to become known. On May 22 it was the turn of eighty young German-Jewish men and women, all of them Zionists, who since 1939 had been living and working on a farm in Germany – at Steckelsdorf, forty-five miles west of Berlin – training for agricultural work in Palestine. That day, they were ordered by the Gestapo to leave. Their destination, they were told, 'lay in a cold region'. They could therefore take with them two blankets each, as well as washing things and food. The young Jews were taken away, never to be seen or heard of again. Three weeks earlier, 2,100 Jews from Dortmund had been sent east, either to Sobibor or to Belzec, where all of them were gassed on arrival; the young pioneers may well have taken the same route, or perhaps one even further east, to Maly Trostenets.

On May 23, British Intelligence, without revealing its source, sent the Soviet High Command the precise details, culled from the Germans' own Enigma messages, of where, and in what strength, the principal German summer offensive would come. The Germans themselves, continually harassed by Soviet partisan operations behind the lines, launched Operation Hanover, to try to clear the partisans from the Bryansk–Vyazma railway; for six days, beginning on May 24, as many as 45,000 German troops, including panzer and ss units, searched for an estimated 20,000 partisans, thousands of whom were caught and killed.

Aid to Russia had continued to be sent eastward across the Arctic Sea, but the hazards were enormous. On May 26, a total of 260 German aircraft struck at Convoy PQ 16, helped in finding their targets by the twenty-four hour Arctic day. Seven of the merchant ships were sunk, and many merchant seamen killed. As the remaining ships and their escorts made their way, battered but unbowed, to Murmansk and Archangel; the Soviet Foreign Minister, Vyacheslav Molotov, was in London, where, on May 26, he signed a twenty-year alliance between Britain and the Soviet Union, whereby both countries undertook 'to afford one another military and other assistance and support of all kinds in the war against Germany and all those States which are associated with her in acts of aggression in Europe'. Both signatories also agreed not to negotiate or conclude any armistice with Germany or her allies 'except by mutual consent'.

The day of the signature of the Anglo-Soviet Treaty marked the first day of Rommel's renewed offensive in the Western Desert. At Bir Hakeim, the desert strongpoint held by Free French forces, many of them members of the Foreign Legion, repeated infantry, tank and air onslaughts could not dislodge the defenders until two weeks had passed. Elsewhere, Rommel pressed back the British line, determined to capture Tobruk and then drive on to the Egyptian border.

On May 27, the second day of Rommel's assault, and while German forces in Russia continued both to crush the partisans in the rear areas and to straighten their front line near Kharkov, Reinhard Heydrich was ambushed and gravely wounded in Prague by Czech patriots. Two of them, Jan Kubis and Josef Gabcik, had earlier been parachuted into German-occupied Czechoslovakia from Britain. 'We shall have no problem', Goebbels noted in his diary on May 28, 'crushing this attempt at creating chaos in the Protectorate and the occupied territories.' Goebbels added: 'My campaign against the Jews in Berlin will be waged along similar lines. I am currently having a Jewish hostage list put together. Sweeping arrests will follow.'

For Goebbels, the attack on Heydrich made no difference to the policy of extermination. 'Ten Jews either in a concentration camp or six feet under', he wrote, 'are preferable to one roaming at large. There is no room for sentimentalism here.' Nor was there any 'sentimentalism' for non-Jews in German-occupied Poland that day, when more than two hundred Poles were taken from Warsaw to the village of Magdalenka and shot, among them three women who had to be brought on stretchers from the Pawiak prison hospital, and fifteen women who had been sent back to Poland from Ravensbrück concentration camp.

On May 29, Hitler, having returned briefly to Berlin from Rastenburg, agreed with Goebbels that all Jews should be removed at once from Berlin. In Paris, the Jews were ordered that day to sew a yellow star on the left side of their coats or jackets. 'The yellow star may make some Catholics shudder,' one French collaborationist newspaper declared, but, it went on, 'it renews the most strictly Catholic tradition.'

As Heydrich lay wounded, deportation and mass murder were being continued. In the Volhynian village of Radziwillow, three thousand Jews were rounded up for slaughter on May 29. A group of young men, among them Asher Czerkaski, organized a breakout. As they ran, fifteen hundred Jews were shot down. The others reached the immediate safety of the nearby forest, but most of them were soon caught and killed.

Still in Berlin on May 30, Hitler told Goebbels, as Goebbels noted in his diary, 'that all restraint be dispensed with, and that the interests of the security of the Reich be placed above the interests of single individuals from whom we can expect little good'. That day, in a mission organized by Admiral Canaris's Intelligence service, Pastor Dietrich Bonhoeffer flew to Sweden. There, he held a secret meeting with a British clergyman, Bishop Bell of Chichester, to whom he spoke of the crimes which his nation was committing, and assured Bell of the growing resistance inside Germany to such evil acts.

Hitler spoke that day in Berlin to a group of recently commissioned German officers. 'I do not doubt for a single second', he told them, 'that we shall win in the end. Fate has not led me this far for nothing, from an unknown soldier to the Führer of the German nation, and the Führer of the German Army. She has not done this simply to mock at me and to snatch away at the last moment what had to be gained after so bitter a struggle'. A thousand years earlier, Charlemagne had used harsh measures to create a German Empire; the German Army, Hitler warned, must now use harsh measures in the East if it were to win the space needed for the new German Empire to survive and flourish.

In the East, however, the Russians, despite all their losses, were regaining strength, and intensifying resistance. On May 30, as Hitler spoke to his young officers, a Central Staff of the Partisan Movement was created, whereby Russian operations behind the German lines could be co-ordinated to the best military and psychological effect. That same night, the Germans suffered a physical and psychological blow from the West, the launching by Britain of Operation Millennium, when more than a thousand British bombers raided Cologne. In this, the first 'thousand bomber raid' of the war, 1,455 tons of bombs were dropped in ninety minutes; thirty-nine of the bombers were shot down by German night fighters and anti-aircraft fire; two had been destroyed when they collided in mid-air.

The principal object of the raid was Cologne's chemical and machine tool industries; these were crippled. More than thirteen thousand houses were destroyed, 45,000 people made homeless, and 469 killed. 'Of course', Hermann Goering wrote in his diary, 'the effects of aerial warfare are terrible if one looks at individual cases, but one has to accept them.'

'I hope you were pleased with our mass air attack on Cologne,' Churchill telegraphed to Roosevelt on the following day, and he added: 'There is plenty more to come. ....'

The repercussions of the Cologne raid were considerable. In the Warsaw ghetto, the captive Jews rejoiced. 'Cologne was an advance payment', Emanuel Ringelblum noted in his diary a few months later, 'on the vengeance that must and shall be taken on Hitler's Germany for the millions of Jews they have killed. So the Jewish population of tortured Europe considered Cologne its personal act of vengeance.' As for himself: 'After the Cologne affair, I walked around in a good mood, feeling that, even if I should perish at their hands, my death is prepaid!'

At Hitler's headquarters at Rastenburg, Albert Speer, a visitor three days after the raid, recalled: 'The excitement over the air raid on Cologne had not yet died down'. Nor did Britain intend that it should do so. 'This proof of the growing power of Britain's bomber force', Churchill told 'Bomber' Harris, 'is also the herald of what Germany will receive, city by city, from now on.' Only William Joyce, Lord Haw-Haw, broadcasting from Berlin in his regular attempt to lower British morale, turned Cologne into a threat for Britain. 'Mr Churchill boasts of the attack on Cologne as an instalment of the hell that Germany is to receive,' Joyce declared, and he added: 'The German attitude is, "Give us more hell, as much as you can, and we shall repay the hell with interest."'

Inside Germany, and German-occupied Europe, it was the aftermath of Heydrich's wounding that was leading to 'hell with interest'. 'Heydrich is in critical condition', Goebbels noted in his diary on May 31. A 'whole crowd of Jews', he wrote, had already been shot in Sachsenhausen concentration camp, and he added: 'The more of this filthy race we eliminate, the better things will be for the security of the Reich.' Two days later, a thousand Jews were deported from Vienna by train to Minsk; they were most probably taken on at once to Maly Trostenets and their death. On 3 June, 110 Jews were rounded up in Warsaw, taken to a prison on the edge of the ghetto, and shot. Those killed included several women, two of whom were pregnant. Three days later, Adolf Eichmann ordered the deportation of 450 Jews from the Koblenz region; the inmates of a mental home in a nearby village were, he said, to be included. To maintain secrecy, and deception, Eichmann's office insisted that the words 'deportation to the East' should not be used in describing these moves, but instead 'people who emigrated elsewhere'.

On the night of May 31, war came briefly to the Australian city of Sydney, when one of two Japanese midget submarines, penetrating the harbour defences, fired its torpedoes at the American cruiser *Chicago*. They missed, hitting instead the Australian depot ship, *Kuttabul*, a converted ferry. Twenty sailors died when the ship went down. All four Japanese submariners also died in the attack, two having committed suicide; the four bodies were cremated in Sydney with full naval honours, and their ashes returned to Japan. That same day, more than six thousand miles to the west, other Japanese midget submarines, reaching Madagascar, sank the British merchant ship *British Loyalty* in Diego Suarez harbour, and damaged the battleship *Ramillies*. All the Japanese submariners were killed; as at Sydney, theirs had been, in effect, a suicide mission.

May 31 also marked the end of the fifth month of the German submarine sinkings off the eastern seaboard of the United States, and the month of heaviest sinkings; the 111 merchant ships sunk that May bringing the total since the start of the year to 377, more than a hundred of them between New York and Miami. But the war at sea took a favourable turn for the United States in the first week of June, when, alerted by their reading of Japan's most secret naval messages, American warships intercepted a Japanese naval assault on Midway Island. The Japanese force was a formidable one, eighty-six warships, including four aircraft-carriers. Four times, American aircraft attacked the Japanese ships in vain, sixty-five of the aircraft being shot down. But the fifth attack, made with fifty-four dive-bombers on the morning of June 5, was successful. Three of the four Japanese carriers, *Akagi, Kaga* and *Soryu*, were sunk. That same afternoon, the fourth carrier, *Hiryu,* was also destroyed, but not before her own aircraft had badly damaged the American carrier *Yorktown,* which was sunk by a Japanese submarine on the following day.

For the Japanese, the Battle of Midway was a disaster; not only did they lose the four aircraft carriers and a cruiser, but also 332 aircraft and 3,500 men. The American losses were one aircraft carrier, one destroyer, 150 aircraft and 307 men. That same week, the Japanese landed 1,800 men on the two most westerly of the American islands in the Aleutian chain, Kiska and Attu. Their aim had been to draw American naval forces away from Midway, but, as this deception was known to the American signals eavesdroppers, it failed.

The Americans rejoiced at their victory, which had been made all the more pleasurable by the fact that three of the Japanese aircraft carriers sunk had been among the five which had taken part in the attack on Pearl Harbor.

The Allies were less fortunate in the Atlantic. In the four weeks beginning on June 1, as a result of their special supply submarines, German submarines had sunk 121 Allied merchant ships off the eastern seaboard of the United States. Helped, however, by intercepted German Naval 'Enigma' messages, the British were able to sink all five of these ships by the end of June. Following strong protests by Britain to Spain, two other German supply ships, the *Charlotte Schliemann* and the *Corrientes,* which had lain at Las Palmas in the Canary Islands since September 1939, were forced to leave the safety of Spanish waters. They too were later sunk.

News of the death camp killings inside German-occupied Poland became public knowledge on 1 June 1942, when a Warsaw underground newspaper, *Liberty Barricade,* the clandestine publication of the Polish Socialist Party, published an extensive account of the gassings at Chelmno. This information had come from Emanuel Ringelblum, who had himself received it from the young Jew,

Jakub Grojanowski, who had escaped from Chelmno in January, after having been forced to participate in the burying of the corpses of those killed in the gas vans. 'Bloodcurdling news', the report began, 'has reached us about the slaughter of Jews.' Six months and three weeks after it had become a site of mass murder, Chelmno was identified by name in the West. The gassings being carried out elsewhere, at Belzec and Sobibor, as well as in gas vans at Belgrade and Riga, and at Maly Trostenets near Minsk, were as yet totally unknown to the Allies.

For the Germans involved in these murders, the problem was one of technology. In an official note dated June 5, a senior civil servant in Berlin gave details of 'technical modifications of special vehicles put into service'. Since December 1941, he explained, 'using three vehicles, 97,000 persons have been "processed", without any defects occurring in these vehicles', and he added: 'The explosion which is known to have occurred in Chelmno should be considered as an isolated case, caused by a technical failure. Special instructions have been sent to the depots involved, in order to prevent such accidents in the future.' There was one more fault that had to be mentioned; the 'merchandise' in the gas van, the civil servant explained, displayed during the operation a regrettable if natural 'rush towards the light' which was hampering the efficiency of the procedure. This fault would be 'rectified'.

In German-occupied Russia, the German Army now launched two major offensives against the Soviet partisans. In the first, Operation Kottbus, begun on June 3, more than sixteen thousand German troops attacked the partisan 'Republic of Palik' which had been set up late in 1942 in the Polotsk Borisov Lepel area. Two days later, on June 5, a further five thousand German troops launched Operation Birdsong, against 2,500 partisans between Roslavl and Bryansk. In a four week sweep, 1,193 partisans were killed, for a loss of 58 German dead. But a German military report expressed dissatisfaction at the results. 'The partisans', one senior officer complained, 'continued their old tactic of evading, withdrawing into the forests, or moving in larger groups into the areas south and south-west of the Roslavl–Bryansk highway and into the Kletnya area.' Although no further partisan attacks were reported in the 'pacified' area, the officer wrote, nevertheless 'mines continued to be planted' and several German vehicles had been damaged. Within two months, Soviet partisans had returned to the 'Birdsong' area in force.

On June 8, while Operation Birdsong was in its early days, three Jews, among them a young woman, Vitka Kempner, left the Vilna ghetto on their first ever sabotage mission. Their target was a German military train, and they succeeded. 'It's been blown up!' – the words spread throughout the ghetto, bringing a sense of achievement, if not of hope. But the reprisals were swift. Thirty-two families were seized by the Gestapo, taken to Ponar, and shot.

Four days before the three Jews had set off from Vilna on their sabotage mission, Reinhard Heydrich had died of his wounds; at his state funeral in Berlin on June 9, Himmler told the assembled SS mourners that theirs was a 'holy obligation' to avenge Heydrich's death, 'and to destroy with even greater determination the enemies of our nation, mercilessly and pitilessly'. On the following day, at the Czech village of Lidice, six miles north-west of Prague, all 199 men in the village were rounded up and shot. The eighty-eight children of the village, and their mothers, sixty women in all, were sent to Ravensbrück, Mauthausen and Auschwitz, where all of them were killed. In a second Czech village, Lezaky, seventeen men and sixteen women were shot, and fourteen children sent to concentration camps. Two of the children survived the war, two survivors out of a total of 394 victims.

The Lidice and Lezaky killings were only the start of what the ss described as Operation Heydrich. On that same June 10, a thousand Jews were deported from Prague 'to the East'. The only survivor was a man who managed to jump from the train early in its journey. There was likewise only one survivor of two further trains, each carrying a thousand deportees, which left the 'model' ghetto of Theresienstadt on June 12 and 13 'to an unknown destination in the East'. All three trains had probably gone to Minsk, and then on to Maly Trostenets, where gas vans operated without respite.

A headline in The Times on June 10 told of 'Mass Butchery in Poland'. This was a reference, not to Operation Heydrich, which was centred upon Czechoslovakia, but to a speech made on the previous day in London by General Sikorski, in which he gave details of the mass murder of Jews on Polish soil during the previous twelve months. 'Massacres of tens of thousands of Jews have been carried out this year,' he said. 'People are being starved to death in ghettos. Mass executions are held; even those suffering from typhus are shot.' As to the Poles, Sikorski added, 'to smash the resistance of the railwaymen at the Upper Silesian junctions, gallows have been erected in eighteen Silesian towns. Members of the educated classes, railwaymen and workers are being hanged there, and all the schoolchildren are herded there to watch this cruel spectacle.'

Only the warning that punishment would follow, Sikorski added, 'and the application of reprisals where these are possible, may stay the fury of German killers, and save further hundreds of thousands of innocent victims from inevitable annihilation'. On June 12, two days after Sikorski's message was published, ten Poles, accused of sabotage in an iron foundry in the Silesian town of Dabrowa Gornicza, were hanged at a street corner, and their bodies left hanging as a warning to all future saboteurs.

In the German Army itself, a young officer, the twenty-five-year-old Michael Kitzelmann, who had won an Iron Cross second class for bravery as a company commander, had spoken out that summer against the atrocities being committed on the Eastern Front. 'If these criminals should win,' he told his fellow officers, 'I would have no wish to live any longer.' Arrested and tried by court martial, Kitzelmann was shot by a firing squad at Orel on June 11.

Within three weeks of Kitzelmann's execution, Himmler addressed the officers of the ss Division 'Das Reich', to explain to them why they, the ss troops, and not the German Army, were the ones who must wage the race war. 'The German soldier', he said, 'has in the past frequently operated under long-outmoded conceptions that once went unquestioned; these he carried with him to the battlefield in 1939.' From the very moment that 'the enemy was taken captive',

Himmler explained, 'this erroneous notion of what war is all about showed itself unmistakably. Thus, for instance, it was thought that one had to say that even a Jew was a human being and that, as such, he could not be harmed. Or, in the case of a Jewess – even if she had been caught harbouring partisans at the time – one couldn't touch her; she was, after all, a lady.' Himmler added that 'the same held for this Eastern campaign too, when the whole German nation took to the field, their heads filled with such absolute rubbish and over-refined, civilized decadence'.

With pride, Himmler declared: 'We ss men were less encumbered, one might even say practically unencumbered, by such rubbish. After a decade of racial education we, the entire cadre of the ss, entered this war as unshakeable champions of our Germanic people'.

'We ought', Himmler concluded, 'to spare neither our own nor foreign blood, if the nation requires. . . .'

On June 13, at Peenemünde, on the Baltic, German scientists tested a twelve-ton rocket with a one-ton warhead, intended to be launched in due course from Germany against England. To watch the test, thirty-five senior officials had come from Berlin, among them the State Secretary for Air, Field Marshal Milch, and the Minister for Armaments, Albert Speer.

It was expected that the rocket, known to the Germans as the 'A4', and later to the Allies as the 'V2', would have a range of up to two hundred miles. The first test, however, was a failure; although the rocket was successfully fired, it crashed to earth less than a mile away, leaving both experts and officials deeply disappointed. Following this failure, however, the research intensified.

In North Africa, Rommel's forces had continued their advance towards the Egyptian border. 'The battle is going favourably for us,' Rommel had written to his wife on June 1, 'about four hundred tanks have been shot up. Our losses are bearable.' By June 5, Rommel was able to announce that he had taken four thousand prisoners. Six days later, his forces broke into the French-held fortress at Bir Hakeim.

Even as Rommel drew closer to the Egyptian frontier, the importance of Egypt as an Allied base was underlined when, on June 12, American bombers based in the Nile Delta flew more than nine hundred miles to bomb the Roumanian oilfields at Ploesti, on which the German war machine was so dependent. But, off the Egyptian coast, a British attempt, Operation Vigorous, to run more supplies to Malta encountered severe difficulties that week, with the British cruiser *Hermione* sunk on June 16, while the British destroyer *Hasty* and the Australian destroyer *Nestor* were both so badly crippled that they had to be scuttled.

Also sunk by the Italians before the action in the eastern Mediterranean ended were three more British destroyers, *Airedale*, *Bedouin* and *Oakley*. The latter, on loan to the Polish Navy, had been renamed *Kujawiak*, and was manned by Polish sailors. Although the Italian heavy cruiser *Trento* was also sunk during the battle, Operation Vigorous was a severe tactical defeat for the British, and an engagement of ill-omen.

On shore, Rommel continued his westward march. 'Enemy resistance crumbled', he later recalled, 'and more and more British troops give themselves up. Black dejection showed on their faces.' 'The battle has been won', Rommel wrote to his wife on June 15, 'and the enemy is breaking up. We're now mopping up encircled remnants of their army. I needn't tell you how delighted I am.'

On June 16, the seven Czechs who had been involved in the assassination of Heydrich were discovered by the Germans hiding in a church in Prague. They had been hiding there for two weeks, and had planned to move on June 19, and to try to reach England. Refusing to give themselves up when they were discovered, they gave battle; fourteen Germans were killed. Jan Kubis, the Czech parachutist from Britain who had thrown the grenade which had mortally wounded Heydrich, was wounded in the battle and died in hospital. Josef Gabcik died in the struggle, as did two other parachutists who had been sent in separately, and three members of the local Czech resistance. They had been betrayed by another Czech, Karel Curda, who had informed the Gestapo of where they were hiding. Curda, like the four parachutists, had been trained in Britain.

The death of the four Czech parachutists, and the betrayal of their group, was not the only disaster for British Intelligence that June. Doing considerable long-term harm was the capture by the Germans of a British agent parachuted into Holland. Using this agent's wireless transmitter, the Germans sent a number of messages back to London. When it became clear that the deception had not been discovered, German counter-Intelligence mounted Operation North Pole, organizing German reception committees for the continuing drop of British agents, radio operators and supplies, including considerable quantities of arms intended for the Dutch resistance. As a result of Operation North Pole, the Germans captured more than fifty Dutch subjects who were parachuted from England; forty-seven of them were murdered in concentration camps.

Soviet Intelligence also suffered a setback that June, with the arrest in Brussels of Johann Wenzel, the Russian-trained wireless operator of the Red Orchestra. After being captured and tortured, Wenzel agreed to co-operate with the Germans; as a result, several hundred Soviet agents in Western Europe were rounded up and executed, among them Hillel Katz who, despite terrible torture, refused to betray his colleagues. The capture of these Soviet agents was, however, kept secret, with the result that all five wireless sets of the Red Orchestra continued to be used by the Germans to convey disinformation to the Soviets for the next nine months.

In spite of these major setbacks to the Allies, there were three British successes that month in the sphere of Intelligence: first, the breaking of two more German Air Force Eastern Front Enigma codes, 'Mosquito' on June 8 and 'Skunk' on June 16; second, the forced landing almost intact on British soil of the most modern version of the German Focke-Wulf 190 combat plane, which British aircraft designers were thus able to study and copy; and, third, the successful work of 'Garbo', the Spaniard, Juan Pujol Garcia, whom the Germans continued to believe was working for them, but who, as a British agent, was providing false military information and developing a whole team of imaginary agents through whom further disinformation was sent to Germany.

On four separate occasions in June, a thousand Jews had been deported from Paris to Auschwitz. At the same time, the killing of Jews in German-occupied Russia had been uninterrupted, and the deportations from southern Poland to Belzec and Sobibor had continued. More than 52,000 Slovak Jews had also been deported to Auschwitz that summer, bringing the Jewish death toll that June to more than 150,000. 'The destruction of the Jewish communities is continuing,' Richard Lichtheim, a Jewish representative in Switzerland, wrote to a colleague in New York on June 15, and he added: 'The whole of Europe is anxiously awaiting the day when the Allied nations will liberate this tortured Continent.'

Not liberation, however, but further setbacks to the Allied cause came in the second and third weeks of June, when, fort by fort, the Germans broke through the Soviet defences of Sevastapol. On June 13, Fort Stalin had fallen, and on June 17, Fort Siberia. One of the biggest of all, Fort Maxim Gorky, fell on June 18, the Germans using flamethrowers to force out, or to burn to death, the tenacious Russian defenders. On June 20, Fort Lenin fell, but still Sevastopol did not surrender its last pockets of resistance. It was to be another thirteen days before, on July 3, the stubborn defenders were finally overrun.

Meanwhile, in North Africa, Rommel had driven the British back behind Bardia, on the Libyan–Egyptian frontier, and at five-thirty in the morning of June 20, began his assault on the besieged fortress of Tobruk. That same evening, at seven o'clock, the first German tanks entered Tobruk. Thirteen hours later, at eight o'clock on the morning of June 21, the commander of the garrison, the South African General Hendrik Klopper, sent his officers forward with the white flag of surrender.

Thirty thousand men surrendered to Rommel at Tobruk. Also surrendered were two thousand vehicles in working order, two thousand tons of petrol, and five thousand tons of rations. That evening, on learning of the victory, Hitler awarded Rommel a field marshal's baton. 'I am going on to Suez,' was Rommel's official reply. Later, however, he remarked to his wife. 'I would rather he had given me one more division.'

Churchill was in Washington with Roosevelt when news of the fall of Tobruk reached him. 'Defeat is one thing,' he later commented, 'disgrace is another'. The silence that greeted the news was broken, however, not by Churchill but by Roosevelt, who asked: 'What can we do to help?'

# 25

# Axis triumphs

JULY 1942

The strong Russian resistance at Sevastopol, although it had been almost broken by 22 June 1942, had forced the Germans to delay their summer offensive. The aircraft needed for the offensive could not be transferred from Sevastopol to Kursk for another four or five days. In North Africa, on June 22, the British fell back across the Egyptian frontier to Mersa Matruh, less than 180 miles from Alexandria. On the Pacific coast of the United States, a Japanese submarine shelled a military depot at Fort Stevens, Oregon, on the estuary of the Columbia river. It was the first attack by any foreign power on a military installation on the continental United States since the British attacks during the war of 1812. The damage done was trivial, however, nor was the attack to be repeated.

In Berlin, on June 22, Adolf Eichmann informed his subordinates of the plan of Operation Heydrich: in the 'first instance', he explained, 40,000 Jews were to be deported from France, 40,000 from Holland and 10,000 from Belgium. They were to be sent to Auschwitz, at a rate of a thousand a day: one train a day. 'No objections to these measures', Eichmann noted, 'had been raised on behalf of the Foreign Office. . . .'

In German-occupied Poland, the euthanasia programme was suddenly accelerated, when Polish and Polish Jewish patients in mental institutions were deported to Auschwitz, the first group on June 23.

In the Far East, in an attempt to by-pass their vulnerable sea lines of communications, the Japanese had begun to plan a railway link between Burma and Thailand, using British, Australian and Dutch prisoners-of-war. On June 23, an advance party of three hundred British prisoners-of-war reached the base at Bampong, in Thailand, with orders to construct their own camp and also a camp for their Japanese guards. Three months later, three thousand Australian prisoners-of-war were to be sent to a camp at Thanbyuzayat, to begin construction of the Burma end of the railway, soon to be known as the 'Railway of Death'.

To help relieve Britain's immediate danger in Egypt, Roosevelt ordered a squadron of light bombers, then in Florida and about to be sent to China, to go instead to Egypt. A further forty Hurricane fighter bombers, then at Basra on their way to Russia, were likewise diverted to Egypt, as were ten American bombers then in India, which were intended for missions over China. A hundred howitzers and three hundred tanks were sent by convoy around the Cape of Good Hope to Suez. The engines for the tanks were sent separately. When the ship carrying them was sunk off Bermuda by a German submarine, Roosevelt and General Marshall at once ordered three hundred more tank engines to be sent in the fastest ship available, so as to overtake the Suez-bound convoy.

In the last week of June, while this American aid was still on its way to Egypt, Rommel launched Operation Aida, pushing the British back as far as El Alamein, and taking six thousand prisoners. Rommel was now only sixty miles west of Alexandria. Mussolini, eager to be seen as a victor and a conqueror, flew to Cyrenaica and prepared for a triumphal entry into Cairo. In nearby Palestine, the Jews, encouraged to do so by the British, worked on schemes to defend the southern approaches to Haifa. Doris May, an Anglo-Catholic friend of the Zionist leaders, wrote on June 25: 'It may yet fall to our handful of half-trained, half-equipped people, to put up the only effective resistance to the advance – to crack the jaws that seek to devour them. I had hoped', she added, 'that the Land of Israel might be spared, but it does not look very like it.'

The Jews of Palestine knew what was in store for them if German occupation was to be their lot. On June 25 the Gestapo ordered the arrest of 22,000 Jews in the Paris region, for deportation 'to the East'. On June 26, the British Broadcasting Corporation broadcast from London an account of the fate of the Jews of Poland, stating that 700,000 had already been murdered. This information had been smuggled out of Warsaw by the Polish underground, which had received it from the Polish Jewish historian Emanuel Ringelblum and his friends. 'Our toils and tribulations, our devotion and constant terror, have not been in vain,' Ringelblum wrote that night. 'We have struck the enemy a hard blow'. Even if the BBC's revelations did not lead Hitler to halt the slaughter, Ringelblum was content: 'We have revealed his Satanic plan to annihilate Polish Jewry, a plan he wished to complete in silence', he wrote. 'We have run a line through his calculations and have exposed his cards. And if England keeps its word and turns to the formidable mass attacks it has threatened – then perhaps we will be saved'.

On the previous night, unknown as yet to Ringelblum, a thousand and six British bombers had cast their bombs on the North Sea port of Bremen. Forty-nine aircraft were shot down, a loss which was considered by many to approach the prohibitive. As to the effectiveness of the raid, cloud cover had made the accurate identification of targets virtually impossible.

Despite the bombing of Bremen, and the broadcast from London, the deportation of Jews continued, and on an accelerated scale. 'You yourself, Reichsführer,' Odilo Globocnik reminded Himmler on June 26, 'once mentioned that you felt the job should be done as quickly as possible, if only for reasons of concealment.' Terror also played its part; on June 27 the German administrator of the Przemysl district, Dr Heinisch, issued a clear public instruction. 'Every Ukrainian or Pole', it read, 'who attempts by any means whatsoever to impede the campaign for the deportation of Jews, will be shot. Every Ukrainian or Pole found in a Jewish quarter looting Jewish houses will be shot. Every Ukrainian or Pole attempting to conceal or helping to conceal a Jew will be shot.'

In the month following this order, 24,000 Jews from Western Galicia passed through Przemysl in trains going eastward. They came from twelve towns and villages within Dr Heinisch's jurisdiction. All were taken to Belzec and killed.

On June 26, as part of their main summer offensive, German troops launched an attack towards Rostov-on-Don. That day, at Rastenburg, Hitler decorated the commander of the SS Death's Head Division, SS General Eicke, with the Oak Leaves to his Knight's Cross, for his bravery in holding out in the Demyansk pocket throughout the previous winter; eleven of Eicke's officers and men were awarded the Knight's Cross for their bravery. But Eicke stressed, in his talk with Hitler, that his men were in a much weakened position as a result of the fighting, had an acute shortage of weapons and vehicles, and wished to be transferred to France.

General Eicke was given home leave. Two days after his appearance at Rastenburg, the German Army launched Operation Blue, the long-awaited summer offensive. That same day, 966 Jews were sent by train from Paris across France, Germany and Silesia, to Auschwitz. One, Adolf Ziffer, who had been born in Belzec itself in 1904, was crossed off the list of deportees at the last moment with the notation: 'Shot attempting to escape'.

In the last three days of June, the German new offensive on the Eastern Front pushed the Red Army back throughout the southern sector. In North Africa, however, Rommel, with only fifty-five tanks still operational, had come to a halt at El Alamein, as South African, New Zealand, British and Indian troops, daily reinforced with American military supplies, stood behind a strongly fortified line, organized by General Auchinleck. Mussolini, cheated of his triumphal ride through Cairo, returned to Italy.

In the Far East, an Australian unit raided the Japanese base at Salamaua, on New Guinea. It was a small act of defiance, but one which boosted the morale of the Allies in the Far East. A few days later a similar raid was carried out on the Japanese supply base at Lae. As so often in the war, however, triumph and disaster marched all too closely together; on July 1, off Luzon, 849 Australian prisoners-of-war, captured by the Japanese in Rabaul six months earlier, were drowned when the Japanese ship carrying them across the Pacific was sunk by an American submarine.

The war at sea knew no pause; at the beginning of July the Allies learned that 124 merchant ships had been sunk in the North Atlantic in June, a loss that constituted the highest monthly toll of the shipping war; these cargoes included the first three hundred American tank engines on their way to Suez to help maintain the Allied line against Rommel.

The part taken by women in the more dangerous tasks of war was highlighted twice in July 1942, first by Yvonne Rudellat, a French-born British agent, who landed by boat on the coast of the French Riviera, travelled northward to Tours, and established an escape route for Allied airmen; and second by Polina Gelman, a history graduate from Moscow University, and a Jewess, who, as a navigation officer in a bombing regiment, embarked that July on the first of many hundreds of missions against German headquarter staffs, trains, vehicles and supply dumps. On one night she was to make eight separate sorties, and, in due course, to be made a Hero of the Soviet Union.

For Soviet soldiers and airmen, capture held terrors not known to the Allied prisoners-of-war taken by the Germans in North Africa. In the Sixth Fort of Kovno, the German's own records for one of the mass graves there gives the precise figure of 7,708 Soviet prisoners-of-war. On July 1, tens of thousands more Soviet soldiers were captured as, finally, and after one of the most tenacious defences of the war, German troops overran the last of the fortresses of Sevastopol. That day, to celebrate this victory, Hitler promoted General Manstein to Field Marshal. Two days later, having flown from his headquarters at Rastenburg to Field Marshal von Bock's headquarters at Poltava, Hitler assured von Bock that the Red Army had 'sapped its last reserves'.

Hitler's confidence in victory was matched by the ruthlessness of his forces in combating partisan activity. On July 3 the German Army in Yugoslavia launched its final assault on the partisans then holding out in the Kozara region. Within a week, as many as two thousand partisans had been killed, for the loss of 150 German soldiers. But it was not against the partisans alone that the German fury turned; tens of thousands of peasants were rounded up and shot, or deported to slave labour. So massive was the scale of deportations, estimated at more than sixty thousand, that special statistical tables had to be drawn up, in order correctly to gauge how many truck and trains would be needed for the deportations. One officer who helped in this statistical work was Lieutenant Kurt Waldheim; on July 22 he was one of five German officers to whom the Croat leader Ante Pavelić awarded the Silver medal of the Crown of King Zvonimir, with Oak Leaves.

In German-occupied Poland, July 3 saw the murder by the Germans of ninety-three Gypsies – women, children and old people among them – in the village of Szczurowa, near Cracow. On the following day, in the Volhynian town of Lutsk, four thousand Jews were driven from their homes to the outskirts of the town, and killed.

The Fourth of July 1942 marked the 166th year of American independence. On that day, for the first time, American aircraft – six in all – joined a British bomber formation in a raid on German airfields in Holland. But in the inner circles of British and American war policy, July 4 saw the beginning of one of the most serious setbacks of the war, the scattering, that night, of the merchant ships of Convoy PQ 17, on its way to Russia with precious war cargoes. PQ 17 had sailed from Iceland on June 27, with twenty-two American, eight British, two Soviet, two Panamanian and one Dutch merchant ship, and an escort of six destroyers, supported by fifteen other armed vessels, and three small passenger ships which had been specially fitted for rescuing the crews of torpedoed merchant ships. This considerable convoy had been spotted by German submarines and aircraft on July 1 and, on the morning of July 4, as the first phase of a long-planned German attack, code-named Operation Knight's Move, four merchant ships had been sunk from the air by the torpedoes of a Heinkel torpedo-bomber. Fearing the imminent arrival of four powerful German warships, *Tirpitz, Scheer, Lützow* and *Hipper* and their destroyers, which, with the exception of *Lützow,* were then at Altafjord, the convoy was told to scatter.

Hitler, nervous about the fate of his finest ships, was to order them back to Altafjord on the following day, within ten hours of their setting sail towards the convoy. But his submarine and air forces wreaked a trail of havoc against the scattered Allied ships, of which nineteen were sunk, and only eleven reached Archangel. Of the 156,492 tons of cargo loaded, 99,316 were sunk, including 430 of the 594 tanks on board, 210 of the 297 aircraft, and 3,350 of the 4,246 vehicles; 153 men were drowned. Had the convoy not been told to scatter, the *Tirpitz* foray might have continued, and all the merchant ships been sunk.

During its voyage eastward, PQ 17 had passed a convoy returning from Russia to Iceland, QP 13. By an ill-fated error of navigation, this convoy, when off Iceland on July 6, ran into a British minefield. Five merchant ships were sunk, as was the British minesweeper *Niger* and the Russian ship *Rodina,* carrying on board the wives and families of Soviet diplomats stationed in London.

On the Eastern Front, July 6 saw the launching of yet another German attack against Soviet partisans. This was Operation Swamp Flower, against the large partisan units in the Dorogobuzh region which had been reinforced earlier in the year by Soviet airborne troops and artillery. In southern Russia, on July 7, despite the capture of Voronezh, the German Sixth Army was unable, in face of a strong Russian counter-attack, to advance further east. It was therefore sent further south, along the southern bank of the River Don, to attack Stalingrad.

Hitler was still confident that he could defeat Russia in 1942. His subordinates were equally confident that, behind the smokescreen of war and victories, they could pursue the Nazi racial policies unimpeded. On July 7, as the battle raged at Voronezh, Heinrich Himmler was in Berlin, presiding over a conference at which only three other men were present: the head of the Concentration Camp Inspectorate, ss General Richard Glueks; the German hospital chief, ss Major-General – and also Professor – Gebhardt; and a leading German gynaecologist, Professor Karl Clauberg. As a result of their discussion, it was decided to start medical experiments in 'major dimensions' on Jewish women at Auschwitz. The experiments would be done in such a way, the notes of the meeting recorded, that a woman would not become aware of what was being done to her. It was also decided to ask a leading x-ray specialist, Professor Hohlfelder, to find out if it were possible to castrate men by means of x-rays.

Himmler warned those present that these were 'most secret matters'. All who became involved in them, he said, would have to be pledged to secrecy. Three days later, at Auschwitz, the first hundred Jewish women were taken from the barracks to the hospital block for sterilization and other experiments.

Deception and concealment remained an essential element of Nazi policy towards the Jews. On July 11, Martin Bormann, head of the Nazi Party Chancellery, informed ss leaders, 'by order of the Führer', that henceforth, 'in public discussion of the Jewish question any mention of a future total solution must be avoided. However, one may discuss the fact that all Jews are being interned and detailed to purposeful compulsory labour forces'.

Two days after his conference in Berlin, Himmler was at Rastenburg. Victory in southern Russia seemed imminent. Himmler and Hitler discussed what to do with the Germans of Italy's South Tyrol once the war was won. The two men were agreed that these German-speaking citizens of Fascist Italy should be resettled in the Crimea. Nor did such a scheme seem far-fetched or fanciful; on July 10, German forces seized Rossosh and crossed to the eastern bank of the River Don. On the following day, Lisichansk, on the River Donetz, was taken. The momentum of attack in the south was growing.

Increasingly confident of victory, on July 11 Hitler issued a directive for the planning of Operation Blücher, a German attack from the Crimea across the Kerch Straits and into the Caucasus. On the following day, Stalin appointed Marshal Timoshenko to be the commander of a new front, charged with the defences of Stalingrad.

From Britain, in an attempt to give the Russians information that would enable them to anticipate future German moves, material culled from the Germans' own Enigma messages was sent on to Moscow. These messages included, on July 13, details of the precise defensive line which the Germans intended to hold in the Voronezh region, while pushing their armoured forces forward between the Donetz and the Don. On the following day, London sent Moscow further details of the objectives that had been laid down for three of the German armies then about to go into action.

In the Far East, Australian forces, advancing from Port Moresby, arrived on July 12 at Kokoda, intent on denying the Japanese any further gains in New Guinea, and determined to prevent them from occupying the northern coastal town of Buna; the plan being made for this was given the code name Operation Providence. At the same time, American troops began their preparations for the liberation of the Solomon Islands. In the Mediterranean, there was considerable relief for Britain on July 13, with the announcement that, in the previous six weeks, a total of 693 German and Italian aircraft had been shot down by the defenders of Malta, while a further 190 German and Italian aircraft had been destroyed by British aircraft based on Malta.

In North Africa, British forces now began to reverse the tide of Rommel's advance, not gaining very much ground, but inflicting heavy losses on German forces which attacked the Ruweisat Ridge, and thereby ending once and for all Rommel's hopes of entering Cairo and Alexandria. 'My expectations for yesterday's attack were bitterly disappointed,' Rommel wrote to his wife on July 14. 'It achieved no success whatever.' The battle on the Eastern Front, he added, 'is going splendidly, which gives us courage to hang on here'.

The German gains on the Eastern Front were now continuous; on July 15 the Red Army was forced to abandon Millerovo, on the Voronezh–Rostov railway, and Kamensk, where the railway line crossed the River Donetz. That day, in

The German offensive, July to November 1942

Britain, British cryptographers widened their mastery of the Eastern Front Enigma by breaking the cypher used by the German anti-aircraft units for their most secret messages; it was given the code name 'Weasel' and was to continue to be broken until the end of the war. The importance of the 'Weasel' Enigmas was considerable. The anti-aircraft units which used it served the dual purpose of engaging both aircraft and tanks; their 88 millimetre dual-purpose gun proved to be one of Germany's most powerful anti-tank weapons.

Unknown to British Intelligence, July 15 saw the despatch from Holland of the first two thousand Dutch Jews deported to Auschwitz. Their departure was known, but not their destination, nor their fate. They had been told by the Germans that they were going for 'labour service in Germany'. On the morning of July 16, as the Dutch deportees were still on their three day journey to Auschwitz, Hitler, with victory over Russia apparently not far off, transferred his headquarters from the 'Wolf's Lair' at Rastenburg to a new site, 'Werewolf', at Vinnitsa. Despite the 'swarming flies and mosquitoes' which so upset him, Hitler was to remain at Vinnitsa for more than two months. On his first day there, he was visited by Himmler, who had driven down from his own headquarters at Zhitomir, eighty miles to the north. The two men discussed the Caucasus, which once again seemed so nearly in the German grasp. 'The Führer's view', Himmler wrote on the following day, 'is that we should not visibly incorporate this territory into the German sphere of power, but only militarily secure oil sources and borders.'

On the following day, July 17, Himmler flew to East Upper Silesia, and to the concentration camp at Auschwitz. There, the first two thousand Dutch Jewish deportees had just arrived. Himmler was in time to watch the unloading of the Jews from the trains, the selection of 1,551 to be tattooed on the forearm and sent to the barracks at Birkenau, and the gassing of the remaining 449, mostly old people, children and the sick. He then watched while the corpses were thrown into pits, and the gas chamber cleaned, ready for the next group of deportees.

That evening, Himmler was the principal guest at a reception for the heads of the SS garrison at Auschwitz. On the following day he was shown over the 'original' Auschwitz, the punitive camp for Poles, and he asked to be shown some beatings in order 'to determine their effects'. At the end of his visit, he urged the expansion of the barracks at nearby Birkenau and of the armaments industry within the camp perimeters, at which the deportees could be put to work. Before leaving, he raised the camp Commandant, Rudolf Hoess, to the SS rank of major. Then, on July 19, he ordered the 'total cleansing' of the entire Jewish population of the General Government 'to be carried out and completed by December 31'.

Himmler's orders were obeyed. Beginning on July 22, many thousands of Jews were rounded up each day in the Warsaw ghetto and sent by train to a camp near the village of Treblinka. There, all but a fragment needed to service the camp were gassed. In the first seven weeks of these Warsaw deportations, more than a quarter of a million Jews were taken to Treblinka and killed; it was the largest, swiftest slaughter of a single community, Jewish or non-Jewish,

Terror in the East, July 1942

in the Second World War. The first Commandant of Treblinka was a German physician, the thirty-two-year-old Dr Eberl. As one of those earlier involved in the German euthanasia programme, he had been responsible for the murder of 18,000 German patients in a year and a half. Now, assisted by ss and Ukrainian guards, he supervised the first month's killing, before being dismissed for inefficiency; his failure to dispose of the bodies quickly had created panic among those in the incoming trains.

Even as the Treblinka gassings began, and Warsaw Jewry was sent unsuspecting to its destruction, Jews from throughout Galicia continued to be killed at Belzec; while Auschwitz received almost daily trains from France, Belgium – beginning on August 4 – Luxemburg and Holland. Jews were not sent, however, from Italian-occupied Croatia, where, in the last week of July, the German Foreign Ministry learned that the Italian Chief of Staff in the region, whose headquarters were in Mostar, 'has declared that he cannot give his approval to the resettlement of the Jews, all inhabitants of Mostar having received assurance of equal treatment'.

In German-occupied Russia, the killing of Jews had continued without protest or respite, by slaughter in fields and ditches just beyond the villages; a thousand Jews had been killed in this way at Bereza Kartuska on July 15, and six hundred at Szarkowszczyzna on July 18, though a further nine hundred had managed to escape that day into the nearby forests.

On July 20 the Germans launched yet another anti-partisan operation in White Russia, Operation Eagle, against Soviet partisans in the Chechivichi region. That same day, in the village of Kletsk, several hundred Jews who were about to be murdered set their ghetto on fire and ran. Most were killed by German machine gun fire. A few, reaching the forests, joined the partisans, where their leader, Moshe Fish, was killed in a battle with the Germans six months later. On the day after the revolt in Kletsk, the Jews of nearby Nieswiez also fought back against their fate. They too were almost all shot down, though one of their leaders, Shalom Cholawski, reaching the forests, set up a 'family camp' of Jews who had managed to escape the daily slaughter, protected the camp against German manhunts, and set up a Jewish partisan unit to harass the German lines of communication.

On the night of July 21, in northern New Guinea, the Japanese, still intent on developing a threat to Australia, forestalled the Australians by landing sixteen thousand troops at Buna and Gona. Then they moved south, along the Kokoda trail, across rugged mountain terrain. The Australians, surprised by the size of the Japanese force, and defeated by the terrain, had to fall back towards Port Moresby. In Burma and Thailand, the Allied prisoners-of-war had been working on the jungle railway. 'The third death in a few days,' Colonel Dunlop noted in his diary on July 23, as he struggled to repair broken bodies with the absolute minimum of medicaments. Fifteen thousand prisoners-of-war were to perish on the railway, their fate recorded not only by diarists like Dunlop, but by artists such as Ray Parkin, whom Dunlop encouraged. 'I hope that it will be a true record', Dunlop wrote of Parkin's work, 'of the manner in which the human spirit can rise above futility, nothingness and despair, since truly we were left here with nothing.'

That night, the prisoners performed Shakespeare's *Julius Caesar*, 'with modern dress', as Dunlop wrote, and he added: 'Audience very sympathetic, with absolutely no frivolity.'

On July 23 the city of Rostov-on-Don was once more occupied by the Germans. That day, Hitler, concerned to secure oil supplies essential to the conduct of any war, issued his Directive No. 45, ordering the seizure of the eastern Black Sea coast from Novorossiisk to Batum, on the Turkish border, and the capture of the Russian oilfields at Maikop, Grozny and Baku, on the Caspian Sea. Stalingrad, on the Volga, was also to be taken, and then, with a German defensive line to be set up on the River Don, the German forces should capture

Leningrad. It was an ambitious plan, which alarmed Hitler's generals, but he ordered it nevertheless. It failed because of the Russian decision to send three reserve armies to the defence of Stalingrad. This defence was so tenacious as to force Hitler to transfer men and materials from the rapidly advancing Caucasus front to the battle at Stalingrad. At the same time, despite the capture of Rostov, the Germans had failed to repeat their successes of 1941 whereby hundreds of thousands of Soviet soldiers were taken prisoner with every major battle. At Rostov, despite severe losses, the bulk of the Soviet forces had escaped the trap, and were thus able to fight again. But, with several units of the German Army only a hundred miles from Stalingrad by July 25, there was little to suggest that Stalingrad could halt the German thrust. That same day, however, to boost the morale of the citizens of Leningrad, several thousand German prisoners-of-war were paraded in the city, 'the only Germans', as one historian has written, 'to reach the heart of Leningrad'.

On July 27 the German Army crossed the River Don south of Rostov, and entered Bataisk. On the following day Stalin issued Order No. 227: 'Panic-makers and cowards must be liquidated on the spot. Not one step backward without orders from higher headquarters! Commanders, commissars, and political workers who abandon a position without an order from higher headquarters are traitors to the Fatherland, and must be handled accordingly.'

The day of Stalin's 'Not one step backward' order was the day on which, behind the German lines in the Leningrad region, local Russian peasants and partisans killed Adolf Beck, a German official of the economic administration of the occupied territories, responsible for sending Russian agricultural produce to Germany, or to the German Army. They also set his barns and granaries on fire. Beck's death, and the destruction of so much foodstuff destined for Germany, gave a boost to partisan morale throughout the Dno and Pskov regions. 'Russians!' declared the partisan pamphlet which announced Beck's death: 'Destroy the properties where the men responsible for your evil fate are hiding. Finish off the German landowners. Don't work for them, but kill every one of them – this is the duty of every Soviet patriot. Drive the Germans from the land of the Soviets!'

In the Warsaw ghetto, from which 66,701 Jews had been deported in a single week, and where 250,000 remained, July 28 saw the setting up of a Jewish Fighting Organization, men and women determined to resist, if possible, the continuing deportations to Treblinka. But on the following day the Germans set a cruel trap, offering the starving Jews of Warsaw – more than four thousand Jews had died that month of hunger – a free issue of three kilogrammes of bread and one kilogramme of jam for each family that would volunteer for 'the East'. For many of those who were starving, the offer was irresistible. Thousands volunteered. All received their bread and jam. And all were then deported to Treblinka, and to their deaths.

On July 29, the Japanese in New Guinea, after four days of fierce jungle fighting, finally wrested Kokoda from the Australians. That same day, the Germans reached Proletarskaya, the gateway to the Caucasus. That day, Stalin created a new military order for the direction of successful operations in the field, the Order of Suvorov, named after Catherine the Great's general who, in 1799, had crossed the Alps. A second military order created that day, for regimental, battalion, company and platoon commanders who showed personal courage and successful leadership in battle, was named after the medieval hero, Alexander Nevsky, who had repulsed an earlier Teutonic invasion.

Meanwhile, German forces pressed on towards the Caucasus, reaching Salsk on August 1, and cutting the railway line between Novorossisk and Stalingrad. Some German units, pushing far ahead of the main force, even reached the Kuban river.

The British and Americans, unable to launch a Second Front on the European mainland to relieve the pressure on Russia in 1942, had decided to strike instead at the Vichy French coastlines of Morocco and Algeria – Operation Torch – and to combine this assault with the attempted destruction of the German and Italian forces now triumphant in the Western Desert. The two operations would, it was hoped, not only drive the Axis from North Africa, thus providing a springboard for an attack on the European mainland of Italy, but would also draw off considerable German resources from the Eastern Front. On August 1, Churchill prepared to fly to Moscow, to meet Stalin and to give him a personal account of this decision and plan. 'The materials for a joyous meeting', Churchill told King George VI, 'are meagre indeed. Still I may perhaps make the situation less edged'.

In order to deceive the Germans as to the true points of landing of Operation Torch, a branch of the British War Cabinet secretariat, known deceptively as the 'London Controlling Section', headed by Colonel John Bevan, submitted on August 1 a series of spurious war plans designed to lure German reinforcements elsewhere. Three principal deceptions were put in train, Operation Solo against Narvik and Trondheim, Operation Overthrow against Calais and Boulogne, and Operation Kennecott against southern Italy, Greece and Crete.

By setting up false Army commands and using double agents such as 'Garbo' to send messages to Germany, reporting fictitious military preparations, Colonel Bevan and his team created doubt in the minds of the German General Staff as to the true destination of the Anglo-American forces, which even then were assembling and training in Scotland for some obvious amphibious landing on a large scale. Bevan also set up two deception schemes, whereby the two commanders of Operation Torch, General Eisenhower and Admiral Cunningham, on their arrival in Gibraltar to take charge of the final planning, were thought respectively to have been 'recalled to Washington' and 'posted to the Far East'.

Whether these plans could come in time to help Russia would depend entirely upon the speed of the German advance. On August 3, the German forces driving into the Caucasus reached Stavropol. On the Stalingrad front, crossing the Don at Tsimlyansky, they pressed eastward to Kotelnikovo, less than a hundred miles south-west of Stalingrad. These German successes threatened not only Russia but also Britain. On August 4, while on his way to Russia, Churchill stopped in Cairo, where, he learned from the Chief of the Imperial General

Staff, General Sir Alan Brooke, that if the German forces succeeded in their drive into the Caucasus, and were able from there to develop a 'serious threat' to the Persian Gulf, it might be necessary, in the view of the British Chiefs of Staff, to consider abandoning Egypt and North Africa altogether, and moving the British forces then in Egypt to the Persian Gulf. This would be necessary, Brooke explained, because if the oilfields of Abadan and Bahrein were lost, Britain would suffer a twenty per cent reduction in her military capability.

On August 5, while Churchill was still in Cairo, German forces crossed the Kuban river at Kropotkin and pressed on towards Armavir; the threat to the oilfields of the Caucasus was now acute. In the Atlantic, the threat to Britain's food and armaments lifeline was likewise acute; that day a homeward bound convoy of thirty-six ships was attacked by German submarines off Newfoundland. One of the attacking submarines was sunk by the convoy escort, but, as the attack continued, five merchant ships were torpedoed in the space of three minutes. Later in the struggle, another German submarine was sunk, but so too were six more merchant ships.

The Germans, using slave labour, had built massive concrete submarine pens in four of the ports on the Atlantic coast of France, Lorient, Brest, St Nazaire and La Pallice. These pens were one of the main construction achievements of the Todt Organization now controlled by Albert Speer. On August 5, as the most recent of the Atlantic submarine attacks was under way, a Japanese submarine docked at the pens in Lorient, a measure of the range and versatility of Axis submarine power. Within six weeks that particular Japanese submarine was back in Malayan waters, where she was sunk.

Among the troops fighting alongside the Germans on the Eastern Front were volunteer units from France, Belgium and Holland. On August 6, the commander of the forces in which the Dutch unit was serving, General Kraus, wrote to Herman Goering: 'We have thousands of Dutchmen in transport regiments in the East. Last week one such regiment was attacked. The Dutch took more than a thousand prisoners and were awarded twenty-five Iron Crosses.' That week, more than a thousand Dutch Jews had been deported from Holland to Auschwitz, followed by 987 on August 7, and 559 three days later; of these deportees, more than half were gassed on reaching the camp. The others were sent to the barracks at Birkenau, to become slave labourers. It was on August 7, as the second of these deportations began, that Goering presided over a meeting to discuss the German Four Year Plan for industrial production. Slave labour was to be an essential part in the plan. But as the notes of the discussion show, there were areas from which Jewish labour could no longer come. In White Russia, the meeting was told, 'Only a few Jews are still alive. Tens of thousands were eliminated.'

On August 7, the German refugee scientist Klaus Fuchs became a British citizen, taking an oath of allegiance to the British Crown. At that time, he was working in Britain on the 'Tube Alloys' project, the Anglo-American research on the atomic bomb. At the same time, he was passing the innermost secrets of the project to the Soviet Union. With the military struggle against Germany at its most intense, the Allies in that struggle remained alert to the basic division of ideology and aim which had pitted their systems against each other before the war, and would dominate their relationship again once they had been victorious against Germany. Even at the moment when such a victory could in no way be guaranteed, the minds that had to focus with all their power on the means to secure that victory were well aware of the conflicts that might come in the post-war era.

# 26

# Guadalcanal, Dieppe, El Alamein

AUGUST–SEPTEMBER 1942

On 7 August 1942 the Americans launched Operation Watchtower, the first Allied counter-offensive in the Pacific. The assault began with the landing of 16,000 American troops on the island of Guadalcanal, in the Solomon Islands. In the course of the landings, four Allied heavy cruisers were sunk, the American warships *Quincy, Astoria* and *Vincennes* and the Australian *Canberra,* leaving more than a thousand Allied dead, 370 of them on the *Quincy,* 332 on the *Vincennes,* 216 on the *Astoria* and 84 on the *Canberra.* Ashore, however, the Americans, often in savage hand to hand fighting, repulsed all Japanese efforts to dislodge them; within two weeks the island's airfield was under American control, but the Japanese, rushing in reinforcements, could not be dislodged from the island. In one month of fighting, nine thousand Japanese soldiers were killed, for the loss of 1,600 American lives. Of the 250 Japanese soldiers manning the garrison at the first American assault, only three had allowed themselves to be taken prisoner; in every engagement, the Japanese fought to the death, or, at the last moment, killed themselves to avoid capture.

At the same time as the landing on Guadalcanal, American Marines also fought their way ashore at four smaller islands, Florida, Tulagi, Gavutu and Tanambogo. Once again, the tenacity of the Japanese defenders shocked those who had to overcome it. 'I have never heard or read of this kind of fighting', Major-General Alexander A. Vandegrift wrote to the Marine Commandant in Washington, and he went on to explain: 'These people refuse to surrender. The wounded will wait till men come up to examine them, and blow themselves and the other fellow to death with a hand grenade.'

On August 9, the third day of the battle of Guadalcanal, German forces in the Caucasus reached the oilfields of Maikop. But Soviet forces having blown up the wells as they withdrew, Hitler was cheated of the oil. That same day, reaching Krasnodar, the Germans again found that the oil installations had been destroyed. Behind the lines, however, there was no impediment to the Germans' own destructive policies. On August 9, a Catholic nun, Edith Stein, the converted daughter of a Jewish timber merchant from Breslau – she had been deported to Auschwitz from Holland because she was of Jewish parentage – was among hundreds of Dutch Jews murdered that day in the gas chamber. Known by her Catholic name of Sister Benedicta, she was considered a martyr by the Catholic Church. Forty-five years later she was sanctified.

On the day after Edith Stein's death, a telegram from Gerhart Riegner, the Secretary of the World Jewish Congress in Geneva, alerted Jews in London and New York to the scale and intention of the killings of Jews. Reports had reached Geneva, Riegner wrote, 'stating that, in the Führer's Headquarters, a plan has been discussed, and is under consideration, according to which all Jews in countries occupied or controlled by Germany, numbering three and a half to four millions, should, after deportation and concentration in the East, be at one blow exterminated, in order to resolve, once and for all the Jewish question in Europe'.

The message sent on by Riegner to the West had apparently been sent to Switzerland by someone who had learned not only of Himmler's July 16 visit to Auschwitz, but also of his order of July 19 for the 'total cleansing' of the Jewish population of the General-Government by the end of the year.

Unknown to those who received the telegram of August 10, the 'plan' of mass murder was not only 'under consideration', but being put daily into practice, as the deportations to Auschwitz from France, Holland and Belgium, and from several Polish cities, continued, as did the deportations from Warsaw to Treblinka, and from central and southern Poland to Chelmno, Sobibor and Belzec. At the same time, more than 87,000 Jews were murdered in the Volhynia and more than 9,000 in White Russia, where, in the towns of Mir and Zdzieciol, five hundred Jews had broken out of the Gestapo cordon to reach the forests and to join the Soviet partisans. But the opportunity to resist was tiny.

On August 10, the day on which Edith Stein was gassed in Auschwitz, a train arrived at Maly Trostenets, the camp near Minsk of which even the name was unknown in the West. From this train, on which were a thousand Jews from the Theresienstadt ghetto on their way to 'the East', forty Jews were taken off at Minsk for work in a labour camp. The remaining 960 deportees were gassed on reaching Maly Trostenets.

Of a thousand Jews sent from Theresienstadt to Maly Trostenets in a further deportation two weeks later, only twenty-two of the younger men were taken to work at an SS farm. The rest were ordered into the vans and killed. Of the twenty-two men sent to the farm, two survived the hard labour and sadism of their overseers, and escaped in May 1943 to join the Soviet partisans. One was killed in action. One survived the war – the only survivor of the thousand.

From Warsaw, each day that August saw more deportations to Treblinka and the destruction of the deportees. 'It gave me great pleasure', SS Lieutenant-General Karl Wolff wrote to the manager of the German Ministry of Transportation on August 13, 'to learn that already, for the last fourteen days, one train goes daily with five thousand passengers of the Chosen People to Treblinka; and we are even in a position to complete this mass movement of people at an accelerated rate.'

On August 10, in a further attempt to reinforce Malta, a British naval convoy had passed through Gibraltar towards Malta, in an operation code-named 'Pedestal'. From the following day the convoy came under sustained German and Italian attack, during which the aircraft carrier *Eagle*, the anti-aircraft ship *Cairo*, the cruiser *Manchester*, and the destroyer *Foresight* were sunk, as were nine of the merchant ships laden with supplies for Malta. But as the escort vessels battled against German and Italian air, sea and submarine assault, five merchant ships reached Malta. For Britain, despite the losses, it was a naval triumph; the 55,000 tons of food and fuel delivered by this convoy saved Malta from surrender, and allowed Malta-based aircraft and submarines to resume their attacks against Rommel's supply lines. Had the Pedestal convoy failed, Malta would have surrendered on September 7.

On August 12, the second day of Pedestal's courageous struggle, Churchill was in Moscow explaining to Stalin that there would be no Second Front in Europe that year, but a landing in French North Africa instead. On first learning the news, as Churchill's interpreter noted, 'Stalin's face crumpled up into a frown.' Why, he asked, were the British 'so afraid of the Germans?' As the North African plan was explained to him, however, Stalin quickly grasped its strategic implications, the opening up of Italy to a joint Anglo-American assault early in 1943, in order, as Churchill phrased it, to 'threaten the belly of Hitler's Europe'. Churchill also told Stalin that, in the air war against Germany, 'we hoped to shatter almost every dwelling in almost every German city'. That, Stalin replied, 'would not be bad', and he went on to advise Churchill to drop Britain's new four-ton bombs 'with parachutes, otherwise they dug themselves into the ground'.

On August 13, while Churchill was still in Moscow, German forces reached the town of Elista, 200 miles south of Stalingrad, and, even more dangerous for the Soviet Union, only 155 miles from the Caspian Sea. That same day, the Caucasian town of Mineralniye Vody fell to the Germans. At his 'Werewolf' headquarters in Vinnitsa, Hitler was thinking that day not only of Russia, but of the Second Front which must surely come sooner or later. In a discussion that day with his Armaments Minister, Albert Speer, Hitler – recognizing for the second time the possibility that his grand strategy might miscarry, and that he might have to fight on two fronts simultaneously – reiterated his call to build up an 'Atlantic Wall' of fortifications against any attempted Anglo-American landing; it was to consist of 15,000 concrete bunkers, set, some at fifty- and others at hundred-yard intervals, to be built without regard for cost. 'Our most costly substance', Hitler explained, 'is the German man. The blood these fortifications will spare is worth the billions!'

The West had to be defended, but it was in the East that danger as well as opportunity loomed most large; on August 14 the Germans launched Operation Griffin against Soviet partisans active in the area of Orsha and Vitebsk. These partisans were threatening to disrupt the German lines of communication along the 'Moscow Highway' from Brest-Litovsk through Minsk to Smolensk. That day, unknown to Hitler, and never to be discovered by him or his commanders, British Intelligence broke the main Enigma key used by the SS; known to the British eavesdroppers at Bletchley as 'Quince', it continued to be read without interruption until the end of the war. Only the Gestapo Enigma, known as TGD after its Berlin call-sign, was to elude them.

On the morning of August 15, the Germans, with their success in the Caucasus dominating Allied fears, intensified their attack on Stalingrad. In Moscow, Stalin asked Churchill for a minimum of 20,000 lorries a month; Russia's production, he said, was only 2,000 a month. Churchill agreed to supply the Soviet needs. His own news that day was good; despite the severe losses to Pedestal, the American oil tanker *Ohio* had managed to reach Malta, with ten thousand tons of oil. The *Ohio* had been so badly damaged during the run that she was declared a total loss, but her oil saved the day – and many days – for Malta.


On August 11 the German authorities began the deportation of Frenchmen needed as further drafts of forced labour for the German war effort, now becoming seriously overstretched. Four days later, a new labour camp was opened in the underground coal mines of Jawiszowice, near Auschwitz. Not only French, and later Belgian labourers were sent to these mines, but also Jews from the barracks at Birkenau. Thousands of labourers died in the harsh conditions. In Holland, anti-German feeling had led to an attempt to blow up a train carrying German troops in Rotterdam. The attempt failed, but on August 15 the Germans shot five civilian hostages as a deterrent to further acts of sabotage. On the battlefield, German troops seemed unbeatable; on August 17 they reached the high valleys of the Caucasus mountains, occupying Kislovodsk, and prepared to climb, as an act of athletic if not military prowess, the 18,000-foot peak of Mount Elbruz.

It was on August 17, as German troops reached the resort towns of the Caucasus, that American morale was lifted by a daring Marine landing on the Makin Atoll, which the Japanese had seized three days after Pearl Harbor. Thirty Marines lost their lives in what one American General, Holland M. Smith, was later to call a 'piece of folly', serving as it did to encourage the Japanese to fortify the Gilbert Islands, making their subsequent capture more costly than it might have been. The Americans withdrew a few days later. Nine Marines, accidentally marooned on the atoll, were captured, taken to Kwajalein, and then beheaded.

Another Allied raid followed the American assault on Makin within forty-eight hours; this was a joint British and Canadian commando raid on August 19 on the French port of Dieppe, a mere sixty-five miles across the English Channel from Britain.

Five thousand Canadian and a thousand British troops took part in the Dieppe raid, as well as fifty American Rangers and two dozen Free French soldiers. The landing, code-named Operation Jubilee, was intended, like that on Makin, to be brief. Its aim was to practise techniques for an eventual invasion of northern Europe. One of the British commandos who took part, Captain Pat Porteous, was awarded the Victoria Cross for his courage in the raid, as was a Canadian officer, Lieutenant-Colonel Merritt. Another Victoria Cross was awarded to a Canadian chaplain, John Foote, who spent many hours tending to wounded men while under fire on the shingle. When the time came to take the men off, Captain Foote carried them to the boat, but himself made no attempt to embark, preferring to stay behind, accept capture, and continue to help the wounded men as a prisoner-of-war.

Unknown to the Germans, a British Flight-Sergeant, Jack Nissenthall, who accompanied the raiders, carried out a foray against a nearby German radar station, thereby taking back crucial knowledge for future British jamming and deception.

The Allied casualty rate at Dieppe was high; just over a thousand of the raiding force were killed and a further two thousand taken prisoner, while all their vehicles and equipment had to be left behind on the beach. 'This is the first time', mocked Hitler, 'that the British have had the courtesy to cross the sea to offer the enemy a complete sample of their weapons.' Later however, Hitler told his commanders: 'We must realize that we are not alone in learning a lesson from Dieppe. The British have also learned. We must reckon with a totally different mode of attack and at quite a different place.'

Twenty-five German bombers and twenty-three fighters had been destroyed during the Dieppe raid, and the German Air Force, by a certain weakening of its air forces on the Eastern Front, increased the size of its fighter force in north-west Europe. As for the Allied lesson learned at Dieppe, this, Admiral Mountbatten told the British War Cabinet on the following day, would be 'invaluable' in planning for the future cross-Channel invasion; many years later he was to say that the Dieppe raid 'gave the Allies the priceless secret of victory'.

It was during the Dieppe raid that the first United States soldier was killed in France, Lieutenant Edwin V. Loustalot.

For the Canadians, Dieppe was a setback and a blow; 907 Canadians had been killed, and 1,874 taken prisoner. The Germans lost 345 men killed, and four taken prisoner and brought back to Britain.

On August 19, with their southern forces approaching Stalingrad and atop the Caucasus, the Germans were themselves attacked outside Leningrad, by Russian forces intent on breaking the German grip on the city. That day, the Nazi leader Martin Bormann wrote, of the Russians and Poles who were being used in their hundreds of thousands as slave labourers for Germany: 'The Slavs are to work for us. In so far as we do not need them, they may die. Slav fertility is not desirable.' That day, the swastika flag was raised on Mount Elbruz, provoking Hitler's irate comment that his Army's ambition should be to defeat the Russians rather than conquer mountains. A hundred and sixty miles east of Mount Elbruz lay Grozny, the principal city and oil centre of the Caucasus; Hitler knew the perils that could lie along the way.

In German-occupied Europe, August 19 saw the deportation to Treblinka, and to their death, of all the mental patients of a Jewish mental asylum at Otwock, near Warsaw, several hundred more victims of a racial policy which wanted neither the Jews nor the mentally ill to survive the triumph of the Reich. Also behind the German lines, the partisan war continued to provoke fierce reprisals. On August 22, in a village in the Bialystok region, Gestapo and ss men rounded up all the men of the village, then selected ten, who were immediately tortured and shot. On the same day, in the nearby Slonim region, after what a Gestapo report called 'an armed fight lasting about six hours', two hundred partisans and villagers, 'half of them Jews', were shot, and two partisan camps 'eradicated'. Gypsies too were being hunted down. Three days after the Slonim action, all German army groups in Russia were warned, by the Army Field Police, that there were also many Gypsy bands roaming the countryside which 'render many services to the partisans, providing them with supplies etc.'. If only a part of the Gypsies were punished, the Field Police added, 'the attitude of the remainder would be even more hostile towards the German forces, and would support the partisans even more than before'. It was therefore 'necessary to exterminate these bands ruthlessly'.

On August 23, at Izbushensky, in the great bend of the River Don, six hundred Italian soldiers of the Savoy Cavalry charged on horseback against two thousand Russians armed with mortars and machine guns. The Italians, using sabres and hand grenades against mortars and machine guns, put the Russians to flight. It was the last successful cavalry charge of the war. Later that day, units of the German Army reached the western bank of the River Volga just north of Rynok, the northernmost suburb of Stalingrad. Six hundred German bombers, on what it was hoped was the eve of the fall of the city, struck at industrial targets and built-up areas.

The city of Stalingrad stood on the border between European and Asiatic Russia, a centre of communications by rail and river, a hub of industry and commerce, a symbol both of the old Russia of trade and the modern Russia of industrialization. The city was not only a symbol of Soviet achievement, but also a symbol of the power of Russia itself – despite the battering of the previous year – to continue to resist, and to survive.

On August 24, as Stalingrad prepared to defend herself, in the Eastern Solomon Islands, the Americans secured another naval victory over the Japanese, sinking the aircraft-carrier *Ryuho*, as well as a light cruiser, a destroyer and a troop transport, with the loss of several thousand Japanese lives. Ninety Japanese aircraft were also shot down, for the loss of twenty American aircraft. On the following day, Japanese transports carrying reinforcements to Guadalcanal were attacked, and forced to turn back. Other Japanese troops, landing on August 25 near Rabi, at the south-eastern end of New Guinea, were attacked by the Australians, and, despite further Japanese reinforcements, forced to withdraw two weeks later. It was their first defeat on land. The main Japanese advance from Buna towards Port Moresby continued, however, with the Australians forced further back along the Kokoda Trail, while in the Pacific, despite their most recent naval setback, Japanese troops occupied Ocean Island, west of the Gilbert Islands.

On August 27 the Germans made plans to round up Jews from the unoccupied zone of France. The Vichy authorities collaborated in the round-ups. But many Frenchmen, and many Catholic priests, sheltered Jews and urged their

Stalingrad besieged, September–November 1942

parishioners to do likewise. On August 28 the Germans ordered the arrest of all Catholic priests who sheltered Jews. With each round-up, the trains to Auschwitz gained new victims; on August 28 the thousand deportees from Paris included 150 children under the age of fifteen. On the day that their train reached

Auschwitz, a new German surgeon, Dr Johann Kremer, who had reached the camp on the previous evening, and was to live in the ss Officers' Home near Auschwitz station, noted in his diary: 'Tropical climate with 28 degrees centigrade in the shade, dust and innumerable flies! Excellent food in the Home. This evening, for instance, we had sour duck livers for 0.40 mark, with stuffed tomatoes, tomato salad etc.'. The water, Kremer added, was infected 'so we drink seltzer water which is served free'.

Two days later Dr Kremer noted: 'Was present for the first time at a special action at 3 a.m. By comparison, Dante's inferno seems almost a comedy. Auschwitz is justly called an extermination camp!' The Jews whom Kremer saw being gassed that day were from France, including the seventy boys and seventy-eight girls under fifteen, deported on August 28. Many of these children had been deported without their parents, among them Helène Goldenberg, aged nine, and her sister Lotty, aged five.

The cruelty of these French deportations, the round-ups for which were done in full view of the public, and the knowledge that children were being separated from their parents, led to considerable revulsion in France, so much so that on August 29 the Swiss Government decided that it would no longer turn back Jewish refugees who sought to cross from Vichy France to Switzerland. On the following day, in all the churches in his diocese, Monsignor Théas, Bishop of Montauban, caused a protest which he had written to be read out, against the 'painful and at times horrible' deportations which were, he said, being carried out 'with the most barbarous savagery'.

Throughout Vichy France, there were those who hid Jews, or who, like the Military Commander of the Lyon region, General de St Vincent, refused to assist in the deportations. But the Vichy police were all too active; by September 5, a total of 9,872 Jews, most of them foreign-born, had been rounded up and sent to Paris, for deportation to Auschwitz as soon as the trains were ready.

On August 30, in the Western Desert, Rommel launched an attack which he hoped would take him on to Cairo. 'The decision to attack today', he told a colleague, 'is the most serious I have taken in my life. Either, the Army in Russia succeeds in getting through to Grozny, and we in Africa manage to reach the Suez Canal, or . . .' and here Rommel made a gesture of defeat.

Unknown to Rommel, the British had been waiting for him in more ways than one. From their reading of the Enigma messages they knew his plan. But, as important, perhaps even more important, Enigma, and the likewise broken Italian cypher c 38m, had also told the British eavesdroppers of the exact times of sailings, routes and cargoes of every ship bringing Rommel munitions and fuel oil. With this knowledge, the British had already attacked and sunk three vital fuel ships. One of these, the *Dielpi,* with 2,200 tons of aircraft fuel, was sunk on August 28. A fourth ship, the *San Andrea,* with essential tank fuel, was sunk on August 30.

'Rommel has begun the attack for which we have been preparing,' Churchill telegraphed to Roosevelt and Stalin on the morning of August 31. Within forty-eight hours, beset by problems of fuel supply, and confronted by the determined defence of British, New Zealand, Australian, South African and Indian troops, Rommel was forced to withdraw from the Alam Halfa ridge in front of El Alamein. The commander of the forces ranged against him was General Montgomery, whose first desert victory this was.

In the Caucasus, as Rommel had feared, the German advance was slowing down; German troops were never to get to Grozny, nor indeed to within thirty miles of it. But as Rommel struggled in vain to push past Alam Halfa, it was upon Stalingrad, not the Caucasus, that all eyes were set. On August 31, after a conference at Hitler's headquarters at Vinnitsa, General Halder noted in his diary: 'The Führer has ordered that, upon penetration into the city, the entire male population be eliminated, since Stalingrad with its one million uniformly Communist inhabitants is extremely dangerous.' The female population, Halder noted, 'must be shipped off' – he did not say to where.

On September 2, as the battle for Stalingrad began, the German Army was forced to launch Operation North Sea against Soviet partisans operating in the Mogilev region, and threatening German's principal lines of communication and supply through Smolensk. Every such anti-partisan operation tied down German forces which might have been used for the main battles.

German and Italian prisoners-of-war held in Britain, or shipped across the Atlantic to Canada, were treated well; none of them died of ill-treatment while in captivity, and none was executed. For the Allied soldiers in Japanese prisoner-of-war camps, however, the situation was almost unbearable. On September 2, in Singapore, after two Australian and two British prisoners-of-war had escaped and been recaptured, the Japanese officer in charge of prisoners-of-war, Major-General Shempei Fukuei, ordered them to be shot, not by his fellow Japanese, but by four Indian Sikhs who were also prisoners-of-war.

The execution duly took place, and the four would-be escapees were killed: they were Corporal Rodney Breavington and Private Victor Gale from Australia, and Privates Harold Waters and Eric Fletcher from Britain.

On the night of September 3, in the Channel Islands, twelve British commandos landed on a German lighthouse which was also being used as a radio station. All seven Germans manning the lighthouse were captured, together with their code books. Their radio equipment was destroyed. Four weeks later, in a conference with von Rundstedt, Goering and Speer, Hitler mocked at the assertion of his advisers that the Atlantic Wall could not be broken. 'Above all', he said, 'I am grateful to the English for proving me right by their various landing attempts. It shows up those who think I am always seeing phantoms, who say "Well, when are the English coming? There is absolutely nothing happening on the coast – we swim every day, and we haven't seen a single Englishman!"'

On September 3, with German troops established on the western shore of the River Volga and just north of Rynok, the most northerly suburb of Stalingrad, Stalin telegraphed to Marshal Zhukov: 'Get the commanders of the troops to the north and north-west of Stalingrad to attack the enemy without delay and get to the relief of the Stalingraders. No delay can be tolerated. Delay at this moment is equivalent to a crime.' On the following day, as Zhukov regrouped his forces for a counter-attack, a thousand German bombers flew repeated sorties over the city. Also on September 4, thirty-two British and Australian bombers flew from Britain to north Russia, to take part, from Soviet airbases, in the protection of the Arctic convoys. Nine of the aircraft never arrived, either running out of fuel and being forced to crash land in Sweden, or, in one case, being accidentally shot down by Russian fighters as they approached the Russian coast. Even in the water, the crew continued to be fired upon, until their shouts of 'Angliski!' were recognized.

One of the bombers on this flight to Russia was damaged by anti-aircraft fire from a German patrol ship. Forced to land on the Norwegian coast, its crew did not have time before they were captured to destroy secret documents about the imminent convoy PQ 18. A week later, the convoy was attacked, as PQ 17 had been in June, by a combined German air and submarine force. Of the forty merchant ships in the convoy, thirteen were sunk, as well as two of the warships escorting the convoy, the destroyer *Somali* and the minesweeper *Leda*. The Germans, however, lost four of their submarines and forty-one aircraft.

On September 5, the first Soviet troops counter-attacked the German forces on the Volga, but were beaten back. On the following day, Soviet air reinforcements reached Stalingrad. A massive German thrust on September 7 was halted. 'Millions of German troops', Roosevelt broadcast that day to the American people, 'seem doomed to spend another cruel and bitter winter on the Russian front.' At his Vinnitsa headquarters, Hitler had attended to another matter on September 7, when he received as his visitor Erich Koch, the Governor of the Ukraine, who was in the process, since early August, of supervising the shooting of seventy thousand Jews in the city of Rovno, and throughout the Volhynia region. That same September 7, as German troops consolidated their position in the Caucasus, eighteen hundred Jews living in the mountain resort town of Kislovodsk were ordered to prepare for a two day journey 'for the purpose of colonizing sparsely populated districts of the Ukraine'. They were taken instead, not to the distant Ukraine, but to the nearby spa town of Mineralniye Vody, where, after being marched two and a half miles to an anti-tank ditch, they were shot, together with two thousand Jews from Essentuki and three hundred from Pyatigorsk. Even as these murders took place, the German Commander-in-Chief of the Caucasus front, Field Marshal Wilhelm List, was being blamed by Hitler for failing to break through to the Caspian Sea, and was dismissed.

On September 8, as Churchill had promised Stalin in Moscow three weeks earlier, British bombers struck with renewed ferocity at a German city, this time Düsseldorf. Among the bombs which they dropped were many which weighed two tons, nicknamed 'block-busters'. That same day, a small Japanese aircraft, launched from a submarine, dropped incendiary bombs near Brookings, in the State of Oregon, setting a forest on fire. This was the only Japanese attack to take place inside the continental United States. It was followed two days later by an American air raid from their newly established airbase at Adak, in the

Aleutian Islands on the Japanese forces occupying Kiska Island, two hundred and fifty miles away.

On September 12 the British launched what they called a 'butcher and bolt' commando raid on the French coast, landing ten men at Port-en-Bessin, a small harbour in Normandy. The raiders killed all seven Germans whom they found in the harbour, but the shooting alerted other soldiers in the area and, as the British embarked, all but one of them were killed. That one, a man by the name of Hayes, who managed to swim along the coast, was aided by a French family, who then passed him to the French Resistance, who helped smuggle him into Spain. There, however, he was caught by General Franco's police, sent back to France, interrogated by the Gestapo in Paris, and shot.

At sea, September 12 saw the sinking of a British troopship, the *Laconia,* by a German submarine, U-156, commanded by Captain Hartenstein. On board were more than 1,500 Italian prisoners-of-war being taken to Canada, together with 180 Polish guards, and 811 British passengers and crew. Learning from survivors that he had been responsible for putting at risk the lives of so many Italians, then clinging desperately to the wreckage, Hartenstein sent a series of signals offering not to attack any ship which came to their rescue. Two British and one French warship hurried to the scene, but, as their rescue work was in progress, an American Army aircraft, flying from the newly established South Atlantic base on Ascension Island, attacked the German submarine with its bombs. As a result, Admiral Dönitz issued an order to every German naval vessel: 'All attempts to rescue the crews of sunken ships will cease forthwith.'

More than a thousand of those on the *Laconia* when she had been sunk were men who had already been rescued from the sea. In all, more than 1,400 of the 2,491 men and sailors on the ship were drowned. Hartenstein, who had done his best to help the survivors, was killed six months later, when his submarine was sunk by American Navy aircraft east of Barbados.

Two British operations were launched on September 13, 'Bluebottle', in which a Royal Navy vessel, the *Tarana,* sailing through the Mediterranean, successfully took off British prisoners-of-war from a beach near Perpignan, and 'Agreement' when, with less success, British troops attacked Tobruk both overland and by sea, in an attempt to destroy Axis supply depots and port installations. During the attack, three British warships were sunk, the valuable Fleet destroyers *Sikh* and *Zulu,* and the anti-aircraft ship *Coventry,* and several hundred Marines were killed. That night, British bombers made their hundredth raid of the war on the German North Sea port of Bremen. Ironically, it was also on September 13 that the much bombed British island of Malta was presented with an award for bravery, the George Cross, normally given to individuals. September 13 was also the day on which the Germans intensified their assault on Stalingrad, driving towards the city's centre; by nightfall, German troops had broken into the Minina suburb in the south, and were also poised to drive the Russian defenders from the Mamayev Kurgan.

The war diary of the German Sixty-second Army noted the timing, though not the ferocity, of the ebb and flow of the struggle for the centre of Stalingrad.

At eight o'clock in the morning of September 14: 'Station in enemy hands.' At 8.40: 'Station recaptured.' At 9.40: 'Station retaken by enemy.' At 13.20: 'Station in our hands.' So close had the Germans now come to the bank of the Volga that they were able to sink ships seeking to carry refugees and the wounded across the Volga; when one such ship, the *Borodino*, was sunk, several hundred wounded soldiers were killed. More than a thousand civilians were drowned when the steamer *Iosif Stalin* was sunk.

That same day, in the Far East, Japanese troops, pressing southwards along New Guinea's Kokoda Trail, drove back the Australians to the Imita Ridge, the last peak in the island's mountain range, and only thirty-two miles from Port Moresby. But there the Japanese were halted by a determined counter-attack.

On September 15, Japanese submarines in the New Hebrides sank the aircraft-carrier *Wasp*, which had earlier played so important a part in the defence of Malta. They also badly damaged the battleship *North Carolina*. That day, as fighting continued on the island of Guadalcanal, the American forces, having driven off a Japanese attack, received reinforcements, and further extended the area of the island under their control. Also on September 15, the first United States troops reached Port Moresby from Australia, to join the Australian defence.

The hegemony of the Rising Sun was no longer assured.

As the battle for Stalingrad became one of hand-to-hand fighting in streets, houses and cellars, the Mamayev Kurgan was taken by the Germans, retaken by the Russians, then defended against repeated German assault. Elsewhere on the Eastern Front, the Germans launched two new anti-partisan operations, 'Triangle' and 'Quadrangle', both of them in the Bryansk region, where the Bryansk to Kharkov railway had been cut repeatedly near Lokot. In a two week action, 2,244 Soviet partisans were killed or captured; but several thousand more escaped the traps set for them, to regroup further north, at Navlya, and to fight again, reinforced by men parachuted in a few weeks later. In the south, another group of 120 partisans were dropped by parachute behind the German line in the area north of Novorossiisk, to replace a group which the Germans had almost totally wiped out. The leader of the second group, Slavin, was believed by the Germans to be a Jew, a fact which seemed to add to the fury of their sweep.

On September 18, Soviet Marines, having reached Stalingrad by ferry across the Volga, took up their positions in the city's giant grain-elevator, beating off ten German attacks in a single day. That day, lunching with Hitler at his Vinnitsa headquarters, one of his headquarters staff, Werner Koeppen, noted that 'the idea was to destroy all Russia's cities as a prerequisite to the lasting German domination of the country'. Also on September 18, Otto Thierack, the German Minister of Justice, who was also a major-general in the SS, came to an agreement with Himmler for the 'delivery of "asocials" for the execution of their sentences'. 'Asocials' meant Jews, Gypsies, homosexuals, Russians, Ukrainians, Poles serving more than three years in prison for civil crimes, and Czechs and Germans serving more than eight years. Their 'sentences' were to

Behind the lines in the East, winter 1942–1943

be forced labour in conditions of such severity and lack of medical help or sustenance that hundreds of thousands were to die. Theirack also advised Himmler that in order to make the newly conquered Eastern territories 'fit' for German settlers and colonization, 'Jews, Poles, Gypsies, Russian and Ukrainians convicted of offences should not be sentenced by ordinary courts but should be executed. . . .'

That September had seen no slackening in the execution, murder and gassing of those whom the Nazis were determined to destroy. That month, fourteen thousand Jews had been sent from France, more than six thousand from Holland, and more than five thousand from Belgium, to Auschwitz. A further twenty thousand Jews had been deported from Eastern Galicia, principally from the town of Kolomyja, and from Brody, to Belzec. When, on September 19, several hundred of the three thousand Jews in the deportation from Brody broke out in fear and desperation from the deportation train, all but a dozen were machine-gunned to death. That same day, as five thousand Jews were deported from the town of Parczew to Treblinka, and gassed, several hundred managed to escape to the relative safety of a 'family camp' which had been set up deep in the Parczew forest. But most of them were to be killed a month later, when German armed units mounted two major sweeps against them.

On September 20, off the coast of Norway, a Free French submarine brought ashore two British commandos, Captain G. D. Black and Captain B. J. Hough-ton. Their target was the hydro-electric power station at Glomfjord, the supplier of electricity to the largest aluminium manufacturing plant in Norway, and an important source of supply for the German war effort. Travelling across difficult mountain country, Black and Houghton reached the power station and blew it up. Then, running by accident into a large German force, they fought back, were wounded and were taken prisoner. They were subsequently shot by the Gestapo.

All over Europe, the tyranny of the occupier was drawing more and more men and women into the resistance. On September 22, in Minsk, Wilhelm Kube, killer of tens of thousands of Jews and Russians, was killed by a bomb planted by his Byelorussian maidservant under his bed. The girl, Elena Mazaniuk, was working for the partisans. After planting the bomb, she succeeded in leaving Minsk, and in reaching a Soviet partisan unit operating nearby.

Also on September 22, German troops reached the very centre of Stalingrad, but the Russians refused to surrender. Hitler, angered by the failure to take either Stalingrad or, as he had hoped to do several weeks earlier, the Caucasian city of Grozny, dismissed General Franz Halder, who since the outbreak of war more than two years earlier had been Chief of the Army General Staff, and replaced him by General Kurt Zeitzler. But Zeitzler was as uneasy as Halder about the German position in Russia, and was also to urge, though unsuccessfully, the need for temporary retreats. Told by Field Marshal Keitel not to upset Hitler by giving him details of German casualties, Zeitzler is said to have replied: 'If a man starts a war he must have the nerve to hear the consequences.'

On the morning of September 23 the Russians launched a counter-attack in the north-west suburbs of Stalingrad. A few hours earlier, two thousand fresh Siberian troops had been ferried across the Volga. Slowly but steadily, amid ferocious hand-to-hand fighting, the Germans were pushed back through the cellars and devastated buildings around the oil storage depot. Also on September 23, in an attempt to renew the advance in the Caucasus, the Germans launched Operation Attica, hoping to drive along the Black Sea shore, through Tuapse to Sochi, Suchumi and Batum. But the Soviet defenders denied them even Tuapse.

Far from the fighting in Russia, and from the continuing struggle between the Japanese and the Americans on Guadalcanal, on September 23 a development took place in Washington which was to seal the fate of Japan. This was the appointment of Brigadier-General Leslie R. Groves to supervise every aspect, from construction to final delivery, of the atomic bomb. Money, he was told, was no object. Requisition and appropriation were his for the asking. The operation, conducted in strictest secrecy, needed a code name; it was given the name 'Manhattan Project'.

On September 24, six hundred Soviet partisans, some dressed in German uniforms and using heavy artillery, burned down the town of Ryabchichi, a German staging and supply post on the Smolensk–Bryansk highway. That same day, Ribbentrop passed on instructions to all German Embassies 'to hurry up as much as possible the evacuation of Jews from the various countries in Europe'. Negotiations should begin at once, his subordinate Martin Luther explained, with the Governments of Bulgaria, Hungary and Denmark, 'with the object of starting the evacuation of the Jews of these countries'. As to what the fate of those Jews would be, the omens that September were clear; of six thousand Jews deported from Theresienstadt to Maly Trostenets in three trains between September 23 and 29, there was not a single survivor. Five death camps were now working at fever pitch: Chelmno, Belzec, Sobibor, Treblinka and Maly Trostenets. At Auschwitz, as many deportees were being killed as were being set aside for slave labour. On September 26, a senior ss officer, Lieutenant-General August Frank, sent the Auschwitz camp administration, as well as the head of administration of Treblinka, Sobibor and Belzec, a note of what was to be done with what he called the 'property of the evacuated Jews'. Foreign currency, jewellery, precious stones, pearls and 'gold from teeth' were to go to the ss for 'immediate delivery' to the German Reichsbank. Smaller personal items such as clocks, wallets and purses were to be cleaned, 'evaluated' and 'delivered quickly' to front line troops.

The troops would be able to buy these small items, although gold watches would be distributed exclusively to the ss. Underwear and footwear would be given mainly to ethnic Germans. Women's clothing, including shoes, as well as children's clothing, was to be sold to ethnic Germans.

Quilts, woollen blankets, thermos flasks, earflaps, combs, table knives, forks, spoons and knapsacks; all were listed by General Frank. So too were sheets, pillows, towels and tablecloths. All were to go to ethnic Germans. Spectacles and eye-glasses were to go to the Medical Officer of the German Army. Gold frames were to go to the ss. 'Valuable furs' were likewise to go to the ss. Everything was priced in meticulous detail: 'for instance', General Frank wrote, 'one pair of used men's trousers, three marks; one woollen blanket, six marks etc.'. It was to be 'strictly observed that the Jewish Star is removed from all garments and outer garments which are to be delivered'. All items should be searched 'for hidden valuables sewn in'.

Within two weeks of General Frank's note, fifty kilogrammes of the dental gold already accumulated were sent to the ss for its own dental needs. Mass plunder and mass murder had led to mass profit, and were to continue to do so for another two years.

# 27

# Stalingrad and 'Torch'

SEPTEMBER–OCTOBER 1942

On 25 September 1942, during a Nazi Party rally in Oslo, British aircraft, flying across the North Sea, attacked the Gestapo headquarters in the city. Their aim was to destroy the Norwegian Resistance records which were being kept in the building, as well as to give a demonstration of Allied power. The building itself was not hit, and in the surrounding buildings four people were killed. There was, however, panic among the Nazis, many of whom fled the city, and their meeting ended in chaos.

That same day, at Stalingrad, German tanks, driving in from Gorodishche, reached the western edge of the Krasny Oktyabr factory, and the south-western corner of the Barrikady factory, on the very banks of the Volga. The heroism of the defenders was typified, at the height of the battle, by Lyuba Nesterenko, a girl nurse who, trapped in a basement, looked after twenty-eight seriously wounded men until she herself died from a chest wound. On September 27, though the swastika flag flew in apparent triumph above the headquarters of the Stalingrad Communist Party, more reinforcements came across the Volga, landing under a murderous shellfire and hurrying forward to retake a cellar or hold the basement of an already pulverized building. That day, Hitler flew back from Vinnitsa to Berlin. He had hoped to announce the capture of Stalingrad, which his troops had indeed penetrated to the very banks of the river; but they had not subdued it. On the northern reaches of the Volga, 680 miles north-west of Stalingrad, Russian troops crossed the Volga near Rzhev, regaining twenty-five villages. On the following day, in Istanbul, a young Jew, Chaim Barlas, overheard two Germans in a restaurant say that Hitler had 'lost the war.'

On September 29, in Berlin, Hitler warned his commanders of the danger of invasion from the West. To try to mitigate the fury of the Anglo-American air raids, he ordered the construction of massive, fort-like, anti-aircraft towers, known as Flak Towers, in Berlin, Munich, Vienna, Linz and Nuremberg.

In Prague, 255 Czechs were sentenced to death on September 29 for supporting, sheltering or refusing to denounce the murderers of Heydrich. At Auschwitz, in the last week of September, four thousand Jews from Slovakia, France, Holland and Belgium were gassed, among them Rene Blum, the brother of the former French Prime Minister, Léon Blum. In Berlin, on September 30, Hitler told a mass meeting gathered to launch the Nazi Party's Winter Aid Programme: 'I said that if Jewry started this war in order to overcome the Aryan people, then it would not be the Aryans but the Jews who would be exterminated. The Jews laughed at my prophecies. I doubt if they are laughing now.' In the Caucasus, on September 30, as a reminder to his troops of what was expected of them, the German commander reissued Field Marshal Manstein's Order of the Day of 20 November 1941, that the German soldier was 'not merely a fighter according to the rules of the act of war, but also the bearer of a ruthless ideology'. He must therefore understand 'the necessity for a severe but just revenge on sub-human Jewry'.

In Britain, the reading of the German Enigma messages was put to good use for the Russians as well as for the British. The total number of Enigma keys now broken, and being read regularly, had reached more than fifty. On September 30 the British cryptographers had broken the Enigma key used by the Todt Organization. Known as 'Osprey', this key was to be read until the end of the war. Also on September 30, Churchill personally passed on to Stalin the information, obtained from the German Enigma messages, that plans had been made in Berlin to establish a German naval flotilla on the Caspian Sea, that its base was to be Makhach-Kala, and that a German admiral had already been selected to command it. Submarines, torpedo craft and minesweepers were to be transported to the Caspian from the Black Sea, by rail from Mariupol. 'No doubt', Churchill commented, 'you are already prepared for this kind of attack.'

The Germans' Caspian plan came to nought; on October 1 the Russian forces in the Caucasus finally brought the German advance to an end. That same day, in Berlin, Rommel told Hitler that British air supremacy, and the shortcomings of the Italian officers under his command, had forced him to give up the march to Cairo.

In the Far East, on October 1, a torpedo hit the Japanese ship *Lisbon Maru*, which began to sink. On board were 1,816 British prisoners-of-war, being taken from Hong Kong to Japan. When the prisoners tried to leave the sinking ship, the Japanese had the hatches battened down. As the ship went down, hundreds attempted to break out. The Japanese fired at them. Those who managed to jump into the water, and tried to climb up the ropes of four other Japanese ships standing by, were kicked back into the sea. More than 840 were killed or drowned. The rest, picked up later by small patrol vessels or by sympathetic Chinese, were taken as prisoners-of-war to Japan.

On the Eastern Front, October 3 saw the launching of a five day German sweep against Soviet partisans, Operation Regatta, near the White Russian town of Gorky, near Smolensk. A day earlier, near Peklina, fifty telegraph poles had been blown up by Soviet partisans. The ceaseless partisan attacks demoralized the German soldiers, who, so far behind the lines, were nevertheless vulnerable.

There was another war, however, the scientific war, where German morale was high. On October 3, at Peenemünde, the Germans were finally successful

The Western Desert; the grave of an Australian soldier, 13 August 1941.

The Western Desert; British troops surrender, 15 August 1941 (*see page 225*).

In Russia, German troops advance. This photograph was taken on 28 October 1941.

October 1941; Russian dead in one of the main streets of Leningrad, after one of the first German artillery bombardments on the city.

Soviet troops, under Stalin's watchful eye, prepare for the defence of Moscow. This photograph shows the presentation of the Banner of Guards to the 1st Moscow Guards Motorized Infantry Division on 22 November 1941. On the following day, German troops reached a village only thirty miles from Moscow (*see page 262*).

Russian women volunteers leave Moscow to dig anti-tank ditches at the front (*see page 246*).

Pearl Harbour, 7 December 1941. Smoke rises from stricken American warships, as the flak from American anti-aircraft guns explodes in the sky (*see page 272*).

The American battleships *West Virginia* and *Tennessee* ablaze at Pearl Harbour, 7 December 1941.

An American bomber destroyed on the ground at Hickham Field, Pearl Harbour, 7 December 1941.

Burying the dead at Pearl Harbour; the ceremony at one of the many mass graves.

A memorial stone at Pearl Harbour to one of those killed, who had been too badly mutilated to be identified.

The Russian front, 7 December 1941: German soldiers pull back from Moscow (*see page 274*).

The Japanese air attack on
Hong Kong, 11 December 1941.

Hong Kong surrenders, 25
December 1941 (*see page 282*).

Japanese troops celebrate victory in Malaya, 31 January 1942.

Japanese troops invade Burma, 31 January 1942. The Union Jack flies on the railway bridge which marks the border between Burma and Thailand.

in firing their twelve-ton rocket, the A4, capable of carrying a one-ton warhead for two hundred miles. This weapon had been the brainchild of a rocket enthusiast, Wernher von Braun. As a result of this success, Hitler, hitherto sceptical, now authorized the rocket's mass production.

Returning from Berlin to his Ukrainian headquarters at Vinnitsa on October 4, Hitler learned of a British commando raid on the Channel Island of Sark, Operation Basalt, during which three German Army engineers had been killed. During the raid, five Germans who were being taken, with their hands tied behind their backs, through the undergrowth, to be spirited back to Britain by sea, realized how few their captors were and began to struggle in an attempt to escape. As they struggled, three were shot. When the Germans found the three bodies with their hands tied behind their backs, it was assumed that they had been deliberately executed in cold blood while being held captive. Hitler at once ordered all British prisoners who had been captured at Dieppe to be manacled as a reprisal. He also drafted an Order of the Day, broadcast on October 7, which was to be obeyed with terrible consequences. 'The terror and sabotage squads of the British and their accomplices', it declared, 'act more like bandits than soldiers. In the future they will be treated as such by German troops and ruthlessly put down in battle, wheresoever they may appear.'

At Stalingrad, two armies were enmeshed in a single city. The Germans, although they had reached the landing stages on the Volga, could not dislodge the Russian defenders from the city's factories, nor could they stop the arrival of reinforcements across the river. Between September 25 and October 5, more than 160,000 Russian soldiers had crossed the Volga. 'Stalingrad must not be taken by the enemy,' Stalin telegraphed from Moscow on October 5, and he added: 'That part of Stalingrad which has been captured must be liberated.' On October 7, in answer to an appeal from Stalin for more fighter aircraft, Churchill arranged, as a matter of urgency, for thirteen merchant ships to sail at once to North Russia, individually and unescorted; five arrived. On the following day, Churchill was able to tell Stalin that, according to his 'latest information', the German plans for sending shipping to the Caspian sea by rail 'have been suspended'. Although Churchill could not say so, this welcome news was derived from the Enigma decrypts. The Germans had now accepted, in their most secret communications at least, that in the Caucasus their plans for 1942 had come to nought.

There had also been an American contribution to the battles at Stalingrad and in the Causasus; in the six months before November 1942, the United States had delivered to the Soviet Union, mostly through Persia, 56,445 field telephones, 381,431 miles of field telephone wire and 81,287 Thompson machine guns. These had proved a timely addition to the Soviet arsenal and means of communication.

In German-occupied Russia, there had been no interruption to the slaughter of the whole Jewish populations of towns and villages. On October 5 a German engineer, Hermann Graebe, had witnessed the murder of fifteen hundred Jews in a pit just outside the town of Dubno. 'I looked round for the man who had shot them,' he later recalled. 'He was an SS man, who was sitting on the edge of the narrow end of the pit, his legs dangling into it. He had a submachine gun across his knees and was smoking a cigarette.' On October 7, at Vinnitsa, Himmler had discussed the work of Odilo Globocnik at the Sobibor and Belzec death camps. Hitler himself had, apparently, seen Globocnik, who later recalled that the Führer had said to him: 'Faster, get the whole thing over with faster!' A month later, Globocnik was appointed to the ss rank of major-general. When, in Hitler's presence, the Ministerial Director of the Ministry of the Interior, Dr Herbert Linden, had suggested that it might be better to burn the corpses of those murdered, rather than to bury them, as perhaps another generation 'will think differently of the matter', Globocnik replied: 'But, gentlemen, if a generation coming after us should be so cowardly and so corrupt as not to understand our deeds, which are so beneficial and so necessary, then, gentlemen, the whole of National Socialism will have been in vain. Rather, we should bury bronze plates with the corpses on which we should write that it was we who had the courage to accomplish this gigantic task!' According to Globocnik, Hitler then replied: 'Yes, my dear Globocnik, that is the truth of the matter. I entirely agree with you.'

It was while this bizarre debate was in progress at Vinnitsa, about whether the corpses of the victims were a cause of shame or pride, that, five hundred miles further west, at Auschwitz, German doctors, trained in pre-war Germany's finest medical schools, were using the corpses of specially murdered Jews for medical experiments. One of the doctors at Auschwitz, Dr Johann Kremer, clearly understood that there was no limit to the experiments he could carry out. 'I took and preserved material from quite fresh corpses', he wrote in his diary on October 10, 'namely, the liver, spleen and pancreas'. Kramer later recalled how one patient was put on the dissecting table 'while he was still alive'. Kremer had then questioned him in detail about his medical history. 'When I had collected my information,' Kremer added, 'the orderly approached the patient and killed him with an injection in the vicinity of the heart'.

After the war, Kremer was to serve ten years in prison in Poland, followed by ten more years in prison in West Germany.

On October 10, the German Air Force began a ten day assault on Malta. Six hundred aircraft, based in Sicily, attacked the island in waves of a hundred. Alerted by the careful reading of the German Air Force's own Enigma messages, the British intercepted each wave of the attackers while they were still over the sea. In the Pacific, an equally careful reading of the most secret Japanese codes enabled the American Navy, on October 11, to intercept off Cape Esperance a Japanese fleet bringing reinforcements to Guadalcanal. In a night battle fought, not by aircraft but by surface ships, one Japanese heavy cruiser, the *Furutaka*, and three Japanese destroyers were sunk, for the cost of a single American destroyer. But during the battle, forty-eight sailors were killed on the American destroyer *Duncan* when she was caught in Japanese and American cross-fire, and more than a hundred American sailors were killed when their light cruiser *Boise* was hit by Japanese shellfire after she had turned on a searchlight to illuminate a Japanese target.

To the amazement of the Americans, when the battle was over many of the Japanese sailors whose ships had been sunk refused to be rescued by the American ships, preferring to be devoured by the sharks that infested the waters of the battlefield.

In the Atlantic, on October 12, a convoy with forty-four merchant ships, SC 104, was attacked by a pack of thirteen German submarines, at the very point, known as the 'black gap', where no air escort could be provided. As the merchant ships continued on their course, the warship escort gave battle. During five days of continuous action, eight merchant ships were sunk, but three German submarines were also destroyed. Among the Allied warships were two Norwegian corvettes whose captains, the British senior officer reported, 'pounced like terriers' whenever opportunity arose.

At Stalingrad, on October 11, after fifty-one days of continuous fighting, no German infantry or tank assaults took place; the Germans were preparing one final, and as they hoped, devastating assault. Meanwhile, on the Moscow front two days later, Soviet partisans blew 178 gaps in the Bryansk–Lgov railway; this had been done by demolition experts specially trained at Tula and parachuted behind the lines for the operation. It was on October 14 that the renewed German assault on Stalingrad came, with an attack aimed at driving the defenders from every nook and cranny, from every cellar and ruin, from the fortified shells of factories and from the river bank. Three hundred German tanks took part in the onslaught. But still the Tractor Factory did not fall, although it was completely surrounded and, between the Tractor and Barrikady factories, buildings were captured by the Germans, then recaptured, and captured again. Fighting took place in every attic, on every floor, on the ruins of floors, and in the cellars.

That night, 3,500 wounded Soviet soldiers were ferried across the Volga to the safety of the eastern bank. Driven almost into the ground, pounded from the air, overrun by wave after wave of German infantrymen, still the defenders of Stalingrad refused to give up. They were still defending their ruins on October 15. The German push, for all its fury, and despite its many successes, had failed. But it was renewed three days later with equal intensity, drawing forth a defence of unprecedented tenacity.

As the battle for Stalingrad moved into its third month, resistance and terror were everywhere in evidence behind the German lines. On October 14, from the Polish city of Piotrkow, the Germans began the deportation of 22,000 Jews to Treblinka; the deportation took seven days. One of these who was deported that week, and killed, was a young girl, Lusia Miller, who wrote to a friend a few days before the deportation: 'It is true that it is terrible; terribly sad that young people die, because everything, everything wants to live in me. And yet, at such a young age, at thirteen, one is only beginning to discover life. And perhaps it is just as well that it is so early. I don't know. But I really do not want to die'.

In German-occupied Warsaw, fifty Polish Communists, members of an underground resistance group, were hanged in public on October 16, their bodies left hanging as a warning to others who might wish to rebel. On October 17, more than ten thousand Jews then in Buchenwald, and seven thousand in Sachsenhausen, some of whom had been prisoners there for four years, were deported to Auschwitz. From Norway, 209 Jews were sent, first by sea and then by train, to Auschwitz. From Holland, five trains that month brought nearly five thousand Jews to the same camp. Also in October, at Belzec, forty-nine thousand Jews were killed, at Sobibor eleven thousand, and at Treblinka more than a hundred thousand, drawn from towns and villages throughout central Poland.

On October 18, at Auschwitz, on a day during which 1,594 Dutch Jews were gassed, Dr Kremer noted in his diary: 'terrible scenes when three women begged to have their lives spared'. They were 'young and healthy women', Kremer later recalled, 'but their begging was to no avail. The ss men taking the action shot them on the spot'.

Thousands of people were killed each day at Auschwitz, where human life had been declared of no value. Elsewhere, the value of each human life was clearly recognized, and individuals were rescued in daring and courageous acts. When, that same October 18, Squadron-Leader Tony Hill, a much-decorated British reconnaissance pilot, was shot down over Le Creusot in south-eastern France, breaking his back, he was not only rescued and hidden by the French Resistance, but a special aircraft was flown from England to land at a clandestine airstrip in France, and then to take him back to England. On November 12, as he was being carried to the plane, he died.

Two days after Squadron-Leader Hill's crash, an Englishwoman, Mary Lindell, was parachuted into France to establish an escape line for Allied airmen and escaped prisoners-of-war. Herself a much decorated Red Cross officer in the First World War, who had won the Croix de Guerre in 1916, she had escaped from France only three months earlier. Hundreds were to owe her their freedom.

At Stalingrad, German and Russian forces now battled in the ruins in heavy rain. The Tractor Factory could hold out no longer, although Soviet troops in the Barrikady and Krasny Octyabr factories beat off all attempt to overrun them. By October 20, however, the Russians held no more than a thousand yards of the western bank. 'The Führer is convinced the Russians are collapsing,' Field Marshal Keitel noted on October 21, and he added: 'He says that twenty million will have to starve.' That day, far behind the lines, a German police company uncovered a Jewish family camp deep in the forest. Such camps were a wonderful attempt at humanitarianism in a brutalized world. Not only did armed men guard hundreds of women, children and old people in the inhospitable forest, but they also foraged for food, and were ever-vigilant against those who sought to destroy the sanctuary. In the attack on October 21, however, the Germans found the camp, and killed 461 people. Only a dozen managed to escape. Two Polish peasant families were also killed, for 'maintaining contact' with the partisans in the region.

Far to the south, at Elista, now the Germans' most easterly outpost, two partisans were captured on October 22; they had been parachuted from Astrakhan, at the mouth of the Volga. In the weeks that followed, many more partisans were to be parachuted into this region. A Cossack cavalry squadron supported the Germans in trying to hunt them down but, a German report admitted, 'Frequently the bands withdrew temporarily, only to make new sallies from their hideouts.'

In North Africa, the Western Allies were a mere two weeks away from Operation Torch, the first Anglo-American amphibious landing of the war. To help prepare it, on October 22 the American General, Mark W. Clark, together with some of his staff, landed secretly by submarine in Algiers, for talks with those senior French officers who supported the Allies, and with the Resistance leaders. On the following day, in the Western Desert, General Montgomery launched an attack at El Alamein on the German and Italian forces.

It was a brave battle on both sides, but also an unequal one. The Germans' own top-secret Enigma messages had revealed to the British every German position, and every German weakness, especially in fuel oil; they had also enabled every essential German supply ship to be shadowed and sunk, including two which reached Tobruk harbour on the second day of the battle. In addition to this advantage derived from Signals Intelligence, Montgomery's tanks included many of the new American Shermans, more than a thousand tanks in all, against his opponents' 480. In manpower, aircraft and guns he was also superior. Rommel, whose presence on the battlefield might also have made a difference, was in Germany on sick leave.

'The battle in Egypt began tonight at 8 pm. . . .' With these words, Churchill announced in a telegram to Roosevelt on October 23 the opening of the desert offensive on which so much depended. 'The whole force of the Army will be engaged', Churchill added. That same day, General Stumme, Rommel's replacement, died of a heart attack, and Rommel was recalled to Egypt, reaching the battlefield on October 25.

On the first day of battle, October 23, General Montgomery had under his command, along a forty mile front, 150,000 men – including Australians, New Zealanders, South Africans and British – 2,182 pieces of artillery, and the use of 500 fighter aircraft and 200 bombers, in addition to his thousand tanks. The battle opened with the simultaneous firing of nearly a thousand of his artillery pieces, an unprecedented barrage of fire on so narrow a front.

There were many moments in the battle of El Alamein when the precious advantage gained by prior Intelligence had to be supplemented on the battlefield by the skills and courage of soldiers and airmen. Throughout October 26, the Allied forces were exposed to a series of cleverly planned German counter-attacks. These however were dispersed by Royal Air Force bombing before they could be put fully into operation. That night, a series of Allied advances along the whole front secured the strategic contour of Kidney Ridge, a geographic feature described by General Alexander to Churchill as 'a small but important spur in this featureless plain'. Montgomery's method of attack – the infantry moving forward to open a path for the tanks – was novel and effective.

The battle of El Alamein lasted for five days. When it was over, the German and Italian forces were in swift retreat. The Italian and German losses were 2,300 killed, and 27,900 taken prisoner.

On October 26, as Montgomery drove to victory at El Alamein, Japanese troops under General Kawaguchi launched a fierce attack on the American positions at Guadalcanal, but were driven off, bringing Japanese losses since the American landing began to more than four thousand. In this most recent attack, more than a hundred Japanese aircraft were shot down, for fifteen American planes. That day, off the Santa Cruz Islands, two small American naval task forces tried to stop a far stronger Japanese fleet, including five aircraft carriers, on its way to Guadalcanal with reinforcements. Once again, as in the Coral Sea five months earlier, the battle was fought entirely by the aircraft of the opposing fleets, neither of which even came within firing range of each other. During the battle, the Americans lost the aircraft-carrier *Hornet*. No Japanese carriers were lost, though a hundred Japanese aircraft were shot down. The American aircraft losses, seventy-four in all, were also heavy. But the Japanese air losses effectively impeded their ability to reinforce Guadalcanal; this was in itself a victory for the United States.

On October 26 the British had tried, by an unorthodox means, to sink the *Tirpitz*, then in a Norwegian fjord, sending a Norwegian naval officer, Leif Larsen, across the North Sea with two manned torpedoes, known as 'Chariots', slung beneath his fishing boat. Larsen reached a point near Trondheim from which his attack could have succeeded, but lost his Chariots in an unlucky squall.

It was also on October 26 that a second deportation took place of Jews in the Theresienstadt ghetto. Already uprooted a year earlier from their homes in Germany, Austria and Czechoslovakia, they were now forced to move again, this time to an 'unknown destination', said to be somewhere 'in the East'. That destination was Auschwitz. In this second Theresienstadt deportation, 1,866 Jews were sent east; on arrival, 350 men under fifty years of age were chosen for forced labour. All the other deportees, the old men, all the women and all the children, were gassed. Of the 350 men chosen for the barracks and forced labour, only twenty-eight were to survive the war. In the next two years, a further twenty-five trains were to leave Theresienstadt for Auschwitz; of more than forty-four thousand deportees, less than four thousand were still alive when the war ended.

On the day after the first deportation of Jews from Theresienstadt to Auschwitz, a seventeen-year-old member of the Hitler Youth, Helmuth Günther Hubener, was executed in Germany; he had been charged with listening to foreign broadcasts and spreading the news which he had heard. German severity was everywhere in evidence. On October 28, the commander of the German forces in the Balkans, General Löhr, instructed his troops to treat all captured partisans with 'the most brutal hardness'. That same day, a 'top secret' ss directive sent from Berlin ordered all children's stockings and children's mittens stored in the death camps to be sent to ss families.

At a public meeting held in London on October 29, leading British churchmen and public figures protested against the persecution of the Jews, and in a message to the meeting, Churchill declared: 'The systematic cruelties to which the Jewish people – men, women and children – have been exposed under the Nazi regime are amongst the most terrible events of history, and place an indelible stain upon all who perpetrate and instigate them.'

'Free men and women' Churchill added, 'denounce these vile crimes, and when this world struggle ends with the enthronement of human rights, racial persecution will be ended'.

Every day, and every region under German rule, had its quota of persecution. In the Polish village of Suchozebry, a monument records the death, in a prisoner-of-war camp just outside the village, of 60,000 Soviet prisoners-of-war who perished there between July 1941 and October 1942. Most of them died of starvation and sickness; there were times when men who were badly ill were stripped of what clothes they wore, and flung, still alive, into ditches where they died. In another Polish village, Ostrowek, 10,000 Soviet prisoners-of-war likewise perished. Ostrowek was less than fifteen miles from Treblinka by rail, Suchozebry less than twenty miles.

Resistance was growing throughout German-occupied Europe, but reprisals were harsh. In Norway, on October 30, a twenty-year-old seaman engaged in anti-German sabotage, and wounded in the legs by his captors, was executed on Hitler's orders. So too was an Englishman captured during the attempted sabotage of the power station at Glomfjord. In Trondheim, ten prominent Norwegian citizens were shot as 'atonement for sabotage'. A further twenty-four Norwegians were later shot 'for transport of weapons and assistance to saboteurs'.

The bravery of individuals could also lead to the saving of lives. On October 30, the Gestapo seized more than a hundred Jewish orphan children from a children's home in Brussels. The staff refused to leave the children and were taken with them to the deportation camp at Malines. There were immediate protests, including one by L.C. Platteau, Secretary-General of the Belgian Ministry of Justice. The protest was successful; the children and staff were sent back to the home.


At the end of October, a British merchant shipping convoy, SL 125, homeward bound from Freetown with thirty-seven cargo ships, ran into a German submarine pack north east of Madeira. For seven days the ten U-boats chased and torpedoed, sinking thirteen ships with a heavy toll of life. On the *President Doumer*, 174 seamen were drowned. It was a disaster, however, which had a beneficial effect on the Allied cause which the Germans could not have foreseen; the U-boats which carried out the attack were unaware that 'assault convoys' carrying troops for the North African landings were at that very moment leaving Scotland for the Atlantic, and for the long southward journey to Gibraltar.

There was another British naval achievement on October 30, when, after a sixteen hour hunt, four British destroyers caught the German submarine U-559 some seventy miles north of the Nile Delta. As the submarine was being scuttled, Lieutenant Tony Fasson, Able Seaman Colin Grazier and a young canteen assistant, Tommy Brown, entered the submarine and succeeded in extracting its Enigma machine, together with documents which were to enable Bletchley Park to break once again into the U-boat Enigma which had eluded them for more than nine months.

A few seconds after Fasson and Grazier had handed this precious booty to Brown, they went down with the submarine. Both were posthumously awarded the George Cross. Brown, who survived, received the George Medal; it subsequently emerged that he was only sixteen years old, having lied about his age to join the Navy. He was immediately discharged and sent home. Two years later he was killed while trying to rescue his two sisters, who had been trapped in their slum tenement during a fire.

The first days of November 1942 saw the conclusion of three decisive battles. At Stalingrad, the Russian defenders continued to cling to the city against a massive German assault. West of El Alamein, British and Commonwealth forces continued to drive the Germans and Italians from their Egyptian conquests. On Guadalcanal, the Americans continued to force the Japanese to cede land over which their conqueror's flag had flown. All three victories were being achieved at a high cost in lives and material; but they represented a decisive turning of the tide.

Germany, Italy and Japan were suffering their first serious setbacks of the war. For the Germans, there was also the mystery of some Allied initiative which their Intelligence services knew to be imminent, but the direction of which was not known. From the moment on November 2 that the Germans sighted the invasion shipping assembling at Gibraltar, and surmised that it might be either for another and major Malta convoy or for the invasion of Sardinia, they began to move long-range bomber units from northern Norway, Russia, France, Holland, Belgium, Germany, Greece and Crete. From the German Air Force's own Enigma messages, these movements were at once made known to British Intelligence, which was thus able to confirm that the Germans knew nothing whatsoever about the 'Torch' landings on the French North African coastline, planned for November 8.

On November 3, from his headquarters at Vinnitsa, Hitler ordered Rommel to 'stand fast' in the Western Desert. 'It would not be the first time in history', Hitler declared, 'that a strong will has triumphed over the bigger battalions. As to your troops, you can show them no other road than to victory or death.' This order, Rommel later commented, 'demanded the impossible. Even the most devoted soldier can be killed by a bomb.' It was issued, nevertheless, and, as Rommel later wrote, 'had a powerful effect on the troops. At the Führer's command they were ready to sacrifice themselves to the last man.' No such sacrifice was to be asked of them, however; within twenty-four hours of receiving Hitler's order not to retreat, Rommel had obtained his permission to withdraw.

'A victory at last,' King George VI wrote in his diary on November 4, and he added: 'how good it is for the nerves'.

There was also good news for the Allied nerves in the messages coming from the Far East, where the Australians had been driving northwards along the Kokoda Trail, denying the Japanese all chance of seizing Port Moresby and, on November 3, retaking Kokoda itself. Four days later, on the Kokoda-Gona trail, Japanese defenders sought in vain to hold up the Australians with a bayonet charge in which 580 Japanese were killed.

On the night of November 5 the British launched Operation Leopard, whose object was to land ten tons of military stores, including a considerable number of Bren guns, on the Algerian coast for use by the Algerian Resistance during the Allied landings in three days time. The British force was unable, however, to make contact with those on shore and the operation had to be abandoned. On the following day, in Operation Minerva, General Giraud, who had earlier escaped after two years in German captivity, was rescued from the coast of southern France by a British submarine, taken to Gibraltar, and briefed about the imminent invasion of French North Africa.

In the Caucasus, on November 6, the Germans made one last attempt to break through to Grozny. But they were halted at the town of Ordzhonikidze, where they were repulsed. Hitler had already made plans, two days earlier, for a switch of strategy if the Caucasus oilfields could not be reached; if occupying Baku were to prove impossible, he would bomb it, denying Russia the use of its own oil. Churchill learned of this decision on November 7, from the Germans' own Enigma messages. He at once passed it on to Stalin. 'Many thanks for your warnings concerning Baku,' Stalin replied. 'We are taking the necessary measures to combat the dangers.'

On the afternoon of November 7, Hitler left the Eastern Front by train for Munich. In the early hours of the morning the train was halted by a signal at a small railway station. There was an urgent message for the Führer from the German Foreign Ministry in Berlin: according to British radio, an American invasion force was disembarking at Algiers, Oran and Casablanca.

The Allied forces which now sought to drive the Germans from French North Africa – Operation Torch – constituted the largest amphibious invasion force thus far in the history of warfare: 300 warships, 370 merchant ships, and 107,000 men. As soon as the beaches were secure, the American officers whose task was to make use of the German Air Force Enigma messages went in. 'Snipers took potshots at us', their senior officer, Lewis F. Powell, later recalled, 'and one of my people was killed the first night we were there'. From a captured senior German Intelligence officer, Powell later learned that the Germans had regarded this landing as a feint, believing even after November 8 that the real effort was either to be against Malta or Sicily, or perhaps the reinforcement of Montgomery in the eastern desert. Hence the Germans' initial failure to attack the landing convoys off Algiers and Oran.

The invasion of French North Africa was swiftly successful. Within seventy-six hours of the first landings, Allied troops were in undisputed control of 1,300 miles of the African coast, from Safi to Algiers. That evening, when Hitler made his annual speech in the Munich beer hall, he focused his attention on Stalingrad, of which he said: 'That was what I wanted to capture, and do you know, modest as we are – we've got it too! There are only a few more tiny pockets!' Hitler also spoke about the Jews, and of his 1939 prophecy that the war would lead to their annihilation. 'Of those who laughed then,' he said, 'countless already laugh no longer today; and those who still laugh today will probably not laugh much longer either.'

From France and Holland, thousands were being deported to Auschwitz that November. In central Poland, tens of thousands more were being deported to Sobibor, Belzec and Treblinka. In the Bialystok region, 110,000 Jews had been seized on November 2 from sixty-five towns and villages. Taken to special camps, they were held there for a few days, before being deported to Auschwitz and Treblinka. In one small village, Marcinkance, all 360 Jews resisted deportation; they were shot down and killed in the village itself.

On November 9, a new name entered the vocabulary of evil: Majdanek, a camp just outside the Polish city of Lublin where, on that day, four thousand Lublin Jews were brought, the first of several hundred thousand to be incarcerated, and murdered. At Majdanek, as at Auschwitz, up to half the deportees in each transport could be taken to the barracks; but the rest were taken to the gas chambers.

In French North Africa, such resistance as there was had been swiftly overcome by the Allied troops. Where the soldiers of Vichy France decided to fight, they were treated as the enemy. At Casablanca and Oran, 115 of the French defenders were killed. At Algiers, Admiral Darlan, the Commander-in-Chief of the Vichy forces, who happened to be in the city visiting his sick son, ordered the defenders to cease firing. Hitler, fearful of an allied drive to Tunis, hurried German troops to Bizerta on November 9. Three days later, British troops landed at Bône. The struggle for Tunisia had begun.

Retaining his grip on Tunisia would enable Hitler to deny the Allies the short sea route to Egypt and India and compel them to continue to use the very much longer route round the Cape. The shipping thus tied down could not then be used by the Allies to make up for the losses in the major Atlantic U-boat offensive then being planned for early 1943.

In the Western Desert, Rommel was being pushed steadily back; on November 9 he was defending Sidi Barrani, two hundred miles west of El Alamein. 'Now this is not the end,' Churchill declared in London at the annual Lord Mayor's Luncheon on November 10, 'it is not even the beginning of the end, but it is perhaps the end of the beginning.'

From his daily reading of the Germans' own top-secret Enigma signals, Churchill knew that his words were more than mere rhetoric. Not only Britain, but the Soviet Union, was proving to be the beneficiary of the North African landings. Four hundred of the five hundred German aircraft moved to Tunisia in the immediate aftermath of the landings on November 8 were brought from Russia, as were several hundred transport aircraft which had been supplying the German forces surrounded at Stalingrad. As a result of the precipitate transfer of these transport aircraft, German bombers had to be pressed into service for Stalingrad in their stead. Goering later commented, of this unforeseen switch of aircraft at Stalingrad: 'There died the core of the German bomber fleet'.

In moving air units from southern Russia – tentatively in the days before Operation Torch, and then massively after it – the Germans also sent to the Mediterranean their torpedo-bomber units based at Banak in northern Norway. These were the very units which had been proving such a threat to the Arctic convoys.

The relief afforded to the Russian forces at Stalingrad by the transfer of German aircraft to Tunisia ought to have been short-lived; the Western Allies had expected to overrun Tunisia within a few weeks. Because the German resistance in Tunisia was far more tenacious than expected, lasting not six weeks but six months, the German need to keep their air forces in the central Mediterranean continued to be a drain on the Russian front for much longer than would have been the case had the Allies succeeded in their initial plan.

On November 11, in the Western Desert, the British forces re-entered Libya, having been driven out, for the second time, five months earlier. The Germans and Italians were in full retreat. That day, in France, Hitler ordered the occupation of the Unoccupied Zone; henceforth, all France, including Vichy France, was under German rule, except for those eastern areas which had been annexed by Italy in July 1940. Even amid the turmoil and danger caused by Torch, Hitler found time to discuss the Jewish question, doing so on November 11 with Arthur Greiser, ruler of the Warthegau. 'In our most recent discussion about the Jews', Greiser told Himmler ten days later, 'the Führer has told me to proceed against them in whatever manner I judge best.'

On the Eastern Front, Hitler's soldiers struggled to fulfil his Munich boast that Stalingrad would soon be German; on November 11 German infantry and tanks, driving forward under the protection of massive artillery and air bombardment, reached the River Volga on a five-hundred-yard front, capturing most of the Krasny Oktybar factory and for the second time virtually cutting it off from the defenders in the Barrikady. That same day, as the Volga began to freeze, floating ice made the evacuation of the wounded almost impossible. When Soviet aircraft dropped food and ammunition, most of it either fell on the German lines or went into the river. But the Russian defenders, their forces now cut in two, and under intense bombardment, would not surrender.

In the Far East, the Americans were being put to one of their most severe tests, a Japanese attempt to land more than 10,000 men on Guadalcanal, in order to create a total Japanese force of 30,000 against the 23,000 Americans already on the island. But the Japanese attempt was foiled. For the cost of two light cruisers, including the *Atlanta*, and seven destroyers, the Americans sank two Japanese battleships, *Hiei* and *Kirishima*, the heavy cruiser *Kinugasa*, two destroyers and, most importantly, seven of the eleven troop transports bound for Guadalcanal. In the end, after two thousand Japanese troops had been killed while trying to land, only two thousand lived to join their comrades already in action, effectively making the island's capture by the Americans a certainty. American losses in the naval battle had been severe, however: 172 of the crew of the *Atlanta* were killed when the warship was struck, first by a torpedo, and then by gunfire which totally demolished the bridge superstructure and most of the gun turrets. After 470 unwounded survivors of the *Atlanta* had been taken off without incident, the crippled cruiser was blown up by a demolition party, and sank beneath the waves.

In the Western Desert, British and Commonwealth forces entered Tobruk on November 13. 'There is a long road still to tread,' Churchill told the Emir of Transjordan that day, 'but the end is sure.' On November 14, the German and Italian forces in Libya had been pushed back to Gazala. 'What will become of the war if we lose North Africa? How will it finish?' Rommel asked that day in a letter to his wife, and he added: 'I wish I could get free of these terrible thoughts.'

On November 15, church bells were rung throughout England to celebrate the victory in Egypt. That same day, on the French North African coast, British forces occupied Tabarka, inside Tunisia, to be followed within twenty-four hours by an American parachute landing at Souk el-Arba, while French troops, hitherto loyal to Vichy, now found themselves in action against the Germans at Beja.

Even as the Germans prepared to defend Tunisia, and to keep their hold in Africa, the Japanese, pushed northward in New Guinea back along the Kokoda Trail, prepared to defend the northern coastal towns of Buna and Gona against Australian and American troops. In New Guinea, as in Tunisia, it was to be no easy victory for the Allies; both wars were beginning to witness what was to become a main feature of the turning of the tide, that both the Japanese and the Germans would fight for every town and for every mile, reinforcing wherever they could, retaking positions whenever advantage could be won. At Stalingrad, this obdurate German refusal to give up ground even when it was clear that the Russians could not be dislodged was a costly feature of the struggle for both sides.

Another emerging feature of the war was the relentless air bombardment by the Allies of every facet of Axis war power. On the eve of Torch, it had been the Italian port city of Genoa that had suffered most. On November 17 it was the German submarine base on the French coast at St Nazaire which was attacked. St Nazaire was one of the first Atlantic coast targets of the United States Eighth Air Force, based in Britain. So fierce were the German anti-aircraft defences at St Nazaire that the port was dubbed 'Flak City' by the bomber crews who were sent against it.

The Japanese were also beginning to feel the impact of air bombardment on their own cities, so much so that on November 16 Japanese newspapers announced that 'the crew of any aircraft raiding Japan will be punished with death.'

As part of the Allied effort to weaken the German war effort, on November 17 a British agent, Michael Trotobas, was parachuted into France. His aim was to set up, on what was his second mission into German-occupied territory, a sabotage circuit based on Lille. Given the code name 'Farmer', this circuit could draw on the growing local hatred of occupation in the one area of France which had also been occupied by the Germans in the First World War.

It was not only in German-occupied lands that the evils of the New Order held sway; on November 17, at a secret conference in Munich, the Bavarian State Commissioner for health, Walther Schultze, explained to the directors of the mental hospitals throughout Bavaria the 'special diet' being introduced for all 'hopelessly ill patients'. This diet, according to Dr Valentin Faltlhauser, director of the Kaufbeuren mental asylum, would lead to 'a slow death, which should ensue in about three months'. Another expert on euthanasia, Dr Pfannmüller, proudly told the meeting 'how he had once grabbed a slice of bread from a nurse who had wanted to give it to a patient.'

In Germany itself, the euthanasia programme was revived that winter by a new method: not gassing, but deliberate starvation. This was made clear in a secret directive to all mental homes, dated November 30, issued from Berlin, which set out that 'in view of the war-related food situation and the health of the working asylum inmates', it was no longer justified to feed all inmates equally. Those who were being cared for in the asylums 'without accomplishing any useful work worth mentioning' must now be subjected to the special diet 'without delay'.

The scale of the euthanasia killings may never be known; the names of many of the victims are likewise lost to history. Even the locations of these killings are forgotten, no plaques marking the sites of such enormities. Elsewhere in German-occupied Europe, where the murder of civilians and civilian hostages never ceased, many thousand monuments have been set up to remember those who were killed; on November 18, for example, two hundred Poles were murdered in the Gestapo prison in Kazimierz Dolny. Today, a monument marks the spot and tells of their fate.

On October 18, the British had launched Operation Swallow, dropping four Norwegian parachutists near Vermork, in Norway, with instructions to prepare the ground for the destruction of the German heavy-water plant at Rjukan. A month later, on November 19, 'Swallow' was expanded to 'Grouse', and thirty-four men were towed across the North Sea in two gliders. Both gliders crashed on landing, as did one of the aircraft.

Seventeen men were killed in these three crashes. Four more, severely injured, were killed by the Gestapo when it was realised that they were too badly injured to be interrogated. A further fifteen were captured shortly after landing, and shot that same day. Four others, who were severely injured during the crash, were taken by the Germans to Stavanger hospital. Too badly injured to be interrogated, they were given lethal injections, and their bodies disposed of at sea.

On every German front, the fate of captured commandos, partisans and resistance fighters was execution. Yet the tide of war was turning. Pressure on the Germans was growing, as Allied bombing increased, and partisan and commando operations gathered momentum. The German failure to take Stalingrad had brought hope to captive peoples everywhere.

# 28

# The turn of the tide for the Allies

WINTER 1942

On 19 November 1942 the Red Army launched a counter-offensive north of Stalingrad, preceded by one of the most intense artillery bombardments of the war, when, to the call sign 'Siren', more than 3,500 guns and mortars opened fire on a fourteen mile front, followed, on one sector of the front, by Soviet martial music blared out by the ninety-strong divisional band. As part of the Russian plan, a particularly fierce assault was made on the Roumanian troops holding part of the line; troops with no previous experience of battle. Within twenty-four hours, 65,000 Roumanian soldiers had been taken prisoner. From London, at Churchill's personal insistence, the Russians were sent operational Intelligence, overheard by the British through Enigma, about German Army and Air Force intentions.

Not only Roumanian, but also Hungarian and Italian forces, fought alongside the Germans during the Russian assault on November 19. All were driven back. Then, on November 20, the Russians attacked south of Stalingrad. Their aim was a bold and dramatic one, to encircle the German forces inside the very city which the Germans themselves were encircling. A sensible German response would have been to break off the siege and withdraw towards the River Don. This proposal was made by General von Paulus on November 21. But Hitler would not allow any withdrawal whatsoever, issuing an order from Berchtesgaden that same day that von Paulus's Sixth Army must stand firm 'despite the danger of its temporary encirclement'.

On November 22 the Russian pincer closed south of Kalach, on the Don, trapping well over a quarter of a million men inside a circle that was to be drawn tighter every day. For the defenders of Stalingrad, so nearly driven into the Volga, the Soviet winter offensive brought the first relief for two months; the city, devastated and almost entirely overrun, had not succumbed, and would not now be lost. 'Hold on!', Hitler broadcast that day to the Sixth Army; but von Paulus saw no hope in holding on, and that same night asked for Hitler's permission to break out of the trap. Hitler did not reply; he was already in his train on his way from Berchtesgaden to Leipzig, from where he flew to Rastenburg. There, he assumed 'personal command' of the German Army, and, on

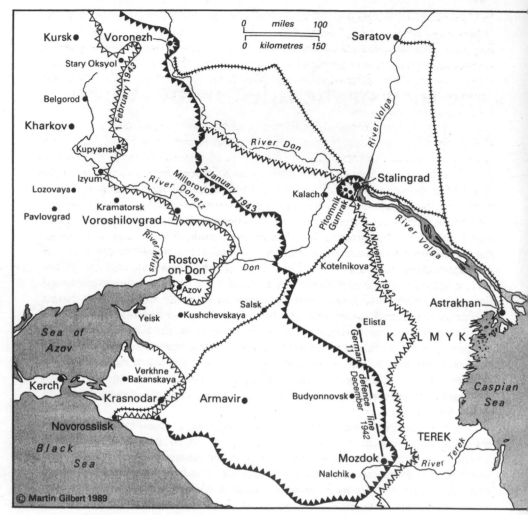

The Soviet reconquest of the Caucasus and the Don, winter 1942–1943

November 24, answered Paulus's request to break out of the encirclement with an emphatic refusal. Stalingrad must not be abandoned.

In the Mediterranean, the Allies had begun to experience, for the first time, the sweet taste of success; on November 20 a convoy of merchant ships, Operation Stone Age, reached Malta from Egypt under the protective umbrella of British aircraft. The siege of Malta was over. As the ships entered Valetta, the islanders lined every vantage point to cheer, while naval bands played in the ships with welcoming music. In the Western Desert, following the loss of Benghazi on November 20, Rommel fell back to El Agheila, more than five hundred miles from the Egyptian frontier across which he had so recently stood in triumph.

In Tunisia, British, Free French and American troops had taken control of the western half of the country, and on November 25 American troops, raiding the airport at Djedeida, destroyed thirty German and Italian aircraft on the ground. But the Allies were not to occupy Tunis, which they had hoped to reach within a month, until the following May. Thus Hitler was able to maintain his formidable pressure on Allied shipping, still forced to use the long and costly Cape of Good Hope route.

In Toulon harbour, fifty-eight French warships now awaited the arrival of the German forces sent to occupy Vichy France. For the Germans, this was a major prize; the seizure of the ships had even been given a code name, Operation Lila. But on the morning of November 27, as ss troops began to take over the naval base, the commander of the French Fleet, Admiral Jean de Laborde, gave orders for the ships to be scuttled. His orders were obeyed, and two battleships, two battle-cruisers, four heavy cruisers, two light cruisers, an aircraft transport, thirty destroyers and sixteen submarines were sunk. Three more submarines managed to put to sea and, avoiding the Germans, to join the Allied forces at Algiers. A fourth, also escaping, was interned by the Germans at Carthage.

The scuttling of the French Fleet at Toulon fulfilled the promise made to the British by Admiral Darlan in June 1940, and partly broken at Oran that same July, that the French Navy would never be allowed to fall into German hands. On November 28, at Rastenburg, Rommel urged upon Hitler the need to abandon the African theatre of war altogether as 'no improvement in the shipping situation could now be expected'. If the Army remained in North Africa, Rommel insisted, 'it would be destroyed'. Hitler refused to accept Rommel's advice, or even to discuss it. It was a 'political necessity', he said, to hold a major bridgehead in North Africa.

Hitler now proposed, not to allow von Paulus to break out of the Stalingrad trap, but to break into the trap from outside. This was Operation Winter Storm. Its planning coincided with yet another Russian counter-attack, this time in the Terek region of the Caucasus. Soviet partisans were also active in this region, as in the area north of Novorossiisk where, on November 29, the Germans murdered 107 villagers at Verkhne-Bakanskaya for 'direct or indirect' connections with the partisans. The partisans themselves, however, escaped. Much further behind the German lines, to the west of the River Dnieper, the end of November saw the establishment of two partisan bands, one led by Sidor Kovpak, the other by Alexander Saburov, who, uniting their forces, and operating from the region of the Pripet Marshes, began to cause havoc to the German lines of communication passing through the Ukraine. The Germans reacted, however, with frequent and savage sweeps, one of which, Operation Munich II, was launched that December against Soviet partisans in the Radoshkovichi region of White Russia, just north of the area of Kovpak's and Saburov's hideaway.

In the Pacific, throughout the last ten days of November, the Japanese tried to re-inforce their isolated and besieged garrison on the island of Guadalcanal. In a series of violent clashes with American warships, there were moments when it looked as if the Japanese attempt would succeed. On November 22, the American warship *Juneau* was sunk, and more than six hundred men were drowned. A hundred more clung to the wreckage. All but ten of them were eaten by sharks, or went mad as a result of the privation and drowned.

The Japanese tried once more, on November 30, to reinforce their now struggling garrison on Guadalcanal. Intercepted by the Americans during a night battle off Tassafaronga, the Japanese transports were forced to turn back. But the battle itself was a blow to the Americans, seriously damaging three heavy cruisers, *Pensacola, New Orleans* and *Minneapolis,* and sinking a fourth, the *Northampton,* fifty-eight crew members of which were killed. In New Guinea, the Australians reached the northern shore, recapturing Buna, but the Japanese, withdrawing to Buna Mission, continued their resistance, nor could the Americans dislodge them from the Soputa–Sanananda track. Thus 15,000 Australians and 15,000 Americans, despite complete mastery of the air, and virtual mastery of the sea, found themselves in vicious combat with less than half of their number of Japanese.

Far from the swamps and jungles of New Guinea, December 2 saw a decisive moment of the war take place, in strictest secrecy, in a rackets court on the campus of the University of Chicago. Here, at ten o'clock that morning, the Italian emigré scientist Enrico Fermi gave the order for an experiment to begin which, by mid-afternoon, had produced the first self-sustaining nuclear chain reaction. All was now set to find and process the necessary uranium for the manufacture of an atomic bomb.

On December 4, in Brussels, members of the Belgian resistance shot dead a Belgian member of the 'Germanic ss', a unit created by the Germans from fascist-inclined Belgians. That same day, in Warsaw, a group of Christian Poles, led by two women, Zofia Kossak and Wanda Filipowicz, set up a Council for the Assistance of the Jews. Their task was one filled with danger; only two days later, at Stary Ciepielow, the ss locked thirteen Poles – men, women and children – into a cottage, and ten more into a barn, and then burned them alive on suspicion of harbouring Jews. That same day, in the Parczew forest, the Germans launched a four-day manhunt against more than a thousand Jews in hiding. 'We fled round and round in terror,' one of those in hiding, Arieh Koren, later recalled, as Germans with machine guns, four small cannon and armoured vehicles penetrated the forest. 'We thought we had run twenty kilometres, but actually we circled an area of half a kilometre.'

In the village of Bialka, near Parczew, Jews found refuge with the villagers. But on the second day of the hunt, December 7, the Germans entered the village and shot ninety-six Poles for helping Jews. Three days later, in the village of Wola Przybyslawska, seven Poles were executed by the Germans for hiding Jews.

Over Italy, British bombers had continued to strike at naval installations. In a raid on Naples on December 4, a light cruiser, *Muzio Attendolo,* was sunk, and 159 Italians killed. That day, however, in the Tunisian battle which these air strikes were intended to help, the Germans counter-attacked, destroying twenty-five British tanks and taking four hundred prisoners. Two days later, on December 6, German armoured forces broke through the American positions at El Guettar.

The Italians, Germany's ally in the Tunisian battle, sought unusual means to advance the Axis cause. On the night of December 7 three Italian manned-torpedoes – known as 'Chariots' – tried to enter Gibraltar harbour. Of the six men who made up their crews, three were killed in action, two taken prisoner, and one returned to the support ship. No damage was done to Gibraltar harbour or to the ships in it. Four days later, however, another three Chariots entered Algiers harbour, sinking four Allied supply ships.

In the Far East, the Japanese made two further unsuccessful attempts to reinforce their troops both on Guadalcanal and New Guinea. Both attempts were repulsed on December 8. On the following day, the Australians overcame the last Japanese resistance in the Gona area. When the final battle ended, more than five hundred Japanese dead lay on the battlefield; once more, they had refused to surrender.

On the Russian front, German efforts to regain the initiative around Stalingrad, on the Don, and in the Caucasus, came to nothing; the German Air Force Enigma messages made it clear that there had been such heavy losses in transport aircraft sent to the Tunisian front that there were no longer enough to satisfy the needs of the Stalingrad defenders. Reading these Enigma messages in London, Churchill asked his Chief of Intelligence, Sir Stuart Menzies: 'Is any of this being sent to Joe?' It was; Stalin was kept well informed by London of deficiencies and setbacks in the German reinforcements being sent to Stalingrad.

In the Caucasus, on December 11, the Germans withdrew to the Mozdok–Elista line, accepting that their bid to reach the Caspian Sea had finally failed. On the following day, in the Kotelnikovo area, less than a hundred miles south-west of Stalingrad, the Germans launched Operation Winter Storm, hoping to break through to the trapped Sixth Army. For two days, it seemed as if the link-up might be made, but then Russian reinforcements hurried forward to check the German thrust, while other Russian troops attacked along the River Don north-west of Stalingrad, wiping out the whole of the Italian Eighth Army, and part of the Roumanian Third Army. The Germans, rushing reinforcements to this weakened sector of the front, were forced to take troops away from Winter Storm, itself under threat. The Stalingrad trap remained closed.

Far from the battleheads of the Volga and the Don, in the quiet waters of the River Gironde, December 12 saw the culmination of a daring commando raid, when twelve British commandos, brought to the river estuary by submarine, went upriver by canoe and, during five consecutive days and nights in enemy waters, placed limpet mines on eight ships. All eight ships were blown up, to Hitler's intense anger, and Britain's delight.

There was an even greater British triumph on the following day, although it had to be kept secret from all but a dozen or so of those at the centre of war direction. This was the breaking of the German U-boat Enigma key, known to the British as 'Shark', which had been unreadable for more than a year. In

November 1942 the Allies had lost 721,700 tons of merchant shipping to German submarine attack, the highest figure for any month of the war. The success of mid-December came none too soon. Whereas, in November, eighty-three Allied ships had been torpedoed, in December the figure fell to forty-four and in January 1943 to thirty-three. It was a triumph of cryptography, and also a testimony to the bravery of the two British seamen, Tony Fasson and Colin Grazier, who, at the end of October, had lost their lives while retrieving an Enigma machine and highly secret signal documents off the Nile Delta.

In Tunisia, the Germans were confronted by one aspect of Italian rule which they did not like. 'The Italians are extremely lax in their treatment of Jews,' Goebbels wrote in his diary on December 13, and he went on to explain: 'They protect Italian Jews both in Tunis and in occupied France and won't permit their being drafted for work or compelled to wear the Star of David.' Nor would the Italians agree to deport to Auschwitz either the Jews in Italian occupied France and Croatia, or those in Italy itself. The Germans could only deport Jews from those countries where the local police force was prepared to co-operate at least in the round-ups and initial incarceration in holding camps; thus, from Westerbork camp in Holland, three trains, with a total of 2,500 Jews on board, were sent eastward to Auschwitz that December. From German-occupied Poland, however, the deportations were almost over. Nearly three million Polish Jews had been murdered in the previous twelve months at Chelmno, Belzec, Sobibor and Treblinka.

During December, the Germans began to 'liquidate' the various labour camps which had been set up at the time of the deportations, killing in each camp the few hundred Jews who had been kept alive to service a factory or a farm. At a camp near Kruszyna, 557 Jews were killed on December 17; a week later the 218 slave labourers at Minsk Mazowiecki were done to death and, a week after that, the four hundred at Karczew. Nor was it the Jews alone who continued to be rounded up and deported; on December 16 Himmler issued an order whereby all individuals of mixed Gypsy blood should be sent to Auschwitz. The only exceptions to this order were Gypsies who agreed to be sterilized. By a cruel coincidence, December 16 was also the day on which, at Auschwitz, ninety castration experiments were made on Polish, non-Jewish, prisoners in the camp, who were subjected to experiments so painful that many of them, as one eye-witness has recalled, 'often crawled on the floor in their pain'. After a long period of suffering, those on whom the experiments were made were sent to the gas chamber.

December 16 also saw the publication of an order issued by the German Commander-in-Chief, Field Marshal Keitel, at Hitler's instigation, intended to curb partisan activity both in Russia and in Yugoslavia. 'If the fight against the partisans in the East, as well as in the Balkans, is not waged with the most brutal means,' the order read, 'we shall shortly reach the point where the available forces are insufficient to control this area. It is therefore not only justified, but it is the duty of the troops to use all means without restriction, even against women and children, so long as it ensures success.' Any 'consideration' for the partisans, the order ended, 'is a crime against the German people'.

On December 17, the three principal Allies – Britain, the Soviet Union and the United States – issued a declaration in each of their capitals, announcing that 'the German authorities, not content with denying to persons of Jewish race in all the territories over which their barbarous rule has been extended the most elementary human rights, are now carrying into effect Hitler's oft-repeated intention to exterminate the Jewish people in Europe'. From all the occupied countries, the Allied declaration continued, 'Jews are being transported, in conditions of appalling horror and brutality, to Eastern Europe. In Poland, which has been made the principal Nazi slaughterhouse, the ghettos established by the German invaders are being systematically emptied of all Jews except a few highly skilled workers required for war industries. None of these taken away are ever heard of again. The able-bodied are slowly worked to death in labour camps. The infirm are left to die of exposure and starvation or are deliberately massacred in mass executions. The number of victims of these bloody cruelties is reckoned in many hundreds of thousands of entirely innocent men, women and children'.

The Allied declaration went on to state that the British, Soviet and American governments, and also General de Gaulle's French National Committee, 'condemn in the strongest possible terms this bestial policy of cold-blooded extermination'.

On the field of battle, the Allies continued everywhere in the ascendant, except in Tunisia, where they were bogged down by wintry conditions and unexpected opposition. On Guadalcanal and in New Guinea, the Japanese were being pushed steadily back. Around Stalingrad, the Russians continued to widen the gap between the encircled German armies and those seeking to break through to them. In Libya, the German and Italian forces were retreating westward. 'We're in heavy fighting again', Rommel wrote to his wife on December 18, 'with little hope of success, for we're short of everything.' Petrol in particular was short, he added, 'and without petrol there's nothing to be done'.

On December 19, German forces which had come to within forty miles of Stalingrad made yet another attempt to link up with the trapped troops under von Paulus. But, despite a massive effort, they were checked by the Russians, and on the following day, at Rastenburg, even Hitler accepted that von Paulus could not be reached. Nor, it seemed, could he now break out; his tanks had fuel for less than fifteen miles.

In the Caucasus, the Russians had succeeded by late December in infiltrating as many as eight hundred partisans behind the German lines near Budyonnovsk. These partisans were active in mining railroads and bridges, destroying fuel oil depots, seizing control of small settlements, recruiting new partisans and killing collaborators. 'We have destroyed about fifty Germans and Cossacks,' one partisan noted in his diary on December 21. When, six days later, Cossack and Kalmyk units, working for the Germans, raided the partisan base, the partisans had already moved elsewhere.

On December 22, an act of defiance was carried out in the very centre of German-occupied Europe, in the Polish city of Cracow, where six members of the Jewish Fighting Organization, which had been set up in Poland five months earlier, attacked a café frequented by the ss and the Gestapo. Armed only with pistols, their attack was bound to fail. The aim of the attack, one of them later wrote, was 'to save what could be saved, at least of honour'. Their leader, Adolf Liebeskind, was killed by German machine-gun fire. 'We are fighting', he had remarked a few weeks before the attack, 'for three lines in the history books.'

Outside Stalingrad, a German armoured column managed on December 23 to come to within thirty miles of the besieged Sixth Army. But with tank fuel for only a fifteen mile movement, von Paulus could no longer plan a breakout with any serious chance of success. Fuel oil was also the cause of Rommel's failure that week to do anything but slowly withdraw to the west. On Christmas Eve, at his Headquarters Company's Christmas Party, Rommel was given as a present a miniature petrol drum, containing, instead of petrol, a pound or two of captured British coffee. 'Thus proper homage was paid', Rommel noted, 'to our most serious problem, even on that day.'

On Christmas Eve, on the Eastern Front, the besieged von Paulus learned ominous news. Because of a swift Russian advance against the German forces already driven south of the Don, towards Millerovo, the 6th Panzer Division was being taken away from the armoured units still seeking to break through to Stalingrad, and transferred to the Don. The only German success that day was a secret one, the successful test launching of the first flying bomb, a jet-propelled, pilotless aircraft, which flew a mile and a half at the test site at Peenemünde. At least a year's more testing and developing would need to be done, as well as the building of suitable sites in north-western France, but at least a German secret weapon now existed, from which a great deal was hoped. As with the American atomic pile at Chicago, so with the German flying bomb at Peenemünde, the most fanciful ideas of pre-war science were being turned into reality, in order to meet the demands of total war.

As science made its slow, experimental progress in laboratory and testing ground, terror advanced with no delays or hesitations; on December 24, in the Parczew forest, the Germans launched a second manhunt. Several hundred Jews in hiding in a 'family camp' were seized and slaughtered. The survivors, unarmed, frightened, freezing and without food, were fortunate: they found a protector, the twenty-four-year-old Yekhiel Grynszpan, from a family of local horse-traders, who, that winter, built up a partisan unit of thirty to forty Jews, foraged for food, acquired arms from the local Polish peasants whom his family had known before the war, and, when German soldiers entered the forest, fought them off. Also on December 24, the day of the Parczew 'sweep', the Germans entered the Polish village of Bialowieza, and executed three hundred Poles for partisan activity. Today, a monument stands in silent testimony on the site of their mass grave.

In Tunisia, throughout December 24, the Allies battled in vain to break through the Axis defences. There was excitement throughout North Africa that day as news spread that Admiral Darlan had been assassinated by a French student in Algiers. 'Darlan's murder,' Churchill later wrote, 'however criminal, relieved the Allies of their embarrassment at working with him, and at the same time left them with all the advantages he had been able to bestow during the vital hours of the Allied landings.' In Darlan's place as High Commissioner and Commander-in-Chief of the French forces in Morocco and Algeria, the Allies appointed General Giraud.

On December 27, at Rastenburg, Hitler listened as General Zeitzler advised him that German forces should withdraw from the Caucasus. If not, Zeitzler warned, 'you will have a second Stalingrad on your hands'. Hitler accepted this advice. Two days later, on December 29, the Russians retook Kotelnikovo, from which the Germans had begun their attempt to spring the Stalingrad trap. 'Outwardly one has to be optimistic about the future in 1943,' King George VI noted in his diary that day, 'but inwardly I am depressed at the present prospect.'

As 1942 came to an end, the Axis powers were in retreat in Libya, on Guadalcanal and New Guinea, and at Stalingrad and in the Caucasus. Partisan activity, though savagely suppressed, was also proving more and more effective. Yet at the same time, as well as maintaining its position in Tunisia, the Axis were still in full control of vast expanses of territory, and of hundreds of millions of captive people throughout Europe and Asia.

In south-east Asia and the Pacific, the forces of Japan were installed over an enormous area, from the borders of India to the islands of Alaska. In Europe, the Germans were masters from the Pyrenees to the North Cape, and from Cape Finisterre to Cape Matapan. Tyranny, too, was uncurbed. On December 29, sixty-nine villagers in tiny Bialowola, in central Poland, had been driven into the school house and shot. But this massacre, terrible as it was, paled into insignificance when seen in the context of the death that December, at nearby Poniatowa, of a total of eighteen thousand Soviet prisoners-of-war; they had died of starvation – prisoners in a camp in which they had been denied all food. On December 31, at Rastenburg, Hitler was shown a report, signed by Himmler, giving a precise statistic of the number of 'Jews executed' for the four months August to November. The figure given was 363,211.

In the Arctic, Captain Robert Sherbrooke, in command of a British destroyer force, beat off a sustained German naval attack led by the battleship *Lützow* and the heavy cruiser *Admiral Hipper*, on a Russia-bound Arctic convoy. During the action, Sherbrooke was hit in the face, losing the use of one eye, but continued to direct the defence to such good effect that not a single merchant ship was lost or damaged. For his defiance and courage, Sherbrooke was awarded the Victoria Cross.

That New Year's Eve, British bombers dropped their bombs on Düsseldorf. They did so on a cloudy night, but with a new device, 'Oboe', a radio beam which enabled bombs to be dropped on target, or as near to target as possible, without anything of the towns being visible from the air. Science, no longer neutral, had come to the aid of deliberate destruction.

# 29

# Casablanca, blueprint for victory

JANUARY 1943

For the Germans, the year 1943 opened badly. In both Tunisia and Libya, the Allies were clearly poised for the destruction of all Axis forces in North Africa. On the Eastern Front, amid the rigours of winter, partisan bands were so active and ubiquitous that three separate operations were about to be launched against them: 'Polar Bear II' between Bryansk and Dmitriev, 'Winter Magic' in Lithuania, and 'Burdock' around Kletnya. On the Eastern Front itself, despite reinforcements brought hurriedly from France, the German forces which had so recently come to within thirty miles of their colleagues trapped in Stalingrad were now pushed back 120 miles south-west of the city, while, in the northern sector of the front, despite a tenacious defence, the Germans were driven from Velikiye Luki.

Despite the setbacks on the battlefield, the Final Solution went on without interruption. At four concentration camps in Yugoslavia, Loborgrad, Jasenovac, Stara Gradiska and Djakovo, more than thirty thousand Jews – men, women and children – had been starved to death or shot by the opening days of 1943. Some were able to escape the round-ups. Of more than four thousand who did so, and who then joined the partisans, 1,318 were killed in battle.

In France, that January, a Frenchman, Joseph Darnard, set up a police force of 25,000 men. Known as the Milice, this force worked in close collaboration with the Gestapo, helping to arrest any Frenchmen suspected of resistance activities, and to round up Jews.

Repression was only one facet of Nazi racial policy; confidence in the race was such that Himmler envisaged replenishing German stock by deliberate means. Seven years earlier, in December 1935, he had established the Lebensborn Organization – its literal meaning was 'Spring of Life' – to pursue his racial theories. The idea was to replenish SS stock lost as a result of the fighting in the East, and to do so by organizing extra-marital procreation between SS men and suitable partners. By January 1943 there were more than twenty Lebensborn houses throughout German-occupied Europe, several of them in Norway, which Himmler felt had special merit as an 'Aryan–Nordic' breeding ground. In Eastern Europe, children from Slavic backgrounds who were thought to have suitably Germanic traits were taken forcibly from their parents, transported to Germany and offered for adoption to childless ss and Nazi Party couples; an estimated 70,000 mothers and children had passed through Lebensborn houses or adoption centres by 1945.

Racial purity was the Nazi ideal; setbacks at Stalingrad and in North Africa were the German reality. In the Far East, 1943 also opened badly for the Japanese, with the decision to evacuate the island of Guadalcanal. All hope of holding the Solomon Islands was now lost, and with it all chance of controlling the approaches to Australia. In New Guinea, the Japanese now gave up their last defensive stronghold, at Buna Mission, with many of the defenders swimming out to sea in order to die, rather than be taken prisoner. The garrison commander, a colonel, committed suicide rather than bear the disgrace of surrender. Even on the Indian frontier with Burma, the British felt confident enough to begin to attempt a reconquest of Burma, launching Operation Cannibal on January 1, from Chittagong towards Donbaik.

In the Philippines, an American Army officer, Captain Ralph B. Praeger, who had escaped into the interior of Luzon when Corregidor fell, transmitted a radio message on January 3, to General MacArthur. He had managed to get together five thousand Filipinos, and needed only an air drop of arms to begin a massive sabotage campaign.

MacArthur refused Captain Praeger's request, partly because his own resources were being strained to the utmost by the campaign in New Guinea, and partly for fear of Japanese reprisals against Filipino civilians. Instead he instructed Praeger to confine his activities to Intelligence gathering. But for many of the Filipinos in Praeger's area, the ambush of Japanese soldiers became a way of life, despite the savage reprisals which each ambush provoked.

On January 4 the Germans were driven from Mozdok, in the Caucasus, the most eastern important town captured during their advance the previous August. The mountain town of Nalchik, fifty miles to the west, was lost on the following day. A swift advance was being replaced by an even swifter retreat.

In German-occupied Europe, the pace of deportation and killing was relentless, often marked by bizarre and effective deception. On January 5, all Jews in the Polish town of Opoczno were told that those with relatives in Palestine would be allowed to leave, as part of an official exchange scheme: Palestinian Jews for German nationals caught in Palestine at the outbreak of war. Five hundred Jews registered for the exchange. They were taken away by train, not to Palestine, but to Treblinka, and to their death. On the following day, the first of fifteen trains to reach Auschwitz that January arrived from Belgium, to be followed by trains from Holland, Berlin, Grodno and the Bialystok region. Of the twenty-four thousand deportees on these trains, all but four thousand were gassed on their arrival at Auschwitz.

On January 8, the commander of the Russian Don front, General Rokossovsky, sent General von Paulus an ultimatum with terms for the surrender of his forces trapped in Stalingrad. Von Paulus, unwilling to disobey Hitler's orders against any surrender, rejected the Russian demand. On the following morning, Rokos-sovsky gave the orders to begin Operation Ring, the direct assault on the trapped German forces. As Soviet troops renewed their assault, the Germans had to continue to fight with less and less chance of airborne supplies reaching them; 490 transport and bomber-transport aircraft were shot down trying to fly in supplies to the two remaining airfields under German control. Inside the trap, 12,000 wounded men were without medical supplies.

As the Red Army's ring closed around Stalingrad, the siege of Leningrad was about to come to an end, as, on January 13, Soviet troops launched Operation Spark, breaking through the German lines, and opening a narrow corridor, only ten miles wide, south of Lake Ladoga. Through this corridor, supplies could travel by land; within a week of the corridor being opened, men, arms, munitions and food were entering the city. But so narrow was the strip over which these supplies could pass, and so ferocious the German artillery bombardment against it, lasting for another year, that it soon became known as the 'Corridor of Death'.

On January 14, Roosevelt and Churchill met at Casablanca, in newly liberated French North Africa, to co-ordinate the next stage of their joint war policy. During their meeting, they publicly reaffirmed that the 'unconditional surrender' of Germany and Japan was their unalterable policy. Also reached at Casablanca was an Anglo-American agreement – made as a result of a clear warning by the Combined Chiefs of Staff of the many problems of supply and preparation – not to launch the cross-Channel liberation of German-occupied Europe until the early summer of 1944. Even the Sicily landing would not take place until later than originally intended. Stalin was not alone in being disappointed at the time lags, especially for the cross-Channel attack. An American observer, the diplomat Averell Harriman, noted during the Conference that Churchill and Roosevelt, while 'much pleased with the meeting', were both 'disappointed by the slowness of the new moves'.

As the Casablanca Conference continued, Soviet forces, driving towards Stalingrad from the north-west, overran the principal German supply airfield at Pitomnik. Only one airfield, the much smaller Gumrak, now linked the Germans with the outside forces that could no longer come to their aid by land.

Behind German lines, on January 15, the German Army launched its fourth offensive against Tito's partisans in Yugoslavia. The campaign, Operation White, was commanded by General Alexander von Löhr, and was the largest military operation conducted by the German forces in Yugoslavia since their invasion in April 1941. Joining the German forces were a considerable number of Italian troops, as well as the Croat Ustache forces of Ante Pavelić, who had earlier been flown to see Hitler at Vinnitsa in order to stiffen his resolve.

Forcing the partisans from their headquarters at Bihac, on the border of Croatia and Bosnia, the troops of Operation White drove them more than two hundred miles southward, to the inhospitable slopes of the 8,290-foot Mount Durmitor, in Montenegro. That same day, in German-occupied Russia, during an anti-partisan sweep near Kletnya, 441 partisans were killed. Also on January 15, in Paris, the thirty-three-year-old Kurt Lishka was appointed commander of the German Security Police, responsible for planning and supervising the continuing deportation of Jews from France to Auschwitz. That same day, in Brussels, the Gestapo began a series of arrests which was soon to break the 'Comet' escape line from Belgium, Holland and France to the Pyrenees, through which more than a hundred Allied airmen had been brought to safety, and in most cases returned to their Air Force tasks. Several hundred of those who had helped organize or guard the escape route were arrested; many of them were killed in captivity, or died of ill-treatment. A few escaped through Spain to Britain. One who stayed behind, Jean Greindl, whose code name was 'Nemo', tried to protect those few still in hiding from arrest; but he himself was arrested three weeks later, and condemned to death. Before the death sentence could be carried out, however, Greindl was killed by an Allied bomb in an air raid.

Air raids were a principal theme of the continuing discussions at Casablanca, where Roosevelt and Churchill agreed that the bombing of Germany both by day and by night, and on a massive scale, should be intensified, in order to achieve not only 'the progressive destruction and dislocation of the German military, industrial and economic system', but also, as their secret directive explained, 'the undermining of the morale of the German people to a point where their capacity for armed resistance is fatally weakened'. On January 16, five days before this directive was finalized, British bombers carried out their first heavy raid on Berlin for more than fourteen months.

In the Far East, in New Guinea, January 16 saw a combined American and Australian attack on Sanananda; after nine days of battle the Japanese forces were destroyed, and three thousand killed. But still the Japanese refused to give up their dwindling hold. Nor would they do so on Guadalcanal, where, despite a decision in Tokyo to withdraw from the island in February, the fighting went on, and an American call by loudspeaker, inviting the Japanese to surrender, was rejected.

It had been nearly four months since the Germans had stopped their daily deportations from Warsaw to Treblinka, but on January 18 a German unit entered the ghetto to start up the deportation again. Six hundred Jews were killed in the streets as the brutal round-up began, and six thousand were deported to Treblinka and their deaths. As the renewed deportations began, a group of Jews who had managed to acquire arms fired back. Several Germans fell. Then the Germans began to return the fire, the machine-gun bullets of the conqueror challenging the pistol shots of the Jews. Nine of the Jewish fighters were killed. 'For the first time since the occupation,' one young Jew, Tuvia Borzykowski, later recalled, 'we saw Germans clinging to walls, crawling on the ground, running for cover, hesitating before taking a step in the fear of being hit by a Jewish bullet'. The cries of the wounded Germans, Borzykowski added, 'caused us joy, and increased our thirst for battle'.

That battle came, on the following day, and again on January 21, when grenades were thrown at the buildings in which Jews sought to resist. 'All through the day,' Borzykowski recalled, 'the ghetto resounded to the explosions in which hundreds of Jews perished.' But the resistance continued, and forty

Jews, going from house to house and rooftop to rooftop, not all of them armed, but taking arms from the Germans, kept up the firing. Then, to the amazement of the fighters, the Germans withdrew from the ghetto. 'At the time,' Borzykowski later wrote, 'we had only ten pistols.' Had the Germans known this, they would probably have continued the raids, and Jewish resistance 'would have been nipped in the bud as a minor, insignificant episode'. 'We obtained faith', another of the Jewish fighters, Yitzhak Zuckerman, later recalled, 'that we can fight; we know how to fight.'

Twelve Germans had been killed in battle with the Jews. The German units withdrew, to leave the ghetto for a later time. On January 18, west of Osipovichi, Operation Harvest Home was launched against Soviet partisans. That same day, in Norway, five Englishmen who had been captured during the glider raid the previous November were taken to a forest outside Oslo and shot.

Inside Germany itself, the effect of the recent setbacks in North Africa and Russia was beginning to be felt. 'The times have grown very grave, in the East also,' Rommel wrote to his wife from Tunisia on January 19, and he added: 'There's going to be total mobilization for every single German without regard for place of residence, status, property, or age.' The supply position, Rommel wrote on January 20, 'is making our situation more difficult every day'. During a meeting that day between Rommel and the Italian Commander-in-Chief, Marshal Cavallero, 'the bad news came in', Rommel later recalled, 'that British torpedo boats had sunk ten out of fourteen petrol barges west of Tripoli'.

Unknown to Rommel or Cavallero, it was their own top-secret Enigma and c 38m radio messages, decrypted at Bletchley, which were enabling the British to locate and then destroy almost every supply ship or barge which set off from Italy carrying fuel and ammunition.

In the Far East, the British launched Operation Bunkum on January 19, landing six men by submarine on the west coast of the Japanese-occupied Middle Andaman Island, a thousand miles south-east of Calcutta. Working their way through dense jungle and mangrove swamps, three of the six, led by Major D. McCarthy, former Commandant of the Andamans Police, reached the capital, Port Blair, and made a detailed study of the defences. For thirty-two days they moved through enemy territory, covering a total of 130 miles. Returning to Ceylon, Major McCarthy reported that 'Japanese brutality, which consists of public beating and limb-breaking at the smallest provocation', made the Andaman Islands a fertile ground for subversion. But it was to be more than a year before their efforts could be followed up.

In reprisal for the two bombing raids on Berlin, German bombers now returned to Britain in force for the first time in almost two years. In a single week of renewed aerial bombardment, 328 British civilians were killed, including thirty-nine schoolchildren on January 20, when a school was hit at Lewisham, in South London. It was also on January 20, from his desk in Berlin, that Himmler sent the German Minister of Transport a top secret letter about 'the removal of Jews' from the General Government, the Eastern Territories and 'the West'.

For this purpose, Himmler wrote, 'I need your help and support. If I am to wind things up quickly, I must have more trains for transports.' 'I know very well', Himmler added, 'how difficult the situation is for the railways and what demands are constantly made of you. Just the same, I must make this request of you: help me get more trains.'

That same day, the deportations from Theresienstadt to Auschwitz were renewed, with two thousand deportees sent 'to the East'. On reaching Auschwitz, 1,760 were gassed.

In a train which left Holland on the day after Himmler wrote his letter on the need for 'more trains', the deportees included several hundred mental patients from the Jewish mental hospital at Apeldoorn. Before the train left Apeldoorn, the commander of the German Security Police in Holland, Ferdinand aus der Fünten, called for volunteers among the hospital nurses to accompany the train. Twenty came forward; he himself chose a further thirty. The 'volunteers' travelled in a separate wagon, at the back of the train. All were offered the choice of returning home immediately after the journey, or working in a 'really modern mental home'. On reaching Auschwitz, nurses and patients alike were sent to the gas chambers. Not one survived: neither the sick, nor those who had been devoted to their care.

On the day after the deportation from Apeldoorn to Auschwitz, thirty Jewish orphans were seized from their orphanage in Marseille, together with their guardian, Alice Salomon, who insisted upon going wherever they were going; it was to Sobibor, and to their deaths. That week, eighty miles east of Marseille, the Germans tried to round up Jews living in the Italian zone of occupation; but on January 23 the Italian authorities refused to co-operate, and no deportations took place.

On January 22, a German Top Secret report gave details of the success of Operation Hamburg, an anti-partisan sweep behind the German lines in Russia, in the area of Slonim. In all, 1,676 partisans had been killed, as well as 1,510 civilians 'on the grounds that they belonged to the gangs'. Four armoured cars and eight machine guns had also been captured, as well as cattle and grain.

Later that month, in Yugoslavia, during the German anti-partisan sweep, Operation White, Tito's partisans agreed to a German request for a limited exchange of prisoners. Among the partisans returned under the exchange was Tito's wife, Herta. As the partisan retreat continued, Tito appealed to Stalin for material help, but Stalin replied that there were 'insurmountable technical difficulties'. When, a few days later, Moscow complained about the partisan-German agreement for the prisoner exchange, Tito replied: 'If you cannot understand what a hard time we are having, and if you cannot help us, then at least do not hinder us'.


On January 21, as Soviet forces continued to drive forward towards Stalingrad and, on the Caucasus front, captured the main German Air Force base and supply centre at Salsk, the British eavesdroppers at Bletchley broke yet another of the Enigma keys, known to them as 'Porcupine', which provided the Allies for the next crucial month with all German Air Force messages relating to ground–air co-operation in south Russia.

On January 22, in the Pacific, off the north-eastern tip of Australia, a Japanese seaplane dive-bombed a boat sailing off Lower Wessell Island. The boat was sunk, and six of those on board were killed. Moments later, the seaplane landed, and its crew seized one of the surviving Australians, Leonard Kentish, a missionary. Kentish was taken away in the seaplane. Later, on one of the Japanese held islands of New Guinea, he was beheaded. By an extraordinary chance, an eye witness to his death survived, and, in August 1948, his executioner, Lieutenant Sagejima Mangan, was brought to trial in Hong Kong, and executed.

In the Far East, both on Guadalcanal and in New Guinea, the Japanese forces were facing the possibility of a defeat on land. It came on January 22, when the American and Australian forces on New Guinea overran the last pockets of Japanese resistance west and south of Sanananda. An estimated seven thousand Japanese soldiers had been killed during the campaign; the American and Australian forces lost three thousand. Almost no Japanese had allowed themselves to be taken prisoner; most of the 350 prisoners taken were Chinese or Korean labourers attached to the Japanese forces.

Even as the Japanese were driven for the first time from one of their principal land conquests, the German and Italian forces in North Africa were driven from Tripoli, in which they had been so powerful less than a year earlier. Falling back towards Tunisia, they were constantly pursued and harassed by Montgomery's forces.

At Casablanca, Roosevelt and Churchill held their final plenary meeting on January 23. Speaking of assistance to Russia, in relation to the other commitments of Britain and the United States, Roosevelt suggested retaining in the next round of supply negotiations the sentence in the Combined Chiefs of Staff report that 'supply to Russia will not be continued at prohibitive cost to the United Nations efforts'. But Churchill replied that aid to Russia 'must be pushed and no investment could pay a better dividend'. The United Nations, Churchill insisted, 'cannot let Russia down'.

In the discussions which followed, however, two of the American Chiefs of Staff, Admiral King and General Marshall, stressed the extent of the shipping losses to the northern convoys. 'Such losses,' Marshall warned, 'made it impossible for us to attack on other fronts and thus eliminate the possibility of forcing the Germans to withdraw ground and air troops from the Russian front.' It must be 'made certain', Marshall added, that, by continuing the convoys to Russia, 'we do not hazard' the success of the Sicily landing.

If 'passage of convoys on the northern route were prohibitive in cost', Churchill agreed, 'they must be stopped'. Whatever was decided, Churchill added, Stalin must be told 'the facts'. The convoys would be stopped 'if the losses are too great'.

The conference then discussed the timing for the Sicily landings. Churchill pressed for the earliest possible date, telling Roosevelt 'that he feared the gap of perhaps four months during the summer when no United States or British troops would be in contact with the Germans'. Roosevelt accepted this argument, commenting that such a gap 'might have a serious effect all over the world'.

Churchill then pressed for a June date for the landings in Sicily. But, after General Marshall warned of the need to avoid any timing which would be 'at the expense of adequate preparation', it was agreed that the July date should stand, 'subject to an instruction that in the next three weeks, without prejudice to the July date, there would be an intense effort made to try and achieve the favourable June moon as the date of the operation'.

The eight days of discussions, 'almost continuously', at Casablanca, of every facet of Anglo-American war policy had been, Churchill reported in his telegram that day to the War Cabinet in London, 'from one point of view, very remarkable'. The priority of 'Hitler's extinction' as against the defeat of Japan had been re-established. Priority had been secured for the Mediterranean, as against the cross-Channel assault that summer, but without prejudice to the 'maximum' development of the build-up in Britain of the forces that would be needed for an eventual cross-Channel landing, in 1944.

On the Eastern Front, on 24 January 1943, the Germans were driven from Voronezh, and in the north Caucasus from Armavir. From Stalingrad, that day, von Paulus asked Hitler for permission to surrender. 'The Sixth Army', Hitler replied, 'will hold its positions to the last man and the last round.' That day, the Russians overran von Paulus's last airfield, at Gumrak. In North Africa, Rommel's troops, retreating continually westward, crossed into Tunisia at Ben Gardane, and began to prepare a defensive line just west of Médenine.

In Germany, from January 26, because of the urgent need on the front line for more men, anti-aircraft batteries in the Reich itself were manned by members of the Hitler Youth from the age of fifteen and upward. On the following day, the United States Eighth Air Force, based in Britain, carried out its first bombing raid over Germany, against warehouses and factories at Wilhelmshaven. In the air battle above the port, twenty-two German aircraft were shot down, for the loss of only three of the sixty-four American bombers which took part in the attack.

After their conference at Casablanca, Churchill and Roosevelt went to Marrakech, where, in a telegram to Stalin, they told the Soviet leader of their decisions which, they believed, together with the 'powerful' Soviet offensive, 'may well bring Germany to her knees in 1943'.

Their 'main desire', Churchill and Roosevelt told Stalin, had been 'to divert strong German land and air forces from the Russian front and to send Russia the maximum flow of supplies'. No exertion would be spared to send Russia material assistance 'by every available route'. Once the Axis had been cleared out of North Africa, a large-scale amphibious operation would be launched in the Mediterranean, while – from the air bases set up in North Africa – Britain and the United States would launch 'an intensive bombardment of important Axis targets in southern Europe'. The allied bomber offensive against Germany from Britain would also be increased 'at a rapid rate'.

Churchill and Roosevelt explained to Stalin: 'We believe an increased tempo and weight of daylight and night attacks will lead to greatly increased material and morale damage in Germany and rapidly deplete German fighter strength. As you are aware, we are already containing more than half the German air force in Western Europe and the Mediterranean. We have no doubt our intensified and diversified bombing offensive, together with the other operations which we are undertaking, will compel further withdrawals of German air and other forces from the Russian front.'

Partisan activities were rapidly becoming an embarrassment to the Germans throughout German-occupied Europe; on January 28, as the battles raged west of Voronezh, Stalingrad and Armavir, German armed forces launched Operation Harvest Home II against Soviet partisan forces west of the Minsk–Slutsk road, two hundred miles behind the front line.

Further behind the lines, far from the battlefield or the partisans, death still came for acts of courage; on January 29, in Wierzbica, near Radom, three Polish families who had been hiding Jews were shot; among the fifteen Poles who were killed that day was a two-year-old girl. Even further west, as several hundred French volunteers left Paris to fight for Germany on the Eastern Front, the words 'Death to the Jews' were scrawled on their railway carriages. That same day, also by train, 869 Jews were taken from Westerbork in Holland, and a thousand Jews from Berlin, for Auschwitz.

To ensure that the process of destruction would run efficiently, on January 30, the tenth anniversary of his coming to power in Germany, Hitler appointed his fellow Austrian, Ernst Kaltenbrunner, as head of the Reich Central Security Office, in charge of co-ordinating the round-ups and deportations. Under him, it was Heinrich Müller who signed the orders whereby the Jews were actually deported; one such order required the delivery to Auschwitz of 45,000 Jews by January 31.

Above Germany, British bombers, carrying out the Casablanca directive of Roosevelt and Churchill, attacked Berlin during the daylight hours of January 30 and Hamburg that same night. The raid on Berlin had been timed to coincide with radio broadcasts by both Goering and Goebbels, on the tenth anniversary of Nazi rule. During his broadcast, Goebbels declared: 'A thousand years hence, every German will speak with awe of Stalingrad and remember that it was there that Germany put the seal on her victory.'

Also on January 31, Hitler appointed von Paulus to be a Field Marshal. It was the very day on which von Paulus surrendered. The German Sixth Army, victors in May 1940 in Holland and Belgium, had now been cut into two separate pockets. Forty-eight hours after von Paulus, in one pocket, surrendered, those in the second pocket also gave up. Of the 284,000 German soldiers originally caught in the Stalingrad trap, 160,000 had been killed in action by January 31. A further 34,000 had been evacuated by air. The survivors, 90,000 frost-bitten and wounded men, were marched eastward, on foot, to Siberia. Tens of thousands died during the march, and tens of thousands more in captivity.

Goebbels's boasting, and Hitler's confidence, had for the first time been held up to mockery. The news of the surrender of so vast a German force, and of Stalingrad's liberation, brought renewed hope to the armies struggling against Germany, and to the captive peoples suffering so cruelly throughout German-occupied Europe. After nearly three and a half years of victories, conquests, advances and the exhilaration of creating fear and uncertainty, the Germans appeared vulnerable. The inevitability of triumph was gone. That day, determined not to lose a single hour of advantage, Allied bombers struck at German airfields and military installations in Sicily.

In the Far East, Japanese troops on New Guinea, with the defeats of Bona and Gona behind them, had tried to reach Port Moresby on January 28 by an attack on the Australian garrison at Wau, but they were beaten off. Near Rennell Island, however, as American reinforcements sailed towards Guadalcanal, Japanese aircraft mounted an attack, sinking the American heavy cruiser *Chicago* on January 30. Twenty-one Americans were killed, but more than a thousand were taken off safely before the ship went down.

On February 1, in Burma, the Japanese successfully repulsed an attack by Indian troops on the garrison at Donbaik. Unknown to the Japanese, February 1 was also the day on which, at Oak Ridge, Tennessee, ground was broken for the first ever manufacturing plant for the uranium-235 needed to build an atomic bomb. To ensure secrecy and seclusion for the ninety-two acre site, a thousand local families were forced to move away. In their place came engineers and scientists whose number was in due course to reach 82,000, as their deadly work drew closer and closer to completion.

As an earnest of the struggle that still lay ahead on the Eastern Front, on February 2 the Soviet Government announced in Moscow the creation of a new medal, 'To a Partisan of the War for the Fatherland', to be awarded by commanders of partisan headquarters to members of their units. On the following day, in Berlin, German radio announced a two day period of mourning for the 'Stalingrad disaster'. Seizing the advantage of the Germans' discomfiture, on February 3 the Red Army entered Kushchevskaya, south of Rostov, and Kupyansk, east of Kharkov; then, on February 4, in an amphibious assault, Soviet forces landed behind the German lines near Novorossiisk, where, for six days, a small force headed by Major Caesar Kunikov held the beachhead until Soviet forces further along the shore could link up with it. Mortally wounded during the battle, Kunikov was posthumously created a Hero of the Soviet Union.

The day of the Novorossiisk landing, February 4, was, for the Germans, a day of revenge in distant Kovno, when forty-five Jews – men and women – were seized in their various workplaces outside the ghetto, and killed. The Germans dubbed these killings the 'Stalingrad Action'.

On February 5, the Germans were driven from Stary Oksyol and Izyum, while a Soviet advance to Yeisk, on the Sea of Azov, cut off the German forces around Novorossiisk from the main body of troops retreating towards Rostov. As the retreats continued, the Germans had to face an intensification of partisan action as far behind the lines as Gomel. It was against these partisans that Operation Hare Chase was launched on February 6, two hundred and fifty miles behind the front line.

It was on February 6, in Berlin, that Himmler received a detailed report on the 'quantity of old garments' collected from Auschwitz, and the death camps in the Lublin region. The list included, amongst many other items, 22,000 pairs of children's shoes, 155,000 women's coats, and 3,000 kilogrammes of women's hair. The women's hair filled a large railway wagon.

The clothing of the victims was to be distributed in Germany, some of it to the Hitler Youth Leadership. The question had also been raised three weeks earlier, by Himmler personally, after a visit to Warsaw, as to what to do with spectacles and eye-glasses, 'of which hundreds of thousands – perhaps even millions' were lying in warehouses in Warsaw.

The Jewish clothing sent to the Reich filled 825 railway wagons. In addition, the amount of foreign currency, gold and silver listed was considerable, including half a million United States dollars, and 116,420 dollars in gold.

Clothes, valuables, hair: these were among the spoils of the German war against the Jews. Children and their parents were stripped of the very last of their possessions at the entrance to the gas chamber. On February 11, in a deportation from Paris to Auschwitz many of the 123 children under twelve were deported without their parents. All of them were killed. Six days later, in London, Churchill was told that leaflets 'setting out German atrocities' had already been dropped over Germany, and would be dropped again 'when next we raid Berlin'.

As the deportation trains travelled from West to East, the Red Army was advancing steadily from East to West, taking both Azov and Kramatorsk on February 7. Reflecting that day on Stalingrad, Hitler told his Gauleiters gathered to hear him in secret conclave at Rastenburg: 'What you are witnessing is a catastrophe of unheard-of magnitude,' and he added: 'The Russians broke through, the Roumanians gave up, the Hungarians didn't even put up a fight.' Hitler then declared: 'If the German people fails, then it does not deserve that we fight for its future; then we can write it off with equanimity.'

For some of his Gauleiters, faithful and senior Nazi Party men, the governors of the provinces of Greater Germany, Hitler's declaration was one which caused a certain unease. 'Not the right attitude of mind', one of them, Herbert Backe, noted – for his wife's eyes only.

On February 8, the Germans were driven from Kursk, a principal centre of north-south communications, and a strongpoint on their winter line. On the following day they were forced from Belgorod. It was a black moment for those who, five months earlier, had reached the western bank of the Volga and stood in triumph on the highest mountain of the Caucasus. Nor was there any comfort for Germany in the performance of her Japanese ally. On February 9, at 4.25 in the afternoon, all organized resistance on Guadalcanal came to an end. More than nine thousand Japanese troops had been killed, for the loss of two thousand Americans.

Stalingrad and Guadalcanal had shown the Allies that the Axis could be defeated in battle. But both places stood on the periphery of the areas under Axis control. The continent of Europe, and the vast island expanses of South-East Asia, were still under the military rule of those who had chosen to make war. The Allies, for all their recent triumphs, stood at the edge of immense regions confronted by hugely powerful forces still to be overthrown, and still capable of prodigious efforts not only of defence but also of attack.

# 30

## The German armies in danger

FEBRUARY 1943

On 12 February 1943, British forces crossed into Tunisia from the south. Throughout the length of western Tunisia, American and British forces already held a line well inside the frontier. But the initial failure to take Tunis at the time of the Operation Torch landings three months earlier was to cost the Allies dear, as Rommel prepared to send his experienced tanks crews and battle-tested tanks against the inexperienced American forces holding the Kasserine Pass. That same day, on the Eastern Front, the Red Army entered Lozovaya, an important junction south of Kharkov. Nor had the Soviet partisan impetus slackened; on 12 February, in the Rogachev region, more than two hundred miles behind the front line, the Germans were forced to launch a four day military sweep, Operation Ursula. Then, on February 14, the Russians retook Rostov, and the city, which had twice been held by Germany, was now lost forever; so too, that day, was the industrial city of Voroshilovgrad. Only in North Africa was there a brief turn of fortune in favour of Germany on February 14, an attack, devised by Rommel, against the British and American forces in western Tunisia. But on the following day, in eastern Tunisia, British forces entered Ben Gardane. Rommel now began to fortify the Mareth Line.

Those of Rommel's forces which attacked westward on February 14 had, however, an immediate success, driving the inexperienced American forces which faced them back across the Kasserine Pass. But Rommel's object, to drive far back across the Algerian border, failed; his troops were halted before Tébessa, and could make no further progress.

The Allied armies in North Africa still had to face the prospect of a long campaign against two Generals, Rommel and von Arnim, who, under orders from Hitler, would cling to Tunisia with skill and tenacity. Unknown to Rommel or von Arnim, however, the most sensitive element of any General's ability to fight, his system of top secret communications to the high command, had been almost totally undermined. The very Enigma machine which gave both Rommel and von Arnim the welcome knowledge that aircraft reinforcements were on the way, and which transmitted to them their tactical directives,

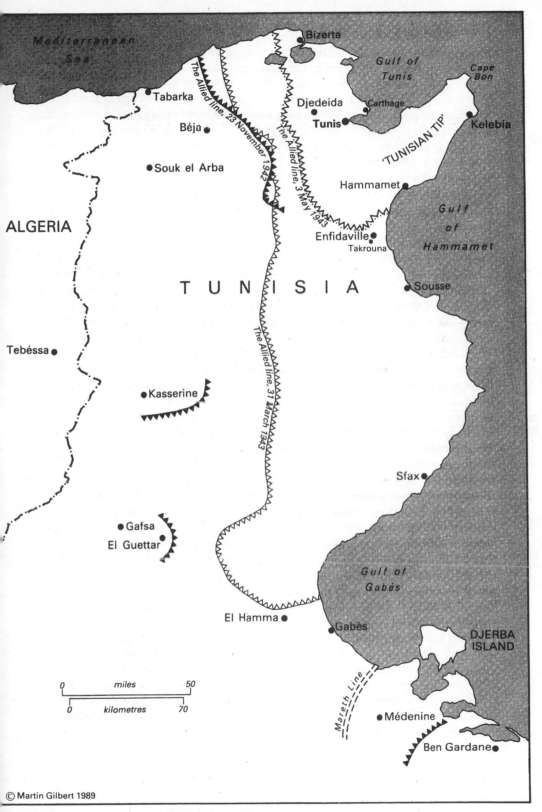

The battle for Tunisia, January–May 1943

enabled their adversaries, from their Signals Intelligence centre in Britain, to monitor their strength and intentions, and to reduce and impede them until the day would come when neither General could hope even to hold a defensive line.

In Burma, on February 14, three thousand British and Gurkha troops of the 77th Indian Brigade, known as the 'Chindits', set off from Imphal towards the inhospitable jungles of Burma, on a mission of sabotage against the Myitkina–Mandalay railway. Crossing into Burma at Tamu, and moving more than five hundred miles into Japanese-held territory, this expedition, code-named 'Loincloth', the brainchild of Brigadier Orde Wingate, blew up the railway between Wuntho and Indaw; three bridges were cut, and a Japanese force which tried to stop the demolitions was driven off. After four weeks of determined marching, and of continued sabotage, five of Wingate's columns crossed the Irrawaddy river. Once over the Irrawaddy, however, and at the limit of air supply, the expedition was forced to return. Before it did so, an ambush was set for the Japanese, in which a hundred Japanese were killed for the loss of a single Gurkha. The aim of Operation Loincloth, to 'stir up a hornets' nest' in Japanese-occupied Burma, had been successful, so much so that the Japanese were later to launch their own imitative attack against India, in the region of Imphal. Wingate, too, was to try again, on a far more substantial scale.

On February 16, the Red Army reached the outskirts of Kharkov. That day, over France, an American airman, Lieutenant T. P. Mayo, was shot down on his way back from an air raid over St Nazaire. As he landed, several French-women came up to him, some of them already carrying plain clothes for him to change into, so that he would all the more easily be able to evade capture. Slowly but surely, the forces of resistance and rescue were gaining in strength and organization. Even an Allied airman lost over France could now expect to be helped, hidden and sent southward to the Pyrenees, and Spain. That same night, over Norway, six specially trained Norwegians were parachuted on to a frozen lake thirty miles north west of Vermork, in a second Allied attempt to destroy the high concentration heavy water plant on which a German atomic bomb would depend. This time, the mission, code named Operation Gunnerside, was a success; nine days after the landing, having been joined by four men from the earlier Swallow mission, the Norwegians blew up the high-concentration plant at the factory. None of the saboteurs was caught; one of them, fully armed and in uniform, went across the snow on skis to neutral Sweden, the other nine remained in Norway and, despite repeated German searches, avoided capture.

In Munich that day, stunned citizens saw the words 'Freedom' and 'Down with Hitler' painted in large white letters on a wall in one of the city's main streets. Two days later, at Munich University, anti-Nazi leaflets were scattered in the main entrance hall. 'Germany's name will remain disgraced for ever', one sentence in the leaflet read, 'unless German youth rises up immediately, takes revenge, and atones – smashes its torturers, and builds a new, spiritual Europe.'

Those responsible for the leaflet, the twenty-four-year-old Hans Scholl, his twenty-one-year-old sister Sophie and their friend Christoph Probst, were members of a small group which called itself the 'White Rose', a rare dissenting voice in Nazi Germany. They were soon arrested and brought to trial. Their judge was Roland Freisler, President of the People's Court. The three were sentenced to death by decapitation, and guillotined. Before putting his head under the guillotine, Hans Scholl called out, with a cry that was heard throughout the prison: 'Long live Liberty!'

Within Munich University, the White Rose had been encouraged by Kurt Hüber, a professor who shared its anti-Nazi views; later he too was arrested and executed, together with two other members of the group, Willi Graf and Alexander Schmorell, both of whom had served on the Eastern Front in 1942, and been shocked at what they had seen there of the barbarity against the Jews, as Hans Scholl had been. Scholl, as a gesture of protest, had shaken the hands of Jews in cattle-trucks at railway stations in eastern Poland.

On February 18, the day of the arrest of Hans and Sophie Scholl in Munich, Goebbels spoke in Berlin of the need for total war. 'Do you want total war?' he asked, and he went on: 'Do you want it, if it has to be, more total, more radical than we can possibly imagine today?' The crowd roared in unison, 'Yes!' Goebbels then asked: 'Is your confidence in the Führer greater, surer, more unshakeable than ever?'

'Yes!' came the echoing cry.

Goebbels also spoke that day about the Jews. 'The Jews are the root of evil in the world,' he declared, 'they are the Devil who pushes the West towards its downfall; they are the carrier of ruin and destruction within the body of Western civilization; they are the instigators of chaos in the world,' and he went on to warn: 'The crocodile tears shed abroad over the treatment of Jews in German-occupied territories will not deter Germany from carrying out its plans and ideas. On the contrary, Germany will pursue its course with more vigour, by lawful means if necessary, in order to implement its plan which provides for the total elimination of Jewry'.

Hitler was at the front on February 18, at Field Marshal von Manstein's headquarters at Zaporozhe, within sound of the Soviet artillery. On the following day he told Manstein's soldiers and airmen, shortly to launch Germany's third offensive against Russia: 'The outcome of a crucial battle depends on you! A thousand kilometres away from the Reich's frontiers the fate of Germany's present and future is in the balance.' The youth of Germany, Hitler told his listeners, was manning the anti-aircraft defences around Germany's cities. More and more divisions were on their way to the East. 'Weapons unique and hitherto unknown are on the way to your front.' He had come to see them, he said, to do everything he could to convert their hitherto defensive battle 'into ultimate victory'.

Immediately after his speech, Hitler flew back to his 'Werewolf' headquarters at Vinnitsa. His troops were ready to launch their new offensive. But even as they made their final preparations, the Russians continued to push forward, retaking Pavlograd, less than sixty miles from the German headquarters at Zaporozhe, on February 20.

For the Dutch living under German occupation, February 20 saw the execution, near Schiphol airport, of several members of the Resistance. It was also the day on which a Dutch member of the Germanic ss, Gerardus Mooyman, became the first foreign volunteer in the ss to be awarded the Knight's Cross to his already awarded Iron Cross, First Class. He had knocked out seventeen Soviet tanks in only two days.

February 21 was Red Army Day, the anniversary of the foundation in 1918 of the Soviet armed forces. That day, it was announced in London that King George VI would present a Sword of Honour to the city of Stalingrad. 'It was the unyielding resistance of Stalingrad', the King declared, 'that turned the tide and heralded the crushing blows which have struck dismay into the foes of civilization and freedom.'

Red Army Day was not to pass, however, without drama of its own on the battlefield; for this was the day chosen by Hitler to launch his third Russian offensive. The aim was no longer the ambitious previous targets of Leningrad, Moscow, Stalingrad or Baku; but in seeking to recapture control of Kharkov, Hitler hoped not only to halt the Soviet advances of the previous three months, but to regain the initiative, and to recapture as much ground in southern Russia as possible. His visit to the troops at Zaporozhe had underlined the importance of the new offensive.

Within twenty-four hours of the renewed German onslaught in the south, however, the Red Army was able to open a counter-offensive towards Rzhev, in the central sector of the front, and against Sumy, in the Ukraine, which was recaptured.

In Tunisia, Rommel was forced that day to break off his attacks on the Allied armies, as British reinforcements began to arrive, but his own fuel supply ships could not get through to Tunis. As British Signals Intelligence was listening into their instructions, action against the ships was swift and sure.

The setbacks to Germany on the battlefield did not affect her behaviour as an occupying power, nor the behaviour of her agents. On February 22, in Oslo, Vidkun Quisling ordered a general mobilization of the whole civilian population. Anyone not registering could lose their ration cards. The first project, road and railway building works, and the construction of military installations, being undertaken by the Todt Organization, called for thirty-five thousand men. When two senior Church leaders, Bishop Berggrav of Oslo and the lay leader, Professor Hallesby, protested, they were arrested and imprisoned at Grini concentration camp.

Also on February 22, the Bulgarian government agreed to a German request to deport the eleven thousand Jews living in those areas of Yugoslavia and Greece which Bulgaria had occupied in 1941. Twenty trains were allocated for those deportations. Within a month of the agreement being signed, all eleven thousand Jews had been taken the length of Europe, some from the Aegean coast, and even from the Aegean islands, through Belgrade and Vienna, to their deaths at Treblinka. No Jewish community, however small, escaped the net; a memorial in Greece records the deportation and death of the three Jews who lived on the remote and beautiful island of Samothrace.

In the Polish town of Zamosc, an act of barbarity took place on February 23, the day after the German–Bulgarian deportation agreement, when thirty-nine Jewish boys, who had been in hiding, were murdered by phenol injections. A further eight were killed by the same method a week later.

For the Jews, a sense of powerlessness was combined with a determination to fight back whenever opportunity arose. Throughout February, a division of the Red Army, the Sixteenth Division, had been training for combat. Many of its twelve thousand men were Jews from Lithuania. On February 23 the division attacked the Germans at Alekseyevka, in the Ukraine, Jewish riflemen and machine-gunners charging on foot across the snow-covered plain. For two days the division struggled against superior German firepower until, its ammunition gone, it was ordered to withdraw. Several hundred Jews lay dead.

Hitler himself broadcast over German radio on February 24, telling his listeners: 'We shall smash and break the might of the Jewish world coalition, and mankind struggling for its freedom will win the final victory in this struggle.' As the German armies struggled to regain the initiative in the East, a sense of hope in victory was renewed. 'Communiqués from the East now sound a little better again,' Rommel wrote to his wife on February 24, and he added: 'That's a ray of light after such bad times.'

On February 23, Stalin issued a second partisan order, urging that the 'flame of partisan warfare shall be kindled and spread'. Fourteen partisans had already been created Hero of the Soviet Union, among them Ivan Nikitin, who, in the course of fifty reconnaissance missions, enabled his unit to attack and kill several thousand Germans. Nikitin himself blew up several bridges and motor vehicles, killing in all more than 350 German soldiers.

The struggle on the Eastern Front was also aided by further British successes in breaking the various German Enigma keys; on February 25 the 'Ermine' key, used by one of the main German Air Force combat units in the East, was broken, followed four days later by the breaking of yet another Enigma key, that of the German Air Force administrative area in the southern Ukraine. This key was known to the British as 'Orchid'.

The day of the breaking of the 'Ermine' key was also the day on which, as a result of the decisions made at the Casablanca conference, a 'round-the-clock' air offensive was launched against Germany, with British bombers attacking by night and American bombers by day, a daylight raid on February 25 against Nuremberg marking the start of this intensification of the air war. Within forty-eight hours, two thousand Allied bombers had dropped their bombs.

In Berlin, on February 27, the Germans rounded up eight thousand Jews, the last remaining Jews in the capital, most of them factory workers hitherto exempt from deportation, hence the round-up's name, the 'Factory Action'. Within twenty-four hours, all were deported to the East, including several Jews who, as converts to Christianity, had married Christian wives. It was this deportation of Christians which led to a protest by the Archbishop of Breslau, Cardinal Bertram. As a result of this protest, a few of the converts were exempted from deportation. Most, however, were sent, like the other deportees, to Auschwitz. Eight of those rounded up on February 27 had earlier been brought to Berlin from Helsinki, as a result of pressure by Himmler on the Finnish Government. Only one was to survive the war. Following protests by churchmen and politicians in Finland against the deportations, the Finnish Cabinet refused to deport any more of its two thousand Jews, several hundred of whom were themselves Germans or Austrians who had fled to Finland as refugees before the war; now, they were safe.

Even in Berlin, there had been protest at the deportations. 'Unfortunately,' Goebbels noted in his diary on March 2, 'our better circles, especially the intellectuals, once again have failed to understand our policy about the Jews and in some cases have even taken their part.' These protests did not affect the deportations from France. That day, of a thousand Jewish deportees sent from Paris to Auschwitz, three hundred were more than seventy years old. They too were gassed.

Also on March 2, in France, the Allied escape line 'Pat' was destroyed, when a British Army deserter, Herbert Cole, betrayed its leader, the Belgian doctor, Captain Guérisse, known as Lieutenant-Commander Pat O'Leary, RN, in Toulouse.

On March 3, on the Eastern Front, the Red Army recaptured Rzhev. That night, British bombers struck at Hamburg. In London, in an area where no bombs were falling, panic struck those entering a Tube shelter at Bethnal Green after an alert had sounded; 173 were killed by suffocation as they fell and were crushed on the steps leading to the shelter.

In the Far East, Operation Cannibal, a British offensive designed to recapture the Burmese port of Akyab by an overland advance from India, came to an unsuccessful end on March 4, when the Japanese forces facing it went over to the offensive. But in the Pacific, in the Bismarck Sea, a Japanese attempt to send seven thousand reinforcements as well as aircraft fuel and spare parts, to Lae and Salamaua, in New Guinea, was routed that day, when 137 American bombers, protected by American and Australian fighters, destroyed all eight of the Japanese troop transports and four Japanese destroyers; 3,500 Japanese troops were drowned. The aircraft fuel and spare parts, both desperately needed by the Japanese at Lae and Salamaua, were also sunk, and 102 of the 150 Japanese aircraft involved in the battle were shot down.

It was exactly ten years since Roosevelt had been inaugurated President for the first time. 'Accept my warmest congratulations', Churchill telegraphed to him that day, 'on your brilliant victory in the Pacific which fitly salutes the end of your first ten years.'

That night, 442 British bombers struck at Essen, in the Ruhr, destroying more than 160 acres of industrial property, and continuing their work of gradual erosion of the German war economy.

Even as the Germans struggled to regain territory in the East, being checked again and again by the tenacity of the Russian defence, the Nazi Governor of the Ukraine, Erich Koch, was speaking with contempt of the Russians under his control. In a speech in Kiev on March 5, he declared: 'We are a master race, which must remember that the lowliest German worker is racially and biologically a thousand times more valuable than the population here.' As to the Russians, they, said Koch, 'will have to work, and work, and go on working'. In fact, the Russians went on fighting, in partisan actions throughout Koch's own empire, as well as at the front; on March 6 the Red Army took Gzhatsk, on the railway line from Moscow to Smolensk, pushing the Germans yet further away from Moscow.

In North Africa, the British ability to eavesdrop on Rommel's most secret messages now reaped one of its most important dividends, with the decrypting on February 28 of Rommel's plan – after his failure to break through against the Americans in western Tunisia – to attack the British Eighth Army instead, driving southward on Médenine with three panzer divisions, in order to encircle the British forces in front of the Mareth Line. Between February 28 and March 4, as Rommel moved troops and tanks from the one front to the other, further decrypts gave the exact size of the forces which he intended to throw into battle. Learning of this through his own secret link with Bletchley, Montgomery was able to rush extra troops, including the New Zealand Division, as well as four hundred tanks and 470 anti-tank guns, two hundred miles along the single surfaced road, to match and exceed the forces being gathered against him.

By the morning of March 6, when Rommel launched his attack, the German and Italian forces had lost both the element of surprise and the advantage of superior numbers. Within a few hours, it was clear that the British tanks and artillery would overwhelm any assaulting force. Nor could the German tanks make progress against the British anti-tank gun fire. At seven o'clock that evening, Rommel ordered 'an immediate cessation of the battle'.

In Berlin there was a minor setback to the Final Solution, when Goebbels was forced to postpone the last deportation of Jews from the German capital. 'Unfortunately,' he wrote in his diary on March 6, 'there have been some regrettable scenes at a home for aged Jews, when a large number of people gathered and some of them even sided with the Jews.' That same day, in Zagreb, the Catholic churchman, Archbishop Stepinac, protested to the Croat leader, Ante Pavelić, against the killing of Jews who were married to Christians. How could the Christian member of the marriage, he asked, be expected to remain silent 'while their beloved are being violently exterminated and their children exposed to an unknown fate'? Pavelić agreed to halt the killing of Jews who were married to Christians. But the killing of the remaining Croat Jews went on; the Archbishop's protective hand did not extend to them.

On the night of March 6, as Churchill and Roosevelt's Casablanca Directive was brought into full effect, British bombers returned to Essen. 'The city of the Krupps has been hard hit,' Goebbels noted in his diary on the following day, and he added: 'The number of dead, too, is considerable. If the English continue their raids on this scale, they will make things exceedingly difficult for us.'

While Goebbels was in Berlin, receiving reports of the increasing severity of the air raids over Germany, Hitler was at his 'Werewolf' headquarters at Vinnitsa, to which Goebbels flew on March 9. It was 'by no means impossible',

Hitler told him, that the Russians might collapse 'sooner or later'.

The vision of a defeated Russia could not be dislodged from Hitler's mind.

That evening, news was telephoned to Vinnitsa that Nuremberg had suffered a heavy air raid. 'The Führer is very much worried about the fate of this city,' Goebbels noted in his diary. 'I telephoned to Nuremberg twice and asked for reports. The damage was not so great as we at first thought.'

For Rommel, who had also arrived at Vinnitsa that day, there was the award of the highest of all orders of the Iron Cross, the Oak Leaves with Swords and Diamonds. There was also advice from Hitler, that he go on sick leave, with the aim, Rommel recalled, 'that I could take command again later for operations against Casablanca'. Rommel added: 'It simply never occurred to him that things could go wrong in Tunisia. Nor would he hear of the front being shortened, for then it would be impossible to take the offensive again.'

On the morning of March 10, German troops began a massive assault on the centre of Kharkov. As Rommel and Goebbels flew back to Germany, Hitler flew eastward once more to Manstein's headquarters at Zaporozhe. Since the start of Manstein's offensive on February 21, more than 23,000 Soviet soldiers had been killed, and 634 Russian tanks destroyed. Now Kharkov lay once more within the German grasp.

That night, British bombers struck at Munich. 'Again one asks: How is this to go on?' Goebbels wrote in his diary on March 11, and he added: 'If the English are in a position night after night to attack some German city, one can easily imagine how Germany will look after about three months unless we take effective countermeasures.' Goebbels was also angry because, he wrote, 'The scheduled arrest of all Jews on one day failed because of the shortsighted behaviour of industrialists who warned the Jews in time.' Now, on Goebbels's instructions, those Jews were being hunted down.

In the defence of the city of Kharkov, the Russians had, as allies, a thousand Czechoslovak troops. Four hundred of the soldiers were Czechs who had fled from Czechoslovakia to Poland in March 1939 and from Poland to Russia in September 1939. Six hundred were Czech Jews who had sought refuge on Soviet soil in 1939, been sent by the Soviets to labour camps in 1940, and in 1942 released to join this Czechoslovak Division.

These Czech troops were first in action between March 8 and 11 at Sokolovo; by the end of the battle, 140 of the Jewish soldiers had been killed in action.

On March 12, Soviet forces liberated Vyazma. In Italy, 100,000 workers, in Turin and Genoa, went on strike, bringing war production to a halt, nor could Mussolini assert sufficient authority to get the men back to work. 'If you show the least weakness in cases like this,' Hitler told his Staff, 'you are finished!'

Since the surrender at Stalingrad, Hitler's own confidence had been shaken. 'He seemed very depressed and upset about the Stalingrad disaster,' Rommel recalled of his conversation at Vinnitsa on March 9. 'He said that one is always liable to look on the black side of things after a defeat, a tendency which can lead one into dangerous and false conclusions.' Not only Hitler, but several senior Army officers, had also been 'upset' by Stalingrad, not so much by the defeat as by Hitler's part in it. As they saw it, his refusal to allow von Paulus

FINLAND

SWEDEN

Gulf of Finland

*Lake Ladoga*

*Lake Onega*

Baltic Sea

Narva

*Lake Peipus*

Leningrad

Riga

*Lake Ilmen*

Narva-Melitopol German defence line,

ARMY GROUP NORTH
ARMY GROUP CENTRE

Velikiye Luki

Rastenburg

Kovno

Polotsk

Durovo

Rzhev

Gzhatsk

Vyazma

Moscow

GREATER
GERMANY

Vilna

Khatyn

Borisov

Lepel

Smolensk

"Panther Line"

Dorogobuzh

Bialystok

Minsk

SOVIET   UNION

Warsaw

Treblinka

Slonim

Osipovichi

12 August 1943

Minsk
Mazowiecki

Slutsk

WHITE RUSSIA

Kletnya

Bryansk

Orel

Miedzyrzec
Wlodawa
Lublin

Rogachev

Gomel

Sobibor

Zamosc

Dmitriev

Kursk

Voronezh

Belzec

Jaworow

Prokhorovka

Lvov

Zolkiew

Sumy

EASTERN

Skalat

ARMY GROUP CENTRE
ARMY GROUP SOUTH

Kiev

Belgorod

Stary Oksyol

GALICIA

SLOVAKIA

Vinnitsa

*River Dnieper*

Kharkov

Sokolovo
Alekseyevka

Kupyansk

Izyum

HUNGARY

Hitler's flight path, 13 March 1943

Lozovaya

Voroshilovgrad

Kramatorsk

Pavlovgrad

Rostov-on-
Don.

Zaporozhe

Odessa

*River Dnieper*

Melitopol

ROUMANIA

Yeisk

Ploesti

*Sea of
Azov*

*Black
Sea*

CRIMEA

Kerch

Krasnodar

Novorossiisk

0        miles        200

0        kilometres        300

ᐯᐯᐯᐯ  *Russian front line,
1 February 1943*

▼▼▼▼  *Russian front line,
4 July 1943*

The German retreats, February to August 1943

to retreat was typical of interference in military matters, leading to disaster. There were also officers who had come to dislike other facets of the regime: its tyranny, the ostentation and dominance of Nazi Party officials, and Hitler's willingness to fight both Russia, whom most of them feared, and the Western Allies, whom some of them would have liked to see outside the conflict. To these officers, the appeal by Goebbels for 'total war' was a call to suicide. The nucleus of a military conspiracy had begun.

On March 13, Hitler was at Vinnitsa, preparing to return to Rastenburg. He had let it be known that, during the flight, he would land briefly at Smolensk, to visit the headquarters of Army Group Centre. At Smolensk, Major-General Henning von Treschkow and his staff officer, Lieutenant Fabian von Schlab-rendorff, leaders of the disaffected officers, had planned to kill Hitler with a parcel bomb. The bomb was given to one of the officers accompanying Hitler during the flight on to Rastenburg; this officer, who was not in the plot, had been told that it was a gift of two bottles of liqueur for a senior officer at Rastenburg.

The parcel was taken on the plane, and Hitler flew westward. In Berlin, other conspirators, among them Colonel Hans Oster, Chief of Staff of the German Armed Forces Counter-Intelligence service, and his deputy, Hans von Dohnanyi, waited for the code word 'Flash', to indicate that they should take control in the capital. The bomb had been timed to go off in the region of Minsk. But, two hours after leaving Smolensk, the plane reached Rastenburg without incident. The conspirators, recovering the parcel, discovered that the detonator had been defective. Operation Flash had failed.

Not only German Army officers and aristocrats, but students and liberals, had been spurred after Stalingrad to protest against the Nazi régime. In Düsseldorf, sixty-one people were arrested that March for distributing anti-Nazi leaflets. Other arrests were made in Dortmund, Görlitz, Chemnitz, Nuremberg, Saar-brücken and Weimar. The local population, a German Security Police report of March 15 complained, was 'no longer meeting such manifestations as before, by, for instance, the prompt removal of the inflammatory writings or the handing over of leaflets, but instead reads the contents and hands them on'.

On March 13, the United States Treasury agreed to a request from Colonel Donovan, to make five million dollars available for Polish resistance behind the German lines. The money, in small denomination bills, was flown from Britain in an aeroplane which landed at night on Polish soil, left the money with members of the Polish resistance, and flew back safely. A further fifteen million dollars was to be sent to Poland during the next fourteen months.

Twenty-four hours after this American decision to help Polish resistance activity, German troops re-entered Kharkov. 'We have shown the Ivans we can withstand their terrible winter,' one ss officer wrote in triumph, and he added: 'It can hold no fear for us again.' Not winter, however, but the coming of spring, hampered further German advance, as the thawing steppes were turned once again into bogs across which tanks and men could move only with considerable difficulty.

On March 15, Goebbels noted in his diary that he had told Hitler 'that I deemed it essential to force the Jews out of the entire Reich as quickly as possible'. Goebbels added: 'He approved, and ordered me not to cease or pause until not a single Jew is left anywhere in Germany.' That day, more than nine hundred miles from Berlin, the deportations began of the Jews of Salonica: an ancient Sephardic community established shortly after 1492 by Jews who had been expelled from Spain. Ten thousand Salonica Jews had been deported from the Aegean port by the end of March, a further twenty-five thousand in April, and ten thousand more in May. They had no idea of their destination, having been told that it was a 'resettlement' area in Poland.

Each deportee from Salonica was allowed to take a food parcel for the journey, and up to fifteen kilogrammes of clothing for the 'resettlement' area. In fact, their destination was Auschwitz.

For many generations the Jews of Salonica had served in the port as stevedores and dock workers: the smooth working of the docks depended upon them. But the Nazi design would allow no exceptions, no logic, no special pleading. Jews from the villages around Salonica were also deported, except from Katerini, where the local Greek head of police gave the Jews three hours to flee after receipt of the deportation order. Thirty-three Jews fled, and were hidden by Greek villagers. Three, who were unable to leave, were shot by the Gestapo.

On March 18, American bombers based in Britain struck at German submarine yards at Vegesack, near Bremen. The bombardier on the lead aircraft, First Lieutenant Jack W. Mathis, despite being severely wounded by anti-aircraft fire when directly over the target, released his bombs on time. Posthumously, he was awarded the Medal of Honour, the first Eighth Air Force recipient. In Warsaw, on March 18, three Polish resistance fighters were in a battle with the Germans. One of them, Hanka Sawicka, was seriously wounded in the fight. All three, after being captured, were tortured to death in Pawiak prison.

On the Eastern Front, the Germans captured Belgorod on March 19; but north of Belgorod, the Russians had created a bulge in the German line west of Kursk which threatened all the German gains in the south. Hitler ordered this Kursk salient to be eliminated. The plan of attack was given the code name Operation Citadel.

In the Atlantic, the British and Americans, whose grip on the u-boat Enigma had become temporarily intermittent, were confronted by a sudden resurgence of German submarine activity. In the three weeks leading up to March 20, a total of 107 Allied merchant ships had been sunk in the North Atlantic, most of them in the mid-Ocean gap between the maximum range of effective air cover from either Canada or Britain. In the first ten days of March, forty-one ships had been sunk, and in the ten days up to March 20, a further fifty-six. The British Naval Staff later recorded that 'the Germans never came so near to disrupting communications between the New World and the Old', so much so, the Naval Staff added, that 'it appeared possible that we should not be able to continue convoy as an effective form of defence'.

On March 20 the Royal Air Force launched Operation Enclose, to try to catch the German submarines while they were in the Bay of Biscay. But, despite twenty-eight sightings in eight days, only a single submarine was sunk. The crisis of the German submarine successes, which had arisen from the problems of decrypting the new German naval Enigma key, was about to be resolved by an outstanding Intelligence success at Bletchley, the successful overcoming of the recent setbacks in reading the U-boat Enigma. Within two months, a mortal danger had passed.

On March 21, on the Eastern Front, the Russians advanced further into the Kursk salient. They were also able that day to push the Germans back further north, capturing Durovo, only fifty-six miles north-east of Smolensk. That day, in Berlin, Hitler was to attend the annual memorial dedication to the dead of the First World War. After the ceremony, he would also be shown a collection of weapons captured from the Russians. The military conspirators, despite their setback at Smolensk, decided to try once more to kill Hitler. One of their number, Major General Baron von Gersdorff, was to be on duty at the exhibition. He proposed the following suicide mission: putting a bomb into his greatcoat pocket, he would detonate it as Hitler passed him. Briefed by Major-General von Tresckow, von Schlabrendorff searched for a bomb with a specially devised short time fuse which would go off after ten minutes, but he could not find one, and the attempt was called off. Ironically, Hitler only stayed at the exhibition for eight minutes after the dedication ceremony ended. As during the Munich Beer Hall assassination attempt in November 1939, he would have left the building just in time.

On March 22 the Germans completed the retreat from a salient in the central sector of the Russian front, giving up a hundred mile stretch of the Vyazma–Moscow–Smolensk railway. The retreat, given the codename Operation Buffalo, considerably shortened the line, as well as giving up areas in which Soviet partisans had been particularly active. That same day, in the village of Khatyn, near Minsk – not to be confused with Katyn near Smolensk – an SS unit formed from German criminals, who had hitherto been imprisoned at Sachsenhausen concentration camp north of Berlin, murdered 149 villagers, and burned the village to the ground. The aim of this action had been to deter villagers from giving help to partisans, but by the end of the year partisans were in control of half the countryside.

On March 23 a German statistician, Dr Richard Korherr, submitted to Himmler a report on the number of Jews who had been subjected to 'total evacuation' and 'special treatment'. The figure he gave was 1,274,166 in the camps in the General Government, and a further 145,301 in the Warthegau.

Although Korherr had no reason to say so, further deportations were continuing that very day, both from Bulgarian-occupied Thrace and Macedonia, and from the Greek city of Salonica. These latter deportations had led to a protest, also on March 23, from Archbishop Damaskinos of Athens to the Greek collaborationist Government in Athens.

Archbishop Damaskinos' protest was to no avail. A week earlier, however, on March 17, the Bulgarian parliament had voted unanimously against any deportation of Jews from pre-war Bulgaria, and this protest was successful, having as it did the support not only of the King of Bulgaria, but also of the Papal Nuncio in Turkey, Angelo Roncalli, who was godfather to the King's son. Fifteen years later, Roncalli was to be elected Pope, as John XXIII.

On March 25, a protest against the treatment of the Jews, written in German, was forwarded by Hans Frank in Cracow to Hitler's Chancellery in Berlin. The letter was anonymous. In it, the writer described his disgust at what he had seen during the liquidation of an eastern ghetto. Jewish children, he wrote, had been thrown to the ground, and had then had their heads deliberately trampled on with boots. This was no exaggeration. But a single, anonymous protest could lead to no change in the pattern of destruction. On March 25, two thousand Jews from the town of Zolkiew, in Eastern Galicia, were driven to a nearby forest and killed. The remnants of Jewish communities throughout Poland, most of whom had been deported to their deaths six months or a year earlier, were now being searched out, or taken from the labour camps to which they had been sent in 1942, and killed.

In the Far East, a Japanese naval squadron seeking to supply the Japanese garrisons on Kiska and Attu islands, in the Aleutians, was intercepted by a smaller American naval force, which courageously engaged it. No capital ships were sunk, but, in the last major naval battle fought with naval guns, the Japanese heavy cruiser *Nachi* and the American heavy cruiser *Salt Lake City* were both badly damaged. The Japanese, however, never again broke the American naval blockade of the Aleutians. The Battle of the Komandorski Islands, as it became known, was a strategic victory for the United States.

In North Africa, with Rommel still recuperating in Germany, his successor, the Italian General Messe, had stood for seven days against a continuous onslaught by the British Eighth Army against the Mareth Line. In scale and ferocity, the Battle of Mareth was comparable with El Alamein. By March 27, Messe could hold the line no longer, and made preparations to withdraw twenty-five miles northward, to El Hamma. 'I hope you will now be able to break and defeat the enemy and completely drive him out of Tunis,' Stalin telegraphed to Churchill from the Kremlin. 'I hope also', Stalin added, 'that the air offensive against Germany will go on inexorably increasing.' That night, the Royal Air Force again raided Germany: 395 heavy bombers, as Churchill telegraphed to Stalin, 'flung 1,050 tons on Berlin in fifty minutes. The sky was clear over the target and the raid was highly successful. This is the best Berlin has yet got. Our loss is nine only.' Twice as many bombs were dropped on Berlin that night as had been dropped by the Germans on London during their heaviest raid, that of 18 April 1941.

From Tunisia, on March 28, Churchill received the first signal of victory: 'After seven days of continuous and heavy fighting', Montgomery telegraphed,

'Eighth Army has inflicted severe defeat on enemy.' Enemy resistance was 'disintegrating'. The Eighth Army was in possession of the whole Mareth Line defences, occupying Gabès and El Hamma on March 29, after a fierce German resistance which was largely overcome by the New Zealand forces.

Hitler's thoughts were not on retreat but retaliation; on March 29 he approved a blueprint submitted to him by Alfred Speer for a massive reinforced concrete missile silo on the Channel coast, from which London could be bombarded. The British were not unaware of this missile development. On March 27, the War Cabinet's rocket expert, Dr R. V. Jones, had been shown the translation of a conversation listened into by British Intelligence, between two German prisoners-of-war, General Cruewell and General von Thoma, both of whom had been captured at El Alamein. During one of their discussions, which had taken place on March 23, von Thoma told his fellow captive that, knowing as he did that their prison was somewhere near London, and hearing no large explosions, he knew that there must have been a hold-up in the rocket programme. 'No progress whatsoever', Thoma said, 'can have been made in this rocket business', and he added, in describing a visit he had once made to an experimental rocket station: 'The Major there was full of hope – he said: "Wait until next year and the fun will start!"' As to the rocket's range, Thoma added, 'There's no limit.'

Germany's much vaunted secret weapon was on its slow way to reality; but, thanks to a hidden microphone and vigilant eavesdroppers, it was no longer secret.

# 31

# 'Drive the enemy into the sea' (Montgomery)

SPRING 1943

In the Far East, Allied prisoners of war continued to suffer in camps without proper medical care, and amid terrible punishments. In the Thailand railway camps, such as his own camp at Konyu, Colonel Dunlop noted in his diary on March 19 that the Japanese intention was 'of just breaking men on this job, with not the faintest consideration for either life or health'. This, Dunlop added, 'can only be regarded as a cold-blooded, merciless crime against mankind, obviously premeditated'. In the nearby prisoner-of-war camp for Dutch soldiers, at Kinsayok, six men had died in six days. For the Japanese, all that mattered was to complete the railway.

On March 29, at Salamaua, on New Guinea, a twenty-three-year-old American flight lieutenant who had been shot down by Japanese anti-aircraft fire, was sentenced to be decapitated. 'The unit commander has drawn his favourite sword,' a Japanese officer noted in his diary. 'He taps the prisoner's neck lightly with the back of the blade, then raises it above his head with both arms, and brings it down with a sweep.' The head was severed with one blow. 'All is over. The head is dead white like a doll's. The savageness which I felt only a while ago is gone, and now I feel nothing but the true compassion of Japanese Bushido. A senior corporal laughs loudly, "Well, he will enter Nirvana now". Then a superior seaman of the medical unit takes the chief medical officer's sword and, intent on paying off old scores, turns the headless body over on its back, and cuts the abdomen open with one clean stroke'.

Fifty miles south east of Salamaue, at Morobe, American infantry units landed and began to prepare a defensive position; these were part of the MacKenzie Force, named after the officer commanding it, which was charged with advancing along the coastline towards Salamaue and Lae.

Over Europe, Allied bombing was now a daily and nightly feature of civilian life. On April 2 a decree issued by Goering made air raid patrol duty compulsory for every able-bodied German, men and women alike. On 3 April, the British had dropped nine hundred tons of bombs on the Krupp factory at Essen, and on April 5, a further 1,400 bombs on Kiel, 'one of the heaviest discharges', Churchill told Stalin, 'we have ever made'. Also on April 5, by day, American bombers had attacked the Renault tank assembly lines near Paris; 228 French civilians were killed. An air raid on port installations at Naples on April 4 left 221 Italians dead.

One of the American bombers on the Naples raid was a Liberator which had recently reached North Africa from the United States, and was on its first wartime mission. Known to its nine-man crew as the 'Lady Be Good', it had taken off from Soluch airfield thirty miles south of Benghazi. On its return flight, it lost its bearings and flew on two hundred miles into the Libyan desert, before its crew, their fuel almost gone, baled out, still believing that they were over the sea. And it was over the sea, two hundred miles away, that the search for the lost bomber took place.

The crew of the 'Lady Be Good' set off across the desert. Two of them kept diaries. Each day, using their parachute harnesses and large stones, they set out arrow markers in the sand. 'Still having prayer meetings for help,' the co-pilot, Second Lieutenant Robert F. Toner, noted in his diary during their fifth day in the desert. 'No signs of anything, a couple of birds; good winds from north. Really weak now, can't walk, pains all over, still all want to die. Nights very cold, no sleep.' On the following day, five of the crewmen could go no further. Only three were able to continue. That night, one of the three, the engineer, Technical Sergeant Harold S. Risplinger, noted in his diary: 'Palm Sunday. Still struggling to get out of dunes and find water.'

The three surviving airmen had walked for more than eighty miles across the desert. One by one they collapsed. The last to be able to walk was one of the gunners, the twenty-six-year-old Staff Sergeant Guy E. Shelley. He walked on a further seven miles, having covered a total distance of ninety miles, the last two or three days without water.

None of this saga was known at the airbase from which the 'Lady Be Good' had set out, and to which she had failed to return. First reported as missing on April 4, the status of the crew was amended on April 5 with the added words 'presumed dead'. That at least was true; but it was to be more than fifteen years before any knowledge or trace of their fate was found.

On April 5, as the crew of 'Lady Be Good' were still struggling across the Libyan desert, American bombers based in Britain launched a daylight raid on Antwerp, intending to destroy the Minerva aircraft factory, plans of which had been smuggled to London by two Belgian Resistance agents. Only a few bombs hit the target, doing far less damage than had been intended. Owing to a navigational error, most of the bombers dropped their bombs on a built-up area of the city, killing 936 civilians, including 209 schoolchildren who were at their school. Within a few weeks, the Minerva factory was back to almost full production. Only the Nazi leaders rejoiced. 'An imposing funeral has been arranged,' Goebbels noted in his diary on April 11, and he added that the British and American silence on the raid 'supports our idea of making a first-class propaganda matter of the Antwerp incident'.

In Berlin, the Gestapo had begun to search out critics of the regime at the highest level. On April 5, the Protestant pastor and theologian, Dietrich Bonhoeffer, who had earlier contacted the British in Sweden, was arrested, charged with 'subverting the armed forces', and imprisoned. Also arrested that day, in his office in German Military Counter-Intelligence, was Hans von Dohnanyi, who had been involved in the attempt to kill Hitler at Smolensk on March 13. Von Dohnanyi revealed nothing, betrayed nobody but, after two years in Sachsenhausen concentration camp, was murdered.

Two days after these arrests in Berlin, Lieutenant Claus von Stauffenberg, one of the leading figures of the discontented German officer corps, was gravely wounded by a mine on the Tunisian front, losing his left eye, his right hand, half his left hand and part of his leg. He was flown to a hospital in Munich, where the sight of his right eye was saved. As he recovered, he resolved to put all his efforts and abilities at the disposal of those Germans – mostly among his fellow officers – who wished to remove Hitler at all costs.

It was on April 7, the day on which von Stauffenberg was wounded in Tunisia, that Hitler met Mussolini at Salzburg. 'I guarantee you that Africa will be defended,' Hitler assured his guest, and he added: 'Verdun stood out against the attack of the best German regiments. I do not see why we should not stand out as well in Africa. With your help, Duce, my troops will make Tunis the Verdun of the Mediterranean.'

As Hitler gave Mussolini this pledge, Italian troops in Tunisia were once again falling back under a further heavy assault from the Eighth Army; during a two day battle, more than half of the Italian Centauro Division were killed or captured before reaching the safety of a new defence line at Enfidaville, less than fifty miles south of Tunis.

In the Far East, on April 7, the Americans were confronted with the largest Japanese attacking air force since Pearl Harbour. The force struck in the area of the recently lost Guadalcanal, and in particular at Tulagi. A total of 188 Japanese warplanes took part, sinking the American destroyer, *Aaron Ward*, a New Zealand corvette, *Moa*, but only a single merchant ship, beneath what had become known as Iron Bottom Bay, because of such a large tonnage of destroyed Japanese and American shipping now lying on the sea bed. Four days later the Japanese renewed their attack, sinking two more Allied merchant ships, but posing no threat to the American forces on Guadalcanal. A Japanese aerial attack on Port Moresby on April 12, made with 177 warplanes, did little serious damage, and was likewise no threat to the Australians in New Guinea.

In Tunisia, German and Italian resistance continued, but in desperation. When, on April 10, the Eighth Army occupied Sfax, General Montgomery told his troops: 'Forward to Tunis and drive the enemy into the sea.' Sousse fell two days later, and Enfidaville on April 13. The Axis forces in Tunisia were trapped in a small and vulnerable pocket, their supply links with Sicily and Italy exposed through Enigma to devastating attack, their air cover virtually destroyed, and all hope of reinforcements gone. It could only be a matter of weeks before they would have to surrender. Like the trap at Stalingrad, that at Tunis was without hope of relief or rescue.

On April 13 the Axis suffered yet another disaster. This was the successful decrypting, by the American Pacific Fleet's Radio Unit, of a Japanese message giving the exact timing and itinerary of a visit being made four days later by the Commander in Chief of the Combined Fleet, Admiral Yamamoto, to the Japanese bases at Ballale and Buin on Bougainville Island. It was decided by the American Chiefs of Staff to shoot down Yamamoto's aeroplane. Thus was launched Operation Peacock, the successful killing of the most illustrious of Japan's war leaders. To protect their secret code-breaking exercise, the Americans made no mention after the attack of Yamomoto's death, treating it as merely another aircraft clash. Only when the Japanese had brought Yamomoto's ashes back to Tokyo on May 21, and publicly mourned his death, did the Americans announce it, but not their deliberate part in it.

That April, a series of lectures by the nuclear scientist, Robert Serber, given to a secret circle of chemists and physicists at Los Alamos in the United States, described the 'Manhattan Project' in detail. Serber described the aim of the Project as 'to produce a practical military weapon in the form of a bomb in which the energy is released by a fast neutron chain reaction in one or more of the materials known to show nuclear fission'. Such an outcome, Serber believed, was obtainable within the next two years. The project would therefore go ahead.

Unknown to the Americans, a meeting of Japanese physicists in Tokyo a month earlier had come to the conclusion that, while an atomic bomb was possible, it could not in practice be produced by any of the warring powers in time to be of use to them in the present war.

The Germans' regular Enigma messages now revealed to the Allies considerable German activity on the northern side of the Kursk salient. One such message was decrypted on April 15, the very day on which Hitler explained to his commanders his detailed plans for Operation Citadel. The attack on the Kursk salient, Hitler wrote, 'must succeed rapidly and totally', in order to give the Germans the initiative for the spring and summer. 'The victory at Kursk', Hitler urged, 'must be a beacon to the world.'

On April 16, Churchill was told that the impending German operation involved launching an attack against the Kursk salient from the Smolensk–Orel area, though British Intelligence was still uncertain whether this was to be a full military offensive or one confined to air attack. It was an uncertainty soon cleared up, however, as more and more of the German orders were decrypted in Britain within a few hours of their reaching those in Smolensk who had to act on them.

At Smolensk itself, it was still Soviet partisan activity behind the lines that was causing the Germans considerable concern. On April 17, in order to curb this activity, the Germans launched Operation Magic Flute, a week-long sweep against partisans who, operating near Minsk, were disrupting the movement of men and supplies to Army Group Centre. It was the task of Army Group Centre to strike at Kursk from the north, as its own top secret Enigma messages were revealing to the British with the greatest precision each day.

Hitler was angered that April by the large number of Jews still alive beyond his grasp. The Italian, Finnish and Bulgarian Governments had each rejected Germany's requests to deport Jews to German camps. Yet the statistics presented to the Wannsee Conference in January 1942 had made it clear that the plans for the Final Solution included the several million Jews who lived scattered throughout Europe in countries over which Germany had no direct control. On April 17, Hitler personally took up this point with the Hungarian Regent, Admiral Horthy, when the two leaders met at Klessheim Castle, near Salzburg.

The Jews, Hitler told Horthy, were 'pure parasites'. In Poland, however, 'this state of affairs had been fundamentally cleared up. If the Jews there did not want to work, they were shot. If they could not work, they had to succumb. They had to be treated', Hitler added, 'like tuberculosis bacilli, with which a healthy body may become infected. This was not cruel, if only it was remembered that even innocent creatures of nature, such as hares and deers, have to be killed, so that no harm is caused by them'. 'Nations', Hitler warned, 'which did not rid themselves of Jews, perished'.

Horthy resisted these arguments and pressures, telling Hitler: 'The Jews cannot be exterminated or beaten to death.' Two days later, unknown to Horthy, 1,400 Jews were deported from Brussels to Auschwitz, followed on April 20 by 1,166 from Holland. But the Jews themselves, despite tyranny, brute force and deception, had twice that month already resisted deportation, first from the Eastern Galician town of Skalat, and then, on April 18, from Jaworow, where 3,489 Jews had been shot during a ferocious German reprisal. But it was on April 19, two days after Hitler's exhortation to Horthy about the need to destroy the Jews like animals, that the most prolonged Jewish revolt of all took place, in the Warsaw ghetto, when the Germans tried to renew yet again the deportations to Treblinka.

With a courage which impressed all who learned of it, 1,200 Jewish fighters battled in the streets, apartments, cellars and sewers of the Warsaw ghetto. Against these Jews, who possessed only seventeen rifles, the Germans brought in 2,100 troops armed with machine guns, howitzers, and 1,358 rifles. Even so, three hundred German soldiers were killed, many by hand-made grenades, before the revolt was crushed three weeks later.

As the German soldiers moved through the Warsaw ghetto street by street, seven thousand Jews were killed, and a further seven thousand deported to Treblinka. More than ten thousand Jews found refuge in the Christian section of Warsaw, though as many as a third of these were later hunted down, or betrayed.

During April 1943, the Germans accelerated the round-up and deportation of forced labourers throughout German-occupied Western Europe. By the beginning of the month, 248,000 labourers were at work constructing the Atlantic Wall. Others were deported to work in Germany, where they were forced to work on average for eleven hours a day, even twelve hours a day, in one of the Krupp factories. For breaches of work discipline, the deportees could face up to a four week deprivation of their ration cards. By the end of April 1943, a total of 1,293,000 forced labourers from the West were working in factories in Germany. Also deported to Germany were those considered actual or potential enemies of the occupation régimes; they were sent to concentration camps. Of a quarter of a million Frenchmen deported to such camps, only 35,000 survived the war. Also deported to concentration camps were 37,000 Belgians, 12,000

Dutchmen, 6,000 Luxemburgers, 5,400 Norwegians and 5,200 Danes. Many of them also died as a result of the terrible conditions in the camps, and the brutal treatment.

Inside France, the arrest of members of the Resistance was sometimes only possible because they were betrayed by fellow-Frenchmen. One Resistance fighter, Olivier Giran, was executed on April 16. On the day of his death, he wrote to his parents: 'Men are cowards, traitors, rotters. But France is pure, clean, vital. I am happy. I am not dying for any faction or man, I am dying for my own idea of serving her, my country, and for you too, whom I adore. I am happy I love you. The door is opening. Adieu'.

In the Atlantic, the Allies now began to reap the benefit of their resumed breaking of the revised German U-boat Enigma key. In mid-April, a convoy of merchant ships being guarded by a combined Anglo-American naval escort force was attacked by a German submarine pack. Only a single merchantman was sunk, but one of the attackers, U-175, was destroyed by depth charges. On April 18 the War Diary of the U-boat Command noted: 'Meagre success, achieved generally at the cost of heavy losses, renders operations in these areas undesirable.' It was a major victory for Signals Intelligence, the hidden arm, and secret ear, of war.

In Tunisia, British Signals Intelligence was given clear warning of the German and Italian defence plans. Even so, each strongpoint had to be fought for. On April 19, at Takrouna, a small New Zealand force, consisting mostly of Maoris, overran a fortified hill which dominated the battlefield. The final assault on the hill was made by thirteen men; one of them, Private H. Grant, took sixty Italian prisoners single-handed. Elsewhere, a Maori soldier, Private T. Heka, advancing alone with two tanks as 'support' at long range, captured an anti-tank gun and three machine guns, killed several Italians and took fourteen prisoners. Having carried the position, Heka held it until reinforcements arrived. For his bravery, he was awarded the Distinguished Conduct Medal.

In the struggle between sovereign States, many national minorities, such as the Maoris, were enlisted to fight or to work. In Thailand, it was Tamils whom the Japanese took, not as volunteer soldiers but as forced labourers. It was said by the local Siamese, Colonel Dunlop noted in his diary at Konyu Camp on April 22, that the Tamils 'require a lot of care and die like flies of pneumonia if exposed to wet'. Dunlop added: 'It was a sad sight to see these poor wretches trudging their way up the deep slushy mud of our road' – guarded by Japanese troops – and he commented: 'Just another of those dreary, homeless, mass migrations of war along a road of sickness and death.'

In Europe, resistance activity was met with swift reprisals. On April 24 one of the organizers of the recently established French Milice, Paul de Gassovski, was killed in Marseille. Less than three weeks earlier, on April 7, a pro-Nazi journalist, Paul Colin, had been killed in Brussels; Colin's killer and his two accomplices were arrested on May 3, tried on May 6 and hanged on May 12. Witnesses of the execution recall that their final agony was increased because the German hangman used a thick rope, so that one of those executed took eight minutes to die after the trap had opened. At their place of execution, Fort Breendonk, one of the forts surrounding Antwerp, at least 187 Resistance fighters and their accomplices were executed during the course of the war, many after prolonged and agonizing torture.

In Holland and Norway, Resistance fighters were likewise active, risking torture and execution if caught. Allied commandos took the same risk. On April 29, six British commandos, led by John Godwin, a sub-lieutenant in the Royal Naval Volunteer Reserve, were taken by motor torpedo boat across the North Sea to Norway where, in Haugesund Fjord, north of Stavanger, they placed limpet mines on several German ships. After being caught, all six commandos were sent to Grini concentration camp near Oslo, and then to Sachsenhausen north of Berlin. One of their number, by name of Mayer, was presumed by the Germans to be Jewish and taken away, never to be seen or heard of again. The other five were forced to walk thirty miles a day, seven days a week, around a closed cobbled track, testing boots for the German Army. 'They cracked jokes with each other,' the historians of their fate have written, 'despised their gloomy guards, knew their own side was going to win the war, and did not brood about their own fate.'

It was on April 26 that, in the Indian Ocean south-east of Madagascar, a German submarine transferred to a Japanese submarine the Indian National Army leader, Subhas Chandra Bose. Within a year 25,000 Indian prisoners-of-war in Japanese camps had volunteered to serve alongside the Japanese army against the British. 'When I appear in Bengal', Bose told his Japanese sponsors that November, 'everyone will rise up in revolt.'

On April 30, in an attempt to deceive the Germans as to where they would strike once Tunis fell, the British launched Operation Mincemeat, floating ashore the body of a man who had recently died. The body was floated ashore from a submarine off the coast of Spain. On it were documents purporting to show that the build-up of activity against Sicily, such as the recent intensified Allied air attacks on Sicilian airfields, was a cover plan to disguise the real Allied intention, a landing in Greece. The Germans, believing the body to be that of an officer shot down during a flight to North Africa, fell into the trap. Only two weeks after the body floated ashore at Huelva, the German High Command in Berlin sent a 'most secret' message to the German Admiral commanding in Greek waters, with information from what it described as an 'absolutely reliable' source, that the 'objective' of an Allied landing in the eastern Mediterranean was Kalamata and Cape Araxos in Greece.

Both these locations had been mentioned in letters found on the body. The German Admiral was also asked 'to reinforce rapidly the defensive strength of the areas which are specifically threatened', including the laying of minefields off Kalamata. He was even given the supposed Allied code name for the Greek landings, 'Husky', which was in fact the code name of the landings in Sicily. The deception had encompassed even the code name.

On account of its extreme secrecy, the message to the German Admiral in

Greece was sent by Enigma. Solely because it was sent by Enigma, it was decrypted in Britain and, on May 14, a telegram sent to Churchill, who was then in Washington, informing him: '"Mincemeat" swallowed rod, line and sinker by the right people, and from best information they look like acting on it.'

To prepare for the non-existent assault on Greece, Rommel was asked to cut short his recuperative leave in Germany, in order to revitalize the Greek defences. A few weeks later, a full strength armoured division, the First Panzer Division, was transferred from France to Greece, and a group of German motor torpedo boats was ordered to proceed from Sicily to the Aegean. The Enigma messages giving these facts were likewise read in Britain, confirming that the deception had succeeded.

An Enigma message at the end of April also confirmed that the German intention on the Eastern Front was to cut off the Soviet forces in the Kursk salient by means of a pincer movement, from Orel in the north and Kharkov in the south, together with a third attack against Kursk itself from the west. These facts were passed from London to Moscow on April 30, together with estimates, also based on the German Army's own Enigma orders, of the strength of the German divisions deployed around the salient.

On the last day of April, the Germans deported two thousand Polish Jews from Wlodawa to Sobibor. On reaching the camp, the Jews, alarmed at what suddenly seemed to be a danger, attacked the SS guards with pieces of wood torn from the carriages. All were shot down by machine gun fire or blown up with grenades. Like the revolt of the Jews in the Warsaw ghetto, and in hundreds of other ghettos throughout eastern Europe, it was a courageous, and also a hopeless act of resistance. The machinery of tyranny, deception and mass murder was by now perfected and overwhelming. The murderers were far too many, their forces far too well armed, and their determination to destroy far too deeply rooted, for them to be overcome.

There continued to be enormous profit, too, in this massive destruction of human life. In the three months to April 30, Hans Frank reported to Himmler from Cracow, a huge amount of personal belongings had been delivered to Germany, including 94,000 men's watches, 33,000 women's watches, 25,000 fountain pens, 14,000 propelling pencils and 14,000 pairs of scissors. The men's watches were being distributed to the combat troops, to the men of the submarine service and to the guards in concentration camps. The five thousand 'most expensive' watches, as well as those in gold or platinum cases or partly fitted with precious stones, were either to go to the Reichsbank in Berlin 'for melting down' or were to be retained by the SS 'for special use'.

On May 3, in Croatia, a final manhunt was launched against Jews who had escaped earlier round-ups, or been exempted from them. Among those seized was Dr Hugo Kohn, the President of the Jewish Community of Zagreb, and Dr Freiberger, the chief Rabbi of Zagreb, a personal friend of Archbishop Stepinac. Despite church protests, however, all those who were seized that day were sent to Auschwitz. In nearby Bosnia, the month of May saw the launching of a double sweep against Yugoslav partisans, 'Black I' and 'Black II'. This sweep, which lasted until mid-June, led to the deaths of several hundred partisans.

The Allied bombing offensive over Europe now combined massive raids, using several hundred bombers, with raids against specific single targets. One such special raid took place on May 3, when a New Zealand pilot, Squadron Leader Leonard Henry Trent, led twelve bombers of a New Zealand squadron on a mission to bomb a power station on the outskirts of Amsterdam. Trent's aircraft was the only one to reach the target: nine of the bombers were shot down and two others were forced to return to England. Trent made a solo attack on the power station before he was himself shot down. He and his navigator survived and were taken prisoner. The full story of the raid did not emerge until after the war, when, in 1946, Trent was awarded the Victoria Cross for his determined leadership and devotion to duty.

In the Atlantic, the fortitude of the Allied merchant seamen and the increasing effectiveness of their naval escorts was at last to be rewarded that May. Success came as a result of the British cryptographers' success in the resumed breaking of the German U-boat Enigma key. Convoy ONS 5 had begun its transatlantic journey on April 22, its escort commanded by Commander Peter Gretton. Tempests beset the convoy's path; by April 30 it was sailing through a full gale. Then, on May 4, the German submarine U-630, about to attack the convoy, was sunk by the depth charges of a Canadian Royal Air Force aircraft. On the following day a second submarine, the U-192, was destroyed by the corvette *Pink*.

As more than thirty German submarines gathered for the attack, it seemed that even prior knowledge could not help. By the evening of May 6, eleven merchant ships had been sunk. One officer of the escort, who knew nothing of the Enigma window on German submarine movements, noted in his log: 'The convoy seemed doomed to certain annihilation.' But then four U-boats were sunk in quick succession and, as a further twenty-five gathered for the kill, local radio direction finding, combat skill, and courage combined to frustrate them. Only one more merchant ship was sunk.

For Grand Admiral Dönitz, the loss of four U-boats in a single attack was a disaster. It was compounded when two more U-boats collided and sank. But worse was to come. On Gretton's next convoy, not a single ship was sunk, but five more U-boats were destroyed, in one of which Dönitz's son was killed.

The Battle of the Atlantic had become a disaster for Germany. So too had the battle for Tunis. On May 4, as a result of the precise details sent, and read, in an Enigma decrypt, British destroyers were able to find and sink a large Italian merchant ship, the *Campobasso*, taking fuel and military supplies to the Axis forces. On the following day, also as a result of an Enigma decrypt, American bombers sank a second merchant ship on its way to Tunis, the *San Antonio*. These were the last two merchant ships of any size to attempt to bring supplies to the beleaguered Axis forces.

On May 6, at dawn, the British First Army began the final assault on Tunis. To the south and north, French and American troops joined in the attack. That same day, Allied bombers attacked the principal harbours in Sicily, as well as the Italian port of Reggio di Calabria, the mainland terminal of the ferry system to Sicily. That day, in an attempt to show the Russians that Britain too had suffered in human terms in the fighting, the British Chiefs of Staff sent the Russian General Staff a note of British deaths between 3 September 1939 and 31 March 1943. These included 38,894 soldiers, 30,540 sailors, 23,588 airmen and more than 20,000 merchant seamen, a total war dead of more than 103,000. This did not include those servicemen who had been reported missing, and made no mention of more than 45,000 civilian dead in air raids over Britain itself.

On May 7, Tunis, the capital of Tunisia, and Bizerta, its principal port, were both taken by the Allies after desperate German and Italian resistance. Such Axis troops as could escape capture withdrew into the Cape Bon peninsula, known to the Allies as the 'Tunisian Tip'. On May 8, three Italian supply ships, hurrying from Sicily to Hammamet with essential fuel, were sunk before they could unload. That day, the German Air Force abandoned its remaining North African airfields, and withdrew to Sicily. In Berlin, however, Goebbels noted in his diary: 'The Führer expresses his unshakeable conviction that the Reich will one day rule all of Europe. We will have to survive a great many conflicts, but they will doubtless lead to the most glorious triumphs. And from then on, the road to world domination is practically spread out before us. For whoever rules Europe will be able to seize the leadership of the world'.

Such was Hitler's confident belief on 8 May 1943, two years to the day before his defeated armies were to surrender unconditionally amid the ruins of the Reich.

On 9 May 1943 the German forces in the Tunisia Tip surrendered unconditionally to the Allies. That same day, the now triumphant Allied forces began to plan Operation Corkscrew, for the capture of the Italian island of Pantelleria, the stepping stone for Sicily. In Berlin, Rommel, when asked for an explanation for the defeat in North Africa, noted in his diary: 'I stressed to both the Führer and Goebbels the meagre fighting quality of the Italians and their reluctance to fight.'

The last pockets of Axis forces between Hammamet and Kelebia, having ignored the surrender two days earlier, capitulated to the Allies on May 11 and 12. In all, in the Tunisian Tip, 238,243 unwounded Germans and Italians were taken prisoner.

On May 12, Churchill and Roosevelt met in Washington to discuss future Allied strategy. That day, on the Aleutian Island of Attu, an American force of 11,000 landed in the face of the determined defence of a mere 2,500 Japanese. Fighting, as in every Japanese encounter, was severe, as Operation Landgrab sought to drive the Japanese from American soil. Two days later, on May 14, in the Pacific, a Japanese submarine torpedoed and sank the *Centaur*, an American ship clearly marked as a hospital ship and brightly lit up; 268 of those on board, including many men badly wounded in action, were drowned.

In Washington, Roosevelt and Churchill agreed that the sequence of Allied war moves should be, first, the invasion of Sicily, second the invasion of Italy, and third, however the situation in Italy might develop, the cross-Channel invasion of northern Europe. It was clear that much planning and much hard fighting remained to be done, but a sense of triumph was nevertheless in the air. 'It is my duty to report that the Tunis campaign is over.' General Alexander telegraphed to Churchill in Washington on May 13. 'All enemy resistance has ceased. We are masters of the North African shores'.

That night, British bombers dropped a thousand tons of bombs on Bochum, in the Ruhr, in forty-five minutes. These devastating air raids had not found the Germans without responses, among them the labour mobilization and the forced labour system, whereby hundreds of thousands of Frenchmen, Dutchmen, Danes, Belgians, Norwegians, Poles, Slovaks and Jews were brought to factory sites throughout Greater Germany, and put to work in conditions of considerable severity.

On May 13, when Hitler was back at Rastenburg awaiting the start of Operation Citadel – the German attack into the Kursk salient – his Armaments Minister, Albert Speer, flew from Berlin to report a substantial increase in German armaments production, in spite of Allied bombing. In the previous four months, German tank production had doubled. 'In the autumn,' Speer told Hitler, 'you instructed us to deliver specific quantities of arms by May 12. Today we can report that we have met every one of those figures and in some cases far exceeded them.' There was another report on May 13, which Goebbels noted in his diary. It was from Croatia, where, in the latest action against partisans, 'more than 13,000 rebels were killed, among them a great many intellectuals'.

On May 14, in Washington, the British and American Chiefs of Staff, meeting as a single body, approved Operation Pointblank, a combined Anglo-American bomber offensive from airbases in Britain. Its aim was set out as 'the progressive destruction and dislocation of the German military and economic system, and the undermining of the morale of the German people to a point where their capacity for armed resistance is fatally weakened', in order – and this was a step forward from previous bombing aims – 'to permit initiation of final combined operations on the continent'.

Six German systems were to be attacked under Operation Pointblank: submarine construction yards and bases, aircraft factories, ball bearing factories, oil production and storage plants, synthetic rubber and tyre factories, and military transport vehicle factories and stores. Nor would the new targets have to wait for any complex procedure of planning or implementation; on the very night that Pointblank was agreed to, British bombers struck at the Skoda munitions factory near Pilsen, deep inside Greater Germany. 'Among other targets the drafting room was destroyed,' Goebbels wrote in his diary on the following morning, and he added: 'This is quite a setback for us. However, the number of planes we shot down is colossal. Within forty-eight hours the English lost seventy-eight four-engined bombers.'

For Hitler, the greatest danger now lay in the defeat of Italy, or in Italy's defection from the Axis. 'Europe must be defended at its margin', he told his generals on May 15, 'we cannot allow a second front to emerge on the Reich's frontiers.' To ensure that the Allies were resisted in Italy, German troops would have to be taken away from Operation Citadel in Russia.

Slowly, and almost imperceptibly, Hitler's successful war and conquest were giving way to defence and withdrawal. Nor was Germany to be given any respite from the now virtually daily air bombardment; on May 16, the day after Hitler's speech to his generals, the British launched Operation Chastise, against the Möhne, Eder and Sorpe dams, which controlled the water level in the Ruhr area.

Led by Wing-Commander Guy Gibson, one of the Royal Air Force's outstanding bomber pilots, and using special 'bouncing' bombs developed by Dr Barnes Wallis, the raid succeeded in breaching two of the three dams, and in causing considerable damage, though not the widespread devastation that had been expected. Eighteen bombers took part, flying at low altitude across the North Sea and Holland. During the raid, six of the bombers were shot down while crossing the Dutch coast and two at the dams, killing 56 of the 133 crew members who had set out. 'If only I'd known,' Barnes Wallis remarked when this death toll was known, 'I'd never have started this.'

In the flood caused by the breaching of the two dams, 1,268 people were killed, including seven hundred Russian inmates in a slave labour camp. For planning and leading the raid, Gibson was awarded the Victoria Cross. 'The Führer is exceedingly impatient and angry about the lack of preparedness on the part of our Air Forces', Goebbels noted in his diary on May 18, and he added: 'Damage to production was more than normal.' To make good the damage, 50,000 workers were brought to the Ruhr from the Todt Organization's force working on the Atlantic Wall, while anti-aircraft guns needed elsewhere were brought to protect dams not only in the Ruhr, but throughout Germany, though none were in fact endangered.

Behind the lines on the Eastern Front, in the Bryansk area, May 16 saw the launching by the German Army of Operation Gypsy Baron, a three week anti-partisan sweep involving five infantry divisions, one armoured division, and aircraft which dropped, not only bombs, but 840,000 leaflets calling on the partisans to surrender. Of the six thousand partisans in the area, 1,584 were killed and a further 1,568 were captured. Twenty-one heavy guns and three tanks were also captured. But, within a few weeks of the end of the sweep, German Intelligence estimated that there were at least four thousand partisans still in the area, including the undestroyed partisan command staffs.

The launching of Operation Gypsy Baron in Russia took place on the very day when SS Brigadier Jürgen Stroop reported to his superiors: 'The Warsaw ghetto is no longer in existence.' The Jewish revolt, which had begun on April 18, had ended that evening, Stroop wrote, 'by blowing up the Warsaw synagogue'. As well as the fourteen thousand Jews killed in the fighting or sent to their deaths at Treblinka, a further forty-two thousand were sent to labour camps in the Lublin district. In recognition of his services, Stroop was awarded the Iron Cross, First Class.

Nearly six months had passed since one of the first American bombers based in Britain, the 'Memphis Belle', had flown her initial sortie over German-occupied Europe. On May 15, she flew on a bombing mission against Wilhelmshaven;

then two days later, in a raid on the German submarine base at Lorient, on the French Atlantic coast, she became the first British-based American bomber to complete twenty-five operational missions. As the 'Memphis Belle' prepared to return to the United States, her crew were filmed receiving combat medals; the filming was part of an exercise in producing a colour feature film of a day in the life of a bomber, to be shown in the United States; the raid on Wilhelmshaven on May 15, was used as the focal point of the film, which included a dramatic sequence showing another bomber, hit by German anti-aircraft fire, falling out of the sky, as one by one its crew, though not all its crew, parachuted out. Included in the film was a sequence showing a bomber returning from what was presumably a combat mission, with much of its tail fin apparently shot away. In fact, the damage had been caused not by German anti-aircraft fire, but in a collision with another American bomber over the English Channel.

Powerful though the film was, as an indication of the risks and perils facing bomber crews, and how they met them, it was to be another eleven months before the 'Memphis Belle' was ready for release. Its final message was that the risks and perils would continue, 'so we can bomb the enemy again and again and again – until he has had enough'.

On May 17, the day on which the 'Memphis Belle' completed her twenty-fifth bombing mission, the higher direction of the Allied war effort was significantly enhanced by an Anglo-American agreement on the full exchange and distribution of Signals Intelligence. To bring the German Enigma, Italian 'c 38m', and Japanese Purple decrypts into a standard form, the code name Ultra was adopted.

Rapid progress had also been made by May 1943, and would continue to be made, in the breaking of many of the signals circuits using the German Geheimschreiber, or secret teleprinter. The task in breaking this vital communications link was in some ways more formidable than breaking the Enigma. Because the teleprinter was used between German military authorities at the highest level, the results for the Allies in reading it were no less important than those of the Enigma; for the most secret messages sent to and from German Army Headquarters at Zossen and the Mediterranean and Eastern Fronts it was even more important. With Enigma as its first triumph, Ultra was now a potent weapon in the Allied ability to make war, and to anticipate danger.

As a result of the agreement of May 17, American cryptographers came to Bletchley to study the British methods and how to operate them, while British cryptographers went to Washington to help with the decrypting of Japanese cyphers. More than five thousand people were now working at Bletchley; the Naval section, which before the war had a staff of twenty-four, now had a thousand.

Many thousands more were working at intercept stations throughout the British Isles where the top-secret signals were intercepted in the form in which they were being transmitted by Axis radio stations. There were also several intercept stations overseas, including those at Socotra and Mauritius in the Indian Ocean, at Brisbane in Australia, and at Abbottabad in northern India, which picked up Japanese signals.

Drawn into this most secret work were professors, linguists, classicists, historians, mathematicians – men and women, British-born and refugees from Germany – a secret army through whose daily intellectual exertions almost the whole pattern of Axis preparations and activities was made known to those who had to direct Allied strategy and tactics.

In the third week of May, Hitler gave instructions to start an anti-Bolshevik Legion made up of British prisoners-of-war. 'These are to take part', Goebbels noted in his diary on May 18, 'in the fight against the Soviet Union, as volunteers'. The prisoner-of-war camps were combed. But the number of volunteers, most of whom merely hoped to exchange their lives as prisoners-of-war for something less onerous, was small: 1,500 had been hoped for, less than fifty came forward to fight against Russia. Not the Russian front, however, but the imminent danger of the opening of an Italian front, was much on Hitler's mind that week. On May 18 he gave orders, in such strict secrecy that he would not even sign a top secret directive to that effect, for Operation Alaric, the German occupation of Italy in the event that his Axis partner either collapsed or defected. To command the troops for Alaric he appointed Rommel, instructing him to assemble eleven divisions for the task.

In May, Churchill was once again in the United States, to co-ordinate Anglo-American war policy for its decisive moment, the cross-Channel invasion of German-occupied northern Europe. Speaking to a joint session of Congress on May 19, he warned: 'The enemy is still proud and powerful. He is hard to get at. He still possesses enormous armies, vast resources and invaluable strategic territories.' There was, Churchill said, 'one grave danger', the 'undue' pro-longation of the war, and he went on to explain: 'No one can tell what new complications and perils might arise in four or five more years of war. And it is in the dragging-out of the war at enormous expense, until the democracies are tired or bored or split, that the main hopes of Germany and Japan must now reside'.

On May 19 Churchill and Roosevelt fixed a date for the cross-Channel landing. It was to take place no later than 1 May 1944, whatever problems or opportunities might be created by the invasion of Italy, and was to be carried out by twenty-nine divisions, with the possibility of a Free French division being added.

At that moment of Anglo-American decision, Tito's partisan forces in Yugoslavia were holding down thirty-four German and Italian divisions; it was to encourage him in his struggle, and to undertake 'joint acts of sabotage' in order to continue to keep the German and Italian forces tied down, that Britain launched Operation Typical on May 22, parachuting into Tito's mountain headquarters a small British mission, headed by two officers, Captain Stuart and Captain Deakin, and two wireless operators, Sergeant Wroughton and Sergeant Rosenberg. Deakin had been Churchill's literary assistant before the war. Rosenberg was a Jewish volunteer from Palestine; later he recalled how the mission arrived in the middle of a battle, the whole area being surrounded by German troops who had 'explicit orders that all partisan forces to be found within were to be destroyed, including civilians, animals – whatever is found within must be destroyed'.

This German partisan sweep was Operation Black I and II, the fifth sweep in Yugoslavia since November 1941. In it, the Germans sent 67,000 German troops, 43,000 Italians and 11,000 Croats, against 16,000 partisans. 'The troops must move against the hostile population', their operational order stated, 'without consideration and with brutal severity, and must deny the enemy any possibility of existence by destroying abandoned villages and securing existing supplies.' Despite considerable losses, the Yugoslav partisans fought a tenacious battle; German brutality against the civilians in the villages through which the partisans had found shelter during their marches served only to strengthen the resolve, not only of the partisans themselves, but of the local population.

The brutality was indeed fearful. Eight days after Operation Black was launched, one of the German combat groups involved issued the order: 'Now that encirclement is complete, let no able-bodied man leave the circle alive.' Of the 498 prisoners whom the Germans took during one particular sweep, 411 were shot. In the fighting itself, and in the slaughter carried out in several hundred villages and hamlets, sixteen thousand Yugoslavs were killed.

On May 22, as the British mission joined Tito's partisans who were struggling to escape the net of Operation Black in Yugoslavia, the Germans in White Russia launched Operation Cormorant, a month-long sweep to try to clear Soviet partisans from the area of the Minsk–Borisov section of the Warsaw–Moscow railway. So effective had the partisans been in reducing the volume of supplies reaching German front-line formations that combat units were having to be taken out of the line in order to undertake security duties along the roads and railways.

In the North Atlantic, German submarine attacks on Allied merchant ships had continued. But the Allies were now masters of the German naval Enigma, including that used between the German u-boats and their command. During the first twenty-two days of May, thirty-one u-boats had been destroyed. On May 23, aircraft from the American aircraft-carrier *Bogue* and the British aircraft-carrier *Archer* drove off an attack on convoy HX 239, sinking two more u-boats. The success of *Archer* marked the very first successful use of air-to-sea rocket projectiles.

For Grand Admiral Dönitz these two sinking were the end of what had so recently been Germany's most successful, and for the Allies most dangerous, war zone. On May 24 he ordered the u-boats to be withdrawn from the North Atlantic convoy routes. Even as the last u-boat packs were recalled to the less dangerous and less fruitful waters of the south Atlantic, and to their Atlantic coast bases in France, eight more were sunk, six of them in the Bay of Biscay as they made for the shelter of their bases.

No setback at sea could halt the relentless momentum of the Nazi New Order. It was on May 24, the day on which Dönitz accepted failure in the North Atlantic, that a new SS doctor reached Auschwitz. His name was Josef Mengele and he had just celebrated his thirty-second birthday. Driven by the desire to advance his medical career by scientific publications, Dr Mengele began to conduct medical experiments on living Jews whom he took from the barracks and brought to his hospital block. Mengele used the pretext of medical treatment to kill several thousand prisoners, personally injecting them with phenol, petrol, chloroform or air, or by ordering ss medical orderlies to do so.

From the moment of his arrival at Auschwitz, Mengele joined the other ss officers and ss doctors, among them Dr Clauberg and Dr Kremer, in the 'selection' of Jews reaching the railway junction from all over Europe. With a movement of the hand or the wave of a stick, he indicated as 'unfit for work', and thus destined for immediate death in the gas chambers, all children, old people, sick, crippled and weak Jews, and all pregnant women.

Between May 1943 and November 1944 Mengele took part in at least seventy-four such selections. He also took an equally decisive part in at least thirty-one selections in the camp infirmary, pointing out for death by shooting, injection or gassing those Jews whose strength had been sapped by starvation, forced labour, untreated illness or ill-treatment by the guards. Always immaculately dressed in a white medical coat, and wearing white gloves at each murderous 'selection', Mengele was known to the Jews at Auschwitz as the 'Angel of Death'.

On May 25, the day after Dr Mengele reached Auschwitz, a further 2,862 Dutch Jews were deported there from Holland; by the end of the month, the camp had received a total of just over eight thousand Dutch Jews, more than two thousand Croat Jews from Zagreb, and ten thousand Greek Jews from Salonica, as well as 395 Jews from Berlin.

On May 26, it was the turn of the Gypsies to suffer death at Auschwitz. They had been brought to the camp from Bialystok two months earlier, and now there was a typhoid epidemic in their barracks. For Dr Mengele, typhoid was not an illness to be cured, but one to be eliminated; that day, all 1,042 Gypsies were dragged out of their barracks and driven to the gas chambers. Against their names in the camp register were put the letters 'SB' – 'Sonderbehandlung', Special Treatment.

The Casablanca and Washington decisions to bomb Germany with increased weight and frequency of bombs continued to be put into effect. On the night of May 24, British bombers attacked Dortmund, 'probably the worst-ever raid directed against a German city', Goebbels noted in his diary on the following day. Industrial and munitions factories, Goebbels wrote, 'have been hit very hard', and he commented: 'One can only repeat about air warfare: we are in a position of almost hopeless inferiority and must grin and bear it as we take the blows from the English and the Americans.' Those Germans living in the western regions, Goebbels added, 'are gradually beginning to lose courage. Hell like that is hard to bear for any length of time, especially since the inhabitants along the Rhine and Ruhr see no prospect of improvement.'

On May 25, in Washington, Roosevelt and Churchill gave a joint press conference, at which Roosevelt told the assembled newspapermen that the combination of the day and night bombing of Germany by United States and British aircraft was achieving 'a more and more satisfactory result'.

The air weapon, Churchill told the assembled journalists, 'was the weapon these people chose to subjugate the world. This was the weapon with which they struck at Pearl Harbour. This was the weapon with which they boasted – the Germans boasted – they would terrorize all the countries of the world. And it is an example of poetic justice that this should be the weapon in which they should find themselves most out-matched and first out-matched in the ensuing struggle'.

# 32

# 'The first crack in the Axis' (Roosevelt)

## SUMMER 1943

In the scientific air war, 26 May 1943 was a double landmark. In Washington, Roosevelt agreed to Churchill's request that the Anglo-American exchange of information on the atomic bomb, suspended for more than a year because of mutual suspicions, should be resumed, and that henceforth the enterprise should be considered a joint one, 'to which both countries would contribute their best endeavours'. That same day, at Peenemünde, on the Baltic coast, Albert Speer, again witnessing a series of demonstrations, agreed that work should go ahead on two different types of long range missile, the pilotless plane – later known as the v1, and the rocket bomb – the v2.

Both the Anglo-American and German secret weapons were still at the experimental stage. On May 27, however, the air war took another step forward along its existing path, when British Bomber Command instructed its planners and pilots to prepare for Operation Gomorrah, the total destruction of Hamburg by 'sustained attack'. Meanwhile, during a British night raid on Wuppertal on May 29, in which the centre of the city was engulfed in a firestorm, a total of 2,450 German civilians were killed and 118,000 people left homeless.

On 28 May 1943 the American attempt to recapture Attu Island from the Japanese reached a bloody climax when the Japanese forces, reduced to a thousand men, launched a suicide attack on the Americans. First, a hundred Japanese were killed. Then, early on May 30, the survivors committed mass suicide with hand grenades, leaving the Americans in possession of the island, and with only twenty-eight wounded prisoners. On May 31, American troops combed the island in search of Japanese survivors. They found only corpses. In three weeks of fighting, 600 Americans, and 2,500 Japanese, had been killed.

The American victory on Attu Island came at a moment when, in German-occupied France, strenuous efforts were being made to bring together all the Resistance groups under a single leadership. It was to achieve this that Jean Moulin had been parachuted into France more than a year before. On May 27 he was finally successful. At a secret meeting in Paris, fourteen Resistance leaders, representing eight separate movements, agreed to accept the overall leadership of General de Gaulle. A month later, however, Jean Moulin was among a number of Resistance leaders arrested by the Gestapo in Lyon. Under terrible torture, he betrayed nobody; broken in body, he died eleven days later, while being taken eastward, already unconscious, to a concentration camp in Germany.

All over the world, total war had dragged hundreds of thousands of human beings into camps where the guards and administrators participated in the torture and death of the inmates. Notorious in this regard were the camps on the Thailand railway. Recording the first death in Hintok camp, that of a private soldier, E. L. Edwards, on June 2, Colonel Dunlop noted in his diary: 'God knows the angel's wings must have been over us in view of the terrible mortality in all other camps up and down this line which seemed to be being built in bones.' As for Konyu camp, Dunlop noted, it was 'a real camp of death these days – at least an average of one death a day, and five in one day recently'. The prisoners-of-war were being made to get up 'in pitch dark and wet, leave with the first light after boiling their morning rice, and return again in darkness after a gruelling day in the rain and mud'.

On June 2 the German Air Force launched a series of attacks on Kursk; on the following day the Russian Air Force struck at German formations in Orel. In Algiers, June 3 saw the final day of the conference between Churchill and the Anglo-American service chiefs at which it was agreed to launch Operation Tidal Wave, the bombing of the Roumanian oilfields at Ploesti. Approval was also given for the bombing of the Italian railway marshalling yards in Rome. The bombing of these yards, advised General Marshall, 'should be executed by a large force of aircraft'.

For the Germans, the problems behind the lines continued. On June 3 they launched Operation Cottbus against Soviet partisans in the Polotsk–Lepel–Borisov region. At Clermont-Ferrand, in France, a Resistance unit struck that day at the Michelin tyre factory, destroying more than three hundred tons of tyres.

The Germans fought against their enemy behind the lines with the same energy as at the front. During Operation Cottbus, five thousand Russian villagers, including many women and children, were killed because partisans had found shelter in or near their villages. Yet only 492 rifles had been captured, in an area in which several thousand partisans were operating; on June 5 a German report noted with alarm that in the largest partisan centres there were airstrips on which it was possible to land two-engined aircraft, to fly in men and arms, and to evacuate fifteen to twenty wounded men on each flight.

The Final Solution also continued to be put into effect day by day. In Warsaw, on June 3, German troops discovered 150 Jews hiding in a bunker under the ruins of the ghetto; the bunker was destroyed. In the town of Michalowice, two Polish farmers, Stefan Kaczmarski and Stanislaw Stojka, were shot on June 3 for hiding three Jews. Two day later, in a slave labour camp at Minsk Mazowiecki, near Warsaw, all 150 Jewish slave labourers were shot dead, and the camp closed.

In German-occupied Western Europe, the escape lines for Allied airmen shot down were ensuring that hundreds of air crew never fell into German hands, but returned to Britain, and flew again, some of them within a few weeks of being shot down or baling out. On June 7, however, final disaster struck one of the main escape routes, the 'Comet' line, as five English airmen and one American were being met in Paris by two members of the line, Frederic de Jongh and Robert Ayle. Betrayed by a young Frenchman, the twenty-two-year-old Jacques Desoubrie, the six airmen were taken to prisoner-of-war camps and the two couriers to a Gestapo prison, where they were shot.

In all, Jacques Desoubrie was to be responsible for the arrest of fifty French and Belgian members of the Resistance, almost all of whom were then executed. On June 7, the day of the betrayal of the airmen in Paris, Professor Clauberg informed Himmler that the method on which he had been experimenting in Auschwitz, for the large-scale sterilization of women by x-rays, was 'as good as ready'. Clauberg added: 'I can now see the answer to the question you put to me almost a year ago about how long it would take to sterilize a thousand women in this way. The time is not far distant when I shall be able to say that one doctor, with, perhaps, ten assistants, can probably effect several hundred, if not one thousand sterilizations on a single day'.

There was no shortage of victims for these experiments; on June 8, more than eight hundred Greek Jews were deported from Salonica to Auschwitz, to be followed before the end of the month by a thousand Jews from Paris, and two thousand from the Upper Silesian city of Dabrowa Gornicza. From Germany, too, the few surviving Jews were being rounded up; that June, seventy Jews from Nuremberg, fifty-seven from Würzburg and eighteen from Bamberg were sent to Auschwitz. Also deported to Auschwitz that month were all the residents of the Jewish Old People's Home in the Czechoslovak city of Moravska Ostrava.

In Lyon, on June 6, the head of the Gestapo there, Klaus Barbie, began the five-day interrogation and torture of a thirteen-year-old girl, Simone Legrange, whose family had been denounced by a neighbour as Jews in hiding. The whole family were then sent to Auschwitz, where Simone Legrange's father was shot in front of her, and her mother sent to the gas chamber after being caught stealing a few discarded cabbage leaves. 'Shot or deported', Barbie told a local Jewish leader about the Jews whom he had arrested, 'there's no difference.' Nor was there any 'difference' as far as the fate of members of the French Resistance was concerned; on June 9, in Paris, the Gestapo arrested Alexander Rochais, the fifty-six-year-old head of the sixth section of the Paris Resistance. Deported to Buchenwald, he was killed there three months later. Today, in the Rue St André des Arts in Paris, a wall plaque marks the house in which Rochais was seized.

In German-occupied Yugoslavia, on June 9, one of the two British officers on the mission to the Yugoslav partisans, Captain Stuart, was killed during an air attack on Tito's headquarters. On the following night, the forces of Operation Black encircled Tito, his staff, an escort battalion and the three surviving members of the British mission. In the breakout, both Tito and the other British officer, Bill Deakin, were wounded, and more than a hundred partisans killed.

From Tunis to Sicily, May–July 1943

But Operation Black had failed; Tito's forces, mauled and scattered, regrouped and fought on.

On June 11, after ten days of air and sea bombardment, British troops based in Tunis launched Operation Corkscrew, landing on the small Italian island of Pantelleria. The Italian garrison at once surrendered. On the following afternoon, after an intense naval and air bombardment, the Italian garrison on the island of Lampedusa surrendered unconditionally. A third Italian island, Linosa, surrendered on June 13, while an uninhabited island, Lampione, was occupied by the Royal Navy that same day. No military obstacle now stood between the Allies in Tunisia and the invasion of Sicily, planned for the second week of July.

In the prisoner-of-war labour camps along the Burma-Thailand railway, the arrival of cholera added to the hardships and perils. 'I have just received news', noted Colonel Dunlop on June 13, 'that 130 British soldiers in the camp across the road died yesterday', and he commented: 'The cholera only hastened the end for these deathmasked men. Dehydration, in a black coat, is taking the victims painfully away'.

Hitler's confidence that he could retain the mastery of Europe was not entirely shared by his subordinates, even in the ss, whose leader, Himmler, decided, in the summer of 1943, to begin the total destruction of the evidence of the mass murder of Jews and Soviet prisoners-of-war. The method chosen was to send special squads to every mass murder site, to dig up the bodies and to burn them. In charge of this massive operation, which was to take more than a year of intense activity, was an ss colonel, Paul Blobel, who had earlier been in command of one of the ss killing squads in German-occupied Russia. Blobel's Special Commando Group No. 1,005, also known as the 'Blobel Commando', began work at the death pits near Lvov on June 15, when several hundred Jewish slave labourers at the adjacent Janowska concentration camp were taken to the pits and forced to dig up the putrefying corpses. Before burning them, the Jews were ordered to extract gold teeth and pull gold rings from the corpses. 'Every day,' one of the few survivors of a Blobel Commando, Leon Weliczker, later recalled, 'we collected about eight kilogrammes of gold.'

On the day on which the Blobel Commando began its gruesome work at Lvov, the head of the German Concentration Camp Inspectorate, ss Major-General Richard Glueks, visited Auschwitz. He was not entirely satisfied with what he saw, noting that the gas chambers, which he described in his report as the 'special buildings', were not well located, and ordered them to be relocated where it would not be possible for 'all kinds of people' to 'gaze' at them. One result of this complaint was the planting of a 'green belt' of fast-growing trees around the two crematoria nearest the camp entrance.

On the day of Glueks's report, a new labour camp was opened in the Auschwitz region, at the coal mines of Jaworzno. On the following day, Himmler's permission was given for eight Jews in Auschwitz to be sent to the concentration camp at Sachsenhausen, near Berlin, for experiments investigating jaundice. Five days later, in what Himmler called the interest of 'medical science', seventy-three Jews and thirty Jewesses were sent, alive, from Auschwitz to the concentration camp of Natzweiler, in Alsace. On reaching Natzweiler, their 'vital statistics' were taken. They were then killed, and their skeletons sent as 'exhibits' to the Anatomical Museum in Strasbourg.

Two hundred and fifty miles west of Natzweiler, in the triangle Orléans–Étampes–Chartres, just south of Paris, a member of the French Resistance was preparing to sabotage German railway and telephone targets. On June 16 a wireless operator was sent into France to join him. Her name was Noor Inayat Khan, an Indian princess, and a direct descendant of Tippoo Sultan. Bilingual in French and English, given the code name 'Madeleine', she did invaluable work until, arrested as a result of a betrayal, she was shot at Dachau in September 1944.

A sense of urgency now gripped the German racial plan. Even as the Blobel

Commando began its task of destroying the physical evidence of mass murder, the process of murder was accelerated. 'Responding to my briefing on the Jewish question,' Himmler noted at Obersalzberg on June 19, 'the Führer declared that the evacuation of the Jews, regardless of the disturbance it will provoke in the next three to four months, must be ruthlessly implemented and endured to the end.'

In Eastern Galicia, more than twenty thousand Jews were murdered in fields and ditches that June, the gas chambers at Belzec having stopped their work to enable a Blobel Commando to burn the bodies, crush their bones with a special machine and scatter the ashes. When this particular Commando, made up entirely of Jewish slave labourers, was sent on to Sobibor, its members, fearing that they were about to be gassed, tried to flee from the station; they were all shot down.


On June 20, British bombers launched Operation Bellicose, the first 'shuttle bombing' raid of the war. Leaving airbases in Britain, the bombers struck at the steel construction works at Friedrichshafen in southern Germany before flying on to airbases in Algeria; then, on their return flight to Britain, they bombed the Italian naval base at La Spezia. Unknown to the British, the Friedrichshafen works also contained the assembly factory for the v2 rockets, with an intended rate of assembly of three hundred rockets a month. So effective was the bombing, that the assembly line was abandoned.

Between the Friedrichshafen and La Spezia flights, a second air raid had been launched against the German industrial city of Wuppertal, in the Ruhr; not only was enormous damage done to factories in the city, holding up industrial production for nearly two months, but, in a second firestorm within two months, a further three thousand of its citizens were killed. Even British newspapers commented on the comparison with the German raid on Coventry, where 568 civilians had been killed and Coventry's factory production halted for a month.

Each day saw a further Allied bombing attack on Germany; on June 22 the United States Eighth Air Force attacked a synthetic rubber factory at Hüls, in the Ruhr, putting it out of action for several months.


In the Pacific, American Marines were slowly extending the range of their operations, landing on June 22 on Woodlark Island in the Trobriand island group, and, also on June 22, reinforcing the existing units which had landed on New Georgia Island. Following up their success on Woodlark Island, American units landed on Kiriwina Island, the largest in the Trobriand group, on the night of June 23. A week later, General MacArthur launched Operation Cartwheel, a series of amphibious assaults with the object of regaining Rabaul. That day, American troops landed on Rendova Island. Beach by beach, island by island, the reconquest of the Pacific had begun. In almost every instance, the Japanese resisted as if they were on their own soil of Japan; but, by the end of June, the Allies had secured the domination of the Solomon Sea.

*          *          *

In the third week of June, Churchill gave orders for air supplies to Tito's partisans to have priority 'even over the bombing of Germany'. The air resources needed to send up to five hundred tons of arms and equipment a month to the Yugoslav partisans would, he told the British Chiefs of Staff on June 23, be a 'small price to pay' for the diversion of German and Italian forces caused by resistance in Yugoslavia. 'It is essential to keep this movement going', Churchill insisted.

On June 23, as Churchill put his authority behind increased help to Tito's partisans in Yugoslavia, Hitler, at Obersalzberg, was justifying the deportation of Jews, following a protest by Henrietta von Schirach – daughter of his photographer Heinrich Hoffman and wife of the Governor of Vienna, Baldur von Schirach – who, on a recent visit to Amsterdam, had seen Jews being loaded into railway wagons. The sight, she told Hitler, was 'horrifying', and she went on to ask him: 'Do you know about it? Do you permit it?' In reply, Hitler told Schirach's wife: 'They are being driven off to work, so you needn't pity them. Meantime our soldiers are fighting and dying on the battlefields!' Hitler added: 'Let me tell you something. This is a set of scales' – and he put up a hand on each side to signify the pans – 'Germany has lost half a million of her finest manhood on the battlefield. Am I to preserve and minister to these others? I want something of our race to survive a thousand years from now.'

Hitler's final injunction was: 'You must learn how to hate!' Two days later, a thousand Jews were deported from Czestochowa to Auschwitz. As the deportation began, members of the Jewish Fighting Organization, led by Mordechai Zylberberg and Lutek Glickstein, distributed their few weapons, and sent their members to prearranged position in the cellars. But the Germans stormed the cellars, and most of the fighters were killed. The Jews had been poorly armed: the Germans captured thirty grenades, eighteen pistols and two rifles. Six fighters, commanded by Rivka Glanc, were cut off by the Germans. They had only two pistols and a single grenade. All six were killed.

Also on June 25, the Germans launched Operation Seydlitz, against Soviet partisans near Dorogobuzh, a vital communication centre for German reinforcements immediately behind the front line. That night, in German-occupied France, the British agent Michael Trotobas, known as Captain Michel, led a raid on the German locomotive works at Fives, on the outskirts of Lille. 'This job will be done with finesse and not with force', was Trotobas's advice to the small Resistance group which he assembled, and which, after bluffing its way into the works, managed to plant and detonate twenty-four powerful explosive charges. In triumph, Trotobas signalled back to London: 'Mission completed'.

That month, in what had become known as the Battle of the Ruhr, British bombers dropped fifteen thousand bombs in twenty nights. On June 27, Australia's representative on the British War Cabinet, Richard Casey, one of Churchill's weekend guests, noted in his diary how, 'in the course of a film showing the bombing of German towns from the air (made up from films taken during actual bombing raids) very well and dramatically done', Churchill suddenly 'sat bolt upright and said to me "Are we beasts? Are we taking this too far?" '

Casey himself had no doubt as to the answer. 'I said that we hadn't started it', he wrote, 'and that it was them or us.' On the following night, British bombers struck at Cologne, as well as at the Italian cities of Livorno and Messina. It was the raids in Italy and Sicily, not those on the Ruhr, which were to have an immediate impact on German strategy. Fearful of Italy's defeat, or defection, the German Air Force moved two operational command stations from southern Russia to Italy. This fact was made known to the British by an Enigma message.

The Russians themselves were now making inroads into Germany's Enigma system, having captured that June a code used by the German Air Force for air-to-ground signalling. In Murmansk, British and Soviet Naval Intelligence experts met to discuss how best to use the German air and naval messages thus procured. Shortly afterwards, the British presented the Russians with a captured Enigma machine, and a book of instructions for its use.

In a broadcast on June 30, Churchill spoke of the impending assault on Italy, and of Italian speculation as to where the assault would come. 'It is no part of our business', he said, 'to relieve their anxieties or uncertainties.' Churchill also spoke of the 'frightful tyrannies and cruelties' with which the German armies, 'their Gauleiters and subordinate tormentors' were now afflicting so much of Europe, and he declared: 'When we read every week of the mass executions of Poles, Norwegians, Dutchmen, Czechoslovaks, Frenchmen, Yugo-slavs, and Greeks; when we see these ancient and honoured countries of whose deeds and traditions Europe is the heir, writhing under this merciless alien yoke, and when we see their patriots striking back every week with a fiercer and more furious desperation, we may feel sure that we bear the sword of justice, and we resolve to use that sword with the utmost severity to the full and to the end'.

On July 1, Hitler returned to his 'Wolf's Lair' headquarters at Rastenburg, where, in a briefing to the commanders of Operation Citadel, he set July 4 as the date for the start of the attack on the Kursk salient. Greater Germany, he explained, 'must be defended far beyond our frontiers'. The principle on which this could be achieved was a simple one: 'Where we are, we stay'—whether in Russia, Sicily, Greece or Crete.

In one last attempt before the Kursk attack to cut down Soviet partisan activity behind the lines, on July 2 the Germans launched Operation Günther in the region of Smolensk. Two days later, Hitler sent a personal message to the soldiers around the Kursk salient. 'This day', it read, 'you are to take part in an offensive of such importance that the whole future of the war may depend on its outcome. More than anything else, your victory will show the whole world that resistance to the power of the German Army is hopeless'. Then, in the very early hours of July 5, at 1.10 a.m., two hours and twenty minutes before the German offensive against Kursk was due to begin, the Russians opened an artillery bombardment on the German forming-up positions and artillery lines. Considerable damage was done, blunting the edge of the German attack and

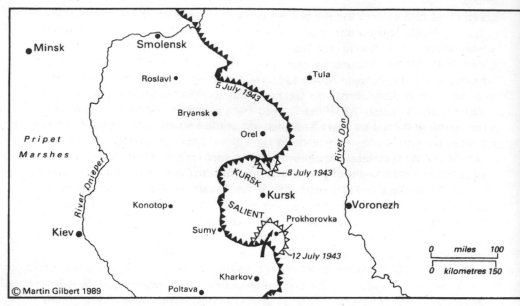

The Battle for the Kursk Salient, July 1943

ending all the intended element of surprise. Then, at 3.30 a.m., exactly on schedule, the German offensive began.

Along a two-hundred-mile front, the battle for the Kursk salient now absorbed the military energies, materials, willpower and hopes of each side; six thousand tanks – the biggest tank battle in history – and four thousand aircraft, were in combat. For Hitler, a relatively small bulge in the line had to be straightened. For Stalin, that same line had to be held, and Kursk retained.

The heroism of individuals was once more a feature of bloody, sordid war. On July 6, a Soviet pilot, Lieutenant Aleksei Gorovets, found himself alone in the sky above the salient facing twenty German aircraft. He decided to attack, and, having shot down the leader, shot down eight more. Then, unseen by Gorovets, four German fighters attacked him from above, and he himself was shot down. He was posthumously awarded the title of Hero of the Soviet Union.

At dawn on July 10, five days after the start of the Battle of Kursk, and while its outcome was still undecided, Allied forces landed on the coast of Sicily, 160,000 men and 600 tanks putting ashore under the cover of an intense naval bombardment. Once again, the heroism of individuals was remarkable. One British officer, Major Richard Lonsdale, who was parachuted with his men too far inland because of high winds, nevertheless remained where he was and with his men fought off successive German attacks, until it was the Germans who withdrew. For his tenacity, he was awarded the Distinguished Service Order.

That night, British units entered Syracuse, the first Italian city to be wrested from Italian rule. Inside German-occupied Europe, the news of this first Allied success in Europe was a cause for rejoicing, and for hope. On July 11, in the Kovno ghetto, Avraham Golub, who had been a lawyer in pre-war Lithuania, noted in his diary: 'Yesterday afternoon the mood in the ghetto was excellent. The British radio had just broadcast the news about the invasion of Sicily by the Allied armies. This news had been brought by workers returning from the city; in no time it spread throughout the ghetto. Everyone was certain that the end is near; deep in our hearts we were very glad. Everyone regarded the invasion of Sicily as a most unusual event which might bring our own liberation closer. Optimists spoke about the surrender of Italy in the near future; about clashes between units of the Italian and German armies, and about the fiasco of the new German offensive in Russia'.

'The Jews, of course,' Golub added, 'were busy drawing up plans for the Allied armies.'

On July 12, in the Kursk salient, the Russians faced their most serious test of the battle, when, at the village of Prokhorovka, they pitted nine hundred tanks against an attack by nine hundred on the German side; the German tanks included a hundred Tiger tanks, which were in many ways superior to the Russian T-34. The Russian officer responsible for holding the line, General P. A. Rotmistrov, later recalled: 'The earth was black and scorched with tanks like burning torches.' At one moment in the battle, Rotmistrov wrote, 'the commander of a Soviet T-34 had been so badly injured by a shell that penetrated the tank and set it on fire that he had to be taken out and laid in the cover of a crater. At that moment, a German Tiger bore down on the already stricken T-34, whereupon Aleksandr Nikolaiev, the driver, clambered back into his damaged and smouldering tank, started up, and charged towards the German tank. The T-34 hurtled across the ground like a fireball; the Tiger halted, but it was too late. The blazing T-34 hit the German tank at full speed, and the explosion made the ground shake'.

At nightfall, the 'slaughter of Prokhorovka' ended. Three hundred German tanks, among them seventy Tigers, were strewn over the battlefield. Even more Russian tanks had been destroyed. But the German thrust had been halted. That same day, north of the salient battle, the Russians launched Operation Kutuzov against Orel, to force the Germans to dissipate their strength, and to deny them the chance of sending reinforcements from Orel to the Kursk salient. Although slow progress was made on the ground, this new Soviet attack showed the extent to which the ability to take strategic and tactical initiatives had now passed, after two years' war in the East, from the attacker to the defender; henceforth, it was to be the defender, the Red Army, which would go over most frequently to the attack.

Far behind the lines, the German slaughters continued. On July 12, in the Polish village of Michniow, German police and Army units killed all two hundred villagers, including babies and expectant mothers, in yet another attempt to try to stamp out Polish patriotic feeling. On the following day, at the village of Sikory Tomkowieta, near Bialystok, a German military detachment executed forty-eight villagers, including fourteen children, for non-delivery of the agricultural produce which each village was obliged to hand over.

In the Pacific, 30,000 American troops were now ashore in the Solomon Islands battling against the fanaticism of the Japanese defenders. In Sicily, American, British and Canadian troops advanced northward across the island, against strong German and Italian opposition. In the Atlantic, British and American air and sea searches led to the sinking of seven German submarines in thirty-six hours, 'the record killing of U-boats yet achieved in so short a time', Churchill informed Roosevelt on July 14.

By July 14, it was clear that the Germans attacking towards Kursk were to be cheated of their prize. More than three thousand German soldiers had been killed and three thousand German tanks destroyed. The Russians had also captured an astonishing total of five thousand motor vehicles, 1,392 aircraft and 844 field guns. Several thousand Russian soldiers had also been killed, but, by holding Kursk, the Red Army had shown that even a relatively limited German aim could now be stopped. Summoning Field Marshals von Kluge and von Manstein to Rastenburg, Hitler told them that Operation Citadel was to be called off.

As Hitler decided, for the first time, to abandon a planned advance after only eight days, the Russians took yet another initiative, with a proclamation by the Soviet Supreme Command on July 14 that a 'Rail War' had been declared on the whole German rail system behind the lines. Six days later, on the Gomel–Bryansk–Orel railway, hundreds of miles of railway track were made impassable.

Not only resistance, but also retribution, now came into prominence, with the opening in Krasnodar on July 14 of the first Russian war crimes trial; eleven Germans were accused of the mass murder of Soviet civilians during the German occupation of the region. Eight Germans were sentenced to death and shot. Their trial, which was attended by several Allied journalists, did much to establish in Western minds the scale and nature of Nazi atrocities, and in particular the use of 'murder vans', inside which the victims were locked, and then gassed. Evidence was produced during the trial to show that some seven thousand civilians had been killed in this way in Krasnodar alone. 'Men, women and children', the court was told, 'were bundled into the van without discrimination,' including most of the patients in the Municipal Hospital. 'The gravely sick patients', one witness stated, 'were brought out on stretchers and the Germans flung them in the van too.' The van was then driven to a specially dug anti-tank ditch on the outskirts of the city. By the time it arrived, all those in it had been gassed. Their bodies had then been dumped into the ditch.

Even as the Krasnodar trial was in progress, killings such as it was revealing to the shocked Western observers continued to be carried out; on July 18, two hundred Jewish slave labourers were killed in the Polish town of Miedzyrzec Podlaski, followed two days later by a further five hundred in Czestochowa.

That month, also, two hundred Jews were deported from Paris to Auschwitz, and a further 1,500 from the camp at Malines, in Belgium, where several thousand Belgian Jews were interned. In the German war against Soviet partisans, during which so many local villagers were also killed as a warning and a reprisal, July 15 saw the launching of Operation Hermann, a month-long sweep between Vilna and Polotsk.

In Sicily, German forces defending Biscari airfield had for three days inflicted heavy casualties on the attacking Americans, before being forced to withdraw. In a final skirmish on July 14, after twelve American infantrymen had been wounded by sniper fire, a group of thirty-six Italians, some of them in civilian clothes, surrendered. On the order of the American company commander they were lined up along the edge of a nearby ravine and shot. That same day, another American infantry company ordered forty-five Italian and three German prisoners-of-war to be sent back to the rear for interrogation. After they had gone about a mile, the sergeant of the escort ordered them to halt, declared that he was going to kill the 'sons of bitches', borrowed a sub-machine gun, and shot the prisoners down.

When General Bradley heard of this incident, and reported it to General Patton, it was Patton who instructed him 'to tell the officer responsible for the shootings to certify that the dead men were snipers or had attempted to escape or something, as it would make a stink in the press and also would make the civilians mad. Anyhow, they are dead, so nothing can be done about it.' Bradley refused, and the two men were court-martialled, the sergeant, Horace T. West, being found guilty and sentenced to life imprisonment, the officer, Captain John T. Compton, being found not guilty. Because of a sustained outcry about unfair discrimination between officers and men, Sergeant West was released from confinement after a year, and returned to active service. Captain Compton had already been killed in action.

In the air above the Kursk salient, the bravery of the Soviet pilots included several whose exploits have entered into legend. One, Alexei Maresyev, had earlier had both his legs amputated, as a result of injuries incurred when he had been shot down over German-held territory. He had managed to crawl back, in eighteen days, to the Soviet lines. Also in action at Kursk were the French pilots of the Normandy Squadron, several of whom were killed in action, and whose commander, Major Jean-Louis Tulasne, shot down a total of thirty-three German planes.

On July 16, the Germans began their withdrawal in the Kursk salient. In Sicily, German forces began to fall back towards Catania. That day, Roosevelt and Churchill issued a joint appeal to the Italian people, urging them to decide 'whether they want to die for Mussolini and Hitler or live for Italy and civilization'. Three days later, on July 19, as American bombers attacked the railway marshalling yards in Rome, Hitler travelled to Italy, to meet Mussolini at Treviso, and to lecture him for two hours on how to fight wars and battles. 'Duce unable to act as he would wish,' Rommel noted in his diary after a talk with Hitler on July 20, and he added: 'I am to take command over Greece, including the islands, for the time being, so that I can pounce on Italy later.' Rommel's Greek assignment had an urgent purpose; German Army Counter-Intelligence still believed that Greece, not Sicily, was the principal and imminent target of the Allied strategists.

In Sicily, a major political objective was secured on July 22, when American troops entered Palermo, the principal town on the northern coast. Two days later, in Rome, the Fascist Grand Council, in a gesture of defiance against Mussolini, asked King Victor Emmanuel to assume 'effective command' of Italy's armed forces, and called for the responsibilities of Crown and Parliament to be 'immediately restored'.

The oldest of the Axis dictatorships was being undermined. Within twenty-four hours, Mussolini had been informed by the King that the Government of Italy had been placed in the hands of Marshal Badoglio.

Benito Mussolini, ruler of Italy since 1922, was suddenly, and with no apparent means of redress, shorn of his powers. Not only that; in an ignominious end to his authority, an ambulance hurried him from Rome to the island of Ponza, 'to safeguard his person against public hostility'.

That July 24, as Italy was in the throes of a sudden, bloodless revolution, Leningrad received the heaviest German shelling of the war; 210 people were killed, including several dozen in a tram on the Liteiny Bridge. In Britain, the civilian death toll from German bombing that July was 167. But on the night of July 24, British bombers set out on the first raid of Operation Gomorrah, against Hamburg, dropping 2,300 tons of high explosive and incendiary bombs in a few hours, as much as the combined tonnage of the five heaviest German air raids on London. 'All Hamburg seems to be in flames,' Berlin radio announced on the following morning. More than 1,500 German civilians had been killed. Nor was that the end of Hamburg's troubles that July; in conjunction with Operation Gomorrah, which continued to pound Hamburg night after night, the American Eighth Air Force launched 'Blitz Week', flying 1,672 sorties over northern Germany, including two raids against Hamburg, two against Kassel and two against Kiel.

In the first of the Gomorrah raids on Hamburg, the British had used a hitherto secret radar-jamming device, 'Window', bales of ten-and-a-half-inch strips of aluminium foil which were pushed out of the bombers as they flew to their target, and as they returned from it, to confuse the German radar watchers by a veritable snowstorm of 'aircraft' on their screens. As a result of the use of 'Window' on July 24, only twelve of the 791 bombers sent on the mission were shot down. On past averages, the new device had saved between seventy and eighty aircraft, and several hundred lives.

For Hitler, this Allied bombing success was part and parcel of a sudden worsening of the war. First, he had been cheated of victory at Kursk, then he had seen, in quick succession, the invasion of Sicily, the fall of his fellow dictator in Rome, and now the massive destruction of a German city. On July 26 he was forced, in order to prepare for the transfer of troops to Italy, to order Marshal von Kluge to begin the evacuation of his troops from the Orel salient. 'The fact is', General Jodl told Hitler that day, 'the whole fascist movement went pop, like a soap bubble.'

Both the King of Italy and Marshal Badoglio, the successor to Mussolini, had declared that Italy would continue to fight the war at Germany's side. But their promise gave no comfort to those at Rastenburg. 'In spite of the King's and Badoglio's proclamation,' Rommel wrote in his diary on July 26, 'we can expect Italy to get out of the war, or at the very least, the British to undertake further major landings in northern Italy.' As for the war itself, Rommel noted, 'The Americans have meanwhile occupied the Western half of Sicily and have broken through'.

Hitler had now to plan for military operations in Italy, in the most unfavourable circumstances, effectively calling a halt to any further advances on the Eastern front, where he had so hoped to reverse the humiliation of Stalingrad. Suddenly, it was in Western Europe, at his own back door, that danger threatened. At Rastenburg, on July 27, he therefore approved Operation Oak Tree for the personal 'liberation' of Mussolini, and Operation Student for the German occupation of Rome and the restoration of a Mussolini government, hoping to forestall an Allied landing as far north, so Rommel feared, as Livorno or even Genoa.

For the Allies, the events of the last week of July were an auspicious omen. 'The massed, angered forces of common humanity', Roosevelt told the American people during his Fireside Chat broadcast on July 28, 'are on the march. They are going forward – on the Russian front, in the vast Pacific area, and into Europe – converging upon their ultimate objectives, Berlin and Tokyo.' As for the events in Italy, Roosevelt declared, 'The first crack in the Axis has come. The criminal, corrupt fascist regime in Italy is going to pieces.'

On the night of July 27, the last Japanese forces on Kiska Island in the Aleutians had slipped away; they had decided not to do battle. On New Georgia Island in the Pacific, however, the Japanese, determined not to yield except at the highest possible cost, continued to fight for every position, forcing the Americans to call for reinforcements on July 28. Nevertheless, everywhere that they were in action, the Japanese were in retreat.

Over Germany, the early hours of July 28 saw the climax of Operation Gomorrah against Hamburg, which had already lost 1,500 of its citizens during the British air raid four days earlier. The raid of July 28, although it lasted only forty-three minutes, was different from any that had proceeded it in more than three years of aerial bombardment. 'The burning of Hamburg that night', one flight lieutenant later recalled, 'was remarkable in that I saw not many fires but one. Set in the darkness was a turbulent dome of bright red fire lighted and ignited like the glowing heart of a vast brazier. I saw no flames, no outlines of buildings, only brighter fires which flared like yellow torches against a background of bright red ash. Above the city was a misty red haze. I looked down, fascinated but aghast, satisfied yet horrified. I had never seen a fire like that before and was never to see its like again'.

A lethal predominance of incendiary bombs in the 2,326 tons of bombs dropped, combined with a warm night with low humidity, and a fire fighting service which had not recovered from its efforts four days earlier, led to a new phenomenon in the history of aerial warfare, described by the Hamburg Fire Department that night in the single word: 'firestorm'. One factory worker engaged in trying to save his factory from the flames later recalled: 'Then a storm started, a shrill howling in the street. It grew into a hurricane so that we had to abandon all hope of fighting the fire. It was as though we were doing no more than throwing a drop of water on to a hot stone. The whole yard, the canal, in fact as far as we could see, was just a whole, great massive sea of fire'.

At the centre of the firestorm, a hurricane style wind was created which uprooted trees. Flames, driven by the wind, burned out eight square miles of the city during an eight hour inferno. By morning, more than forty-two thousand German civilians were dead. This was more than the total British civilian deaths for the whole of the Blitz.

More than thirty-five thousand residential buildings, a third of those in Hamburg, were totally destroyed. Remarkably, however, within a few weeks, Hamburg's war production began to exceed that of the pre-firestorm levels.

In the early hours of July 29, Churchill and Roosevelt spoke on the telephone about their imminent armistice negotiations with Italy, secret contacts for which had already been made. 'We do not wish', Churchill told Roosevelt, 'to come forward with any specific armistice terms before we are asked in so many words,' to which Roosevelt replied: 'That is right'. 'We can wait one or two days', Churchill said, to which Roosevelt answered: 'Right.' The two leaders then discussed the problem of British prisoners-of-war in Italy, in order to forestall their transfer to what Churchill described as 'the land of the Hun'. He would communicate on this directly to the King of Italy, Churchill explained; Roosevelt agreed to do likewise.

This telephone conversation, revealing how close the Allies must be to taking Italy out of the war, was intercepted by German Intelligence, and shown to Hitler on the morning of July 29. Then, on the morning of July 30, he was shown a message from the German Security Police chief in Zagreb, Siegfried Rasche, reporting that the Chief of the Italian General Staff, General Roatta, had confided to a senior Croat general that 'Badoglio's assurances are designed merely to gain time for the conclusion of negotiations with the enemy'.

There was further distressing news for Hitler on the morning of July 30. In the third of the Gomorrah raids on Hamburg, mostly on suburban areas, a further eight hundred civilians had been killed, including 370 asphyxiated in a bomb shelter underneath a department store where the reserves of coke kept there caught fire. If three or four more cities were bombed as Hamburg had been, Albert Speer told Hitler, it could lead 'to the end of the war'.

Blow after blow seemed now to fall on Germany's war-making effort; on July 31, Churchill informed Roosevelt that eighty-five German submarines had been sunk in the previous ninety-one days of battle in the Atlantic. In Russia, behind German lines, the 'War of the Rails' intensified in the first days of August 1943, with Soviet partisans placing 8,600 explosive charges on the railway lines of Army Group Centre. On August 1, as part of Operation Tidal Wave, 177

American bombers flew from bases at Benghazi to the Roumanian city of Ploesti, putting forty per cent of the oil-refining plants out of action. For Hitler, the loss of this oil, not too serious in itself, as it took only a few days to restore production to the level needed by Germany, was nevertheless an ill omen of things to come. For the Americans, there was little comfort in a mission which resulted in the loss of fifty-four bombers and 532 aircrew. But a further twenty raids were to go ahead, until Tidal Wave brought production to a halt twelve months later.

In the Pacific, on August 1, Japanese aircraft bombed the American PT – fast patrol – boat base at Rendova Island, one of the Solomon Island chain, killing two men. The aim of the raid had been to deter PT activity against a force of four Japanese destroyers which were taking essential war supplies to the Japanese forces at Vila, on the southern tip of Kolombangara Island. Undeterred, fifteen PT boats set out from Rendova that evening, but failed to halt or harm the destroyers, despite a series of torpedo attacks upon them. During the engagement, one of the PT boats, PT-109, was rammed by the Japanese destroyer *Amaqiri* and cut into two pieces. So violent was the explosion at the moment of impact that the other PT boats assumed that PT-109 had been destroyed, and, returning to Rendova, prepared to hold a memorial service for the lost crew.

The crew had, however, survived, and, during a five-hour ordeal, clinging to some heavy timber from the boat, made for the shore of a small coral island. That evening, one of the eleven surviving crew members decided to swim out to sea, in the hope of being able to flag down any of the PT boats that might pass that way during the night. His name was John Fitzgerald Kennedy. When no PT boats came by, he began to swim back to the coral island, but was swept off course by the current. Returning with difficulty to the island, Kennedy was taken ill; two days later, he and his fellow crewmen decided to swim to a larger island, in fact Cross Island, which they believed to be Nauru Island. There, two native Solomon islanders agreed to take a message southward; Kennedy scratched it on a coconut shell. The message read: 'Nauru Is. Native knows posit. He can pilot. 11 alive need small boat.'

Kennedy hoped that the coconut message would be taken to one of the Australian coast watchers who, working for Allied Intelligence, and amid daily risk and danger, kept a vigilant eye along the enormous and predominantly unguarded island coastlines in the Solomons and New Guinea island chains, and who were themselves largely dependent for their survival on the goodwill of the native islanders. His hope was fulfilled; the coconut was handed to Lieutenant Arthur Evans, a coast watcher on the unoccupied Gomu Island, next to the Japanese held island of Wana Wana. Evans at once replied: 'Have just learned of your presence on Nauru Island and also that two natives have taken news to Rendova. I strongly advise you return immediately to here in this canoe and by the time you arrive here I will be in radio communication with authorities at Rendova, and we can finalize plans to collect balance of your party'.

This message reached Kennedy on August 7; that afternoon, a Solomon islander, Benjamin Kevu, paddled him and his crewmen to Gomu Island. From there, a PT boat took them back to Rendova. Later, Lieutenant Kennedy was awarded the Navy and Marine Corps Medal, for gallantry in action. Later still, when President of the United States, he welcomed both Arthur Evans and Benjamin Kevu to the White House, where the coconut with its scratched message, and Evans's reply, had pride of place among his trophies and souvenirs.

In German-occupied Europe, the destruction of the evidence of mass murder had become a priority. But its gruesome course was not always easy. At the death camp of Treblinka, August 2 saw a revolt by those Jews who were being forced to dig up the corpses and to burn them; men who knew that once their task was done, they too would be killed. Of the seven hundred Jewish slave labourers in the camp, more than five hundred were shot down during the revolt by the SS and Ukrainian guards, but more than 150 managed to escape. Some were subsequently hunted down by German and Ukrainian units and shot; others found safety in Polish homes, or went into hiding. As they did so, the Red Army launched an offensive against the German forces withdrawing from Orel, breaking into the city on August 4. Then, to the south, Soviet forces drove towards Kharkov, retaking Belgorod on August 5.

In Sicily, British troops entered Catania on August 5. On the following day, off Kolombangara Island, the Americans sank three Japanese destroyers bringing reinforcements to the island, drowning 1,500 soldiers and seamen. There were no American losses. Over Italy, throughout the second week of August, British bombers dropped more than six thousand tons of bombs on Milan, Turin and Genoa, killing several hundred Italian civilians. In Germany, a small group of officers, academicians, churchmen and professional men, about twenty in all, shocked by both the military setbacks and the moral turpitude of Hitler's regime, drafted a document on August 9 in which they dedicated themselves to the overthrow of Nazism, and to its replacement by a new political and social ethic. Led by two members of the old German military aristocracy, Count Helmut von Moltke and Count Peter Yorck von Wartenburg, the group met at Moltke's family estate in Kreisau, Silesia; hence its name, the Kreisau Circle.

'German hopes of victory are completely dwindling,' the Swiss newspaper *Neue Züricher Zeitung* commented on August 10. 'They have been replaced by a deep anxiety, as the people are convinced that the Party will not give in, even if more towns like Hamburg are erased.' It was not only the Nazi Party that had set its heart against surrender. On August 9, Rommel had written to his wife: 'The casualties in Hamburg must have been very high. This must simply make us harder.'

Such hardness was seen, not only in internal reaction to Allied bombing, but in external action against the continuing efforts of partisans and resistance fighters. On August 10, in Yugoslavia, General Löhr ordered retaliation 'with shooting or hanging of hostages' to each partisan attack, as well as the 'destruction of the surrounding localities'. Against Greek partisans a similar severity was to be shown. When, on August 12, German troops found an arms cache in the village of Kuklesi, ten civilians were shot in reprisal, and the village burned

down. Two days later, in a so-called 'cleansing' operation in the Paramythia–
Parga region, eighty partisans were caught and killed, in reprisal for the death
of a single German soldier.

In the Pacific, Japanese propaganda had begun to undermine the faith of the
Filipinos that the Americans would ever be able to liberate them. On August
10, General MacArthur was asked to agree to a proposal to send in to the
Philippines packets of cigarettes, matches, chewing gum, sewing kits and pen-
cils, individually wrapped with the American and Philippine flags, and with
MacArthur's facsimile signature below the words, 'I shall return'.

MacArthur noted on this suggestion, 'No objections. I *shall* return!' Several
million Victory Packages were made up, and sent in by submarine.

On August 11, the German Army began the evacuation of its forces in Sicily.
For six days, a total of seventy naval vessels, and a further fifty rubber boats,
took 60,000 German troops across the Straits of Messina, together with a high
proportion of their vehicles and weapons. The Allies, although warned by Ultra
of the German withdrawal, no longer had the necessary reserve strength to stop
this movement. As a result, the Allied armies' task was to be the more difficult
when, less than a month later, they invaded the Italian mainland.

On the Eastern Front, Hitler gave permission for the start of work on the
construction of the 'Panther Line', a defence line to run from Narva on the Gulf
of Finland to the Sea of Azov near Melitopol. Not only German Army engineers
and rear-echelon troops, but slave labourers drawn from all over Europe, were
to be used for the task: a massive bulwark of earthworks, concrete, barbed wire
and mines.

For the Germans, the sense of ever-impinging Allied activity was heightened
on August 13, when American bombers struck at the industrial city of Wiener
Neustadt, twenty-seven miles from Vienna. This was the first Allied air raid
over Austria. That same day, under conditions of strictest secrecy, a United
States physicist, Norman F. Ramsey, organized the dropping of a scale model
of the atomic bomb at the Dahlgren Naval Proving Ground in Virginia. Known
as the 'Sewer Pipe Bomb', its test was a failure; but it was not long before the
problem, stability in descent, was mastered.

In the Pacific, six thousand Americans landed on August 15 on Vella Lavella
Island; there were not enough Japanese troops to impede their landing or
seriously to hold up their advance. That same day, landing on the Aleutian
island of Kiska, 29,000 Americans and 5,300 Canadians, supported by a hundred
ships specially designed for the transport of tanks and armoured vehicles, landed
at dawn, only to discover that the Japanese had gone.

That week, Churchill was Roosevelt's guest for two nights at the President's
Hyde Park home. On August 13, using the code name 'Boniface' to disguise
Enigma, he gave Roosevelt a document about the daily German killings of
Yugoslav civilians: 'I am not sure that your people have quite realised all that
is going on in the Balkans and the hopes and horrors centred there. You might

find it convenient to keep it by you. Much of it is taken from the Boniface sources, and it certainly makes one's blood boil.' 'I must add,' Churchill continued, 'that I am not in any way making a case for the employment of an Allied Army in the Balkans but only for aiding them with supplies, agents and Commandos. Once the Adriatic is open we should be able to get into close contact with these people and give them aid sufficient to make it worth their while to follow our guidance.'

It was while Churchill was at Hyde Park that he and Roosevelt reached agreement on the full sharing of all work being done by British and American scientists on the atomic bomb. This agreement, signed by both men and shown to no one outside their most secret circle, placed the research and manufacture of the bomb in the United States, but as a joint project with no secrets withheld from either side. The first of the four Articles of Agreement laid down that Britain and the United States 'will never use this agency against each other'. The second article stated: 'We will not use it against third parties without each other's consent'; the third, 'that we will not either of us communicate any information about Tube Alloys to third parties except by mutual consent'. In the fourth article of agreement, covering the post-war industrial and commercial advantages of atomic research and development, Churchill, as the article noted, 'expressly disclaims any interest in these industrial and commercial aspects beyond what may be considered by the President of the United States to be fair and just in harmony with the economic welfare of the world'.

From Hyde Park, Roosevelt and Churchill travelled to Quebec, where they and their most senior advisers, including the Combined Chiefs of Staff, agreed to allow General Eisenhower to negotiate with the Italian Government for the unconditional surrender of Italy. Then, on August 19, the combined Chiefs of Staff presented Roosevelt and Churchill with their conclusions, which the two leaders accepted. Germany was to be defeated before Japan. The cross-Channel landing, Operation Overlord, was to constitute the 'primary United States-British ground and air effort against the Axis in Europe', with its D-Day set for 1 May 1944. Its aim was not only to be a landing in northern France, but the undertaking of further operations from northern France 'designed to strike at the heart of Germany and to destroy her military forces'.

One condition was set in the planning of Operation Overlord. If there were more than twelve German mobile divisions in France at the intended moment of the Allied landing, it would not take place. Nor would there be a landing if the Germans were thought to be capable of a build-up of more than fifteen extra divisions in the two months following the landing.

It was also decided at Quebec that the invasion of Italy would take place before the end of the month, with Naples as its objective. In the Balkans, Allied activity would be limited to sending supplies by air and sea to the partisans, to minor Commando raids, and to the bombing of strategic objectives.

On the morning of August 17, American forces entered Messina. After only thirty-nine days of fighting, the whole island of Sicily was under Allied control, and mainland Europe was within sight of the soldiers who crowded on the cliffs overlooking the Straits of Messina. That same day, American bombers based in Britain carried out heavy raids on the German ball-bearing factory at Schweinfurt and the Messerschmitt works at Regensburg. In the two raids, sixty of the five hundred attacking aircraft were shot down and more than a hundred aircrew killed, but both factories were badly damaged. During the bombing raid on Schweinfurt, 565 Germans, and 86 forced labourers of six different nationalities were killed. In Regensburg, there were 402 civilian dead, of whom 78 were foreign workers, most of them from Belgium, others from France, Russia, Czechoslovakia, and Hungary. The total Allied air crew deaths in the two air raids were 112 Americans, one Englishman and one Canadian.

That night, nearly six hundred British bombers carried out Operation Hydra, a long-planned raid on the German rocket and flying bomb construction centre at Peenemünde. During the raid, as a result of a deliberate decision by its planners, 130 German scientists, engineers and technical staff were killed in the housing estate on which they lived, among them Dr Thiel, who was responsible for the design of the rocket's propulsion unit. Owing, however, to a mistake in the dropping of two of the marker bombs, a substantial proportion of the actual bombs fell on a nearby camp housing the foreign labourers; six hundred of them were also killed. Technically, the raid was a success, setting back production of the rocket by at least two months, forcing its production to be transferred to an underground factory being constructed by foreign labourers at Nordhausen, south-west of Berlin, and leading to the majority of the launching trials being moved to Blizna in Poland.

Goebbels was particularly angered by the Peenemünde raid, as a result of which, he wrote, 'we can't possibly count on reprisals before the end of January'. That night, the Chief of the German Air Staff, General Hans Jeschonnek, already under fire from Hitler for the Schweinfurt and Regensburg raids, committed suicide.

Despite the destruction at Peenemünde, one more rocket test was made from the Baltic coast. It took place on August 22, with a rocket which had been fitted with a dummy concrete warhead. The rocket came down, not in the sea, where it would have sunk without trace, but on the Danish island of Bornholm. There, the Danish naval officer in charge on the island, Lieutenant-Commander Hasager Christiansen, immediately photographed the rocket and managed to smuggle the photograph to Britain, together with some sketches which he had made. Two weeks later, Christiansen was arrested by the German occupation forces on Bornholm, and so severely tortured that he had to be transferred to hospital. After two weeks in hospital, a Danish resistance group smuggled him to Sweden. He was subsequently awarded the Distinguished Service Cross.

On August 18 one of the more bizarre operations of the war took place. This was Plan Bunbury, the destruction of an electricity generating station at Bury St Edmunds, in East Anglia. A news item in *The Times* gave a brief description of this act of sabotage, which a German radio broadcast claimed to have resulted in the deaths of more than a hundred and fifty workmen. In fact, there had been no sabotage and no deaths; the news item had been a plant by British Military

The Eastern Front and the Red Army advance, July–August 1943

Intelligence, to give credence for their German 'masters' to two German agents, 'Jack' and 'OK', who had long before agreed to work for Britain, and whom their British masters knew as 'Mutt' and 'Jeff' – after the popular cartoon characters.

On August 22, after several days of stubborn fighting, German forces withdrew from Kharkov, and, for the fourth time in two years, the Ukrainian city changed hands. On the following evening, in Moscow, 224 guns each fired twenty salvoes to salute the troops who had liberated the city.

In a further discussion with Churchill at Quebec on August 23 Roosevelt seemed to take alarm at the turn of the tide in eastern Europe, telling Churchill that he 'desired' the troops of the Western Allies 'to be ready to get to Berlin as soon as did the Russians'. On that day, the American and Russian troops were almost identical distances from Berlin, the Americans at Messina were 1,000 miles from Berlin, the Russians at Orel 950 miles away; yet, despite these great distances, which could surely not be covered for more than a year, Roosevelt showed concern about an eventual conflict of goals between the Soviet Union and the West. Churchill did not disagree.

Berlin was not merely a talking point that August 23; following the destruction of Hamburg, and the death of forty-four thousand of its citizens, at the end of July, British bombers had planned a new series of attacks, this time on Berlin, which were intended to wreak similar havoc. The first of these raids, in what the British were to call the Battle of Berlin, took place on the night of August 23, carried out by more than seven hundred bombers. When the raid was over, 854 people were dead, 102 of whom were foreign workers, and two of whom were Allied prisoners-of-war. British losses among the bomber crews were also high, with 298 airmen killed, and a further 117 taken prisoner and sent to prisoner-of-war camps.

More fortunate than those shot down over Berlin was Staff Sergeant Claude Sharpless, shot down near Toulouse on August 24. As he landed, thirty or more Frenchmen surrounded him, spirited away his tell-tale flying suit, and produced a suit of civilian clothes for him to change into, so that he could go into hiding and be guided southward to the Pyrenees, Spain, and safety.

On the Eastern Front, the Red Army followed up the recapture of Kharkov by continuing its advance, capturing Kotelva, sixty miles west of Kharkov, on August 27, and, west of Kursk, entering Sevsk that same day. Also on August 27, a total of 185 American bombers made a massive raid on the German rocket launching site at Éperclecques, on the Channel coast. The moment chosen for the raid was after the concrete had been poured, but before it had time to set; as a result, it was a mass of twisted steel reinforcing girders which hardened within a few days into a useless, distorted mass. The Germans had therefore to begin the construction all over again, and to do so at a new site. Following a meeting between Hitler and Albert Speer a month after the raid, the Chief Engineer of the Todt Organization, Xavier Dorsch, was authorized to build a million-ton concrete dome at nearby Wizernes. This project, embarked on when the strain of German resources was mounting to a climax, epitomized the hopes which Hitler placed in his novel weapons.

In Yugoslavia, Tito's partisans, driven from Durmitor, had set up their head-quarters at Jajce, two hundred miles to the north. There, on the night of August 27, they held their first national assembly, in the presence of Soviet, American and British officers. The session was held at night because of the danger of German air attack.

On the morning of August 28, a Yugoslav partisan leader, Ivo-Lola Ribar, and two British officers, Major Robin Weatherley and Captain Donald Knight, were about to fly from partisan headquarters to Cairo when a single German reconnaisance plane flew over the airstrip and dropped two bombs. The three men were killed. A month earlier, Ribar's younger brother Jurica, an artist, had been killed fighting the Četniks in Montenegro; their mother was later murdered by the Germans for refusing to betray the men who had earlier helped her to flee from Belgrade. Ivo-Lola Ribar's fiancée, Sloboda Trajkovic, who had refused to betray his whereabouts, had already been murdered by the Germans, together with her mother, her sister and her brother, at Banjica concentration camp, just outside Belgrade.

Since the fall of Mussolini in the last week of July 1943, the people of Denmark had felt a sense of excitement at the prospect of an eventual end to the tyranny of occupation. Resistance, especially strikes and sabotage, had increased since the defeat of von Paulus at Stalingrad; now it accelerated. On August 28, Hitler's representative in Denmark, Dr Karl Rudolf Werner Best, presented an ultimatum to the Danish Government, demanding an end to strikes and meetings, as well as the introduction of a curfew, Press censorship and the death penalty for harbouring arms, and for sabotage. The Danish Government, supported by the King, refused the German demands. On August 29, without further negotiation, the German Army reoccupied Copenhagen, disarmed the Danish Army, and confined the King to his palace. For those Danes who had been active in the resistance, the German move provided a welcome end to Denmark's existence as what they called 'Hitler's little canary'. But there were hardships too which would now have to be borne, and evils to be combated.

On August 30, the Red Army, advancing towards Smolensk, reoccupied Yelnya; in the south, on the Sea of Azov, the city of Taganrog was recaptured. On the following day south of Bryansk, after four days of fighting, two hundred villages and hamlets were liberated. That night, above the German capital, 613 British aircraft carried out the second raid of the Battle of Berlin. A total of 225 aircrew were shot down and killed, and a further 108 taken prisoner-of-war. The German deaths were only eighty-seven, a tenth the number of those killed in the city a week earlier, and a third of the British deaths. This reversal of the order of casualties was not, however, to impede or to delay the bombing of Berlin.

Four years had passed since the German invasion of Poland, the first military step of the Second World War. On that day, the war had been a conflict limited to two States. Within three days, Britain and France had joined as Poland's allies. Now Poland was approaching a fifth terrible year of German occupation; and France had known more than three years of occupation. Yet Italy, which had joined in the war against France only when it was clear that France would fall, was now herself on the verge of defeat, and disaster. On September 1, the Italian Government replied to an Allied demand that its armistice terms should be accepted: 'The answer is affirmative, repeat affirmative. Known person will arrive Thursday morning, 2 September, time and place arranged.'

In the Pacific, after a year and nine months of war, the United States was steadily regaining the ground which had been so swiftly and decisively lost. On September 1, American units landed on Baker Island, intent on transforming it into a base for air operations against the Japanese in the central Pacific. That same day, in an air attack launched from the decks of an aircraft carrier, American aircraft bombed Marcus Island, severely damaging Japanese military installations. All this was accomplished despite the priority given by the Americans to the war in Europe. On the following day, on the Eastern Front, the Red Army occupied the important railway junction of Sumy which, although recaptured from the Germans earlier, had then been lost.

Hitler did not intend to give up the struggle against any of his enemies. He was hoping to retrieve German fortunes through the tenacity of his soldiers, the disunity of the Allies, and the impact of various untried but novel weapons which included not only the V1 flying bomb and the V2 rocket, but also jet aircraft, and two revolutionary types of ocean-going submarines, one designed for high underwater speeds using conventional battery–diesel propulsion, the other powered by hydrogen peroxide, and both designed for operations against Atlantic convoys. Smaller versions of these submarines were also designed for operating nearer home against potential invasion forces.

On September 2, in an attempt to recover from the effect of the Anglo-American bombing raids on German industrial targets, Hitler appointed Albert Speer to be the head of a single controlling authority for industrial production, with authority even over the Minister of Economics, Walther Funk, who had hitherto controlled Germany's raw material supply.

On September 3, the fourth anniversary of Britain's declaration of war on Germany, the Western Allies launched Operation Baytown, the invasion of mainland Italy. At half past four that morning, formations of the British Eighth Army, commanded by General Montgomery, crossed the Straits of Messina to land at Reggio di Calabria. As British and Canadian troops came ashore, the Italian Government adhered to the terms of the armistice conditions, that no Italian troops would go into action against the invading forces. The armistice itself was signed in Sicily that afternoon, to come into public and formal effect in five days' time. The German Army was now committed to defending a second front on the continent of Europe.

# 33

# Germany and Japan in retreat

AUTUMN 1943

August 1943 had seen many setbacks for Germany's war-making machine. September was to see many more. The first of them that month was particularly of Germany's own making, the mutiny of Muslim volunteers in the 13th SS Division. These Muslims, living in Sarajevo and its surrounding villages and valleys, wished to further their own aspirations by fighting alongside Germany in the Balkans. But they were belittled and maltreated by their German officers, who despised them, and, during the mutiny, several Germans were killed. From Berlin, the Mufti of Jerusalem, Haj Amin el-Husseini, who had cast his lot with the Germans against Britain, hurried to Bosnia, where, with some difficulty, he helped to restore order among the mutineers.

Similar discontent in the Ukraine could not be so easily quelled; many Ukrainian nationalists had looked to the Germans to create an independent Ukraine, protected by German arms from a return of Soviet rule. Hundreds had volunteered to serve in SS and police units, and as concentration camp guards and tormentors. But once again, the scorn in which Slavs were held, and by some Germans even the hatred, turned a potential ally into a cowed, sullen but vengeful foe.

The military situation in the East was now turning seriously against Germany; on September 3, with the 800,000 German soldiers of Army Group South outnumbered two to one in manpower and even more in tanks and guns, both Field Marshal von Manstein and Field Marshal von Kluge protested to Hitler about the neglect of the Eastern Front, now that German forces were also in daily action and retreat in southern Italy. That night, the British launched their third bomber raid against Berlin in eleven nights, sending just over three hundred bombers to drop 965 tons of bombs. The German death toll was 346; the British lost 130 aircrew killed during the mission. The only German victories were those forecast on the radio; on September 4, William Joyce, Lord Haw Haw, broadcasting to Britain from Hamburg, declared: 'Now that we have arrived in the fifth year of the war, I will only say that German victory is certain. The German people know that while many blows are yet to be struck, the final blow will be struck by Adolf Hitler.'

On September 5, in the Pacific, nearly two thousand American and Australian parachutists seized Nazdab, in New Guinea, at which an airstrip was quickly built, for the continuing assault on Lae. Among those jumping successfully at Nazdab were thirty-four Australian field gunners, together with their twenty-five pounder guns; they had only been added to the assault a week before, and had not had time for more than a single practice jump.

The Japanese fell back towards Lae. On the Eastern Front in Europe, the Germans were also in retreat; on September 6 the Red Army seized Konotop, an important railway junction. The Germans, now forced to give up the Don Basin, instituted a policy of scorched earth, destroying coal mines, factories and industrial installations. On September 7, Stalino was evacuated, its mines left in ruins.

On September 7, Allied bombers struck at German military targets in the Brussels area. One bomb, falling on an artillery barracks, hit the cell in which Jean Greindl, organizer of one of the Allied escape routes, was awaiting execution; he was killed at once. That same day, from Westerbork camp in Holland, a further 987 Jews were deported eastward to an 'unknown destination'. One of the deportees, a teenage girl, Etty Hillesum, managed to write a postcard to a friend and throw it out of the train while it was still on Dutch soil. 'We left the camp singing,' she wrote, 'Father and Mother firmly and calmly, Mischa too. We shall be travelling for three days.' The train's destination was Auschwitz, where most of the deportees were gassed on arrival. Etty Hilversum, sent to the barracks in the women's camp, died there on the last day of November.

In five further deportations that month, two thousand more Dutch Jews, 1,400 Belgian Jews and a thousand French Jews were sent to their deaths.

Early on the morning of September 8, Hitler flew from Rastenburg to the headquarters of Army Group South at Zaporozhe. There, Field Marshal von Manstein gave him a grim account of the numerical superiority of the Soviet forces, and of the pace and pattern of their advance. Shortly after midday, Hitler flew back to Rastenburg; he was never again to be on Russian soil. On his return, he emulated Churchill's habit of a late afternoon sleep, only to be woken up with the news that, according to the BBC, Italy had surrendered.

That evening, Hitler issued orders for Operation Axis, the German occupation of Italy. At the same time, the Allies gave orders for the launching of Operation Avalanche, a landing on the Italian coastline, at Salerno. That night, German forces entered Rome. As they did so, Marshal Badoglio and the Italian Royal Family drove across Italy to the Adriatic port of Pescara, where they were taken by sea to Brindisi, and at once set up an anti-fascist Italian government. There were no plans, however, for a general Italian uprising against the Germans; the Allies were therefore forced to cancel a plan, Operation Giant, devised by General Eisenhower, for an airborne assault near Rome, 'as no, repeat no, arrangement for its reception has been made by the Italians' – General Alexander explained to Churchill – 'and we have reason to believe the Germans are in occupation of airfields'.

Throughout southern Europe and the Aegean, Italian soldiers surrendered to their German allies of the previous week. Where Italian troops resisted German efforts to disarm them, there was bloodshed; on Cephalonia, in Greece, in a vicious massacre, 1,646 Italian soldiers were killed. The remaining five thousand then surrendered; after laying down their arms on September 22, they were shot. Three thousand more, sent by ship to prisoner-of-war camps in Germany, drowned when the ships taking them were sunk by the Allies, who had no knowledge of their human cargo.

At La Spezia and Genoa, the Italian naval forces under the command of Admiral Carlo Bergamini, so recently the object of Allied air attack, set sail on September 8 for the Allied ports of North Africa. German bombers attacked them, sinking the battleship *Roma* with a novel type of radio-controlled bomb; 1,552 of the two thousand crewmen of the *Roma* were drowned, including Bergamini and his staff. The rest of his squadron, twenty-eight ships in all, reached Malta, where they joined the Allies. 'Now,' wrote one of the historians of Malta's wartime struggle, 'the bulk of the large and strong Italian fleet nestled within the waters of the small island it had once sought to subdue.' Elsewhere, a hundred Italian merchant ships sought sanctuary in Allied ports, while a further 168 were scuttled, to avoid capture by the Germans.

With Italy's defection, the Germans removed 50,000 Allied prisoners from Italy; they also took 268,000 Italian soldiers back to Germany as prisoners-of-war, to work in labour camps throughout Germany. Some British and American prisoners-of-war managed to flee southward as German forces moved into Italy. A special British unit, commanded by Captain Christopher Soames, was set up with instructions to 'utilize all known available means to produce a network of helpers behind the enemy lines, and make local plans for the early rescue of ground troops and air crews at large within enemy territory'. At least a thousand prisoners-of-war were brought to the Allied lines by this means. Several hundred more stayed in Italy, to join the local partisan units which quickly formed in northern Italy.

It was against partisans in Russia that the Germans were forced, that October 8, to divert still more troops from the fighting front, in launching yet another anti-partisan sweep, Operation Jacob, in the area north of Uzda.

On the morning of September 9, German troops in Athens seized the docks and railway yards, hitherto guarded by the Italians. All Italian troops in the Greek capital were seized, disarmed and deported to Germany. That morning, the Allied troops of Operation Avalanche landed near Salerno, while British airborne troops carried out Operation Slapstick, seizing the southern Italian port of Taranto. On September 10, after a brief skirmish with Italian troops, the Germans occupied Rome. In Germany itself, a group of Germans, led by a Protestant teacher, Elizabeth von Thadden, met to discuss the evils of the Nazi regime; they were betrayed to the Gestapo, and arrested.

The German regime remained as vigilant as ever, both inside and outside Germany. At Kiev, when 355 Soviet prisoners-of-war and Jews tried to escape from a unit whose task was to dig up the corpses of the victims of Nazi armies and burn them, all but fourteen were hunted down and shot. That same week, five thousand German, Austrian and Czech Jews reached Auschwitz from the Theresienstadt ghetto; a further fifteen thousand Jews had already reached Auschwitz that month from the Czech city of Moravska Ostrava, and from several cities in Western Galicia.

On September 11, as the impact of the Italian surrender continued to be felt, the French launched Operation Vesuvius, for the recapture of Corsica. Hitler, unwilling to become embroiled on the island, ordered all 27,347 German troops to be evacuated. But in the eastern Mediterranean, it was Hitler who went over to the offensive, ordering his seven thousand troops on the island of Rhodes to seize control from the much larger Italian garrison. This they did, thereby forestalling a British plan, Operation Handcuff, to seize the island.

On September 12, the Germans were sufficiently well recovered in Italy to make their first attack on the Allied bridgehead at Salerno, cutting off the bridgehead from the forces battling towards it from the south. But it was only to be a short setback. Nor were the German troops holding the islands around the Bay of Naples able to resist for long the Allied efforts to dislodge them. On September 12 the German garrison on the island of Capri surrendered without firing a shot; the Anglo-American island-hopping force, which had already taken the island of Ventotene, included a United States lieutenant, Douglas Fairbanks Junior, who, before joining the Navy, had been a leading Hollywood film star. For his part in these island operations he was awarded the Silver Star.

For Germany, the loss of Capri on September 12 was offset, at least in terms of morale, by the spectacular success of Operation Oak, the seizure of Mussolini from the isolated mountain hotel on the 9,000-foot high Gran Sasso d'Italia, in the Abruzzi mountains, where he was being held by Italians loyal to the King. Using ninety soldiers in gliders, and a small plane, the German commando leader, Captain Otto Skorzeny, landed on the mountain, outwitted the Italian garrison of 250 men, and flew off with a bewildered Mussolini to a small hamlet in the Rome province, whence Mussolini was flown northward, first to Vienna, then to Munich, and finally to Hitler's headquarters at Rastenburg.

Over France, the night of September 12 was the night of Operation Battering Ram, when three British pilots flew eight members of the French Resistance to a rendezvous between Saumur and Chinon, and took off with eight more back to Britain. The passengers brought to France included Colonel Marchal, who was arrested ten days later, and who avoided interrogation by taking his cyanide pill. Another of the passengers, Colonel Jarry, was later arrested, tortured and shot.

In a further clandestine operation, on September 14, the British parachuted Major Philip Worrall into the Pindus mountain area of Greece, to make contact with Greek partisans. There, he found himself protecting Italian soldiers both from the Greeks who wanted revenge on them, and from the Germans who wanted to capture them: by the end of the month, 100,000 Italian soldiers had been deported from Greece to labour camps in Germany. At one point, Worrall was forced to leave behind ninety sick Italians whom he was protecting. He put them, for safety, in a makeshift hospital, assuming that Red Cross conventions would apply to them, and would protect them. The Germans, reaching the hospital, took out all ninety Italians, and shot them dead.

Partisans were now active against the Germans in Italy, Greece, Yugoslavia and Russia. In the General Government of Poland also, so Goebbels noted in his diary on September 17, 'acts of sabotage and terrorism have increased enormously'. In Yugoslavia, on September 17, the British parachuted Brigadier Fitzroy Maclean to Tito's headquarters, to command the Allied Mission and co-ordinate Allied help to the partisans. In France, Resistance groups had begun to embark on acts of sabotage, including the execution of collaborators and members of the Milice, four of whom were killed that September.

On the Eastern Front, following a further meeting with von Manstein and von Kluge on September 14, Hitler agreed to a substantial withdrawal, involving the imminent loss of Smolensk, Roslavl and Klintsy, and to the strengthening of the Panther Line defence, between Vitebsk and Kiev. The area to be given up was almost half the territory captured by Army Group Centre since July 1941. On September 15, the day after this German decision to withdraw, Soviet forces captured Nezhin, less than sixty miles north-east of Kiev.

The daily budget of news reaching Hitler at Rastenburg made it clear that the massive blood letting and sacrifice of his 1941 and 1942 offensives had been in vain; on September 16, Soviet forces entered the Black Sea port of Novorossiisk, as the remnants of the German forces which a year earlier had raised the swastika flag on the highest mountain of the Caucasus now crossed the Kerch Strait for the comparative safety of the Crimea. That same day, September 16, the Germans evacuated Bryansk.

Only Nazi racial plans seemed to be rolling forward, unimpeded. Indeed, with the German occupation of Italy, new areas of deportation were opened up where, under Mussolini, no Jews had been deported or killed. Now, on September 16, the first twenty-four Jews were deported by the Germans from the northern Italian town of Merano, direct to Auschwitz. One of them was a child of six. He was gassed on arrival.

In the Pacific, September 16 saw the Japanese garrison of 7,500 men abandon the town of Lae, in New Guinea, and slip away to the north. In a year's fighting on New Guinea, 12,161 Australians had been killed – nearly ten per cent of the total Australian population of New Guinea. On the following day, determined to drive the Japanese from the northern coast, further Australian troops prepared to land at Finschhafen. Port by port and beach by beach, New Guinea was to be reconquered. As they assembled for the assault, Japanese bombers struck at Western Australia, missing the Allied airstrip which was their target, but destroying the Drysdale River Mission a mile away.

On the Thailand to Burma railway, a case of cholera had broken out at Kinsayok camp. The Japanese decided to deal with the case by shooting, as in target practice, at the sick man from outside the tent, hoping to hit him in due course. To spare the soldier this cruel end, the British adjutant of his battalion, Lieutenant Primrose, killed him with a single shot.

In Italy, the Allied forces, advancing northward, linked up on September 19

A British naval gun at Singapore fires a practice volley. The guns were specifically placed to defend the port from the sea. The Japanese, who came overland, destroyed the guns in an aerial attack on 13 February 1942.

British soldiers in Singapore marching into captivity, 15 February 1942 (*see page 300*). Japanese soldiers are standing in the background.

Hitler meets wounded soldiers in Berlin, 15 March 1942. In a speech that day, he forecast that Russia would be 'annihilatingly defeated' (*see page 308*).

Bataan, Philippines. American soldiers taken captive after the Japanese conquest of the Bataan Peninsula on 9 April 1942 (*see page 316*).

Prague, 27 May 1942. The car in which SS General Heydrich was travelling, when it was ambushed by Czech patriots. Heydrich died eight days later (*see page 327*).

Chelm, Poland, 28 May 1942; the execution of four Jews.

Jewish women being deported to 'the East', and to their deaths.

British soldiers surrender at Tobruk, the Libyan desert fortress overrun on 21 June 1942 (*see page 335*).

Japanese soldiers occupy the American island of Attu, in the Aleutian Island chain, off Alaska, in June 1942. The twenty-five American troops killed during the Japanese landing had only reached Attu on the previous day (*see page 330*).

Soviet soldiers in German captivity, part of 30,000 taken captive at Sevastopol in July 1942.

German troops with Canadian dead and a British tank, on the beach at Dieppe, after the Allied landing on 19 August 1942 (*see page 353*).

British troops advance in the Western Desert, 3 November 1942 (*see page 374*).

The Eastern Front; the Russian mud and a German motorcyclist, a photograph taken on 13 November 1942.

German wounded being evacuated from an airfield near Stalingrad.

The swastika flies over one of
the buildings of Stalingrad
University.

The swastika decorates two
German war graves; both Joan
Socodol and Bairamon-Schereb
were killed on 31 December
1942.

with the troops at the Salerno beachhead. Italy had now become a source of constant strain for the German forces, and a persistent claimant for men, munitions and fuel. Meanwhile, at Split, on the Adriatic, it took the Germans seven days of attack, including the use of dive-bombers, to drive the partisan forces of General Mihailović out of the port, which they had seized on September 20.

It was on the evening of September 20 that the British launched Operation Source, a submarine attack against the German battleship *Tirpitz*, then in the apparent safety of Norwegian waters, at Altafjord. This powerful ship not only threatened the movement of urgently needed stores to Russia through Arctic waters, but tied down large British naval forces which the British Government wished to send to the Pacific.

In an attempt to destroy the *Tirpitz*, six midget submarines, each with a four-man crew, were towed to northern Norway by submarines, and released; one disappeared on the way and was never seen again. A second, becoming unserviceable, was scuttled. A third was damaged and two of its crew drowned. Three of the submarines reached their objective, and their crews went into action. The *Tirpitz*, although not sunk, was severely disabled by explosive charges laid on the sea bed underneath her keel, and put out of action for at least six months. Two of the submarine commanders, Lieutenant Place and Lieutenant Cameron, were awarded the Victoria Cross. Both had been captured and, with the four other survivors, spent the rest of the war in captivity. The two drowned crewmen whose bodies were recovered were buried at Tromsö by the Germans, with full military honours.

It was on September 20 that senior German Government officials received details of German losses on the Eastern Front. Since the start of the war, until the last day of August 1943, a total of 548,480 German soldiers had been killed, and almost two million wounded. 'It is a curious thing', Goebbels noted that day in his diary, 'that although every individual soldier returning from the Eastern Front considers himself personally superior to the Bolshevik soldier, we are still retreating and retreating. The Soviets are able to publish new and justified reports of victories every day.' The front had not actually broken down, Goebbels added, 'nor been torn up, but that is meagre comfort considering the extremely valuable industrial and agricultural terrain and the tremendous quantities of supplies which we have had to abandon'.

On September 21 the Red Army entered Chernigov, less than forty miles from the River Dnieper, and the Panther Line. On the following day, the Germans evacuated Poltava, one of the principal industrial cities of the Ukraine. In Italy, partisans prepared to take control of rural and mountain areas throughout the northern region, proclaimed by Mussolini on September 23 as the 'Italian Social Republic'. Direct German administration was set up in the Trieste, Istria and Trentino regions.

On the Channel coast, September 23 marked the near completion of fifty-eight flying bomb sites. But a British agent, the Frenchman Michel Hollard, who had already reported on several of the new constructions, was able to send in a recently qualified engineer, André Comps, to work as a draftsman at one of the sites; Comps made copies of the site-design blueprints, which Hollard then smuggled back to Britain, crossing with them into Switzerland on one of his forty-eight clandestine wartime crossings. As soon as the design reached Dr R. V. Jones in Britain, models were prepared from which it was possible to make detailed plans of the buildings, although it was still not known precisely what weapons the sites were intended to house, or to launch.

After the war, Hollard was awarded the Distinguished Service Order, the highest British military decoration for which a non-British subject is eligible. In the First World War, having joined the French Army at the age of sixteen, he had won the Croix de Guerre. Now his efforts were to engage the detailed scrutiny of Britain's scientists, searching for Hitler's 'secret weapon', and determined to find and if possible to destroy it.

On September 24, German forces withdrew from Smolensk after bitter fighting; on the following day, Stalin announced the city's recapture. In southern Russia, Red Army units crossed the River Dnieper between Kremenchug and Dnepropetrovsk. In Italy, Allied troops were advancing northwards towards Naples; on September 27, after German soldiers began to loot a shop in the centre of Naples, its citizens rose in revolt. In Paris, on September 27, Resistance fighters shot and killed Dr Julius Ritter, the German official responsible for rounding up Frenchmen for forced labour in Germany. 'We shall have to take extremely severe measures', Goebbels wrote in his diary two days later, 'to make the French de Gaullist population understand there is a limit to German patience, even in our present military situation.' The measures chosen were indeed 'severe'; fifty Parisians were arrested in reprisal, held for a while as hostages, and then shot.

In Naples, the Germans fought throughout September 28 to regain control. On the Adriatic side of Italy, the allies captured Foggia, by far the most important airport in the region, giving the possibility of eventual air attacks on targets in the Balkans, the Danube basin, southern Germany and even Silesia. 'They hope to use it', Goebbels noted disconsolately in his diary on September 29, 'as a jumping-off place for targets in southern Germany.'

In Denmark, there were rumours that the Germans intended to arrest and deport all Denmark's seven thousand Jews. One of these Jews was the atomic scientist, Niels Bohr; he and his wife escaped to Sweden by boat on the night of September 29. Bohr went at once to Stockholm, to plead with the Swedish Government to help the Jews. The Swedes had already decided to do so; twenty-four hours before the round-up was to begin, almost all Denmark's Jews were smuggled by Danish fishermen across the water to the safety of neutral Sweden. Already safe from deportation were the three thousand Jewish refugees from Germany, Austria and Czechoslovakia who had reached Sweden as refugees before the outbreak of war.

At Auschwitz, the tortures continued; on October 3, an ss doctor, as part of a regular inspection in the camp's barracks, selected 139 Jewish labourers whom he judged too sick to work. They were taken away and gassed.

October 3 was also the day on which the Gestapo in Athens issued an order for all Athenian Jews to register. In response, a Greek underground newspaper

called on the local population to ridicule the German measures and to offer
asylum to the Jews. Three thousand Athenian Jews fled from their homes, and
were given shelter. Among those who hid Jews in her home was Princess Andrew
of Greece, a great-granddaughter of Queen Victoria. Princess Andrew's son,
Prince Philip, was then serving in the Royal Navy.

Among the Greek Jews who left Athens that October was the Chief Rabbi
of Athens, Elias Barzalai; he went to Thessaly, where he joined the Greek
partisans, as did hundreds of other Jews. Many Jews were also smuggled by the
partisans by boat across the Aegean Sea, to the coast of Turkey, from where
they could make their way to Palestine.

Greece was also a focal point of Allied concern during the first week of
October, as German troops launched Operation Polar Bear. Since the defection
of Italy from the Axis nearly a month earlier, British troops had been in
occupation of several of the Dodecanese Islands. One by one, the Germans now
attacked them, landing their first parachute troops on the island of Kos on
October 3. Within twenty-four hours the British were beaten; of the garrison
of 1,500, only a hundred men were brought off to safety. The rest had either
been killed or taken prisoner. The Germans, who had shown a remarkable and
unexpected power to hit back, lost only eighty-five men.

On October 2, in New Guinea, after the Australian capture of Finschhafen, a
Japanese counter-attack was driven off, with the loss of a thousand Japanese
lives. On the Russian front, two days later, the leader of the Spanish volunteer
Blue Division, Esteban Infantes, was awarded the Knight's Cross of the Iron
Cross. In all, 4,500 Spanish volunteers were to die on the Eastern Front, and
several thousand more taken prisoner. Also on October 4, at Poznan, Heinrich
Himmler spoke to the ss group leaders, many of whose special squads had in
the second half of 1941 and throughout 1942 murdered more than a million
Jews in the ditches of German-occupied Russia. 'Most of you know what it
means', he said, 'to see a hundred corpses lying together, five hundred, or a
thousand. To have stuck it out and at the same time – apart from exceptions
caused by human weakness – to have remained decent fellows, that is what has
made us hard. This is a page of glory in our history which has never been
written and shall never be written'.

Himmler went on to tell his listeners: 'We have fulfilled this most difficult
duty for the love of our people. And our spirit, our soul, our character has not
suffered injury from it.' This abuse of language – the proud boastings of 'spirit',
'soul' and 'character' – was one of the tools of tyranny, creating a state of mind
which made possible unimaginable horrors. On the day after Himmler's speech
in Poznan, 1,260 children who had been sent in August from the Bialystok
ghetto to Theresienstadt, together with the fifty-three doctors and nurses who
had accompanied them, were sent from Theresienstadt to Auschwitz. They had
been told that their destination was Palestine, or Switzerland.

In his speech at Poznan, Himmler did not limit his reflections and exhortations
to the mass murder of Jews. He also spoke of other civilian victims of the ss.
'What happens to the Russians, what happens to the Czechs,' he said, 'is a

matter of utter indifference to me', and he added: 'Such good blood of our own kind as there may be among the nations we shall acquire for ourselves, if necessary by taking away the children and bringing them up among us. Whether the other peoples live in comfort or perish of hunger interests me only in so far as we need them as slaves for our *Kultur*. Whether or not 10,000 Russian women collapse from exhaustion while digging a tank ditch interests me only in so far as the tank ditch is completed for Germany'.

Himmler spoke of decency: 'We shall never be rough or heartless', he said, 'where it is not necessary; that is clear. We Germans, who are the only people in the world who have a decent attitude to animals, will also adopt a decent attitude to these human animals, but it is a crime against our own blood to worry about them and to bring them ideals.'

On October 6, Himmler once more addressed the senior SS men gathered at Poznan. Once more, he spoke of the mass murder of the Jews. 'Then the question arose', he said, 'What about the women and children?', and he went on to explain: 'I decided to find a perfectly clear-cut solution to this too. For I did not feel justified in exterminating the men – that is, to kill them or have them killed – while allowing the avengers, in the form of their children, to grow up in the midst of our sons and grandsons.'

As Himmler spoke, the 1,260 Jewish children who had just reached Auschwitz from Bialystok were being taken to their deaths.

In the Pacific, on October 6, the Americans landed unopposed on the Central Solomon Island of Kolombangara; once more, the Japanese had chosen not to fight. But they still held out on Vella Lavella, forcing the Solomon Islands battle, in which 1,100 Americans and 2,483 Japanese had already been killed, to continue. On October 7, on Wake Island, which the Americans had decided not to invade, but to leave its Japanese garrison to its own devices and starvation, all ninety-six Allied prisoners of war on the island were made to sit down in a long line with their backs to the sea. Blindfolded, and with their hands tied behind their backs, they were then shot.

In Norway, October 7 saw an act of sabotage by a Norwegian Communist resistance group. Two Germans, and a large number of Norwegians, were killed when a main line train was attacked. In reprisal, the Gestapo executed five hostages. In Italy, in reprisal for the capture of two German soldiers, the Gestapo killed thirty Italian civilians at Boves. That same week, it was the round-up of Italian Jews which dominated much of the Gestapo's work. On October 9, the Day of Atonement in the Jewish calendar, and the holiest day in the Jewish year, a hundred Jews were deported by train from Trieste to Auschwitz. None survived the war. That same day, however, in Ancona, a Catholic priest, Don Bernardino, warned the local Rabbi, Elio Toaff, of the impending deportation; the Jews went into hiding, most of them with Christian families. Only ten were caught and deported, one of whom survived the war. At Auschwitz, on that Day of Atonement, a thousand men and women, judged too sick to work any more, were taken from the barracks and gassed. Two days later, in the Polish villages of Sokolka and Laznie, fifty-six villagers, including women and children, were shot; the villagers had been accused of sheltering Soviet partisans.

Those who lived under terror had no alternative but to submit to it, if they were to avoid reprisals and the murder of hostages. Yet for the slave labour gangs now being used at several hundred mass murder sites to dig up the bodies of those who had been killed, and to burn them, death was also to be their end. Revolt, however hopeless, represented at least an outside chance of survival. So it was, at the former Sobibor death camp, that the six hundred Jewish slave labourers being forced to dig up and burn the bodies of those killed there in 1942 decided, on October 13, to attack their armed guards with such knives and hatchets as they could find beforehand. Led by a Soviet prisoner-of-war, Alexander Pechersky, and a Polish Jew, Leon Felhendler, they turned on their guards on the following day, killing nine SS men and two Ukrainians, and then breaking through the camp wire. Three hundred of the prisoners managed to get beyond the wire. Two hundred of them were shot down as they ran. The three hundred who could not get beyond the wire were killed by German military and police units hurried to the camp from the nearby town of Chelm. The hundred who escaped took their chances in the forests and swamps of eastern Poland; many were able to reach Soviet partisan units, and fight with them against their former tormentors. Some joined the Red Army, among them Semyon Rozenfeld, who was in Berlin on the day of victory.

On October 13, the Government of Italy, based in Brindisi, declared war on Germany. On the battlefield, Italian soldiers joined the Allied forces in trying to break through towards Rome. But Hitler ordered his troops to hold the line. As they did so, 228 American bombers, flying in tight formation without fighter protection, carried out a daylight raid, on October 14, on the German ball bearing factory at Schweinfurt. Little damage was done to the factory, but sixty-two of the attacking aircraft were shot down, and more than a hundred American airmen killed. The American commanders realized that such a scale of loss was unacceptable, both in human and in material terms. No further such raids could therefore take place, until adequate fighter escorts became available. Thus Schweinfurt obtained a three-month reprieve, and German ball-bearing production, vital to the construction of many different types of weapons, was brought up to full capacity.

In Italy, Allied troops were engaged in a daily battle to try to force the Germans northward. By October 16 they were only ninety miles from Rome. That day, in Rome, SS troops seized more than a thousand of Rome's seven thousand Jews. Two days later those who had been rounded up were deported to Auschwitz. Eight hundred of the deportees were gassed on arrival, among them a baby born after the round-up. Of the three hundred deportees who were tattooed on the forearm and taken to the barracks, only sixteen survived the war. But in Rome, more than four thousand Jews had been given shelter in private homes, monasteries and convents, 477 of them in the Vatican itself. Thus the Germans were cheated of most of their intended victims. The same happened also in Milan, when two hundred Jews were arrested by the SS on the evening of October 16, and a further six hundred a few days later; they too were deported to Auschwitz; but more than six thousand other Jews, both Italian-born and pre-war refugees from central Europe, found shelter in Christian homes in Milan, and survived.

The night of October 16 also saw the rescue, by a British aircraft, of seven Frenchmen, picked up from a large meadow near Mâcon. They were one of three groups picked up that night, on what had become regular rescue sorties from the Royal Air Force base at Tangmere. Among the seven taken off that night was General de Lattre de Tassigny, who had escaped six weeks earlier from a German prison at Riom, having been condemned to ten years' imprisonment for trying to resist the German occupation of Vichy France in November 1942. These acts of rescue brought out several hundred Resistance fighters, soldiers, administrators and agents.

The future of France was much thought of on October 17, when a British naval, air and Army exercise, Exercise Pirate, was carried out at Studland Bay, in southern England. The aim of the assaulting force was to make use of naval gunfire, including rocket fire from special vessels, and self-propelled artillery fire from the tank landing craft, during the actual run in to the beach. Slowly but surely, the preparations for a cross-Channel invasion were advancing. Earlier that month, the code name 'Mulberry' had been chosen for the huge artificial harbour made of concrete which was to be an essential part of the invasion plan.

On the Eastern Front, the Russians attacked yet again, east of Vitebsk, driving a deep salient into the German lines, behind which, as a German Army report noted on October 18, Soviet partisans were carrying out 'strong, disruptive activities', so much so that the destruction of road and rail bridges 'has occurred in assembly line fashion'. That same day, far to the south, in the fighting for Melitopol, a nineteen-year-old Red Army lieutenant, Abram Zindels, led his men into one sector of the town, destroying twenty-three machine gun points. As Zindels ran out of ammunition, the Germans called on him to surrender. 'A Soviet officer will not be taken prisoner,' he replied, blowing up himself and the Germans near him with his last grenade. Zindels was posthumously created Hero of the Soviet Union.

In Moscow, the three principal Allied Foreign Ministers, Cordell Hull, Eden and Molotov, met on October 18 to confirm that America, Britain and Russia would not consider any separate peace negotiations with Germany. On the following day, in Washington, agreement was reached on the scale of American aid to Russia over the next eight months; 2,700,000 tons of supplies would be sent through the Russian Pacific ports and a further 2,400,000 tons through the Persian Gulf, in addition to nearly a million tons sent through the Arctic route. In a final session with Cordell Hull, at which a film was shown which included scenes of the defeat of Japan at Khalkin Gol in August 1939, Stalin made it clear that the Soviet Union also considered Japan as an enemy. 'Now I see, Marshal Stalin,' said Hull, 'that you have accounts to settle with the Japanese, which you will undoubtedly present in good time. I understand you, and am confident of success.'

It was on October 19, at Stanley Jail in Hong Kong, that the Japanese executed, without trial, a British prisoner-of-war, Douglas Waterman, a member of the clandestine British Army Aid Group, which encouraged prisoners to escape and tried to smuggle medical supplies into the various prisoner-of-war camps in the Colony. That same day, in the North Borneo capital, Jesselton, local Chinese and native Suluks rose up in revolt against the Japanese occupation; forty Japanese were killed. In reprisal, the Japanese razed many Suluk villages to the ground, arrested and tortured thousands of civilians, and on one occasion put 189 suspects to death without trial. In a further execution, several dozen Suluk women and children, their hands tied behind their backs, were then attached by a rope to the pillars of a mosque. A machine gun was then set up, and the captives shot down in cold blood.

Knowledge of such atrocities culminated in the Allies setting up, on October 20, a United Nations War Crimes Commission, to investigate and bring to trial all individuals responsible for 'war crimes'. Among the members of the Commission were the Governments-in-exile of Poland, Czechoslovakia, Greece and Yugoslavia, on whose soil the murder of civilians had become the daily practice of occupation and reprisal.

Over Germany, on the night of October 22, a British bomber raid on the industrial city of Kassel destroyed essential German aircraft and rocket production facilities. In the ensuing firestorm, 5,300 of Kassel's citizens died.

On October 23, six British destroyers, accompanied by the new light cruiser *Charybdis,* embarked upon Operation Tunnel, hoping to catch a German merchant ship on its way from Brest to the English Channel. They were surprised, however, by the merchant ship's escorts. *Charybdis,* struck by two torpedoes, sank with the loss of 462 men, while on one of the destroyers, the *Limbourne,* forty-two men were killed. Many of the bodies, washed up on the beaches of the Channel Islands, were buried by the Germans with full military honours. Five thousand Channel Islanders also made their way to the cemetery, to pay their respects, and as a mark of passive defiance.

Another act of defiance took place on October 23 at Auschwitz, following the arrival there of 1,750 Polish Jews, holders of South American passports, who had been told that they were being sent out of Europe altogether, to the safety of South America. On reaching Auschwitz, the women among the deportees were ordered to undress. As they did so, the German guards, as usual, seized rings from fingers and watches from wrists. During this activity, an SS sergeant-major, Josef Schillinger, ordered one of the women to undress completely. This woman, who according to some reports was a former Warsaw dancer by the name of Horowitz, threw her shoe in Schillinger's face, seized his revolver, and shot him in the stomach. She also wounded another SS man, Sergeant Emmerich. The shooting of Schillinger served as a signal for the other women to attack the SS men at the entrance to the gas chamber. One SS man had his nose torn off, another was scalped.

Schillinger died on the way to the camp hospital. The other SS men fled. Shortly afterwards the camp Commandant, Rudolf Hoess, entered the chamber, accompanied by other SS men carrying machine guns and grenades. They then removed the women one by one, and shot them outside.

The revolt of the Jewish women at Auschwitz was recorded by two prisoners who worked in the camp. One of them, a Jew, Stanislaw Jankowski, remembered only one other such attempt, when a Soviet prisoner-of-war, who was about to be shot with four of his comrades, snatched the gun of an ss man, 'but did not manage to make use of it and was overpowered'. The second prisoner, a Polish medical student, Jerzy Tabau, who later escaped from Auschwitz and passed news of the episode to the West, noted that, after October 23, 'the extermination of Jews continued relentlessly'. On October 25, it was the turn of 2,500 Jewish women and girls, including eight hundred from Salonica, who had been locked in a barrack without food, and with almost no water, for three days and nights, to be taken to the gas chamber and killed.

One of those Jewish girls from Salonica was the eleven-year-old Lillian Menasché. Her father, who survived Auschwitz, was later to recall 'that cursed day'. But for most of the victims of that particular killing, no one was to know or mourn their fate. All but a tiny minority of Hitler's victims went to their deaths behind a fog of anonymity; they were numbers, not names; a part of the daily and anonymous statistics of death.

On October 25, the Japanese celebrated the completion of the Burma–Thailand railway. Of the 46,000 Allied prisoners-of-war who had been forced to build it, sixteen thousand had died of starvation, brutality and disease. Also dying on the 'Railroad of Death', in conditions even worse than those imposed upon the prisoners-of-war, were more than fifty thousand Burmese labourers, for whom neither their race nor their lowly status had been any protection against the imperial ambitions of Japan.

# 34

# 'Bleeding to death in the East' (Goebbels)

WINTER 1943

On 25 October 1943, Soviet forces, crossing the lower Dnieper in a surprise attack, entered Dnepropetrovsk, one of the largest and most important cities of southern Russia. That same day, Dneprodzherzhinsk, another of the cities on the western bank of the Dnieper, fell to the advancing Russians. From Berlin came a radio broadcast, admitting that the German military position in Russia was 'extremely grave'. On the following day, Field Marshal von Kleist, on his own initiative, ordered the evacuation of the Crimea. Hitler had not been consulted. That evening, at Hitler's insistence, the order was cancelled. In the Pacific, the Japanese were less reluctant to accept the need to withdraw. When New Zealand troops landed on Stirling Island, in the Central Solomons, on October 27, they found the island undefended. Landing that same day on nearby Mono Island, the New Zealanders did discover a small Japanese garrison, but it was soon overcome, two hundred Japanese defenders being killed, for the loss of fifty-two New Zealanders and Americans.

On Choiseul Island, an officer in the Australian navy, Alexander Waddell, and his colleague Sergeant Seton, both of whom had been carrying out Intelligence tasks on the Japanese-held island for almost a year, were able to guide an American force ashore. During a diversionary attack, Lieutenant John F. Kennedy's PT boat was among those sent to bring American troops away from their beach-head; when one of the boats, hitting a coral reef, began to sink, he rescued eight of those on board, including three wounded men, one of whom, Corporal Schnell, died before he could be brought to safety. Three days later, Kennedy and his boat were in action against Japanese barges off Moli Island.

On October 28, the sixty-first deportation train in less than a year and a half left Paris for Auschwitz. Among those on it, and later killed at Auschwitz, was the thirty-nine-year-old Roumanian-born Arno Klarsfeld. In 1939 he had volunteered to fight with the French Army. Taken prisoner by the Germans, he had escaped. Reaching Nice, he had joined the Resistance group 'Combat'. Arrested by the Gestapo, he had been sent to Auschwitz with a thousand other Jews, of whom only forty-two survived the war. Of the 125 children of seventeen years and under on this train, including a five-month-old girl, Michele Nathan, not one survived.

German forces on the Eastern Front succeeded, in the last week of October, in halting the Red Army's westward thrust. In one German counter attack, north of Krivoi Rog, three hundred Soviet tanks and five thousand soldiers were captured, and the Russians driven back halfway to the Dnieper. Further north, a tenacious German defence was preventing Vitebsk from falling into Soviet hands. On October 28, Field Marshal von Rundstedt gave Hitler an assessment of the danger in Western Europe, indicating the Channel coast, the French Riviera and the Bay of Biscay as three possible areas for an Allied landing. Hitler, realizing that the presence of Allied troops on Italian soil marked only the first stage of Anglo-American endeavour on European soil, issued on November 3 his Directive No. 51, stating that Germany was now in greater danger from the West than from the East, that the German forces in the West should not be reduced, and that more tanks and artillery should be sent to the armies in the West.

In Italy, meanwhile, the Allies struggled in vain to break through to Rome. The Germans gave up even the smallest sector of the line only after the most furious of battles. In the eastern Mediterranean, German aircraft based on Rhodes disrupted British attempts to reinforce the two smaller islands of Samos and Leros, seized by Britain after Italy's surrender. On October 30, in the Aegean, forty-three British sailors were killed during a German dive-bomber attack on the cruiser *Aurora*. One of the ship's officers, Lieutenant Kenneth More, an actor and film star in civilian life, later recalled how, that night, 'My turn came round to be on watch and I had the dreadful, melancholy job of probing the shattered decks with a torch, retrieving torn-off limbs from corners, and even from the rigging.'

Behind German lines, the power of partisan and anti-Nazi forces was growing. In German-occupied Poland, November 1 saw the publication in an underground journal of a death sentence on Waclaw Noworol, a farmer from the Nowy Sacz region accused of betraying Jews and Poles who were in hiding from the Germans. Also on November 1, German forces north of Vitebsk were forced to launch two anti-partisan sweeps, Operation Snipe and Operation Wild Duck, in order to protect the supply lines of both Army Group Centre and Army Group North. That same day, Field Marshal von Weichs, the German Commander-in-Chief in the Balkans, noted in his diary: 'The grim partisan situation puts a completely different complexion on things. Not that you can speak of "partisans" any more – under Tito, a powerful Bolshevik army has arisen, rigidly led, acting on directives from Moscow, moving from strength to strength, and growing deadlier every day.' In addition, Weichs added, 'It has strong British support.'

In nine days in mid-October, Goebbels noted in his diary on November 2, more than nine thousand German soldiers had been killed on the Eastern Front. 'We cannot stand such a drain for long', he wrote. If it went on, 'we are in danger of slowly bleeding to death in the East'.

On the day that Goebbels wrote these words, a blood-letting of a different sort had begun at the Majdanek concentration camp near Lublin. Within a week, forty-five thousand survivors of the Warsaw ghetto were killed, shot by machine gun fire in ditches behind the gas chamber, eighteen thousand of them on a single day. Also killed that week were five thousand former Jewish soldiers of the Polish Army. These soldiers had been held in a prisoner-of-war camp in Lublin for the previous four years – since October 1939. In mocking imitation of a military operation, this mass killing was given the code name Harvest Festival.

On November 3, in Italy, two hundred Jews from Genoa, and a further hundred Jewish refugees from central Europe who had found a haven in Genoa before the war, were deported to Auschwitz. Among them was the Rabbi of Genoa, Riccardo Pacifici, who was killed with his congregation. That same day, in Germany, the Catholic pastor, Bernhard Lichtenburg, who had been held in prison in Berlin for just over two years, as a result of having prayed publicly for the Jews, was transferred to Dachau; he died during the journey.

On November 5, the Red Army approached Kiev; the Soviet Union's third largest city after Moscow and Leningrad. As the battle for Kiev raged, demolition charges were set off, and many ancient churches and public buildings destroyed. That evening, Czechoslovak soldiers of the 1st Czechoslovak Independent Brigade, urged by their commander, Colonel Svoboda, to fight for Kiev as if they were fighting 'for Prague and Bratislava', captured the main railway station. On the following morning, Kiev was once more in Russian hands, after more than two years of German rule. For Hitler, the loss of Kiev was a blow. Nor did the Red Army halt at Kiev, but, still driving the Germans before it, advanced a further thirty miles on November 7, taking the town of Fastov, an important railway junction for German supplies moving south-east towards the Dnieper bend. Fastov lay to the west of the 'Panther' defence line which Hitler had established less than two months earlier.

For the Red Army, even amid the devastation of Kiev, a sense of victory had now emerged; indeed, on November 8 an 'Order of Victory' medal was created, for senior commanders who successfully carried out such military operations on one or several fronts 'as to result in a radical change of the situation to the enemy's disadvantage'. The Order, made of platinum, contained ninety-one diamonds; a roll of honour with the names of the recipients was to be set up in the Kremlin. That same day, an 'Order of Glory' was created for the lower ranks, and for Air Force lieutenants, to reward deeds of personal valour; those holding the Order would have the right to a pension for life, and free education for their children.

On November 8, in Munich, Hitler made his annual beer hall speech. 'Even if for the present we cannot reach America', he said, 'thank God that at least one country is near enough for us to tackle, and on that State we are going to concentrate.' Hitler's scientists had assured him that the rocket bomb would be ready by the end of the year, but on November 8, Albert Speer noted that 'the research is not as complete as the development team would have people believe'.

It was also on November 8, in Britain, that scientists and military experts, having studied the drawing of one of the sites smuggled out by Michel Hollard, decided to re-examine existing aerial photographs of the whole of northern France, and to take as many new photographs as possible, in order to try to work out what was happening at them; the existence of an actual rocket, or of a flying bomb, had yet to be proved.

That same day, the first of the new reconnaissance flights took place. Breaking the secret of the 'Ski' sites was now a British priority. That day, in Italy, a train left Florence for an 'unknown destination'. The four hundred Jews on the train had been rounded up in Siena and Bologna as well as Florence. Not one is known to have survived.

On the battlefield, the scale of casualties had risen during the second week of November; in the Pacific, where on November 9 the Americans began their advance into the interior of Bougainville; in Italy, where the Allied forces had now to accept that Rome was beyond their grasp; and on the Eastern Front, where the Germans were blocking any further Soviet advance west of Kiev, but further north were forced to give up Zhitomir, only seventy-five miles from the pre-war Polish–Soviet frontier. In the Eastern Mediterranean too the clash of arms suddenly intensified, when a landing by German forces on the island of Leros on November 11 was resisted by ten thousand British and Italian troops, with heavy casualties on both sides, until, after five days, the defenders were overwhelmed.

On November 14, during an American daylight air raid over Germany, twenty German fighters, hitherto the scourge of such raids, were shot down. 'The Americans are now flying in by day with fighter protection,' Goebbels noted in his diary. This, he commented, was 'a thing that is naturally very hard for our anti-aircraft to cope with'. On the Eastern Front, too, Goebbels saw the danger looming for Germany, despite the recapture of the western Ukrainian city of Zhitomir on November 15, and the death in action that week of as many as twenty thousand Russian soldiers. 'Where will it ever end!' Goebbels wrote. 'The Soviets have reserves of which we never dreamed in even our most pessimistic estimates.'

Himmler was determined that it would not 'all end' until the racial theories of Nazism had been put fully into practice. On November 15, an order was published whereby nomadic Gypsies and 'part-Gypsies' were to be put 'on the same level as Jews and placed in concentration camps'. In 'cases of doubt', local police commanders would decide 'who is a Gypsy'. Following this order, several hundred Gypsies then in labour camps were deported to Auschwitz: the first twenty being brought from Grodno. Also deported to Auschwitz, on November 15, were 1,149 Dutch Jews, followed a day later by 995 more. Of this later group, 531 were gassed on reaching the camp, including 166 children. At the same time, 164 Poles were brought to the gas chamber and killed; twelve of them were women members of a Polish resistance group.

Dutch Jews and Polish patriots perished together, their deaths witnessed by a Jewish slave labourer who managed to note down, and to hide, the exhortation of one of the Polish women on the threshold of death: 'Tell our brothers, our nation, that we went to meet our death in full consciousness and with pride'. Thus she died; the slave labourer was also killed not long afterwards. But his note, and her words, survived.

Another eye-witness of the extermination that November was Josef Reznik, a Polish Jew who had been held prisoner-of-war by the Germans since his capture on the battlefield in September 1939. With three hundred other Jews, his life had been spared during the 'Harvest Festival' killings which began at Majdanek on November 2, in order to create a further Blobel Commando, digging up and then burning the corpses of those who had earlier been murdered. This particular Commando was sent to a camp in the Borki woods outside Chelm. Reznik later recalled how he and his fellow captives dug up more than thirty thousand corpses in the Borki woods that winter. Most of them were former Soviet soldiers who had been taken prisoner in 1941. There were also several thousand Jews, among them many children from the nearby town of Hrubieszow. The most 'recent' corpses, Reznik noted, were those of Italian soldiers, brought to Borki as prisoners-of-war after Italy's defection, and likewise murdered.

On the night of November 15, British Special Operations Executive carried out Operation Conjuror, flying in six agents from Tangmere, in southern England, to a hilltop landing strip in France, near Angers. One of these brought in was Victor Gerson, organizer of the 'Vic' escape line for Allied prisoners-of-war and air crew evaders. Three of those brought in were arrested on reaching Paris. Leaving the field on the return flight were twelve people; one of them, François Mitterand – using the code name 'Monier' – had for more than a year been in charge of the 'Morland' group, active in maintaining links with French prisoners-of-war and civilian deportees; in 1940, he had himself escaped from a prisoner-of-war camp in Germany.

Two months later, Mitterand returned to France, being taken by depot ship from Dartmouth to a motor gunboat out at sea, and then across the Channel by night to a small beach at Beg-an-Fry. Back in France, he formed a new Resistance committee to organize help for all French prisoners-of-war and deported labourers. Thirty-eight years later, he was elected President of France.

As British reconnaissance flights continued to search out and photograph the mysterious 'Ski' sites in northern France, the hopes placed in another of Hitler's potential victory weapons were finally eliminated when, in Norway, on 16 November, 160 American bombers, flying from bases in Britain, struck at the hydro-electric power station and heavy water factory at Vermork. Twenty Norwegian civilians were killed in the raid, which, although missing the factory, did such serious damage to the power station that no further heavy water could be produced there. Such stocks of heavy water as existed were ordered to be brought back to Germany. Norwegian secret agents passed this information back to London, where plans were made to destroy these stocks on their journey.

On November 18, two days after the American daylight raid on Vermork,

440 British bombers struck by night at Berlin. The raid, intended to hit at industrial areas, killed 131 Berliners, but did little damage to factories. Nine British bombers were shot down, and fifty-three of the aircrew killed, among them Wing Commander John White, who had earlier played a vital part in the raid on Peenemünde, placing his markers in exactly the right place, and drawing the bombing back from the camp for foreign workers on to the correct target.

On November 20, in the Pacific, the Americans launched Operation Galvanic, against three atolls in the Gilbert Islands, Makin, Tarawa and Abemana. On Makin, where more than six thousand Americans landed, there were a mere three hundred Japanese soldiers and five hundred Korean labourers; but the Japanese were determined to fight to the bitter end; 550 of the defenders were killed before the rest – almost all of the surviving Koreans – surrendered. Sixty-four Americans lost their lives during the assault, thirty-five of them as 'non-battle' casualties. But an American escort carrier, Lisome Bay, was torpedoed by a Japanese submarine, and, in a terrible explosion which blew the ship apart, 644 of her crew of nine hundred were killed. A further forty-three Americans were killed on the battleship Mississippi, when a turret accidentally exploded during the pre-landing bombardment.

The native islanders on Makin were effusive in their welcome of the Americans. Lieutenant Clarence B. Selden, the Navy Beachmaster, later recalled meeting a native chief who said to him in a single breath: 'I-am-so-glad-you-have-come-we-have-waited-many-months-we-are-happy-you-have-come-may-I-get-your-men-coconuts?'

On Tarawa Atoll, more than five thousand Japanese defenders met a similar number of American attackers on the beaches of Betio Island. At the end of seventy-six hours of savage fighting, only one Japanese officer and sixteen men, and 129 Korean labourers, were still alive. A thousand Americans – a fifth of the invasion force – had been killed in overcoming the fanatical resistance of the five thousand. The battle on Tarawa greatly shocked American opinion, indicating, as it did, how costly the total defeat of Japan would be. Nor was it a shock confined to statistics; newspaper photographs of American corpses floating with the tide, or piled up on the beaches next to burned out landing craft, shocked an American public which had hitherto been protected by censorship from such scenes.

Against the small Japanese garrison on Abemana, it was decided, after one Marine had been killed during an attempted landing, to use only naval gunfire. This was effective, a native islander reporting to the Americans on November 25 that all the Japanese defenders were dead. Fourteen had been killed by naval gunfire; the rest had committed suicide.

On November 22, as the Americans struggled to overcome Japanese resistance on Makin and Tarawa, the British had carried out another night raid on Berlin, with 764 bombers sent against the German capital. To Hitler's chagrin, considerable damage was done to the Government section of the city, including the Admiralty, the Air Ministry, and the Ministry of Armaments and War Production. Even Hitler's Chancellery was damaged, as was much of his train,

*Amerika,* then in a railway siding; Hitler himself was at Rastenburg.

For the Berliners, this raid involved two civilian disasters, a hundred people being crushed to death trying to get down the steps of an underground shelter, and five hundred being killed when a four thousand pound bomb exploded just outside a public shelter in the basement of a school. In all, 1,737 civilians were killed that night in Berlin. 'Hell itself seems to have broken loose over us,' Goebbels noted in his diary that night. 'Mines and explosive bombs keep hurtling down upon the Government quarter. One after another of the important buildings begins to burn.'

Although 167 British aircrew had been shot down and killed in the raid over Berlin on November 22, a further raid took place on the following night, when 127 more aircrew died. For Berliners, this second raid was hardly less severe than the one the night before, with 1,315 recorded deaths, a total for the two consecutive nights of more than three thousand. 'The second air raid equalled the first in intensity', Goebbels noted in his diary. 'Though at first we thought it might be weaker, this hope was not realized.' His own official residence had been hit, and its upper rooms destroyed. 'Gradually, we are learning to accustom ourselves again to a primitive standard of living'; in his own house that morning there was 'no heat, no light, no water', and he added: 'One can neither shave nor wash. One must get up in the shelter by the light of a burning candle.'

On the morning of November 23, in Lille, two hundred German soldiers surrounded the house in which the British Agent Michael Trotobas was hiding. In the ensuing fight, Trotobas killed the Gestapo officer who had come to arrest him, and then kept on firing until he himself was killed. His fellow agent, Denise Gilman, received a wound in the stomach from which she too died. After the war, a Resistance medal was named after Trotobas – Le Croix du Capitaine Michel – the only medal awarded to the French Resistance which was dedicated to the memory of a British officer. Despite Trotobas's death, his 'Farmer' group remained active, harassing German installations throughout north-eastern France.

In the Far East, the Japanese suffered a blow to their prestige on November 25, when American bombers attacked Shinchiku airfield, on Formosa. In all, forty-two Japanese aircraft were destroyed, some in combat, others while still on the ground. That same day, in New Guinea, after an eight-day battle, Australian forces captured the 2,400-foot-high Sattelberg summit on the Kokoda Trail; the turning point in the battle being an attack on the last day, led by Sergeant Thomas Derrick. For his courage in action, he was awarded the Victoria Cross.

In the slave labour camps on the now completed Burma–Thailand railway, disease still took a heavy toll. At Tarsao camp, on November 25, Colonel Dunlop recorded 364 deaths in the previous four months, noting in his diary: 'The "captains of the man of death" were dysentery, cholera, malaria, deficiency diseases and tropical ulcers. Dysentery was much the most common cause.'

\* \* \*

On November 26, on the Eastern Front, the Russians captured Gomel, only four hundred miles from Hitler's headquarters at Rastenburg. That night, British bombers struck again at Berlin, destroying the main workshops of the Allkett tank factory. Hitler, learning of the raid, ordered fire engines to rush to Berlin from as far away as Potsdam and Brandenburg, but these efforts were in vain. As well as Allkett, several other weapons and munitions factories were badly damaged, as was a factory making radar sets. During this raid, the fourth in a month, 196 British and Canadian aircrew were shot down and killed, or died in crashes and accidents; 470 Berliners were also killed, 92 of them when a bomber crashed on to a building, destroying the building's air raid shelter.

On the Eastern Front, 6,473 German soldiers had been killed in action in the previous ten days; the civilian deaths in Berlin in the same period totalled 3,653. Of the military deaths, Goebbels noted in his diary on November 27: 'That is bearable. On the other hand, sickness has increased, and, above all, the troops' morale has sunk, physically and spiritually, because of our continuous retreats.'

November 28 saw a brief turn of the tide on the Eastern Front, when Field Marshal von Manstein's Army Group South surrounded a large Russian force in the Korosten area, north-west of Kiev, inflicting heavy casualties on them.

At this moment of Soviet setback, Stalin was not in the Soviet Union. He had travelled outside Russia for the first time since the Bolshevik Revolution of 1917, to meet both Roosevelt and Churchill at Teheran. There, amid tight security, Churchill outlined the Anglo-American plans for a cross-Channel invasion the following spring or summer.

On November 29, during the discussion at Teheran of Operation Overlord, Churchill told Stalin, somewhat to the Soviet leader's unease, of the conditions, decided upon three months earlier, upon which the launching of Operation Overlord depended: first, that there must be a 'satisfactory reduction' in the strength of the German fighter forces in north-west Europe before the assault; second, that German reserves in France and the Low Countries must not on the day of the assault be more than 'about twelve full-strength first-quality mobile divisions'; and third, that it must not be possible for the Germans to transfer from other fronts more than fifteen first-quality mobile divisions during the first sixty days of the operation.

In response to this, Stalin asked Churchill if 'the Prime Minister and the British Staffs really believe in "Overlord"', to which Churchill replied that, provided these conditions were met, 'it will be our stern duty to hurl across the Channel against the Germans every sinew of our strength'.

Also on November 29, at Teheran, Stalin told Roosevelt and Churchill that the Soviet Union would enter the war against Japan 'the moment Germany was defeated'. This, Churchill told the British Chiefs of Staff, was a 'momentous decision'. It was also one which had to be kept absolutely secret, so much so that it was not recorded even in the secret record of the Teheran talks.

As the Teheran conference continued on November 29, Stalin was not told, however, that the American scientists working on the atomic bomb had reached that day a decisive stage, the modification of a B-29 bomber to enable it to carry, and to drop, the bomb. Four days later, fifteen atomic scientists arrived in the

United States from Britain to join the American atomic bomb team; one of the fifteen, Klaus Fuchs, was a Soviet spy.

Unknown to any of the Big Three that November, there had been an attempt earlier in the month to kill their principal enemy, when a German Army officer, Baron Axel von dem Bussche, undertook to 'model' a new type of Army greatcoat which Hitler wished to see. Von dem Bussche proposed putting a bomb in one of the pockets, and, while Hitler was examining the coat, to detonate the bomb, killing both himself and Hitler. Unfortunately for the conspirators, the demonstration dates were repeatedly postponed until, by even greater mischance, the prototypes of the coats were destroyed in one of the November air raids on Berlin. Von dem Bussche, meanwhile, had returned to active service on the Eastern Front, where he was severely wounded.

Hitler now seldom left Rastenburg, but on November 26 he had driven the forty-five miles to Insterburg airfield, to inspect a flying bomb which had been brought specially from its test site at Peenemünde. The test site itself was photographed by a British pilot on November 28. Two days later, a photographic reconnaissance expert, Flight Officer Constance Babington Smith, looking at earlier pictures as part of the November 8 directive, thought she saw, in what had earlier been interpreted as 'dredging equipment', a possible flying bomb launch site. The November 28 photograph confirmed that an actual pilotless plane could be seen on a ramp.

In the erroneous belief that the warhead of this new secret weapon might weigh as much as seven tons, the British Government made urgent plans to set aside several million hospital beds for those who might be injured once the flying bombs began to arrive. But plans were also made to try to minimize, and even to avert, the danger.

On December 4, the whole northern French coast containing the mysterious 'Ski' launch sites, now mysterious no longer, was re-photographed from the air, to make sure that no sites had been overlooked. On the following day, the systematic bombing of the sites began, code-named Operation Crossbow.

Another air raid on Berlin had taken place on the night of December 2. During the raid, 228 British airmen were killed, and also two Allied war correspondents. The Berliners' death toll was 150. One bomber, falling behind the others and missing the target, dropped its bombs on Cottbus, fifty miles south-east of Berlin. On the night of December 3, Leipzig was the target. 'The centre of the city was especially hard hit,' Goebbels noted in his diary. 'Almost all public buildings, theatres, the university, the Supreme Court, exhibition halls etc., have either been completely destroyed or seriously damaged.'

In German-occupied Poland, the cowing and terrorizing of the local population continued. On December 3, in Warsaw, the ss and Gestapo publicly executed a hundred municipal tramway workers, as reprisal against a recent act of sabotage. Six days later, Polish underground forces announced the condemnation and death by shooting of two Poles, Tadeusz Karcz and Antoni Pajor, accused of betraying Jews to the Gestapo, and denouncing Poles who were sheltering Jews.

Helped by information smuggled into Allied prisoner-of-war camps in

Germany, Allied soldiers, sailors and airmen made repeated attempts to escape, and to return to active duty. One such attempt, made on December 9, was remarkable because of the clothing in which the escapee, Lieutenant D. P. James, Royal Navy, chose to make his way to the Baltic Sea. 'Owing to the large number of uniforms to be seen in Germany', he later explained, 'I resolved to attempt to escape in full British naval uniform, carrying a card purporting to be a Bulgarian naval identity card.' The name and initial which Lieutenant James chose for his card contained a scarcely concealed message: 'I. Bagerov'. Changing his disguise in due course to that of a Swedish sailor, James eventually boarded a Finnish ship at Danzig, for neutral Stockholm.

At his Rastenburg headquarters, 110 miles from Danzig, Hitler found time on December 10 to design, for his Bavarian retreat at Obersalzberg, a special protective tunnel against bomb blast. He was particularly concerned, one of his staff noted, to design an effective barrier, or baffle, against the blast created by an explosion.

No day passed without some crime being committed in German-occupied Europe; on December 14, nine members of the Polish Communist Party were taken from a local prison at Herby, near Czestochowa, and shot. To this day, a memorial cross marks the site of their execution.

As the Russian forces moved forward, they uncovered more and more German atrocities, and on December 15, at Kharkov, four ss men were brought to trial, accused of using gas vans to murder Soviet civilians. One of the accused was a twenty-four year old ss lieutenant, Hans Ritz. On first having heard the words 'gas van' mentioned in Kharkov, Ritz told the prosecutor, 'I remembered the vehicle from my stay in Warsaw, when I witnessed the evacuation in it of the unreliable sections of the Warsaw population.' While in Warsaw, Ritz added, 'I got to know that part of the Warsaw population were evacuated by railway and another part were loaded into the "gas vans" and exterminated.'

Hans Ritz also gave evidence of the mass shooting, in sandpits and stone quarries, of tens of thousands of people in the Soviet cities of Krasnodar, Vitebsk and Taganrog. During the shooting of some three hundred people at a village near Kharkov, Ritz recalled, a woman, trying to save her child, 'covered it with her body. But this did not help her, because the bullet went through her and the child.'

After three days of hearings, Lieutenant Ritz and his three fellow ss men were found guilty, and condemned to death; they were executed publicly on December 19.

On the battlefronts, the third week of December saw yet another intensification of military activity. On the Eastern Front, Soviet forces launched an offensive on December 14 in the central sector of the front against Nevel. In Italy, Allied troops renewed their assault on the German line east of Cassino; on December 15 a German panzer battalion, defending the village of San Pietro Infine, inflicted heavy casualties on the American attackers before being forced to withdraw; in the artillery bombardment, the village itself was almost completely destroyed.

A year later, a film made by John Huston about the battle gave such a stark picture of the terrible reality of war that it had to be cut from five reels to three.

In the Pacific, American troops landed on December 15 on the Arawe Peninsula, at the western end of the island of New Britain, the capital of which, Rabaul, although much bombed, remained a formidable Japanese strongpoint. Three days later, in Hong Kong, the Japanese executed four prisoners-of-war, members of the British Army Aid Group, who had managed to smuggle messages out of the Colony to the Allied forces. After the war, three of them were awarded the George Cross. Despite terrible torture, all four had refused to betray their colleagues.

Above Berlin, a further bombing raid on December 16 resulted in the deaths of 294 British and Canadian aircrew, 438 Berliners and 279 foreign forced labourers, of whom 186 were women. Seventy of the foreign labourers were Poles and Ukrainians, killed when their train was hit at the Halensee station. Railway stations and marshalling yards had been the main targets of the raid; as a result of it, an estimated thousand railway trucks with weapons and munitions for the Eastern Front were blocked in the city. On being given details of this latest air raid, including the fact that twenty-five of the 482 bombers had failed to return, Churchill instructed the Secretary of State for Air: 'Compliment officers and crews, from me, on all this series of great attacks.'

Four days after this Berlin raid, Bishop Wurm, a leading German churchman, protested about the mass murder of Jews, in a letter to Dr Hans Lammers, the State Secretary of Hitler's Chancellery. 'We Christians', he wrote, 'consider the policy of exterminating the Jews as a grave injustice and of fatal consequences for the German people. Our people see the suffering imposed on us by the air raids as an act of punishment for what was done to the Jews.'

In Warsaw, on December 22, two days after Bishop Wurm's protest, the Polish underground reported that the Gestapo had discovered sixty-two Jews in hiding in a cellar in Warsaw; all sixty-two were killed.

On Christmas Eve, 1943, the British again bombed Berlin. The most serious damage was done by bombs which fell at Erkner, fifteen miles south-east of the aiming point, severely damaging a ball-bearing factory. That night, 178 Berliners were killed, and 104 aircrew. Sixteen aircrew were taken prisoner. On Christmas Day, in one of a series of air attacks on flying bomb sites in northern France, American bombers attacked twenty-four sites; seven were totally destroyed. More than half of the aircrew who were shot down were able to avoid capture and go into hiding. Many were then able to join one of the escape lines into Spain, returning in due course to fly again. But at one site, thirty French civilian workmen were killed.

'The war is now reaching the stage', Roosevelt warned the American people that Christmas Day, 'when we shall have to look forward to large casualty lists – dead, wounded and missing,' and he added: 'War entails just that. There is no easy road to victory. And the end is not yet in sight.'

On Sunday, December 26, on the day after Roosevelt's broadcast, American troops in the Pacific launched Operation Backhander, a landing at Cape Gloucester, on the extreme western tip of New Britain. Within a week, the Americans had secured an important airfield for their attacks on the as yet unconquered half of New Guinea. But once again, the Japanese fought for every mile of the inhospitable, marshy ground, which the Americans soon named the 'green hell' and the 'slimy sewer'.

That same Sunday, German warships, including the battle-cruiser *Scharnhorst*, embarked upon Operation Rainbow, an attack on two Anglo-American convoys in the Arctic, between Bear Island and the North Cape. But British warships, alerted by the Germans' own naval Enigma signals, moved in to attack the attackers, and *Scharnhorst* was sunk. Two thousand of her officers and men were drowned, including forty cadets on board for training. Only thirty-six men were rescued. 'The Arctic convoys to Russia have brought us luck,' Churchill telegraphed to Stalin on the following morning.

In Italy, British and Canadian forces captured the coastal town of Ortona on December 28, after a five-day struggle. On the night of December 29, in yet another British air raid on Berlin, 182 Berliners were killed, and eighty-one aircrew. A particular 'success' that evening was scored by a German Air Force night-fighter ace, Lieutenant Schnaufer, who shot down two bombers, one over Holland and the other over Germany, to reach a total of forty-two bombers shot down thus far; two days later he was awarded the Knight's Cross. Later in the war, with 121 successes, he was to receive the Oak Leaves with Swords and Diamonds, only one of two night-fighter pilots to be awarded this highest of all the grades of the Iron Cross.

There was nothing heroic in German actions in occupied Poland as 1943 came to an end. On December 31, at Karpiowka, as a reprisal for the participation of individual villagers in anti-occupation activities, fifty-nine villagers were locked into a granary, which was then set on fire. All fifty-nine were burned to death.

Death had also come that year, on Polish soil, to several hundred thousand Soviet prisoners-of-war, whom the Germans had imprisoned in several dozen camps, subjecting them to brutal forced labour, deliberate starvation and the denial of even the most primitive of medical help. A traveller through Poland today will constantly come across monuments to these Russian victims; ten thousand at Bukowka, a further ten thousand at Blizyn, twelve thousand at Swiety Krzyz, seven thousand at Barycz, seven thousand more at Skrodow, forty-six thousand at Krzywolka, twelve thousand at Zambrow, and at least ten thousand more at Tonkiele. An obelisk in Tonkiele, overlooking peaceful meadows running gently down the banks of the River Bug, is one of many monuments throughout Poland to these frequently forgotten victims of Hitler's tyranny.

In Italy, in front of Cassino, the German forces could not be dislodged, despite a renewed American attack on December 31. It was now clear that the battle for Italy would be a long and costly one, and not only for the armies; in the

Some mass murder sites of Soviet prisoners-of-war, 1943

Some execution sites of Polish civilians, 1943

Some of the camps in which Soviet prisoners-of-war, Poles and Jews were murdered in 1943

Baltic Sea

Stutthof

Rastenburg
*Hitler's East Prussian headquaters*

Laznie

Sokolka

Bialystok

River Narew

Grady

Zambrow

River Vistula

Sikory

Treblinka

Ostrowek

Tonkiele

Suchozebry

River Bug

Warsaw

Hola

Tuliszkow

Mledzyrzec Podlaski

Krzywolka

Poniatowa

Bialawola

Skrodow

Michniow

Majdanek

Barycz

Blizyn

Chelm

Borki

Czestochowa

Bukowka

Karpiowka

Herby

Swiety Krzyz

Zamosc

Michalowice

River Vistula

miles        50

Auschwitz    Plaszow

kilometres   75

© Martin Gilbert 1989

Nowy Sacz

Some execution sites of Soviet prisoners-of-war, Poles and Jews, 1943 previous three months, more than six thousand Italian civilians had been killed in Allied air raids on the peninsula. In south-western France, now under direct German rule for more than a year, December 31 saw the first major act of resistance, a sabotage operation organized from London, carried out simultaneously against several key railway centres, including Eymet and Bergerac. One of the organizers of the explosive charges was 'Edgar', Baron Philippe de Gunzbourg, a grandson of one of Tsarist Russia's leading Jewish philanthropists. His controller was 'Hilaire', a British agent, George Starr. Both were to play an active part in sabotage efforts behind the lines at the time of the cross-Channel invasion six months later.

As 1943 came to an end, Germany and Japan could look forward only to further and relentless attacks, both from the unconquered nations ranged against them, and from the rising tide of partisan and resistance activity. The United States alone now had 1,600,000 servicemen ready to be deployed against Germany, and 1,800,000 more in action against Japan. Yet both Germany and Japan were determined to fight on, still believing that they could break the power of those 'United Nations' whose armies, navies and air forces had vowed to fight them until unconditional surrender.

# 35

# Anzio, Cassino, Kwajalein

JANUARY–FEBRUARY 1944

The New Year of 1944 opened with the establishment of yet another German concentration camp on Polish soil, at Plaszow, a suburb of Cracow. A forced-labour camp since March 1943, ruled by a notorious sadist, Amnon Goeth, it now joined the ranks of those places at which tens of thousands of people were toiled and tortured to death. The total death toll at Plaszow was to reach 80,000; Poles, Jews, Gypsies, Italians, Hungarians and Roumanians. A special branch camp was set up near by specifically for Soviet prisoners-of-war, thousands of whom likewise perished.

Not only death, however, but also resistance, characterized the world behind the lines that New Year's Day. On the Eastern Front, as the Red Army battled for Vitebsk and Orsha, more than sixty thousand partisans were active in five widespread areas, a constant threat to the German troops and supplies moving up to the front; in another partisan area, near Mogilev, on the very axis of Hitler's 'Panther' defence line, six thousand partisans had at their disposal five underground hospital bunkers, and two more underground bunkers for men with contagious diseases.

In the Philippines, an American mining engineer, Wendell Fertig, who in May 1942 had decided to go into the jungle rather than surrender, had built up a force of several thousand Filipinos, willing to suffer the considerable privations and hazards of jungle life in order to harass the Japanese, whose rule had become increasingly tyrannical. In Burma, it was an Englishman, Hugh Seagrim, who organized a guerrilla force of two hundred native Karens and, for two years, struck at Japanese outposts and lines of communication. So savage were the Japanese reprisals against the Karen tribes that Seagrim decided to spare them further slaughter by giving himself up. The Japanese executed him. But the reprisals continued. So too did Karen resistance.

The British had planned a further air raid over Berlin for the first night of the New Year. Bad weather forced its brief postponement, until the early hours of January 2. More than four hundred bombers took part; twenty-eight were shot down or crashed, and 168 crewmen killed. The Berliners had seventy-nine dead, twenty-one of whom died when there was panic at the entrance to their shelter, although no bombs fell anywhere near it. For failing to control the panic, several police officers were transferred to the Eastern Front.

It was on the Eastern Front that a dramatic Soviet advance now caught the headlines of all Allied newspapers. 'Russians 27 Miles from Poland', was the banner headline in the *Sunday Express* on January 2, followed by a second line: '300 more towns taken in great surge towards frontier'. Along a two hundred mile front, the newspaper added, Field Marshal von Manstein's forces were reported to be 'everywhere falling back in disorder, leaving vital bridges intact and villages unscorched'. Even as Western newspaper readers rejoiced at this news, Russian forces captured Radovel, a mere eighteen miles from the 1939 border.

The Allied planners were less exultant than the newspapers, for they knew, through their clandestine reading of neutral diplomatic telegrams, that Hitler's deliberate policy was to yield space in the East in order to build up his forces and defences in the West.

That night, in yet another air raid on Berlin, 383 British bombers dropped more than a thousand tons of high explosive and incendiary bombs. Twenty-six bombers were shot down, mostly by German night fighters which were able to exploit the bombers' radar transmissions. A total of 168 aircrew were killed, but only seventy-seven Berliners.

Those who had to carry out these regular air attacks had begun to fear such a high rate of attrition. When the aircrews walked into their briefing room and saw that Berlin was to be their target for the second night running, there was then, one flight commander recalled, 'the nearest thing I ever saw to mutiny', 'a rumble of what I might call amazement, or horror, or disbelief'.

The raid had gone on; on every front, the war with all its terrors, was uninterrupted and insatiable. On January 2, in the Pacific, the Americans launched yet another seaborne landing, Operation Dexterity, against the Japanese fortified bastion of Saidor, on New Guinea. In capturing Saidor, fifty-five Americans were killed, for the cost of 1,275 Japanese lives. The success of the landing brought an even greater disaster for the Japanese than the loss of a single garrison; twenty thousand Japanese troops and civilians, who had earlier retreated from Lae and Salamaua, were now forced to begin a two hundred mile inland retreat through the jungle to Madang. Starving, dispirited, attacked by the Australian forces based on Finschhafen, ten thousand perished on the march.

The American forces, steadily advancing in New Guinea and New Britain, were still a long way from Japan. But with every day the Red Army drew closer and closer to Germany. On January 3 it reached Olevsk, only ten miles from the 1939 Polish border, and 280 miles from the border of East Prussia. On the following day, American and British aircraft began Operation Carpetbagger, the dropping of arms and supplies to resistance groups in France, Belgium, Holland and Italy. Hitler with his mind as much on the problem of a cross-Channel invasion as on that of a Russian breakthrough, now put his faith in jet aircraft. Allied aerial photographic reconnaissance had already revealed that the development of the German jet was more advanced than that of Britain or the

The Eastern Front, winter 1943–1944

United States; nor did the Soviet Union have any jet designs sufficiently advanced for operational use in 1944 or 1945.

'If I get the jets in time,' Hitler told Albert Speer and Field Marshal Milch on January 4, 'I can fight off the invasion with them'. More than a momentary respite was at stake. 'If I get a few hundred of them to the front line,' Hitler remarked a few days later, 'it will exorcise the spectre of invasion for all time'.

German propaganda broadcasts were beginning to reflect concern about a possible cross-Channel invasion. 'Can the ordinary British soldier understand', William Joyce, Lord Haw-Haw, asked on January 4, 'why he should have been expected to die in 1939 or 1940 or 1941 to restore an independent Poland on the old scale, whilst today he must die in order that the Soviets may rule Europe?'

On January 6, the Red Army crossed the 1939 Polish-Soviet border, and advanced twelve miles inside it, to capture the Volhynian town of Rokitno. Five days earlier, Stalin had established a Polish National Council to be the 'supreme organ of democratic elements' in Poland. It was to have its own armed forces and its own administration, in direct challenge to the Polish Government-in-exile in London.

To combat the growing resistance to German rule in Denmark, a German group headed by Otto Schwerdt, had arrived in Denmark to carry out a series of terror killings. The first of these took place on January 4, when the victim was the clergyman and poet, Kaj Munk. Far from deterring resistance, Munk's death served only to stimulate it. His funeral a few days later, at Vederso, was a powerful demonstration of Danish national unity and defiance. The murder of Danish patriots also continued, including the shooting of four doctors in Odense, and of eleven members of the Resistance, killed after their capture.

On January 9, two German soldiers were shot dead in the French city of Lyon. In reprisal, twenty-two Frenchmen held in Lyon prison were shot dead. 'We were in the right,' the Gestapo chief in Lyon, Klaus Barbie, commented many years later, 'because they shouldn't have shot our soldiers in the back. It was against all the laws.' On the day after the shooting, the chief of the French Milice in Lyon, Joseph Lecussan, arrested the former National President of the League of Human Rights, the eighty-four-year-old scholar and philosopher, Victor Basch, and his seventy-nine-year-old wife. They were shot a day later, and a placard hung on Basch's corpse with the words: 'Terror against terror – the Jew pays with his life for the death of a National.'

Payment of a very different kind was exacted that week on five former Italian Fascist leaders, brought to trial in Verona by the remnants of the Fascist régime, Mussolini's Republic of Salò. All five were executed on January 11, including Mussolini's own son-in-law and former foreign minister, Count Ciano, and his former military commander, Marshal De Bono. On the following day, with the connivance of local Fascist militia, thirty-two Jews were deported from Trieste to Auschwitz.

Still determined to break the German front line in Italy, and to reach Rome, the Allied forces launched an assault on January 12 on the heights of Monte

Cassino. The attack was led by the French Corps under General Juin. Progress was made, but not enough; the combination of a determined German defence, and appalling winter weather, made the capture of the town of Cassino impossible. That night, a new Allied bombing offensive was begun, aimed at the total destruction of the German aircraft industry. Three aircraft factories were hit that night, at Halberstadt, Braunschweig and Aschersleben, and considerable damage was done. But, as with the British bomber raids over Berlin, the cost was high; of the 650 American bombers which took part in the raids, 60 were shot down.

On January 14, the Red Army resumed the offensive in the Leningrad region, determined once and for all to break the German grip on the city. That same day, in the central sector, Russian troops drove the Germans from Mozyr and Kalinkovichi, on the eastern edge of the Pripet Marshes, creating a deep salient in the German front line. Hitler, pressed by his commanders to make a tactical withdrawal, refused to do so. Instead, he ordered a series of counter-attacks. 'Our armies have indeed achieved success of late,' Stalin wrote to Churchill that day, in thanking Churchill for his congratulations on the most recent advances, 'but', he added, 'we are still a long way from Berlin. What is more, the Germans are now launching rather serious counter-attacks.' What was now needed, Stalin told Churchill, was that Britain 'should not slacken, but intensify the bombing of Berlin as much as possible.'

In France, January 14 saw the arrest by the Gestapo of Captain Gustave Bieler, a Canadian who had been parachuted into the Montargis region in November 1942. Although seriously hurt on landing, he had managed to set up a sabotage network near the Belgian frontier, disrupting German rail movements. Repeatedly tortured, he revealed nothing. After three months in prison at Fresnes, he was taken to the Flossenbürg concentration camp, and held there, in the prison section, in solitary confinement, for three more months. Taken out of his cell one day, and led to the prison courtyard, Captain Bieler was executed by a firing squad.

Elsewhere in German-occupied Europe, partisan and resistance activity was continually on the increase: in France, in Yugoslavia, in Greece, even in Albania. In each area, British agents were parachuted in, to try to co-ordinate the work of sabotage. German reprisals were fierce, particularly in the Balkans, where whole villages were burned to the ground, and villagers shot almost daily.

In yet another attempt to crush the Yugoslav partisans, on January 15 the German Army launched its sixth offensive in just over three years. Tito's headquarters at Jajce were attacked, and he was forced to move forty miles westward, to Drvar. By now, however, he was receiving considerable aid by air from the British and Americans.

On January 15, the Red Army finally broke the German ring around Leningrad, the city's defenders and those driving towards it from the east linking up at the village of Ropsha, scene long before of the assassination of Tsar Peter III, the 'Prussomaniac'. 'The fierceness of the fighting was such', one Soviet soldier later recalled, 'that we didn't take many prisoners'. Within hours, Pushkin, Slutsk and Gatchina, to the south of the city, and Mga in the east, fell to the Red Army. As the whole Leningrad Province was cleared of the Germans, more than sixty thousand German soldiers were killed. That same day, in Italy, the first allied shells fell on the monastery above Cassino.

British troops now joined the French in the assault on Cassino, launching Operation Panther on the morning of January 17, and crossing the Garigliano river between Cassino and the sea. But a further assault on Cassino itself was repulsed. Behind German lines, the second week of January saw no diminution in terror. On January 18, a German military sweep, using tanks, searched in the Buczacz area of Eastern Galicia for Jews who had escaped deportation nine months earlier and were still in hiding; three hundred were found, and killed. That same day, in Greece, a German Intelligence officer, Lieutenant Kurt Waldheim, reported that there were as many as 25,000 Greek partisans active in northern Greece, as well as four thousand Italian soldiers. Operations against these forces were continuous, as were reprisals against the villages which sheltered them.

Also on January 18, in Paris the Gestapo arrested the twenty-three-year-old Baron Jean-François de Nothomb, who for almost a year had been organizing, under the code name 'Franco', an escape route to Spain for Allied airmen and escaped prisoners-of-war. Tortured, and then imprisoned, he was to survive the war. On the day after Nothomb's arrest, two British saboteurs, Captain George Hiller and Lieutenant Cyril Watney, both of whom had been parachuted into France, organized the destruction of an aircraft propeller factory at Figeac. Production was never resumed. That day, in further preparation for an invasion which they knew must soon come, the German Armed Forces High Command designated as 'fortresses' all the principal ports along both the Atlantic and Channel coasts. Each fortress was given a commander, who took an oath to defend his fortress to the death.

On January 20, in Italy, the armies of which President Roosevelt was Commander-in-Chief reached the Rapido river, and were in action north of Cassino; they were also in the final forty-eight hours of planning for a landing from the sea at Anzio, just south of Rome. That night, as more than a thousand Jews were deported from Paris to Auschwitz, crossing Germany by rail from west to east, 759 British bombers, also flying from west to east, across the North Sea, struck at Berlin. Their 2,456 tons of bombs was the heaviest load for two months. Thirty-five of the bombers were shot down, and 172 aircrew killed. During the raid, the main railway line to Hamburg was cut, and a factory making radar components for the German Air Force was put out of action completely. A total of 243 Berliners were killed during the raid, and a further 13 people outside the city. One bomber, dropping its bombs thirty miles from the target, possibly because the pilot was not prepared to risk a flight through the centre of the target area, caused considerable damage, entirely by mistake, to a Todt Organization depot and workshop.

In London, on January 21, General Eisenhower, the Commander-in-Chief

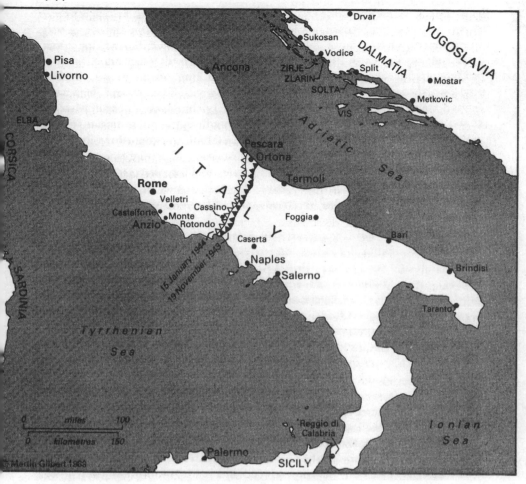

The Italian Front, 1943–1944

designate of the Allied cross-Channel invasion forces, held his first meeting with his commanders. The long-awaited Operation Overlord was now little more than four months away. As the commanders began their discussion, British and American troops, escorted by twenty-eight warships, were sailing from Naples for Operation Shingle, the landing at Anzio, designed to turn the German flank in Italy, and open the way to Rome. A few minutes after midnight, in the early hours of January 22, the first troops went ashore. They were unopposed. The Germans having been taken by surprise, 227 of them, who were based in the landing area, surrendered. Within twenty-four hours, more than 36,000 Allied troops were ashore; only thirteen had been killed.

On January 21, when the British bombers' target was the city of Magdeburg, two German fighter aces died. One of them, Major Heinrich Prinz zu Sayn-

Wittgenstein, a descendent of Franz Liszt's celebrated mistress, had eighty-three British, American and Russian bombers on his 'kill' list; during the Magdeburg raid he shot down four more, but was himself shot down while attacking a fifth. At the time of his death, Prince Wittgenstein was already a legendary figure in Germany; Hitler recognized this by conferring on him, posthumously, the Oak Leaves with Swords to his existing Knight's Cross with Oak Leaves. The second German ace who was killed that night over Magdeburg was Captain Manfred Meurer. As the third highest scoring German night-fighter pilot, he had already shot down sixty-five Allied aircraft. As he was about to shoot down his sixty-sixth, it blew up above him, causing him to crash. That night, 447 German bombers attacked London, the first of a series of short, sharp raids – all that the German Air Force was now capable of – code-named Operation Ibex. But of five hundred tons of bombs carried, only thirty-two were dropped on the capital.

On January 23, German aircraft struck at the Anzio beachhead forces and their supplies, sinking the British destroyer *Janus*. On the following day, the hospital ship *St David's* was also sunk. On land, the American commander, General Lucas, hesitated to advance before tanks and heavy artillery had been landed; as he waited, the Germans were able to rush up reinforcements. On January 24, in a special Order of the Day, Hitler instructed his troops to hold the front line in Italy at all costs; in a counter-attack that day, they retook Castelforte and Monte Rotondo from the British, but with heavy loss of life. That same day, Hitler told the Japanese Ambassador to Germany that he was now having to conduct the war in Russia on the principle of not jeopardizing the defence of Western Europe; he had been obliged, he told the Ambassador, to reinforce his armies in Italy and the Balkans by thirty-five German divisions, at the expense of the Eastern Front.

Using his most secret method of radio communication, the Japanese Ambassador sent Tokyo a full account of his interview with Hitler; as with all his most secret messages, this one was intercepted and read in Britain and the United States. Also intercepted were most of the actual German Army and Air Force movements, both to the Anzio bridgehead and to the front line, as well as to the Balkans. These intercepts became of additional importance from January 25, when the Anglo-American Combined Chiefs of Staff agreed to Plan Jael, a comprehensive scheme to lure German attention away from Normandy. This was to be done by creating several entirely fictitious land, sea and air operations, intended to force the Germans to divert troops and resources.

For several months, in preparation for the cross-Channel invasion, British and American deception experts had sought to give the Germans the impression that it was not Normandy, but the Pas de Calais, which was to be the Overlord landing area. One plan involved the creation of a vast military formation, the First United States Army Group – FUSAG – which did not in fact exist. It was given a commander – General Patton – bases, training grounds, a communications network, plans, orders of battle and a specific target, the French coast between Calais and Boulogne. The first indication that the deception was working came in two Enigma messages, sent on February 9, in which, through

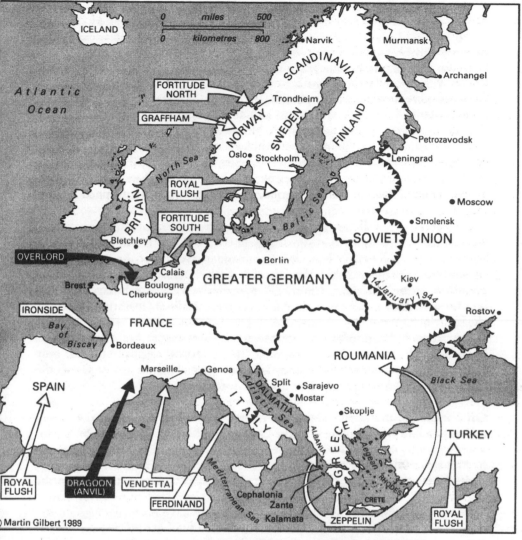

The Normandy and South of France deception plans

the Germans' own most secret method of communication, German troops in the Balkans were ordered from Split to Skoplje, and from Mostar to Sarajevo, in order, the message explained, to be available for rapid movement in the event of an Allied landing in Greece. Further messages, decrypted at Bletchley two weeks later, revealed to the British planners of the Normandy landings that, for the Germans, the First United States Army Group was a reality. The phantom Army could therefore go on 'threatening' Calais.

Not only was a fictitious United States Army Group to participate in these operations, but also an equally fictitious Twelfth British Army, containing among its forces the 15th British Motorized Division, the 34th British Infantry Division, the 8th British Armoured Division and the 7th Polish Infantry Division, all to be equipped, deployed, moved, trained and communicated with, and all existing only on paper.

It was by reading Germany's own top-secret messages that the Combined Chiefs of Staff would know whether the Germans had fallen for these deceptions, intended to ensure the widest possible dispersion of German forces, and to do so by skilfully leaked preparation of nine separate, but each of them spurious, British landings: Operation Fortitude North against central Norway, centred on Trondheim; Graffham against central Sweden; Royal Flush against the triply deceptive coastlines of southern Sweden, Spain or Turkey; Zeppelin, a triple assault against the Roumanian Black Sea coast, Crete, and the western coastline of Greece and Albania; Ironside against Bordeaux; Vendetta against Marseille; Ferdinand against Rome; and Fortitude South against Calais.

A careful scrutiny at Bletchley of the Ultra decrypts revealed just how seriously the Germans were taking these non-existent threats. Reports had been received, Churchill told General Wilson, the Commander-in-Chief of the British forces in the Mediterranean, 'that the islands off the Dalmatian coast are being equipped with naval guns'. Churchill's telegram was dated February 13; Ultra was his source. That same day, the Allied planners finalized Operation Fortitude, that part of Operation Jael intended to persuade the German Army 'to make faulty strategic dispositions in north-west Europe' before the cross-Channel invasion, and also to induce it to make 'faulty tactical dispositions' not only during, but even after the Normandy landings, by making the Pas de Calais the apparent location of the principal invasion force.

On January 26, in Poznan, Heinrich Himmler spoke to three hundred German generals, admirals and officers of the General Staff. One of his listeners, Count von Gersdorff, later recalled Himmler's declaration that day, that when Hitler had given him the order 'to carry out the total solution of the Jewish question', he had hesitated, 'uncertain whether I could demand of my worthy ss men the execution of such a horrid assignment'. But, Himmler added 'this was ultimately a matter of a Führer order, and therefore I could have no misgivings. In the meantime, the assignment has been carried out, and there is no longer a Jewish question.' This was indeed true as far as Poland was concerned, since almost all Poland's three million Jews had been murdered. From Western Europe, however, the deportations to Auschwitz, part of a monthly quota, continued. From France, almost a thousand Jews were being deported every week. From Italy, 563 were to be deported from Milan on January 30 and a further 462 from Fossoli three weeks later. Nor, as yet, had the three quarters of a million Jews of Hungary, or the six thousand Jews of central Greece, or the Jews of Corfu, Rhodes or Kos, come within the Nazi deportation net. This did not lessen, however, the chilling note of Himmler's message; his own speech notes contained the words: 'Racial struggle. – Total solution. Don't let avengers arise to take revenge on our children.'

On the battlefield, the Allies were now in constant motion. On January 26,

German troops were being attacked at all points still held by them on the Moscow–Leningrad railway, between Tosno and Lyuban. In Italy, American troops crossed the Rapido river, establishing a small bridgehead north of Cassino. In the Pacific, more than two hundred American bombers and fighters struck so forcefully at the Japanese airbases at Rabaul that the Japanese were no longer capable of launching any effective air counter-strike on General MacArthur's forces in the Solomon Islands or on New Guinea.

On January 27, the Moscow–Leningrad line was cleared. The 880-day siege of Leningrad was finally at an end. That night, the Soviet warships anchored in the Neva fired a salute of 324 rockets.

Determined to crush the rising tide of resistance throughout German-occupied Europe, Hitler told his generals on January 27: 'You can't smash terror by philosophizing, you have to smash it by using even greater terror.' Twenty-four hours later, in Warsaw, 102 Poles were executed publicly on Jerusalem Avenue.

At Anzio, the Allies were now pinned down by the Germans to a bridgehead from which they could neither link up with the main Allied force to the south, nor drive on Rome. On January 27, over Berlin, thirty-three British bombers were shot down, and 182 aircrew killed. Of the 474 dead in Berlin, 132 were foreign workers. In a further British raid on the following night, 254 aircrew were killed. On January 29, off the Anzio bridgehead, German bombers sank the British cruiser *Spartan* and the cargo ship *Samuel Huntington*, on which four crew died. That night, German bombers struck at London, their second raid of Operation Ibex. In contrast to the 1,887 tons of bombs dropped on Berlin the night before, the tonnage of German bombs dropped on London was less than forty. That day, eight hundred American bombers struck at industrial targets in Frankfurt-on-Main. Fifty were shot down.

In this shooting down of American airmen over Germany, several hundred, surviving the crash-landing of their plane or parachuting to the ground, avoided capture and sought out the various escape lines which were in operation. So confident were airmen that these escape lines could help them, that when on January 25, a British Flying Officer, H. Furniss Roe was shot down over France for the second time in five months, he sent back a final radio message from his cockpit to his base in England: 'Back in two months'; he was back, in fact, only three weeks later than the date he set himself.

On January 29, a new Allied escape organization, code named 'Shelburne', involved a motor boat run from the Channel port of Dartmouth to the French beach resort of Plouha. In the five months before 'Shelburne' was discovered by the Germans, 135 Allied airmen were brought back to Britain; the first nineteen, brought back on January 29, were thirteen American airmen and four British airmen. With them were two French civilians who wanted to join the allied forces.

One particularly successful evasion line was in the Aegean, where A. C. – 'Tony' – Simonds organized a large number of clandestine journeys by small boats which, wending their way among the Greek islands, brought to safety in Turkey more than seven hundred people in December 1943 and January 1944. These seven hundred included 425 Greeks, 121 Britons, 41 Jews and 39 Americans, as well as several hundred wounded Allied soldiers taken off the German-occupied islands of Kos, Leros and Samos.

Far more Allied servicemen were captured than could escape; in the British bombing raid on Berlin on January 30, a total of 193 aircrew were killed, and forty-three taken prisoner-of-war. More than 2,400 Berliners perished, nearly half of them under rubble so deep that they could not be dug out that night, or for many nights to come. Among the buildings damaged in the raid was Goebbels's Propaganda Ministry. Industrial production, however, suffered little.

On the day of the Anzio landings, a British soldier, Christopher Hayes, had found a six-year-old Italian girl wandering in one of the minefields behind the beach. Her name, she told him, was Angelita. She did not know where her mother had gone, and stayed with Hayes' unit for ten days. Then, on February 1, she was riding with the unit on a lorry when it was hit by a shell, and all its occupants thrown out. 'My rifle was shattered', Hayes later recalled. 'I lifted Angelita out of the trench. She died and I left her by the roadside'.

Three Allied offensives were launched on the first day of February 1944. The first, an attempt at a series of American landings on three of the Marshall Islands in the Pacific, Kwajalein, Roi and Namu, succeeded after four days of fighting, when, on Roi and Namu, 3,742 Japanese were killed and ninety-nine taken prisoner, for a loss of less than two hundred American dead. On Kwajalein 7,870 of the eight thousand Japanese defenders were killed, for the loss of 372 Americans. Although the eight thousand Japanese on Kwajalein, and the 3,841 on Roi and Namu had been numerically overwhelmed from the outset – on Kwajalein by more than forty thousand Americans – they had chosen once more to fight, literally, to the end.

The second Allied offensive begun on February 1, on the Eastern Front, saw the Red Army reach the town of Kingisepp, cross the River Luga, and push on to within a mile of the Estonian frontier of 1940. The third Allied offensive, in Italy, brought the Allied forces even closer to Cassino than before, although the break-through still eluded them.

Behind the lines, the pattern of killing continued; on February 1, three Gypsies were killed at Auschwitz as they tried to escape from a labour gang. At Dachau, a group of Soviet prisoners-of-war, all officers, was shot by a firing squad. In Warsaw, on February 2, Polish partisans killed ss General Franz Kutschera, the commander of the Warsaw ss and of the District Police; in reprisal, three hundred Poles were executed in the city on the following day.

Poland was much on Churchill's mind that week, as news reached London that two former Polish towns, Rovno and Lutsk, had both been liberated by Soviet troops. 'Now that the Russians were advancing into Poland,' Churchill told his senior military advisers, 'it was in our interest that Poland should be strong and well-supported. Were she weak, and overrun by the advancing Soviet armies, the result might hold great dangers in the future for the English-speaking peoples.'

A prospect of post-war conflict was now quickly opening up, with the Soviet

Union on one side of the divide and the Anglo-American alliance on the other; a divide of conflicting ideology, backed by territorial control. On the day of the fall of Rovno and Lutsk, Churchill argued in favour of diverting some of the Royal Air Force's 'responsibilities' over Germany to helping the Polish resistance movement being organized by the Polish Government in London. At the same time, Churchill was spending endless, patient hours trying to persuade the 'London' Poles to give up their claim to a return of Polish sovereignty over eastern Poland. This substantial territory had been secured by Poland in 1921, under the Treaty of Riga, following the Polish victory in the Polish–Soviet war. It was a Treaty which pushed the Polish border eastward from the proposed Curzon Line along the River Bug, to the Pripet Marshes and into White Russia.

Stalin welcomed this pressure on Poland to give up as much as one third of the territory of pre-war Poland, the very towns and villages from which his armies were even then driving the Germans; during the first week of February several Red Army units had come to within fifty miles of Brest-Litovsk, and of the post First World War Curzon Line, which Stalin wished to see as the new post-war border between Poland and the Soviet Union. Stalin did not intend, however, to rely upon Churchill to persuade the London Poles to accept this considerable reduction of Poland's inter-war territory. He was also supporting the claims of the Polish National Council, a predominantly Communist group, still based in Russia, to be the post-war Government of Poland. This Council had already accepted the Curzon Line.

Churchill, meanwhile, stood by the legitimacy of the London Poles to return to Poland as the country's post-war Government, pointing out to Stalin in a telegram sent to Moscow on February 5 that a Polish Division established by the London Poles 'had already entered the line against the Germans in Italy', and that a second Polish Division was at that very moment under training in England as part of the Allied forces preparing for the cross-Channel invasion.

That cross-Channel invasion had become a massive commitment of planning, energy and resources, absorbing the combined skills of soldiers, sailors, airmen, scientists and technical experts of all sorts, as well as a formidable Intelligence effort which had begun in 1941. 'Overlord' was also a cause for daily concern to those who knew of its detailed planning. 'The more one goes into it,' King George VI wrote in his diary on February 3, 'the more alarming it becomes in its vastness.' That day, in Italy, the Germans showed that they still had considerable reserves of force and willpower, launching Operation Fish Trap against the Allied forces on the Anzio beachhead, pushing back the borders of the bridgehead, and ensuring that a landing which was originally intended to break the German line in Italy, would remain little more than an irritant. On the main front, similar German tenacity still denied the Allies control of Cassino, even though, on February 4, American troops came within a thousand yards of the monastery which dominated the town.

On February 5, in France, the Gestapo arrested Michel Hollard, the man who had done so much to alert the British to the dangers, and indeed to the existence, of the German flying bomb. After terrible tortures, to which he did not

497

succumb, he was sent to a concentration camp. Unlike so many who were caught and imprisoned, Hollard survived the war.

In German-occupied Poland, resistance brought rapid and violent retribution; on February 9, at Lesno, sixty Polish women railway workers were killed as a reprisal for a local act of sabotage, while on the following day 140 Poles were executed in the Warsaw suburb of Ochota as a further reprisal for the murder of ss General Franz Kutschera nine days earlier.

For the Germans, these acts of sabotage had for a long time made it a clear sign that it was not only the Allied armies, but the captive peoples, who were making progress and gains. On February 10, French Resistance fighters so seriously damaged a Peugeot factory making aircraft parts at Sochaux-Montbéliard that production was halted for five weeks; when replacement machine tools were sent from Germany, they were destroyed on arrival. The public mood in Germany was the subject of a German Security Service report on February 10. 'In spite of all his stupidity and obtuseness,' the report read, 'the enemy is getting his claws upon us and no one can imagine how we can shake him off again, however often he has been or may be "cracked over the head".'

Such moods led to no relaxation of terror; on February 11, on the German-occupied Channel Island of Guernsey, the Gestapo arrested Charles Machen, founder of a clandestine news bulletin. Deported to the mainland, Machen died in prison in Germany, at Naumburg-on-Saale, eight months later; he had been betrayed.

In Italy, the second week of February saw no progress in the battle for Cassino, yet without the capture of Cassino there could be no Allied advance on Rome, and no linking up with the now trapped bridgehead at Anzio. On February 12, leaflets were dropped on Cassino, addressed to 'Italian friends', warning that the monastery on Monte Cassino, hitherto exempt from shelling, was about to become a target. 'The time has come', the leaflets declared, 'when we must train our guns on the monastery itself. We give you warning so that you may save yourselves. We warn you urgently: Leave the monastery. Leave it at once. Respect this warning. It is for your benefit.'

In northern Italy, there was a setback to the allies on February 13, when the Germans attacked one of the main Italian partisan formations, numbering about five hundred men under the leadership of Filippo Beltrami, who was killed in the action. It was to be more than six weeks before the routed units could be regrouped. Two days after Beltrami's death, Allied bombers struck at the monastery on Monte Cassino. In four hours, more than four hundred tons of bombs were dropped on one of the shrines and showpieces of early medieval Christian culture, killing the bishop, who had remained in the monastery despite the warning leaflets, and some 250 civilian refugees who were sheltering in the upper levels. The monastery itself was reduced to ruins. An infantry assault later that day, however, in which Maori, Indian and Gurkha troops fought with bayonets against the German defenders on the slopes, failed to dislodge them; indeed, the Germans, having driven off the assault, managed to find the strength to counter-attack, forcing two Maori companies back across the Rapido river.

That night, 875 British bombers attacked Berlin; of the Allied aircrews, 265 were shot down and killed. Five hundred Berliners also died, as did eighty foreign slave labourers. As with the Korean labourers killed in every Pacific battle, so, in Europe, those whom the Germans had forced from their homes, and brought to the Reich, suffered both as victims of the Germans and as victims of the Allied bombing of Germany.

On February 16, the Germans launched a second attack on the Anzio bridge-head, and did so with sufficient forces to drive the Allies back to the sea shore. Their detailed plans were sent to the troops, however, over their top-secret Enigma communication system, and were thus known to the Allied defenders, who were able to halt the new offensive, and then to throw it back.

Elsewhere on February 16 the Allies were massively victorious. On the Eastern Front, at least twenty thousand German soldiers were killed – the Soviet estimate was 55,000 – as, at Korsun, Soviet forces destroyed the last German forces in the Dnieper bend. In the Pacific, on the island of Truk, in the Carolines, American bombers and torpedo planes, launching Operation Hailstorm, destroyed fifteen Japanese warships, twenty-five merchant ships and 265 aircraft – 220 of them on the ground – for the cost of only twenty-five American aircraft, while, on Eniwetok Island, in the Marshalls, in Operation Catchpole, American Marines overwhelmed the 2,677 Japanese defenders, all but sixty-four of whom were killed, at the cost of 195 American lives.

On the Eastern Front, on February 18, Soviet forces drove the Germans from Staraya Russa, south of Lake Ilmen. That same day, in Germany, Admiral Canaris was dismissed from his post as head of German Military Counter-Intelligence, his responsibilities being transferred to Ernst Kaltenbrunner, already in charge of the Gestapo and concentration camp system. Canaris went on extended leave. That day, on the eve of the intended execution of twelve members of the French Resistance then in prison at Amiens, German Intelligence suffered a blow to its prestige and rule when nineteen British bombers carried out Operation Jericho, breaching the walls of the prison and enabling fifty members of the Resistance to escape. Ninety-six prisoners were, however, killed in the raid, including fifty-six members of the Resistance; a heavy toll.

The pilot who led the Amiens raid, Group Captain Charles Pickard, who two years earlier had led the raid on the Bruneval radar installations, was also killed, together with his observer, Flight Lieutenant Alan Broadley. The third airman killed was one of the navigators on the raid, Flight Lieutenant Sammy Sampson, of the Royal New Zealand Air Force. Among those who did escape from Amiens was Louis Vivant, leader of the Resistance in the Department of the Somme; the Germans were never to catch him again.

On the following night, more than eight hundred British bombers struck at Leipzig, followed within twelve hours by an American daylight raid; in this twin assault, of a type which was to become increasingly frequent, 969 German civilians were killed and more than fifty thousand made homeless. But during the raid, seventy eight of the attacking aircraft were lost and nearly four hundred aircrew were killed, the largest aircrew deaths so far in any bombing raid over Germany.

*         *         *

In the Pacific, the American death toll at sea rose on February 21, when, off Iwo Jima, two American warships were hit by Japanese torpedo bombers. On one of the warships, the *Bismarck Sea*, 119 men were killed; a further 123 died on the *Saratoga*.

To those survivors who had no means of defending themselves, the Japanese showed no mercy; on February 22, two boats and four rafts containing survivors of a British merchant ship, the *British Chivalry*, torpedoed in the Indian Ocean, were machine-gunned by the same submarine which had torpedoed them; four days later, the survivors of the merchant ship *Sutlej* were likewise machine gunned as they clung to the rafts and wreckage of their ship.

Three days later, another British merchant ship, the *Ascot*, was torpedoed in the Indian Ocean, on its way from Colombo to Diego Suarez. Four of the crew were killed when the ship was hit, but the remaining fifty-two managed to get away in two of the ship's boats. The Japanese submarine which had sunk the *Ascot* then surfaced, and, as had happened twice before that week, began to machine gun the survivors. Ten survivors were killed. The submarine then left the scene, but returned half an hour later, and once more opened fire. Only eight survived this second ordeal.

On February 20, in Norway, Norwegian saboteurs, acting on instructions from London, blew up the ferry-boat *Hydro*, as it carried all Germany's existing supplies of heavy water across Lake Tinnsjo, on their way to Germany. The sinking of the ferry, in which four German guards and fourteen Norwegian civilians were killed, was yet another setback to Germany's ability to produce an atomic bomb. That same day, over Germany, American bombers launched Operation Argument, a week-long series of massive attacks, also known as 'Big Week', against German aircraft and ball-bearing factories, and port installations, within the triangle Brussels–Rostock–Pola.

On the first night of the Anglo-American 'Big Week' raids, the Germans were also bombing London; four people were killed just outside the Prime Minister's residence at 10 Downing Street, although Churchill himself was out of London that night. Returning to London two days later, he revealed to the House of Commons that, since the beginning of the war, 38,300 British pilots and aircrew had been killed, and ten thousand aircraft lost. The most recent four raids, including the one on Leipzig, 'constitute', he said, 'the most violent attacks which have yet been made on Germany, and they also prove the value of saturation in every aspect of the air war'. The air offensive, he added, 'constitutes the foundation upon which our plans for overseas invasion stand', and he went on to tell the House of Commons, in words which summed up the feeling of millions of people on the Allied side, as they contemplated the daily and nightly rain of bombs on Germany: 'The air power was the weapon which both the marauding States selected as their main tool of conquest. This was the sphere in which they were to triumph. This was the method by which the nations were to be subjugated to their rule. I shall not moralise further than to say that there is a strange, stern justice in the long swing of events'.

As Churchill spoke, 248 American bombers, guarded by 185 fighters, struck

'Big Week' air raids, 20–26 February 1944

at the German aircraft-factory in Regensburg, on the upper Danube, while a further 288 bombers and 596 fighters attacked aircraft factories at Fürth, as well as the German airfield at Graz, railway lines at Zell-am-See, and harbour installations, warehouses and storage sheds in the Adriatic ports of Fiume, Pola and Zara. In the air battles above the targets, more than 170 American aircraft were shot down. On the following day, two further raids, on a similarly heavy scale, were made on German aircraft and ball-bearing factories at Steyr, Gotha and Schweinfurt. The 'main tool of conquest' had been turned against the would-be conqueror. Yet the considerable damage done during Big Week was, in many of the bombed factories, quickly repaired. At Augsburg, the main aircraft factory was back in full production in little more than a month. At Aschersleben, however, production of aircraft engines remained at only half its pre-bombing capacity for the whole of March and the first half of April. Nevertheless, whereas the average German monthly production of single-engine fighters was 851 in the last half of 1943, it rose to a monthly average of 1,581 in the first half of 1944. Despite the massive damage done by air attack, Germany's aircraft factories continued to produce substantial numbers of aircraft, though in the end this productivity was not matched by the training of sufficient pilots.

For the Americans, the losses during Big Week were considerable, with 2,600 crewmen either killed in action or seriously wounded, or taken prisoner.

# 36

# Bombing, deportation, and mass murder

FEBRUARY–MARCH 1944

On the Eastern Front, the Germans were now in retreat in every sector. In the north, German ss units recruited outside Germany had been thrown into the battle; on February 20 the commander of the Walloon Legion of Belgian ss volunteers, Léon Degrelle, was awarded the Knight's Cross to add to his Iron Cross after the Legion was in action near Narva. But on the following day, the Germans were driven from Kholm, nearly two hundred miles south of Leningrad. Twenty-four hours later, they were driven from Dno. Further south and west, the Red Army was consolidating its positions inside the pre-1939 Polish frontier; but it was still three hundred miles away from East Upper Silesia, too far to help the hundreds of thousands of slave labourers in southern Poland. On February 22, a German survey noted that there were 73,669 Jewish slave labourers in the Auschwitz region alone, 24,637 of them women, working in ten separate industrial enterprises, more than six thousand of them at IG Farben's petrochemical factory at Monowitz, the Buna Works, located only six miles from the gas chambers of Auschwitz. Also working at Monowitz were several hundred British prisoners-of-war, held in special camps adjacent to the Jewish one; it was for his exceptional courage in helping to save the lives of Jews at Monowitz that one of the British prisoners, Sergeant Charles Coward, was later awarded a high honour by the State of Israel.

At Dachau, on February 22, thirty-one Soviet prisoners-of-war, all of them officers, were taken from the barracks and executed. The two youngest were both twenty-one years old, Anatoly Dunov and Konstantin Atamasov. Their names, and those of the other twenty-nine victims, are known because a Polish priest, Jan Domagala, a clerk in the camp, later took away several hundred lists of such executions, to ensure that the facts would be preserved.

On the night of February 25, in the Barents Sea, fourteen German submarines attacked a convoy of forty-three merchant ships on their way to Russia; one of the submarines torpedoed an escort vessel, the British destroyer *Mahratta*; of the ship's crew of more than two hundred, only seventeen could be saved from the icy waters by another destroyer, *Impulsive*. In the battle of the escorts, two

German submarines were also sunk. The convoy continued intact.

In Germany, bizarre ideas were now being thought up in a search for some way out of a losing war; on February 28, when the test pilot Hanna Reitsch visited Hitler at Berchtesgaden to receive the Iron Cross, First Class, she suggested the creation of a 'Suicide Group' of pilots, to fly specially designed suicide planes. Hitler's first instinct, she later recalled, was to reject the idea 'completely', but he did agree to her request to start experimental work on the type of plane that would be most suitable, and effective. Shortly afterwards, when a Suicide Group was set up, Hanna Reitsch was one of the first to sign the pledge: 'I hereby voluntarily apply to be enrolled in the suicide group as pilot of a human glider-bomb. I fully understand that employment in this capacity will entail my own death.'

That February, Hitler had a more personal problem to deal with. For nearly a year his meals had been cooked by Frau Marlene von Exner, a Viennese dietician originally recommended to him by the Roumanian dictator, Marshal Antonescu. In due course, Frau von Exner became engaged to an SS adjutant at Hitler's headquarters, whereupon it was discovered that she had a Jewish great grandmother. 'You will understand', Hitler told her, 'that I must pay you off. I cannot make one rule for myself and another for the rest.'

Frau von Exner left Hitler's employ, and her relatives were forced to leave the Nazi Party. But there were no further repercussions. Meanwhile, on February 23, in Warsaw, twenty-six Jews were discovered in hiding and deported to Auschwitz, followed two days later by thirty-seven Jews from Vienna, Frau von Exner's own city. Nor did the deportations end there; on March 3 it was the turn of 732 Dutch Jews to be deported, followed on March 7 by 1,501 Jews from France. Nearly two thousand of them were gassed.

On March 1, the German Air Force resumed its bombing offensive over Britain; in six raids that month, 279 British civilians were killed. The principal raids were over London, Hull, North-East England, and South Wales. But they were small compared to the British bomber raids on Germany that month, in which six thousand bombers dropped 27,000 tons of bombs on Stuttgart, Frankfurt, Essen, Nuremberg and Berlin. It was during these raids that the British dropped 4,000-pound bombs for the first time.

British agents also continued to be parachuted into occupied Europe; on March 2, Alec Rabinovitch, code named 'Arnaud', dropped near Nancy, his second mission into German-occupied France, to set up a sabotage network. With him was a French Canadian, Roger Sabourin. By mischance, the dropping zone was under German control, and both men were arrested. Rabinovitch was sent to a concentration camp at Rawicz, in Poland; Sabourin was sent to Buchenwald, where, after six months as a prisoner, he was hanged. Also captured that March, and later executed, were two other members of the French Resistance, Robert Benoist, the pre-war motor racing champion, hanged at Buchenwald, and Denise Bloch, code name 'Ambroise', executed at Ravensbrück.

March 2 saw the first Allied bombing mission, from bases in southern Italy, in support of the Yugoslav partisans. In an attack on the rail junction and marshalling yards at Knin, the lines were hit. That same day, a strafing mission along the Dalmatian coast struck at German petrol supply dumps at Vodice, and along the coasts of Zlarin and Zirje islands and destroyed five motor vehicles at Sukosan. That same night, from a field near Châteauroux, in France, a British agent, the French barrister Jean Savy, was flown back to Britain with information about a German ammunition dump near the town of Creil which contained two thousand flying bombs, being made ready to fly against London. Thus pinpointed, they were later bombed and destroyed. Meanwhile, on March 3, another bomb was dropped, a dummy atomic bomb, at Muroc Army Air Force Base in California. It was the first of a series of tests that were to culminate five months later in the setting up of a special Air Force unit, the 393rd Bombardment Squadron, which would be given the task of delivering the real bombs once they were ready for action.

That March 3, as the American atomic bomb reached yet another stage in its long evolution, two more war trials took place, one in Africa and one in Europe. The trial in Africa, in Algiers, was of two Germans accused of the brutal killings in 1941, in a German punishment camp in the Sahara, of nine Jewish and non-Jewish prisoners. The camp, at Hajjerat m'Guil, had contained many German and Austrian refugees from Nazism who had fled to France, joined the Foreign Legion in 1939, fought against Germany in 1940 and been sent as prisoners to the Sahara after the Franco-German armistice. The accused guards were both sentenced to death.

The second trial of March 3 took place in German-occupied Poland, when a Polish woman, Anna Zwarycz, was accused, for the second time, of sheltering a Jewish child. Eight months earlier, in a lower court, she had been acquitted of this charge because she had 'kept the child openly and made known to everyone that it was Jewish'. This acquittal had been challenged by Dr Josef Ganser, a senior official in the Ministry of Justice in the General Government. 'It would be most unjust', he said, 'if one who granted shelter openly and audaciously should go unpunished, while one who does the same thing secretly incurs the death penalty.' Dr Ganser's challenge was successful. On March 3, Anna Zwarycz was sentenced to death. Twenty years later, her accuser was Senate President of the Patent Court of the German Federal Republic.

'The Jews are a race which must be wiped out,' Hans Frank told a meeting of Nazi Party speakers in Cracow on March 4. 'Whenever we catch one', he warned, 'he will be exterminated.' That same day, in Warsaw, four Jewish women, caught in the city, were shot in the ruins of the ghetto, together with eighty non-Jews. The bodies of those who had been shot, some of whom had not been killed but wounded, were thrown into the basement of a ruined house. The basement was then doused with an inflammable liquid and set on fire. 'For four to six hours', the historian of this episode has written, 'there could be heard the screams of the wounded as they burned alive.'

The names of the four Jewish women killed in Warsaw that day are unknown, like so many of the millions who perished in the war, of every race, nationality and creed. Some of the victims of these terrible times, their names and careers are a part of the history of their people; of their national struggles, their fate, and their aspirations. Thus, on March 5, at the Drancy deportation centre in Paris, awaiting deportation, was the sixty-year-old Jewish poet, Max Jacob. That day he died of bronchial pneumonia. Jacob had been baptized in the Catholic Church in his late thirties. Picasso had been his godfather. Despite his devout Catholicism of more than thirty years, Max Jacob had been forced to wear the yellow star, and had been sent to Drancy for deportation.

On March 4, in Moscow, Soviet Intelligence and military experts gave their approval to the Anglo-American deception plans for the Normandy landings. Fictitious Soviet military activity would make its contribution to the Allied plan for a spurious landing on the coast of Norway. By a coincidence of timing, March 4 was also the day on which a German Intelligence document, discussing the Allied plans for the 'decisive Atlantic front', noted that the Allied strategists, having been 'successful' in the creation of an active 'subsidiary front' in Italy, might have come 'to a like decision in the Scandinavian area'.

As the British and American cross-Channel planners prepared what was to be the largest amphibious landing in the history of modern war, the battles on the Eastern Front, in Italy, in Burma and in the Pacific continued with all their previous severity. On March 5, British, Indian and Gurkha forces were sent in by glider to a site behind Japanese lines in Burma, as part of Major General Orde Wingate's second Chindit Expedition. Their first landing was at 'Broadway', a clearing more than a hundred miles inside Japanese-occupied Burma, and nearly three hundred miles from the nearest Allied supply base. During the first landings, twenty-three men were killed, but more than four hundred reached the landing area safely. On the next day, as further gliders landed at 'Broadway', a second glider landing was made at 'Chowringhee', across the Irrawaddy river, followed by a third landing at 'Aberdeen' two and a half weeks later.

More than nine thousand officers and men were behind the Japanese lines in Burma by early April. These glider-borne forces were then joined by a fourth Chindit brigade, which had set off early in February, marching overland from the Naga Hills, across precipitous, six-thousand-feet mountain ranges, and across the Chindwin river. Two more land forces, one of American and Chinese troops, the other of Gurkhas and Kachins, were at the same time making their way through upper Burma, from Ledo and Fort Herz respectively towards Mogaung and Myitkyina. 'We have inflicted a complete surprise on the enemy,' Wingate told his men when the landings were done. 'All our columns are inside the enemy's guts. The time has come to reap the fruit of the advantage we have gained.'

Wingate himself was killed in an air crash before the end of March.

On the Eastern Front, beginning on March 2, four Soviet armies had advanced against the Germans along the whole southern sector, from the Pripet Marshes to the lower Dnieper. While the line remained static north of the Pripet Marshes, the Germans in the south were driven steadily back, and with such force, that within a month they had been forced back across the Southern Bug, the Dniester and the Pruth. The former Roumanian city of Czernowitz – once part of the

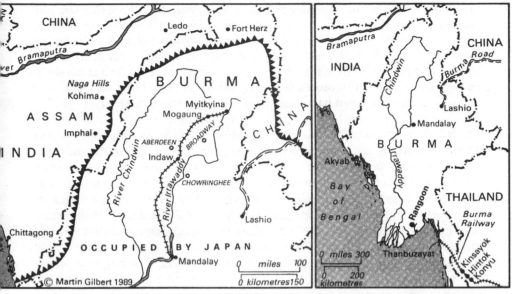

Burma, 1944

Austro-Hungarian Empire – was now under the control of the Red Army, its German masters driven southward. Of the German conquests of the summer of 1941 in southern Russia, stretching from the Pruth to the Don, only Odessa and the Crimea remained under German occupation. Hitler's dream of a colonial empire, with its Russian slaves, its motorways and its German settlers was over; now there remained little more than the nightmare of continual battle, devastation, retreat and retribution.

On the night of March 6, in preparation for the Normandy landings, now only three months away at the most, 263 British bombers dropped more than a thousand tons of bombs on the railway centre at Trappes, to the south-west of Paris. Tracks, engine sheds, engines and railway wagons were so badly damaged that the centre was unable to function for more than a month. During that month, eight other rail centres were attacked with similar effect.

The prospect of a third battleground in Europe did not deter the continued killing of Jews; on March 7, at Auschwitz, 3,860 Czech and Slovak Jews, including hundreds of children, brought to the camp some months earlier from the Theresienstadt ghetto and put in a special barrack, were taken to the undressing room next to one of the four gas chambers. Realizing that they were about to be killed, those among them who were strong enough, after the terrible privations of Theresienstadt and Auschwitz, tried to resist, attacking the s s guards with their bare hands. All but thirty-seven were killed; those thirty-seven included eleven pairs of twins, kept alive on the orders of Dr Mengele, so that he could perform medical experiments on them.

507

Also on March 7, Hitler received a report from Poznan, from Artur Greiser, Gauleiter of the Warthegau, informing him that not only had a million Germans been settled in the region and seven hundred thousand Poles been forced to leave it, but that the number of Jews in the Warthegau was 'down to a very insignificant remnant'. In Warsaw that day, thirty-eight Jews, in hiding since the destruction of the ghetto nearly a year earlier, had been betrayed; seized in their hiding place in 'Aryan' Warsaw, they were taken away and killed. Among them was the historian Emanuel Ringelblum, his wife and son.

In the Pacific, March 8 marked the start of a massive Japanese counter-attack on Bougainville, in the Solomon Islands, designed to drive the Americans from their positions around Empress Augusta Bay, which they had secured four months earlier. In three days of violent fighting, the Americans drove off their attackers. A further Japanese thrust on the following day was likewise repulsed. In four days, five thousand Japanese were killed, for the deaths of less than three hundred Americans. Once more, fanaticism in attack had served only to prolong and intensify the conflict, ensuring that, wherever the opposing forces met, men would die in their thousands, on remote islands far from either homeland.

In the lands under German rule, perversity and killing knew no pause. On March 9, Professor Hallervorden, a German neurologist, wrote to Professor Nitsche, who was in charge of the euthanasia programme: 'Dear Colleague, I have received 697 brains in all, including those which I took out myself in Brandenburg. Those from Dosen' – a mental hospital near Leipzig – 'are included in this figure. The greater proportion of them have already been studied, but whether I will be able to make a histological study of them all, only time will tell.' Professor Hallervorden's method was to remove the victims' brains immediately after they were killed. 'There was wonderful material among those brains,' he later told his American interrogators, 'beautiful mental defectives, malformations and early infantile diseases.'

After the war, Professor Hallervorden continued to use these brains in his researches, publishing the results of one particular case in 1949. Part of his collection later went to the University of Frankfurt.

Plans for mass killing were also being discussed that week, as part of the preparations for Operation Margaret, the imminent German military occupation of Hungary. On March 10, Adolf Eichmann and his principal subordinates met at Mauthausen concentration camp to work out a programme for the deportation of three quarters of a million Jews from Hungary to Auschwitz.

The German plan to occupy Hungary arose from the imminent arrival of the Red Army on Hungary's eastern border. A British plan was also being prepared at that time, Operation Chicken, to set up an evasion line through Hungary to Yugoslavia, for Allied airmen now being shot down deeper inside Europe than before, as the bombing itself went deeper. To establish this line, twenty-five Allied agents were parachuted into Yugoslavia, the first group of them on March 15, at Metlika, and made their way toward the Hungarian border. Most of these agents were Jewish volunteers from Palestine, among them the twenty-two-year-old Hannah Szenes, who had emigrated from Hungary to Palestine in

September 1939. Code-named 'Minnie', she arrived at the Hungarian border four days after landing at Metlika. Her arrival coincided by tragic chance with the German occupation. On crossing the border she was immediately arrested, and later, after being imprisoned in Budapest, she was taken out of her cell and shot.

In Italy, the Allies tried once again, on March 15, to capture Monte Cassino. The infantry attack was preceded by one of the heaviest aerial bombardments of the war on a single building, 992 tons of bombs in three and a half hours; but many of the bombs fell, not on the monastery, but several miles away, killing 96 Allied soldiers, and 140 Italian civilians. The air strike was followed by an artillery bombardment of 195,000 rounds, yet again one of the heaviest attacks on a single building. But in the bitter hand to hand fighting that followed, in which British, Maori, Indian and Gurkha troops were the main Allied participants, the Germans could still not be dislodged. Their tenacity in defence amazed even their adversaries. 'I doubt if there are any other troops in the world', General Alexander told Churchill, 'who would have stood up to it' – the artillery barrage – 'and then gone on fighting with the ferocity they have.'

By the end of the battle, with Monte Cassino still in German hands, 863 New Zealanders and more than a thousand Indians had been killed. Both Anzio and Rome were still beyond the reach of Alexander's army.

Against the German forces on the Dalmatian coast, a combined British, South African, American and Yugoslav partisan operation was launched on March 17, when a raid was carried out on Solta island. At the same time, German units in the port of Split and on the Metkovic–Mostar road were attacked from the air. Also on March 17, on the Eastern Front, the Red Army entered Dubno, a road and rail junction twenty-five miles inside Poland's pre-war borders, and only 170 miles from the eastern border of Hungary. On the following day, Hitler summoned the Hungarian Regent, Admiral Horthy, to Klessheim Castle, south of Salzburg. There, Horthy was forced to accept Hitler's terms: a new government headed by Dome Sztojay – a former Hungarian chargé d'affaires in Berlin, the entry of German troops into Hungary, German control of Hungary's oil and other raw materials – including the oil wells at Nagykanizsa – and the deportation to Auschwitz of Hungary's three quarters of a million Jews, who had up until then survived four and a half years of war unharassed and unharmed, apart from the deportation of nearly twenty thousand to slave-labour and eventual execution of Kamenets Podolsk in the autumn of 1941, and a further ten thousand, at Hitler's insistence, to the copper mines at Bor, one of Germany's essential raw material sources.

In the early hours of March 19, German troops entered Hungary. Horthy returned to Hungary several hours later, to be received at his residence in Budapest by a German guard of honour.

At Anzio, on March 17, more than fifty men were drowned when the ship they were unloading was hit by German shell-fire. On the following day, in the Indian Ocean, a Japanese submarine sank the British cargo ship *Nancy Moller*.

Her crew took to two lifeboats and got safely away from the sinking ship. A few minutes later, the submarine rammed the lifeboats, smashing both of them to pieces. The survivors were then machine-gunned as they swam in the sea or clung to life rafts. Of the sixty-nine crewmen, only sixteen survived.

Also on March 18, off Okinawa, Japanese aircraft severely damaged the American warship *Franklin*; several hundred of those on board were drowned.

In Russia, as the Red Army continued its advance in the south, taking Vinnitsa, on the Southern Bug, on March 20, and crossing the Dniester north of Kishinev, there was particular cause for celebration that day when the regular 'Red Arrow' express train resumed services between Moscow and Leningrad. Two days later, over the Baltic, a Soviet Air Force major, Victor Kashtankin, attacking a German naval task force, and finding his plane on fire, drove it at full throttle towards the deck of one of the German ships. His last words, carried over the plane radio to his divisional headquarters, were: 'Dying is simple. We must win.' For his final act, Kashtankin was posthumously made a Hero of the Soviet Union.

On the day of Kashtankin's heroic deed, a revolt broke out against dire odds in a slave labour camp at Koldyczewo, in German-occupied White Russia. The revolt was led by a Jew, Shlomo Kushnir. During the revolt, ten Nazi guards were killed, and hundreds of labourers reached the forests, and the partisans. Kushnir and twenty-five others were caught: Kushnir committed suicide before he could be tortured and shot. On the following day, in the Bialystok region, a Soviet partisan group, led by a Jew, Sergeant Andrei Tsymbal, with a large number of Jewish fighters under him, destroyed a German military train carrying armoured cars to the Eastern Front.

On March 23, the German authorities in Greece began the deportation to Auschwitz of more than four thousand Greek Jews, seized in towns and villages throughout Greece. But for every Jew caught and taken away, another was able to find shelter and safety with local peasants, or to join the Greek partisans. The largest number taken to their deaths were the 1,687 Jews of Yanina. In Rome, on March 23, Italian partisans threw a bomb at an SS unit; thirty-three of them were killed. In reprisal, 335 Italians were taken on the following day to the Ardeatine caves and shot; 253 were Catholics and 70 were Jews. The remaining twelve victims were never identified.

On the night of March 24, as part of the continuing British air raids over Berlin, 811 bombers struck at the German capital; seventy-two of them were shot down or crashed, and 392 aircrew killed, the largest death toll of any of the nineteen raids on Berlin. Less than eighty Berliners died that night, though much damage was done, including direct hits on the Swedish Embassy, three breweries, a butter warehouse, five hospitals, a gasworks and Himmler's personal bunker. Himmler himself, however, was unhurt.

Even as British bombers were over Berlin, seventy-nine Allied prisoners-of-war, all airmen, escaped through a tunnel from their prisoner-of-war camp at Sagan. Three of the escapees, a Dutch pilot, Flight Lieutenant van der Stok, and two Norwegians, Sergeant Bergsland and Second Lieutenant Miller, managed to reach Stettin, go by boat to Sweden and thus return to Britain. All the rest were captured, three close to the exit of the tunnel, and one, Roger Bushell, as far west as Saarbrücken.

Hitler learned of the escape on the morning after the Berlin air raid. He was outraged at the thought of so many aircrew on their way back to Britain, and to their bombers, telling Himmler: 'You are not to let the escaped airmen out of your control!'

Fifty of the escaped airmen, handed over to the ss after their recapture instead of to the German Air Force, were shot – without trial.

German fury was also evident on March 25, when eight thousand German soldiers, supported by two air squadrons, launched an attack on 450 members of the French Resistance on the Plateau des Glières, high above Annecy; more than four hundred of the Resistance fighters were killed.

On the Eastern Front, on March 25, the Germans were driven from Proskurov, less than fifty miles from Eastern Galicia; that day, Field Marshal von Manstein asked Hitler's permission to retreat further westward. He was at once dismissed from command of Army Group South, and retired to his estate. On the following day, Russian troops reached the River Pruth on a fifty-six mile front. The Red Army had advanced more than nine hundred miles in the past year. Its advances, Churchill told his listeners in a broadcast on March 26, 'constitute the greatest cause of Hitler's undoing'.

In Paris, March 27 saw a meeting of two German officers who were so disturbed at Hitler's leadership as to be determined, despite the risks, to discuss the need for his overthrow. One of the two, Ernst Junger, noted in his diary how the other, Caesar von Hofacker, 'was not at his ease in my workroom and begged me to accompany him to the Avenue Kléber so that he could speak freely. While we were pacing up and down between the Trocadero and the Étoile, he confided a number of details coming from men he could trust.'

As conspirators talked, neither military setbacks nor civil tyranny abated. At the front, on March 27, the Red Army entered Kamenets-Podolsk, on the border of Eastern Galicia. To protect the southern flank of Greater Germany, the German Army, already in occupation of Hungary, moved into Roumania. All military energies had now to be put into the protection of the borders of Greater Germany. But even as Soviet troops overran the sites of previous mass murder, the killings continued. That same March 27, in the Kovno ghetto, two hundred miles behind the front line, all surviving Jewish children below the age of fourteen were seized by the ss, thrown into trucks and driven off to their deaths. Thirty-seven Jewish policemen, among them the commander of the Jewish ghetto police and his two deputies, refused to take part in this round-up of children. They were killed on the spot.

The 'children's action' in Kovno took two days to complete. Several thousand children were rounded up, driven off in trucks and shot. Only a tiny fragment survived, among them the five-year-old Zahar Kaplanas. This young boy was saved by a non-Jew, a Lithuanian, who smuggled him out of the ghetto in a sack.

The Red Army now thrust forward in the south across the frontier of Greater

Germany, occupying Kolomyja on March 29. On the following day, Soviet forces reached to within sixteen miles of the Hungarian frontier. That night, Churchill left London by train for Yorkshire, for a visit to British troops preparing for the cross-Channel invasion. As his train travelled northward, eight hundred British bombers carried out Operation Grayling, a night raid over Nuremberg; but ninety-five were shot down or crashed on landing and 545 aircrew were killed, the largest death toll of aircrew on any Allied raid over Germany. The Germans lost 110 civilian and nineteen Air Force dead; fifty-nine foreign slave labourers were also killed. Three airmen had died for every person on the ground. Hardly any damage was done to Nuremberg's war industries, though 256 buildings were damaged, and several thousand citizens made homeless.

On the return flight from Nuremberg, Pilot Officer Cyril Barton sought in vain to bring his badly damaged Halifax bomber back to its airfield. Crossing the Durham coast at Ryhope, Barton skillfully avoided hitting four rows of miners' cottages. His plane finally crashed in the yard of a coal mine, killing one miner. Barton himself was also killed. For his exceptional skill and courage in avoiding the miners' cottages he was posthumously awarded the Victoria Cross, the only one awarded to a Halifax crew member throughout the war.

At the same time as the Nuremberg raid, and using it as cover, a British bomber flew to Belgium on a resistance mission. During the flight it was shot down, and five of the ten people on board were killed. One of the dead was a Belgian Resistance leader, Robert Deprez. Three of the survivors were captured and sent to prisoner-of-war camp. Two others, the pilot and co-pilot, were sheltered by Belgian families in the village of Zelzate, on the Belgian–Dutch border, where forty-seven other Allied airmen were already in hiding, waiting the opportunity to join an escape line. Jews, too, were being taken to safety by the escape lines, one of which, run by John Weidner, a Dutch Seventh-Day Adventist, passed on his escapees from Holland to Switzerland. As many as 150 people helped Weidner to operate his line; forty of them were arrested by the Gestapo and killed, including his own sister Gabrielle.


In the Far East, the Japanese, advancing on March 30 across the Indian border, began the siege of Imphal. The garrison, supplied by air, held out; by the time the siege was lifted three months later, thirteen thousand Japanese soldiers had been killed. An even larger number of German soldiers were killed, in a far shorter time, when, on April 1, they were surrounded in the East Galician town of Skala; in the course of a nine-day battle, twenty-six thousand were killed.

That same April 1, sixteen members of various Polish resistance groups were hanged in Suwalki, including a fourteen-year-old boy. On the following day, in France, as a reprisal for the derailment of a German troop train at the village of Ascq, near Lille, in which no one was killed, eighty-six villagers were taken from their homes and shot. One of the victims, Lucien Albert, was a former prisoner-of-war who, a month earlier, had been allowed by the Germans to return home because of illness. Another victim was Abbé Henri Gilleron, shot down outside his church; his curate, Abbé Maurice Cousin, was beaten to death in the street outside.

Three weeks after the reprisal massacre at Ascq, an informer, who has never been identified, gave the Gestapo the names of eight local civilians; six of them were found guilty of the sabotage and shot.

In Operation Tungsten, on April 3, British carrier-borne aircraft struck at the German battleship *Tirpitz* – now recovering from the damage inflicted six months earlier by British midget submarines – at Kaafjord, its Norwegian haven; 128 German sailors were killed, but the *Tirpitz* remained afloat. It was, however, too badly damaged to put to sea again under her own steam.

On April 4, a South African Air Force reconnaissance plane, coming from Foggia in southern Italy, flew, at 26,000 feet, over the IG Farben synthetic oil and rubber plant at Monowitz. This plant was a known factor in the German war effort, and one of the potential Allied bombing targets in East Upper Silesia. The technique of aerial photography then in use involved the pilot turning on his camera shortly before reaching the site to be photographed, and turning it off when he judged that he had flown past his objective.

Monowitz lay two and a half miles east of Auschwitz. The pilot turned on the camera when he was approaching his target, and turned it off some six kilometres later. The result: twenty exposures, on three of which Auschwitz itself appeared for the first time.

The Intelligence personnel who developed and studied the photographs of April 4 at the Royal Air Force station at Medmenham, in the Thames Valley west of London, were looking for specific industrial installations. These were quickly identified, including 'a power station, carbide plant, synthetic rubber plant and synthetic oil (Bergius) plant'. Each of these plants was then analysed in detail. The oil-production method was seen to be similar to that already in use at Blechhammer–South, one of the existing high priority bombing targets.

Both the synthetic oil and rubber plants at Monowitz were clearly in 'partial production' already, and, while work was still in progress to complete both plants, they were already producing the oil and rubber on which, because the Russian advance was now threatening all Germany's sources of natural petroleum, the German war machine depended. Monowitz would soon be capable of producing synthetic oil on a scale similar to the largest of the plants elsewhere.

The Monowitz interpretation report of April 4 was sent to both American and Royal Air Force Intelligence. With so much relevant and important detail visible in the factory zone, the interpreters found no need to comment on the row upon row of huts at Auschwitz; huts which resembled hundreds of other barracks, army camps, prisoner-of-war camps and labour camps in the Silesian region. Nor did these first photographs include the gas chambers and crematoria, and the far more extensive hutted area, of the Birkenau section of Auschwitz, where at that moment some 52,000 Jews were being held captive, in addition to the 15,000 Jews in barracks at Monowitz itself. It was not for another seven weeks, until May 31, that Birkenau itself was to be photographed from the air.

At Birkenau itself, the process of gassing continued without respite. On April 4, the day on which its huts were so nearly photographed, a train reached the camp from Trieste. Of its 132 deportees, most of them Italian Jews, 29 were sent to the barracks, registered and tattooed, while the remaining 103 were gassed.

In India, April 4 saw the unexpected arrival of Japanese troops at Kohima, where the local garrison of 1,500 held on tenaciously to as much of the town as possible, before being relieved two and a half weeks later. To help the defenders, before reinforcements could arrive by land, British bombers from bases in Assam flew more than two thousand sorties against the Japanese besiegers, whose losses were in the thousands.

As the Kohima battle began, the British public were told of the scale of the war casualties so far. It was Churchill who gave the figures, in the House of Commons: 120,958 British soldiers, sailors and airmen had been killed, as had 49,730 civilians in German bombing raids, and 26,317 merchant seamen, killed at sea. In addition, the British Commonwealth deaths were made known: 12,298 Australian servicemen, 9,209 Canadians, 5,912 Indians, 5,622 New Zealanders and 3,107 South Africans, a total British and Commonwealth death toll, in just over four and a half years of more than 232,000.

On April 5, death lay in wait for both soldiers and Jews. The soldiers were six British commandos, who set off that day for the German-occupied Alimnia Island, in the Aegean Sea. Intercepted by a German patrol boat and taken prisoner, they were first interrogated and then sent for 'special treatment'. Also designated for 'special treatment' on April 5 were 559 Jews deported from northern Italy to Auschwitz, including several small children, among them the five-year-old Rosetta Scaramella, born in Venice, and the three-year-old Roberto Zarfatti, born in Rome.

In France, even children being cared for in remote villages were found and taken away. On April 6, German soldiers and French Milice drove from Lyon to the remote and tiny village of Izieu, where it was alleged that Jewish children were being hidden in a school run by a Jew, Miron Zlatin. There were forty-three Jewish children in the village; all were taken away, together with the ten adults – five men and five women – who were looking after them. Zlatin and two of the children were deported to the Estonian city of Tallinn, where they were shot; the others were sent to Auschwitz, where all but one, a young woman helper, Lea Feldbaum, were gassed.

As the Izieu round-up was taking place, Hitler, at Berchtesgaden, was agreeing to send 2,500 ss men, of the 2nd Panzer Division, from the Eastern Front to southern France. 'In this uneasy period of waiting for invasion and retribution, and also for a change of fortunes in the East' a Security Service 'Report from the Reich' noted that day, 'many are wondering what would happen if we could not hold out. People are asking themselves whether the many severe sacrifices and hardships which the war demands, and will continue to demand, are worth it.' The people of Germany, the report concluded, 'are gradually beginning to long for peace'.

The British effort to sustain and stimulate the French Resistance was continuous; on April 6 a French-Canadian from Montreal, Jean-Paul Archambault, was parachuted into France near Lyon. As an agent of Britain's Special Operations Executive, SOE, he helped to form three groups of local saboteurs; one, in the Bourges area, consisted of 250 men.

For Eisenhower, as Supreme Commander, and for Montgomery, as Commander-in-Chief, whatever disruption could be made to the movement of German troops and supplies in France gave a welcome added element of strength.

On April 7, a further German sweep against French Resistance fighters was launched in the hills around Gex and Oyonnax, in the Jura mountains. Code-named Operation Spring, it involved six German regiments, and also a regiment of Cossacks – Soviet citizens who, having been taken prisoner-of-war in south Russia 1941 and 1942, had volunteered to fight for the Germans. On the first day of the sweep, five members of the Resistance were killed and thirteen captured. That same week, in northern France, near Angers, German agents captured twenty Frenchmen who, a month earlier, had pieced together for the British a detailed fifty-five foot map of the German defences in the Cotentin peninsula, on the eastern edge of which a part of the cross-Channel invasion was to take place. All twenty were executed once the invasion began.

On the Eastern Front, the Russians now prepared to drive the German Army from the Crimea, the last of Russia's inter-war territory still under German rule. The attack, under the overall command of Marshal Tolbukhin, began on the morning of April 8. Within four days, two German defensive lines had been broken, and German and Roumanian troops quickly put to flight. Only Sevastopol, the fortress which the Russians had themselves defended with such tenacity in 1942, held out against its would-be liberators. April 8, the first day of the Crimean offensive, was also the first day of Operation Gardening, when three American and nineteen British bombers, flying low along the river Danube near Belgrade, dropped forty mines in the river. Within ten days, the total number of mines dropped had risen to 177, their purpose being to disrupt the barge traffic bringing Roumanian oil from the oil wells at Ploesti, to Germany. This disruption was to be achieved with conspicuous success.

On April 19, American bombers began a series of attacks on German shore batteries along the Normandy coast, in preparation for the cross-Channel landings. They also bombed anti-aircraft batteries between Rouen and Dunkirk, to ensure that the deception of a landing in the Pas de Calais should be maintained. Indeed, in order to maintain this deception, it had been laid down that two batteries had to be bombed elsewhere for every battery bombed in the actual assault area. Also bombed that week, on April 11, in a precision raid, was a five-storey building in The Hague which contained the principal Gestapo records about their captive Dutch population; six British aircraft of No. 613 Squadron, led by Wing-Commander R. N. Bateson, approaching the building at only fifty feet, destroyed almost all of the Gestapo's card-index system. During the raid, sixty-one Dutch officials were killed; it had been impossible to warn them without endangering the plan. But the lives of many more Dutch patriots were saved by the destruction of the files through which those active in the Resistance were being monitored and tracked down.

On the day of this British air raid on The Hague, a fourteen-year-old Jewish girl in nearby Amsterdam, Anne Frank, a refugee from Germany now in hiding in Holland with her parents and her sister, wrote in her diary: 'Who has inflicted this upon us? Who has made us Jews different to all other people? Who has allowed us to suffer so terribly up to now?', and she went on to answer her own question with the words: 'It is God that has made us as we are, but it will be God, too, who will raise us up again.'

Four months after writing these words, Anne Frank and her family were betrayed, and then deported; she was to die in Belsen concentration camp, together with her sister Margot, early in 1945, at about the same time that her mother died in Auschwitz. Her father alone survived.

Behind the lines on the Eastern Front, mid-April marked the beginning of another German anti-partisan sweep, between Lepel and Borisov, and Lepel and Polotsk, where ss troops, advancing village by village, destroyed everything in their path. According to the Germans' own estimates, seven thousand Soviet partisans were killed. Many of those killed were ordinary villagers.

This anti-partisan sweep did not go unopposed; as it proceeded, Soviet aircraft flew over the region, attacking the partisan hunters. Even after this major sweep, within a few weeks, railway demolitions by partisans throughout the region had regained their former intensity. Further north, on April 15, sixty Jewish slave labourers, who for several months had been forced to dig up and burn the corpses of Jews who had been murdered at Ponar, outside Vilna, in the summer and autumn of 1941, rose up in desperate revolt; only fifteen managed to break out to the woods, and to join the Soviet partisans; the rest were killed. Further south, across the former Polish border, April 15 saw the capture by the Red Army of Tarnopol, one of the principal cities of Eastern Galicia.

In the Pacific, on April 15, the United States began the planning stage of Operation Wedlock, against the Kurile Islands of northern Japan. Like Operations Jael and Fortitude in Europe, it was a totally spurious plan, devised to deceive the Japanese into diverting men and resources away from the actual operation being planned against the Marianas Islands.

Operation Wedlock involved a fictional force of American and Canadian troops, complete with their own supplies, signals and staging posts. As well as giving the actual staging post and communications centre in Hawaii the appearance of an integral part of the Kurile Island attack, a largely phantom Ninth Fleet was also created, and began sending and receiving messages from the very real Third and Fifth Fleets, as well as carrying out entirely fictitious practice manoeuvres. To add to the credibility of the deception, American bombers were instructed to bomb Japanese military, air and naval installations on the Kurile Islands 'every day, weather permitting'.

\*          \*          \*

On April 16, on the Eastern Front, Soviet forces entered the Black Sea coastal resort of Yalta. On the following day, in Britain, to protect the secrecy of the preparations for the cross-Channel landings, all foreign diplomats were forbidden to send or receive any uncensored message, or to leave Britain. That day, Grand Admiral Dönitz issued a proclamation to Germany's armed forces, warning that a large-scale landing could come at any moment: 'Throw yourself recklessly into the fight,' he declared, and went on to warn: 'Any man who fails to do so will be destroyed in shame and ignominy.' Far worse than 'shame and ignominy' was meted out in Germany that April 17 to a Catholic priest, Max Josef Metzger, who had written privately to a fellow clergyman about the need for a new government. Found guilty of 'assisting the enemy', he was executed in Brandenburg.

In the Pacific, April 18 marked the beginning of Operation Stamina, an air lift to the British and Indian troops besieged in Imphal. By the end of the month, 1,479 men and 1,929 tons of supplies had been flown in by air. By the end of June, 12,561 men and 18,824 tons had been delivered, and, on the return flights, 13,000 wounded men and 43,000 non-combatants flown out of the Japanese trap. On April 19th, British, American and French warships bombarded Japanese positions at Sabang, in the Dutch East Indies; a warning to the Japanese that they no longer had naval mastery in the Indian Ocean.

Hitler, too, received a setback that week, when the Turkish Government declared on April 20 – Hitler's fifty-fifth birthday – that it would no longer send chrome to Germany. The Soviet reconquest of the Crimea made it dangerous for Turkey to continue with her absolute neutrality; now, more than a year after Churchill had gone specially to Adana in southern Turkey to try to persuade the Turks to enter the war, it was announced that Turkey was no longer a neutral, but a 'pro-Allied' nation – though not a belligerent.

As of April 1944, Germany's stocks of chrome were sufficient for no more than a year and a half's further production of the high grade steel needed for the manufacture of tanks. Yet Hitler had hopes that new tanks, faster and more powerful, some of which were demonstrated to him on April 20 at Klessheim Castle, could halt the Soviet thrust on the Eastern Front, and check any cross-Channel invasion at the shore. Perhaps he never saw the Security Police 'Report from the Reich' of April 20, in which it was stated that 'developments in the East and the continually deferred hope of "a saving miracle" are gradually producing signs of weariness among the people'. He certainly had no inkling that one of his own most top secret Ultra messages, setting out the Western itinerary of General Guderian as Inspector General of Panzer Troops, had not only enabled the German tank commanders to prepare for the visit, but gave British Intelligence, who also read it, a clear picture of the location and distribution of Germany's armoured forces, less than two months before the Normandy landing was due to take place.

The first lap of Guderian's itinerary was the tank headquarters at Mailly-le-Camp, near Reims; even as Guderian moved on to his next stop, at Amiens, British bombers struck at Mailly-le-Camp, killing as many as a hundred soldiers,

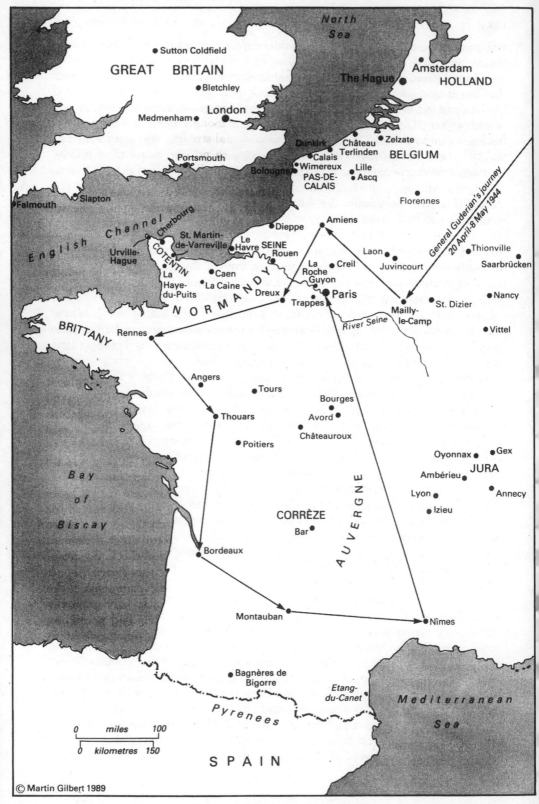

France, 1 February–5 June 1944

and injuring many more. But it was not always the Germans who suffered from the intensification of Allied bombing over France that month; when, on April 21, a heavy night raid over Paris struck at the marshalling yards of St Denis and the Gare de la Chapelle, 640 Parisians were killed.

The growing number of German divisions known through Ultra to be in north-western France was now causing alarm among the Allied leaders. But Intelligence was also able to show that their actual strength was not excessive, and that the scale of German strength needed to postpone or cancel D-Day would not be reached. Guderian's journey had helped to confirm this.

On April 22, in the Pacific, the Americans launched Operation Persecution, landing 84,000 men in a twin assault on Hollandia and Aitape, on the northern coast of New Guinea. The Japanese, whose total strength did not exceed 15,000, many of them administrative troops, ought, if logic ruled, to have abandoned the fight. Instead, they prolonged the battle for more than three months. But it was at a terrible cost even by European standards: 12,811 Japanese dead, for the loss of 527 American lives.

In western Europe, it was French civilians who had begun to suffer, as Allied bombers carried out the 'Transportation' plan for the destruction of German railway yards and junctions throughout the Normandy, Seine and Pas de Calais regions; on April 24, four hundred people were killed during an American daylight raid on the railway yards at Rouen, when many bombs fell on the centre of the town. That same day, two South African Air Force pilots, Lieutenant Charles Barry and Lieutenant I. McIntyre, flying an aerial reconnaissance mission from southern Italy deep across eastern Roumania, photographed German and Roumanian Army defences in the Galatz Gap between Focsani and Galatz. So clearly did the photographs reveal the nature and scale of the defences which would confront the Red Army about to attack the Gap, that they were flown to Russia by special courier.

On April 25, an American bomber was shot down over northern Italy. One of its crewmen, Lieutenant Charles F. Kingsman, was injured when he landed by parachute. An Italian family hid him; while in hiding, he gave secret lessons to Italian partisans in how to use and maintain the machine guns which they had collected from other crashed Allied aircraft. Also behind the lines, in German-occupied Crete, plans were being made by British Special Operations to kidnap the German General commanding the island, General Heinrich Kreipe. One British agent, Major Patrick Leigh-Fermor, was parachuted into Crete; another, Captain Stanley Moss, with two Greek partisans, was brought ashore by boat. Helped also by three Greek partisans on the island, the agents ambushed and captured the General on the morning of April 26, as he was driving from his headquarters at Arhanes to his villa on the road to Heraklion. General Kreipe's captors then crossed Crete on foot with him, and, after a seventeen day trek covering seventy-five miles, brought him to a remote beach near Rodakino. He was then taken by boat across the Mediterranean to Mersa Matruh, flown to Cairo, thence to Gibraltar and on to London. After interrogation, he was sent by ship across the Atlantic and by train across Canada, to a prisoner-of-war camp near Calgary. For their remarkable exploit, Major Leigh-Fermor and Captain Moss were awarded the Distinguished Service Order.

There were no immediate reprisals following General Kreipe's capture; the British made it clear that this would affect the General's safety. Four months after his capture, however, German military units in Crete destroyed the town of Anoya and the village of Kedrous, killing more than five hundred of their inhabitants.

In Britain, during March and April 1944, the preparations for the cross-Channel invasion had reached the stage of practice landings on various beaches in southern England. One such practice, Exercise Tiger, was carried out at Slapton Sands, near Dartmouth, between April 26 and 28. The mass of Allied shipping assembled to make the simulated assault was observed by seven German torpedo boats on a routine patrol from Cherbourg, whereupon two Tank Landing Ships were torpedoed and sunk, one other badly damaged, and 639 American soldiers killed. Many of them were specialist engineers who could not easily be replaced.

For mounting the attack on the Slapton forces, the German commander of the naval patrol, Captain Peterson, was awarded the Oak Leaves to the Knight's Cross which he had won in 1940.

Ten of the American officers drowned off Slapton Sands on April 28 were in possession of secret information relevant to the actual cross-Channel invasion; information given under the code name 'Bigot' only to those who needed to know it. In order to ensure that none of the ten had been picked up at sea by the Germans, a vast search was carried out, and all the corpses which could be recovered were carefully examined. Although more than a hundred bodies were never recovered, those of each of the ten Bigot officers were found. The cross-Channel secrets were safe.

In the Pacific, on April 28, in their second attack on the island of Truk in ten weeks, thirty American aircraft were shot down, but twenty-five of their pilots were saved. With the almost total destruction of Japanese fuel and ammunition depots on the atoll, any possible flank attack on the American forces in north-western New Guinea was removed.

On the last day of April 1944, more than two hundred Jews were gassed at Auschwitz; they were originally from Poland, but had been sent to Vittel, in France, supposedly as the first stage in being allowed to proceed, with South American passports, to Lisbon, and on to safety. Instead, after being held at Vittel for several months, they were deported back eastward and killed; among them was the poet Yitzhak Katznelson, author of songs and poems which, reflecting youthful pleasures and the joys of life, had been particularly popular among Polish Jewish children before the war. He was gassed at Auschwitz with his eighteen-year-old son. His wife, and his two younger sons, had been deported from Warsaw to Treblinka more than a year and a half earlier. Thus perished, amid separation, deception and horror, yet another talented family among the millions of victims of the Second World War.

# 37

# Resistance, sabotage and deception

## SPRING 1944

During May 1944, the Germans intensified their efforts to crush resistance activity in Europe. In France, a 'Blood and Ashes' campaign against Resistance fighters in the Auvergne led to the public hanging of ninety-nine of those caught. But as many as 35,000 active members of the French Resistance had now been identified, region by region, by British Intelligence, which sent them regular supplies of arms in preparation for a general uprising in support of the cross-Channel attack. In Yugoslavia, Tito's partisans launched their own offensive that May, Operation Bearskin, to disrupt German road and rail communications northward through Slovenia, in an effort to make it more difficult for the Germans to move troops from the Balkans to France once the landings had begun.

In Britain on May 2, despite the disaster four days earlier at Slapton Sands, the last of the practice landings, Operation Fabius, was held at the same Assault Training Area, which included Slapton.

On May 2, in Germany, the journalist Erich Knauf, who had declared publicly not only that 'a German victory would be the greatest misfortune', but also that Himmler 'only keeps his job by ordering between eighty and a hundred executions a day', was himself executed. On the previous day, in London, a British court had sentenced to death a Belgian subject, Pierre Richard Neukermans, found guilty of having flown from Lisbon to Britain in order to spy against Britain; he was executed at the end of June.

The Allies continued to use the Germans' own top-secret Ultra radio messages to improve their invasion plans. On May 3, a newly formed German division reached France; four days later, as a result of reading the German Army's Ultra signals, the Anglo-American planners knew, not only of its existence, but of its strength – defensive only, and location – at the base of the Cotentin Peninsula.

Thus the most secret triumph of British Intelligence, and the hard, often laborious work of more than five thousand cryptographers and their helpers – work which four years earlier had been fraught with uncertainty and difficulty – reached a high point of decisive achievement, averting all danger of a 'blind' landing in France. One by one, every German military formation was precisely located.

On May 5, in a further success for their Intelligence services, the Germans were again able to eavesdrop on a telephone conversation between Churchill and Roosevelt. Something was in preparation, but what it was or where, or when, they could neither overhear nor deduce. Particularly galling for those who read the transcript of the discussion were Roosevelt's final words: 'Well, we will do our best – now I'll go fishing.'

Allied 'fishing' was of a high order; also on May 5, as a result of clues received by Enigma, South African Air Force pilots flew a reconnaissance mission from Italy deep over southern Poland, to Blizyn, where they photographed a German flying bomb assembly and test centre. Both the rocket and its firing platform were identified by the Photographic Reconnaissance Unit at Medmenham, in Britain. To accelerate flying bomb production, on May 6 German rocket scientists, including Wernher von Braun, and senior SS officers, agreed that 1,800 skilled workers should be brought from France to work in the underground tunnels and facilities at Nordhausen; they were to be housed at the nearby Dora concentration camp, and treated as concentration camp inmates. Few of them were to survive the war.

On May 7, against Hitler's wishes, General Schörner, commander of the South Ukraine Army Group, realizing that his forces could no longer hold the Crimean city of Sevastopol, ordered it to be evacuated by sea and air. More than thirty thousand soldiers were taken off before, on May 11, the last of the strongpoints was given up. But already, on May 10, the city was sufficiently in Soviet hands for Marshal Tolbukhin to report its capture to Stalin. That same day, in a somewhat disingenuous communiqué, the German High Command announced: 'The ruins of Sevastopol were evacuated in the course of a disengaging move.' Defeat had become disengagement.

In Western Europe, the planning and deception for Overlord were in their final month. On May 9, United States bombers struck at the principal German airfields in north-west Europe – Laon, Florennes, Thionville, St Dizier, Juvincourt, Orléans and Avord. That same day, in Stockholm, a deliberate British manipulation of the Swedish Stock Exchange, whereby Norwegian stocks rose by almost twenty per cent, was intended, as part of Operation Graffham, to give the impression that the liberation of Norway was near; that Norway, not France, was one of the destinations of the Allied forces being assembled in Britain.

Even the imminence of the landing was hidden from the Germans; on May 9, Admiral Dönitz told the Japanese Ambassador in Berlin, Count Oshima, that the Allies would not be able to invade 'for some time'. Oshima's radio report of this conversation, sent to Tokyo, was decrypted at Bletchley on May 13, providing welcome relief to the Anglo-American planners.

At eleven o'clock on the evening of May 11, in Italy, nearly two thousand Allied guns opened fire in a simultaneous artillery barrage from Cassino to the sea. Forty-five minutes later, the infantry began their attack – Indian, British, French, Polish and Moroccan troops among them. In this, the fourth battle for Cassino and its monastery, General Alexander had assembled a numerical superiority of three to one; but it was to take seven days before even this advantage could overcome the tenacious German defence. Meanwhile, on May 12, the United States Air Force launched a massive attack on German synthetic oil plants. The seven plants which were bombed that day produced together far more than a third of Germany's total output of synthetic oil, on which the German forces were now almost entirely dependent for their capacity to continue at war.

Only eighty German fighters were available to meet this air onslaught by eight hundred bombers; since the beginning of the year, the Germans had lost more than three thousand fighter pilots either killed in action, or taken prisoner after their planes were shot down. Nevertheless, the German fighter pilots fought with skill and determination, shooting down forty-six bombers for the loss of thirty fighters. All seven targets were hit, three of them so seriously that they were temporarily shut down. The German's own Ultra messages revealed to the Allies the extent of the German alarm.

Acts of sabotage were also accelerated as the cross-Channel invasion drew nearer; on May 13, at Bagnères-de-Bigorre, in the Pyrenees, a factory producing the carriers for self-propelled guns was put out of action for six months, after an attack by British agents and French Resistance fighters. That day, along the Channel coast, Rommel completed two formidable lines of underwater obstacles; altogether, 517,000 obstacles had been laid down in six feet of water for high tide and half tide, 31,000 of which were fitted with mines. But two further lines of obstacles, intended for six feet of water at low tide, and for twelve feet of water at low tide, were not yet in place.

On May 8, Rommel had warned the German High Command that the systematic Allied destruction of railways throughout northern France had begun to disrupt his supplies and troop movements; this most secret signal was decrypted in Britain on May 14. This was certainly an encouragement for the Americans to continue their attacks. The bombing of German airfields had also been effective, so much so that Goering ordered the Todt Organisation to carry out work at airfields which were no longer used, or hardly used, so as to deceive the Allies into diverting bomber resources against them. Unfortunately for Goering, his order, sent by a top-secret Ultra radio signal, was decrypted by British Intelligence on May 14, exposing the ruse.

The Germans were far more vulnerable to deception than the Allies; on May 15, the German High Command was informed that 'A good Army Intelligence source' had reported the presence of units of the First United States Army Group in Yorkshire and Norfolk. The 'good' source was in fact a former German agent who had long been working for Britain; the army group on which he was reporting so assiduously existed only in the minds of Britain's deception planners. Yorkshire and Norfolk were the starting points for the fictitious attacks on Norway and the Pas de Calais.

On May 15, after two months of careful preparation, and amid massive and successful deception, the Germans began the deportation of hundreds of thousands of Jews from Hungary to Auschwitz. Four thousand were deported every

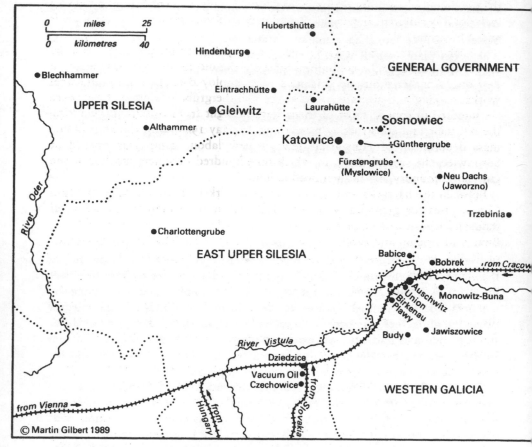

Slave labour camps in Eastern Silesia, 1944

day; on their arrival at Auschwitz, sometimes two-thirds, sometimes a half, would be gassed. Those who were not killed were sent to the barracks, to swell the ranks of slave labourers, including Polish, British, Yugoslav, French and Soviet prisoners-of-war, forced to work, and to suffer appallingly cruel privations, in the many factories set up specially around Auschwitz, or already in existence there.

At the Upper Silesian industrial city of Gleiwitz, four factories received slave labourers from Auschwitz; one for the production and packing of black smoke for smoke screens, had been opened on May 3. The others were for repairing railway carriages and oil wagons, for making railway bogies and gun carriages, and for repairing and remodelling military motor vehicles.

In the East Upper Silesian power station and coal mine at Neu Dachs, known also by its Polish name, Jaworzno, more than sixteen hundred prisoners were employed by May 1944. At the synthetic-petrol plant at Blechhammer, opened on April 1, four thousand prisoners were employed. At Bobrek, from April 22, the two hundred and fifty prisoners employed by the Siemens Schuckert works included fifty children: all were employed making electrical apparatus for aircraft and submarines.

A further labour camp at Myslowice provided thirteen hundred slave labourers for the Fürstengrube coalmines, working the old mine and constructing a new one. Another thousand prisoners were employed at the Laurahütte steel works, making anti-aircraft guns. At the Günthergrube coalmines there were six hundred prisoners, most of them Jews brought from Auschwitz, working the old mine and constructing a new one. In May 1944, with the start of the mass deportation of Hungarian Jews, a new labour camp was opened at Sosnowiec, the second there, in which nine hundred prisoners worked at the gun-barrel foundry and in shell production.

Between the barracks and gas chambers at Birkenau, and Auschwitz Main Camp, fuses for grenades were manufactured at the Union factory. Several thousand Jewish women prisoners were employed there. At Monowitz, the vast Buna synthetic oil and rubber factory was already absorbing tens of thousands of Jewish workers, as well as some British prisoners-of-war, all non-Jews. Hungarian Jews were also to be sent from Auschwitz to the labour camp on the site of the Warsaw ghetto, to clear the rubble, and to search for valuables.

It was not only in the Auschwitz region that slave labour was being used for the German war effort. On May 15, the day of the first deportation of Hungarian Jews, a thousand Jews already at Auschwitz were sent to a factory at Wüstegiersdorf; others were to go to factories at Brünnlitz, Schwarzheide and Hamburg, as well as to a building site at Ullersdorf, south-east of Berlin, which was even then under construction as an ss recreation and rest centre.

It was on that fateful May 15, as the wheels of death began to roll from a thousand Hungarian towns and villages towards Auschwitz, that a Palestinian Jew, Enzo Sereni, who had been born in Italy, was parachuted by British Intelligence into the German-occupied half of the Italian peninsula. His mission was to contact Italian partisan groups near Florence, collect maps and military information for the eventual Allied advance into Tuscany, and help British prisoners-of-war who had escaped captivity. Immediately on landing, Sereni was captured; after four days of interrogation and torture at Verona, he was sent to a prison camp at Gries, then on to Dachau. There, six months after his capture, he was summoned from his barracks, and was never seen again.

From the Italian city of Fossoli, 575 Jews were deported to Auschwitz on May 16. When they reached Auschwitz seven days later, 518 were taken to their deaths, and only 57 to the barracks. Among those who were gassed immediately on their arrival was a baby girl, Gigliola Finzi, born at Roccastrada two and a half months earlier. Also gassed that day was Carolina Calo and her four small children, the youngest of whom, a boy, had been born on the first day of the seven day journey to death. Carolina Calo's husband, Eugenio, a prominent Italian partisan leader, was even then capturing German soldiers in Tuscany, and preparing to take them southwards across the war zone to the Allied lines, before returning to German-occupied Italy to continue the fight behind the lines.

*          *          *

On the morning of May 18, after almost a week of continuous fighting, Polish troops raised their flag over the ruins of the monastery of Monte Cassino. The six month struggle to push beyond Cassino was over. In the final battle, 4,267 Allied troops were killed, and a further 4,068 'missing': their bodies so pounded by shell fire that they were never found. On the following day, the Polish commander, General Wladyslaw Anders, visited the battlefield. 'Corpses of German and Polish soldiers', he wrote, 'sometimes entangled in a deathly embrace, lay everywhere, and the air was full of the stench of rotting bodies.' As Anders walked over the battlefield, he noted that 'crater after crater pitted the sides of the hills, and scattered over them were fragments of uniforms and tin helmets, tommy guns, Spandaus, Schmeissers and hand grenades.'

That day, from Washington, came the announcement that in the most recent campaign for the successful capture of the Admiralty Islands, 326 American soldiers had been killed, and 3,820 Japanese. Only seventy-five Japanese had been taken prisoner, mostly those who were too gravely injured to be able either to fight to the death or to kill themselves rather than surrender. Two days later, on May 20, an American task force completed the conquest of Wadke Island, all eight hundred Japanese defenders having been killed for the loss of fifty-three American lives.

On May 20, a mere seventeen days before the Normandy landings, the Germans still did not know where those landings would be. The Germany Navy was even then mining the Bay of Biscay. When Rommel asked that it should start mining the Bay of the Seine, his request was refused. He was also refused troop dispositions which could cover Normandy and Brittany at the same time, a refusal that was due, he later wrote, 'to fears of a possible enemy airborne landing in the neighbourhood of Paris'.

The Allied preparations now moved into high gear. On May 21, British and American aircraft launched Operation Chattanooga Choo-Choo, a systematic attack on railway engines and rolling stock throughout northern Europe, including Germany. So effective were these attacks that within twenty-four hours German municipalities were urgently seeking foreign slave labourers, and even Jews from concentration camps, to help repair the bomb damage.

For the Allies, secrecy remained the key to the possibility of success on the day of the Normandy landings – 'D-Day' in military parlance. On May 23, at Sutton Coldfield, in Britain, an American officer in an Army Postal Unit who was privy to some of the Bigot secrets disclosed the objectives of the United States First Army to a member of the Adjutant General's department who was not in the know. He was sentenced to confinement for one year, with hard labour, at the United States Disciplinary Barracks at Greenhaven, New York, to be followed by dismissal from the service.

The capture of Monte Cassino on May 18 had opened the way for a rapid Allied advance northwards, first to link up with the Anzio beachhead, and then to drive on to Rome. At Anzio, on May 23, more than 150,000 Allied soldiers broke out of the perimeter in which they had been trapped for four months.

Along the coastline of those areas under German occupation, British and American patrol boats searched for escaped prisoners-of-war whom they could take off from danger and return to the Allied armies. On the night of May 24, in one such operation, 'Darlington II', two boats, setting off from Termoli to the mouth of the River Tenna, rescued a total of 153 escaped prisoners-of-war and airmen who had managed to avoid capture altogether after having been shot down; by the end of November, 2,156 escapees had been recovered by such means.

Behind the lines in Greece, German forces were being increasingly harassed by Greek guerrillas. On May 24 the entire population of the village of Pogonion was deported to a camp near Yanina, to be held as hostages. When, shortly afterwards, a German division was attacked by guerrillas, all 325 hostages were shot. In German-occupied Yugoslavia, May 25 saw the launching of Operation Knight's Move, an attempt, by use of parachute and glider-borne troops, to seize the partisan leader, Tito, while he was at the village of Drvar. As the German troops moved in, one partisan, shot through the head, died in agony at Tito's feet. Tito escaped; but the villagers in whose midst he had been living were almost all killed, women and small children as well as men.

In Italy, on May 25, the troops who had broken out at Anzio linked up with the advancing Allied forces. That day, American troops entered Velletri, less than twenty-five miles from the centre of Rome. In German-occupied Greece, a young Intelligence officer, Kurt Waldheim, was writing to his superior, General Schmidt-Richberg, with criticism of the most recent sweeps against the guerrilla bands, and the reprisals that accompanied them. 'The reprisal measures imposed in response to sabotage and ambush', he wrote, 'have, despite their severity, failed to achieve any noteworthy success, since our own measures have been only transitory, so that the punished communities or territories soon have to be abandoned once more to the bands. On the contrary' – Waldheim added – 'exaggerated reprisal measures undertaken without a more precise examination of the objective situation have only caused embitterment and have been useful to the bands. It can be demonstrated that the population broadly supports the bands and supplies them with excellent information'.

From each German report, one can see the extent of the terror, and of resistance. On the same day that Lieutenant Waldheim was sending this report from Greece, SS Brigadier-General Edmund Veesenmayer was reporting to the German Foreign Office in Berlin that 138,870 Jews had been deported to their 'destination' in the past ten days. That destination was Auschwitz. At Auschwitz itself, on the evening of Veesenmayer's report, as several hundred Hungarian Jews were being led to one of the two more distant gas-chamber buildings in Birkenau, they sensed that something was wrong, and scattered into the nearby woods. Special searchlights, installed around the gas chamber, were at once switched on by the SS, who opened fire on those seeking to flee. All were shot. A similar act of revolt, similarly suppressed, took place three days later.

'Hungary!' Hitler exhorted his generals at Obersalzberg on May 26. 'The entire country subverted and rotten, Jews everywhere, Jews and still more Jews right up to the highest level, and the whole country covered by a continuous network of agents and spies waiting for the moment to strike, but fearing to do so in case a premature move drew us in. Here too I intervened, and this problem is now going to be solved too'.

As the Germans were more and more pressed back in the war zones, so, in Hungary and in other regions of central Europe – in Italy, Holland, France and Greece – Hitler and his subordinates hastened to 'solve' the Jewish question, by deporting every Jew they could find to Auschwitz, several thousand every day. At the same time, the western Allies, while on the verge of a cross-Channel invasion of northern Europe, were almost at the gates of Rome and were bombing German industrial centres and war factories without respite. As the outcome of the war became more starkly apparent, it was as if two victories were on offer; for Germany a victory over the Jews, and for the Allies a victory over Germany. There could no longer be victory for Germany, that was clear. Even Goebbels had declared, in a newspaper editorial on May 24: 'Germany must be made more desolate than the Sahara.' Nothing must be left which the Allies – and in particular the dreaded 'Bolsheviks' – could plunder.

On May 25, British Intelligence decrypted a top secret message from Rommel, sent six days earlier to Berlin, in which he revealed that one SS panzer division had no tanks, and was not expecting any; it was seriously short of officers, motor transport and vehicle spares. Its transport included horses and bicycles. A further decrypt, of a German Air Force Enigma message, showed that it was expected that it was in the region of Dieppe that, in the German view, the landing would most probably come. It was the continual bombing attacks on the bridges over the River Seine which had led to this conclusion.

On May 26, in a daylight air raid on Lyon, intended to block the German re-inforcement routes from the South, railway lines, power stations and military installations were massively bombed, and 717 French civilians killed.

Despite a protest by the regional Resistance leader, Alban Vistel, that the local population were 'painfully indignant', resistance continued; on the day after the Lyon bombing, in an ambush set by the Maquis, twelve members of the collaborationist Milice were killed. There were also many acts of sabotage. At Ambérieu, a railway engine depot was destroyed and fifty-two railway locomotives made unusable. At Bar, in the Corrèze, a hydro-electric station was so badly damaged on May 26 that it was put out of action for the next four months. That day, British Intelligence decrypted a message from Rommel, sent to Berlin sixteen days earlier, warning that the locomotive situation had become so serious that forced labour, and even prisoners-of-war, would have to be used at the repair shops; the French civilian work force was 'not responding'.

Not only did the Ultra decrypts reveal to the Anglo-American planners the German Army's weaknesses and problems in France, and the strength of individual units; they also showed precisely where those units were still being sent. A series of decrypts between May 24 and May 27 showed a sudden and considerable transfer of troops to the Cotentin peninsula, to the very area around La Haye-du-Puits where it was intended to drop American parachute troops, in order to protect the landing beaches from attack from the Cherbourg peninsula. On the evening of May 27, scarcely a week before the date originally set for the landings, the Americans had therefore to abandon the plan to drop men at La Haye-du-Puits; they had also to put back the date for the capture of Cherbourg itself by seven days. Ultra had saved the Allies from the potential disaster of landing men at a point strongly held by German troops.

On May 28, American bombers made their second raid on five of the German synthetic oil plants which they had already damaged on May 12. That night, British bombers attacked the reinforced concrete fortifications at St Martin de Varreville, overlooking the invasion beaches; a block house, command posts and signals equipment were destroyed. The air bombardment of railway marshalling yards had also continued, resulting not only in the disruption of German military movements by rail, but also in a total of three thousand French civilian deaths in forty-eight hours. 'Terrible things are being done', Churchill wrote to Eden on May 28. On the following day, after reading the reports of the attacks during May 28, Churchill wrote again, to Air Chief Marshal Tedder, the Deputy Supreme Commander of the Allied Expeditionary Force: 'You are piling up an awful load of hatred.'

Hatred or not, the bombing was effective. On May 28, the destruction of the German naval wireless station at Château Terlinden, near Bruges, made it much more difficult for German Intelligence to 'hear' the extra volume of Allied wireless traffic, which would indicate the imminence of an Anglo-American land, air and sea assault.

The German air force, once so boastful under Goering, and capable of sustained and devastating bomber attacks, no longer had the resources both to bomb Britain and to prepare for the inevitable air battles of a cross-Channel attack. For their part, the Allies had continued with Operation Crossbow, attacking the flying bomb 'Ski' sites from the Pas de Calais to Dieppe. By the end of May, these sites were protected by 520 heavy guns and a further 730 guns of lighter calibre. In the Crossbow attacks, 154 Allied aircraft had been shot down by the end of May, with 771 aircrew dead or missing. But as many as two thirds of the 'Ski' sites had been put out of action.

An Allied air raid over northern France on May 31 was effective in another way; by cutting the German Air Force overland telephone cable at a point between Paris and Rouen, it interrupted telephonic communication between German headquarters in Paris and Air Force bases around both Rennes and Caen for three crucial days.

On May 31, a South African Air Force reconnaissance plane made its first flight over Auschwitz since the beginning of April, to photograph once more the German synthetic-oil plant at Monowitz. Two of the frames of its photographic cover showed, for the first time, not only the main camp at Auschwitz, but also the gas chambers, crematoria and extensive barracks of the Birkenau section, where tens of thousands of Jews were being held, and more than a million and a half Jews had already been killed. But the barracks and installations at Birkenau were not examined by the Photographic Reconnaissance Unit in

Britain, whose only task was to identify, in as much detail as possible, the oil production process at Monowitz, with a view to bombing it. At Auschwitz, on the day of this reconnaissance flight, the ss camp administration recorded that a total of forty kilogrammes of gold had been taken from the teeth of the corpses of Hungarian Jews, who had been gassed in the fifteen days between May 17 and the end of the month. This included those gassed on May 31 itself, from two trains, out of which a thousand men and a thousand women had been sent to the barracks, and more than six thousand gassed, among them the two thousand Jews deported from the Hungarian city of Baja; during their three and a half day journey in sealed wagons, without food or water beyond that which they had managed to take with them, fifty-five had died, and two hundred had gone mad.

On June 1, the Anglo-American planners of the Normandy landings, now set for June 4, were shown the decrypt of a telegram from the Japanese Ambassador in Berlin, Count Oshima, to Tokyo. In it, Oshima reported on a conversation which he had had with Hitler four days earlier, when Hitler told Oshima that the Allies had completed their preparations; that they had assembled eighty divisions, eight of which had combat experience and were 'very good troops'; that after diversionary operations in Norway, Denmark, south-west France and on the French Mediterranean coast, they would establish a bridgehead in Normandy or Brittany; and that after seeing how things went, they would embark on establishing a real second front in the Dover Strait.

Several things were clear from Hitler's conversation; that while the Germans regarded an invasion either in Normandy or Brittany as definite, they did not know which it would be, nor did they regard it as imminent; several diversionary operations elsewhere were expected to come first. Also, it was believed in Berlin that the Pas de Calais would be the true focus of the main assault on Fortress Europe.

On the night of June 2 British bombers again bombed the French railway marshalling yards at Trappes. This raid marked the culmination of the 'Transportation' Plan, begun on March 6, whereby more than eight thousand British bombers had dropped forty-two thousand tons of bombs on railway marshalling yards in France and Belgium. American bombers had dropped a further eleven thousand tons of bombs in May alone. June 2 also saw the first of a new series of bombing operations over central Europe, when American bombers, flying from Foggia and other airbases in southern Italy, struck deep into the industrial regions of Silesia, Hungary and Roumania, and then flew on to Soviet airbases in and around Poltava. By flying straight on to Poltava, the bombers did not have to face a return flight which their fuel consumption would have made impossible.

Devised to help the Red Army during its Roumanian offensive, as a result of an urgent appeal from Stalin, these flights were given the code-name Operation Frantic Joe. To avoid offending Stalin, this was quickly modified to Operation Frantic. On the first run, the railway marshalling yards at Debrecen were hit on the way out, and the airfield at Focsani on the return flight.

*          *          *

On June 2, the Normandy landings were fixed for June 5. But bad weather seemed to make a postponement inevitable. In a most secret radio signal to Berlin, Field Marshal von Rundstedt had stated that the Allies would need four consecutive days of good weather in order to carry out a cross-Channel assault. No such four day clear period was forecast. He, Rundstedt, was therefore certain that the invasion could not take place in the first week of June.

The secret communications code which von Rundstedt had used for his message about the weather was in a cypher which the British had broken. His message was therefore decrypted at Bletchley, where more than six thousand people were now employed, and passed on immediately to Eisenhower. From that moment, as a result of reading not only the message but the mind of his opposite number, Eisenhower knew that if he could launch the invasion in conditions ruled out by von Rundstedt, he would catch the Germans unawares.

The weather over the Channel, bad on June 2, began to deteriorate in the early afternoon of June 3. The German forecasters predicted bad weather for the next three or four days. This ruled out June 5 or June 6 as days on which an assault would be launched. Increased Allied wireless traffic might have caused this confident assumption to be reviewed, but on June 3 the German wireless intercept station on the Cherbourg peninsula, at Urville-Hague, was destroyed by air attack. Ironically, it had not been identified as an intercept station, but only as an 'important installation of a special character'. That was enough, however, for it to become a target. Thus the two chief intercept stations covering the landing area – Château Terlinden and Urville-Hague – were out of action.

Eisenhower knew that the bad weather made it impossible to go ahead on June 5. But both the juxtaposition of the moon positions, plus the knowledge that the Germans expected no assault anywhere for the next three to four days, made it desirable that too great a delay beyond June 5 should be avoided.

On the morning of June 4, there was a forecast of a brief spell of better weather. But it was not the four clear days which the Germans regarded as the Allied minimum; it was therefore unlikely that the Germans would be alerted or alarmed. Thanks to knowledge provided by Ultra, the risks to the Allies of launching the invasion under the poor prevailing weather conditions would be more than compensated for.

On the evening of June 4, American troops reached the centre of Rome. 'How magnificently your troops have fought!' Churchill telegraphed that day to Roosevelt. On the following day, after a formal and triumphal entry into the Italian capital, the Allied troops continued their northward pursuit of the retreating Germans. But for those in charge of the Allied fortunes, the thrill of the fall of the first Axis capital to Allied arms was offset by the knowledge that on the morning of June 6, the largest amphibious operation of all time was to be launched, and the lives of hundreds of thousands of men put at risk. 'I feel so much for you', Churchill's wife Clementine wrote to her husband on June

5, 'at this agonizing moment – so full of suspense, which prevents one from rejoicing over Rome!'

Waking on the morning of June 5, Eisenhower knew that within twenty-four hours the die would already have been cast. That same morning, confident that the continuing bad weather meant that no invasion was imminent, Rommel left his headquarters at La Roche Guyon, by car, on his way to Germany, where he intended to speak to Hitler personally, and to impress upon him 'the extent of the man-power and material inferiority we would suffer in the event of a landing', and to request the despatch to northern France of two further panzer divisions, an anti-aircraft corps, and other reinforcements.

It was the bad weather on June 5 which kept almost all the German Air Force reconnaissance aircraft grounded. Five reconnaissance sorties were flown, but none reported any unusual activity in the ports of southern England. At 9.30 that evening a coded British wireless message, sent openly on the BBC, instructed French Resistance operatives to cut railway lines throughout France. German Intelligence, which had partially broken the code, warned Rommel's headquarters at La Roche Guyon; but in Rommel's absence no notice seems to have been taken of the warning. Of 1,050 planned breaches of the railway lines, 950 were carried out.

A message sent by the German Air Force High Command shortly before midnight on June 5, showed the extent of German weakness in the air as a result of the growing shortage of fuel oil. The message was an instruction to the First Parachute Army, based at Nancy, to conserve its consumption of aircraft fuel as much as possible. 'With reduction of aircraft fuel by Allied action,' the message read, 'most essential requirements for training and carrying out production plans can scarcely be covered by quantities of aircraft fuel available.' Wherever possible, the High Command added, the supply of goods to air units, and 'duty journeys in general', must be made by rail.

On the night of June 5, more than a thousand British bombers struck at the ten most important German gun batteries in the assault area, dropping five thousand tons of bombs. That same night, more than three thousand ships – British, American, Polish, Dutch, Norwegian, French and Greek – Operation Neptune – were crossing the Channel. As this vast armada drew closer and closer to the Normandy beaches, a series of deceptions was launched on other possible destinations; the largest of all, Operation Taxable, involved the dropping of dummy parachutists near Boulogne, and the dropping of a vast number of radar-jamming strips in such a way as to produce on German radar screens the appearance of a large, slow-moving convoy edging its way across the Channel towards the Pas de Calais. A further spurious raid, using motor launches and electronic deception to simulate the movement of a large convoy, was made towards the beaches between Le Havre and Dieppe. A third deception that night, by motor launches off Harfleur, was designed to suggest a similar threat east of Le Havre. So successful was one particular dummy parachute drop, Operation Titanic, at Marigny, that, as its planners intended, it drew a whole German infantry regiment from its position in reserve at Bayeux, a mere six miles from the real landing beaches, as far west as the Carentan-Isigny area.

Deception had played its part to the end, Ultra having revealed in detail just who needed to be deceived, now revealed that the deception had been successful.

At 11.55 on the evening of June 5, British infantrymen, members of the 6th Airborne Division, landed by gliders at the village of Bénouville, six miles north of Caen. Operation Overlord had begun.

# 38

# D-Day

June 1944

By dawn on June 6, eighteen thousand British and American parachutists were on the ground in Normandy, capturing essential bridges and disrupting German lines of communication. At 6.30 that morning the first troops landed, Americans, coming ashore at 'Utah' beach with amphibious tanks. Less than an hour later, at 7.25, the first British soldiers were ashore at 'Gold' and 'Sword' beaches, followed, at 'Juno' beach, by 2,400 Canadians, supported by seventy-six of the amphibious tanks. At 10.15 that morning the news of these landings was brought to Rommel, who was still in Germany. He at once flew back to France, instructed by Hitler to drive the invaders 'back into the sea' by midnight.

By midnight, 155,000 Allied troops were already ashore. Only at 'Omaha' beach had the German defenders been able to pin down the American assaulting force of nearly 35,000 men to a perimeter no more than a mile deep. At all the other landing grounds, much greater progress inland had been made. Hitler, convinced that the Normandy landing was not the 'real' Second Front, hesitated to commit his full resources to the bridgehead. That day, German naval units were warned to be prepared for surprise attacks elsewhere; this message was decrypted by the British that evening, giving the Allied commanders some assurance that even on June 7, D-Day plus one, the full force of the German military might would not be thrown against them.

The Allied casualties on D-Day itself had been relatively low; 355 Canadians had been killed in action or died of wounds, as compared with more than nine hundred Canadian dead at Dieppe in 1942. Both the Americans and the British each lost more than a thousand men killed during the first day of battle. That same day, in the Mediterranean, the Germans on Crete took four hundred Greek hostages, three hundred Italian prisoners-of-war and 260 Jews by boat a hundred miles out to sea, where the boat was scuttled. None of the captives survived.

On June 7, as the Allies consolidated their positions on the Normandy beach-head, and sought to enlarge them, the German Air Force High Command was still warning its units in western Europe that further landings could be expected either for a thrust towards Belgium, or in Norway, or near Lorient on the French Atlantic coast, or on the western coast of the Cotentin peninsula.

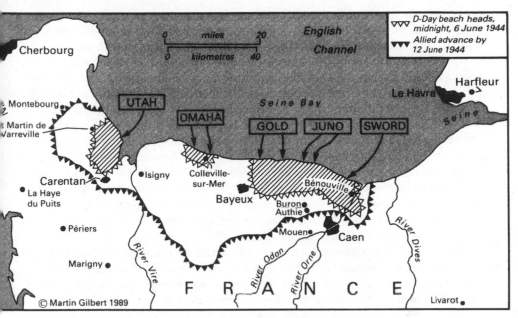

The Normandy landings, June 6 1944

During the second day's fighting in Normandy, on June 7, a German Waffen ss unit captured thirty-four Canadian soldiers near the villages of Buron and Authie. Most of the Canadians were wounded, some of them badly so. All thirty-four were then shot or bayoneted to death. A local stonemason, Constance Raymond Guilbert, later recalled seeing one of the wounded Canadians, who was lying under a tree, move his arm and leg a little. 'One of the German soldiers took a bayonet and hit him, opening his head. . . .' Forty three more Canadian prisoners-of-war were killed in the following forty-eight hours. One of them, Rifleman D.S. Gould, still wearing his Red Cross armband, was a stretcher-bearer. 'What should we do with these prisoners?' the ss commanding officer, Lieutenant-Colonel Kurt Meyer, had asked. 'They only eat up our rations.'

It was on June 7 that British Intelligence decrypted the German Air Force Enigma message, sent to the First Parachute Army at Nancy, about the growing shortage of aircraft fuel. On the following day the Chief of the Air Staff, Sir Charles Portal, informed Churchill that he regarded this 'as one of the most important pieces of information which we have yet received'. In the light of it, there seemed 'little doubt', in Portal's view and that of the War Cabinet's Joint Intelligence Committee, that Britain's strategic bomber offensive should be 'turned over to synthetic oil plants as soon as Overlord can spare them'.

Churchill noted on Portal's suggestion: 'Good'. That same day, the head of the American bomber forces, General Spaatz, directed that the German oil plants should be first priority targets for the United States Strategic Air Forces.

Henceforth, the installations for the most crucial element in Germany's ability to make war – fuel oil – were to be bombed with mounting force and effectiveness, a sustained aerial bombardment which was to be as instrumental in the defeat of Germany as the amphibious landings in Normandy. Four days after Portal's letter to Churchill, a British night bombing raid on the German oil installations at Gelsenskirchen was so effective that the plant was put out of action for several months, and five thousand tons of stored oil destroyed.

On June 8, British troops from Gold Beach reached the American troops on Omaha beach at Colleville-sur-Mer. Above the battlefield, the Germans had less than a hundred operational aircraft. On the ground, crucial secret orders were being decrypted; one, on June 8, enabled the British to pinpoint the exact location of the headquarters of Panzer Group West. Two days later the headquarters, at La Caine, was bombed so severely, and so many staff officers – seventeen in all – killed, that the heavy counter-attack being planned for the following day had to be put off for twenty-four hours.

'"Overlord" is a source of joy to us all', Stalin telegraphed to Churchill on June 8; and he promised to launch Russia's own summer offensive shortly, in accordance with the agreement at Teheran at the end of 1943, whereby the Soviet Union would bring its own forces into action along the whole Eastern Front once the western Allies were ashore, thus preventing the Germans from transferring extra forces to Normandy, just when such a transfer would be most needed.

For the Russians, the human cost of the war had already become almost unbearable, with an estimated ninety per cent of all young men between the ages of eighteen and twenty-one already killed in action. With concern for the future, on June 8 the Praesidium of the Supreme Soviet adopted a decree 'On mothers of large families and motherhood care'. Mothers of more than ten children were to receive a new title, 'Heroine Mother'. Special family allowances would be given to large families. Even unmarried mothers would receive benefits.

On June 9, in the town of Tulle, in the Corrèze, the ss Das Reich Division carried out a widespread reprisal against civilians in the town, for acts of sabotage committed against the Division by French Resistance fighters nearby. A woman from Tulle later recalled: 'I came home from shopping on 9 June 1944 to find my husband and my son hanging from the balcony of our house. They were just two of a hundred men seized at random and killed in cold blood by the German ss. The children and the wives were forced to watch while they strung them up to the lamp-posts and balconies outside their own homes. What else is there for me to say?'

It was on June 9 that Stalin informed Churchill: 'Tomorrow, June 10, we begin the first round on the Leningrad Front.' The artillery preliminaries had already begun, 240 Soviet guns bombarding the Finnish defences to the north-west of the city. The Germans were already in action against the Russians in Roumania, and against the Western Allies in Italy and Normandy. But they remained convinced that a further Western assault was imminent, and that Normandy was a diversion. At 10.30 on the evening of June 9, German Intelligence chiefs received, and at once passed on to Hitler, a message from Juan Pujol Garcia in Britain, their trusted agent 'Arabel', that, after 'consultation on 8th June in London with my agents Donny, Dick and Dorick', he was of the opinion that the Normandy landings were 'a diversionary manoeuvre designed to draw off enemy reserves in order to make a decisive attack in another place'.

This report, Hitler was told by German Intelligence, 'confirms the view already held by us that a further attack is to be expected in another place'. That other place, Intelligence felt, was possibly Belgium. Britain's agent 'Garbo' had thus successfully maintained the Fortitude deception three full days beyond the Normandy landings. Just over three years had passed since Garcia had set up his 'Arabel' network, with at various times twenty-seven spurious agents working under him. The three agents mentioned by him on June 9 each had a carefully built up history: 'Donny', recruited in December 1943, was an ex-seaman and leader of the World Aryan Order; 'Dick', recruited in February 1944, was 'an Indian fanatic'; and 'Dorick', also recruited in February 1944, was a civilian living at the North Sea port of Harwich.

At German Army Headquarters in Zossen, it was likewise felt that Normandy was only a diversion. 'The main thrust', Colonel Alexis von Roenne, Chief of the Army General Staff's Intelligence Division, informed General Jodl on June 9, 'must be expected at any moment in the Pas de Calais.' That same day, the German Admiral commanding in the Atlantic suggested to Admiral Dönitz that the 'hesitant and slow' progress of the Allied landings in Normandy might indicate 'an intended second landing at another point'. This message was decrypted in Britain on June 10. Not only was deception continuing to keep a protective shield over the Allied armies, but the fact that the deception was working was known to the Allied commanders.

During June 10, there was fighting on six battlefronts: in Normandy, in Italy, on the Leningrad front in Finland, in New Guinea, in Burma and in China, where the Japanese had launched an overland offensive along the River Liu-yang, towards Changsha. Tens of thousands of soldiers fought not only far from home, but in diverse causes; among the soldiers fighting alongside German troops in Normandy were Cossack troops from Russia, and Indian troops loyal to Subhas Chandra Bose who were committed to the violent overthrow of British rule in India. Thousands of soldiers were killed each day in these struggles, each so distant from the other, each with its own catalogue of dangers and torments.

In Europe, the additional torments behind the lines knew no pause. On June 10, in German-occupied Poland, more than forty villagers were killed in the tiny hamlet of Pikule as a reprisal for sheltering Polish partisans, three thousand of whom were trying to escape a German force of thirty thousand which had been sent against them, Operation Hurricane. That same day, in the tiny French village of Oradour-sur-Glane, as a reprisal for a Resistance attack on a military formation moving towards the Normandy beachhead, ss troops murdered 642 villagers, including 190 schoolchildren. Only two villagers managed to escape, a woman, Madame Rouffanche, and an eight-year-old boy, Roger Godfrin.

Among those killed were several Jews to whom the villagers had given refuge, including the forty-five-year-old Maria Goldman, who had been born in Warsaw, and the eight-year-old Serge Bergman, born in Strasbourg.

That day, at Salon-la-Tour, a British agent, Violette Szabo, who had been dropped into German-occupied France on D-Day, was captured by the Gestapo. Interrogated and tortured, she was then sent to Ravensbrück concentration camp.

On the Normandy beachhead, the Allies had consolidated their landings and continued to advance inland. They had done so despite yet another of Hitler's secret weapons, an unscupperable mine known to the Allies as the 'Oyster', and showing a technology far more advanced than the Allied mines. These Oysters had been laid on the Normandy beaches after D-Day, causing grave inconvenience by forcing ships to limit their speed virtually to one mile an hour. The new weapon was defeated because of the sheer numerical and technical superiority of Allied resources, which enabled the losses to be sustained.

On the beach-head itself, the Allied forces met strong opposition, but its organizer knew its limitations. 'During the day', Rommel wrote on June 10, 'practically our entire traffic – on roads, tracks and in open country – is pinned down by powerful fighter-bomber and bomber formations, with the result that the movement of our troops on the battlefield is almost completely paralysed, while the enemy can manoeuvre freely. Every traffic defile in the rear areas is under continual attack and it is very difficult to get essential supplies of ammunition and petrol up to the troops'.

Rommel sought to focus his attacking forces against the American bridgehead in the Carentan–Montebourg area, a move which could prevent the cutting off of the German forces in the Cotentin peninsula. Hitler, however, intervened to veto this plan, and ordered Rommel to attack instead from Caen against the British bridgehead. The British troops, however, were reinforced more quickly than Rommel's, and were able to advance against him before his own attack was ready.

The Allied D-Day objective – the vital communications centre at Caen through which German reinforcements to the bridgehead would pass – was not taken on that day, however; nor indeed for another two months. The German reinforcements thus brought in were to tie down the Allies in bloody fighting in a region which they had expected to overrun on their first day, and were to prevent them from breaking out.

By the night of June 10, more than 325,000 Allied soldiers were ashore on the Normandy beaches. That night, and on the following night, in a desperate attempt to halt the flow of men and materials, German motor torpedo boats broke into the Utah beach anchorage, sinking the American destroyer Nelson. In the Channel itself, several components of the Mulberry artificial harbour were sunk before they could reach their anchorages. But of the fifteen German motor torpedo boats operational on June 6, nine had been put out of action a week later, a fact known to British Intelligence through the Ultra decrypts.

Also known to British Intelligence, as a result of eavesdropping on the German

Ultra messages, was a German plan to launch a motor torpedo boat attack from Le Havre against the invasion fleet; forewarned, 344 British bombers were made ready for a sustained daylight operation against the German torpedo boat pens at Le Havre.

On June 11, in Normandy, there was yet another episode when Allied troops, in this instance British, were pushed up against a wall after being captured, and shot. One man, feigning death, was able to escape; it was through him that details of the massacre became known. On June 12, Canadian prisoners-of-war being marched towards Rennes were accidentally strafed by American fighters; fifteen were killed.

On the Indian border on June 12, a Gurkha soldier, Ganju Lama, the son of a priest, sent on a tank-hunting mission against the Japanese forces besieging Imphal, knocked out two tanks with his anti-tank gun. Wounded in both arms and the leg, but still able to throw his grenades, Ganju Lama called out: 'Give me some grenades', and then killed the surviving Japanese crewmen. He was awarded the Victoria Cross.

In the early hours of June 13, the Germans at last launched their long-awaited and – by those who knew that it was in preparation – much-feared 'secret weapon', a small, pilotless, jet-propelled plane, carrying a ton of explosives that detonated on contact. Known to the Germans as the V1, 'Vergeltung' or 'Reprisal' 1, and by the British as the 'flying bomb', its first efforts were dismal. Of the ten that were fired, from Watten, near the Channel Coast, five crash landed almost immediately in the vicinity of the launch site. One 'went missing', probably crashing in the Channel. Four reached England. Only one caused any casualties: six people killed in London, at Bethnal Green.

The Germans had intended to mount a bombing offensive at the same time as the first flying bombs were launched, to add to the alarm and terror. By a coincidence, the bomber force involved was destroyed on the ground on the afternoon of June 12 when Allied bombers, on a systematic raid of German airfields, bombed their airfield at Beauvais.

By another chance, June 13 was the day on which an experimental V2 rocket, fired from the Baltic test site at Peenemünde, fell, not in the Baltic Sea as intended, to sink without trace, but at Backebo in Sweden. Two British officers examined the rocket in Stockholm. It was an advanced type, designed to answer to a controller, and with a device which would have prevented outside interference. Fortunately for the Allies, the rocket was never used.

In Italy, on June 13, Italian partisans blew up road bridges used by German military traffic between La Spezia and Reggio Emilia; this was known in London four days later, as a result of a decrypted German signal. In Thessaly, Greek partisans were in action against the Germans on June 14, as they tried to deny the Germans the use of the Greek harvest; among the partisans was Leon Sakkis, a Greek Jew, killed by machine gun fire as he tried to help a wounded colleague.

\*          \*          \*

As the Normandy battle entered its eleventh day, two German armoured divisions remained in the South of France. The Ultra eavesdroppers at Bletchley scrutinized their decrypts to see if they would be ordered to move north. But the decrypts made it clear, as the War Cabinet's Joint Intelligence Committee reported in London in June 14, that the Germans still feared 'subsidiary operations' not only in the South of France, but in the Pas de Calais, south-west France and Norway, with the Dutch–Belgian coast, to the east of the Pas-de-Calais, still seen as the intended landing place of the main invasion force.

Determined to forestall the planned German motor torpedo boat attacks on Allied supply ships crossing the English Channel to the Normandy beaches, the British air raid was carried out on June 14 against the torpedo boat pens at Le Havre. The raid was led by Leonard Cheshire, who had already received the Victoria Cross for his outstanding leadership in many earlier raids. Not only did Cheshire and his fellow pilots destroy the pens, but of the sixteen torpedo boats then at Le Havre, only a single one remained serviceable.

In the Pacific war, June 14 saw the first American 'Super-Fortress' raid on the Japanese mainland, when sixty of these new heavy bombers, based on the Chinese city of Chengtu, attacked the iron and steel works at Yawata, on Honshu Island. Not very much material damage was done, but the announcement of the raid in Washington gave a boost to American morale.

In Europe, June 14 saw an episode in the partisan war in Italy, when two Italian partisans, helping two British soldiers to blow up a bridge at Norcia, were surprised by a German patrol. The two British soldiers escaped. One of the partisans, Sergio Forti, a twenty-four-year-old Jew from Trieste, then persuaded the Germans to let the other partisan go off in order to 'bring in' the British. As prearranged, neither the partisan nor the British came back. Forti was tortured and killed that same day; he was posthumously awarded the Gold Medal of the Resistance.

Not resistance, but bewilderment, was in the minds of the 1,800 Jews of Corfu on June 14, as they were deported by ship to mainland Greece, then taken by truck across Thessaly to Larissa, then on by sealed train through Salonica, northwards, more than seven hundred miles, to Auschwitz. They had been told that they were to be 'resettled' in Poland. On reaching Auschwitz, 1,600 were sent at once to the gas chambers, two hundred to the barracks.

Hitler's war against the Jews was to continue, even as his war against the Allies reached its most critical stage. Three groups of armies were now on soil once controlled by Germany: in Eastern Galicia, where the Red Army awaited its order to renew the offensive; in Italy, where the Americans had reached the River Ombrone; and in Normandy, where the Cotentin peninsula was in imminent danger of being overrun. But Hitler's ability to take the initiative had not entirely been lost. On June 15, the German 'Ski' site commander, Colonel Wachtel, launched a second flying bomb raid on Britain. This came much closer to the scale and impact that had been intended. In all, 244 missiles were fired from Watten that day. Forty-five of them crash landed immediately after being launched, destroying nine of the launch sites, and killing ten French civilians.

Of the missiles which reached Britain, twelve were shot down by anti-aircraft fire and eight by fighters. But seventy-three flying bombs reached London, killing more than fifty civilians. To deny the Germans statistical evidence of the effect and location of the hits, the British Government ordered that the number of newspaper obituary notices for people killed by enemy action should be limited to three 'from the same postal district' on any one day.

On June 15, in the Pacific, the Americans began Operation Forager, against the Marianas Islands. On Saipan Island, twenty thousand American soldiers came ashore, meeting the same Japanese refusal to surrender that they had come to know, and to fear, on almost every island. Robert Sherrod, correspondent of *Time,* wrote of one episode, typical of many, when a Japanese sniper, found under some logs, came out into the open waving a bayonet. 'An American tossed a grenade and it knocked the Jap down', Sherrod wrote. 'He struggled up, pointed his bayonet into his stomach and tried to cut himself open in approved hara-kiri fashion. The disemboweling never came off. Someone shot the Jap with a carbine. But, like all Japs, he took a lot of killing. Even after four bullets had thudded into his body he rose to one knee. Then the American shot him through the head and the Jap was dead.'

In the three-week battle for Saipan, twenty thousand Japanese and 3,426 Americans were killed. Then, on July 9, three days after the suicide of the Japanese commander, Lieutenant-General Yoshitsugu Saito, a further seven thousand Japanese committed suicide. On Guam, 2,124 Americans were to be killed, and on Tinian, 290; few Japanese survived on either island, several thousand being killed in battle, and several thousand more either dying in deliberately suicidal 'banzai' charges, or committing suicide.

Similar Japanese fanaticism was being shown at Imphal and Kohima, inside the Indian frontier; there, in three and a half months, 2,700 British and Indian troops were killed, for the loss of thirty thousand Japanese.

Behind German lines, on June 16, the Jews working as slave labourers for the German war production in the Lodz ghetto were asked to volunteer for 'labour outside the ghetto'. They were needed, so the Germans themselves said, for 'the clearing away of debris in cities that have been bombed'. The first three thousand would go to Munich. Those who volunteered for this work could 'collect their rations immediately, without waiting their turn'. The three thousand left the ghetto, but 'Munich' was a deception. They were taken to Chelmno, where, in gas chambers built on the site of the former death camp, all of them were gassed.

In German-occupied France, two Jews were shot on June 16: Marc Bloch, the historian, who had been active in the resistance, and Jean Zay, a former Minister of Education in pre-war France. These killings came as the Allies launched Operation Gain, a parachute landing near Orléans, by a British Special Air Service unit, to cut the railway lines along which the Germans were now sending reinforcements to Normandy. But even with the need to reinforce Normandy, the German High Command still believed that the Normandy landings were only a diversion. Early that week there were fears in Berlin of a landing on the west coast of Denmark, and on June 16, the German Naval Group West reported strong indications of an imminent Allied invasion against Holland and Belgium. These indications, including the jamming of radar, and air activity, were deliberate, the last brilliant efforts of the Fortitude deception. On June 17, as Hitler travelled to Soissons to see his commanders, Juan Pujol Garcia, his best agent in Britain, 'Arabel', was awarded the Iron Cross.

Hitler's visit to Soissons, his first return to France since he had travelled there in triumph four years earlier, led to a clear order: 'The fortress Cherbourg is to be held at all costs.' At the same time, the German Fifteenth Army, then at the Pas-de-Calais, was not to be moved to Normandy, but was to stay near Calais, to await the still expected 'main' invasion.

On June 17, Free French Forces carried out Operation Brassard, capturing the Italian island of Elba. That same day, General de Gaulle made a one day visit to the Normandy beach-head, his first visit to French soil for four years. In the Normandy battle zone, at the village of Mouen, seven Canadian soldiers, taken prisoner by the ss troops opposing them, were interrogated for several hours, marched to the outskirts of the village, and shot.

Over Britain, a third flying bomb attack was launched on June 17. At St John's Hill, near Clapham Junction, twenty-four shoppers and passers-by were killed. At St Mary Abbots Hospital, Kensington, thirteen patients, most of them children, and five members of the staff, were killed. These figures were kept secret for the next three months. One flying bomb, going wildly off course, and turning southward, fell near Hitler's headquarters in Soissons.

Rommel saw considerable advantage in the flying bombs. 'The long-range action', he wrote to his wife on Sunday June 18, 'has brought us a lot of relief.' That Sunday, in London, a flying bomb hit the Guards Chapel at Wellington Barracks, killing 121 of the congregation: fifty-eight civilians and sixty-three servicemen. A second flying bomb, falling that same morning in Battersea, killed nineteen civilians, while a third, falling in Putney, killed twenty-eight. This brought the flying bomb deaths in the three days of attacks so far to more than two hundred and fifty.

Behind the German lines in Poland, the Germans launched a second Operation Hurricane on June 18, against Polish partisans, killing seven hundred partisans in a six day sweep in the region of Osuchy, near Lublin. In China, on June 18, Japanese forces captured Changsha, the first success of the Japanese Operation Ichigo, against the towns being used by the Americans to launch their air attacks on Japan itself.

On June 19, off the north-western coast of New Guinea, General Eichelberger launched an American attack against the defenders of Biak Island, who, since the American landings three weeks earlier, had resisted all attempts to dislodge them. The Japanese, defeated in open battle, retreated to caves, where they could only be destroyed by flame-throwers. By the end of the struggle, there were 5,093 Japanese dead on the island, killed for the loss of 524 Americans.

As Eichelberger's troops renewed their assault on Biak on June 19, two new

Japanese carrier-borne aircraft, 'Jill' and 'Judy', led an attack on American naval forces protecting the landing force on Saipan Island, in the Marianas. But, despite the increased range of 'Jill' and the faster speed of 'Judy', 346 Japanese aircraft were shot down, for the loss of only thirty American aircraft. In the ensuing naval battle, three of the nine Japanese aircraft-carriers involved, *Taiho*, *Shokaku* and *Hiyo*, were sunk, and four thousand Japanese sailors drowned.

On the afternoon of June 6, the 2nd ss Panzer Division, equipped with the latest German heavy tanks, had been ordered to move from Toulouse, where it was based, to Normandy. But what should have been a three-day journey, reaching the still-struggling Allied forces on June 9 or 10, took seventeen days. The extra two weeks, which relieved the Normandy bridgehead of a major danger, had been forced upon the Division, in part, by the successful Allied destruction of all the bridges on the Loire between Orléans and the sea. The Division, however, as a veteran of the Russian front, had its own bridging train, and ought to have been able to cross all the rivers in its path without undue delay. Its efforts were frustrated, nevertheless, by repeated acts of sabotage along its road. First, the British agent George Starr, alias 'Hilaire', was so successful in blowing up the petrol dumps on which the Division's tank transporters depended that it had to abandon its road journey and go by rail. Then it was the turn of another British agent, Baron Philippe de Gunzbourg – 'Edgar' – and those under his command, to blow up the railway bridges between Bergerac and Périgueux, forcing the Division further east, where another Special Operations Executive circuit, led by Jacques Poitier – 'Nestor' – set up a series of ambushes around Brive and Tulle. All this exceptional effort was combined with the continuing Allied air attack on the Division, as its own top-secret Ultra signals, many of them about its urgent need for fuel, alerted the Allies to its whereabouts and movements. On June 15 it was at Champsecret, still twenty miles from the Normandy bridgehead. Not until June 18 had the Division reached its reserve positions in the area of Torigni, Canisy and Tessy.

On June 19, a British bombing raid on Watten destroyed a large number of flying bombs as they were being prepared for launching. Three days later, American bombers were equally effective against a suspected flying bomb supply railhead at Nucourt, fifteen miles north-west of Paris. But the flying bombs were now reaching Britain every day; in the twenty-four hours up to six in the morning on June 20, twenty-six flying bombs had reached London, and a further twenty-seven had been shot down.

For two weeks, the Allied air forces had patrolled the Channel and struck at the V1 launch sites, averting two dangers: the arrival of German submarines off Normandy, and the bombardment of the embarkation points by flying bombs.

By midnight on June 20, half a million Allied soldiers were ashore in Normandy; in the first two weeks of fighting, four thousand had been killed. From German-occupied France, news reached London that the French Resistance forces had declared a 'general uprising'; Churchill at once instructed the Special Operations Executive – soe – to fly in whatever was needed in the way of arms and ammunition 'to prevent the collapse of the movement and to extend it'.

Behind the German lines on the Eastern Front, ˜n the night of June 19, more than ten thousand demolition charges laid by Soviet partisans damaged beyond immediate repair the whole German rail network west of Minsk. On the next two nights, a further forty thousand charges blew up the railway lines between Vitebsk and Orsha, and Polotsk and Molodechno. The essential lines for German reinforcements, linking Minsk with Brest-Litovsk and Pinsk, were also attacked, while 140,000 Soviet partisans, west of Vitebsk and south of Polotsk, attacked German military formations.

All this was but a prelude to the morning of June 22, when the Red Army opened its summer offensive. Code-named Operation Bagration, after the tsarist General, it began on the third anniversary of Hitler's invasion of Russia, with a force larger than that of Hitler's in 1941. In all, 1,700,000 Soviet troops took part, supported by 2,715 tanks, 1,355 self-propelled guns, 24,000 artillery pieces and 2,306 rocket launchers, sustained in the air by six thousand aircraft, and on the ground by 70,000 lorries and up to a hundred supply trains a day. In one week, the two-hundred-mile-long German front was broken, and the Germans driven back towards Bobruisk, Stolbtsy, Minsk and Grodno, their hold on western Russia broken for ever. In one week, 38,000 German troops had been killed and 116,000 taken prisoner. The Germans also lost two thousand tanks, ten thousand heavy guns, and 57,000 vehicles. German Army Group North, on which so much depended, was broken into two segments, one retreating towards the Baltic States, the other towards East Prussia.

On the first day of the Soviet offensive, a group of German socialists and Army officers, members of the clandestine Kreisau Circle, decided to make contact with the German Communists, whom hitherto they had shunned. Count Claus von Stauffenberg approved of these contacts, which were initiated by the former Social Democratic politician and teacher, Adolf Reichwein, and the Social Democrat leader Julius Leber. As a result of their discussions, it became clear that the German 'masses' were not ready for action against Hitler; if such action was to be taken, it would have to be through the agency of senior Army officers. Count von Stauffenberg agreed. Nine days later, he was appointed Chief of Staff to General Fromm, the Commander of the Reserve Army, who was also privy to the conspiracy. Von Stauffenberg's new appointment gave him access to Hitler's headquarters at both Rastenburg and Berchtesgaden. But Reichwein and Leber, betrayed by one of the three Communists whom they had met on June 22, were arrested.

Behind the German lines in Italy, near Arezzo, on June 24, Italian partisans took on German forces, attacking units on their way to the front line further south. In fierce reprisals, more than a hundred partisans were killed. In Britain, the flying bombs had revived the terrors of the Blitz; on June 24, fifty-one soldiers were killed when a flying bomb, shot down by anti-aircraft guns at Newlands in Kent while on its way to London, fell on their barracks and exploded.

In France, on June 25, American troops reached the suburbs of Cherbourg. The German commander of the fortress, General Karl Wilhelm von Schlieben,

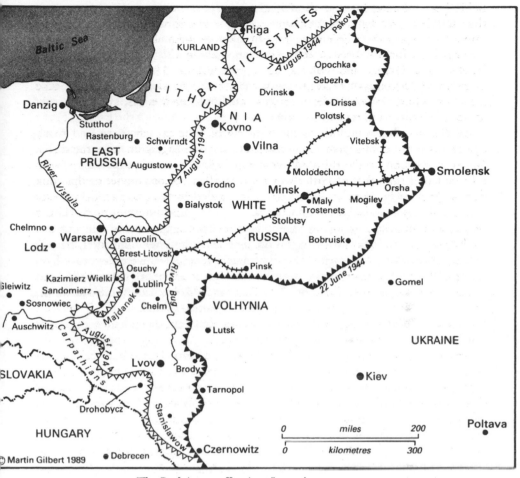

The Red Army offensive, June–August 1944

appealed to Rommel to be allowed to surrender. 'Among the troops defending the town', von Schlieben explained, 'there are two thousand wounded who cannot be treated,' and he went on to ask: 'Is the sacrifice of the others still necessary?' Rommel replied: 'In accordance with the Führer's orders, you are to hold out to the last round.' That day, more than a hundred German fighters flew from their bases in France to support von Schlieben's defence; all were beaten back, whereupon Allied warships, now masters of the Channel, began to bombard von Schlieben's positions from the sea.

Field Marshal von Rundstedt was still not convinced that Normandy was more than a diversion. On June 25, in his weekly situation report, he referred to the non-existent First United States Army Group, which, he believed, was in Britain ready to embark. This force, in his view, was even larger than Montgomery's 21st Army Group, and might be used at any moment for landings between the right bank of the Somme and the mouth of the Seine, to encircle and capture Le Havre. With this fear in mind, von Rundstedt kept in the Pas-de-Calais area many thousands of German soldiers who might otherwise have tipped the balance in Normandy.

On June 26 the German naval commander at Cherbourg, Admiral Hennecke, ordered the total destruction of all port facilities; for this act, Hitler awarded him the Knight's Cross to add to his Iron Cross. That day, on the Eastern Front, after an aerial attack by seven hundred bombers, the Red Army entered Vitebsk; the bodies of six thousand German soldiers were found in the streets. The German forces at Vitebsk, like those at Cherbourg, had been ordered by Hitler to fight to the last; but after the fight came defeat. In Germany, that day, Professor Walther Arndt, a physician and zoologist, was executed; his crime was to have remarked, after a particularly heavy Allied bombing raid: 'This is the end of the Third Reich, and the guilty can now be brought to punishment.'

The 'guilty' still had work to do; on June 26, from Fossoli and Verona, 485 Jews were sent to Auschwitz; four days later, 1,153 Jews were deported from Paris. At the beginning of the month, 496 had been deported from Holland, while from Hungary a total of 381,000 Jews had reached Auschwitz in six weeks, and more than a quarter of a million of them gassed.

It was to alert the world to these killings that four Jews had managed to escape from Auschwitz, with extraordinary luck and courage, and had brought news of its gas chambers to Jews in Slovakia. They, in turn, had managed to get the news to neutral Switzerland, from where the terrible details had been sent, on June 24, to both Washington and London, with an appeal that the Allies should bomb the railway lines leading to Auschwitz. The names of twenty stations on those lines was included in the appeal. On June 26, the revelations about the mass murder of Jews at Auschwitz were being studied in London and Washington. When, on the following day, Churchill himself read the report, he wrote, to Anthony Eden: 'What can be done? What can be said?' Eden's answer was the one which had just been put to him by two Zionist leaders, Chaim Weizmann and Moshe Shertok. This was a request for the bombing of the railway lines, as asked for in the telegrams from Switzerland on June 24. Churchill's reply was sympathetic and immediate. 'Get anything out of the Air Force you can', he wrote to Eden, 'and invoke me if necessary'.

The response to Churchill's appeal was, however, negative. The British Air Ministry were sceptical of losing British airmen's lives 'for no purpose', as one official noted in the secrecy of his departmental correspondence. The bombing would in any case have to be done in daylight, that is, by the Americans. But, in Washington, the American Assistant Secretary of War, John J. McCloy, rejected four separate appeals to bomb the lines; his instruction on getting each request was, as his deputy noted, 'to "kill" this'. The deportations continued. But no plans were made to bomb the lines.

*         *         *

In Burma, on June 26, British, Indian, Gurkha and American troops captured Mogaung. This was the first Japanese-held town in Burma to be wrested back from them. Eight days later, Myitkyina was also captured. On every front – in Burma, in the Pacific, in Italy, in Normandy, and most dramatically of all, in White Russia – the Axis powers were now firmly in retreat.

# 39

# Germany encircled

JULY 1944

On 27 June 1944, the Cherbourg dockyard surrendered, leaving only a few strongholds still in German hands around the port. But the German power of retaliation elsewhere was not yet over. In Britain, 1,600 civilians had now been killed by flying bombs. 'After five years of war', the Minister of Home Security, Herbert Morrison, told the War Cabinet in London, 'the civil population were not as capable of standing the strains of air attack as they had been during the winter of 1940–41.' That day, a flying bomb, falling on Victoria Station in London, killed fourteen people.

In Russia, June 27 saw the first ton of steel produced by the rebuilt Izhorsky steel mill in Leningrad. That day, as Mogilev was liberated in White Russia, Soviet troops on the Karelian front entered Petrozavodsk, releasing several thousand Soviet citizens held in a concentration camp there.

On June 28, as the Normandy battle continued, with the last German strongpoints in Cherbourg on the verge of surrender, but with Caen still held by the Germans, the figures of Allied dead since June 6 were calculated: 4,868 of the deaths were American, 2,443 British and 393 Canadian.

In Paris, on June 28, in an act of revenge by the Resistance, the Milice leader Philippe Henriot was shot dead. On the Eastern Front, that day, the advancing Soviet troops approached the Maly Trostenets concentration camp near Minsk. Russian aircraft attacked the camp itself. That day, the camp guards, Latvian, Ukrainian, White Russian, Hungarian and Roumanian ss auxiliaries, were replaced by a special ss detachment, all German, under German ss officers. This detachment locked all the surviving prisoners, Russian civilians, Jews from the Minsk ghetto, and Viennese Jews who had been brought from Theresienstadt, into the barracks, and then set the barracks on fire.

All those who were able to flee from the blazing buildings were shot. About twenty of the Jews from Theresienstadt managed to escape the blaze and the bullets, and to hide in the forest until the arrival of Soviet forces six days later.

On June 28 the Red Army entered Bobruisk, killing 16,000 German soldiers and taking 18,000 prisoner. 'This is the moment', Churchill telegraphed to Stalin three days later, 'for me to tell you how immensely we are all here impressed with the magnificent advances of the Russian Armies which seem, as they grow in momentum, to be pulverizing the German Armies which stand between you and Warsaw, and afterwards Berlin. Every victory that you gain is watched with eager attention here.'

Churchill went on to tell Stalin: 'I realize vividly that all this is the second round you have fought since Teheran, the first which regained Sevastopol, Odessa and the Crimea and carried your vanguards to the Carpathians, Sereth and Pruth.'

That day, in Italy, General Alexander continued to push the German forces northward. In Normandy, more than three-quarters of a million British and American troops were now ashore, and 40,000 Germans had been taken prisoner. 'The enemy is burning and bleeding on every front at once,' Churchill telegraphed to Stalin, 'and I agree with you that this must go on to the end.'

On June 29, the last German strongpoints in Cherbourg surrendered. That day, Rommel and von Rundstedt went to see Hitler at Berchtesgaden, to demand massive reinforcements, particularly of aircraft and anti-aircraft guns, for Normandy. Both of them also asked Hitler 'how he imagined the war could still be won'. Within three days, von Rundstedt was relieved of his post, to be replaced by Field Marshal von Kluge.

On the Eastern Front, by June 29, more than 130,000 Germans had been killed in a week of fighting, and 66,000 had been taken prisoner. In Berlin, Heinz Bello, a twenty-five-year-old sergeant in the German Army Medical Corps, and a holder of the Iron Cross, Second Class, the East Medal, and the Badge for wounded soldiers, had expressed, while on fire-watching duty, his hostility to Nazism and militarism; denounced by two 'friends', he was found guilty of 'undermining morale' and sentenced to death. He was executed on a machine-gun range.

In the Far East, June 29 saw the execution by the Japanese of a leading Malayan resistance fighter, General Lim Bo Seng.

Over London, the flying bombs continued to wreak their havoc; on June 30, in the Strand, 198 people were killed, while at Westerham in Kent, twenty-four babies under a year old, and eight staff, at a children's home were killed when a flying bomb was brought down by anti-aircraft fire on their rural refuge. Five of the babies were only one month old. They had mostly been evacuated to Kent for safety. In sixteen days of bombardment, the flying bomb had killed 1,935 British civilians.

On the last day of June, the 1,795 Jews deported from Corfu reached Auschwitz. An eye-witness of their fate was a Hungarian Jewish doctor, Miklos Nyiszli, himself a deportee, who later recalled that these Greek Jews had travelled for twenty-seven days in sealed railway wagons, with only the food and water that they had taken with them at the start of the journey. 'When they arrived at Auschwitz's unloading platform', Nyiszli wrote, 'the doors were unlocked, but no one got out and lined up for selection. Half of them were already dead, and the other half in a coma. The entire convoy, without exception, was sent to number two crematorium.'

*       *       *

In Denmark, on the last day of June 1944, a strike began against the curfew and other occupation restrictions; by the time it ended four days later, a hundred Danes had been killed. In Belgium, however, the lack of reprisals led to the recall of the German Military Governor, General von Falkenhausen: accused of being too lenient, he was placed under arrest, and then sent to Dachau.

In Italy, an anti-partisan sweep began on July 1. That day, Field Marshal Kesselring, the Commander-in-Chief of the German forces in Italy, issued an order stating that his earlier warning of 'severest measures' against the Italian partisans must not prove to have been an empty threat. Two hundred partisans were killed during this sweep, carried out between Parma and Piacenza. Forty-three of the partisans, captured alive, were brutally tortured, and then shot.

On the night of July 1, sixty-four British and American bombers renewed Operation Gardening – a general code-name for aerial minelaying – dropping a total of 192 mines in the River Danube near Belgrade; sixty more mines were dropped on the following night. Further north, in Budapest, Admiral Horthy now demanded a halt to the deportation of Hungarian Jews to Auschwitz. On the morning of July 2, Budapest was already under air bombardment, oil refineries and oil storage tanks being hit by American bombers flying from southern Italy, and set ablaze. Hundreds of bombs had fallen on residential areas; several hundred Hungarian civilians had been killed, as were a hundred Hungarian Jews holding British or American nationality, when the villa in which they were confined received a direct hit.

As well as bombs, the Americans dropped leaflets over Budapest, informing 'the authorities in Hungary' that the United States Government was closely following the persecution of the Jews 'with extreme gravity', and warning that 'all those responsible' for carrying out orders to persecute Jews would be punished.

Within forty-eight hours of the American raid and its leaflets, Admiral Horthy informed the Germans that the deportations would have to stop. As a result of publicity given to the report of the four escapees from Auschwitz, protests had been made to him by the International Committee of the Red Cross, the King of Sweden, and Pope Pius XII. The Germans, whose deportation plans depended upon the support of Hungarian policemen and railway workers, had no choice but to halt the deportations. A total of 437,000 Hungarian Jews had already been deported from the provinces and countryside. But more than 170,000 remained in Budapest, saved from deportation on the very eve of their intended departure.

The deportation of Hungarian Jews stopped on July 8. On the following day, a Swedish diplomat, Raoul Wallenberg, reached Budapest from Sweden with a list of 630 Hungarian Jews for whom Swedish visas were available. No longer in danger of deportation to Auschwitz, these Jews were desperate nevertheless for whatever protection they could receive.

Raoul Wallenberg, the man who now sought to protect the Jews of Budapest from further disasters, was the great-great-grandson of Michael Benedics, one of the first Jews to settle in Sweden, at the end of the eighteenth century, and a convert to Lutheranism.

\* \* \*

In Germany, the Army officers close to Count von Stauffenberg were nearing their planned assassination of Hitler, calling it Operation Valkyrie. Their first idea was to kill Hitler, Goering and Himmler with a single bomb at Berchtesgaden on July 2. As, however, Hitler was alone that day, the attempt was called off. Meanwhile, the build-up of Allied forces on the Normandy beach-head continued; by July 2, a million men were ashore, together with 171,532 vehicles. Even in the narrow perimeter under Allied control, 41,000 Germans were being held prisoner-of-war.

On the Eastern Front, the German position had become precarious by the beginning of July, with twenty-eight German divisions encircled on July 2; and more than 40,000 soldiers killed fighting inside the trap, or trying to break out of it. On July 3, Soviet forces entered Minsk, the capital city of White Russia. More than 150,000 German soldiers were taken prisoner, and two thousand tanks captured. That day, Count von Stauffenberg went to Berchtesgaden. There, within Hitler's own headquarters, he was given, by the chief of the Organization Branch of the Army High Command, Major-General Helmuth Stieff, a bomb with a silent fuse, small enough to hide inside a briefcase. Stauffenberg took the bomb away, determined to use it on July 11, when he would have to return to Berchtesgaden.

Since the first day of the Normandy landings, a British Special Air Service team, headed by J. E. Tonkin, had been parachuted into the Poitiers region; for nearly a month the team, eventually nearly fifty strong, and code-named Operation Bulbasket, hampered German rail traffic between Poitiers and Tours, as well as providing valuable information for the Royal Air Force, including the 'best petrol fire' of the campaign, at Châtellerault. But on July 3 the team was trapped by an ss infantry battalion, and a third of them captured, and then shot. Tonkin was also captured, but survived torture and captivity. The other survivors of Operation Bulbasket were brought out of France by a Special Operations Executive flight. For his successful sabotage activities, Tonkin was awarded the Military Cross.

Over London, throughout the first week of July, the flying bombs continued to cause damage and death. On the morning of July 3, a flying bomb fell in Lambeth. From across the river, twenty-nine American servicemen then at their Central Base Section at Turk's Row, in Chelsea, were loaded into a truck to go to the aid of the wounded, while seventy others waited for more trucks to arrive. At that moment, a flying bomb fell on Chelsea, hitting the loaded truck and bringing down the fronts of the buildings on either side of the road. Sixty-four of the Americans were killed, and ten British civilian passers-by.

The British Chiefs of Staff, alarmed at the rate of deaths from the flying bombs, and their possible adverse effect on morale in London, authorized the diversion of bomber resources from the Normandy beachhead to the flying bomb sites. On July 4, in a precision bombing attack using deep penetration bombs, an underground storage depot at St Leu was hit, and two thousand flying bombs buried in the ruins. A German top-secret message, decrypted in Britain, indicated that flying bombs intended for the store at St Leu would be diverted to Nucourt; six days after the St Leu raid, Nucourt was therefore the target of a similar bombing attack. After two attacks, Nucourt's flying bombs were also buried. Meanwhile, the death roll continued to rise; by six o'clock on the morning of July 6, as Churchill told the House of Commons that day, 2,754 flying bombs had been launched, and 2,752 people killed – 'almost exactly one person one bomb'. The drug penicillin, Churchill added, which had hitherto been restricted to military use, would be made available to treat all those wounded by flying bombs.

The Germans were also taking special measures to deal with the effects of bombing. On July 4, a thousand Jewish women, then in the barracks at Auschwitz, were sent away from Auschwitz altogether, and taken by train to Hamburg, where they had to demolish houses which had been too badly bombed to be repaired. Throughout German-occupied Europe, slave labourers were being used to clear rubble and repair roads and railways. Also on July 4, more than two hundred prisoners in a camp on the Channel Island of Alderney, most of them Jews who had been deported from France, were put on board ship to be sent to tasks on the mainland. The ship was attacked by British warships, and sunk. All the prisoners on board were drowned.

By July 4, as Ultra decrypts revealed, the Germans were still concerned that further Allied landings might be imminent, between the Seine and the Somme, against one of the ports in Brittany or on the French Mediterranean coast. This latter landing was in fact being planned, using forces from Italy. In Northern France, the only activity outside the Normandy bridgehead was sabotage; in Operation Gain, a British Special Air Service group, commanded by Ian Fenwick, a popular cartoonist, was attacking German supply columns thirty to fifty miles south of Paris, between the Loire and the Seine. On the night of July 4, however, a reinforcing party from England arrived to find their dropping zone under fire. Fenwick was killed during the struggle. A dozen of his men, unable to get away, were captured, interrogated for a month by Josef Kieffer of the German Security Service, and then shot. One of them managed to escape. His testimony was later fatal to his captor.

Executed on July 6, in a wood outside Paris, was the former French Minister of Colonies, Georges Mandel, a leading Government opponent of the capitulation in 1940, and a Jew. 'To die is nothing,' he said as he was handed over by the German Security Service to the French Milice. 'What is sad is to die without seeing the liberation of the country and the restoration of the Republic.'

French soldiers were already fighting on French soil to liberate France when Mandel, a French patriot, was murdered by Frenchmen. The murderers in their turn, were later brought to trial, found guilty, and executed.

In the Pacific, on Saipan Island, on July 7, the 4,300 surviving Japanese troops threw themselves against the Americans in a final 'banzai' charge; in bitter hand-to-hand fighting, almost all 4,300 Japanese were killed, for the loss of 406 American lives. A few hundred Japanese soldiers managed to swim out to the coral reefs. A small flotilla was sent across to persuade them to surrender, but, clinging to the reef, the Japanese opened fire on the Americans, who returned the fire with devastating effect. On one reef, the Americans saw a Japanese officer beheading his men with his sword. He was shot by the Americans before he could commit suicide himself.

As the Americans on Saipan searched the caves for Japanese survivors, but found none, they came across the remains of the bodies of two senior officers who had committed suicide rather than surrender. General Saito had opened his artery with a sword, after which his adjutant shot him in the head. Admiral Nagumo, the former commander of the Pearl Harbour Striking Force, had killed himself with a pistol shot.

That day, in northern France, British bombers dropped 2,500 tons of bombs on Caen in preparation for an attempt to capture the town. On the following day, as Caen was bombarded by sixteen-inch shells from the British battleship *Rodney*, from a safe anchorage in the Channel, Hitler issued a new directive, warning that the Normandy bridgehead must not be allowed to increase in size, 'otherwise our forces would prove inadequate to contain it, and the enemy will break out into the interior of France, where we do not possess any comparable tactical mobility with which to oppose him'.

'Every square kilometre must be defended tenaciously', this was the final message of Hitler's directive of July 8. It was certainly obeyed, as the Americans found on the following day as they tried to advance from La Haye-du-Puits towards Périers. After a month of fighting, the bridgehead had still not turned into a spearhead. But, for the Germans, the spectre, not only of retreat but of defeat, had begun to loom. Hardly had Hitler's new directive to fight for every kilometre reached the German commanders who had to carry it out, when an SS general, Kurt Meyer, ordered his men to pull back from their forward positions into the suburbs of Caen. In the previous month's fighting, every one of Meyer's battalion commanders had been killed. 'Officers and men know that the struggle is hopeless,' Meyer wrote that day, and he added: 'Silent but willing to do their duty to the bitter end, they wait for their orders.'

On July 9, the day of Meyer's order to withdraw into Caen, the German military conspirators, their date for Hitler's assassination only three days away, contacted Rommel at his headquarters at La Roche-Guyon. Their emissary was Colonel Caesar von Hofacker, a member of the staff of the German Military Command in Paris. Another of the conspirators of the group centred in Paris was Major von Falkenhausen, the nephew of the German Military Governor in Brussels who had just been arrested for leniency.

On the Eastern Front, the evening of July 10 marked the start of the Soviet offensive against the German Army Group North. Within forty-eight hours the Soviet commander, General Yeremenko, had torn a fifty mile gap in the German line, and was advancing deep into German held territory. One by one the German strongpoints fell, first Drissa, then Opochka, then Sebezh. Germany's last line of defence inside Russia was broken.

On July 11, Count von Stauffenberg was ordered to Berchtesgaden, to report to Hitler on the military situation. He took his bomb with him, but did not use it; Hitler was about to go to his East Prussian headquarters at Rastenburg, and the Count had been summoned there also. On the day that Stauffenberg was at Berchtesgaden, Churchill, in London, was shown further details, based on the information set down by the four escapees from Auschwitz, of the murder there of 1,700,000 Jews, some gassed, some shot, some buried alive, in the previous two years. 'There is no doubt', Churchill wrote that day to Anthony Eden, 'that this is probably the greatest and the most horrible crime ever committed in the whole history of the world, and it has been done by scientific machinery by nominally civilized men in the name of a great State and one of the leading races in Europe. It is quite clear' – Churchill added – 'that all concerned in this crime who may fall into our hands, including the people who only obeyed orders by carrying out the butcheries, should be put to death after their association with the murders has been proved'.

Against any partisans or resistance fighters who were caught, German savagery continued. On July 8, thirty captured Polish partisans had been shot in public at Garwolin, outside Warsaw. That same day, in France, the Resistance leader Lieutenant Joly, code name 'Valentin', had been killed in an anti-Maquis sweep around Ecot. On July 12, forty-eight Italian partisans, led by Eugenio Calo, were captured near Arezzo. After being cruelly tortured for two days, but having revealed nothing, they were forced to dig a deep pit, then buried in it up to their necks. Sticks of dynamite were put next to their heads, but still no one talked. The dynamite was then ignited.

Eugenio Calo was posthumously awarded the Italian Gold Medal for Military Valour.

On July 12, a German spy was hanged at Pentonville Prison in London. Joseph Jan Vanhove was a Belgian waiter who had claimed to have escaped from German-occupied Europe to Sweden, in order to enlist in the Allied armies. While in northern France, his job had in fact been to betray French and Belgian forced labourers who were sympathetic to the Resistance. He had been taken into custody on reaching Scotland in February 1944. Tried at the Old Bailey in May, Vanhove was found guilty of treachery. His appeal had been dismissed in June. He was the sixteenth German spy to be executed in Britain during the war, and the last.

On July 13 a Russian Army under General Koniev began a two-pronged offensive to cross the River Bug and to capture the East Galician city of Lvov. As the Red Army advanced to the town of Brody, it encircled forty thousand German soldiers, of whom, after a seven day battle, thirty thousand were killed. The River Bug marked the Curzon Line, which Stalin, with Churchill's support, wished to establish as the western border of the Soviet Union. Lvov, one of the principal cities of pre-war Poland, lay on the Soviet side of the new line. To the north of Koniev's assault, July 13 saw the fall of Vilna, another city which pre-war Poland claimed, but which now lay within the Soviet sphere. With each military victory, the post-war political map of Europe was being drawn.

On July 14, Soviet forces entered Pinsk, less than two hundred miles from East Prussia. That very day, Hitler left Berchtesgaden for his East Prussian headquarters at Rastenburg. In Kovno, a mere 130 miles from Rastenburg, more than a hundred Jews then in hiding in a cellar were discovered by the Gestapo, who locked them in the house beneath which they had been hiding, and set the house on fire. None survived. Nor, on July 14, Bastille Day in France, were there any survivors of the twenty-eight French prisoners at the Santé Prison in Paris, who rose up in defiant revolt on that day of historic defiance; all were put up against the prison wall and shot.

It was at this time also that four British women agents, Vera Leigh, Diana Rowden, Andrée Borrel and Sonia Olschanesky, who had been held in prison at Karlsruhe since their capture, were taken to Natzweiler concentration camp in Alsace. Two British agents already at Natzweiler, among them the Belgian doctor, Colonel Guérisse, saw them arrive; that same evening, all four were taken to the camp crematorium, given a lethal injection, and put into the ovens.

By July 15, by a strange coincidence which Churchill pointed out to his War Cabinet, 3,582 flying bombs had fallen on Britain, and 3,583 British civilians had been killed by flying bombs. But the rising death toll in London was of no solace to the Germans fighting in France. On July 15, Rommel wrote to Hitler of the enormous casualties and material losses, the lack of adequate reinforcements, and the danger that with the Allied air and artillery superiority 'even the bravest army will be smashed piece by piece, losing men, arms and territory in the process'.

Rommel also wrote of how no new forces could be brought up to the Normandy front 'except by weakening Fifteenth Army front on the Channel, or the Mediterranean front in southern France'. 'Fifteenth Army front on the Channel' was still in place to meet the non-existent threat of the First United States Army Group, as the Allied deception plan, more than five weeks after the Normandy landings, still influenced German strategy. A telegram from the Japanese Ambassador in Berlin, sent to Tokyo and decrypted at Bletchley on July 15, reiterated that the Germans still thought that this fictional formation would be sent across the Straits of Dover, and used to cut off the German forces in Normandy by an attack in the rear. As Churchill wrote to Eisenhower, in sending him the decrypt of the Japanese Ambassador's telegram: 'Uncertainty is a terror to the Germans. The forces in Britain are a dominant preoccupation of the Huns.'

Unknown to Churchill, July 15 was the day on which Count von Stauffenberg and his fellow Army conspirators had decided to carry out Operation Valkyrie, the assassination of Hitler. In Berlin, one of the conspirators, the Chief of Staff of the Reserve Army, General Friedrich Olbricht, confident that the attempt would be made as planned, gave orders two hours before the 'assassination' for his troops to march on Berlin. At the last moment, because Hitler shortened the length of the conference, Stauffenberg decided to postpone the attempt until his next visit to Rastenburg in five days' time. Meanwhile, General Olbricht's troops continued to march towards Berlin. Quickly halting them, Olbricht explained to his superior, General Fromm, that it was a 'surprise exercise'.

On July 16, a massive German gun on the Channel coast, known as the 'England' gun, was almost ready to fire its heavy shells against the British south coast towns. That day, in a sustained bombing attack, the gun's site, at Marquise-Mimoyecques, was destroyed. That day, over the Russian front, a French pilot, Maurice de Seynes, a member of the Free French fighter regiment, which had been active on the Eastern Front for the past nine months, was blinded in his cockpit during an action over the German lines. He refused to bail out, however, because his co-pilot, mechanic Vladimir Belozub, a Russian, was trapped in his seat. 'Nobody', wrote Soviet Air Force General Georgi Zakharov, 'could force Maurice de Seynes to save his own life.' The plane exploded in mid air; had de Seynes tried merely to save himself, his mother wrote, 'it would have been a stain upon the whole of our family. My son acted nobly'.

Forty-two French pilots gave their lives fighting on the Eastern Front; four were made Heroes of the Soviet Union. De Seynes' heroic act of July 16 entered into the annals of Soviet history.

On July 16, Colonel Caesar von Hofacker was in Berlin, where he went to Count von Stauffenberg's home in the suburb of Wannsee. There, the decision was made to go ahead in four days' time with the assassination of Hitler. During the meeting, Hofacker told the conspirators of the imminent collapse of the Normandy defence perimeter, and the inevitable subsequent failure of the German armies in the West. Rommel, indeed, in whose name Hofacker partly spoke, had stated bluntly, in his letter to Hitler on the previous day: 'The troops are everywhere fighting heroically, but the unequal struggle is approaching its end.' Rommel also sought Hitler's permission to bring over to Normandy most of the 28,000 German troops still stationed in the Channel Islands, and badly needed in France, but Hitler refused.

The conspirators needed Rommel's support and prestige, if they were to win over the support of the German officers in the West. But, as Rommel was being driven from south of Caen to his headquarters at La Roche-Guyon on July 17, and had reached Livarot, he was severely wounded by machine gun fire from a low-flying fighter-bomber, piloted by a South African air ace, Squadron Leader J. J. Le Roux. Rommel's wounds were dressed by a French pharmacist in Livarot. Later, he was taken to a German Air Force hospital at the nearby town of Bernay, his roles both as commander and conspirator brought prematurely to an end.

For Squadron Leader Le Roux – with twenty-three 'kills' to his credit, the top scoring pilot over Normandy since D-Day – the identity of his victim was unknown. Le Roux himself was to disappear over the Channel during a flight back to England eight weeks later.

In Moscow, on July 17, more than 57,000 German prisoners-of-war were marched through the streets of the city. These were some of the men captured in the White Russian offensive which had opened on June 22. Nineteen German generals led the parade, each still wearing his Iron Cross; at their head, wearing his Knight's Cross, was General Friedrich Gollwitzer, commander of an army corps, who had been captured near Vitebsk.

On the day after this Moscow parade, Soviet forces reached Augustow, on the Polish side of the East Prussian border, and only eighty miles from Rasten-burg. There, they were halted by a ferocious counter-attack. Behind German lines, July 18 saw the first day of a massive sweep by ten thousand German troops against French Resistance forces in the Vercors. Five hundred Resistance fighters, and two hundred civilians, were killed. 'As the Germans overran the plateau,' one historian has written, 'they behaved with customary barbarity, burning and torturing, slaying everyone they could reach as nastily as they could.'

In London, the evacuation of civilians had begun to exceed the numbers evacuated at the time of the Blitz in 1940. By July 17, more than half a million Londoners had left the capital, and within the next two months the number had risen to more than a million. Among those who were aware of German rocket developments, this seemed prudence rather than panic; among the senior Government scientists and Intelligence experts, there was concern on July 18 that the Germans would soon launch a successor to the flying bomb that would be even more lethal. That day Dr R. V. Jones warned the War Cabinet's 'Crossbow' Committee that as many as a thousand v2 rockets might already exist, each weighing more than eleven tons, and capable of an unprecedented speed of about four thousand miles an hour. This rocket would only take three to four minutes to travel from its launching site in northern Europe to its target – London.

If such a rocket attack should develop, Churchill told the committee, 'he was prepared, after consultation with the United States and the USSR, to threaten the enemy with large-scale gas attacks in retaliation, should such a course appear profitable'.


It was on July 18 that the Western Allies launched the first phase of Operation Goodwood, for the capture of Caen, an attack by a hundred bombers over the German defences. Much of the city was destroyed, and as many as three thousand Frenchmen killed. Then the artillery opened fire, four hundred guns in all, supported by the naval gunfire of two British cruisers, and the monitor *Roberts*, whose fifteen-inch guns had last been fired in action at the Battle of Jutland in 1916. British and Canadian armoured forces then moved forward. That same day, but too late to save Caen, Hitler at last agreed to move such units of the Fifteenth Army as were mobile from the Pas-de-Calais, and rush them to the Normandy battle zone. The deception of Operation Fortitude was over; but Operation Goodwood was won.

As British and Canadian troops fought throughout July 20 to capture Caen and push the Germans back from the Normandy bridgehead, Hitler was at Rastenburg, in one of his headquarters' wooden huts, being given an account of the worsening situation on the Eastern Front. As he studied the map, there was a violent explosion. A bomb, left in a briefcase by Count von Stauffenberg, had gone off, devastating the room in which Hitler and his generals had gathered. But Hitler survived the blast, saved at the last moment because one of those present, General Brandt, in trying to get a better look at the map laid out on the table, had pushed the briefcase to the far side of the frame holding up the table.

As the bomb went off, at 12.42 p.m., von Stauffenberg was already about two hundred yards away; looking back, he saw the hut blown up into the air. Assuming that Hitler was dead, he hurried from the 'Wolf's Lair' to the airport at Rastenburg, and flew back to Berlin. All now seemed set for Operation Valkyrie to come into effect – the military overthrow of a leaderless Nazi régime. At 4.30 p.m. von Stauffenberg's plane reached Berlin; there, he learned that, although four officers in the hut had been killed, Hitler was alive. Nevertheless, the conspirators still hoped to activate their plan, and within an hour, von Stauffenberg and General Olbricht arrested the Commander of the Reserve Army, General Fromm. Plans had been made by the conspirators to surround the Government offices in the Wilhelmstrasse, and orders were given by the Berlin Fortress commander, General von Hase, for this to be done. The officer chosen for the task was Major Otto Ernst Remer; but, from his office in the Wilhelmstrasse, Goebbels telephoned Remer, and persuaded him, before taking action, to speak by telephone to Hitler. Having done so, Major Remer declined to support the conspirators further. At 6.45 p.m. that same evening, Goebbels broadcast over German radio that Hitler was alive and well.

Too late, at 8.10 p.m., was a telegram sent out in the name of Field Marshal von Witzleben, which began: 'The Führer is dead. I have been appointed Commander-in-Chief of the Armed Forces, and also ...' At this point, the message broke off. The conspiracy had failed.

Believing that Hitler had been killed, the conspirators in Paris had ordered the arrest of all senior Gestapo and Security Service officers. By nightfall, however, it was learned in Paris that Hitler was alive. General von Stuelpnagel, the commander of the Paris garrison, was ordered back to Berlin. Driving as far as Verdun, the battlefield on which he had fought in the First World War, he tried to commit suicide, but succeeded only in blinding himself.

A terrible revenge was now exacted against the conspirators, and against all those associated with them. General Fromm, having earlier been released by Olbricht and von Stauffenberg, who had both assumed that he would join their cause, turned swiftly against them; that evening, Olbricht and von Stauffenberg were shot in the courtyard of the War Ministry in Berlin.

More than five thousand Germans were to be executed in the months ahead. Others, like Major-General Henning von Treschkow, committed suicide. Before killing himself, he declared: 'God once promised Abraham to spare Sodom, should there be ten just men in the city. He will, I hope, spare Germany because of what we have done, and not destroy her.'

Another of those who committed suicide was General Ludwig Beck, whom the conspirators had designated Head of State in place of Hitler. Beck had resigned as chief of the Army General Staff in 1938, in protest against Hitler's plans to invade Czechoslovakia. On July 20, he was given by General Fromm the opportunity to shoot himself. Twice he tried, unsuccessfully, to blow out his brains; finally, and already gravely wounded, he was shot by an Army sergeant.

\*         \*         \*

The German V1 rocket, the first of these rockets was successfully tested on 24 December 1942.

A German top-secret teleprinter, *Geheimschreiber*, whose messages, codenamed 'Fish', were, from the end of 1942, to transmit top-secret high level communications from Berlin to German field commanders, especially in Russia. This machine was broken by Bletchley Park and its messages read by British Intelligence almost uninterruptedly until the end of the war.

Soviet units link up at Volkhov, on the Leningrad front, 13 January 1943, enabling supplies to reach Lake Ladoga by rail, and then cross the frozen lake to the besieged city (*see page 392*).

Italian troops, Germany's allies on the Eastern Front, retreating from the Don, January 1943.

Italian war dead on the Eastern Front, January 1943.

Admiral Yamamoto and his staff at Rabaul, in New Guinea. Behind them is a Japanese Zero fighter.

The fuselage and tailplane of Admiral Yamamoto's Betty bomber, shot down on 17 April 1943 as a result of information gained by Ultra, the Allies' eavesdropping on German, Italian and Japanese top secret radio messages (*see pages 419–20*).

American Liberator bombers
drop incendiary bombs on the
shipyards in the German port of
Kiel, 14 May 1943, while, from
a higher altitude, Boeing
bombers drop high explosives.
This was the first day of
Operation Pointblank (*see page
427*).

The crew of a British Lancaster
bomber set off for an air raid
over Germany, a photograph
published in *Picture Post* on 15
May 1943.

The British 'bouncing' bomb on a test drop.

The effect of the 'bouncing' bomb in action: the Möhne Dam in the Ruhr, 16 May 1943 (*see page* 428).

American warships at anchor
during the reoccupation of
Kiska Island, in the Aleutians,
16 August 1943 (*see page 451*).

American Marines examine the
wreckage of Japanese aircraft on
Tarawa, the principal Japanese
airbase in the Gilbert Islands, 20
November 1943 (*see page 476*).

Roosevelt, Churchill and Stalin at the Teheran Conference, 30 November 1943. The birthday cake is to celebrate Churchill's 69th birthday. The conference had begun on the previous day (*see page 478*).

British soldiers, captured by the Germans on the island of Kos, reach the Greek mainland, 28 December 1943, on their way to an internment camp. They had been taken prisoner nearly three months earlier (*see page 465*).

American troops go ashore at Anzio, 22 January 1944 (*see page 491*).

Anzio, 30 January 1944; three Grave Registration Assistants place the body of a dead American soldier on a stretcher. A double row of other dead soldiers lies behind them.

In the explosion at Rastenburg, Hitler had been badly shaken and scratched, but was otherwise unhurt. At the moment of the explosion he had been leaning right across the table, to look at the situation in Kurland, which lay at the extreme north-east corner of the map. The table top, and the table frame behind which the briefcase had been pushed, saved his life. During the afternoon he showed the shattered hut to his first visitor, Benito Mussolini.

That midnight, Hitler broadcast to the German people. He was alive and well, and the war would go on. At the same time, Admiral Dönitz telegraphed to all naval commanders that only orders from Himmler 'were to be complied with'. Similar messages were sent out to the German Air Force and Army commanders. Hitler, Himmler and Goebbels were now in effective control of the German war machine. One by one, their enemies, even on the furthest fringes of the conspiracy, were eliminated; among those executed was the Kaiser's former Private Secretary, Freiherr von Sell, who after his master's death in Holland in 1941 had returned to Germany, and had joined those who feared that Hitler's excesses would lead to Germany's destruction.

The bomb plot also led to honours; Major Remer, who, after speaking to Hitler on the telephone, had declined to help the conspirators, was awarded the Knight's Cross with Oak Leaves.

On July 21, as the German Army accepted that Hitler would continue to lead it, American forces landed on Guam. In the Japanese conquest of the island in December 1941, only a single Japanese soldier had lost his life; now, in a twenty day battle, 18,500 Japanese defenders were killed, for the cost of 2,124 American lives. Three days after the Guam landings, American troops landed on Tinian Island. Once more, the Japanese refused to accept that they could not win; 6,050 Japanese soldiers died, and 290 Americans, before Tinian was overrun.

The pace of the Allied advance was now accelerating on all fronts. On July 22, Soviet forces crossed the River Bug, to capture the town of Chelm, inside the area which Russia had accepted as part of a future post-war Poland. That same day, Radio Moscow announced the establishment, on Polish soil, of a Polish Committee for National Liberation.

On the Baltic front, Pskov fell to the Russians on July 23. That day, Hitler appointed Goering as Reich Commissar for Total War Mobilization.

In Poland, Soviet troops, reaching the outskirts of Lublin, overran the German concentration camp at Majdanek, finding there hundreds of unburied corpses, and seven gas chambers. This was the first death camp to be reached by the Allies. More than a million and a half people had been murdered at Majdanek in the previous two years, among them Polish opponents of German rule, Soviet prisoners-of-war, and Jews. Photographs of the corpses at Majdanek provided the West with the first visual evidence of the horrors of the concentration camp system. Hitler, who had been told that all such evidence of mass murder had been destroyed, spoke angrily of 'the slovenly and cowardly rabble in the security services' who had not erased 'the traces' in time.

Even as Majdanek's barbarities were being revealed, the 1,700 Jews living in the island of Rhodes, in the Eastern Mediterranean, and the 120 Jews on the nearby island of Kos, were taken by boat to Salonica, then by train to Auschwitz. Soviet troops were only 170 miles away. But with the gas chambers at Majdanek, Treblinka, Sobibor and Belzec no longer in operation, those at Auschwitz worked harder and faster. On July 24, despite Admiral Horthy's order two weeks earlier that no more Hungarian Jews were to be deported, 1,500 Jews from the Hungarian town of Sarvar were taken away; they were the last Hungarian Jews to be sent to Auschwitz; Adolf Eichmann, his work completed as far as he had been able, was awarded the Iron Cross, Second Class.

# 40

# The battles for Poland and France

SUMMER 1944

On 25 July 1944, the Americans launched Operation Cobra in Normandy. Within a few days, American troops succeeded in breaking out of the Cherbourg peninsula, enabled to do so by a major British assault on the far more heavily defended German positions between Caen and Falaise. That week, behind the German lines in Poland, an experimental v2 rocket failed to explode, was hidden in a river by the Polish underground, salvaged, dismantled, and then flown out of Poland, together with a Polish engineer. The flight was in a Royal Air Force Dakota which made the dangerous journey across German-occupied Hungary from southern Italy, for that sole purpose. Flown back to Britain, the parts of the bomb revealed essential details about the imminent heavy German rocket attack, although there was nothing the British could do to forestall it. The Polish engineer was flown back to Poland. Later he was caught by the Gestapo, and shot.

In the former Polish capital, Warsaw, the presence of Soviet troops west of the River Bug led to a decision, by Poles loyal to the Government-in-exile in London, to try to throw off the German yoke before the Soviets arrived. 'We are ready to fight for the liberation of Warsaw at any moment,' the Home Army's commander, Lieutenant General Tadeusz Bor-Komorowski, telegraphed to London on July 25, and he added: 'Be prepared to bomb the aerodromes around Warsaw at our request. I shall announce the moment of the beginning of the fight.' On the following day, a senior Home Army officer in Warsaw, General Tadeusz Pelczynski, telegraphed to the expectant forces in Warsaw: 'It might be necessary to begin the battle for Warsaw at any time.'

On July 26, eleven Soviet partisans, led by Captain P. A. Velichko, were parachuted into German-occupied Slovakia, near Ruzomberok, with weapons and radio-transmitters. Their task was to prepare the way for a drop of substantial numbers of partisans and supplies, to create a network of anti-German bases and activity. That day, in Lyon, a bomb was thrown at a restaurant frequented by the Gestapo. No one was seriously hurt. But on the following day five prisoners of the Gestapo, including the Resistance leader Albert Chambonnet, were shot, and their bodies left in the street as a warning.

On July 27, as American troops broke out of the Normandy bridgehead, a Special Air Service force parachuted into Mazignen, behind German lines, to disrupt German road communications to the battle zone. That same day, Périers fell at last to American assault. In Italy, the Germans had fallen back as far as Florence. On the Eastern Front, the Red Army entered Dvinsk, Bialystok, Lvov and Stanislawow, driving back the Germans at every point along a five-hundred-mile front.

Over London, two flying bombs on July 28 did considerable damage; the first, at Lewisham, killing fifty-one people, the second, at the corner of Earls Court Road and Knightsbridge, killing forty-five; the first had fallen on a busy shopping centre, the second on a Lyons Corner House tea shop.

In the Pacific, the United States completed its New Guinea campaign with Operation Globetrotter, the capture on July 30 of the town of Sansapor, for the loss of only two American soldiers; yet in once more defending their indefensible positions, 374 Japanese soldiers were killed.

As the Anglo-American forces broke out of the Normandy beach-head, opening the road to central France, yet another deportation train left Paris. On it were 1,300 deportees, among them three hundred children and young people under eighteen, including a fifteen-day-old baby boy, deported in the wooden box that had served as his cradle. In Auschwitz itself, towards which this train was bound, July 31 saw the gassing of 750 Gypsy women whose barrack had been reported to Dr Mengele as being infected with lice. Within the next three days, two thousand more Gypsies were killed. The rest, 1,408 in all, were sent westward by train, some to Buchenwald, others to Ravensbrück, to yet more barracks, beatings and slave labour. Some were used for sea-water experiments. Others were sent on, yet again, to Mittlebau-Dora and Flossenbürg, to work in the underground factories of the disintegrating Reich.

On July 29, in central Poland, units of the Red Army crossed the River Vistula, capturing the town of Sandomierz. That day, with Soviet tanks already at Wolomin, twelve miles east of Warsaw, Radio Moscow broadcast to the people of the Polish capital: 'the hour of action has already arrived'. On July 31, Soviet forces entered Radzymin, to the north-west of Warsaw, and Otwock to the south-east. The battle was so close that it could be heard in Warsaw. But with German reinforcements being hurried across the Vistula, on August 1, the Soviet commander, Major-General Radzievskii, realizing that his tank forces were considerably outnumbered, ordered a defensive line to be held between Kobylka and Milosna. That day, inside Warsaw, members of the Polish Home Army, members of the Communist-led People's Army, and armed civilians of no political persuasion, in all 42,500 men and women, seized two-thirds of the city from the Germans. For three days they awaited a German counter-attack, confident that they could hold it off, and achieve the liberation of their capital city before the Red Army could cross the Vistula.

As Warsaw rose in revolt, the Germans were everywhere in retreat: in Normandy, on August 1 the Americans entered Vire. On the Eastern Front,

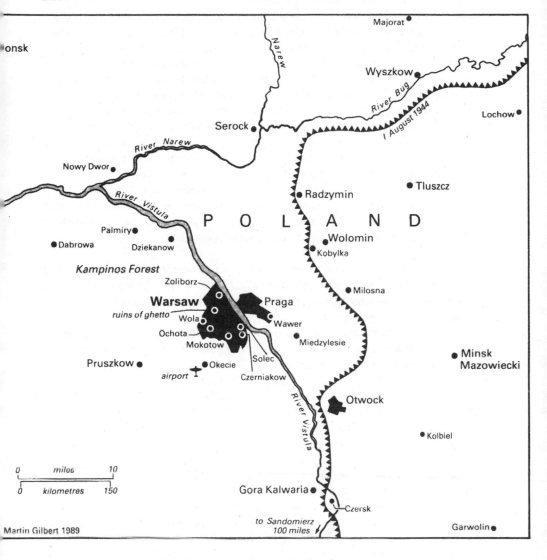

The Warsaw uprising, July–October 1944

the Russians entered Kovno. But the Germans were determined to crush the insurgents in Warsaw. 'Destroy tens of thousands,' was Himmler's order to General Geibel on August 1. His order was obeyed, with brutal savagery. Entering a hospital on Plocka Street, the Germans killed the head doctor, then ordered the patients to leave the building. All the patients were then shot.

On the other side of the world, on Tinian Island in the Pacific, August 1 saw a collective act of self destruction. As one American soldier later wrote, it was after the fighting had ceased that, as Marines 'watched in amazement', a Japanese soldier 'leaped off the plain into the sea, a sheer drop of more than a hundred feet. In a few minutes another jumped. For half an hour the suicide leaps of the soldiers continued.' The American soldier's account went on: 'In the caves overhead an intermittent puff of grey smoke from hand grenades told of other Japs who preferred that form of suicide. The drama was coming to its destructive conclusion. Several soldiers had succeeded in gathering a group of thirty-five or forty civilians around them. The Marines looked on helplessly as two of the soldiers tied the group together with a long rope. Suddenly a puff of smoke from a grenade went up from among the tightly packed group. This was only the beginning. The grenade had been used to detonate a larger charge of high explosives. A terrific blast shook the ground. The bodies of the victims were thrown twenty-five feet in the air. Their arms, legs, and hands were scattered across the plain. The remaining soldiers committed suicide with hand grenades'.

Only after this massacre did the surviving civilians make for the American lines. Within two weeks, 13,262 had surrendered. 'We had literally saved these people from their own protectors,' the soldier reflected.

On August 2, as the Allies advanced northward in Italy, the Germans deported 222 Italian Jews from Verona to Auschwitz. That day, in London, Churchill told the House of Commons that 4,735 people had been killed by the flying bombs. In Warsaw, the commander of the Polish resistance forces, General Bor-Komorowski, sent an assault group to capture Okecie airport, through which he hoped to obtain arms and ammunition from the West. The attackers were mown down by German machine-gun fire. Two days later, the German forces went over to the offensive. As well as SS troops, commanded by Hitler's most ruthless anti-partisan general, von dem Bach Zelewski, the German troops included the Kaminski Brigade of Russian prisoners-of-war who had thrown in their lot with the Germans, and the Dirlewanger Brigade of German former criminals, who had been offered their release from prison if they agreed to fight. The fighting was savage, from the first days; it was to last for two months.

That August 4, the insurgents in Warsaw appealed for Allied help. 'At urgent request of Polish Underground Army,' Churchill telegraphed to Stalin, 'we are dropping, subject to weather, about sixty tons of equipment and ammunition into the south-west quarter of Warsaw, where it is said a Polish revolt against the Germans is in fierce struggle. They also say that they appeal for Russian aid, which seems to be very near. They are being attacked by one and a half German divisions. This may be of help to your operation'.

Stalin replied at once, an answer, Churchill later described it, 'both prompt and grim'. The Soviet Union would not help the insurgents. 'I think that the information that has been communicated to you by the Poles', Stalin declared, 'is greatly exaggerated and does not inspire confidence.' Stalin went on to tell Churchill: 'The Home Army of the Poles consists of a few detachments, which they incorrectly call divisions. They have neither artillery nor aircraft nor tanks. I cannot imagine how such detachments can capture Warsaw, for the defence of which the Germans have produced four tank divisions, among them the Hermann Goering Division.'

That night, thirteen British bombers flew from Foggia in southern Italy to central Poland, which lay at the extreme limit of their range. Five out of the thirteen failed to return. Two of the planes reached as far as Warsaw, where they dropped twenty-four containers of arms and ammunition. Twelve of the containers fell into the hands of the insurgents; twelve fell into German controlled parts of the city.

It was on that same August 4, in Amsterdam, that Anne Frank and her family, German Jewish refugees in hiding for more than two years, were betrayed to the Gestapo, seized and deported. In Australia, on the following morning, a thousand Japanese prisoners-of-war in Cowra camp, west of Sydney, staged a mass breakout. Two Australian privates, Benjamin Hardy and Ralph Jones, who tried to hold the Japanese back with their machine gun, were overwhelmed and killed; both were subsequently awarded a posthumous George Cross. In the ensuing chase, 183 Japanese were killed, and a further twenty-nine committed suicide.

In Warsaw, on August 5, German bombers flew, shortly after dawn, over the suburb of Wola, dropping high-explosive and incendiary bombs. Later that day, the Polish insurgents liberated a German forced labour camp on Gesiowka Street, near the ruins of the former ghetto, freeing 348 Jews who were working there clearing the vast mounds of rubble. These liberated prisoners included Greek, Belgian, French, Roumanian and Hungarian, as well as Polish, Jews. One of the prisoners at Gesiowka, Hans Robert Martin Korn, was one of the eight Jews deported in the summer of 1942 from Finland to Auschwitz. German born, he had been a volunteer in the Winter War between Finland and the Soviet Union in October 1939. He did not survive the events of 1944.

All of the Jews released from the Gesiowka camp joined the Warsaw uprising. Those who were technicians, like Korn, formed a special platoon for the repair of captured German tanks. The first of these Jews to fall in battle was David Edelman, a deportee from France to Auschwitz.

By August 5, more than fifteen thousand Polish civilians had been murdered by German troops in Warsaw. At 5.30 that evening, General von dem Bach Zelewski gave the order for the execution of women and children to stop. But the killing continued of all Polish men who were captured, without anyone bothering to find out whether they were insurgents or not. Nor did either the Cossacks or the criminals in the Kaminski and Dirlewanger Brigades pay any attention to von dem Bach Zelewski's order: by rape, murder, torture and fire, they made their way through the suburbs of Wola and Ochota, killing in three days of slaughter a further thirty thousand civilians, including hundreds of patients in each of the hospitals in their path.

On August 6, less than eighty miles south-west of Warsaw, the Germans began the deportation of the remaining 70,000 Jews from the Lodz ghetto; all of them were sent to Auschwitz, where more than half of those deported were taken straight to the gas chambers and killed.

That same day, in northern France, Hitler ordered a counter-attack against the base of the Cherbourg peninsula, determined to reach Avranches and cut off the American armies already moving southward out of the bridgehead. But a determined American defence at Mortain blunted the impetus of the attack, which within forty-eight hours was halted more than ten miles short of its objective. In the air, three hundred German fighters were in action on the first day of the counter-attack, against more than a thousand Allied aircraft; by August 8, only 110 were still in action.

For Hitler, August 8 marked the first of what were to be many days of vengeance for the bomb plot, when eight German Army officers were hanged at the Plötzensee Prison in Berlin. The method of their execution was designed to create shock and fear; each of them was placed underneath a meathook on the ceiling and then, with a running noose – not of rope but of wire – around the hook and around his neck, was pulled slowly up, and strangled. Among those executed that day was General Erich Hoepner, who had been dismissed in 1941 for carrying out a withdrawal on the Russian front in defiance of Hitler's orders, and Count Peter Yorck von Wartenburg, a cousin of Count von Stauffenberg and one of the founders of the Kreisau Circle. Also hanged on August 8 was the sixty-three-year-old Field Marshal, Erwin von Witzleben, whom the conspirators had chosen to be Commander-in-Chief of the German Army once Hitler had been overthrown. 'I believe I have gone some way', he wrote to his wife in a final letter, 'to atone for the guilt which is our heritage.'

In Poland, as the Warsaw insurgents continued their fight, five German armoured divisions blocked the Soviet forces within striking distance of the capital, three at the Praga suburb on the eastern side of the Vistula, and two around the Russian troops which had crossed the Vistula thity miles south of the capital, near Gora Kalwaria. That day, the Anglo-American Combined Chiefs of Staff rejected an appeal from Warsaw for the despatch of a Polish Parachute Brigade by air to the city.

Polish tank crews were in action in Normandy on August 8, when, together with Canadians, they launched Operation Totalize, striking along the Caen–Falaise road at the ss armoured forces which had so effectively kept in the beachhead. That day, the commander of the ss division's armoured regiment, ss Major Max Wünsche, who had recently been decorated with the Oak Leaves to his Knight's Cross, was captured, and ss Captain Michael Wittman killed. Wittman, who held the higher decoration of Oak Leaves with Swords, had been credited with the destruction of 138 Allied tanks and 132 anti-tank guns in less than two years.

As the German forces began to withdraw, British Intelligence followed their plans and orders through Ultra, decrypting the German's own most secret messages and then acting to disrupt the moves as they were being carried out. It was still, of course, the Allied soldiers and airmen who had to go into battle in order to reap the fruits of Ultra; on August 9, in an attack on a German anti-aircraft battery near Ste Marguerite-de-Viette, Flight Sergeant Reginald Thursby was shot down behind the German lines. He had become a pilot only after the Normandy landings; it was his sixteenth sortie. In Britain, his fiancée Doreen Young learned only that he was 'reported missing'. Like thousands of others who received similar messages about their children, husbands or friends, she could only live in hope that he might still be alive, either a prisoner-of-war or an evader. But it was not to be. Thursby had been killed.

At six o'clock on the evening of August 9, Hitler personally ordered the renewal of the German attack on Mortain. His signal, sent by Ultra, was decrypted at Bletchley shortly before four in the morning of August 10, giving more than twenty-four hours' warning of the impending attack. The Germans therefore withdrew, not amid secrecy, but carnage, their way back from Mortain becoming known to the Canadians who pursued them as 'Dead Horse Alley'. At the height of the battle, one Canadian officer, Major David Currie, finding that all the officers under him had been either killed or wounded, took personal command of all his tanks and their hundred and fifty crewmen. After three days of combat at St Lambert-sur-Dives, he and his small force of 175 men had destroyed seven German tanks, killed or wounded eight hundred Germans, and taken more than a thousand prisoners. 'When his force was finally relieved,' read Currie's citation for the Victoria Cross, 'and he was satisfied that the handover was complete, he fell asleep on his feet and collapsed.'

To the south and west of the Falaise pocket, the Americans had swept the Germans to the Atlantic coast, and were advancing towards the River Loire. On August 10, in Paris, now less than 140 miles from the nearest Allied armies, a strike by railwaymen paralysed all German troop and supply movements in and out of the capital.

On August 12, American forces occupied Mortain; the German attempt to hold back the Allied advance in Normandy was over. That same day, a French military unit reached Alençon, 112 miles from Paris. That morning, in London, Churchill received the copy of an appeal sent by the Poles in Warsaw to the Allies. It was their tenth day of fighting against the Germans. 'We are conducting a bloody fight,' the message read. 'The town is cut by three routes.' Each route was 'strongly held' by German tanks, and the buildings along them 'burned out'. Two German armoured trains on the city's periphery, and artillery from the Praga suburb on the east bank of the Vistula, 'fire continuously on the town, and are supported by air forces'.

The Polish message noted that only one 'small drop' had come from the Allies. 'On the German–Russian front silence since the 3rd. We are therefore without any material or moral support....' The message continued: 'The soldiers and the population of the capital look hopelessly at the skies, expecting help from the Allies. On the background of smoke they see only German aircraft. They are surprised, feel deeply depressed, and begin to revile.'

Churchill at once sent on this message to Stalin, several of whose operational airfields were within only ten or twelve minutes' flight from Warsaw. 'They implore machine guns and ammunition,' Churchill telegraphed. 'Can you not give them some further help, as the distance from Italy is so very great?'

Determined to help the Polish insurgents, Churchill personally authorized the despatch two nights later of twenty bombers from their base at Foggia in southern Italy, each carrying twelve containers of arms and ammunition. In fact, twenty-eight bombers set out, of which fourteen reached Warsaw. Of those fourteen, three were shot down by German anti-aircraft fire. Of more than thirty-five tons of supplies, less than five tons reached the insurgents; but for them, every ton was a means of continuing the fight for another day.

The German armies, battling in Warsaw, on the Eastern Front, in Italy and in Normandy, had also to fight an increasingly active war behind the lines. The response continued to be brutal; on August 12, in the French mountain village of Sospel, fifteen members of the Maquis, captured in an ss sweep, were tortured and then shot. Throughout France, village memorials and wayside markers record these moments of cruel revenge. But the Resistance was determined to give the Allied forces whatever help it could.

In Normandy, the ebb and flow of battle had given way to a flood; on August 13 American forces reached the River Loire at Nantes. That same day, French parachutists, carrying out Operation Barker, landed at Salornay, to disrupt the German retreat.

As the Germans struggled, in chaos, inside the Falaise pocket, Hitler ordered them to fight on. And so they did, day after day, to the bitter end.

On August 14, the Allies launched Operation Tractable, the drive into Falaise itself, and simultaneously a westward thrust towards Paris. On the previous evening a Canadian officer, losing his way, had driven into the German lines and been killed. On his body the Germans found plans of the Tractable attack. As a result, they were able to stiffen their defences. The Allies also suffered when, by accident, a preliminary bombing raid against the German forward positions fell instead on the Allied lines, killing sixty-five Canadian and Polish troops. But the offensive, once launched, could not be held back. Within four days, Allied soldiers stood on the banks of the River Seine, at Mantes, thirty miles from the centre of Paris. But inside the Falaise pocket the German defenders continued to fight against the remorselessly closing gap.

As this drive towards Paris began, Allied air, sea and land forces launched Operation Dragoon, landing 94,000 men and 11,000 vehicles between Toulon and Cannes on the Mediterranean coast of France in a single day. Within twenty-four hours these troops had pushed nearly twenty miles inland. That day, in Paris, amid the excitement of the news of this fresh landing, the city's police force, hitherto a reluctant arm of German civic control, agreed to put aside its uniforms, keep its arms and join the active resistance on the streets. But the revenge of the occupier was still not ended. That day, five French prisoners, among them de Gaulle's clandestine military representative in Paris, Colonel André Rondenay, were taken by the Gestapo to the village of Domont, twelve miles north of Paris, and shot. Their killers then returned to Paris for an 'executioners' banquet', of champagne.

There was yet another execution that August 15, this one in Berlin, when Count von Helldorf, the former Chief of Police in the German capital, was hanged for his part in the plot against Hitler.

For the Poles still struggling in Warsaw, the American landing in the South of France was another blow. 'In view of the unfeasibility of day operations to

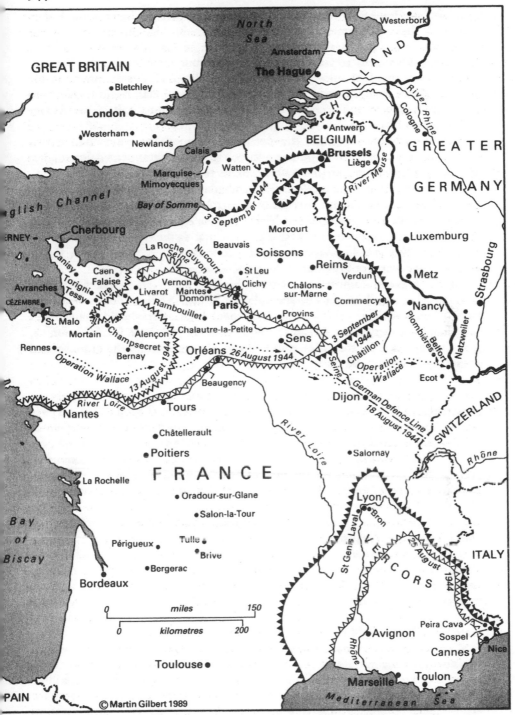

The battle in France, summer and autumn 1944

Warsaw,' the Joint Staff Mission in Washington reported to London on August 15, 'and the commitment of all available xvth Air Force resources to "Dragoon",' the American chiefs of Staff were of the opinion that the 'best solution' with regard to 'acceptance of responsibility for helping the Poles in Warsaw' was that it should be undertaken by Stalin. As far as the efforts by the Western Allies were concerned, the American Chiefs of Staff could recommend only 'the minimum night effort' of the special operations unit of the Anglo-American air force.

Thus Operation Dragoon, the diversion of troops to which had earlier undermined British plans to pursue a more vigorous military campaign against the German armies in Italy, now also took its toll of Warsaw.

In Moscow, the British and American ambassadors had both gone, on August 15, to see the Soviet deputy Foreign Minister, Andrei Vishinsky, to seek Soviet help for the Warsaw uprising. But Vishinsky – as Averell Harriman, the American Ambassador, reported to Washington – 'clung' to the view that the outbreak in Warsaw 'was an ill-advised and not a serious matter, and that the future course of the war would not at all be influenced by it'.

On the night of August 15, a further bomber flight left southern Italy for Warsaw. Ten bombers set off; six failed to return. Among those killed were twenty South African aircrew. One, Lieutenant J. J. C. Groenwald, managed to parachute to safety near Kazimierz Wielka; he stayed there for five months, given false papers by the Poles, and living as a worker under the unsuspecting eyes of the German guards.

On August 16, Hitler reluctantly accepted that Normandy was lost; angrily, he now replaced Field Marshal von Kluge with Field Marshal Model. But the pace of the Allied advance could not be slowed down. On August 17, the town of Falaise was entered by the Canadians, while American forces entered the port of St Malo, in Brittany. The German commander of St Malo, Colonel von Aulock, had given orders for the port to be held to the last man. Anyone who deserted or surrendered, he declared, 'is a common dog!' Hitler, much impressed by von Aulock's determination not to give up St Malo, awarded him the Oak Leaves to his Knight's Cross. But so swift was the battle that the award was actually made on August 18, the day after von Aulock's surrender.

Despite the surrender of St Malo, a young German Lieutenant, Richard Seuss, with 320 men, continued to defend the fortified islet of Cézembre, which lay only four thousand yards offshore. Seuss refused to surrender, despite a leaflet appeal to do so, followed by a heavy American air bombardment in which napalm was used in Europe for the first time. Only after the destruction of his water-distillation plant two weeks later did he raise the white flag.

Surrender and retreat in France did not deter the Germans from their efforts to undermine the morale of France's ally, Britain. At midday on August 17, a flying bomb fell on Lavender Hill, in the London borough of Battersea, killing fourteen people in a passing bus, and fourteen more in the street and the surrounding buildings. This was only one of more than forty flying bombs which did serious damage in London that month. At Morden Hill, in south-east London, a flying bomb, landing almost exactly where another one had fallen eight hours earlier, killed several rescue workers who were still searching for the victims of the earlier one.

On August 17 Hitler ordered the evacuation of southern France. Two top-secret messages to this effect were decrypted by the British at Bletchley, giving the troops already ashore near Toulon a major advantage, as they learned the exact line to which the Germans were to withdraw; it ran from Sens to Dijon to the Swiss frontier.

At Lyon, now itself within the area which Hitler had decided to abandon, the Gestapo and French Milice took 109 prisoners on August 17 from the Montluc prison to Bron airport, on the outskirts of the city. There, the prisoners were shot. In Paris, that day, the German forces began to pull out: 'the great flight of the Fritzes', one Parisian called it. As the Germans left, by train and road, the Gestapo commandeered three railway carriages, on which they deported fifty-one Jews to Auschwitz. One of them, Marcel Bloch-Dassault, a leading French aircraft manufacturer, was then sent to Dachau, and survived the war. Also deported was Armand Kohn, head of the Rothschild hospital, together with his twelve-year-old son Georges-André Kohn, and a twelve-year-old girl, Jacqueline Morgenstern. Both these twelve-year-olds were later sent from Auschwitz to Neuengamme concentration camp near Hamburg, where they were subjected to sadistic medical experiments.

When these deportation carriages reached Morcourt, near St Quentin, fifteen of the fifty-one deportees managed to escape.

It was on the morning of August 17, as the German Army and Gestapo began their flight from Paris, that, on the Eastern Front, two Soviet infantry battalions, commanded by Captain Georgi Gubkin and Captain Pavel Yurgin, reached the border of East Prussia. In front of them were the tiled roofs of a German town, Schirwindt. A small group of men crossed a narrow bridge across the river which marked the border; then, on the far bank, Sergeant Alexander Belov raised the Red Flag. 'Woe to this land of evil-doers!' the Soviet writer Ilya Ehrenburg declared in a newspaper article when the German frontier was reached. 'We say this as we stand on Germany's threshold – woe to Germany!'

# 41

# The bitter-sweet path of liberation

AUTUMN 1944

On 18 August 1944, the Communist-controlled National Council in Poland declared Lublin to be the temporary capital of Poland. In Warsaw, the insurgents fought on with growing desperation, against considerable German reinforcements, and without Soviet aid. That same day Churchill telegraphed to Roosevelt: 'The refusal of the Soviets to allow US aircraft to bring succour to the heroic insurgents in Warsaw, added to their own complete neglect to fly in supplies when only a few score of miles away, constitutes an episode of profound and far reaching gravity. If as is almost certain the German triumph in Warsaw is followed by a wholesale massacre no measure can be put upon the full consequences that will arise'.

Anglo-American aid continued to be flown to Warsaw from southern Italy, but, of a total of 182 aircraft sent, 35 of them failed to return. Stalin, asked repeatedly to allow these aircraft to land at Soviet controlled airstrips to the east of Warsaw, refused. Angrily, Churchill wrote to his wife on August 18 of 'the various telegrams now passing about the Russian refusal either to help or allow the Americans to help the struggling people of Warsaw, who will be massacred and liquidated very quickly if nothing can be done'.

There was no hesitation on the German side as to how to combat their enemies. On August 18 a train pulled out of Nancy railway station with 2,453 French political prisoners, locked into its wagons. They had come from the Gestapo prisons in Paris, and were on their way to Ravensbrück and Buchenwald. Less than three hundred of them were to survive their imprisonment there.

Thirty miles north of Nancy, a train reached Metz from Paris on August 19. In it was the body of Field Marshal von Kluge. He had committed suicide by taking a cyanide pill. In a final letter to Hitler, von Kluge wrote: 'If your new weapons, in which such burning faith is placed, do not bring success, then, my Führer, take the decision to end the war,' and he added: 'The German people have suffered such unspeakable ills, that the time has come to put an end to these horrors.'

On the day of von Kluge's suicide, Canadian, Polish and American troops launched their final attack to close the Falaise pocket.

On August 19, in Paris, the French police force, now loyal to the Resistance, seized the Préfecture de Police. A tricolour flag was raised, and the Marseillaise sung. When a single German armoured vehicle appeared, and opened fire with an automatic weapon, the police returned the fire. The battle for Paris had begun. A remnant of the German occupation forces was trapped by an increasingly active Resistance force, prepared to drive off any attempt by German soldiers to dislodge them. By nightfall, more than six hundred Germans had been taken prisoner. On the following morning, August 20, sixty members of the Resistance entered the Hôtel de Ville. Once inside it, they fired with rifles and pistols at any German vehicle which tried to approach. When two German trucks accidentally collided at Clichy, on the northern outskirts of the capital, the Resistance were able to get away with nine machine guns and twenty sub-machine guns; within forty-eight hours, there were more than seven thousand armed members of the Resistance, awaiting only the arrival of the Allies.

That same day, August 20, a British Special Air Service force, of sixty men and twenty jeeps, set off eastward from Rennes, working its way through the German lines to carry out a series of attacks on German units in a wide swathe behind the lines. Codenamed Operation Wallace, and commanded by Major Roy Farran, a veteran of similar exploits in Italy, it fought its way eastward through the forests of German-occupied France from just north of Orléans to Belfort. 'I was most impressed', Farran later recalled, 'by the bellicose air of the French partisan' – and also by the sense of imminent liberation. During one skirmish, just east of Orléans, Farran noted, 'a pretty girl with long black hair and wearing a bright red frock put her head out of a top window to give me the "v" sign. Her smile ridiculed the bullets.'

On several occasions, the men of Operation Wallace joined forces with the local French Resistance, to do battle with the retreating Germans. At Châtillon-sur-Seine one of Farran's men, Parachutist Holland, was killed during a joint attack on the Germans in the town; today, a monument there recalls his sacrifice. Two more of Farran's men were killed at nearby Villaines.

On August 20, in Lyon, 100 French men and women being held by the Gestapo were taken from prison to a disused fort of St Genis Laval, and shot. The bodies were then doused in petrol and set on fire. 'While the fire was raging', a French member of the Milice, Max Payot, later recalled, 'we saw a victim who had somehow survived. She came to a window on the south side and begged her executioners for pity. They answered her prayers by a rapid burst of gunfire. Riddled with bullets and affected by the intense heat, her face contorted into a fixed mask, like a vision of horror. The temperature was increasing and her face melted like wax until one could see her bones. At that moment she gave a nervous shudder and began to turn her decomposing head – what was left of it – from left to right, as if to condemn her executioners. In a final shudder, she pulled herself completely straight, and fell backwards'.

In Paris, on August 20, the citizens awaited the arrival of the Western Allies. In the Falaise pocket, individual German units still fought on, in a series of suicidal attacks against units of the Polish forces. Inside Warsaw, the citizens fought on with increasing helplessness against overwhelming German force and brutality. On the Eastern Front, Soviet forces launched their offensive against Roumania along a three-hundred-mile front. At the end of its first day, five German divisions had been shattered, and three thousand German soldiers taken prisoner. The Roumanian forces in the line, commanded by General Abramescu, sought permission to withdraw to a more defensible line, but the Roumanian dictator, Marshal Antonescu, insisted that they remain in action. As a result, the Roumanian forces were crushed. After six days of continual advancing, the Red Army was poised to enter Focsani.

In what was left of the Falaise pocket, August 21 saw the last German effort to break out of the trap. In a final attack, on the Polish forces holding the trap closed, more than three hundred Poles were killed, but the position held, and a thousand Germans were taken prisoner. In all, during the Falaise battles, more than fifty thousand German soldiers had been taken prisoner, and ten thousand killed. Visiting the battleground two days after the last engagements had been fought, General Eisenhower later recalled: 'Roads, highways and fields were so chocked up with destroyed equipment and with dead men and animals, that passage through the area was extremely difficult.' It was, he added, 'literally possible to walk for hundreds of yards at a time, stepping on nothing but dead and decaying flesh'.

On August 21, the Foreign Ministers of the Allied powers met at Dumbarton Oaks, a suburb of Washington, to establish a post-war system of collective security, designed to prevent future wars. Known as the United Nations Organization, its inner body was to be a Security Council, whose five member states – Britain, the Soviet Union, the United States, France and China – would each have the right of veto on any proposed measure to which they were opposed.

At that moment, however, it was not the possibility of future dissension among the Allies, but their impending victories, which were influencing the daily course of events. On August 22, as Soviet forces burst across the Roumanian frontier, capturing Jassy, King Michael of Roumania summoned Marshal Antonescu to the royal palace in Bucharest and ordered him to come to an immediate armistice with the Allies.

Antonescu refused, and was arrested. Also arrested was the German Ambassador, and the chief German military liaison officer in Bucharest. The King then ordered his troops to cease firing on the Russians. Hitler, caught by surprise, and unable to put into effect a recently prepared plan to occupy Roumania in the event of its defection, ordered his air units at Ploesti to bomb Bucharest. But the onward march of the Soviet forces could not be halted, and within a week more than 105,000 German soldiers had been killed, and an equal number taken prisoner.

As Roumania signed its armistice with Russia, the Finnish Government, which in the autumn of 1941 had helped the Germans to draw the ring of siege around Leningrad, announced that it too was ready to make peace with the Allies. Germany had lost its Axis partners at both the southern and northern

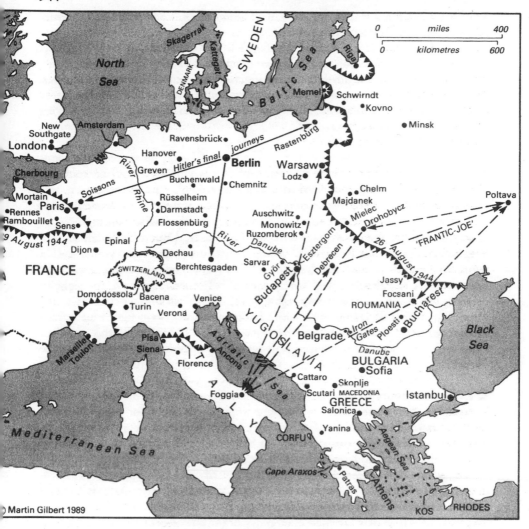

Europe at war, September 1944

extremities of the Eastern Front. In the Balkans, Greek and Yugoslav partisans intensified their attacks on German lines of communication, as the German forces in Greece and southern Yugoslavia, vulnerable to a Soviet thrust through Roumania, struggled to pull back from Athens, Salonica and Skoplje, to a defensive line between Scutari on the Adriatic coast and the Iron Gates on the Danube.

In Italy, too, the partisan movement now felt strong enough to wrest whole valleys from German and Italian Fascist control; after a three day struggle, the Fascist stronghold in the mountain village of Bacena fell to the partisans on

575

August 23. Within a week, all four valleys between Domodossola and the Swiss frontier were under partisan control.

In London, August 23 saw another flying-bomb incident, at New Southgate, when a single bomb fell on a factory manufacturing Bailey bridges, teleprinters, tank and fighter radios, air–sea rescue launches and aircraft blind-landing gear. 'Lie down!' one of the factory look-outs, Reg Smith, had called over the factory loudspeakers, 'For God's sake, lie down'. But it was too late; 211 factory workers were killed.

Churchill was in Italy on August 23, when, near Siena, he visited the troops who, despite the considerable diversion of forces and weaponry to southern France, were planning a new offensive in three days' time. That day, it was agreed by the War Cabinet in London that Jewish soldiers in the Allied armies, and above all in Palestine, could serve in a specifically Jewish fighting unit, to be known as the Jewish Brigade Group. This force, Churchill explained in a telegram that day to Roosevelt, would constitute 'what you would call a regimental combat team', and he added: 'This will give great satisfaction to the Jews when it is published and surely they of all other races have the right to strike at the Germans as a recognisable body. They wish to have their own flag which is the Star of David on a white background with two light blue bars. I cannot see why this should not be done. Indeed I think that the flying of this flag at the head of a combat unit would be a message to go all over the world'.

The German ability to continue the war now depended, not on the tenacity of its soldiers, but on the ability to continue to provide fuel oil for their tanks and vehicles, as well as the oil needed for every other aspect of war-making: aircraft fuel, anti-aircraft gun lubrication, and the fuel oils needed to maintain the production of arms and ammunition. Since June 8, the bombing of German oil installations had been an Anglo-American priority. At the end of July, British Intelligence learned that German fighter production was recovering; this was one more reason to intensify the oil campaign. Another reason was the knowledge reaching the Allies of a German emergency organisation which had been set up specifically to repair oil installations. Beginning on August 7, an intensified Allied oil offensive had been launched, during which, by the end of the month, sixty bombing raids had taken place, against oil targets throughout Germany and south-eastern Europe. Half of these raids were against oil storage plants, a quarter against synthetic oil plants, and a quarter against synthetic oil refineries.

That this strategy was the correct one was made clear on August 12, when British Intelligence decrypted a German Air Force Enigma message, sent two days earlier from German Air Force headquarters, ordering a general curtailment of operational activity because of further damage to German fuel production by air attacks. Reconnaissance was to be flown only when it was essential. Four-engined aircraft were to fly only after application to headquarters. Other aircraft were only to fly when action could be decisive, or when the chances of success were good. This first curtailment of German operational, as opposed to non-

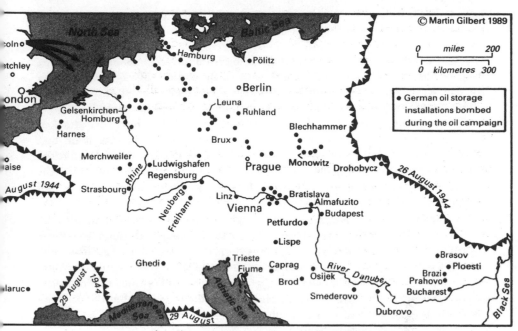

The oil campaign, August 1944: oil targets

essential flying, was followed a few days later, on August 16, by what had been von Kluge's last appeal to German Army headquarters, asking permission to withdraw from Falaise in view of tank deficiencies and shortage of fuel, which was in his words 'the decisive factor'. This dramatic admission, sent by top-secret Ultra, was, as a result of its high secrecy, made known almost at once to the vigilant listeners at Bletchley.

On August 20, four days after von Kluge's appeal, American bombers struck at the synthetic oil plant at Monowitz. During the raid, several hundred British prisoners-of-war, as well as tens of thousands of Jewish slave labourers, watched as the bombs fell on the oil installations. During the raid, thirty-eight of the British prisoners-of-war were killed.

In a further American bombing raid on August 22, the synthetic oil plant at Blechhammer was the target; three days later, it was the synthetic oil plant at Pölitz. That same week, on August 27, British bombers carried out a daylight raid on the synthetic oil plant at Homberg, the first ever raid in which British bombers had penetrated as far as the Rhine by day. That same day, British Intelligence decrypted a German Air Force Enigma message, in which the German Air Force High Command had warned the principal air fleet on the Western Front that its fighting activities must be even further curtailed, so as to release aircraft fuel for the training of 120 air-crews a month for the Western Front. The alternative, warned the High Command, was that the existing extremely low allocation of fuel oil for training for the Western Front would

577

have to be accepted, in which case only one-third of the replacement needs of the German Air Force in the West could be met.

On August 23, a French armoured division began its advance on Paris, reaching Rambouillet, thirty miles to the south west of the capital, by nightfall. During the day, Resistance forces, now established as the French Forces of the Interior under General Koenig, freed all French civilian captives in the capital.

The Germans, in one last effort to show their ability to hit back, attacked Resistance forces which had taken over the Grand Palais, and set it on fire. Elsewhere in the centre of the city, heavily armed German patrols attacked Resistance groups, killing many, and forcing others to withdraw from the streets. But this demonstration of strength came too late to influence the fate of the capital.

On the morning of August 24, a French armoured force commanded by Colonel Pierre Billotte entered the city from the south, through the Porte d'Orléans. Tens of thousands of Parisians came out to welcome their liberators with flags, food, flowers, wine and kisses. Yet still there were German strong-points and barricades which were strongly defended; soldiers died on both sides of the barricades. Civilians died too, caught up in the cross-fire. But the delirium of liberation quickly swept aside such obstacles as remained, while the bells of Paris rang out their victory peals.

As the Germans retreated on all the war fronts, on August 24, in the slave-labour camp at Mielec, in southern Poland, the SS murdered three thousand Jewish slave labourers that day, before evacuating the camp. Three weeks earlier, two thousand Jews had been murdered in the labour camp at Ostrowiec. Also on August 24, the crew of an American bomber, shot down over Greven, as they returned from an air raid on Hanover, were taken south by train, for interrogation. On reaching the town of Rüsselheim, where the railway line had been blocked by a British bombing raid a few hours earlier, and where the streets were full of hundreds of people evacuating that part of town, they were set upon by an irate mob, beaten with clubs, rocks, bricks and stones. Six of the Americans were killed. Two survived.

The Allied bombing of Germany led to several such incidents. On August 24, in a raid on the Gustloff armament factory outside Buchenwald, bombs fell both on the factory and on the SS barracks, killing four hundred prisoners and eighty SS men. As a retaliation, the camp Commandant, SS Major Pfister, ordered the execution two weeks later of sixteen British and French officers, all of them Special Operations Executive agents who had been captured while on missions in France. All sixteen were hanged. Eleven days after the first executions, another twelve were hanged.

On August 25, Allied reconnaissance aircraft again flew over Auschwitz from their base in southern Italy. Once more their task was to photograph the Monowitz synthethic-oil plant so necessary now to the German ability to carry on the war. Once more, the camera also took pictures of Auschwitz Main Camp, of Birkenau, of the railway sidings, the gas chambers and the crematoria. One of the photographs of August 25 actually shows (in a 1960 enlargement) Jews on

The Eastern Front, September–December 1944

the way from a train to a gas chamber and crematorium, the gate of which is seen open to receive them.

No attempt was made to identify any of the locations or activities at Birkenau as they appeared in the photograph, even though a plan of the camp, and a full description of what went on there, had reached the British Foreign Office in London on August 22, sent by a Zionist official, Joseph Linton, who had received it from Jerusalem. It had been compiled there from the reports of the four escapees.

Not the mass-murder site at Birkenau, but the oil installations at Monowitz, were again the intended subject of the photographs, as plans for the continuing bombing of Monowitz were made, in an attempt totally to destroy Germany's oil-producing capacity. The first bombing raid on the synthetic-oil plant had been made on August 20.

The sole purpose of the photographic reconnaissance over Auschwitz on August 25 was to look at the damage done during the raid of August 20, and to see what further repairs were being made. The result was disappointing. 'The damage received', the report concluded, 'is not sufficient to interfere seriously with synthetic fuel production, and should not greatly delay completion of this part of the plant.'

Shortly after seven o'clock on the morning of August 25, General Jacques Philippe Leclerc, commander of the French 2nd Armoured Division, entered Paris. There was one more day of confusion: snipers firing, small groups of Germans resisting, fifty German soldiers killed trying to defend the French Foreign Office building on the Quai d'Orsay, and dozens of captured Germans being attacked after they had surrendered, including a column of prisoners who were machine gunned as they were being marched around the Arc de Triomphe.

At two thirty in the afternoon the German Commander of Paris, General von Choltitz, surrendered. An hour and a half later, General de Gaulle reached the city, making his way through a vast crowd to the Hôtel de Ville. It was a day of triumph, but at a cost; more than five hundred Resistance fighters had been killed during the liberation of the city, as well as 127 civilians. In the elation of freedom restored, many of those who had collaborated with the Germans were killed, without trial or debate.

South of Paris, as the capital rejoiced, Resistance fighters in Lyon were still struggling to liberate their city. Forty miles to the north-west of Paris, at Vernon, British troops crossed the Seine. In southern France, American troops entered Avignon. Eight hundred miles to the east, in German-controlled Slovakia, Soviet partisans commanded by Captain Velichko, seized the town of Turciansky Sv Martin, as part of a general Slovak uprising against German rule; two days later the German General commanding the region was seized, and shot. In Estonia, Soviet forces captured Tartu, breaching the German fortified line. That same day, Roumania declared war on Germany. The Axis was in disarray. But in Warsaw, where the insurgents were still fighting after three weeks and four days, Stalin still refused to allow British or American aircraft to use Soviet airstrips in an effort to increase the dwindling Allied aid. Almost in despair,

Churchill telegraphed to Stalin on August 25: 'We do not try to form an opinion about the persons who instigated this rising which was certainly called for repeatedly by Radio Moscow. Our sympathies are however for the "almost unarmed people" whose special faith has led them to attack German guns, tanks and aircraft. We cannot think that Hitler's cruelties will end with their resistance. On the contrary it seems probable that that is the time when they will begin with full ferocity. The massacre in Warsaw will undoubtedly be a very great annoyance to us when we all meet at the end of the war. Unless you directly forbid it therefore we propose to send the planes'.

If Stalin failed to reply to this appeal, Churchill told Roosevelt, 'I feel we ought to go, and see what happens.' British and American aircraft would make the journey without Stalin's approval. 'I cannot conceive', Churchill added, 'that he would maltreat or detain them'.

Roosevelt rejected Churchill's suggestion. One reason, he told Churchill on August 26, was Stalin's 'definite refusal' to allow Soviet airfields to be used by Allied planes seeking to drop supplies in Warsaw. The other reason was the 'current American conversations' with the Soviet Union about the future use of Soviet airbases, in Siberia, for use by American bombers on their way to bomb Japan. 'I do not consider it advantageous to the long range general war prospect', Roosevelt explained, 'for me to join with you in the proposed message to Uncle J.'

Thus, over aid to Warsaw, the Anglo-American unity was broken, leaving Britain alone to take, if she so wished, a step that would greatly anger the Soviet Union.

On August 28 it was learned in London and Washington that, as the Red Army advanced through Poland, leaders of the underground Polish Home Army were being arrested. On the following day, the British and American Governments issued a public declaration, that the Polish Home Army was a 'responsible belligerent force'. The future of Poland had become the principal cause of contention among the Allies.

On August 26, General de Gaulle walked in triumph down the Champs Élysées. That same day, crossing the Seine over the Vernon bridgehead, Canadian and British troops advanced swiftly towards Calais and Brussels. In Italy, the British Eighth Army attacked the German defences of the Gothic Line, but, despite the capture of Pisa, a German counter-attack enabled the line to be restored, and it was to remain intact for the rest of the year.

In Berlin, August 26 saw another execution in the Plötzensee Prison; the hanging of Adam von Trott zu Solz, a German Foreign Office official who had held secret talks with British and American diplomats in Switzerland at the beginning of the year, and who, while a strong German patriot, was also an anti-Nazi; he was descended, on his mother's side, from John Jay, the first Chief Justice of the United States.

On August 27 there was a further execution, not of German conspirators but of French civilians, seized by German troops as they retreated through the village of Chalautre-la-Petite, fifty-three miles south-east of Paris. That day, American troops had entered the nearby town of Provins, and an advance party had, briefly, entered Chalautre and then withdrawn, taking two German soldiers prisoner. The soldiers escaped, and the Germans returned to Chalautre in search of 'partisans'. No one was found; the Americans had moved elsewhere. But the Germans took twenty-two villagers and led them out of the village; some succeeded in breaking away, but thirteen were shot. Four days later, after the Americans had liberated the village, six German prisoners, 'donated' by the Americans who had captured them, were shot in revenge, not by the villagers, but by people from the neighbourhood.

At his 'Wolf's Lair' headquarters in East Prussia, on August 27, Hitler personally conferred the Oak Leaves to the Knight's Cross on the Flemish fascist leader and Commander of the Walloon SS Assault brigade, Léon Degrelle. This was a rare award and a rare honour for a foreign volunteer. Only 632 of Degrelle's two thousand volunteer troops survived the war.

On the day after Degrelle was honoured by Hitler, the former German Communist leader, Ernst Thaelmann, who in 1932 had contested with Hitler for the Presidency, was shot at Buchenwald, after more than ten years in captivity. He was fifty-eight years old. Also killed in Buchenwald that day, by Allied bombs dropped accidentally on the camp, were Princess Mafalda, the daughter of the King of Italy, and Marcel Michelin, the tyre manufacturer.

At Auschwitz, while Jews continued to be murdered inside the camp, other Jews were being sent to slave labour outside it. Simultaneously with the arrival of trains bringing Jews from the Lodz ghetto, Rhodes, Kos and Slovakia, most of whom were gassed on their arrival at Auschwitz, other trains continued to take Jews away from the barracks at Auschwitz to factories and labour camps inside Germany. On August 29, while seventy-two sick Jewish adults and youths and several pregnant women from a labour camp at Leipzig were brought to Auschwitz and gassed, 807 Jews were sent from Auschwitz to the concentration camp at Sachsenhausen, just north of Berlin, for work in a dozen nearby factories. On August 30, a further five hundred Hungarian Jews were sent by train from Auschwitz to Buchenwald, to be sent on to a Junkers aircraft factory at Markkleeberg. Other Jews were kept in Buchenwald, from where, as one young Jew from the Lodz ghetto, Michael Etkind, later recalled, 'no one escaped. No one was missing – except the dead.'

On August 28, the British defences in southern England finally got the better of the flying bomb. That day, ninety-seven bombs were sent across the Channel. Thirteen were destroyed by British fighters over the water. Sixty-five were then shot down by anti-aircraft guns over land. Another ten were shot down by fighters over land. Nine reached the outskirts of London, where two collided with barrage balloons and three came to earth before reaching the capital. Only four fell on London.

That day, in southern France, Allied forces entered Toulon and Marseille, taking 47,000 German prisoners. In the north, on the following day, Reims and Châlons-sur-Marne fell to the Americans, who were now less than 110 miles from Germany's western border. Also on August 29, British bombers flew across

The Slovak uprising, August–October 1944

the whole of northern Germany, to the East Prussian city of Königsberg. For the loss of four of the 175 attackers, 134,000 citizens of Königsberg were made homeless. The city was a mere fifty-five miles from Hitler's headquarters at Rastenburg. That same day, above Belgium, an American pilot, Major J. Myers, forced down a German jet fighter: it was a new weapon, but one which was arriving too late to alter the course of the war.

The only initiative which the Germans now seemed able to take was in the war behind the lines. On August 29, German reinforcements entered Slovakia, where they were in action against Slovak partisans at Zilina, Cadca, Povazska Bystrica and Trencin. The partisans reacted by declaring a Czechoslovak Republic and taking virtual control of the city of Banska Bystrica, as well as much of the area between Banska Bystrica and Brezno, Zvolen and Ruzomberok.

On August 30, Soviet forces occupied the Roumanian city of Ploesti, Germany's only remaining source of crude oil. That day, in Berlin, General Kurt von Stuelpnagel, the former Military Governor of Paris, who, after the July Plot, had tried to commit suicide but had succeeded only in blinding himself, was led by the hand to the gallows at Plötzensee Prison, and hanged.

Broadcasting from Germany on August 30, William Joyce, who was about to be awarded the Cross of War Merit, First Class, blamed the conspirators for having kept essential troops away from the front; these conspirators, he said, 'have paid the just penalty'. Germany was now in a position, 'not only to defend itself, but, with the aid of time, to win this war'. The chief purpose of German strategy 'at the moment', said Joyce, was to gain time.

Time was not to be allowed to Germany by the ever advancing Allies: on August 31, in France, American troops crossed the Meuse at Commercy, less than sixty miles from Germany; in Italy, Canadian and British troops penetrated the Gothic Line, while American troops crossed the River Arno; in the Balkans, Bucharest fell to the Red Army. In the Pacific, August 31 saw the American capture of Numfoor Island, off the northern coast of New Guinea; during the battle, 1,730 Japanese were killed, for the loss of sixty-three American lives.

In the march to victory, success and tragedy went side by side; on August 31, as American forces in southern France drew near to the mountain village of Peira Cava, inland from Nice, twelve young men, most of them teenagers, were murdered by the ss. A memorial records their fate.

On September 1, the Royal Air Force and Tito's partisans launched Operation Ratweek, a seven-day joint attack on German road and rail routes through Yugoslavia, aimed at preventing the evacuation of German troops from Greece and the Balkans. Several railway bridges on the evacuation route were totally destroyed, as were many kilometres of track. At the same time, an unexpectedly rapid advance by the Red Army to the Danube at Turnu Severin made it certain that, in conjunction with the success of Operation Ratweek, the Germans would be unable to withdraw any substantial number of troops from the Balkans to assist their troops elsewhere, either in Italy or in Central Europe.

As Ratweek disrupted all German road and rail movement northward through Yugoslavia, Greek guerrillas launched Operation Noah's Ark, to harass 315,000 German troops who were trying to get back to Yugoslavia, particularly those on the roads into and out of Yanina. Those Germans who sought a more westerly line of retreat through Albania were no more fortunate; Albanian partisans were active along all the mountain routes leading to Scutari and Cattaro. As many as 30,000 German troops were left on the Greek islands, unable to be evacuated as Allied air and sea patrols now dominated the waters of the Aegean.

On September 2, in the Pacific, American aircraft based on the light carrier *San Jacinto*, set off on a bombing mission against a Japanese radio station on Chichijima. One of the pilots, the twenty-year-old George Bush, was on his fifty-eighth mission. When six hundred miles from Japan, his plane was shot down, and he ditched into the sea. Forty-four years later he was elected President of the United States.

British forces crossed the border into Belgium on September 2. In Warsaw, the insurgents, after a month of fighting, were forced to abandon their positions in the Old Town, and descend into the sewers. In the village of Majorat, northeast of Warsaw, the Germans murdered more than five hundred villagers that day, including women, children and old people.

From Holland, on September 3, a thousand Jews were deported to Auschwitz, and a further 2,087 the following day. British forces, now less than two hundred miles away from the Dutch deportation camp of Westerbork, entered Brussels on September 3, the fifth anniversary of Britain's declaration of war on Germany. On the following day, Antwerp was liberated. That same week, as a result of a suggestion first put forward by Churchill's son Randolph, the evacuation began, by air, of 650 German, Austrian and Czech Jews from the partisan-held areas of Yugoslavia, to Allied-occupied Italy. Also in Italy, in the German-held port of Fiume, the Gestapo arrested a senior Italian police officer, Giovanni Palatucci, who had helped more than five hundred Jewish refugees who had reached Italy from Croatia, giving them 'Aryan' papers and sending them to safety in southern Italy. Palatucci was sent to Dachau, where he died.

On September 4, ninety Red Army officers were executed at Dachau, including the fifty-year-old Vassily Borisienko and the twenty-year-old Vassily Gajduk. September 4 also saw another execution at Plötzensee Prison in Berlin, when General Erich Fritz Fellgiebel was hanged. His task during the July Plot had been to close down the signal circuits at Rastenburg, where, as Chief of Communications for the Armed Forces, he was present at Hitler's headquarters.

Hitler now appointed Field Marshal von Rundstedt to command the retreating German forces in the West. It was he who, in May 1940, had led the main thrust of the German armies into France. Hitler had dismissed him from his command on 2 July 1944, for failing to stop the Allied invasion of Normandy; two months later, he was again in command. But von Rundstedt saw at once how little could be done to halt the Allied armies. Watching a specially created Hitler Youth Division retreating over the Meuse, near the Belgian town of Yvoir, on September 4, he commented: 'It is a pity that this faithful youth is sacrificed in a hopeless situation.'

Yet Hitler did not intend to give up France without a considerable fight. In a directive on September 3, which was issued to his Army commanders on the following day, he ordered Boulogne, Dunkirk and Calais to be held. In addition, by holding Walcheren Island and Breskens, at the mouth of the Scheldt, the port of Antwerp, although in Allied hands, could be made unusable for the landing of troops or supplies. 'It must be ensured', Hitler said, 'that the Allies cannot use the harbour for a long time.' The Allies were thus forced to rely on long lines of communication, stretching back to their original Normandy beach-head.

Hitler's determination to hold on to the Scheldt was known to the Allies, through Ultra, within forty-eight hours, making clear that there was to be no speedy German retreat from Holland. But so swift had the Allied advance been so far, since the breakout from Falaise less than two weeks earlier, that the British Joint Intelligence Committee predicted, on September 5, that German resistance might end altogether by December 1, if not earlier. Churchill was sceptical of this prediction. 'It is at least as likely', he commented, 'that Hitler will be fighting on 1st January as that he will collapse before then.'

Even though the Polish insurgents had been forced to abandon the Old City, Churchill still hoped to be able to drop more air supplies to those Warsaw suburbs in which the insurgents were still holding out: Zoliborz, Solec and

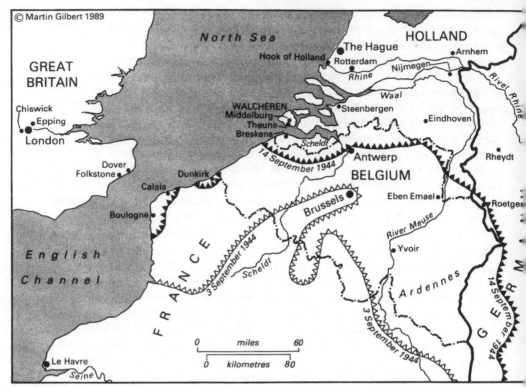

The battle for north-west Europe, September 1944

Czerniakow. To this end he had sent two telegrams on September 4, one to Roosevelt and one to Stalin. The 'only way' to bring material help to the Poles, he wrote in his telegram to Roosevelt, was for American aircraft to drop supplies, 'using Russian airfields for the purpose', and he went on to urge the President to 'authorize your air forces to carry out this operation, landing if necessary on Russian airfields without their consent'. Churchill's second telegram, sent to Stalin 'in the name of the War Cabinet', stated that the Soviet Government's action in preventing help from being sent to the Poles 'seems to us at variance with the spirit of Allied co-operation to which you and we attach so much importance both for the present and for the future'.

Roosevelt's reply was a negative one. 'I am informed by my Office of Military Intelligence', he wrote, 'that the fighting Poles have departed from Warsaw and that the Germans are now in full control.' Roosevelt added: 'The problem of relief for the Poles in Warsaw has therefore unfortunately been solved by delay and by German action, and there now appears to be nothing we can do to assist them.'

On September 5, it was announced on Brussels radio, amid the euphoria of liberation, that Germany had surrendered. The news immediately spread through Britain. 'People left their surburban homes', the *Daily Herald* reported, 'and came to town to join the celebrations. There were taxis full of singing soldiers.'

Not surrender, however, but yet another effort at intensifying the war, was Germany's intention on September 5, when Heinkel bombers flew across the North Sea with the first of 1,200 flying bombs which they were to launch from the air. In four months, sixty-six bomber-borne flying bombs were to fall on London, but at the cost of twenty German bombers shot down, and a further twenty crashing into the North Sea as they flew to their missile-launch positions at low altitude, to avoid being detected by British coastal radar. September 5 also saw two British initiatives. The first was the intensive bombing of German dock installations and military strongpoints at Le Havre, during which the bombs started a firestorm in which 2,500 French civilians died. The second initiative was Operation Brutus, dropping the Belgian Independent Parachute Company of the Special Air Service behind the German lines, near Yvoir, to help the local Belgian Resistance.

Italian resistance was also being helped by British special forces, and had gained in both momentum and scale. On September 6, the Japanese Embassy to Mussolini's Italy reported to Tokyo, from Venice, that although the Germans had recently achieved considerable success in their large scale punitive sweeps against Italian partisans, guerrilla activity was still increasing, especially around Turin and along the Franco-Italian frontier. This information, read by British Intelligence through Ultra, gave satisfaction to those who were in charge of the British units fighting behind German lines in Italy.

At Buchenwald, on September 6, fifteen Englishmen and Frenchmen who had been caught earlier in France helping the French Resistance were put to death. Three days later, sixteen more were summoned from the barracks, and killed. Although every day now brought liberation to several towns and villages, the execution and death of captives continued to the end.

On the afternoon of September 6, Soviet forces, crossing the Danube opposite the Yugoslav town of Kladovo, entered the first Yugoslav village in their path. For Tito and his partisans, now numbering tens of thousands, the time had come to liberate their own land, and to fight side by side with Soviet troops against German military strongpoints. Hitler, seeing clearly that the time could not be long distant before one or other of the Allies was on German soil, ordered an editorial in the Nazi Party newspaper, *Völkischer Beobachter*, which declared, on September 7: 'Not a German stalk of wheat is to feed the enemy, not a German mouth to give him information, not a German hand to give him help. He is to find every footbridge destroyed, every road blocked — nothing but death, annihilation and hatred will meet him.'

Hitler's adherents had no doubt as to the need to fight on to the end, and to terrorize those who stood in their path. On September 7, German troops searched a farm near the Dutch town of Middelburg, where four British evaders had been in hiding for more than four months. Three of the evaders escaped. The Germans then took four Belgians who were living on the farm, and a fifth from a neighbouring farm, drove them to the nearby sand dunes, forced them to dig their own graves in the sand, tied them to the stake, and shot them. One of those shot was a teenage boy, Yvon Colvenaer. When offered his life if he would talk, he replied that he did not want to be a traitor; before he was shot, he cried out: 'Long live Belgium!'

On September 7, off the Philippine island of Mindanao, an American submarine sank a large Japanese freighter, the *Shinyo Maru*. Unknown to those in the submarine, there were 675 Americans on board, prisoners-of-war since the fall of the Philippines in 1942, and now being evacuated to Japan. Only eighty-five survived the sinking; swimming to the shore, they were found and sheltered by Filipino guerrillas.

# 42

# Into Germany; towards the Philippines

SEPTEMBER 1944

On 7 September 1944 the British Government announced that the flying bomb danger was over. Seven days had passed since the last missile had been sent across the English Channel. On the morning of September 8, the British newspaper headlines proclaimed the end of the assault. That very evening, however, the first two V2 rocket bombs reached Britain; both fell on the outskirts of London, one near Epping, the other in Chiswick, killing three people. Both V2s came from the area around the Hook of Holland, which lay within two hundred miles of London, and less than sixty miles from the Allied front line. So as not to give the Germans cause for comfort, or improved aim, news of the rockets was kept secret for almost a month, until details were revealed in the *New York Times*.

As London braced itself for the onslaught of a new weapon, the Belgian Government-in-exile returned from London to Brussels. That same day, the Russians completed their occupation of Bulgaria, the Government which was formed in Sofia on September 9 being pledged to a total break with Germany and friendship with the Soviet Union. Later that day, all 'pro-German members' of the previous Government were arrested.

In Berlin, there were several more executions on September 8, in the continuing aftermath of the July Plot. Among those hanged that day was a woman, Elizabeth von Thadden, at whose home the anti-Nazi tea party discussion of 10 September 1943 had taken place. Also hanged that day was the diplomat Ulrich von Hassell, the Army officer Captain Count Ulrich von Schwerin-Schwanenfeld, and the lawyer Joseph Wirmer.

Revenge was also being taken on those who had fought for the Allies behind German lines. On September 9 a group of thirty-nine Dutchmen, as well as one American and seven Englishmen, all of whom had been active in the anti-Nazi underground, or in sabotage activities behind the lines, were brought to the concentration camp at Mauthausen, in Austria. After spending the night inside the bunker, they were driven, barefoot and in their underclothes, to the quarry, where, the historian of Mauthausen has written, the 186 steps were lined on both sides by SS men and guards 'swinging their cudgels and anticipating a spectacle'. The forty-seven prisoners were 'loaded with stone slabs of up to sixty pounds in weight, and then forced to run up the steps. The run was repeated again and again, and the blows fell faster and faster as the exhausted prisoners stumbled on the uneven steps'. One of the prisoners was a British Jew, Marcus Bloom, who had operated a clandestine radio in German-occupied France. He was shot in the head at point-blank range. Then the others were killed.

On September 9, in northern Italy, two hundred miles behind Allied lines, the German army and the Italian Fascist forces signed an agreement with the Italian partisans, whereby all German and Fascist forces were to be pulled out, at once, from Domodossola and the valleys around it.

On September 10, at the village of Roetgen, the first Allied soldier crossed into Germany; he was an American, Charles D. Hiller, and with him in his jeep was a Belgian passenger, Henri Souvée. It was an historic moment. It was also a moment at which the western Allies were closer to Berlin than the closest Soviet troops. The western Allies were also bombing deep into Germany. An arms factory at Chemnitz was hit by 132 American aircraft during a daylight raid on September 11. That night, more than two hundred British bombers struck at Darmstadt. In the resulting firestorm, an estimated 12,300 people died, about a fifth of them children. Only twelve British bombers were lost.

By midnight on September 10, American troops were in control of the Fort of Eben-Emael, which in May 1940 had been the most formidable obstacle in Belgium's front-line defence against German attack. Then it had been defended tenaciously; now it surrendered without a fight. On September 12, the German garrison in Le Havre surrendered. That day, Roumania signed an armistice with the Soviet Union, Great Britain and the United States; she would take part in the war against Germany and Hungary, would pay 300 million dollars' worth of goods and raw materials in reparations to the Soviet Union, and would go back to the Roumanian–Soviet frontier of June 1940. The Roumanians thus paid the price of defeat; for the Soviet Union, the price of victory over Roumania had been 46,783 men killed.

The price of clandestine work was also death; on September 12, in Dachau, the Germans shot four British women agents, Noor Inayat Khan, Yvonne Beekman, Elaine Plewman and Madeleine Damerment.

On September 9, Stalin at last agreed both to send air support to the Warsaw insurgents and to allow the western Allies to do so, using Soviet airstrips. On the night of September 13, the first Soviet air drops, of food, were made over Warsaw. The pilot of the first Soviet plane to drop food was a Pole, Alexander Danielak.

Less than 170 miles south-west of Warsaw, that same September 13, American bombers attacked synthetic oil plants at both Blechhammer and Monowitz. At Monowitz they met intense and accurate anti-aircraft fire, but hit their target, which lay within five miles of the still active gas chambers of Auschwitz–Birkenau.

They also, by mistake, dropped a number of bombs on Auschwitz Main

Camp, accidentally hitting and destroying the ss barracks there, and killing fifteen ss men. A further twenty-eight ss men were badly injured. The clothing workshop was also hit and destroyed, and forty camp inmates working there, including twenty-three Jews, were killed. During the raid, a further sixty-five inmates were severely injured.

During this same bombing attack of September 13, a cluster of bombs was dropped in error on Birkenau. One of the bombs damaged the railway enbankment leading into the camp, and the sidings leading to the crematoria. A second bomb hit a bomb shelter located between the crematoria sidings, killing thirty Polish civilian workers.

For the Jews themselves, trapped as slave labourers at Monowitz, the impact of the raid had been considerable. Among those who witnessed it was Shalom Lindenbaum, who had been sent from Birkenau to Monowitz only a few days before. As the American bombers appeared in the sky, he later wrote: 'We ceased to work, and the German soldiers and civilians ran to the shelters. Most of us didn't. So probably, we expressed our superiority feeling, and a kind of revenge. We had nothing to lose, only expected to enjoy the destruction of the big factory which we were building for the IG Farben Industrie. It was naturally so. This happy feeling didn't change after the Americans indeed, began to bomb, and obviously we had casualties too – wounded and dead. How beautiful was it to see squadron after squadron burst from the sky, drop bombs, destroy the buildings, and kill also members of the Herrenvolk'.

Lindenbaum added, of the raid of September 13 and those which soon followed it: 'Those bombardments elevated our morale and, paradoxically, awakened probably some hopes of surviving, of escaping from this hell. In our wild imagination we also saw a co-ordination between the Allies and the indeed small underground movement in the camp, with which I was in touch. We imagined a co-ordinated destruction and escape; destruction from above by the bombers, and from our own hands while escaping, even if we have to be living bombs....'

On the day of the Monowitz air raid of September 13, the Allies learned of the success of their oil campaign. In a signal sent to Tokyo that day from the Japanese Naval Mission in Berlin, and decrypted at Bletchley, the Japanese reported that although – despite Allied bombing – German fighter and rocket aircraft production was progressing, the German oil shortage, also the result of Allied bombing, had been one of the reasons for the defeat of the German Army in France, and would henceforth prevent the German Air Force from 'attaining the anticipated objective of regaining control of the air'.

At Hanford, in the United States, 230 miles from the Pacific Ocean, September 13 saw the start of a final, crucial series of experiments to activate an atomic pile, the essential preliminary to an atomic bomb. Supervised by the Italian-born physicist, Enrico Fermi, the experiment was first successful two weeks later.

On September 14 the Red Army, already in possession of the village of Miedzylesie, advanced northward to the Warsaw suburb of Praga, across the river from the suburbs in which the insurgents were still fighting, and to which, ten days earlier, Churchill had wished to drop supplies by air. That day, September 14, a Soviet aircraft flew low over one of the suburbs, Zoliborz, dropping a container in which was a letter naming the places where supplies were to be dropped. Within forty-eight hours, the Soviets had dropped two heavy machine guns, fifty automatic pistols and fifty thousand rounds of ammunition.

As the Polish insurgents fought their final, heroic but hopeless battles against the German Army, Churchill was in Quebec with President Roosevelt. They had before them a proposal by the American Secretary of the Treasury, Henry Morgenthau, that, once Germany was defeated, the industries of both the Ruhr and the Saar would be 'completely dismantled'. The Russians, Churchill explained in a personal and top secret telegram to the British War Cabinet, would 'claim the bulk' of the machinery of these two industrial regions, 'to repair their own plants' devastated by the war. In addition, Churchill explained, 'some international Trusteeship and form of control would keep these potential centres of rearmament completely out of action for many years to come'. The consequences of this, Churchill noted, 'will be to emphasize the pastoral character of German life, and the goods hitherto supplied from these German centres must to a large extent be provided by Great Britain. This may amount to three hundred to four hundred million pounds a year.' Churchill added: 'I was at first taken aback at this but I consider that the disarmament argument is decisive and the beneficial consequences to us follow naturally.'

The 'Morgenthau Plan', as it soon became known, was agreed to by Churchill and Roosevelt on September 15, when both men signed a programme 'for eliminating the war-making industries in the Ruhr and in the Saar' and 'looking forward to converting Germany into a country primarily agricultural and pastoral in its character'. Eden later told Churchill that he and the American Secretary of State, Cordell Hull, were both 'horrified' when they found out what Churchill and Roosevelt had initialled, Eden telling Churchill that the British War Cabinet would never agree to such a proposal. In the event, it was the State Department which rejected it.


On September 14, in the Pacific, American troops landed on Morotai Island, in the Moluccas, its airfields needed for any sustained air bombardment both of the Philippines and of Japan. In the battle for the island, 325 Japanese and forty-five American soldiers were killed. More costly in men on both sides was the American landing, that same day, on the Palau Islands, in the western Carolines. The casualty rate in the conquest of one of these islands, Peleliu, was to prove the highest of any amphibious attack in United States history, with 9,171 Americans being killed in eleven days, for the cost of 13,600 Japanese lives.


On September 16, Dunkirk, which the Germans had cut off in June 1940, was now bottled up by the Allies, and effectively besieged. That day, at Beaugency, on the Loire, 754 German officers and 18,850 German soldiers surrendered to the Americans. A further 30,000 Germans were able, however, to avoid the closing American pincers and to escape eastwards. Hitler, despite the collapse of his forces in France and Belgium, and the crossing of the German frontier, had every intention of regaining the military initiative; on September 16, the day of the surrender at Beaugency, he informed his senior generals, including Jodl and Guderian, that he intended to take the offensive against the Western Allies before the end of the year; it was to be made, he explained, through the Ardennes, with the port of Antwerp as its objective.

That night, on the Eastern Front, a Polish general nominally under Russian command, General Berling, authorized two battalions of the Polish Infantry Regiment to cross the Vistula west of Miedzylesie, and to enter the southern Warsaw suburb of Czerniakow. Once across the river, however, the attacking soldiers were pinned down by heavy German artillery fire, and then pressed back towards the river in repeated German tank and infantry attacks.

Equally unsuccessful, but far more costly, was Operation Market Garden, an attempt by the Western Allies on the following day, September 17, to land three airborne divisions, British and American, at Nijmegen, Eindhoven and Arnhem, behind German lines in Holland, with the aim of seizing a bridge over the Rhine at Arnhem. After an eight-day battle, in which, on the fifth day, a brigade of Polish parachute troops managed to link up with the original force, the bridge over the Rhine at Arnhem was retaken by the Germans.

In all, more than six thousand of the original airborne force of 35,000 men were taken prisoner; just over two thousand succeeded in recrossing the Rhine to safety. A total of 1,400 airborne troops had been killed. The casualties would have been higher, but for the efforts of Major Richard Lonsdale, commanding a small force of men who had become separated from their units. This force secured a small portion of the perimeter through which many survivors of the airborne attack were able to escape back across the Rhine. When the force itself eventually withdrew, Lonsdale was the last to leave.

In northern Italy, on September 17, German and Italian Fascist soldiers attacked a group of fifteen Italian partisans whose hiding place, in Verona, had been betrayed. The commander of the group, Rita Rosani, a twenty-four-year-old Jewish girl from Trieste, had already fought in several actions in the Verona region. Wounded in the attack, she fell, only to be found by an Italian Fascist officer and shot.

On September 18, two unusual flights took place over German-occupied Europe. One was of 107 American bombers which, leaving their bases in Britain, flew to Warsaw, dropped their supplies to the insurgents in the city, and flew on to the Soviet airbase at Poltava, with Stalin's knowledge and agreement. So small was the area now controlled by the insurgents that, of the 1,284 containers of arms and supplies dropped, nearly a thousand fell into German hands. But only two of the American bombers were shot down.

The second flight was a part of Operation Amsterdam, an Allied escape line which made use of a small grass airstrip at Tri Duby, in central Slovakia, between Zvolen and Banska Bystrica, then under Slovak partisan control. On September 18 two B-17 Flying Fortresses, flying from Bari in southern Italy, landed at the Slovak airstrip, with a forty-one Mustang fighter escort which remained in the air above the strip during the twenty-five minutes while the two bombers were on the ground. On this occasion, the airborne Operation Amsterdam had flown in four and a half tons of military stores for the Slovak and Soviet partisans in the area. Flying back to Italy, the bombers took with them twelve American and three British airmen, and a Czech.

A third noteworthy flight on September 18 was part of an airlift of supplies to the British troops still beleaguered at Arnhem; that day, Flight Lieutenant D.S.A. Lord's aircraft, a Dakota, was twice hit as it approached Arnhem, and one of its engines set on fire. Lord continued, nevertheless, on his mission, managed to drop most of his containers, and finally ordered his crew to jump. Shortly afterwards, the Dakota crashed in flames, and Lord was killed; he was awarded a posthumous Victoria Cross, one of five Victoria Crosses – four of them posthumous – to be awarded at Arnhem.

Also on September 18, a German v2 rocket, falling on the London suburb of Southgate, killed seventeen civilians; in all, fifty-six civilians were killed in London that week. Heavy cross-Channel shelling of Dover and Folkestone by German gun batteries set up on the clifftop near Calais led to a further twenty-two British civilian deaths.

On September 18, Hitler authorized the withdrawal of his armies from Estonia. That same day, he agreed that the British Government should be approached, with a request to help feed the civilians on the German-occupied Channel Islands. On the following day, the Americans captured the Atlantic port of Brest, and its commander, General Hermann Ramcke.

Less successful for the Allies, on September 19 two more Polish battalions crossed the Vistula to try to make contact with the insurgents still holding out in the suburb of Czerniakow, against a ferocious German onslaught. There was no way, however, to reach the defenders. General Berling's action in trying to do so, Stalin told the American Ambassador in Moscow, Averell Harriman, four days later, 'went against the better judgement of the Red Army'.

Almost at once, Berling was removed from his command, as was General Galicki, the commander of the battalions which had crossed the Vistula.

On September 19, Churchill and Roosevelt were at Roosevelt's home, Hyde Park, on the River Hudson. Both men had been told by their scientific advisers that an atomic bomb, the equivalent to between 20,000 and 30,000 tons of TNT, would 'almost certainly' be ready by August 1945. Indeed, such a bomb might have three or four times such an explosive power. British scientists and technicians, Churchill had earlier been told, were 'co-operating in the design and erection of the American plants'.

Churchill and Roosevelt agreed, and initialled an aide-memoire to that effect, that 'when a "bomb" is finally available, it might perhaps, after mature consideration be used against the Japanese, who should be warned that this bombardment will be repeated until they surrender'.

The nature of what might be used against the Japanese was at least clear in terms of its explosive power. Here was a single bomb of at least 20,000 tons of explosive power; during the week Churchill and Roosevelt learned this, it had taken 2,600 sorties by British and American bombers to drop 9,360 tons of bombs.

On the day that Churchill and Roosevelt agreed that the atomic bomb might be used against the Japanese, two members of an American Air Force bomber crew, having been asked to remove their Air Force insignia, and to use Corps of Engineers emblems instead, were given, at Los Alamos, in New Mexico, an account of what the atomic bomb might do, and of the hazards which they, as part of the delivery crew, might face in dropping it. 'The shock waves from the detonation could crush your plane,' Robert Oppenheimer, in charge of the project, told the senior officer, Colonel Paul Tibbets, and he added: 'I am afraid that I can give you no guarantee that you will survive.'

Among those to whom the second crew member, Lieutenant Beser, was introduced at Los Alamos was a young technician, David Greenglass. Unknown to anyone working on this top-secret project, Greenglass had just stolen the first of many blueprints which, for a few hundred dollars, he passed on to the Russians.

A patriot who died on September 19 was Guy Gibson, awarded the Victoria Cross for his skill in leading the raid on the Möhne dam in 1943; at his own request, he had left his desk job to go on a bombing raid against a German communications centre at Rheydt in the Ruhr. Returning from the raid, his plane was shot down over the Dutch village of Steenbergen; both he and his navigator, Squadron Leader J. B. Warwick, were killed. They were buried in a single coffin in the local Roman Catholic cemetery.

On September 19, as the Germans began the evacuation of Estonia, three thousand Jews at the slave labour camp at Klooga were taken from their barracks, as if to be evacuated, and shot. A further 426 were shot at the nearby camp of Lagedi. On the following day, a further deportation began of four thousand Jews from the Theresienstadt ghetto to Auschwitz. Before being deported, they had been made to appear in a film, designed to be shown throughout Germany, with the title: 'The Führer donates a town to Jews'.

Inmates of Theresienstadt were shown in the library, by a swimming pool, at a tea dance, in a bank, and working at tailoring, shoe repairing, leatherwork and sewing. Children were shown in a playground, at a football match and in a canteen with plenty of bread, cheese and tomatoes. There were also scenes of wounded German soldiers at the front, with the comment: 'While the Jews in Theresienstadt enjoy their coffee and cakes and dance, our soldiers bear the brunt of this terrible war, suffering death and deprivation in defence of the homeland.'

Almost all the Jews who appeared in the film were among those deported to Auschwitz; hardly any survived. Kurt Gerron, whom the Germans had appointed scriptwriter and director, died at Auschwitz that November.

On September 20, the last attempt to drop air supplies over Warsaw, to a Polish resistance group still holding out in the woods ten miles west of the city, was made from Foggia in southern Italy, when twenty aircraft, flown by Polish volunteers, crossed the Adriatic, Hungary, Slovakia and southern Poland. Five of the twenty were shot down. Only the 'Frantic' route across Europe to Soviet airfields now remained; but on October 2, Stalin vetoed the use of Poltava for any further British or American flights in support of the Warsaw uprising.

On September 21, evading the British security men who were guarding him at his hideaway on the Adriatic island of Vis, the Yugoslav partisan leader, Marshal Tito, flew by Soviet Dakota to a Soviet airfield in Roumania. From there, he went to Moscow, to sign an agreement for the 'temporary entry of Soviet troops into Yugoslav territory'. He also secured a proviso, that the Red Army would leave Yugoslavia once its 'operational task' was completed. Nor would the Russians have any power over the partisans once the two forces were fighting together inside Yugoslavia.

In Rome, on September 20, the trial took place of Pietro Caruso, the former Italian police chief who had prepared a supplementary list of fifty names for execution by the Germans in the Ardeatine caves. Found guilty, he was executed by firing squad on the morning of September 21.

In the Pacific, September 21 saw the first American air raid on the Philippines, in preparation for the attempt to retake the largest of the Japanese conquests of American territory. The aircraft set off from carriers more than 145 miles from their targets in and around Manila. In two days, 405 Japanese aircraft were destroyed or damaged, 103 ships sunk or damaged. Only fifteen American aircraft were lost. It was a prelude to General MacArthur's pledge of more than two and half years earlier: 'I shall return'.

In northern Europe, the liberation of France was almost completed during the third week of September; on September 22 the German garrison at Boulogne surrendered to the Canadians. In Italy, Allied troops had pushed past the Gothic Line, and by September 25 were in control of their own line across the peninsula from Pisa to Rimini. On the Eastern Front, the Red Army had entered the Estonian capital, Tallinn, that week. In Greece, the Germans were pulling out of the Peloponnese; when a British commando unit was parachuted on to Cape Araxos on September 23, it found that the Germans had gone.

Only in Warsaw did the fortunes of war continue to favour the Germans. On September 23, German troops were in control of the whole western bank of the Vistula, and on the following day they moved against the last substantial pockets of resistance, in the suburbs of Mokotow and Zoliborz. That day also saw one of the last of the Allied air drops over the city, as the insurgents retreated to cellars and sewers, and had no open space under their control sufficient to enable supplies to be dropped. The final air drop was made three days later, when a Polish pilot, shot down over Dabrowa, and badly injured, was captured by the Germans, interrogated, and shot. Near the village of Dziekanow, an American crewman was beaten to death by his German captors. In all, 306 Allied aircraft had flown over Warsaw, with Polish, British, American and South African crews; forty-one of those planes had been shot down, and at least two hundred airmen killed.

*          *          *

In the prisoner-of-war camp at Colditz, Allied officers were driven by both hope and despair to seek to escape. But the obstacles were formidable. One would-be escapee, Michael Sinclair, known to the Germans as the 'Red Fox', tried three times. At the first attempt he had been shot through the chest, the bullet passing right through him, two inches from his heart. After a spell in hospital, he tried again, but was caught when only two days short of the Dutch frontier. On September 25, he made his third attempt; while on a heavily guarded walk in the park below the castle with other prisoners-of-war, he made a dash for the wire surrounding the park. He was shot as he climbed it, and killed.

On September 26, the Allied troops trapped at Arnhem surrendered to the Germans. That day, at Rastenburg, Hitler signed a decree establishing a People's Army, for the defence of German soil, by means of the conscription of every able-bodied man between the ages of sixteen and sixty. Hitler's unshaken determination to defend every yard of German soil was in sharp contrast to his physical appearance. A general who visited him that day, Nikolaus von Vormann, noted how 'it was a tired, broken man who greeted me, then shuffled over to a chair, his shoulders drooping, and asked me to sit down'. Vormann added: 'He spoke so softly and hesitantly, it was hard to understand him. His hands trembled so much he had to grip them between his knees.'

Hitler had cause to tremble later that day, when Himmler visited him, bringing a 160-page dossier of documents which the Gestapo had discovered at German Army headquarters in Zossen, implicating Admiral Canaris, the former head of Secret Intelligence Service of the German Armed Forces, in plots against Hitler going back to the earliest days of the war, including the warnings to the West about Hitler's military intentions in 1940. Also implicated in the documents brought by Himmler were two senior members of Canaris's Intelligence staff, General Oster, and Hans von Dohnanyi, as well as the former Mayor of Leipzig, Karl Goerdeler. It was a plot whose ramifications appeared to have no end.

On September 26, a three-man American mission, code-named Mongoose, was dropped behind German lines in Italy, near Stresa. Led by Major William V. Holohan, it quickly set up an Italian partisan Intelligence network. Further south, however, at Marzabotto, near Bologna, German forces commanded by ss Major Walter Reder, began an anti-partisan sweep that week, in which four hundred partisans were killed.

In Warsaw, the last of the insurgents fighting in the suburb of Mokotow surrendered to the Germans on the afternoon of September 27. That evening, Himmler telephoned to the commander of the German forces in the city, General von dem Bach Zelewski, to say that Hitler had awarded him, and also General Dirlewanger, the Knight's Cross. During the next five days, a terrible vengeance was wrought on all who had been captured. During the fighting itself, fifteen thousand Polish resistance fighters had been killed, for a cost of at least ten thousand German dead. In savage reprisals, both during the fighting and after it, an estimated 200,000 Polish civilians were killed.

On September 27, the Japanese transport ship *Ural Maru* was torpedoed off the Japanese island of Okinawa by an American submarine, while on its way from

Singapore to Japan. More than 2,000 of the 2,350 passengers on board were drowned. One of those who drowned was Bishan Singh, a young Indian who had volunteered to serve with the forces of Imperial Japan against the British Empire, and who, almost a year earlier, on 24 October 1943, had received the blessing of the Indian National Army founder, Subhas Chandra Bose, for his chosen path. Nine of Bishan Singh's fellow volunteers were rescued from the sea. In due course they reached Japan and achieved their aim of fighting against Britain, alongside the Japanese forces in Burma.

On September 28, two hundred Gypsies, who had earlier been sent from Auschwitz to Buchenwald, were sent back to Auschwitz, where they were immediately gassed. That same day, in Theresienstadt, ss Lieutenant-General Heinrich Müller asked for volunteers to leave the privations of the ghetto and to work in factories in Germany. Some 2,300 Jews chose what they hoped would be the path of work and survival. They too were sent to Auschwitz, where nine hundred of them were gassed within a few hours of reaching the camp.

Many of the deportees from Theresienstadt to Auschwitz were German Jews, deported up to two years earlier to Theresienstadt from Berlin and from other German cities. Also murdered that week, on September 29, was Wilhelm Leuschner, a former trade union leader, who was hanged for his adherence to the July Plot. Two days later, Rudolf Schmundt, Hitler's principal Army adjutant, who had been grievously wounded by the bomb, died of his wounds.

In Germany, all those declared 'Enemies of the People' for relatively minor offences were now in danger of more than imprisonment. In Vienna, seventeen Post Office employees who were found guilty that October of taking chocolate and soap from badly wrapped Army gift parcels were marched to a central square and publicly executed.

In Buchenwald, October saw two sets of medical experiments carried out on homosexuals, the first, on seven men, took place on October 1, the second, on eleven more, nine days later. The experiments involved castration; several of those operated on died as a result.

On October 3, as a prelude to the Allied advance into Holland, 247 British aircraft attacked the dykes which protected the Dutch island of Walcheren from the sea. Using the same type of bombs which had earlier breached the Möhne dam in the Ruhr, more than a hundred yards of dyke were destroyed, and the sea rushed in. During the raid, 125 islanders were killed, forty-seven of whom had been sheltering in a mill at Theune which collapsed on top of them. For a month, the air attacks on German strongpoints on Walcheren continued; only after more than eight thousand tons of bombs had been dropped on German radar stations, ammunition dumps and artillery batteries did British and Canadian forces cross the River Scheldt from Breskens, to occupy the island.

On October 4, in Greece, British parachute troops landed at Patras, in an operation, code-named 'Manna', intended to liberate the whole of the Peloponnese and, in due course, Athens. That same day, in Yugoslavia, the Red

Army drove the Germans from the town of Pancevo, on the east bank of the Danube, less than ten miles downriver from Belgrade. That night, twenty-two British and American bombers, flying from southern Italy, laid fifty-eight mines in the Danube, both north of Györ and east of Esztergom, to impede German military supplies being brought south by barge through Hungary.

The British had been at war with Germany for more than five years, the Russians for more than three years, and the Americans for nearly three years. The strain of so prolonged a conflict had long been evident to the commanders of every army. On October 4, General Eisenhower distributed to all his combat units in Europe a report by the Office of the United States Surgeon General, which set out these hazards without equivocation. 'The key to an understanding of the psychiatric problem', the report explained, 'is the simple fact that the danger of being killed or maimed imposes a strain so great that it causes men to break down. One look at the shrunken, apathetic faces of psychiatric patients as they come down stumbling into the medical station, sobbing, trembling, referring shudderingly to "them shells" and to buddies mutilated or dead, is enough to convince most observers of this fact'.

There was 'no such thing', the report continued 'as "getting used to combat" ', and it went on to explain that: 'Each man "up there" knows that at any moment he may be killed, a fact kept constantly before his mind by the sight of dead and mutilated buddies around him. Each moment of combat imposes a strain so great that men will break down in direct relation to the intensity and duration of their exposure. Thus psychiatric casualties are as inevitable as gunshot and shrapnel wounds in warfare'.

In Italy, the American forces estimated that an infantryman could 'last' for about two hundred regimental combat days. The British commanders, who pulled their men out of the line after every twelve days of combat, for a four day rest period, estimated that their men could remain unaffected for up to four hundred days of combat. The American report, which gave these figures, continued: 'A wound or injury is regarded, not as a misfortune, but a blessing. As one litter bearer put it, "Something funny about the men you bring back wounded, they're always happy ... they're sure glad to be getting out of here". Under these circumstances it is easy for a man to become sincerely convinced that he is sick or unable to go on. This in turn leads to the premature development of genuine psychiatric disability and to needless loss of manpower. It also leads to self-inflicted wounds and to misbehaviour before the enemy'.

On October 6, over Nijmegen, on the Dutch–German border, a Royal Canadian Air Force squadron found itself confronted by a new adversary, a German jet aircraft. This was another of Hitler's secret weapons. As, however, the jet was flying five hundred feet below the Canadians, it presented them with an ideal target, and was destroyed.

There was another Allied success in the air on the following day, when, as part of Operation Amsterdam, yet more Allied airmen, most of them Americans, were flown out of central Slovakia in an aircraft sent specially to take them out.

In Auschwitz, on October 7, about 450 Jews who were being forced to take the bodies of the victims from the gas chambers to the furnaces, rose up in revolt. Using explosive smuggled to them from Jewish women working in the nearby Union armaments factory, they blew up one of the four gas chambers, and set fire to another, before trying to break out of the camp's wire perimeter. Two hundred and fifty managed to get beyond the wire; all were hunted down and shot. The two hundred who had failed to get beyond the wire were also shot. The SS also arrested five Jewish women in the Union factory. Despite terrible torture, they betrayed nobody. One of the women, Roza Robota, managed to smuggle out a message from the cell in which she was being held: 'You have nothing to fear – I shall not talk.' Three months after the revolt, the women were hanged, all the other women then at Auschwitz being assembled to watch the execution. Recalled one eye-witness: 'They went calmly to their deaths.'

In northern Italy, the Germans, assisted by two thousand Cossack troops, continued their anti-partisan sweeps throughout the second and third weeks of October, freeing 336 Italian fascists and Germans being held by the partisans, capturing large quantities of rifles and ammunition, and killing, near Tolmezzo, 3,633 partisans in the self-proclaimed partisan Republic of Carnia.

At a meeting in Moscow on October 9, Churchill and Stalin talked not only about the final phases of the war against Germany, but also about their own countries' respective positions in liberated Europe once the war was won. At Churchill's urging, the two men discussed the Soviet Union's future influence in those countries from which the Germans were even then being driven by the Red Army. He was 'not worrying very much about Roumania', Churchill told Stalin. That, he said, 'was very much a Russian affair'. Over Greece, where, as Churchill put it, 'Britain must be the leading Mediterranean power', he hoped that Stalin would let Britain have 'first say' in the same way as Russia could in Roumania.

Only in Greece did Churchill seek a major influence for Britain. Over Yugoslavia, he proposed a 'fifty-fifty' divide of influence between East and West. Churchill also told Stalin that he envisaged the removal of the German population of Silesia and East Prussia into central Germany; East Prussia could then be divided between Russia and post-war Poland, and Silesia given to Poland as compensation for the eastern areas of inter-war Poland which Russia had already occupied, and intended to annex.

Churchill also told Stalin, at a second meeting on October 10, that the western Allies wanted every country to have 'the form of government which its people desire'. No ideology should be imposed on any small States, Churchill asserted. 'Let them work out their own fortunes during the years that lie ahead.' There were fears in every country in western Europe, he told Stalin, of 'an aggressive, proselytizing Communism' once Nazism had been overthrown.

As Churchill and Stalin talked in Moscow, American forces in northern Europe encircled the German city of Aachen, the western gateway to Germany.

In the Pacific, an American task force, in action off the Japanese island of Okinawa, destroyed more than a hundred Japanese aircraft. On the Eastern Front, the Red Army had reached the Baltic coast of Lithuania, and was besieging Memel, the city which Hitler had annexed to Germany in March 1939.

At Auschwitz, October 10 saw the arrival in the camp of eight hundred Gypsy children who had been held previously at Buchenwald. Among them were more than a hundred boys aged from nine to fourteen, who had earlier been sent from Auschwitz to Buchenwald, but had been found unsuitable for work. All were gassed in one of the two gas chambers which had not been destroyed or damaged in the Jewish revolt three days earlier.

In Italy, New Zealand troops crossed the River Rubicon on October 11, thus echoing Julius Caesar's phrase, crossing in the other direction: 'The die is cast'. That same day, Soviet forces crossed the River Tisza, at Szeged, Hungary's southernmost city. Further east, Russian forces besieged both Debrecen and Cluj, where a combined Hungarian and German defence faced a combined Roumanian and Soviet attack. On the following day, the Red Army entered the Transylvanian city of Oradea; Hungary was now under Soviet attack along almost the whole length of its southern and south-eastern border. Desperately, the Germans pulled back their troops from northern Greece and southern Yugoslavia, but everywhere along the way they met the resistance of Greek and Yugoslav partisans. On October 12, a German Intelligence report, sent by Lieutenant Waldheim from Salonica, spoke of increased partisan activity on the road between Stip and Kocani. Two days later, German troops withdrew from Salonica; as they hurried northwards, they set fire to three villages along the threatened road, killing 114 of their civilian inhabitants. In all, according to Waldheim's own final report of November 7, a total of 739 partisans and civilians were killed in Macedonia during the German withdrawal.

In the Pacific, the American preliminaries to the return to the Philippines continued, on October 12, with a massive air raid on Formosa, lasting for three consecutive days, in which five hundred Japanese aircraft, and forty Japanese warships, were destroyed, for the cost of eighty-nine American aircraft. Many of the Japanese pilots who were killed had only just been trained, a serious loss to the Japanese carrier fleet.

Another Berlin execution took place on October 12, that of Carl Langbehn, a lawyer, who had tried more than a year earlier to involve Himmler in the plot against Hitler. He had also made enquiries through Switzerland, in September 1943, about a possible negotiated peace with the Allies. It was then that he had been arrested.

On the morning of October 13, a German V2 rocket fell on Antwerp, killing thirty-two civilians. That afternoon, a V1 flying bomb fell on Antwerp's municipal slaughterhouse, killing a further fourteen civilians, many of them butchers who had come for the weekly meat distribution. Six days later, forty-four civilians were killed by a second flying bomb. The agony of Antwerp had begun.

In Moscow, on October 13, Stalin indicated to Churchill that the Soviet Union would enter the war against Japan as soon as Germany was defeated. That same day, British troops entered Athens; the Germans had evacuated the city during the night. Also on October 13, after a violent three day struggle, Soviet troops entered Riga. The battle for the Baltic States was ended. 'Riga and Athens are ripe plums fallen,' Churchill's wife Clementine wrote to her husband in Moscow, and she added: 'How I wish we could wrench Rotterdam and Cologne.'

City by city, the German mastery of Europe was being ended. But there was to be no easy road to victory. On October 13 the Americans began a sustained assault on Aachen, already besieged for three days.

On October 14, two German generals went to see Field Marshal Rommel at his home in Herrlingen, where he was slowly recuperating from the head injury he had received in Normandy. They offered him, from Hitler personally, the choice of suicide, or a public trial. He chose suicide, taking the cyanide which the two generals had brought with them. Three days later, he was given a State funeral in Ulm. The German public were to be shielded from knowledge of the full extent of the opposition to Hitler, and of his revenge.

# 43

# Fighting for every mile

WINTER 1944

On 14 October 1944, Soviet and Yugoslav forces began their assault on the German troops holding the Yugoslav capital, Belgrade. In hand-to-hand fighting, lasting for almost a week, they pressed towards the city centre. The Germans, once again determined not to yield easily, rejected a Soviet ultimatum to surrender; within forty-eight hours of this rejection, they were obliterated.

In the Arctic, Soviet forces drove the Germans from Petsamo on October 15. That same day, the Transylvanian city of Cluj was overrun after a four-day siege. Hitler now took steps to strengthen Germany's hold over Hungary, launching Operation Mickey Mouse, the abduction of Admiral Horthy, who was seized on October 15 by troops under the command of two SS Generals, Otto Skorzeny and von dem Bach Zelewski, the latter of whom had just come from Warsaw, having crushed the last of the insurgents there. Horthy, seized in his palace in Budapest, was taken, as a prisoner, to Weilheim in Bavaria. On the following day, October 16, a pro-German government was set up by Major Szalasi, head of the fascist military organization, the Arrow Cross.

Twenty-four hours after the German Army entered Hungary, Adolf Eichmann returned to Budapest, where he at once demanded fifty thousand able-bodied Jews to be marched on foot to Germany, to serve as forced labourers there. Eichmann also wanted the remaining Jews of Budapest to be assembled in ghetto-like camps near the capital. 'You see', he told the Hungarian Jewish leader, Rudolf Kastner, 'I am back again. You forgot Hungary is still in the shadow of the Reich. My arms are long and I can reach the Jews of Budapest as well.' The Jews of Budapest, Eichmann added, 'will be driven out on foot this time'.

These deportations began on October 20. Even as Soviet troops approached Budapest from the south-east, Jews from Budapest were marched westward, away from the advancing Soviet forces, to dig anti-tank trenches. Beginning on October 22, twenty-five thousand men and boys, and ten thousand women and girls were taken, in four days, for this task; thousands were shot as they marched, or left to die where they fell.

On October 16, the Red Army broke in force into East Prussia, advancing

603

towards both Gumbinnen and Goldap. The roads around Hitler's headquarters at Rastenburg were suddenly crowded with refugees fleeing westward. At Gumbinnen, the Soviet forces outnumbered the Germans by four to one, sweeping them aside. The Red Army was only fifty miles from the 'Wolf's Lair'.

On October 18, American forces in the Pacific shelled Japanese coastal defences on the island of Leyte, the first step in their most ambitious scheme yet, the reconquest of the Philippines. In Europe, German troops were seeking to crush the Slovak revolt, driving the partisans from the valleys which they had held for more than a month, and capturing Banska Bystrica, self-proclaimed capital of 'Free Slovakia'. There was much butchery, carried out by the Dirlewanger Brigade, which less than three weeks earlier had completed the suppression of the Warsaw uprising. A hundred and twenty miles to the east of the valleys in which the slaughter was taking place, Soviet and Czechoslovak troops battled to break through the German defences in the Carpathians; in a month of fighting, twenty thousand Soviet soldiers were killed. Also killed were 6,500 members of General Ludwik Svoboda's Czechoslovak Corps; one Czech commander, General Vedral, was only a few yards over the frontier of his native soil when he was blown up by a German mine.

On October 19, Soviet and Yugoslav forces entered Belgrade. The battle had cost fifteen thousand German dead. The Red Army and the Yugoslav partisans had also suffered heavy losses. On the following day, the Adriatic port of Dubrovnik fell to Tito's partisans, while, inside the Hungarian frontier, a combined force of Soviet, Roumanian and Bulgarian troops, now linked in unaccustomed alliance, drove the Germans from Debrecen. Inside Germany itself, now pierced both from West and East, the Red Army captured the East Prussian border town of Eydtkuhnen, while, in the West, Aachen fell after a seven day siege. More than three thousand German soldiers were taken prisoner inside Aachen, and a further eight thousand outside it. Unit by unit, the Germans had been drawn into the defence of this, the first German city to fall into Allied hands, and to do so 1,875 days after the first German soldiers had crossed the borders of their State, in the first act of a war which, at that time, they had been so confident of winning.

On October 20, the day of Aachen's surrender, Adolf Reichwein was tried in Berlin for his part in the July Plot. A professor of history before Hitler came to power, he had served as a link between the Kreisau Circle and resistance groups among German industrial workers. Found guilty on October 20, he was hanged that same day.

At five minutes past ten on October 20, in the Philippines, more than 100,000 American soldiers began to land on two separate beachheads, on the east coast of Leyte Island, near the town of Tacloban. There was much heroism; when everybody else in Private Harold Moon's platoon had been killed, he continued to fire his machine gun for four hours, alone, killing at least eighteen Japanese before his dugout was overrun. Moon was awarded the Congressional Medal of Honour – posthumously.

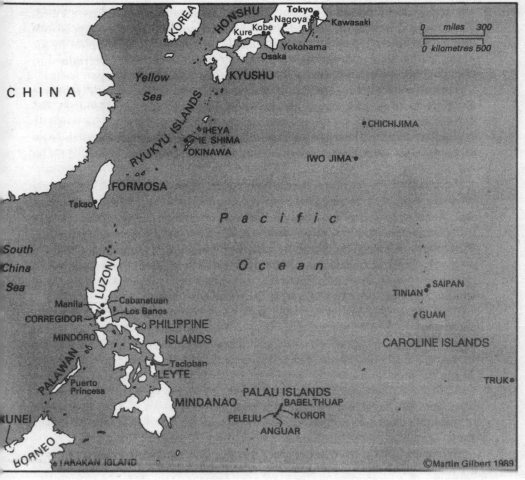

The Eastern Pacific, October 1944–March 1945

For sixty-seven days the Americans fought to conquer Leyte, whose Japanese garrison of 80,000, by their prolonged resistance, forced General MacArthur to delay his planned invasion of Luzon by a further week. In all, 55,344 Japanese were killed on Leyte. Even after the island was conquered, Japanese units continued to emerge from hiding and to fight on, rather than surrender. In what were euphemistically called 'mopping up' operations in the first four months of 1945, a further 24,294 Japanese soldiers were killed, bringing the total Japanese death toll on the island to almost eighty thousand, virtually the whole of the original garrison. The Americans lost 3,508 men in action against the eighty thousand. It was said by the Americans who witnessed this unequal slaughter that 'the Japanese fought to die, and the Americans fought to live'.

On October 21, on Anguar Island, in the Palaus, the Japanese garrison was overcome, after a month of fighting. In all, 1,300 Japanese soldiers were killed, as against 265 Americans. Henceforth, the Americans left the remaining islands unmolested; their Japanese garrisons, unable any longer to get supplies by air or sea, presented no danger to the American forces, who were determined to take the Philippines, and then to move on against the islands of Japan itself.

Three days after the American landings on Leyte, three separate Japanese naval forces, almost the entire Japanese fleet, sought to disrupt the landings and drive off the American warships accompanying it. Two of the first three Japanese cruisers sent against Leyte from Brunei Bay were torpedoed off the north coast of Borneo; 582 sailors were drowned, but the rest of the force continued on its way.

The greatest sea battle in history had begun. It was a battle full of carnage; when the American carrier *Princeton* was hit and sunk by a single bomb, more than five hundred men drowned; the loss on the cruiser *Birmingham* was 229. But American warplanes, unopposed, rapidly tilted the balance of destruction. When the giant 72,800 ton Japanese battleship *Musashi* was sunk by a massive air onslaught of thirteen aerial torpedoes and seven bombs, more than a thousand of her sailors were drowned, including her captain, Toshihei Inoguchi, who, standing on the bridge to the end, chose to go down with his ship.

After a three-day battle, thirty-six Japanese warships had been sunk, totalling 300,000 tons. The Americans lost six warships, totalling 37,000 tons. It was, Churchill telegraphed to Roosevelt, a 'brilliant and massive victory'. It was also a turning point in the nature of Pacific warfare, with the appearance, on the last day of the battle, of a special Japanese suicide corps, the Kamikaze, or 'divine wind'. In their first day's work, on October 25, one kamikaze pilot drove his plane into the flight deck of the American aircraft carrier *St Lo*, igniting the bombs and torpedoes stored below decks. Half an hour later, the *St Lo* had sunk.

By the end of the war, more than five thousand kamikaze pilots had died, and thirty-four American ships sunk. But neither heroism, tenacity, skill nor suicide had been able to avert the Japanese naval disaster at Leyte Gulf, when four aircraft carriers and three battleships had been among the Japanese losses, virtually eliminating the Imperial Japanese Navy as a fighting force.

On October 25, the first day of the kamikaze attacks in Leyte Gulf, the leading Japanese air ace, Hiroyoshi Nishizawa, who had shot down eighty-seven American aircraft, died, not in combat, but as a passenger aboard a Japanese transport plane, intercepted and shot down by American fighters.

In western Europe, with the fall of Aachen after its virtual destruction street by street, there were those in the West who thought that the Germans might accept defeat. But Hitler's authority, still exercised from his remote headquarters at Rastenburg, remained absolute. On October 22, the Red Army was halted at Insterburg, a mere forty-five miles from the 'Wolf's Lair', by a determined German effort, while on the following day, on the Western Front, German forces held St Dié against a sustained American assault.

On October 24, in East Prussia, German troops recaptured Gumbinnen. Also

The Western and Italian fronts, October 1944

on October 24, three hundred Italian Jews were deported from Bolzano to Auschwitz; 137 were gassed on arrival. On the following day, as French forces approached Strasbourg, Himmler ordered the destruction of the skeleton collection at the Anatomical Institute; a collection created as a result of the deliberate killing of Jews in Auschwitz.

Even as the evidence of evil was being destroyed, further tests were being made of the v2 rocket. With the Allied advance into Holland, the launch unit was withdrawn northward to Overveen, on the North Sea; on October 27 it tested a rocket which rose to a height of three hundred feet before falling back on the launch crew, killing twelve of them. The launch site was then abandoned, and transferred to The Hague. On the following day, seventy-one Belgian civilians were killed in Antwerp by a flying bomb.

Also on October 28, the last deportation took place from the Theresienstadt ghetto to Auschwitz, when two thousand Jews were sent eastward; after a number of men and women were sent to the barracks, the remaining 1,689 deportees were gassed. There then followed the systematic destruction of the evidence of mass murder, with the files about individual prisoners, and the death certificates of hundreds of thousands of people, Jews and non-Jews alike, being brought to one of the two remaining crematoria and burned. All trace of the documents, as all trace of the corpses, was to be obliterated. Not only the documents and the corpses, but also the buildings of destruction were to be destroyed. When a train with more than five hundred Jews reached Auschwitz on November 3, from the Slovak labour camp at Sered, the Auschwitz administration office telephoned to Mauthausen: 'We have a transport here; could you handle it in your gas chambers?' The answer was, 'That would be a waste of coal burned in the locomotive. You should be able to handle the load yourself.'

But Auschwitz no longer had the apparatus for mass murder, and on November 6 the men from Sered were given their tattoo numbers, followed on November 7 by the women and children. The men were then sent to the factory zone at Gleiwitz, the women and children to the barracks. A twelve-year-old girl who survived this Sered transport later recalled that there were about a hundred and fifty children in the transport.

On October 31, the Red Army crossed the River Tisza and reached the outskirts of Kecskemet, fifty miles from Budapest. But in Slovakia, 160 miles to the north, the last resistance was being crushed; at the battle of Kremnica, one of those captured by the Germans was Haviva Reik, a Palestinian Jewess who had been parachuted into Slovakia by the British, to help the uprising. Of the 2,100 Slovak partisans killed in action, 269 were Jews.

The Slovak uprising, like the Warsaw uprising, had broken out before the arrival of the Red Army; both were signs of an intense national identity, and desire for post-war independence. Both had been crushed by the Germans with ruthless severity, the Slovak uprising by ss General Gotlob Berger, an expert on the cowing of subject people and the organisation of Quisling States.

From Denmark, in mid-October, Danish resistance had appealed to London to bomb the Gestapo headquarters at Aarhus, in order to destroy the Gestapo

The Eastern front, October 1944

records, which were about to be used in a drive to eliminate the Danish Resistance altogether. This involved a 900-mile round trip across the North Sea. In the raid, launched on October 31 by twenty-four British aircraft commanded by Group Captain Wykeham-Barnes, and made at roof-top height, the Gestapo headquarters was hit, and more than 150 Germans were killed. Also killed in the raid were more than twenty Danes, most of them informers. The Gestapo records were destroyed. One bomb, falling on a nearby private house, killed a Danish civilian.

During the confusion of the Aarhus raid, a number of Danes were released from the prison inside the Gestapo headquarters. Among these prisoners was Pastor Harald Sandbaek. Repeatedly tortured, he had reached the end of his tether; the raid had begun during what could well have been his final interrogation. Hardly had his interrogators fled, in terror, at the sound of the raid, than Pastor Sandbaek was buried under the rubble. Pulled clear by Danish forced labourers, he made his escape to Sweden.

On November 1, British and Canadian troops crossed the Scheldt in Operation Infatuate, the attempt to seize the island of Walcheren, in order to free both banks of the River Scheldt and open the port of Antwerp to Allied military transports. For eight days, as the landings proceeded, a total of ten thousand air sorties were made by rocket-firing aircraft against the remaining German positions on the island, already the object of earlier and sustained air attack. During this renewed bombardment, fifty-one British aircraft were shot down and thirty-one pilots killed. But already, on November 4, the first minesweepers had sailed the length of the Scheldt from the sea to Antwerp, and by the end of the month the first Allied shipping convoy had reached the port.

In Yugoslavia, Tito's partisans drove the Germans from the Italian Adriatic port of Zara on November 2. That day, in Budapest, more than fifty thousand of the city's Jews were driven westward, towards Austria. Bludgeoned, whipped and frequently shot at by their SS guards, as many as ten thousand perished during the six-day march. A further thousand, however, were saved by the determined personal intervention, even as the march was in progress, of the Swedish diplomat, Raoul Wallenberg, who had earlier extended the protection of the Swedish flag to several thousand Jews inside Budapest.

On November 4, the Red Army captured Cegled, just under forty miles from the Hungarian capital. But, from that moment, the road to Budapest was strongly defended. Nor was the advance going as swiftly on the Western Front as the Allies had hoped. In Belgium and Holland, Churchill telegraphed to Stalin on November 5, there had been 'very hard fighting', which had led to more than 40,000 killed and wounded. In Italy, Churchill added, 'tremendous torrential rain' had resulted in the sweeping away of a 'vast number' of bridges, so that all movement of troops and supplies was at a standstill.

The coming of winter, Hitler's fanaticism, and German tenacity, were ensuring that the war would not be over in 1944. Yet British Intelligence knew how desperately the German war effort was under strain. On November 2, a top-secret directive issued in Berlin called for greater use of Germany's canals and inland waterways in order to relieve pressure on the railways. This directive was decrypted at Bletchley six days later. Also in November, it was learned in Britain, from a further Ultra message, that the destruction of the German railway system had been so effective that Berlin had ordered an emergency mobilization of lorries to help maintain supply lines to the Western Front.

The Allies were now virtual masters of the European air; yet every raid had its element of risk. On 6 November 1944, in a raid by South African Air Force fighters against German troop trains on the Brod–Sarajevo railway line in Yugoslavia, one of the ten aircraft was shot down, and its pilot, Lieutenant R. R. Linsley, killed. That same day, in an American bombing raid on Hamburg, a much decorated American airman, Jay McDonough, from Chicago, was wounded. He already had the Air Medal with four Oak Leaf Clusters; having been wounded, he received the Purple Heart. Within six weeks, he was again in action.

On November 7, Franklin Roosevelt was elected President of the United States for a fourth term. That day, in Tokyo, one of Russia's most successful wartime spies, Richard Sorge, was executed. He had been held in prison for more than two years. Twenty years later, he was posthumously awarded the title of Hero of the Soviet Union. In Budapest, the parachutist Hanna Szenes was executed that day by the Germans, her mission from Palestine unfulfilled, but her name a beacon for Jewish youth in the years to come. Of her fellow parachutists, Enzo Sereni was killed in Dachau eleven days later, followed on November 20, in Kremnica, by Haviva Reik, Raffi Reiss and Zvi Ben Ya'acov. Another Jewish parachutist from Palestine, Peretz Goldstein, perished in Sachsenhausen.

On November 8, Canadian forces completed the capture of Walcheren Island. That day, in northern Europe, Walther Nowotny, the fifth-ranking ace of the German Air Force, was shot down and killed. He was one of only eight pilots to win the Knight's Cross with Oak Leaves, Swords and Diamonds. As little known as Nowotny was well known, a thirty-eight-year-old German physician, Dr Kurt Heissenmeyer, was experimenting on November 8 on four recently hanged inmates at Neuengamme. Three of those killed to help his experiments were Poles; the fourth was a Russian, Ivan Tschurkin, a former locksmith from Kalinin, who was just twenty-two years old.

Speaking in London on November 9, Churchill commented that the French Governor of Paris and the Belgian Burgomaster of Brussels, who were both present to hear him speak, were 'living representatives' of 'the splendid events which have so recently taken place'. The Allies now stood 'on the threshold of Germany'. But the war was not yet won: 'supreme efforts' had yet to be made. 'It is always in the last lap', Churchill warned, 'that races are either gained or lost. The effort must be forthcoming. This is no moment to slacken.'

Reaching Antwerp by air from Paris on November 10, an American officer, Brigadier General Clare H. Armstrong, set up an Anti Flying Bomb Command consisting of several thousand American, British and Polish troops, with six hundred anti-aircraft guns and a communication system designed to spot the bombs as far from the city as possible. At least half, and at times three-quarters, of the flying bombs which came over Antwerp were thus to be shot down; against the faster-than-sound V2 rocket there was, however, no possible anti-aircraft defence. Of these Allied defenders of Antwerp, thirty-two were killed while at their posts.

For many weeks, the German army had been infiltrating spies across the American lines, in an attempt to ascertain as best they could the strengths of the Allied positions. All of these infiltrators were caught. Among them were two Poles, Josef Wende and Stefan Kotas, both of whom had earlier been drafted into the German army and forced to serve as spies. Wende and Kotas had crossed the front line in civilian clothes, posing as Polish slave labourers working as coal miners. Their mission was to observe the strengths of certain American units and to return that same day with their report. After being caught, both men were tried and sentenced to death. They were executed by an American firing squad at Toul on November 11.

That same November 11, the day of the First World War armistice in 1918, Winston Churchill and Charles de Gaulle drove together through Paris to the Arc de Triomphe, where both men laid a wreath to the Unknown Soldier of that first of the century's world wars. On the following day, in the remote Norwegian inlet of Tromsö Fjord, above the Arctic Circle, thirty-two British bombers, operating from Lossiemouth in Scotland, attacked the *Tirpitz*, Germany's last surviving battleship.

If the *Tirpitz* could be sunk, the big ships of the British Home Fleet could at last be released to the Pacific.

Each of the British bombers carried a single, 12,000 pound 'Tallboy' bomb. At least two bombs hit the ship, which capsized. Of her crew of 1,800, just over eight hundred were rescued, eighty-two of them when a hole was cut in the exposed underside of the ship thirty hours after it had capsized; in all, a thousand men had drowned.

As the *Tirpitz* capsized, many of the men inside were heard singing the German national anthem, 'Deutschland über Alles'. 'What a tragedy it was', commented the British scientist R. V. Jones, 'that men like that had to serve the Nazi cause.'

One German who had refused to serve the Nazi cause, Bernard Letterhaus, a former Catholic labour leader, was sentenced to death on November 13, for his part in the July Plot; he was hanged on the following day.

On November 14, the Japanese destroyer *Ushio*, the last surviving warship of those which had struck at Pearl Harbour, was among the ships attacked by American aircraft in Manila Bay. Severely damaged by a bomb, she was never to be in action again. Also on November 14, in the Balkans, Bulgarian and Yugoslav troops entered Skoplje. Germany's three-and-a-half year control of the Balkans was over. In Scandinavia, German rule was also under threat, with the landing of a Norwegian Army officer, Colonel Arne Dahl, north of the Arctic Circle, to work with Soviet forces in Karelia against the Germans, who had already been forced to abandon the port of Kirkenes and withdraw westward.

In northern Italy, a German sweep against more than a thousand partisans near Mondovi was unsuccessful; the partisans escaped the net, although their British liaison officer, Captain Neville Temple, was killed in a car accident on November 15, during the escape. He had been parachuted into the area three months earlier, as head of the 'Flap' mission, to attack German troops and supply convoys on the move.

On the Italian front, the Germans were holding firm to their line south of La Spezia and Bologna; repeated Allied efforts to dislodge them had failed. In Western Europe, slow but steady advances were being made both north and east of Aachen, and against Alsace and Lorraine. From behind their ever diminishing lines, the Germans were still able to send flying bombs against Antwerp; on November 16, a total of 263 civilians were killed when ten flying bombs hit the city; thirty-two of the deaths were in an orphanage which had been converted into an emergency hospital. On the following day, thirty-two nuns died when a flying bomb hit their convent.

In the Far East, November 17 saw a further Japanese advance into mainland China, towards Kweiyang. But that same day, in the Yellow Sea, an American submarine sank one of Japan's few remaining escort carriers, the *Jinyo*, while, in Tokyo, unknown to the Americans, a secret meeting of atomic scientists heard a report that 'since February of this year there has not been a great deal of progress'. It had become clear, those at the meeting realized, that Japan could not build an atomic bomb in time to affect the outcome of the war.

From the eastern frontiers of India, the British, now masters of Imphal and Kohima, launched Operation Extended Capital on November 19, to drive into Burma on a wide front; within two weeks, the Chindwin river had been crossed at three separate points. In Western Europe, French forces reached the Rhine on November 19, at Rosenau, near the border of France and Switzerland. Further north, the Germans were rapidly being driven from Alsace and Lorraine, losing Sarrebourg on November 20. That day, Hitler left Rastenburg for Berlin. He was never to see East Prussia again.

On the day that Hitler returned to his capital, a man who had helped to impose the worst evils of Nazism on the captive peoples of Europe was being brought to trial; he was a Belgian collaborator, Fernand Daumeries. Tried at Charleroi on November 20 for inhumane behaviour at Breendonk camp, on the outskirts of Antwerp, Daumeries was sentenced to death.

On November 22, American troops entered the town of St Dié, in the foothills of the Vosges; it was in flames, having been set on fire by the retreating Germans. 'For the second time in twenty-five years,' an emotional Mayor Evrat told his liberators, 'our brave American friends have come to the rescue of their grandmother, aged Europe, and of their godmother, the city of St Dié.'

During the First World War, for four years, St Dié had been less than ten miles from the German front line.

On November 23, French and American troops entered Strasbourg, which in

1940 the Germans had made the capital of annexed Alsace. Reaching the Reich
Anatomical Institute of Himmler's friend Professor Auguste Hirt, the Americans
found a supply of headless bodies in his storeroom. The Professor himself had
disappeared, and was never found. He was forty-six years old.

On November 25, the city of Metz fell to General Patton's Third Army. That
day, at Auschwitz, the Germans began the demolition of the remaining gas
chambers. On the following day, all two hundred Jews who had been forced to
drag the corpses into the crematoria were themselves murdered. 'I am going
away calmly,' one of them, Chaim Herman, had written three weeks earlier to
his wife and daughter in France, 'knowing that you are alive, and our enemy is
broken.'

In the Far East, the Allied armies were still a long way from victory. On
November 24, Japanese troops entered the Chinese city of Nanning, only 120
miles by rail from their forces in French Indo-China. On the following day, in
the Gulf of Leyte, every available Japanese aircraft was sent against the Americans, many of them on suicide missions, in the first of a series of hopeless yet
damaging attacks. In this first attack, three aircraft carriers were damaged; on
board the *Intrepid*, sixty-five men were killed.

Over London, on November 25, a V2 rocket hit a Woolworth's department
store in New Cross Road, Deptford, killing 160 lunchtime shoppers. 'I remember
seeing a horse's head in the gutter,' a thirteen-year-old girl, June Gaida, later
recalled, and she added: 'Further on there was a pram all twisted and bent, and
there was a little baby's hand still in its woolly sleeve. Outside the pub, there
was a bus and it had been concertinaed, with rows of people sitting inside, all
covered in dust – and dead.'

On the day of the Deptford rocket bomb, a British submarine, HMS *Sturdy*,
on its way from Australia to Indonesian waters, stopped a Japanese cargo ship
by surface shellfire. The Japanese crew having abandoned their ship, the only
people left on board were fifty women and children, all of them Indonesians.
In order to deny the Japanese any use of the ship's cargo, the submarine
commander ordered the ship to be sunk, despite a protest from the officer who
had to lay the explosive charges. 'Get on with it', was the commander's response.
The cargo ship and its passengers were then blown up, together with the ship's
war supplies.

On November 26, the first Allied shipping convoy sailed through the Scheldt
unimpeded to Antwerp. That day, Hitler put Heinrich Himmler in full military
command of all German troops, as well as all German air forces, on the Upper
Rhine. On November 27, at Auschwitz, nearly six hundred of Himmler's men,
the camp SS guard, were decorated with the Iron Cross for their 'bravery' in
suppressing the slave labourers' revolt of the previous month, in which four SS
had been killed.

In Antwerp, the full brunt of the V2 rockets was now being felt; on November
27, when one of the rockets fell at a busy road junction near the central railway
station, just as a military convoy was passing, 157 people were killed, including

twenty-nine Allied servicemen from the convoy. That same day, in Britain, at Fauld in Staffordshire, an accidental explosion in an underground bomb store, in a gypsum mine ninety feet below the surface, killed sixty-eight civilians in the farms and factories above. German propaganda at once claimed that the explosion was the work of saboteurs. For their part in the rescue work, three men were awarded the George Medal.

On November 29, German troops in Albania abandoned the port of Scutari, falling back to a new defensive line through Mostar and Visegrad to the River Drina. In Hungary, the Red Army entered the southern cities of Pecs and Mohacs. Across the Atlantic Ocean, two German agents, Eric Gimpel and William Colepough, were landed that day on the coast of Maine, at Crabtree Neck, by German submarine. Colepough, a former sailor, had with him 60,000 dollars to pay for espionage activities. Both men were arrested within the month, their mission having been given away by Ultra even before they were put ashore.

In Berlin, on November 30, there were still further executions as a result of the failure of the July Plot; that day Lilo Gloeden, a forty-one-year-old housewife who had given shelter for six weeks to one of the plotters, General Fritz Lindemann, was beheaded with an axe, as were her husband and her mother, at two-minute intervals. Their fate was then publicized, as a warning to anyone else who might try to shelter the enemies of the Third Reich.

The fate of that Reich could not, however, be seriously in doubt. On the day of Lilo Gloeden's execution, American troops drove the Germans from Mackwiller, in the Saar, inside Germany's pre-war frontier. In Hungary, the Red Army entered Eger, less than twenty-five miles from the central Slovak frontier. Despite these advances, no mile of territory was yielded by the Germans without a severe fight, often from house to house.

On December 1, as the Jewish slave labourers in the barracks at Auschwitz–Birkenau were being evacuated by foot and train to factories and camps in western and central Germany, Josef Kramer, the Commandant at Birkenau, was himself transferred westward, to Belsen. Although there were no gas chambers in his new camp, he was determined not to do anything there which might lengthen by a single day the lives of those who were dying of starvation or disease.

The camp at Belsen was less than two hundred miles from Germany's western frontier, and from the River Maas, along whose western bank the Allies now stood. The American commanders were confident that they could continue with their advance into Germany; on December 2, General Eisenhower noted that the American forces were destroying about three-quarters of a German division every day on the long battle front. 'This,' he noted, 'is about twenty a month.' But Hitler had plans to retake the initiative, by driving westward through the Ardennes, to Antwerp, now reopened as a principal port for Allied supplies.

Usually so alert to each impending German move, British Intelligence failed to foresee the Ardennes offensive. Yet the Enigma decrypts since mid-November had suggested some unusual German preparations in the North European war zone. There had, for example, been a number of Enigma indications of a movement of German troops westward across the Rhine and their subsequent concentration on the western side. There had also been indications of an impending large-scale air attack.

These indications, arriving over a prolonged period, were not, however satisfactorily brought together, partly because the German troop movements thus revealed were seen as an attempt to meet an impending Allied attack, and partly because those who interpreted them did not feel that the Germans were any longer capable of a serious counter-attack. Churchill was not convinced, asking the Joint Intelligence Committee, on December 3, if there was 'any further news'. He was told that nothing was amiss. That same day, Montgomery's chief Intelligence Officer, Brigadier Williams, commented on the most recent decrypt that the Germans' 'bruited sweep to Antwerp is clearly beyond his powers'.

The principal effort to cripple Germany's warmaking powers remained the persistent and sustained attacks on synthetic oil factories and oil storage depots. On December 3, the Japanese Naval Attaché in Berlin reported to Tokyo that the transfer of German oil plants to underground locations was 'very much behind schedule' despite strenuous effort, and that although aircraft production was good, the fighter aircrews were losing many opportunities for combat on account of oil shortage.'

British Intelligence decrypted this message five days after it was sent. Also decrypted in mid-December was a top-secret telegram sent to Tokyo from the Japanese Ambassador in Berlin, dated December 6, with the information that the oil repair squads now employed 72,000 workers, that oil production underground was unlikely to start before March; and that total German output was running at only 300,000 tons a month. 'Oil', the Ambassador added, 'was clearly Germany's greatest worry'.

Despite the emphasis on attacking oil targets, December 4 saw, at the insistence of the head of Bomber Command, Sir Arthur Harris, a renewal of the British fire bomb attacks on German cities, when more than two thousand tons of incendiary bombs were dropped on Heilbronn. 'We estimated that there were some two hundred planes,' a British prisoner-of-war in a nearby camp later recalled, and he added: 'They came circling over, wave upon wave, black shadows gliding across the floodlit ceiling, releasing their hissing bombs and slowly veering away. The flames were replenished from time to time and the countryside for miles around was flooded with yellow light. Windows could be heard tinkling to the ground all over the camp. I was in the slit trenches. A plane screamed to earth in the east'.

During the Heilbronn firestorm, 7,147 German civilians were killed.

On the Eastern Front, Soviet forces, avoiding the strongly fortified region around Budapest, cut off the city in the north, and, shortly before midnight on December 4, began crossing the Danube at Vac, a mere fifteen miles from Hungary's pre-war northern border with Czechoslovakia. Three days later, Soviet forces driving from the south reached Lake Balaton, occupying the town of Adony, twenty-five miles south of Budapest. The Hungarian capital, now a German stronghold, was almost entirely cut off from the rest of Hungary. Hitler, determined not to yield this former royal city of the Austro-Hungarian Empire into which he had been born, ordered German troop reinforcements both from Italy and from the Western Front.

In the Pacific, the American fleet off Leyte had continued to be beset by Japanese suicide pilots. On December 7, the third anniversary of Pearl Harbour and of America's entry into the war, a kamikaze pilot struck just above the waterline of the destroyer transport *Ward*, which, in the first American engagement of the war, had sunk a Japanese midget submarine three years earlier. Now she too was doomed; so badly damaged that she had to be sunk by naval gunfire. The commander of the ship which sank her was, by a strange coincidence, the man who had been her commanding officer in December 1941. No lives were lost. But on board the destroyer *Mahan*, also hit by a kamikaze pilot, ten men were killed, before she too had to be sunk.

In further suicide attacks, Japanese pilots killed thirty-six men on the carrier *Cabot*, thirty-one on the battleship *Maryland* and thirty-two on the destroyer *Aulick*. So heavy and continuous were these casualties, that General MacArthur and Admiral Nimitz ordered a complete news blackout, with the twofold aim of preventing panic in the United States and of denying to the Japanese commanders any knowledge of the scale of damage and loss of life which their suicide pilots were inflicting.

On December 10, Hitler left Berlin for the Western Front, returning to the 'Eagle's Nest' bunker at Bad Nauheim, a bunker which he had last used in the triumphant days of 1940. There, that same afternoon, he spoke to his senior generals about the coming offensive against the Ardennes. He also spoke, that week, to Hitler Youth leaders who had been brought to hear him from throughout the war zone. 'Never since the Napoleonic wars', Hitler told them, 'has an enemy devasted our country, and we shall decimate this enemy also at the very gates to the Fatherland.' It was on the Western Front, he declared, 'where we are going to turn the tide and split the American–British alliance once and for all'.

Hitler was also in a reflective mood. In a further speech to his generals on December 12, he told them: 'You can't extract enthusiasm and self-sacrifice like something tangible, and bottle and preserve them. They are generated just once in course of a revolution, and will gradually die away. The greyness of day and the conveniences of life will then take hold on men again and turn them into solid citizens in grey flannel suits'.

That day, American forces entered the German town of Düren, twenty miles east of Aachen, and less than twenty-five miles from Cologne.

On December 12, in the Pacific, an American battle fleet and invasion force left Leyte Gulf on its 350 mile sea voyage to the island of Mindoro. On the following day, Japanese suicide pilots struck again. Their first target was the cruiser *Nashville*, on which 131 men were killed. Two hours later, the destroyer *Haraden* was hit, and fourteen sailors killed. Reaching Mindoro, the landing itself was a success, but on the following day, in a ferocious storm, with ninety-mile an hour winds and seventy-five foot waves, three destroyers capsized. On the *Spence*, 280 men were drowned; on the *Hull*, 195; and on the *Monaghan*, 244: a total death toll of 719 men, the victims of nature's fury.

As American forces fought their way ashore on Mindoro, many thousand American, Dutch and British prisoners-of-war were being taken by ship from the Philippines to Japan. The conditions on these ships were appalling. On board the *Oryoku Maru*, 40 of the 1,650 prisoners died in forty-eight hours. Locked below decks, and allowed only one canteen of water for every thirty-five men, some drank urine to try to assuage their thirst, others cut themselves so as to be able to moisten their lips with their own blood. Many hundreds went mad. Then, when the ship was sunk by an American aeroplane on December 15, and more than a thousand prisoners-of-war were in the water, the Japanese opened fire on them with machine guns. Two hundred were killed during the sinking and the shooting. More than a thousand of the survivors died later, when a ship to which they had been transferred, the *Enoura Maru*, was bombed in Takao harbour, in Formosa. Of the 1,650 who had set off, only 450 eventually reached Japan.

On the Philippine island of Palawan, 150 American prisoners-of-war in a camp at Puerto Princesa were ordered into deep air raid shelters on December 14, warned by their Japanese captors that an American air raid was on its way. The warning was a trick. As soon as the men were in the shelters, more than fifty Japanese soldiers attacked them, throwing in buckets full of petrol and then lighted torches. As the Americans fled, burning, from the shelters, they were shot, bayoneted and clubbed to death. Badly burned men, some moaning in agony, were buried alive. Only five survived.

On December 16, the German Army launched its counter-offensive, Operation Autumn Mist, against the Allied forces in the Ardennes, seeking to push the Allied line back through Belgium to Antwerp and the River Scheldt. A German attempt on the previous night to drop parachute troops in the rear, near Belle Croix, to disrupt Allied communications at the moment of the attack was, however, a failure; within twenty-four hours, most of the paratroops had been captured, without causing any disruption.

In all, a quarter of a million German soldiers were thrown into the Ardennes assault. Opposite them were 80,000 men, unprepared for an attack, let alone such a massive one. At Hitler's suggestion, thirty-three English-speaking German commandos, led by Otto Skorzeny, infiltrated through the Allied lines dressed in American uniforms and driving captured American jeeps and trucks. They were able to cause considerable confusion and, once the trick was discovered, a frenzy of suspicion. 'Three times I was ordered to prove my identity by cautious GIs,' General Bradley later recalled. 'The first time by identifying Springfield as the capital of Illinois (my questioner held out for Chicago); the second by locating the guard between the centre and tackle on a line of scrimmage; the third time by naming the then current spouse of a blonde named

The German counter-offensive in the Ardennes, December 1944

Betty Grable. Grable stopped me, but the sentry did not. Pleased at having stumped me, he nevertheless passed me on'.

For ten days the Germans drove forward. At one point in the battle, at the Schnee Eifel, nearly nine thousand Americans, surrounded, outnumbered and outgunned, surrendered; after Bataan, this was the largest single mass surrender in American history. More than nineteen thousand Americans were killed in the battle, as were forty thousand Germans.

On the first day of the Ardennes offensive, disaster struck Antwerp, when a v-2 rocket hit a cinema, killing 567 people; 296 of them were Allied servicemen. The rocket had been fired from near Enschede, in Holland, 130 miles away. There was a slaughter of another sort on the following day, December 17, when seventy-two American soldiers, having been captured by a German ss unit south of the Ardennes town of Malmédy, were led into an open field, lined up, and machine-gunned. About twelve of the men managed to escape the massacre and hide in a café. The Germans surrounded the café, set it on fire, and then shot the men as they fled from the flames.

The news of the Malmédy massacre spread rapidly through the battlefield. After the surprise and panic of the first German attack, the Americans quickly found a sterner mood, with 'Avenge Malmédy' as its cry. There were also several other massacres by the same ss unit: at ten other places along its line of march, at least 308 American soldiers and 111 Belgian civilians were killed after being captured or arrested.

The commander of the ss unit which carried out these killings was ss Lieutenant-Colonel Joachim Peiper. For his work in November 1943, during an action against Soviet partisans near Zhitomir, Peiper had received the Oak Leaves to his Knight's Cross. During that particular sweep, an estimated 2,500 Russians had been killed, and only three taken prisoner.

The German murderers in the Ardennes were mostly soldiers in their early twenties. Their whole upbringing and education had been in the Hitler Youth. They were imbued with the ss belief that mercy was a crime. On December 19, near Stavelot, they killed 130 Belgian civilians; forty-seven women, twenty-three children and sixty men, whom they systematically executed on the charge of sheltering American soldiers. When one of the villagers appealed to Peiper to stop the killing, he replied: 'All you people in this region are terrorists.'

The atrocities committed in the Ardennes were parallelled and surpassed by those taking place in the Philipinnes, where Japanese soldiers acted with terrible brutality towards the Filipinos. 'Taking advantage of darkness', a Japanese private noted in his diary on December 19, 'we went out to kill the natives. It was hard for me to kill them because they seemed to be good people. The frightful cries of the women and children were horrible.' 'I myself,' the soldier added, 'killed several persons.'

On December 20, the German forces in the Ardennes surrounded the town of Bastogne, trapping several thousand American soldiers. That same day, in Berlin, the German industrialist Caesar von Hofacker was executed for complicity in the July Plot. He was one of those who, on July 16, had made the final decision to kill Hitler – four days before the actual assassination attempt.

As the battle in the Ardennes continued, the repercussions of the Malmédy massacre were quickly felt. On December 21, at Chenogne, as German soldiers emerged from a burning house carrying a Red Cross flag, they were shot down in the doorway; twenty-one were killed.

In Antwerp, sixteen people were killed on December 21 when a V2 rocket hit a hospital; on the following day, at almost exactly the same spot, three Belgian workmen were killed by a second rocket, as they were clearing the rubble created by the first.

In all, 3,752 Belgian civilians were killed by V2 rockets in Antwerp that winter. In addition, 731 Allied servicemen were killed by the rockets on Antwerp. Not occupation, but liberation, had brought death to the city's streets.

On December 18, American bombers had struck again at the German synthetic oil factory at Monowitz. Three days later, a South African photographic reconnaissance aircraft flew over the factory. Its sole aim was to photograph the damage done to the oil-producing system, but once again, within the full frame of one of the photographs, many of the electrified fences and guard towers of Auschwitz–Birkenau can be seen to have been dismantled.

All gassing at Auschwitz had now ceased, but Auschwitz Main Camp remained, as did the camp for Jewish women in Birkenau: in December, more than 20,000 women were being held captive there.

In strictest secrecy, December 21 saw the award of the MBE – Member of the British Empire – to Germany's leading spy in Britain, Jean Pujol Garcia, the German agent 'Arabel' who, as 'Garbo', had served British Intelligence for more than two years, including the D-Day deception plan. The presentation was made, not at Buckingham Palace, where secrecy might well have been difficult to maintain, but at the headquarters of the Security Services, where a short speech of appreciation was made to Garcia by the head of the Service.

On December 22, despite the German success, so far, in the Ardennes, Field Marshal von Rundstedt asked Hitler to authorize a withdrawal to the Eifel Mountains. Hitler refused. Behind the American lines in the Ardennes, Otto Skorzeny was still causing havoc with his teams of English-speaking commandos around the still American-held town of Malmédy, causing considerable damage, blowing up bridges and embankments, and adding to the discomfort of the Americans. Hitler's faith in the offensive remained. But when, that same day, the Germans called on Major-General Anthony McAuliffe, the American commander besieged in Bastogne, to surrender, they received a single word answer: 'Nuts!' Asked what this answer meant, they were told, with scarcely less brevity, that its meaning was: 'Go to hell.'

On December 22, General Eisenhower issued an Order of the Day to all Allied troops in the Ardennes. 'Let everyone hold before him a single thought', he said, 'to destroy the enemy on the ground, in the air, everywhere to destroy him.' In fact, Allied operations in the air had been virtually impossible since the Ardennes offensive had begun, because of low lying fog; the fog only cleared on December

23. But once it cleared, Allied air superiority was quickly established; hardly a single German train, vehicle or group of soldiers could move without being seen and attacked. Bastogne, too, could now be supplied by air, effectively ending the perils, if not the geography, of the siege.

With the lifting of the fog, Allied bombers struck at the German railway stations through which supplies would have to come: the railway yards at Koblenz, Gerolstein and Bingen were attacked until they were unusable. At the same time, Allied fighters could now follow clearly the line of advance of the most forward German tanks, as they reached to within five miles of the River Meuse. Not only could these tank formations now be attacked from the air, but, even more inhibiting, they had begun to run out of fuel. British bombers having now joined the American oil offensive, the Germans had not been able to accumulate enough oil to maintain a sustained offensive. German air cover was likewise of little avail to them; on December 23 the German Air Force commander for the offensive, General Peltz, was complaining that his pilots were breaking off their attacks without good reason, jettisoning their extra fuel tanks, and heading back to Germany. That day, twenty per cent of one squadron's aircraft had turned back in this way.

On December 23, American forces launched their first counter-attack against the southern flank of the Ardennes 'bulge'. That day, three of Skorzeny's commandos, who had been captured wearing their American uniforms, were shot by an American firing squad. Fifteen other commandos later suffered the same fate. Fifteen returned to Germany.

At midday on December 24, sixteen German jet aircraft, known as 'Blitz' bombers, were in operation against a ball-bearing factory and tool-die warehouse in Liège. They then flew on to attack railway marshalling yards supplying the Allied forces in the Ardennes. It was the first jet bomber operation in history.

By Christmas Eve, the German offensive towards Antwerp had been halted; after an advance of less than sixty miles, at its furthest point, it had nowhere reached closer than seventy miles to its objective, although coming close to the Meuse. On Christmas Eve, in the Ardennes village of Bande, a Gestapo unit, calling itself the 'Special Himmler Troops', shot thirty-two Belgians; thirty as a reprisal for three Germans killed three months earlier by the Belgian Resistance, and two in reprisal for the killing of a Belgian collaborator.

There were many other murders that Christmas Eve; a British prisoner-of-war, Corporal Rowley, recalled one such killing in his prisoner-of-war camp at Hartmannsdorf. 'I was in the compound', he wrote, 'when I saw two German guards carry the dead body of a Russian POW into the camp and dump the body on the floor of the wash house. I asked the Russian interpreter what he was going to do about it and he said "leave well alone". I went into the wash house and examined the body. He had been shot through the chest. There was also a bullet embedded in his elbow; it appeared that he had been shot by a drunken guard'.

Also on Christmas Eve, the Germans launched a final flying bomb attack on England. As well as warheads, the bombs contained letters from British prisoners-of-war; these letters were scattered like confetti when the bombs exploded. 'Dearest,' read one of them, 'This is an unexpected and extra letter card that we have been permitted to send off with our Xmas greetings.'

One of these Christmas Eve flying bombs hit a workers' hut near Gravesend, killing all twelve of its occupants. At Oldham, twenty-eight people were killed, including a woman of seventy-nine and a six-month-old child. These were the last large-scale deaths caused by a flying bomb in Britain.

On Christmas Day 1944, the first irradiated slugs of uranium were turned out by a reactor at the atomic research centre at Hanford, in the United States, and, a month later, the first plutonium was ready for shipment. The atomic bomb was even nearer to becoming a reality.

In Greece, the arrangement which Churchill had made with Stalin two months earlier, that this would be the one Balkan country not to come within the Soviet sphere of influence, seemed about to be breached. Greek Communist forces, hitherto active as an anti-German guerrilla movement, were, that Christmas, in partial control of Athens itself. Churchill, in a dramatic move, flew to Athens, where, on December 25, amid sniper fire and the threat of an imminent Communist take-over of the city, he prevailed upon the Greek Communist leaders to join the Government of the Regent, Archbishop Damaskinos. The Soviet representative at the discussions, Colonel Popov, encouraged the Greek Communists to accept Churchill's terms. 'If we had not intervened', Churchill told the British War Cabinet on his return to London, 'there would have been a massacre'. There might also have been a Communist presence in the Aegean Sea.

On December 26, as part of the continuing offensive against Germany's oil resources, United States bombers again attacked the German synthetic-oil factory at Monowitz. By accident, a cluster of bombs fell on the ss sick bay at Auschwitz-Birkenau, killing five ss men. The raid of December 26 was judged a success; photographs of the factory taken a few days later by a high-flying reconnaissance plane showed 'a good concentration of hits'. But several important parts of the synthetic oil production processes, although much damaged, were still working after the raid of December 26, and the slave-labour camp at Monowitz, as well as the dozens of other factories in the Auschwitz region, continued to employ thousands of Jewish men and women from Auschwitz.

During December, 2,093 women died in Auschwitz, leaving 18,751 on the camp roll-call on December 27. Three days later, a further roll-call established that there were 2,036 women working in the Monowitz group of factories, and 1,088 at the Union explosives factory nearby. Of the male inmates at Auschwitz 35,000 were working at Monowitz, and another 31,000 in other factories throughout the region.

It was still not clear how long the Germans would continue to control these regions beyond the 1939 frontiers of Germany. On December 26, Soviet forces, after a three-day battle, succeeded in surrounding Budapest, cutting off the German garrison from its last remaining supply route from Austria. Inside the city, the persecution of Jews had continued, as had the attempts, by Raoul Wallenberg and others, to protect them. On December 27, two Hungarian Christians, Sister Sara Salkhazi and the teacher Vilma Bernovits, were executed by the Hungarian Arrow Cross for hiding Jews.

In Budapest, as fighting continued in every suburb, two Soviet officers went forward on December 29, under a white flag of truce, to offer the Germans terms for the surrender of the city. The first of the officers, Captain Miklos Shteinmetz, a Hungarian by birth, was killed as he approached the German lines. The second of the officers, Captain Ostapenko, was killed by a shot in the back as he returned to the Russian lines. The Germans declined to surrender, or to parley. Two days later, Hungary declared war on Germany. The last remnant of the European Axis was broken.

In the air above Germany, British and American bomber attacks continued. 'Large numbers of Allied aircraft flew over,' Able Seaman Walker noted on the last day of December, in his prisoner-of-war camp, Marlag, across the River Elbe from Hamburg, and he added: 'I saw them return later, presumably after attacking Hanover and Hamburg. Four hit and down in flames. One American baled out, parachute failed to open. Fell just outside wire at noon.'

These bombing attacks were proving disastrous for the German war machine. On December 29 a top-secret German Air Force message reported that Allied fighter-bomber attacks throughout the Saar region had destroyed road and rail installations on a massive scale, eliminating telephone facilities, and making it impossible to re-route military supply trains. An Ultra decrypt three days later gave the Allies knowledge of this – for them highly successful – state of affairs.

On the last day of 1944, more than two years after their earlier attempt, British bombers again attacked the Gestapo Headquarters in Oslo. Although a substantial part of the building was destroyed, the damage to nearby buildings was considerable, and there were also civilian deaths; during the raid a tram-car full of people was hit. Only four of the passengers survived.

Surveying the war zones in Europe and Asia, it was clear that the year 1944 had ended disastrously for both Germany and Japan. In Europe, almost every square mile of territory conquered by Germany between 1939 and 1942 had been wrenched away. In the Pacific, the vast island empire conquered by Japan in 1942 was being slowly but inexorably eroded. Only Japan and Germany remained as effective war making powers on the once diverse Axis side; Roumania, Bulgaria and, on the last day of the year, Hungary, had cast their lot with the Allies. It was clear that neither Germany nor Japan was prepared to surrender. Both were determined to fight, not only on conquered soil, but on their own native land, and to do so to the bitter end, town by town and mile by mile. The Allies had no choice but to go on fighting the war on these terms, knowing that the cost in the lives of their soldiers, and of their airmen – already high – was likely to continue to climb. Yet the secret weapons of which Hitler had so boasted, and threatened, in the past, had proved, while capable of killing thousands of civilians, to be nevertheless quite indecisive in terms of the outcome of the war.

By contrast, the still secret atomic weapon of the Western allies was giving those who knew about it a sense of impending triumph.

There was, however, one further German secret weapon in which, as 1944 came to an end, Hitler put his faith. When he had spoken of a 'secret' weapon in 1939, he had meant no more than the German Air Force, in itself a formidable instrument of war. Since then, he had been able to cause a certain short-lived havoc with several inventions, from the magnetic mine in 1939 to the flying and rocket bombs in 1944. Now he had a device of which the Allies had known since 1940, when Dutch submarines then using it had escaped to Britain, but to which the Allies had no answer. It was the Schnorchel submarine breathing tube – known to the Allies as the 'Schnorkel' – which, in conjunction with a considerably increased electrical battery performance, a rapid pre-fabricated system of submarine construction, and torpedo tubes capable of firing many torpedoes at a time, could sink eight ships at once. Yet the new submarines could not easily be sunk while at sea, for, once they were ready to enter Atlantic waters, they would have been extremely difficult to find. Even when the submarines' own naval Enigma signals would have given away their location, the aircraft of coastal command would not have been able to find them on the surface to sink them; the revolutionary breathing tube would see to that.

The moment of greatest Allied expectations on land thus coincided with a new and grave anxiety at sea, as the new prefabricated submarines, being assembled at Kiel, Hamburg and Danzig, began exercising in the Baltic. It was this very exercising, however, which proved their undoing, as their own top-secret Enigma messages revealed to the British just where the exercises were taking place, and Bomber Command, from its bases in East Anglia, struck into the Baltic. Thus good Intelligence and skilful bombing, as well as one or two lucky hits on the dock facilities at Kiel, enabled what might have been a real danger to be averted. Only in May was Hitler's final secret weapon ready to go to sea. By then it was too late.

# 44

## Flying bombs, suicide pilots, death marches

JANUARY 1945

Twelve minutes after midnight on 1 January 1945, a German flying bomb fell on Antwerp, killing thirty-seven civilians. Later that day, almost a thousand German fighters attacked Allied airfields throughout northern France, Belgium and western Holland. As many as 156 Allied aircraft were destroyed, many of them on the ground, but 277 German planes were also lost, a formidable toll. This was the attack which the Germans had planned to make when the Ardennes offensive began, but which had been delayed by the bad weather.

Neither the flying bomb, nor German air attacks, could any longer weaken the Allied supremacy. On that first day of 1945, in the Ardennes, the Americans, attacking the 'Bulge' in a fierce drive from the south, pushed the Germans out of Moircy, Tenneville and Chenogne. In Alsace, a German offensive by the Nineteenth Army was thrown back, with the virtual destruction of the Army which had launched it. On the Eastern Front, from Memel on the Baltic to Lake Balaton in the Hungarian plain, just over three million German soldiers faced six million Russians. Against an additional two and a half million German soldiers in reserve, the Russians could pit a further five and a half million men. Against the 4,000 German tanks, the Russians had 12,900. The disparity in combat aircraft was even greater, 1,960 German planes as against 15,540 Russian aircraft. Hitler, all too aware on January 1 of this enormous disparity of forces, was under considerable pressure to agree to withdraw his most experienced ss division from the Eifel mountains south of Aachen, and to transfer them to the Eastern Front. This would clearly end any chance of maintaining the Ardennes offensive, even in a limited form.

That night, German 'Blitz' jet bombers launched their first night attack, when four of them attacked military targets in the Brussels area. But, despite their considerable advantage of speed, there were too few of them to make any change in the balance of air power, now resting securely and massively with the Allies.

In the Far East, New Year's Day 1945 saw a human tragedy for the Allies along the Burma–Thailand railway when, in a raid on Nong Pladuk, ninety-five Allied prisoners-of-war were accidentally killed by Allied bombers hitting at Japanese petrol, ammunition and supply trains in the railway sidings. Unknown to the Allies, these prisoners-of-war had been left at Nong Pladuk to repair the track.

Off Formosa and the Ryukyu Islands, aircraft from a fast American aircraft-carrier task force commanded by Vice-Admiral Mitscher, began, on January 3, a sustained two-day attack against Japanese ships and aircraft; twelve Japanese ships were sunk, and 110 aircraft shot down, for the loss of eighteen American planes. But in yet another suicide attack, by a Japanese kamikaze pilot off Luzon on January 3, the escort carrier *Ommaney Bay* was sunk, and ninety-three American sailors killed. During the ten day battle, an Australian heavy cruiser, the *Australia*, was hit by kamikaze pilots on two separate days; although she did not sink, forty-four of her crew were killed. Kamikaze pilots also killed twenty-two sailors on the American escort carrier *Manila Bay*, forty-five on the battleship *California* and thirty on the battleship *New Mexico*, including General Lumsden, Churchill's personal liaison officer with General MacArthur.

By the end of the tenth day of sustained kamikaze attack, 53 American ships had been hit, out of a total force of 164, and 625 sailors killed.


In the Ardennes, the German forces were being pushed steadily backward. They were further weakened on January 4 by Hitler's final decision to send the 6th SS Panzer Division to the Eastern Front. But for the Americans the battle was nevertheless a hard one: 'The 11th Armoured Division is very green', General Patton wrote in his diary on 4 January, 'and took unnecessary losses to no effect'. There were also, Patton added, 'some unfortunate incidents in the shooting of prisoners (I hope we can conceal this)'.

In Germany, the execution of Germans opposed to Hitler's regime continued. On January 4, at Sachsenhausen, the SS executed Fritz Elsas, who in 1931 had been Mayor of Berlin, and who was a friend of Karl Goerdeler. A day later, Julius Leber was executed at the Plötzensee Prison in Berlin; a leading Social Democrat, the conspirators had chosen him to be Minister of the Interior once Hitler was overthrown.

Since December 16, the front line in Poland had been static, with Warsaw still behind the German lines. On January 5, in anticipation of an imminent Russian forward thrust into Poland, the Soviet Government announced that it now recognized the pro-Soviet Lublin Committee as the Provisional Government of Poland. This excluded, as it was intended to, the Polish leaders then in London – and with a Government-in-exile of their own since October 1939 – from any say in the post-war government of their State. 'Naturally', Churchill telegraphed to Stalin that day, 'I and my War Cabinet colleagues are distressed at the course events are taking.' There was little, if anything, however, that Churchill could do, to alter the reality which Stalin and his armies had created on the ground. That same day, in Washington, President Roosevelt issued a directive which recognized the wider aspects of that reality. 'Russia', he wrote, 'continues to be a major factor in achieving the defeat of Germany. We must, therefore, continue to support the USSR by providing the maximum amount of supplies which can be delivered to her ports. I consider this a matter of utmost importance, second only to the operational requirements in the Pacific and the Atlantic'.

On January 6, German ss troops launched an attack on the Americans still trapped in Bastogne, but were driven off. In the Pacific, despite the death of more than 150 men, killed by kamikaze attacks that day off Luzon, no ships were sunk. On board the troop transport *Callaway*, where twenty-nine crewmen were killed in one such attack, the 1,188 troops on board were unharmed. On board one of the escort vessels, the destroyer *Walke*, the ship's commander, George F. Davis, continued to control operations after he had been covered in petrol during a kamikaze attack and was turned into a human torch. In terrible pain, he directed both the fire fighters, and the guns which managed to shoot down a second kamikaze before it could hit the ship. Davis died a few hours later. He was posthumously awarded the Medal of Honour. On board the cruiser *Louisville*, thirty-one sailors were killed in a kamikaze attack that same day. Here again, the ship's captain, Admiral Ted Chandler, although hideously burned, continued to direct the fire-fighting. He died on the following day.

In the United States, James B. Conant, the man whom Roosevelt had put in charge of the 'Manhattan Project' in 1942, noted that the dropping of an atomic bomb would be possible that year, and wondered 'whether the month will be July, August or September'.

Shortly after nine o'clock on the morning of January 9, more than sixty thousand American troops began their landing on Luzon. As they did so, the Japanese launched a new form of suicide attack, an explosive boat piloted by the equivalent of the airborne kamikaze. In the first of these attacks, the light cruiser *Columbia* was hit, and twenty-four crewmen killed. A second kamikaze pilot then succeeded in hitting the battleship *Mississippi*, killing twenty-five of her crew. On the battleship *Colorado*, eighteen crewmen were killed when the ship was mistaken for an enemy vessel by another American ship. But these, though tragic episodes in the lives of individuals, were minor incidents in the battle itself, and by nightfall the Americans had secured a bridgehead seventeen miles long and four miles deep. On the following day, those who had landed were greeted by runners from one of the American officers, Captain Ray Hunt, who, for more than two years, having escaped from the death march on Bataan, had maintained a substantial Filipino guerrilla force behind Japanese lines. Henceforth, Hunt and his men were able to provide regular information about Japanese troop movements and preparations.

On January 12, three days after the American landings on Luzon, the Red Army, already fighting in the streets of Budapest, reopened its offensive in central Poland. In all, 180 Soviet divisions were in action. Hitler could only match them with seventy-five; thirty more German divisions were trapped in the Memel and Kurland pockets, with a further twenty-eight embattled in Hungary. In an attempt to redress the balance as far as he could, Hitler ordered the immediate transfer of sixteen more German divisions, and considerable quantities of artillery, from the Western to the Eastern Front.

As Hitler awaited news of the next Soviet offensive, his judges in Berlin were bringing to trial the twenty-seven-year-old Gertrud Seele, a nurse and public health worker who had expressed her loathing of Nazism during a conversation at a private party. It subsequently emerged that she had helped individual Jews to escape persecution. Found guilty of being 'a recognized enemy of the State', Gertrud Seele was executed at Plötzensee Prison on January 12.

It was on January 12, that the United States Office of War Information announced the number of American war dead on all fronts since the Japanese attack on Pearl Harbour, and Hitler's declaration of war against America, three years earlier. A total of 138,393 Americans were known to have been killed on all fronts, at sea, and in the air. A further 73,594 were missing, presumed dead; a total death toll of more than two hundred thousand. Four days later, Churchill announced the British figures for the five years and one month of war up to the end of November 1944; 199,497 United Kingdom military, naval and air force deaths. In addition, 28,040 Canadians, 18,015 Australians, 17,415 Indians, 8,919 New Zealanders and 5,783 South Africans had been killed in action; more than a quarter of a million British and Commonwealth dead.

On the day that these figures were issued, giving in all an Allied death toll of almost half a million, a further 129 American sailors were killed off the Philippines as a result of a kamikaze attack on the troopship *Kyle V. Johnson*.

However high the cost in human life, the Allies were committed to the unconditional surrender of both Germany and Japan; nor did either adversary show any sign of being willing to give up the fight. Yet it was a fight whose outcome could no longer be in doubt, as two more Allied initiatives were launched on January 14, when, in the Ardennes, the Americans reached Bastogne, freeing those who were trapped, and ending any German hopes of holding even a fragment of the area which had been reoccupied since the start of their counter-offensive a month earlier. That same day, on the Eastern Front, Marshal Zhukov launched the attack which was to drive the Germans from their very first conquest of the war, western Poland. So swift was the Russian advance that by the time Hitler ordered a panzer corps to be brought from East Prussia to Lodz, in order to take part in the defence of Kielce on January 15, Kielce was already in Russian hands.

As the battles raged, the brutalities continued behind the lines. In Cracow, on January 15, as the Red Army approached, the Gestapo shot seventy-nine Poles in an act of terror. In Budapest, in the second week of February, with the city surrounded, Hungarian fascists attacked Jews in hiding or in hospitals and old people's homes; in one such attack, ninety-two Jews were shot, in another, more than two hundred.

On the evening of January 15, Hitler returned by train from his headquarters at Bad Nauheim, on the Western Front, to the Reich Chancellery in Berlin. As the train travelled towards Germany, one of his staff, an ss colonel, remarked in Hitler's hearing: 'Berlin will be most practical as our headquarters: we'll soon be able to take the streetcar from the Eastern to the Western Front!' Hitler laughed.

That same evening, another train set off on an equally historic journey; a boat train which left Victoria Station in London, bound for the English Channel coast, and Paris. It was the first regular civilian link between the two capitals since May 1940.

Another European capital was about to be liberated in the third week of January; but Warsaw, whose uprising had been crushed three and a half months earlier, was in ruins. No city in Europe had suffered such a combination of human and physical destruction, or been so long under the heel of the conqueror; more than five years. In the towns north and west of Warsaw, last minute slaughter continued. At Mlawa, 320 Poles were shot on January 17, most of them captured Polish partisans, as well as many Soviet prisoners-of-war brought to Mlawa from a nearby camp. That same day, at Chelmno, the ss prepared to murder the surviving members of the Jewish forced-labour squad which, for the previous two and a half months, had been forced to dismantle the crematoria and remove all signs that there had ever been a camp on the site. A hundred Jews had been put to this work. By mid-January only forty-one were still alive. There had been no work that final day, one of the labour squad, Mordechai Zurawski, later recalled, 'and we were placed in a row; each man had a bottle on his head and they amused themselves shooting at the bottles. When the bottle was hit, the man survived, but if the bullet landed below the mark, he had had it'.

On the night of January 17 the ss entered the barracks at Chelmno and one of them, waving his flashlight, demanded: 'Five men follow me!' Five people were taken out, Zurawski later recalled, 'and we heard five shots'. Then someone else came in and shouted, 'Five more – out!' More shots; then a third group of five was taken out. Further shots, then a fourth group was called, among them Zurawski. 'The ss man came in,' he recalled. 'I hid behind the door – I had a knife in my hand; I jumped on the ss man and stabbed him. I broke his flashlight and stabbed right and left, and I escaped.'

Running from the camp, Zurawski was shot in the foot. But he managed to reach the safety of the dense woods.

A second Jew of the forty-one had also survived. Unknown to Zurawski, in the first group that had been taken out to be shot, one had been gravely wounded, but had not died. His name was Shimon Srebnik. He too was later to give witness to the horrors of Chelmno, first at Eichmann's trial in Jerusalem in 1961, then, twenty-five years later, in the film *Shoa*, when he returned to Chelmno to meet again the local Poles, one of whom had given him shelter after his escape.

On January 18, after five days of continuous street-fighting, the German forces trapped inside Budapest could fight on no more; 35,840 had been killed. The remaining 62,000 surrendered. Six of the capital cities into which Hitler's armies had marched in triumph since September 1939 were now free from German rule: Warsaw, Paris, Brussels, Belgrade, Athens and now Budapest. Only The Hague, Copenhagen and Oslo still awaited their day of liberation, as did Prague, which German forces had entered in March 1939.

At Auschwitz, the surviving inmates were also awaiting the imminent arrival of the Red Army. But the ss were determined not to allow the liberation of so many thousands of people, all of them emaciated, sick, and struggling to survive. In the barracks at Birkenau, on January 17, there remained 15,058, mostly Jews; at Auschwitz Main Camp, 16,226, mostly Poles brought there after the Warsaw uprising the previous August; at Monowitz, 10,233, Jews, Poles and forced labourers of a dozen nationalities, including British prisoners-of-war; and in the factories of the Auschwitz region, another 16,000 Jews and non-Jews. On January 18 the order was given: immediate evacuation. The captives were sent, on foot, to nearby railway junctions, from which they were taken to a hundred different camps and sub-camps in western Germany, but sometimes by foot for hundreds of miles.

Throughout January 18 and 19 enormous columns, some with as many as 2,500 prisoners, set off on foot, in the freezing weather, westwards towards the cities of Silesia. Anyone who fell, and could not rise again, was shot. The slightest protest was met with savage brutality from the armed guards. The European 'death marches' had begun. In one column of eight hundred men, only two hundred survived the eighteen days of marching and savagery. In another column of 2,500, a thousand were shot during the first day's march.

As the marchers continued westwards on January 19, Allied bombers, in continual search of Germany's oil reserves, struck once more at the Monowitz synthetic-oil factory. As a result of the bombardment, the 850 sick slave labourers who had been left behind were without water or light. In the week to come, two hundred of them died.

Not only from Auschwitz, but from all the slave-labour camps of Upper Silesia, Jews and non-Jews were being marched away. At the same time, United States bombers continued to strike at the whole region. On January 20 they hit the synthetic-oil plant at Blechhammer, were nearly four thousand Jews worked as slave labourers: all of them former inmates of Auschwitz. During the bombing, the ss abandoned the watch-towers, and forty-two Jews were able to escape through a hole made in the wall by one of the bombs. One of the escapees was shot, but the rest managed to reach the shelter of a nearby wood, from where they were able to make contact with an outlying unit of the advancing Soviet forces.

British prisoners-of-war were also among those who had been taken from their camps and put on to the roads. There, marching as much as twenty miles a day, many collapsed by the wayside, as columns of concentration camp prisoners – and of a new phenomenon, German refugees – crowded the same roads and fought for the same shelter. 'Marching all night to cross the Oder before bridges blown,' Sergeant Webster noted on January 20. 'Intense cold, six refugee children died on route – many falling out of ranks exhausted – frostbite gets a grip'.

At Birkenau, on January 20, the ss blew up two of the three remaining crematoria. That same day, they shot two hundred of the 4,200 Jewish women who had been too sick to leave the camp on foot two days earlier. Day by day, the death marches continued into Silesia, with hundreds being shot each day, as well as those who were too weak even to stand up when morning came. Reaching the large cities, the marchers were then put in trains, and sent to the concentration camps at Gross Rosen, Ravensbrück, Sachsenhausen, Nordhausen, Buchenwald and Bergen–Belsen. Often they were forced to travel in open goods wagons. Each night the temperature fell far below zero. Of four thousand men sent by train from Gleiwitz to Nordhausen on January 22, six hundred died on the journey. That same day, sixty men and women, who were among the sick Jews who had been left at Birkenau, set off on foot, in search of safety. An hour later a Gestapo unit went after them, and opened fire. Ten managed to find their way back to Birkenau. The rest were killed.

As these death marches continued, under ss guard and gun, the Red Army was advancing steadily towards Auschwitz and Chelmno. On the night of January 19, Soviet forces entered Cracow. That same day, Lodz fell to General Chuikov's Army. On the Western Front, on January 20, the German armies had been pushed back to the starting point of their Ardennes offensive; 15,600 American soldiers had been killed in the battle, but so also had 25,000 Germans. A further 75,000 Germans had been taken prisoner.

On January 20, the Red Army entered East Prussia in force. In Czechoslovakia, Soviet troops had broken through the Carpathians, and advanced northwards from Hungary, to take Bardejov, Presov and Kosice. On January 21, in East Prussia, German troops evacuated Tannenberg, the site of Germany's greatest victory over Russia in the First World War; as they left, they disinterred the remains of Field Marshal Hindenburg and his wife, who were buried there, and took their bodies back to Berlin.

While the Red Army swept all before it in East Prussia, more than two million German civilians took to the roads, fleeing westward. Even as the war of armies continued, the flight of refugees had become a flood.

On January 22, Hitler ordered the evacuation of Memel by sea. There was to be no order to the besieged city to fight to the death. That same day, north-west of Oppeln, the Red Army crossed the River Oder, seizing a bridgehead on the western bank. The Soviet forces in Silesia were now less than 250 miles from Berlin. That night, further north, units of the Red Army, pushing through the 1939 Polish frontier town of Rawicz, reached the village of Göben, on the eastern bank of the Oder, a mere 150 miles from Berlin.

In Berlin, the trials and execution continued of those who had been arrested at the time of the July Plot. On January 23, Count Helmuth von Moltke, the former legal adviser to the German High Command, was hanged at Plötzensee Prison. The founder and leader of the Kreisau Circle, which had first met in his family home at Kreisau, in Silesia, Moltke was thirty-seven years old at the time of his execution; an eye-witness of his last moments described him as 'steadfast and calm'.

There were two other executions at Plötzensee Prison on January 23: Nikolaus Gross, who had been an active anti-Nazi in trade union and Catholic working-ingmen's associations, and Erwin Planck, son of the Nobel Prize winning physicist Max Planck, and a former Under Secretary at the Reich Chancellery before Hitler came to power. He was fifty-one years old.

On the battlefield, on January 23, the German Fourth Army, which had guarded the frontiers of East Prussia, withdrew from the fortress of Lötzen. Hitler was furious, dismissing the Army's commander, General Hossbach, and all his staff, as well as the Army Group commander, General Hans Reinhart. But dismissals could not hold the Red Army at bay. With Lötzen lost, Soviet troops swept into nearby Rastenburg, overrunning Hitler's 'Wolf's Lair', scene of his exhilaration during the spectacular advances of July 1941, and of the Bomb Plot in July 1944. Now it was but one more ruin in the lost and abandoned territories which had been German for centuries. On January 26, when the Red Army reached the Prussian coast at Elbing, more than half a million German soldiers were cut off, and East Prussia severed from Germany.

In the Pacific, on January 24, as the battle for Luzon continued, British aircraft launched Operation Meridian, against the Japanese oil refineries at Palembang, on Sumatra. From these refineries came three-quarters of the aviation fuel needed by the Japanese Air Force. Five days later, a second strike completed the damage begun by the first, reducing the output of the refineries by three-quarters. In northern Burma, a combined Chinese and American force was overrunning the last Japanese positions on the Burma Road.

As German forces continued to fall back on the Eastern Front, more and more concentration camps and slave-labour camps were evacuated. Again and again, those who were too sick to leave, or who stumbled or fell on the march, were shot. On January 25, the SS ordered the evacuation of Stutthof, where 70,000 inmates had been murdered since September 1939. On the day of the evacuation, there were 25,000 prisoners in the camp; at least 12,000 were killed as the evacuation began. Once on the march, those unfit to continue were shown no mercy; at Nawcz, 538 prisoners who had typhus were murdered.

One girl, Sara Matuson, who had escaped from this death march, was saved near Marienburg, when a British prisoner-of-war, Stan Wells, found her freezing and starving in the barn where he was working. Wells and his nine fellow British prisoners-of-war took turns to feed her and to care for her. As the march itself continued, Sara Matuson's mother and sister were among the thousands who died. Her father had been murdered in the Siauliai ghetto soon after the German invasion of Russia.

'God punish Germany', Wells wrote in his diary on January 26, and he went on: 'Never again will I help a German, never again will I speak well or defend them in speech! I have seen today the filthiest foulest and most cruel sight of my life. God damn Germany with an everlasting punishment. At 9 a.m. this morning a column straggled down the road towards Danzig – a column far beyond the words of which I am capable to describe. I was struck dumb with a miserable rage a blind coldness which nearly resulted in my being shot. Never in my life have I been so devoid of fear of opening my mouth. They came straggling through the bitter cold, about 300 of them, limping, dragging footsteps, slipping and falling, to rise and stagger under the blows of the guards – SS swine. Crying loudly for bread, screaming for food, 300 matted haired, filthy objects that had once been – Jewesses! A rush into a nearby house for bread resulted in one being clubbed down with a rifle butt, but even as she fell in a desperate movement she shoved the bread she'd got into her blouse.'

On January 25, in the sick bay at Auschwitz, the ss shot 350 Jews: 150 men and two hundred women. On the following day, the last of the camp's five gas chambers and crematoria was blown up. The ss then left. Behind them was a pitiful remnant of the sick and dying. One of those who remained, an Italian Jew, Primo Levi, later a Nobel Laureate, recalled: 'We lay in a world of death and phantoms. The last trace of civilization had vanished around and inside us. The work of bestial degradation, begun by the victorious Germans, had been carried to its conclusion by the Germans in defeat.'

On January 26, at Ravensbrück, the ss shot Violette Szabo, the British agent who had been caught after she had parachuted into France. That same day, on French soil near Colmar, the last German resistance was being overcome; among the American soldiers who fought and were wounded that day was a twenty-year-old Lieutenant, Audie Murphy. It was an action which won him the Congressional Medal of Honour. Murphy, who was later to re-enact his own exploits in the film *To Hell and Back*, subsequently featured on the cover of *Life* magazine as the 'most decorated soldier'.

Undecorated, and unsung, on the night of January 26 a friend of Primo Levi, a Hungarian Jew by the name of Somogyi, died in the barracks at Auschwitz. On the following morning, Levi and another of his friends were carrying his body away from the barrack on a stretcher. 'He was very light,' Levy later recalled. 'We overturned the stretcher on the grey snow'. As they did so, the Russians arrived.

Entering Auschwitz, the Soviet troops found 648 corpses and more than seven thousand starving and skeletal survivors: 5,800 Jews at Auschwitz–Birkenau, 1,200 Poles in Auschwitz Main Camp and 650 slave labourers of many nationalities at Monowitz. The liberators also found the charred ruins of twenty-nine enormous storehouses, which the ss had set on fire before leaving. But six storehouses had escaped destruction; in them were 836,255 women's dresses, 348,000 sets of men's suits, and thirty-eight thousand pairs of men's shoes.

Even in defeat, the German Army continued to resist ferociously, and at times to counter-attack; that same January 27, in East Prussia, eight German divisions halted the advance of the Soviet troops near Marienburg. In Hungary, too, a German counter-attack had retaken Szekesfehervar. But the Red Army was strong enough to encircle towns, besieging the Germans inside them, and then to move on. Both Poznan and Torun were encircled on January 27, as Soviet troops advanced towards the 1939 German–Polish border. Two days later, the frontier was crossed, and two Pomeranian towns, Schönlanke and Woldenberg, fell to the Russians. But Küstrin, on the east bank of the Oder, only forty-eight miles from Berlin, held out against repeated Soviet attacks.

In a desperate attempt to hold the eastern frontier of Germany, Hitler appointed Himmler to command the recently created Vistula Army Group. It was ill-named; the Vistula itself was almost entirely overrun. But around Breslau, a massive German plan of defence was in place.

On the Western Front, three American divisions launched an attack on the Siegfried Line on January 30. That day, in Kiel harbour, a Soviet submarine sank the German transport ship *Wilhelm Gustloff,* which was bringing eight thousand soldiers and refugees from East Prussia. More than six thousand of them were drowned, the worst single maritime disaster of the Second World War.

Not disaster, but heroism, was the theme of the German film *Kolberg,* the first showing of which was on January 30. Shot in colour, the most expensive film ever made in Nazi Germany, making use in one scene of 187,000 soldiers specially withdrawn for the purpose from active service, it told of the miraculous triumph of the defenders in the besieged Baltic port of Kolberg in 1807. Copies of the film were sent to German garrisons everywhere. The besieged garrison at La Rochelle, on receiving the film by air, promised 'to emulate the historic struggle at home, and not to fall short of them in our perseverance and initiative'. Shortly afterwards, La Rochelle fell. So too did the real Kolberg, overrun by the Red Army; but this fact was kept from the German public while the film was still showing.

On Luzon, sixty-five miles behind Japanese lines, January 30 saw a dramatic raid to rescue more than five hundred American prisoners-of-war, captives for the past three years, from a camp at Cabanatuan. A hundred members of the Sixth Ranger Infantry Battalion carried out the raid, which was helped on its course by more than four hundred Filipino guerrillas; in a twenty minute battle, all 225 Japanese soldiers in the camp garrison were killed, and 531 prisoners freed. On the way back to the American lines, one Ranger and twenty-six Filipino guerrillas were killed. In the United States, news of the rescue electrified the nation; for Mrs Caryl Picotte, of Oakland, California, who had been notified two days earlier of the death of her brother in action on Leyte, there was now the news that her husband was among those brought out to safety from Cabanatuan.

In Borneo, the Allied prisoners-of-war were less fortunate than those on Luzon; of two thousand Australian and five hundred British prisoners, only six survived the death marches and mass executions carried out by their guards as the prospect of an Allied invasion loomed.

Throughout the Japanese occupied islands of the Dutch East Indies, conditions in the prisoner-of-war and civilian internment camps worsened during January 1945, as the Japanese, confronted by the prospect of continuing military losses and naval disasters, treated their prisoners with contempt. By the end of January, in the prison camp at Muntok, on Sumatra, seventy-seven Dutch, Australian and British women internees died of starvation and disease. This pattern of deliberate death was repeated throughout hundreds of similar camps.

On the Eastern Front, Soviet tanks crossed the Oder on January 31, seizing a bridgehead at Kienitz, less than fifty miles from Berlin. So unexpected was their crossing that they found German soldiers strolling in the streets, and trains still running on the Kienitz–Berlin line. But so swift, and deep, was the Russians' own advance that several Red Army brigades had begun to run out of fuel, and even of ammunition.

That day, at a meeting of the British Chiefs of Staff, the Chief of the Air Staff, Sir Charles Portal, told his Army and Navy colleagues that the Air Staff would shortly be submitting an appreciation 'of the assistance to the Russian advance which might be effected by the strategic bomber force'. This could be done because the Allied armies in the West were stalled after the Ardennes. Portal also spoke of rearranging the Anglo-American bombing priorities in such a way as to make it possible to attack both Berlin and the German tank factories, 'in relation to the present Russian offensive'. If the forces employed on bombing German lines of communication in the West could be reduced, Portal added, it would be possible both to attack German tank factories, 'and, also to make heavy attacks in the four cities, Berlin, Dresden, Leipzig and Chemnitz', where the 'resulting confusion' was 'most likely to hamper enemy efforts to transfer forces between the Western and Eastern fronts'.

British bombers were now to be used to help the Red Army.

On January 31, at Ste Marie-aux-Mines, an American private soldier, Eddie E. Slovik, was taken before an American firing squad, and shot for desertion, the first American to suffer this punishment since the American Civil War, and the only American deserter to be executed in the Second World War. Five months earlier, Slovik had left his unit while on active service. Later, he had been arrested in Brussels, and court-martialled. An almost illiterate man, he had written in his confession, with innocent honesty: 'I'll run away again if I have to go out there.'

To have stated that he would desert again sealed Slovik's fate.

In every Army, there were tens of thousands of soldiers for whom the stress of battle proved too much to bear. Hundreds – even thousands – were shot on the battlefield itself, without a court-martial. They too were the victims of war.

# 45

# Berlin, Manila, Dresden, Tokyo

FEBRUARY–MARCH 1945

On 1 February 1945, with the Red Army less than fifty miles away, Berlin was declared a Fortress City. Young and old were now set to work to build fortifications – trenches, earthworks, strongpoints and tank traps. On walls and buildings the old slogan: 'Wheels must roll for victory', was replaced by a new one: 'Victory or Siberia'. At the Plötzensee Prison, anti-Nazis were still being put to death; among those who were hanged on February 2 were the Jesuit priest and member of the Kreisau Circle, Alfred Delp. Also hanged that day were Johannes Popitz, Hitler's Reich Commissioner for Prussia and holder of the Nazi Party Golden Badge of Honour, who had tried to persuade his fellow conspirators to restore the monarchy after Hitler's overthrow; and Carl Goerdeler, the former Lord Mayor of Leipzig, the leading non-military figure in the conspiracy against Hitler, and the man whom the generals had wanted to succeed Hitler as Chancellor.

At Sachsenhausen, on February 2, there was an act of heroism by one of Hitler's prisoners, a British naval officer, Sub-Lieutenant John Godwin, who had been held prisoner with six other sailors since his capture on a clandestine mission to Norway in April 1943. Returning from the day's forced labour, Godwin and the other six were taken, not to the barracks, but to an execution site. Seizing the pistol from the commander of the firing party, Godwin shot the commander dead, before he himself was shot down.

On February 3, the Berlin People's Court met yet again to sentence further conspirators, each day's trial being dominated by the unyielding severity, and personal abuse, of the President of the Court, Roland Freisler. That day, while the trial was taking place of Fabian von Schlabrendorff, of the widow of Wilhelm Solf, and of her daughter, the Countess Ballestrem – at whose home on 10 September 1943 many conspirators had been present – there was an American bombing raid on Berlin. The court was adjourned, and the prisoners were rushed, in manacles, to the cells. Freisler, clutching the files of the cases under consideration, each of which was about to be resolved with a sentence of death, was in the cellar of the courthouse when the building received a direct hit. He was killed by a falling beam.

Von Schlabrendorff, Frau Solf and the Countess Ballestrem, survived. Indeed, the Solf dossier having been destroyed with Freisler, their trial could not continue even in the reconstituted court, and they were later, through an oversight, released.

On February 4, near Brandschied, American forces breached the outer defences of the Siegfried Line. That day, in the Crimean resort town of Yalta, Stalin, Roosevelt and Churchill met to discuss the political problems of post-war Europe, and in particular Poland. After considerable pressure from the two Western leaders, Stalin gave a series of assurances that free elections would be held, and that all Polish political parties could participate. These assurances were to prove valueless.

The Big Three also heard a plea on February 4 by the Deputy Chief of Staff of the Soviet forces, General Antonov, for British and American bombing help, 'to prevent the enemy from transferring his troops to the East from the Western front, Norway and Italy'. What Antonov asked for was 'air attacks against communications'. This Soviet request for Anglo-American air support was presented to the Big Three at their meeting on the afternoon of February 4, when Antonov told the meeting that the Germans were even then transferring to the Eastern Front eight divisions from the interior of Germany, eight from Italy, three from Norway and a further twelve from the Western Front, in addition to six already transferred. Antonov's exaggerated assessment – only four divisions were transferred from Italy, for example – led Stalin to ask what Churchill and Roosevelt's wishes were 'in regard to the Red Army', to which Churchill replied that they would like the Russian offensive to continue.

The urgency of the need for some Anglo-American air action to help that offensive continue was made clear by a sentence in the British Cabinet's War Room Record that day, in which it was pointed out that 'between the Oder bend north west of Glogau and the Carpathians all Russian attacks failed in the face of strengthened German resistance'. On the following day, in a memorandum for the Combined Chiefs of Staff, the British Chiefs of Staff agreed 'to do what is possible to assist the advance of the Soviet Army'. That same day, at a meeting of the joint British, United States and Russian Chiefs of Staff, General Antonov went so far as to warn the Western generals that if the Allies 'were unable to take full advantage of their air superiority they' – the Russians – 'did not have sufficient superiority on the ground to overcome enemy opposition'.

The British and American Chiefs of Staff at once agreed to deflect some of their bomber forces from the attack on Germany's oil reserves and supplies, then the current priority, to an attack on the German Army's lines of communication in the Berlin–Dresden–Leipzig region. They also agreed, at Antonov's suggestion, that these three specific cities should be 'allotted to the Allied air forces', leaving the Russian bombers to attack targets further east.

Thus, at Yalta, in an attempt to help the Red Army halt the flow of German troops through Dresden and other cities to the Eastern Front, the fate of Dresden – which for 'Bomber' Harris remained one of the few major unbombed cities – was sealed. It was Harris who, in his capacity as head of Bomber Command, had for so long resisted the call to focus his strength against Germany's oil resources, preferring to put his faith, which all Allied Intelligence including Ultra had shown to be misplaced, in the creation of firestorms and rubble.

Discussing the military balance of forces, Stalin pointed out to Roosevelt and Churchill, at their meeting on February 5, that the Red Army had put 180 divisions in the field, against 80 German divisions, 'a preponderance of over two to one', and went on to ask: 'How did we stand as regards preponderance of troops in the West?' Churchill, answering, explained that neither in France nor Italy did the Anglo-American forces have 'any large preponderance' in infantry, although they had 'an overwhelming preponderance in the air, and also in tanks at those points at which we had decided to concentrate force'. On the Western Front, General Marshall told the Big Three, the Germans had seventy-nine divisions, albeit greatly under strength, as against seventy-eight Allied divisions.

That night, the Red Army again crossed the Oder, this time at Brieg, twenty-five miles below Breslau. Further north, two days later, Soviet troops crossed the river at Fürstenberg, sixty miles from Berlin, The Germans were dismayed. 'The troops are pretty well fed up to the back teeth' was von Rundstedt's private comment that day. Yet the fanaticism of the German soldier continued to amaze those whose armies had come so far and won so many battles; in Poznan, and in Glogau, the German garrisons refused to surrender, while in Breslau, not yet besieged, more than 40,000 troops prepared to resist the Russian attack.

On the Western Front, on February 8, Canadian forces launched Operation Veritable, aimed at driving south from Nijmegen, to capture the area between the River Maas and the River Rhine, and thus force the Germans from the western bank of the Upper Rhine. On the following day, General de Lattre de Tassigny completed Operation Cheerful, against the Germans trapped in a pocket at Colmar. During the battle, which had lasted twenty days, 1,600 French and 540 American soldiers were killed; when the battle ended, and the Germans pulled back across the Upper Rhine, 22,000 German soldiers were taken prisoner.

That night, in Berlin, Hitler was shown an architectural model for the reconstruction of Linz once the war was over. To ss General Kaltenbrunner, who had reported on the sharp fall in public morale, Hitler remarked: 'do you imagine I could talk like this about my plans for the future if I did not believe deep down that we really are going to win this war in the end!'


In Manila, on February 9, Japanese troops rounded up more than twenty girls, whom they proceeded to rape over the next three days. Some were raped more than thirty times. Only when the building in which the girls were being confined was hit by American shell fire did some of them manage to escape. One of them, Esther Gracia Moras, was later to give evidence of this atrocity at the Tokyo War Crimes trial.

*          *          *

At Yalta, Roosevelt, Churchill and Stalin agreed on February 10 that Germany should pay reparation for the damage done by her occupation. At Stalin's request, all Russians who had been captured fighting in the ranks of the German Army were to be repatriated – 'sent to Russia as quickly as possible' were Stalin's words. Many of these troops had opposed the Allies during the Normandy landings. It was also agreed that the Soviet Union would enter the war against Japan two or three months after Germany had been defeated, and to receive in return both southern Sakhalin, annexed by Japan from Russia in 1905, and the Kurile Islands, acquired by Japan – in part from Russia and in part from China – in 1875.

On the day of these decisions, a renewed Soviet offensive was launched against the Germans in East Pomerania, where Himmler's Vistula Army Group was still holding on at the lower reaches of the river, south of Danzig. In Budapest, a German force of 16,000 was still trying to break out of the city; encircled at Perbal, it was destroyed; only a few hundred soldiers were able to escape. Inside Buda, that part of the capital which lay on the western bank of the Danube, all German resistance was coming to an end, as 30,000 Germans surrendered, their ammunition, strength and willpower gone.

In the first two months of 1945, German rocket bomb attacks on Britain had continued, with 585 civilians being killed in January and a further 483 in February. Among those who died in Britain on February 13 was Leading Seaman Tommy Brown, who, two years earlier, had been awarded the George Medal for bravery at sea. When two of his sisters were trapped in a burning tenement building, he tried to rescue them, but was killed in the attempt.

On the night of February 13, as part of the Anglo-American plan, agreed at the Yalta Conference, to delay for as long as possible German troop reinforcements being transferred from Norway, Italy and Holland to the Eastern battle zone around Breslau, 245 British bombers struck at the city of Dresden, followed three and a half hours later by 529 more. Their purpose was to destroy the city's railway marshalling yards. During the first of the two raids, a firestorm, created in a single hour's bombardment, burnt through eleven square miles of the city.

The British raid on Dresden was followed the next morning by an American raid, also aimed at the marshalling yards, in which 450 bombers took part. Dresden, whose ancient city centre had hitherto been untouched by war, was now on fire; some of the fires were to burn for seven days and nights. Of the total of more than 1,200 bombers which had cast their bombs on the city, only eight were shot down. For the British bombers, this was the lowest ever 'chop rate' over Germany; it was also their deepest ever penetration into Germany. Most of Dresden's anti-aircraft defences had been sent to the Western Front, to defend the Ruhr, and to protect Germany's synthetic-oil plants.

On the morning of their February 14 raid on Dresden, American bombers also dropped 642 tons of bombs on Chemnitz and 752 tons on Magdeburg. That morning, Churchill, who was on his way back to Britain from the Crimea, received a telegram from the War Cabinet Office in London reporting on eleven aspects of the previous day's military events. On the Western Front, he learned, six thousand German soldiers had been captured. In North Russia, a British convoy of twenty-eight ships had arrived without loss. In central Burma, a series of Japanese attacks had been beaten back. In central Europe, Budapest had been entered by Russian troops, and tens of thousands of German soldiers killed in the battle. In the air – and this was the tenth item in the list of eleven – Bomber Command had despatched a total of 1,252 aircraft over Germany, of which 805 had been sent to Dresden, 368 against the Böhlen synthetic-oil factory, 71 against Magdeburg and eight against the oil refinery at Misburg.

The eleventh and final item in this War Cabinet Office telegram concerned the continuing v2 rocket attacks on Britain. In the fifteen hours before daybreak on February 14, fourteen rockets had fallen in the London area, killing twelve civilians at Wood Green, twelve at Romford, twenty-eight at West Ham and three at Bexley. The total number of rocket bomb deaths in the week ending February 15 was 180, the highest since the rocket attacks had begun.

That same day, the first British report on the Dresden raid was prepared, based on an analysis of aerial photographs. Although it gave no casualty figures, the report noted the 'great material damage' to be seen in the photographs, adding that it was 'apparent, from the many blocks of buildings seen gutted, that fires have already destroyed part of the city'. Interpretation of further photographs taken on February 15 was 'rendered difficult', the Chiefs of Staff Committee learned a week later, 'by the haze from fires still burning more than thirty-six hours after the last attack'.

On the morning of February 15, less than thirty-six hours after the first British bombers had flown over Dresden, a second wave of two hundred American bombers attacked the still burning city, on the assumption that even more havoc could be caused if an attack were made while fire-fighting equipment and personnel were at work in the streets, and could themselves be hit.

The death toll at Dresden has never been calculated with precision. In all, 39,773 'officially identified dead' were found in the city and registered, most of them burned to death. At least twenty thousand more bodies were buried beneath the ruins, or incinerated beyond recognition, even as bodies. The inscription on the mass grave in Dresden's main cemetery asks: 'How many died? Who knows the number?' It hazards no answer.

For miles around, the glow of Dresden had been seen in the night sky, an incredible sight in the heart of Germany. In a labour camp at Schlieben, one of the Jewish slave labourers, Ben Helfgott, who in September 1939 had witnessed the burning of Sulejow in Poland, later recalled the red sky above Dresden: 'Not only could we see it, the earth was shaking. We were out watching it. We were in heaven. It was like a boon for us. We didn't have to work. The Germans were running for their lives. We knew that the day of our liberation must be drawing nearer. To all of us, it was absolute salvation. That was how we knew that the end was near'.

British and American prisoners-of-war were brought into Dresden to dig out the bodies. One of these prisoners, Kurt Vonnegut, later a distinguished American novelist, recalled: 'Every day we walked into the city and dug into basements and shelters to get corpses out, as a sanitary measure. When we went into them, a typical shelter, an ordinary basement usually, looked like a streetcar full of people who'd simultaneously had heart failure. Just people sitting there in their chairs, all dead'.

Such unusual occurences had been seen in a number of Germany's bombed cities since the Hamburg firestorm two and a half years earlier, when 42,000 had died.

In the Philippines, American forces, having driven a wedge between the Japanese forces, now pressed in upon Manila. On February 15, American carrier-based aircraft attacked the Japanese home islands for the first time, as the most powerful naval force that had ever put to sea – twenty aircraft-carriers escorted by ninety warships – steamed off Honshu Island.

On February 16, an American parachute regiment landed on Corregidor. That same day, as American carrier-based aircraft began the bombardment of Japanese installations on the island of Iwo Jima, an American expeditionary force set sail for Iwo Jima from Saipan.

In the battle for Manila, the Japanese soldiers, refusing to surrender, turned every street and every building into a savage battleground, reducing a once beautiful city to ruins and carnage. In an orgy of killing, nearly a hundred thousand Filipino civilians were murdered by the Japanese; in some cases, hospitals were set on fire after the patients had been strapped to their beds. The killing of Filipino civilians had reached a frenzy. 'In various sectors', a Japanese soldier noted in his diary on February 17, 'we have killed several thousand (including young and old, men and women), and Chinese'.

On February 17, two thousand Japanese soldiers took up position inside Manila's ancient walled city. With them were five thousand Filipino hostages. Over a loudspeaker, the American commander, General Oscar Griswold, urged the Japanese to surrender. They would not do so; six days and six nights later, with the ancient city in ruins, and almost every one of the Japanese and the Filipinos dead, yet another Allied victory had been secured.

At dawn on February 19, American marines landed on Iwo Jima, an eight square mile barren island, and an airbase judged essential for the bombing of Japan. After three days of violent fighting, in which hundreds of Americans were literally blown to pieces by the Japanese artillery, the American flag was raised above Mount Suribachi, the highest point on the small island. It was 10.20 in the morning. Of the dozen flag raisers, two – Lieutenant Colonel Chandler W. Johnson and Sergeant Ernest T. Thomas – were subsequently killed in action, Thomas on his twenty-first birthday.

A Marine photographer, Sergeant Louis R. Lowery, photographed the scene, but his photograph, sent back by ordinary army post to Marine headquarters in the United States, took a month to arrive. Meanwhile, a second flag raising, which had taken place an hour after the first, was photographed by an Associated Press photographer, Joe Rosenthal. His photograph, sent by seaplane to Guam, and on from there by radio-photo to the United States, was immediately acclaimed as extraordinary, so much so that President Roosevelt ordered the six flag raisers seen in it to come home to share their glory with all their fellow-Americans.

By the time Roosevelt's order reached Iwo Jima, three of the six – Captain Harlon Block, Sergeant Michael Strank and Private Franklin R. Sousley – were already dead. Joe Rosenthal won a Pulitzer prize for his photograph, and, while the struggle against Japan still raged, the United States Post Office Department issued a three-cent Iwo Jima Flag Raising Stamp, the first United States stamp of the war to show a Second World War scene. The photograph of this second flag raising was to become the most frequently-reproduced photograph of the Pacific war.

The flag had been raised, but the battle for Iwo Jima went on, across strongly contested ridges and ravines such as 'Bloody Gorge', the 'Meat Grinder', and the 'Mincer'. Victory on Iwo Jima did not come until the end of March, after the death of 6,821 American marines, and of 20,000 of the Japanese defenders. Only 1,083 Japanese had allowed themselves to be captured.

Nearly nine hundred American sailors were also killed during the battle for Iwo Jima, 218 of them when the escort carrier *Bismarck Sea* was sunk by a Japanese suicide aircraft.

Following the capture of Iwo Jima, American bombers, based on the island, began the regular and relentless bombing of the Japanese home islands. On Luzon, with Manila at last under American control, the fighting continued, as did the attempts to rescue American prisoners-of-war. In a raid by American troops and Filipino guerrillas on Los Banos prison camp, south of Manila, the whole Japanese garrison was killed, and 2,100 prisoners-of-war rescued, for the loss of only two Americans.

In Germany, the sound of artillery fire could now be heard at Peenemünde, home of the V2 rocket. On February 17, the rocket scientists left the centre by train, their equipment sent westward by barge. By the end of the month, both had reached Oberammergau, in Bavaria, rumoured to be the region to which Hitler would retreat for the final fight. In Silesia, Breslau was now besieged.

On February 19, at this moment of crisis for the German Army in the East, Heinrich Himmler, acting behind Hitler's back, met a Swedish Red Cross official, Count Folke Bernadotte, to ask the Swede if it might be possible to open negotiations with the Western Allies. Bernadotte, a skilful negotiator, suggested that as a first step the concentration camps might be transferred to the International Committee of the Red Cross. Himmler was willing to allow the inmates to receive Red Cross food parcels – but only the 'Nordic' inmates, not Slavs or Jews. The two men agreed to meet again.

On February 21, Hitler's military advisers urged him to pull back all German troops from Pomerania. He refused to do so, insisting that the railway line from Stettin to Danzig be held at all cost. On the following day, the German garrison in Poznan surrendered, their commander having committed suicide. There was now no way that Pomerania could be retained.

643

One last Allied bombing effort was about to be made to destroy German communications throughout the Reich: Operation Clarion. Two early but accidental victims, on February 22, were the two Swiss border towns of Stein am Rhein and Rafz, in which seventeen Swiss civilians were killed.

In all, nine thousand aircraft took part in Operation Clarion, hitting at railway yards, canal locks, bridges and vehicles without pause for twenty-four hours. In a raid on Pforzheim on the night of February 23, Captain E. Swales held his crippled bomber in the air for long enough to allow his crew to parachute to safety; he died when the bomber crashed, and was awarded a posthumous Victoria Cross. Captain Swales was one of 2,227 members of the South African Air Force who were killed in action during the Second World War.

On February 24, as the Operation Clarion bombing raids were in progress, Hitler met his Gauleiters in Berlin. 'You may see my hand tremble sometimes today,' he told them, 'and perhaps even my head now and then; but my heart – never!' On the Western Front, no Allied soldiers had yet crossed the Rhine. On the Eastern Front, the Oder, although bridged in several places, was still serving as an effective barrier to any Russian attempt to move closer to Berlin.

On February 26, the Americans on Corregidor Island prepared for victory. For two weeks, they had fought to defeat the Japanese on the island fortress from which they had been driven three years earlier. In the struggle to retake the tiny island more than three thousand Japanese soldiers, all but a handful of the garrison, had been killed. Then, in a final act of mass defiance and suicide, the Japanese hiding in the tunnels under Monkey Point blew up the largest ammunition dump on the island; fifty-two American soldiers were killed in the explosion. The two hundred Japanese in the tunnel were also dead and 196 Americans injured. 'As soon as I got all the casualties off,' wrote Captain Bill McLain, a battalion surgeon, 'I sat down on a rock and burst out crying. I couldn't stop myself and didn't even want to. I had seen more than a man could stand, and still stay normal.'

By nightfall on February 27, when organized resistance on Corregidor ended, some six thousand Japanese were dead. Earlier that day, while fighting was still going on in Manila's walled city, General MacArthur had reached the Mala-canan Palace, where he told the Filipinos present that their country was 'again at liberty to pursue its destiny to an honoured position in the family of free nations'. As for Manila itself, MacArthur added: 'Your capital city, cruelly punished though it be, has regained its rightful place – citadel of democracy in the East.' He then broke down and wept. Later he was to write: 'To others it might have seemed my moment of victory and monumental personal acclaim, but to me it seemed only the culmination of a panorama of physical and spiritual disaster. It had killed something inside me to see my men die.'

On February 28, American forces landed at Puerto Princesa, on Palawan Island, where they immediately began to search for the prisoners-of-war who had been held there for the past three years. What they found were only a few identity discs and personal belongings. Two weeks later they were to find seventy-nine skeletons, twenty-six of them in a mass grave. Bullets had pierced the skulls, which had also been crushed with blunt instruments.

The landing at Puerto Princesa was the first of thirty-eight assaults against the 450,000 Japanese soldiers in the islands of the southern Philippines. Six principal islands were invaded within two weeks, culminating on March 10 with Mindanao. Other landings continued until July, the reconquest of these islands costing more than thirteen thousand American lives.

On February 28, British Intelligence informed the Soviet Military Mission in London of the German Army's order of battle on the Eastern Front. This information had come from Ultra. That same day, after German documents captured at Strasbourg had confirmed that the Auer Factory at Oranienburg, north of Berlin, was involved in the manufacture of uranian metals for atomic energy, orders were given to bomb the factory as a matter of priority.

On the Western Front, American forces reached the Rhine opposite Düsseldorf on March 2, but found that all the bridges had been destroyed. That day, as German forces still held the Russians at bay in Breslau, American bombers again struck at Dresden, their target once more the marshalling yards through which the Breslau front was being fortified and reinforced. One of the casualties that day was a hospital ship on the Elbe, crowded with injured from the earlier raids.

On March 3, Finland declared war on Germany. Turkey had already done so ten days earlier. By these two declarations, Finland and Turkey both earned their place at the table of the victor powers. In Germany itself, Churchill, visiting the Western Front, was in Jülich that day, the first time a British Prime Minister had been on German soil since Neville Chamberlain had gone to Munich in September 1938, to concede the Sudetenland regions of Czechoslovakia to Germany.

In Berlin, which had celebrated with such enthusiasm the bloodless success of those early annexations, March 3 saw yet another execution of a German who had tried to overthrow the Nazi regime. The victim that day was Ernst von Harnack, a former Prussian civil servant and Social Democrat who, when Hitler came to power in 1933, had denounced the new Government as one 'without goodness or grace'.

On March 3, the Germans launched the first v1 flying bombs against London since the previous September. Twenty-one missiles were fired from aircraft. Seven of them reached the London area. Fears for the state of morale in London if the v2 raids were intensified led, that same day, to a British bombing raid on the rocket launching site near The Hague. By accident, many of the bombs fell on residential areas, and 520 Dutch civilians were killed.

On the following day, March 4, American bombs, falling accidentally on Zurich, killed five Swiss civilians. The bombers responsible were on their way from bases in Britain to bomb the German industrial city of Pforzheim.

On March 4, American bombers hit the Musashino aircraft factory in Tokyo. This was their last precision bombing raid over Japan; henceforth, the Americans were to resort only to 'carpet' bombing, of the sort that had devastated Dresden in February. In Burma, British and Indian troops were advancing both along the Arakan coast – driving the Japanese from Tamandu on March 4 – and towards Mandalay.

On March 5, the German Army began to enrol all boys born in 1929, even before they reached their sixteenth birthdays. That day, in northern Hungary, German forces launched Operation Spring Awakening, to try to push the Red Army back from the approaches to Vienna. Despite the scepticism of his generals, Hitler was convinced that Budapest could be recaptured, followed by the Hungarian oilfields, which, only a few months earlier, after the loss of the Roumanian oilfields at Ploesti, had provided more than three-quarters of the oil available to Germany.

Ironically, lack of fuel was one of the reasons why the German offensive in search of oil failed. Spring Awakening also coincided with the spring thaw, exceptionally muddy conditions making it particularly hard to advance.

In Holland, a senior SS officer, General Rauter, was accidentally killed on March 6, during an attempt by some young members of the Dutch Resistance to hijack a truck near Apeldoorn. The fact that Rauter's death had been an accident did not avert reprisals; in the week that followed, 263 Dutchmen were shot. Many of them were so-called 'Death Candidates', Resistance fighters and others who had been held for some time in prison in Amsterdam and Utrecht. Before the executions started, a member of the German police firing squad, Helmuth Seijffards, refused to take part. He was arrested, and later shot. During the execution itself, Jan Thijssen, leader of one of the main Dutch Resistance groups, tried to escape; he was caught, and shot with the others.

News of executions of another sort reached London on March 6; the killing in Poland, by the Russians, of Poles loyal to their London Government-in-exile. According to these reports, there had been 'mass arrests' in the Cracow area of Poles loyal to the London Government or active in the Home Army underground. Two train loads 'of two thousand persons each' had been deported from Poland to labour camps in the Soviet Union. As many as six thousand former Home Army officers were in a camp near Lublin directed by Soviet officials. 'Prisoners are badly treated,' the report asserted, 'and many are removed every few days to an unknown destination.' Home Army men arrested in Bialystok 'are starved, beaten and tortured, and accused of spying for Great Britain and for the Polish Government in London as well as of collaboration with the Germans. There are many deaths.' Refugees were now beginning to trickle home from the liberated camps and regions. A few weeks earlier, twenty Jews returned to their home in the small village of Sokoly, near Bialystok, now liberated from the Nazi yoke. But the local Poles did not want them back, and seven of the Jews were killed, among them a four-year-old orphan girl.

On the morning of March 7, American troops reached the River Rhine at the town of Remagen, whose inhabitants quickly hung out white flags to avert a conflict. Spanning the river at Remagen was a railway bridge – intact. It was the Ludendorff bridge, one of the great railway bridges of Germany built during

Crossing the Rhine, March 1945

the First World War. As the Americans approached it, German engineers on the far bank set off the first of their explosive charges, but the bridge remained intact. The main charge had failed to go off.

Disconnecting the charge, the American soldiers set off across the bridge. 'We ran down the middle of the bridge,' Sergeant Alexander A. Drabik, from Ohio, later recalled, 'shouting as we went. I didn't stop because I knew that if I kept moving they couldn't hit me. My men were in squad column, and not one of them was hit. We took cover in some bomb craters. Then we just sat and waited for the others to come.' By early evening, a hundred American soldiers had crossed the Rhine.

The Western Allies now stood on the eastern bank of the Rhine. No enemy or invader had crossed the Rhine into Germany since Napoleon had done so in 1805.

That night, as the Americans consolidated their bridgehead on the eastern bank of the Rhine, Hitler dismissed Field Marshal von Rundstedt from his post of Commander-in-Chief of the German forces in the West. 'He is finished,' Hitler declared. 'I don't want to hear any more about him.'

In Italy, a senior German Army officer, ss General Karl Wolff, had decided to negotiate the surrender of all German forces in Italy. On February 25, he had sent an emissary to Switzerland, to open talks with the American Secret Service Chief in Berne, Allan Dulles. As proof of his seriousness, Wolff agreed on March 8 to release two men imprisoned by the Germans in Italy, the Italian Resistance leader Ferruccio Parri, and an American agent, Major Antonio Usmiani. Both were taken from their prison cells to the Swiss border on March 8, together with General Wolff himself and three other German officers. They went to Zurich, scene of the recent accidental bombing by the Americans, and began negotiations. 'I control the ss forces in Italy,' Wolff told Dulles, 'and I am willing to place myself and my entire organization at the disposal of the Allies, to terminate hostilities.' He would have, however, as he explained, to persuade the German commanders in the field to agree. Promising to seek their approval, Wolff returned to Italy.

On March 8, when a v2 rocket bomb fell on Smithfield market in London, 110 people were killed. In Germany, the Allies were completing their conquest of the west bank of the Rhine. On March 9, American troops entered Bonn. Far to the West, five hundred miles behind the battle front, German troops on the Channel Islands made a swoop, from their own beleaguered garrison, on the French port of Granville. Ultra had given warning of the Granville raid, but had been given insufficient attention, so improbable did such a raid seem at this stage of the war. At a cost of four men killed, the Germans landed on French soil, blew up several port installations and released sixty-seven German prisoners-of-war being held at Granville by the Americans. During the raid, the commander of a British merchant ship was also killed, and a British civilian, John Alexander, taken prisoner; Alexander was the Principal Welfare Officer of the United Nations Relief and Rehabilitation Administration, UNRRA, which, from its headquarters at Granville, was sending its personnel to all the liberated areas of Europe, to co-ordinate a massive relief programme, as well as arranging to house displaced persons in Granville itself. Alexander was imprisoned in the Channel Islands until the end of the war, together with five American soldiers captured that same day. Fifteen American and eight British servicemen had been killed, as well as six French civilians. One of those killed was Lieutenant Frederick Lightoller, the Port Liaison Officer, whose brother Pilot Officer Herbert Brian Lightoller had been one of the very first Englishmen killed in the war, during a raid on Wilhelmshaven in September 1939.

The Americans were shocked by the Granville raid; during it, according to the official American report, the enemy 'had complete control of the Granville area, and were his objective that of conquest, he was the conqueror'.

In the Pacific, the Americans' own road to conquest was marked, on March 9, with the first day of a new bombing offensive against Japan itself, when, in a raid lasting less than three hours, 334 American bombers, flying from Tinian Island, dropped two thousand tons of incendiary bombs on Tokyo. In a firestorm of even greater proportions than that of Dresden three weeks earlier, almost sixteen square miles of Tokyo were burned out, and 83,793 Japanese civilians killed. That was the official minimum death toll; later, 130,000 deaths were 'confirmed' by the Japanese authorities.

The March 9 raid on Tokyo was the most destructive single bombing raid yet known. But it was only the first of the firestorm raids. In the next three months, the cities of Nagoya, Osaka, Kobe, Yokohama and Kawasaki were likewise attacked and pulverized, and more than a quarter of a million Japanese civilians killed, for the loss of only 243 American airmen – the same number of airmen as had been lost a year and a half earlier during a single British bombing raid on Berlin.

On March 11, Hitler drove from Berlin to the western bank of the River Oder, to see for himself the defensive preparations being made between the Oder and the capital. He was never to leave Berlin again. On the following day, as the Americans completed the occupation of the west bank of the Rhine, having taken 343,000 German prisoners-of-war, the Red Army entered Küstrin, eliminating one of the last bridgeheads held by the Germans on the eastern bank of the Oder, and coming to within fifty miles of Berlin.

Before attempting to cross the Rhine in force, the British and Americans sought to pulverize the German lines of communication leading up to the river. On March 14 the Bielefeld railway viaduct linking Hamm and Hanover was destroyed. A new type of bomb, exceeding in size any hitherto dropped, was used in the attack. On the previous three days, massive attacks had already been made by British and American bombers on railway marshalling yards and bridges at Essen, Dortmund, Münster, Soest, Osnabrück and Hanover, as well as on the Ruhr towns of Rheine, Borken, Dorsten and Dülmen.

Since the American seizure of the bridge over the Rhine at Remagen, German troops had fought in vain to destroy the narrow bridgehead. There had also been a series of attempts to destroy the bridge, including the firing of eleven V2 rockets from their base at Hellendoorn, in Holland. One rocket landed only three hundred yards from the bridge; another fell twenty-five miles away, near Cologne. On March 15, during one of the daily German Air Force raids on the bridge, sixteen out of the twenty-one German bombers were shot down. Many of those shot down were jets.

Also on March 15, American bombers, at the urgent request of Major-General Leslie R Groves, the head of the American atomic bomb 'Manhattan' Project, dropped nearly 1,300 tons of high explosive and incendiary bombs on the German thorium ore processing plant at Oranienburg. All the above-ground parts of the plant were completely destroyed, and German atomic bomb research brought to a halt.

On March 16, American units further extended the Remagen bridgehead, cutting the Cologne–Frankfurt autobahn. Then, on March 17, worn out by the pounding of American artillery units nearby, the bridge collapsed; twenty-five American engineers were killed. By then, however, two temporary bridges had been thrown across the river, and several thousand troops were on the far side. Not knowing that the bridge had collapsed, on the night of March 17, six German frogmen entered the Rhine upstream and, using oil drums, floated explosive charges towards the bridge. All six were seen, and captured.

Hitler was still confident that he could avert defeat. On March 17 a new submarine set sail for the eastern seaboard of the United States. It was one of many that were now able to remain under water almost indefinitely, using the Schnorchel breathing tube. Jet aircraft were now a regular component of German Air Force assaults. The line of the Oder, and the line of the Rhine, although both had been crossed, were still serving as effective barriers. Even Churchill was worried that week about the extent to which Hitler might still be able to prolong the war. 'I should like the Intelligence Committee', he informed the Chiefs of Staff on March 17, 'to consider the possibility that Hitler, after losing Berlin and Northern Germany, will retire to the mountainous and wooded parts of Southern Germany and endeavour to prolong the fight there.' The 'strange resistance' which the Germans had made at Budapest, and were now making at Lake Balaton, and the retention for 'so long' of Kesselring's Army in Italy seemed, Churchill wrote, 'in harmony with such an intention'. He added: 'But of course he is so foolishly obstinate about everything that there may be no meaning behind these moves. Nevertheless the possibilities should be examined.'

In the Pacific, as American carrier-borne aircraft struck at the Japanese fleet in the Kure–Kobe area on March 18, a new Japanese suicide weapon was launched, a flying bomb with a pilot who guided it on to its target, and died in doing so. During the first of these suicide bomb attacks, the aircraft carrier *Enterprise* was accidentally damaged by shrapnel from another American warship, while 101 men were killed on board the new aircraft carrier *Wasp*. Japanese losses, however, were formidable; of 193 aircraft committed to the battle, 161 were shot down. Two days later, British and Indian forces in Burma entered Mandalay.

In Germany, the third week of March saw the execution in Berlin of yet another senior Army officer, General Friedrich Fromm. He was shot by a firing squad on March 19. At the time of the July Plot, he had shown his loyalty to Hitler by arresting Count von Stauffenberg. But he had earlier intimated that he would join the conspiracy once it had shown that it could succeed.

That day, in Belsen, a roll-call showed that there were 60,000 inmates in the camp. Deprived of adequate food or medical help, overrun by disease, tormented by lice and dysentery – those who were dead mixed with the living, and even the living attacked by rats – several hundred inmates, most but not all of them Jews, were dying every day, their corpses left to rot where they lay.

In liberated Poland, commissions of enquiry were taking evidence of the atrocities and mass murders in every town and in hundreds of camps. On March 19, Chaim Hirszman, one of only two survivors of Belzec death camp, gave testimony in Lublin. He had so much to say that he was asked to come back on the following day. But on his way home he was attacked by Polish anti-Semites and murdered, because he was a Jew.

Inside Germany, on the day after Chaim Hirszman's murder, a British Special Operations agent, Francis Suttill, was hanged in Sachsenhausen concentration camp. Before his capture in France two years earlier, he had been in charge of the 'Prosper' escape and evasion route.

In a low flying precision raid on March 21, eighteen British and twenty-eight American planes carried out a raid on the former Shell Petroleum Company headquarters in Copenhagen, on three floors of which the Gestapo kept the records of what it had found out about the Danish resistance. On the top floor of the building, the Gestapo had imprisoned thirty-two Resistance fighters. In the basement, Danish citizens were being held and tortured. The attackers had therefore to hit only the three middle floors of the building. They did so. Nearly a hundred Germans and their collaborators were killed, but only six of the Danish prisoners on the top floor. The rest of the prisoners were smuggled out of Copenhagen and spirited away by ship to Sweden.

Nine aircraft were lost on the raid, and ten airmen killed. In the target area, one of the attacking aircraft hit a power line and crashed on to a school, where it exploded, setting fire to the school building. Other aircraft, thinking that the blazing building was their intended target, dropped their bombs on it. In all 112 Danish civilians were killed as a result of this mistake, including eleven nuns and eighty-six children.

Also on March 21, an Allied air attack was launched against all the main German jet airfields, many of which were made unusable. That same day, after having urged Hitler to conclude an immediate armistice in the West, General Guderian was dismissed. In 1940 and 1941, it was Guderian's Blitzkrieg techniques that had secured Hitler the sequence of victories whereby Nazism had crushed most of Europe.

Hitler would not listen even to Guderian. On March 22, American forces secured two further bridgeheads over the Rhine, seventy miles south of Remagen, the first at Nierstein, the second at Oppenheim, only twenty miles from Frankfurt. 'Don't tell anyone,' General Patton telephoned General Bradley on the morning of March 23, 'but I'm across. I sneaked a division over last night. But there are so few Krauts around there, they don't know it yet.'

Against the two new bridgeheads, the Germans did in fact send almost all their available jet aircraft, fifty of them on the night of March 23. But within twenty-four hours, shortage of fuel, and lack of undamaged airfields to land on, cut even this number by half. During March 23, in Hungary, the Red Army broke down the German defences at Szekesfehervar, ending any chance of a German reconquest of the Hungarian oilfields. That same night, on the Rhine, Canadian and British forces launched Operation Plunder, crossing the Rhine at

Rees and Wesel, the crossing points being illuminated, and the German defenders blinded, by specially designed tank-borne searchlights, capable of thirteen million candlepower, and known, in tribute to the Army's commander, as 'Monty's Moonlight'.

Montgomery's two crossings were a success; they were followed, within forty-eight hours, by six more in the north, and seven more in the American zone of operations to the south. As the Germans pulled back from the river, the decrypters in Britain who continued to read the Germans' own secret cypher messages learned exactly where the next German points of resistance were to be set up, as well as Hitler's plan to drive back the bridgeheads north of the Ruhr by a counter-attack at Haltern and Dülmen. Knowing this, the Allies were able to forestall the intended counter-attack before it began.

On March 24, during the battle for Wesel, on the eastern bank of the Rhine, a Canadian medical orderly, Corporal F. G. Topham, saw two fellow orderlies killed while trying to get to a wounded man who had been hit in open ground. Topham managed to reach the man and then, although himself wounded in the face and in considerable pain, carried him back through heavy fire to safety. On being sent to the rear for treatment, Topham begged to be allowed to return to the front, where he once more went forward over open ground under fire, to help three men who had been badly wounded in an armoured carrier. For his 'gallantry of the highest order', Topham was awarded the Victoria Cross.

The Allied forces now thrust forward to encircle the Ruhr. As they did so, all possibility of Hitler's jets being effective was brought to an end on March 25, as American forces overran the principal jet airfields in the regions of Darmstadt and Frankfurt. That day, Churchill, while visiting the Twenty-first Army Group, flew from a British airstrip at Straelen for more than an hour along the Rhine and east of the Meuse, for about 140 miles, at a mere 500 feet, unescorted, in a tiny Messenger aircraft. Churchill's pilot, Flight-Lieutenant Trevor Martin, later recalled 'seeing the flashes from our own artillery to the west of us' as, in the cramped plane, with no radio, Churchill looked down on the German defensive positions east of the Meuse and the areas of British and American attacks east of the Rhine. 'I was worried', Martin recalled, 'that the Americans in particular would not know that it was one of our aeroplanes.'

Returning safely to Straelen, Churchill was driven to Büderich, on the western bank of the Rhine, where he crossed the river in an American landing craft, setting foot briefly on the eastern side. Then, after crossing back, he clambered over the twisted girders and broken masonry of the road bridge at Büderich, while German shells fell into the river a hundred yards away. On the following day, Churchill crossed the Rhine again, spending more than an hour on the eastern side. It was a moment of deep satisfaction after five and a half years of struggle and setbacks, dangers and unceasing war. 'The Rhine and all its fortress lines lie behind the 21st Group of Armies,' he wrote in Montgomery's autograph book on March 26, and he added: 'A beaten army not long ago Master of Europe retreats before its pursuers. The goal is not long to be denied to those who have come so far and fought so well under proud and faithful leadership. Forward all on wings of flame to final Victory.'

On March 27, Argentina declared war on Germany and Japan, becoming the fifty-third nation to be at war. That same day, the Germans fired the last v2 rockets of the war, from their one remaining launching site near The Hague. One of the rockets, falling on London at 7 o'clock that morning, killed 134 people in a block of flats at Vallance Road, Stepney. Another, falling in Antwerp, killed twenty-seven people. In the afternoon, at Orpington in Kent, an Englishwoman was killed by a third rocket; she was the last civilian casualty in Britain. Two days later, the v2 crew retreated eastward, taking with them sixty unfired rockets. In England, 2,855 people had been killed, and in Belgium 4,483, by this particular 'secret weapon' since the previous September. On this, as on his other types of new weapon and scientific advance, Hitler had set great hopes. But in that same period, his mastery of Europe had been destroyed.

# 46

# The Axis in disarray; the Allies in conflict

MARCH–APRIL 1945

Throughout March 1945, the Red Army had fought in both East Prussia and Hungary against German forces which, however battered and weakened, were determined not to yield, but only to be annihilated. On the Baltic coast, on March 27, Gdynia, Danzig, and Königsberg were all under siege. In Hungary, tens of thousands of German soldiers were surrounded at Esztergom on the eastern bank of the Danube north of Budapest; on March 28, on the western bank, the Red Army entered Györ, only seventy-five miles south-east of Vienna.

Hitler's more fanatical followers still spoke in terms of victory. On March 28, as American troops entered Marburg and Lauterbach – only two hundred miles from Berlin – the thirty-one year old Hitler Youth Leader, Arthur Axmann, told the Hitler Youth now under arms: 'It is your duty to watch when others are tired; to stand fast when others weaken. Your greatest honour, however, is your unshakeable faithfulness to Adolf Hitler.'

'Faithfulness' was a much abused word in the spring of 1945. On March 28, at Pruszkow, near Warsaw, the second of two groups of Polish political leaders, non-Communists, went under safe conduct for consultations with senior Soviet officers. They were immediately arrested, and taken as prisoners to Moscow. Also sent to prison was Raoul Wallenberg, who had earlier done so much in Budapest to help save Jews from deportation to Germany. He too went to parley with the Russians when they reached the city, and he too was arrested. According to one Soviet account, he died a few years later in prison in Moscow.

On March 29, Soviet troops captured the Hungarian city of Kapuvar, and advanced into Austria, only fifty miles from Vienna. In Germany, American troops captured Frankfurt. That same day, at Flossenbürg concentration camp, several dozen Allied agents – Englishmen and Frenchmen among them – were executed. Many sang the Marseillaise on their way to the scaffold, and cried out 'Vive la France!' or 'Vive l'Angleterre!' as their last words. Among the British agents killed that day was Captain Isadore Newman who, in the weeks after the Normandy landings, had, from behind German lines, transmitted and received hundreds of messages to and from Supreme Allied Headquarters and French Resistance fighters in northern France. After his capture, despite abom-

Hitler greets the German woman aviator, Hanna Reitsch, 28 February 1944. Marshal Goering, head of the German Air Force, looks on (*see page 504*).

Soviet forces renew their westward offensive in the Ukraine, 2 March 1944 (*see pages 506–7*).

Churchill and Eisenhower visit American troops in England, 23 March 1944. The troops are in training for the cross-Channel Normandy landings on 6 June 1944.

Rommel inspecting German low-tide defences along the Channel Coast.

Soviet forces land on the Kerch Peninsula, 11 April 1944, to begin the reconquest of the Crimea.

The Italian village of Cassino, after the nearby monastery had finally been occupied by the Allies on 18 May 1944 (*see page 526*).

German war graves at Cassino.

The artificial, sea-borne 'Mulberry Harbour', built for the Normandy landings of 6 June 1944, and seen here in use a month later, after the bridgehead had been secured.

A German flying bomb falls on central London. The first of these 'V1' bombs was launched from across the English Channel on 13 June 1944 (*see page 539*). The first rocket bomb, or 'V2', was launched on 8 September 1944 (*see page 589*).

The American heavy cruiser *Indianapolis*, during the pre-invasion bombardment of Tinian Island, 14–15 June 1944. On 26 July 1945, the *Indianapolis* carried the atomic bomb to Tinian; three days later she was torpedoed by a Japanese submarine, with the loss of 883 lives.

Hitler immediately after the attempt on his life, 20 July 19 holding his injured right arm (*see pages 557–8*).

*Left*
Carl Goerdeler, former Mayor of Leipzig, on trial in Berlin. He was later executed.

*Right*
Judge Roland Freisler addressing one of the accused during the bomb-plot trial. He was killed when an Allied bomb fell on the courthouse (*see page 637*).

*Left*
Ulrich von Hassell, a German diplomat, one of the accused in the bomb-plot trial. He was later executed.

*Right*
Julius Leber on trial in Berlin; he was later executed.

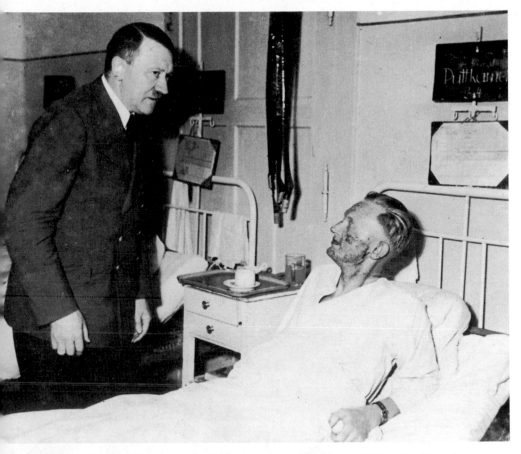

Hitler visits Admiral von
Puttkamer, one of those
severely injured in the bomb
blast on 20 July 1944.

Private William J. Cook, of Pine
Bluff, Arkansas, guards more
than six hundred German
soldiers, after their surrender at
St Malo, on the French Channel
coast, on 17 August 1944 (*see*
*page 570*).

Hungarian Jews reach Auschwitz, summer 1944 and are divided into those (in the foreground), mostly women and children, who will be sent at once to the gas chamber, and those (nearer the train) who will be sent to the barracks and used as slave labourers. On the far left can be seen several inmates, in their striped concentration camp clothes.

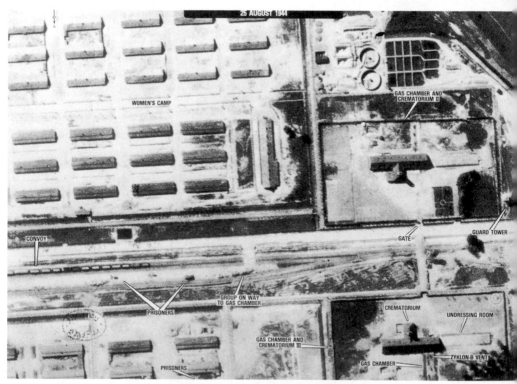

A British air reconnaissance photograph, taken above Auschwitz on 25 August 1944. In it can be seen – as identified after the war – a train on the sidings (left), groups of people, two gates to the gas chamber compounds (one of them open), the roofs of two underground dressing rooms, the roofs of two gas chambers (with vents in the ceilings through which poison gas was dropped), two of the crematoria (with their high chimneys) and the huts of the women's camp (*see pages 578 and 580*).

inable tortures, Newman had refused to betray any of his vital secrets.

Another British agent, the Canadian Gustave Bieler, who had been severely injured when he had parachuted into France, was also executed that day. He was said by one German eye-witness to have made such a powerful impression on his captors that when the time came for his execution, they mounted a guard of honour to escort him, as he limped to his death.

At Buchenwald that same March 29, the Germans ordered Captain Maurice Pertschuk to go to the camp guard-room. Pertschuk had been held prisoner in Buchenwald for three years, having also been captured in France while on special operations for British Intelligence. When a friend tried to stop him answering the order to go to the guard room, he replied: 'You know what happens when someone refuses to go, they take a hundred hostages and murder them'. Captain Pertschuk went, as ordered. He too was hanged.

At Buchenwald, out of a prisoner population of 82,000, a total of 5,479 had died that March of illness, starvation and ill-treatment, bringing the total deaths there to 17,570 in three months.

At Ravensbrück, on March 30, a number of Jewish women who were being led to their execution struggled with the ss guards. Nine managed to escape, but were soon recaptured, and then executed.

Over Germany, Allied bombers continued to fly virtually unchallenged. On March 30, in an American daylight raid on the German submarine base at Wilhemshaven, the U-96 was sunk, the latest of hundreds of U-boats to be destroyed. Among those killed was its Captain, Heinrich Lehmann-Willenbrock, who in his time had sunk twenty-five Allied merchant ships, with a total tonnage of 183,253. Another ace, the fighter pilot Hans-Ulrich Rudel, was shot down that month, and badly injured, losing his right leg. The most highly decorated soldier in the Third Reich, Rudel was the only holder of the Knight's Cross with Golden Oak Leaves, Swords and Diamonds. The Golden Oak Leaves, awarded in January 1945, were unique to him. Rudel had been credited with having destroyed 532 Russian tanks from the air, during the course of 2,530 operations. In March 1944 he had been shot down by the Russians and captured, but had escaped.

On March 31, French forces crossed the Rhine at Speyer and Germersheim. That day, in the Pacific, the Americans completed their five day conquest of the Kerama island group, in the Ryukyu chain; 530 Japanese had been killed on Kerama Retto, for the cost of thirty-one American dead. During the battle, 350 Japanese 'suicide boats' had been found, and captured intact. Then, on the following day, April 1, also in the Ryukyus, the Americans launched the greatest land battle of the Pacific war, Operation Iceberg, the invasion of Okinawa.

Fifty thousand American troops landed on Okinawa on the morning of April 1, Easter Sunday, on an eight-mile-long beachhead. Twice that number of Japanese were entrenched on the island. The landing, however, was unopposed, leading the American troops to change their slogan from 'The Golden Gate in '48' to 'Home Alive in '45'. But then the Japanese attacked the bridgehead, with all the ferocity of men defending their homeland. In twelve days of ruthless

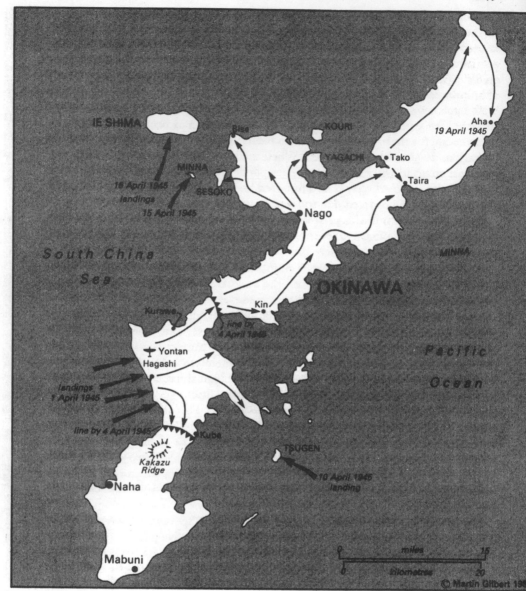

The landings on Okinawa, 1 to 23 April 1945

fighting, the Americans gained less than two miles. But the capture of Okinawa was an essential prelude to the invasion of Japan, which was a mere 360 miles away, to the north-east.

The battle of Okinawa was to last for eighty-two days, with 180,000 American combat troops involved, and a further 368,000 American troops in support. The fighting was ferocious – hand to hand and bayonet against bayonet. Once more the Japanese soldiers fought until killed; but, in the last days of the battle, more than seven thousand were willing to be taken prisoner. Almost every American soldier who was captured by the Japanese was killed after being captured. At sea off Okinawa, thirty-four American warships were sunk, many as a result of attacks by individual Japanese suicide pilots. A total of 1,900 kamikaze attacks were launched, and a further 5,900 Japanese aircraft shot down in combat, for the loss of 763 American warplanes.

At least 107,500 Japanese soldiers were known to have been killed on Okinawa, an average of just over thirteen hundred a day. A further 20,000 Japanese are thought to have perished in caves sealed by American assault teams, using flame throwers and explosives. It has also been calculated that 150,000 local Okinawan civilians were killed. American losses were 7,613 killed on land and 4,900 at sea.

In all, more than a quarter of a million human beings died in and around Okinawa in the spring and early summer of 1945.


On April 1, in Berlin, Hitler moved his headquarters from the Chancellery building to a bunker system behind the Chancellery, and deep below it. That same day, in Moscow, Stalin asked his commanders: 'Well, now, who is going to take Berlin, will we or the Allies?' and he set April 16 as the day on which the Soviet campaign against the German capital should begin. Also on April 1, in Hamburg, Himmler told the City Council that disagreements among the Allies, as well as the imminent use of German jet aircraft in large numbers, would give Germany decisive breathing space.

No such breathing space, however, was to be allowed; the Western Allies, albeit with reluctance, agreed to make central Germany and Czechoslovakia their main target, allowing the Red Army to reach Berlin first. As for the German jet aircraft, they were to be shot out of the skies.

As the Red Army prepared for its attack on Berlin, Soviet forces on the Danube front reached the Austrian border at Hegyeshalom, less than seventy miles from Vienna. That same day, April 2, Soviet and Bulgarian troops captured Nagykanizsa, the centre of the Hungarian oilfields. Germany's last hope of an adequate fuel supply to make war was lost. A counter-attack that day in the Ruhr, led by General Student, had to be postponed because of a lack of tank fuel; this fact was known to the Allies through Ultra.

Not only fuel oil, but essential medical supplies, were now virtually unobtainable within the dwindling confines of the Reich; on April 2 the head of Germany's medical services, Dr Karl Brandt, warned Hitler personally that one-fifth of all medicines needed no longer existed, and that stocks of two-fifths would run out completely in two months. But Hitler refused to accept even the possibility of surrender, and in a message to Field Marshal Kesselring, sent on April 2, he ordered the replacement of every commander in Italy who failed to stand firm.

*          *          *

In London, Churchill looked uneasily at the Soviet advance, and in particular at what was happening in Poland, where it had become clear that the free elections, promised by Stalin at Yalta less than three months earlier, would not take place. As early as March 23, having read the reports from Averell Harriman in Moscow, Roosevelt had told a close friend: 'Averell is right. We can't do business with Stalin. He has broken every one of the promises he made at Yalta.' On April 2, Churchill telegraphed direct to General Eisenhower, suggesting that it might even be possible for the Western Allies to advance eastward to Berlin. 'I deem it highly important', he wrote, 'that we should shake hands with the Russians as far to the East as possible.'

On April 3 the Anglo-American forces completed their encirclement of the Ruhr. Prisoners were being taken at the rate of between 15,000 and 20,000 a day. The conquest of Germany could now be only a matter of two months at the most. That day, Churchill gave May 31 as the date 'towards which we should now work', but he added: 'it may well be that the end will come before this', possibly 'on 30th April'. But the political and ideological clash over Poland cast a dark cloud over the imminence of victory. 'The changes in the Russian attitude and atmosphere since Yalta are grave,' Churchill wrote to the Chiefs of Staff Committee on April 3. To the Dominion and Indian representatives who attended the War Cabinet in London that day, Churchill warned: 'Relations with Russia, which had offered such fair promise at the Crimea Conference, had grown less cordial during the ensuing weeks. There had been grave difficulties over the Polish question; and it now seemed possible that Russia would not be willing to give full co-operation at the San Francisco Conference on the proposed new World Organization. It was by no means clear that we could count on Russia as a beneficent influence in Europe, or as a willing partner in maintaining the peace of the world. Yet, at the end of the war, Russia would be left in a position of preponderant power and influence throughout the whole of Europe'.

Fears of Soviet predominance in Europe did not stop the signature, on April 3, of a final package of British and American aid to Russia, code-named 'Milepost'. Under this agreement, Russia was to receive, and did receive, more than a thousand fighter aircraft and 240,000 tons of aircraft fuel, as well as 24,000 tons of rubber from Britain, and more than three thousand aircraft, three thousand tanks, nine thousand jeeps, sixteen thousand weapon carriers and 41,436 trucks from the United States, as well as nearly two thousand million dollars worth of machinery and equipment.

On April 3, an American armoured division was approaching the German town of Gotha. Among the war correspondents attached to the division was a Jewish novelist, Meyer Levin, who later recalled how he and his companions came upon some 'cadaverous refugees' along the road. 'They were like none we have ever seen,' Levin wrote: 'Skeletal with feverish sunken eyes, shaven skulls.' They identified themselves as Poles and asked Levin and the others to come to the site where they had been held prisoner. They spoke of 'People buried in a Big Hole' and 'Death Commando'.

On the following morning, American troops entered the site of which the refugees had spoken. The name of the place was Ohrdruf, and just inside the camp entrance were hundreds of corpses, all in striped uniforms, each with a bullet hole at the back of the skull. In a hut were more corpses, naked, stacked up, as Levin recalled, 'flat and yellow as lumber'.

It soon became clear the Ohrdruf was neither a labour camp nor a prisoner-of-war camp, but something else: a camp in which four thousand inmates had died or been murdered in the previous three months. Hundreds had been shot on the eve of the American arrival. Some of the victims were Jews, others were Polish and Russian prisoners-of-war. All had been forced to build a vast underground radio and telephone centre, intended for the German Army in the event of a retreat from Berlin.

Among those who had been held at Ohrdruf was a young Polish Jew, Leo Laufer. Four days before liberation, he had managed to escape, as the evacuation of the camp began, running off with three fellow prisoners. For four days they had hidden in the hills above Ohrdruf. When the American forces and war correspondents arrived, Laufer accompanied them into the camp. Many of the corpses which they found there were of prisoners who had been in the camp sick bay four days earlier.

The sight of the emaciated corpses at Ohrdruf created a wave of revulsion which spread back to Britain and the United States. Eisenhower, who visited the camp, was so shocked that he telephoned Churchill to describe what he had seen, and then sent photographs of the dead prisoners to him. Churchill, shocked in his turn, circulated the photographs to each member of the British Cabinet.

On April 4, as American troops entered Ohrdruf, opening up a horrific vista of what had gone on in wartime Germany, General Student was forced, through lack of fuel, to cancel altogether the counter-attack, postponed two days earlier, against the Allied forces in the Ruhr. There was now no section of the front line through which the Western Allies could not break. At the same time, by a careful scrutiny of the Germans' own Ultra messages, it was possible for the Allies to anticipate each change of German plan and each intended counter-attack; top-secret details of one particularly strong German counter-attack, from Mühlhausen towards Eisenach, intended to begin on April 6, were decrypted in time for the counter-attack to be met and defeated.

The Red Army was now fighting in the suburbs of Vienna, and making its final plans for the assault on Berlin. In the air, the last of Germany's once dominant Air Force struggled in vain against the daily mass of Allied bombers and fighters. On April 4, over the Eastern Front, Hermann Graf was shot down; he had to his credit a total of 202 Soviet aircraft destroyed on the Eastern Front, for which he had been awarded the coveted Knight's Cross with Oak Leaves, Swords and Diamonds. Now he too, taken eastward into captivity, was a witness to the destruction of German military and air power.

Churchill had seen April 30 as a possible date for the end of the war in Europe. The war in the Pacific was going to be a far longer struggle. On April 5, the Americans began planning for Operation Olympic, the invasion of the southernmost Japanese island of Kyushu, set for 1 November 1945, to be followed by Operation Coronet, the invasion of the principal Japanese island of Honshu, to take place on 1 March 1946, using troops to be brought from Europe after the defeat of Germany. Both operations were expected to be exceptionally violent and bloody, an expectation which was heightened on April 6, when, off Okinawa, the Japanese Air Force launched its own Operation Floating Chrysanthemum, the use, instead of single suicide pilots, of 355 such pilots in a single stroke. So successful was this initial attack that two American destroyers, two ammunition ships and a tank landing ship were sunk; but at the loss of 355 Japanese aircraft and pilots.

On April 7, there was yet another suicide attack at Okinawa. It was made by the largest battleship in the world, the 72,800-ton *Yamato*, which, with only enough fuel to reach Okinawa, carried out a suicide mission against the American transport fleet. Its eighteen-inch guns never achieved their object however; struck by nineteen American aerial torpedoes, the *Yamato* was sunk, and 2,498 of her crew drowned. In the same suicide attack, the cruiser *Yahagi* and four destroyers were likewise sunk, with a further loss of 446 men on the cruiser and 721 on the destroyer. Of 376 American aircraft taking part in the operation, only ten were lost.

Even over Germany, a virtual suicide operation now took place, with 133 aircraft being lost, and seventy-seven pilots killed, in a mass German attack on American bombers, in which only twenty-three of the bombers were shot down. That same day, April 7, in Yugoslavia, German forces evacuated Sarajevo and began their withdrawal from the Dalmatian coast. In Czechoslovakia, Bratislava fell to the Red Army. In Austria, the battle for Vienna continued. In Silesia, the Germans holding out in Breslau were being systematically destroyed.

To the bitter end, Hitler was determined that his enemies would not survive. On April 8, Hans von Dohnanyi was murdered in Sachsenhausen, and on the following day Admiral Canaris, General Oster and Dietrich Bonhoeffer were hanged at Flossenbürg, less than 150 miles from the American spearhead moving eastward from Gotha. Also on April 9, at Plötzensee Prison in Berlin, Ewald von Kleist-Schmenzin was beheaded. As early as 1932 he had denounced Nazism as 'lunacy' and 'the deadly enemy of our way of life'. In 1944 he had invited several German resistance groups to meet at his country estate, at Schmenzin.

In Dachau, among tens of thousands of prisoners awaiting liberation, was Johann Elser, the carpenter who had tried to assassinate Hitler in November 1939; he too was now to die, murdered on April 9 on Himmler's orders.

In Italy, April 9 saw a renewed Allied attack on the German 'Gothic Line' defences, with British, American, Polish, Indian, New Zealand, South African, Brazilian and Jewish Brigade Group troops taking part. That evening, on the Baltic, the fortress commander of Königsberg, General Otto Lasch, ordered his troops to surrender; 42,000 of his men had been killed and 92,000 captured during the battle to hold the city. Also killed were 25,000 German civilians, a quarter of the city's inhabitants, whom the Nazi authorities in Königsberg had refused to allow to be evacuated. On the following night, Hitler telegraphed to the few German radio units still operational in East Prussia: 'General Lasch is to be shot as a traitor immediately.' But Lasch was already a prisoner-of-war.

In western Germany, on April 9, the Allied forces were confronted by a German Army, commanded by General Wenck, which had taken up a strong defensive position in the Harz mountains. Hitler, in Berlin, had great hopes of Wenck, both in holding up the Allied advance and in being able, if necessary, to hurry back the hundred miles to Berlin, should the Russians get much closer to the city. Within nine days, however, Wenck's forces were surrounded, as the Allied armies, leaving him encircled, drove on eastward to Halle and to the River Elbe.

North of Berlin, on April 10, American pilots began what came to be known as the 'Great Jet Massacre', shooting down fourteen German jets over Oranienburg. That same day, the British public learned from their Prime Minister of the scale of British war deaths between September 1939 and February 1945: 216,287 fighting men on land, sea and air; 59,793 civilian casualties in Britain from air raids, flying bombs and rockets; and 30,179 merchant seamen – a total of more than 300,000 deaths.

On April 11, the Soviet Union signed a treaty of friendship, mutual aid, and post-war collaboration with Tito's Yugoslavia. The Red Army was now master of Hungary, and of eastern Czechoslovakia. In Vienna, Soviet troops had reached the city centre. The Western Allies, too, were not without resources; on 11 April American forces reached the Elbe just south of Wittenberge, less than eighty-five miles from the centre of Berlin. Yet Eisenhower now agreed, in consultation with the Soviet High Command, that American forces would not move on to the German capital, but would push south and east.

On April 11, the Gestapo headquarters at Weimar telephoned the camp administration at Buchenwald camp, to announce that they were sending up explosives to blow up the camp and its inmates. But the camp administrators had already fled, and the inmates were in charge of the camp; answering the telephone, they told the Weimar Gestapo: 'Never mind, it isn't necessary. The camp has been blown up already'.

Thus the inmates of Buchenwald were saved; at the eleventh hour, luck had protected those whom evil had sought to destroy. A few hours later, American troops entered Buchenwald, where a scene of terrible deprivation confronted them: a sickening picture of emaciated corpses and starving survivors. One of those whom they liberated there, Elie Wiesel, later wrote: 'You were our liberators, but we, the diseased, emaciated, barely human survivors were your teachers. We taught you to understand the Kingdom of Night.'

# 47

# The deaths of Roosevelt, Mussolini and Hitler

APRIL 1945

On 12 April 1945 President Roosevelt died at his home in Warm Springs, Georgia. Battle-hardened American soldiers wept when they heard the news. The Nazi leaders rejoiced: 'This', said Goebbels, 'is the turning point.' His view was shared by the Hitler Youth leader, Alfons Heck, who, at Wittlich, was already far behind the American lines, and who learned of Roosevelt's death on an American soldier's radio. 'I shared Josef Goebbels's short-lived illusion', he later wrote, 'that his demise might persuade his successor, Harry Truman, to settle for an armistice or even to join us against the Soviets.'

On Okinawa, the Japanese hailed Roosevelt's death as a sign that their suicide ventures were effective. 'Sudden death of President Roosevelt', a Japanese leaflet announced gloatingly, and it went on to ask: '"Suicide" holding himself responsible for the defeat at Okinawa? "Assassination" laying the blame on him for the defeat?'

No such defeat was, however, in prospect, despite the ferocity of the battle on land and the continuing kamikaze attacks at sea. By coincidence, April 12 marked the day on which news about the very existence of the kamikaze, hitherto kept a strict military secret, was released to the American public.

That night, on Okinawa, Staff Sergeant Beaufort T. Anderson, in an attempt to stave off a Japanese counter attack on Kakazu Ridge, single-handedly advanced throwing his grenades and then, when he had no more grenades, took mortar shells and – having no mortar with which to fire them – banged each shell against a rock in order to release its pin, and then threw fourteen shells by hand against the advancing Japanese. Anderson survived. For his success in holding off that particular attack, he was awarded the Congressional Medal of Honour.

Also awarded the Congressional Medal of Honour during the fighting for the Kakazu line was a medical orderly, Desmond T. Doss, who, as a Seventh Day Adventist, refused to carry a weapon. Under heavy fire, the only unwounded man on a high point on the ridge, Doss carried fifty wounded men one by one to the edge of a thirty-five foot drop, and then lowered them by rope to safety.

In Germany, on the day of Roosevelt's death, at Stadtilm near Erfurt the Americans captured one of Germany's two heavy-water piles. As a result, no German atomic bomb could be developed in the months ahead. On the following day, April 13, from his underground bunker in Berlin, Hitler issued a proclamation to the German troops on the Eastern Front. Deliverance was at hand. Berlin would remain German. Vienna – which the Russians had finally captured that very day – would be German again. 'A mighty artillery is waiting to greet the enemy,' Hitler promised, and he added, mendaciously: 'Our infantry losses have been made good by innumerable new units.'

Even at this desperate eleventh hour for Germany's armed forces, many units were still employed guarding, moving and killing Jews. 'One night we stopped near the town of Gardelegen,' Menachem Weinryb, a survivor of the death march from Auschwitz later recalled, of the events of April 13. 'We lay down in a field and several Germans went to consult about what they should do. They returned with a lot of young people from the Hitler Youth and with members of the police force from the town. They chased us all into a large barn. Since we were five to six thousand people, the wall of the barn collapsed from the pressure of the mass of people, and many of us fled. The Germans poured out petrol and set the barn on fire. Several thousand people were burned alive'. Those who had managed to escape, Weinryb added, lay down in the nearby wood 'and heard the heart-rending screams of the victims'.

Trapped in the barn, the Jews had tried to escape by burrowing under the foundation walls. But as their heads appeared on the outside, they were shot by the Germans surrounding the barn.

'More than an end to war,' Roosevelt had intended to tell the annual Jefferson Day dinner in Washington on April 13, 'we want an end to the beginnings of all wars – yes, an end to this brutal, inhuman and thoroughly impractical method of settling the differences between governments.' Not only differences between governments, however, but fierce racial hatreds, had been unleashed during the two thousand days of war which had already passed between Hitler's invasion of Poland and Roosevelt's death. This became all too clear in the third week of April, as camp after camp was overrun, including Gardelegen, where the Americans discovered the charred bodies of those burned in the barn, and Belsen, whose sadistic commandant, Josef Kramer, took the British soldiers who reached his camp on a 'tour of inspection', untroubled by the revolting nature of the scene with which he was confronting them.

It was on April 15 that the first British tanks entered Belsen. By chance, three of the British soldiers in the tanks were Jews. But the survivors could not grasp what had happened: 'We, the cowed and emaciated inmates of the camp, did not believe we were free,' one of the Jews there, Josef Rosensaft, later recalled. 'It seemed to us a dream which would soon turn again into cruel reality.'

The 'cruel reality' came swiftly at Belsen, as those first British tanks moved on, in pursuit of the German forces. For the next forty-eight hours the camp remained only nominally under British control, with 1,500 Hungarian soldiers, who had been stationed in the camp as guards, remaining in command. During that brief interval, seventy-two Jews and eleven non-Jews were shot by the

Hungarians, for such 'offences' as taking potato peel from the kitchen.

There were 30,000 inmates in Belsen at this moment of liberation postponed; 1,500 Jewish survivors from Auschwitz; a thousand Germans sent there for anti-Nazi activities; several hundred Gypsies; 160 Luxemburg civilians who had been active against the German occupation; 120 Dutch anti-fascists; as well as Yugoslavs, Frenchmen, Belgians, Czechs, Greeks, and, most numerous of all, Russians and Poles – a veritable kaleidoscope of Hitler's victims.

When, after forty-eight hours, British troops did enter Belsen in force, the evidence of mass murder on a vast scale became immediately apparent to them. Of ten thousand unburied bodies, most were victims of starvation. Even after liberation, three hundred inmates died each day during the ensuing week from typhus and starvation. Despite the arrival of considerable quantities of British medical aid, personnel and food, the death rate was still sixty a day after more than two weeks.

'People were falling dead all around,' a British officer, Patrick Gordon-Walker, wrote of the scene as he entered the camp, '– people who were walking skeletons', and he went on to relate a story told to him by the British soldier who had witnessed it. 'One woman came up to a soldier who was guarding the milk store and doling the milk out to children, and begged for milk for her baby. The man took the baby and saw that it had been dead for days, black in the face and shrivelled up. The woman went on begging for milk. So he poured some on the dead lips. The mother then started to croon with joy and carried the baby off in triumph. She stumbled and fell dead in a few yards.'

About 35,000 corpses were counted by the British at Belsen, five thousand more than the number of living inmates. Among those living inmates were many who were too weak even to stand up to greet their liberators. One of these, Harold Le Druillenec, a Channel Islander, had been sent to the camp for sheltering two Russian prisoners-of-war. His sister, Louisa Gould, who had likewise been sent to concentration camp for helping to shelter the two Russians, had been sent to Ravensbrück, where she died.

On the day that British tanks first reached Belsen, seventeen thousand women and forty thousand men were being marched westwards from Ravensbrück and Sachsenhausen. A Red Cross official, who was present by chance as the marchers set off from Ravensbrück, wrote in his report: 'As I approached them, I could see that they had sunken cheeks, distended bellies and swollen ankles. Their complexion was sallow. All of a sudden, a whole column of those starving wretches appeared. In each row a sick woman was supported or dragged along by her fellow detainees. A young ss woman supervisor with a police dog on a leash led the column, followed by two girls who incessantly hurled abuse at the poor women'.

Many hundreds of women died of exhaustion in the march from Ravensbrück. Hundreds more were shot by the wayside. Others were killed by Allied bombs falling on the German lines of communication. Among these bomb victims was Mila Racine, a twenty-one-year-old French girl who, in October 1943, had been caught by the Gestapo while on clandestine courier duty, escorting a group of

From the Rhine to the Elbe, April 1945

children to the Swiss border. Later she had been deported to Auschwitz. Now, having survived so long, she lay dead by a German roadside.

On April 15, Canadian forces captured Arnhem, scene of the abortive Allied parachutists' attack seven months earlier. That day, Hitler's mistress Eva Braun arrived in Berlin to join him in his bunker, telling a friend, as she left the comparative safety of Munich: 'A Germany without Adolf Hitler would not be fit to live in.'

Beginning on April 15, the German Army launched a counter attack against the Americans, south of Uelzen, hoping to reopen the road for General Wenck's Army, or at least its remnants, to break out from the Harz Mountains and to join in the battle for Berlin. But it was a forlorn attempt, halted and then driven back by the Americans, who used not only artillery and tanks, but white phosphorous weapons, to end all hope even of a German defensive line. Conscious that this was to be virtually their last battle in Europe, the Americans gave it the code name Operation Kaputt.

Almost all Germany's ammunition factories and ammunition dumps were now in Allied hands. 'There may shortly occur the most momentous consequences for our entire war effort,' Hitler was warned by Alfred Toppe, the Army Quartermaster General on April 15.

At five o'clock on the morning of April 16, with the firing of half a million shells, rockets and mortar bombs, the Red Army opened its offensive against Berlin, when three thousand tanks of the highest quality and firepower drove westwards from their bridgeheads over the River Oder. Sixty German suicide planes crashed on the Oder bridges, or as close to them as they could, but were powerless to halt the massive thrust of Soviet troops and armour. On the southern front, Soviet forces, already masters of Vienna, drove westward to St Pölten and Fürstenfeld. In the air above Berlin, American fighters shot down twenty-two German jet aircraft, almost the last jets that were capable of action. From his bunker in Berlin, Hitler issued an Order of the Day to his commanders facing the Red Army: 'He who gives the order to retreat is to be shot on the spot.'

Pressing into the last German pockets of resistance in the Ruhr, the Americans had taken 20,000 prisoners by April 16. That same day, American forces liberated both Fallingbostel and Colditz, two camps from which Allied prisoners-of-war now joined more than a quarter of a million other prisoners-of-war freed from captivity during April. In Berlin on April 16, Hitler dismissed his personal physician, Germany's Minister for Health and Sanitation, Karl Brandt; he had just learned that Brandt had sent his wife and child to Thuringia, where they could give themselves up to the Americans.

In the Pacific, on April 16, the Americans landed on the small Ryukyu island of Ie Shima. The Japanese suicide planes were still a daily threat to every move at sea; that day, one such attack killed eight crewmen on board the aircraft-carrier *Intrepid,* which had already lost nearly a hundred men in earlier attacks. Also on April 16, on the Philippine island of Leyte, where some Japanese forces had continued fighting since the American conquest of the island more than three months earlier, the Japanese commander, General Suzuki, was killed, and the resistance dwindled. In the southern Philippines, even on central Luzon, the Japanese had also continued to fight; on April 17, further American forces landed on Mindanao.

Throughout Germany, April 17 saw the collapse of all Hitler's hopes of holding either the Western or the Eastern Front. In the West, American troops reached the outskirts of Nuremberg, scene of the greatest pre-war Nazi rallies and triumphs; now the city was deluged in a barrage of artillery fire.

In the East, the Red Army crossed the Oder in force, driving towards Berlin, and reaching Seelow. As it did so, 572 American bombers struck for the sixth time at the marshalling yards in Dresden. From his bunker under the Chancellery, Hitler ordered all autobahn bridges in the Berlin area blown up, and declared, at a midday conference of his commanders: 'The Russians are in for the bloodiest defeat imaginable before they reach Berlin.'

Not the Russians, but the Germans, were on the verge of bloody defeat; on April 17, American bombers destroyed 752 German aircraft on the ground, virtually the last air forces of the Reich. That same day, however, Hitler refused a request by General von Vietinghoff, in Italy, to withdraw his armies northward. Also on April 17, Hitler ordered his armies in the West to attack the weakest points of the Anglo-American flanks and supply lines; on the following day, Field Marshal Kesselring urged the German troops to stand firm in the Harz Mountains.

On April 18, nearly a thousand British bombers struck at German fortifications on the island of Heligoland, in the North Sea. That day, Churchill instructed General Montgomery to make, not for Berlin, but for the Baltic port of Lübeck. 'Our arrival at Lübeck,' Churchill told Eden, 'before our Russian friends from Stettin, would save a lot of argument later on. There is no reason why the Russians should occupy Denmark, which is a country to be liberated and to have its sovereignty restored. Our position at Lübeck, if we get it, would be decisive in this matter'.

On the same theme, Churchill told Eden that it would be 'well' for the Western Allies to 'push on to Linz to meet the Russians there'. He also suggested 'an American circling movement to gain the region south of Stuttgart before it is occupied by the French'. In this region, Churchill pointed out, were the main German installations connected with 'their research into "TA"' – Tube Alloys, the atomic bomb – 'and we had better get hold of these in the interests of the special secrecy attaching to this topic.' These suggestions, Churchill added, 'are for your own information and as background in deep shadow'.

In Burma, on April 18, as part of the plan to recapture Rangoon, a substantial commando force, led by Major Tulloch and a group of British officers, attacked Japanese positions behind the lines. Known as Operation Character, it also provided Intelligence for the bomber forces engaged in the Rangoon offensive, and assisted special groups parachuted into the region, with whom, in a series of joint attacks on troop trains, marching columns and isolated bases, it killed an estimated ten thousand Japanese troops, for the loss of less than sixty of its own officers.

On the island of Ie Shima, off Okinawa, April 18 saw the death of one of America's most popular war correspondents, Ernie Pyle, killed by a Japanese machine gun bullet. His body was recovered, under fire, by some of the infantrymen whose daily existence in war he had tried to convey to the American public. In his pocket they found the draft of a newspaper column which he had intended to publish at the end of the war in Europe. In it, he wrote of how, in the 'joyousness of high spirits' brought about by victory, 'it is easy for us to forget the dead. Those who are gone would not wish themselves to be a millstone of gloom around our necks. But there are many of the living who have had burned into their brains forever the unnatural sight of cold dead men scattered over the hillsides and in the ditches along the high rows of hedge throughout the world. Dead men by mass production – in one country after another – month after month and year after year. Dead men in winter and dead men in summer. Dead men in such familiar promiscuity that they become monotonous. Dead men in such monstrous infinity that you come almost to hate them'.

Pyle added: 'These are the things that you at home need not even try to understand. To you at home they are columns of figures, or he is a near one who went away and just didn't come back. You didn't see him lying so grotesque and pasty beside the gravel road in France. We saw him, saw him by the multiple thousands. That's the difference. . . .'

Ernie Pyle was killed six days after Roosevelt's death. 'The nation is saddened again', said President Truman, 'by the death of Ernie Pyle.'

On April 19, the day after Pyle's death on Ie Shima, American forces entered Aha, completing their conquest of central and northern Okinawa. But in the south, around Naha, the Japanese prepared to hold the land yard by yard, as they had earlier done on Iwo Jima.

On April 19, American troops entered Leipzig. That same day, the Red Army broke through the German defences at Forst, on the River Neisse, seventy-five miles south-east of Berlin. In Bayreuth, the Gauleiter of Bavaria, Fritz Waechtler, was executed that day by the ss on a charge of defeatism. Also on April 19, at Dachau, the ss executed four French and eleven Czech officers, who had been captured several years earlier on clandestine missions in German-occupied France and Czechoslovakia.

Nuremberg, the city of the pre-war Nazi rallies, fell to the Americans on April 20 with 17,000 German soldiers taken prisoner, as, on the Eastern Front, Soviet forces entered Kalau, only sixty miles from Berlin. That day, Hitler celebrated his fifty-sixth birthday, in a Berlin which suddenly reverberated to the sound of Soviet artillery, which had opened fire on the capital at eleven o'clock that morning.

As Hitler's birthday party progressed, Allied bombers made their last massive raid on his capital. That afternoon, during a lull in the bombing, Hitler came up from his bunker to inspect the teenage soldiers of the Hitler Youth, and older men of a recently formed ss division, which was to defend the capital. Wishing them all well, he returned underground, to a birthday tea-party, at which his guests gained the impression that he was considering the possibility of leaving Berlin for Berchtesgaden, to continue the fight in an Alpine redoubt south of Munich. He also spoke to his guests of his determination to hold both Bohemia–Moravia and Norway. From the German administrators of Norway and Denmark, he had just received a birthday telegram: 'Norway shall be held!'

Hitler now remained in his bunker, fifty feet below ground, with his staff and secretaries, as Berlin took a daily pounding from Soviet artillery, and as the Red Army drew closer every day. Himmler, who had been one of the guests at the birthday party, made contact later that day with the Swedish Red Cross, and in the hope of favourably impressing the Western Allies, agreed to send seven thousand women, half of them Jews, from Ravensbrück to Sweden.

In Italy, on April 20, in an attempt to cut off the German lines of retreat, Allied bombers launched Operation Corncob, a three-day attack on the bridges over the rivers Adige and Brenta. In Yugoslavia, the last German forces were moving northward through Croatia, towards Zagreb, and on to Austria; among the medals given out on Hitler's birthday was a War Merit Cross, First Class, with Swords, awarded to Lieutenant Waldheim, for his work on the staff of General Löhr.

Hitler's birthday also saw a continuation of the terror which had made his rule hated throughout Europe. That day, at Bullenhuser Damm, near Neuengamme, the Gestapo hanged a Dutchman, Anton Holzel, from the town of Deventer. Holzel had earlier been arrested for distributing underground Communist newspapers. Also killed on Hitler's birthday, by hanging, were twenty Russian prisoners-of-war, and twenty Jewish children, each of whom had earlier been taken from Auschwitz to Neuengamme for medical experiments. British forces were already a few miles away, at Harburg. Before they reached Bullenhuser Damm, the bodies of both the adults and the children had been taken to Neuengamme and cremated.

Seven of the twenty children have never been identified. The thirteen whose names are known included two five-year-olds, Mania Altman and Eleonora Witonska, as well as Eleonora Witonska's seven-year-old brother Roman, and the seven year old Rywka Herszberg, all from Poland. Also murdered were the seven-year-old Sergio de Simone from Italy; the eight-year-old Alexander Hornemunn from Holland and his twelve year-old brother Eduard; and two twelve-year-olds from France, Jacqueline Morgenstern and Georges André Kohn, who had been on the very last of the deportations from Paris, in August 1944.

In Germany, on April 21, French forces entered Stuttgart. In Italy, Polish forces entered Bologna. That same day, the Germans launched an anti-partisan sweep in the region around Gorizia; more than 170 Italian partisans were killed. In Berlin, where Soviet troops had now reached the extreme southern and eastern suburbs, Hitler ordered ss General Steiner to move north to Eberswalde, break through the Soviet flank and re-establish the German defences to the north-east of Berlin. 'You will see', he told Steiner, 'the Russians will suffer the greatest defeat of their history, before the gates of Berlin,' but he went on to warn his General: 'It is expressly forbidden to fall back to the West. Officers who do not comply unconditionally with this order are to be arrested and shot immediately. You, Steiner, are answerable with your head for execution of this order.'

In what was once the Ruhr pocket, 325,000 German troops, including thirty generals, had surrendered by April 21; that day, their commander, Field Marshal Model, shot himself in a forest between Düsseldorf and Duisburg.

In the British zone of battle, in the village of Wistedt, between Bremen and Hamburg, April 21 saw a twenty-four-year-old Guardsman, Edward Colquhoun Charlton, win the last Victoria Cross of the war in Europe, for saving the lives of several men who had been trapped in their tank. He himself was so badly wounded that he died shortly after being taken prisoner. His principal adversary in this battle, Lieutenant Hans-Jürgen von Bulow, was awarded the Iron Cross, First Class.

To the south of Berlin, during April 21, the Red Army reached, and overran, the headquarters of the German High Command, at Zossen. The chief opposition now to the Soviet entry into Berlin were small 'battle groups' of Hitler Youth, teenage boys with anti-tank guns which had been placed in parks and prominent buildings and suburban streets. At Eggersdorf, on April 21, seventy such defenders with three anti-tank guns between them, were typical of the last minute efforts to keep the Russians out of Berlin. They were mown down by tanks and infantry.

Heinrich Himmler was now in command of both the Rhine and Vistula armies. On April 22, at a further meeting with Count Folke Bernadotte, this time in Lübeck, he offered to surrender to the Western Allies, but not to the Russians. Germany would continue fighting the Russians, Himmler explained, 'until the front of the Western powers has replaced the German front'. The Western powers had no intention, however, of turning against Russia; they would allow no separate negotiations, only a surrender without conditions: total and complete surrender of all armies on all fronts. Until the German surrender, Churchill assured Stalin – in reporting Himmler's approach – 'the attack of the Allies upon them, on all sides and in all theatres where resistance continues, will be prosecuted with the utmost vigour'.

Inside Greater Germany, the imminence of defeat led to the first relaxation of concentration camp security. On April 22, when two Swiss representatives of the International Committee of the Red Cross reached Mauthausen with trucks and food, they were allowed to take away with them 817 French, Belgian and Dutch deportees.

In his bunker on April 22, Hitler learned that General Steiner had failed to move a single man to attack the Russians at Eberswalde. He at once told those who were with him in the bunker that the war was lost. All thought of an Alpine redoubt south of Munich was abandoned. He would remain in Berlin, Hitler declared, and would shoot himself when the end came. Hitler's entourage were appalled; General Jodl, in a burst of optimism quite at variance with the reality of the situation, spoke of new military moves designed to defend

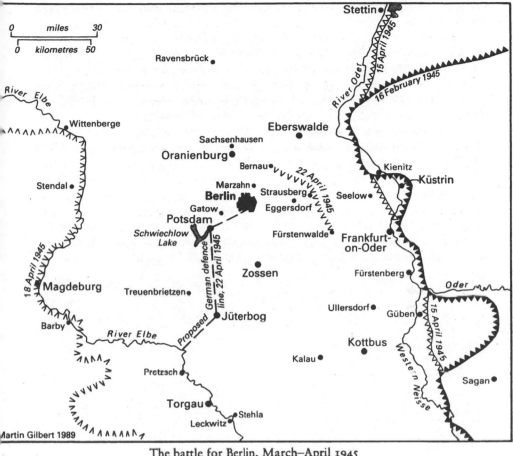

The battle for Berlin, March–April 1945

Berlin, declaring that the Army on the Elbe, which faced the British and Americans, could be brought eastward to hold a defensive line from the Elbe, to Jüterbog and Potsdam.

That same day, however, a Soviet mechanized corps reached Treuenbrietzen, forty miles south-west of Berlin and fifteen miles west of Jodl's proposed defence line; there, they found a prisoner-of-war camp, in the liberation of which a Red Army officer, Lieutenant Zharchinski, was killed while breaking through the camp defences. Among those freed that day was Major General Otto Ruge, the former Commander-in-Chief of the Norwegian Army, who had been captured by the Germans five years earlier.

From Treuenbrietzen, the Soviet mechanized corps moved eastward to Jüterbog, reaching an aerodrome on which it found 144 damaged aircraft, 362 aircraft engines without aircraft, and three thousand bombs. Long before Jodl's plan for German forces to regroup at Jüterbog could be put into action, the town was in Soviet hands, and a Soviet ring established to the south and south-west of the capital.

To the north-east and east of Berlin, Soviet troops now stood on the line Fürstenwalde–Strausberg–Bernau. That night, at the Prinz Albrechtstrasse Prison in Berlin, an ss firing squad shot Rüdiger Schleicher, whose office at the Institute for Aviation Law at the University of Berlin had been a meeting place for German anti-Nazis, including his brothers-in-law, Dietrich Bonhoeffer and Hans von Dohnanyi, both of whom had already been executed.

In Yugoslavia, German troops were falling back to Zagreb: on April 22 they were still in control of the region of Jasenovac, the concentration camp in which tens of thousands of Serbs and Jews had been murdered. Only a thousand inmates were still alive. Fearful that they would be murdered on the eve of the German retreat, they rose up in revolt. Six hundred of them turned on their guards; more than five hundred of them were shot down. But sixty of the Serbs, and twenty of the Jews, escaped – yet more witnesses of barbarities, the full details of which were yet to be made known to a world which was suddenly becoming exposed to tales of previously unimagined barbarity.

On April 23, Hitler assumed personal command of the defence of Berlin. Policemen, members of the Hitler Youth, old men, and women of all ages, were enlisted to help keep the Russians from entering the capital. That day, Goering sent Hitler a telegram proposing, as Hitler's current deputy, to assume full control of Germany. 'If no reply is received by ten o'clock tonight,' Goering added, 'I shall take it for granted that you have lost your freedom of action.'

Hitler at once dismissed Goering from all his offices of State, and ordered his arrest. In Goering's place as head of the German Air Force, Hitler decided to appoint Robert Ritter von Greim, one of Germany's most highly decorated pilots, and, since February 1943, commander of the German Air Force on the Eastern Front. Greim, who was then in Munich, was summoned to Berlin.

In Berlin, during April 23, two more of the imprisoned conspirators were executed: Dietrich Bonhoeffer's brother Klaus, and the geographer and writer Albrecht Haushofer, who had wished to see a restoration of the monarchy once Hitler was overthrown.

In Belsen, on April 23, eight days after the camp's liberation, one of the hundreds of emaciated former prisoners who died that day was a Frenchwoman, Yvonne Rudellat, who, as the British agent 'Jacqueline', had been smuggled by boat into France in July 1942, and who had been arrested eleven months later.

In Italy, Allied forces had crossed the River Po, and on April 24, the Italian Committee for National Liberation ordered a general uprising through the areas still under German control. German columns in retreat were everywhere attacked, and on April 25, Italian partisans liberated Milan. That morning, more than three hundred British bombers attacked Hitler's Berghof headquarters at Berchtesgaden; Goering, who was already under arrest in his home on the mountain, was unhurt, but many buildings were badly damaged, and six people killed.

As British bombs fell on Berchtesgaden, General Ritter von Greim flew from Munich to Berlin. With him was Hanna Reitsch, one of Germany's leading test pilots, and advocate of a pilots' suicide squad. On the last lap of their journey, von Greim flew a tiny plane from Gatow to the Chancellery, with Hanna Reitsch stuffed into the tail of the plane. During the flight, von Greim was injured in the foot by Russian anti-aircraft fire; Hanna Reitsch managed to lean across him and land the plane a few hundred yards from Hitler's bunker.

In the bunker's surgery, while von Greim's wound was being dressed, Hitler told the astonished airman: 'I have called you because Hermann Goering has betrayed both me and the Fatherland. Behind my back he has made contact with the enemy. I have had him arrested as a traitor, deprived him of all his offices, and removed him from all organizations. That is why I have called you.'

Hitler then informed von Greim that he was the new Commander-in-Chief of the German Air Force, and a Field Marshal.

That same day, April 25, Hitler ordered the arrest of General Karl Weidling, commander of a panzer corps, accusing him of desertion. Weidling, whose troops were in fact still defending the outskirts of Berlin, hurried to the bunker and protested his innocence; Hitler then appointed him 'Battle Commandant' of Berlin itself. Eight Soviet armies were now closing in on the city. But the most dramatic development of April 25 came shortly after midday, when an American Army officer, Lieutenant Albert Kotzebue, moving forward near the village of Leckwitz, on the western bank of the Elbe, met a solitary Soviet soldier. Crossing the river, Lieutenant Kotzebue met more Soviet soldiers, encamped near the village of Stehla. The Soviet and American armies had linked up. Germany was cut in two. Four hours later, ten miles north-west of Stehla, another American patrol, led by Lieutenant William D. Robinson, came upon yet more Soviet soldiers at the village of Torgau.

The Allies rejoiced to have linked forces. Himmler's last minute hopes of turning one against the other were utterly broken. In Moscow, 324 guns fired a twenty-four salvo in celebration of the Torgau meeting. In New York crowds danced and sang in Times Square.

As the Americans and Russians joined forces on the Elbe, the French Army was sweeping through Württemberg. On April 25 it reached the upper Danube village of Tuttlingen, where it found the mass grave of eighty-six Jews, brought there six months earlier from ghettos in the East, and killed. In four other villages in the region, including Schomberg and Schörzingen, a further 2,440 bodies were found. That same day, in the Italian town of Cuneo, the Gestapo shot six Jews. At Ravensbrück, April 25 saw the execution of Anna Rizzo, who, with her husband, had helped organize one of the largest Allied escape and evasion lines through France, the 'Troy' line. At Johanngeorgenstadt that day, the Gestapo executed Paul d'Ortoli, the town clerk of the small French village of Contes, who had been arrested in October 1943.

In the Pacific, the struggle for Okinawa continued. At the same time, American bombers intensified their attacks on the Japanese islands, hoping to create the disruption needed for a successful invasion, planned for that November. But on

April 25, the Secretary for War, Henry L. Stimson, went to see President Truman with news which could conceivably alter the whole timetable of the final assault on Japan. 'Within four months', Stimson told Truman, 'we shall in all probability have completed the most terrible weapon ever known in human history, one bomb of which could destroy a whole city.'

The Berlin defence perimeter, which Hitler had ordered to be held at all cost, was now pierced in the north, the east and the south east. The suburbs of Moabit and Neukölln were both in Russian hands by nightfall on April 26. That same day, British Intelligence decrypted a top-secret message, sent to Himmler by the ss, warning that food for the civilian population still under German control would not last beyond May 10. On the day of this message, Russian forces, entering Potsdam, completed the encirclement of Berlin. German forces in the city were now restricted to an area less than ten miles long from west to east, and only one to three miles wide. That day, unaware that Hitler had decided never to leave Berlin, units of the Red Army seized his last avenue of escape, the airfield of Tempelhof.

Camp after camp was now being liberated; not far from Berlin, Soviet forces freed Edouard Herriot, a former Prime Minister of France. At Landsberg, where Hitler had been imprisoned for just over a year in 1923 and 1924, an American officer, Colonel Yevell, secured one of the strangest trophies of the war, the plaque above the door of Hitler's former prison cell. 'Here', it read, 'a dishonourable system imprisoned Germany's greatest son from November 11, 1923 to December 20, 1924. During this time Adolf Hitler wrote the book of the National Socialist Revolution, Mein Kampf.' Today, the plaque is on display in the Kentucky Military Museum at Frankfort, Kentucky.

In the Landsberg region, the Americans found six concentration camps; German civilians living near by were forced to bury the hundreds of emaciated corpses that lay on the barren, filthy ground. Thousands of slave labourers were also liberated around Landsberg, including Russians, Poles, Yugoslavs and Frenchmen.

The days of liberation were also days of massive casualties, as German units, especially those facing the Red Army, refused to abandon the battlefield. On April 26, after a prolonged battle, Soviet forces captured the Moravian city of Brno, and drove on northward to Olomouc; 38,400 Red Army men had been killed in the Czechoslovak campaign. In Berlin, three-quarters of the city was in Soviet hands by the end of April 27. Near Zossen, Red Army troops foiled an attempt by the German Ninth Army to fight its way back to Berlin.

At Marienbad, in western Czechoslovakia, a thousand Jews, originally from Buchenwald, and on the road for nearly two weeks, were killed on April 27 by machine gun fire and grenades; their guards had turned on them at Marienbad railway station. That same day, at Mauthausen, Himmler's deputy, Kurt Becher, was told by the camp Commandant that Ernst Kaltenbrunner, the head of the Security Service, 'instructed me that at least a thousand men must still die every day in Mauthausen'.

That April 27, in Turin, Italian partisans took up arms against the Germans,

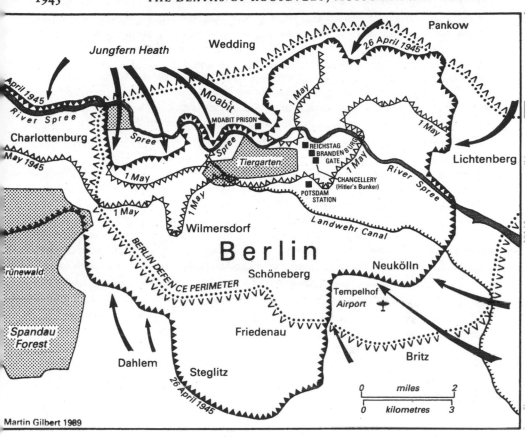

Berlin besieged, April 1945

as they had done two days earlier in Milan. Among the partisans killed that day in Turin was a young Jew, Giorgio Latis, whose mother, father and sister had been deported to Auschwitz the previous September, and never heard of again. That same day, in the Baltic Sea, off Rostock, several thousand Jewish women from Stutthof concentration camp, who had been evacuated by sea a week earlier, were caught in an Allied bombing raid; five were killed. The ss and Ukrainian guards who were accompanying them on board, had already thrown overboard several hundred of the sick and injured, mostly women from Kovno and Lodz ghettos. On April 28, in a second Allied bombing raid, several hundred women were killed.

President Truman and his advisers now discussed what city the atomic bomb should be dropped on; a special Target Committee was looking for one which had not already been badly damaged. Although Tokyo was a 'possibility', the Committee wrote on April 27, 'it is now practically all bombed and burned out, and is practically rubble with only the Palace grounds left standing'. The

675

committee concluded: 'Hiroshima is the largest untouched target not on the 21st Bomber Command list. Consideration should be given to this city'.

In Berlin, a motley crew of defenders still tried to keep the Russians from the inner city. One such defender, Reginald Leslie Cornford, was a British volunteer in the British Free Corps. Hiding in a church, on April 27 he knocked out a Russian tank with his anti-tank gun; then defended himself for half an hour, before being killed. On the following day, a French ss volunteer, Eugene Vaulot, destroyed six Russian tanks; he was awarded the Knight's Cross.

During April 28, a Red Army rifle regiment, commanded by Colonel Zinchenko, seized the Moabit Prison, on the edge of the Tiergarten; seven thousand prisoners, including many Allied prisoners-of-war, were released. Within a few hours, Soviet troops were fighting in the Tiergarten itself. Not only the sound of battle, but its acrid fumes, now penetrated Hitler's bunker. From the bunker, orders were still flowing, including one to General Wenck, who, with a few shattered remnants of the men he had managed to bring away from encirclement in the Harz Mountains, had been ordered to advance to Berlin. But there were now fewer and fewer people who were either able or willing to obey the new spate of orders. That day, General Gotthard Henrici, Himmler's successor as Commander of the Vistula Army Group, was dismissed for not having carried out a 'scorched earth policy' in front of the advancing Russians. When General Weidling proposed that all those in the central area, and in Hitler's bunker, break out to the West of the city, Hitler refused. Only the newly promoted Field Marshal von Greim was allowed to leave, ordered to do so by Hitler, in order, not to reactivate the shattered German Air Force, but to arrest Himmler, whose negotiations with the Allies had become known in the bunker that afternoon. 'A traitor must never succeed me as Führer,' Hitler declared.

Now anyone close to Himmler was suspect. On April 26, Eva Braun's brother-in-law, Hermann Fegelein, Himmler's representative in the bunker, had slipped away, unnoticed, to his home in the Charlottenburg district of Berlin, itself now partly under Russian control. But on April 28, Hitler noticed Fegelein's absence, and an armed ss search party was sent to find him. Brought back to the bunker, he was stripped of his ss lieutenant-general's rank, taken into the Chancellery yard, and shot.

In Italy, April 28 saw the ignominious end to the Fascist rule which had begun twenty-three years earlier; for on that day, near the lakeside village of Dongo, Mussolini was shot dead by Italian partisans. Also shot, in reprisal for the killing of fifteen Italian partisans in Milan nine months earlier, were fifteen of those who had been captured with Mussolini, including Alessandro Pavolini, the Secretary of the Fascist Party, four Cabinet Ministers, and several of Mussolini's friends. His mistress, Clara Petacci, was also shot. Her body, and that of Mussolini, were taken to Milan and hanged there, upside down, on the morning of April 29. Early that afternoon, at Caserta, General von Vietinghoff's representatives signed the unconditional surrender of all German troops in Italy.

As Mussolini's body was being taken from Dongo to Milan, Hitler, in his bunker in Berlin, was writing his political testament and making plans to marry Eva Braun. In his testimony, he explained how much her loyalty, and her decision to stay with him in the bunker, had meant to him. He also wrote that he was expelling both Goering and Himmler from the Nazi Party, and announced the setting up of a new Government, with Admiral Dönitz as President and Dr Goebbels as Chancellor.

Much of Hitler's testimony consisted of his reflections on the origins of the war. Neither he, nor 'anyone else in Germany', he wrote, had wanted a second war against Britain and America, and he went on to explain: 'Centuries will go by, but from the ruins of our towns and monuments the hatred of those ultimately responsible will always grow anew against the people whom we have to thank for all this: international Jewry and its henchmen.'

Hitler then declared that the war had been caused solely by those international statesmen 'who either were of Jewish origin or worked for Jewish interests'. The Jews were 'the real guilty party in this murderous struggle' and would be 'saddled' with the responsibility for it. Hitler added: 'I left no one in doubt that this time not only would millions of children of European Aryan races starve, not only would millions of grown men meet their death, and not only would hundreds of thousands of women and children be burned and bombed to death in cities, but this time the real culprits would have to pay for their guilt even though by more humane means than war'.

The 'more humane means' had been the gas chambers.

Stating that he could not 'abandon' Berlin, and that the city's resistance was being 'debased by creatures who are as blind as they are lacking in character', Hitler explained that he wished to share his fate 'with that which millions of others have also taken upon themselves by remaining in this city'. He had therefore decided to stay in Berlin 'and there to choose death voluntarily when I determine that the position of the Führer and the Chancellery itself can no longer be maintained. I die with a joyful heart in the knowledge of the immeasurable deeds and achievements of our peasants and workers and of a contribution, unique in history, of our youth which bears my name'.

Hitler added: 'Through the sacrifices of our soldiers and my own fellowship with them unto death, a seed has been sown in German history that will one day grow to usher in the glorious rebirth of the National Socialist movement in a truly united nation.'

After setting out the names of the members of the new Government, Hitler ended his testimony with one more denunciation of the Jews. 'Above all,' he concluded, 'I enjoin the Government and the people to uphold the race laws to the limit and to resist mercilessly the poisoner of all nations, International Jewry.'

What those race laws had led to was once again brutally revealed, later that same day, when, shortly after three o'clock in the afternoon, American forces entered Dachau. An inmate in the camp, the Belgian doctor and British agent, Albert Guérisse, later recalled how, as the first American officer, a major, descended from his tank, 'the young Teutonic Lieutenant, Heinrich Skodzensky, emerges from the guard post and comes to attention before the American officer. The German is blond, handsome, perfumed, his boots glistening, his uniform well-tailored. He reports, as if he were on the military parade grounds near Unter den Linden during an exercise, then very properly raising his arm he salutes with a very respectful "Heil Hitler!" and clicks his heels. "I hereby turn over to you the concentration camp of Dachau, 30,000 residents, 2,340 sick, 27,000 on the outside, 560 garrison troops".'

The American major did not return the German lieutenant's salute. 'He hesitates for a moment', Albert Guérisse later recalled, 'as if he were trying to make sure that he is remembering the adequate words. Then, he spits into the face of the German, "Du Schweinhund!" And then, "Sit down here!" – pointing to the rear seat of one of the jeeps which in the meantime have driven in. The major turns to me and hands me an automatic rifle. "Come with me". But I no longer had the strength to move. "No, I stay here – " The major gave an order, the jeep with the young German officer in it went outside the camp again. A few minutes went by, my comrades had not yet dared to come out of their barracks, for at that distance they could not tell the outcome of the negotiations between the American officer and the ss men. Then I hear several shots'.

Lieutenant Skodzensky was dead. Within an hour, all five hundred of his garrison troops were to be killed, some by the inmates themselves, but more than three hundred of them by American soldiers who had been literally sickened by what they saw of rotting corpses and desperate, starving inmates. In one incident, an American lieutenant machine-gunned 346 of the ss guards after they had surrendered, and were lined up against a wall. The lieutenant, who had entered Dachau a few moments earlier, had just seen the corpses of the inmates piled up around the camp crematorium, and at the railway station.

None of those who saw Dachau in the days after its liberation were to forget its horrors. As at Belsen two weeks earlier, the Allied journalists accompanying the troops were shattered by what they saw. Sam Goldsmith, a Jewish journalist from Lithuania who had gone to Britain before the war, and who had earlier been at Belsen, noted down his first sight of Dachau: 'On a railway siding there is a train of fifty wagons – all full of terribly emaciated dead bodies, piled up like the twisted branches of cut-down trees. Near the crematorium – for the disposal of the dead – another huge pile of dead bodies, like a heap of crooked logs ready for some infernal fire. The stench is like that of Belsen; it follows you even when you are back in the Press camp'.

There were 2,539 Jews among the 33,000 survivors in Dachau. Of those survivors, 2,466 were to die in the following month and a half.

Everywhere, the ss troops continued to fight with fear of capture ever balancing the desire to live. At Dachau itself, as many as thirty guards had been killed when they opened fire on the Americans from the camp watchtowers. That same day, less than five miles away, at Webling, after an American soldier had been killed by ss sniper fire, all seventeen ss men who then surrendered were lined up against an earthen bank, and shot.

The only mercy on April 29 came from the air, when three thousand British bombers launched Operation Manna, parachuting more than six thousand tons of supplies to the Dutch behind German lines in Rotterdam and The Hague. where shortages of food were leading to starvation throughout German-occupied Holland. In all, 16,000 Dutch civilians starved to death.

In Berlin, General Weidling reported to Hitler on the evening of April 29 that the Russians had reached the nearby Potsdam Station. In addition, there were no longer any anti-tank guns available for the defence of the Chancellery area. What, asked Weidling, were his men to do once they had run out of ammunition? 'I cannot permit the surrender of Berlin,' Hitler replied. 'Your men will have to break out in small groups.'

That afternoon, the Citadel Commandant of Hitler's bunker, ss Major-General Mohnke – who in 1940 had been the senior officer involved in the massacre of British prisoners-of-war at Paradis, near Dunkirk – made the last two presentations of the Knight's Cross. One was to the French ss volunteer, Eugene Vaulot, for destroying six Russian tanks on the previous day, the other was to the commander of the tank troops defending the Chancellery, Major Herzig. That night, at eleven o'clock, Hitler telegraphed from the bunker: 'Where are Wenck's spearheads? When will they advance? Where is the Ninth Army?' British cryptographers at Bletchley, ever-vigilant, read these last desperate questions on their Enigma machine.

At one o'clock on the morning of April 30, Field Marshal Keitel informed Hitler that General Wenck's forces were 'stuck fast' south of the distant Schwiechlow Lake, and had no way of moving towards the capital, while the Ninth Army was completely encircled.

As Hitler, in Berlin, contemplated the imminent destruction of his capital and his life's work, Churchill, in London, was looking with anguish as Stalin imposed full Soviet control on Poland. 'I have been much distressed', Churchill telegraphed to Stalin on April 29, 'at the misunderstanding that has grown up between us on the Crimean Agreement about Poland.' Britain and America had agreed to allow the Lublin Government to become a 'new' Government, 'recognized on a broader democratic basis with the inclusion of democratic leaders from Poland itself and from Poles abroad'. For this purpose, a Commission had been set up in Moscow 'to select the Poles who were to come for consultations'. Britain and America had excluded from their nominees those who they thought 'were extreme people unfriendly to Russia'. They had not selected anyone 'at present in the London Government', but chose instead 'three good men' who had earlier gone into opposition to the London Government 'because they did not like its attitude towards Russia, and in particular its refusal to accept the eastern frontier', the Curzon Line, 'which you and I agreed upon, now so long ago, and which I was the first man outside the Soviet Government to proclaim to the world as just and fair', together with the territorial compensations for Poland in the west and north.

Churchill went on to point out to Stalin that not one of the three British and American nominees had been invited to Moscow to come before the Commission. As to the plan, agreed upon at Yalta, to establish a government based on 'universal suffrage and secret ballot', with all the democratic and anti-Nazi parties having the right to take part and put forward candidates, 'none of this has been allowed to move forward'. The Soviet Government had signed a Twenty Years' Treaty with the former Lublin Committee, now called by Stalin the 'new Government' of Poland, 'although it remains neither new nor reorganized'.

'We have the feeling', Churchill wrote, 'that it is we who have been dictated to and brought up against a stone wall upon matters which we sincerely believed were settled in a spirit of friendly comradeship in the Crimea.' He went on, after referring to the Communist predominance in the Yugoslav Government with which Stalin had just signed a treaty, to tell the Soviet leader, with deep foreboding: 'There is not much comfort in looking into a future where you and the countries you dominate, plus the Communist Parties in many other States, are all drawn up on one side, and those who rally to the English-speaking nations and their associates or Dominions are on the other. It is quite obvious that their quarrel would tear the world to pieces and that all of us leading men on either side who had anything to do with that would be shamed before history'.

Churchill's telegram to Stalin continued: 'Even embarking on a long period of suspicions, of abuse and counter-abuse and of opposing policies would be a disaster hampering the great developments of world prosperity for the masses which are attainable only by our trinity. I hope there is no word or phrase in this outpouring of my heart to you which unwittingly gives offence. If so, let me know. But do not, I beg you, my friend Stalin, under-rate the divergencies which are opening about matters which you may think are small to us but which are symbolic of the way the English-speaking democracies look at life'.

On the morning of April 30, American troops entered Munich; in Italy, they entered Turin. That same day, General Eisenhower informed the Soviet Deputy Chief of Staff, General Antonov, that American troops would not advance further into Austria than the 'general area of Linz' and the River Enns. In Istria, British and American forces hurried to reach Fiume, Pola and Trieste before Tito did. Churchill, angered by Eisenhower's promise to Antonov, and fearful of the westward march of Communism to the Adriatic, telegraphed to Truman on April 30: 'There can be little doubt that the liberation of Prague and as much as possible of the territory of Western Czechoslovakia by your forces might make the whole difference to the post-war situation in Czechoslovakia, and might well influence that in nearby countries. On the other hand, if the Western Allies play no significant part in Czechoslovakian liberation that country will go the way of Yugoslavia'.

To Churchill's disappointment, Truman replied that he would leave the tactical deployment of troops to the military. In passing on the British request that United States forces liberate Prague, General Marshall told Eisenhower: 'Personally and aside from all logistic, tactical or strategical implications, I would be loath to hazard American lives for purely political purposes.'

Prague was to be liberated by the Red Army, and Istria by Tito's partisans; there was nothing Churchill could do to prevent these developments. The same day, April 30, in Berlin at half-past two in the afternoon, a Red Army soldier,

Sergeant Kantariya, waved the Red Banner from the second floor of the Reichstag. German troops were still on the floor above. Less than a mile away, Hitler
was in his bunker, all hope of a counter-attack long abandoned. At half-past
three that afternoon, having finished his lunch, he sent those who were with
him – Goebbels, Bormann, and his personal staff – out into the passage. As they
stood there, they heard a single shot. Hitler had shot himself in the mouth.

Waiting for a few moments, Goebbels, Bormann and the others entered
Hitler's room. The Führer was dead. So too was Eva Braun; she had swallowed
poison.

With a single pistol shot, the Thousand Year Reich was at an end, in ignominy,
a mere twelve years since it had been launched in triumph. It had been twelve
years of bloodshed, war and evil on a scale which almost defies imagination.
As Soviet shells still fell around the Chancellery, Hitler's body, and that of Eva
Braun, were taken up from the bunker to the courtyard above, doused in petrol,
and set on fire.

At ten minutes to eleven that night, the Red Banner flew on the roof of the
Reichstag.

# 48

# The end of the war in Europe

MAY 1945

Hitler was dead, but the war in Europe still had eight days to run; eight days of battle, death, confusion, fear, exhilaration and exhaustion. On 1 May 1945, the German garrison in Rhodes surrendered. That day, in Berlin, negotiations began between General Krebs and General Zhukov. Krebs asked for a truce. Zhukov insisted upon unconditional surrender. Krebs returned to the bunker, where he found Martin Bormann, the Head of the Nazi Party Chancellery, and Goebbels, both determined not to give in. General Weidling, however, decided that there was no option but to surrender, and, on his own initiative, issued an order to his garrison troops, and to the people of Berlin, to cease all resistance.

Inside the bunker, Goebbels arranged for his six children to be poisoned with a lethal injection by an ss doctor; then he had his wife Magda and himself shot by an ss orderly. General Krebs committed suicide. Bormann tried to escape, but was most probably killed within a mile or so of the bunker.

Another of those who committed suicide on May 1 was Professor Max de Crinis, one of the main advocates of the euthanasia programme at the beginning of the war; it was he who was thought to have provided Hitler with the actual wording of the Euthanasia Decree of September 1939.

In the Far East, May 1 saw the launching of Operation Dracula, a British attempt to recapture Rangoon. In one skirmish, where thirty Japanese resisted a Gurkha parachute unit, only a single wounded Japanese soldier survived. But the Japanese had decided not to fight in Rangoon itself; a British pilot, flying over the city that morning, saw written in large letters above the Royal Air force prisoner-of-war camp the words: 'Japs gone. Exdigitate.' The British forces did indeed 'pull their finger out', and within seventy-two hours Rangoon was liberated.

During Operation Dracula, British bombers flew from their base at Salboni, east of Calcutta, to bomb Japanese military targets around Rangoon, breaking their near-thousand-mile journey at Baranga Island. On board one of these bombers, on its second flight to Rangoon in twenty-four hours, was Wing Commander James Nicolson, the only fighter pilot to have won the Victoria

Cross during the Battle of Britain. Now in charge of training at South East Air Force headquarters, he had been selected as a prospective candidate at the next British General Election. On the flight to Baranga, however, the bomber crashed into the sea; Nicolson and nine of the eleven crew members were drowned.

In Borneo, on May 1, Australian troops landed on Tarakan Island; after eighteen days, the Japanese were defeated. But on Luzon and Mindanao in the Philippines, and on Okinawa, continued Japanese resistance made the capture of every mile a fierce and bloody struggle.

At a quarter to seven on the morning of May 2, Marshal Zhukov accepted the surrender of Berlin; the ceasefire came into effect at three o'clock that afternoon. That day, the Red Army took 134,000 German soldiers prisoner. Also on May 2, the Mayor of Hamburg began negotiations for the unconditional surrender of the city. That evening, Churchill told the House of Commons that more than a million German troops had now laid down their arms in northern Italy and southern Austria.

In the northern Italian village of Biella, the German soldiers were astounded to see that the American tank crews who entered the village after the German surrender were Japanese; members of a Japanese–American Task Force of American-born Japanese who had fought throughout the Italian campaign. Also surrendering to the Western Allies on May 2, at Oberammergau, in southern Germany, was Dr Herbert Wagner, a guided missile designer. With him were two senior members of the Peenemünde rocket research staff, Wernher von Braun and General Walter Dornberger. All three were hurried to Paris, and then to the United States. 'We were interested in continuing our work', von Braun later wrote, 'not just being squeezed like a lemon and then discarded.'

On May 2, a German bomber, piloted by Lieutenant Rolf Kunze, left the German air base at Trondheim in northern Norway, ostensibly for the even more northerly air base at Bardufoss. It flew instead across the North Sea to Britain, where Kunze and his four fellow-airmen sought asylum. By chance, they landed their plane a few miles from Fraserburgh, in Scotland, not far from where the first German aircraft to be shot down over Britain in October 1939 had crash-landed. Theirs was the first wartime defection of an armed German bomber.

In Dublin, on May 2, the President of Eire, Eamon de Valera, called on the senior German diplomat in the capital, to express his condolences on the death of Hitler. Eire had preserved a tenacious neutrality through more than five and a half years of war.

In Lübeck harbour, still controlled by the Germans, May 2 saw the attempt to transfer 850 Jewish women who had earlier been evacuated by sea from Stutthof, to three large ships in the harbour, the *Cap Arcona*, the *Athena* and the *Thielbeck*. The captains of these ships refused to take them, however; between them, they already had more than nine thousand Jews, political prisoners and Russian prisoners-of-war on board. The small boats were ordered back to the shore. But, as they neared land in the early hours of May 3, and the starving Jews tried to clamber ashore, ss men, Hitler Youth and German marines opened fire on them with machine guns. More than five hundred were killed. Only three hundred survived.

As the British bombardment of Lübeck harbour continued, all two thousand prisoners on board the *Athena* had managed to get ashore. Of the 2,800 on board the *Thielbeck*, however, only fifty were saved. Of the five thousand men on the *Cap Arcona*, which was first set on fire and then sunk by British bombs, only 350 were saved. On the lowest deck, seven hundred gravely ill and dying men were burned to death. Several hundred Russian prisoners-of-war had been put into the ship's banana coolers; most of them perished.

A Jewish girl born in Lodz, who had survived all the travails of Hitler's war against the Jews, and who was one of the fifty survivors rescued that day from the *Thielbeck* and picked up by another German boat, later spoke of the last stage of the journey of the survivors, from Lübeck to Kiel. 'We kept hearing deafening bombardments along the way,' she recalled, 'and fantastic explosions lighting up the horizon. We saw countless numbers of burning ships and huge cargo steamers packed full of people everywhere we passed. The soldier convoys were all on fire and the Germans were jumping into the burning waters. It was all one huge conflagration.'

The prisoners reached Kiel after two days at sea. Three hours after they arrived, British tanks reached the dockside. 'The English treated us really well,' the girl from Lodz later recalled. 'They kissed us and tried to give us new hope and said to us: "Just you wait, luvs. We won't be a moment and we'll get us all some food!"'

At 11.30 on the morning of Thursday, May 3, just outside the village of Wendisch Even, Grand Admiral Hans Georg von Friedeburg – Dönitz's successor as Chief of the Naval Staff – and General Hans Kinzel – Chief of Staff to the German North West Army Command – arrived at Field Marshal Montgomery's headquarters. 'Who are these men?' Montgomery asked. 'What do they want?'

The two German officers had come to surrender three German armies then facing the Russians. Montgomery rejected their offer. Surrender of the forces facing the Russians, he said, must be made to the Russians, and to the Russians alone. They could surrender to him only those armies facing the British; that is, all the German forces in Holland, north-west Germany and Denmark. If they did not agree, Montgomery told them, 'I shall go on with the war, and will be delighted to do so, and am ready,' and he went on to warn: 'All your soldiers will be killed'.

The German officers crossed back through the lines and returned to Flensburg, where they put Montgomery's conditions to Dönitz. At half past five on the following afternoon they returned; an hour later, they signed the instrument of surrender. In western Austria, the cities of Innsbruck and Salzburg surrendered that day to the Americans, who also entered Hitler's former mountain retreat of Berchtesgaden, capturing two thousand prisoners.

Also on May 4, the Americans entered Flossenbürg concentration camp. Among those liberated there was the former Prime Minister of France, Léon

Europe from war to peace, May 1945

Blum, whose brother René had been deported to Auschwitz in September 1942, and had perished there. Also liberated that day were the former Chancellor of Austria, Kurt von Schuschnigg, whose challenge to Hitler in March 1938 had exposed the strength of democracy in Austria; and one of the leading figures of German decency, Pastor Martin Niemöller, the former leader of the Confessional Church in Germany who had been held, first in Sachsenhausen then in Dachau, and finally at Flossenbürg, for more than seven years.

German armies were still fighting north of Berlin, and in Czechoslovakia; Allied bombing raids against them also continued. On May 4, in one such raid, a bomb killed Field Marshal von Bock, the Commander of German Army Group Centre during the invasion of the Soviet Union in June 1941, whom Hitler had dismissed when the offensive against Moscow was halted. That same May 4, in Zagreb, the ruler of Croatia, Hitler's former ally, Dr Ante Pavelić, made a final appearance in the streets of his capital. 'If we must die,' he declared, 'let us fall as true heroes, not as cowards crying for mercy'. But then, leaving most of his followers behind him, he hurried northward to the comparative safety of the Austrian border.

On May 4, at the United Nations conference which had recently opened in San Francisco, the Soviet Foreign Minister, Vyacheslav Molotov, revealed to a startled American Secretary of State, Edward R. Stettinius, that the sixteen Polish negotiators who had met with the Soviet Colonel Pimenov at Pruszkow near Warsaw on March 27 had 'been arrested by the Red Army' on charges of having earlier caused 'the death of two hundred Red Army officers'. This figure, Eden telegraphed to Churchill from San Francisco, 'I seem to remember was the same figure Stalin quoted at Yalta'. The effects on American opinion, Eden added, 'are likely to be serious, and I have no doubt that they will be so at home'.

Churchill replied at once to Eden: 'The perfidy by which these Poles were enticed into a Russian conference and then held fast in the Russian grip is one which will emerge in great detail from the stories which have reached us, and there is no doubt that the publication in detail of this event upon the authority of the great western Allies, would produce a primary change in the entire structure of world forces'.

At the moment of victory over Germany, the fate of Poland gave Western leaders cause for grave alarm. It was likely, Churchill telegraphed to Truman on May 4, that the territories under Russian control once all the German armies had surrendered 'would include the Baltic Provinces, all of Germany to the occupational line, all Czechoslovakia, a large part of Austria, the whole of Yugoslavia, Hungary, Roumania, Bulgaria, until Greece in her present tottering condition is reached. It would include all the great capitals of middle Europe including Berlin, Vienna, Budapest, Belgrade, Bucharest and Sofia.' This, Churchill went on to warn the President, 'constitutes an event in the history of Europe to which there has been no parallel, and which has not been faced by the Allies in their long and hazardous struggle. The Russian demands on Germany for reparations alone will be such as to enable her to prolong the occupation almost indefinitely, at any rate for many years, during which time Poland will sink with many other States into the vast zone of Russian-controlled Europe, not necessarily economically Sovietised but police-governed'.

Churchill had every intention of trying to forestall what could be prevented of the Soviet military advance. On May 5, he explained to Anthony Eden that, in addition to sending Montgomery to Lübeck to cut off any Soviet advance from the Baltic to Denmark, 'we are sending in a moderate holding force to Copenhagen by air, and the rest of Denmark is being rapidly occupied from henceforward by our fast-moving armoured columns. I think therefore, having regard to the joyous feeling of the Danes and the abject submission and would-be partisanship of the surrendered Huns, we shall head our Soviet friends off at this point too'.

The Red Army was still in fierce combat on May 5, in northern Germany between Wismar and Schwerin, in East Prussia on the narrow strip of shore between Danzig and Königsberg, in Czechoslovakia near Olomouc, in Austria near St Pölten, and in Silesia, around Breslau. Near Wansen, twenty miles south of Breslau, a monument records the death of 469 Russian soldiers that day, when the German Seventeenth Army launched one last desperate counter-attack.

Several more German surrenders were signed on May 5; one, at Wageningen in The Netherlands, led to the surrender of all German forces in Holland. The surrender was signed shortly after four o'clock in the afternoon, in the presence of a senior Canadian officer, Lieutenant-General Charles Foulkes; also present, in his capacity as Commander-in-Chief of the Netherlands forces of the Interior, was Prince Bernhard of the Netherlands, to whom the commander of the German forces in Holland, General Blaskowitz, showed unexpected deference. The Prince ignored him.

At Baldham, in southern Germany, a further unconditional surrender was signed at half past two in the afternoon of May 5. This time it covered all German forces between the Bohemian mountains and the Upper Inn river. The German officer agreeing to the surrender was General Hermann Foertsch, to whom the American General, Jacob L. Devers, explained that this was not an armistice, but unconditional surrender. 'Do you understand that?' Devers asked Foertsch. 'I can assure you, Sir,' Foertsch replied, 'that no power is left at my disposal to prevent it'.

Although the war was virtually over, yet at Ebensee, near Mauthausen, a hundred miles east of Baldham, the ss made plans to kill several thousand Jews, most of them survivors of Auschwitz, who had been marched to Ebensee from Mauthausen. The prisoners were ordered into one of the tunnels of the Ebensee mine. It was, their guards explained, to protect them from Allied bombing.

Among the prisoners at Ebensee was a forty-six-year-old Russian Jew, Lev Manevich, who had been a prisoner in Germany since 1936, when he had been arrested for spying for the Soviet Union. In September 1943 he had been released, briefly, by the Americans, when a small American front line unit had entered the prison of San Stefano, in Italy, but, extremely weak, Manevich had been recaptured by the Germans within forty-eight hours. Now, emaciated, and anonymous, he answered the German order to enter the mine by crying out, in several languages: 'No one will go. They will kill us.'

Manevich's warning was effective. To a man, the prisoners refused to move. The SS guards, as the historian of this last revolt, Evelyn le Chêne, has written, 'were paralysed with indecision. The hordes of humans swayed and murmured. For the first time since their arrest, the prisoners who were not already dying saw the possibility that they might just survive the war. Understandably, they neither wished to be blown up in the tunnel, nor mown down by SS machine guns for refusing. But they knew that in these last days, many of the SS had left and been replaced by ethnic Germans'.

A quick consultation with some of the officers under his command made it clear to the German Commandant 'that they too were reluctant either to force the men into the tunnel, or to shoot them down. With the war all but over, they were thinking of the future, and the punishment they would receive for the slaughter of so many human beings was something they still wished – even with their already stained hands – to avoid. And so the prisoners won the day.'

Among those at Ebensee that day was Meir Pesker, a Polish Jew from Bielsk Podlaski who had been deported first to Majdanek, then to Plaszow, and finally to Mauthausen. 'We saw that the Americans were coming,' he later wrote, 'and so did the Germans.' His account continued: 'Suddenly a German guard appeared, a bloated primeval beast whose cruelty included the bare-handed murder of dozens of Jews. Suddenly he had become weak and emotional and he began to plead with us not to turn him in for he had "done many favours for the Jews to whom that madman Hitler had sought to do evil". As he finished his pleading three boys overpowered and killed him, there in the same camp where he had been sole ruler'.

Meir Pesker added: 'We killed every one of the German oppressors who fell into our hands, before the arrival of the Americans in the enclosure of the camp. This was our revenge for our loved ones whose blood had been spilled at the hands of these heathen German beasts. It was only by a stroke of luck – even if tainted luck – that I had survived'.

Also at Ebensee on May 5, as the Germans prepared to flee, was Dr Miklos Nyiszli, an eye-witness of Dr Mengele's brutality at Auschwitz. Like all his fellow prisoners at Ebensee, he too had survived the death marches, including one from central Germany to Mauthausen on which three thousand had set off, and one thousand been killed on the march. 'On May 5th,' he later recalled, 'a white flag flew from the Ebensee watch-tower. It was finished. They had laid down their arms. The sun was shining brightly when, at nine o'clock, an American light tank, with three soldiers on board, arrived and took possession of the camp. We were free.'

Once again, the moment of freedom was one of deep shock for the liberators. When American troops reached Mauthausen, they found nearly ten thousand bodies in a huge communal grave. Of the 110,000 survivors, 28,000 were Jews. More skeletal bodies, and more emaciated survivors, were found at nearby Ebensee, including Lev Manevich. Like hundreds of those who were liberated, Manevich was too weak to survive; he died four days after his act of defiance.

On May 6, in Berlin, the final awards were made of the much coveted Swords to the Knights Cross of the Iron Cross. The last award of all was made to one of the most highly-decorated and popular of all the s s officers in the fighting units of the s s, Otto Weidinger. It is probable that it was Weidinger's defence of Vienna that was responsible, at least in part, for this award. But in those final, confused and catastrophic moments of the war, the message announcing the award was lost; indeed, it was only six years later, after his return to Germany following six and a half years of capitivity in France, that Weidinger himself learnt of his award. It had been granted to him three weeks after his forces had been forced to leave Vienna.

The last acts of the European war were about to take place. At six o'clock on the evening of May 6, the commander of the German forces besieged in Breslau, General Nickhoff, accepted the Soviet terms for the surrender of his forces, and of the city. Half an hour later, in the West, General Jodl flew from Flensburg to Reims, to sign the capitulation of all German forces still fighting or facing the Western Allies. At first, Jodl was determined to limit the surrender to the German forces facing westward. But, without prevarication or debate, General Eisenhower made it clear to him that either the Germans agreed to a complete surrender of all their forces, East as well as West, or he would break off all negotiations, and seal the Western Front, thus preventing any more Germans transferring from East to West in order to give themselves up. General Jodl passed back this ultimatum by radio signal to Grand Admiral Dönitz at Flensburg. Shorly after midnight, Dönitz replied, authorizing Jodl to make a final and complete surrender of all German forces on all fronts. At 1.41 on the morning of May 7, watched by General Ivan Susloparov of Russia and by General François Sevez of France, General Jodl signed. General Bedell Smith then signed for the Allied Expeditionary Force and General Susloparov for the Soviet High Command. Finally, General Sevez signed as a witness. The surrender was to come into effect at fifty-nine minutes to midnight on May 8. The war in Europe still had twenty-one hours and eighteen minutes to run.

In Czechoslovakia, throughout May 7, German forces continued to fight the Red Army north of Olomouc and in the town itself. On the long spit of land between Danzig and Königsberg, German troops continued to fight the Russians near the village of Vogelsang. Just off the coast of Scotland, in the Firth of Forth, one mile south of the Isle of May, the German submarine U-2336, commanded by Captain Emil Klusmeier, sank two merchant ships, the Norwegian *Sneland* 1 and the British *Avondale Park*. On the *Sneland* 1, seven Norwegian merchant seamen were killed; two British seamen died on the *Avondale Park*. These nine merchant seamen were the last Allied naval deaths of the European war.

In five years and eight months of submarine war, 27,491 officers and men on German submarines had been killed. Of the 863 U-boats that had gone on operational patrols, 754 had been sunk, or damaged beyond repair while in port. Their success had been considerable, however, with 2,800 Allied merchant ships and 148 Allied warships being sunk. Their own end was ignominious; under Operation Rainbow, launched in that first week of May, 231 U-boats scuttled themselves, rather than fall into Allied hands. Among those scuttled were many which had never put to sea, including, at Lübeck, several which were to have been powered by the new hydrogen-peroxide method. One of their inventors, Helmuth Walter, captured by the British on May 5, agreed two days later to give the Allies details of all new submarines and torpedoes then under construction at the nearby research stations at Eckernförde. One of the new type of submarines was shipped to America for trials, another to Britain.

In Prague, Czechoslovak resistance forces had taken up arms against the German forces in the city on May 7; that day, three American Army vehicles arrived. But so did the Russians, who insisted that, under Eisenhower's agreement with the Soviet High Command, the Americans withdraw to Pilsen. The Americans complied.

Throughout May 7, the fighting in Prague continued. Then, at four minutes past five on the morning of May 8, the German forces in the city surrendered unconditionally. In the battle for Prague, more than eight thousand Soviet soldiers, and considerably more German soldiers, had been killed, the last substantial blood-letting of the German war.

In Britain and the United States, May 8 was VE-Day – Victory in Europe Day. As both nations rejoiced, their cities were bedecked with flags and banners. In the once captive capitals of Western Europe – The Hague, Brussels and Paris – there was a renewal of the excitement and relief of their days of liberation. In Copenhagen and Oslo, the Germans laid down their arms. That same day, the last of the German forces in eastern Germany signed an instrument of surrender to the Russians at Karlshorst, near Berlin. That day, the German troops cut off for many months in northern Latvia likewise surrendered, as did those in the Dresden–Görlitz area. Only around Olomouc did the Germans fight on, but it was a brief and hopeless resistance; Olomouc fell during the day, as did Sternbeck, further north.

At two in the afternoon of May 8, the German garrison at St Nazaire, on the Atlantic surrendered to the Americans. An hour later, the Dame of the small Channel Island of Sark raised both the British Union Jack and the United States Stars and Stripes over her tower. There were still 275 Germans on the island, and not a single Allied soldier. The British Army, three officers and twenty men, arrived two days later.

In Berlin, half an hour before midnight on May 8, a further signing took place of the Reims surrender; the signatories for the German High Command being Grand Admiral von Friedeburg, signing his third instrument of surrender in four days; General Hans-Jurgen Stümpff, Head of the German Air Force, and Field Marshal Keitel. Four Allied witnesses added their names to the surrender document: Air Chief Marshal Sir Arthur Tedder for the Allied Expeditionary Force, Marshal Zhukov for the Supreme High Command of the Red Army, General de Lattre de Tassigny, General Commanding-in-Chief of the First French Army; and General Carl Spaatz, commanding the United States Air Forces.

Even as the Berlin surrender ceremony was in progress, the German forces in western Czechoslovakia were in receipt of a call by Marshal Koniev, issued at eight o'clock that evening, that they too surrender. When, by eleven o'clock, they had made no reply, Koniev ordered his artillery to launch a new barrage, and his troops to resume military operations. As they did so, the German guards in charge of one of those many groups of Jews who were still being shunted by rail through the Sudeten Mountains, towards Theresienstadt, suddenly fled. 'We can't believe it's over!' Alfred Kantor, one of the deportees, recalled of that moment at eleven o'clock on the night of May 8 when they were no longer being guarded. Of the thousand men who had begun that particular terrible rail journey less than two weeks earlier, only 175 were still alive. 'Red Cross trucks appear,' Kantor wrote, 'but can't take 175 men. We spend the night on the road – but in a dream. It's over.'

# 49

# Germany in defeat, Japan unbowed

MAY–JULY 1945

During 9 May 1945 there were several further surrenders; the 30,000 German troops on the Channel Islands; the German garrisons on the Aegean islands of Milos, Leros, Kos, Piskopi and Simi; the German garrison on the Baltic island of Bornholm, a part of Denmark; the German troops still holding out in East Prussia and around Danzig; Germans in western and central Czechoslovakia who fought on against the Russians during much of May 9; German troops likewise still fighting in Silesia, where local memorials record the death on May 9 of more than six hundred Soviet soldiers; and the German garrison which had been surrounded at Dunkirk for more than six months, most recently by Czechoslovak troops commanded by Major General Alois Liska. To the surprise of the Czech, British and French officers who accepted the surrender, the German fortress commander, Vice-Admiral Friedrich Frisius, arrived at General Liska's headquarters with his own surrender document already signed.

In Moscow, May 9 was Victory Day, welcomed by a salvo of a thousand guns. 'The age-long struggle of the Slav nations for their existence and independence', Stalin declared in a radio broadcast that evening, 'has ended in victory. Your courage has defeated the Nazis. The war is over.'

Throughout Europe, former prisoners-of-war were being brought home. On May 8, more than thirteen thousand former British prisoners-of-war were flown from Europe to Britain; on May 9, when one of the aircraft crashed on its way across the Channel, twenty-five men on their way home were killed.

In the Pacific, the war knew no abatement or relaxation. On Okinawa, on May 9, sixty Japanese soldiers who broke into the American lines were killed in hand-to-hand fighting. Hundreds of Americans died that day in battles to capture Japanese strongpoints; hundreds more were the victims of battle fatigue and could fight no longer. On Luzon, more than a thousand Japanese soldiers barricaded themselves in caves. Attacked by flame throwers and explosives when they refused to surrender, all of them were killed after a few days. In Indo-China, it was the Japanese who still had the upper hand; at Lang Son, sixty French soldiers and Foreign Legionnaires, who had managed to hold out since the Japanese occupation, were killed when their fort was overrun; the few survivors, put up against a wall, were machine-gunned as they defiantly began to sing the Marseillaise. Afterwards, the Japanese bayoneted any who showed signs of life. Even so, a few survived the massacre. One of them, a Greek legionnaire by the name of Tsakiropolous, was caught three days later, and decapitated, together with two Frenchmen, the Political Resident at Lang Son, and the local commander, General Lemonnier.

In Europe, the first days of Germany's defeat saw the suicides of many of those who feared the already announced war crimes trial should they be captured, or recognized after capture. On May 10, Konrad Henlein, who had been Governor of Bohemia and Moravia since May 1939, committed suicide in an Allied internment camp. That same day, in a naval hospital at Flensburg, ss General Richard Gluecks was found dead; it is not known whether he committed suicide, or was killed by some group, possibly Jews, who sought to avenge the concentration camp savageries over which he had presided for more than five years.

From Britain, soldiers were now being flown across the North Sea, to Oslo, to assist in the disarming of the German occupation forces in Norway. In one aeroplane, which crashed near Oslo on May 10, all twenty-four soldiers and airmen on board were killed.

In the Pacific, off Okinawa, seven American ships had been hit by Japanese suicide aircraft on May 4, and 446 sailors killed. On May 11, a further 396 men were killed on the aircraft carrier *Bunker Hill* – three times the American death toll in the 1775 battle which the carrier's name commemorated.

There was still fighting in Europe on May 11, when Soviet troops overran several pockets of German resistance east of Pilsen. Further south, German troops in Slovenia, near Maribor, continued to fight against Tito's forces. In East Prussia and northern Latvia, several hundred thousand Germans were still refusing to surrender. But it was now no longer military defeat, but possible future retribution, which loomed; in Oslo, on May 11, the former German ruler of Norway, Josef Terboven, committed suicide by blowing himself up with a stick of dynamite.

Every German concentration camp was now in Allied hands, but many thousands of the inmates were too weak or too sick to survive, despite the food and medical care which were now rushed to them. On May 12, at Straubing, in Bavaria, a forty-two-year-old German lawyer, Adolf von Harnier, died of typhoid fever. Denounced in 1939 as an anti-Nazi by a Gestapo informer, von Harnier had been imprisoned since then. Liberation had come a few days too late to save him.

That day, in mid-Atlantic, a German submarine, the U-234, which had left Norway nearly a month earlier to sail to Japan with General Kessler, the newly appointed German Air Attaché to Tokyo, on board, surrendered to the Americans. In the North Sea, German motor torpedo boats were making their way from Rotterdam to Felixstowe, likewise to surrender. Peter Scott, the son of the polar explorer Robert Falcon Scott, was one of the British naval officers who went aboard to escort the German craft to the shore. 'With some difficulty,' he later recalled, 'we persuaded the Germans to fall their crew in on deck as they entered harbour, where a great crowd of spectators was assembled on all the piers and jetties. All at once the armed guards filed on board and the Germans were hustled off the boats. It was the end!'

On Okinawa, May 12 saw a renewed American attack against the fortified Shuri line across the southern part of the island. Hundreds died on both sides. 'Conical Hill', on Okinawa, fell to the Americans on May 13, nor could the Japanese drive them off again. On the day after the capture of Conical Hill, American atomic scientists and bombing experts examined possible targets for the atomic bomb. A report discussed by a special top-secret Target committee meeting at Los Alamos that day noted that the hills around Hiroshima, one of the most favoured targets, were 'likely to produce a focusing effect which would considerably increase the blast damage'. According to the report, the one drawback was Hiroshima's rivers, which made the city 'not a good incendiary target'. Another target under consideration on May 14 was Hirohito's palace in Tokyo, but this was not one of the four targets which were chosen that day for further study; these were Kyoto – the Japanese holy city – Hiroshima, Yokohama and the Kokura arsenal.

Six days had passed since Germany's formal surrender to the Allies; on May 14, 150,000 Germans surrendered to the Red Army in East Prussia, and a further 180,000 in northern Latvia. Only one German force, some 150,000 men, the remnants of the German forces in Yugoslavia, was still under arms that day; on May 15 it surrendered to the Russians and Yugoslavs at Slovenski Gradec. For the Yugoslavs, May 15 is Victory Day. In the previous two months' fighting in Yugoslavia, the Germans had lost 99,907 men killed in action. The Yugoslavs had lost 30,000 men killed during those same final months, a small proportion of the 1,700,000 Yugoslavs who had died since April 1941 in battle, in concentration camps, or in captivity in Germany.

In Burma, the nationalist leader Aung San, who had earlier co-operated with the Japanese, offered his services to the British on May 15. His services were accepted. 'If the British sucked our blood,' one of his leading followers told General Slim, 'the Japanese ground our bones!'. Hence Aung San's change of side. After Burma's liberation, Aung San was to be assassinated by political rivals. Two days after Aung San's change of side, a Canadian member of the British Special Operations Executive, Jean-Paul Archambault, was killed behind the Japanese lines in Burma, when he accidentally detonated one of his explosive charges. Only a year earlier, Archambault had been carrying out similar clandestine duties behind the lines in German-occupied France.

On Okinawa, the ferocity of the fighting reached a climax that day, with the battle for the 'Sugar Loaf', a battle which was to last for ten days, and in which nearly three thousand Marines were killed or wounded. Among the dead was Major Henry A. Courtney, who led a charge to the very top of the hill, but was killed after several hours of hand-to-hand fighting on the crest. Courtney was posthumously awarded the Medal of Honour. In a Japanese suicide attack on American positions on May 19, more than five hundred Japanese were killed.

As the battle raged for Sugar Loaf, American Marines were caught up in mortar and grenade battles of exceptional ferocity. When a popular company commander, Bob Fowler, bled to death after being hit, his orderly, 'who adored him', as a fellow Marine – William Manchester – later recalled, 'snatched up a submachine gun and unforgivably massacred a line of unarmed Japanese soldiers who had just surrendered.' Manchester added: 'Even worse was the tragic lot of eighty-five student nurses. Terrified, they had retreated into a cave. Marines reaching the mouth of the cave heard Japanese voices within. They did not recognize the tones as feminine, and neither did their interpreter, who demanded that those inside emerge at once. When they didn't, flamethrowers, moving in, killed them all. To this day, Japanese come to mourn at what is now known as the "Cave of the Virgins".'

On Luzon and Mindanao in the Philippines, as well as on Okinawa, the third week of May saw bloody battles, in which even the massive use of flame throwers could not dislodge the Japanese defenders, but could only destroy them yard by yard and cave by cave. Off Okinawa, on May 24, Japanese suicide pilots sank a fast troop transport and damaged six warships, while ten Japanese pilots, in a daring landing on Yontan airfield, destroyed seven American aircraft and damaged twenty-six more, as well as igniting 70,000 gallons of aircraft fuel, before being killed. Theirs had also been a suicide mission.

In Germany, on May 21, the last of the hundreds of wooden barracks at Belsen was burned down by flame throwers. 'The swastika and a picture of Hitler were displayed on that last barrack', Anita Lasker, a survivor of Auschwitz, later recalled, 'and there was a little ceremony. We all stood there and watched as this last trace of the camp was devoured by the flames'.

On May 22, Hitler's most senior surviving military Intelligence officer, Reinhard Gehlen, gave himself up to the Americans at Oberursel, north of Darmstadt. In due course, he was to return to Intelligence work against the Russians in post-war West Germany. Also on May 22, an American major, William Bromley, who had earlier been sent to Nordhausen for the express purpose of aiding future rocket research in the United States, began to despatch four hundred tons of German rocket equipment to Antwerp, for shipment across the Atlantic to White Sands, in New Mexico. Requisitioning railway wagons from as far west as Cherbourg, Bromley completed his task before June 1, when – according to the wartime agreement establishing the precise borders of the British, American, French and Russian zones of occupation – the Russians entered Nordhausen.

On May 23, the Russians ordered the arrest of all the Cabinet members of Admiral Dönitz's Government. That same day at Mürwik, Admiral von Friedeburg, who just over two weeks earlier had been the signatory of three of the German Army's instruments of surrender, committed suicide. That evening, Heinrich Himmler, who had been arrested by the British on the previous day, committed suicide by biting a cyanide capsule, while undergoing a medical examination at Lüneburg. He had revealed his identity four hours earlier. 'The bastard's beat us!' was one British sergeant's comment when the deed was done.

On the following day, May 24, Field Marshal von Greim, whom Hitler had made head of the German Air Force in the last days of April, committed suicide in prison in Salzburg.

On May 24, more than four hundred American bombers dropped 3,646 tons of bombs on central Tokyo, and on the industrial areas in the south of the city. More than a thousand Japanese were killed. Also killed in the raid were sixty-two Allied airmen, prisoners-of-war; it was later alleged that they had been deliberately locked into a wooden cell block for the duration of the raid, while all 464 Japanese prisoners and their jailers were taken to a safe shelter.

On the day following this Tokyo raid, the United States Joint Chiefs of Staff confirmed November 1 as the date for the start of Operation Olympic, the invasion of the most southerly Japanese island of Kyushu.

On May 26, the Japanese evacuated the Chinese city of Nanning, losing their direct land link with Indo-China. Chinese soldiers quickly reoccupied the city. Two days later, off Okinawa, the Japanese mounted their last major air offensive against American warships, losing a hundred planes without sinking a single ship.

On May 28, at Flensburg, near the German frontier with Denmark, two British officers arrested William Joyce, the broadcaster 'Lord Haw-Haw'. On him they found not only a German civilian document made out in the name of Wilhelm Hansen, but a German military passport in his real name. He was placed under arrest, and sent back to Britain. Three days later, at Weissensee in Carinthia, a British patrol arrested a man whom they identified as the death camp organizer, Odilo Globocnik; a few minutes after his arrest, he committed suicide by biting a cyanide capsule.

On May 31, those who had to decide on when and where – and if – the atomic bomb was to be dropped on Japan, met in the Pentagon. Speaking for the scientists, Robert Oppenheimer stated, as the official minutes of the meeting record, 'that the visual effect of an atomic bombing would be tremendous. It would be accompanied by a brilliant luminescence which would rise to a height of 10,000 to 20,000 feet. The neutron effect of the explosion would be dangerous to life for a radius of at least two-thirds of a mile.' There was a long discussion that day as to what the targets ought to be, and what effect the bomb might have on them. As the meeting came to an end, the Secretary for War, Henry Stimson, 'expressed the conclusion', as the minutes noted, 'on which there was general agreement, that we could not give the Japanese any warning; that we could not concentrate on a civilian area; but that we should seek to make a profound psychological impression on as many of the inhabitants as possible'. At the suggestion of Dr Conant, Stimson agreed 'that the most desirable target would be a vital war plant employing a large number of workers and closely surrounded by workers' houses'.

It was James Byrnes, the American Secretary of State, who, that same day, took this decision to President Truman, for his approval. Byrnes noted, of their conversation, 'Mr Truman told me he had been giving serious thought to the subject for many days, having been informed as to the investigation of the committee and the consideration of alternative plans, and that with reluctance he had to agree that he could think of no alternative and found himself in accord with what I told him the Committee was going to recommend'.

The alternative plan, to invade Kyushu Island in November, and the far larger Honshu Island in the following spring, had been judged so costly in the lives of the invading force as to make the use of the atomic bomb the preferable plan. If it led to Japan's surrender before the November invasion, so the argument went, as many as a million American lives might be saved, and the war shortened by as much as a year.

Meanwhile, both on Luzon and Okinawa, considerable Japanese opposition was overcome in the first three days of June. On Okinawa, an extreme shortage of rations for the Japanese troops was causing considerable discontent among them, something hitherto unknown. On June 3, American Marines seized the Iheya Islands, north of Okinawa; then, on Okinawa itself, they landed on June 4 on the Oroku peninsula, where a Japanese Naval Base Force of five thousand men was defending the Naha airfield. For ten days they fought with flame-throwers, flame-throwing tanks and explosives against a fanatical and tenacious Japanese defence – men, willing to die in their hundreds in flames rather than give up a single cave. In the ten day battle, four thousand Japanese were killed, at a cost of 1,608 American lives. When the Americans finally penetrated the Japanese headquarters cave, which had also served as a hospital, they found that more than two hundred wounded soldiers and headquarters staff had committed suicide, including the commander of the Naval Base Force, Admiral Minoru Ota.

On June 5, a typhoon off Okinawa damaged many American warships, including four battleships and eight aircraft-carriers. To compound the injury, the battleship *Mississippi* and the heavy cruiser *Louisville* were both seriously damaged by Japanese suicide aircraft. But with every set of suicide attacks, the Japanese power to sustain such a course was further diminished.

In Tokyo, at a Government conference held in the presence of Hirohito on June 8, the Japanese Cabinet resolved 'to prosecute the war to the bitter end'. That day, on Okinawa, the Americans advanced once more, at the southern end of the island, against the Japanese fortified positions on Yuza Hill and the Kunishi Ridge; but once more they were confronted with a ferocious defender whose power to drive back the attackers was still formidable. Despite a massive American artillery bombardment, the Japanese again dug deep into the hillside; the napalm bomb was virtually the only effective means of dislodging them, or, rather, of destroying them. Yet the Japanese determination to fight back led to an enormous number of casualties among the Marines. On average, an American rifleman could expect to fight for only about three weeks before becoming a casualty. In many front line companies, every soldier was wounded, and their replacements then wounded in their turn. Some replacements were killed before they could fire a single shot.

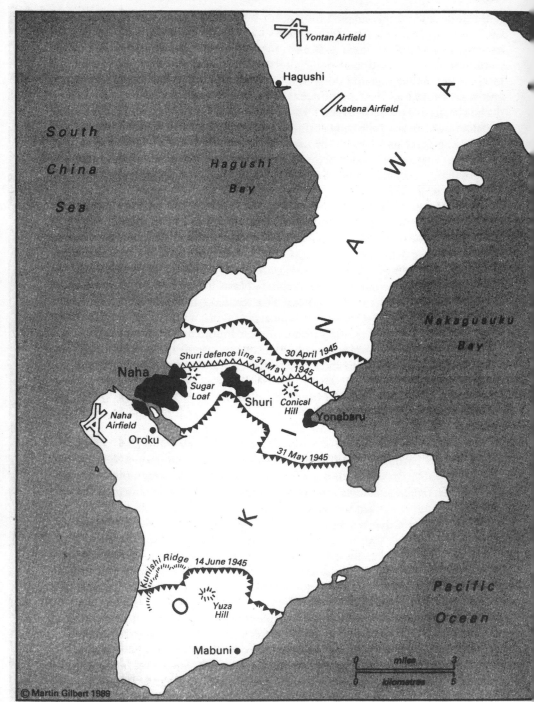

The fall of Okinawa, 30 April to 21 June 1945

On June 10, the assault on the Japanese defences on the southern tip of Okinawa was renewed. One Marine, Charles J. Leonard, later recalled a typical incident in the fight for Hill 69, the last major Japanese outpost before Kunishi ridge. 'I had only one grenade left,' he wrote, 'and it was white phosphorous. I threw it in and stood back. A huge cloud of smoke and burning phosphorous roared out of the shallow cave. A piece landed on my arm and quickly burned through the cotton cloth and started burrowing into the skin. I pulled my bayonet from my rifle and started to scrape the phosphorous off. The smell of burning flesh was nauseating'.

Leonard's account continued: 'I was so occupied with this problem I did not notice that a Japanese soldier was squeezing through the cave opening. He saw me and charged with his bayonet-tipped rifle aimed at my stomach. I dropped my bayonet and grabbed my rifle. I squeezed off four rounds before he hit me. By then he was dead but his bayonet slapped into the webbing of my back pack strap which was over my right shoulder. It glanced off the heavy webbing and slashed across my chest. Since my bullets had slowed his lungs there was no significant weight behind the bayonet and it did not enter my body – just cut me superficially. He had been knocked off balance and slumped beside me. I shot him four more times and continued jerking on the trigger even after the clip had been ejected past my ear'.

Thirty-nine years later, Leonard was to write of how he had looked directly into the dark eyes of the Japanese soldier as his bullets had hit him. 'I carry that vision still', he wrote, 'like a photograph in my brain. I have no regrets. We were two soldiers whose job was to kill. I had done my job. He had failed to do his. At least on me. Perhaps, he had killed some of my friends. If so, they were now avenged.'

On June 10, as the Americans struggled to defeat the Japanese in the southern-most hills of Okinawa, Australian forces landed at Labuan Island, in the first stage of the defeat of the Japanese in North Borneo. In Burma, local Burmese guerrillas, led by British officers, drove the Japanese from Loilem, in the Shan mountains. In China, Chinese troops liberated I-shan, and pursued the Japanese towards Liuchow.

In Europe, the war of armies was over, but the mass movement of refugees and displaced persons had only just begun. At Soviet insistence, tens of thousands of Russians who had either fought in German units, or had been taken prisoner by the Western Allies, were returned forcibly to the Soviet Union. At the same time, from the areas under Soviet control, millions of Germans were expelled westward, as their cities and farms changed ownership and sovereignty. On June 11, the mass expulsion began, from the Sudeten mountain regions of Czechoslovakia, of more than 700,000 Sudeten Germans, who were literally beaten across the border. These men, women and children had been Hitler's excuse in October 1938 to dismember Czechoslovakia; now the new Czecho-slovak State was determined to be rid of them. Thousands had already fled, starting from the last days of the war. Hundreds had been killed on the roads as they fled, or were thrown into the rivers of their ancestral lands. What had begun as a great adventure for German-speaking people all over Europe, during the euphoria of Hitler's early victories, was now one more tragic ending in a war which had seen every variety of tragedy and disaster.

In Germany, the Allied search for Germany's wartime leaders continued; on June 14, the former Foreign Minister, Joachim von Ribbentrop, was arrested in a Hamburg boarding house by British soldiers. Together with many of his senior colleagues of the Third Reich, he was held in prison, while preparations were made to bring him to trial.

Preparation also continued, under the supervision of the American Army, to move as much German scientific equipment, and the scientists themselves, out of those areas of the proposed Russian zone which were temporarily under American control; it was not until a few hours before the Russians were due to arrive at Nordhausen and Bleichrode, on June 20, that the last German scientists and their families were brought by train into the American zone. Within three weeks, on July 6, the American Joint Chiefs of Staff authorized Operation Overcast, to 'exploit' from among the German scientists 'chosen, rare minds whose continuing intellectual productivity we wish to use'. Under Operation Overcast, 350 German and Austrian scientists were to be brought within a few months to the United States.

In the Far East, as part of Operation Oboe III, the Australians had liberated the town of Brunei on June 13. On the Philippine island of Mindanao, all organized resistance ended on June 18; for some while, the Japanese defenders had been forced to live on roots, and on the bark of trees. Also on June 18, American bombers began a series of attacks against twenty-three Japanese towns.

On Okinawa, the last Japanese resistance on Kunishi Ridge was being slowly overcome. On June 18 the commander of the American forces on the island, Lieutenant-General Simon Buckner, left his headquarters in the north of the island to observe the final phase of the battle in the south. As he watched the battle, he was killed by a Japanese anti-tank shell. Two other senior American officers were killed within the next twenty-four hours, the Marine Commander, Colonel Harold C. Roberts, hit by a sniper's bullet, and Brigadier-General Claudius M. Easley. But by the evening of June 21, the Marines had reached the entrance to the Japanese command cave at Mabuni. That night, the two Japanese generals in the cave, Generals Ushijima and Sho, were served a special feast; then, before daylight, dressed in full field uniform, with swords and medals, both men knelt on a clean sheet, faced north in the direction of Hirohito's palace in Tokyo, and, using a sharp sabre, committed suicide. In a final message, General Sho had written: 'I depart without regret, shame, or obligations.'

More than 127,000 Japanese soldiers had been killed on Okinawa, and a further 80,000 Okinawan civilians. The Japanese had also inflicted massive American casualties during the battle; 7,613 Americans had been killed on land, and a further 4,907 in air and kamikaze attacks at sea, when thirty-six American warships had been sunk. The Japanese had lost an extraordinary number of aircraft over Okinawa, 7,800, for the cost of 763 American aircraft.

Elsewhere in the Pacific, the death toll was lower. When, on July 20, Australian troops landed at Miri, in Sarawak, as part of the reconquest of North Borneo, they were quickly able to overcome a small and already demoralized garrison. In the reconquest of the whole area, 1,234 Japanese were killed, at a cost of 114 Australian and four American lives.

Whether in a blood-bath, as at Okinawa, or with considerable slaughter, as on Luzon or Mindanao, or more easily, as in North Borneo, the Japanese were being driven slowly but relentlessly from their conquests. It was clear to the Japanese Government that the prospect of a heavy loss of American lives was not going to deter the continuing advance, or prevent new landings, including those clearly under preparation against mainland Japan. On June 20, Hirohito summoned his Prime Minister, Foreign Minister and military chiefs to an Imperial conference, at which he took an unusual initiative, urging them to make all possible efforts to end the war by diplomatic means. Even the War Minister and the Army Chief of Staff recognized the logic of their Emperor's appeal.

In order to seek a negotiated peace, the Japanese Government decided to approach the Soviet Government, and to ask it to act as an intermediary. These approaches were made by the Japanese Foreign Minister, Togo, through his Ambassador in Moscow, Sato Naotake; unknown to Togo, his top-secret messages, sent by radio through Japan's apparently unbreakable Magic system, were read by American Intelligence. Unfortunately for Japan, these intercepts made it clear to the Americans that, while Japan did want to negotiate peace with the United States, it was not prepared to accept unconditional surrender. Knowing this, the Americans were all the more determined to force Japan to its knees.

On June 24, in Thailand, British bombers destroyed the two railway bridges over the notorious 'River Kwai' which had been built under appalling conditions of slave labour by Allied prisoners-of-war as part of the Burma–Thailand railway.

In Moscow, June 24 saw a Victory march-past in Red Square, during which two hundred Soviet soldiers carried into the square two hundred captured German military banners, and, to the solemn roll of drums, threw them at the foot of the Lenin Mausoleum. Two days later, in San Francisco, the United Nations conference came to an end with the signature of the United Nations Charter. The maintenance of peace would be the responsibility of the Security Council, on which each of the five Great Powers, Britain, the Soviet Union, the United States, China and France, would have an effective veto.

In Prague, Emil Hacha, the President of Czechoslovakia in 1938, whom Hitler had made State President of Bohemia and Moravia, died in prison on June 27. Two days later, the new Czechoslovak Government signed a treaty with the Soviet Union, ceding its most easterly region, Ruthenia, to Russia. This was the first formal transfer of territory as a result of the Second World War; the Polish borders awaited the decision of Stalin, Truman and Churchill, who were preparing for a Big Three conference at Potsdam.

In the Far East, the Japanese continued to move Allied prisoners-of-war away from the areas on which they thought the Allies might land. Of 2,000 Australian prisoners-of-war who had been taken out of their camp at Sandakan, in North Borneo, in February, only six were still alive by the end of June, when the march reached Ranau, a hundred miles inland. On the first day of July, Australian forces, their assault preceded by a massive American aerial bombardment, landed near Balikpapan, which with its oil installations fell to them two days later; the Japanese, however, had prepared strong defensive positions in the interior; they were determined not to give up Borneo easily.

In the Philippines, a further American landing on Mindanao, near the southern port of Davao, on July 4, further restricted the area under Japanese control. On the following day, General MacArthur announced that the liberation of the Philippines was completed. That same week of Allied success against the Japanese saw the tragic end of a once twenty-three strong British Special Operations group, led by Lieutenant-Colonel Ivan Lyon, which had begun its operations behind Japanese lines on Merapas Island, near Singapore, the previous September. In a series of clashes with the Japanese, twelve of the group, including Lyon, had been killed, and eleven captured. One of the eleven died of his wounds. After six months in captivity, the surviving ten were beheaded, on July 7.

In Canada, on July 9, a British physicist working on research into nuclear fission, Dr Alan Nunn May, handed to Colonel Zabotin, a member of the Soviet Embassy in Ottawa '162 micrograms of Uranium 233, in the form of acid, contained in a thick lamina' – as Zabotin described it in his telegram to Moscow. From Klaus Fuchs, the Soviet atomic scientists already knew of the American experiments being carried out for the final manufacture of an atomic bomb.

Another recently developed type of bomb, the napalm bomb, was already in use against the Japanese; on July 11, and again on July 12, several thousand tons of napalm bombs were dropped on the Japanese forces still holding out on the Philippine island of Luzon, 40,000 of them in the area around Kiangan.

On July 12, on mainland China, in Operation Apple, a Chinese Nationalist commando force dropped near Kaiping, to cut the Japanese lines of communications. At all its margins, even those that had seemed most secure, the Japanese New Order in Asia and the Pacific was being eroded.

In Berlin, on July 12, Field Marshal Montgomery invested four Soviet commanders, including Marshals Zhukov and Rokossovsky, with British medals. That day, in London, the British Air Ministry launched a peacetime plan, Operation Surgeon, designed to 'cut out the heart' of German aviation expertise. Not only was German equipment to be brought to Britain, from the German Air Force research centre at Volkenrode, now in the British zone of Germany, but also to be brought to Britain were several German experts; two of them, Wernher Pinsche and Dietrich Kuchemann, were among more than twenty German aviation experts who were eventually employed at the Royal Air Force research establishment at Farnborough. Another German aviation expert, Adolf Busemann, was later to leave Britain in order to continue his research in the United States.

Those of Germany's leading Nazis who had been captured by the Allies were now awaiting trial. On July 14 the *Chicago Daily News* revealed that they were being held, not in prison, but at a hotel in Luxemburg, the Palace Hotel, Mondorf. The newspaper was critical of what it saw as far too pleasant a setting for such evil men. Radio Moscow, picking up this news item, translated the hotel into 'a Luxemburg palace', where the Nazi leaders were 'getting even fatter and more insolent'. In fact, they were receiving standard Allied prisoner-of-war rations, and were living amid the strictest security of stockade, floodlights, and guards with machine-guns.

As Germany's former leaders awaited trial, one of Germany's former allies, Italy, declared war on Japan, a final, ignominious end to the Axis which had once been so formidable a war-making combination.

The American target date for the initial invasion of mainland Japan was still November 1, a mere three and a half months away when, on July 14, American warships, among them the *Massachusetts*, began a series of bombardments of specific targets on the Japanese home islands. The target that day was the Imperial Ironworks at Kamaishi. On the following day, from distant Naples, the first shipload of American troops who had served in the European theatre set sail for the Pacific. They too were a part of the build-up to the November invasion.

The Japanese, aware only that the day of American landings on Kyushu and Honshu could not be very far distant, made preparations to meet the invaders, not only with the stubborn defences which they had used throughout the Pacific, but with an intensification of suicide tactics. Thousands more men were being trained for 'kamikaze' aircraft attacks and the equally destructive 'kaiten' torpedo suicide missions. In addition, a third type of suicide weapon, a suicide mine, had been devised, whereby a diver would place the mine on the hull of a ship, and detonate it, blowing himself up with the ship.

The suicide divers who were to carry these mines were known as 'fukuryu' – crouching dragons. Their principal task would be to swim out to sea to place their mines on the hulls of the landing craft and supply ships at each invasion beach. That November, the Fukuryu began their training, walking out to sea with their mines to depths of up to fifteen metres. At the same time, experiments were made into sunken concrete shelters in which six-man squads of Fukuryu could be waiting offshore under the water up to ten hours before the invasion barges arrived.

# 50

# Alamogordo, Potsdam, Hiroshima

JULY–AUGUST 1945

At half past five in the morning of 16 July 1945, the first atomic bomb was successfully tested at Alamogordo, New Mexico, in the United States. 'The sun can't hold a candle to it!' was the reaction of one of the physicists as he watched the light of the explosion dazzle with its reflection on the surrounding hills. At Ground Zero, the temperature at the moment of explosion had been three times hotter than the interior of the sun, and ten thousand times the heat of the sun on its surface. As had never happened before, the steel scaffold on which the experimental bomb had stood had been transformed into gas by the intense heat, and had dispersed. Within a mile radius of the explosion, all plant and animal life had vanished.

It was immediately clear that something quite extraordinary had happened. As far away as two hundred miles, windows had been blown out. A hundred and fifty miles away, bewildered citizens reported that the sun had come up and then gone down again. Many of the measuring devices and instruments set up in the desert had been swept away. Most of the film in the scientists' cameras had been completely fogged – by radiation. That same day, in Berlin, the Allied leaders were gathering for their final conference on the future of the defeated Germany; that day, Churchill was given a guided tour through the ruins of Hitler's Chancellery.

The Big Three conference opened at Potsdam on July 17, to discuss the continuing war against Japan, and the post-war settlement in Europe. As the conference began, Allied bombers, taking off from American and British ships, attacked military installations and airfields around Tokyo, while other American bombers hit at the industrial towns of Mito and Hitachi, on Honshu Island. But it was the news of the successful testing of the atomic bomb which led to the most dramatic information sent to Potsdam that day. 'Operated on this morning,' a top-secret telegram informed the American Secretary for War, Henry Stimson, and it continued: 'Diagnosis not yet complete, but results seem satisfactory and already exceed expectations.'

It was also necessary, Stimson was told, for a local press release to be issued, 'as interest extends great distance'. The local press release stated that an ammunition dump had exploded, 'producing a brilliant flash and blast', which had been observed more than two hundred miles away.

At noon that day, Stimson, at lunch with Churchill, handed him a sheet of paper on which was written: 'Babies satisfactorily born.' Churchill had no idea what the message meant. 'It means', Stimson explained, 'that the experiment in the Mexican desert has come off. The atomic bomb is a reality.'

Later that day, Churchill and Stalin held a private conversation, during which Stalin told the British Prime Minister that, when he was leaving Moscow for Berlin, a message had been delivered to him through the Japanese Ambassador. 'It was from the Emperor of Japan,' Stalin explained, who had '– stated that "unconditional surrender" could not be accepted by Japan but that, if it was not insisted upon, "Japan might be prepared to compromise with regard to other terms".' According to the message, Stalin added, 'the Emperor was making this suggestion "in the interests of all people concerned".'

Churchill pointed out to Stalin that, while Britain shared America's aim 'of achieving complete victory over Japan', at the same time people in America 'were beginning to doubt the need for "unconditional surrender". They were saying: was it worth while having the pleasure of killing ten million Japanese at the cost of one million Americans and British?'

The Japanese realized the Allied strength, Stalin commented, and as a result they were 'very frightened'. They could see what unconditional surrender meant in practice 'here in Berlin and the rest of Germany'.

On the battlefront, the Japanese were now trying to limit their commitments. But on July 20, as Japanese troops tried to escape from Burma through Moulmein, British bombers flew 3,045 sorties against them in nine days, when more than ten thousand Japanese were killed. Since the British had started on the reconquest of Burma a year earlier, more than 100,000 Japanese soldiers had lost their lives in action; thousands more had died of disease and privation in the hostile jungle.

In Berlin, on July 21, during a short break in the Potsdam Conference, Churchill took the salute of the British forces in the city. That morning's parade, he told them, 'brings back to my mind a great many moving incidents in these last, long, fierce years. Now, here in Berlin, I find you all established in this great centre, from which, as from a volcano, fire and smoke and poison fumes have erupted all over Europe twice in a generation. And in bygone times also German fury has been let loose on her neighbours, and now it is we who have our place in the occupation of this country'.

At Potsdam, considerable areas of disagreement had opened up among the former Allies. During the discussions of the Big Three on the afternoon of July 21, Churchill told Stalin that the situation in Vienna and Austria was 'unsatisfactory'; Britain had not been allowed even now to take up her zone in Vienna or in Austria, although three or four months had passed since discussions started. In reply, Stalin informed the Conference that he had agreed 'the previous day' to the recommendations of the European Advisory Commission, so that the way was 'now free' to fix the date for the entry of the British and American

Post-war Europe

troops into their zones; 'so far as he was concerned this could start at once'.

The discussion then turned to Poland. In a memorandum submitted to the Conference, the Soviet delegation had argued that Poland's western frontier should run to the west of Swinemünde, as far as the River Oder, leaving the city of Stettin on the Polish side, then up the River Oder to the confluence with the Western Neisse, and from there along its course to the northern border of Czechoslovakia.

It was Truman who protested that this movement of the Polish frontier so far westward was the equivalent of giving Poland a zone of occupation of her own in Germany. But the agreement to divide Germany into four zones of occupation, British, American, French and Soviet, was based upon the 1937 frontiers. The frontier now proposed for Poland was well inside this area.

He wished it to be 'clearly understood', declared Truman, 'that Germany should be occupied in accordance with the zones stated at Yalta'. But Stalin replied that the Germans had fled from the eastern regions which Poland now intended to occupy.

On July 22, at Potsdam, Henry Stimson brought Churchill a detailed account of the effect of the atomic bomb test at Alamogordo. Inside a one-mile circle, Stimson reported, the devastation had been absolute. Churchill went at once to see Truman. 'Up to this moment,' Churchill later recalled, 'we had shaped our ideas towards an assault upon the homeland of Japan by terrific air bombing and by the invasion of very large armies'. Churchill added: 'We had contemplated the desperate resistance of the Japanese fighting to the death with Samurai devotion, not only in pitched battles, but in every cave and dug-out. I had in my mind the spectacle of Okinawa Island, where many thousands of Japanese, rather than surrender, had drawn up in line and destroyed themselves by hand-grenades after their leaders had solemnly performed the rite of hara-kiri. To quell the Japanese resistance man by man and conquer the country yard by yard might well require the loss of a million American lives and half that number of British – or more if we could get them there: for we were resolved to share the agony'.

Now, Churchill recalled 'all this nightmare picture had vanished. In its place was the vision – fair and bright indeed it seemed – of the end of the whole war in one or two violent shocks. I thought immediately myself of how the Japanese people, whose courage I had always admired, might find in the apparition of this almost supernatural weapon an excuse which would save their honour and release them from their obligation of being killed to the last fighting man'.

On July 24, while still at Potsdam, Churchill, Truman, and the representatives of China agreed to send a message to Japan, offering her 'an opportunity to end the war'. What had happened in Germany, the message read, 'stands forth in awful clarity as an example to the people of Japan'. The 'full application' of Allied military power, 'backed by our resolve, will mean the inevitable and complete destruction of the Japanese forces, and just as inevitably the utter devastation of the Japanese homeland'. It was now for Japan to decide 'whether she will continue to be controlled' by those who had brought her 'to the threshold of annihilation', or whether she would follow 'the path of reason'.

The Big Three then set out their 'terms', adding that there were no alternatives, and that 'We shall brook no delay.' The influence and authority of those who had 'deceived and misled' the people of Japan would have to be 'eliminated for all time'. The Japanese forces would have to be 'completely disarmed'. Japanese sovereignty would be limited to the four main islands of Japan 'and such minor islands as we determine'. Freedom of speech, of religion and of thought, 'as well as respect for fundamental human rights', would be established. In return, Japan would be allowed to maintain 'such industries as will sustain her economy' and would be permitted 'eventual participation in world trade relations'. The message ended: 'We call upon the Government of Japan to proclaim now the unconditional surrender of all the Japanese armed forces, and to provide proper and adequate assurances of their good faith in such action. The alternative for Japan is complete and utter destruction.'

The Japanese had failed to involve the Russians as peace-makers. They had also failed to undermine the Russian pledge, made five months earlier at Yalta, to enter the war against Japan within two to three months of the end of the war in Europe.

Hardly had this call for unconditional surrender been agreed to between America, Britain and China, than Truman approached Stalin, to tell him privately that the United States had just tested a bomb of extraordinary power. During that same day, Truman also discussed with Stimson when this new bomb was to be dropped, and on what sort of target. 'The weapon is to be used against Japan between now and August 10th,' Truman wrote in his diary on July 24, and he added that he had instructed Stimson 'to use it so that military objectives and soldiers and sailors are the target and not women and children. Even if the Japs are savages, ruthless, merciless and fanatic, we as the leader of the world for the common welfare cannot drop this terrible bomb on the old capital or the new'.

Truman went on to confide to his diary that he and Stimson were 'in accord' about the use of the atomic bomb on a military target, and he explained that: 'The target will be a purely military one and we will issue a warning statement asking the Japs to surrender and save lives. I'm sure they will not do that, but we will have given them the chance. It is certainly a good thing for the world that Hitler's crowd or Stalin's did not discover this atomic bomb. It seems to be the most terrible thing ever discovered, but it can be made the most useful'.

On July 24, as these decisions were made at Potsdam, American carrier-based bombers attacked the Kure naval base on mainland Japan, as well as Japanese airfields at Nagoya, Osaka and Mito. They repeated their attack on the following day, when twenty-two British warships, including two carriers and their aircraft, launched Operation Cockpit against Japanese port and oil installations on Sabang Island, off the northern tip of Sumatra. Considerable damage was caused. Also on July 25, the Americans announced that all organized Japanese resistance had ceased on the Philippine island of Mindanao.

On July 25, a war crimes trial began at Darmstadt, in the American zone of Germany. The eleven accused, nine men and two women, were those who, in Rüsselheim in August 1944, were believed to have participated in the killing of six American airmen, who had earlier been shot down and were on their way to a prisoner-of-war camp. Seven of the accused were found guilty, including the two women. The five men were hanged, the sentences being carried out by the United States military executioner, Master-Sergeant John C. Wood.

While the Darmstadt trial was in its second day, the British Government set up a Missing Research and Enquiry Service, to try to locate the 42,000 British airmen who had not returned from air missions over wartime Europe, but whose fate was still unknown.

On July 26, at seven in the evening, President Truman's staff issued the Potsdam

Declaration on Japan to the newspapers. That same day, in the Pacific, the American cruiser *Indianapolis* arrived at Tinian Island with the atomic bomb on board. Waiting for it were the scientists who would assemble it and the aircrew who would drop it. Even the aircraft which would carry the bomb to Japan had been chosen and made ready; she was the 'Enola Gay'.

At a specially called press conference on the afternoon on July 26, the Japanese Prime Minister, Admiral Kantaro Suzuki, rejected the Potsdam Declaration. 'As for the Government,' he said, 'it does not find any important value in it, and there is no other recourse but to ignore it entirely and fight resolutely for the successful conclusion of the war.'

On July 28, American carrier-based aircraft struck again at the Japanese naval base at Kure. Five Japanese warships were sunk, including the aircraft carrier *Amagi* and the heavy cruiser *Tone*; of the twenty-five Japanese warships involved in the attack on Pearl Harbour, the *Tone* was the twenty-fourth to be sunk. Only one, the destroyer *Ushio*, was to survive the war.

Air and sea bombardment of the Japanese home islands was now an almost daily event. On July 29, an American naval squadron shelled an aircraft factory at Hamamatsu, on Honshu Island. That same day, however, disaster struck for the American cruiser *Indianapolis*, torpedoed just before midnight between Tinian and Guam, while she was on her way, unescorted, first to Guam and then to Okinawa, to train for the still-projected invasion of Japan on November 1. Amid fire and darkness, more than 350 of her crew of 1,196 were killed in the explosion or went down with the ship. More than eight hundred were pitched or slid into the sea. Fifty of them, mostly those who had been injured during the submarine attack, died during the night. On the following morning, sharks attacked the survivors. There were no ships near to rescue the desperate men, nor had there been time for any distress call; the sun blinded them; sea water, which many drank in their desperation, drove them mad. Not until the morning of August 2 were those who still survived spotted from the air. Until then, the ship had not even been missed. Now, after the men had been eighty-four hours in the water, a rescue operation began. Only 318 sailors were still alive; 484 had died in the water, either eaten by sharks or drowning in the ocean.

In all, 883 men had died in the *Indianapolis* disaster, the greatest loss at sea in the history of the United States Navy, and the last major warship to be lost at sea in the Second World War. For the Japanese, it was a welcome success in a losing struggle. The officer who had been in charge of the Japanese submarine, Lieutenant-Commander Mochitsura Hashimoto, a veteran of the Japanese attack on Pearl Harbour, later recalled how, on the day after the sinking of the *Indianapolis*, 'we celebrated our haul of the previous day with our favourite rice with beans, boiled eels, and corned beef (all of it tinned)'.

Commander Hashimoto also sent a radio message to Tokyo, stating that he had sunk 'a battleship of *Idaho* class', and giving the exact latitude and longitude. Although no radio message reached the Americans from the stricken *Indianapolis*, Commander Hashimoto's victorious signal was intercepted as a matter of routine by American Signals Intelligence, and decoded. By the morning of July 30, a copy of the decoded message had been sent to American naval headquarters on Guam. The Seventh Fleet also received a copy. But, as Japanese claims of sinkings were almost always absurdly exaggerated, no one thought to ascertain what ship it might be, or to check the area by air search. Had that been done, rescue efforts might have been started a full three days before they were in fact begun.

On July 30, in connection with the plans for the dropping of the atomic bomb on the four target cities earlier agreed, General Carl Spaatz telegraphed to Washington that Hiroshima, 'according to prisoner-of-war reports', was the only one of the four 'that does not have Allied prisoner-of-war camps'. He was told, by return of signal, that it was too late now to change the targets, 'however, if you consider your information reliable, Hiroshima should be given first priority among them.'

The Japanese had continued to work for Soviet mediation, hoping to circumvent the Anglo–American–Chinese call for unconditional surrender by the opening up of negotiations for a compromise peace. On August 2, an American Intelligence analysis based on the Magic intercepts noted that Japan was 'still balking at the term unconditional surrender', and also 'still determined to exploit fully the possible advantage of making peace first with Russia'. After reading the Magic intercepts on which these conclusions were based, Secretary of the Navy, James R. Forrestal, commented that the Japanese Cabinet seemed to have decided 'that the war must be fought with all the vigour and bitterness of which the nation is capable, so long as the only alternative is unconditional surrender'.

In the early hours of July 31, two British midget submarines, having been towed by submarine from the Philippines, entered Singapore dockyard. Emerging from one of the submarines only with difficulty, and then working underwater for half an hour, amid great risk, Leading Seaman Mick Magennis, an Irishman from Belfast, scraped the seaweed and barnacles from the hull of the Japanese cruiser *Takao*, in order to fix six limpet mines to its hull. For his exceptional courage, both he and the midget submarine's captain, Lieutenant Ian Fraser, were awarded the Victoria Cross.

A large hole was blown in the hull of the *Takao*, but, being in shallow water, she settled on the sea bed. No doubt had she been in deep water she would have sunk. Somewhat to the chagrin of the British submariners, it was later learned that an American submarine had already damaged the cruiser's stern at sea.

On August 2, the Potsdam Conference came to an end. Among the agreements which it reached was 'the removal of Germans from Poland, Czechoslovakia and Hungary'. Many of these Germans were already on the move. The Conference also transferred all of eastern Germany between the 1937 border and the Oder–Neisse line to Poland. Churchill had been uneasy at the Russian insistence upon the Western and not the Eastern Neisse; but in mid-conference he had returned to London to learn the British General Election results, in which his Conservative Party had been defeated. It was the new Labour Prime Minister,

Clement Attlee, who had returned to Potsdam to conduct the final negotiations.

As well as Poland's gain of Pomerania and Silesia from Germany, she also divided the German province of East Prussia between herself and the Soviet Union. Hitler's 'Wolf's Lair' at Rastenburg was now on Polish soil. Under Soviet sovereignty fell the eastern regions of pre-war Poland, including the once predominantly Polish cities of Vilna and Lvov. Just as several million Germans moved westward from the new Poland to Germany, so millions of Poles now moved westward from the new Russia to Poland; many of these Poles were to be settled on land taken from Germany, and Germany's eastern cities acquired new names. Stettin became Szczecin; Breslau, Wroclaw; Kolberg, Kolobrzeg; Allenstein, Olsztyn; and Rastenburg, Ketrzyn.

At the end of the First World War, when, instead of unconditional surrender, the Germans and their allies had been allowed to accept an armistice, the terms of peace had been negotiated. During the course of these negotiations, the victors had nevertheless effectively imposed their wishes on the defeated States. Territory was taken away, reparations were secured, and armies disbanded in the guise of a negotiated peace. This peace had soon been denounced as a 'dictated' one, and political agitators, among them Hitler, had stirred up intense nationalism through these denunciations. The Allies were determined not to allow that situation to recur; hence their insistence on unconditional surrender. The boundaries and the conditions to be created in the post-war world would be subject neither to negotiation nor discussion with those who had been defeated. By this method, the Allies intended that Potsdam would not repeat what had been seen as the errors and weaknesses of Versailles. The Germans would not be able to feel that their leaders had let them down at the negotiating table; the negotiations at Potsdam had been conducted without any German representation.

President Truman, returning home to the United States, lunched with King George VI at Plymouth, on board the battleship *Renown*. Much of the conversation revolved around the atomic bomb. One member of Truman's party, Admiral Leahy, was sceptical of the effect the bomb would have. 'It sounds like a professor's dream to me' was his comment, whereupon the King remarked: 'Would you like to lay a little bet on that, Admiral?'

The Japanese had become concerned lest Russia, unwilling to negotiate with them, were to join in the attack against them. But on August 4, the operations section of the 700,000 strong Japanese Army in Manchuria concluded that no Soviet attack was possible until September, nor was such an attack probable, the section believed, until the spring of 1946.

That August 4, at a naval base in Singapore, the Japanese executed seven captured American airmen. One of the Japanese cooks at the base, Oka Harumitzu, later recalled that, previously, fourteen or fifteen other prisoners-of-war had been similarly executed.

*        *        *

In preparation for an American amphibious landing on Kyushu, the Japanese had trained considerable numbers of kamikaze suicide pilots, kaiten suicide human torpedoes and fukuryu suicide divers. By August 1945, as many as 1,200 suicide divers had been trained, with a further 2,800 under training. Their task would be to position themselves off shore, in underwater concrete shelters with iron hatches, ready to emerge as the landing craft arrived, and to fix their mines on the hulls. The landing craft, their men and tanks, and the diver, would then all be blown up together.

On the night of August 5, seven groups of American bombers set off to bomb mainland Japan. Thirty of the bombers flew through the night to drop mines on the Inland Sea; sixty-five were on their way to bomb Saga; 102 were on an incendiary raid on Maebashi; 261 were to strike at the Nishinomiya–Mikage area; 111 were on their way to Ube; sixty-six were flying against Imabari; and one was flying, with two back-up planes, to Hiroshima.

This seventh mission was Operation Centreboard. It began at a quarter to three in the early hours of August 6, when the B-29 bomber, the 'Enola Gay', which had been especially adapted to carry an atomic bomb, took off from Tinian Island in the Marianas. Five and a half hours later, at a quarter-past eight in the morning Japanese time, it dropped its atomic bomb on the Japanese city of Hiroshima. Among the messages scrawled on the bomb was one which read: 'Greetings to the Emperor from the men of the *Indianapolis*.'

Captain Robert A. Lewis, the aircraft commander on the 'Enola Gay', saw the massive, blinding flash of the explosion, his fellow crewmen heard him call out: 'My God, look at that son-of-a-bitch go!' In that instant, 80,000 people were killed, and more than 35,000 injured.

Of the 90,000 buildings in Hiroshima when the bomb fell, 62,000 were destroyed. Of the two hundred doctors in the city, 180 were killed or badly injured. Of the city's fifty-five hospitals and first aid centres, only three could still be used. Of the city's 1,780 nurses, less than 150 could attend to the sick. Several American prisoners-of-war being held in Hiroshima castle since they had been shot down over the city eight days earlier were also killed. The city burned: 'I am starting to count the fires,' Staff Sergeant Caron recorded as he looked back. 'One, two, three, four, five, six ... fourteen, fifteen ... it's impossible. There are too many to count.'

'It's pretty terrific,' another of the crewmen, Jacob Beser, commented, and he added: 'What a relief it worked.'

The scale and nature of the destruction of human life at Hiroshima was eventually to alter the whole nature of how mankind looked at wars, power, diplomacy and the relationships between states. In the days when its reality was only slowly becoming apparent, it was the terrifying human aspects which each survivor could not shake out of his or her nightmares. 'Mother was completely bedridden,' a nine-year-old boy later recalled of the days following the bomb. 'The hair of her head had almost all fallen out, her chest was festering, and from the two-inch hole in her back a lot of maggots were crawling in and out. The place was full of flies and mosquitoes and fleas, and an awfully bad smell

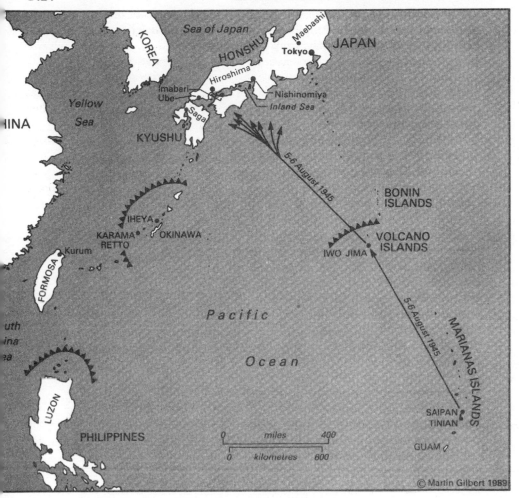

The seven bombing missions of 5–6 August 1945

hung over everything. Everywhere I looked there were many people like this who couldn't move. From the evening when we arrived mother's condition got worse and we seemed to see her weakening before our eyes. Because all night long she was having trouble breathing, we did everything we could to relieve her. The next morning grandmother and I fixed some gruel. As we took it to mother, she breathed her last breath. When we thought she had stopped breathing altogether, she took one deep breath and did not breathe any more after that'.

That was thirteen days after the bomb had exploded over Hiroshima; by then, the death toll had risen by a further twelve thousand, reaching 92,233. It was to rise still further in the following years from the illnesses resulting from radiation. In 1986, the number of identified victims was given on the Cenotaph in Hiroshima as 138,890. People were still dying from the effects of radiation, nearly half a century after the bomb was dropped.

# 51

# The defeat of Japan

AUGUST 1945

On 7 August 1945, before the full extent of the destruction at Hiroshima had become known, American officers met on Luzon to prepare for the first stage of the invasion of Japan, set for November 1. On the following day, in London, agreement was signed between Britain, the United States, the Soviet Union and France, establishing an International Military Tribunal for the trial and sentencing of those who had committed 'crimes against humanity'. That same day, August 8, the Soviet Union declared war on Japan, hurling its armies into Japanese occupied Manchuria, pitting more than a million Soviet soldiers against the 700,000 men of the Japanese Kwantung Army.

The Americans had planned to drop a second atomic bomb on Japan on August 11, if, after the Hiroshima bomb, the Japanese did not surrender unconditionally. Because of predicted bad weather, however, that date was brought forward by two days. Thus it was, that at four minutes before two o'clock on the morning of August 9, as several hundred American bombers set off on a massive air raid over military targets on Honshu Island, a second specially adapted B-29 bomber, 'Bock's Car', took off from Tinian Island with a second atomic bomb. Bock was the name of the bomber's usual commander, Frederick Bock. But on this flight its pilot was Major Charles W. Sweeney. His target was to be the city of Kokura, but, if Kokura was obscured by cloud, an alternative target, Nagasaki, had been set. Reaching Kokura, 'Bock's Car' found the city covered in industrial haze. As Sweeney's orders were that he could drop the bomb only on a visual target, he flew on to Nagasaki. At two minutes after eleven o'clock, nine hours after the bomb had left Tinian, it was released, exploding 1,650 feet above the city.

In a few moments, more than 40,000 people had been killed. Five thousand were to die before the end of the year; thirty years later, the full death toll at Nagasaki was calculated at 48,857.

Among those who looked down on Nagasaki as the bomb exploded was the British pilot, Leonard Cheshire, present as an observer. He was later to recall the writhing cloud, 'obscene in its greedy clawing at the earth, swelling as if with its regurgitation of all the life that it had consumed'.

At the very moment when the Nagasaki bomb exploded, the Japanese Supreme War Direction Council was meeting in Tokyo. News of the bomb led to a renewed discussion as to whether Japan should accept unconditional surrender. The Council was evenly divided; three generals were for surrender, three for continuing the war. The Foreign Minister, Shigenori Togo, cast his vote for surrender, as did the Prime Minister, Admiral Suzuki. But the Minister of War, General Anami, was emphatic that there should be no surrender. 'It is far too early to say that the war is lost,' he told his colleagues, and he added: 'That we will inflict severe losses on the enemy when he invades Japan is certain, and it is by no means impossible that we may be able to reverse the situation in our favour, pulling victory out of defeat. Furthermore, our Army will not submit to demobilization. And since they know they are not permitted to surrender, since they know that a fighting man who surrenders is liable to extremely heavy punishment, there is really no alternative for us but to continue the war.'

The impasse was complete; but Togo and Suzuki were determined to end the war at once, and, in a secret meeting with Hirohito, prevailed upon him to summon a further meeting of the Supreme War Direction Council, and to preside over it himself.

The meeting took place shortly after midnight, in the Emperor's underground bomb shelter. First, Suzuki read out the Potsdam Declaration. Then, Togo urged its acceptance, provided that the position of the Emperor and the throne could be respected. Suzuki supported Togo, General Anami opposed him. For nearly two hours, the discussion continued. Then Hirohito spoke. 'Continuing the war', he said, 'can only result in the annihilation of the Japanese people and a prolongation of the suffering of all humanity. It seems obvious that the nation is no longer able to wage war, and its ability to defend its own shores is doubtful.'

The time had come, Hirohito told the council, 'to bear the unbearable'. He therefore gave his sanction to Togo's proposal that Japan should accept unconditional surrender. The message to that effect, a formal acceptance of the Potsdam Declaration, was sent out from Tokyo, early on August 10, to the Japanese ambassadors in Switzerland and Sweden, for transmission to the Allies. 'The Japanese Government', read the message, 'are ready to accept the terms enumerated in the Joint Declaration which was issued at Potsdam on 26 July, 1945, by the heads of government of the United States, Great Britain, and China, and later subscribed to by the Soviet Government, with the understanding that the said Declaration does not comprise any demand which prejudices the prerogatives of His Majesty as a sovereign ruler'.

On the morning of August 10, President Truman and his advisers discussed whether the proviso about the Emperor negated the acceptance of 'unconditional' surrender. A formula was devised, drafted by Secretary of State Byrnes, whereby Japan would have to agree that, from the moment of surrender, 'the authority of the Emperor and the Japanese Government to rule the State shall be subject to the Supreme Commander of the Allied Powers'. That morning, as the diplomatic exchanges began, Truman gave orders for the atomic bombing to stop. 'He said', noted Secretary of Commerce Henry Wallace in his diary, that 'the thought of wiping out another 100,000 people was too horrible. He didn't like the idea of killing, as he said, "all those kids".'

In Manchuria, the Red Army continued its advance against the Japanese; in heavy fighting at Pingyanchen on August 10, of 850 Japanese engaged, 650 were killed or wounded. On August 11, Soviet naval forces began the bombardment of the southern part of Sakhalin Island.

The diplomatic exchanges between Tokyo and Washington, still conducted through neutral powers, continued throughout August 11 and August 12. On the evening of August 12, east of Okinawa, a Japanese submarine sank the American landing ship *Oak Hill* and the destroyer *Thomas F. Nickel*. That day, in Manchuria, Soviet forces, after a fierce and prolonged struggle, overran the Japanese defenders of the fortress of Hutou, in the final phase of the battle pouring petrol into the exhaust vents of the fortress and setting the fuel alight, thereby asphyxiating all the fortress defenders who were sheltered underground.

During August 12, the Japanese used kamikaze infantrymen to try to halt the Soviet tanks. But at Hualin, on the following day, the tanks were able to fire at the infantry reinforcements while they were still on their train, killing nine hundred as they tried to leave their carriages.

During the morning of August 14, more than eight hundred American bombers struck at military installations throughout the island of Honshu. That afternoon, the official Japanese news agency sent out an overseas radio bulletin, stating that an Imperial Proclamation was soon to be made, 'accepting the Potsdam Proclamation'. Unknown to the radio listeners, the Emperor had already recorded the Proclamation. That evening, more than a thousand Japanese soldiers attacked the Imperial Palace, hoping to find the proclamation, and to prevent it being transmitted. They were successful only in assassinating the commander of the Imperial Guards Division, as troops loyal to the Emperor drove the attackers away. That night, General Anami, who still opposed surrender, but who had nevertheless refused to join the revolt, committed suicide. He was killing himself, he explained, in order to be spared listening to the Emperor's Proclamation, and to 'atone' for the Army's defeats.

By midnight on August 14, Soviet forces had advanced up to 250 miles into Manchuria, occupying Mukden; at the same time, Soviet troops were already ashore on Sakhalin and the Kurile Islands.

At midday on August 15, a Japanese radio announcer asked all listeners to stand 'respectfully' in front of their radio sets. There followed the music of the Japanese national anthem, and then, heard over the radio for the first time ever, the voice of the Emperor. He was reading the message which he had recorded on the previous day. The enemy, he said, 'has begun to employ a new and most cruel bomb, the power of which to do damage is indeed incalculable, taking the toll of many innocent lives'. This was the reason 'why we have ordered our Government to communicate to the Governments of the United States, Great Britain, China, and the Soviet Union, that our Empire accepts the provisions of their Joint Declaration ...'

In the United States there was, as the historian Samuel Eliot Morison has written, a 'sour note to the glad news' when, that same August 15, the United States Navy Department made public for the first time news of the torpedoing of the *Indianapolis*, sunk more than two weeks earlier with the loss of 883 men.

The Second World War was over, although not everybody engaged in it was to learn the news that day. Lieutenant-Commander Hashimoto, who had sunk the *Indianapolis* just over two weeks earlier, reached his naval base on the Inland Sea in happy mood, expecting to receive an ovation. Instead, he was handed a despatch containing the Imperial order to cease fire. Over Tokyo, American bombers, part of a fast carrier-based force that had not heard the news, struck once more at military targets. That day, in Nakom Paton prisoner-of-war camp, near Bangkok, the Australian surgeon, Colonel Dunlop, noted in his diary: 'There are now wild and persistent rumours that the war is over.'

Those rumours were not to be confirmed for a further forty-eight hours; until, just after six o'clock on the evening of August 17, Dunlop was among several hundred prisoners who were summoned to the Japanese Army compound in the camp, and told, through an interpreter: 'An armistice is now being held between all nations. All fronts are at peace and we have received instructions that we are to cease to regard you as prisoners-of-war. Therefore we cease to guard you. The maintenance of discipline is your own responsibility. Your repatriation will be soon. I advise you to keep your health, and to cultivate the papaya trees!'

Dunlop commented: 'So many had suffered and died; even now, some would never see home; but the momentous day had come.'

The 'momentous day' had come to hundreds of thousands of Allied prisoners-of-war, scattered and confined throughout the unconquered Empire. Kenneth Harrison, an Australian soldier who had been captured at Singapore and had worked on the 'Death Railway' in Thailand, was, at the time of the Japanese surrender, in a prisoner-of-war camp in Japan itself. Later he recalled how 'the tremendous exultation of our first night as free men was followed by a most unsatisfactory and unsettled week that came somewhat as an anti-climax. The Japanese made no official admission that they had surrendered, and they still controlled the camp "to keep out angry civilians". For this reason we were warned not to sing and dance, although this admonition came rather late and was completely ignored. It was a strange twilight period in which we were neither free men nor captives, and the balance of power between us and the Japanese was a delicate thing'. Only on August 22, Harrison noted, 'just as the pessimists were lapsing back into gloom and doubt, we had the first official admission that the mightiest conflict the world had known had indeed ended. A haggard, white-faced Japanese Camp Commandant addressed the assembled prisoners-of-war and said that hostilities had ended on 18 August. He asked us to stay quietly in the camp until we could be taken home. Alas, we were to shatter these fond hopes, for Camp Nakamura became unique in that its occupants were to flow over half of Japan with all the happy zeal of tourists'.

The Ardennes offensive, 16 December 1944 (*see page 618*). German soldiers file past a burning American half-track.

Three German infiltrators captured driving an American jeep and wearing American uniforms, executed by an American firing squad. The Germans were (from left to right), Corporal Wilhelm Schmidt, Officer Cadet Guenther Billings, and Sergeant Manfred Parnass.

Bodies of seventy-two American soldiers, massacred near Malmedy on 17 December 1944, and discovered by the Americans a few days later (*see page* 620).

An American pontoon bridge across the Rhine. The first Rhine crossing was at Remagen on 7 March 1945 (*see pages 646–8*). The photograph was taken near the village of Wallach.

Japanese-Americans, serving in the American army in Italy.

An accident of war; the American aircraft carrier *Enterprise*, after being hit on 20 March 1945 by shrapnel from another American ship, during a Japanese suicide bomb attack (*see page 650*). In three and a half years, aircraft from the *Enterprise* sank 71 Japanese ships and shot down 911 Japanese aircraft.

Hitler says farewell to young soldiers, on his 56th birthday, 20 April 1945, in the courtyard of the Chancellery of Berlin (*see pages 668–9*).

After capturing Munich on 29 April 1945, American soldiers march past the entrance to the Beer Hall in Munich, the 'cradle of Nazism', where, in 1925, Hitler had re-organized the Nazi movement. On the day of Munich's capture, Hitler was in his bunker in Berlin, writing his political testimony (*see page 677*).

oviet soldier raises the
mer and Sickle on the roof
e Reichstag, Berlin, 30 April
(see pages 680–1).

d Marshal Keitel (right, with
n), General Stumpf
tre), and Grand Admiral
Friedeburg (behind Keitel)
e Russian Headquarters in
lin, having just signed the
fied, unconditional terms of
ender, 8 May 1945 (see page
).

Hiroshima; the scene near the centre of the atomic explosion of 6 August 1945 (*see pages 71 4*).

After the Japanese surrender o 15 August 1945, former British prisoners-of-war continue wor on the memorial crosses to the fellow prisoners-of-war who died in captivity, or, like Lieutenant Godward (cross on left), had survived for only a fe days after liberation, dying on 27 August 1945.

On board the American battleship *Missouri*, in Tokyo Bay, on 2 September 1945 (*see page 722*), General Umezu signs the instrument of surrender for Japan. General MacArthur is standing at the microphone.

General MacArthur adds his signature to the instrument of surrender, 2 September 1945. Behind him (left) is General Wainwright, who had been a prisoner of the Japanese since the fall of Bataan, and (right) General Percival, who had been held captive since the fall of Singapore.

Marshal Goering on trial at Nuremberg, 13 March 1946. Sentenced to death, he committed suicide on 15 October 1946 (*see pages 730–1*).

General Tojo on trial at Tokyo, 24 December 1947. Sentenced to death, he was executed on 23 November 1948 (*see page 733*).

The skeleton of one of the crewmen of the American bomber 'Lady be Good', which crashlanded in the Libyan desert on 5 April 1943 (*see page 418*). The remains of the plane and its crew were found by chance on 9 November 1958 (*see page 739*).

Among the cities visited by Harrison and many of his fellow prisoners-of-war was Hiroshima. 'The reality', he wrote, 'was the girl with scarred features who passed with averted face. And the listless people who went by so dully; the scarred people; the burnt people; the apathetic people. And the people who even now showed not the slightest sign of hostility or resentment. Saddened and depressed beyond words at the magnitude of the tragedy, and feeling like ghouls, we decided to leave Hiroshima that same day. There was little to keep us there; nothing to see; no place to rest; nothing to eat; nothing to drink'. Harrison added: 'Fortunately for our peace of mind we knew nothing of such atomic age refinements as radiation sickness, and although we occasionally picked up a statue or kicked over a strangely fused piece of metal for a closer look, we were never tempted to take a souvenir. One does not rob a tomb.'

# 52

## Retribution and Remembrance

1945–1952

In the immediate aftermath of war, many efforts were made to cover up its traces. Near Singapore, where seven American prisoners-of-war had been executed eleven days before the surrender of Japan, Oka Harumitzu was told that as soon as one of the officers who had carried out those executions heard the news of the surrender, on 15 August 1945, he and the other executioners went at once to Niyusun airport, dug up the airmen's bodies, brought them back to camp, cremated them on a big fire on the barrack square and threw the ashes into the sea. 'The flames did not attract any undue attention', Harumitzu later recalled, 'as there were fires lit at all the different naval and military establishments at that time to burn all military documents and records before the Allied forces arrived'.

In Manchuria, and in particular around Mutanchiang, Japanese forces continued the struggle from August 16 until August 19 against the Soviet advance. When the Manchurian battles were over, 8,219 Soviet troops were dead. The Japanese had lost more than 40,000 men. On the night of August 19, after further Soviet advances at Hutou, several hundred Japanese blew themselves up with grenades, to avoid the disgrace of being captured.

On August 19, four days after the surrender of Japan, the Vietnamese Communist guerrilla leader, Ho Chi-minh, seized power in northern Indo-China; three days later, British aircraft parachuted a Free French military team into southern Indo-China. A new conflict had begun.

On August 23, the Russians occupied Port Arthur; their defeat at the hands of the Japanese Army forty years earlier had been avenged. The Russian conquest of southern Sakhalin was completed two days later. Russia, like the United States, was now a victor in the Pacific.

New conflicts were everywhere about to begin. On August 25, in China, a four-man American Special Services team, headed by Captain John Birch, was ordered to halt by a patrol of Chinese Communist troops; a tussle ensued, insults were exchanged, and Birch was shot. In the United States, there were those who called him, with pride, 'the first casualty in the Third World War between Communists and the ever shrinking Free World'. The right-wing Society founded in his name was to become a leading opponent of Communism in all its aspects, not only in Europe and Asia, but also in the United States.

Over northern Malaya, Burma and Siam, under Operation Birdcage, thirty-three million leaflets were dropped on ninety prisoner-of-war camps, and on 150 other localities, to explain that the war was over, and that help was on its way. There followed, in the last week of August, Operation Mastiff, the dropping by parachute of medicines, principally Atabrine – the prophylactic against malaria – of which more than a million tablets were dropped in one week. Allied aircraft had also begun to bring back prisoners-of-war from the Far East; four thousand were flown back in that last week of August alone. In Britain, 394,000 German prisoners remained in captivity; more than half of them were engaged in agricultural work. Churchill's farm in Kent was among those which were brought back into use with the help of German prisoners-of-war.

On August 25, ten days after the Japanese surrender, American troops entered a prisoner-of-war camp at Haichow, on Hainan Island. Of the original 273 Australian prisoners-of-war in the camp when it was set up, only 130 were still alive. Of the survivors, only eight were strong enough to be able to join the last burial parties.

No Allied soldier had yet set foot on the soil of mainland Japan. On August 28, the first American soldier did so; he was Colonel Charles Tench, one of General MacArthur's staff. Landing with a small task force of 150 men at Atsugi airfield, near Yokohama, he telegraphed to MacArthur's headquarters in Manila: 'No hostile action encountered.' On the following day, an American airborne division landed at the Yokosuka naval base. The occupation of Japan had begun. In Tokyo Bay, off Yokohama, Allied warships had begun to gather, among them, on August 29, the American battleship *Missouri* and the British battleship *Duke of York*.

On August 30, a British naval squadron reached Hong Kong. That day, British medical officers were parachuted into Changi prisoner-of-war camp, in Singapore; British troops were still on their way to Singapore by sea. As the doctors worked, the former Japanese guards remained on duty, in the service of their recent captives. Also on August 30, General MacArthur arrived in Japan; in an extraordinary scene, which alarmed many of the Americans who were with him, as MacArthur drove the fifteen miles from Atsugi airport to Yokohama, more than thirty thousand Japanese soldiers lined both sides of the road, with bayonets fixed.

On MacArthur's second day in Yokohama, he was shocked by the sudden and emaciated appearance of Lieutenant-General Jonathan M. Wainwright, the officer whom he had left in command of Bataan and Corregidor in 1942, when he, MacArthur, had been ordered by Roosevelt to move his headquarters to Australia. General Wainwright had been found by the Russians in a prisoner-of-war camp in Manchuria, had travelled by train to Mukden, then by bomber to Chungking and on to Manila, then back by air across the Pacific to Yokohama. His four years in captivity had left him haggard and emaciated, with snow white hair and parchment-like skin. Deeply shocked, MacArthur could not eat that night, or sleep.

On August 31, the remote Japanese garrison on Marcus Island surrendered to the Americans. On September 1, Soviet troops completed their occupation of the Kurile Islands, which stretched from the northernmost island of Japan to the tip of the Soviet Far Eastern peninsula of Kamchatka. On September 2, the Japanese garrisons on Truk Island in the Carolines, on Pagan and Rota in the Marianas, and on the Palau Islands, surrendered to the Americans. That same day, in Tokyo Bay, on board the American battleship *Missouri,* the new Japanese Foreign Minister, Mamoru Shigemitsu, and the Chief of Staff of the Japanese Army, General Yoshijiro Umezu, signed the instrument of surrender in the presence of General MacArthur, who then signed it in the name of the Allies. At MacArthur's wish, the signing was watched both by General Wainwright, and by General Percival, the British General who had surrendered to the Japanese at Singapore. 'We are gathered here,' MacArthur began, 'representatives of the major warring powers, to conclude a solemn agreement whereby peace may be restored. The issues, involving divergent ideas and ideologies, have been determined on the battlefields of the world, and hence are not for our discussion or debate. ....'

Among the 250 Allied warships in Tokyo Bay that September 2 was the British destroyer *Whelp*; its First Lieutenant, Prince Philip of Greece, was about to ferry British prisoners-of-war from the small boats which had brought them from the shore to the Escort Carriers which were to take them home. Three days later, Indian troops reached Changi prisoner-of-war camp in Singapore, taking the Japanese guards into custody.

Another island surrender took place in the Pacific on September 4, when 2,200 Japanese soldiers on Wake Island laid down their arms. During the nearly two years during which the Japanese garrison on Wake had been left unchallenged, 1,300 soldiers had died from starvation, and a further 600 from occasional American air attacks. Three days after the surrender of Wake Island, the Japanese forces on the Ryukyu Islands surrendered.

The evacuation of prisoners-of-war was now in full swing. On September 7, Allied warships entered port Kiirun, on Formosa, to take off 1,200 prisoners. Eighty-nine of those liberated were survivors of the Bataan 'Death March' of 1942. On the southern coast of Burma, near Moulmein, Japanese soldiers continued to fight against British Special Operation forces, part of Operation Character, until September 8; several hundred Japanese were killed in this conflict in the first month of peace.

As Operation Character came to an end in Burma, Operation Masterdom began in Indo-China, the attempt by the French, with British and Indian troops, starting on September 8, to forestall the local Communist guerrillas, and to restore the French colonial administration. In this first direct anti-Communist struggle of the post-war world, the French commander, Colonel Cedile, made use of 1,400 Japanese troops, former prisoners-of-war, who had just been released. The British commander, Major General D. D. Gracey, also enlisted large numbers of Japanese troops, who until three weeks earlier had been the occupying power. Two weeks after Operation Masterdom had been launched, French troops overthrew the interim Vietnamese Government in Saigon; Vietnamese retaliation was swift, with more than a hundred Westerners, including the commander of the wartime clandestine American forces, being killed. By the time the British troops had left Indo-China, in May 1946, a civil war was raging.

On September 12, in Singapore, Lord Louis Mountbatten was the senior Allied officer present at the signing of the Japanese surrender document by the Japanese General, Seishiro Itagaki. 'I have come today', Mountbatten declared, 'to receive the formal surrender of all Japanese forces within South East Asia Command. I wish to make this plain; the surrender today is no negotiated surrender. The Japanese are submitting to superior forces, now massed here.'

As Mountbatten was speaking, General Slim, whose forces had carried out the long, arduous, costly reconquest of Burma, 'looked', as he later recalled, 'at the dull impassive masks that were the faces of the Japanese generals and admirals seated opposite. Their plight moved me not at all. For them, I had none of the sympathy of soldier for soldier, that I had felt for Germans, Turks, Italians, or Frenchmen that by the fortune of war I had seen surrender. I knew too well what these men and those under their orders had done to their prisoners. They sat there apart from the rest of humanity'.

General Slim's account continued: 'If I had no feeling for them, they, it seemed, had no feeling of any sort, until Itagaki, who had replaced Field Marshal Tarauchi, laid low by a stroke, leant forward to affix his seal to the surrender document. As he pressed heavily on the paper, a spasm of rage and despair twisted his face. Then it was gone and his mask was as expressionless as the rest. Outside, the same Union Jack that had been hauled down in surrender in 1942 flew again at the masthead. The war was over'.

On September 18, General MacArthur moved his command headquarters to Tokyo, where, in the former Japanese Army headquarters for the Tokyo region, he established his Supreme Command Allied Powers. Nine days later, he was visited there by the Emperor Hirohito. 'You are very, very welcome, Sir!' was MacArthur's greeting. 'It was the first time I had ever heard him say "Sir" to anyone,' MacArthur's aide–interpreter, Faubion Bowers, later recalled.

Hirohito, no longer divine, was to remain Emperor of Japan. His country, guided towards democracy and modernity, gradually outstripped in productivity and wealth each of its wartime adversaries. In western Germany, new leaders were chosen to restore democracy and the economic and international fortunes of the now divided State. Eastern Germany, like Poland, Czechoslovakia, Hungary, Roumania, Bulgaria and Albania, became an integral part of the Soviet bloc; only Yugoslavia broke away, in 1948, to pursue its own form of Communism.

In the aftermath of so destructive a war, there were many claims for reparations and restitution. On September 20, the senior member of the Jewish Agency for Palestine, Dr Chaim Weizmann, whose son had died on active service in 1943 fighting for Britain, sent a letter to the victorious powers, asking for 'restitution, indemnification and compensation' from Germany, for the crimes committed against the Jews. Nine days after Dr Weizmann's request, the *New York Times* reported the disembarkation of sixteen 'Reich technicians' from a troop ship in Boston harbour. One of the sixteen was the German rocket expert, Dr Wernher von Braun.

The British, as well as the Americans, had begun to examine and to build upon the German technical expertise of war. On October 2, in Operation Backfire, a German v2 rocket was launched under British direction, at Altenwalde, in the British zone of Germany. But it was the United States, not Britain, which continued to offer the rocket scientists the most interesting prospects of research and achievement. In all, 457 German scientists went to the United States in the two and a half years following the end of the war in Europe.

But it was punishment, not research, which dominated the autumn and winter months of 1945. On October 6, at Pentonville Prison in London, five Germans, found guilty of the murder of a fellow prisoner after an attempted prisoner-of-war breakout in 1944, were hanged. They had believed the man they killed to have been an informer. On October 6, in a prison cell at Nuremberg, Dr Leonardo Conti, one of the German doctors who had conducted medical experiments on concentration camp inmates, committed suicide. The former French Foreign Minister, Pierre Laval, found guilty of treason by a court in Paris, also tried to commit suicide that October; he failed, and was shot by a French firing squad on October 15.

Three days after Laval's execution, the International Military Tribunal met in Berlin, where American, British, French and Russian representatives agreed to proceed with four indictments against the leading Nazis now in captivity. The four indictments were: '1. A common plan or conspiracy to seize power and establish a totalitarian regime to prepare and wage a war of aggression. 2. Waging a war of aggression. 3. Violation of the laws of war. 4. Crimes against humanity, persecution and extermination.'

On October 20, twenty-two Nazis were indicted on these charges. As there was no building in Berlin large enough and sufficiently undamaged to serve as a courthouse, it had been decided to hold the principal War Crimes Trials in Nuremberg, and other trials at particular concentration camp sites. Meanwhile, national trials, like that of Laval in France, continued; on October 24, Vidkun Quisling, found guilty of 'criminal collaboration' with Germany, was shot by a Norwegian firing squad in Oslo. That same day, in his prison cell at Nuremberg, Robert Ley, one of Hitler's earliest supporters, committed suicide.

In India, the British were determined to bring to trial the leading members of the Indian National Army. Subhas Chandra Bose could not be charged; he had been killed in an air crash over Formosa in the closing days of the war. For Indian nationalists, the imminent trial of these men, despite their having joined the Japanese war effort, created considerable unease. 'India adores these men,' wrote Gandhi, while Nehru, who in 1942 had strongly opposed the Indian National Army's alliance with Japan, now described what its followers had done as 'a brave adventure', sprung from 'a passionate desire to serve the cause of India's freedom'.

The first of the Indian National Army trials began on November 5, at the Red Fort in Delhi. Three of those charged, Shah Nahwaz, P. H. Sahgal and G. S. Dhillon, were found guilty of 'waging war' against the King, and were sentenced to transportation. Their sentences were subsequently remitted, and they were released. In protest against the original sentences, there were several acts of violence in Calcutta, Bombay and Delhi, when Hindus and Muslims joined forces to set lorries and tramcars on fire. In the riot in Calcutta, forty-five Indians were killed, and martial law imposed on the city. Within three months, 11,000 Indian National Army soldiers had been released from internment. They returned to their homes as heroes. 'The hypnotism of the INA has cast its spell upon us' was Gandhi's comment.

Throughout October 1945, and into November, Japanese commanders on isolated islands and in coastal enclaves had been surrendering. On October 6, the Japanese garrison at Jesselton, in Borneo surrendered; on October 9, the garrison on the Andaman and Nicobar Islands; on October 19, the Japanese naval forces at Mergui, in Burma; on October 21, the forces at Padang, on Sumatra; on October 25, the forces at Thaton, in Burma. Some small forces remained in isolated parts of the jungles; it was not until February and March of 1946 that the last of these were able to find an Allied officer to whom they could offer their swords, and their capitulation.

On October 30, in an American shipyard, at Portland, Maine, the *Albert H. Boe* was ready for sea. She was the last of 2,742 Liberty ships, built on the production line system. More than two hundred Liberty ships had been sunk by enemy action. Now they were among the ships that helped to bring home Allied prisoners-of-war from the Far East; within nine months, 96,575 military prisoners and civilian internees had been returned.

November 1 marked the day on which the Americans had intended to launch Operation Olympic, against the Japanese home island of Kyushu. That day marked the seventy-eighth day since Japan's surrender. Japanese civilians were still dying every day in Japan, as a result of the atomic bombs dropped on Hiroshima and Nagasaki. Former Allied prisoners-of-war were also dying, though far fewer, as a result of the treatment which they had received while in Japanese captivity, the victims of deliberate, prolonged and sadistic cruelty. Details of such cruelty were beginning to be documented. On November 5, sixteen Japanese officers and men, suspected of the execution of American prisoners-of-war on Wake Island, were taken to Kwajalein for trial. During the voyage, two of them committed suicide. The third, Lieutenant Commander Torashi Ito, wrote while in prison a statement describing the executions in full. He then also took his own life.

Atrocities in Europe were also being documented in the course of the many war crimes trials. In Germany, on November 15, the trial began of the Commandant, forty guards, and one civilian doctor, from Dachau camp. The trial was held at Dachau. During the course of the trial, the doctor, Klaus Karl

Schilling, a former professor of parasitology at the University of Berlin and, before the war, a member of the Malaria Commission of the League of Nations, pleaded to be allowed to write up the result of his medical experiments, in the interests of medical science. Those experiments had been carried out on human beings. Dr Schilling was sentenced to death.

From the liberated concentration camps, and from the newly established Displaced Persons camps throughout central Europe, Jews were on the move, some returning to towns which had been destroyed, or in which they were no longer welcome, others seeking new havens in Western Europe and the United States. But most desired to go to Palestine. On November 13, however, the British Foreign Secretary, Ernest Bevin, announced that the pre-war British immigration restrictions would continue; 13,000 Jews would be allowed into Palestine that year, and no more. But at least 100,000 Jewish survivors, determined not to remain in what they considered the cemetery of Europe, were on the march, travelling in groups across the frontiers, rivers and mountain passes of Europe. This exodus, known as Operation Flight, was organized by Jews who had survived inside German-occupied Europe, and by Jews from Palestine who were serving in the British Army. 'We dressed our people in uniforms,' one of them, Abba Geffen, later recalled, 'with the insignia "CAJR" on the left sleeve. Neither the Austrians nor the Americans knew much about what it was. We gave them certificates, bearing their pictures in uniform, with an official seal. And we sent off the transports. At the borders they were sometimes sent back because some stamp or other was missing. We didn't argue. We would ask the border guards to explain things to us precisely, and perhaps even give us a genuine certificate with the required stamp as an example. We would go back, summon our two stamp-makers, and make sure that the next time, we'd have the stamps we needed – and it worked!'

'CAJR' meant, simply, 'Committee for Assistance to Jewish Refugees'.

As Jews tried to leave Europe, those of their persecutors who failed to slip through the net continued to face trial. At Lüneberg, a British military court was trying the thirty-eight-year-old Commandant of Belsen, Josef Kramer, who had earlier served at Auschwitz, Mauthausen and Dachau. During his trial, Kramer had described how, at Auschwitz, he had participated in the gassing of a group of eighty women in August 1943. Asked how he had felt about it at the time, he told the Court: 'I had no feelings in carrying out these things because I had received an order. That, incidentally, is the way I was trained.'

Kramer was sentenced to death, and hanged. Also on trial, and later sentenced to death, were thirteen of the twenty-two leading Nazis whose trial opened at Nuremberg on November 20, and was to continue for almost a year, bringing before the court, and the world, documentary evidence of mass murder and atrocities throughout German-occupied Europe. More than 100,000 captured documents had been examined before the trial began; of these, 4,000 had been translated from German into English, Russian and French, and were to be used in evidence.

*          *          *

Beginning on November 25, the British naval authorities carried out Operation Deadlight, the assembling and sinking of German submarines. Eighty-six U-boats were assembled in western Scotland, in Loch Ryan, and twenty-four off Lisahally, in Northern Ireland; they were then sunk by air attack. Throughout Britain, and Europe, bomb disposal experts were risking their lives to defuse the thousands of unexploded bombs and shells of the war years; on November 27, British experts removed the last bomb from the underground bomb storage chambers at Fauld, which had blown up a year earlier.

No day passed during the winter of 1945 without the newspapers reporting on a war crimes trial; on December 10, at Aurich in Germany, SS General Kurt Meyer was charged by a Canadian court martial with the massacre of at least forty-one Canadian prisoners-of-war in June 1944. That same day, in an American prison camp at Bad Tölz, Theodor Dannecker, one of the Nazi officials responsible for the deportation of Jews from both France and Greece, committed suicide. In London, a young Englishman, John Amery, was being brought to trial. His father Leo had been a member of Churchill's wartime administration. His brother Julian had parachuted behind German lines in Albania, to play an active part in the rallying of guerrilla forces and the disruption of the German lines of communication. John Amery was charged with trying to persuade British prisoners-of-war in Germany to join the British Free Corps. After he had pleaded guilty, he was hanged on December 19.

With retribution came reconstruction; on December 27, an International Bank for Reconstruction and Development was set up, the aim of which was to provide both government and private financing for 'the restoration of economies destroyed or disrupted by war, the reconversion of productive facilities to peacetime needs and the encouragement of the development of productive facilities and resources in less developed countries'.

The employment of German scientists by both East and West was another aspect of reconstruction; eight days after the establishment of the International Bank, a group of eight German submarine experts, headed by Helmuth Walter, reached the British naval research station at Barrow-in-Furness; they were preceded by one of Germany's most recent hydrogen-peroxide powered sub-marines, which had been scuttled on Germany's surrender, but then raised.

On 1 January 1946, on Corregidor, a soldier in the American Graves Registration Company was surprised to see a file of about twenty Japanese soldiers coming towards him, waving white pieces of cloth in a gesture of surrender; since the end of the war four and a half months earlier, they had been living in one of the deep underground tunnels on the island, unaware that the war had ended. It was while coming out one night, to look for water, that one of the soldiers had found a newspaper from which it was clear that Japan had surrendered.

The pace of retribution did not slacken with the coming of the first New Year of full peace for six years. On 3 January 1946, in London, the broadcaster William Joyce, Lord Haw-Haw, was hanged. So, too, was a former member of the British Union of Fascists, Private Church, who had deserted to the Italians in North Africa, and offered his services to Italian Intelligence. His claim to be a Swiss citizen having been dismissed, he was hanged on January 5. Across the English Channel, in Lille, Jacques Desoubrie, who had betrayed his fellow Frenchmen to the Gestapo in the summer of 1943, was also hanged that winter. On January 9, in Paris, two French policemen came to question Harold Cole, the man who had betrayed the wartime 'Pat' escape and evasion line. Cole opened fire, wounding one of the policemen; the other shot him dead.

Honours, too, came in the aftermath of war to those whose suffering and courage only became known in detail as eye-witnesses came forward with testimony. On 16 January 1946, the Croix de Guerre with Gold Star was awarded posthumously to the British Agent, Noor Inayat Khan who, although betrayed to the Gestapo shortly after her arrival in France in 1943, had refused to co-operate with her captors in any way, and had been shot a year later. Three years after this French award, Britain awarded Noor the George Cross.

In Tokyo, on January 19, General MacArthur established the International Military Tribunal for the Far East; eleven nations were to participate in its prosecutions. That day, in Dachau, five hundred American and Polish troops used tear gas to help them carry out Operation Keelhaul, the forcible repatriation of 339 Soviet citizens who, having served in the German forces during the war, were being held in Dachau as prisoners-of-war. The Russians fought against being sent back to the Soviet Union, but were overpowered.

In the Philippines, in the town of Los Banos, General Tomoyuki Yamashita was hanged on February 23, having been found guilty by an American Army tribunal of brutality against Americans and Filipinos. A week later, in the same courtyard, General Masaharu Homma was executed by firing squad. He had been found guilty of responsibility for the Bataan 'Death March'.

American anxieties had turned from the four year long focus on Germany and Japan to a new focus on the Soviet Union. On February 28, the day before the Americans would – but for the atom bomb – have launched Operation Coronet against the principal Japanese island of Honshu, James F. Byrnes, United States Secretary of State, in a speech in New York, declared: 'If we are to be a great power, we must act as a great power, not only to ensure our own safety but to preserve the peace of the world.' Six days later, at Westminster College, Fulton, Missouri, Winston Churchill pointed out the danger of Soviet pressures against Turkey and Iran, and warned: 'From Stettin in the Baltic to Trieste in the Adriatic, an iron curtain has descended across the Continent. Behind that line lie all the capitals of the ancient states of Central and Eastern Europe. Warsaw, Berlin, Prague, Vienna, Budapest, Belgrade, Bucharest and Sofia, all these famous cities and the populations around them lie in what I must call the Soviet sphere, and all are subject in one form or another, not only to Soviet influence but to a very high and, in many cases, increasing measure of control from Moscow. Athens alone – Greece with its immortal glories – is free to decide its future at an election under British, American and French observation'.

Churchill went on to advocate the need for 'a new unity in Europe', from which no nation should be 'permanently outcast'; a 'grand pacification of Europe', he called it, 'within the structure of the United Nations and in accordance with its Charter'. The need for it was, he believed, an urgent one. Even 'in front of the iron curtain', in Italy and in France, in places far from the Russian frontiers, and 'throughout the world', including the Far East, Communist parties or Communist fifth columns 'constitute a growing challenge and peril to Christian civilization'. As for the Soviet aim, 'I do not believe', he said, 'that Soviet Russia desires war. What they desire is the fruits of war and the indefinite expansion of their power and doctrines. But what we have to consider here today, while time remains, is the permanent prevention of war and the establishment of conditions of freedom and democracy as rapidly as possible in all countries'.

New alliances, and new groups of confronting States, were already emerging dominated by the 'Eastern' and 'Western' blocs, the West setting up a defence system under a North Atlantic Treaty Organization in 1949, of which the United States was by far the strongest member, the East under the Warsaw Pact, signed six years later, in which the Soviet Union was predominant.

Meanwhile, the retribution which had become an integral part of victory and defeat continued; on April 27, in Singapore, Major-General Shempei Fukuei, found guilty of the murder of Allied prisoners-of-war, was taken to the exact location of one of the executions which he had ordered, and shot. His last word, like that of so many hundreds of thousands of Japanese soldiers as they had charged the Allied lines, was 'Banzai!' – 'Ten Thousand Years!', a reference to the longevity of the divine Emperor. Now the Emperor was no longer divine. Like Hitler's Thousand-Year Reich, his New Order in Asia had been a short-lived but devastating era.

The victor nations, and the former captive peoples, found some small solace in the continuing trials and sentences of the immediate post-war years, although there was no way in which those trials and executions could ever bring back those who had been murdered against all the accepted rules and codes of war. On 7 May 1946, Anton Mussert, founder of the Dutch National Socialist Movement, and a staunch supporter of Nazi rule in Holland, was hanged in The Hague. Two weeks later, on May 22, Karl Hermann Frank, Hitler's former Chief of Police in Bohemia and Moravia, found guilty of several hundred murder charges, was hanged in Prague, his execution witnessed by five thousand spectators. In the Polish city of Poznan, on June 20, Artur Greiser, the former Gauleiter of the German province of the Warthegau, was sentenced to death, paraded around Poznan in a cage, and then hanged in the square in front of his former palace.

Not only trials, but celebrations, marked the transformation from war to peace; on June 8, in London, a victory parade was held. But Soviet, Polish and Yugoslav representatives had refused to come.

The weapon with which Japan had been defeated was not to be buried together with the debris which it had created; on 1 July 1946, the United States exploded its first post-war atomic bomb at Bikini Atoll, in the Marshall Islands. Among the warships on whom the impact of the new bomb was being tested was the

German warship, *Prinz Eugen*. She survived the blast, unlike five other ships in the test. Five months later, she was scuttled.

On 4 July 1946, on American Independence Day, the Republic of the Philippines was inaugurated as an independent State after more than fifty years of American rule. She thus became the first of the Far Eastern victims of Japanese attack in 1941 to obtain their freedom from those who had ruled them before the war, and whose forces had subsequently defeated Japan. British-ruled Burma, Malaya and Singapore, Dutch-ruled Indonesia and Borneo, Australian New Guinea and French Indo-China, were each to become independent in the following decades.

As well as independence – often achieved only after bitter and violent civil war – the events of the immediate post-war years produced many of what Churchill had called, after the First World War, the 'ugly creatures of the aftermath'. July 4 was a day of tragedy for forty-two Jews in the Polish town of Kielce, all of them survivors of Nazi tyranny, and now killed by an anti-Semitic mob. One of those murdered had no identification on him. The only clue to his past was the tattoo number on his arm, B 2969. The numbers B 2903 to B 3449 had been given to those Jews who reached Auschwitz on 2 August 1944 from the Polish town of Radom, fifty miles from Kielce. At least five hundred other Jews on that train, mostly women, children and old people, had been gassed that day. Now the unknown survivor had himself become a victim, fourteen months after the end of the war in Europe, and nearly two years since the Germans had been driven from Kielce.

On 1 August 1946, in Washington, in an attempt to make constructive use of the vast mass of American war surplus, an amendment was passed to the Surplus Property Act of 1944, to enable American wartime supplies to be sold, and their proceeds to be used for a world-wide scholarship programme. This diversion to educational purposes of resources created for war purposes was the brainchild of Senator J. William Fulbright, whose name the scholarships were to bear; educational exchange agreements were subsequently signed with more than sixty States, of which China, the Philippines and Greece were the first.

Throughout 1946, the trial and execution of war criminals had continued throughout Germany's former conquered territories. On August 14, Robert Wagner, the wartime Chief of the German Civil Administration in Alsace, who in 1940 had carried out the deportation of German Jews to camps in the Pyrenees, was sentenced to death by a French military court in Strasbourg, and hanged.

That September, the Allies began the repatriation of German prisoners-of-war; 394,000 were repatriated from Britain alone. In Cyprus, where more than five thousand Germans were held, their last task was to build a light railway from Nicosia to the Caraolos camp, where thousands of Jewish survivors were being detained behind barbed wire, having been caught by the British authorities while trying to enter Palestine illegally, by boat.

As the German prisoners-of-war began to go home, the International Military

Tribunal at Nuremberg sentenced twelve German wartime leaders to death. On October 8, after a separate trial, four of those who had murdered the Jewish children at Bullenhuser Damm were hanged in Hameln Prison by the British executioner, Albert Pierrepoint. At Nuremberg, Herman Goering escaped the hangman by committing suicide on October 15. The rest of those sentenced to death were hanged on the following day, among them Ernst Kaltenbrunner, who in 1943 and 1944 had been in charge of the concentration camp system; Field Marshal Keitel, who in 1941 and 1942 had authorized the execution of Soviet commissars and the mass killing of women and children in German-occupied Russia; Hans Frank, the 'slayer of Poles' and murderer of Jews; Julius Streicher, whose virulently anti-Semitic magazine, *Der Stürmer,* had done so much to stir up race hatred; General Jodl, Chief of the Operations Staff of the High Command of the German Armed Forces from 1939 to 1945; and Joachim von Ribbentrop, the German Foreign Minister from 1938 to 1945. Their hangman was the American Master Sergeant, John C. Wood. On the following morning, the bodies of those who had been hanged were taken to Dachau, where the crematorium ovens were ignited and the bodies cremated; that night their ashes were dropped into a river on the outskirts of Munich.

On October 26, Otto Thierack, Reich Minister of Justice from 1942 to 1945, hanged himself in Neumunster internment camp, to avoid being brought to trial. Six weeks later, on December 9, the trial began in Nuremberg of twenty-three ss physicians and scientists who were accused of carrying out medical experiments on the inmates of concentration camps, including Jews, Gypsies and Russian prisoners-of-war. Seven of the twenty-three were sentenced to death, and hanged, among them Victor Brack, Chief Administrative Officer at Hitler's Chancellery, and holding the rank of colonel in the ss; Dr Karl Brandt, Hitler's personal physician and also Minister for Health and Sanitation and a major-general in the ss; and Dr Karl Gebhardt, personal physician to Himmler, Chief Surgeon to the ss, and President of the German Red Cross.

'This is nothing but political revenge,' Dr Brandt declared on the scaffold. 'I served my Fatherland as others before me. ...' As he was speaking these words, the black hood was placed over his head, and he was hanged.

The Nuremberg Trials were to become the object of much controversy. In particular, the charge of 'waging a war of aggression' was to be criticized as one which could have been applied equally to the Soviet Union for its attack on Finland. There was anger, too, in some Western circles, that the Katyn Forest massacre of Polish prisoners-of-war was, at Soviet insistence, excluded from the investigations. There were also those who argued that Britain and France, by their acquiescence, albeit reluctant, in Hitler's annexations of Austria and the Sudetenland in 1938, and Bohemia and Moravia in 1939, had been parties to the initial phases of aggression. But, despite these controversies, the evidence of specific and deliberate acts of war and terror was overwhelming. Men like Dr Brandt, who had been involved at the highest level in Germany's euthanasia programme, could speak of 'political revenge', but for the millions who had suffered and survived, and for the liberators who had been given a glimpse of the results of the Nazi racial policies, his protestations were hypocritical and absurd.

On 11 December 1946, as a measure designed to try to heal the massive deprivations caused throughout the world between 1939 and 1945, the United Nations established a Children's Emergency Fund, UNICEF, to aid both mothers and children in need as a result of war. The trials and executions also continued; among those executed in 1947 were Karel Curda, the Czech whose treachery had led to the death of his fellow Czechs who had assassinated Heydrich in 1942; Max Knipping, head of the French Milice in northern France, and the man responsible for the murder of the former French Minister of the Colonies, Georges Mandel; and General Helmuth von Pannwitz, hanged in Moscow on 16 January 1947, for his part in the mass murder of tens of thousands of Russian civilians behind the lines on the Eastern Front.

On April 7, Rudolf Hoess, the former Commandant at Auschwitz, was hanged next to the house inside the camp where he had lived with his wife and five children. On April 12, in Belgium, sixteen Belgian citizens who had participated in sadistic tortures at Breendonk camp, near Antwerp, were executed; because of the nature of their crimes, they were shot in the back. In Prague, on May 4, Paul Rafaelson, a former labour camp prisoner, and a Jew, was sentenced to death and hanged for cruelties perpetrated on his fellow prisoners. 'He is the first Jewish criminal', noted a Press Agency report from Prague, 'to be hanged for atrocities.'

Also on May 4, the first of 82,000 German prisoners-of-war were sent back to Germany from camps in Egypt. 'Those who are still enthusiastic Nazis and Fascists,' the *Palestine Post* reported on May 4, 'numbering 5,000, will be the last to be removed.'

Not all those sentenced to death for war crimes were in fact executed. Field Marshal Kesselring, sentenced to death by a British court-martial on May 6, for having allowed the shooting of 335 Italian civilians as a reprisal against an Italian partisan action, later had his penalty commuted to life imprisonment, and, five years after his initial sentence, was pardoned and freed. Less fortunate was General Friedrich-Wilhelm Müller, recipient of the Knight's Cross with Oak Leaves and Swords, found guilty by a Greek court of brutality towards civilians in Greece, and executed in Athens on May 20. That same day also saw the execution in Athens of Bruno Brauer, the former Governor of Crete, who had waged a ruthless war against the Cretan partisans.

In seeking to rebuild both the ruins and the security of Europe, defence and material help went hand in hand. On 4 March 1947, the French and British Governments signed a treaty, at Dunkirk, binding the two signatories to come to each other's aid if attacked by Germany. At the same time, the former Chief of the American Defence Staff, now Secretary of State, General George C. Marshall, launched a comprehensive plan to bring American economic aid to Europe. On June 5, this aid was offered to all the former warring nations; not only did the Soviet Union refuse to accept American help, but it prevailed upon all the Communist bloc countries, including Czechoslovakia which had hitherto enjoyed a degree of independence, to do likewise. The Czechoslovak Cabinet had actually voted unanimously, on July 7, to accept Marshall Aid, but its leaders, summoned at once to Moscow, then turned it down. This example of the nature of Soviet leadership in the Eastern bloc was not lost on Western observers. The division of the victors into opposing blocs was complete.

In the Far East, there were likewise new, and increasingly bloody alignments. On July 29 the self-styled 'Indonesian Republican Air Force' carried out its first combat operations against the Dutch, bombing two towns in Java, Semarang on the north coast and Salatiga in the eastern sector. During the Semarang raid, seven Indonesians were killed.

The Dutch, who, except for a brief period during the Napoleonic wars, had ruled the Netherlands East Indies since the early seventeenth century, first fought against the Indonesian nationalist movement and then negotiated with it. Three years after these first bombing raids, a United States of Indonesia were inaugurated, and one more of the former European Colonial territories conquered by Japan in 1942 achieved its independence. Burma was to do so, from the British, on 4 January 1948, and Malaya on 31 May 1957.

On 25 October 1947, the coffins of the first 6,300 American war dead to leave Europe from their graves in France reached New York aboard ship. Five days later, a second ship, with several thousand more coffins, left Antwerp for the United States. But the bodies of many of the dead were never found; of the 42,000 British airmen reported missing over Europe between 1939 and 1945, nearly 20,000 were still undiscovered four years after the end of the war, despite thorough searches by the specially established Missing Research and Enquiry Service, in which 118 searchers were employed.

In Europe, 1948 saw more trials, and more escapes from justice. On February 5, in his prison cell in Nuremberg, the Commander of the German forces in Holland at the time of the surrender, General Blaskowitz – who at the end of 1939 had protested to Hitler about Nazi atrocities in Poland – committed suicide shortly before he was to be brought to trial. On the following day, in the Cherche–Midi Prison in Paris, the first Military Governor of Paris, Otto von Stuelpnagel, committed suicide rather than face trial for his actions while he was effective ruler of the French capital.

On 12 November 1948, in the former War Ministry building in Tokyo, before the International Military Tribunal for the Far East, seven Japanese wartime leaders, including General Tojo, were sentenced to death, and sixteen others to life imprisonment. The sentences, reviewed by General MacArthur two weeks later, were upheld in their entirety, and the death sentences carried out, by hanging, on 23 November 1948.

On 28 January 1949, after a British Military trial in Hamburg, Fritz Knoechlein, who had been responsible for the shooting down in cold blood of British prisoners-of-war at Paradis in 1940, was hanged in the Hamburg garrison prison. His Defence Counsel's appeal – 'Spare the life of the accused. He has a wife and four children who are dependent upon him for support. Consider the fact that he is a soldier, and the Court is composed of members of the British Army' – had been in vain.

Also executed that day was Joseph Kieffer, Knoechlein's deputy at Gestapo headquarters in Paris in 1943 and 1944, found guilty of the execution of British paratroopers in Normandy in 1944. It was Kieffer who had interrogated Noor Inayat Khan, the British agent captured in France in 1943; following her interrogation, she had been sent to Dachau and shot.

A trial of a different sort took place early in 1950, that of Klaus Fuchs, the German refugee scientist and Soviet spy who, during the war, had worked on the Anglo-American atomic bomb programme. On 1 March 1950 he was sentenced to fourteen years' imprisonment; after serving his sentence, he went to live in East Germany, becoming a member of the Communist Party establishment.

In the search for reparations, the German Government refused to recognize the Gypsies as meriting compensation. 'It should be borne in mind', the Interior Ministry of the West German province of Württemberg wrote on 9 May 1950, 'that Gypsies have been persecuted under the Nazis not for any racial reason but because of an asocial and criminal record.'

In the forty and more years following the end of the Second World War, the discovery of documents, and the writing of testimonies, was continuous. On 1 December 1950, Polish building workers discovered part of an eye-witness report of the mass murder at Treblinka; the report had been hidden there by the Polish Jewish historian, Dr Emanuel Ringelblum, in 1943.

Even as more and more perpetrators of crimes were brought to trial, more and more were able to evade prosecution. On 19 December 1950 the principal German organizer of the massacre of Jews in Kovno, Helmut Rauca, left the German port of Bremerhaven for St John, New Brunswick, becoming a Canadian citizen. Other killers who fled as he did, to most of the countries of the Western world, were never brought to trial; Rauca himself was extradited to Germany thirty-three years later. He died in a prison hospital in Frankfurt-on-Main while awaiting trial.

On 15 January 1951, Ilse Koch was sentenced to prison in West Germany for the second time. In 1947 she had received a four-year sentence for her activities at Buchenwald, as the sadistic wife of the camp's Commandant, Karl Koch, whom the SS had themselves executed for corruption in 1944. In her second trial, Ilse Koch was sentenced to life imprisonment; sixteen years later, she committed suicide in prison.

Three weeks after Ilse Koch's second sentence, the American High Commissioner in Germany, John J. McCloy, issued a general amnesty for all convicted industrialists who had used slave labour, and for all generals. Among those released as a result of the amnesty was Alfred Krupp von Bohlen, whose Krupp factories had employed, and terribly ill-treated, slave labour, on a vast scale. Originally sentenced at Nuremberg in July 1948 to twelve years' imprisonment, he became a free man two and a half years later.

On 7 March 1951, in Brussels, General Alexander von Falkenhausen, the former German Military Governor of Brussels, was found guilty of ordering the execution of several hundred Belgian hostages and the deportation of 25,000 Belgian Jews to Auschwitz. He was sentenced to twelve years' imprisonment, then released after three weeks as an act of clemency, and in recognition of the fact that he had also protected Belgians from the SS. In July 1944 he had been imprisoned by Hitler for alleged leniency as Military Governor. Indeed, in May 1945, he was liberated by the Americans just as he was about to be executed by the SS in Dachau for having sympathized with those who had organized the July Plot. Between his arrest by Hitler in July 1944 and his release by the Belgians in April 1951, he had been confined in forty-three different prisons.

Oswald Pohl, the man who had been in charge of the goods and chattels of those murdered in concentration camps, and who had supervised the melting down of gold teeth taken from the corpses of the dead at Auschwitz, was tried by a United States military tribunal and hanged at Landsberg Prison on 8 June 1951. That same day Otto Ohlendorf was also hanged; he had been in charge of several special killing squads in German-occupied Russia which had murdered 90,000 people, most of them Jews. In his defence, he cited the historical precedence of the killing of Gypsies in the Thirty Years' War. Also executed by the Americans that June 8 was another special killing squad commander, Wernher Braune. Following his execution, the Bavarian welfare authorities gave him the status of 'war victim', thus qualifying his widow for an automatic pension.

Reconciliation and retribution continued to march hand in hand. On September 8, in Warsaw, the commander of the SS troops who suppressed the Warsaw ghetto uprising, Jürgen Stroop, was executed, on the site of the former ghetto. Before being extradited from Germany to Poland, he had already been sentenced to death by an American military tribunal for shooting American pilots and hostages in Greece.

On 28 August 1951, Japan had become a beneficiary of a bi-national agreement with the United States, as a member of the Fulbright educational exchange programme. Eleven days later, in San Francisco, a peace treaty was signed between Japan and most of the nations which had been at war with her, but not by the Soviet Union. In the treaty, the Japanese Government declared that 'the Japanese people forever renounce war as a sovereign right of the nation, and the threat and use of force as a means of settling international disputes'. That same day, a security treaty was signed between Japan and the United States, allowing the United States to maintain armed forces 'in and about Japan'.

The Jewish search for reparation reached its fulfilment that same year, when, after a secret meeting in a London hotel between the West German Chancellor, Dr Konrad Adenauer, and the head of the World Jewish Congress, Dr Nahum Goldmann, Dr Adenauer agreed to the principle of a substantial payment by the West German Government. The Government of East Germany declined to make any similar commitment, then or later.

In the spring of 1952, the west German territory occupied by the Western Allies became a separate State. The Transition Agreement of 26 May 1952, which established this, included a clause recognizing West Germany's obligation to make amends. Later that year, on 1 August 1952, as part of the integration of the new Federal German Republic with Western Europe, Britain and Germany signed the London Debt Agreement, resolving Germany's long outstanding First World War reparations debts which had been first agreed in 1930, on the eve of Hitler's coming to power. In 1935 Hitler had declared a moratorium on these debt repayments. Now the West German Government agreed to make token repayments, thus clearing the way for future economic loans designed to revive the West German economy.

On 10 September 1952, in Luxemburg City Hall, at a silent ceremony lasting only thirteen minutes, Israel and West Germany signed an agreement, known as the Luxemburg Treaty, under which the West German Government agreed to pay 3,000 million German marks to the recently established State of Israel, and a further 450 million German marks to Jewish organizations, as reparation for 'material damage' suffered by the Jews at the hands of the Nazis.

There was much for reparations money to be used for; that summer there were still 1,845 Displaced Persons, among them five hundred children, living in what – seven years earlier – had been Dachau concentration camp.

# 53

# 'Unfinished business'

1953–1989

By 1953, more than thirteen years had passed since the outbreak of the Second World War, and more than seven since it had ended. But what one survivor of Auschwitz, Hugo Gryn, has called the 'unfinished business' of the war remained. It existed in many forms, opening old wounds or aggravating those which had never been fully healed. For some, it was a simple bureaucratic act which shocked, such as the extension of the patent, on 5 January 1953, to J. A. Topf and Son, of Wiesbaden, for a crematorium furnace in which to burn corpses; it was this same furnace which had burned so many bodies in Auschwitz. For others, there was the shock of a spate of exonerations for wartime crimes, such as the posthumous pardon granted on 28 February 1953 by a German De-nazification Court to General Jodl, hanged as a war criminal at Nuremberg scarcely six years earlier.

For yet others, the unfinished business related to accusations of military incompetence or failure. On 20 July 1953 Admiral Halsey, commander of an aircraft-carrier group in 1941, wrote to Admiral Kimmel, about the latter's failure to be ready for the Japanese surprise attack on Pearl Harbour when he was Commander-in-Chief of the Pacific Fleet: 'Certainly we did not discard the possibility of an attack on Pearl, but with the evidence we had, the most logical inference was that the attack would be against the Philippines and to the southward. Knowing what I did, I felt I was just as responsible as you or anyone else in the higher command position.'

Admiral Halsey continued, in defence of his superior: 'Had we been in possession of the "Magic" messages with clear implication from the Japs, by their anxiety to be constantly informed of ships berthing, that an attack on Pearl was intended, and the further pointed fact that the date was Dec. 7th, the *Enterprise* and *Lexington* would never have gone on their missions to Wake and Midway. And further, the Fleet would not have been in Pearl Harbour on that date'.

Admiral Kimmel was to continue to feel aggrieved that his case, even as supported by Admiral Halsey, had not been heard; that he was considered primarily responsible for the disaster. In his memoirs, he expressed his feelings with the bitter words: 'I cannot excuse those in authority in Washington for what they did. And I do not believe that thousands of mothers and fathers whose sons perished on that tragic seventh day of December Nineteen Hundred and Forty-one will excuse them. They will be judged at the bar of history. In my book they must answer on the Day of Judgment like any other criminal'.

In Europe, those judged in the post-war trials to have been criminals were returning home. At the beginning of 1954, ss General Kurt Meyer had his life sentence reduced by the Canadian Government to fourteen years, with further time off for good behaviour; on September 7 he was back in his home village of Niederkrüchten. A month later, on October 9, Helmut Knochen, of the feared and hated Paris Gestapo, was sentenced to death; three and a half years later, his death sentence was reduced to forced labour for life; a year and half after that, it was reduced again to twenty years' penal servitude; and in 1963, within nine years of his death sentence, he was released and sent home to Baden Baden.

On 5 May 1955, the Federal German Republic became an independent sovereign state. Four months later, on 9 September 1955, the Federal German Chancellor, Dr Adenauer, was the guest of the Soviet Government in Moscow. During a gala dinner on the evening of September 12, he and the Soviet leader, Marshal Bulganin, came to an agreement that all German prisoners-of-war still detained in the Soviet Union should be sent home. By the end of the month, the repatriation of 8,872 German soldiers had been decreed by the Supreme Soviet. They were released in October; among them was General Friedrich Gollwitzer, who had headed the group of nineteen German generals paraded through the streets of Moscow in July 1944.

Indictments and trials continued, with the Federal German Republic initiating many of the prosecutions; on 22 November 1955 the police in Kiel arrested Dr Karl Clauberg, one of the doctors who had carried out the sterilization of Jewish and Gypsy women at Auschwitz; while a free citizen of West Germany, he had openly boasted of his wartime scientific achievements. Two years later, on the eve of his trial, Clauberg died in a Kiel hospital.

The 1950s were also a time of memorials; on 11 September 1956, religious delegates from twenty-one countries inaugurated a memorial at Dachau. On 30 May 1958, at Arlington Cemetery, Virginia, a memorial was unveiled to America's Unknown Soldier of the Second World War. So long had it taken to prepare this memorial that a second coffin had to be buried at the same cemetery, to represent the unknown soldier of the Korean War which, beginning in the summer of 1950, pitted American against North Korean and Chinese Communist soldiers, and left 33,629 American dead.

More than a decade had now passed since the end of the Second World War. Memories were merged into, and overtaken by, the claims of a new age. On 1 July 1957 a hundred-mile section of the once notorious Burma railway, built at such a high cost in the lives of Allied prisoners-of-war, was reopened to civilian traffic. It became a regular route of pilgrimage for the widows and children of prisoners-of-war visiting the Allied cemetery at Kanchanaburi; thirty years later, a special tourist train of the State Railway of Thailand left Bangkok every morning to make the hundred mile journey. The rest of the railway, over the mountains into Burma, had long since been swallowed up by the jungle.

The relics and remains of war were found everywhere: there were unexploded bombs on all the battlefronts, and in the cities and towns which had been under repeated air attack. As I write these words – on 4 February 1989 – the British newspapers report the discovery of yet another unexploded bomb at Whitechapel, in the East End of London, and the evacuation of several thousand people as the bomb was made safe.

The remains of human beings were also found, long after the war's end, in the fields that were once the front line, on beaches and landing grounds, in the mass murder sites of Eastern Europe, in jungles, and in deserts. On 9 November 1958 a pilot flying across the Sahara desert south of Tobruk saw a crashed aircraft lying in the sand. It was the American bomber 'Lady Be Good' which had disappeared in 1943 while on its return flight to its base in Libya from a bombing raid over southern Italy. Its radio, guns and ammunition were found in working order. Later, the skeletons of five of its crew members were discovered in the desert sand, including that of Lieutenant Robert Toner. Also found was Lieutenant Toner's diary, describing their final, fateful days in the desert.

It was in the 1960s that West Germany began to pay money to States which had suffered from German occupation during the Second World War, having signed what were called Global Accords on reparation payments with eleven European countries. On 18 March 1960, Greece was paid 115 million German marks under one such accord, and France four hundred million that same July. Payments were also made to Poland, which received one hundred million, and, on a much smaller scale, seven and a half million to Russia and eight million to Yugoslavia.

For Western Germany, it was the existence of a divided Europe, with all its fears and uncertainties, that provided an opportunity to enter a new world of defence systems facing the East; on 11 September 1960, the officers, men and tanks of a West German panzer battalion began a three week training programme in Britain, at Castlemartin in South Wales. Nine days later, journalists were invited to watch the German tanks in action, sending their shells into the battered hulks of five British wartime 'Churchill' tanks.

Not only retribution and reconciliation, but, for the Soviet Union, rehabilitation of individual reputations, was a feature of the post-war years. In 1962, ten years after Stalin's death, the Leningrad Military District Court rehabilitated Captain Vyacheslav Kaliteyev, commander of the troop transport *Kazakhstan* during the evacuation of Tallinn in August 1941. Following the decision of the court, Kaliteyev's widow, the actress Vera Tutcheva, was informed that the charges against her husband, of deserting his ship at its moment of need – charges for which he had been shot – were totally without foundation.

On 31 May 1962, Adolf Eichmann, the principal organizer of the deportation of Jews to the death camps, was hanged at Ramle Prison in Israel. Two years earlier he had been tracked down to Buenos Aires, abducted to Israel, and brought to trial. During his trial, which lasted for just over four months, eye-witnesses gave testimony, not only about Eichmann's part in the deportation process, but about every aspect of that process itself, from the initial round-ups to the very gates of the gas chamber. Within five months of Eichmann's execution, further details about the final moments of Jews sent to the gas chambers at Auschwitz were discovered within a few yards of one of the gas chambers itself: on 17 October 1962 a Polish worker at the camp site discovered the notes hidden by a Jew, Salmen Lewental, who had been forced to take the bodies of those killed out of the gas chamber and into the crematorium. Lewental's notes, which had been hidden in a jar, included an account of the last-minute remarks of several Jewish women as they were about to die, one of whom, in January 1942, had asked him: 'I am still so young, I have really not experienced anything in my life, why should death of this kind fall to my lot? Why?'

No one could answer that question in 1942; no one could answer it twenty years later. Yet the question continued to be asked at every war crimes trial. On 30 December 1963, in Frankfurt-on-Main, twenty-two former Auschwitz guards were put on trial. 'I knew only one mode of conduct', Wilhelm Boger told the court, 'to carry out the orders of superiors without reservations.' Found guilty of 144 murders, and complicity in the deaths of a thousand more, Boger was sentenced to life imprisonment. 'I believed in the Führer,' another of the guards, Hans Stark, explained, and he added: 'I wanted to serve my people.' Found guilty of forty-one separate instances of joint murder, one involving two hundred people, Stark was sentenced to ten years in prison.

On 30 September 1964, ss General Wolff, who in a letter on August 1941 had written that he was 'particularly gratified with the news that each day for the last fortnight a trainload of five thousand members of the "Chosen People" has been sent to Treblinka', was sentenced to fifteen years' penal servitude. In view of what the court called Wolff's 'otherwise blameless life', and of his part in the negotiations for the surrender of the German Army in Italy, he was released seven years after being sentenced.

Honour as well as shame came to those who had been active in the torments and struggles of the Second World War; on 19 December 1964, what were believed to be the remains of the French Resistance hero, Jean Moulin, were placed in the Panthéon in Paris, as part of the twentieth anniversary celebrations of France's liberation. This was but one of tens of thousands of memorials and monuments set up throughout Europe and Asia. On 26 October 1968, in the British city of Leamington Spa, a monument was unveiled to all Czechs and Slovaks who had died during the war, and in particular to the seven Czech patriots who had been killed after their successful attempt to assassinate the ss General Reinhard Heydrich, Hitler's Deputy Reich Protector for Bohemia and Moravia.

Stories arising from the Second World War became a regular feature, long after the war had ended, of newspaper and magazine articles, and film and television presentations. Some of these stories were bizarre, as when, on 7 February 1972, the American magazine *Newsweek* reported the discovery in the jungles of Guam of a Japanese army sergeant, Shoichi Yokoi, twenty-eight years after he had fled into the forest to avoid the shame of surrender. With two other soldiers, Sergeant Yokoi had hidden in a cave by day, emerging at night to forage for mangoes, nuts, snails, pigeons and rats. His two fellow fugitives had died of malnutrition in 1964, the year in which they had learned, from an old leaflet, that the war was over. Still Yokoi was determined not to surrender, and had maintained his determination by thinking: 'I am living for the Emperor, and for the spirit of Japan'.

Not only monuments, but relics, became a part of the aftermath of war; in 1975, under Operation Harvest, British and Dutch researchers recovered the wrecks of eight aircraft shot down over the Zuider Zee in Holland. Similar recoveries, of aircraft, tanks and even warships, were made in every war zone, even in the remotest corners of Borneo and New Guinea.

The advent of films, plays, even tournaments recalling the war years could not entirely eclipse the continuing war crimes trials, which, after the rebuilding of the cities, had become one of the most visible legacies of the war, despite a widespread public reluctance to pursue them. Such sentences as were imposed were often for only that fragment of a major crime that could be proved so long after the event. On 26 November 1975 the trial began in Düsseldorf of fourteen SS men, accused of mass murder at Majdanek concentration camp near Lublin, in Poland; the trial was to last for more than five years. One of the accused, SS Lieutenant Arnold Strippel, found guilty of participation in the deaths of forty-one Russian prisoners-of-war, was sentenced to three and a half years in prison. Being over seventy years old, he did not have to serve it. Earlier, Strippel had spent six years in prison for complicity in murders at Buchenwald and Neuengamme. For his time spent in prison, he was awarded compensation, a cash payment of 121,000 German marks, seven times more than the amount his concentration-camp prisoners would have received as reparations for the same period, had they lived. But Strippel's trials were not over; on 12 December 1983 he was charged with the murder of twenty Jewish children at Bullenhuser Damm and twenty-two adults at Neuengamme concentration camp.

In France, a law passed in 1964, enabling charges to be brought for 'crimes against humanity', was first used in March 1979, when Jean Leguay, who had been actively involved in the round-up and deportation of Jews from Paris to Auschwitz, was indicted. Seven months later, in October 1979, three Germans were put on trial in Cologne, charged with actually arranging those deportations. The sentences were of twelve, ten and six years in prison respectively. But one observer at the trial, David Pryce-Jones, the historian of Paris in the war years, commented: 'Public opinion was hardly touched'.

As the Second World War receded in time, there remained much 'unfinished business' to fuel controversies. In 1971 the Emperor Hirohito visited Europe. He was seventy-seven years old. His journey provoked considerable protest among those who had been prisoners-of-war in the notorious prison camps throughout Japanese-occupied South East Asia. On October 5, Hirohito was in London, where the Queen and the Duke of Edinburgh – who in 1945 had witnessed Japan's surrender in Tokyo Bay – met him at Victoria Station. During his visit, the Emperor was invested with the Order of the Garter. In outrage, a former prisoner-of-war on the 'Death Railway', John Marsh, then Director-General of the British Institute of Management, returned his Mentioned in Dispatches certificate. 'We cannot pretend', the Queen told her Imperial guest at a banquet at Buckingham Palace, 'that the relations between our two peoples have always been peaceful and friendly. However, it is precisely this experience which should make us all the more determined never to let it happen again'.

The 'unfinished business' of the Second World War has continued even into the 1980s. On 15 June 1981, the survivors of what had become known as the Holocaust – the German murder of six million Jews – held their first international reunion, on a hilltop on the outskirts of Jerusalem. Hundreds of people who had not seen each other since 1945 met again, to share memories not only of torment, but of loved ones and friends who had been killed.

Other echoes of the war abounded, from all aspects of the conflict. When, on 2 May 1982, during the Falklands War, the Argentine light cruiser *General Belgrano* was sunk by a British submarine, there were not many who knew, or could remember, that she was in fact the American light cruiser *Phoenix*, which had survived the Japanese attack on Pearl Harbour with a single bullet hole in the shield of a range-finder. A veteran of the Pacific war, she had met her watery grave, as did 368 of those on board, in a war in the Atlantic.

Three months after the sinking of the *General Belgrano*, another warship of the Second World War, the United States aircraft carrier *Intrepid*, came to a very different final berth when, having been moored at Pier 86 in New York City's Hudson River, she was opened to the public as an Air, Sea and Space Museum.

The mid-1980s saw other echoes of a war that had ended four decades earlier. In February 1985, the widow of Judge Roland Freisler, who had condemned to death the Germans found guilty of plotting against Hitler in July 1944, was granted a pension from the Government of Bavaria, on the grounds that, had her husband not been killed by the Allied bomb which struck his courthouse, he would have been able to accept a high position in post-war West Germany, with the result that she would have been entitled to a substantial widow's pension. Not a widow, but a former fiancée, Doreen Young, was present on 5 November 1985 for the burial near Caen of Reginald Thursby, shot down in Normandy in August 1944, whose remains had been found earlier that year at Ste Marguerite-de-Viette.

Forty years after the end of the Second World War, there was a sudden upsurge in concern at the number of former Nazi war criminals who, undetected, had found a safe haven in the West. The United States took the lead in deporting those who could be shown to have had a Nazi past. In Britain, Australia and Canada, official commissions of enquiry examined how such people had been allowed in, and asked if trials should be begun again. On 30 December 1986, the Canadian Deschenes Commission of Inquiry on War Criminals was outspoken in its assertion that, since 1948, 'Canada devoted not the slightest energy to the search and prosecution of war criminals'.

Suddenly, with the beginning of the fifth decade since the war had ended, its wounds were again being opened up, as happened on 24 April 1988, when a

British newspaper, the *Sunday Times,* reported that Wilhelm Mohnke, the officer responsible for the massacre of British prisoners-of-war at Wormhout, near Dunkirk, in May 1940, was living, as a retired businessman, near Hamburg. An official British post-war report, stating that it was Mohnke who 'gave the order the prisoners were to be shot', was, however, not to be open to the public until the year 2011, seventy-one years after the event.

The relics of war had continued to be a source of curiosity, and even of looting, for more than four decades. On 3 September 1988, the forty-ninth anniversary of the outbreak of the war, three British deep-sea divers were being held by police in Germany on suspicion of trying to loot the *Wilhelm Gustloff* in German Baltic waters. More than six thousand soldiers and refugees had drowned when the ship was sunk during the last months of the war – the greatest loss of life in any sea disaster.

The search for a reconciliation of former adversaries continued to exercise the world's leaders. 'You and I are about the same age', the Federal German Chancellor Helmut Kohl told the Soviet President, Mikhail Gorbachev, on 26 October 1988, at a banquet in the Kremlin, and he added: 'In our youth we experienced the horror of war. Your father was seriously wounded, my brother was killed in action. We saw how many women waited for their husbands, how many mothers waited for their sons – often in vain'. Now was the time, with the debris of war removed and the towns and villages rebuilt, 'to bring the people closer together in heart and mind'. In this, Kohl declared, 'I perceive a common, a profoundly human obligation, in spite of the fact that we live in different political and social systems'.

Yet, more than four decades after the end of the Second World War, such sensitive and sane words were not universally accepted. Within a month, in Chancellor Kohl's own West Germany, when a group of sixteen Jews, then living in Holland, Britain, the United States and Israel, revisited their former home town of Xanten in the second week of November 1988, some local residents were so angered by the visit that they painted slogans on the walls of two schools and a museum. One slogan read: 'That's the way to the gas chamber,' and another, 'Auschwitz is too small.'

That same week, in Bonn, in the Federal German parliament, the Speaker, Philipp Jenninger, recalling the pre-war years and the beginning of Nazi persecution, asked, during a memorial meeting to commemorate German anti-Jewish pogrom of November 1938: 'And as far as the Jews were concerned: hadn't they in the past measured themselves for roles that did not suit them? Didn't they finally have to accept restrictions? Didn't they perhaps even deserve to be shown their place? And above all: apart from wild exaggerations which were not to be taken seriously, didn't basic points of the propaganda reflect one's own speculation and convictions?'

'Wasn't Hitler', the Speaker went on to ask, 'someone selected by Providence, a leader who would only be given to a people once in a thousand years?'

Forty-eight hours after asking these questions, Philipp Jenninger resigned. His questions, which had been intended merely to recall the German mood of the pre-war years, offended many Germans, as well as Jews. The emotions of

743

the past had remained vivid in the minds of those who lived through it. Even if physical wounds had healed, other wounds remain. Although the Second World War is now far distant, its shadows are long, its echoes loud. How else could it be with an event, lasting for nearly six years, in which courage and cruelty, hope and horror, violence and virtue, massacre and survival, were so closely intertwined?

One example of these shadows and echoes was reflected early in 1988, when the United States Government decided to reduce the number of countries whose citizens would need a visa to enter. On 26 May 1988 a pilot visa waiver programme was launched in which, instead of presenting a visa, visitors had to answer certain questions on entry. These questions listed, among the grounds for exclusion to the United States, one of which applied to those individuals 'who were in any way connected with the persecution of others in association with the Nazi government.'

Thus the unfinished business of war remained on the legal agenda of the victor States fifty years after the war had begun.

For the leaders of West Germany, there was a continual and courageous effort to face up to the past. On 12 October 1988, in opening a congress of German historians at Bamberg, the Federal German President, Richard von Weizsäcker – whose father had been a senior diplomat in the Nazi era – declared that the German nation 'cannot make others responsible for what it and its neighbours endured under National Socialism. It was led by criminals, and allowed itself to be led by them. It knows this to be true'.

The unfinished business of war concerned all the warring nations, and all the war zones; even areas beyond those zones. On 25 January 1989, the Governor-General of Australia gave the Royal Assent to an Australian act of Parliament, the War Crimes Amendment Act, which in its preamble stated that 'concern has arisen that a significant number of persons who committed serious crimes in Europe during World War II may since have entered Australia and become Australian citizens or residents'. It was 'appropriate', the Act continued, 'that persons accused of such war crimes be brought to trial in the ordinary criminal courts in Australia'. Under the Act, a procedure was set up to find these people as quickly as possible and to prepare a legal case against them. Two days later on 27 January 1989 the Dutch Parliament discussed the proposed release earlier that week of two German war criminals, Ferdinand aus der Fünten and Franz Fischer, from prison in the Dutch town of Breda. Both men had been sentenced to death – later commuted to life imprisonment – in 1945 for their part in the deportation of Jews from Holland to Auschwitz. Fischer was now eighty-seven years old and aus der Fünten seventy-six; amid considerable protests and world-wide publicity, it was agreed by a vote of 85 to 55 that they should both be allowed to return to Germany.

The controversy about the release of the two men came at a time when the Dutch, as well as the British, public, were much exercised over the question of who should represent them at the funeral of the Emperor Hirohito, who had died earlier that same month. The British Government were under much criticism for deciding to send Prince Philip, who as a young naval officer had been present at the formal surrender of Japan in Tokyo Bay. The Dutch Government had as

744

yet made no decision, but, as it studied the question, and as survivors of the Japanese prison camps protested against any royal emissary, a Dutchman who had collaborated with the Japanese in the war, Jan Olij, was in prison in Argentina, awaiting extradition to Holland. He was later released by the Argentine authorities.

The unfinished business of the Second World War was seen again on 29 January 1989, the year of the fiftieth anniversary of the outbreak of the war, when, in parliamentary elections in West Berlin, a new extreme right wing party, the Republicans, won eleven of the 138 seats. The leader of the Republicans, Franz Schönhuber, then aged sixty-five, had joined the Waffen SS in 1942 at the age of nineteen, and had fought both on the Eastern front and, in 1944, in Normandy. In reaction to Schönhuber's success, ten thousand Berliners marched through the streets of their city carrying placards which read: 'No more fascists' and chanting the slogan: 'Nazis out'.

It was controversy over Hirohito's funeral which was proved the most pronounced of those which were heard in the early months of the year which marked the fiftieth anniversary of the Second World War. 'I have before me', John Hart, a former prisoner-of-war of the Japanese, wrote to *The Times* on 4 February 1989, 'a list of 300 names of those POWs who died on the tiny island of Haroekoe, in far western Indonesia. Ragged and emaciated, they stumbled daily to build an airstrip, until abandonment of hope, or disease, brought them release. They died under unspeakable, degrading conditions.' John Hart added: 'Pleas for help from the Red Cross, its patronage claimed by the Imperial Family, were ignored and the very mention of the Geneva Convention brought hysterical reaction. But we had surrendered and thus, in accordance with Japanese military custom, we had forfeited all rights. We buried our dead without ceremony, save for a hurried prayer, under the bayonets of impatient guards. Now, kings and princes will assemble, trumpets will sound and troops march, in memory of a man who must carry the ultimate responsibility for so much inhumanity'.

The bitterness evoked by reflections such as these brought back to public prominence the scale of the slaughter of the Second World War, both in the Pacific and in Europe. As many as a quarter of a million slave labourers – Javanese, Burmese, Malays, Chinese and Indians – had died while working for the Japanese on the Thailand–Burma 'Death Railway', forced amid constant brutality and near starvation to move earth and rock along the route. A further 50,000 Allied prisoners-of-war – Australian, Dutch, English and American – had also died on this railway, of disease, starvation and deliberate killing. In Japanese prison camps, 10,500 Dutch civilian internees and 8,500 Dutch prisoners-of-war had perished.

The number of those who died in the Second World War will never be known with precision. Tens of millions of men, women and children were killed without any record being made of their names, or of when or how they died. Millions of soldiers were killed in action without anyone recording their names, or marking the place where they fell.

Many calculations have been made of the number of war dead. In the war between China and Japan, which began two years before the war in Europe, it has been estimated that six million Chinese civilians were killed. The Soviet Union suffered ten million deaths in action, on land, in the air and at sea. A further 3,300,000 Soviet soldiers were killed after they had become prisoners-of-war. Seven million Soviet civilians also died; a death toll in excess of twenty million Soviet citizens. The Germans calculate 3,600,000 civilians dead, and 3,250,000 soldiers. The Japanese calculate two million civilians and a million military deaths, the largest single toll being the 138,890 deaths recorded at Hiroshima as a result of the dropping of the first atomic bomb. Six million Polish citizens were killed while Poland was under German occupation, three million of them Polish Jews. A further three million Jews from other parts of Europe were killed, bringing the Jewish death toll to six million. More than a million and a half Yugoslavs were also killed after the German conquest. In this listing only of those groups that suffered a million dead or more, a total is reached in excess of forty-six million.

In every war zone, and behind every front line, loss of life was enormous. The British, who had entered the war in September 1939, suffered 264,433 army, navy and air force deaths, as well as 60,595 civilian deaths from bombing, and 30,248 merchant navy deaths. The total number of British Commonwealth deaths in actions was 129,196, making a total British and Commonwealth death toll of 484,472.

In Greece, which was first attacked, by Italy, in October 1940, and then, in April 1941, by Germany, 260,000 civilians died from privation and hunger between 1940 and 1945, 70,600 were executed by the occupying forces in reprisals, and 50,000 were killed in the Resistance: a total civilian death toll – not counting the 60,000 Jews deported to their deaths – of 380,600. A further 79,743 Greek soldiers were killed in action in 1940 and 1941. In all, 420,343 Greeks lost their lives.

The United States, which entered the war in December 1941, suffered 362,561 army, navy and air force and Marine Corps deaths.

In Holland, 185,000 civilians perished as a result of war and occupation, more than 104,000 Jews, and 16,000 civilians from hunger and disease during the famine in the northern part of the Netherlands, when, still under German rule, it was cut off from the war zone at the end of 1944.

The number of Indian war dead was 36,092, killed in action in the Far East, North Africa and Italy. The number of Australians killed on the same battlefields, and in New Guinea, was 27,073.

Every warring country suffered losses; even small countries on the periphery, and far from the war zone, could not avoid losses which were heavy for them. Finland, for example, lost 27,000 soldiers in the winter war of 1940. The Spanish Legion lost 4,500 dead during its action alongside the Germans during the siege of Leningrad. The South African Air Force lost 2,227 pilots killed in action over Europe.

There were also deaths from among the soldiers brought from black Africa, including 1,105 Basutos who volunteered to fight for Britain in Syria, Sicily and

Italy; and 498 Askaris from Southern Rhodesia, who fought in the Mediterranean, Europe and Burma.

With the return of the soldiers, sailors and airmen from the war zones, and from the prisoner-of-war camps, it became clear that the legacy of the battlefield was far more than its heroism, statistics and victories. Of the Australian servicemen who returned to Australia in 1945, among them her own father, Germaine Greer has written: 'Thousands of them came home to live out their lives as walking wounded, carrying out their masculine duties in a sort of dream, trying not to hear the children who asked "Mummy, why does that man have to sleep in your bed?" '

No one has been able to calculate the number of wounded, certainly amounting to several millions, whose lives were permanently scarred as a result of the war. Physical scars, from the severest disability to disfiguring wounds, and mental scars, accompanied these millions for the rest of their lives. Many died as a direct result of them. Others lived in pain, discomfort, fear or remorse. For those civilians who were fortunate to survive privation, deportation and massacre, similar scars, physical, mental and spiritual, remained – and still remain – to torment them. The greatest unfinished business of the Second World War is human pain.

# Bibliography

In the course of my historical work on the war-years volumes of the Churchill biography – *Finest Hour 1939–1941* (London 1983) and *Road to Victory 1941–1945* (London 1989) – and on my history of the Jews of Europe in the Second World War, *The Holocaust, The Jewish Tragedy* (London 1986), I assembled a substantial amount of documentary and factual material for use in this book. I also consulted and used specific material from the following published works:

Abyzov, Vladimir: *The Final Assault, Memoirs of a Veteran Who Fought in the Battle of Berlin*, Moscow 1980.

Abrahamsen, Professor Samuel: 'The Rôle of the Norwegian Lutheran Church During World War II', *Remembering for the Future, Jews and Christians During and After the Holocaust*, Oxford 1988.

Ainsztein, Reuben: *Jewish Resistance in Nazi-Occupied Eastern Europe*, London 1974.

Air Ministry: *The Rise and Fall of the German Air Force (1933 to 1945)*, London 1948.

Allen, Louis: 'The Indian National Army, Renegades or Liberators?', *World War II Investigator*, volume 1, number 4, London, July 1988.

Amery, Julian: *Sons of the Eagle, A Study in Guerrilla War*, London 1948.

Amipaz-Silber, Gitta: *La Résistance Juive en Algérie 1940–1942*, Jerusalem 1986.

Antosyak, Alexei: *Operations in the Balkans 1944*, Moscow 1980.

A Polish Doctor: *I saw Poland suffer*, London 1941.

Apenszlak, Jacob (editor): *The Black Book of Polish Jewry*, New York 1943.

Appleman, Roy E., Burns, James M., Gugeler, Russell A., and Stevens, John: *United States Army in World War II, The War in the Pacific, Okinawa, The Last Battle*, Washington D.C. 1948.

Arad, Yitzhak: *Ghetto in Flames, the Struggle and Destruction of the Jews in Vilna in the Holocaust*, Jerusalem 1980.

Arad, Yitzhak: *Belzec, Sobibor, Treblinka – the Operation Reinhard Death Camps*, Bloomington and Indianapolis 1987.

Archer Clark (editor): *Paratroopers' Odyssey, A History of the 517th Parachute Combat Team*, Hudson, Florida, 1985.

Armstrong, John A. (editor): *Soviet Partisans in World War II*, Madison, Wisconsin, 1964.

Aron, Robert: *The Vichy Regime 1940–44*, London 1958.

Arseyenko, Oleg: *An Attempt on Culture*, Kiev 1987.

Ash, Bernard: *Norway 1940*, London 1964.

Auty, Phyllis, and Clogg, Richard (editors): *British Policy Towards Wartime Resistance in Yugoslavia and Greece*, London 1975.

Bader, Douglas: *Fight for the Sky, The Story of the Spitfire and the Hurricane*, London 1973.

Balabkins, Nicholas: *West German Reparations to Israel*, New Brunswick, New Jersey 1971.

Baldwin, Hanson: *Battles Lost and Won, Great Campaigns of World War II*, London 1967.

Bankier, David: 'Hitler and the Policy-making process on the Jewish Question', *Holocaust and Genocide Studies*, volume 3, number 1, Oxford 1988.

Bar-Adon, Dorothy and Pesach: *Seven Who Fell*, Tel Aviv 1947.

Barker A. J.: *Waffen S.S. at War*, London 1982.

Barker, Ralph: *Children of the 'Benares', A War Crime and its Victims*, London 1987.

Barkley, Alben W.: *Atrocities and Other Conditions in Concentration Camps in Germany*, Washington DC 1945.

Bartoszewski, Wladyslaw, and Lewin Zofia: *Righteous among Nations, How Poles Helped the Jews 1939–45*, London 1969.

Bartov, Omer: *The Eastern Front, 1941–45, German troops and the barbarisation of warfare*, London 1985.

Bartz, Karl: *The Downfall of the German Secret Service*, London 1956.

Baudouin, Paul: *The Private Diaries, March 1940 to January 1941, of Paul Baudouin*, London 1948.

Bauer, Yehuda: *Flight and Rescue, 'Brichah', The organized escape of the Jewish survivors of Eastern Europe, 1944–1948*, New York 1970.

Baukh, Efrem (editor): *Babi Yar, Kiev 1941–61*, Jerusalem 1981.

Baumbach, Werner: *Broken Swastika, The defeat of the Luftwaffe*, London 1960.

Bauminger, Arieh L: *Roll of Honour*, Tel Aviv 1971.

Bauminger, Arieh L.: *The Fighters of the Cracow Ghetto*, Jerusalem 1986.

Beaumont, Joan: *Comrades in Arms, British Aid to Russia 1941–1945*, London 1980.

Belgian Ministry of Foreign Affairs, The: *Belgium, The Official Account of what happened 1939–1940*, London 1941.

BenGershôm, Ezra: *David, The Testimony of a Holocaust Survivor*, London 1988.

Bennett, Ralph: *Ultra in the West, the Normandy Campaign 1944–45*, London 1979.

Ben-Tov, Arieh: *Facing the Holocaust in Budapest, The International Committee of the Red Cross and the Jews in Hungary, 1943–45*, Geneva 1988.

Best, Captain S. Payne: *The Venlo Incident*, London 1950.

Bezwinska, Tadwige, and Czech, Danuta (editors): *Amidst a Nightmare of Crime, Manuscripts of Members of Sonderkommando*, Oswiecim 1973.

Bhargava, Dr M. L.: *Indian National Army, Tokyo Cadets*, New Delhi 1986.

Biegański, Stanislaw (editor): *Documents on Polish–Soviet Relations 1939–1945, volume 2, 1943–1945*, London 1967.

Birn, Ruth Bettina: 'Guilty Conscience, Anti-semitism and the Personal Development of some SS Leaders', *Remembering for the Future, Jews and Christians During and After the Holocaust*, Oxford 1988.

Blumenson, Martin: *Rommel's Last Victory, The Battle of Kasserine Pass*, London 1968.

Boelcke, Willi A.: *The Secret Conferences of Dr. Goebbels, October 1939–March 1943*, London 1970.

Bois, Elie J.: *Truth on the Tragedy of France*, London 1940.

Bond, Brian: *France and Belgium, 1939–1940*, London 1975.

Boothroyd, Basil: *Philip (an approved biography of HRH the Duke of Edinburgh)*, London 1971.

Boozer, Jack S.: 'The Political, Moral, and Professional Implications of the "Justifications" by German Doctors for Lethal Medical Actions 1938–1945', *Remembering for the Future, Jews and Christians During and After the Holocaust*, Oxford 1988.

Borkin, Joseph: *The Crime and Punishment of I. G. Farben*, New York 1978.

Bower, Tom: *Klaus Barbie, Butcher of Lyons*, London 1984.

Bower, Tom: *The Paperclip Conspiracy, The Battle for the Spoils and Secrets of Nazi Germany*, London 1987.

Bowman, Steven: 'Greek Jews and Christians During World War II', *Remembering for* the Future, Jews and Christians During and After the Holocaust, Oxford 1988.

Brackman, Arnold C.: The Other Nuremberg, the Untold Story of the Tokyo War Crimes Trials, New York 1987.

Braddon, Russell: Cheshire V. C., A Story of War and Peace, London 1954.

Braham, Randolph L.: The Politics of Genocide, The Holocaust in Hungary, 2 volumes, New York 1981.

Breuer, William B.: Hitler's Fortress Cherbourg, The Conquest of a Bastion, New York 1984.

Breuer, William B.: Retaking the Philippines, America's Return to Corregidor and Bataan, October 1944–March 1945, New York 1986.

Browning, Christopher R.: 'Genocide and Public Health, German doctors and Polish Jews, 1939–41', Holocaust and Genocide Studies, volume 3, number 1, Oxford 1988.

Bruce, George: The Warsaw Uprising, 1 August–2 October 1944, London 1972.

Bruce Lockhart, Sir Robert: The Marines Were There, The Story of the Royal Marines in the Second World War, London 1950.

Buechner, Colonel Howard A.: Dachau, the Hour of the Avenger, An Eyewitness Account, Metairie, Lousiana, 1987.

Bullock, Alan: Hitler, A Study in Tyranny, London 1952.

Butcher, Captain Harry C.: Three Years with Eisenhower, The Personal Diary of Captain Harry C. Butcher, London 1946.

Butler, J. R. M.: Grand Strategy, Volume II, September 1939– June 1941, London 1957.


Calder, Angus: The People's War, Britain 1939–45, London 1969.

Calvocoressi, Peter, and Wint, Guy: Total War, The Causes and Courses of the Second World War, London 1972.

Cammaerts, Emile: The Prisoner at Laeken, King Leopold, Legend and Fact, London 1941.

Campbell, Vice-Admiral Sir Ian, and Macintyre, Captain Donald: The Kola Run, A Record of Arctic Convoys 1941–45, London 1958.

Campion, Joan: In the Lion's Mouth, Gisi

Fleischmann and the Jewish Fight for Survival, London 1987.

Carsten, Professor F. L. (editor): The German Resistance to Hitler, London 1970.

Cartland, Barbara: Ronald Cartland, London 1945.

Casey, Lord: Personal Experience 1939–1946, London 1962.

Chant, Christopher: Kursk, London 1975.

Chant, Christopher: The Encyclopedia of Codenames of World War II, London 1986.

Chary, Frederick B.: The Bulgarian Jews and the Final Solution 1940–44, Pittsburgh 1972.

Churchill, Winston S.: The Second World War, 6 volumes, London 1948–1954.

Ciechanowski, Jan M.: The Warsaw Rising of 1944, London 1974.

Clark, Alan: Barbarossa, The Russian–German Conflict 1941–1945, London 1965.

Clissold, Stephen: Whirlwind, An Account of Marshal Tito's Rise to Power, London 1949.

Clive, Nigel: A Greek Experience 1943–1948, Salisbury, Wiltshire, 1985.

Coates, W. P., and Coates, Zelda K.: A History of Anglo-Soviet Relations, London 1943.

Cole, Hugh M.: United States Army in World War II, The European Theater of Operations, The Ardennes, Battle of the Bulge, Washington D.C. 1965.

Collier, Basil: The Defence of the United Kingdom, London 1957.

Collier, Richard: 1940 The World in Flames, London 1979.

Collier, Richard: 1941, Armageddon, London 1981.

Collins, Larry, and Lapierre, Dominique: Is Paris Burning?, London 1965.

Commission de Crimes de Guerre: Bande, Liège 1945.

Connell, John: Wavell, Scholar and Soldier, To June 1941, London 1964.

Cooper, Alan W.: Bombers over Berlin, The RAF Offensive November 1943–March 1944, London 1985.

Cooper, R. W.: The Nuremberg Trial, London 1947.

Costello, John: *The Pacific War*, London 1985.

Council for the Preservation of Monuments to Resistance and Martyrdom: *Scenes of Fighting and Martyrdom Guide, War Years in Poland 1939–1945*, Warsaw 1968.

Cox, Geoffrey: *The Red Army Moves*, London 1941.

Craven, Wesley Frank, and Cate, James Lea (editors): *The Army Air Forces in World War II*, 7 volumes, Chicago 1953–65.

Cruickshank, Charles: *The German Occupation of The Channel Islands*, London 1975.

Cruickshank, Charles: *Deception in World War II*, Oxford 1979.

Cruickshank, Charles: *SOE in the Far East*, Oxford 1983.

Czarnomski, F. B. (editor): *They Fight for Poland, The War in the First Person*, London 1941.

Czech, Danuta (editor): 'Kalendarium der Ereignisse im Konzentrationslager Auschwitz-Birkenau', *Hefte von Auschwitz*, Oswiecim 1960–64.

Dallek, Robert: *Franklin D. Roosevelt and American Foreign Policy, 1932–1945*, New York 1979.

Dallin, Alexander: *German Rule in Russia 1941–45*, New York 1957.

Dalton, Hugh: *The Fateful Years, memoirs 1931–1945*, London 1957.

Dawidowicz, Lucy S. (editor): *A Holocaust Reader*, New York 1976.

Deacon, Richard: *The Silent War, A History of Western Naval Intelligence*, London 1988.

Deakin, F. W.: *The Brutal Friendship, Mussolini, Hitler, and the Fall of Italian Fascism*, New York 1966.

Deakin, F. W., and Storry, G. R.: *The case of Richard Sorge*, London 1966.

Dedijer, Vladimir: *Tito speaks, his self portrait and struggle with Stalin*, London 1953.

De Gaulle, Charles: *War Memoirs, Volume One, The Call to Honour, 1940–1942, Documents*, London 1955.

De Gaulle, Charles: *War Memoirs, The Call to Honour, 1940–1942*, New York 1955.

De Jong, L.: *Holland Fights the Nazis*, London 1941.

Delmer, Sefton: *The Counterfeit Spy*, London 1973.

Denfield, D. Colt: 'The Air Raid on Dutch Harbour', *After the Battle*, Number 62, London 1988.

Derry, T. K.: *The Campaign in Norway*, London 1952.

Deschner, Günther: *Heydrich, The Pursuit of Total Power*, London 1981.

D'Este, Carlo: *Bitter Victory, The Battle for Sicily, July–August 1943*, London 1988.

Distel, Barbara: '29 April 1945, The Liberation of the Concentration Camp at Dachau', *Dachau Review*, volume 1, Dachau 1988.

Divine, A. D.: *Dunkirk*, London 1945.

Djilas, Milovan: *Wartime*, London 1977.

Djurović, Gradimir: *The Central Tracing Agency of the International Committee of the Red Cross*, Geneva 1986.

Dodds-Parker, Douglas: *Setting Europe Ablaze, Some Account of Ungentlemanly Warfare*, London 1984.

Donnison, F. S. V.: *British Military Administration in the Far East 1943–46*, London 1956.

Douglas-Hamilton, James: *Motive for a Mission, The Story Behind Hess's Flight to Britain*, London 1971.

Douglas-Hamilton, Lord James: *The Air Battle for Malta, The Diaries Of A Fighter Pilot*, Edinburgh 1981.

Drozdov, Georgii, and Ryabko, Evgenii: *Russia at War, 1941–45*, London 1987.

Dulles, Allen: *The Secret Surrender*, New York 1966.

Dunand, Georges: *Ne perdez pas leur trace!*, Neuchâtel 1951.

Dunin-Wąsowicz, Krzysztof: *Resistance in the Nazi Concentration Camps 1933–1945*, Warsaw 1982.

Dunlop, E. E.: *The War Diaries of Weary Dunlop, Java and the Burma–Thailand Railway 1942–1945*, Wheathampstead, Hertfordshire 1987.

Eckman, Lester, and Lazar, Chaim: *The Jewish Resistance, The history of the Jewish partisans in Lithuania and White*

*Russia during the Nazi occupation, 1940–1945*, New York 1977.

Egbert, Lieutenant-Colonel Lawrence D. (Editor of the Record): *Trial of The Major War Criminals Before the International Military Tribunal, Nuremberg 14 November 1945–1 October 1946*, 42 volumes, Nuremberg 1947–1949.

Ehrman, John: *Grand Strategy, Volume V, August 1943–September 1944*, London 1956.

Ehrman, John: *Grand Strategy, Volume VI, October 1944–August 1945*, London 1956.

Eiler, Keith E. (editor): *Wedemeyer on War and Peace*, Stanford, California, 1987.

Eisenhower, Dwight D.: *Crusade in Europe*, London 1948.

Ellis, Major L. F.: *The War in France and Flanders, 1939–1940*, London 1953.

Erez, Tsvi: 'Hungary, Six Days in July 1944', *Holocaust and Genocide Studies*, volume 3, number 1, Oxford 1988.

Erickson, John: *The Road to Stalingrad, Stalin's War with Germany, Volume 1*, London 1975.

Erickson, John: *The Road to Berlin, Stalin's War with Germany, Volume 2*, London 1983.

Erickson, John (editor): *Main Front, Soviet Leaders Look Back on World War II*, London 1987.

Farago, Ladislas: *The Game of the Foxes, British and German intelligence operations and personalities which changed the course of the Second World War*, London 1971.

Farran, Roy: *Winged Dagger, Adventures on Special Service*, London 1948.

Favez, Jean-Claude: *Une Mission Impossible, Le Comité international de la Croix-Rouge, les déportations et les camps de concentration nazis*, Lausanne 1988.

Federation of Jewish Communities in Yugoslavia: *Studies, Archival and Memorial Materials about the Jews in Yugoslavia*, Belgrade 1979.

Ferrell, Robert H. (editor): *The Eisenhower Diaries*, New York 1981.

Fest, Joachim C.: *Hitler*, London 1974.

Fleischner, Eva: 'Can the Few become the Many? Some Catholics in France who saved Jews during the Holocaust', *Remembering for the Future, Jews and Christians During and After the Holocaust*, Oxford 1988.

Fleming, Gerald: *Hitler and the Final Solution*, London 1985.

Foot, M. R. D.: *S.O.E. in France, An Account of the Work of the British Special Operations Executive in France 1940–1944*, London 1966.

Footitt, Hilary, and Simmonds, John: *France, 1943–1945*, Leicester 1988.

Foster, Tony: *Meetings of Generals*, Toronto 1986.

Franco, Hizkia M.: *Les Martyrs Juifs de Rhodes et de Cos*, Elizabethville 1952.

Frank, Anne: *The Diary of Anne Frank*, London 1954.

Frank, Hans: *Hans Frank Diary*, Warsaw 1961.

Freeman, Julie D.: 'German Views of the Holocaust as Reflected in Memoirs', *Remembering for the Future, Jews and Christians During and After the Holocaust*, Oxford 1988.

Freeman, Michael: *Atlas of Nazi Germany*, Beckenham, Kent 1987.

Friedhoff, Herman: *Requiem for the Resistance, The Civilian Struggle Against Nazism in Holland and Germany*, London 1988.

Friedländer, Saul: *Pius XII and the Third Reich*, New York 1966.

Friedman, Philip: *Roads to Extinction, Essays on the Holocaust*, New York and Philadelphia 1980.

Fuller, Jean Overton: *Noor-un-nisa Inayat Khan (Madeleine), George Cross, MBE, Croix de Guerre with Gold Star*, London 1988.

Fursdon, Major-General Edward: 'The Japanese Surrender', *After the Battle*, Number 50, London 1985.

Gadja, Stan: 'Air-raid on Broome', *After the Battle*, Number 28, London 1980.

Gander, T. J.: 'The Fukuryu, Japanese Suicide Divers and the Defence of Japan, 1945', *World War II Investigator*, volume 1, Number 4, London, July 1988.

Gaon, Solomon, and Serels, M. Mitchell:

*Sephardim and the Holocaust*, New York 1987.

Georg, Enno: *Die Wirtschaftlichen Unternehmungen Der SS*, Stuttgart 1963.

Geraghty, Tony: *March or Die, France and the Foreign Legion*, London 1986.

Ghosh, K. K.: *Indian National Army*, Meerut 1969.

Gilbert, Martin: *Auschwitz and the Allies*, London 1981.

Gilbert, Martin: *The Holocaust, the Jewish Tragedy*, London 1986.

Gilbert, Martin (editor): *Surviving the Holocaust, the Kovno Ghetto Diary*, Cambridge, Massachusetts, 1989.

Gill, Anton: *The Journey Back From Hell, Conversations with Concentration Camp Survivors*, London 1988.

Ginns, Michael: 'The Granville Raid', *After the Battle*, Number 47, London 1985.

Gjelsvik, Torge: *Norwegian Resistance 1940–1945*, London 1979.

Gladkov, Teodor: *Operation Bagration, 1944*, Moscow 1980.

Glantz, David M.: *August Storm, Soviet Tactical and Operational Combat in Manchuria, 1945*, Combat Studies Institute, Leavenworth Papers No. 8, Fort Leavenworth, Kansas, June 1983.

Glantz, Lieutenant Colonel David M.: *The Soviet Airborne Experience*, Combat Studies Institute, Research Survey No. 4, Fort Leavenworth, Kansas, November 1984.

Goldberg, Anatol: *Ilya Ehrenburg, Writing, Politics and the Art of Survival*, London 1984.

Goldberger, Leo (editor): *The Rescue of the Danish Jews, Moral Courage Under Stress*, New York 1987.

Gorlitz, Walter (editor): *The Memoirs of Field-Marshal Keitel*, London 1965.

Graham, Dominick: 'For you the war is over', *World War II Investigator*, volume 1, number 9, London, December 1988.

Gray, Brian: *Basuto Soldiers in Hitler's War*, Maseru, Basutoland, 1953.

Green, Colonel John H.: 'The Battles for Cassino', *After the Battle*, Number 13, London 1976.

Green, Colonel J. H.: 'Anzio', *After the Battle*, number 52, London 1986.

Grenville, J. A. S.: *The Major International Treaties 1914–1973, A history and guide with texts*, London 1974.

Gretton, Vice-Admiral Sir Peter: *Convoy Escort Commander*, London 1964.

Griess, Thomas E. (editor): *The Second World War, Asia and the Pacific*, Wayne, New Jersey, 1984.

Griess, Thomas E. (editor): *The Second World War, Europe and the Mediterranean*, Wayne, New Jersey, 1984.

Griffith, Hubert: *R.A.F. In Russia*, London 1942.

Gross, Jan Tomasz: *Polish Society Under German Occupation, The General gouvernement 1939–1944*, Princeton, New Jersey, 1979.

Groves, Leslie R.: *Now It Can Be Told, The Story of the Manhattan Project*, New York 1962.

Guedalla, Philip: *Middle East 1940–1942, A Study in Air Power*, London 1944.

Guillain, Robert: *I Saw Tokyo Burning, An Eyewitness Narrative from Pearl Harbor to Hiroshima*, London 1981.

Gurdus, Luba Krugman: *The Death Train, A Personal Account of a Holocaust Survivor*, New York 1978.

Gutman, Yisrael: *The Warsaw Ghetto, 1939–1943*, Bloomington, Indiana, 1985.

Gutman, Yisrael, and Krakowski, Shmuel: *Unequal Victims, Poles and Jews During World War Two*, New York 1986.

Gwyer, J. M. A., and Butler, J. R. M.: *Grand Strategy, Volume III, July 1941–August 1942*, London 1964.

Hachiya, Michihiko: *Hiroshima Diary, The Journal of a Japanese Physician, August 6–September 30, 1945*, London 1955.

Hall, J. W. (editor): *Trial of William Joyce*, London 1946.

Hamilton, Charles: *Leaders and Personalities of the Third Reich, Their Biographies, Portraits and Autographs*, San Jose, California, 1984.

Handel, Michael I. (editor): *Strategic and Operational Deception in the Second World War*, London 1987.

Hansell, Major-General Haywood S.: *Strategic Air War Against Japan*, Washington DC 1980.

Hanson, Joanna K. M.: *The civilian population and the Warsaw Uprising of 1944*, Cambridge 1982.

Harriman, W. Averell, and Abel, Elie: *Special Envoy to Churchill and Stalin 1941–46*, London 1976.

Harris, Roger.: *Islanders Deported*, Channel Islands 1980.

Harrison, D. I.: *These Men are Dangerous, The Special Air Service at War*, London 1957.

Harrison, Kenneth: *The Brave Japanese*, Adelaide 1966.

Harrison-Ford, Carl (editor): *Fighting Words, Australian War Writing*, Melbourne 1986.

Hashimoto, Mochitsura: *Sunk, The Story of the Japanese Submarine Fleet 1942–1945*, London 1954.

Hastings, Max: *Das Reich, Resistance and the march of the 2nd SS Panzer Division through France, June 1944*, London 1981.

Haswell, Jock: *The Intelligence and Deception of the D-Day Landings*, London 1979.

Hawkins, Desmond, and Boyd, Donald (Editors): *War Report, A Record of Dispatches Broadcast by the BBC's War Correspondents with the Allied Expeditionary Force, 6 June 1944–5 May 1945*, London 1946.

Herzstein, Robert Edwin: *Waldheim, The Missing Years*, London 1988.

Hilberg, Raul: *The Destruction of the European Jews*, New York 1981.

Hilberg, Raul (editor): *Documents of Destruction, Germany and Jewry 1933–1945*, London 1971.

Hillesum, Etty: *Letters from Westerbork*, London 1987.

Hinsley, F. H., with Thomas E. E., Simkins C. A. G. and Ransom, C. F. G.: *British Intelligence in the Second World War, Its Influence on Strategy and Operations*, 3 volumes, London 1979–1988.

His Majesty's Stationery Office: *Indictment presented to the International Military Tribunal sitting at Berlin on 18th October 1945*, London 1945.

His Majesty's Stationery Office: *British Merchant Vessels Lost or Damaged by Enemy Action During Second World War*, 3rd September, 1939 to 2nd September, 1945, London 1947.

His Majesty's Stationery Office: *Ships of the Royal Navy, Statement of Losses During the Second World War, 3rd September, 1939 to 2nd September, 1945*, London 1947.

Hoffenberg, Sam: *Le camp de Poniatowa, la liquidation des derniers Juifs de Varsovie*, Paris 1988.

Höhne, Heinz: *The Order of the Death's Head, The Story of Hitler's SS*, London 1969.

Hosking, Geoffrey: *A History of the Soviet Union*, London 1985.

Howard, Michael: *Grand Strategy, Volume IV, August 1942–September 1943*, London 1972.

Hughes, John Craven: *Getting Hitler into Heaven, Based on the previously untranslated memoirs of Heinz Linge, Hitler's valet and confidant*, London 1987.

Hunt, Ray C., and Norling, Bernard: *Behind Japanese Lines, An American Guerrilla in the Philippines*, Lexington, Kentucky, 1986.

Hyde, A. P.: 'Pearl Harbor, Then and Now', *After the Battle*, Number 38, London 1982.

Hyde, H. Montgomery: *The Quiet Canadian, The Secret Service Story of Sir William Stephenson*, London 1962.

Hyde, H. Montgomery: *Stalin, The History of a Dictator*, London 1971.

Hyde, H. Montgomery: *The Atom Bomb Spies*, London 1980.

Hymoff, Edward: *The OSS in World War II*, New York 1986.

Inber, Vera: *Leningrad Diary*, London 1971.

International Committee of the Red Cross: *Documents relating to the work of the International Committee of the Red Cross for the benefit of civilian detainees in German Concentration Camps between 1939 and 1945*, Geneva 1975.

International Military Tribunal: *The Trial of the War Criminals*, 42 volumes, Nuremberg 1947–9.

Iranek-Osmecki, Kazimierz: *He Who Saves One Life*, New York 1971.

Irving, David: *Hitler's War*, London 1977.

Isely, Jeter A., and Crowl, Philip A.: *The U.S.*

*Marines and Amphibious War, Its Theory, and Its Practice in the Pacific*, Princeton, New Jersey, 1951.

Jacobsen, Dr Hans-Adolf, and Rohwer, Dr Jürgen (editors): *Decisive Battles of World War II: the German View*, London 1965.

Jaksch, Wenzel: *Europe's Road to Potsdam*, London 1963.

Jankowski, T., and Weese, E. (Editors): *Documents on Polish–Soviet Relations, 1939–1945*, volume 1, London 1961.

Johnson, Brigadier G.D.: 'The Battle of Hong Kong', *After the Battle*, Number 46, London 1984.

Jones, Robert Huhn: *The Roads to Russia, United States Lend-Lease To The Soviet Union*, Norman, Oklahoma, 1969.

Jones, R.V.: *Most Secret War, British Scientific Intelligence 1939–1945*, London 1978.

Jones, Vincent C.: *Manhattan, The Army and the Atomic Bomb*, Washington DC 1985.

Joseph, Francis: 'Flying the World's First Jet Bomber', *World War II Investigator*, volume 1, number 8, London, November 1988.

Jurado, Carlos Caballero: *Resistance Warfare 1940-45*, London 1985.


Kagan, Lord: *Knight of the Ghetto*, London 1975.

Kahn, David: *Hitler's Spies, German Military Intelligence in World War II*, London 1978.

Katz, Robert: *Death in Rome*, London 1967.

Kedward, H.R.: *Resistance in Vichy France, A Study of Ideas and Motivation in the Southern Zone 1940–1942*, Oxford 1978.

Keegan, John (editor): *Who was Who in World War II*, London 1978.

Keegan, John: *Six Armies in Normandy, From D-Day to the Liberation of Paris*, London 1982.

Kennedy, Ludovic: *Menace, The Life and Death of the Tirpitz*, London 1979.

Kennett, Lee: *G.I., The American Soldier in World War II*, New York 1987.

Kenrick, Donald, and Puxon, Grattan: *The Destiny of Europe's Gypsies*, London 1972.

Kermish, Joseph: *The Destruction of the Jewish Community of Piotrkow by the Nazis During World War II*, Tel Aviv 1965.

Kermish, Joseph (editor): *To Live with Honor and Die with Honor! Selected Documents from the Warsaw Ghetto Underground Archives*, Jerusalem 1986.

Kersaudy, François: *Churchill and de Gaulle*, London 1981.

Kimmel, Rear-Admiral Husband E.: *Admiral Kimmel's Story*, Chicago 1955.

King George's Jubilee Trust: *The Royal Family in Wartime*, London 1945.

Kitroeff, Alexandros: 'Greek Wartime Attitudes Towards the Jews in Athens', *Forum*, Issue No. 60, Jerusalem, Summer 1987.

Klarsfeld, Serge: *Memorial to the Jews Deported from France, 1942–1944*, New York 1983.

Klarsfeld, Serge: *The Children of Izieu, A Human Tragedy*, New York 1985.

Klarsfeld, Serge (editor): *The Struthof Album, Study of the Gassing at Natzweiler-Stuthof of 86 Jews whose bodies were to constitute a collection of skeletons, A photographic document*, New York 1985.

Klarsfeld, Serge: 'The Upper Echelons of the Clergy and Public Opinion Force Vichy France to put an end, in September 1942, to its Broad Participation in the Hunt for Jews', *Remembering for the Future, Jews and Christians During and After the Holocaust*, Oxford 1988.

Klarsfeld, Serge, and Steinberg, Maxime: *Mémorial de la Déportation des juifs de Belgique*, Mechelen, Belgium, 1982.

Klenfeld, Gerald R., and Tambs, Lewis A.: *Hitler's Spanish Legion, The Blue Division in Russia*, Carbondale and Edwardsville, Illinois, 1979.

Kless, Shlomo: 'The Rescue of Jewish Children in Belgium During the Holocaust', *Holocaust and Genocide Studies*, volume 3, number 3, Oxford 1988.

Knightley, Phillip: *The Second Oldest Profession, The Spy as Bureaucrat, Patriot, Fantasist and Whore*, London 1986.

Knott, Richard C.: *Black Cat Raiders of WWII*, New York 1981.

Knox, MacGregor: *Mussolini Unleashed,*

*1939–1941, Politics and Strategy in Fascist Italy's Last War*, Cambridge 1982.

Koch, H. W.: *The Hitler Youth, Origins and Development 1922–45*, New York 1976.

Kochan, Miriam: *Britain's Internees in the Second World War*, London 1983.

Koliopoulos, John S.: *Greece and the British Connection 1935–1941*, Oxford 1977.

Konev, I.: *Year of Victory*, Moscow 1969.

Krakowski, Shmuel: *The War of the Doomed, Jewish Armed Resistance in Poland, 1942–1944*, New York 1984.

Kulka, Erich: *Escape from Auschwitz*, South Hadley, Massachusetts 1986.

Laffin, John: *Brassey's Battles, 3,500 Years of Conflict, Campaigns and Wars from A–Z*, London 1986.

Lanzmann, Claude: *Shoah, An Oral History of the Holocaust*, New York 1985.

Laqueur, Walter, and Breitman, Richard: *Breaking the Silence*, New York 1986.

Leach, Barry A.: *German Strategy Against Russia 1939–1941*, Oxford 1973.

Le Chêne, Evelyn: *Mauthausen, the History of a Death Camp*, London 1971.

Leiser, Erwin: *Nazi Cinema*, London 1974.

Leonard, Charles J.: 'Okinawa', *After the Battle*, Number 43, London 1984.

Le Tissier, Tony: *The Battle of Berlin*, London 1988.

Levi, Primo: *Survival in Auschwitz*, New York 1959.

Levin, Nora: *The Holocaust, the Destruction of European Jewry 1933–1945*, New York 1968.

Lewis, Laurence: *Echoes of Resistance, British Involvement with the Italian Partisans*, Tunbridge Wells, Kent, 1985.

Liddell Hart, B. H. (editor): *The Rommel Papers*, London 1953.

Lifton, Robert Jay: *The Nazi Doctors, Medical Killing and the Psychology of Genocide*, New York 1986.

Lindsay, Captain Martin, and Johnston, Captain M. E.: *History of 7th Armoured Division, June 1943–July 1945*, Germany, September 1945.

Littlejohn, David: *Foreign Legions of the Third Reich, volume 2, Belgium, Great Britain, Holland, Italy and Spain*, San Jose, California, 1981.

Littman, Sol: *War Criminal on Trial, The Rauca Case*, Toronto 1983.

Lochner, Louis P. (editor): *The Goebbels Diaries*, London 1948.

Lockwood, Douglas: *Australia's Pearl Harbor, Darwin 1942*, Melbourne 1966.

Longhurst, Henry: *Adventure in Oil, the Story of British Petroleum*, London 1959.

Longmate, Norman: *The Doodlebugs, The Story of the Flying Bombs*, London 1981.

Longmate, Norman: *The Bombers, The RAF Offensive Against Germany 1939–1945*, London 1983.

Longmate, Norman: *Hitler's Rockets, The Story of the V-2s*, London 1985.

Lucas Phillips, C. E.: *Victoria Cross Battles of the Second World War*, London 1973.

Lund, Paul, and Ludlam, Harry: *PQ 17, Convoy to Hell, the Survivors' Story*, London 1968.

Macdonald, John: *Great Battles of World War II*, London 1986.

Macdonald, J. F.: *The War History of Southern Rhodesia*, 2 volumes, Salisbury, Southern Rhodesia, 1947 and 1950.

Macintyre, Donald: *The Battle of the Atlantic*, London 1961.

Macintyre, Donald: *The Battle for the Pacific*, London 1966.

McKee, Alexander: *Caen, Anvil of Victory*, London 1984.

Mackenzie, Compton: *Mr Roosevelt*, London 1943.

MacLaren, Roy: *Canadians Behind Enemy Lines 1939–1945*, Vancouver 1981.

Maclean, Fitzroy: *Disputed Barricade, The Life and Times of Josip Broz-Tito, Marshal of Yugoslavia*, London 1957.

Mack, Joanna, and Humphries, Steve: *The Making of Modern London 1939–1945, London at War*, London 1985.

Madeja, W. Victor: *The Russo-German War, Summer–Autumn 1943*, Allentown, Pennsylvania, 1987.

Manchester, William: *The Arms of Krupp, 1587–1968*, Boston 1964.

Manchester, William: *American Caesar, Douglas MacArthur, 1880–1964*, London 1979.

Manchester, William: *Goodbye, Darkness,*

*A Memoir of the Pacific War*, New York 1979.

Manning, Paul: *Hirohito, The War Years*, New York 1986.

Manstein, Field-Marshal Erich von: *Lost Victories*, London 1958.

Manus, Ukachukwu Chris: 'Roman Catholicism and the Nazis, A Review of the Attitude of the Church during the Persecutions of the Jews in Hitler's Europe', *Remembering for the Future, Jews and Christians During and After the Holocaust*, Oxford 1988.

Manvell, Roger, and Fraenkel, Heinrich: *The Canaris Conspiracy, The Secret Resistance to Hitler in the German Army*, London 1969.

Maresch, Boguslaw (editor): *Stutthof Historic Guide*, Gdansk 1980.

Margry, Karel: 'The Ambushing of SS-General Hanns Rauter', *After the Battle*, Number 56, London 1987.

Marrus, Michael R., and Paxton, Robert O.: *Vichy France and the Jews*, New York 1981.

Martin, Lieutenant-General H. J., and Orpen, Colonel Neil D.: *Eagles Victorious, The Operations of the South African Forces over the Mediterranean and Europe, in Italy, the Balkans and the Aegean, and from Gibraltar and West Africa*, Cape Town 1977.

Martin, Ralph: *World War II, A Photographic Record of the War in the Pacific, From Pearl Harbor to V-J Day*, Greenwich, Connecticut, 1955.

Martin, Ralph G.: *The G.I. War, 1941–1945*, Boston 1967.

Maser, Werner (editor): *Hitler's Letters and Notes*, London 1974.

Mason, John T., Jr., (Editor): *The Pacific War Remembered, An Oral History Collection*, Annapolis, Maryland, 1986.

Masterman J. C.: *The Double-Cross System In the War of 1939 to 1945*, London 1972.

Matsas, Joseph: *The Participation of the Greek Jews in the National Resistance (1940–1944)*, Janina 1982.

Mayer, S. L. (editor): *The Japanese War Machine*, London 1976.

Mead, Peter: *Orde Wingate and the historians*, Braunton, Devon, 1987.

Messenger, Charles: *The Commandos, 1940–1946*, London 1985.

Messenger, Charles: *Hitler's Gladiator, The Life and Times of Oberstgruppenführer and Panzergeneral-Oberst der Waffen-SS Sepp Dietrich*, London 1988.

Michelis, Meir: *Mussolini and the Jews, German–Italian Relations and the Jewish Question in Italy*, Oxford 1978.

Middlebrook, Martin: *The Nuremberg Raid 30–31 March 1944*, London 1973.

Middlebrook, Martin: *The Peenemünde Raid, The Night of 17–18 August 1943*, London 1982.

Middlebrook, Martin: *The Schweinfurt-Regensburg Mission, American Raids on 17 August 1943*, London 1983.

Middlebrook, Martin: *The Berlin Raids, RAF Bomber Command, Winter, 1943–44*, London 1988.

Milazzo, Matteo J.: *The Chetnik Movement and the Yugoslav Resistance*, Baltimore 1975.

Military Intelligence Division, US War Department: *German Military Intelligence, 1939–1945*, Frederick, Maryland, 1984.

Millar, George: *The Bruneval Raid, Flashpoint of the Radar War*, London 1974.

Miller, John, Jr.: *United States Army in World War II, The War in the Pacific, Guadalcanal, The First Offensive*, Washington D.C. 1949.

Mills, Walter: *This Is Pearl! The United States and Japan, 1941*, New York 1947.

Ministry of Information: *Front Line, 1940–41, The Official Story of the Civil Defence of Britain*, London 1942.

Ministry of Information: *The Campaign in Greece and Crete*, London 1942.

Ministry of National Defence: *The Canadians in Britain 1939–1944*, Ottawa 1945.

Mitcham, Samuel W., Jr.: *Hitler's Field Marshals and their Battles*, London 1988.

Mocq, Dr Jean-Marie: *Ascq 1944, La Nuit La Plus Longue*, Lille 1984.

Modelski, Tadeusz: *The Polish Contribution to the Ultimate Allied Victory in the Second World War*, Worthing, Sussex, 1986.

Molho, Michael: *In Memoriam, Hommage*

*aux Victimes Juives des Nazis en Grèce*, Salonica 1973.

Mollo, Andrew: 'Dachau', *After the Battle*, Number 27, London 1980.

Molony, Brigadier C. J. C.: *The Mediterranean and Middle East, Volume V, The Campaign in Sicily 1943 and the Campaign in Italy, 3rd September 1943 to 31st March 1944*, London 1973.

Molony, Brigadier C. J. C.: *The Mediterranean and Middle East, Volume VI, Victory in the Mediterranean*, London 1984.

Morgan-Witts, Max, and Thomas, Gordon: *Ruin from the Air, The Atomic Mission to Hiroshima*, London 1977.

Morison, Samuel Eliot: *History of United States Naval Operations in World War II*, volumes 1–15, London 1948–1962.

Morton, Louis: *United States Army in World War II, The War in the Pacific, The Fall of the Philippines*, Washington D.C. 1968.

Moss, Norman: *Klaus Fuchs, The Man who Stole the Atom Bomb*, London 1987.

Mrazek, James E.: *The Fall of Eben Emael, Prelude to Dunkirk*, London 1972.

Mueller, Ralph, and Turk, Jerry: *Report After Action, The Story of the 103$^D$ Infantry Division*, Innsbruck 1945.

Muggeridge, Malcolm (editor): *Ciano's Diary 1939–1945*, London 1947.

Müller-Hill, Benno: *Murderous Science, Elimination by scientific selection of Jews, Gypsies, and others, Germany 1933–1945*, Oxford 1988.

Neave, Airey: *Saturday at M.I.9, A history of underground escape lines in North West Europe in 1940–5 by a leading organiser at M.I.9*, London 1969.

Nichols, David (editor): *Ernie's War, The Best of Ernie Pyle's World War II Dispatches*, New York 1986.

North, John: *N-W Europe 1944–5, The Achievement of 21st Army Group*, London 1953.

Novitch, Miriam: *Sobibor, Martyrdom and Revolt, Documents and Testimonies*, New York 1980.

Nussbaum, Chaim: *Chaplain On The River Kwai, Story of a Prisoner of War*, New York 1988.

Pabst, Helmut: *The Outermost Frontier, A German Soldier in the Russian Campaign*, London 1986.

Padfield, Peter: *Dönitz, The Last Führer*, London 1984.

Pallud, Jean Paul: 'SDE Operation Pimento', *After the Battle*, Number 26, London 1979.

Pallud, Jean Paul: 'Budapest', *After the Battle*, Number 40, London 1983.

Pallud, Jean Paul: 'Operation Merkur, The German Invasion of Crete', *After the Battle*, Number 47, London 1985.

Papagos, General Alexander: *The Battle of Greece 1940–1941*, Athens 1949.

Parton, James: *'Air Force Spoken Here', General Ira Eaker and the Command of the Air*, Bethesda, Maryland, 1986.

Pavlov, Dmitri, V.: *Leningrad 1941, The Blockade*, Chicago 1965.

Pedersen, Bent: 'The Aarhus Attack', *After the Battle*, Number 54, London 1986.

Perrault, Gilles: *The Red Orchestra*, London 1968.

Phayer, Michael: 'Margarete Sommer, Berlin Catholics, and Germany's Jews 1939–1945', *Remembering for the Future, Jews and Christians During and After the Holocaust*, Oxford 1988.

Plant, Richard: *The Pink Triangle, The Nazi War Against Homosexuals*, New York 1986.

Playfair, Major-General I. S. O.: *The Mediterranean and Middle East, Volume I, The Early Successes against Italy (to May 1941)*, London 1954.

Playfair, Major-General I. S. O.: *The Mediterranean and Middle East, Volume II, 'The Germans come to the Help of their Ally' (1941)*, London 1956.

Pogue, Forrest C.: *George C. Marshall, Ordeal and Hope, 1939–1942*, London 1968.

Polish Air Force Association: *Destiny Can Wait, The Polish Air Force in the Second World War*, London 1949.

Polish Ministry of Information: *The German New Order in Poland*, London 1941.

Porter, Cathy, and Jones, Mark: *Moscow in World War II*, London 1987.

Posner, Gerald L., and Ware, John: *Mengele, The Complete Story*, London 1986.

Presser, Jacob: *The Destruction of the Dutch Jews*, New York 1969.

Price, Billy F.: *Adolf Hitler, The Unknown Artist*, Houston, Texas, 1984.

Prittie, The Hon. T. C. F., and Edwards, Captain W. Earle: *South to Freedom, A Record of Escape*, London 1946.

Pryce-Jones, David: *Paris in the Third Reich, A History of the German Occupation, 1940–1944*, New York 1981.

Putney, Diane T. (editor): *ULTRA and the Army Air Forces in World War II*, Washington DC 1987.

Puvogel, Ulrike: *Gedenkstätten für die Opfer des Nationalsozialismus, Eine Dokumentation*, Bonn 1987.

Quigley, Harold S.: *Far Eastern War 1937–1941*, Boston 1942.

Raiber, Dr R.: 'The Führerhauptquartiere', *After the Battle*, Number 19, London 1977.

Ramsey, Winston G.: 'Normandy 1944–1973', *After the Battle*, Number 1, London 1973.

Ramsey, Winston G.: 'Arnhem', *After the Battle*, Number 2, London 1973.

Ramsey, Winston G.: 'The Battle of the Bulge', *After the Battle*, Number 4, London 1973.

Ramsey, Winston G.: 'Eben-Emael', *After the Battle*, Number 5, London 1974.

Ramsey, Winston G.: 'German spies in Britain', *After the Battle*, Number 11, London 1976.

Ramsey, Winston G.: 'Crossing the Rhine', *After the Battle*, Number 16, London 1977.

Ramsey, Winston G.: 'The Assassination of Reinhard Heydrich', *After the Battle*, Number 24, London 1979.

Ramsey, Winston G.: 'The Lady be Good', *After the Battle*, Number 25, London 1979.

Ramsey, Winston G.: 'Christmas Eve 1944, Massacre at Bande', *After the Battle*, Number 30, London 1980.

Ramsey, Winston G.: 'The Execution of Eddie Slovik', *After the Battle*, Number 32, London 1981.

Ramsey, Winston G.: 'St Malo 1944', *After the Battle*, Number 33, London 1981.

Ramsey, Winston G.: 'Germany Surrenders', *After the Battle*, Number 48, London 1985.

Ramsey, Winston G.: 'Europe's Last VC', *After the Battle*, Number 49, London 1985.

Ramsey, Winston G.: 'The Rüsselheim Death March', *After the Battle*, Number 57, London 1987.

Rashke, Richard: *Escape from Sobibor*, Boston 1982.

Rautkallio, Hannu: *Finland and the Holocaust, The Rescue of Finland's Jews*, New York 1987.

Ready, J. Lee: *The Forgotten Axis, Germany's Partners and Foreign Volunteers in World War II*, Jefferson, North Carolina, 1987.

Reed, John: 'Operation Jericho, The Amiens Raid', *After the Battle*, Number 28, London 1980.

Reed, John: 'The Cross-Channel Guns', *After the Battle*, Number 29, London 1980.

Reed, John: 'Assault on Walcheren, Operation Infatuate', *After the Battle*, Number 36, London 1982.

Reitlinger, Gerald: *The Final Solution, The Attempt to Exterminate the Jews of Europe 1939–45*, London 1953.

Rely, Achiel: 'Disaster at Antwerp, April 5, 1943', *After the Battle*, Number 42, London 1983.

Rely, Achiel: 'The Notorious Fort Breendonk', *After the Battle*, Number 51, London 1986.

Reynaud, Paul: *In the Thick of the Fight 1930–1945*, London 1955.

Rhodes, Richard: *The Making of the Atomic Bomb*, New York 1988.

Richards, Denis: *Royal Air Force 1939–1945, The Fight at Odds 1939–1941*, London 1953.

Richards, Denis, and Saunders, Hilary St. George: *Royal Air Force 1939–1945, The Fight Avails 1941–1943*, London 1954.

Rings, Werner: *Life with the Enemy, Collaboration and Resistance in Hitler's Europe, 1939–1945*, New York 1982.

Robertson, John: *Australia at War 1939–1945*, Melbourne 1981.

Robinson, Nehemiah: *Indemnification and Reparations, Jewish Aspects*, New York 1944.

Rohwer, Jürgen: *Axis Submarine Successes 1939–1945*, Cambridge 1983.

Rolf, David: *Prisoners of the Reich, Germany's Captives 1939–1945*, London 1988.

Romanus, Charles F., and Sunderland, Riley: *United States Army in World War II, China–Burma–India Theater, Stillwell's Mission to China*, Washington D.C. 1966.

Roskill, Captain S. W.: *The War at Sea 1939–1945*, 3 volumes, 1959–61.

Rowe, Vivian: *The Great Wall of France, The Triumph of the Maginot Line*, London 1959.

Royal Institute of International Affairs: *Chronology of the Second World War*, London 1947.

Rubenstein, Philip (editor): *Report on the entry of Nazi war criminals and collaborators into the UK 1945–1950*, London 1988.

Ruby, Marcel: *F Section SOE, The Buckmaster Networks*, London 1988.

Russell of Liverpool, Lord: *The Scourge of the Swastika, A Short History of Nazi War Crimes*, London 1954.

Russell of Liverpool, Lord: *The Knights of the Bushido, A Short History of Japanese War Crimes*, London 1958.

Salisbury, Harrison E.: *The 900 Days, The Siege of Leningrad*, London 1986.

Salmaggi, Cesare, and Pallavisini, Alfredo: *2194 Days of War, An illustrated chronology of the Second World War*, London 1979.

Saunders, Andy: 'The Last Flight of the only Battle of Britain VC', *After the Battle*, Number 30, London 1980.

Saunders, Hilary St George: *Combined Operations, The Official Story of the Commandos*, New York 1943.

Saunders, Hilary St George: *Royal Air Force 1939–1945, The Fight is Won*, London 1954.

Sawyer, L. A., and Mitchell, W. H.: *The Liberty Ships, The History of the 'Emergency' type Cargo ships constructed in the United States during the Second World War*, London 1980.

Schäfer, Ernst (editor): *Ravensbrück*, Berlin 1960.

Schmidt, Maria: 'Margit Slachta's Activities in Support of Slovakian Jewry 1942–43', *Remembering for the Future, Jews and Christians During and After the Holocaust*, Oxford 1988.

Schneider, Gertrude: *Journey into Terror, Story of the Riga Ghetto*, New York 1979.

Schneider, Gertrude (editor): *Muted Voices, Jewish Survivors of Latvia Remember*, New York 1987.

Schofield B. B.: *The Russian Convoys*, London 1964.

Schwarberg, Günther: *The Murders at Bullenhuser Damm, The SS Doctors and the Children*, Bloomington, Indiana, 1984.

Scutts, Jerry: *Lion in the Sky, US 8th Air Force Fighter Operations 1942–45*, Wellingborough, Northamptonshire, 1987.

Selwyn, Francis: *Hitler's Englishman, The Crime of 'Lord Haw-Haw'*, London 1987.

Seth, Ronald: *Jackals of the Reich, The Story of the British Free Corps*, London 1982.

Sevillias, Errikos: *Athens – Auschwitz*, Athens 1983.

Sharipov, Akram: *War Heroes, Stories about the heroism of Soviet soldiers 1941–1945*, Moscow 1984.

Sharp, Tony: *The Wartime Alliance and the Zonal Division of Germany*, Oxford 1975.

Shelah, M.: 'The Catholic Church in Croatia, the Vatican and the Murder of the Croatian Jews', *Remembering for the Future, Jews and Christians During and After the Holocaust*, Oxford 1988.

Sherwood, John M.: *Georges Mandel and the Third Republic*, Stanford, California, 1970.

Sherwood, Robert E.: *The White House Papers of Harry L. Hopkins*, 2 volumes, London 1948, 1949.

Shirer, William L.: *Berlin Diary, The Journal of a Foreign Correspondent 1934–1941*, London 1941.

Shirer, William L.: *The Rise and Fall of the Third Reich, A History of Nazi Germany*, London 1960.

Shores, Christopher, and Cull, Brian, with Malizia, Nicola: *Air War for Yugoslavia, Greece and Crete 1940–41*, London 1987.

Shortal, John F.: *Forged by Fire, General Robert L. Eichelberger and the Pacific War*, Columbia, South Carolina, 1987.

Simpson, Christopher: *Blowback, U.S. Recruitment of Nazis and Its Effects on the Cold War*, New York 1988.

Slim, Field Marshal Sir William: *Defeat into Victory*, London 1956.

Sloan, Jacob (editor): *Notes from the Warsaw Ghetto, the Journal of Emanuel Ringelblum*, New York 1958.

Slowe, Peter, and Woods, Richard: *Battlefield Berlin, Siege, Surrender and Occupation, 1945*, London 1988.

Smolen, Kazimierz (Editor): *From the History of KL Auschwitz*, Oswiecim 1967.

Smolen, Kazimierz (editor): *KL Auschwitz seen by the SS*, Oswiecim 1978.

Snyder, Louis L.: *Encyclopedia of the Third Reich*, London 1976.

Snydor, Charles W., Jr.: *Soldiers of Destruction, The SS Death's Head Division 1933–1945*, Princeton, New Jersey, 1977.

Solovyov, Boris: *The Battle on the Kursk Salient (The Crushing of Operation Citadel)*, Moscow 1979.

Spaight, J. M.: *The Battle of Britain 1940*, London 1941.

Spector, Ronald H.: *Eagle Against the Sun, The American War with Japan*, New York 1984.

Speer, Albert: *Inside the Third Reich*, London 1970.

Stacey, Colonel C. P.: *The Canadian Army 1939–1945, An Official Historical Summary*, Ottawa 1948.

Stein, George H.: *The Waffen SS, Hitler's Elite Guard at War 1939–1945*, London 1966.

Steinberg, Lucien: *Not as a Lamb, the Jews against Hitler*, Glasgow 1974.

Stewart, Adrian: *Guadalcanal, World War II's Fiercest Naval Campaign*, London 1985.

Stewart, I. McD. G.: *The Struggle for Crete 20 May–1 June 1941, A Story of Lost Opportunity*, London 1966.

Strong, Major-General Sir Kenneth: *Intelligence at the Top, The Recollections of an Intelligence Officer*, London 1968.

Swinson, Arthur: *Kohima*, London 1966.

Szajkowski, Zosa (editor): *Analytical Franco-Jewish Gazeteer 1939–1945*, New York 1966.

Taylor, Fred (Editor): *The Goebbels Diaries 1939–1941*, London 1982.

Taylor, James, and Shaw, Warren (editors): *A Dictionary of the Third Reich*, London 1987.

Taylor, Telford: *The Breaking Wave, The German Defeat in the Summer of 1940*, London 1967.

Tec, Nechama: *When Light Pierced the Darkness, Christian Rescue of Jews in Nazi-Occupied Poland*, New York 1986.

Tennyson Jesse F., and Harwood, H. M.: *London Front, Letters written to America, August 1939–July 1940*, London 1940.

Terraine, John: *The Right of the Line, The Royal Air Force in the European War 1939–1945*, London 1985.

Thomas, David A.: *Battle of the Java Sea*, London 1968.

Thomas, David A.: *Nazi Victory in Crete 1941*, New York 1973.

Thomas, Nigel, and Abbott, Peter: *Partisan Warfare 1940–45*, London 1985.

Thorne, Christopher: *The Far Eastern War, States and Societies, 1941–1945*, London 1986.

Tillion, Germaine: *Ravensbrück*, Garden City, New York, 1975.

Toland, John: *Adolf Hitler*, New York 1976.

Toynbee, Arnold, and Toynbee, Veronica M. (editors): *The Initial Triumph of the Axis*, London 1958.

Tregenza, Michael: 'Belzec Death Camp', *The Wiener Library Bulletin*, volume 30, London 1977.

Tremlett, P. E. (editor): *Thomas Cook Overseas Timetable*, London, November–December 1988.

Trepper, Leopold: *The Great Game, The Story of the Red Orchestra*, London 1977.

Trevor-Roper, H. R.: *The Last Days of Hitler*, London 1947.

Trevor-Roper, Hugh R. (editor): *Hitler's Table-Talk, 1941–1944*, London 1953.

Trevor-Roper, H. R. (editor): *Hitler's War Directives 1939–1945*, London 1964.

Trunk, Isaiah: *Jewish Responses to Nazi Persecution, Collective and Individual Behavior in Extremis*, New York 1979.

Tusa, Ann, and Tusa, John: *The Nuremberg Trial*, London 1983.

Tyrnauer, Gabrielle: *Gypsies and the Holocaust, A Bibliography and Introductory Essay*, Montreal 1989.

United Nations Relief and Rehabilitation Administration: *Death Marches (Marches de la Mort), Routes and Distances*, Central Tracing Bureau, 28 May 1946.

United States Strategic Bombing Survey: *The Effects of the Atomic Bomb on Hiroshima, Japan*, Washington DC 1947.


Verity, Hugh: *We Landed by Moonlight, Secret RAF Landings in France 1940–1944*, Shepperton, Surrey, 1978.

Voronkov, Nikolai: *900 Days – the Siege of Leningrad*, Moscow 1982.

Vrba, Rudolf, and Bestic, Alan: *I Cannot Forgive*, London 1963.


Warhaftig, Zorach: *Uprooted, Jewish Refugees and Displaced Persons After Liberation*, New York 1946.

Warlimont, Walter: *Inside Hitler's Headquarters 1939–45*, London 1964.

Warmbrunn, Werner: *The Dutch under German Occupation 1940–1945*, Stanford, California, 1963.

Warner, Geoffrey: *Iraq and Syria 1941*, 1974.

Warner, Philip: *The Secret Forces of World War II*, London 1985.

Warner, Lavinia, and Sandilands, John: *Women Beyond the Wire, A Story of Prisoners of the Japanese 1942–45*, London 1982.

Watson, Betty: *Miracle in Hellas, The Greeks Fight On*, London 1943.

Watts, Franklin (editor): *Voices of 1942–43, Speeches and Papers of Roosevelt, Churchill, Stalin, Chiang, Hitler and other leaders, Delivered During 1942*, New York 1943.

Webster, Sir Charles, and Frankland, Noble: *The Strategic Air Offensive Against Germany, 1939–1945*, volumes 1–4, London 1961.

Werth, Alexander: *The Last Days of Paris, A journalist's Diary*, London 1940.

Werth, Alexander: *Moscow '41*, London 1942.

Werth, Alexander: *Leningrad*, London 1944.

Werth, Alexander: *The Year of Stalingrad, An Historical Record and a Study of Russian Mentality, Methods and Policies*, London 1946.

Werth, Alexander: *Russia at War 1941–1945*, London 1964.

West, Nigel: *MI5, British Security Service Operations 1909–1945*, London 1981.

West, Nigel: *MI6, British Secret Intelligence Service Operations 1909–45*, London 1983.

West, Nigel: *GCHQ, The Secret Wireless War 1900–86*, London 1987.

Wheeler, Harold: *The People's History of the Second World War September 1939–December 1940*, London 1941.

Wheeler, Richard: *Iwo*, New York 1980.

Wheeler-Bennett, John W.: *King George VI, His Life and Reign*, London 1958.

Whiting, Charles: *Massacre at Malmédy, The Story of Jochen Peiper's Battle Group Ardennes, December 1944*, London 1971.

Willis, John: *Churchill's Few, The Battle of Britain Remembered*, New York 1987.

Willoughby, Major General Charles A.: *Sorge, Soviet Master Spy*, London 1952.

Willoughby, Major-General Charles A., and Chamberlain, John: *MacArthur 1941–1951, Victory in the Pacific*, London 1956.

Wills, Henry: 'British Invasion Defences', *After the Battle*, Number 14, London 1976.

Wilmot, Chester: *The Struggle for Europe*, London 1952.

Winant, John G.: *A Letter from Grosvenor Square, An Account of a Stewardship*, London 1947.

Winn, Godfrey: *'P.Q.17'*, London 1947.

Winton, John: *Ultra at Sea*, London 1988.

Wiskemann, Elizabeth: *Europe of the Dictators 1919–1945*, London 1966.

Wistrich, Robert: *Who's Who in Nazi Germany*, London 1982.

Woodward, Sir Llewellyn: *British Foreign Policy in the Second World War*, London 1962.

Worm-Muller, Professor Jacob: *Norway's Revolt Against Nazism*, London 1941.


Yeremyev, Leonid: *USSR in World War Two, Through the Eyes of Friends and Foes*, Moscow 1985.

Yerger, Mark C.: *Otto Weidinger, Knights Cross With Oak Leaves and Swords*, Winnipeg, Manitoba, 1987.


Zawodny, J. K.: *Nothing but Honour, The*

*Story of the Warsaw Uprising, 1944*, London 1978.

Zee, Henri A. van der: *The Hunger Winter, Occupied Holland 1944–5*, London 1982.

Zevin, B. D. (editor): *Nothing to Fear, The Selected Addresses of Franklin Delano Roosevelt 1932–1945*, London 1947.

Zhukov, Marshal of the Soviet Union G.: *Reminiscences and Reflections*, 2 volumes, Moscow 1985.

Ziegler, Philip: *Mountbatten*, London 1985.

Zuccotti, Susan: *The Italians and the Holocaust, Persecution, Rescue and Survival*, London 1987.

# Regional Maps

1 **Germany**

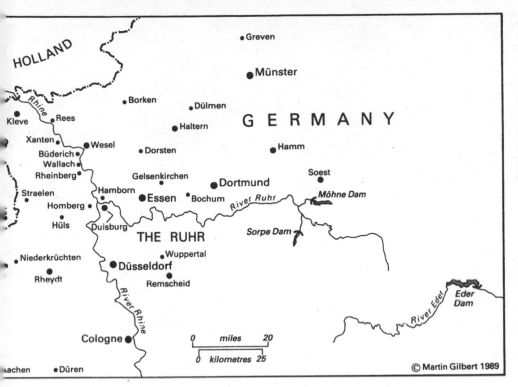

2 The Ruhr

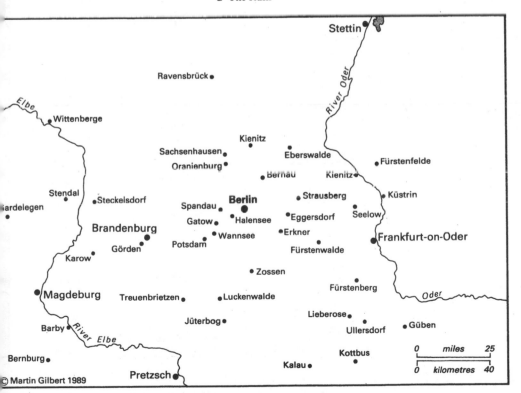

3 Germany from the Elbe to the Oder

4 Eastern Germany, East Prussia, Poland and the Baltic States

FINLAND

Helsinki
Viipuri
Lake
Onega
Lake
Ladoga
Petrozavodsk
Vytegra
Gulf of Finland
Tallinn
Lagedi
Klooga
Narva
KRONSTADT
Leningrad
Schlüsselburg
Volkhov
Tikhvin
Vologda
Luga
Novgorod
Pskov
Dno
Staraya Russa
Lake Ilmen
Kholm
Kalinin
Yaroslavl
Kostroma
River Volga
Dvinsk
Sebezh
Velikiye
Luki
Rzhev
Klin
Zagorsk
Gorky
Kazan
Drissa
Polotsk
Nevel
Mozhaisk
WHITE
Lepel
Vitebsk
Vyazma
Moscow
Smolensk
Dorogobuzh
Kolomna
RUSSIA
Minsk
Orsha
Ryazan
Maly
Trostenets
Mogilev
Roslavl
Kaluga
Shilovo
Kuibyshev
Rogachev
Bryansk
Tula
SOVIET  UNION
Slutsk
Bobruisk
Klintsy
Orel
Mozyr
Gomel
Yelets
Olevsk
Korosten
Chernigov
Lgov
Kursk
Voronezh
Saratov
Marxstadt
Engels
Zhitomir
UKRAINE
Stary Oksyol
Strassburg
Kiev
Belgorod
Rossosh
Berdichev
Kharkov
Vinnitsa
Poltava
River Don
Uman
River Dnieper
Kremenchug
Izyum
River Dniester
Dneprodzerzhinsk
River Donetz
Kalach
Stalingrad
Balta
Dnepropetrovsk
Igren
Stalino
River Volga
Krivoi Rog
Zaporozhe
Taganrog
Kotelnikovo
Kishinev
Odessa
Nikolayev
Mariupol
Rostov- on-Don
Astrakhan
Kherson
Berdyansk
Yeisk
Salsk
Elista
Sea of
Azov
KALMYK
Izmail
Perekop
Kerch
Kropotkin
Simferopol
Krasnodar
Stavropol
Caspian
Sevastopol
Feodosiya
Armavir
TEREK
Yalta
Novorossiisk
Maikop
Kislovodsk
Mozdok
Sea
Tuapse
Caucasus
Nalchik
Grozny
Black  Sea
Sochi
Mountains
Makhach-Kala
Suchumi
Ordzhonikidze
GEORGIA
Batum
Tiflis
Baku
TURKEY
ARMENIA
© Martin Gilbert 1989
IRAN

NORTH SEA

GREAT BRITAIN

London

English Channel

HOLLAND

The Hague

GERMANY

Ostend
Dunkirk
Calais
Epercleques
Fives
Brussels
Antwerp
BELGIUM
Liège
Wimereux
Boulogne
Hardelot
Wizernes
Lille
Ascq
Namur
Dinant
Malmédy
LUX
Mondorf
Dieppe
Abbeville
Bastogne
Bruneval
Amiens
Cherbourg
Le Havre
Rouen
Beauvais
Compiègne
Soissons
Sedan
ALDERNEY
GUERNSEY
SARK
JERSEY
COTENTIN
Creil
La Roche Guyon
Reims
Verdun
Caen
Beg-an-Fry
CEZEMBRE
Port-en-Bessin
Granville
Falaise
Trappes
Fresnes
Paris
Melun
Provins
Châlons-
sur-Marne
Mailly-le-Camp
St Dizier
Metz
Spicheren
Strasbourg
Nancy
Natzweiler
Colmar
Brest
Plouha
St Malo
River Seine
Chartres
Etampes
Vittel
Rennes
Laval
Le Mans
Mazignen
Orléans
Montargis
Sens
Rosenau
Lorient
Montoire
Tours
Beaugency
Briare
Villaines
Belfort
Montbéliard
Nantes
Angers
Saumur
Chinon
FRANCE
Dijon
SWITZERLAND
St. Nazaire
Thouars
Châtellerault
Bourges
River Loire
Le Creusot
Salornay
Poitiers
Mâcon
Gex
Rhône
La Pallice
La Rochelle
Vichy
Riom
Oyonnax
Ambérieu
Annecy
Bay of
Biscay
Oradour-sur-
Glane
Clermont
Ferrand
Lyon
Blyes
Salon-la-Tour
Bar
AUVERGNE
River Rhône
VERCORS
Périgueux
Tulle
Brive
ITALY
Bergerac
Bordeaux
Eymet
Figeac
Peira Cava
Contes
Montauban
Nîmes
Avignon
Toulouse
Marseille
Toulon
Hendaye
Gurs
Bagnères de Bigorre
Perpignan
Gulf of Lions
Etang-du-Canet
Pyrenees
Mediterranean
Sea
SPAIN

0    miles    100
0    kilometres    150

© Martin Gilbert 1989

6 France

North Sea

TEXEL

• Leeuwarden

Assen •

• Westerbork

*Z u i d e r*
*Z e e*

• Hellendoorn

Ijmuiden
Overveen
Amsterdam
✈ Schiphol

• Deventer
• Apeldoorn

Enschede •

H O L L A N D

• Leiden

Utrecht •
Doorn • Wageningen
Arnhem • Rhoden

**The Hague**
• Delft

*River Rhine*

Rotterdam

*River Waal*
Nijmegen

*River Maas*

G E R M A N Y

*River Maas*

• Steenbergen  • Breda

• Eindhoven
Venlo •

*River Rhine*

*River Scheldt*

Antwerp
Fort Breendonk

*Maas*

Eik •

B E L G I U M

• Malines

Mechelen-sur-Meuse •

| 0 | miles | 20 |
| 0 | kilometres | 30 |

• Maastricht

© Martin Gilbert 1989

7 Holland

8 Great Britain

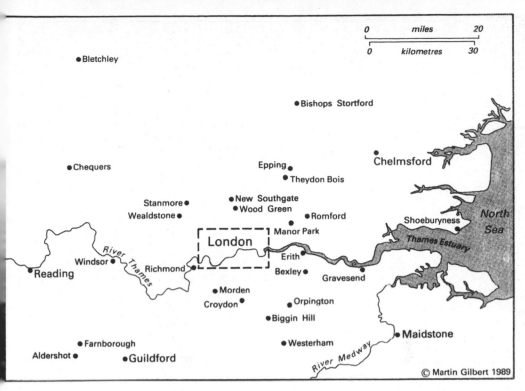

9 The Thames Valley

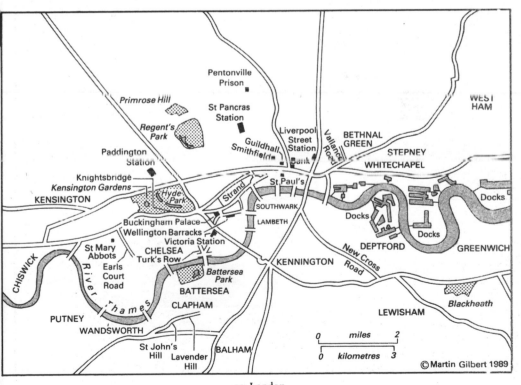

10 London

© Martin Gilbert 1989

11 Northern Italy

12 Austria, Slovakia, Hungary and Yugoslavia

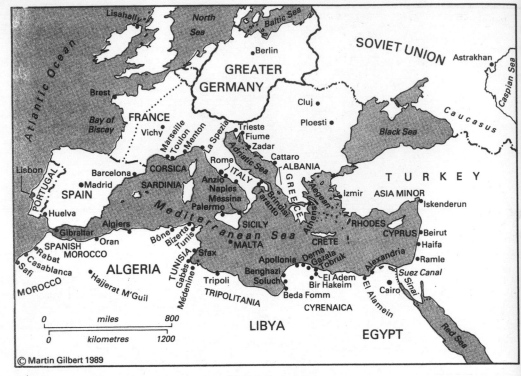

13 The Mediterranean

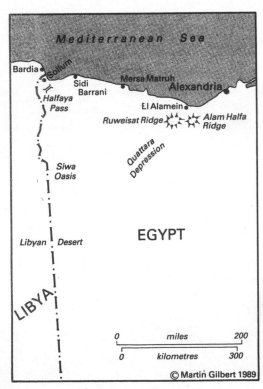

14 The Egyptian–Libyan border

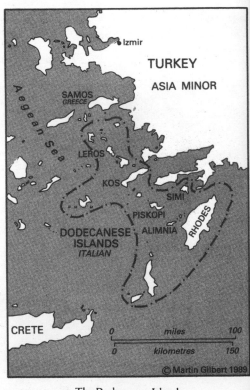

15 The Dodecanese Islands

16 Southern Yugoslavia, Bulgaria, Greece and Crete

17 Scandinavia and the Baltic

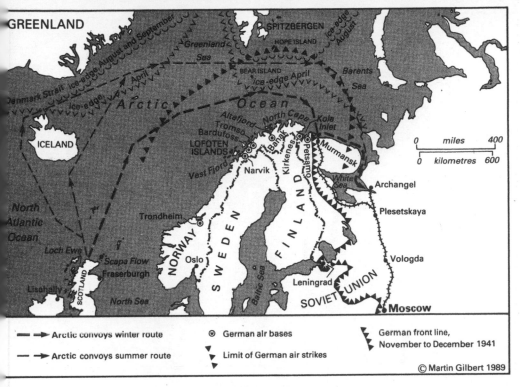

© Martin Gilbert 1989

18 The Arctic Convoys

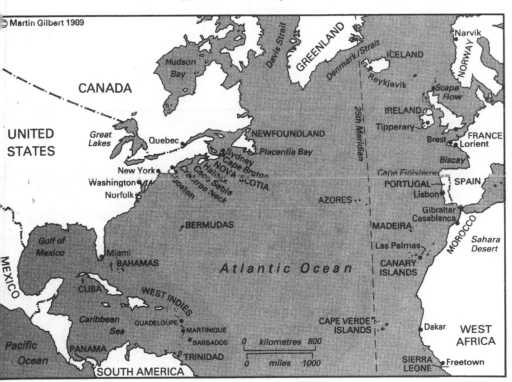

© Martin Gilbert 1989

19 The Atlantic Ocean

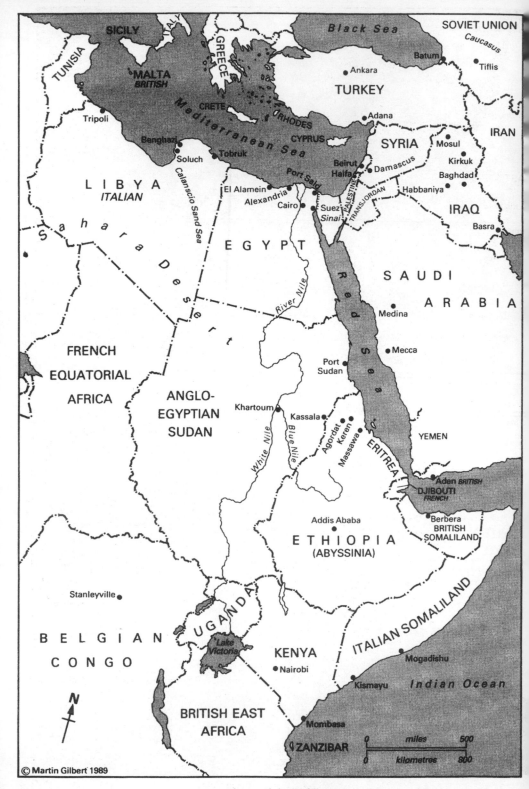

20 East Africa and the Middle East

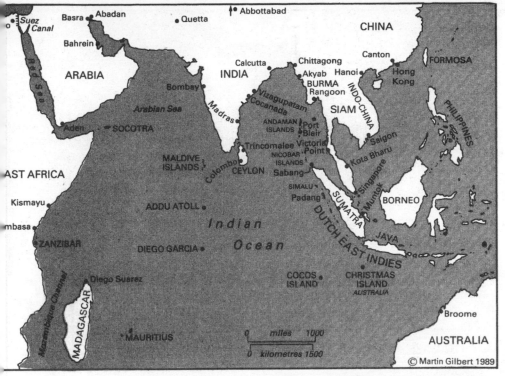

The following place names are visible on the first map:

Suez Canal, Basra, Abadan, Quetta, Abbottabad, Bahrein, CHINA, Calcutta, Chittagong, Canton, FORMOSA, ARABIA, INDIA, Akyab, Hanoi, Hong Kong, BURMA, Bombay, Vizagupatam, Rangoon, INDO-CHINA, Madras, Cocanada, SIAM, Aden, SOCOTRA, ANDAMAN ISLANDS, Port Blair, Saigon, Trincomalee, Victoria Point, NICOBAR ISLANDS, Kota Bharu, EAST AFRICA, MALDIVE ISLANDS, Colombo, CEYLON, Sabang, Singapore, Kismayu, SIMALU, Muntok, BORNEO, ADDU ATOLL, Padang, SUMATRA, mbasa, Arabian Sea, Red Sea, Mozambique Channel, ZANZIBAR, DIEGO GARCIA, Indian Ocean, DUTCH EAST INDIES, JAVA, Diego Suarez, COCOS ISLAND, CHRISTMAS ISLAND AUSTRALIA, Broome, MADAGASCAR, MAURITIUS, AUSTRALIA

miles 1000
kilometres 1500

© Martin Gilbert 1989

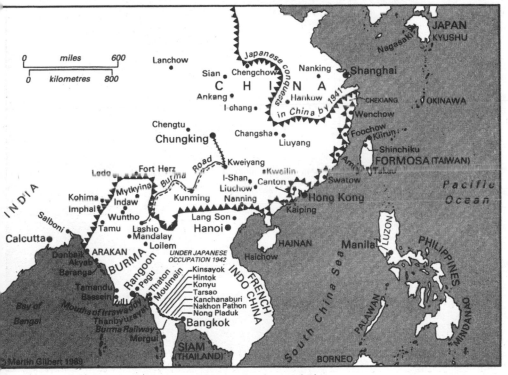

The following place names are visible on the second map:

JAPAN, KYUSHU, Lanchow, Nagasaki, Sian, Chengchow, Nanking, Shanghai, CHINA, Ankang, Hankow, CHEKIANG, OKINAWA, I-chang, Japanese conquests in China by 1941, Wenchow, Chengtu, Changsha, Foochow, Kiirun, Chungking, Liuyang, Shinchiku, FORMOSA (TAIWAN), Fort Herz, Kweiyang, Ledo, Burma Road, Kweilin, Kohima, Mytkyina, I-Shan, Canton, Swatow, Pacific Ocean, Indaw, Liuchow, INDIA, Imphal, Wuntho, Kunming, Nanning, Hong Kong, Tamu, Lashio, Lang Son, Kaiping, Calcutta, Salboni, Mandalay, Hanoi, HAINAN, Manila, LUZON, PHILIPPINES, Loilem, ARAKAN, BURMA, UNDER JAPANESE OCCUPATION 1942, Haichow, Donbaik, Akyab, Beranga, Rangoon, Pegu, Thaton, Moulmein, Kinsayok, Hintok, Konyu, Tarsao, Kanchanaburi, Nakhon Pathon, Nong Pladuk, FRENCH INDO-CHINA, Tamandu, Bassein, Mouths of Irrawaddy, Thanbyuzayat, Burma Railway, Bangkok, Mergui, SIAM (THAILAND), South China Sea, PALAWAN, MINDANAO, Bay of Bengal, BORNEO

miles 600
kilometres 800

© Martin Gilbert 1989

23 The Philippines and the Dutch East Indies

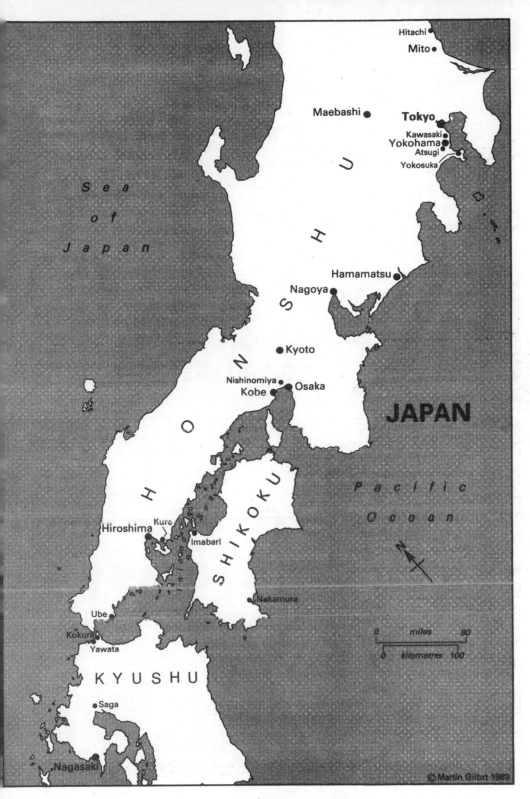

Hitachi
Mito

Maebashi
Tokyo
Kawasaki
Yokohama
Atsugi
Yokosuka

*S e a*

*o f*

*J a p a n*

H

O

N

S

H

U

Hamamatsu
Nagoya

Kyoto

Nishinomiya
Kobe
Osaka

**JAPAN**

*P a c i f i c*

*O c e a n*

N

Hiroshima
Kura
Imabari

S H I K O K U

Nakamura

Ube

Kokura
Yawata

**K Y U S H U**

Saga

Nagasaki

0        miles        80
0      kilometres     100

© Martin Gilbrt 1989

24  Japan

25 The United States

26 The Eastern Seaboard of the United States

27 The Pacific Ocean

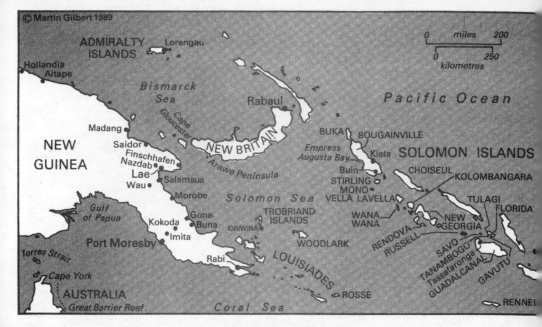

28 New Guinea and the Solomon Islands

# Index

*Compiled by the author*

'A4': the German rocket bomb, 333, 366–7

A5 (Belgian fishing vessel): at Dunkirk, 81

A-54: an Allied agent inside Germany, 25, 120

Aachen (Germany): encircled, 600; falls, 604, 606; Allies push eastward from, 613

Aarhus (Denmark): air attack on Gestapo headquarters at, 608, 610

Aaron Ward (US destroyer): sunk, 419

Aba (a British hospital ship): attacked, 184

Abadan (Iran): threat to oil at, 348

Abbeville (France): Germans reach, 69; British hold line near, 87

Abbottabad (India): a listening post, 429

Abdullah, Emir of Transjordan: and 'the end is sure', 378

Abemana Atoll (Gilbert Islands): attacked, 476

'Aberdeen' (Burma): landing at, 506

Abetz, Otto: in Paris, 144; at Rastenburg, 235

Abraham: God's promise to, 558

Abramescu, General: refused permission to withdraw, 574

Abusch, Walter: executed, 27

Acasta (British destroyer): sunk, 89

Achilles (British destroyer): sunk, 89

Adak (Aleutian Islands): American bombers attack from, 359–60

Adana (Turkey): Churchill's mission to, 517

Addis Ababa (Ethiopia): British advance to, 153; evacuated, 169; the Emperor returns to, 179

Addu Atoll (Maldive Islands): 314

Aden: bombed, 90

Adenauer, Dr Konrad: and reparations for Jews, 735; and the return of German prisoners-of-war in Russia, 738

Adlon Hotel (Berlin): and a British air raid, 128

Admiral Graf Spee (German pocket battleship): sinks a British merchant ship, 18; scuttled, 34

Admiral Hipper (German heavy cruiser): beaten off, 287

Admiral von Scheer (German pocket battleship): attacks a convoy, 138; in the Arctic, 340

Admiralty (Leningrad): spires of, 233

Admiralty Islands (Pacific): captured, 526

Adony (Hungary): Red Army occupies, 616

Adriatic Sea: and help for Yugoslav partisans, 451

Adventure (British destroyer): damaged, 29

Aegean Islands: Jews deported from, 406; and an escape line, 495–6; Germans trapped on, 584

Africa: 'will be defended' (Hitler), 419

Afridi (British destroyer): hit, 58

Aftermath, the: the 'ugly creatures' of, 730

Agordat (Eritrea): occupied, 155

Aha (Okinawa): Americas enter, 668

Aid to Russia Appeal: launched, 240

Air Medal (with Oak Leaf Clusters): awarded, 611

Air power: and 'poetic justice', 433; and 'a strange, stern justice', 500

Airedale (British destroyer): sunk, 333

Aisne River (France): battle on, 83, 86

Aitape (New Guinea): landings on, 519

Ajax (British destroyer): in action, 5, 34

Akagi (Japanese aircraft carrier): sunk, 330

Akulovo (near Moscow): Germans driven from, 267

Akyab (Burma): reconquest of, fails, 408

Alam Halfa (Western Desert): Rommel forced to withdraw from, 358

Alamogordo (New Mexico): an atomic bomb tested at, 704, 707

Albania: invasion of Greece from, 135; Greek troops advance into, 143, 148; an Italian counter-attack in, fails, 162; Italians advance from once more, 172–3; declares war on Russia, 207; resistance activity in, 489, 727; and an Allied deception plan, 494; partisans in, harass Germans, 594; Germans fall back from, 615; in the Soviet bloc, 723

Albert Canal (Belgium): attacked, 61

Albert H. Boe (US Liberty Ship): ready for sea, 725

Albert, Lucien: killed, 512

Alderney (Channel Islands): forced labourers on way from, drowned, 552

Aldershot (England): bombed, 108

Alekseyevka (Ukraine): a Jewish unit in action at, 407

Alençon (France): Free French troops reach, 567

Ålesund (Norway): plan to land at, 55; Norwegians arrested at, shot, 321

Aleutian Islands: landings on, 330; Japanese reinforcements to, intercepted, 415

Alexander Nevsky: an Order named after, 347

Alexander, General Sir Harold: at Dunkirk, 82, 83; at Rangoon, 306; falls back to India, 325; and El Alamein, 371; and Tunisia, 426–7; in Italy, 459, 509, 522–3, 549

Alexander, John: taken prisoner, 648

Alexander of Yugoslavia, King: and the Cetniks, 181

Alexandria (Egypt): French warships at, 109; British re-inforcements reach, 122, 143; Hitler's thoughts on, 135; a threat to, 145; an Italian manned-torpedo raid on, 280; British fall back towards, 336, 337; Rommel denied capture of, 341

Alexandrovka (Leningrad): captured, 233

Algeria: Allied landing on, in prospect, 347, 371, 374, 375; Rommel fails to regain border of, 402; used for British 'shuttle bombing' raids, 439

Algiers (Algeria): a secret landing at, 371; Allied forces disembark at, 376; a French warship reaches, 383; a manned-torpedo attack on, 385; a war crimes trial at, 505

Aliakhmon Line (Greece): Germans advance on, 173; Germans overrun, 174

Alimnia Island (Aegean Sea): commandos captured near, 514

Allen, Captain: shot, 78–9

Allenstein (East Prussia): acquired by Poland, 711

Allied Declaration (of 17 December 1942): and the fate of the Jews, 387

Altman, Mania: murdered, 669

Alor Star (Malaya): 249, 278

Alsace (France): Allies advance towards, 613

Altafjord (northern Norway): a German warship at, 340

Altenwalde (West Germany): a German rocket tested at, by the British, 724

'Altona': the code word to postpone 'Barbarossa', 192

Altmark (German auxiliary ship): boarded, 42

Aluminium: the search for, to make aircraft, 110

Alytus (Lithuania): battle at, 199

Amagi (Japanese aircraft carrier): sunk, 709

Amaquiri (Japanese destroyer): in action, 449

787

Ambérieu (France): sabotage at, 528
Amboina (Dutch East Indies): fate of prisoners-of-war on, 297
American-British-Conversations (ABC): held in Washington, 154; agreement reached during, 167
American Civil War: the first execution for desertion since, 636
American Rangers: participate in Dieppe raid, 353
American Red Cross: Roosevelt's appeal for, 76
*Amerika* (Hitler's train): 4, 133, 134, 147, 172, 279; damaged, 476–7
Amery, Julian: active behind German lines in Albania, 727
Amery, John: his trial and execution, 727
Amiens (France): Germans reach, 69; executions in, 499
Amsterdam (Holland): children flee, 67; strikes, and reprisals, in 158; an execution in, 160; Jews expelled into, 288; a bombing mission against, 425; a 'horrifying' scene in, reported to Hitler, 440; Anne Frank in, 516; Anne Frank deported from, 565; 'Death Candidates' in, 646
Anami, General: against surrender, 716; commits suicide, 717
Ancona (Italy): Jews of, warned in time, 466
Andalsnes (Norway): landing at, 55; withdrawal from, 57
Andaman Islands (Bay of Bengal): Japanese occupy, 312; a clandestine landing on, 394; Japanese on, surrender, 725
Anders, General Wladyslaw: describes a battlefield, 526
Anderson, Staff Sergeant Beaufort T.: his courage, 662
Andrew of Greece, Prince: 148, 166, 465
Andrew of Greece, Princess: hides Jews, 465
'Angel of Death': at Auschwitz, 432
Angelita (an Italian girl): at Anzio, 496
Angers (France): a clandestine landing near, 475; arrests near, 515
Anglo-Egyptian Sudan: Italians withdraw from, 153
Anglo-French Purchasing Board: set up in Washington, 25
'Anglo-French Union': proposal for, 97
Anglo-Soviet Treaty: signed, 327
Anguar Island (Palaus): fighting on, 605–6
Anin (Poland): hostages from, killed, 36
Annecy (France): an anti-Resistance attack near, 511
Anoya (Crete): and a reprisal action, 520
Anti-Comintern Pact: celebrated, in Berlin, 262
Antonescu, Marshal Ion: comes to power in Roumania, 124; warns Germany of Soviet preparations, 179; meets Hitler, 188; and Hitler's cook-housekeeper, 504; refuses a request to withdraw, 574; arrested, 574
Antonov, General: requests Anglo-American bombing support, 638; and the American-Soviet demarcation line, 680
Antwerp (Belgium): demolitions at, 67; falls to Germans, 68; a punishment

camp near, 127; bombing raid on, 418; liberated, 585; to be cut off, 585; 'Flying Bomb' attacks on, 601, 608, 613, 626; help for, 611–2; Hitler's plan to recapture, 615; a rocket bomb attack on, 620.621; rocket equipment despatched to America through, 695
Anzio (Italy): a planned landing at, 490; landing at, 491, 492; Allies pinned down at, 495; and Angelita, 496; and a German offensive, 497; the bridgehead at, trapped, 498; continuing battle at, 499, 509; a break-out from, 526–7
Aosta, Duke of: evacuates Addis Ababa, 169
Aparri (Philippines): Japanese land at, 276
Apeldoorn (Holland): Jewish mental patients sent to Auschwitz from 395; a hijack attempt near, followed by reprisals, 646
Arab Legion, the: 'will fight anybody', 182
'Arabel': a double agent, 212, 537, 542, 621
Arakan Coast (Burma): advance along, 646
*Arandora Star* (luxury liner): sunk, 106
Arawe Peninsula (New Britain): an American landing on, 481
Arc de Triomphe (Paris): swastika on, 94; prisoners-of-war machine gunned at, 580; Churchill and de Gaulle at, 612
Archambault, Jean-Paul: his sabotage mission, in France, 515; his mission behind Japanese lines in Burma, 694
Arctic Circle: British troops north of, 62
Archangel (Soviet Union): planned German advance to, 115, 147; British aid to Russia through, 214, 123; British convoys to, 239, 242, 325, 327
*Archer* (British aircraft carrier): in action, 431
Arctic Convoys: 223, 239, 242, 324, 325, 327, 339–340, 359; a welcome relief for, 377; continuation of, discussed, 396
Ardeatine Caves (Rome): executions in, 510; a trial concerning, 596
Ardennes (Belgium, Luxemburg): Germans reach (1940), 64, 65, 66; Germans recapture (1944), 615–6, 617, 618, 620, 621, 621–2; and a German air attack on Allied airfields, 626; Germans pushed back in, 627, 629, 632; Allied forces stalled at, 636
*Ardent* (British destroyer): sunk, 89
Arendal (Norway): German plans to land at, 45
Argentina: declares war on Germany and Japan, 653; releases a wanted man, 745
*Argus* (British aircraft carrier): helps Malta, 114; goes to North Russia, 223
Arhanes (Crete): a kidnapping near, 519
*Arizona* (US battleship): 1,177 men killed on, 272
*Ark Royal* (British aircraft carrier): torpedoed, 255
Arlington Cemetery (Virginia): a burial at, 204; a memorial unveiled at, 738
Armavir (Caucasus): Germans

approach, 348; Germans driven from, 397; battles west of, 398
Armenia: German plans for, 193
Armstrong, Brigadier General Clare H.: at Antwerp, 611–2
Armstrong, George: hanged, 132
'Arnaud' (Alec Rabinovitch): his sabotage mission, 504
Arndt, Professor Walther: executed, 546
Arnhem (Holland): a parachute landing at, 593; air supplies to, 594; Canadian forces reach, 666
Arnim, General von: in Tunisia, his losing battle, 402
Arras (France): a British counter-attack at, 70
Arezzo (Italy): partisans near, in action, 544; partisans near, captured, 554
Arno River (Italy): American troops cross, 584
'Aromatic' (Edward Rizzo): a British agent, 177
Arrow Cross, the: in Budapest, 603; executions by, 604
Artois (France): British troops in, 73
'Aryan' superiority: 24, 366, 390–91, 408–9
Ascension Island (South Atlantic): and the sinking of the *Laconia*, 360
Asché (a French secret agent): and Enigma, 39
Aschersleben (Germany): bombed, 489, 501
*Ascot* (British merchant ship): torpedoed, 500
Ascq (France): a reprisal in, 512–3
Asia: Stalin's possible withdrawal into, 235; and terror, 297
*Asia* (Goering's train): at Calais, 123
'Asia for the Asiatics': and the Indian National Army, 278
Asiatic Russia: a barrier to be erected against, 147
'Asiatics': Stalin's comment (on the Russians and Japanese), 173
Askaris: war dead of, 746
Assam (India): and the siege of Kohima, 514
*Astoria* (US heavy cruiser): sunk, 350
Astrakhan (Russia): Soviet reinforcements at, 267; Soviet partisans parachuted from, 370–1
Atamasov, Konstantin: executed, 503
Atabrine (a prophylactic): dropped in the Far East, 721
*Athena* (a German refugee ship): 683–4
*Athenia* (British passenger liner): sunk, 4
Athens (Greece): British aid to, 148; German troops enter, 178; German troops seize docks in, from Italians, 460; fate of Jews in, 465; Germans pull back from, 575; British troops enter, 602; Churchill flies to, 623; 'free to decide its future', 728; war crimes trials in, 732
*Atlanta* (US light cruiser): sunk, 377
Atlantic Charter, the: issued, 222
'Atlantic Wall': to be built, 352, 358; labourers deported to work on, 421; labourers sent from, to repair Ruhr dams, 427
*Atlantis* (a German commerce raider): 35; ready to sail, 51; in action, 140; sunk, 261–2

Atomic Bomb: and uranium (1941), 167, 212; secrets of, passed on, 241, 348; to be produced, 271, 363, 384, 399, 420, 434, 505; and attacks on German supplies of heavy-water, 319, 379, 404; Anglo-American exchange of information on, 434; a scale model of, dropped, 451; and Anglo-American sharing of work on, 452; Stalin not told of (November 1943), 478; Stalin's spy, privy to, 478–9; Germany's hopes for, sunk, 500; activated (September 1944), 591; 'almost certainly' ready (by August 1945), 594–5; Japanese unable to complete, 613; and Allied strength, 625; ready in 1945 ('July, August or September'), 628; and German installations, to be overrun, 667; the 'probability' of, 673–4; the decision to drop, 696–7; successfully tested, 704, 707, 708; 'a professor's dream', 711; and Hiroshima, 675–6, 694, 710, 712–4, 715; and Nagasaki, 715–6
Atomic Energy: German plans for (1939), 14; American plans for (1939), 20–21; German progress in (1945), 645; a German plant for, bombed, 649–50
Atsugi (Japan): an American officer lands at, 721
Attlee, Clement: at Potsdam, 710–11
Attu Island (Aleutians): Japanese land on, 330; Americans regain, 426, 434
Auchinleck, General Sir Claude: attacks, 262; defends, 338
Augsburg (Germany): Jews deported to their deaths from, 315; bombing raids on, 317, 501
Augustow (Poland): troop movements near, 194; Red Army reaches, 556–7
Aulock, Colonel von: determined not to surrender, 570
Aulick (US destroyer): hit by a kamikaze pilot, 617
Aung San: offers his services to the British, 694
Aurich (northern Germany): a war crimes trial in, 727
Aurora (British cruiser): attacked, 472
Aurora (Russian cruiser): in action, 228
Auschwitz (Poland): a punishment camp for Poles at, 43, 57; Poles and Jews deported to, 95; Poles deported to, 127, 147, 168; an escape from, and reprisals, 219; gassing experiments at, 220, 228, 230; and the gas chambers at Birkenau, 310, 322, 343, 344, 348, 350–1, 365, 464, 466, 507, 520, 527, 560, 631; and the nearby Monowitz synthetic oil plant, 326, 503, 513–4, 529–30, 578, 590; Czech women and children (from Lidice) killed at, 332; deportations of Jews to, 335, 336, 338, 343, 356, 362, 364, 370, 372, 386, 391, 395, 398, 400, 407, 408, 413, 421, 436, 440, 456, 461, 462, 465, 467, 470, 471, 473, 474, 488, 490, 494, 504, 510, 514, 520, 523–4, 525, 527, 540, 546, 549, 559–60, 562, 564, 565, 571, 582, 585, 595, 598, 608; medical experiments at, 340, 368, 431–2, 436; and euthanasia, 437; Himmler visits, 343, 351; and forced labour, 353, 364, 503, 525; a refusal to deport Jews to, 386; use of clothes collected at, 400; a 'green belt' camouflage to be created at, 438; Jews

taken from, for medical experiments elsewhere, 438; acts of defiance at, 469, 470; and the Gypsies, 474, 496, 562, 598, 601; air reconnaisance flights over, 513–4, 529–30, 578, 579, 621; the appeal to bomb railway lines leading to, 546; and the Jews of Hungary, 523–4, 527, 530, 546, 550; Jews sent away from, to forced labour elsewhere, 552, 565; the truth about, reaches the West, 554; a deportee from, killed in the Warsaw uprising, 565; a bombing raid near, 590–1; a revolt at, 600; evidence of mass murder being destroyed at, 608; last murders at, 614; Jews deported from, 615; Jews still held at, after gassing ceases, 621; bombs fall on, 623; mass evacuation of, 631–2; final executions at, 634; Red Army reaches, 634; survivors of, at Gardelegen, 663; survivors of, at Belsen, 663; a former officer at, brought to trial, 726; a survivor of, murdered after the war, 730; the former commandant at, executed, 732; a survivor of, speaks of the 'unfinished business' of the war, 737; and the renewal (in 1953) of a crematorium patent, 737; evidence concerning, discovered hidden in the ground, 740; guards from, brought to trial, 740; said to have been 'too small', 743
Australia: troops from, in France, 81; a naval action, in the Pacific, 91; and a German commerce raider, 101; troops from, reach Britain, 115; troops from, in North Africa, 148, 149, 153, 156, 172, 259, 316, 358, 371; troops from, in Greece, 173, 175; troops from, reach the safety of Crete, 180; troops from, in action on Crete, 184, 186; troops from, in action in Syria and Lebanon, 189; the Sydney sunk, off the coast of, 259; declares war on Finland, Hungary and Roumania, 270; Hitler envisages Japanese conquest of, 280; troops from, in action in Malaya and the Far East, 293, 296, 297, 300, 683; Japanese threat to, 296; fate of nurses from, 301; MacArthur transfers headquarters to, 302; part of, 'may fall', 303; fate of prisoners-of-war from, 305, 306, 336, 355; a town in, bombed, 305; MacArthur reaches, 307; MacArthur's orders sent from, 315; Japanese draw closer to, 315, 322; and a submarine attack on Sydney, 329; in action, in New Guinea, 341, 345, 346, 355, 361, 375, 378, 384, 391, 459, 462, 486; a Mission in, bombed, 462; war dead of, 514; a Japanese prisoner-of-war breakout in, 565; forces from, land on Labuan, 699; forces from, liberate Brunei, 700; forces from, land at Miri, 701; prisoners-of-war, liberated, 718–9, 721; and Nazi war criminals, 742, 744; and the 'walking wounded' who returned to, 747
Australia (Australian heavy cruiser): hit in suicide attacks, 627
Austria: and possible peace talks (1940), 50; first Allied bombing raid on (1943), 451; aircraft factories and airfields in, bombed (1944), 500–1;

battle for, 666; German soldiers in Yugoslavia retreat to, 669; Americans advance through, 684; Churchill fears part of will be 'police-governed', 686; continued fighting in, 687; its future, discussed at Potsdam, 705–6
Authie (Normandy): prisoners-of-war murdered at, 535
Automedon (British steamer): attacked, 140
Auvergne, the (France): hangings in, 521
'Avenge Malmédy': a battle cry, 620
Avignon (France): American troops enter, 580
Avord (France): airfield at, bombed, 522
Avondale Park (British merchant ship): sunk, 689
Avranches (Normandy): a counter-attack to, ordered, 565
Axis, the (the Rome-Berlin Axis): extended to Japan, 129; Franco refuses to join, 134; and the British Empire, 141; its first setback (in Albania), 143; Bulgaria declines to join, 149; Yugoslavia refuses to join, 157; Bulgaria joins, 160; Yugoslavia joins, 165; Japan urged to withdraw from, 264; the 'United Nations' to combat, 286; and America's new arms programme (January 1942), 287; Allies capture a capital of, 531; Finland defects from, 574; Roumania turns against, 580, 590; Bulgaria turns against, 589; Hungary turns against, 624
Ayle, Robert: betrayed, and shot, 436
Axmann, Arthur: 'unshakeable faithfulness' to Hitler, 654
Azerbaidjan: German plans for, 193; and a celebration, 246
Azov (southern Russia): Red Army enters, 400
Azov, Sea of (southern Russia): German forces reach, 242; Soviet forces return to, 399

B a369: a Jew murdered after war, 730
Babington Smith, Constance: and the German 'Flying Bomb'. 479
Babi Yar (Kiev): Jews murdered at, 239
Bačka Province (Yugoslavia): offered to Hungary, 166, 169; Hungarians enter, 172
Bacena (Italy): partisans occupy, 575–6
Backe, Herbert: uneasy at a Hitler declaration, 400
Backebo (Sweden): a V2 rocket falls on, 539
Baden (Germany): Jews deported from, 133
Badayev Warehouse (Leningrad): bombed, 231
Baden Baden (Germany): a former Gestapo chief sent home to, 738
Bad Nauheim (Germany): Hitler at, 617; Hitler returns to Berlin from, 629
Bad Tölz (Bavaria): suicide in, 727
Bader, Douglas: and the fall of France, 98; and the Battle of Britain, 119
Badoglio, Marshal Pietro: replaces Mussolini, 446, 459
'Baedeker Raids': over Britain, 319
Bagac (Philippines): a Japanese landing south of, 293; a Japanese setback near, 295

Baghdad (Iraq): and Rashid Ali, 168, 175, 182; killing of Jews in, 187

Bagnères-de-Bigorre (France): sabotage at, 523

Bahrein (Persian Gulf): threat to oil fields at, 348

Baikal Lake (Siberia): and Japan, 312

Baja (Hungary): Jews deported from, 530

Baker Island (Pacific Ocean): Americans land on, 456

Bakopoulos, General: ordered to surrender by his superiors, 171

Baku (Soviet Union): Anglo-French proposal to bomb oil fields at, 51; German plans against, 114, 135, 345; Hitler's plan to bomb, revealed to the Allies, 375

Balakin, Vyacheslav: a partisan diary by, 298

Balanga (Philippines): a death march from, 316

Balaton, Lake (Hungary): Red Army reaches, 616; German resistance at, 650

Balbo, Marshal Italo: killed, 104

Baldham (near Munich): German forces sign an unconditional surrender at, 687

Balham (London): sixty-four people killed at, 132

Balikpapan (Borneo): Japanese about to land at, 293; battle at, 294; occupied, 294; Australians land at, 702

Balkans, the: Germany's hopes for, 114; severity urged in, 372, 386; Allies to help partisans in, 452; the 'grim partisan situation' in, 472; a German anti-partisan sweep in, 489; Hitler reinforces, 492; and the Normandy Landings deception plan, 492–3; German traffic through, to be disrupted, 521; Red Army reaches, 584; Germans harassed in, 584

Ballale (Bougainville Island): Yamamoto's journey to, 419–20

Ballestrem, Countess: her trial, and lucky escape, 637–8

Baltic Military District: 'state of readiness' in, 168

Baltic Sea: mining of (June 1941), 189

Baltic States: 23, 114; and the 'Final Solution', 216–7

Baltimore (Maryland): a 'Liberty' ship launched in, 239

Baltiski (Estonia): Soviet Union to occupy, 16

Bamberg (Germany): Jews deported to Auschwitz from (1943), 436; a congress in, hears a denunciation of Nazism (1988), 744

Bampong (Thailand): and the Burma railway, 336

Banak (northern Norway): German aircraft diverted from, 377

Bande (Ardennes): reprisals in, 622

Bandarjarmasin (Borneo): Japanese land at, 300

Bandung (Dutch East Indies): fate of prisoners-of-war at, 318; rumours circulate among prisoners-of-war in, 324

Bangkok (Thailand): Japanese land at, 276

Bank Underground Station (London): more than a hundred killed at, 149

Banska Bystrica (Slovakia): partisans take control of, 583; an escape line near, by air, 593; Germans capture, 604

'Banzai': a death charge cry, 552; called, on the eve of execution, 729

Bar (France): sabotage at, 528

Baranga Island (Burma): and the bombing of Rangoon, 682

Baranowicze (eastern Poland): a Soviet signals centre, 192; overrun, 201; partisan activity near, 292; Jews murdered at, 304–5

Barbados: the U-156 sunk near, 360

Barbarossa, Emperor: his twelfth century conquests, 145; the anniversary of his death, 189

Barbie, Klaus: in Lyon, 432, 488

Barclay, Cecil: in Moscow, 202, 238

Bardejov (Slovakia): Red Army enters, 632

Bardia (Libya): attacked, 148; an attack on, driven off, 175; Rommel takes, 335

Bardufoss (Norway): and the defection of a German bomber, 683

Barents Sea (Arctic): a convoy attacked in, 503–4

Barham (British battleship): crosses Mediterranean, 139; sunk, 262

Bari (southern Italy): an escape line from, to Slovakia, by air, 593–4

Barlas, Chaim: overhears that Hitler has 'lost the war', 365

Bartolomeo Colleoni (Italian cruiser): sunk, 205

Barrow-in-Furness (England): German submarine experts work at, 727

Barry, Lieutenant Charles: an aerial reconnaissance by, 519

Barton, Pilot Officer Cyril: his courage, 512

Barycz (Poland): Soviet prisoners-of-war murdered at, 482

Barzylai, Elias, Chief Rabbi of Athens: joins Greek partisans, 464

Basch, Victor: shot, together with his wife, 488

Bastille Day (1940): 110

Basutos: war dead of, 746

Basra (Iraq): British troops land at, 174–5; aid to Egypt diverted from, 336–7

Bastogne (Ardennes): besieged, 621, 622, 628, 629

Bataan Peninsula (Philippines): Japanese advance down, 286. 288, 291; Americans withdraw down, 293; the 'battling bastards' of, 294; an American-Filipino success on, 297; last battles on, 315, 316; survivors of death march on, liberated, 722; the General responsible for the death march on, executed, 728

Bataisk (southern Russia): Germans reach, 346

Batan Island (Philippines): Japanese land on, 275

Batavia (Dutch East Indies): tea from, dropped on Holland, 161; the cruel fate of evacuees from, 305–6; final evacuation of, 306

Bateson, Wing-Commander RN: and a precision bombing raid, 515–6

Bath (England): bombed, 319

Battersea (London): a 'Flying Bomb' at, 542, 570

Battle of Britain, the: 117–25

'Battle Commandant' (of Berlin): appointed, 673

Batum (Black Sea): to be occupied, 222, 345, 363

Baudouin, Paul: and the French Fleet, 99

Baum, Herbert: shot, 325

Baum, Marianne: shot, 325

Bavaria (Germany): the Gauleiter of, executed for defeatism, 668

Bayeux (Normandy): and an Allied deception, 532

Bayreuth (Germany): a Gauleiter executed in, 668

Bear Island (Arctic Ocean): and the Arctic convoys, 325; and the sinking of the Scharnhorst, 482

Beaugency (France): a German surrender at, 592, 593

Beauvais (France): an unarmed airman shot near, 70; German bombers destroyed at, 539

Beaverbrook, Lord: in Moscow, 223, 239

Becher, Kurt: visits Mauthausen, 674

Beck, Adolf: killed by Soviet partisans, 346

Beck, General Ludwig: 50. 58; commits suicide, 558

Beda Fomm (Libya): Italians pushed back at, 156

Bedouin (British destroyer): sunk, 333

Bedzin (Poland): Jews murdered at, 7

Beekman, Yvonne: shot, 590

Begué, Georges: parachuted into France (1941), 180

Beg-an-Fry (France): a clandestine mission to, 475

Beirut (Lebanon): to be conquered, 188–9

Bela Crkva (Yugoslavia): an armed clash in, 208

Belfort (France): German troops at, 89; a sweep to, behind German lines, 573

Belgium: and Hitler's war plans, 20, 29, 38, 59; Anglo-French plans concerning, 51, 54; invasion of, 61; battles in, 62, 65–74, 76; surrender of, 77; fishing vessels from, at Dunkirk, 80–1; troops of, in Britain, 113; under German rule, 127; art taken from 130; and an escape line, 177; deportation of Jews from, 336, 344, 351, 362, 365, 373–390, 444, 459; volunteers from, on the Eastern Front, 348; German bombers move from 374; an ill-fated bombing raid on, 418; forced labourers from, 421, 427; and a betrayal, 436; forced labourers from, killed in an Allied air raid, 453; an Allied helper, killed in an air raid in, 459; air supplies to resistance in, 486; sabotage near, 489; a resistance mission to, 512; and Allied deception plans, 534, 542; leniency in, and an arrest, 550; British troops reach, 584; Allied help to Resistance in, 587; 'very hard fighting' in, 610; civilians murdered in, 620, 622; rocket bomb deaths in, 653; torturers from, executed, 732

Belgorod (Russia): Germans enter, 245; Germans driven from, 400; Germans capture, 413; Russians retake, 450

Belgrade (Yugoslavia): vulnerable, 166; to be destroyed, 167; bombed, 170;

German troops advance towards, 170–1, 173; Germans occupy, 173; surrender of Yugoslavia signed in, 174; resistance and reprisals in, 217; Jews killed by gas vans in, 331; mines dropped in Danube near, 515, 550; battle for, 603; Germans driven from, 604; and Soviet control, 686, 728

Belle Croix (Ardennes): Germans parachute landing at, 618

Bello, Heinz: executed in Berlin, 549

Belomorsk (Russia): 206

Belov, Sergeant Alexander: reaches German border, 571

Belsen (Bergen-Belsen, Germany): deaths in, 516; a new commandant at, 615; mass evacuations to, 632; daily deaths in, 650; British troops enter, 663–4; deaths in, after liberation, 672; the barracks at, burnt, 695; the Commandant of, brought to trial, 726

Beltrami, Filippo: a partisan, killed in action, 498

Belzec (Poland): forced labour camp at, 129; a death camp at, 292, 307–8, 310, 315, 322, 331, 335, 344, 351, 361, 370; a Jew born in, deported to Auschwitz, 338; the evidence of mass murder at, to be destroyed, 439; a survivor of, gives testimony, 651

Ben Gardane (Tunisia): Rommel driven back to, 397; British forces enter, 402

Ben Ya'acov, Zvi: killed, 611

Benedicta, Sister: see index entry for Stein, Edith

Benedics, Michael: a descendant of, protects Jews, 550

Bengal (India): a forecast of revolt in, 423

Bengal, Bay of: merchant ships sunk in, 315

Benghazi (Libya): bombed, 141; captured, 155; evacuated, 169; fuel ships sunk on way to, 262; Rommel occupies, 296; Rommel loses, 382; American bombers use, as a base to bomb Ploesti, 448

Benoist, Robert: captured, and executed, 504

Bénouville (Normandy): British glider landing at, 549

Berbera (British Somaliland): occupied, 120

Berchtesgaden (Bavaria): Hitler issues a 'Hold on!' order from, 381; Hitler at, orders troops to France, 514; a possible German redoubt in, 669; bombed, 672; American forces enter, 684

Berdichev (Russia): Jews killed in, 219, 235; Hitler at, 221

Berdyansk (Russia): Germans enter, 242

Beresina River (Russia): battle on, 205

Bereski (Russia): an ambush in, 298

Bereza Kartuska (eastern Poland): Jews killed at, 345

Berezovka (Russia): a macabre scene at, 290

Berg, Mary: in the Warsaw ghetto, 261, 276

Bergamini, Admiral Carlo: sails for Allied ports, 460

Bergé, Georges: returns to Britain, 163

Bergen (Norway): Allied action at, 42, 45, 48, 52, 53

Berger, SS General Gotlob: crushes

Slovak uprising, 608

Bergerac (France): sabotage at, 482; sabotage near, 543

Berggrav, Bishop: imprisoned, 406

Berghof (Berchtesgaden): bombed, 672

Bergman, Serge: killed, 538

Bergonzoli, General: retreats, 148; captured, 156

Bergsland, Sergeant: escapes, 510

Bergson, Henri: registers, 129

Beria, Lavrenti: and Destruction Battalions, 201

Bering Strait: and a German commerce raider, 109

Berlin: a broadcast from, 10; and the war at sea, 13; and nuclear power, 14; leaflets dropped on, 18; Hitler's appeal from, 19; future of Poles, as seen from, 29; and Enigma, 39; leaflets dropped on, 46; and the fate of Denmark, 53; and lack of enthusiasm for the war, 57; bombed (1940–1942), 102, 121, 124, 128, 136, 141, 147, 172, 210, 222, 254; Hitler's building plans for, 102, 104, 225, 247–8; Hitler's triumphant return to (July 1940), 108; Hitler's 'peace offer' from (July 1940), 110; British bombing raid north of, 121; and British bombing policy, 132; news of Gurs camp reaches, 133; an anti-Semitic film shown in, 144; and the 'crucial year' (1941), 155; Hitler's post-war plans for, 102, 174, 196, 235; and the Jews of, 224, 230, 245, 263, 266, 391, 409, 410; a protest in, and its consequences, 228; two further protests to, 250–1; Hitler speaks of Moscow battle in, 242; a conference at, on the 'future' of the Jews, 279; anti-Nazi posters in, 325; Flak Towers to be built in, 365; renewed bombing of (1943), 393, 397, 415, 455, 456, 458, 475–6, 476, 477, 478, 479, 481, 482; (in 1944), 485–6, 486, 490, 495, 496, 499, 504, 510; two days mourning declared in, for Stalingrad, 399; and a leaflet detailing 'German atrocities' to be dropped on, 400; Jews deported from, 407, 432; Roosevelt wants Western Allies to reach, 454; a critic of Nazism executed in, 549; and the Bomb Plot, 558, 566, 568, 589, 645 Western Allies nearer to, than Soviet forces, 590; fate of Jews deported from, 598; 'most practical as our headquarters', 619; Hindenburg's remains brought to, 632; Red Army 150 miles from, 632; Red Army less than fifty miles from, 635–6; proposed 'heavy' bombing of, 636; declared a Fortress City, 637; 'allotted' to the Allied air forces, 638; Hitler leaves, for the last time, 648; Hitler moves to a bunker beneath, 657; a possible Anglo-American advance to, 658; battle for, 666, 668–9, 670–1, 672, 673, 674, 676; falls to the Red Army, 680–1; surrender of, 682, 683; and Churchill's fear of Soviet control in, 686; a final award in, 688–9; a final surrender ceremony in, 690; Churchill in, 704, 705; in the 'Soviet sphere', 728

'Berlin-Tiflis Axis': to be established, 193; map showing, 195

Berling, General: crosses Vistula, 593, 594

Bermuda: a supply ship sunk off, 337

Bernadotte, Count Folke: Himmler approaches, 643, 670

Barnardino, Don: warns Jews, 466

Barnatowicz, Pelagia: sentenced to death, 158

Bernau (near Berlin): Red Army at, 672

Bernay (Normandy): Rommel in hospital at, 556

Bernburg (Germany): Jews gassed at, 263, 267

Bernhard of the Netherlands, Prince: and the surrender of the German forces in Holland, 687

Bernovits, Vilma: executed, 624

Bertram, Cardinal Archbishop of Breslau: a protest to, 250; a protest by, 407

Beser, Lieutenant Jacob: and the atomic bomb, 595; 'What a relief it worked', 712

Bessarabia (Roumania): ceded by the Soviet Union, 104, 105, 108; Roumanian desire for return of, and Germany, 124, 188

Best, Dr Karl Rudolf Werner: and Danish resistance, 452

Best, Captain: kidnapped, 27; his kidnapper's promotion, 94

Bethnal Green (London): a tunnel near, for shelter, 130; a disaster at, 408; 'Flying Bomb' deaths at, 539

Béthouart, General: lands in Norway, 64

Béthune (France): a small German withdrawal near, 73

Betio Island (Tarawa Atoll): savage fighting on, 476

Bevan, Colonel John: and deception, 347

Bevin, Ernest: and Jewish refugees, not to be allowed into Palestine, 726

Bexley (southern England): rocket bomb deaths at, 641

Biak Island (New Guinea): battle for, 542

Biala Podlaska (Poland): Soviet prisoners-of-war murdered at, 282

Bialka (Poland): Poles in, shot for helping Jews, 384

Bialowola (Poland): Poles murdered at, 389

Bialowieza (Poland): Poles murdered in, 388–9

Bialystok (Poland): Soviet troops in, put on alert, 193; Poles shot near, 354–5; Jews from region of, murdered, 376, 391; children from, reach Auschwitz, 465; partisans in action near, 510; Red Army enters, 562; Home Army members in, arrested by the Russians, 646

Biarritz (British steamship): troops evacuated on, 96

Bielefeld (Germany): viaduct at, bombed, 649

Bieler, Captain Gustave: arrested, 489; executed, 655

Biella (northern Italy): Japanese-American troops in, 683

Bielsk Podlaski (Poland): a Jew from, liberated at Ebensee, 688

'Big Week': against German armament factories, 500–2

Biggin Hill (England): airfield at, attacked, 111, 122

'Bigot': a code for secret knowledge, 520, 526

Bihac (Yugoslavia): partisans driven to, 323

Billancourt (Paris): bombed, 306

Bikini Atoll (Marshall Islands): a post-war atomic test at, 729–30

Billotte, Colonel Pierre: enters Paris, 578

Bingen (Germany): bombed, 622

Bingel, Lieutenant Erwin: an eye-witness to mass murder, 236

Bir Hakeim (Libya): siege of, 187; renewed battle at, 327

Birch, Captain John: shot, in China, 720

Birkenau (Auschwitz): *see* index entry for Auschwitz

Birmingham (England): bombed, 142

*Birmingham* (US cruiser): sunk, 606

Birzai (Lithuania): Soviet parachutists land at, 307

Biscari (Sicily): battle for airfield at, 445

Biscay, Bay of: and 'Fortress Europe', 283; and an offensive against German submarines, 414; German submarines sunk in, 431; and a possible Allied landing, 472; mined, 526

Bishan Singh: drowned, 598

*Bismarck* (German battleship): its blueprints, 44; in preparation, 114; in action, 185; damaged and then scuttled, 186

Bismarck Archipelago (Pacific): Japanese bomb, 288

Bismarck Sea: naval battle in, 408

*Bismarck Sea* (US escort carrier): deaths on, 500; sunk by a suicide aircraft, 643

*Bison* (French destroyer): hit, 58

Bitner, Czeslaw: lands in France (1941), 177

Bizerta (Algiers): Hitler hurries troops to, 376; captured by the Allies, 426

Bjerkvik (Norway): landing at, 64

Black, Captain G. D.: his mission, and fate, 362–3

Black Sea: and Hitler, 120

Blaney, Captain M. F.: killed, 146

Blankenberge (Belgium): attack on, 74

Blaskowitz, General Johannes von: his protests, 19, 24, 29, 43; surrenders the German forces in Holland, 687; commits suicide, 733

Blechhammer (Silesia): an oil target in, 513; slave labour at, 524; oil installations at, bombed, 590, 631

Bleichrode (Germany): scientists spirited away from, 700

Bleichrode, Heinrich: attacks Atlantic voneoys, 132

Bletchley Park: and Enigma, 45, 56, 71–2, 82, 159, 161; and Purple, 154, 182; and Rashid Ali's revolt in Iraq, 182; and the German advance into Russia, 202; and the war at sea, 218; and a promise by Hitler to Japan, 226; and the German orders for the attack on Moscow, 231, 239; and German air weakness on the Eastern Front, 257; five Enigma keys broken at (1–2 January 1942). 287; a failure and a success at, 297; further successes at, 334, 394, 395–6; and the Battle of Médenine, 409; an outstanding success at, 414; and the 'Ultra' system, 429; and the Normandy Landings deception plans, 494; and German assessments of the cross-Channel timing, 522, 531; and the continuing

Normandy deception, 540, 555; and the battle in Normandy, 567; and Hitler's order to withdraw from southern France, 571; and 'the decisive factor' of German fuel shortages, 577, 591; and the pressure on German railways, 610–11; and Hitler's final questions, 679

'Blitz', the: the German bombing of London, 124, 127, 131, 135, 136; German losses during, 137; British losses during, 148; and British morale, 150, 155; to continue, 156; renewed, over London, 162; civilian deaths in, 167; renewal, over Bristol, 173; over Plymouth, 178–9; over Clydeside and Liverpool, 181; and a comparison with the Hamburg firestorm (of 28 July 1943), 448; its terrors revived (by the 'Flying Bomb'), 544, 557

'Blitz' (German jet aircraft): in action, 622, 626

'Blitzkrieg': the method of 'lightning war', 2

Blizyn (Poland): Soviet prisoners-of-war murdered at, 482; and the German 'Flying Bomb', 522

Blobel, ss Colonel Paul: and the destruction of the evidence of mass murder, 438

'Blobel Commando': destroys evidence of mass murder, 438, 439, 475

Bloch, Denise ('Ambroise'): captured, and executed, 504

Bloch, Marc: shot, 541

Bloch-Dassault, Marcel: deported, 571

Block, Captain Harlon: and an Iwo Jima photograph, 643

Blomberg, Major Axel von: killed, 181

'Bloody Gorge' (Iwo Jima): fighting at, 643

Bloom, Marcus: shot, 590

Blum, Léon: his brother's fate, 365–6; liberated, 684, 686

Blum, René: gassed at Auschwitz, 365–6, 686

Blyes (France): supplies parachuted to, 312, 314

Bobrek (East Upper Silesia): slave labour at, 524

Bobruisk (Russia): captured, 205; Jews murdered in, 280; Soviet partisans near, 308; an anti-partisan sweep near, 308–9; Germans driven back to, 544; Red Army enters, 548

Bochum (The Ruhr): bombed, 427

Bock, Field Marshal Fedor von: 221, 247, 304, 339; killed by an Allied bomb, 686

'Bock's Car' (US bomber): flies to Kokura and then on to Nagasaki, 715

Bodö (Norway): British troops at, 62; troops on their way to, attacked, 65; evacuation from, 78

Bogen (Norway): landing at, 55

Boger, Wilhelm: and 'only one mode of conduct', 740

Bogorodisk (near Moscow): 'panic' reaches, 259

*Bogue* (US aircraft carrier): in action, 431

Bohemia-Moravia: 7; Hitler determined to hold, 669; battles in, 674

Böhlen (Germany): bombed, 641

Bohr, Niels: escapes from Denmark, 464

*Boise* (US light cruiser): hit, 368

Bologna (Italy): fate of Jews of, 474; Germans hold, 613; Polish forces enter, 669

Bomb Plot (against Hitler): planned, 412, 414, 551, 553; carried out, 557–8, 559; repercussions of, 566, 581, 583, 585, 597, 598, 601, 604, 615, 620, 639, 645, 650, 660

Bombing policy: (of Britain), in 1940, 108, 120, 132, 136, 142, 146; in 1941, 208, 210; in 1942, 308, 314, 319, 329, 352, 359; in 1943, 439, 440, 447–8, 448; (of the Allies), in 1942, 378; in 1943, 393, 398, 407, 409, 427, 432; in 1945, 636, 638–9, 644; and 'Operation Pointblank', 427; 'Are we beasts?', 440–1

*see also* index entries for, Leaflets, 'Blitz', 'Flying Bomb', V1, V2 and Atomic Bomb

Bonhoeffer, Dietrich: flies to Sweden, 328; imprisoned, 418–9; hanged, 660; his brother-in-law shot, 672

Bonhoeffer, Klaus: executed, 672

'Boniface': the code name for Enigma Signals Intelligence, 451

Bolzano (Italy): Jews deported to Auschwitz from, 608

Bombay (India): violence in, 725

Bône (Algeria): British forces land at, 376

Bonn (Germany): American troops reach (1945), 648; questions concerning Jews asked in (1988), 743

Bonsergent, Jacques: executed, 147

Bor-Komorowski, Lieutenant General Tadeusz: and the Warsaw uprising, 561, 564

Bordeaux (France): French Government moves to, 93, 86–7; heavy water evacuated from, 95; assurances to Britain from, 99; French delegates reach Compiègne from, 101; a British commando raid on, 316; and an Allied deception plan, 494

Boris, King of Bulgaria: declines to join the Axis, 149; joins the Axis, 160, 165; opposes the deportation of Bulgarian Jews, 415

Borisienko, Vassily: executed, 585

Borisov (Russia): Germans temporarily halted near, 205; Hitler at, 221; Jews 'liquidated' at, 251; Soviet partisans near, 331; an anti-partisan sweep near, 431, 435, 516

Borken (Ruhr): bombed, 649

Borki Woods (near Chelm, Poland): corpses in, dug up, 475

Bormann, Martin: 136, 340–1; and the Slavs, 354; and Hitler's suicide, 681; wants to fight on, 682

Borneo: fate of Allied prisoners-of-war on, 635; Allied landings on, 683, 699; a Japanese surrender on, 725; becomes independent, 730; war's debris recovered in, 741

Bornholm (Baltic Sea): bombed in error, 49–50; a German rocket falls on, in error, 453; German troops on, surrender, 692

Borodino (Russia): battle at, 245; Soviet troops from the Far East in action, 251

*Borodino* (Soviet naval vessel): sunk, 361

Borrel, Andrée: a British agent, killed, 555

Borzykowski, Tuvia: and Jewish resistance, 393–4

Bose, Subhas Chandra: in Germany, 303; goes to Japan, 423; soldiers loyal to, in action, 537; followers of, rescued, 598; killed in an air crash, 724; followers of, brought to trial, 724–5

Bosnia (Yugoslavia): anti-partisan sweep in, 424–5; a Muslim revolt in, 458

Bosphorus (Turkey): 137

Boston (Massachusetts): a spy arrested in, 132; Roosevelt's pledge in, 135; 'Reich technicians' arrive in, 724

Bouler, Dr Philipp: and euthanasia, 11, 20, 147

Bougainville Island (Solomons): Americans begin advance into, 474; Japanese counter-attack at, 508

Boulogne (France): embarkation from, 73; a raid on, 102; an attack on the docks at, 125; Hitler at, 147; and a deception plan, 347; and further deception plans, 492, 532; to be held, 585; surrenders, 596

Bourges (France): sabotage near, 515

Boves (Italy): burned down as a reprisal, 463

Bowers, Faubion: and a 'Sir' to Hirohito, 723

Bouhler, Dr Joseph: and the 'Final Solution', 292

Bourrasque (French destroyer): sunk, 80

Brack, Dr Victor: and euthanasia, 105, 147, 224; and the killing of human beings by poison gas, 249–50; hanged, 731

Bradley, General Omar N.: and the killing of German prisoners-of-war, 445; in the Ardennes, 618,620

Brandenburg (Germany): Jews gassed at (1940), 105; three Germans imprisoned in (1941); fire engines rushed to Berlin from (1943), 478; medical experiments at, 508; an execution in, 517

Brandenburg Division, the: and 'cleansing' measures, 8; and a 'Jewish action', 12

Brandschied (Siegfried Line): Americans reach, 638

Brandt, Dr Karl: and euthanasia, 11; warns Hitler of Germany's shortage of medicines, 657; dismissed, 666; hanged, 731

Brandt, General: saves Hitler, 557–8

Bratislava (Slovakia): and the Jews, 230; falls to the Red Army, 660

Brauchitsch, General Walther von: 6, 14, 25, 43, 114, 145, 155; and the Commissar Decree, 188; overruled, 224

Braunschweig (Germany): bombed, 489

Brauer, Bruno: executed, 732

Braun, Eva: joins Hitler in Berlin, 666; marries Hitler, 677; swallows poison, 681

Braun, Dr Wernher von: and German rocket research, 367, 522; surrenders to the Americans, 683; reaches Boston, 723

Braune, Pastor Paul-Gerhard: protests to Hitler, 109

Braune, Wernher: executed for war crimes, 735

Brauns, Dr Moses: an eye-witness to murder, 223

Brazil: 154; troops of, in action in Italy, 660

Brazzaville Declaration, the: 135

Breavington, Corporal Rodney: executed, 358

Breda (Holland): war criminals released from, 744

Breendonk, Fort (Belgium): prisoners at, 127; a prisoner dies at, 158; executions at, 423; and a war crimes trial, 613; torturers at, executed, 732

Bretagne (French battleship): sunk, 107

Brenner Pass: Hitler and Mussolini meet at, 130

Bremen (Germany): leaflets dropped on, 46; bombed, 100, 207; Jews deported from, 254; renewed bombing of, 337, 360

Bremerhaven (Germany): a Nazi escapes through, 734

Breskens (Holland): to be held, 585; Allied advance to, 598

Breslau (Germany): and an anti-Semitic film, 151; Jews deported from, 262; a German defence line at, 634–5; Red Army approaches, 639; German reinforcements sent to, 640; besieged, 643, 645, 660; fighting near, 687; surrender of, 689; acquired by Poland, 711

Brest (France): Germans advance to, 97; Allied troops embarked from, 98; Germans enter, 100; a German radio station at, 104; German warships attacked in, 216; Churchill's aircraft approaches, in error, 391; a naval dash from, 300; German submarine pens at, 348; captured, 594

Brest-Litovsk (Poland): Germans capture, 214; Hitler and Mussolini at, 277; the Red Army approaches, 497; a partisan success near, 544

Bretons: at Bir Hakeim, 187

Brezno (Slovakia): partisans seize areas near, 583

Briare (France): French Government at, 91; Churchill at, 93; Churchill's words at, echoed, 99; occupied by the Germans, 100

Bridge, Jill: killed, 46

Bridge, Doris: killed, 46

Brieg (Oder): Soviet troops reach, 639

Brien, Colin F.: witnesses a war crime, 305

Brighton Belle (British holiday resort paddle steamer): sunk, 78

Brindisi (Italy): Italian Government in, declares war on Germany, 467

Brisbane (Australia): an 'Ultra' listening post, 429

Bristol (England): bombed, 125, 173

Britain: declares war on Germany, 4; action by, 5; and German spies, 15; and Hitler's Directive No. 5, 16; and Hitler's war planes, 20, 30; and Canadian volunteers, 25, 35; and the Russo-Finnish War, 34, 46; and 'Enigma' (in 1940), 39, 45, 56, 71, 82, 83, 87, 88, 104, 104–5, 108, 117, 119, 121, 138–9; and air weakness, 47–8; a peace mission to, 48; and Norway, 48,

50–1, 52; supports Belgium, 61, 62; and the battles for France, Belgium and Holland, 64; and the battle of Britain, 117–25; and the 'Blitz', 124, 127, 131, 136, 148, 150, 155, 156, 162, 167, 173, 178–9, 181; and Anglo-American strategy, 154, 167, 282; Hitler's 'main enemy' (June 1941), 191; and the atomic bomb, 212; and Japan, 216; and Iran, 226, 296; and aid to Russia, 239–40, 247, 296, 314, 658; and Intelligence from, sent to Russia, 202, 210, 213, 237, 239, 366, 375, 381, 385; and the cross-Channel landing, 392, 397, 426, 430, 452, 472, 486, 488, 490–1, 497, 507, 512, 515, 517, 520, 521, 526, 528–9, 533, 534–6; to have a post-war veto, 574, 701; and the German rocket bomb (V2): 330, 434, 457, 474, 539, 557, 561, 589, 594, 614, 640, 641, 648, 724; and the 'Flying Bomb' (V1): 434, 457, 463–4, 474, 479, 505, 522, 529, 539, 542, 543, 544, 548, 549, 551, 552, 555, 564, 570–1, 582, 587, 622–3, 624, 645; and the political future of Poland, 496–7, 594, 627, 679–80; and Victory in Europe Day (VE Day), 690; and French Indo-China, 722–3; and the Treaty of Dunkirk (1947), 732; wartime death toll of, 746

see also index entries for Churchill, 'Enigma', 'Ultra', London, Blitz, Bombing Policy

British Army Aid Group (Hong Kong): a member of executed, 469

British Broadcasting Corporation (BBC): and the bombing of the Ruhr, 69; and the bombing of Munich, 139; and German losses in Russia, 243; and the fate of the Jews of Poland, 337; and the fall of Italy, 459; and the Normandy Landings, 532

British Chivalry (merchant ship): torpedoed, 500

British East Africa: 89

British Empire: not to be demolished (Hitler), 98

British Free Corps: a member of, in the battle for Berlin, 676; a recruiter for, hanged, 727

British Loyalty (merchant ship): sunk, 330

British Merchant Navy Code Book: captured, 140

British Somaliland: 90, 120

British Union of Fascists: leaders, of, arrested, 70

Britannic (British merchant ship): brings supplies to Britain, 107

Brittany (France): a possible stand in, 90, 91; 'too late' to hold, 93; and Hitler's view of Allied strategy, 530; and the Normandy Landings deception, 552

Brive (France): ambushes near, 543

Brize Norton (Britain): an air attack on, 118

Brno (Czechoslovakia): Red Army enters, 674

Broadley, Flight Lieutenant Alan: killed, 499

'Broadway' (Burma): a landing at, 506

Broch, Theodor: and the future of Norway, 92

Brod (Yugoslavia): railway at, bombed, 611

Brody (Poland): Jews from, murdered, 362; Red Army approaches, 554

*Broke* (British destroyer): and an evacuation, 89

Bromley, Major William: and American rocket research, 695

Brooke, General Sir Alan: in France, 93; and the German advance into the Caucasus, 347–8

Brookings (Oregon): Japanese bombs fall near, 359

Broome (Australia): bombed, 305

*Broompark* (a British collier): evacuates heavy water, 95

Brown, Tommy: his courage, 374; dies, 640

Broz, Herta (Tito's wife): and an exchange of prisoners, 395

Brückmann, Else: and Hitler, 35

Bruges (Belgium): the road to, open, 76

Brûly-de-Pesche (Belgium): Hitler at, 86, 97

Brunei (Borneo): Japanese land on, 288; Australians liberate, 700

Brunei Bay (Borneo): cruisers sent from, sunk, 606

Bruneval (France): a commando raid on, 304

Brünnlitz (Germany): slave labour at, 525

Bruskina, Maria: executed, 251

Brussels (Belgium): Germans enter, 68; Hitler at, 82; an act of resistance at, 384; an escape line in, broken, 392; Jews deported to Auschwitz from, 421; a pro-Nazi executed in, 422; bombing near, 459, 500; Allied advance towards, 581; British forces enter, 585; Belgian Government returns to, 589; Burgomaster of, in London, 611; a German night Jet attack near, 626; rejoicing in, 690; a war crimes trial in, 734–5

Bryansk (Russia): 208; Russians driven back to, 242; Russians forced to abandon, 243; partisans near, 326, 327, 331; anti-partisan sweep near, 361; renewed partisan activity near, 363, 369; further anti-partisan sweeps near, 390, 427; partisans still active near, 444; Soviet successes south of, 456; Germans evacuate, 462

Bucharest (Roumania): transfer of power in, 124; Jews killed in, 151; Hitler orders bombing of, 574; Red Army enters, 584; and Soviet control, 686, 728

Buchenwald (Germany): Jews executed in, 27; a prisoner dies in, 51–2, 210; Jews deported to, from Amsterdam, 158, 205; gassing experiments at, 260; Jews sent to their deaths from, 263, 267, 370; French Resistance leaders killed in, 436, 504; a deportation to, from Paris, 572; Allied bombing near, and a reprisal, 578; deliberate and accidental deaths in, 582; Jews sent to, from Auschwitz, 582; Englishmen and Frenchmen executed at, 587; medical experiments at, 598; Gypsy children sent to Auschwitz from, 601; a British agent executed at, 655; deaths at, 655; American troops reach, 661; Jews deported from, killed at Marienbad, 674; tormentors from, brought to trial, 734, 741

Buckie (Scotland): German agents land at, 129

Buckingham Palace (London): and an air raid, 155; and Hirohito's visit to Britain (1971), 742

Buckner, Lieutenant-General Simon: killed, 700

Buczacz (Eastern Galicia): Jews in hiding in, killed, 490

Budapest (Hungary): German occupation of, 509; a demand in, to halt deportation of Jews, 550; bombed, 550; Horthy abducted from, 603; Jews driven westward from, 610; a parachutist executed in, 611; Red Army draws close to, 616; Red Army surrounds, 623; fighting in, 624, 628; murder of Jews in, 629; surviving German forces in, surrender, 630; Germans encircled near, 640; report of surrender of, reaches London, 641; Hitler confident of recapture of, 646; and Churchill's fear of Soviet control in, 686; in the 'Soviet sphere', 728

Büderich (Germany): Churchill crosses Rhine at, 652

Budyenny, Marshal Semyon: and the battle for Kiev, 231, 232

Budyonnovsk (Caucasus): Soviet partisans in, 387–8

Buenos Aires (Argentina): Eichmann abducted from, 739

Buin (Bougainville Island): 419–20

Bug River (Poland): Soviet withdrawal to, 16; Jews expelled across, 23; Germans masters up to, 103; fortifications built on, 129; German troop movements along, 179; last-minute Soviet plans for, 192; last two trains cross, 196; Soviet prisoners-of-war murdered on the banks of, 482; and Poland's post-war frontiers, 497; Red Army approaches, 554; Red Army crosses, 559

Buka Island (Solomons): occupied, 307

Bukovina (Roumania): ceded in part to the Soviet Union, 104

Bukowka (Poland): Soviet prisoners-of-war murdered at, 482

Bulganin, Nikolai: and the battle for Moscow, 243; and the return of German prisoners-of-war (1955), 738

Bulgaria: and German design on Greece, 148, 149, 160; joins the Axis, 160, 165; offered Macedonia, 166; invades Greece, 176; declares war on the United States, 280; and German demands for the 'evacuation' of Jews, 363–4, 406; refuses to deport Jews, 415, 420; Red Army occupies, 589; troops from, in action against Germany, 604, 657; to be 'police-governed', 686–7; in the Soviet bloc, 723

'Bulge', the (in the Ardennes): attacked, 626

Bullenhuser Damm (near Neuengamme): executions at, 669; executioners from, themselves hanged, 731; an SS officer from, brought to trial, 741

Bullwinkel, Sister Vivien: eye witness to a massacre, 301

Bulow, Lieutenant Hans-Jürgen von: in action, 670

Buna (New Guinea): planned defence of, 341; Japanese land at, 345, 355; Japanese pushed back to, 378; Australians capture, 384

Buna Mission (New Guinea): Japanese hold, 384; Japanese give up, 391

Bunker Hill (Massachusetts): battle of (1775), 693

*Bunker Hill* (US aircraft carrier): deaths on, 693

Buraki (Soviet-German border): a reconnaissance mission at, 194

Burma: pressures on, 108, 131; in danger, 303; Japanese invasion of, 306, 321; 'Railway of Death' to, 336; a British attack on, repulsed, 399; sabotage columns cross into, 404; glider troops land in, 506; Allied advance in, 547, 633, 641, 646, 650, 667–8, 682, 699; nationalist forces in, join the British, 694; Japanese try to withdraw from, 705; end of the war in, 721; continued fighting in, 722; final surrenders in, 725; becomes independent, 730, 733

Burma Road (between Burma and China): closed, 108, 111; reopened, 129; in use, 131; Japanese reach, 321; Chinese and Americans recapture, 633

Burmese: their deaths, as forced labourers, 470

Buron (Normandy): prisoners-of-war murdered at, 535

Bursche, Dr Edmund: dies, 113

Bury St Edmunds (England): an act of sabotage-deception in, 453

Busemann, Adolf: brings his aviation expertise to the West, 703

Bush, George: shot down, 584

Bushido: the 'true compassion' of, 417

Bushell, Roger: escapes, but captured, 511

Bussche, Baron Axel von dem: hopes to kill Hitler, 479

Butrimonys (Lithuania): Jews killed at, 241

Bydgoszcz (Poland): Poles murdered at, 5, 12; and 'the German cause', 27

Byrnes, James: and the atomic bomb, 696–7; and the surrender of Japan, 716; 'we must act as a great power', 728

Bzura River (Poland): battle at, 7

*Bzura* (Polish destroyer): badly damaged, 73

C38m (Italian secret cypher): broken, 218, 254, 357, 394; and the Anglo-American exchange agreement (of May 1943), 429

'CAJR': an impressive, innocuous insignia, 726

Cabanatuan (Philippines) a dramatic rescue from, 635

*Cabot* (US carrier): hit by a kamikaze pilot, 617

Cadca (Slovakia): uprising in, 583

Cadzow, Lieutenant: and Operation XD, 67

Caen (Normandy): a telephone link to, cut, 529; an Allied objective, 538; battle for, 548, 553, 557, 561, 566

Cahn, Ernst: executed, 160

Caibobo Point (Philippines): Japanese land at, 295

Cairo (Egypt): Mussolini prepares for triumphal entry into, 337; Mussolini not to enter, 338; Rommel denied capture of, 341; Rommel's renewed thrust toward, 357–8; Rommel tells Hitler why he failed to reach, 366

*Cairo* (British anti-aircraft ship): sunk, 352

Cajnice (Yugoslavia): hostages killed in, 323

Calais (France): besieged, 75–6; a raid on, 102; and a deception plan, 347; and two other deception plans, 492, 493, 494, 542; Allied advance towards, 581; to be held, 585; cross-Channel shelling from, 594

Calcutta (India): in danger, 303; alarm in, 315; violence in, 725

*Calcutta* (British anti-aircraft cruiser): sunk, 186

Calgary (Canada): General Kreipe sent to, 519–20

*California* (US battleship): hit in a suicide attack, 627

*Callaway* (US troop transport): suicide attack on, 628

Calo, Carolina: her fate, 525

Calo, Eugenio: a partisan, 525; killed, 554

Cam Ranh Bay (French Indo-China): 216

Cambodians: fight at Bir Hakeim, 187

Cambrai (France): Germans reach, 67, 68; Germans in action near, 69; Hitler at, 80

Cameron, Lieutenant: his act of bravery, 463

*Cameronia* (British merchant ship): brings aircraft to Britain, 106

*Campobasso* (Italian merchant ship): sunk, 431

Canada: German prisoners-of-war in, 25; soldiers from, in Britain, 25, 35, 115, 178; and American aircraft for Britain, 67; pilots from, in action, 75 paintings not to go to, from Britain, 82; soldiers from, to go to France, 93; soldiers from, in France, 95–6; German and Italian internees sent to, 103, 106; Klaus Fuchs reaches, 106–7; soldiers from, killed by German bombs, 108; pilots from, in the Battle of Britain, 124; evacuees to, torpedoed, 126; an officer from, wins the George Cross, 126–7, evacuees to, attacked from the air, 132; a German airman escapes from, 154; soldiers from, killed in London Blitz, 174; commandos from, in action, 228; pilots from, confront the German Jet aircraft, 599; and a war crimes trial, 727; and war criminals, 742 troops from, and Hong Kong, 262, 280, 282; declares war on Finland, Hungary and Roumania, 270; troops from, in Malaya, 296; troops from, in cross-Channel assaults, 318–9, 353–4; and the Atlantic convoys, 413; forces from, land in the Aleutian Islands, 451; troops of, in Italy, 457, 482, 584; parachutists from, in France, 489, 515; war dead of, 514, fictional troops from, and a deception plan, 516; troops from, in Northern Europe, 534, 535, 548, 567, 568, 572, 581, 596, 610, 639, 666 fate of prisoners-of-war from, 535, 542

Canal d'Aire (France): a battle at, 73; an atrocity at, 74

Canaris, Admiral Wilhelm: an eye-witness, 8; and his staff, 25, 59; and the German war against Russia, 213–4, 218, 253; and a secret meeting in Sweden, 328; dismissed, 499; and the Hitler Bomb Plot, 597; hanged, 660

Canary Islands (Spain): 141

Canas Point (Philippines): Japanese land at, 295

*Canberra* (Australian heavy cruiser): sunk, 350

Canisy (Normandy): a Panzer Division reaches, 543

Cannes (South of France): Allied landing near, 568

Canstein (Deputy President of the Berlin police): and German atrocities, 57

*Cap Arcona*: a German refugee ship, 683–4; sunk, 684

Cape Araxos (Greece): and an Allied deception, 419; British commandos land on, 596

Cape Bon Peninsula (Tunisia): Axis forces withdraw into, 426

Cape Esperance (Pacific Ocean): battle off, 368–9

Cape Gloucester (New Britain): an American landing on, 481

Cape of Good Hope (South Africa): aid to Egypt sent via, 337; remains an essential route, 376, 383

Cape Sable (Nova Scotia, Canada): 159

Cape Verde Islands (Portuguese): 159

Cape York (Australia): Japanese 800 miles from, 315

Capra, Frank: a film by, 322

Capri, Island (Italy): surrenders, 461

Cardiff (Wales): bombed, 125

Carentan (Normandy): and an Allied deception, 493; battle at, 538

Caribbean, the: and a destroyers-for-bases deal, 117; German submarines in, 301–2. 318

Carl, Dr: protests about murder of Jews and White Russians, 250

Carol of Roumania, King: abdicates 124

Caron, Staff Sergeant: and the fires at Hiroshima, 712

Carpathian Mountains: battle for, 604; German strength near, 638

Carter, Able Seaman: a survivor, 89

Carthage (Tunisia): a French submarine interned at, 383

Cartland, Ronald: and 'a comparatively peaceful war', 55; and the Belgians, 62; 'horror and tribulation ahead', 66; 'a rum war', 73; killed, 80

Caruso, Pietro: shot, 596

Casablanca (French Morocco): 100, 101, 103, 109; Allied forces disembark at, 375, 376; Churchill and Roosevelt meet at, 392, 393, 396–7, 397; bombing policy directive of, 393, 398, 407; Hitler envisages an assault on, 410

Caserta (Italy): a German unconditional surrender at, 676

Casey, Richard: and British bombing policy, 440

Caspian Sea: and Hitler, 120, 135, 345; German forces approach, 352; German forces fail to reach, 359; Intelligence concerning, sent by Churchill to Stalin, 366

Cassel (France): Germans advance towards, 75

Cassino (Italy): battle for, 480, 482, 490, 496, 497, 498, 522–3, 526

Castelforte (Italy): Germans retake, 492

Castlemartin (Wales): German tank crews train in (1960), 739

Catania (Sicily): Germans fall back to, 445; British troops enter, 450

Cathedral of the Dormition (Kiev): blown up, 253

Catherine the Great: 347

Catholic Church, the: a victim, 8, 14; protests by, 39–40; warned, 59; a protest to, 250; protests by, 355–6; Jews sheltered by, 467

Cattaro (Dalmatian Coast): Albanian partisan activity near, 584

Caucasus, the (Soviet Union): proposal to bomb oil fields in, 50, 51; German designs on, 120, 142, 224, 312, 341; German forces approach, 260; Hitler's plans after conquest of, 265, 343; German troops transfered from, 346; Germans battle for, 347, 352, 353, 358, 366, 375; turn of the tide in, 383; Soviet partisans in, 387; Germans driven from, 397

Cavallero, Marshal: in North Africa, 394

Cavalry Assault Badge: award of, 225

'Cave of the Virgins' (Okinawa): fate of Japanese student nurses in, 695

Cavell, Edith: her monument destroyed, 102

Cedile, Colonel: uses Japanese troops against Vietnamese, 722

Cegled (Hungary): Red Army reaches, 610

Cenotaph (London): wreaths laid at, 110

Cephalonia (Greece): Italian soldiers massacred on, 460

*Centaur* (US hospital ship): sunk, 426

Četniks: in Yugoslavia, 181, 255, 392, 456

Ceylon: in danger, 303; a raid on, 314–5

Cézembre (off St Malo): holds out, 570

*Chacal* (French destroyer): sunk, 73

Chad: troops from, at Bir Hakeim, 187

Chalautre-la-Petite (France): civilians murdered at, 581–2; German prisoners-of-war shot at, 582

Châlons-sur-Marne (France): Americans reach, 582

Chamberlain, Neville: 6, 34, 42, 48; urges 'active measures', 51; and Norway, 52; succeeded by Churchill, 61–2; recalled, 645

*Chambly* (Canadian corvette): in action, 231

Chambonnet, Albert: shot, 561

Champs Elysées (Paris): German troops march down, 93; a French parade down, recalled, 110; de Gaulle walks in triumph down, 581

Champsecret (France): a Panzer Division reaches, 543

Chancellery, the (Hitler's Chancellery, Berlin): 22, 24, 25; and euthanasia, 105, 109, 249–50; and Hitler's eastern plans, 135–6; and Hitler's Berlin plans, 248, 260; a protest sent to, 415; Hitler's return to, after the Ardennes, 629; Hitler moves to a bunker at, 657, 663; Eva Braun joins Hitler at, 666;

Chancellery, the—*contd.*
von Greim and Hanna Reitsch reach, 673; an SS Lieutenant General shot in, 676; a final presentation of the Knight's Cross in, 679; Churchill visits, 704

Chandler, Admiral Ted: his courage, 628

Changi Camp (Singapore): medical officers reach, 721; Indian soldiers reach, 722

Changsha (China): a Japanese attack towards, 537; Japanese capture, 542

'Channel Dash': and Enigma, 300

Channel Islands: evacuated, 100; occupied by Germans, 105; commando raids on, 358, 367; bodies washed up on, given full military honours, 469; Hitler refuses to transfer troops from, 556; civilians on, to be helped, 594; a German swoop from, 648; deportees from, die in Germany, 664; German forces on, surrender, 692

Chantilly (France): 817

'Chariots': manned torpedoes, in action, 216, 280, 385; on a mission to Norway, 372

Charlemagne: and harsh measures, 328

Charleroi; (Belgium): a war crimes trial at, 613

Charleville (France): Hitler at, 83

'Charlie': a double agent, 15–16; his brother's death, 106

*Charlotte Schliemann* (German supply ship): forced to leave safety, 330

Charlottenburg (Berlin): an unsuccessful flight to, 676

Charlton, Guardsman Edward Colquhoun: his courage, 670

*Charybdis* (British light cruiser): sunk, 469

Château Terlinden (Belgium): bombed, 529; out of action, 531

Château-Thierry (France): German troops at, 88–9; reached by the Germans in 1870, 92

Châteauroux (France): a British agent reaches, 180; a British agent returns from, 505

Châtellerault (France): sabotage near, 551

Châtillon-sur-Seine (France): a parachutist killed at, 573

Chechivichi (White Russia): an anti-partisan sweep in region of, 345

Chekiang Province (China): occupied by Japan, 318

Chelm (Poland): Jews deported from, 23; mental patients murdered at, 32; Jews from, killed near, 326; Red Army enters, 559

Chelmno (Poland): a death camp at, 274–5, 279, 292, 304, 310, 322, 330–1, 351; renewed deportations to, 541; murder of a forced-labour squad at, 630; Soviet forces approach, 632

Chelsea (London): a 'Flying Bomb' on, 551

Chelyabinsk (Siberia): evacuations to, 199, 230

Chemnitz (Germany): arrests in, 412; bombed, 590; proposed 'heavy attacks' on, 636; bombed, 640

Chengtu (China): American air raids from, 540

Chennault, Colonel Claire L.: goes to

China, 276; in action, 280, 282

Chenogne (Belgium): German soldiers killed in, 621; Germans driven from, 626

Cherbourg (France): troops evacuated from, 89; troops land at, 93; Germans advance to, 97; evacuations from, 98; occupied by German troops, 100; a German radio station at, 104; a German naval patrol from, in action, 520; and the imminent Normandy Landings, 528–9; 'to be held at all costs', 542; Americans reach suburbs of, 544–5; dockyard at, surrenders, 548; final surrenders in, 549; a counter-attack towards, ordered, 565–6; railway wagons found at, for despatch of rocket equipment from Germany, 695

Cherche-Midi Prison (Paris): a suicide in (1948), 733

Chernigov (Russia): Red Army enters, 463

Cherven (Russia): partisan camps near, 303

Cheshire, Leonard: his leadership rewarded, 540; an observer above Nagasaki, 715

Chiang Kai-shek: at 129; in Burma, 325–6

*Chicago* (US heavy cruiser): a failed attack on, 329; sunk, 399

*Chicago Daily News*: and Nazi war criminals, 703

Chicago University: and the atomic bomb, 384

Chichester, Bishop of (Bishop Bell): in Sweden, 328

Chichijima (Volcano Islands): air raid on, 584

China: and the Burma Road, 108, 321; and the United States, 129, 264; and medical help, 326; forced labourers from, in New Guinea, 396; Japanese advance in, 537, 542, 613, 614; to have a post-war veto, 574, 701; soldiers from, enter Nanning, 696; soldiers from, enter I-shan, 699; soldiers from, land by parachute near Kaiping, 702; and an offer of peace to Japan, 707; American post-war help for, 730; slave labourers of, 745; war time toll of, 745–6

Chindits: in action, 404, 506

Chindwin River (Burma): crossed, 613

Chinese: massacred, in Malaya, 301; wartime death toll of, 746

Chinon (France): Resistance fighters land near (1943), 461

Chiswick (London): a rocket bomb hits, 589

Chittagong (India): British advance from, 391

Chocz (Poland): a priest from, executed, 22

Choiseul Island (Solomons): battle on, 471

Cholawski, Shalom: and the fate of a prisoner-of-war, 203; and a 'family camp' in the forests, 345

Choltitz, General Dietrich von: surrenders Paris, 580

Chorostkow (Eastern Galicia): Jews killed in, 219

'Chosen People', the: their fate gives 'pleasure', 351–2; and a fifteen year prison sentence, 740

'Chowringhee' (Burma): a landing at, 506

Christen, SS Corporal Fritz: his bravery in action, 237–5

Christian X, King of Denmark: orders a cease-fire, 54

Christiansen, Lieutenant-Commander Hasager: photographs a rocket, 453

Christmas Island (Australian): Japanese conquer, then evacuate, 314

*Chrobry* (a Polish liner): attacked, 65

Chrzanowski, Professor Ignatius: dies at Sachsenhausen, 26

Chudovo (near Leningrad): bombed, 224; captured, 225

Chuikhov, Political Commissar: dismissed, 233

Chuikov, General: enters Lodz, 632

Church, Private: hanged, 727–8

Churchill, Clementine: and aid to Russia, 240; and an 'agonizing moment', 531–2; and 'ripe plums fallen' (Riga and Athens), 602

Churchill, Randolph: suggests a rescue operation, 585

Churchill, Winston S: and the war at sea, 5, 10; and plans for 1940, 6–7; and the magnetic mine, 29, 35; and Finland, 46; and Narvik, 49; and leaflet bombing, 49 and Enigma (his 'golden eggs'), 56, 262, 300, 308; becomes Prime Minister, 61; and northern Norway, 62, 64–5; and Iceland, 63; offers 'blood, toil, tears and sweat', 64; and the battle in France, 66, 67, 68, 69, 72–3, 77–8; and Operation XD, 67; and the surrender of Belgium, 77; and Dunkirk, 77–78, 80; and the fall of France, 81–3, 87, 88, 89, 91, 93, 94, 97, 98, 101; 'we shall not flag or fail', 86; and the munitions programme for 1941, 92; and the sinking of the *Lancastria*, 98; and the defiance of Britain, 101–2, 103, 133; and the *Arandora Star*, 106; and Mers-el-Kebir, 107; and bombing policy, 108, 120, 132, 136, 142, 146, 208, 209, 319, 329, 352, 415, 417, 434–3; and a commando raid on Guernsey, 110; and the 'War of the Unknown Warrior', 110; and the Battle of Britain, 119–20; and the Blitz, 124, 125, 179, 181; and Dakar, 127; and De Gaulle, 135; and Hitler's eastern plans, 135, 192; and American military supplies, 136, 172; and Greece, 136–7, 623; and Turkey, 517; and the French Resistance, 141, 190, 396, 543; and the Western Desert war, 147, 175, 357; and Roosevelt's emissary, 151, 155; and Anglo-American cooperation, 154, 173, 319; and Hitler's designs on Britain, 157; and British aid to Russia, 190, 208, 223, 239–40, 242, 247, 308, 353, 367, 396; and British Intelligence for Russia, 202, 210, 213, 237, 239, 366, 375, 381, 384; and Roosevelt, 35, 93, 127, 136, 222, 223, 261, 282, 286, 287, 300, 326, 336, 392, 426, 451, 478–9, 576, 594, 638; and Japan, 222, 261, 275–6; and German atrocities in Russia, 226, 256; and Pearl Harbour, 272; and Hitler's declaration of war on the United States. 277–8; and Hitler's 'outstanding blunder', 278;

and the Anglo-American alliance, 282, 434; and the United Nations, 286, 396, 728–9; approaches German-occupied France, in error, 291; and the fall of Singapore, 300, 303; and the bombing of Cologne, 329; and the fall of Tobruk, 335; and Stalin, 347, 352, 353, 366, 367, 385, 415, 417, 489, 536, 600, 610, 679–80: and El Alamein, 371, 376; and the Jews of Europe, 372–3; and the murder of Darlan, 389; at Casablanca, 392, 393, 396–7; and a leaflet detailing 'German atrocities', 400; congratulates Roosevelt, 408; and the Battle of Kursk, 420; and the Allied deception plan for Sicily, 423–4; and a discussion of Allied strategy (May 1943), 426; addresses the United States Congress, 430; and Tito, 440; and Italy, 441, 445, 448, 452, 459, 509; eavesdropped telephone conversations of, 448, 522; and the U-boat war, 444; and Roosevelt's desire to reach Berlin, 455; at Teheran, 478–9; and the bombing of Berlin, 481; and the sinking of the Scharnhorst, 482; and the political future of Poland (1944–5), 496–7, 554, 627, 679–80; and preparations for the Normandy Landings, 452, 478, 512, 529; and British war casualties, 514; and 'an awful load of hatred', 529; and the capture of Rome, 531; and the German shortage of fuel oil, 535; and the request to bomb the railways to Auschwitz, 546; and the Russian advance (from June 1944), 548–9; and the truth about Auschwitz, 554; and the Curzon Line, 554; and the Normandy Landings deception, 555; and the V2 rocket, 557; and gas 'in retaliation', 557; and the Warsaw uprising, 564, 567, 572, 580–1, 585–6, 592; in Italy, 576; and the Jewish Brigade Group, 576; and the future of Germany, 592; in Moscow (October 1944), 600, 601; and a 'brilliant' American victory, 606; and the 'last lap', 611; in Paris (November 1944), 512; and the Ardennes, 615; and British and Commonwealth war dead (by the end of November 1944), 629; and the Allied balance of forces (by the end of November 1944), 629; and the Allied balance of forces (February 1945), 639; and German reparations, 640; and Dresden, 640–1; and Hitler's possible move to southern Germany, 650; views the battle (on the Rhine), 652; crosses the Rhine, 652 unease at at Soviet advance, 658; and the corpses of Ohrdruf, 659; and British war dead (by February 1945), 661; and a British drive to the Baltic, 667; and Himmler's offer to surrender, 670; and the imminent Communist – non–Communist divide, 579–80, 686–7; and the American–Soviet military demarcation line, 680; and the German surrender, in Italy and southern Austria, 683; in Berlin, 704, 705; and the atomic bomb test, 705, 707; and a possible negotiated peace with Japan, 705, 707–8; and Austria, 705–6; and German prisoners-of-war, 721; the 'iron curtain' speech of, 728–9

Ciano, Count Galeazzo: and Hitler, 98, 142; executed, 488
Ciechocinek (Poland): Polish prisoners-of-war in, 27
City of Benares (British passenger liner): torpedoed, 126
Clan Fraser (British merchant ship): blows up, 170
Clapham Junction (London): a 'Flying Bomb' near, 542
Clark, General Mark W.: his secret landing, 371
Clauberg, Professor Karl: and medical experiments, 340, 432; dies on the eve of his trial, 738
Clermont-Ferrand (France): 95; an act of sabotage in, 435
Clement (British merchant ship): sunk, 18
Cluj (Hungary): beseiged, 601; overrun, 603
Clydeside (Scotland): bombed, 181
Coconada (India): bombed, 315
Codex Judaicum: issued in Slovakia, 232
Cohen, Major P. A.: reaches Crete, 180
Colditz Castle (Germany): escapes from, 288, 597; American forces reach, 666
Cole, Sergeant Harold: his treachery, 275, 408; shot dead, 728
Colepough, William: a German agent, arrested, 615
Colin, Paul: killed, 422
Colleville-sur-Mer (Normandy): American troops link up at, 536
Cologne (Germany): leaflets dropped on, 461 Jews deported from, 245; bombed, 254, 328–9, 440; still under German control, 602; American forces approach, 617; a rocket bomb falls near, in error, 649; an autobahn to, cut, 650; a war crimes trial in, 741
Colorado (US battleship): hit by accident, 628
Colombo (Ceylon): bombed, 314; merchant seamen, on their way from, machine-gunned after being torpedoed, 500
Colmar (France): at, 97; occupied, 100; liberated, 634; battle near, 639
Colvenaer, Yvon: shot, 588
Columbia (US cruiser): hit by a suicide boat, 628
Combat: the psychological hazards of, 599
'Combat': a Resistance group, 471
Combined Chiefs of Staff: established, in Washington, 282
'Comet': an escape line, betrayed, 393; broken, 426
Commandant Teste (French aircraft carrier): escapes, 107
Commercy (France): American troops cross Meuse at, 584
'Commissar Decree': and the German invasion of Russia, 160, 167–8, 183, 191, 200–1, 205, 218
Compiègne (France): and peace negotiations, 70; and the armistice of June 1940, 100–1
Comps, André: and the 'Flying Bomb', 463–4
Compton, Captain John T.: court-martialled, 445

Conant, Professor James B.: and the atomic bomb, 241, 628, 696
Congressional Medal of Honour: see index entry for Medal of Honour
'Conical Hill' (Okinawa): captured, 694
Conte Rosso (Italian troopship): sunk, 185
Contes (southern France): a deportee from, executed, 673
Conti, Dr Leonardo: and euthanasia, 11; a protest to, 228; commits suicide, 724
Copenhagen (Denmark): occupied, 54; re-occupied, 456; Gestapo headquarters at, bombed, 651; a British 'holding force' to be sent to, 687; Germans lay down their arms in, 690
Cor Jésu (Belgian fishing vessel): at Dunkirk, 81
Coral Sea: battle of, 322
Corfu (Greece): and Italy, 135, 494; Jews deported to Auschwitz from, 540, 549
Cork, Lord: and northern Norway, 64–5
Cornford, Reginald Leslie: and the battle for Berlin, 676
Cornish, Mary: her courage, 126
Cornwall (British cruiser): in action, 180; sunk, 314
Corregidor (Philippines): MacArthur reaches, 282; Japanese bomb, 284; defence of, 316; surrenders, 323; Americans return to, 642; battle for, 644; last Japanese soldiers surrender on (January 1946), 727
'Corridor of Death': at Leningrad, 391
Corrientes (German supply ship): forced to leave safety, 330
Corsica (Mediterranean): Hitler orders evacuation of, 461
Cossack (British destroyer): the success of, 42
Cossacks: in action against the French Resistance, 515; in action against Italian partisans, 600
Cotentin Peninsula (France): defences of, 515, 528; an Allied landing expected on, 534; Allies about to overrun, 540
Cottbus (near Berlin): bombs dropped on, 479
Council for the Assistance of Jews: established, in Warsaw, 384
Courageous (British aircraft carrier): torpedoed, 10
Cousin, Abbé Maurice: killed, 513
Courtney, Major Henry A.: his courage, 694–5
Coventry (England): bombed, 142–3; repercussions of bombing of, 146; renewed bombing of, 171; a comparison with, 439
Coventry (British anti-aircraft destroyer): in action, 184; sunk, 360
Coward, Sergeant Charles: his courage, 503
Cowra (Australia): a mass breakout at, 565
Cox, Geoffrey: an eye-witness, 31, 42, 47, 49
Crabtree Neck (Maine): German agents land at, 615
Cracow (Poland): Germans enter, 6; slave labour camps near, 23; Poles

Cracow (Poland)—*contd.*
seized in, 26; and the Jewish star, 28; a Pole shot in, 47; and German atrocities, 57; a deportation to Auschwitz through, 95; Poles from, executed at Dachau, 140; and German moves prior to 'Barbarossa', 164; a Jewish act of defiance in, 388; a German act of terror in, 629; Soviet forces enter, 632; 'mass arrests' near, 646

Creil (France): and the 'Flying Bomb', 505

Crerar, Brigadier H. D. G.: reaches Britain, 25

Creswell, Michael: helps escapees, 288

Crete: and Italy, 135; British troops reach, 147; British troops evacuated to, 175, 176; German preparations for invasion of, 180, 183; bombardment of, 183, 184; invaded, 184; evacuation of, 186; losses on, 186–7; and a deception plan, 347; German bombers move westward from, 374; Germany to 'stay' on, 441; and an Allied deception plan, 494; a kidnapping on, 519–20; reprisals on, 520; killing of hostages on, 534; a former Governor of, executed, 732

Crimea, the: German designs on, 120; German aspirations for, 207, 236; to be occupied, 222; and Hitler's strategy, 224; a motor road to be built to, 235; German advance towards, 238, 239; Germans reach, 245; Hitler's new name for, 253; German conquest of, 254; executions in, 267–8, 296, 301; Soviet troops land on, 283; German counter-offensive on, 323; German speakers from South Tyrol, to be settled in, 341; an attack into the Caucasus from, 341; to be evacuated, 471; Germans retain control of, 507; liberation of, 515; effect of liberation of, on Turkey, 517

Crinis, Professor Max de: commits suicide, 682

Croatia: declared an independent State, 172; persecutions in, 182, 306; to be a 'tourist' paradise', 207; Jews not to be deported from, 344–5, 386; Jews sent to Auschwitz from, 424, 432; an anti-partisan action in, 427; troops from, fight Tito's partisans, 431; Jews from, reach safety in Italy, 585; German forces retreat through, 669

Croats: political assurances to, 167

Croix de Guerre: awarded, 370, 464

Croix de Guerre with Gold Star: awarded, 728

Croix du Capitaine Michel: created, 477

'Cromwell': codeword for an imminent invasion, 123

Cross Island (Solomons): J. F. Kennedy reaches, 449

Cross of War Merit: awarded, 583

Cross-Channel landing: planning of, 392, 397, 426, 430; to be the 'primary ... effort' of Britain and the United States, 452; Hitler warned about, 472; discussed at Teheran, 478; German concern with, 486, 488; planning for (January–May 1944), 490–1, 497, 507, 512, 515, 517, 520, 521, 526, 528–9; deception plans for, 492–3, 494, 506, 522, 532; and a map of German

defences, 515; and General Guderian's visit to France, 517, 519; and Ultra, 517, 519, 521, 530, 533; launched, 533; carried out, 534–6

Crown of King Zvonimir: awarded, 339

Croydon (England): fifty people killed at, 136

Cruewell, General: and the German rocket bomb, 416

Cuneo (Italy): Jews shot in, 673

Cunningham, Admiral Sir John: 184, 347

Cunnington, Captain D. W.: his courage, 126–7

*Cumberland* (British cruiser): hit, 127

Curda, Karel: an informer, 334; executed, 732

Currie, Major David: his courage, 567

Curzon Line: and Poland's post-war borders, 497, 554, 679

Cvetković, Dragiša: refuses to join Axis, 157; join Axis, 164

*Cyclops* (British merchant ship): torpedoed, 290

Cyprus: German prisoners-of-war and Jews in camps on, 730

Cyrenaica (Libya): Australian troops advance in, 153; Rommel advances in, 168; Rommel completes reconquest of, 170; Rommel reconquers a second time, 299; Mussolini flies to, 337; Mussolini returns to Italy from, 338

Czechoslovak Republic: declared, 583

Czechoslovakia: an agent of, 25; forces of, in Britain, 113, 124; a clandestine mission to, 283–4; Jews from, deported to their deaths, 324, 507; troops of, in action at Kharkov, 410; forced labourers from, killed in an Allied air raid, 453; and war crimes, to be punished, 469; troops of, in action at Kiev, 473; troops from, reach the Carpathians, 604; Red Army approaches pre-war borders of, 616; Red Army enters, 632; Red Army advances through, 661; officers from, executed in Dachau, 668; battles in, 674, 686; to be 'police-governed', 686; continued fighting in, 689; final military operations in, 691; German troops surrender in, 692; troops from, and the surrender of Dunkirk, 692; German-speaking inhabitants expelled from, 699–700, 710; in the Soviet bloc, 723; rejects the Marshall Plan, 733

Czechs: imprisoned, 7; sent to Germany for forced labour, 40; 'bludgeoned', 69; their fate 'a matter of utter indifference', 466; a monument to, unveiled, 740

Czertaski, Asher: and an act of resistance, 328

Czerniakow (Warsaw): holds out, 586; Polish troops enter, 593, 594

Czernowitz (Roumania): Red Army reaches, 506–7

Czestochowa: German orders in, 9; forced labourers taken from, 129; Jewish resistance in, 440; Jews killed in, 444

'D-Day' (the Normandy Landings): 526, 534; and an air ace, 556

Dabie (western Poland): Jews from, gassed, 279

Dabrowa (near Warsaw): a Polish pilot shot in, 596

Dabrowa Gornicza (Eastern Silesia): Poles executed in, 332; Jews deported to Auschwitz from, 436

Dachau (Germany): Czech prisoners at, 7; a would-be assassin imprisoned at, 26; a mass execution of Poles at, 140; prisoners from, used for medical experiments, 184; a courageous Pastor, dies on way to, 228; a Resistance heroine, shot at, 438; Soviet prisoners-of-war shot at, 496, 503; a parachutist sent to, 525; a German general sent to, 550; an Italian police officer sent to, 585; Red Army officers executed in, 585; British agents executed in, 490; a parachutist from Palestine executed in, 611; Hitler's would-be assassin, murdered in, 660; further executions in, of Allied officers, 668; American forces enter, 677–8; a war crimes trial at, 725–6; forcible repatriation from, 728; war criminals cremated at, 731; Displaced Persons at, 736; a memorial inaugurated at (1956), 738

Dahl, Colonel Arne: lands in Karelia, 612–3

Dahlerus, Birger: his peace mission, 19–20

Dahlgren (Virginia): and a scale model atomic bomb, 451

*Daily Express*: 'Shakespeare beats Hitler', 131

*Daily Herald*: reports on a false announcement of victory, 586–7

Dakar (French West Africa): 109; plans for the seizure of, 127; and France's 'honour', 133

Daladier, Edouard: and Finland, 34; falls from power, 50; Foreign Minister, 54

Dalmatian Coast (Adriatic Sea): islands off, being fortified, 494; islands off, bombed, 505; Germans begin evacuation of, 660

Dalton, Hugh, urged to 'Set Europe ablaze', 106

Damascus (Syria): battle for, 188–9; surrender of, 194

Danube River: mines dropped in, 515, 550, 599; Red Army reaches, 584; Red Army crosses, 587, 616; battles near, 640

Damaskinos, Archbishop of Athens: protests against deportation of Jews, 414; leads a government, 623

Dame of Sark, the: raises the Allied flags, 690

Damerment, Madeleine: shot, 590

Danielak, Alexander: drops supplies on Warsaw, 590

Dankowski, Stefanek: shot, 36

Dannecker, Theodor: and the Jews, 129, commits suicide, 727

Danzig: Hitler enters, 11; Germans deported to, 23; an escape through, 480; a new submarine being fabricated in, 625; a 'death march' on the road towards, 640; Germans in action near, 640; Hitler demands railway line to, to be held, 643; besieged, 654; fighting near, 687, 689

'Danzig': code word for an invasion, 60

Dardanelles (Turkey): 137

Darlan, Admiral Jean: and the French

Fleet, 99, 106, 383; and the Allied landings in North Africa, 376; assassinated, 389

Darling, Donald: helps escapees, 288

Darmstadt (Germany): bombed, 590; jet airfields at, bombed, 652; a war crimes trial at, 708

Darnard, Joseph: collaborates, 390

Dartmouth (southern England): a mission from, 475; and an Allied escape line, 495; an invasion exercise attacked off, 520

Darwin (Australia): Japanese attack on, 302; MacArthur reaches, 307

Das Reich (magazine): and the Jews, 257

Daumeries, Fernand: sentenced to death, 613

Davao (Philippines): an American landing at, 702

Davis, Commander George F.: his bravery, 628

'Day of the Eagle, The': the air war against Britain, 114–5; launched, 116, 117; fails, 124; and the Blitz, 127; German air losses after, 130

Day of Judgement, the: and the responsibility for Pearl Harbour, 738

Dayan, Moshe: in action, 189

Dayton (Ohio): Roosevelt speaks in, 131

De Bono, Marshal Emilio: executed, 488

De Gaulle, Charles: in action, 68; becomes Under-Secretary of War, 86; supports a stand in Brittany, 90, 91; broadcsts from London, 99; pledges to fight on, 110; and the Dakar expedition, 127; sets up the Empire Defence Council, 134; takes Gabon from Vichy, 141; and Jean Moulin's mission, 287, 434; denounces 'war crimes', 290; denounces 'bestial policy' of killing Jews, 387; his influence in France, to be combatted, 464; returns to France, 542; his representative in Paris, shot, 568; returns to Paris, 580, 581, 612

De Ruyter (Dutch light cruiser): sunk, 303

De Tassigny, General de Lattre: his escape, 468; and the battle for Colmar, 639; witnesses the final German instrument of surrender, 690

De Valera, Eamon: a protest from, 295; sends condolences on Hitler's death, 683

'Dead Horse Alley': in Normandy, 567

Deakin, Captain William: in Yugoslavia, 430, 432

'Death Candidates': killed in a reprisal action, 646

'Death Commando': reports of, 658

'Death marches': westward from Auschwitz and its labour camps, 631, 631–2; westward from Stutthof, 633

Death's Head Division (of the S.S.): in Poland, 2–3, 32; in action in France, 69, 70, 73, 74, 76–7, 100; moves to East Prussia, 188, 191; in action against Russia, 201–2, 204, 237–8, 238; and the first heavy snowfall (October 1941), 244; complaints of cowardice in, 257; and Soviet partisans, 264–5

Debica (Poland): fate of Polish children at, 37

Deblin (Poland): 115

Debrecen (Hungary): bombed, 530; beseiged, 601; falls, 604

Deception: and Hitler, 59; and Russia, 130–1, 159; and the Normandy landing, 492–3, 494, 506, 522, 532

Degrelle, Léon: awarded the Knight's Cross, 503; awarded the Oak Leaves, 582

Delft University (Holland): a protest at, 144

Delhi (India): violence in, 725

Delp, Alfred: hanged, 637

Demyansk (Russia): Hitler refuses withdrawal from, 208; Hitler awards commanding General in, 338

Dendre River (Belgium): British fall back to, 68

Denée (Belgium): battle at, 66

Denmark: plans for, 45, 46; invasion of, 53; overrun, 54; its future, 85; and a German demand for the evacuation of Jews, 363–4; forced labour from, 421, 427; resistance in, and a German ultimatum, 456; rescue of Jews from, 464; terror killings in, 488; and Hitler's view of Allied strategy, 530; and the Normandy deception plan, 542; a strike in, and reprisals, 550; Allied raids, on Gestapo headquarters in, 608, 651; Russians to be prevented from entering, 667, 687

Dentz, General Henri: defends Beirut and Damascus, 188–9

Deprez, Robert: killed, 512

Deptford (London): a rocket bomb hits: 614

Der Stürmer: the editor of, hanged, 731

Derby (England): a bombing raid on, foiled, 181

Derna (Libya): evacuated, 155

Dekanozov, Vladimir: his place of honour, 179

Derrick, Sergeant Thomas: his courage in action, 477

Deschenes Commission of Inquiry on War Criminals: its rport, 742

Desoubrie, Jacques: hanged, 728

Destruction Battalions: to be set up, in Russia, 201

'Deutschland über Alles': sung as the Tirpitz sank, 612

Deventer (Holland): a Dutchman from, hanged, 669

Devers, General Jacob L.: accepts an unconditional surrender, 687

Devil, the: in Lille, 104; and the Jews, 405

Devonshire (British cruiser): King Haakon embarks on, 87; sinks the Atlantis, 261–2

Diamonds (to the Knight's Cross): awarded, 87

'Dick': and the Normandy deception, 537

Dieppe (France): Germans advance towards, 88; an Allied commando raid on, 353–4; fate of prisoners-of-war captured at, 367; and a possible Allied landing, 528; an Allied deception at, 532

Diego Suarez (Madagascar): attcked, 323; a submarine raid on, 330

Dielpi (Italian fuel ship): sunk, 357

Dietrich, Otto: Russia 'vanquished', 242

Dietrich, Sepp: in hiding, 78

Dijon (France): Germans enter, 97; ss

in action near, 100; Germans withdraw from, 571

Dinant (Belgium): German troops reach, 64

Dimitrov (near Moscow): Germans reach, 262; Soviet reinforcements gather near, 265

Dirlewanger, General: his award, 597

Dirlewanger Brigade: in Warsaw, 564, 565; in Slovakia, 604

Diskin, Efim: his heroism, 259

Displaced Persons (D.P.s): throughout Europe, 726; remnants of (in 1952), 736

Distinguished Conduct Medal: awarded, 422

Distinguished Flying Cross: awarded, 5

Distinguished Service Cross: awarded, 279, 453

Distinguished Service Medal: awarded, 64

Distinguished Service Order: awarded, 45, 64, 442, 464, 520

Djakovo (Yugoslavia): Jews murdered at, 392

Djedeida (Tunisia): raid on, 383

Djilas, Milovan: a partisan, 208

Dmitriev (Russia): an anti-partisan sweep near, 390

Dnepropetrovsk (southern Russia): Germans capture, 226; Russians in action near, 242; executions in, 298; Red Army approaches, 464; Red Army enters, 471

Dneprodzherzinsk (southern Russia): Russians enter, 471

Dnieper River (Russia): 181, 219, 227; Soviet partisans east of, 303; Soviet partisans west of, 383; Red Army approaches, 463; Red Army crosses, 464, 471; Germans defeated at, 499

Dniester River (Russia): Germans forced back across, 506

Dno (Russia): partisans active near, 346; Germans driven from, 503

Dobromil (Eastern Galicia): Jews killed in, 209

Dodecanese Islands (Aegean Sea): 161; battle for, 465

Dohnanyi, Hans von: and the first Bomb Plot against Hitler (March 1943), 412; arrested, 419; implicated, 597; murdered, 660; his brother-in-law shot, 672

Dolfuss, Dr Engelbert: 211

'Dolphin': a German cypher key, recovered, 45

Domagala, Jan: saves evidence of executions, 603

Domodossola (Italy): partisans control region near, 575–6, 590

Domont (near Paris): five Frenchmen shot in, 568

Don Basin (Russia): Germans forced to give up, 459

Don River (Russia): German attack towards, 340; reached, 341; a defensive line to be held on, 345–6; Germans cross, 347; Italian cavalry in action on, 355; Germans not allowed to withdraw across, 381; Germans driven south of, 388

Donat, Alexander: 'victory ... certain', 199

Donbaik (Burma): British advance to, 391; attack on, repulsed, 399

Donetz Basin (Ukraine): a German objective, 222

Donetz River (Ukraine): Germans reach, 341

Dongo (Italy): Mussolini killed in, 676

Dönitz, Admiral Karl: and the *Courageous*, 10; and German submarine losses, 281; and the Channel Coast, 299; and rescue work to stop, 360; and the Battle of the Atlantic, 425, 431; warns of a cross-Channel invasion, 517; doubts an imminent invasion, 522; and the Normandy deception, 537; and the failure of the Bomb Plot, 559; and the German surrender, 684, 689

'Donny': a double agent, and the Normandy deception, 537

Donovan, Colonel William J.: and the Balkans, 157–8; and national security, 192; and money for the Polish resistance, 412

Doolittle, Lieutenant-Colonel James H.: leads a bombing raid against Japan, 317

Doorman, Admiral Karel: killed in action, 303

Dora (Germany): concentration camp 'at, 522; Gypsies at, 562

'Dorick': a double agent, and the Normandy deception, 537

Dornberger, General Walter: surrenders to the Americans, 683

Dorogobuzh (Russia):-Soviet partisans in region of , 296, 308, 318, 340; an anti-partisan sweep near, 440

Dorsch, Xavier: builds a rocket launching site, 455

*Dorsetshire* (British cruiser): rescues survivors, 184; sunk, 314

Dorsten (Ruhr): bombed, 649

Dortmund (Ruhr): Jews deported from, 326–7; bombed, 432, 649

'Dortmund': the codeword to start 'Barbarossa', 192

D'Ortoli, Paul: executed, 673

Dosen (near Leipzig): and euthanasia, 508

Doss, Desmond T.: his courage, 662

'Double Cross' system: established, 15–16

Dover (England): and the Dunkirk evacuation, 75, 78; cross-Channel shelling of, 594

Dover Strait: and Hitler's view of Allied strategy, 530; and the Normandy Landings deception plan, 555

Dowding, Sir Hugh: and Britain's weakness in the air, 85

'Down with Hitler': painted on a wall in Munich (1943), 404

Downing Street (London): awaits a parachute attack, 69

Drabik, Sergeant Alexander A.: crosses the Rhine, 647–8

Drancy (Paris): Jews deported to Auschwitz from, 310; a Jew dies at, 506

Dresden (Germany): proposed 'heavy attacks' on, 636; 'allotted' to the allied airforces, 638; bombing of, 640–2, 667; German troops still fighting near (on 8 May 1945), surrender, 690

Drina River (Yugoslavia): Germans fall back to, 615

Drissa (Russia): a Soviet defence line at, 201, 205; Germans driven from, 553

Drohobycz (Eastern Galicia): Soviet annexation of, 16; Jews killed in, 211, 218

Drugge, Karl: hanged, 129

Drvar (Yugoslavia): Tito moves to, 489; a German move against, 527

Drysdale River Mission (Australia): bombed, 462

Dublin (Eire): condolences on Hitler's death expressed in, 683

Dubno (Poland): overrun, 201; Jews murdered in, 322, 367–8

Dubnov, Simon: his last words, 266

Dubrovnik (Yugoslavia): Tito's partisans enter, 604

*Duchess of York* (British passenger liner): German prisoners-of-war on, 154

*Duilio* (Italian battleship): sunk, 140

Dudin (a partisan): in action, 209

Dulles, Allan: negotiates with an ss general, 648

Dülmen (Ruhr): bombed, 649; a planned German counter-attack at, 652

Dumbarton Oaks (Washington): and the United Nations Organization, 574

*Duncan* (US destroyer): caught in cross-fire, 368

*Dunkerque* (French battle cruiser): sunk, 107

Dunkirk (France): and the British Expeditionary Force, 72–4; 75–83; to be held, 585; Germans besieged in, 592; Germans in, surrender, 692; an Anglo-French treaty signed in (1947), 732

Dunlop, Colonel Edward: a prisoner-of-war of the Japanese, his daily record, 318, 345, 417, 422, 435, 437–8, 477; and liberation, 718

Dunov, Anatoly: executed, 503

Duquenne-Créton, Madame: helps two survivors, 77

Düren (Germany): American forces enter, 617

Durmitor, Mount (Yugoslavia): Tito's partisans driven to, 392; partisans driven from, 455

Durovo (Russia): Russians reach, 414

Düsseldorf (Germany): a Dutch officer dies in, 27; bombed, 146; Jews deported from, 245; bombed, using two-ton bombs, 359; bombed, using a new device, 389; anti-Nazi leaflets distributed in, 412; American troops ,reach Rhine opposite, 645; a war crimes trial in, 741

Dutch Council of Churches: a protest by, 288

Dutch East Indies: and Japan, 216, 253, 290; overrun, 303–4, 305–6, 306–7; fate of internees and prisoners of war on, 635; civil insurgency in, 733

Dutch Volunteer Legion: on the Leningrad front, 296

Dvina River (the Western Dvina): 181; Germans reach, 201

Dvinsk (Latvia): Germans enter, 201; Jews shot in, 209; 'insane persons' murdered at, 235; Red Army enters, 562

Dyle River (Belgium): Anglo-French plan for, 59; advance to, 61

Dzhankoi (Crimea): executions at, 295

Dziekanow (near Warsaw): an

American airman beaten to death in, 596

*Eagle* (British aircraft carrier): in action, 109; and aid to Malta, 323; sunk, 352

'Eagle's Nest' (Bad Nauheim): Hitler at, 617

Easley, Brigadier Claudius M.: killed, 700

East Anglia (England): bombers strike into Baltic from, 625

East Germany: in the Soviet bloc, 723; an atom spy to live in, 734; declines to pay reparations to Jews, 735

East Grinstead (England): burns treated at, 131

East Prussia (Germany): a concentration camp in, 14; German mental patients in, rounded up and killed, 70; Hitler's search for a headquarters in, 117; German troops move to (June 1941), 188, 191; Germans driven back towards (June 1944), 544; Red Army reaches (August 1944), 571; to be divided between Russia and Poland, 600; Red Army enters, 603–4; Hitler leaves, 613; Red Army enters in force, 632; Germans counter-attack in, 634; soldiers and refugees from, drowned, 635; continued fighting in, 654, 687; surrenders in, 692; some Germans refuse to surrender in (11 May 1945), 693; final surrender in, 694

East Upper Silesia (Poland): Poles expelled from, 27; slave labour in, 503; 524–5; aerial photography over, 513–4

'East Wall': to be built along the Volga, 312

Eastern Galicia (Poland): 9, 307, 310, 315, 362, 439, 490; Red Army approaches, 511

Eben-Emael (Belgium): attacked, 61; surrenders, 62; American troops capture, 590

Ebensee (Austria): and the intended murder of several thousand Jews, 687–8; an act of defiance in, 688

Eberl, Dr Irmfried: and euthanasia, 105; and the Treblinka death camp, 344

Eberswalde (near Berlin): and the German defence of Berlin, 669–70; General Steiner's lack of action at, 670

Eckernförde (Germany): 'activity' at, 52; details of new submarines at, to go to the Western Allies, 690

Ecot (France): an anti-Maquis sweep at, 554

Edelman, David: falls in battle, 565

Eden, Anthony: 134, 159, 278, 468, 529, 546, 554; 'horrified' by Morgenthau Plan, 592; and Churchill's wish to forestall the Russians, 667, 687; and the missing Polish negotiators, 686

'Edgar' (Philippe de Gunzbourg): sabotage by, 484, 543

Edgers, Mrs Dorothy: and Pearl Harbour, 271

*Edinburgh* (British cruiser): sunk, 325

Edmondson, Corporal Jack: his courage, 316

Edwards, Private E. L.: dies in captivity, 435

Edwards, Hughie: wins the Victoria Cross, 207

Eger (Hungary): Red Army enters, 615
Egersund (Norway): a German ship boarded near, 42
Eggersdorf (near Berlin): defence of, 670
Egypt: 90, 104; vulnerability of British forces in, 122; Hitler's thoughts on, 135, 143; reinforcements for, 149, 175; danger to, 157; Rommel plans to conquer, 177; Rommel enters, 178; supplies for, 180; aircraft transferred to, from Crete, 184; King of the Hellenes evacuated to, 186; renewed threat to, 296; a successful Italian naval action off, 333; renewed danger in, 335, 336–7; and the German advance into the Caucasus, 348; setback to, 376; German prisoners-of-war repatriated from, 732
Ehrenburg, Ilya: and Stalin, 176; 'woe to Germany!' 571
Eichelberger, General: and the battle for Biak Island, 542–3
Eichmann, Adolf: and the Jews, 129, 249. 251; and the 'Final Solution', 292; and medical experiments, 299; and the deportation of Jews, 329, 336, 508, 560; returns to Budapest, 603; brought to trial in Israel, 739–40
Eicke, SS General: in Poland, 2, 4, 12; in East Prussia, 191; at Sachsenhausen, 243; complains of cowardice on the Eastern Front, 257; decorated by Hitler, 338
Eifel Mountains (Germany): Hitler refuses a withdrawal to, 621; troops withdrawn from, to the East, 626
Eik (Belgium): German troops reach, 61
Eindhoven (Holland): a parachute landing at, 593
Einstein, Albert: 20, 21
Eire: the President of, and Hitler's death, 683
Eisenach (Germany): a counter-attack towards, defeated, 659
Eisenhower, General Dwight D.: 'we must win in Europe', 295; and a deception plan, 347; and the surrender of Italy, 452; and a plan to land near Rome, 459; and the Normandy landings, 490–1; 515, 531, 532; and the Normandy Landing deception, 555; visits the Falaise battlefield, 574; and the human hazards of combat, 599; and German losses, 615; and the Ardennes, 621–2; and Berlin, 658, 661; and the corpses of Ohrdruf, 659; and the American-Soviet demarcation line, 680; and the German surrender, 689; and Prague, 690
Eisiskes (Lithuania): Jews killed in, 239
El Agheila (Libya): British driven from, 165; Rommel driven from, 259; Rommel, again master of, falls back to, 382
El Alamein (Egypt): Rommel reaches, 337, 338; Rommel unable to take, 358; Rommel defeated at, 371; Rommel pushed back towards Libya from, 374, 376
El Greco: paintings by, evacuated, 206
El Guettar (Tunisia): Germans break through at, 385
El Hamma (Tunisia): General Messe withdraws to, 415; German and Italian forces driven from, 416
Elba (Italy): captured, 542
Elbe River: a secret meeting on, 188; a

hospital ship on, sunk, 645; western Allies reach, 661; a proposed defence line from, towards Berlin, 670–1; Americans and Russians link forces at, 673
Elbing (East Prussia): Soviet forces reach Baltic at, 633
Electra (British destroyer): sunk, 303
Eliasberg, Karl: conducts in Leningrad, 255
Elista (southern Russia): Germans reach, 352; Soviet partisans at, 370; Germans withdraw to, 385
Elizabeth, Queen: and an air raid, 155
Elizabeth II, Queen: and Hirohito's visit to London (1971), 741–2
Elsas, Fritz: executed, 627
Elser, Johann Georg: tries to kill Hitler, 26; murdered, 660
Empire Defence Council: set up by De Gaulle, 134
Empress Augusta Bay (Solomon Islands): battle in, 508
Empress of Asia (British troopship): sunk, 299
Empress of Britain (British passenger liner): attacked at sea, 132
Empress of Canada (British passenger liner): Russians evacuated on, 226
Emmerich, SS Sergeant: wounded, at Auschwitz, 469
Emmons, General Delos C.: reaches London, 120
Encounter (British destoyer): sunk, 304
Endrass, Captain: lost without trace, 281
'Enemies of the People': executed, 598
Enfidaville (Tunisia): defence line at, 419
Engel, Captain Gerhard: and a protest to Hitler, 19; and Hitler's 'nightmare' (25 November 1941), 263
'England Gun': destroyed, 555–6
English Channel: a British convoy attacked in, 109; and the 'Day of the Eagle', 117; and a possible German invasion, 123; and the movement of German air forces to the Balkans, 166; and the movement of German air forces to Poland, 176; a Commando raid across, 304; decoy air raids across, 315–6; pre-invasion practice attacks across, 318–9, 353–4
Enigma machine: its secrets broken, 39; three rotors of, recovered, 45; its Norway key broken, 58; and the German plans in May 1940, 58; and the breaking of the German Air Force key, 71, 82; and an understanding of German priorities, 82, 83; enables British re-inforcements to be sent to France, 83, 87, 88; restriction of secrets of, 85–6; and the bombing of Britain, 104, 104–5; and German bomber strength, 108; and German intentions (August 1940), 117, 119, 121; and Hiter's eastern plans, 136, 142, 148, 164, 181, 191, 192; confirms that no invasion of Britain is in prospect (November 1940), 138–9; and 'Purple', 154; further success in keybreaking of, 154; and the Battle of the Atlantic, 159; and 'Operation Claymore', 161; and the North African battles, 174, 183, 259, 262, 357; and German plans for Crete, 180, 183; and the recovery of cypher material

from a U-boat, 180; and the 'Vulture' key used by the Germans in Russia, 202, 237; and Soviet Intelligence, 208; an Eastern Front key, broken, 207, 209; sent to Russia, 208, 210, 213, 238, 327, 341, 366, 367, 381, 385, 424; and SS atrocities, 213, 221, 226, 233, 256; and German operational orders on the Russian front, 232, 238, 257, 287, 297, 308, 327, 334, 341, 343, 381, 385, 395–6, 407, 420, 424; five keys of, broken (1–2 January 1942), 287; a setback to the decrypting of, in the Atlantic and Mediterranean, 297; further keys of, broken at Bletchley, 297; and the 'Channel Dash', 300; and the Tirpitz, 307; and a naval success off the United States, 330; further keys of, broken, 334, 353, 366, 385–6, 395–6, 407; and Malta, 368; and El Alamein, 371; and an act of courage off the Nile Delta, 373–4; and the 'Torch' landings in French North Africa, 374, 376; and the German plan to bomb Baku, 375; and the diversion of transport aircraft from Stalingrad, 376–7, 385; and the destruction of Rommel's oil fuel supplies, 387, 388, 394, 406; and the battle in Tunisia, 402; and the Battle of Médenine, 409; and the battle of the Atlantic, 413–4, 422, 425, 431; and Rommel's supply links with Sicily, 419, 425; and the Allied deception plan for Sicily, 423–4; and the battle of Kursk, 424; and an Anglo-American agreement concerning, 429; and the Geheimschreiber secret teleprinter, 429; and the German transfer of air forces from Russia to Italy, 441; Soviet use of, 441; and the Balkans, 451; and the sinking of the Scharnhorst, 482; and the Normandy Landings deception plans, 492–3; and a German attack at Anzio, 499; and the 'Flying Bomb', 522; and German preparations to meet a cross-Channel landing, 528; and the German fuel shortage in France, 535; and the German fuel shortage on all fronts, 576; and a curtailment of German air activity on the Western Front, 577; and the Ardennes, 625–6; and a new German submarine, 625; and Hitler's final questions, 679
see also Index entry for 'Ultra'
Eniwetok Island (Pacific Ocean): Americans land on, 496; American victory on, 499
'Enola Gay' (US bomber): and the atomic bomb, 70, 712
Enoura Maru (Japanese freighter): bombed, 618
Enschede (Holland): a rocket fired on Antwerp from, 620
Enterprise (US aircraft carrier): at Pearl Harbour, 268; damaged in the Marshall Islands, 297; a flying bomb suicide attack on, 650; an earlier mission of, recalled, 737
Eperclecques (Channel Coast): rocket site on, bombed, 455
Epping (London): a rocket bomb raid, 589
Erdman, Lothar: killed, 10
'Ermine': German communication key, broken, 407

Erith (Kent): an incident in, 183
Eritrea: 90; bombing attack on, 90–91; British advance in, 153, 155, 165; overrun, 170
Erkner (near Berlin): bombed, 481
Essen (Germany): bombed, 139, 308, 408, 409, 417, 504, 648
Essentuki (Caucasus): Jews murdered at, 359
Estonia: its treaty with Russia, 16; Soviet bases in, 44; Soviet troops to enter, 94; annexed, 111; 'no more Jews', 252–3, 267; Soviet troops approach frontier of, 496; Germans to withdraw from 594; Jews murdered in, 595
Estreicher, Professor Stanislas: dies at Sachsenhausen, 26
Esztergom (Hungary): mines laid in Danube near, 599; Germans surrounded at, 654
Etang du Canet (France): British agents land at, 177
Ethiopia: war comes to, 90, 153, 169
Etkind, Michael: at Buchenwald, 582
Ettrick (British passenger liner): reaches Canada, 106
Euskirchen (Germany): Hitler at, 60
Euthanasia: German plans for, 11–12, 20, 39, 105; protests against, 109, 224; a report on, reaches London, 302; continuation of (June 1942), 336; new methods for (November 1942), 379; and medical experiments, 508; an advocate of, brought to trial, 731
Euthanasia Decree (of October 1939): 11–12, 160; the probable author of, commits suicide, 682
Evacuation Council: set up, in Moscow, 199
Evans, Lieutenant Arthur: a coast watcher, 445
Evrat (Mayor of St Dié): and St Dié's liberators, 613
Export Control Act: and Japan, 108
'Exercise Pirate': preparation for invasion, 468
'Exercise Tiger': an invasion practice, 520
Exeter (England): bombed, 319
Exeter (British cruiser): and the Graf Spee, 34; sunk, 303–4
Exner, Frau von: dismissed, 504
Eydtkuhnen (East Prussia): captured, 604
Eymet (France): sabotage at, 482

'Fabien': and a reprisal action in Paris, 225–6
'Factory Action': against the Jews of Berlin, 407
Faggioni, Lieutenant Luigi: his exploit, 165
Fairbanks, Douglas, Jr: in action, 461
Falaise (Normandy): battle of, 561, 566, 568; entered by the Canadians, 570; attacks on Poles at, 573, 575
Falkenhausen, General Alexander von: accused of leniency, 550; his nephew a conspirator, 553; his trial, 734–5
Falkenhausen, Major von: a conspirator, 553
Falkenhorst, General Nikolaus von: and Norway, 45, 54
Falkenhorst, Corporal: loses faith in Hitler, 316–7
Falkland Islands: and the sinking of the Belgrano (1982), 742

Fallingbostel (Germany): prisoners-of-war in, liberated, 666
Falmouth (England): heavy water reaches, 96
Faltlhauser, Dr Valentin: supports 'a slow death', 379
'Family Camp': Jews in hiding in, 345, 362, 370; Jews killed in, 388
'Farmer': a sabotage circuit, 378, 477
Farnborough (England): German aviation experts at, 703
Farran, Major Roy: commands a sweep behind German lines, 573
Fascist Grand Council: turns against Mussolini, 446
Fasson, Lieutenant Tony: his courage, 374, 386
Fastov (Ukraine): Jews killed in, 232; Germans driven from, 473
Fateh Khan: found guilty, 725
Fauld (England): an explosion at, 615; the last bombs removed from, 727
Faulhaber, Cardinal Michael von: and Hitler's 'miraculous escape', 26
Federal German Republic: becomes an independent sovereign State (1955), 738; war crimes trials initiated by, 738, 741; the President of, recalls the Nazi past, 744
Fegelein, SS Lieutenant-General Hermann: shot, 676
Fegen, Captain Edward: his courage, 138
Feldbaum, Lea: deported, and killed, 514
Felhender, Leon: leads a revolt, 467
Felixstowe (England): German motor torpedo boats sail to, to surrender, 693
Fellgiebel, General Erich Fritz: executed, 585
Fenwick, Ian: leads a sabotage mission, 552
Feodosiya (Crimea): Soviet troops land at, 283, 284; Russian partisans killed at, 295, 306
Fermi, Enrico: and the atomic bomb, 384, 591
Fertig, Wendell: organizes resistance, in the Philippines, 485
Fidelity (British armed merchantman): lands agent in France (1941), 177
Figeac (France): sabotage at, 490
Fiji (British cruiser): sunk, 185
Filipinos: Japanese brutality towards (in the Philippines), 620; a substantial guerrilla force of (on Luzon), 628; and the rescue of prisoners-of-war, 635, 643; their fate, in Manila, 642; their 'destiny', 644; a tormentor of, hanged, 728
Filipowicz, Wanda: helps Jews, 384
Film: and the German occupation of Warsaw (1939), 18; and the British bombing of Germany, 216; and the Battle of San Pietro Infine, 480–1; and the Theresienstadt ghetto, 595; and the testimony of a survivor, 630; and a soldier's story, 634; and the heroism of a port, 635
Filzinger, Major Friedrich: his award, 66
'Final Solution', the: under discussion, 188; anticipated, 216; 'more than deserved', 257; discussed, at Wannsee, 292; and Berlin, 409; and Hungary, 420–1; and the Warsaw Ghetto, 435;

to be 'ruthlessly implemented', 439; and a 'Führer order', 494
Finland: attacked, 31–2; defends herself, 34, 36, 38–9; negotiates, 40–2, 47; help for, 46; 'in extremis', 48; and the planned German invasion of Russia, 146, 192; declares war on Russia, 201; invades Karelia, 204, 206; and the siege of Leningrad, 228, 230; granite from, Hitler's plans for, 234; and North Russia, 241; occupies Hango, 268; Britain declares war on, 270; fate of the Jews in, 407–8, 420; a Jew from, in the Warsaw uprising, 565; defects from the Axis, 574; declares war on Germany, 645; the Soviet attack on, recalled, 731; war dead of, 746
Finschhafen (New Guinea): Australians land at, 462; a Japanese counter-attack on, unsuccessful, 465; Australians advance from, 486
Finzi, Gigliola: her fate, 525
Firestorm: its first appearance (at Hamburg on 28 July 1943), 447–8; at Kassel, 469; at Darmstadt, 590; at Heilbronn, 616; at Dresden, 640–2; at Tokyo, 648; and Ultra, 639
First United States Army Group (FUSAG): fictitious, but effective, 492, 493; 523; 545–6, 555
Fischer, Franz: released from prison (1989), 744
Fish, Moshe: joins partisans, 345
Fiume (Italy): bombed, 500–1; an arrest in, 585
Fives (Lille): an act of sabotage at, 440
'Flak City': a defended port, 378
Flak Towers: to be constructed, 365
Flanders (Belgium): British troops in, 72, 73
Flensburg (northern Germany): and the German surrender, 684, 689; William Joyce arrested at, 696
Flerov, Captain: and a new weapon, 210
Fletcher, Private Eric: executed, 358
Flinn, John: in action, 272
Florence (Italy): Hitler meets Mussolini at, 135; Jews deported from, 474; partisan groups near, and a parachute mission, 525; Germans fall back to, 562
Florennes (France): bombed, 522
Florida (United States): aid to Egypt from, 336
Florida Island (Solomons): landing on, 350
Flossenbürg (Germany): an execution at, 489; Gypsies at, 562; Allied agents executed at, 654–5; Canaris, Oster and Bonhoeffer hanged at, 660; American forces enter, 684
'Flying Bomb': Hitler's 'secret weapon', 434, 457, 463–4, 474, 479, 497, 505, 522, 529; launched 539, 542, 543, 544; growing death toll from 548, 549, 551, 552, 555, 564, 570–1; mastered, 582; carried by bombers, against London, 587, 645; scatters leaflets as well as explosives, 622–3; against central and northern England, 624; falls on Antwerp, 601, 608, 613, 626; a suicide version, launched by Japan, 650
Flying Fortresses: and an escape line from Slovakia, by air, 593–4
'Flying Tigers': in action, 280, 282

Foca (Yugoslavia): Tito reaches, 288; Tito forced out of, 323

Focke-Wulf (combat plane): forced landing of, 334

Focsani (Roumania): an aerial reconnaisance near, 519; airfield at, bombed, 530; Red Army approaches, 574

Foertsch, General Hermann: accepts an unconditional surrender, 687

Foggia (Italy): Allies capture, 464; American bombing raids from, 530; aid to Warsaw from, 564–5, 567–8, 595–6

Folkestone (England): cross-Channel shelling of, 594

Fontainbleau (France): 114

Foote, John: his courage, 354

'Force Z': reaches Singapore, 268

Foreign Legion: in Norway, 55, 65; at Bir Hakeim, 187, 327; at Lang Son (Indo-China), 692–3

Foresight (British destroyer): sunk, 352

Formosa (Taiwan): Japanese troop transports off, 264; Japanese troop transports head towards Malaya from, 268; an airfield on, bombed, 477; a massive air raid on, 601; a ten-day naval battle off, 627

Forrestal, James R.: and the Japanese rejection of 'unconditioned surrender', 710

Forst (River Neisse): Red Army enters, 668

Forster, Albert: and German rule in Poland, 22, 27

Fort Herz (Burma): 323; an attack from, 506

Fort Lenin (Sevastopol): falls, 335

Fort Maxim Gorky (Sevastopol): falls, 335

Fort Siberia (Sevastopol): falls, 335

Fort Stalin (Sevastopol): falls, 335

Fort Stevens (Oregon): shelled by a Japanese submarine, 336

Forti, Sergio: tortured and killed, 540

'Fortress City': Berlin declared a, 637

'Fortress Europe': Hitler orders the creation of, 283; 'fortresses' to be created for, 490

Fortune, Major-General, V. M.: in action, 89; surrenders, 92

Fossoli (Italy): Jews deported to Auschwitz from, 494, 525, 546

Foster, Tony: and the air battles above Britain, 123

Foulkes, Lieutenant-General Charles: and the surrender of the Germans in Holland, 687

Fowler, Bob: his death, on Okinawa, 695

Fragonard: his paintings, stolen, 130

France: declares war on Germany, 4; action by, 6; British troops land in (1939), 10–11; and Hitler's Directive No. 5, 16; and Hitler's war plans, 20, 38; and Finland, 34; German invasion of, 61; battle in, 63–101; under German occupation, 104; and Mers-el-Kebir, 106, 107; fate of the Jews in, 129, 310, 336, 344, 351, 362, 365, 459, 494, 504; works of art taken from, 130; Churchill's broadcast to, 133; former prisoners-of-war of, liberated, 226; reprisals in, 247, 306, 512–3; and the Billancourt raid, 306; volunteers from, on the Eastern Front, 348, 394;

forced labour from, 353; 421, 427; Germans bring aircraft from, 377; Germans bring troops from, 390; and the Milice, 390; 'pure, clean and vital', 422; and the cross-Channel landing, 452; air supplies to Resistance in, 486; to have a post-war veto, 574, 701; troops of, cross Rhine, 655; troops of, to be forestalled, 667; officers from, executed in Dachau, 668; slave labourers from, liberated, 674; and the conflict in Indo-China, against the Communists, 720, 722–3; and the 'challenge' of Communism in, 729; American war dead returned to the United States from, 733; and war crimes trials, 741

Franco-Prussian War (1870–1): 92

Frampton, Commander: dies, 307

Franco, General Francisco: Hitler meets, 133–4; again rejects Hitler's pressure, 145–6; rejects Mussolini's pressure, 157; the police of, and the fate of a British commando, 360

'Franco' (Baron de Nothomb): arrested, 490

Frank, Anne: in Amsterdam, 516; betrayed, 565

Frank, SS Lieutenant-General August: and the belongings of 'evacuated' Jews, 364

Frank, Dr Hans: and Polish 'slaves', 19, 22; and Jewish slave labour, 23; and the Jewish star, 28; and the Jewish fate, 35; and the deportation of Poles to Germany, 40; angered, 43; and the 'Final Solution', 279; a protest forwarded by, 415; and the belongings of murdered Jews, 414; and the continued killing of Jews, 505; hanged, 731

Frank, Karl Hermann: hanged, 729

Frank, Margot: dies, 516

Frankfort (Kentucky): a trophy in, 674

Frankfurt-on-Main: an institute set up at, to study the 'Jewish question', 130; bombed, 210, 495, 504; Jews deported from, 245, 254, 263; jet airfields at, bombed, 652; American forces reach, 654; a war crimes trial at, 740

Franklin (US warship): sunk, 510

Fraser, Lieutenant Ian: his courageous exploit, 710

Fraserburgh (Scotland): a German bomber flies to, instead of to a base in Norway, 683

Free French Movement (and forces): pledges to fight on, 110; in French West Africa, 127; sets up an Empire Defence Council, 134–5; takes Gabon from Vichy, 141; and the invasion of Syria and Lebanon, 188–9, 194; and the Dieppe raid, 353; and the cross-Channel landing, 430; the Normandy Squadron of, in action in Russia, 445, 556; and the capture of Elba, 542; and the liberation of France, 567, 578; in Indo-China, 692–3, 720

'Free Slovakia': proclaimed, 604

'Freedom': painted on a wall in Munich (1943), 404

Freetown (West Africa): a convoy from, attacked, 373

Freiberger, Chief Rabbi (of Zagreb): sent to Auschwitz, 424

Freisler, Roland: and the 'Final

Solution', 29; and the 'White Rose' protest group, 405; killed, 637; his widow receives a pension, 742

French Equatorial Africa: 134

French Indo-China: and Japan, 108, 111, 206, 216, 249, 264; Japanese troops in, attack Malaya, 273; Japanese approach from China, 614; continued fighting in, 692–3; a new conflict in, 720, 722–3; becomes independent (as Vietnam, Cambodia and Laos), 730

French Morocco: 100

French National Committee: established in London, 103

French North Africa: 81, 93, 97, 98, 101; Allies plan to land in, 347, 371, 374; landings in, 375, 376

French Resistance: 65, 370, 397, 422, 434–5, 435, 436, 438, 461, 464, 471, 475, 477; its activities intensified (1944), 498, 523, 528, 532; and the Amiens raid, 499; members of, captured, 504; attacks on, 511; Allied aid to, 515, 543; and SS reprisals, 536, 537–8; an act of revenge by, 548; sweeps against, 554, 557; and the liberation of Paris, 573, 580; and a British sweep behind German lines, 573; helpers of, executed, 587

French Riviera: Italian advance into, 101; a British agent lands on, 338–9

French West Africa: 'Operation Menace' against, 127

French West Indies: 107

Frenkel, Getzel: shot, 9

Frentz, Walter: and Hitler's jump of joy, 97

Fresnes (Paris): a parachutist, imprisoned at, 489

Freud, Sigmund: his pupil's suicide, 95

Freyberg, Lieutenant-General Sir Bernard: on Crete, 180, 186

Fricke, Rear-Admiral Kurt: plans for the post-war years, 85

Friedeburg, Grand Admiral: and the German surrender, 684, 690; commits suicide, 695

Friedrichshafen (southern Germany): bombed, 439

Frisius, Vice-Admiral Friedrich: and the surrender of Dunkirk, 692

Fritsch, SS Captain Karl: and gassing experiments, 220

'Fritzes': Russian girls machine-gunned by, 246; the 'great flight' of, 571

Fromm, Dr Benjamin: killed with his family, 201

Fromm, General Friedrich: and the opposition to Hitler, 544; not a conspirator, 558; shot, 650

Fuchs, Klaus: reaches Canada, 106–7; gives Russia atomic secrets, 241, 348; reaches the United States, 478–9, 702; imprisoned, 734

Fujiwara, Major Iwaichi: and 'Asia for the Asiatics', 277

Fukuei, General: orders an execution, 358; executed, 729

'Fukuryu': suicide mine, 703, 712

Furutaka (Japanese heavy cruiser): sunk, 368

Fulbright, Senator J. William: his magnanimous idea, 730; Japan a beneficiary of, 735

Fulton (Missouri): Churchill's 'iron curtain' speech at, 728

Funk, Walther: and German raw material supply, 457

Fünten, Ferdinand aus der: and the deportation of Jews to Auschwitz, 391; released from prison, 744

Furniss Roe, Flying Officer H.: shot down, returns to Britain, 495

Fürstenberg (Oder): Red Army reaches, 639

Fürstenfeld (Austria): Red Army approaches, 666

Fürstengrube Mines (East Upper Silesia): slave labour at, 525

Fürstenwalde (near Berlin): Red Army at, 672

Fürth (Germany): Jews deported to their deaths from, 310; aircraft factories at, bombed, 500–1

'GGG': a German cypher, broken, 297

Gabès (Tunisia): Germans driven from, 416

Gabcik, Josef: his mission behind German lines, 283–4, 327; killed, 334

'Gadfly': a German air corps key, broken, 287

Gaida, June: and a V2 rocket attack, 614

Gainsborough: paintings by, stolen, 130

Gajduk, Vassily: executed, 585

Gajowniczek, Francis: saved, 219

Galatos (Crete): battle at, 185–6

Galatz Gap (Roumania): an aerial reconnaisance over, 519

Gale, Private Victor: executed, 358

Galen, Bishop (of Münster): denounces enthanasia, 224

Galicki, General: replaced General Berling, 594

Gallipoli Peninsula (Turkey): and Dunkirk, 83

Gällivare (Sweden): iron ore at, 42; plans to seize, 48, 50, 55

Gamelin, General Maurice Gustave: orders French to leave Belgium, 67

Gandhi, M.K.: and the Indian National Army, 724, 725

Ganju Lama: his courage in action, 539

Ganser, Dr. Josef: calls for death penalty, 505

'Garbo': a double agent, 212, 334, 347, 537, 621

Garcia, Juan Pujol: a double agent, 212, 334; and the Normandy deception, 537, 542; his award, 621

Gardelegen (Germany): Jews killed at, 663

Garigliano River (Italy): crossed, 490

Garwolin (Poland): an execution in, 554

Gassovski, Paul de: killed, 422

Gatchina (Leningrad): defence works at, 217; captured, 225; partisan activity near, 246; liberated, 490

Gatow (Berlin): a flight through, 673

Gaudo Island (Crete): an Italian naval defeat off, 166

Gauger, Martin: dies, 210

Gauleiters: Hitler addresses, 399

Gaultherot, Henry: executed, 222–3

Gavrilović, Ambassador (of Yugoslavia): in Moscow, 169–70

Gavutu Island (Solomons): landing on, 350

Gazala (Cyrenaica): Italians pushed back to, 378

Gdynia (Poland): bombed, 2; Poles

expelled from, 22; a labour camp near, 27; beseiged, 654

Gebhardt, Professor Karl: and medical experiments, 340; hanged, 731

Geffen, Abba: recalls the journey of Jewish refugees to Palestine, 726

Geheimschreiber (secret teleprinter): its secrets broken into, 429

Geibel, General: and the Warsaw uprising, 563

Gehlen, Reinhard: gives himself up to the Americans, 695

Gelman, Polina: her bombing missions, 339

Gelsenkirchen (Germany): bombed, 77, 147, 536

General Belgrano (Argentine light cruiser): a survivor of Pearl Harbour, 742

'General Commissariats': German plan to establish, in the Caucasus, 193

General Government, the: 19, 24, 28; forced labour in, 34–5; starvation in, 37; Poles to be sent to Germany from, 40; the future of the Poles in, 79, 105; the future of Jews in, 279, 292, 343, 351, 394–5; a death camp in, 307–8; statistics of the murder of Jews in, 414; sabotage in, 462

Geneva (Switzerland): and the Russo-Finish War, 34; a report of German intentions sent from, 351

Geneva, Lake of: and the French Resistance, 398

Genoa (Italy): bombed, 90, 378; an Allied landing at, feared, 447

Genoa (Italy): a strike in, 410; bombed, 450; Italian ships set sail from, 460; Jews deported to Auschwitz from, 473

Genzken, Dr. Karl: his experiments, 32

George, King of the Hellenes: 174, 185

George VI, King: and the Queen of Holland, 64; and the battle in France, 73; welcomes the Polish Government-in-Exile, 101; and Britain with 'no allies to be polite to', 104; and Germany's 'aggressive spirit', 115; and the London Blitz, 124, 155; and the sinking of Italian warships, 140; and Roosevelt's 'encouragement', 186; and further American help, 255; 'depressed', 304; and Churchill's first meeting with Stalin, 347; and El Alamein, 374; and 'the future in 1943', 389; and Stalingrad, 406; and the Normandy landings, 497; and the atomic bomb, 742

George Cross: awarded (to a bomb disposal officer), 126–7, 146, 183 (to Malta), 360; (to two seamen), 374; (to two Australian soldiers), 565; (to a British agent), 728

George Medal: awarded, 374, 615; the death of a recipient of, 640

'George One': a British agent, in France, 180

Georges, General Joseph: and French losses in battle, 91

Georges, Pierre: kills a German, 225–6

Georgia (Soviet Union): German plans for, 193

German Four Year Plan: and slave labour, 348

German Railways: Enigma key of, broken, 154

German Secret Service: hand cypher of, broken, 154

German-Soviet Boundary and Friendship Treaty (September 1939): 16

'Germanic SS': an act of resistance against, 384; an act of bravery in, 405–6

Germany: and the invasion of Poland, 1–14; and euthanasia, 11–12, 20, 39, 105, 109, 224, 336, 379, 508; and the annexation of western Poland, 22; and a peace mission, 48; an unexpected landing in, 49; and British bombing policy, 108, 120, 132, 136, 142, 146, 208, 210, 308, 314, 319, 329, 352, 259, 439, 440, 447–8, 448; and Allied bombing policy, 378, 393, 398, 407, 409, 427, 432, 636, 638–9, 644; and the Battle of Britain, 117–25; and the 'Blitz' against Britain, 124, 127, 131, 135, 136, 137, 156, 162, 173, 178–9, 181; and the 'Berlin-Tiflis Axis', 193; and the invasion of the Soviet Union, 198; declares war on the United States, 277–8; presses Japan for action against Russia, 312; Protestant and Catholic protest in 315; and the fall of Mussolini, 446, 448; and the atomic bomb, 14, 319, 379, 404, 500, 645, 649–50, 667; and the Axis (Rome-Berlin-Tokyo), 129, 134, 141, 143, 149, 157, 160, 165, 264, 286, 287, 531, 574, 580, 590, 589, 624; and the plots against Hitler, 412, 414, 551, 553, 557–8, 559; and the destruction of the evidence of mass murder, 438, 439, 475; 'Big Week' (bombing raids) against, 500–2; Jet aircraft of, 599, 622, 626, 649, 650, 651, 652, 657, 661, 666; 'led by criminals', 744; wartime death toll of, 746; see also index entries for 'Enigma', Gestapo, Hitler, Jews, SS, 'Ultra'

Germersheim (Germany): French cross Rhine at, 655

Gerolstein (Germany): bombed, 622

Gerron, Kurt: dies in Auschwitz, 595

Gersdorff, Major General Baron von: and a second military attempt to kill Hitler (March 1943), 414

Gerson, Victor: flown in to France (1943), 475

Gesiwka Street Camp (Warsaw): Jews from, in the Warsaw uprising, 565

Gestapo, the: and the German invasion of Poland, 1; and executions in Poland, 22, 104, 379, 561; seize Poles in Cracow, 26; 'public shootings' by, 29; arrests by, 7, 39, 460; its 'grip', 85; in Paris, 94, 279, 337, 558, 568, 571; a refugee handed over to, 151–2; in the Crimea, 295; and General Giraud, 317; its secret communications key, unbroken, 353; and the fate of a British commando, 360; Headquarters of, in Oslo, bombed, 365; in Brussels, 373; in Norway, 379, 466; in France, 390, 489, 497, 513, 538; in Greece, 413; in Berlin, 418; in Lyon, 434–5, 436, 561, 571; in Italy, 466; in Warsaw, 479; in the Channel Islands, 498; in Holland, 512, 515–6; in Kovno, 555; in Fiume, 585; and the Bomb Plot conspirators, 597; a headquarters of, in Denmark, bombed, 608, 610; headquarters of, in Oslo, bombed, 624; go after Jews who had left

Birkenau in search of safety, 632; headquarters of, in Copenhagen, bombed, 651; at Weimar, 661; and Buchenwald, 661; in Italy, 673

Gex (France): German anti-resistance sweep near, 515

Ghormley Rear-Admiral Robert L.: Reaches London, 120

Gibraltar: and the battle of Malta, 114; an Italian air attack on, 120; aid to Egypt through, 122, 139, 143; Hitler offers, to Spain, 134; possible bombing of, 135; Hitler's proposed seizure of, 141, 143, 145; aid to Greece through, 148; convoys from, attacked, 157, 381; British to be driven from 189; a convoy to, attacked, 237; *Ark Royal* torpedoed off, 255; a spy from shot, 325; North African invasion force, on way to 373; Germans sight invasion force at, 374; General Giraud brought to, 375; a manned-torpedo attack on, 385

Gibson, Wing-Commander Guy: and the Ruhr dams, 428; shot down, 595

Gilbert, Captain: killed, 66

Gilbert Islands (Pacific): Japanese land on, 276; Japanese fortify, 353

Gilleron, Abbé Henri: shot, 512–3

Gilman, Denise: dies, 477

Gimpel, Eric: a German agent, arrested, 615

Giorgione: paintings of, evacuated, 206

Giran, Olivier: executed, 422

Giraud, General Henri: captured, 68; escapes from captivity, 317; rescued from France, 375; to command in North Africa and Algiers, 389

Gironde River (France): a commando raid on, 385

Gitter, Asscher: shot, 8–9

Glanc, Rivka: commands a small resistance group, 440

Glasgow (Scotland): American aid reaches, 106; Roosevelt's emissary in, 151

Gleiwitz (East Upper Silesia): and the outbreak of war, 1, 26; slave labour at, 524, 608; a mass evacuation from, 632

Glickstein, Lutek: a resistance leader, 440

Glières, Plateau des (France): an attack on, 511

*Gleaner* (British minesweeper): and Enigma, 45

Global Accords: and reparations payments, 739

Globocnik, Odilo: and the Jews, 27, 311, 337; and the evidence of mass murder, 368; commits suicide, 696

Gloeden, Lilo: executed, 615

Glomfjord (Norway): a sabotage mission to, 362–3, 373

Glogau (Silesia): Russian attacks fail near, 638; German troops hold out in, 639

*Glorious* (British aircraft carrier): sunk, 89

*Gloucester* (British cruiser): sunk, 184–5

Glubb, Major: enters Iraq, 182

Gluecks, ss Major-General Richard: and medical experiments, 32, 340; and the establishment of Auschwitz, 43; and the need for a 'green belt' at

Auschwitz, 438; found dead, 693

*Gneisenau* (German battle cruiser): 153; in action, 159, 162; an attack on, 216; its dash, and damage to, 300

Göben (on the Oder): Red Army reaches, 632

God: Hitler gives thanks to, 11, 473; and Hitler's image in Germany, 133; and the Book of Ruth, 151; and the 'final victim', 257; his 'sovereignty' above ideology, 315; and Sodom, 558; '... punish Germany', 633

Godfrin, Roger: survives, 537

Godwin, Sub-Lieutenant John: his mission, and his fate, 423; shot down, 637

Goebbels, Dr Josef: and the Jews, 24, 32, 87, 224, 257, 301, 306, 310, 311–2, 327, 328, 329, 386, 405, 408, 409, 410, 413; and a British bomb, 124; and an anti-Jewish film, 128; and British bombing raids, 128, 314, 319, 321, 409, 410, 427, 428, 432, 464, 474, 477, 479; reports 'considerable losses', 147; and Norway, 161; and Hitler's moods, 172, 409; and 'John Bull', 178; and the German invasion of Russia, 198, 199, 201, 217; and euthanasia, 224; and Subhas Chandra Bose, 304; and reprisals, 306, 321; and Soviet partisans, 308, 326; and General Giraud, 317; and the assassination of Heydrich, 327, 329; and the 'interests of security', 328; declares 'victory' at Stalingrad, 398; calls for 'total war', 405, 412; arranges 'an imposing funeral', 418; and Hitler's confidence in victory (May 1943), 422; and anti-partisan warfare, 427; and an anti-Bolshevik Legion, 430; and growing resistance, in Poland, 462; and the war on the Eastern Front, 463, 472, 478; and the need for 'extremely severe measures' in France, 464; his Ministry bombed, 496; and the future of Germany (to be made 'desolate'), 528; and the July 1944 Bomb Plot, 558, 559; and Roosevelt's death, 662; and Hitler's suicide, 681; wants to fight on, 682; has himself shot, 682

Goebbels, Magda: shot, 682

Goerdeler, Carl: and Germany's 'brutal conduct', 8; and possible peace talks, 50, 51; implicated in the Bomb Plot, 597; hanged, 637

Goering, Hermann: his 'intention', 6; and a peace mission, 19; and the Dunkirk perimeter, 72; and the air war against Britain, 115, 119, 123; and German plans against Russia, 142; and the looting of art treasures, 161; and the Jews, 219; and a future Office for, in Berlin, 260; and the bombing of Cologne, 329; and foreign volunteers on the Eastern Front, 348; and slave labour, 348; Hitler mocks, 358; and the diversion of transport aircraft from, 376–7; and compulsory air raid patrol duty, for civilians, 417; and the cross-Channel danger, 523; and a hollow boast, 529; to be killed, 551; and Total War Mobilization, 559; seeks control of Germany, 672; under arrest, 672; 'a traitor', 673; expelled from the Nazi Party, 677; commits suicide, 731

Goeth, Amnon: a camp commandant, 485

Goethals, Colonel: warned, 38

Goethe Medal: awarded, 158

'Gold' Beach (Normandy): landing at, 534, 536

Gold Medal for Military Valour: awarded, 554

Gold Medal of the Resistance: awarded, 540

Goldap (East Prussia): Red Army reaches, 603–4

Golden Oak Leaves: awarded, 655

Golden Badge of Honour: a holder of, hanged, 637

Goldenberg, Hélène: deported to her death, 357

Goldenberg, Lotty: deported to her death, 357

Goldman, Marie: killed, 538

Goldmann, Dr. Nahum: and reparations for Jews, 735

Goldsmith, Sam: enters Dachau immediately after its liberation, 678

Goldstein, Peretz: a parachutist, dies, 611

Golikov, General: and 'rumours' of war, 164

Gollwitzer, General Friedrich: paraded in Moscow, 556; returns to Germany, 738

Golta (South Russia): concentration camps near, 290

Golub, Avraham: and the invasion of Sicily, as seen from the Kovno ghetto, 443

Gomel (Russia): 201, 210; Soviet partisan activity near, 399, 444; Russians capture, 478

Gomu Island (Solomons): a coast watcher on, 449

Gona (New Guinea): Japanese land at, 345; Japanese defeat near, 375; continued fighting for, 378, 385

Gonzaga (Philippines): Japanese land at, 276

Gora Kalwaria (Poland): Red Army crosses Vistula near, 566

Gorbachev, Mikhail: and an appeal to, 'to bring the people closer together', 743

Görden (Germany): euthanasia at, 11–12, 105

Gordon-Walker, Patrick: enters Belsen, 664

Gorizia (Italy): partisans killed near, 669

Gorky (Volga): planned German advance to, 113; Soviet reinforcements gather at, 267; death of an evacuee in, 325

Gorky (White Russia): Jews murdered in, 255; a German sweep against Soviet partisans near, 366

Gorky Street (Moscow): Soviet troops march to the Front from, 254

Görlitz (Germany): anti-Nazi leaflets distributed in, 412; German troops still fighting near (on 8 May 1945), surrender, 690

Gorovets, Lieutenant Aleksei: his tenacity 442

Gort, Field Marshal Lord: and the battle in Belgium, 74; and the battle in France, 80

Gospić (Yugoslavia): Italians occupy, 225

Gotha (Germany): bombed, 501; 'cadaverous refugees at', 658
Gothenburg (Sweden): 153, 314
'Gothenland': Hitler's proposal for the Crimea, 253
Gothic Line (Italy): Germans hold, 581; penetrated, 584; a section of, pushed past, 596; renewed Allied attack on, 660
Gould, Rifleman D. S.: witnesses an atrocity, 535
Gould, Louisa: dies at Ravensbrück, 665
Goya: the fate of his paintings, 130, 162
Grabow (Poland): a witness to mass murder reaches, 292
Grable, Betty: and the Ardennes, 618, 620
Gracey, Major General D. D.: enlists Japanese troops against Vietnamese, 722–3
Graebe, Hermann: witnesses the murder of Jews, 367–8
Graf, Hermann: shot down, 659
Graf, Willi: executed, 405
Grafeneck (near Stuttgart): its director, at Auschwitz, 228
Grafton (British destroyer): attacked, 79
Gran Sasso d' Italia (Italy): seizure of Mussolini at, 461
Grant, Private H.: in action, 422
Granville (France): a German swoop on, 648–9
Gravesend (London): a 'Flying Bomb' hits, 623
Graz (Austria): Hitler in, 178; bombed, 500–1
Grazier, Able Seaman Colin: his courage, 374, 386
Great Britain: see index entry for Britain
'Great Jet Massacre' (near Berlin): 661
Greater Danzig – West Prussia: 22, 27, 39
Greece: invaded by Italy, 135; British help for, 136–7, 159–161; repulses the Italian forces, 143; German designs on, 146, 148, 157, 160; and Roosevelt, 157–8, 162; invaded by Germany, 170–2; Italians re-enter, 172–3; British troops evacuated from, 175; surrenders, 175–6; Allied forces evacuated from, 176; losses in the battle for, 178; reprisal actions in, 243; an anti-partisan sweep in, 321–2; and a deception plan, 347; German bombers move westward from, 374; fate of the Jews of, 406, 432, 436, 465, 510, 549; and an Allied deception, 423, 445; Germany to 'stay' in, 441; severity against civilians in, 450–1; massacre of Italians in, 460; activities of a British officer in, 461–2; resistance in, 465, 490; and war crimes, to be punished, 469; and an Allied deception plan, 494; partisans active in, 527, 539, 575, 584, 601; British landings on, 598; its future, discussed in Moscow, 600; Churchill's flight to, 623; 'tottering', 686; American post-war help for, 730; war crimes trials in, 732; receives German reparations, 739; wartime death toll in, 746
Greenhaven (New York): an officer imprisoned at, 526

Greenland (Danish Colony): occupied by the United States, 173
Greer, Germaine: and the 'walking wounded', 747
Greer (US submarine): attacked, 230
Greim, Robert Ritter von: ordered to fly to Berlin, 672; flies to Berlin, 673; allowed to leave Berlin, 676; commits suicide, 696
Greindl, Jean: escapes, 392; killed in an Allied air raid, 459
Greenglass, David: and the atomic bomb, 595
Greiser, Artur: and German rule in Poland, 22, 127, 133; and Hitler's eastern plans, 135–65; proposes 'special treatment' for sick Poles, 322; and the Jews, 377, 508; paraded, and then hanged, 729
Gretton, Captain Peter: on convoy escort duty, 425
Greven (Germany): American airmen shot down over, 578
Grierson, John: and Hitler's jump of joy, 97
Gries (Italy): a parachutist imprisoned at, 525
Grini (Norway): imprisonments in, 406, 423
Griswold, General Oscar: urges a Japanese surrender, 642
Grodno (Poland): and Soviet defence plans, 168; Russian resistance near, 204; Jews deported to Auschwitz from, 391; Gypsies deported to Auschwitz from, 474; Germans driven back to, 544
Groenwald, Lieutenant J. J. C.: parachutes to safety, 570
Grojanowski, Jakub: a witness to mass murder, escapes, 292, 330–1
Grom (a Polish destroyer): hit, 58
Gross, Nikolaus: executed in Berlin, 632
Gross-Rosen (Silesia): concentration camp at, 256; evacuations to, 632
Groves, Brigadier-General Leslie R.: and the atomic bomb, 363; and German atomic research, 649–50
Grozny (Caucasus): a German objective, 345, 354, 357, 363, 375
Grüber, Pastor Heinrich: news of Gurs camp reaches, 133
Grudziadz (Poland): a Polish woman sentenced to death in, 158
Gryn, Hugo: and the 'unfinished business' of the war, 737
Grynspan, Yekhiel: protects fellow Jews, 388
Guadalcanal Island (Solomon Islands): landing on, 350; fighting on, 361, 363; reinforcements on way to, attacked, 368; a renewed Japanese assault on, repulsed, 372; further fighting on, 374, 377, 383–4, 385, 387; to be evacuated, 391; still fought for, 393, 396; reinforcements to, attacked, 399; organized resistance on, ends, 400; a Japanese attack towards, 419
Guam (Pacific): a warning concerning, 262; bombed, 272; Americans forced to surrender on, 278; Americans return to, 541, 559; a photograph sent to, 642–3; a Japanese army sergeant emerges on (1972), 740–1
Gubkin, Captain Georgi: reaches East Prussia, 571

Guderian, General Heinz: reaches the Meuse, 64, 65; east of Sedan, 67; enters St. Quentin, 68; in Russia, on the Beresina River, 205; at Borisov, 221; near Kiev, 233; in France, 517; and the Ardennes, 593; dismissed, 651
Guérisse, Albert-Marie (Lieutenant-Commander Pat O'Leary RN): lands in France (1941), 177; betrayed (1943), 408; sees four British agents on the eve of their deaths (1944), 555; and the liberation of Dachau, 677–8
Guernsey (Channel Islands): Germans occupy, 105; a British commando raid on, 110; an arrest in, 498
Gurkhas: in action, 404, 498, 506, 509, 539, 547
Guilbert, Constance Raymond: witnesses an atrocity, 535
Guildford (England): German aircraft shot down near, 119
Giulio Cesare (Italian battleship): badly damaged, 109
Guggenberger, Lieutenant: torpedoes Ark Royal, 255
Gulf of Finland: Soviet coastline on, 40
Gumbinnen (East Prussia): Red Army reaches, 603–4; Germans recapture, 606
Gumrak (Stalingrad): Germans hold, 392; Germans lose, 393
Günther, Hans: his birthday celebrated, 158
Günthergrubbe Mines (East Upper Silesia): slave labour at, 525
Gurs (France): Jews deported to, 133, 310
Gunzbourg, Baron Philippe de ('Edgar'): organizes sabotage, 484, 543
Gustav of Sweden, King: and a negotiated peace, 115; protests, 550
Györ (Hungary): mines laid in Danube near, 599; Red Army reaches, 654
Gypsies: shot, 268; a 'double danger', 282; murdered, 292, 297, 298, 306, 339, 355, 565; their fate discussed, 361–2; to be sent to Auschwitz, 386, 432, 474, 496; at Plaszow, 485; used for medical experiments, 562; returned to Auschwitz, 598; at Belsen, 664; persecutors of, brought to trial, 731; not to receive compensation, 734; their earlier killing, cited as a precedent for mass murder, 735
Gzhatsk (Russia): Red Army enters, 409

HG 76 (a convoy from Gibraltar): attacked, 281
HX 239 (an Atlantic convoy): an attack on, 431
Haakon, King (of Norway): goes into exile, 85, 87
Haapsalu (Estonia): to be occupied, 16
Habbaniya (Iraq): Britons trapped in, 178; a force reaches, from Transjordan, 182
Hacha, Emil: dies in prison, 701
Hague, The (Holland): attacked, 61; Queen Wilhelmina leaves, 64; a precision bombing raid on, 515; V2 rockets launched from, 608; rocket site at, bombed, 645; last rockets launched from 653; food supplies for, 679; rejoicing in, 690; an execution in, 729
Haichow (Hainan Island): a prisoner-of-war camp on, 721

Haifa (Palestine): Rommel's threat to, 337

Haile Selassie, Emperor of Abyssinia: returns to his capital, 180

Hainan Island (China): a prisoner-of-war camp on, 721

Hajjerat m' Guil (Sahara): war crimes at, 505

Halban, Hans von: leaves France, 94

Halberstadt (Germany): bombed, 489

Halder, General Franz: 6, 7–8, 51, 68, 73, 111, 114, 117, 137; and the Russian soldier, 145; and Russian tanks, 155; and the need for a 'surprise attack', 189; and the coming of war with Russia, 198; and the course of the battle in Russia, 204, 207, 208, 209, 210, 236, 260, 265, 267, 281, 304, 358; dismissed, 363

Halifax, Lord: and a peace mission, 19; and Norway, 37; and Finland, 46; and Narvik, 49; and the fall of France, 94; and Hitler's 'peace offer' (July 1940), 111

Halensee Station (Berlin): bombed, 481

Halfaya Pass (Egypt): Rommel withdraws from, 182; Rommel recaptures, 187

Halifax (Nova Scotia): American destroyers handed over to Britain at, 122; convoys sail from, 132, 138, 236, 251

Halle (Germany): Allied armies reach, 661

Hallervorden, Professor: and euthanasia, 508

Hallesby, Professor: imprisoned, 406

Hals, Frans: a painting of, stolen, 162

Halsey, Vice-Admiral William 'Bull': and Pearl Harbour, 737

Haltern (Ruhr): a planned German counter-attack at, 652

Hamamatsu (Japan): shelled, 709

Hamar (Norway): evacuation to, 54

Hamborn (Germany): bombed in error, 308

Hamburg (Germany): and the 'Double Cross' system, 16; Jews seized in, 23; leaflets dropped on, 46; an SS officer hanged in, 77; bombed, 100, 142–3, 143, 210, 398, 408, 446, 447, 448, 611; Hitler's rebuilding plans for, 104; Jews deported from, 245, 254; a German student executed in, 373; a firestorm in, 447–8; repercussions of bombing in (August 1943), 450; a broadcast from, 458; Jews sent to, to demolish damaged buildings, 552; a new submarine being fabricated in, 625; an autobahn to, cut, 650; Himmler, in, 657; negotiations for unconditional surrender in, 683; Ribbentrop arrested in, 700; a war crimes trial in, 733; a former SS officer living near, 743

Hameln (Germany): executions at, for war crimes, 731

Hamm (Germany): viaduct to, bombed, 649

Hammamet (Tunisia): ships on way to, sunk, 426

Hanford (Washington State): an atomic bomb activated at, 591; further atomic bomb research at, 623

Hango (Finland): attack on, repulsed, 34; leased to Russia, 49; Russians forced to evacuate, 268

Hanoi (French Indo-China): an air raid from, 280

Hanover (Germany): Hitler sends code word from, 59; a British bomber crashes near, 69; bombed, 210, 649; a viaduct to, bombed, 649

Hansteen, Viggo: executed, 232

Haraden (US destroyer): hit by a suicide pilot, 617

Harburg (near Hamburg): British forces reach, 669

Hardelot (France): a raid on, 318

Hards, Fred: in France, 95; killed, 183

Hardy, Private Benjamin: killed, 565

Harfleur (Normandy): an Allied deception at, 532

Haringzelles (France): a gun battery at, 299

Harnack, Ernst von: executed, 645

Harnier, Adolf von: dies, after liberation, 693

Haroekoe Island (Dutch East Indies): a prisoner-of-war on, recalls conditions there, 745

Harrer, Captain: kills a wounded soldier, 74

Harriman, Averell: in Moscow, 223, 239; at Casablanca, 392; and the Russian view of the Warsaw uprising, 570, 594; and Stalin's untrustworthiness, 658

Harris, Air Marshal Sir Arthur: and British bombing policy, 142, 314, 329, 616, 638–9

Harrison, Kenneth: a prisoner-of-war in Japan, liberated, 718–9

Harstad (Norway): landing at, 55, 56; bombed, 62, 65

Hart, John: and Hirohito's funeral, 745

Hartenstein, Captain: and the sinking of the Laconia, 360

Hartle, General Russell P.: reaches Britain with his troops, 291

Hartmannsdorf (Germany): prisoners-of-war at, 622

Harumitzu, Oka: recalls executions, 711; recalls the destruction of evidence of an execution, 720

Harwich (England): a fictitious German agent at, 537

Harwood, H.M.: irate, 48

Harz Mountains (Germany): a German army in, 661; and the battle for Berlin, 666, 667, 676

Hase, General von: and the July bomb plot, 558

Hashimoto, Lieutenant-Commander Mochitsura: sinks the Indianapolis, 709–10; cheated of an ovation, 718

Hasty (British destroyer): crippled, 333

Hassell, Ulrich von: and possible peace talks, 50, 51; and rumours of war (June 1941, 192; hanged (September 1944), 589

Hauge, Eiliv: and the German invasion of Norway, 54

Haugesund (Norway): a resistance group near, 151; a commando mission to, 419

Haushofer, Albrecht: executed, 672

Hawaii: a telegram to, causes no alarm, 268; and an American deception plan, 516

Hayate (Japanese destroyer): sunk, 278

Hayes (a commando): his fateful saga, 360

Hayes, Christopher: at Anzio, 496

Hearst Press, the: Hitler's interview with, 93

Heaven: the wrath of, 9

Heavy-water: plant manufacturing, to be attacked, 319, 379, 404; plant bombed, 475; German supplies of, sunk, 500; German manufacturing site of, overrun, 663

Hecht, Gerhard: on Poles and Jews, 29

Heck, Alfons: and Roosevelt's death, 662

Hector (British armed merchant cruiser): sunk, 314

Hegyeshalom (Hungary): Soviet forces reach, 657

'Heil Hitler!': Poles forbidden to greet each other with, 24

Heilbronn (Germany): bombed, 616

Heilmann, Ernest: dies, 51–2

Heinisch, Dr.: and the deportation of Jews from Przemysl, 337–8

Heissenmeyer, Dr. Kurt: Medical experiments by, 611

Heka, Private T.: in action 422

Hel Peninsula (Poland): battle at, 13, 18

Helfgott, Ben: 'the sky was red', 4; 'in heaven', 641

Heligoland (Germany): naval activity near, 52; bombed, 667

Helldorf, Count Wolf Heinrich von: and German atrocities, 57; hanged, in Berlin, 568

Hellendorn (Holland): rocket bombs launched from 649

Helsinki (Finland): bombed, 31, 41; volunteers reach, 34; Soviet troops approach, 47; fate of eight Jews from, 407

Hendaye (France): Hitler at 133–4

Henlein, Konrad: commits suicide, 693

Hennecke, Admiral: at Cherbourg, 546

Henrici, General Gotthard: dismissed, 676

Henriot, Philippe: shot dead, 554

Heraklion (Crete): attacked, 184; a kidnapping near, 519, anti-partisan operations south of, 534

Herby (Poland): executions at, 480

Hereward (British destroyer): Queen Wilhelmina embarks on, 64

Hering, General: and the fall of Paris, 92

Herman, Chaim: 'our enemy is broken', 614

Hermann Goering Division: in Warsaw, 564

Hermes (British aircraft carrier): sunk, 315

Hermione (British cruiser): sunk, 333

Hermitage, the (Leningrad): art treasures evacuated from, 106, 214

Hero City: award of, 323

Hero of the Soviet Union: awarded, 205, 259, 323, 339, 399, 407, 442, 468, 510, 556, 611

'Heroine Mother': award of, 536

Herriot, Edouard: liberated, 674

Herrlingen (Germany): Rommel receives two emissaries at, 602

Herszberg, Rywka: murdered, 669

Herzen, Alexander: his words recalled, 227

Herzig, Major: wins the Knight's Cross, 679

Hess, Rudolf: flies to Britain (May 1941), 181

Hewel, Walther: on Hitler's moods, 172, 178, 186; in Russia with Hitler, 209, 221; and the 'secret' of what was happening to the Jews, 267; and Hitler's reaction to Pearl Harbour, 273–4

Heyde, Professor Werner: and euthanasia, 11; and gassing experiments, 258; and the sick, to be gassed, 276–7

Heydrich, Reinhard: 6, 12, 14, 40, 109; and the 'Final Solution', 188, 219, 246, 257, 266, 279, 292; ambushed, 327, 329; death of, 331–2, 334, 365; a monument to the assassins of, unveiled, 740

*Hiei* (Japanese battleship): sunk, 372

'Hilaire' (George Starr): sabotage by, 484, 543

Hildebrandt, Dr.: and mass 'elimination', 39

Hilferding, Rudolf: dies, 151–2

Hilkovec, Kurt: and the death of her three children, 295

Hill, Squadron-Leader Tony: rescued, 370

Hiller, Captain George: his sabotage mission, 490

Hiller, Charles D.: crosses into Germany, 590

Hillesum, Etty: deported, 459

Himmler, Heinrich: 4, 18, 22, 24, 28, 32, 39, 43; and the future of Poland, 79, 105; and the death of a Pole, 127; and an anti-Jewish film, 128; and euthanasia, 147; and the German invasion of Russia, 168–9; and medical experiments, 184; and the 'Final Solution', 188, 257, 317, 337, 389, 394–5, 414, 439; and the killings in East, 207, 213, 217–8, 218, 220, 333; and the Jews of Berlin, 224, 266; and an end to Jewish emigration, 246; and homosexuals, 256; and forced labour, 270; and a new category of victim, to be gassed, 276–7; Hitler's musings to, 280, 293, 341, 343; and medical experiments, 299, 340, 386, 436, 438; and 'Germanic blood', 315; and Giraud, 317; and the fate of Poles, 322; and the death of Heydrich, 331–2; addresses the ss, 332–3; visits Auschwitz, 343, 351; and the fate of 'asocials', 361; at Vinnitsa with Hitler, 368; and the fate of the Gypsies, 386, 474; and 'Aryan-Nordic' stud farms, 390–1; and the use of the clothes of Auschwitz victims, 400; receives statistics of mass murder, 414; and the property of murdered Jews, 424; and the destruction of the evidence of mass murder, 438; and a German 'page of glory', 465–6; has 'no misgivings', 494; personal bunker of, bombed, 510; and Allied escapees, 511; a critic of, executed, 521; to be killed, 551; and the failure of the Bomb Plot, 559, 597, 601; and the Warsaw Uprising, 563, 597; orders skeleton collection destroyed, 608, 614; given command on Upper Rhine, 614; given command of Vistula Army Group, 634, 640; seeks negotiations with the Western Allies, 643; expresses confidence in a 'breathing space', 657;

seeks to impress Western Allies, 669; offers to surrender, 670; his hopes of dividing West and East broken, 673; and a grave food shortage, 674; Hitler orders arrest of, 676; expelled from the Nazi party, 677; commits suicide, 695–6; his personal physician, hanged, 731

Hindenburg, Field Marshal: 'greetings' to, 10; his remains taken to Berlin, 632

Hintok Camp (Burma-Thailand railway): the first death in, 435

*Hipper* (German heavy cruiser): in the Arctic, 340, 389

Hirohito, Emperor of Japan: his palace, a possible atomic bomb target, 694; and the Japanese resolve to fight 'to the bitter end', 697; his palace, and the suicide of two generals on Okinawa, 700; urges a negotiated end to the war, 701, 705; 'Greetings to', 712; willing to accept unconditional surrender, 716; broadcasts the Potsdam Declaration, 717; no longer divine, 723, 729; a Japanese army sergeant still 'living for' (1972), 741; visits Europe, 741–2; his death and funeral, 744–5, 745

Hiroshima (Japan): to be an atomic bomb target, 675–6, 694, 710; an atomic bomb dropped on, 712–4; and a possible second bomb (on a second city), 715; recently liberated prisoners-of-war, visit, 719; continuing deaths at, 725, 746

Hirsch, Alice: shot, 325

Hirsch, Hella: shot, 325

Hirszman, Chaim: his evidence, and his death, 651

Hirt, Professor Auguste: his medical experiments, 299; disappears, 614

*Hiryu* (Japanese aircraft carrier): sunk, 330

Hitachi (Japan): bombed, 704

Hitler, Adolf: and the coming of war, 1, 2, 4; and 'Blitzkrieg', 2; and 'police and security' measures behind the lines in Poland, 2–3; and the Jews, 6, 28, 36–7, 100, 145, 151, 160, 177, 207, 209, 224, 232, 245, 257, 267, 284, 293, 295, 296, 301, 310, 311, 328, 340–1, 366, 368, 375–6, 377, 386, 389, 398, 407, 413, 420–1, 438–9, 439, 508, 527–8, 595, 677; visits Poland, 6, 9; and 'racial extermination', 8; in Danzig, 11; and the Polish borderlands, 16; signs a secret amnesty for ss men, 18–19; in Warsaw, 19; protests to, 19, 29, 36; a peace emissary visits, 19–20; plans a Western offensive, 20, 25, 29, 30, 34, 38, 59 and euthanasia, 20, 147; and the magnetic mine, 35; visits the Western Front, 35–6; plans an Eastern offensive, 23, 83, 111, 113, 114, 117, 120, 123, 124, 135, 137, 141, 142, 144–5, 146–7, 160, 164, 167, 176, 178, 188, 189, 191, 197; in Munich, 26, 35, 99, 139, 254, 375–6, 414, 473; and the magnetic mine, 29; and the 'Night and Fog' decree, 32; and Mussolini, 37–8, 50, 90, 99, 130, 134, 135, 149, 153, 227, 318, 410, 419, 445, 558; and a protest against the ss, 40; and the Soviet Union, 44; and Scandinavia, 45, 46–7; a peace mission to, 48; and Norway, 52, 54, 55, 56, 58; and Denmark, 54; and the invasion of France, Belgium,

Holland and Luxemburg, 61, 62, 65, 68, 69, 72, 75, 80, 82, 83, 88–9; awards given personally by, 62, 66, 154, 238, 338, 582; and Himmler, 79, 147, 315; and Italy, 90, 492; his interview with the Hearst Press (1940), 91; and a possible invasion of Britain, 99, 107, 110, 113, 122, 123, 125; and the fall of France, 101, 103; and the art treasures of Paris, 105; his building plans, 104, 109, 174, 260, 291, 325, 639; and the air war against Britain, 144–5; postpones the invasion of Britain, 125, 138–9; Churchill's broadcast about, 133; meets Laval, 133; meets Franco, 133–4; meets Pétain, 134; meets Ciano, 143; meets Horthy, 176, 421, 509; meets Antonescu, 188; meets the Mufti of Jerusalem, 265; meets Pavelić, 392; and Greece, 146, 149, 156, 165, 166; and Yugoslavia, 157, 165, 166; and *The Eternal Jew* (1941), 155; and the 'crucial year' (1941), 155; and Rommel, 156, 335, 374, 383; at Cambrai, 80; in Brussels, 82; at Charleville, 83; at Brûly-de-Pesche, 86, 97, 102, 104; at Rethondes, 101; visits Paris, 102; visits the Western Front (of 1914–18), 104; in Lille, 104; returns to Berlin (July 1940), 108; at Montoire, 133; at Hendaye, 133–4; at Florence, 135; at Boulogne, 147; in Vienna, 160; at Mönichkirchen, 172, 174, 176, 178; at Maribor and Graz, 178; at Borisov, 220; at Berdichev, 221; at Brest-Litovsk, 227; at Uman, 227; at Poltava, 339; at Vinnitsa, 343, 352, 358, 367, 392, 405, 409, 410, 412; at Zaporozhe, 405, 406, 410, 459; returns to Rastenburg via Smolensk, 412; at Treviso, 445; at Insterburg, 479; at Soissons, 542; at Berchtesgaden, 381, 514, 549, 553, 554; at Klessheim, Castle, 421, 509, 517; at Bad Nauheim ('Eagle's Nest'), 617; at Rastenburg (*see* index entry for Rastenburg); and the Commissar Decree, 160, 167, 183, 188, 191; postpones invasion of Russia, 166; spends night in air raid shelter, 172; plans invasion of Crete, 176; learns of Soviet defence preparations, 177; and the Thousand Year Reich, 179; 'has his problems', 180; and Hess, 181; his priorities (in May 1941), 185; and the loss of the *Bismarck*, 186; and the 'main enemy' (June 1941), 191; and the invasion of Russia, 194, 196, 198, 208–9, 209, 210, 212, 214, 219, 233, 241, 242, 253, 255; an important conversation of, intercepted, 226; and Dr Todt, 245, 266, 283, 299, 301; his 'evils' denounced, 255; and North Africa, 262, 366; and the Arabs, 265; and the battle for Moscow, 263, 266, 268, 270; and forced labour, 270, 283, 310; and Pearl Harbour, 273–4; and scorched earth, in Russia, 275; declares war on the United States, 277–8; refuses a withdrawal from Leningrad, 279, 288; his 'halt' orders 279, 281, 287, 381; and 'Fortress Europe', 289; and the war on the Eastern Front (1942–4), 308, 312, 316, 340, 346; 'in a black rage', 317; angered, 319; forecasts 'great victories', 320; 'we shall win in the end', 328; and the war at sea, 340;

cheated of oil (in the Caucasus), 350, 363; and the 'Atlantic Wall', 352, 358; and Dieppe, 354; and Stalingrad, 363, 365, 370, 381, 387, 391, 397, 398, 400, 410; and Sark, 367; and a debate over the destruction of the bodies of murdered Jews, 368; and the battle for Tunisia, 376, 377, 382, 410; and the occupation of Vichy France, 377; accepts a withdrawal in the Caucasus, 389; his 'extinction', agreed upon at Casablanca, 397; the third Russian offensive, of 406, 409; and British bombing raids, 410; disaffection with, 410, 412; the first military bomb plot against (March 1943), 412; and the second assassination attempt (of March 1943), 414; bomb plot against (July 1944), 551, 553; and the Kursk Salient, 413, 420, 441, 444; and the rocket bomb, 416, 455, 463–4, 473–4, 479, 653; his continuing confidence in victory (May 1943), 426; and the danger and consequences of the defeat of Italy, 427, 446, 448, 458, 459, 467, 462; and an anti-Bolshevik Legion, 430; and Sicily, 441; and Greece, 441; and Crete, 441; and Turkey, 517; and a Churchill-Roosevelt telephone conversation, 448, 522; Generals protest to, about Eastern Front neglect, 458; the 'final blow' will be struck by, 458; and the Red Army's advances, 458, 459, 473; orders evacuation of Corsica, 461; accepts withdrawals from large areas of Russia, 462; cancels order to evacuate the Crimea, 471; and the coming cross-Channel landing, 472; and bombing raids on Berlin (November 1943), 476–7, 478; a further attempt on the life of, fails (November 1943), 479; yields space in East, to prepare in West, 486, 492, 514; and the jet aircraft, 486, 488; again rejects a tactical withdrawal (January 1944), 489; 'terror' and 'greater terror', 495; and Hanna Reitsch, 504; and Frau von Exner, 504; the Russian colonial empire of, lost, 507; and Allied escapee airmen, 511; and the Red Army the 'undoing' of, 511; and the evacuation of Sevastopol, 522; and the coming cross-Channel landing, 530, 532; and D-Day, 534; and the Normandy deception, 536–7; and the 'Oyster' mine, 538; and the battle in Northern Europe (1944–5), 545, 546, 549, 553, 556, 557, 565–6, 567, 568, 570, 585, 587, 592–3; and the Bomb Plot (July 1944), 557–8, 559, 566; and the photographs of Majdanek, 559; orders evacuation of southern France, 571; von Kluge's suicide letter to, 572; and the defection of Roumania, 574; and the Warsaw uprising, 581; authorizes withdrawal from Estonia, 594; 'donates a town to the Jews', 595; and 'tired, broken man', 597; and the Jet aircraft, 599; and Rommel's death, 602; remains at Rastenburg (October 1944) 606; leaves Rastenburg (never to return), 613; gives Himmler command on Upper Rhine, 614; and the Ardennes offensive, 615, 617, 621; and the defence of Hungary, 617; and the

failure of his 'secret weapons', 624–5; the final 'secret weapon' of, 625, 650; transfers roops from West to East, 626, 627, 628; orders troops from East Prussia to central Poland, 629; orders evacuation of Memel, 632; and the loss of East Prussia, 633; gives Himmler command of Vistula Army Group, 634; rumoured last redoubt of, 643; advised to pull back from Pomerania, 643; 'You may see my hand tremble...', 644; convinced Budapest can be recaptured, 646; dismisses von Rundstedt, 648; visits the Oder, 648; dismisses Guderian, 651; descends to his bunker, 657; warned, about shortage of medicines, 657; and General Lasch, 660–1; and General Wenck, 661; and the defence of Berlin, 663, 667; Eva Braun joins, 666; warned of munition shortages, 666; his fifty-sixth birthday, in the bunker, 668; and the battle for Berlin, 668–9, 669, 669–70, 670–1, 672, 673, 674, 677; his testimony, 677; refuses to allow the surrender of Berlin, 679; commits suicide, 681; condolences on his death, sent from Dublin, 683; his picture, burnt, 695; and 'unconditional surrender', 711; one of the earliest supporters of, commits suicide, 724; his personal physician, hanged, 731; reparations debts unpaid by, finally resolved (1952), 736; and 'Providence', 743

Hitler Youth, the: and an anti-Jewish film, 128; and a 'Year of Service' in the East, 286; a member of, executed, 372; to man anti-aircraft batteries, 397; and the clothing of Germany's victims, 400; 'sacrificed', 585; and the Ardennes offensive, 617; an exhortation to (March 1945), 654; a leader of, and Roosevelt's death, 662; members of, and the murder of Jews at Gardelegen, 663; Hitler inspects soldiers of, 668–9; and the defence of Berlin, 670, 672; at Lübeck, open fire on refugees, 687–8

Hitler Youth Division: in Belgium, 585
'Hitler's little canary' (Denmark): resistance in, 456
Hiyo (Japanese aircraft carrier): 543
Ho Chi-minh: seizes power, 720
Hoepner, General Erich: hanged, 556
Hoess, Rudolf: at Auschwitz, 57, 343, 469–70; executed, 732
Hofacker, Colonel Caesar von: his opposition to Hitler, 511, 553, 556; executed, 620
Hola (Poland): Soviet prisoners-of-war murdered at, 282
'Hold on!': Hitler's broadcast order, 381
Holland (a parachutist): killed, 573
Holland: a double-agent in, 15; a kidnap in, 26; and Hitler's war plans, 29, 38, 59; invasion of, 61, 62; battle in, 64, 65, 66; motor vessels from, at Dunkirk, 83; its future, 85; under German occupation, 103; soldiers of, in Britain, 113; works of art taken from, 130; a protest in, 144; anti-Jewish measures in, 151; executions in, 160, 161, 405; Jews deported from, 205, 317, 343, 344, 348, 350–1, 351, 362, 365, 370, 386, 391, 395, 398, 421,

432, 459, 474, 504, 546, 584; the fate of a British agent in, and the consequences, 331; a merchant ship from, attacked, 343; volunteers from, on the Eastern Front, 348; attempted sabotage, and reprisals, in, 353; German bombers move southward from, 374; soldiers of, in Japanese captivity, 417; forced labour from, 421, 427; air supplies to resistance in, 486; Jews smuggled from, 512; Gestapo records in, destroyed, 515–6; and the Normandy deception plan, 542; to be held, 585; Allied parachute landings in, 593; attacks on dykes in, 598; V2 rockets launched from, 608; 'very hard fighting' in, 610; German troops in, being moved to the Silesian Front, 640; a mass reprisal in, 646; anti-fascists from, in Belsen, 664; food supplies for, 678–9; Germans sign surrender in, 687; Jews from, revisit Germany, 743; war criminals released from, 744; the Far Eastern death toll of, 745; wartime death toll in, 746
Hollandia (New Guinea): landings on, 519
Hollard, Michel: and the 'Flying Bomb', 463–4, 474; arrested, 497–8
Holocaust: survivors of, meet in Jerusalem (1981), 742; see also index entries for 'Final Solution' and Jews
Holohan, Major William V.: behind the lines in Italy, 597
'Holy Trinity': killed, 183
Homberg (Ruhr): bombed, 577
Hong Kong: 108, 140; Canadian troops on way to, 262; Japan attacks, 171, 273; Japanese land at, 280, 282; surrenders, 282–3; the fate of prisoners-of-war from 366; a post-war execution in, 396; a prisoner-of-war executed in, 468–9; a British naval squadron enters, 721
Honshu Island (Japan): attacked, 642; invasion plans for, 659–660; and the atomic bomb, 697; continued preparations for the invasion of, 763; bombed, 704; shelled, 709; massive air raids on, 715, 717; the day of the planned invasion of, 728
Hood (British battle-cruiser): sunk, 185
Hook of Holland (Holland): rocket bombs launched from, 589
Hoizel, Anton: hanged, 669
'Home Alive in Forty-Five': an American soldiers' slogan, 655
Home Army (A.K.): revolts, in Warsaw, 562, 564; leaders of being arrested, 581; arrests of members of, by the Russians, 646
Homma, General Masaharu: executed, 728
Homosexuals: to be executed, 256, 361–2; medical experiments on, 598
Hopkins, Harry: Roosevelt's emissary, 150, 151, 155, 167; in Moscow, 218, 219; at Placentia Bay, 220
'Hornet': a German air corps key, broken, 287
Hornet (U.S. aircraft carrier): and the first American bombing of Japan, 317; sunk off Santa Cruz Islands, 372
Hornum (Germany): bombed, 49
Horodenka (Eastern Galicia): Jews deported to their deaths from, 315

Horowitz (a dancer): her act of defiance, 469

Hornemunn, Eduard: murdered, 669

Hornemunn, Alexander: murdered, 669

Hôtel Crillon (Paris): Germans at, 94

Horthy, Admiral Miklos: aligns Hungary with Germany, 169; visits Hitler, 176, 232, 421; demands halt to deportation of Hungarian Jews, 550, 560; abducted, 603

Hossbach, General Friedrich: dismissed, 633

Hötz, Lieutenant-Colonel: assassinated, 247

Houghton, Captain J.B.: his mission, and fate, 362–3

House of Commons (London): and the surrender of Belgium, 77–8; and the Battle of Britain, 119–20; bombed, 181; and British military aid to Russia, 239; Churchill speaks about 'air power' in, 500; and the 'Flying bomb' death toll, 552, 564; and the German surrender in Italy and southern Austria, 683

Houston (U.S. heavy cruiser); sunk, 303

Hualin (Manchuria): battle at, 717

Hubener, Helmuth Günther: executed, 372

Hüber, Kurt: executed, 405

Hudson, Colonel D.T.: lands in Yugoslavia, 236

Hudson River (New York): a museum at, 742

Huelva (Spain): and an Allied deception, 423

Hull, Cordell: and the fall of France, 94; and Japanese intentions, 263; and no separate peace, 468; 'horrified' by Morgenthau Plan, 592

Hull (U.S. destroyer): losses on, 618

Hulme, Sergeant Clive: in action, 184

Hüls (Ruhr): bombed, 439

Humberside (England): bombed, 181

Humbie (Scotland): a German bomber shot down at, 25

Hungary: and the German invasion of Yugoslavia, 166; and the German invasion of Greece, 169; treatment of Jews and Serbs by, 174; declares war on Russia, 202; Jews from, killed at Kamenets-Podolsk, 227; Britain declares war on, 270; and a German demand for the 'evacuation' of Jews, 363–4; troops from, at Stalingrad, 400; forced labourers from, killed in an Allied air raid, 453; German occupation of, 508, 509; Jews deported to Auschwitz from, 523–4, 527, 530, 546, 550, 560; and slave labour, 525; and Allied bombing raids, 530, 550; and Allied mining, of the Danube, 599; Red Army advances through, 616; declares war on Germany, 624; Germany's need for the oil of, 646, 651; final battles in, 651, 654, 657; Red Army master of, 661; troops from, at Belsen, 663–4; to be 'police-governed', 686–7; German speaking peoples in, to be 'removed', 710; in the Soviet bloc, 723

Hunt, Captain Ray: and the American landings on Luzon, 628

Husseini, Haj Amin el- (Mufti of Jerusalem): meets Hitler, 265; and a Muslim revolt, 458

Huston, John: his film, cut, 481

Hutou (Manchuria): battle at, 717; mass suicide at, 720

Hyde Park (New York State): Churchill and Roosevelt at, 451, 594

Hydro (Norwegian ferry boat): sunk, 500

I-23 (Japanese submarine): sunk, 303

'I. Bagerov': escapes from captivity, 480

Iceland: occupied, 63; defence of, to be taken over by the United States, 190, 208; and the Russian convoy route, 239, 314, 325

Ie Shima (Ryukyu Islands): American landing on, 666; Ernie Pyle killed on, 668

Igren (south Russia): inmates of mental hospital at, murdered, 298

Iheya Islands (Okinawa): seized, 697

Ihler, General: surrenders, 92

Ijmuiden (Holland): British troops land at, 67

Ijssel River (Holland): Germans cross, 62

Ilja (White Russia): Jews murdered in, 305

Illustrious (British aircraft carrier): reaches Egypt, 121; in action, 140; badly damaged, 149, 150

Ilmen Lake (Russia): partisans in action near, 264–5; a rumour concerning, 324

Ilomantsi (Finland): defended, 34

Imita Ridge (New Guinea): Australians driven back to, 361

Imabari (Japan): bombed, 712

Imperial Guards Division (Japan): commander of, assassinated, 717

Imphal (India): a retreat to, 325; an advance from, 404; besieged, 512; an air lift to, 517; continuing fighting on, 541; Japanese driven from, 613

Impulsive (British destroyer): its efforts at rescue, 503

Inber, Vera: in Leningrad, 227, 266

Indaw (Burma): and a sabotage mission, 404

India: troops needed from, 68; Hitler's admiration for British rule in, 83; and the possibility of Hitler at the 'gates' of, 120; troops from, in action in Malaya, 284, 296, 300; and the Empress of Asia, 299; and Japan, 316; General Stilwell withdraws to, 321; aid to Egypt diverted from, 336–7; troops from, in North Africa, 338, 358; a setback to communications with, 376; troops from, in Burma, 399, 646; troops from, in action in Italy, 498, 509, 522, 660; troops of, besieged in Imphal, 517; war dead of, 746

Indian National Army: and 'Asia for the Asiatics', 278; and Japan, 419, 598; members of, brought to trial, 724–5

Indian Ocean: 100, 101, 140; a Japanese attack across, 314; survivors, machine-gunned in, 500, 509–10; end of Japanese mastery in, 517

Indianapolis (U.S. cruiser): brings atomic bomb across the Pacific, 709; sunk, 709–10; 'Greetings . . . from the men of', 712; news of the sinking of, made public, 718

Indomitable (British aircraft carrier): runs aground, 268

Indonesia: independence of, 730, 733

Infantes, Esteban: on the Eastern Front, 465

Inland Sea (Japan): mines dropped in, 712; a naval commander, cheated of his ovation in, 718

Innsbruck (Austria): surrenders to the Americans, 684

Inoguchi, Captain Toshihei: goes down with his ship, 606

Ionian Sea: naval action in, 140

Inönü, Ismet: a message of support to, 157

Insterburg (East Prussia): Hitler sees a rocket bomb at, 479

International Bank for Reconstruction and Development: established, 727

International Military Tribunal: established, 715; the four indictments of, 724; to be set up in Tokyo, 728; its sentences (at Nuremberg), 731; verdicts of (in Tokyo), 733

Intrepid (U.S. aircraft carrier): losses on, 614, 666; becomes a museum, 742

Iosif Stalin (Soviet steamer): sunk, 361

Ipswich (England): and a possible German invasion, 123

Iran (Persia): pressure on, 189; Anglo-Soviet occupation of, 226; Anglo-Soviet Treaty with, 296; an American aircrew reach, 324; threat to oil fields in, 348; American aid to Russia through, 367; Soviet pressure on, 728

Iraq: a blow to Britain in, 168; British troops land in, 174–5; surrender of Rashid Ali in, 187; planned German expedition to, 189

Iron Bottom Bay (Solomon Islands): battle in, 419

Iron Cross: awarded, 62, 126, 205, 332, 348, 428, 504, 542, 560, 614, 670; not suitable for executioners, 256; a winner of, executed, 332, 549; winners of, paraded in Moscow, 556

'Iron Curtain': and the 'permanent prevention of war', 729

Iron Gates (Danube): Germans pull back to a defensive line at, 575

Iron Guard, the: attack Jews (in Roumania), 151

Irrawaddy River (Burma): glider landings across, 506

I-shan (China): liberated, 699

Isigny (Normandy): and an Allied deception, 532

Isle of May (Scotland): two merchant ships sunk off, 689

Ismay, General Sir Hastings: and Swedish neutrality, 78; and the Battle of Britain, 118–9; and the Blitz, 173

Israel: accepts reparations payments from West Germany, 736; the trial of Eichmann in, 739–40; Jews from, revisit Germany, 743

Istra (near Moscow): German troops reach, 262; Germans driven from, 278

Istria (Italy): Italians to march from 170; Germans take control of, 463; to be liberated by Tito's partisans, 680

Itagaki, General Seishiro: signs a formal surrender, 722

'Italian Social Republic': established, 463

Italy: fate of a merchant ship from 29; and Finland, 34; declares war on France and Britain, 90; occupies Menton, 101; naval battle off toe of, 109; occupies Berbera, 120; and Japan,

129; invades Greece, 135, 143; approaches the Suez Canal, 135; a setback to, in Egypt, 145; setbacks to, in East Africa, 153, 165; fails to redress military balance in Albania, 162; a successful exploit by, 165; a naval victory over, 166; lands on Crete, 186; assets of, in the United States, frozen 190; declares war on Russia, 199; and an attack on Malta, 216; top secret cypher of, broken, 218, 254, 357; and a raid on Alexandria, 280; and reprisals in Yugoslavia, 323; and a successful naval action off Egypt, 333; soldiers from, on the Eastern Front, 355, 381, 385; and the Jews of Tunisia, 386; prospect of defeat or defection of, 427, 430; troops from, fight Yugoslav partisans, 431; driven from the islands between Tunisia and Sicily, 437; Allied bombing of, 441; and the fall of Mussolini, 445–6, 448, 452, 456; Allied invasion of, 457; further Allied landing on, 459; and the German occupation of Italy, 460; Jews deported from, 462, 466, 473, 494, 514, 564; declares war on Germany, 467; soldiers from, in action against Germans, 474, 490; and Allied bombing raids, 482; air supplies to resistance in, 486; to be reinforced, by Hitler, 492; partisans in, 498, 519, 525, 539, 544; fate of prisoners-of-war from, 461–2, 475, 534; anti-partisan sweeps in, 550, 554, 597; renewed partisan activity in, 575–6, 587, 589; partisans in, betrayed, 593; partisans in, receive an American mission, 597; and the hazards of combat, 599; partisans in, escape a sweep, 613; German troops in, being moved to the Silesian front, 638, 640; German troops in, and a possible surrender, 648; Hitler urges his troops in, to 'stand firm', 657; Hitler rejects an appeal to withdraw in, 667; final battles in, 669; partisans killed in (near Gorizia), 669; a general uprising in, 672; and communism, 729

Italian Alpine Division (in Greece): 'will be crushed', 139–40

Ito, Lieutenant Commander Torashi: confesses, then commits suicide 725

'Ivans': the terrible winters of, 412

Iwo Jima (Pacific): a naval engagement off, 300; aerial bombardment of, 642; battle for, 642–3

Izbushensky (southern Russia): a cavalry battle at, 355

Izhorsky Steel Mill (Leningrad): rebuilt, 548

Izieu (France): Jews deported from, 514

Izmail (Bessarabia): Soviet troops enter, 105

Izyum (south Russia): Russians poised to retake, 293; Germans capture, 325; Germans driven from, 399

'Jack': a double agent, 255

Jacob, Max: dies, 506

Jacobi, Harry: saved, 67

'Jacqueline' (Yvonne Rudellat): her clandestine mission, 338–9; dies, 672

Jadovno (Yugoslavia): mass murder at, 225

Jaeckeln, s.s. General Franz: and the killing of Jews from Hungary, 227;

and a sweep against Soviet partisans, 305

Jaeger, s.s. Colonel Karl: and the Jews of Lithuania, 267, 298

Jajce (Yugoslavia): Tito's partisans move to, 455; Tito's partisans driven from, 489

Jakobs, Josef: executed, 155

James, Lieutenant D.P.: his escape from captivity, 480

James, Lieutenant: killed, 146

Jankowski, Stanislaw: recalls two acts of defiance, 470

Janowska Camp (Lvov): evidence of mass murder to be destroyed at, 438

Janus (British destroyer): sunk, 492

Japan: Soviet espionage in, 45; and French Indo-China, 108; joins the Axis, 129; and the British naval victory over Italy, 140; and Soviet fears, 149; its eventual defeat envisaged (March 1941), 167; signs neutrality pact with Soviet Union, 173; and its 'Magic' cypher system broken, 178–271; urged to enter war against Germany, 206; occupies French Indo-China, 216; a warning to, 222; an assurance from Hitler to, 226; and the Togo government, 245; air defences in, 249; Pearl Harbour preparations by, 249, 253, 254, 263; American demands to, 264; imminent attacks by, 268; attacks Pearl Harbour, 272; first victories throughout South-East Asia, 273–80; and Australia, 280; German pressure on, 312; bombed, 317, 321; cyphers of, read, 322; a submarine from, docks at Lorient, 348; and the battle for New Guinea, 308, 322, 338, 341; 345, 346, 355, 361, 375, 378; and the battle of Guadalcanal, 350, 361, 363, 368, 372, 374, 377, 383; continuing bombing of, 378, 645, 648, 696, 718; and Allied priorities, agreed at Casablanca, 397; and the Indian National Army, 423; and the Suluk revolt, 469; and the Soviet Union, 478, 602, 640; and the fate of Allied merchant seamen, 500, 509–10; Argentina declares war on, 653; and the atomic bomb on Hiroshima, 675–6, 694, 710, 712–14, 715; and a possible negotiated peace with, 701, 705, 707–8, 710; and the Soviet Union (in 1945), 711, 715, 717, 720; and the effect of the atomic bomb, on continuing the war, 716; signs peace treaties, 735; wartime death toll of, 746

see also index entries for
Hirohito, Hiroshima, Prisoners-of-War, Tokyo, 'Magic', 'Purple'

Jarocin (Poland): evacuations from, 2

Jaroslaw (Poland): Hitler at, 9

Jarry, Colonel: flown to France, 461

Jasenovac (Yugoslavia): Jews murdered at, 390; a revolt at, 672

Jassy (Roumania): Jews murdered in, 204; Soviet forces enter, 574

Java (Dutch light cruiser): sunk, 303

Java (Dutch East Indies): evacuated, 302, 303, 306; battles off, 303–4, 305–6

Java Sea: naval battle in, 303–4

Jawiszowice (East Upper Silesia): a forced labour camp at, 353

Jaworow (Eastern Galicia): Jews of, resist deportation, 421

Jaworzno (East Upper Silesia): a labour camp at, 438

Jay, John: his descendant hanged, 581

Jean Bart (French battleship): sailed to safety, 100; put out of action, 109

'Jeff': a double agent ('O.K.'), 255, 453

Jervis Bay (armed merchant cruiser): attacked, 138

Jenninger, Philipp: his questions, recalling the past, 743

Jersey (Channel Islands): Germans occupy, 105

Jerusalem (Israel): a survivor gives evidence in, 630; survivors gather in, 742

Jerusalem Avenue (Warsaw): an execution on, 495

Jeschonnek, General Hans: commits suicide, 453

Jesselton (North Borneo): a revolt in, 469; Japanese garrison at, surrenders, 725

Jet aircraft (German): shot down, 599; in action, 622, 649, 650; airfields for, bombed, 651, 652; Himmler's confidence in, 657; 'massacre' of, 661; final air battle of (above Berlin), 666

'Jewish Bolshevism': and National Socialism, 191

Jewish Brigade Group: established, 576; in action in Italy, 660

Jewish Chronicle (London): and 'unspeakable evils', 254, 255

Jewish Council: in Warsaw, 28

Jewish Fighting Organization: established in Poland, 346; acts of defiance by, 388, 440

Jews: Hitler's obsession with, 6, 28, 36–7, 100, 14, 151, 160, 179, 107, 209, 224, 232, 245, 257, 267, 284, 293, 295, 296, 301, 310, 311, 328, 340–1, 366, 368, 376, 377, 386, 389, 398, 407, 413, 420–1, 438–9, 439, 508, 507–8, 595, 677; murdered (1939), 4, 5, 7, 8, 9, 12, 27, 28, 32; murdered (1940), 39, 43, 56–7, 105, 145; murdered (1941) 151, 182, 201, 204, 209, 213, 214–5, 216, 217, 218, 218–9, 219–20, 223, 225, 227, 228, 228–9, 232, 235, 139, 141, 243, 246, 247, 249, 250, 251, 252, 254, 255, 257, 260, 263, 266, 268; (in 1942) 290, 293, 295, 296, 297, 305, 306, 308, 315, 322, 324, 326–7, 328, 329, 331, 332, 336, 345, 355, 367–8; (in 1943), 390, 406–7, 435, 444, 460–1, 481; (in 1944), 490, 578, 595; (in 1945) 669, 672, 683–4; their 'annihilation' threatened, 6, 151; and the 'Commissar Decree', 160, 168–9; and Himmler, 188, 107, 213, 217–8, 218, 220, 257, 317, 333, 337, 368, 394–5; and the execution of a Pole, 12; deported, 22–3, 27, 49, 133, 244, 245; indignities against, 24; reprisals against, 28; future of, as seen from Berlin, 29, 40; and forced labour, 43, 460–1; and Dr Goebbels, 87, 128, 224, 257, 301, 306, 310, 311–2, 327; and euthanasia, 105, 336; and the spread of anti-Jewish measures, 127, 129, 151; and an anti-Jewish film, 128, 144; in Belgrade, 173; in Hungarian-occupied Yugoslavia, 174; in Baghdad, 187; in Norway, 205; in Slovakia, 232; the 'destroyer', 245; and the decision to kill by gassing, 249–50; protests on behalf of, 250, 288, 481; sympathy for, 255, 256, 633;

Jews—contd.
resistance by, 256, 308, 328, 341, 345, 376, 388, 393–4, 421, 424, 440, 460–1, 467, 516, 600; and the Mufti of Jerusalem, 265; and the death camps (Chelmno), 274–5, 279, 364, 541, 630; (Belzec), 292, 307–8, 310, 315, 322, 351, 362, 364, 370, 386; (Auschwitz-Birkenau), 322, 335, 340, 343, 351, 356–7, 362, 365, 369–70, 372, 386, 391, 395, 398, 400, 407, 408, 413, 424, 432, 436, 440, 444, 459, 462, 465, 467, 470, 471, 474, 488, 490, 494, 504, 507, 510, 514, 520, 523–4, 525, 527, 540, 546, 550, 559–60, 562, 564, 571, 582, 584. 595, 598, 608; (Sobibor), 322, 326, 351, 364, 370, 386, 395, 424, 467; (Maly Trostenets), 324, 332, 351, 364; (Treblinka), 343–4, 346, 252, 354, 364, 369, 370, 386–91, 393, 406, 421, 428; (Majdanek), 376, 559; and Gypsies, 282, 297; in Yugoslavia, 225, 295, 390, 672; and the British bombing of Cologne, 329; and the assassination of Heydrich, 329, 331–2; and medical experiments, 340, 356–7, 368, 370, 431–2, 436; a declaration on behalf of (17 December 1942), 387; 'warned ... in time' (in Berlin), 410; rescued (from Denmark), 464; of Hungary (in 1944), 508, 509, 527, 603; rescued (from Holland), 512; killed, in Crete, 534; in the Warsaw uprising (August 1944), 565; rescue of (from Yugoslavia), 585; a helper of, arrested, 585; killed by Allied bombs (at Auschwitz), 591; marched out of Budapest, 603; a helper of, executed in Berlin, 629; mass graves of, discovered in southern Germany, 673; shot, in Italy, 673; shot, at Marienbad, 674; killed during evacuations, 675; and Hitler's testimony, 677; possible revenge by, 693; seek 'compensation' from Germany, 723–4; killed, after the war, 730; survivors, held in camps on Cyprus, 730; and reparations from Germany, 723–4, 735; survivors among, meet in Jerusalem, 742; former German citizens, return to Germany, 743; historical questions concerning (asked in 1988), 743; wartime death toll of, 746

'Jill': a Japanese warplane, in action, 542–3
Jinyo (Japanese escort carrier): sunk, 613
Jodl, General Alfred: 69, 75, 113, 145, 160; and German execution plans for Russia, 183; and the war with Russia, 199; and the fall of Mussolini, 446; and the Normandy deception, 537; and the Ardennes, 593; and the defence of Berlin, 670–1; and the German surrender, 689; hanged, 731; posthumous pardon for, 737
Johanngeorgenstadt (Germany): a French deportee executed at, 673
John Birch Society: opposes Communism, 720–1
'John Bull': to be brought to his knees, 177
Johnson, Lieutenant-Colonel Chandler W.: raises the flag, 642
Johore Straits (Malaya): Japanese cross, 299
Joint Basic War Plan Number One (Anglo-American): agreed, 166

Joint Intelligence Committee (British): and German intentions, 30, 311
Joly, Lieutenant ('Valentin'): killed, 554
Jones, Private Ralph: killed, 565
Jones, Dr R. V.: and the German rocket bomb, 416, 464, 557; and the German sailor, 612
Jonge Jan (Belgian fishing vessel): at Dunkirk, 81
Jongh, Frederic de: betrayed, and shot, 436
Jösing Fjord (Norway): a victory in, 42
Jovanovic, Mara: and the killings of Sabac, 225
Joyce, William ('Lord Haw-Haw'): his broadcasts, 10, 115, 119, 329, 458, 488, 583–4; arrested, 696; hanged, 727
Jud Süss (film): shown in Berlin, 128; shown in Breslau, 151
'Judy': Japanese warplane, in action, 542–3
Jülich (Germany): Jews deported to their deaths from, 310; Churchill on German soil at, 645
Julius Caesar: 'The die is cast', 601
Julius Caesar (Shakespeare): performed on the 'Railway of Death', 336, 345
Jung, Dr Edwin: his experiments, 32
Junger, Ernst: seeks Hitler's overthrow, 511
'Juno' Beach (Normandy): landing at, 534
Jupiter (British destroyer): sunk, 303
Jüterbog (south of Berlin): a proposed defence line at, 671; Red Army enters, 671–2
Jutland, Battle of (1916): guns used at, in use in 1944, 557
Juvincourt (France): bombed, 522
Juvisy (France): Germans to enter, 92

Kaafjord (Norway): Tirpitz, bombed in, 513
Kachins: in action in Burma, 506
Kaczmarski, Stefan: shot, 435
Kafka, Franz: his friend's suicide, 95
Kaga (Japanese aircraft carrier): sunk, 330
Kagan, Joseph: and the fate of 534 Jews in Kovno, 224–5
Kagoshima Bay (Japan): and a Pearl Harbour practice run, 254
Kain, Flying Officer, E.J.: his victory, 21–22
Kainz, Ludwig: in Paris, gives information to a spy, 150
'Kaiten': Japanese suicide torpedo, in action, 703, 712
Kakazu Ridge (Okinawa): fighting on, 662
Kalach (Russia): battle at, 380
Kalamata (Greece): evacuation from, 175; and an Allied deception, 423
Kalau (Germany): German forces enter, 668
Kalinin (Russia): falls to the Germans, 244, 265; battle near, 270; Russians recapture, 279, 287; a locksmith from, killed at Neuengamme, 611
Kalinovichi (White Russia): Germans driven from, 489
Kalisz (Poland): an execution in, 22; Jews murdered by gas van in, 250

Kaliteyev, Captain Vyacheslav: executed, 227; rehabilitated, 739
Kallmeyer, Dr: an expert in gassing, 250
Kalmyk Region (of southern Russia): German plans for, 193
Kaltenbrunner, S.S. General, Ernst: to co-ordinate deportations, 398; to run Military Counter-Intelligence, 499; and Hitler's confidence in victory (February 1945), 639; 'a thousand men must still die every day' (in Mauthausen), 674; hanged, 731
Kaluga (Russia): Germans seize, 243; Germans evacuate, 283; heavy German losses near, 296
Kamaishi (Japan): bombarded, 703
Kamchatka (Russia): 722
Kamenets-Podolsk (Russia): partisans organized in, 202; Jews killed in, 225, 509; Red Army enters, 511
Kamensk (Russia): abandoned, 341
Kamikaze ('divine wind'): suicide pilots, 606, 617, 627, 657, 697, 700, 712, 717; and other suicide devices, 703, 712
Kaminski Brigade: in Warsaw, 564, 565
Kampar (Malaya): battle at, 284
Kanchanaburi (Thailand): an Allied cemetery at, 738
Kandalaksha (Russia): German attack on, 206
Kantariya, Sergeant: takes the Red Banner into the Reichstag, 681
Kantor, Alfred: 'It's over', 691
Kantorovich, Lev: killed in action, 205
Kaplan, Chaim: in Warsaw, 28, 32, 47, 145, 257
Kaplanas, Zahar: saved, 511
Kapuvar (Hungary): Soviet troops enter, 654
Karasev (Soviet historian): and the coming of war (in June 1941), 198–9
Karcz, Tadeusz: shot, 479
Karczew (Poland): Jews killed at, 386
Karelia (Finland): Soviet control of, 40; attacked, 204; a Norwegian mission to, 612–3
Karens: resist the Japanese, 485
'Karl': a new German mortar, 214
Karlshorst (near Berlin): German forces sign a surrender at, 690
Karlsruhe (Germany): and mines in the Rhine, 64; four British agents imprisoned in, 555
Karpiowka (Poland): villagers murdered in, 482
Kashira (near Moscow): Germans draw near to, 262
Kashtankin, Victor: 'Dying is simple', 510
Kassala (Anglo-Egyptian Sudan): Italians withdraw from, 153
Kassel (Germany): bombed, 446, 469
Kasserine Pass (Tunisia): battle at, 402
Kastner, Rudolf: and Adolf Eichmann, 603
Katerini (Greece): Jews saved in, 413
Katowice (Poland): anti-Jewish measures in, 12; mass execution of Poles in, 46
Kattegat: the Russian interest in, 141; mining of approach to, 189
Katyn (Soviet Union): and Polish prisoners-of-war, 53, 731
Katyusha rocket: in action, 210
Katz, Hillel: a Soviet spy, 150, 334

Katznelson, Yithak: gassed at Auschwitz, 520

Kaufbeuren (Bavaria): euthanasia at, 379

Kawaguchi, General: at Guadalcanal, 372

Kawasaki (Japan): bombed, 648

Kazakhstan (Soviet Central Asia): evacuations to, 199, 240

*Kazakhstan* (Soviet troop transport): heroism on, 227; the captain of, rehabilitated, 739

Kazan Railway Station (Moscow): Stalin's remarks at, 173

Kazinets, Isai: hanged, 323

Kazimierz Dolny (Poland): Poles murdered at, 379

Kazimierz Wielka (Poland): a pilot in hiding near, 570

*Kearney* (U.S. destroyer): torpedoed, 244-5

Kecskemet (Hungary): Red Army reaches, 608

Kedainiai (Lithuania): Jews killed in, 214-5, 228

Kedrous (Crete): reprisals at, 520

Keeble, Lieutenant: killed, 114

Keitel, General Wilhelm: and the execution of Polish civilians, 8; and the German plans in the West, 20; and the future of Poland, 22; and the French armistice, 101; and the German invasion of Russia, 212, 230, 233; and scorched earth, 275; and German casualties, 363; and the fate of Russia, 370; and anti-partisan activity, 386; and the battle for Berlin, 679; signs the final instrument of surrender, 690; hanged, 731

Kelebia (Tunisia): Axis forces at, continue to fight, 426

*Kelly* (British destroyer): in action at Namsos, 58; crippled, 59; sunk, off Crete, 185

Kempner, Vitka: her sabotage mission, 331

Kendari (Celebes): Japanese about to land at, 293

Kennedy, John F.: in action in the Solomon Islands, 449, 471

Kennedy, Joseph P.: contradicted, 120, 150

Kennington (London): a pilot bales out over, 125

Kensington (London): a 'Flying Bomb' at, 548

Kent (England): 'Flying Bomb' deaths in, 549

Kentish, Leonard: abducted, and killed, 396

Kentucky Military Museum (Kentucky): a trophy at, 674

Kerama Retto (Ryukyu Islands): battle for, 655

Kerch (Crimea): Jews murdered at, 260; battle on, 320, 325

Kerch Straits (Russia): 222; Soviet troops land on, 283, 284, 286; German plans to advance through, 341; Germans retreat back across, 462

Keren (Eritrea): Italians driven from, 165

Kesselring, Field Marshal Albrecht von: his anti-partisan order, 550; in Italy, 650; Hitler's 'stand firm' message to, 657; urges a stand in the Harz Mountains, 667; sentenced to death, pardoned, and freed, 732

Kessler, General: surrenders to the Americans, while on his way to Tokyo, 693

Kevu, Benjamin: takes American crewmen to safety, 449

Key, José: a spy, shot, 326

Khalkin Gol (Soviet Far East): Japanese defeated at, 2; a film of, 468

Kharkov (Ukraine): factory evacuations from, 205, 275; a German objective, 222, 238; Germans enters, 249; German reserves sent from, 266; Russians seek to isolate, 293; a rumour concerning, 324; a Russian attack near, 325, 327; Red Army reaches outskirts of, 404; Hitler seeks recapture of, 406; Red Army assault on centre of, 410; German troops re-enter, 412; and the battle of Kursk, 424; Soviet forces approach, 450; German forces withdraw from, 454; Red Army liberates, 454; a war crimes trial in, 480

Kharkov Tank Works: relocated, 275

Khatskilevich, General: killed in action, 201

Khatyn (White Russia): villagers murdered at, 414

Kherson (South Russia): Jews and Russians murdered in, 239

Khmelnik (Ukraine): Jews murdered in, 235

Khimki (near Moscow): German troops reach, 267

Kholm (Russia): Germans driven from (1942), 293; Germans driven from (1944), 503

Khota Baru (Malaya): 249

Khrushchev, Nikita: in the Ukraine, 191; and the defence of Kiev, 194, 233; and the organization of partisans, 203

Kiangan (Luzon): napalm used at, 702

Kidney Ridge (El Alamein): secured, 371

Kieffer, Josef: and the shooting of British commandos, 552; executed, 734

Kiel (Germany): leaflets dropped on, 46; bombed, 132, 417, 446; a new submarine being fabricated in, 625; dock facilities at, bombed, 625; six thousand soldiers and refugees drowned off, 635; refugee ships reach, 684; a war criminal dies in, on the eve of his trial (1957), 738

Kielce (Poland): labour camps near, 23; German troops sent to, too late, 629; Jews murdered in, after the war, 730

Kienitz (River Oder): Soviet tanks reach, 635-6

Kieta (Solomon Islands): Japanese about to land at, 293

Kiev (Soviet Union): German plan against, 114, 147; Soviet defences in area of, 168, 170-1, 177; Soviet troop concentrations near, 179; last-minute plans for, 192, 194; on the eve of war, 196; factory evacuations from, 206; a Soviet counter-attack from, 209; Germans poised to enter, 231, 232; Russians withdraw from, 236; Germans enter, 237; Jews murdered in, 239, 290; 'Germanization' in, 253; partisans killed near, 460; slave labourers shot near, 460; a defence line, to be strengthened near, 462;

Germans driven from, 473

Kiirun (Formosa): prisoners-of-war liberated in, 722

*Kimberley* (British destroyer): damaged, 55

Kimmel, Admiral: and Japanese intentions, 263; and American alertness, 737

King, Admiral: and the Arctic convoys, 396

King, Mackenzie: and Britain's future, 102

King's Award for Bravery: won by an eleven-year-old boy, 126

Kingisepp (Russia): abandoned, 217; Red Army returns to, 496

Kingsman, Lieutenant Charles F.: and the Italian partisans, 519

Kinsayok Camp (Thailand): deaths in, 417, 462

*Kinugasa* (Japanese heavy cruiser): sunk, 377

Kinzel, General Hans: and the German surrender, 684

*Kirishima* (Japanese battleship): sunk, 377

Kiriwina Island (Pacific Ocean): Americans land on, 439

Kirkenes (Norway): and a German war correspondent, 191; Stalin's request concerning, 214; Germans abandon, 613

Kirponos, General: told 'Do not move', 192; orders a new defence line, 205; receives Stalin's orders, in Kiev, 232; killed in action, 236

*Kisaragi* (Japanese destroyer): sunk, 278

Kishinev (Bessarabia): Jews murdered in, 219; Red Army approaches, 510

Kiska Island (Aleutians): Japanese land on, 330; American bombers attack, 359-60; a naval battle off, 415; Japanese abandon, 447; Americans and Canadians land on, 451

Kislovodsk (Caucasus): Germans enter, 353; Jews murdered at, 359

Kita, Nagai: and Pearl Harbour, 163, 238, 249, 268, 271

'Kite': the German army's most secret supply key to the East, broken, 287

Kitzelmann, Michael: his protest, and execution, 332

Kladovo (Yugoslavia): Soviet forces reach, 587

Klarsfeld, Arno: deported to Auschwitz, 471

Klein, Sergeant Zigmund: killed, 145

Kleist, General Paul von: and the British forces around Dunkirk, 72; east of Kiev, 233; forbidden to retreat, 266; orders the evacuation of the Crimea, 471

Kleist-Schmenzin, Ewald von: beheaded, 660

Klessheim Castle (Salzburg): Hitler meets Horthy at, 421, 509; Hitler sees a tank demonstration at, 517

Kletnya (Russia): Soviet partisans regroup near, 331; an anti-partisan sweep near, 390, 392

Kletsk (Russia): murder of Jews at, 252; Jews flee from, 345

Klimovskikh, General: and the imminence of war, 194; shot, 217

Klin (near Moscow): Germans reach, 262; Germans driven out of, 279

Klintsy (Russia): mass murder at, 306; Germans to withdraw from, 462

Klissura (Greece): Italians driven back to, 149; Italians drive out of, 149

Klooga (Estonia): Jews murdered at, 595

Klop, Lieutenant Dirk: dies of his wounds, 27

Klopper, General Hendrik: surrenders Tobruk, 335

Kluge, General Günther von: in Paris, 94; and Hitler's visit to Paris, 102; and Hitler's visit to Lille, 104; and the German opposition to Hitler, 218; and the Kursk battle to end, 444; and the evacuation of Orel, 446; a protest from, 458; urges a withdrawal, 462; replaces von Rundstedt, 549; is himself replaced, 570; commits suicide, 572; his final appeal, about tank deficiencies and shortages of fuel, 576–7

Klusmeir, Captain Emil: sinks two Allied merchant ships (on 7 May 1945), 689

Knauf, Erich: executed, 521

Knight, Captain Donald: killed in Yugoslavia, 455

Knight's Cross (to the Iron Cross): award of, 66, 87, 154, 238, 405–6, 465, 482, 503, 546, 556, 676, 679; a winner of, paraded in Moscow, 556

Knightsbridge (London): a 'Flying Bomb' at, 562

Knin (Yugoslavia): bombed, 505

Knipping, Max: executed (in 1947), 732

Knochen, Helmut: his award, 26–7; heads the Paris Gestapo, 94–5, 242; tried, sentenced, and later released, 738

Knochlein, SS Captain Fritz: orders a massacre, 77; hanged, 733

Knox, Frank: and Pearl Harbour, 140, 154

Kobe (Japan): bombed, 317, 648; Japanese fleet at, attacked, 650

Koblenz (Rhineland): Jews deported from, 329; bombed, 622

Kobona (Lake Ladoga): supplies, 261

Kobryn (Poland): a signals centre, 192; two last trains through, 196

Kobylka (Poland): a defence line at, 562

Kocani (Greece): partisan activity near, 601

Koch, Erich: visits Hitler, 359; his contempt for Russians, 408–9

Koch, Karl: an SS man, executed by the SS, 734

Koch, Karl: an S.S. man, executed by the S.S., 734

Koedel, Marie: a German agent, 37

Koenig, General Marie-Pierre: and the liberation of Paris, 578

Koeppen, Walter: and Hitler's plans for Russia, 361

Kohima (India): besieged, 514, 541; Japanese driven from, 613

Kohl, Helmut: and the 'horror of war', 743

Kohn, Armand: deported, 571

Kohn, Georges-André: deported, 571; murdered, 669

Kohn, Dr Hugo: sent to Auschwitz, 424

Kokkorevo (Lake Ladoga): supplies reach, 260

Kokoda (New Guinea): Australians

defend, 341; Australians fall back from, 345; Japanese seize, 346; Australians forced further back from 355, 361; Australians move back to, 375, 378; reconquest of heights on trail to, 477

Kokura (Japan): a possible atomic bomb target, 694; obscured by cloud, 715

Kolbe, Father Maximilian: his sacrifice, 219

Kolberg (East Prussia): its heroic past, 635; acquired by Poland, 711

Kolberg (film): portrays heroism, 635

Koldyczewo (White Russia): a slave labour camp revolt at, 510

Kolo (Poland): bombed, 2; Jews deported from, to their deaths, 274

Kolombangara Island (Solomons): a skirmish off, 449; a naval action off, 450; Americans land on, 466

Kolomyja (Eastern Galicia): Jews from, murdered, 362; Red Army enters, 511–2

Kolomna (near Moscow): battle at, 267

Komandorski Islands: Battle of, 15

Komet (German commerce raider): sets sail, 109

Koniev, General: advances westward, 554; orders the final artillery barrage of the Second World War in Europe, 691

Königsberg (Germany): to be bombed, 198; Hitler's plans for, 291; bombed, 582–3; beseiged, 654; surrenders, 660; fighting near, 687, 689

Königstein (Saxony): an escape from, 317

Konotop (southern Russia): Germans driven from, 459

Konoye, Prince Fumimaro: comes to power in Japan, 111; resigns, 245

Konstanz (Germany): a would-be assassin caught in, 26

Konstruktor (Soviet gunboat): crosses Lake Ladoga, 253

Konyu Camp (Thailand): 'breaking men' in, 417; Tamils 'die like flies' near, 422; a 'real camp of death', 435

Kopec, Professor: shot, 162

Korbokov, General: shot, 208–9

Korea: forced labourers from, in New Guinea, 396

Koreans: surrender, on Makin Atoll, 476

Koren, Arieh: and a German manhunt, 384

Korherr, Dr Richard: and the statistics of mass murder, 414

Koritsa (Albania): Greeks reach, 143

Kormoran (German ocean raider): in action, 259

Korn, Hans Robert Martin: his saga, and fate, 565

Korobkov, General: shot, 217

Korosten (Russia): a defensive line at, 205; a Soviet counter-attack, at 209; Jews killed in, 232; a Russian attack at, 478

Korsun (southern Russia): Germans defeated at, 499

Koryzis, Alexander: commits suicide, 174

Korzec (Volhynia): Jews murdered at, 326

Kos (Dodecanese Islands): Germans land on, 465; and an escape line, 495–

6; Jews of, deported to Auschwitz, 559–60, 560; German forces on, surrender, 692

Kosciuszko, General: his monument blown up, 27

Kosice (Slovakia): Red Army enters, 632

Kosmodemianskaya, Zoia: hanged, 265

Kossak, Zofia: helps Jews, 384

Kostroma (Russia): reinforcements gather at, 267

Kosygin, Alexsei: and the removal of factories, 199

Kostas, Stefan: executed, 612

Kotelnikovo (southern Russia): Germans reach, 348; Germans attacked at, 385; Russians recapture, 389

Kotevla (Ukraine): Russians enter, 455

Kott, Andrzej: captured, 39

Kotzebue, Lieutenant Albert: on the Elbe, 673

Kovner, Abba: an eye-witness, 229

Kovno (Líthuania): frontier violated near, 194; bombed, 198; a battle near, 199; Jews murdered in, 204–5, 207, 223, 224–5, 239, 242, 250, 263, 308, 399, 511; a protest about the murder of Jews in, 250; Jews in ghetto at, 267; Jewish deportees murdered in, 263, 290; Soviet prisoners-of-war murdered at, 339; the Allied invasion of Sicily, as seen from, 443; Jews in hiding in, discovered, and killed 555; Red Army enters, 562–3; Jewish women from, killed by their S.S. guards, 675; a killer of Jews in, extradited, 734

Kovpak, Sidor: a partisan leader, 383

Kowale Panskie (Poland): Jews from, gassed, 279

Kowalke, Gottlieb: killed, 25

Kowarski, Lew: leaves France, 95

Kozara Mountains (Yugoslavia): an anti-partisan sweep in, 339

Kozelsk (Soviet Union): and Polish prisoners-of-war, 53; Germans driven from, 284

Kragujevac (Yugoslavia): a massacre in, 247

Kraljevo (Yugoslavia): and a reprisal action, 243; a massacre at, 247

Kramatorsk (southern Russia): machine-works evacuated from, 241, 247; Red Army re-enters, 399

Kramer, Lieutenant Commander Alvin: and Pearl Harbour, 271

Kramer, Josef: transferred to Belsen, 615; and the arrival of British troops, at Belsen, 663; brought to trial, 726

Krancke, Captain Theodor: and Norway, 45; sinks the Jervis Bay, 138

Kraslava (Russia): Soviet troops move to (May 1941), 183

Krasnaya (Russia): reprisals at, 237

Krasnodar (Caucasus): German plans for, 193; Germans reach, 350; a war crimes trial at, 444; an eye witness to mass murder at, 480

Krass, SS Captain: awarded the Iron Cross, 62

Kraus, General: and Dutch volunteers on the Eastern Front, 348

Krebs, Colonel (later General): Stalin's remark to, 173; and the surrender of Berlin, 682

*Krebs* (German armed trawler): boarded, 161

Kreipe, General Heinrich: kidnapped, 519–20

Kreisau Circle: opponents of Nazism in, 450, 544; and the Hitler Bomb Plot, 566, 604, 632, 637

Kreiser, General Jakov: in action, 205

Kremenchug (Soviet Union): Soviet troops move to (May 1941), 183; the Mayor of, shot, 239; Red Army approaches, 464

Kremer, Dr Johann: at Auschwitz, 356–7, 368, 370, 432

Kremer, Simon Davidovich: receives atomic secrets, 241

Kremlin (Moscow): spires of, 197; bombs near, 217; German elation concerning, 242; Germans twelve miles from, 266; a telegram to Churchill from 415; the 'horror of war' spoken of in, 743

Kremnica (Slovakia): battle at, 608, 611

Kretshchmer, Captain Otto: captured, 162

Kriesshaber, Theodor: executed, 27

Krimchak Jews: executed, 267

Kristiansand (Norway): 45, 52, 53

Krivoi Rog (Ukraine): Hitler's plan for, 235; Jews murdered in, 235; a German counter-attack at, 472

Kronstadt (Leningrad): bombed, 237

Kropotkin (southern Russia): Germans reach, 348

Krosniewice (Poland): Jews from, murdered, 304

Krotoszyn (Poland): evacuation from, 2

Krupp Armament Factories (at Essen): bombed, 139, 308, 408, 409, 417

Krupp von Bohlen, Alfred: sentenced, then amnestied, 734

Kruszyna (Poland): Jews killed at, 386

Kryukovo (near Moscow): the 'final point of withdrawal', 262

Krzywolka (Poland): Soviet prisoners-of-war murdered at, 482

Ksiazki (Poland): Poles murdered at, 6

Kuala Lumpur (Malaya): abandoned, 288

Kuantan (Malaya): Japanese land at, 276; battle at, 284; occupied, 286

Kuban River (Caucasus): Germans reach, 347; Germans cross, 348

Kube, Wilhelm: forwards a protest, 250–1; killed, 363

Kubis, Jan: his mission behind German lines, 283–4, 327; killed, 334

Kublichi (White Russia): Jews murdered at, 291

Kuchemann, Dietrich: brought to Britain, 702–3

Kuczynski, Ruth: receives atomic secrets, 241

Kuhmo (Finland): defended, 34, 36

Kuibyshev (Russia): evacuation to, 244

*Kujawiak* (British destroyer, manned by Poles): sunk, 333

Kuklesi (Greece): reprisals in, 450

Kulik, General: and the cavalry, 44

Kummert, SS Corporal: recalls a massacre, 79

Kunikov, Major Caesar: holds a beach-head, 399

Kunishi Ridge (Okinawa): fighting for, 697, 699, 700

Kunming (China): 276, 280

Kuntsevo (near Moscow): an anti-tank ditch at, 246

Kunze, Lieutenant Rolf: flies to Scotland, 683

Küpfinger, Lieutenant-Commander Hans: and Enigma, 161

Kupyansk (southern Russia): Red Army enters, 399

Kure (Japan): Japanese fleet near, attacked, 650; bombed, 708, 709

Kurgan (Soviet Union): evacuations to, 199

Kurile Islands: and Pearl Harbour, 261, 264; and an American deception plan, 516; Soviet Union to acquire, 640; Soviet troops land on, 717; Soviet troops complete their occupation of, 722

Kurland (Baltic): a map showing, saves Hitler, 559; German forces trapped in, 628

Kursk (Russia): Germans to withdraw to, 274; effect of resistance at Sevastopol on, 336; Germans driven from, 400; a Soviet salient around, 413, 414, 420, 424, 427; bombed, 434; German plans to conquer, 441; battle for, 441–2, 443, 445

Kushchevskaya (southern Russia): Red Army enters, 399

Kushnir, Shlomo: leads a revolt, 510

Küstrin (on the Oder): holds out, 634; falls, 648

*Kuttabul* (Australian depot ship): hit, 329

Kutschera, SS General Franz: killed, 496; reprisals after death of, 496, 498

Kuznetsov, Admiral: at Libava, 164; tries to arouse Stalin, 191; and last-minute preparations, 193

Kwai River (Thailand): bridges on, destroyed, 701

Kwajalein (Marshall Islands): American air attacks on, 297; American Marines beheaded on, 353; American Marines land on, 496; a war crimes trial on, 725

Kwantung Army (Manchuria); Red Army attacks, 715

Kweilin (China): 326

Kweiyang (China): Japanese advance towards, 613

Kyoto (Japan): a possible atomic bomb target, 694

*Kyle V. Johnson* (U.S. troopship): suicide attack on, 629

Kyushi Island (Japan): planned invasion of, 659, 696, 725; and the atomic bomb, 697; continued preparations for the invasion of, 703; preparations for the defence of, 712

Laborde, Admiral Jean de: scuttles ships, 383

Labuan Island (Borneo): Japanese land on, 288; Australians land on, 699

La Caine (Normandy): bombed, 536

*Laconia* (British troopship): sunk, 360

Ladoga, Lake (Leningrad): Germans reach, 230; a Russian gunboat crosses, 253; supplies for Leningrad cross, 261, 266, 283; wounded soldiers evacuated across, 296; 'Corridor of Death' to, 392

'Lady Be Good' (US bomber): its ill-fated flight, 418; the remains of, found in the desert, 739

Lae (New Guinea): Japanese land at, 296; occupied, 308; raided, 338; reinforcements to, sunk, 408; an American force lands near, 417; Americans and Australians advance to, 459; Japanese abandon, 462; Japanese trek from, 486

Lagedi (Estonia): Jews murdered at, 595

La Haye-du-Puits (France): German troops moved to, 528, 529; battle at, 553

Lahousen, Colonel: and Soviet prisoners-of-war, 247; and 'indescribable' scenes of mass murder, 251; and German sabotage in Britain, 255

Lambeth (London): a 'Flying Bomb' on, 551

Lammers, Dr Hans: and euthanasia, 20, 109; records a protest, 481

Lampedusa Island (Mediterranean): surrenders, 437

Lampione Island (Mediterranean): occupied, 437

*Lancastria* (British passenger liner): sunk, 98

Landau, SS Sergeant Felix: and the murder of Jews, 211, 218

Landsberg (Bavaria): American troops reach, 674; a war crimes trial at, 735

Lang Son (French Indo-China): Free French forces in, overrun, 692–3

Langbehn, Carl: executed, 601

Langeron, Roger: defies the Germans, 94; arrested, 151

Langley, Jimmy: escapes, 131

*Langley* (US support ship): sunk, 303

Langsdorff, Captain Hans: and the *Graf Spee*, 34

Laon (France): bombed, 522

La Pallice (France): troops embarked from, 98; German warships attacked at, 216; German submarine pens at, 348

Larissa (Greece): deportations through, 540

La Roche-Guyon (France): Rommel leaves, 532; Rommel contacted at, 553; Rommel wounded on the way to, 556

La Rochelle (France): the German garrison at, shown in heroic film, 635

Larsen, Leif: his torpedo mission, 372

Lasch, General Otto: surrenders Königsberg, 660–1

Lashio (Burma): supplies pass through, 131; Japanese reach, 321

Lasker, Anita: and the burning of Belsen, 695

Las Palmas (Canary Islands): German ships forced to leave safety of, 330

La Spezia (Italy): bombed, 439; Italian ships set sail from, 460; partisan action near, 539; Germans hold, 613

Latsis, Giorgio: a partisan, killed in action, 675

Latvia: its treaty with Russia; Soviet bases in, 44; Soviet forces to enter, 94; annexed, 111; fate of Jews in, 266; German forces in, surrender, 690; some Germans in, still refusing to surrender (11 May 1945), 693; final German surrender in (14 March 1945), 694

Laufer, Leo: accompanies Americans into Ohrdruf, 659

Laurahütte Works (East Upper Silesia): slave labour at, 525

Lauterbach (Germany): American troops enter, 654

Laval (France): Canadian troops reach, 95–6

Laval, Pierre: Hitler meets, 133; tried, and shot, 724

Laznie (Poland): villagers shot in, 466–7

Leaflets: dropped over Germany, 4–5, 18, 34, 46, 48; dropped over Warsaw, 49; dropped over Berlin, 121; give details of 'German atrocities', 400

League of Human Rights: the President of, shot, 488

League of Nations: Soviet Union expelled from, 34; a former official of, found guilty of war crimes, 725–6

Leahy, Fleet Admiral William D.: and the atomic bomb, 711

Leamington Spa (England): and a monument to Czechs and Slovaks, 740

Lebanese: at Bir Hakeim, 187

Lebanon: battle for, 188–9

Lebel, Reb Bunem: shot, 5

Lebensborn (human stud farms): 24, 390–1

Leber, Julius: and the opposition to Hitler, 544; executed, 627

Le Cateau (France): Germans in, 68

Le Chêne, Evelyn: describes an act of defiance, 688

Leckwitz (Elbe): an American and a Soviet soldier meet at, 673

Leclerc, General Jacques Philippe: enters Paris, 580

Le Creusot (France): a pilot shot down over, 370

Le Crotoy (France): Germans reach, 70

Lecussan, Joseph: an arrest by, 488

Leda (German minesweeper): sunk, 359

Ledo (India): troops fall back to, 326; an attack from, 506

Le Druillenec, Harold: at Belsen, 664

Leeb, Field Marshal Wilhelm Ritter von: besieges Leningrad, 230, 231; his protest, 233; has to send tanks to Moscow front, 237; refused permission to withdraw, 279, 288

Légion d'Honneur: award of, 66

Legrange, Simone: the fate of her family, 436

Leguay, Jean: brought to trial, 741

Le Havre (France): to be evacuated, 89; evacuation at, 93; a Commando raid near, 304; an Allied deception near, 532; a German attack from, forestalled, 538–9, 540; Allied bombing of, 587; surrenders to the Allies, 590

Lehmann-Willenbrock, Captain Heinrich: killed, 655

Lehmkühl, Kurt: captured, 25

Lehoux, Captain Jacques: killed, 66

Leibstandarte Regiment (of the ss): and a massacre, 78–9

Leiden (Holland): attacked, 61

Leigh-Fermor, Major Patrick: on Crete, 519, 520

Leigh, Vera: a British agent, killed, 555

Leikina, Fania: 'liquidated', 256

Leipzig (Germany): troops in, 148; Hitler on way to, 381; bombed, 479, 499; Jews deported to Auschwitz

from, 582; proposed 'heavy attacks' on, 636; 'allotted' to the Allied air forces, 638; American troops enter, 668

Le Mans (France): Allied troops at, 93; Germans occupy, 100

Le Matin (Paris): a seller of, and Hitler, 102

Lembicz, Edward: sentenced to death, 162

Lemelsen, General: his protest, 200; and the Commissar Decree, 200–1

Lemnos (Greece): Germans occupy, 176

Lemonnier, General: decapitated, 693

Lemp, Julius: and the Athenia, 4; drowned, 180

Lend-Lease: 139, 149, 156–7, 162, 251–2, 254

Lenin's Mausoleum (Moscow): a place of honour by, 173; Stalin reviews troops from, 254; German military banners thrown at foot of, 701

Leningrad: protection of, 40; German troops go through, 62; planned German advance to, 115, 144, 147; air defences of, 172; German engineers leave, 192; the defence of, 201; a poster in, 202; a writer from, killed in action, 205; art treasures evacuated from, 206; factories evacuated from, 206; German forces approach, 208, 214, 217, 224, 225; first volunteers leave for front line from, 209; siege of, 225, 228, 230, 231, 232, 233; to be razed to the ground, 235; bombardment of, 237; partisan activity near, 241; starvation in, 243, 267; first snow falls in (1941), 244; a celebration in, 246; mass evacuation from, completed, 252; leaflets dropped on, 254; a concert in, 255; bombed, 255; supplies for, 261, 275; shelled, 266; and Hitler's 'halt' order, 279; continued starvation in, 283, 285, 296, 304, 317, 325; partisans behind the lines near, 298; trams run again in, 316; to be a German objective in late 1942, 345–6; Germans attacked outside, 354, 392; receives heaviest shelling of the war (July 1943), 446; Red Army renews offensive at, 489; siege of, ends, 495; railway services with Moscow resumed, 510; Soviet offensive near (June 1944), 536; Spanish Legion deaths during siege of, 746

Leonard, Charles J.: recalls the fighting on Okinawa, 699

Leonardo da Vinci: two paintings by, evacuated, 206

Leopold of the Belgians, King: exhorts his soldiers, 73–4; bows to German pressure, 77

Lepel (Russia): Soviet partisans near, attacked, 331, 435, 516

Leros (Aegean Sea): struggle for, 472, 474; and an escape line, 495–6; German troops on, surrender, 692

Le Roux, J. J.: and Rommel, 556

Les Milles (France): Jews at, 310

Les Petites Dalles (France): Rommel reaches, 90; recalled, 170

Lesno (Poland): reprisals at, 498

Les Préludes (Liszt): Hitler listens to, 196

Letterhaus, Bernard: hanged, 612

Leuna (Germany): bombed, 98

Leuschner, Wilhelm: murdered, 598

Levi, Primo: in 'a world of death and phantoms', 634

Levin, Meyer: 'cadaverous refugees' seen by, 658–9

Levinson-Lessing, Vladimir: and Leningrad's art treasures, 206

Lewenthal, Salmen: his notes, and his question, dug up at Auschwitz (1962), 740

Lewi, Israel, shot, 4

Lewi, Liebe, shot, 4

Lewis, Captain Robert A.: and a 'son-of-a-bitch', 712

Lewisham (South London): bombed, 393; a 'Flying Bomb' at, 562

Lexington (US aircraft carrier): sunk, 322; an earlier mission of, recalled, 737

Ley, Robert: commits suicide, 724

Leyte Gulf (Philippines): battle of, 606, 617

Leyte Island (Pacific): Americans shell, 604; landings on, 604–5, 606; deaths on, 635; last fighting on, 667

Lezaky (near Prague): a reprisal action in, 332

Lgov (Russia): partisan activity near, 369

Libava (Lithuania): a German aircraft over, 164; bombed, 198; executions of Jews halted in, 256

Liberty Barricade (Warsaw): publishes account of Chelmno killings, 330

Liberty ships (US merchant ships): the first one launched, 239; the last one launched, 725

Libesis, Lance-Corporal: and the Commissar Decree, 205

Libreville (French Equatorial Africa): Free French forces enter, 141

Libya: 90, 104; Italian forces in, 122; Italian forces cross into Egypt from, 125, 145; British forces cross into, 148; British forces return to, 259, 260; British forces return yet again to, 377, 386, 389, 390

Lichtheim, Richard: and the destruction of the Jews, 335

Lichtenburg, Pastor Bernard: his protest, and his death, 228, 473

Lida (Poland): a signals centre, 192; overrun, 201

Lidice (near Prague): a reprisal massacre at, 332

Liebehenschel, ss Lieutenant-Colonel: and awards for executioners, 256

Liebeskind, Adolf: killed, 388

Liège (Belgium): bombed by German Jets, 622

Life magazine: and the 'most decorated soldier', 634

Lightoller, Commander C. H. (RN, retd): at Dunkirk, 82

Lightoller, Lieutenant Frederick: killed, 648

Lightoller, Pilot Officer H. B.: killed, 5; recalled, 82

Lille (France): Hitler visits, 104; an Englishman escapes from, 131; a sabotage circuit based on, 378, 477; a reprisal action near, 512; a traitor hanged in, 728

Lim Bo Seng, General: executed by the Japanese, 549

Limbourne (British destroyer): deaths on, 469

Lindell, Mary: parachuted behind German lines, 370

Lindemann, General Fritz: and the Hitler Bomb Plot, 615

Linden, Dr Herbert: wants to destroy evidence of mass murder, 368

Lindenbaum, Shalon: and the bombing of Monowitz, 591

Linosa Island (Mediterranean): surrenders, 437

Linsley, Lieutenant R. R.: killed, 611

Linton, Joseph: and a plan of Auschwitz, 580

Linz (Austria): Hitler's rebuilding plans for, 104, 109, 196, 325, 639; Flak Towers to be built in, 365; Churchill's wish 'to meet the Russians there', 667; and the American-Soviet demarcation line, 680

Lisahally (Northern Ireland): post-war sinking of German submarines off, 727

Lisbon (Portugal): a false destination, 520; a spy reaches Britain from, 521

Lisbon Maru (Japanese merchant ship): sunk, 366

Lishka, Kurt: and the deportation of Jews from Paris, 392–3

Lisichansk (southern Russia): Germans enter, 341

Liska, Major General Alois: and the surrender of Dunkirk, 692

Liskof, Alfred: a deserter, 194, 202

Lisome Bay (US escort carrier): torpedoed, 476

List, Field Marshal Wilhelm: dismissed, 359

Liszt, Franz: and the death of a German air ace, 491–2

Liteiny Bridge (Leningrad): civilians killed on, 446

Lithuania: and the Soviet Union, 16, 44, 94; annexed, 111; Jews murdered in, 204–5, 267, 298; a German anti-partisan sweep in, 390; Jews from, in action, 407; Red Army reaches Baltic coast of, 601

Liuchow (China): Japanese driven back towards, 699

Liuyang River (China): a Japanese offensive in, 537

Livarot (Normandy): Rommel severely wounded at, 556

Liverpool (England): 4, 7; bombed, 125, 181; a ship sailing from, attacked, 133

Liverpool Street Station (London): a tunnel near, 131

Livorno (Italy): bombed, 440; possible Allied landing at, 447

Ljubljana (Slovenia): Germans enter, 171

Loborgrad (Yugoslavia): Jews murdered in, 390

Loch Ryan (Scotland): post-war sinking of German submarines in, 727

Lodeinoye Polye (Lake Ladoga): Finns reach, 334

Lodz (Poland): battle for, 7; Jews of, 24, 27, 27–8; a ghetto established in, 57; starvation in the ghetto of, 179; deportations to, 244, 245; deportations from, and a deception, 541; final deportations from, 565, 582; German troops sent through, too late, 629; Red Army enters, 632; Jews women from, killed in the Baltic, 675; recollections of a girl from, on the sea journey from Lübeck to Kiel, 684

Lofoten Islands (Norway): a naval raid on, 161

Löhr, General Alexander: urges severity, 372; conducts an anti-partisan sweep, 392; orders retaliation against civilians, 450

Lohse, Hinrich: and the 'Final Solution', 216; and measures restricting Jews, 223–4; and the killing of Jews by gas, 249–50; halts killings for economic reasons, 256; and the Gypsies, ' a double danger', 282

Loilem (Burma): Japanese driven from, 699

Loire River (France): retreat to, 90; French Government evacuated to, 91; proposed action on, 93; bridges destroyed on, 543; German supply columns attacked near, 552; Americans advance to, 567, 568; a German surrender on, 592

Loknya (Russia): Jews and Gypsies murdered in, 297

Lokot (Russia): anti-partisan sweep near, 361

London (England): and the threat of bombing, 19; children return to, 37; awaits a parachute attack, 69; German bombs fall on (1940–1941), 121, 122, 123, 124, 125, 127, 131, 135, 142, 149, 162, 174, 181; (1943), 492, 495, 500, 504; 'bad days for' (Goebbels), 178; 'boundless wrath' in, 304; the bombing of Hamburg and a comparison with, 446; the VI 'Flying Bomb' falls on, 539, 541, 542, 543, 548, 549, 551, 552, 562, 576, 645; news of Auschwitz reaches, 546; evacuations from (July 1944), 557; the 'Flying Bomb' no longer a threat to, 582; a renewed 'Flying Bomb' offensive against, 587; a rocket bomb offensive against, 589, 594, 614, 641, 648, 653; a victory parade in, 729; and an unexploded bomb, 739; Hirohito visits, 741

'London Controlling Section': and deception, 347

London Debt Agreement (1952): resolves Germany's reparations debts of 1914–18, 736

London Declaration (1942): on 'war crimes', 290–1

'Long live Belgium!': a cry, during an execution, 588

'Long live Poland!': a cry, during an execution, 27

Longoskayan Point (Philippines): Japanese land at, 294; Japanese bridgehead at, destroyed, 296

Lonsdale, Major Richard: his heroism, in Sicily, 441; at Arnhem, 593

'Lord Haw-Haw' (William Joyce): his broadcasts from Germany, 10, 115, 119, 329, 458, 488, 583–4; arrested, 696; hanged, 727

Lord, Flight Lieutenant D. S. A.: over Arnhem, 594

Lorengau (Admiralty Islands): Japanese land at, 315

Lorraine (France): Allies advance towards, 583

Lorient (France): a German submarine base, 132, 348; bombed, 428; a landing expected at, 534

Los Alamos (New Mexico): and the atomic bomb, 595, 694

Los Banos (Philippines): a rescue mission to, 643; a war crimes trial in, 728

Lossiemouth (Scotland): a raid from, on the Tirpitz, 612

Lötzen (East Prussia): German troops withdraw from, 633

Louisville (US cruiser): suicide attack on, 628, 697

Loustalot, Lieutenant Edwin V.: killed in action, 354

Lower Wessell Island (Australia): raided, 396

Lowery, Sergeant Louis R.: the fate of a photograph by, 642–3

Lozovaya (southern Russia): Red Army enters, 402

Lübeck (Germany): leaflets dropped on, 46; bombed, 314, 319; British thrust to, 667, 687; Himmler meets Bernadotte in, 670; fate of refugee ships at, 683–4; new submarines at, never put to sea, 690

Lublin (Poland): Jews deported to, 22–23, 49; Jewish tribulations in, 28; Jews deported to their death from, 308, 312, 376; declared the temporary capital of Poland, 572

Lubny (Ukraine): battle near, 231

Lucas, General John P.: hesitates, 492

Ludendorff Bridge (Remagen, Rhine): Americans cross, 646–7

Luknitsky (a Russian writer): and the burial of the dead in Leningrad, 285

Luleå (Sweden): mines to be laid off, 78

Luga (Russia): Soviet partisans near, 209; Soviet defence line at, 217

Lüneburg (Germany): Himmler's suicide at, 695–6; a war crimes trial at, 726

Lushno (Russia): German bravery at, 237

Luteyn, Tony: escapes, 288

Luther, Martin: and the 'Final Solution', 292, 363–4

Lütjens, Vice-Admiral: in action, 159, 161, 185; scuttles the Bismarck, 186; goes down with his ship, 186

Lutsk (Poland): Germans enter, 201; Jews murdered in, 209, 339; Red Army reaches, 496

Lützow (German battleship): beaten off, 286; in the Arctic, 340

Luxemburg: 20, 38; invaded, 61; laws against Jews introduced in, 127–8; Jews deported from, 245, 344; forced labour of, 421; civilians from, at Belsen, 664; war criminals held in a hotel in, 703

Luxemburg Treaty (1952): and reparations to the Jews, 736

Luzon (Philippines): bombed, 275; Americans land at, 276, 282; President Quezon leaves, 302; loss of life off, 338; sabotage activities on, forbidden, 391; American naval losses off, 627, 628; American landing on, 628; battle for, 633; prisoners-of-war on, rescued, 635, 643; continued fighting on, 667, 683, 692, 695; napalm used on, 702; plans for the invasion of Japan, made on, 715

Lvov (Poland): Polish surrender at, 9; Soviet annexation of, 16; Soviet preparations near, 177; German troop movements near, 179; and a partisan group, 202; and Russian resistance,

Lvov (Poland)—*contd.*
204; overrun, 204; withdrawal behind, 205; Jews murdered in, 209, 216; evidence of mass murder destroyed in, 438; Red Army approaches, 554; Red Army enters, 562; acquired by Russia, 711

*Lydie Suzanne* (Belgian fishing vessel): at Dunkirk, 80–1

Lyon, Lieutenant-Colonel Ivan: killed, 702

Lyon (France): s s in action near, 100; Jean Moulin arrested in 434–5; tortures in, 436; executions in, 488; a deportation near, 514; sabotage near, 515; bombed, 528; reprisals in, 561; a mass execution in, 571; further executions at, 573; Resistance fighters in, 580

Lyuban (near Leningrad): fighting at, 495

Maas River (Holland): Allies reach, 615; Allied plans to advance from, 639

Mabuni (Okinawa): suicides at, 700

MacArthur, General Douglas: and Japan, 215, 253, 264; reaches Corregidor, 282; says 'Help is on the way', 291; orders a withdrawal, 293; 'I intend to fight it out', 294; ordered to leave the Philippines, 302; leaves Luzon, 307; in Australia, 316; forbids sabotage activities, 391; seeks to regain Rabaul, 439; agrees to 'I shall return' packets, to be sent in to the Philippines, 451; his pledge to be honoured, 596; and the battle for Leyte, 605; and a news blackout, concerning kamikaze pilots, 617; returns to Manila, 644; announces liberation of the Philippines, 702; and the defeat of Japan, 721–2; moves to Tokyo, 723; upholds death sentences, 733

McAuliffe, Major-General Anthony: refuses to surrender, 621

McCarthy, Major D.: a clandestine landing by, 393

McCloy, John J.: an appeal to, 546; issues a general amnesty, 734

McDonough, Jay: wounded, 611

McIndoe, Archibald: his healing work, 131

McIntyre, Lieutenant I.: an aerial reconnaisance by, 519

Mackesy, Major-General Pierse Joseph: in Norway, 56

McLain, Captain Bill: on Corregidor, 644

Maclean, Brigadier Fitzroy: parachuted into Yugoslavia, 462

Macedonia (Yugoslavia): offered to Bulgaria, 165; deportation of Jews from, 414

Machen, Charles: arrested and deported, 498

Machines: 'will beat machines', 91, 99

Mackwiller (Saar): Germans driven from, 615

Mâcon (France): a rescue from, 468

Macva (Yugoslavia): a massacre at, 247

Madagascar: and the Jews, 100; a British landing on, 323; a Japanese submarine attack on, 330; Subhas Chandra Bose transferred to a Japanese submarine near, 423

Madang (New Guinea): Japanese withdraw to, 486

'Madeleine': helps the French Resistance, 438

Madeira (Portugal): 141; German submarines near, attack a convoy, 373

Madras (India): 'may fall', 303; bombs near, 315

Madrid (Spain): Franco returns to, 134

Maebashi (Japan): bombed, 712

Mafalda, Princess: killed by an Allied bomb, 582

Magdalenka (Poland): Poles murdered at, 328

Magdeburg (Germany): bombed, 491–2, 640; bombing of, reported, 641

Magennis, Mick: his courageous exploit, 710

'Magic': Japanese diplomatic messages, being read by the United States, 178, 271, 701, 710; and Pearl Harbour, 737

Magnetic mine: a new weapon, 29–30; loses its terror, 35

Magnitogorsk (Urals): evacuation to, 206

*Mahan* (US destroyer): hit by a kamikaze pilot, 617

*Mahratta* (British destroyer): torpedoed, 503

Maidstone (England): German aircraft show down near, 119

Maikop (Caucasus): a German objective, 345; Germans reach, 350

Mailly-le-Camp (France): bombed, 517

Maine (United States): German agents land at, 615

Mainz (Germany): and mines in the Rhine, 64

Maisky, Ivan: and a 'saga of heroism', 214

Majdanek (Poland): a concentration camp at, 376; mass murder at, 473, 475; Red Army reaches, 559; and a war crimes trial, 741

Majorat (Poland): murders at, 584

Makhach-Kala (Caspian Sea): German plans for, sent by Churchill to Stalin, 366

Makin Island (Pacific): Japanese land on, 276; an unsuccessful American landing on, 353; final invasion of, 476

Malaya: 107. 140; a Japanese air reconnaisance over, 249; to be a target, 253; Japanese troops head for, 263, 268; Japanese invasion of, 271, 272–3, 275, 278, 284, 286; executions in, 301, 549; end of the war in, 721; becomes independent, 730, 733

Maldegem (Belgium): a gap near, 76

Maleme (Crete): attacked, 184

Malines (Belgium): Jews deported to Auschwitz from, 310, 373, 444

Malmédy (Ardennes): American soldiers massacred at, 620

Maloelap (Marshall Islands): American air attacks on, 297

Malöy (Norway): a commando raid on, 283

Maloyaroslavets (Russia): occupied, 246

Malta: bombed, 90; air battles of, 114, 341; Hitler seeks to isolate, 143; supplies reach, 143, 149, 180, 318, 324, 353, 382; bombed, 150, 183; a torpedo boat attack on, 216; supplies to, sunk, 312; fears for, 319–20; naval escort for, attacked, 333; attacks made from, 341; to be reinforced, 352; receives George Cross, 360; a renewed air

assault on, 368; thought to be the real object of the 'Torch' landings, 375; Italian ships reach safety of, 460

Maly Trostenets (Russia): a German concentration camp at, 210; a death camp at, 324, 329, 331, 332, 364; a revolt at, 548

Manado (Dutch East Indies): Japanese capture, 290

Manchester (England): Churchill speaks in, 40; bombed, 125

Manchester, William: recalls an incident on Okinawa, 695

*Manchester* (British cruiser): sunk, 352

*Manchester Guardian*: and the Jews of Poland, 43

Manchuria: Japanese army in, 711; Soviet troops advance through, 715, 717, 720

Mandalay (Burma): 276; bombed, 315; and a sabotage mission, 404; British and Indian troops advance towards, 646; falls, 650

Mandel, Georges: fights subversion, 68; prevents flight of public officials, 85; wants to fight on, 93, 101; executed, 552; his executioner executed, 732

Manevich, Lev: his act of defiance, 687–8; dies, 688

Mangan, Lieutenant Sagejima: an executioner, 396

Mangin, General: his statue destroyed, 102

'Manhattan Project': the atomic bomb, 363, 420, 628

Mannerheim, Marshal Carl: and a 'holy war', 201

Mannerheim Line (Finland): attacked, 41; breached, 42; by-passed, 47

Manila (Philippines): 216, 239, 282; evacuated, 284; Japanese forces enter, 287; Japanese send reinforcements from, 295; American targets near, 596; the *Ushio* damaged off, 612; atrocities in, 639; American forces approach, 642; battle for, 642, 643

*Manila Bay* (US escort carrier): hit in a suicide attack, 627

Mannheim (Germany): bombed, 146, 210, 254, 326

*Manoora* (Australian armed merchant cruiser): in action, 91

Manor Park (London): bomb at, 146

Manstein, General Fritz Erich von: and Hitler's musings, 245; and the Jews, 259, 366; promoted Field Marshal, 339; Hitler visits, 405, 410, 459; visits Hitler, 444; a protest from, 458; a warning from, 459; urges a withdrawal, 462; a success of, on the Eastern Front, 478; troops of, fall back, 486; dismissed, 511

Mantes (France): Allies reach, 568

*Maori* (British destroyer): rescues survivors, 186

Maoris: in action, 422, 498, 509

Maquis, the: in France, 397, 398, 528; sweeps against, 554, 568

*Marat* (Soviet battleship): in action, 231

Marburg (Germany): American troops enter, 654

'March of Death': in the Philippines, 316; survivors of, liberated, 722; the officer responsible for, executed, 728

Marchal, Colonel: flown to France (1943), 461

Marcinkance (eastern Poland): Jews in, murdered, 376

Marcks, General Erich: and German plans against Russia, 111, 115

Marcus Island (Pacific Ocean): an attack on, in retaliation, 302; Americans bomb, 457; Japanese garrison on, surrenders, 722

Maresyev, Alexei: his exploit, 445

Mareth Line (Tunisia): Rommel fortifies, 402; Rommel attacks from, 409; British Eighth Army attacks, 415

Margerie, Roland de: wants to fight on, 81

Mariampolé (Lithuania): Jews murdered at, 213

Marianas Islands: planned conquest of, 516; landings on, 541; battles for, 543; Japanese surrenders on, 722

Maribor (Yugoslavia): Hitler visits, 178; German troops still in action near (11 May 1945), 693

Marienbad (Czechoslovakia): Jews killed in, 674

Marienburg (East Prussia): Hitler meets Horthy at, 232; British prisoners-of-war encounter a 'death march' near, 633; Red Army halted near, 634

Marienwerder (East Prussia): German troops reach, 188

Marigny (Normandy): an Allied deception at, 532

Marinenko, Captain: sights German troop transports, 194

Maritza (Italian fuel ship): sunk, 262

Mariupol (southern Russia): evacuation from, 206; Germans reach, 242; Germans retreat to, 267; and Germany's Caspian Sea plans, 366

Mariveles Mountains (Philippines): 294

Markkleeberg (near Leipzig): slave labour at, 582

Marlag (near Hamburg): and an Allied air raid, nearby, 624

Marquise-Mimoyecques (near Calais): bombed, 556

Marseille (France): an escapee reaches, 131; Jewish orphans sent to their deaths from, 395; a member of the Milice killed in, 422; Allies enter, 582

Marseillaise, the: sung in Paris (August 1944), 573; sung in Indo-China (May 1945), 692–3

Marsh, John: and Hirohito's visit to London (1971), 741–2

Marshall, General George C.: and aid to Britain, 81; and preparations against Japan, 253; and the Philippines, 288; and aid to Egypt, 337; and aid to Russia, 396; and the bombing of Rome, 435; and the liberation of Prague, 680; his comprehensive aid plan, 732–3

Marshall Aid: launched, 732–3

Marshall Islands: American air attacks on, 297; American landings on, 496

Martel, Major-General G. le Q.: in action, 70

Martin, Flight-Lieutenant Trevor: Churchill's flight to view the battle, 652

Marxstadt (Volga): deportations from, 231

Mary, Queen: 104

Maryland (US battleship): hit by a kamikaze pilot, 617

Marzabotto (Italy): a clandestine mission to, 597

Massachusetts (US warship): bombards Japan, 703

Massawa (Eritrea): Italian naval setback near, 168; surrenders, 170

Mastiff (British minesweeper): blown up by a magnetic mine, 29

Matabele (British destroyer): sunk, 291

Matapan, Cape (Greece): Italian naval defeat off, 166

Mathis, First Lieutenant Jack W.: in action, 413

Matsuoka, Yosuke: Stalin's remark to, 173

Matuson, Sara: sheltered and saved, 633

Mauban-Abucay Line (Philippines): Americans withdraw from, 293

Mauritius (Indian Ocean): 101; troops from, fight at Bir Hakeim, 187; an 'Ultra' listening post at, 429

Mauthausen (Austria): concentration camp at, 113; Poles sent to, 127; Jews sent to, 158, 205; Czech women and children sent to, 332; a mass execution in, 589; 'handle the load yourself', 608; Red Cross at, 670; 'a thousand men must still die every day' in, 674; American troops reach, 688

'Max': parachuted into France, 287

Maxim Gorky (Soviet cruiser): in action, 231

Maximov, Ivan: crosses Lake Ladoga, 261

May, Dr Alan Nunn: passes on uranium, 702

May, Doris: and Rommel's threat to Palestine, 337

Mayakovsky Metro Station (Moscow): Stalin speaks in, 253

Mayer (a British commando): his fate, 423

Mayo, Lieutenant T. P.: shot down, but evades capture, 404

Mazaniuk, Elena: kills a killer, 363

Mazignen (France): parachutists at, 562

'Meat Grinder' (Iwo Jima): fighting at, 643

Meaux (France): Germans to enter, 92

Mechelen-sur-Meuse (Belgium): a plane crash near, 38

Medal of Honour: awarded, 272, 322–3, 413, 604, 628, 634, 662, 694–5

Médaille Militaire: awarded, 317

Médenine (Tunisia): a defence line at, 397; Rommel defeated at, 409

Medmenham (England): photo interpretation at, 513, 522

Medyn (Russia): Germans to withdraw to, 274; a battle west of, 284

Megara (Greece): evacuation from, 176

Mein Kampf (Hitler): and Communism, 36

Meindl, Major-General: wounded, 184

Meknès (French merchant steamer): sunk, 111

Melitopol (southern Russia): a German defence line at, 451

Melun (France): sabotage near, 324

Member of the British Empire: awarded, 621

Memel: and Hitler's 'mission', 11; to be bombed, 198; besieged, 601; German forces trapped in, 628; Hitler orders evacuation of, by sea, 632

'Memphis Belle': bombing missions of,

428–9; her crew filmed, 429

Menasché, Lillian: and 'that cursed day', 470

Mengele, Dr Josef: at Auschwitz, 431–2, 507, 562; an eye witness of the brutality of, liberated, 688

Menin (Belgium): 73

Mennecke, Dr Fritz: his medical experiments, 168, 260, 263, 267

Mental patients: murdered, 32, 39, 70, 235, 243, 253, 298, 329, 354, 379, 395

Menton (France): occupied by Italy, 101; anti-Italian posters in, 143

Menzies, Sir Stuart: and Intelligence for Stalin, 385

Merano (Italy): Jews deported to Auschwitz from, 462

Merapas Island (Singapore): clandestine operations on, 702

Merchant seamen: attacked after being torpedoed, 500, 509–10

Mergui (Burma): Japanese surrender at, 725

Mermagen, Tubby: and the French surrender, 98

Merritt, Lieutenant-Colonel: at Dieppe, 354

Mers-el-Kebir (Algeria): French naval base at, 106; British bombardment of, 107; and France's 'honour', 133

Mersa Matruh (Egypt): a body washed ashore at, 185; British fall back to, 336; General Kreipe brought to, 519

Messe, General: in Tunisia, 415

Messina (Italy): bombed, 440; American forces enter, 452

Messina, Straits of (Sicily–Italy): Germans withdraw to Italy across, 451; Allies invade Italy across, 457

Messmer, Captain Pierre: at Bir Hakeim, 187

Metaxas, General John: and the liberation of Albania, 143

Metkovic (Yugoslavia): German units attacked near, 509

Metlika (Yugoslavia): and a planned Allied escape line, 508

Metz (France): German troops at, 89; von Kluge commits suicide on the way to, 572; Americans enter, 614

Metzger, Max Josef: executed, 516

Meurer, Captain Manfred: shot down, and killed, 492

Meuse River (Belgium, Holland): German troops cross, 61, 64; Allies cross, 584; Germans drive towards, 622; Churchill views battle east of, 652

Mexico: an escapee returns to Germany through, 154

Mexico, Gulf of: and German submarines, 318

Meyer, SS Lieutenant-Colonel Kurt: and the killing of prisoners-of-war, 535; withdraws into Caen, 553; tried, 727; released, 738

Mga (near Leningrad): Germans occupy, 228; Russians recapture, 230; Germans in renewed occupation of, 266; liberation of, 490

M.I.9: and escapees, 326

Miami (Florida): German submarines off, 330

Michael, King of Roumania: and the Soviet-Roumanian armistice, 574

Michalowice (Poland): Poles shot in, 435

Michelin Marcel: killed by an Allied bomb, 582

Michniow (Poland): Poles executed in, 443

Michiels, General: and the defeat of Belgium, 76

Middelburg (Holland): a reprisal at, 587–8

Midway Island (Pacific): to be reinforced, 263, 737; bombed, 272; a raid on, forestalled, 330; a 1941 mission to, recalled, 737

Miedzylesie (near Warsaw): Red Army reaches, 591; Vistula crossed west of, 593

Miedzyrzec Podlaski (Poland): Jews killed in, 444

Mielec (Poland): Jews deported to their death from, 307; Jewish slave labourers murdered at, 578

Mierzwa, Pilot Officer Boguslaw: killed, 174

Mieth, Major-General Friedrich: his protest, 40

Mihailović, Colonel Draža: a focus of revolt in Yugoslavia, 182; a British agent reaches, 236; attacks Tito's partisans, 255; defends Split, 463

Mikolajczyk, Jan: sentenced to death, 162

Milan (Italy): bombed, 450; Jews deported from, to Auschwitz, 467–8, 494; partisans liberate, 672; Mussolini's body hanged in, 676

Milice: a member of, killed, 418; members of, executed, 462; help round up Jews, 514; twelve members of, killed, 528; an act of revenge against, 548; and the execution of Georges Mandel, 552; in Lyon, 571; a member of, recalls an execution, 573; a member of, executed (1947), 732

Milch, Field Marshal Erhard: and the German rocket, 333; and the German jet aircraft, 488

Military Cross: awarded, 551

Miller, Second Lieutenant: escapes, 510

Miller, Lusia: 'I really do not want to die', 370

Millerovo (southern Russia): abandoned, 341; Germans driven back to, 388

Milos (Aegean Sea): German troops on, surrender, 692

Milosna (Poland): a defence line at, 562

'Mincer' (Iwo Jima): fighting at, 643

Mindanao (Philippines): Japanese land on, 281; MacArthur reaches Australia through, 307; a freighter sunk off, 588; American landing on, 645, 667; continued fighting on, 683, 695; organized resistance on, ends, 700; a further landing on, 702; last resistance on, ends, 708

Mindoro Island (Philippines): American landing on, 618

Mineralniye Vody (Caucasus): German forces enter, 352; Jews murdered at, 359

Minerva Factory (Antwerp): bombed, 418

Minneapolis (US heavy cruiser): damaged, 384

'Minnie' (Hannah Szenes): her parachute mission, 508–9

Minsk (White Russia): a Soviet signals centre, 192; bombed, 198; battle for,

202; the front near, 204; mopping up operations near, 209; a German concentration camp near, 210; Jews murdered in, 220, 252, 304; mass murder in region of, 221; measures against Jews promulgated in, 223–4; action against partisans near, 244, 420; a public execution in, 251; partisan activity near, 292, 303, 323, 397; a death camp near, 324; Jews deported to, 330; an assassination in, 363; a planned assassination against Hitler near, 412; an anti-partisan sweep near, 431; a partisan success at, 544; Soviet forces enter, 551

Minsk Mazowiecki (Poland): Jews killed at, 386, 435

Mir (White Russia): Jews murdered in, 351

Mir (Sarawak): Japanese land at, 279; Australians land at, 701

Misburg (Germany): bombed, 641

Missing Research and Enquiry Service: established, 708

Mississippi (US battleship): accidental explosion on, 476; hit by a suicide pilot, 628, 697

Mito (Japan): bombed, 704, 708

Mitscher, Vice-Admiral Marc: and a ten-day naval battle, 627

Mitterand, François: flown in to Britain, from France (1943), 475

Mius, River (southern Russia): Germans withdraw behind, 265–6

Mlawa (Poland): murders on the road to, 298; further murders at, 630

Moa (New Zealand corvette): sunk, 419

Moabit (Berlin): Russians reach, 674

Moabit Prison (Berlin): Russians enter, 676

Model, Field Marshal Walther: replaces von Kluge, 570; commits suicide, 670

Modlin (Poland): battle at, 13

Mogaung (Burma): an advance to, 506; captured, 547

Mogilev (western Russia): a signals centre, 192; on a defence line, 201; and the establishment of partisan groups, 206; Jews murdered in, 255; resistance, and reprisals, in, 256; an anti-partisan sweep near, 358; continued partisan activity at, 485; liberated, 548

Mohacs (Hungary): Red Army enters, 615

Möhne Dam: bombed, 428

Mohnke, ss Captain (later Major-General) Wilhelm: and a massacre, 79; makes two final Knight's Cross presentations, 679; his whereabouts reported, 742–3

Moircy (Ardennes): Germans driven from, 626

Mokotow (Warsaw): Polish resistance in, 596; Poles in, surrender, 597

Molders, Werner: shot down, 87; killed, 257

Moli Island (Solomons): a skirmish off, 471

Molodechno (White Russia): a partisan success at, 544

Molotov, Vyacheslav: and the partition of Poland, 9, 13; and Finland, 49; and the Tripartite Pact, 141; a military warning to, 158; and a warning from

Washington, 160; replaced as Soviet Premier by Stalin, 180–1; signs Anglo-Soviet Alliance, 327; and no separate peace, 468; and the fate of Polish negotiators, 686

'Molotov cocktail': 31, 34

Moltke, Count Helmut von: opposes Nazism, 450; hanged, 632

Mona's Isle (British pleasure steamer): rescues soldiers, 77

Monaghan (US destroyer): losses on, 618

Monastir (Yugoslavia): 170; British troops near, 172

'Monday': helps escapees, 288

Mondovi: (northern Italy): an anti-partisan sweept near, 613

Mondorf (Luxemburg): war criminals held in a hotel at, 703

Monemvasia (Greece): evacuation from, 175

Mongols, the: their successors, 226

Mönichkirchen (Austria): Hitler at, 172, 174, 176, 178

'Monier': Mitterand's code name, 475

Monkey Point (Corregidor): an act of mass suicide on, 644

Mono Island (Solomons): battle on, 471

Monowitz (near Auschwitz): a synthetic oil and rubber factory at, 326; slave labourers at, 503, 525; photographed from the air, 513–4, 529–30; oil installations at, bombed, 577, 590, 621, 623, 631; mass evacuations from, 631; Red Army reaches, 634

Montargis (France): a parachutist reaches, 489

Montauban, Bishop of (Monsignor Théas): his protest, 357

Monte Cassino (Italy): assault on heights of, 488–9; monastery on, bombed, 498; battle for, 509, 526

Montebourg (Normandy): battle at, 538

Montenegro (Yugoslavia): resistance in, to be organized, 207–8

Monte Rotondo (Italy): Germans retake, 492

Montgomery, General Bernard L.: in Belgium, 68; at El Alamein, 358; launches his attack on Rommel, 271; occupies Tripoli, 396; defends Médenine, 409; overruns Mareth Line, 415–6; occupies Sfax, 419; invades Italy, 453; in northern Europe, 515, 616, 652, 667; and the German surrender, 684; and Lübeck, 687; invests Soviet generals with British medals, 702

Montoire (France): Hitler at, 133

Montreal (Canada): 4; a saboteur from, in France, 515

'Monty's Moonlight': and the crossing of the Rhine, 652

Monument of Liberation: to be built, in Linz, 260

Moon, Private Harold: his heroism, 604

Moosejaw (Canadian corvette): in action, 231

Mooyman, Gerardus: his bravery, 405–6

Moras, Esther Gracia: her evidence of an atrocity, 639

Moravska Ostrava: Jews deported from, 22–23, 436, 461

Morcourt (France): an escape at, 571

Morden, Miss: in France, 94; killed, 183
Morden Hill (London): a 'Flying Bomb' at, 570
More, Lieutenant Kenneth: in action, 472
Morgenstern, Jacqueline: deported, 571; murdered, 669
Morgenthau, Henry: his 'goodwill', 66; and the future of Germany, 592
'Morgenthau Plan', the: and the future of Germany, 592
Morison, Samuel Eliot: and a 'sour note' to victory, 718
Morobe (New Guinea): Americans reach, 417
'Morland': a clandestine group, in France, 475
Morocco: troops from, in action, 69, 100, 522; an Allied landing on, 347
Moron (Philippines): Japanese troops sent from, 295
Morotai Island (Moluccas): American landing on, 592
Morrison, Herbert: and the 'Flying Bomb', 548
Mortain (Normandy): American defence at, 566; Hitler orders attack on, 567
Moscow: Ribbentrop in, 16; a German-Soviet commercial treaty signed in, 44; a report to Tokyo from, 45; negotiations with Finland in, 47; Russo-Finnish Treaty signed in, 48, 49; German plans against, 114, 144, 147; air defences of, 172; Soviet-Japanese Neutrality Pack signed in, 173; Soviet defence preparations seen, on journey to, 177; evacuation of factories from, 179; prepares for war, 194; an Evacuation Council set up in, 199; German advance towards, 204; factory evacuations from 206; to 'disappear', 207, 208–9; German advance towards 210, 212; bombed, 217, 227, 252; and Hitler's strategy, 225, 230, 232, 239; German assault on, 241–2, 243–4, 245; defence of, 246, 251 temperature falls to below zero at (12 November 1941), 255; continuing battle for, 259–60, 262, 263, 264, 265, 267, 268, 270; German losses in battle for, 281; supplies to, arrive from Archangel, 284–5; a complaint to, from Tito, 395; a partisan medal issued in, 399; an agreement reached in, for no separate peace, 460; German prisoners-of-war in, 556; Churchill and Stalin discuss the post-war Europe in, 600; Poles and a Swede taken as prisoners to, 654; celebrations in, 673, 701; Dr Adenauer reaches agreement in, on return of German prisoners-of-war, 738
'Moscow Highway': partisans active along, 352–3
Moscow University: heroism of a graduate from, 339
Moscow Young Communist League: members of, executed, 281
Mosjöen (Norway): British troops at, 62
Mosley, Sir Oswald: imprisoned, 70
'Mosquito': an Enigma key, broken, 334
Moss, Captain Stanley: on Crete, 519, 520
Mostar (Yugoslavia): Jews not to be

deported from 344–5; and an Allied deception plan, 492–3; German units at, attacked, 509; a German defence line at, 615
Mouen (Normandy): prisoners-of-war killed at, 542
Moulin, Jean: parachuted into France, 286–7; arrested, 434–5; dies, 435; his remains honoured (1964), 740
Moulmein (Burma): Japanese try to escape through, 705; continued fighting near, 722
Mount Elbruz (Caucasus): German troops climb, 353, 354
Mount Suribachi (Iwo Jima): American flag raised on, 642–3
Mountbatten, Lord Louis: at Namsos, 58; off Holland, 59; his nephew in action, 148; off Crete, 185; and the Dieppe raid, 354; and the surrender of Japanese forces in South-East Asia, 723
Mozdok (Caucasus): Germans withdraw to, 385; Germans driven from, 391
Mozhaisk (Russia): battle near, 245; ablaze, 246; Russians recapture, 291
Mozyr (Russia): and a Soviet defence line, 201, 205; Germans driven from, 489
Mrocza (Poland): an atrocity at, 6
Mstislavl (Russia): murder of Jews in, 255
Mud: on the Eastern front, impedes the Germans, 244, 254
Mühlhausen (Germany): a counter-attack from, defeated, 659
Mukden (Manchuria): Soviet forces occupy, 717
'Mulberry': an artificial harbour, 468, 538
Müller, General Friedrich-Wilhelm: executed, 732
Müller, ss Lieutenant-General Heinrich: and mass murder, 221, 398; asks for volunteers, 598
Müller, Dr Joseph: the secret mission of, 58–9
Munich: an attempt on Hitler's life in, 26, 29; Hitler returns to, 35, 99, 139, 473; Hitler's rebuilding plans for, 104; bombed, 139, 410; and an anti-Semitic film, 151; Jews deported from, 263; Flak Towers to be built in, 365; Hitler learns of Allied North African landings while on his way to, 375; anti-Nazi leaflets in, 404; a second attempt on Hitler's life in, 414; a possible stronghold south of, abandoned, 670; von Greim ordered to fly to Berlin from, 672, 673; American troops enter, 680
'Munich': a deception, 541
Munk, Kaj: murdered, 488
Münster (Germany): the bishop of, protests, 224; bombed, 649
Munthe-Kaas, Colonel: and the Norwegian surrender, 88
Muntok (Sumatra): fate of civilian internees at, 635
Murillo: paintings by, taken to safety, 206
Murmansk (northern Russia): German troops pass through, 62; German plan to seize, 206; British pilots reach, 223, 233; railway line to, cut, 230; a convoy to, its escort sunk, 291; further

convoys to, 325, 327; Anglo-Soviet Intelligence co-operation in, 441
Muroc (southern California): a dummy atomic bomb dropped at, 505
Murphy, Audie: wounded, 634
Mürwick (northern Germany): a suicide at, 695
*Musashi* (Japanese battleship): sunk, 606
Muslims (of Bosnia): mutiny by, 458
Mussert, Anton: hanged, 729
Mussolini, Benito: nervous of war, 37–8; meets Hitler, 50, 98, 130, 135, 153, 415, 445, 559; declares war on France and Britain, 90; Hitler confides in, 134; invades Greece, 135; his troops driven back into Albania, 143; setbacks to, in the Mediterranean and North Africa, 143, 149, 156; fails to persuade France, 157; and the German invasion of Russia, 194, 201; at Brest-Litovsk with Hitler, 227; at Uman with Hitler, 227; and Malta, 318; a rumour concerning, circulates in the Warsaw Ghetto, 324; flies to Cyrenaica, 337; returns to Italy, 338; 'weakness' of, 410; Hitler 'rescues', 447, 461; shot, 676
Mutanchiang (Manchuria): battle at, 720
'Mutt': a double agent ('Jack'), 255, 453
*Muzio Attendolo* (Italian light cruiser): sunk, 384
Myers, Major J.: forces down a German jet aircraft, 583
Myitkyina (Burma): 326; a sabotage mission towards, 404; an advance to, 506; captured, 547
Myslowice (East Upper Silesia): a slave labour camp at, 525

*Nachi* (Japanese heavy cruiser): badly damaged, 415
Naga Hills (India): an attack on Burma from, 506
Nagasaki (Japan): an atomic bomb dropped on, 715–6; continuing deaths at, 725
Nagoya (Japan): bombed, 317, 648, 708
Nagumo, Admiral: has himself killed, 553
Nagykanizsa (Hungary): oil wells at, 509; captured, 657
Naha (Okinawa): Japanese defend, 668, 697
Nakagawa, Lieutenant: recalls executions of prisoners-of-war, 297, 302
Nakamura Camp (Japan): prisoners-of-war in, liberated, 718
Nakom Paton (Thailand): liberation comes to, 718
Nalchik (Caucasus): Germans driven from 391
Nalewki (Warsaw): bombed, 8; a reprisal in, 28
Namsos (Norway): landing at, 55; evacuation of, 58
Namu Island (Marshall Islands): Americans land on, 496
Namur (Belgium): 'lost', 67
Nancy (France): bombed, 61; a clandestine mission near, 504; German aircraft based at, short of fuel, 532, 535; deportees leave, 572
*Nancy Moller* (British cargo ship): sunk, 509

Nanking (China): 264

Nanning (China): Japanese enter, 614; Japanese evacuate, 696

Nantes (France): troops embarked from, 98; Germans occupy, 100; reprisals in, 247; American forces reach, 568

Naotake, Sato: and Japan's willingness to end the war (June 1945), 701

Napalm bomb: in use against the Japanese, 702

Naples (Italy): a warship sunk at, 384; bombed, 418; an Allied objective, 452; a revolt in, 464; an Allied task force sails from, 491; American troops leave, for the Pacific, 703

Naples, Bay of (Italy): battle for Islands in, 461

Napoleon: Hitler visits tomb of, 102; his march to Moscow (1812), 197; his crossing of the Rhine (1805), 648

Napoleonic Wars: Hitler's reference to, 617

Naro-Fominsk (near Moscow): an anti-tank ditch at, 246; Germans driven back from, 266

Narva (Estonia): 16; a German defence line at, 451

Narvik (Norway): and German iron ore, 37, 42; plans and counterplans for, 45, 48, 50; German landings at, 53; naval attack on, 54; British landings near, 55, 56; a French landing near, 64; a British landing at, 78; evacuation from, 83, 86, 89, 93; and a deception plan, 347

*Nashville* (US cruiser): hit by suicide pilots, 617

Natzweiler (Alsace): medical experiments at, 438; four British agents (all women) killed in, 555

Naujocks, Alfred: and a successful kidnap, 26

Naumburg-on-Saale (Germany): a deportee dies at, 498

Nauplia (Greece): evacuation from, 175

Nauru Island (Pacific): a naval skirmish near, 91; shelled, 144

Nautsi (Finland): successfully defended, 34

Navlya (Russia): Soviet partisans regroup near, 361

Navy and Marine Corps Medal: awarded (to J. F. Kennedy), 449

Nawcz (Poland): sick evacuees murdered at, 633

Nazdab (New Guinea): Allies seize, 459

Nazi–Soviet Non-Aggression Pact: 9, 62, 179

Nazism: leaflets denounce evils of, 46; its tyranny, 51; its anti-Semitic ideology, 144; an appeal for the overthrow of, 450; a critic of, executed, 549

Neave, Airey: escapes, 288

Nebe, SS General Arthur: and methods of mass murder, 220; Hitler to be kept informed by, 221

Neisse River (Western Neisse): Red Army crosses, 668; and Poland's post-war borders, 706, 710

Nehru, Jawaharlal: alarmed, 316; and a 'brave adventure', 724–5

*Nelson* (US destroyer): sunk, 538

Neman River: Napoleon's crossing of (1812), 198; battle at (1941), 199

'Nemo': escapes, 392

*Nerissa* (a troop transport): sunk, 178

Nesterenko, Lyuba: her heroism, 365

'Nestor': a sabotage circuit, 543

*Nestor* (Australian destroyer): crippled, 333

Netherlands, the: *see index entry for Holland*

Nettelton, John Dering: his skill rewarded, 317

*Neue Züricher Zeitung* (Zurich): reports 'deep anxiety' in Germany, 450

Neutrality Act: partly repealed (November 1939), 25; bypassed (May 1940), 67

Neva River (Leningrad): naval guns in action on, 228; German troops fail to cross, 231; a salute on, 495

*Nevada* (US battleship): at Pearl Harbour, 268

Nevel (Russia): 214; a Soviet offensive against, 480

Nevers (France): occupied, 100; fighting near, 100

New Britain (Pacific): an American landing on, 481; advances on, 486

New Georgia Island (Pacific): American reinforcements to, 439; Japanese tenacity on, 447

New Guinea (Pacific): struggle for, 307, 322, 338, 341, 345, 346, 355, 361, 375, 378, 384, 387, 391, 393; resistance in, gradually overcome, 396, 408, 459, 477, 481, 486, 495; further landings on, 519, 542; a flank attack on, forestalled, 520; naval engagement off, 521; last battle on, 562; an island off, captured, 584; becomes independent, 730; war's debris recovered in, 741

New Hebrides (Pacific): naval action in, 361

New Jerusalem (near Moscow): Germans reach, 262

*New Mexico* (US battleship): hit in a suicide attack, 627

New Orleans (US heavy cruiser): damaged, 384

New Southgate (London): a 'Flying Bomb' at, 576

New World: sea communications with Old World endangered, 413

New York: aid to Britain sails from, 106, 107; a German spy in, 132; a German escapee in, 154; German submarines off, 302, 330; singing and dancing in, 673; a speech in, asserting 'we must act as a great power', 728; American war dead brought back to, 733; a museum opened in, on the aircraft carrier *Intrepid*, 742

*New York Times*: reveals details of German rocket bomb attacks, 589; describes arrival of 'Reich technicians' in Boston, 724

New Zealand: troops from, in Greece, 174, 175; troops from, on Crete, 180, 184, 186; troops from, in North Africa, 259, 338, 358, 371, 409, 416, 422; declares war on Finland, Hungary and Roumania, 270; a pilot from, wins the Victoria Cross, 425; troops from, in the Far East, 471; troops from, in Italy, 509, 601, 660; war dead of, 514

Newlands (Kent, England): a 'Flying Bomb' shot down over, 544

Newman, Captain Isadore: his exploits,

and his death, 654–5

Newport (Wales): a bomber crashes on, 125

Neumann, Peter: witnesses an atrocity, 205

Neu Dachs (East Upper Silesia): a labour camp at, 524

Neuengamme (near Hamburg): medical experiments at, 571, 611; an execution near, 669; an SS officer from, brought to trial, 741

Neukermans, Pierre Richard: executed, 521

Neukölln (Berlin): Russians reach, 674

Neumunster (Germany): a suicide in, 731

Newfoundland: 67, 222; German submarine attack off, 348

*Newsweek* (New York): and a Japanese army sergeant on Guam (1972), 740–1

Nezhin (Ukraine): battle near, 231; Soviet forces enter, 462

*Niblack* (US destroyer): drops depth charges, 172

Nice (France): a Resistance group in, 471

Nichiporovich, Colonel: forms a partisan unit, 209

Nicholas II, Tsar of all the Russias: 188

Nicholson, Brigadier C. N.: at Calais, 75–6

Nickhoff, General: surrenders, 689

Nicolson, Flight Lieutenant James: his bravery rewarded, 118; killed on a bombing mission, 682–3

Nicosia (Cyprus): German prisoners-of-war at work near, 730

Niederkrüchten (Germany): an SS General returns home to, 738

Niedzialkowski, Mieczyslaw: killed, 104

Niedzinski (a Polish miller): his punishment, 127

Niehoff, Rolf: captured, 25

Niemöller, Pastor Martin: liberated, 686

Nieswiez (eastern Poland): the fate of a prisoner-of-war in, 202; Jews escape from, 345

Nierstein (Rhine): a bridgehead at, 651

Nieuport (Belgium): attack on, 74

*Niger* (British minesweeper): sunk, 340

'Night and Fog' decree: 32

Nijmegen (Holland): a parachute landing at, 593; German Jets in action over, 599; a plan to advance from, 639

Nikitin, General: killed in action, 201

Nikitin, Ivan: a partisan, in action, 407

Nikolaiev, Alexander: in action at Prokhorovka, 443

Nikolayev (southern Russia): Russians evacuate, 224; Jews and Russians murdered in, 239, 246

Nile Delta (Egypt): a German submarine sunk off, 373–4

Nimi, Vice-Admiral Masaichi: no surrender to, 280

Nimitz, Admiral Chester: orders a news blackout, 617

Niš (Yugoslavia): 170

Nishinomiya-Mikage (Japan): bombed, 712

Nishizawa, Hiroyoshi: dies, 606

Nissenthal, Jack: at Dieppe, 354

Nitsche, Professor: and the gassing of concentration camp inmates, 277; and euthanasia, 508

Nizami (a poet): his 800th anniversary, 246

Nobel Prize, the: 129, 634

Noé (France): Jews at, 310

Noguès, General A.P.: accepts armistice, 103

Nong Pladuk (Thailand): Allied prisoners-of-war accidentally killed at, by Allied bombs, 626–7

Noor Inayat Khan: her Resistance activities, 438; shot, 590; her posthumous awards, 728; her interrogator hanged, 734

Norcia (Italy): sabotage at, 540

Nordhausen (Germany): underground rocket factory built at, 453, 522; mass evacuations to, 632; rockets despatched to America from, 695; scientists spirited away from, 700

Norfolk (England): and a deception plan, 523

Norfolk (British heavy cruiser): attacked, 49

Norland regiment (SS): established, 56

Normandy (France): and a deception plan, 492; and Hitler's view of Allied strategy, 530; landings on, postponed, 531; and the D-Day deceptions, 532–3; and the first glider landings in, 533; battle in, 534–6; the continued deception in, 536–7, 541–2, 545–6, 555; Allied reinforcements for, 543, 549, 551; Hitler refuses German reinforcements for, 556; last phase of battle in, 561, 566, 567; continued use of beachhead at, 585

Normandy Squadron: in action on the Eastern Front, 441, 556

North America: Hitler denies designs on, 93

North Atlantic Treaty Organization (NATO): established, 729

North Cape (Norway): 103

North Carolina (US battleship): badly damaged, 361

North Caucasus (Soviet Union): Soviet reinforcement from, 183; German plans for, 193

North Sea: a British air raid across, 5

Northampton (US heavy cruiser): sunk, 384

Northern Prince (British merchant ship): sunk, 170

Norway: and German iron ore, 37; a protest from, 42–3; German plans for, 46, 52; Anglo-French plans for, 50; invaded, 53–4; unable to fight on, 57–8; last Allied resistance in, 62, 64–5, 65, 78, 83; future of, 85; Allied troops on their way to France from, 86; fighting ends in, 87, 89; 'strangers' in, 92; soldiers of, in Britain, 113; an act of defiance in, 147; a resistance group in, 151; demonstrations in, 172; German troops advance from, 204; Jews deported from, 205, 370; commandos from, land on Spitzbergen, 226; mass arrests in, and executions, 232; granite from, Hitler's plans for, 235; and 'Fortress Europe', 183; Prinz Eugen torpedoed off, 302–3; Lutheran clergy in, protest, 315; and heavy-water, 319, 379; resistance and reprisals in, 321; sabotage missions to,

362–3, 379, 404; warships from, pounce 'like terriers' 369; further executions in, 373; German bombers move from, 374, 377; and 'Aryan-Nordic' stud farms, 390–1; forced labour from, 441; and the fate of the Tirpitz, 463; resistance, and reprisals in, 466; and German heavy water, 319, 379, 404, 475, 500; and an Allied deception plan, 494, 506, 522, 523, 534, 540; and Hitler's view of Allied strategy, 530; German troops in, being moved to the Silesian Front, 638, 640; Hitler determined to hold, 669; former Army Commander-in-Chief of, liberated, 671

'Norwegian Front': creation of, as a focus of resistance, 128–9

Norwich (England): bombed, 319

Nothomb, Baron Jean-François de ('Franco'): arrested, 490

Novaya Ladoga (Lake Ladoga): trucks abandoned near, 261

Novgorod (Russia): a Soviet counter-offensive launched near, 288

Novgorod-Volynsk (western Russia): on the eve of war, 196; a defence line at, 205

Novi Sad (Yugoslavia): Hungarians enter, 172; Jews and Serbs murdered at, 293

Novorossiisk (southern Russia): a German objective, 345; Soviet partisans near, 361, 383; a Soviet landing near, 399; Soviet forces enter, 462

Nowotny, Walther: killed, 611

Noworol, Waclaw: sentenced to death, 472

Nowy Sacz (southern Poland): a death sentence in, 472

Nuclear fission: German plans for (1939), 14; American plans for (1939), 20–21; see also index entry for Atomic Bomb

Nucourt (France): bombed, 543, 551–2

Numfoor Island (New Guinea): Americans capture, 584

Nuremberg (Bavaria): Hitler's rebuilding plans for, 104, 235, 288; Flak Towers to be built in, 365; bombed, 407, 410, 504, 512; anti-Nazi leaflets distributed in, 412; Jews deported to Auschwitz from, 436; American forces reach outskirts of, 657; American forces occupy, 668; suicides in, 724, 733; war crimes trials held in, 724, 731, 734

Nuremberg Laws (of 1935): introduced in Luxemburg, 127–8; one of their authors, and the 'Final Solution', 292

'Nuts!': in answer to a call to surrender, 621

Nyiszli, Dr Miklos: an eye-witness, 549; liberated, 688

'OK': a double agent, 255

ONS 5: a transatlantic convoy, 425

Oahu (Hawaii): warships to be sent away from, 263

Oak Hill (US landing ship): sunk, 717

Oakland (California): bad news, and good, arrive at, 635

Oak Leaves (to Knight's Cross): awarded, 87, 338, 492, 520, 559, 566, 570, 582, 620

Oak Leaves with Swords (to Knight's

Cross): awarded, 492, 566; a recipient of, executed for war crimes, 732

Oak Leaves with Swords and Diamonds (to Knight's Cross): awarded to Rommel, 406; awarded to an air ace, 482, 611, 659

Oakley (British destroyer): sunk, 333

Oak Ridge (Tennessee): and the atomic bomb, 399

Oberammergau (Bavaria): rockets and scientists reach, 643; scientists surrender to the Americans at, 683

Obersalzberg (Bavaria): Hitler at, 109, 111, 113–4, 143, 153, 438–9, 440; Hitler designs a shelter for, 480; Hitler's outburst against the Jews at, 527–8

Oberursel (Germany): an Intelligence officer surrenders at, 695

'Oboe': a radio beam bombing device, first use of, 389

O'Callagan, Private William: survives a massacre, 76–7

Ocean Island (Pacific): Japanese occupy, 355

Ochota (Poland): reprisals at, 498; subjugated, 565

October Revolution (Soviet battleship): in action, 231

Odense (Denmark): murders in, 488

Oder River: a 'death march' towards, 631; Soviet troops cross, 632; Soviet tanks cross, 635–6; a further Soviet crossing of, 639; Hitler's last visit to, 648; Red Army drives towards Berlin from, 666, 667; and the post-war borders of Poland, 706, 710

Oder-Neisse Line: established, 710

Odessa (Soviet Union): Soviet troop preparations near, 179; bombed, 198; 'not to be surrendered', 222; evacuation of, begins, 244; Jews murdered in, 246; Jews deported from, 290; Germans remain in control of, 507

Oerhn, Captain: attacks convoys, 157

Ohio (US oil tanker): reaches Malta, 353

Ohlendorf, Otto: hanged, for war crimes, 735

Ohrdruf (Germany): Americans enter, 659

Oil: Soviet acquisition of, 16; targets in Germany, bombed, 67, 77, 98, 99, 102, 119, 147; German designs on, in the Caucasus and at Baku, 114, 343, 345, 350, 354, 375; to have primacy as a British target, 146, 159; and Japan, 279, 288, 633, 708; and Malta, 312; synthetic preparation of, by Germany, 326; installations for, at Ploesti, bombed, 333, 435, 448; threat to, in the Persian Gulf, 348; and Rommel, 357–8, 371, 387, 388, 394, 406; and the German forces at Stalingrad, 388; and the battle for Tunis, 425, 426; and the German occupation of Hungary, 509; and Auschwitz-Monowitz, 513–4, 529–30, 578, 580, 590–1, 621, 631; and the mining of the Danube, 515; American air assaults (May 1944), 523, 529; and Ultra, 523, 591, 616; shortage of, among German units in France (June 1944), 532, 535, 536; targets throughout Germany, bombed (August 1944), 576–7; and the Soviet occupation of Ploesti, 583; and Germany's

Oil: Soviet acquisition of—*contd.* 'greatest worry'. 616, 622; and the Ardennes offensive, 622; and the switch of Allied air priorities to Berlin-Dresden-Leipzig, 638, 640; and the continued bombing of German synthetic plants for, 641; and the German counter-offensive towards Budapest, 646, 651; Germany's last hope of (in Hungary) lost, 657; and the cancellation of the Ruhr counter-offensive, 659

Oise River (France): Germans reach, 68

Oka River (Russia): battle near, 262, 265

Okecie airport (Warsaw): battle for, 564

Okinawa Island (Japan): a transport ship torpedoed off, 597–8; a naval action off, 601; American landings on, 655–7; mass suicide attacks at, 660; continuing battle on, 662, 673–4, 683, 692, 694; naval losses off, 693; and the 'Sugar Loaf' battle, 694–5; and a final Japanese air offensive, 696; continuing Japanese opposition on, 697–9, 700; death toll on, 700–1; and the atomic bomb, 707; a surrender ceremony on, 722

*Oklahoma* (US battleship): at Pearl Harbour, 268

Olander, Sven: his act of rescue, 138

Olbricht, General Friedrich: and the July Plot, 555, 558

Oldham (England): 'Flying Bomb' deaths at, 624

O'Leary, Patrick, Lieutenant-Commander RN (Albert-Marie Guérisse): a Belgian, operating a British escape line, 177

Olevsk (western Russia): Red Army reaches, 486

Olij, Jan: wanted for trial, but released, 745

Olomouc (Czechoslovakia): Red Army approaches, 674; fighting at, 687, 689; overrun, 690

Olovo (Yugoslavia): Tito driven from, 288

Olschanesky, Sonia: a British agent, killed, 555

'Omaha' Beach (Normandy): landing at, 534

Ombrone River (Italy): Americans reach, 540

*Ommaney Bay* (US aircraft carrier): sunk in suicide attack, 627

Onega, Lake (northern Russia): Finns advance to, 228, 241; reinforcements group near, 267

'Operation Abercrombie': against the French coast, 318–9

'Operation Agreement': an attack on Tobruk, 360

'Operation Aida': Rommel's thrust into Egypt, 337

'Operation Alaric': the German occupation of Italy, 430

'Operation Alphabet': the Allied evacuation of Narvik, 78

'Operation Ambassador': against Guernsey, 110

'Operation Amsterdam': an Allied escape line, by air from Slovakia, 593–4, 599–600

'Operation Anthropoid': contact with the Czech resistance, 283–4

'Operation Apple': against Japanese forces in China, 702

'Operation Archery': against western Norway, 283

'Operation Argument': against German aircraft factories, 500

'Operation Ariel': French coast evacuations, 98

'Operation Attica': along the Black Sea shore, 363

'Operation Attila': against Vichy France, 146; postponed, 169

'Operation Autumn Mist': German Ardennes offensive, 618

'Operation Avalanche': Allied landing in Italy, 459, 460

'Operation Axis': the German occupation of Italy, 459

'Operation Backfire': a British launching of a German rocket, 724

'Operation Backhander': an American landing on New Britain, 481

'Operation Bagration': the Red Army offensive of June 1944, 544

'Operation Bamberg': a German sweep against Soviet partisans, 308–9

'Operation Barbarossa': the German invasion of Russia, 145, 146, 156

'Operation Barker': a parachute mission, in France, 568

'Operation Basalt': against the Island of Sark, 367

'Operation Battering Ram': members of French Resistance, flown to France, 461

'Operation Battleaxe': against the Germans in Libya, 192–3

'Operation Baytown': the Allied invasion of Italy, 453

'Operation Bearskin': a Yugoslav partisan offensive, 521

'Operation Bellicose': a British 'shuttle bombing' raid, 439

'Operation Birdcage': announcing that the Japanese war was over, 721

'Operation Birdsong': against Soviet partisans, 331

'Operation Biting': a cross-Channel raid, 304

'Operation Black I and II': an anti-partisan sweep in Yugoslavia, 424, 430–1, 436

'Operation Blood and Ashes': against French Resistance fighters, 521

'Operation Blücher': German offensive into the Caucasus, 341

'Operation Blue': German summer offensive in Russia, 1942, 310, 338

'Operation Bluebottle': rescuing prisoners-of-war, 360

'Operation Bowery': aircraft for Malta, 323–4

'Operation Brassard': the capture of Elba, 542

'Operation Brevity': against Rommel, 183

'Operation Brutus': a parachute drop in Belgium, 587

'Operation Buffalo': a German tactical retreat in Russia, 414

'Operation Bulbasket': sabotage in France, 551

'Operation Bunkum': a landing on a Japanese-occupied island, 394

'Operation Burdock': a German anti-partisan sweep, 390

'Operation C': against Ceylon, 314

'Operation C3': possible German occupation of Malta, 318

'Operation Calendar': to reinforce Malta, 318

'Operation Cannibal': reconquest of Burma, 391; fails, 408

'Operation Carpetbagger': air supplies to resistance forces in Western Europe, 486

'Operation Cartwheel': recapture of Rabaul, 439

'Operation Castigo': bombing of Belgrade, 170

'Operation Catapult': against the French Fleet, 105, 107

'Operation Catchpole': against the Japanese on Eniwetok, 499

'Operation Centreboard': against Hiroshima, 712

'Operation Cerebus': a German naval exploit, 300

'Operation Character': an Intelligence mission, before the recapture of Rangoon, 667–8; continued operations of (until 8 September 1945), 722

'Operation Chariot': against St Nazaire, 312

'Operation Chastise': against Ruhr dams, 428

'Operation Chattanooga Choo-Choo': attack on German railway stock, 526

'Operation Cheerful': against the Germans at Colmar, 639

'Operation Chicken': a planned Allied escape line, 508

'Operation Citadel': against the Russian-held Kursk Salient, 413, 420, 427, 441–2, 443; called off, 444

'Operation Clarion': against German lines of communications, 644

'Operation Claymore': against Lofoten Islands, 161

'Operation Coast': against Warsaw, 13

'Operation Coat': to reinforce Egypt, 139

'Operation Cobra': a break-out from the Cherbourg Peninsula, 561

'Operation Cockpit': against Japanese oil installations, 708

'Operation Collar': war supplies to Malta and Egypt, 143

'Operation Colossus': against an Italian viaduct, 157

'Operation Conjuror': flying in agents to occupied France, 475

'Operation Corkscrew': Allied capture of Pantelleria, 426, 437

'Operation Cormorant': a German anti-partisan sweep in White Russia, 431

'Operation Corncob': against bridges in northern Italy, 669

'Operation Coronet': the planned invasion of Honshu Island (Japan), 659–660, 728

'Operation Cottbus': against Soviet partisans and villagers, 435

'Operation Countenance': Anglo-Soviet occupation of Iran, 226

'Operation Crossbow': bombing 'Flying Bomb' sites, 479, 529

'Operation Crusader': against Rommel, 259

'Operation Darlington II': rescue of Allied prisoners-of-war, 527

'Operation Deadlight': post-war

sinking of German submarines, 727

'Operation Demon': evacuation of Allied troops from Greece, 176

'Operation Dexterity': an American landing in New Guinea, 486

'Operation Disclaim': aid to Yugoslav partisans, 298

'Operation Dracula': to take Rangoon, 682

'Operation Dragoon': against southern France, 568; its side effects (on Warsaw and in Italy), 570

'Operation Drum Roll': a German submarine offensive, 290, 304

'Operation Dynamo': the Dunkirk evacuation, 75–83

'Operation Eagle': against Soviet partisans, 345

'Operation Enclose': against German submarines, 414

'Operation Excess': aid to Greece, 148

'Operation Exporter': against Syria and Lebanon, 188–9

'Operation Extended Capital': into Burma, 613

'Operation Fabius': an invasion practice landing, 520

'Operation Felix': the seizure of Gibraltar, 141, 145

'Operation Fish Trap': against the Allies at Anzio, 497

'Operation Flap': behind German lines in northern Italy, 613

'Operation Flash': codeword for the assassination of Hitler (March 1943), 412

'Operation Flight': Jewish refugees set off for Palestine, 726

'Operation Floating Chrysanthemum': a Japanese mass suicide pilot plan, 660

'Operation Forager': against the Japanese in the Marianas Islands, 541

'Operation Fortitude': and an Allied deception, 494, 537, 542; ends, 557

'Operation Fortitude South': an Allied deception plan, 494

'Operation Frantic Joe': American bomber offensive, 530; and the Warsaw uprising, 596

'Operation Fritz': the German invasion of Russia, 145

'Operation Gain': a British landing behind the lines in France, 541, 552

'Operation Galvanic': American, against three Pacific atolls, 476

'Operation Gardening': Allied minelaying in the Danube, 515, 550

'Operation Gauntlet': commando raid on Spitzbergen, 226

'Operation Giant': an Allied landing near Rome, 459

'Operation Globetrotter': capture of Sansapor, New Guinea, 562

'Operation Gomorrah': the bombing of Hamburg, 434, 446, 447, 448

'Operation Goodwood': the capture of Caen, 557

'Operation Graffham': an Allied deception plan, 494, 522

'Operation Grayling': bombing of Nuremberg, 512

'Operation Griffin': against Soviet partisans, 352–3

'Operation Grouse': parachutists into Norway, 379

'Operation Gunnerside': an attack on a heavy-water plant in Norway, 404

'Operation Günther': a German anti-partisan sweep, near Smolensk, 441

'Operation Gypsy Baron': a German anti-partisan sweep, in Russia, 428

'Operation Hailstorm': against the Japanese on Truk, 499

'Operation Hamburg': a German anti-partisan sweep, 395

'Operation Hanover': against Soviet partisans, 329

'Operation Harvest Home': a German anti-partisan sweep, 394

'Operation Hare Chase': against Soviet partisans, 399

'Operation Handcuff': a British plan, to seize Rhodes, 461

'Operation Harvest': recovery of wartime aircraft (1975), 741

'Operation Harvest Home II': against Soviet partisans, 398

'Operation Hats': reinforcements to Egypt, 122

'Operation Hermann': a German anti-partisan sweep, 445

'Operation Heydrich': against Czechs and Jews, 332, 336

'Operation Himmler': a border deception, 1

'Operation Hurricane': a German anti-partisan sweep, in Poland, 537

'Operation Hurricane II': against Polish partisans, 542

'Operation Husky': Allied landings on Sicily, 423

'Operation Hydra': air raid on German rocket establishment, 453

'Operation Ibex': German air raids on London and southern England, 492, 495

'Operation Iceberg': the invasion of Okinawa, 655–7

'Operation Indigo': a landing on Iceland, 208

'Operation Infatuate': the seizure of Walcheren Island, 610

'Operation Ironclad': against Madagascar, 313

'Operation Ironside': an Allied deception plan, 494

'Operation Isabella': Spanish and Portuguese coastlines, 189

'Operation Jacob': a German anti-partisan sweep, 460

'Operation Jael': and the Normandy Landings deception plan, 464

'Operation Jericho': against Amiens prison, 499

'Operation Jubilee': a raid on Dieppe, 353–4

'Operation Judgement': against the Italian Fleet, 140

'Operation Kaputt': against the Germans in the Harz Mountains, 666

'Operation Karlsbad': against Soviet partisans, 244

'Operation Keelhaul': forcible repatriation, after the war, 728

'Operation Kennecott': and a deception plan, 347

'Operation Knight's Move': a German attack against Arctic convoys, 339–40

'Operation Knight's Move': a German attempt to seize Tito, 527

'Operation Kottbus': against Soviet partisans, 331

'Operation Kutuzov': a Soviet offensive against Orel, 443

'Operation Landgrab': against the Japanese on Attu Island, 426

'Operation Leopard': landing arms in Algeria, 375

'Operation Lila': seizure of ships at Toulon, 383

'Operation Loincloth': behind Japanese lines in Burma, 404

'Operation Lustre': British troops to Greece, 161

'Operation Magic Flute': against Soviet partisans, 420

'Operation Malaria': against Soviet partisans, 298

'Operation Manna': British landings in Greece, 598

'Operation Manna': Allied food supplies for Holland, 678–9

'Operation Margaret': German occupation of Hungary, 508

'Operation Marita': against Greece, 146

'Operation Market Garden': to seize a bridge on the Rhine (at Arnhem), 593

'Operation Marsh Fever': against Soviet partisans, 305

'Operation Masterdom': to forestall Communists in Indo-China, 722

'Operation Mastiff': medicines by parachute, in the Far East, 721

'Operation Menace': the seizure of Dakar, 127

'Operation Mercury': the invasion of Crete, 176

'Operation Meridian': against Japanese oil refineries, 633

'Operation Millenium': bombing of Cologne, 328

'Operation Mickey Mouse': German seizure of Admiral Horthy, 603

'Operation Milepost': final Anglo-American military aid to Russia, 658

'Operation Mincemeat': on Allied deception plan, 523–4

'Operation Minerva': the rescue of General Giraud, 375

'Operation Mongoose': an American mission behind the lines in Italy, 597

'Operation Munich': a German sweep against Soviet partisans, 308

'Operation Munich II': against Soviet partisans, 383

'Operation Neptune': the cross-Channel armada (5–6 June 1944), 532

'Operation Noah's Ark': against the Germans in northern Greece, 584

'Operation North Pole': against British agents in Holland, 334

'Operation North Sea': against Soviet partisans, 358

'Operation Oak Tree': Hitler's 'liberation' of Mussolini, 447, 461

'Operation Oboe III': liberation of Brunei, 700

'Operation Olympic': the planned invasion of Kyushu Island (Japan), 659, 696, 725

'Operation Olympus': against Greek partisans, 321–2

'Operation Otto': fortifications on the Bug, 129, 181

'Operation Overcast': to 'exploit' German scientific knowledge, 700

'Operation Overlord': the cross-Channel (Normandy) landings, 452,

'Operation Overlord'—contd.
478, 490–1, 497, 522, 533; 'a source of
joy' to Stalin, 536
'Operation Overthrow': a deception
plan, 347
'Operation Panther': an assault on
Cassino, 490
'Operation Paul': mining the Baltic, 78
'Operation Peacock': shooting down
Admiral Yamamoto, 420
'Operation Pedestal': to reinforce
Malta, 352, 353
'Operation Performance': a merchant
ship break-out, 314
'Operation Persecution': landings on
New Guinea, 519
'Operation Plunder': crossing the Rhine
below Cologne, 651–2
'Operation Pointblank': Allied
bombing policy, 427
'Operation Polar Bear': against the
Dodecanese Islands, 465
'Operation Polar Bear II': a German
anti-partisan sweep, 390
'Operation Providence': defence of
northern New Guinea, 341
'Operation Quadrangle': against Soviet
partisans, 361
'Operation Rainbow': against Allied
Arctic convoys, 482
'Operation Rainbow': the scuttling of
German submarines, to avoid
surrender, 689–690
'Operation Ratweek': against the
Germans in Yugoslavia, 584
'Operation Regatta': against Soviet
partisans, 366
'Operation Ring': against the Germans
trapped at Stalingrad, 392
'Operation Royal Flush': an Allied
deception plan, 494
'Operation Rubble': rescue of merchant
ships, 153
'Operation Salmon Trap': against the
Murmansk railway, 206
'Operation Savannah': behind the lines
in France, 162–3
'Operation Sea Lion': the German plan
to invade Britain, 110, 113–4;
abandoned, 130–1
'Operation Seydlitz': a German anti-
partisan sweep, 440
'Operation Shelburne': an Allied escape
line, 495
'Operation Shingle': an Allied landing,
at Anzio, 491
'Operation Silver Fox': against
Murmansk, 206
'Operation Slapstick': the Allied seizure
of Taranto, 460
'Operation Snipe': a German anti-
partisan sweep, 472
'Operation Solo': a deception plan,
347
'Operation Source': against the Tirpitz,
463
'Operation Spark': against the
Germans besieging Leningrad, 392
'Operation Spring': a German anti-
resistance sweep, in France, 515
'Operation Spring Awakening': against
the Red Army as it approached
Vienna, 646
'Operation Stamina': an airlift at
Imphal, 517
'Operation Stone Age': a convoy to
Malta, 381

'Operation Student': the German
occupation of Rome, 447
'Operation Sunrise': against German
warships, 216
'Operation Surgeon': to obtain German
aviation expertise, 702–3
'Operation Swallow': parachutists into
Norway, 379, 404
'Operation Swamp Flower': against
Soviet partisans, 340
'Operation Taxable': an Allied
deception, near Boulogne, 532
'Operation Tidal Wave': against the
Ploesti oil fields, 435, 448
'Operation Tiger': to reinforce Egypt,
175, 180
'Operation Tiger': an invasion exercise,
disrupted, 520
'Operation Titanic': an Allied dummy
parachute drop, 532
'Operation Tooth': decreed by
Himmler, 128
'Operation Torch': Allied landings in
North Africa, in prospect, 347, 371,
384, 375; launched, 375; fails in its
immediate objective, 402
'Operation Totalize': a Normandy
beachhead breakout, 566
'Operation Tractable': Allied drive into
Falaise, 568
'Operation Triangle': against Soviet
partisans, 361
'Operation Trio': against Yugoslav
partisans, 323
'Operation Tungsten': against the
Tirpitz, 513
'Operation Tunnel': to catch a German
merchant ship, 469
'Operation Typhoon': assault on
Moscow, issued, 231; its operational
orders read by British Intelligence,
232; given priority, 232–3; its top
secret orders, to be sent to Stalin, 239;
launched, 241–2
'Operation Typical': a British mission
to Tito, 430
'Operation Ursula': a German anti-
partisan sweep, 402
'Operation Valkyrie': the assassination
of Hitler, 551, 555, 557–8
'Operation Veritable': against the
Germans south of Nijmegen, 639
'Operation Vesuvius': French
liberation of Corsica, 461
'Operation Vigorous': supplies to
Malta, 333
'Operation Wallace': a sweep behind
German lines, 573
'Operation Warzburg': German mine-
laying in the Baltic, 189–90
'Operation Watchtower': against
Guadalcanal, 350
'Operation Wedlock': against the
Kurile Islands, 516
'Operation Weser' ('Weser-Exercise'):
against Scandinavia, 46
'Operation White': against Tito's
partisans, 392, 395
'Operation Wild Duck': a German anti-
partisan sweep, 472
'Operation Wilfred': against Narvik,
48, 49
'Operation Winter Magic': a German
anti-partisan sweep, 390
'Operation Winter Storm': to relieve
German forces at Stalingrad, 383;
launched, 385

'Operation XD': mouth of Scheldt, 61,
67
'Operation Yellow': Hitler's Western
war plan, 20, 37, 38, 58, 121
'Operation Z': the attack on Pearl
Harbour, 261
'Operation Zeppelin': an Allied
deception plan, 494
Opochka (Russia): Germans driven
from, 553
Opoczno (Poland): Jews from,
deceived, and killed, 390
Oppeln (Silesia): Red Army crosses
Oder near, 632
Oppenheim (Rhine): a bridgehead at,
651
Oppenheimer, J. Robert: and the
atomic bomb, 595, 696
Oradea (Transylvania): Red Army
enters, 601
Oradour-sur-Glane (France): a reprisal
action in, 537–8
Oran (Algeria): 106, 107; Allied forces
disembark at, 375, 376
'Orange II': a German cypher, broken,
297
Oranienburg (north of Berlin): and
German atomic energy research, 645;
bombed, 649–50; Jet 'massacre'
above, 661
Orbeli, Professor Iosif: and a brief
celebration, 246
'Orchid': German communication key,
broken, 407
Order No. 227: 'Not one step
backward', 346
Order of the Garter: Hirohito invested
with, 741–2
Order of Glory: created, 473
Order of Lenin: awarded (to four
Englishmen), 233; awarded (to eight
victims of Nazi terror), 281
Order of the Red Banner: awarded, 227
Order of Suvurov: created, 346–7
Order of Victory: created, 473
Ordzhonikidze (Caucasus): German
plans for, 193; Germans halted at, 375
Oregon (United States): a Japanese
submarine off, 336; Japanese bombs
fall on, 359
Orel (Russia): Soviet reinforcements at,
208; captured, 242; Germans to
withdraw to, 274; a battle west of,
284; a German officer court-
martialled and executed at, 332; and
the battle of Kursk, 424, 435, 443;
Soviet partisans active near, 444;
German forces withdraw from, 450
Organization Todt: and the labour
camp system, 46; and a Soviet spy,
150; workers of, drowned, 303; and
German submarine pens, 348; top
secret communications code of,
broken, 366; mobilization for labour
by, in Norway, 406; and the bombing
of the Ruhr dams, 428; and the rocket
bomb, 455; damage done to a depot
of, 490; and a proposed German ruse,
523
Orion (Philippines): a Japanese setback
at, 295
Orion (British cruiser): dive-bombed,
186
Origny (France): Germans reach, 68
Orléans (France): airfield at, bombed,
522; a parachute landing near, 541;
bridges destroyed near, 543; a sweep

near, behind German lines, 573

Orpington (Kent): a rocket bomb falls on, 653

Oroku Peninsula (Okinawa): landing on, 697

Orsha (western Russia): a signals centre, in 201; a defence line on, 201; and a new Soviet weapon, 210; Soviet partisans near, 352–3; battle for, 485; a partisan success at, 544

Ortona (Italy): captured, 482

Oryoku Maru (Japanese freighter): fate of Allied prisoners-of-war on, 618

Osaka (Japan): bombed, 648, 708

Osborn, Sergeant-Major, J. R.: his courage, 280

Oshima, General Count Hiroshi: in Berlin, 165, 312, 492, 522, 530; and the Normandy Landings deception, 555

Osinovets (Lake Ladoga): refugees leave, 253

Osipovichi (White Russia): an anti-partisan sweep at, 394

Oslo (Norway): 45, 52, 53, 54, 58; and a German deception, 172; demonstrations in, 172; state of emergency in, 232; a protest in, 315; a British air raid on, 365; five Englishmen shot near, 394; general mobilization for labour in, 406; Gestapo headquarters in, bombed, 624; Germans lay down arms in, 690; British soldiers on their way to, killed in an air crash, 693; Quisling shot in, 724

Osnabrück (Germany): bombed, 649

Ostapenko, Captain: shot in the back, 624

'Osprey': a top secret German cypher key, broken, 366

Ostend (Belgium): attack on, 74; invasion barges at, 121

Oster, Colonel Hans: warns the West, 25, 38, 52, 53, 58; and possible peace talks, 50; and German atrocities, 57; and the first Bomb Plot against Hitler (March 1943), 412; implicated, 597; hanged, 680

Ostrow (Poland): Jews deported from, 23; Jews shot in, 28

Ostrowek (Poland): fate of Soviet prisoners-of-war in, 373

Ostrowiec (Poland): Jews murdered at, 578

Osuchy (Poland): an anti-partisan sweep at, 542

Oswiecim (Poland): see index entry for Auschwitz

Ota, Admiral Minoru: commits suicide, 697

Othmer, Waldemar: a German spy, 155

Otranto, Straits of: naval battle in, 140

Ott, Major-General Eugen: and Russian resistance, 204

Ottawa (Canada): Churchill in, 284; uranium handed to a Soviet diplomat in, 702

'Otto Line': under construction, 129; completed, 181

Otwock (Poland): Jews deported to their death from, 354; Soviet forces enter, 562

Overveen (Holland): V2 rockets launched from, 608

Ovruch (Russia): Jews murdered at, 233

Owens, Arthur: a double agent, 15–16, 126

Oxford (England): and a possible German invasion, 123

Oyonnax (France): German anti-resistance sweep near, 515

'Oyster': a cypher key, 45

PQ-1: the first British convoy to Russia, 239

PQ-13: a convoy, attacked, 314

PQ-16: a convoy, attacked, 327

PQ-17: attacked, 339–40

PQ-18: attacked, 359

PT-109 (US fast patrol boat): rammed, presumed lost, 449

Pabianice (Poland): battle at, 7

Pacific Ocean: and a German commerce raider, 109, 144; American naval expansion on (July 1940), 111; a British success in (May 1941), 180; the slow but steady reconquest of, (from June 1943), 439

Pacifico, Rabbi Riccardo: deported to Auschwitz, 473

Paderewski, Ignacy: dies, 204

Pag Island (Yugoslavia): occupied by Italy, 225

Pagan Island (Marianas): Japanese on, surrender, 722

Pajor, Antoni: shot, 479

Palatinate, the (Germany): Jews deported from 133

Palatucci, Giovanni: arrested, 585

Palau Islands (Carolines): Americans land on, 592; severity of fighting on, 605–6; Japanese surrender on, 722

Palawan Island (Philippines): fate of prisoners-of-war on, 618

Palembang (Sumatra): Japanese land at, 300; oil refineries at, bombed, 633

Paleohora (Crete): evacuation from 186

Palermo (Sicily): American troops enter, 445

Palestine: troops needed from, 68; danger to, 157; Jews from, in action, 188–9; British to be driven from, 189; and the Mufti of Jerusalem, 265–6; and the approach of Rommel, 337; and a deception scheme in Poland, 391; a volunteer from, parachutes into Yugoslavia, 430; volunteers from, set off for Hungary, 508–9; a volunteer from, parachutes into Italy, 525; Jews from, to serve as a special Allied unit, 576; fate of parachutists from, 608, 611; Jewish survivors wish to go to, 726, 730

Palestine Post: and the repatriation of German prisoners-of-war, 732

Pallas Athena (sculpture): evacuated, 206

Palm Sunday: Yugoslavia invaded on, 170

Palmiry (Poland): executions at, 39, 104

Pan-American Security Zone: Germans to operate in, 276

Panama: 154; Japanese agents at, 238; merchant ships from, attacked, 339

Panama Canal: closed to Japanese shipping, 216

Pancevo (Yugoslavia): Germans driven from, 598–9

Panevezys (Lithuania): German moves near, 194

Pannwitz, General Helmuth von: executed, 732

Pantelleria Island: Allied plans to capture, 426; Allied landing on, 437

Panthéon (Paris): a Resistance hero's remains placed in, 740

Pantheon of the Army: to be built in Berlin, 248

'Panther Line': German defence line on the Eastern Front, 451, 462, 463; Red Army crosses, 473; partisans on an axis of, 485

Papagos, Marshal: contemplates the surrender of Greece, 174

Paradis (France): a massacre at, 76–7; the executioner at, himself executed, 733

Parczew (Poland): Jews from, murdered, 362

Parczew Forest (Poland): hunts against Jews in, 384, 388

Parga (Greece): reprisals in, 450

Park, John Mungo: killed in action, 200

Parkin, Ray: on the 'Railway of Death', 345

Parkinson, Flight Lieutenant: shot down, 65

Parichi (Russia): Jews murdered in, 280–1

Paris: a Polish Government-in-Exile set up in, 18; and the threat of bombing, 19; a peace mission to, 48; Churchill flies to, 67; panic in, 68; a round-up in (to prevent subversion), 68; French troops fall back to, 72; Belgian Government-in-exile in, 77; bombed, 85; battle for, 87, 88; French Government leaves, 91; declared an open city, 92; Germans enter, 94; Hitler visits, 102; German occupation of, 105, 129; an act of defiance in, 140–1; German contempt for culture of, 144; executions in, 147, 221–3, 279; Soviet spies in, 150; an arrest in, 151; art looted from, 162; reprisals in, 175; a novel about the fall of, to be published in Moscow (1941), 177; a German killed in, 225–6; reprisals in, 226, 306, 464; six synagogues dynamited in, 242; Jews in, to wear a yellow star, 328; Jews deported to Auschwitz from, 335, 337, 338, 356, 357, 391–2, 400, 408, 436, 444, 471–2, 546, 562, 571; an American air raid near, 414; an arrest in, 436; 'severe' measure in, 464; anti-Hitler conspirators in, 511; bombing raids on (April 1944), 519; Germans fear parachute landings near, 526; an act of revenge in, 548; and the Bomb Plot (July 1944), 558; a railwaymen's strike in, 567; police in, join Resistance, 568; Germans begin withdrawal from, 571; a final deportation from, 572; liberation of, 573, 478, 580; Governor of, in London, 611; a boat train to, from London, 630; rejoicing in, 690; a traitor shot dead in, 728

Parit Sulong (Malaya): murder at, 293

Parma (Italy): an anti-partisan sweep near, 550

Pärnü (Estonia): Russians acquire right to occupy, 16

Parramatta (Australian sloop): sunk, 262

Parri, Ferruccio: released, 648

Pas de Calais (France): Goering at, 123; and the Normandy Landings deception plans, 492, 494, 515, 523, 530, 532, 537, 540, 542, 546, 557

'Pat Line': a route for Allied escapees and evaders, 177; betrayed, 408; its betrayer, shot dead, 728

Patani (Thailand): a landing at, 276

Patras (Greece): British troops land at, 598

*Patrick Henry* (US merchant ship): launched, 239

Patton, General George S.: and the killing of German prisoners-of-war, 445; and a Normandy deception plan, 492; enters Metz, 614; and 'some unfortunate incidents' in the Ardennes, 627; crosses the Rhine, 651

Patton, Lieutenant J. M. S.: his courage, 126

Paul, Prince Regent of Yugoslavia: support for, 157; joins the Axis, 165

Paulus, General Friedrich von: at Stalingrad, 381–2, 382; trapped, 387, 388; refuses to surrender, 391–2; asks to surrender, 397; surrenders, 398; repercussion of Hitler's 'no retreat' order to, 410

Pavelić, Ante: ruler of Croatia, 172; awards German officers, 339; visits Hitler, 392; a protest to, 409; 'let us fall as true heroes', 686

Pavlov, General G. D.: his warning, 158–9; shot, 217

Pavlovgrad (southern Russia): Russians retake, 405

Pawiak Prison (Warsaw): Poles from, shot, 328; Poles tortured to death in, 413

Pawlowski, Father: shot, 22

Pawlowski, Leon: sentenced to death, 183

Payot, Max: recalls a woman's death, 573

Pearl Harbour (Hawaii): Japanese plans for, 140; a warning concerning, 154; information about, sought by Japan, 164, 238; plans to attack, go ahead, 249, 253, 253–4, 268; not mentioned, during a general warning, 262; warships to be sent away from, 263; attacked, 271, 272–3; relief to Wake Island sent from, 282; Japanese warships which had been at, sunk, 303, 330; and the evolution of bombing as a method of war, 432–3; the Japanese Striking Force commander at, has himself killed, 553; the last surviving Japanese warship from, put out of action, 612; the twenty-fourth (of twenty-five) Japanese naval vessels at, sunk, 709; a veteran of, sinks the *Indianapolis*, 709; retrospective discussions concerning, 737–8; a naval survivor of, sunk (1972), 742

*Peary* (US destroyer): sunk, 302

Pecs (Hungary): Red Army enters, 615

Pechersky, Alexander: leads a revolt, 467

Pedang (Sumatra): Japanese surrender at, 725

Peenemünde (Baltic Coast): rocket experiments at, 333, 366–7, 388, 434; bombed, 449, 476; a rocket from, shown to Hitler, 479; a rocket falls on Sweden from, 539; scientists leave, 643

Pegu (Burma): Japanese enter, 306

Peiper, SS Lieutenant-Colonel Joachim: and the Malmédy massacre, 620

Peira Cava (France): young men murdered in, 584

Peklina (Russia): Soviet partisans active near, 366

Pelczynski, General Tadeusz: and the Warsaw uprising, 561

Peleliu Island (Palaus): battle for, 592

Peloponnese (Greece): Germans withdrawing from, 596

Peltz, General: and Germany's lack of aircraft fuel, 622

Penang (Malaya): bombed, 278

Penicillin: its use to be extended, 552

*Pensacola* (US heavy cruiser): damaged, 384

Pentagon, the (Washington): and the atomic bomb, 696

Pentonville Prison (London): a spy hanged in, 554; five German prisoners-of-war hanged in, 724

People's Army (in Poland): revolts, in Warsaw, 562

People's Army (in Germany): established by Hitler (September 1944), 597

*People's Avenger* (a Soviet partisan newspaper): 298

Perbal (Hungary): Germans encircled at, 640

Percival, Lieutenant-General Arthur Ernest: in Singapore, surrenders, 299; in Tokyo Bay, witnesses Japan's surrender, 722

Perekop (southern Russia): occupied, 239

Peretz, Dr. Aharon: and the fate of Jewish deportees to Kovno, 263

Périers (Normandy): battle at, 553, 562

Périgueux (France): sabotage near, 543

Perpignan (France): prisoners-of-war rescued from, 360

Persia (Iran): *see index entry for* Iran

'Persian Corridor': and aid to Russia, 296

Persian Gulf: British troops land at head of, 174–5; and the German advance into the Caucasus, 347–8; and American aid to Russia, 468

*Perth* (Australian cruiser): sunk, 303

Pertschuk, Captain Maurice: hanged, 655

Pescara (Italy): Italian Royal Family leaves through, 459

Peshki (near Moscow): Germans reach, 262

Pesker, Meir: liberated at Ebensee, 688

Petacci, Clara: shot, 676

Pétain, Marshal Philippe: and the fall of France, 81, 91, 97; and the armistice, 98; establishes his Government at Vichy, 106; breaks off relations with Britain, 107–8; negotiates with Japan, 108; Japanese pressure on, 111; abrogates the pre-war race hatred laws, 127; Hitler's meeting with, 134

Peter III, Tsar: the 'Prussomaniac', 489

Peterson, Captain: attacks an invasion exercise, 520

Petrishchevo (near Moscow): an execution at, 265

Petrovac (Dalmatian Coast): a British agent lands at, 236

Petrozavodsk (Lake Onega): Finnish troops reach, 241; Red Army

liberates, 548

Petsamo (Finland): overrun, 34; German war supplies to, 214; Germans driven from 603

Petter, Robert: hanged, 129

Peter the Great: treasures of, evacuated, 206

Petzel, General: protests, 29

Pfanmüller, Dr.: and euthanasia, 11, 379

Pfister, SS Major: orders an execution, 578

Pforzheim (Germany): bombed, 644, 645

Philip of Greece, Prince (later Duke of Edinburgh): in action, 148, 166, 185; his mother saves Jews, 465; on board ship in Tokyo bay, 722; and Hirohito's visit to London (1971), 741; and Hirohito's funeral (1989), 744–5

Philippines, the: and Japan, 216, 253; a warning concerning, 262; a possible attack on, 263; attacked, 271, 275; MacArthur leaves, declaring, 'I shall return', 307; sabotage activities forbidden in, 391; resistance in, 485; preparations for liberation of, 592, 596, 601; invasion of, 604–5, 606; becomes independent, 730; American post-war help for, 730

Phillips, Malcolm: trapped, 125

Phillips, Myrtle: trapped, 125

*Phoenix* (US light cruiser): a survivor of Pearl Harbour, sunk (in 1972), 742

Piacenza (Italy): an anti-partisan sweep near, 550

Piasnica (Poland): and euthanasia, 20

Piatnitsa (near Moscow): Russians driven back to, 262

'Pigs' (manned torpedoes): in action, 216, 280

Picasso, Pablo: the death of his godson, 506

Pickard, Squadron Leader (later Group Captain) Charles: and a war film, 216; killed in the Amiens raid, 499

Picotte, Mrs Caryl: her brother's death, her husband's rescue, 635

Pierrepoint, Albert: hangs war criminals, 731

'Pike': a cypher key, 45

Pikule (Poland): a reprisal at, 537

Pilar-Bagac Road (Philippines): Americans withdraw to, 293; Japanese attack, 294–5

Pilsen (Czechoslovakia): armaments works at, bombed, 143, 427; a clandestine mission near, 283; German troops still in action near (11 May 1945), 693

Pilva (Russia): Jews murdered in, 235

Pimenov, Colonel: and the arrest of Polish negotiators, 686

Pindus Mountains (Greece): a British officer reaches (1943), 461–2

*Pinguin* (German commerce raider): sets sail, 101; its successes, 169; sunk, 180

Pingyanchen (Manchuria): fighting at, 717

'Pink': a German Air Force key, broken, 287

Pinsk (White Russia): a partisan success near, 544; Soviet forces enter, 554

Pinsche, Wernher: brought to Britain, 702–3

Piotrkow (Poland): Jews murdered at,

5, 9; indignities at, 13; Jews deported to their deaths from, 369
Piraeus (Greece): 161, 170
Pirgos (Crete): Germans driven back at, 186
Pisa (Italy): Germans driven from 581; an Allied line at, 596
Piskarevsky Cemetery (Leningrad): bodies on the road to, 285
Piskopi (Aegean Sea): German troops on, surrender, 692
Pitomnik (Stalingrad): Russians overrun, 392
Pius XII, Pope: protests, 39–40; warns, 58–9; protest again, 550
Place, Lieutenant: his act of bravery, 463
Place de la Concorde (Paris): Germans reach, 94
Placentia Bay (Newfoundland): 222
Plakias (Crete): evacuation from, 186
'Plan Bunbury': an act of German sabotage (in fact, a British deception), 453
'Plan Guy Fawkes': fictitious sabotage, 16
'Plan Jael': a deception plan, for the Normandy landings, 492
Planck, Erwin: executed in Berlin, 632
Planck, Max: his son executed, 632
Plaszow (Poland): fate of Poles at, 37; a concentration camp set up at, 485
Platteau, L. C.: his protest, 373
Plewman, Elaine: shot, 590
Pljevlja (Yugoslavia): hostages killed at, 323
Ploesti (Roumania): oil wells in, and Germany, 124, 142, 143, 159; bombed, 333, 435, 448; barges from, and the mining of the Danube, 515; Hitler orders air units at, to bomb Bucharest, 574; Soviet forces reach, 583
Plötzensee Prison (Berlin): hangings at, 566, 581, 583, 585, 589, 604, 612, 620, 627, 632, 637, 660
Pohl, Oswald: hanged, 735
Plouha (France): and an Allied escape line, 495
Pluto: and plutonium, 167
Plutonium: and heavy water, 319; ready for shipment, 623
Plymouth (England): bombed, 178
Po River (Italy): Allies cross, 672
Pogonion (Greece): hostages from, killed, 527
Poitiers (France): sabotage near, 551
Pola (Italy): bombed, 500–1
Poland: German invasion of, 1–14; German-Soviet partition of, 16; German occupation of, 22; expulsions from, 23; executions in (in 1934), 4–9, 16, 22, 24, 32, 36, 40, 46, 47; deportations from, 40, 152; Jews of, and Madagascar, 100; Government-in-exile of, reaches London, 101; German plans for, 105; forces of, in Britain, 113, 115–6; troops from, in Greece, 176; forced labourers from, 299, 427; American money for resistance in, 412; the Jewish problem in, 'fundamentally cleared up', 421; a resistance group in, and its fate, 474; its post-war frontiers, and the Allies, 488, 496–7, 554, 559; troops from, in Italy, 522, 526; an anti-partisan action in, 542; a V2 rocket, smuggled to

England from, 561; troops from, in Normandy, 566, 568, 572– 573, 574; the political future of, and the Red Army's advance, 559, 572, 627, 658, 679–80, 686; pilots from, aid Warsaw, 596; a German act of terror in (January 1945), 629; deportations from, to Russia, 646; forces of, in Italy, 660, 669; slave labourers from, liberated, 674; its future, discussed at Potsdam, 706–7; Germans in, to be 'removed', 710; new frontiers of, 710–11; in the Soviet bloc, 723; Jews murdered in, after the war, 730; receives reparations, 739; wartime death toll of, 746; see also index entries for Poles, Warsaw
'Poland Has Not Yet Perished': a Pole executed for singing, 47
Poles: murdered (1939), 4, 5, 6, 7, 8, 9, 19, 22, 24, 27, 32, 36; their cruel fate (1940), 37, 39, 40, 43, 46, 56, 127, 144; executions of (in 1941), 162, 168, 298; (in 1942), 299, 308, 309–10, 322, 328, 332, 336, 354–5, 369, 379, 384, 388–9, 389; (in 1943), 389, 443, 479, 480, 482; (in 1944), 496, 498, 505, 512, 537, 554, 584; (in 1945), 629; to be 'slaves)', 19, 133, 354; expelled, 22, 23, 27; rules for, 23–4; future of, as seen from Berlin, 29, 79, 105; to be deported to Germany, 40; 'bludgeoned', 69; expelled from parts of Warsaw, 129; in action (in France), 75, 86; in action (in Norway), 78, 83; embarked from France, 98; in action (during the Battle of Britain), 124; in action (against Boulogne), 125; against Germany, 144, 174; prisoners-of-war, in Germany, 151; and a British agent, landed in France (1941), 177; killed, 'for helping Jews', 308; warned not to help Jews, 337–8; sentences on, as 'asocials', 361–2; their fate, for helping Jews, 384, 398, 435, 505; medical experiments on, 386; fate of, for sheltering Soviet partisans, 466–7; and a deportee to Auschwitz, her last words, 475, killed, by Allied bombs, 591; arrested (by the Russians), 654; a 'slayer of', hanged, 731
Polish Committee for National Liberation: announced in Moscow, 559
Polish National Council: established, by Stalin, 488, 497, 572
Pölitz (Germany): bombed, 577
'Polonism': to be eradicated, 27
Polotsk (White Russia): 201, 214; partisans near, 309, 331; an anti-partisan sweep near, 435, 516; a partisan success at, 544
Poltava (Ukraine): mass murder at, 253; Hitler visits, 339; Germans evacuate, 463; American bombers use, 530, 593
Polyarnoe (North Russia): British submarines at, 223
Pomerania (Germany): fate of mental patients in, 39; Red Army reaches, 634; a Soviet offensive in, 640; Hitler advised to pull back from 643; transferred to Poland, 710
Ponar (near Vilna): murder of Jews at, 213, 217, 219, 249, 331; a revolt at, 516
Poniatowa (Poland): Soviet prisoners-of-war murdered at, 389

Ponza Island (Italy): Mussolini seeks refugee on, 446
Pook, ss Lieutenant-Colonel Hermann: and 'Operation Tooth', 128
Pooley, Private Albert: eye-witness to a massacre, 76
Pope (US destroyer): sunk, 304
Popitz, Johannes: hanged, 637
Popov, Colonel: in Athens, 623
Porchunov, Major: and supplies for Leningrad, 261
'Porcupine': German communications key, broken, 395–6
Port Arthur (Manchuria): Russians occupy, 720
Portal, Sir Charles: and the German shortage of fuel oil, 535; and bombing support for the Russian advance, 636
Port Blair (Andaman Islands): a clandestine mission to, 394
Port-en-Bessin (France): a British raid on, 360
Porteous, Captain Pat: at Dieppe, 354
Portland (Maine): the last Liberty Ship launched at, 725
Portland Bill (England): radar station at, attacked, 116
Port Moresby (New Guinea): Japanese attack as, 322; Australians advance from, 341; Australians fall back to, 345, 355, 361; American troops reach, 361; Japanese pushed further back from, 375; Japanese try to reach, 399; Japanese air raid on, 419
Port Swettenham (Malaya): abandoned, 288
Port Rafti (Greece): evacuation from, 176
Port Sudan (Anglo-Egyptian Sudan): bombed, 90; an Italian naval defeat on way to, 168
Portugal: and Jewish emigration, 187; Hitler's plan for, 189
Porvoo (Finland): attack on, repulsed, 34
Potenza (Italy): a commando raid near, 157
Potsdam (near Berlin): fire engines rushed from, 478; a proposed defence line to, 671; Red Army reaches, 674; the Big Three conference at, 702, 704, 705–9, 710–1
Potsdam Declaration: agreed to by the Allies, 707–8; issued to Japan, 708–9; rejected, 709; accepted, 716; broadcast by the Emperor, 717
Potsdam Station (Berlin): Russians reach, 679
Povazska Bystrica (Slovakia): uprising in, 583
Powell, Lewis F.: and the North African landings, 375
Powers, Lieutenant John James: a hero, 322–3
Poznan (Poland): a battle near, 7; a concentration camp at, 14; Poles deported from, 23; Jews deported from, 35; and the future of the Poles in, 127; Poles sentenced to death in, 163, 183; Himmler tells of German 'page of glory' in speech at, 465–6; Hitler speaks in, of the fate of the Jews, 494; encircled, 634; German troops in, hold out, 639; surrenders, 643; an execution in, 729
Praeger, Captain Ralph R.: sabotage activities by, forbidden, 391

Praga (Poland): Jews expelled from, 130; and the Warsaw uprising, 566, 567; Red Army reaches, 591–2

Prague (Czechoslovakia): 7; leaflets dropped over, 48; Jews deported from, 245, 266, 332; assassination of Heydrich in, 331–2, 334; death sentences in, 365; to be liberated by the Red Army, not by the Americans, 680; uprising in, 690; in the 'Soviet sphere', 728; a public hanging in, 729; a former prisoner, hanged in, 732

*President Doumer* (merchant ship): sunk, 373

Presov (Slovakia): Red Army enters, 632

Prestissimo, Colonel: captured, 187

Pretzsch (Germany): and the 'Final Solution', 188

Price, Lieutenant-Commander Hugh: his award, 45

Prien, Günther: sinks *Royal Oak*, 21; sinks *Arandora Star*, 105; attacks Atlantic convoys, 132; sunk with his submarine, 162

Primrose, Lieutenant: his cruel fate, 462

*Prince of Wales* (British battleship): reaches Singapore, 268; sunk, 276

*Princeton* (US carrier): sunk, 606

*Prinz Eugen* (German heavy cruiser): in the Atlantic, 185; an attack on, 216; its dash to the North Sea, 300; torpedoed, 302–3; used in a post-war atomic test, 729–30

Pripet Marshes (western Russia): partisans near, 383; Red Army reaches, 489; and Poland's post-war frontiers, 497; front line static at, 506

Prisoners-of-war: shot after capture (Poles), 6, 27; indignities against (Poles and Jews), 13; fate of (Poles), 37, 53, 731; liberated (British), 42; at Dunkirk (British), 83; on the Dieppe-Paris road (French), 87; after the fall of France (French), 101, 134, 226; taken by Greece in Albania (Italians), 143; aid to (Poles), 151; taken in North Africa (Italians), 153; cross the Atlantic (Germans), 154; a German, escapes, 154, 172; Yugoslavs, 174; an escape line for, 177; cruel fate of (Soviet), 200, 202, 210, 228, 230, 243, 260, 266, 281, 282, 298, 399, 373, 389, 460–1, 475, 483, 485, 496, 503, 524, 559, 585, 622, 630, 669, 683; and the building of the new Berlin, 260; not taken, in Hong Kong, 280, 282; escapes of (Allied), 288, 326, 370, 475, 510; executed (by the Japanese), 290, 293, 297, 302, 305, 316, 318, 353, 358, 417, 435, 466, 468–9, 635, 711, 725; forced labour of, in the Far East, 336, 345, 417, 462, 470; death of, at sea, 338, 366; to be manacled (British and Canadian), 367; taken, in Tunisia (German and Italian), 426; recruited for Germany (British), 430; killed, in Sicily (Germans), 445; drowned off Greece (Italians), 460; mass movement of (Allied and Italians), 460; fate of, in Greece (Italians), 461–2; acts of defiance by, 467, 470; killed at Majdanek (Jews), 473; killed at Borki (Italians), 475; at Plaszow (Soviet), 485; rescued (Allied), 527; killed, off Crete (Italians), 534; killed in Normandy (Canadians), 535, 542,

(British), 539; paraded in Moscow (Germans), 556; a mass breakout by (Japanese), 564; killed by Allied bombing (British), 577; killed in reprisal for an Allied bombing raid (Americans), 578; machine gunned in Paris (Germans), 580; shot in revenge (Germans), 582; killed in Dachau (Russians), 585; drowned after an American submarine attack (Americans), 588; their fate while on the *Oryoku Maru* (American, Dutch and British), 618; mass murder of (American), 618; accidental death of by Allied bombs (Allied), 626–7; shot in the Ardennes (Germans), 627; and the mass evacuation of Upper Silesia (British), 631; save a Jewish girl from a 'death march' (British), 633; rescue of (American), 635, 643; mass executions of (Australian and British), 635, on the Rhine (Germans), 648; two Channel Islanders die, for sheltering (Soviet), 664; liberated (Allied), 666; killed, while returning home (British), 692; machine gunned on Okinawa (Japanese), 695; killed in Allied bombardment (Americans), 696; returned to the Soviet Union (Russian, Cossacks), 699; and a death march in North Borneo (Australians), 702; and the decision to use the atomic bomb on Hiroshima, 710; executed (Americans), 711; liberated (Allied, in Japanese camps), 718, 721, 722; remain in captivity (German), 721; used in a new conflict (Japanese), 722–3; hanged in London (Germans), 724; resist repatriation (Russians), 728; repatriated (Germans), 730, 732, 738; build a railway (Germans), 730; persecutors of, brought to trial, 731; and a route of pilgrimage, in Thailand, 738–9; and a war crimes trial (Russians), 741; conditions on a Japanese-held island recalled by (Allied), 745

Probst, Christoph: his courageous protest, 404

*Procida* (Italian fuel ship): sunk, 262

Prokhorovka (Kursk): battle at, 443

Proletarskaya (Russia): Germans reach, 346

Proskurov (Russia): 205; Jews killed in, 218; Germans driven from, 511

'Prosper' (an escape and evasion route): its organizer hanged, 651

*Provence* (French battleship): sunk, 108

Providence: Hitler's praise for, 26; Hitler possibly 'selected by', 743

Prussic acid: used to kill Soviet prisoners-of-war, 230

Pruth, River: Germans forced back across, 506; Red Army establishes Front on, 511

Pruszkow (Warsaw): arrests in, 654; repercussions of arrests in, 686

Pruzhany (Poland): overrun, 199

Pryce-Jones, David: observes a war crimes trial, 741

Pryor, General: against a cease-fire, 54

Przemysl (Poland): Jews killed at, 8–9; Jews deported to their deaths from, 337–8

Pskov (Russia): Germans enter, 208; Soviet partisans near, 209; Jews murdered at, 213; partisans active

near, 346; Red Army enters, 559

Puerto Princesa (Philippines): fate of American prisoners-of-war at, 618; American landing at, 644–5

Pulford, Air Vice Marshal C. W.: dies, 307

Pulkovo Heights (Leningrad): naval guns at, 228

Pultusk (Poland): Jews deported from, 23

Purkayev, General: and the eve of war, 194

'Purple' (Japanese coding machine): reaches Britain, 154; becomes part of the 'Ultra' system, 425

Purple Heart: awarded, 611

Purvis, Arthur: 25, 65–6, 67, 81, 139; killed, 223

Purvis, George: his courage, 126

Pushkin (Leningrad): captured, 233, liberated, 490

Putney (London): a 'Flying Bomb' at, 542

Puttkammer, Lieutenant Karl von: Hitler confides in, 125

Pyadyshev, General: shot, 216

Pyle, Ernie: killed, 668

Pyatigorsk (Caucasus): Jews murdered at, 359

Pyrenees, the: 103, 133; an escape line over, 288; an escape line over, broken, 393; further escapes over, 404, 455

QP-13 (Arctic convoy): attacked, 340

Quebec (Canada): Allied strategic decisions made at, 452, 454; and the future of Germany, 592

*Queen Elizabeth* (British battleship): badly damaged, 280

Quetta (India): an American aircrew reach, 324

Quezon, President Manuel: leaves Luzon, 302

'Quince': the main SS communications key, broken, 353

Quincuan Point (Philippines): Japanese land at, 295

*Quincy* (US heavy cruiser): sunk, 350

Quisling, Vidkun: in Norway, 53, 54, 56, 406; and the future of Britain, 103; shot, 724

Rabaul (Bismarck Archipelago): Japanese bomb, 288; battle for, 293; prisoners-of-war massacred near, 297; bombed, 302; fate of prisoners-of-war captured at, 338; the planned recapture of, 439; Japanese remain at, 481; American bombing of, 495

Rabi (New Guinea): Japanese landing at, 355

Rabinovitch, Alec ('Arnaud'): parachuted into France, 504

Racine, Mila: killed by an Allied bomb, 664

Radio Bremen: a broadcast over, 115

Radio Brussels: a false victory announcement over, 586

Radio Moscow: and Poland, 559; and Warsaw, 562, 581; and 'a Luxemburg palace' for Nazi war criminals, 703

Radio Paris: transmitter of, blown up, 324

Radom (Poland): fate of Jews from, 113; forced labourers taken from, 129; a Jew from, murdered after the war, 730

Radomyshl (Russia): Jews murdered in, 235

Radoshkovichi (Russia): an anti-partisan sweep near, 383

Radovel (Russia): Red Army captures, 486

Radzievskii, Major-General: east of Warsaw, 562

Radziwillow (Poland): Jews killed in, 328

Radzymin (Poland): Soviet forces enter, 562

Raeder, Admiral Erich: 99; and the invasion of Britain, 113–4, 123; and Hitler's plans for Trondheim, 196; on the Channel Coast, 299

Rafaelson, Paul: executed, 732

Rafina (Greece): evacuation from, 176

Rafz (Switzerland): bombed in error, 644

'Railway of Death' (Thailand-Burma): 336, 345, 417, 437–8, 462, 470, 477; accidental deaths on, caused by Allied bombs, 626–7; bridges on, bombed, 701; a survivor of, liberated in Japan, 718–9; becomes a route of pilgrimage, 738–9; a protest, by a former prisoner-of-war on, 741–2; the death toll on, 745

Rakov (White Russia): Jews murdered at, 297

Rambouillet (near Paris): a French armoured unit reaches, 578

Ramcke, General Hermann: captured, 594

Ramillies (British battleship): damaged, 330

Ramle Prison (Israel): Eichmann hanged in, 739

Ramsay. Vice-Admiral Bertram: and Dunkirk, 75

'Ramsay': a Soviet spy's codename, 45

Ramsbottom-Isherwood, Wing Commander: in North Russia, 223, 233

Ramsey, Norman F.: and the atomic bomb, 447

Ranau (North Borneo): a death march reaches, 702

Rangoon (Burma): bombed, 281; evacuated, 306; plans to capture, 682

Raphael: paintings by, evacuated, 206

Rapido River (Italy): Allies approach, 490; Americans cross, 495; Maoris forced back over, 498

Raritan (New Jersey): American aid sails from, 91–2

Rasche, Siegfried: and the defection of Italy, 448

Rascher, Dr Sigmund: medical experiments by, 184, 305

Rashid Ali al Gailani: seizes power, 168; British moves against, 174–5; besieges Habbaniya, 178; continues to hold Baghdad, 182; surrenders, 187

Rastenburg (East Prussia): Hitler's headquarters in (June-December 1941), 199, 207, 208–9, 209, 212, 213–4, 219, 221, 224, 225, 230, 233, 235, 242, 243, 244, 245, 247, 249, 253, 266, 273, 275, 279, 280, 283, 284; (January-December 1942), 295, 299, 310, 312, 315, 328, 329, 338, 341; Hitler leaves (July 1942), 343; Hitler returns to (November 1942), 381, 383, 387, 389, 400, 412, 427, 441, 444, 447, 462, 477, 479, 553–4, 554–5, 557–8, 582, 597; first snow flurries at (1941), 242; snow

reports reach, 245; Hitler leaves, for 'Werewolf', 343; an attempt to kill Hitler on his way to, 412; Mussolini flown to, 461; Red Army draws closer to, 478, 556–7; bomb plot at, 557–8; Mussolini at, 559; British bombers strike near, 583; Red Army approaches, 604; Hitler remains at, 606; Hitler leaves, never to return to, 613; Soviet forces enter, 633; acquired by Poland, 711

Rauca, Helmut: extradicted, 734

Rauter, General Hanns Albin: opens fire on strikers, in Amsterdam, 158; killed in error, 646

Ravensbrück (north of Berlin): deaths at, 332; a British agent sent to, 538; a deportation to, from France, 572; mass evacuations to, 632; an execution at, 634; an unsuccessful escape from, 655; deaths at, 664; a 'death march' from, 664; and an evacuation to Sweden, 669; a further execution at, 673

Ravna Gora (Yugoslavia): a focus of revolt at, 182

Rawalpindi (British armed merchant cruiser): sunk, 30

Rawicz (Poland): a concentration camp at, 504; Soviet troops reach, 632

Reading (England): and a possible German invasion, 123

Récébédou (France): Jews at, 310

'Red Arrow' (railway train): resumes services, 510

Red Banner: flies over the Reichstag, 681

Red Cross: (International Committee of the Red Cross): its Conventions ignored, 461–2; a protest by, 550; the flag, no protection (to German soldiers), 621; an approach to, by Himmler, 643; and a 'death march' from Ravensbrück, 664; and Himmler's attempt to impress the Western Allies, 669; reaches Mauthausen, 670; trucks of, on the road to Theresienstadt, 691; pleas for help from, bring 'hysterical reaction' (from the Japanese), 745

Red Fort (Delhi): trials at, 725

'Red Fox' (Michael Sinclair): killed, 597

'Red Orchestra': Stalin's spy ring, 233; the destruction of, 334

Red Square (Moscow): Soviet troops march to the Front from, 254; German military banners paraded in, 701

Reder, SS Major Walter: an anti-partisan sweep commanded by, 597

Rees (Rhine): Allies cross Rhine at, 652

Regensburg (Germany): Messerschmitt works in, bombed, 453, 500–1

Reggio di Calabria (Italy): bombed, 425; Allies land at, 457

Reggio Emilia (Italy): partisan action near, 539

Reichenau, General Walther von: enters Brussels, 68; on the Eastern Front, 23; and the shooting of prisoners-of-war, 247

Reichstadt, Duc de: Hitler returns remains of, 102

Reichstag (Berlin): Hitler speaks of 'duties' in, 320; Soviet soldiers reach, 680–1; Red Banner flies over, 681

Reichwein, Adolf: and the opposition to Hitler, 544; hanged, 604

Reik Haviva: captured, 608

Reimann, Bruno: killed, 25

Reims (France): German's reach, 91; Americans reach, 582; and the final German surrender, 689, 690

Reinhart, General Hans: dismissed, 633

Reiss, Raffi: killed, 611

Reinberger, Major Helmut: crashes, 38

Reitsch, Hanna: proposes a 'Suicide Group', 504; reaches Hitler's bunker, 673

Rejewski, Marian: and Enigma, 39

Remagen (Rhine): American forces reach, 646–7; unsuccessful German counter-attack at, 649; bridgehead at, extended, 650; further bridgeheads south of, 651

Rembrandt: the fate of his paintings, 130, 162, 206

Remer, Major Otto Ernst: declines to support conspirators, 558; his reward, 559

Rendova Island (Pacific Ocean): American landing on, 439; bombed by the Japanese, 449

Rennell Island (Solomon Islands): a naval action off, 399

Rennes (France): Canadian troops pass through, 95; Germans occupy, 100; a telephone link to, cut, 529; Canadian prisoners-of-war accidentally killed near, 539; an operation begins from, behind German lines, 573

Republic of Carnia (Italy): an anti-partisan sweep at, 600

'Republic of Palik' (Russia): an attack on, 331

Republic of Salò (Italy): executions in, 488

Repulse (British cruiser): reaches Singapore, 268; sunk, 276

Resolution (British battleship): the rescue, 58; hit, 127

Rethondes (France): armistice signed at, 100

Reuben James (US destroyer): torpedoed, 251

Reynaud, Paul: becomes Prime Minister of France, 50; proposes to bomb Soviet oil fields, 50, 51; in London, 54; and the German breakthrough at Sedan, 66, 67; and the fall of France, 81, 83, 87, 89, 90, 91, 97, 101; and the French Fleet, 106

Reza Pahlavi, Shah of Iran: abdicates, 226

Reznik, Josef: his grim task, 475

Rheinburg (Germany): decoy fires at, 308

Rheine (Ruhr): bombed, 649

Rheydt (Ruhr): bombed, 595

Rhineland, the (Germany): and Hitler's 'mission', 11; industrial targets in, bombed, 189; Jews deported from, 254

Rhine River (Germany): plan to drop mines in, 51; mines dropped in, 61, 64; and the bombing of Rotterdam, 65; Germans cross, at Colmar, 97; Allies seek to seize a bridge over, at Arnhem, 593; Himmler given command on, 614; German troops move westward from, 616; military operations against, 639; American troops reach, 644; American troops

Rhine River—contd.
cross, 646–7; further crossings of, 651, 651–2
Rhodes (Dodecanese islands): 161; Germans seize, 461; Germans use, as a base of attack, 472; Jews of, deported to Auschwitz, 559–60, 582; the German garrison on, surrenders, 682
Rhône River (France): and the French Resistance, 398
Ribar, Ivo-Lola: killed, 455
Ribar, Jurica: killed, 455
Ribbentrop, Joachim von: 13, 16; a 'resounding slap' for, 137; in his air-raid shelter, with Molotov, 141; a telegram from, sent from Tokyo to Moscow, 161; and Japan, 206, 312; and the Jews, 363; arrested, 700; hanged, 731
Richelieu (French battleship): put out of action, 109; at Dakar, 127
Ride, Lieutenant-Colonel Lindsay: heads an escape organization, 326
Rieff, Georges: escapes from a deportation train, 310
Riegner, Gerhart: reports killing of Jews 'under consideration', 351
Riga (Latvia): Germans enter, 206; and the fate of Jewish deportees to, 249, 266; Jews killed by gas vans in, 331; Red Army enters, 602
Riga, Treaty of (1921): and Poland's post-war borders, 497
Rimini (Italy): an Allied line at, 596
Ringelblum, Emanuel: in Warsaw, 130, 144, 145, 152, 257, 279, 329; his death 'prepaid', 329; and the truth about Chelmno, 330–1; 'our toils ... have not been in vain', 337; betrayed, and killed, 508; his hidden documents, discovered, 734
Riom (France): an escape from, 468
Risplinger, Sergeant Harold S.: dies in the desert, 414
Ritter, Dr Julius: killed, 464
Ritz, ss Lieutenant Hans: an eye-witness to mass murder, 480
Rivesaltes (France): Jews at, 310
Rizzo, Anna: executed, 673
Rizzo, Edward: lands in France (1941), 177
Rjukan (Norway): a sabotage objective, 379
Roatta, General: and the Italian armistice, 448
Robert E. Peary (merchant ship): constructed in four days, 239
Roberts, Colonel Harold C.: killed, 700
Roberts (British monitor ship): and the battle for Caen, 557
Robinson, Lieutenant William D.: and the link-up of American and Soviet forces, 673
Robota, Roza: 'I shall not talk', 600
Robotnik (Poland): the editor of, killed, 104
Roccacastrada (Italy): fate of a girl from, 525
Rochais, Alexander: arrested, later killed, 436
Rodakino (Crete): General Kreipe sails from, 519
Rodina (Russian passenger ship): sunk, 340
Rodney (British battleship): bombards Caen, 553

Roenne, Colonel Alexis von: and the Normandy deception, 537
Roetgen (Germany): Allies reach, 590
Rogachev (Russia): 208; Soviet partisans near, 402
Rohland, Corporal: shot, 175
Rokitno (Volhynia): Red Army enters, 488
Rokossovsky, General Konstantin: on the eve of war, 6; in the battle for Moscow, 262; and the battle for Stalingrad, 391–2; receives British medals, 702
Roma (Italian battleship): sunk, 460
Rome (Italy): a peace mission to, 48; to be a target, 136; marshalling yards in, to be bombed, 435; bombed, 445; Mussolini forced to leave, 446; German occupation of, 447; planned Allied landing near, cancelled, 459; Germans occupy, 460; Jews deported to Auschwitz from, 467; German defence of, 472, 488; Allied move to capture, 491, 509; reprisals in, 510; Allied advance to, 526; Allies enter, 531
Romford (London): rocket bomb deaths at, 641
Rommel, General Erwin: and Hitler's 'resolution', 29; and the coming war in the West, 30; and Hitler's 'genius', 56; on the Western Front, 63, 66, 67, 68, 69, 70, 73, 80, 85, 88; reaches the Channel Coast, 90; at St Valery-en-Caux, 92; at Cherbourg, 100; at Rennes, 100; advancing towards Spain, 103; sees Hitler, 156, 366, 410, 549; in North Africa, 157, 165, 168, 169, 170, 175, 177; enters Egypt, 178; in Egypt, 183, 187; an attack against, fails, 192; and 'wonderful news' from Russia, 244; reinforcements to, attacked, 254; driven back (November-December 1941), 259, 262, 265, 279; takes the offensive, 293, 299; hopes war will end in 1942, 324–5; renews the offensive, 327, 333, 334; retakes Tobruk, 335; reaches El Alamein, 337, 338; checked at Ruweisat Ridge, 341; supply lines under attack, 352; a renewed offensive by, 357–8; and El Alamein, 371, 374; ordered to 'stand fast', 374; pushed steadily westwards, 376, 378; his advice rejected by Hitler, 383; continuing fuel oil shortage of, 387, 388, 394, 406; driven from Tripoli, 396; forced back to Tunisia, 397, 402; and a 'ray of light' from the East, 407; finds Hitler 'depressed', 410; recuperates in Germany, 415; sent to Greece, 424; blames the Italians, 426; to be sent to Italy, 450; to 'pounce on Italy later', 445; and the fall of Mussolini, 447; and the bombing of Hamburg, 450; and the cross-Channel defences, 523, 526, 528; returns to Germany (5 June 1944), 532; returns to France (6 June 1944), 534, 538; and the 'Flying Bomb', 542; and Cherbourg, 544–5; and the battle in Normandy, 549; and the conspiracy against Hitler, 553; warns Hitler of the imminent fate of his troops, 555, 556; gravely wounded, 556; commits suicide, 602
Romolo (Italian merchant ship): attacked, 91
Ronarch, Captain: his skill, 100

Roncalli, Angelo: opposes the deportation of Jews from Bulgaria, 415
Rondenay, Colonel André: shot, 568
Roosevelt, President Franklin D.: and American neutrality, 4, 25, 135; and atomic energy, 20–21; and the atomic bomb, 594; and the magnetic mine, 35; and a peace mission, 48; and military supplies from Britain, 66, 67, 92, 136, 139, 148; and the battle in France, 66, 68, 76, 93, 94, 97; and Italy's attack on France, 90; urges 'resistance not appeasement', 110–1; and a destroyers-for-bases deal with Britain, 117; and Churchill, 35, 93, 127, 136, 222, 223, 261, 282, 286, 287, 300, 326, 336, 392, 426, 451, 478–9, 576, 594, 638; 'we will continue to help', 130; 'we are mobilizing our citizenry', 132; re-elected (November 1940), 138; and the 'arsenal of democracy', 148; and the 'four essential human freedoms', 148–9; his emissary to Britain, 150, 151, 155; and Anglo-American cooperation, 154, 173; and the Balkans, 157; and Lend-Lease, 162; 'The only thing we have to fear is fear itself', 186; freezes German and Italian assets, 200; told of imminent German invasion of Russia, 192; and the death of Paderewski, 204; and Japan, 216, 222, 226, 260, 263; and aid to Russia, 223, 254, 396, 627; and United States naval losses (September-October) 1941, 230, 244, 251; and a further amendment to the neutrality act (November 1941), 255; and Pearl Harbour, 272, 275; and Germany's declaration of war on the United States, 276, 277–8; and the Anglo-American alliance, 282, 319; and the United Nations, 286; and American arms production, 287; and General MacArthur, 302; and 'the final battles', 302; and the bombing of Tokyo, 221; and the Battle of the Coral Sea, 322–3; a rumour concerning, circulates in the Warsaw ghetto, 324; and the fall of Tobruk, 335, 336, 337; and the Eastern Front, 359; at Casablanca, 392, 393, 396–9; Churchill congratulates, 408, 531; Churchill discusses Allied strategy with (May 1943), 426, 430; and Allied bombing policy, 432; and the Italian surrender, 445, 447, 448, 452; eavesdropped telephone conversations of, 448, 552; and the Balkans, 451; wants Western Allies to get to Berlin, 454; at Teheran, 478–9; warns of 'large casualty lists', 481; his armies in action in Italy, 490; and the Warsaw uprising, 572, 581, 586; and the future of Germany, 592, 640; his fourth term, 611; and Russia's role in the defeat of Germany, 627–8; and the future of Poland, 638; and an Iwo Jima photograph, 642–3; and Stalin, 658; dies, 662; his last, undelivered speech, 663
Ropsha (near Leningrad): Soviet forces link up at, 489–90
Rosani, Rita: shot, 593
Rosenau (France): French forces reach (on Rhine), 613

Rosenberg, Alfred: 54, 130, 158, 193, 212; a protest about mass murder forwarded to, 250; and the demands of the economy to be 'ignored', 256

Rosenberg, Sergeant Peretz: in Yugoslavia, 430

Rosensaft, Josef: and the British entry into Belsen, 663

Rosenthal, Joe: his Iwo Jima photograph, 642–3

Roskiskis (Lithuania): Jews murdered at, 223

Roslavl (Russia): 201; partisans near, 326, 331; Hitler agrees to withdraw from, 462

Rosler, Major: an eye-witness to mass murder, 219–20

Ross, Sergeant Wilhelm: shot, 70

Rossosh (southern Russia): Germans enter, 341

Rosten, Captain Leo: and 'Purple', 154

Rostock (Germany): troops to embark from, 52; bombed, 320, 322, 500; Jews at, killed by Allied bombs, 675

Rostov-on-Don (southern Russia): planned German advance to, 114; Germans reach, 260; Germans forced to give up, 265; Germans recapture, 338, 345; Soviet forces escape from, 346; Soviet forces draw near to, 399; Soviet forces enter, 402

Rota Island (Marianas): Japanese on, surrender, 722

Rotmistrov, General P. A.: and the Battle of Kursk, 443

Rotterdam (Holland): attacked, 61; Queen Wilhelmina embarks from, 64; bombed, 65; surrenders, 66; attempted sabotage in, 353; still held by the Germans, 602; food supplied for, 679; German motor torpedo boats sail from, to surrender, 693

Rouen (France): German troops approach, 89; anti-aircraft batteries near, bombed, 515; railway yards at, bombed, 519; a telephone cable to, cut, 529

Rouffanche, Madame: survives, 537

Roulers (Belgium): a gap near, 76

Roumania: and Germany, 48; Poles escape through, 86; joins the Axis, 108; German Counter-Intelligence in, 120; German army and air force missions in, 124; German occupation of, 130; and the German invasion of Russia, 142; joins Tripartite Pact, 143; as a German base against Greece, 146, 148, 157, 160, 166; and the German invasion of Russia, 188, 192; and the Yugoslav frontier, 169; declares war on the United States, 280; troops from, in Russia, 381, 385, 400, 515; and an Allied deception plan, 494; German Army enters, 511; an aerial reconnaissance over, 519; American bombing of, 530; Soviet offensive against, 573; declares war on Germany, 580; signs armistice, 590; its future, discussed in Moscow, 600; troops from, in action against Germany, 601, 604; to be police-governed, 686–7; in the Soviet bloc, 723

Rovno (Poland): a German aircraft forced down by Russians at, 174; bombed, 198; a partisan group at, 202;

Jews killed in, 242, 359; Red Army reaches, 496

Rowden, Diana: a British agent, killed, 555

Rowley, Corporal: and the fate of a Russian, 622

Rowley, Captain Henry Aubrey: killed, 185

Royal Oak (British battleship): sunk, 21

Rozenfeld, Semyon: goes from Sobibor to Berlin, 467

Rubens: the fate of his paintings, 130, 162, 206

Rubicon River (Italy): crossed, 601

Rudel, Hans-Ulrich: shot down, 655

Rudellat, Yvonne ('Jacqueline'): lands in German-occupied France, 338–9; dies in Belsen, after liberation, 672

Rudin, Professor Ernst: praises Hitler's 'racial-hygenic measures', 113

Rudnya (Russia): Jews murdered in, 281; Soviet partisans near, 309

Ruge, Major General Otto: in Norway, 57–8; taken prisoner, 88; liberated, 671

Ruhr, the (Germany): 5, 20, 48; bombed, 67, 68–9, 77, 99, 115, 139, 189, 427, 428, 432, 439, 440; to be 'dismantled', 592; anti-aircraft units sent to, 640; German counter-attacks north of, forestalled, 652; a final German counter-attack in, postponed, 657; encircled, 658; final counter-attack in, cancelled, 659; German resistance in, broken, 666; German troops in, surrender, 670

Ruma (Yugoslavia): a death march from, 295

Rumbuli Forest (Riga): Jews shot in, 266

Rundstedt, General Gerd von: and the Dunkirk perimeter, 72, 73, 74, 75; and Hitler's Eastern plans, 83; Hitler visits (at Uman), 227; Hitler mocks, 358; warns Hitler, 472; and the Allied cross-channel plans, 531; and the Normandy deception plans, 545; relieved of his post, 549; put in command of German forces in the West, 585; urges a withdrawal, 621; his troops 'fed up', 639; dismissed, 648

Russel Island (Pacific): Japanese land at, 296

Rüsselheim (Germany): American airmen murdered at, 578; the guilty from, hanged, 708

Ruth, Book of: quoted, 151

Ruthenia (Czechoslovakia): ceded to the Soviet Union, 701

Ruweisat Ridge (Western Desert): attacked, 341

Ruzomberok (Slovakia): Soviet partisans near, 561; Slovak partisans seize area near, 583

Ryabchichi (Russia): Soviet partisans destroy, 363

Ryazan (Russia): reinforcements at, 265

Ryder, Major Lisle: and an SS massacre, 76

Ryder-Richardson, Colin: his act of bravery, 126

Ryhope (England): an act of courage at, 512

Rynok (Stalingrad): German soldiers reach, 355, 358

Rypin (Poland): Poles shot in, 24

Ryti, Risto: negotiates, 40, 47

Ryuho (Japanese aircraft carrier): hit, 317; sunk, 355

Ryukyu Islands (Japan): a ten-day naval battle off, 627; landings on, 655; Japanese on, surrender, 722

Rzeszow (Poland): labour camps near, 23

Rzhev (Russia): a defence line near, 218; Germans enter, 245; Germans to withdraw to, 274; a Russian success near, 287; Russians encircle, 293; a Russian offensive near, 302; Germans cross Volga near, 365; Russian counter-offensive towards, 406; Russians recapture, 408

'S-1': and the atomic bomb, 271

'SB' ('Sonderbehandlung' – Special Treatment): and the fate of the Gypsies, 432

SC-104 (Atlantic convoy): attacked, 369

SL-125 (British merchant shipping convoy): attacked, 373

SS, the: 'Spring of Life' stud farms of, 24, 390; criticized, 40, 43; expanded, 56; repeated atrocities of, 57, 76, 78–9, 257, 367, 383, 414, 578; in action in France, 69, 70, 73, 74, 76, 78–9, 100; and the future of Poland, 79; in Belgium, 127; and an anti-Jewish film, 128; and Operation Tooth, 128; in Amsterdam, 158; and Operation Barbarossa, 168–9, 194, 201, 204, 213, 302; and homosexuals, 256; and Soviet partisans, 264–5, 516; secret cyphers of, broken, 297, 353; Hitler's exhortation to, 301; and Operation Heydrich, 332; 'unshakeable', 332–3; at Treblinka, 344, 450; and the property of 'evacuated' Jews, 364, 372, 424; and the 'Ivans', 412; at Sobibor, 424, 467; and the destruction of the evidence of mass murder, 438; and a Muslim revolt, 458; in Italy, 467; at Auschwitz, 469, 507, 591, 600, 614, 623, 631, 634; in Warsaw, 479, 564; and escapee Allied airmen, 511; in Kovno, 511; a recreation centre for, built by slave labour, 525; reprisals by, in France, 536, 568; at Maly Trostenets, 548; troops of, in Normandy, 535, 543, 553, 566; at Buchenwald, 578; at Peira Cava, 584; in Budapest, 610; and the Malmédy massacre, 620; troops of, transferred from West to East, 626; at Chelmno, 630; at Blechhammer, 63; at Ravensbrück, 655, 664; and a grave food shortage in Germany, 674; in the Baltic, throw Jews overboard, 675; deaths of, at Webling (Bavaria), 678; at Lübeck, open fire on refugees, 683–4; at Ebensee, and a Jewish act of defiance, 687–8

Saar, the (Germany): Jews deported from, 133; industry in, to be 'completely dismantled', 592; American forces enter, 615; bombed, 624

Saarbrücken (Germany): action at, 6; arrests in, 412; an escapee captured at, 511

Saarlouis (Germany): action at, 6

Sabac (Yugoslavia): Jews and Serbs killed at, 225; fate of a child born in, 295

Sabang (Dutch East Indies): bombarded, 517, 708

Sabourin, Roger: his sabotage mission, 504

Saburov, Alexander: a partisan leader, 383

Sachs, Alexander: and atomic energy, 20–21

Sachsenhausen (north of Berlin): a concentration camp at, 2, 10; Poles die in, 26; 'Hitler's special prisoner' in, 26; experiments at, 32; criminals from, sent to Auschwitz as barrack chiefs, 57; a German pastor sent to, 133; medical experiments at, 169; Russian prisoners-of-war murdered at, 243; Jews killed in, 329; Jews sent to Auschwitz from, 370; criminals from, murder villagers in Russia, 414; British commandos sent to, 423; medical experiments at, 438; Jews sent to, from Auschwitz, 582; a parachutist from Palestine dies in, 611; an opponent of Hitler executed at, 627; mass evacuations to, 632; executions at, 637, 651, 660; a 'death march' from, 664

Safi (French Morocco): Allies in control of, 376

Sagan (Germany): an escape from, 510

Sahara Desert: a crash in, 414; a concentration camp at, 505; Germany to be made 'more desolate than', 528; the remains of American crewmen found in, 739

Saidor (New Guinea): a landing at, 486

Saigon (French Indo-China): Japanese enter, 216; Vietnamese government in, overthrown, 723

St Davids (British hospital ship): sunk, 492

St Denis (France): bombed, 519

St Dié (France): German forces hold, 606; liberated, 613

St Dizier (France): bombed, 522

St Genis Laval (France): executions at, 573

St Germain (France): Germans to enter, 92

St John (New Brunswick): sanctuary found in, for thirty-three years, 734

St John Ambulance Brigade: three men of, shot, 280

St Lambert-sur-Dives (France): battle at, 567

St Leu (France): 'Flying Bomb' storage depot at, bombed, 551–2

St Lo (American aircraft carrier): sunk, by a kamikaze pilot, 606

St Malo (France): troops embarked from, 96; further evacuations from, 98; surrenders to the Americans, 570

St Martin de Varreville (France): fortications at, bombed, 99

St Maur (France): Germans to enter, 92

St Nazaire (France): evacuations from, 98; Germans approach, 100; a naval and commando raid on, 312; German submarine pens at, 348; bombed, 378; an American airman shot down over, evades captures, 404; German garrison on, surrenders, 690

St Paul's Cathedral (London): bombs near, 148

St Pölten (Austria): Red Army approaches, 666; fighting near, 687

St Quentin (France): German forces near, 68

St Valery-en-Caux (France): troops cut

off at, 89; troops evacuated from, 90; surrender at, 92

St Vincent, General de: refuses to assist in deportations, 357

Ste Marguerite-de-Viette (France): a pilot shot down near (1944), 566; a pilot's remains found near (1985), 742

Ste Marie-aux-Mines (France): an execution at, 636

Saipan Island (Marianas): American landing on, 541, 543; the final battle on, 552–3; a fleet sails from, for Iwo Jima, 642

Saito, Lieutenant-General Yoshitsugu: commits suicide, 541, 543

Sajmiste (Yugoslavia): Jews murdered at, 295

Sakai, Lieutenant-General: no surrender to, 280

Sakamaki, Ensign Kazua: taken prisoner, 272

Sakhalin Island: Soviet Union to acquire southern section of, 640; Soviet naval forces bombard, 717; Soviet troops land on, 718; Soviet forces conquer, 720

Sakkis, Leon: a partisan, killed, 539

Sakowicz, W.: an eye witness to mass murder, 217, 219

Salamaua (New Guinea): occupied, 307; raided, 338; reinforcements to, sunk, 408; an execution at, 417; Japanese retreat from, 486

Salangen (Norway): landing at, 55

Salatiga (Java): bombed (1947), 733

Salboni (India): a bomber base, against Rangoon, 682

Salerno (Italy): landing at, planned, 459; carried out, 460; bridgehead at, attacked, 461; Allied success at, 462–3

Salkhazi, Sister Sara: executed, 624

Salomon, Alice: shares the fate of her charges, 395

Salon-la-Tour (France): a British agent captured in, 538

Salonica (Greece): 170; Germans occupy, 171; Jews of, deported to their deaths, 413, 414, 432, 436, 470; Germans pull back from, 575; a report from, about Greek partisan activity, 601

Salornay (France): a parachute mission to, 568

Salsk (southern Russia): Germans reach, 347; Russians recapture, 395

Salt Lake City (US heavy cruiser): badly damaged, 415

Salvation Army, the: its methods cited, 19

Salzburg (Austria): Hitler meets Mussolini at, 419; surrenders to the Americans, 684; von Greim commits suicide in, 696

Samat Mountain (Philippines): 294

Samos (Aegean Sea): struggle for, 472; and an escape line, 495–6

Samothrace (Greece): Germans occupy, 176; Jews deported from, 402

Sampson, Flight Lieutenant Sammy: killed, 499

Samuel Huntington (US cargo ship): sunk, 495

Sanananda (New Guinea): battle at, 393, 396

San Andrea (Italian fuel ship): sunk, 357

San Antonio (Italian merchant ship): sunk, 425

Sandakan (North Borneo): a 'death march' from, 702

Sandbaek, Pastor Harald: escapes, 610

Sandomierz (Poland): Red Army reaches, 562

San Francisco (California): Molotov at, 686; United Nations Charter signed in, 701; Japanese peace treaties signed in, 735

San Francisco Conference (of the United Nations): 658

San Jacinto (US light carrier): and a Pacific bombing raid, 584

San River (Poland): killing near, 8; fighting near, 9

San Pietro Infine (Italy): battle in, 480–1

Sansapor (New Guinea): captured, 562

San Stefano (Italy): a prisoner recaptured near, 687

Santa Cruz Islands (Pacific Ocean): naval battle off, 372

Santé Prison (Paris): a revolt in, 555

Santos, José Abad: executed, 323

Sapozhnikova, Olga: and the defence of Moscow, 246

Sarajevo (Yugoslavia): a British mission near, 297; a mutiny near, 458; and an Allied deception plan, 492–3; German forces evacuate, 660

Saratoga (US warship): deaths on, 500

Saratov (Volga): reinforcements at, 267

Sarawak: Japanese land on, 279

Sardinia: and the battle for Malta, 114; a naval action off, 143–4; a possible invasion of, 374

Sark (Channel Islands): a commando raid on, 367; raises the Allied flags, 690

Sarrebourg (Alsace-Lorraine): Germans driven from, 613

Sarvar (Hungary): Jews deported to Auschwitz from, 560

Sas, Colonel Jacobus: and German war plans, 25, 38, 52, 53, 58

Sattelberg Summit (New Guinea): captured, 477

Satzkis, Lily: not allowed to leave Germany, 251

Sauckel, Fritz: and forced labour, 310

Saumur (France): Resistance fighters land near, 461

Savicheva, Tanya: her family's fate, and hers, 325

Savoy Cavalry: in action on the Don, 355

Savy, Jean: and the 'Flying Bomb', 505

Sawicka, Hanka: her courage, and death, 413

Sayn-Wittgenstein, Major Heinrich Prinz zu: shot down, 491–2

Scapa Flow (Orkney Islands): 21, 49, 52, 153, 214

Scaramella, Rosetta: deported, 514

Scharnhorst (German battle cruiser): sinks the Rawalpindi, 30; in the North Sea, 155; in action, 159, 162; an attack on, 216; its dash, and damage to, 300; sunk, 482

Scheldt River (Belgium, Holland): mined, 61; British retreat from, 66; mouth of, to be held, 585; Allied advance to, 598; Allies cross, 610; Allies control, 614

Schellenberg, Walter, and Jewish emigration, 188

Schepke, Captain Joachim: drowned, 162

Schijvenschuurer, Leen: shot, 160

Schillinger, ss Sergeant Josef: attacked at Auschwitz, 469

Schiphol Airport (Holland): an execution near, 405

Schirach, Henrietta von: protests to Hitler, 440

Schlabrendorff, Lieutenant Fabian von: 217; and the first German Army bomb plot to kill Hitler (March 1943), 412; and the second attempt, 414; on trial, 637

Schilling, Dr Klaus Karl: tried for war crimes, 725–6

Schleicher, Rüdiger: shot, 672

Schlieben (Germany): 'We were in heaven', 641

Schlieben, General Karl Wilhelm von: defends Cherbourg, 544–5

Schlüsselburg (Lake Ladoga): Germans capture, 230; recapture of, judged impossible, 234; Germans in control of, 266

Schmidt, Wulf: becomes a double agent, 126

Schmidt-Richberg, General: and reprisals in Grece, 527

Schmitt, Philip: receives his first prisoners, 127

Schmorell, Alexander: executed, 405

Schmundt, Colonel Rudolf: and Hitler's triumphs, 11; and the Jews, 207; dies of his wounds, 598

Schnaufer, Lieutenant: a German air ace, 482

Schnee Eifel (Ardennes): Americans surrender at, 620

Schneidemühl (Germany): Jews deported from, 49; Germans troops embark at, 52

Schnell, Corporal: rescued, but dies, 471

Schniewind, Admiral: and the invasion of Britain, 113

Schnorchel ('Shnorkel'): a secret weapon of quality, 625, 650

Scholl, Hans: courageous protest of, 404

Scholl, Sophie: courageous protest of, 404

Schomberg (southern Germany): a mass grave discovered at, 673

Schönhuber, Franz: a former ss officer, wins a parliamentary seat (1989), 745

Schönlanke (Pomerania): Red Army reaches, 634

Schörner, General: evacuates Sevastopol, 522

Schörzingen (southern Germany): a mass grave discovered at, 673

Schuhart, Lieutenant: and the Courageous, 10

Schulenburg, Friedrich Werner, Count von der: reports from Moscow, 180–1

Schumann, Dr Horst: and murder by gassing, 228

Schuschnigg, Kurt von: liberated, 686

Schutlze, Walther: and a 'special diet', 379

Schwarzheide (Germany): slave labour at, 525

Schweinfurt (Germany): bombed, 452, 467, 501

Schwerdt, Otto: terror killings by, 488

Schwerin (Germany): fighting near, 687

Schwerin-Schwanenfeld, Captain Count Ulrich von: hanged, 589

Schwiechlow Lake (near Berlin): an army 'stuck fast' south of, 679

Schwirndt (East Prussia): Red Army units reach, 571

Scotland: German bombers shot down over, 21, 25; gales off, 55; troops in, 83; an invasion force, leaves from, 373; a spy lands in, 554

Scott, Lieutenant-Commander Peter: helps an evacuation, 90; and the surrender of German motor torpedo boats (May 1945), 693–4

Scutari (Albania): Germans pull back to a defensive line at, 575; partisan activity near, 584; Germans abandon, 615

Scott-Ford, Duncan: captured and hanged, 37

Scott, Robert Falcon: 90, 693

'Sea Lion': the German plan to invade Britain, 110, 113–4; abandoned, 130–1

Sea Witch (British aircraft carrier): its abortive mission, 304

Seagrim, Hugh: organizes resistance, in Burma, 485

Seal, Eric: and British morale, 155

Seattle (Washington State): and Japanese agents, 238

Sebezh (White Russia): Germans driven from, 553

'Second Front': Stalin seeks, in Europe, 352; Allies open (in Italy), 457; Allies open (in northern France), 534

Sedan (France): Germans near, 64, 65; German breakthrough at, 66, 67

Seela, ss Captain Max: in action, 238

Seele, Gertrud: executed, 629

Seelow (east of Berlin): Red Army reaches, 667

Seijffards, Helmuth: shot, 646

Seine River (France): retreat across, 89–90; and Allied cross-Channel plans, 528; and the Normandy deception plans, 546, 552; German supply columns attacked near, 552; Allies reach, 568

Selective Training Act (USA): registration under, 132

Selizharovo (Russia): 201

Sell, Freiherr von: and the Hitler Bomb Plot, 559

Semarang (Java): bombed (1947), 733

Sens (France): a German withdrawal to, 571

Sephton, Petty Officer Alfred: in action, 184

Serai (Brunei): Japanese land at, 279

Serber, Robert: and the atomic bomb, 420

Serbs: persecuted, 182; executed, 174; murdered, 225; killed in reprisal actions, 243; massacres of, 247, 293; 'fifty Serbs for one German', 309; revolt of, at Jasenovac, 672

Sered (Slovakia): Jews deported from, 608

Sereni, Enzo: his parachute mission, 525

Serokomla (Poland): murders near, 56

'Set Europe ablaze!': a motto and an aim, 106

Seuss, Lieutenant Richard: determined not to surrender, 570

Sevastopol (Russia): to be defended, 146; bombed, 198; an evacuation to, 244; Jews murdered at, 260; besieged, 283, 284, 323; overrun, 335; effect of resistance at, 336; Germans evacuate, 522

Seventh-Day Adventist, a: saves Jews, 512; wins Congressional Medal of Honour, 662

Sevez, General François: and the German surrender, 689

Sevsk (Russia): Red Army enters, 455

'Sewer Pipe Bomb': a scale model atomic bomb, tested, 451

Seyne, Maurice de: his heroism on the Eastern Front, 556

Seyss-Inquart, Dr Arthur: in Holland, 103

Sfax (Tunisia): Eighth Army occupies, 419

Shah Nawaz Khan: found guilty, 725

Shakespeare: 'beats Hitler', 131; performed on the 'Railway of Death', 345

Shanghai (China): Japanese action at, 275

Shaposhnikov, Marshal Boris Mikhailovich: and Soviet partisans, 206; and Intelligence from Britain, 238

'Shark': German U-boat communications key, broken, 385

Sharpless, Staff Sergeant Claude: shot down, reaches safety, 455

Shcherbakov, General: dismissed, 233

Shcherbatseyvich, Volodya: executed, 251

Sheffield (England): bombed, 146

Shelley, Staff Sergeant Guy E.: dies in the desert, 418

Shepetovka (Russia): a Soviet defence line at, 205; Jews killed in, 219

Sherbrooke, Captain Robert: in action, 287

Sherrod, Robert: and the American landing on Saipan Island, 541

Shertok, Moshe: appeals to Eden, 546

Shigemitsu, Mamoru: signs instrument of surrender, 722

Shilovo (Russia): reinforcements brought from, 265

Shinchiku Airfield (Formosa): bombed, 477

Shinyo Maru (Japanese freighter): sunk, 588

Shirer, William, in the Ruhr, 68–9; in Berlin, 121; reports on effect of British bombing, 121–2, 128; hears Hitler speak, 122; reports on the death of a Pole, 127; and Roosevelt's re-election, 138

Shklarek, Moshe: a survivor of mass murder, 317

Shklov (Russia): Jews 'liquidated' in, 243

Sho, General: commits suicide, 700

Shoa (a film by Claude Lanzmann): a survivor's recollections, 630

Shoeburyness (Britain): and the magnetic mine, 29–30

Shoho (Japanese aircraft carrier): sunk, 322

Shokaku (Japanese aircraft carrier): sunk, 543

Short, General: and Pacific naval movements, 263

Shteinmetz, Captain Miklos: killed, 624

Shumyachi (Russia): mentally ill murdered in, 281

Shuri Line (Okinawa): attack on, 694
Siauliai (Lithuania): Jews in ghetto of, 267; the fate of a family from, 634
Siberia: Soviet troop movements from, 179; American use of air bases in, 581
'Siberia': code name for the Indian Ocean, 101
Sicily: German bombers at, 149; Germans bomb Malta from, 368; thought to be the real object of the 'Torch' landings, 375; proposed landing on, 392, 396–7; bombed, 399; Rommel's supply links with, attacked, 419; and an Allied deception, 423; German air force withdraws to, 426; Allied invasion of, in prospect, 437, 441; Allied landing on, 442; battles for, 446, 447; Germans begin evacuation of, 451; under Allied control, 452; Italian armistice signed in, 457
Sidi Barrani (Egypt): Italian forces at, 136, 145; German dive bombers in action off, 205; Rommel defends, 376
Siedlecki, Professor Michael: dies at Sachsenhausen, 26
'Siege of England': Hitler's plan for, 189
Siegfried Line (Germany): Americans breach, 638
Siemens works (Berlin): hit by British bombs, 123
Siemiatycze (Poland): on the eve of war, 197
Siena (Italy): fate of Jews of, 474; Churchill visits Allied troops at, 576
Siena (Poland): troop movements near, 194
Sierra Leone: a convoy on way to, attacked, 237
Sieradz (Poland): Poles and Jews shot in, 9
Sierpc (Poland): Jews expelled from, 28; Jews from, murdered, 299
Siilasvuo, Colonel Hjalmar: and 'the road of glory', 36
Sikhs: forced to carry out an execution, 358
Sikh (British destroyer): sunk, 360
Simonds, A. C.: organizes an escape line, 495–6
Sikorski, General Wladyslaw: sets up Polish Government-in-Exile, 18; denounces 'war crimes', 290; describes the fate of Poles and Jews, 332
Sikory Tomkowieta (Poland): Poles executed in, 443
Silver Star: award of, 461
Simferopol (Crimea): murder of Jews in, 301
Simi (Aegean Sea): German troops on, surrender, 692
Simone, Sergio de: murdered, 669
Simović, General Dusan: denounces Tripartite Pact, 166
Sinclair, Michael (the 'Red Fox'): an escapee, killed, 597
Singapore: vulnerable, 140; more vulnerable, 215; British warships reach, 268; bombed, 273, 293; battle for, 293; heavy loss of life in, 293; surrenders, 300; fate of four prisoners-of-war in, 358; a courageous exploit off, 710; captured American airmen executed in, 711; a former captive in, liberated in Japan, 718–9; and the destruction of evidence of an execution in, 720; and the surrender

of Japanese forces in South-East Asia, 723; a war crimes trial in, 729; becomes independent, 730
Singh, Major Mohan: and 'Asia for the Asiatics', 278
Singhara Singh: found guilty, 725
Singora (Thailand): a landing at, 276
Sinkov, Major Abraham: and 'Purple', 154
'Siren': a call sign, near Stalingrad, 381
Sitia (Crete): Italian landing on, 186
Skagerrak, the: Russian interest in, 141; merchant ships escape through, 153, 314
Skala (Eastern Galicia): battles of, 512
Skalat (Eastern Galicia): Jews of, resist deportation, 421
'Ski' sites: and the V1 and V2 'secret weapons', 474, 475, 479; bombed, 529; in operation, 540
Ski troops (Russian): in action on the Eastern Front, 257; gather in reserve, 265
Skoda Armaments Works (Pilsen, Czechoslovakia): bombed, 143
Skodzensky Lieutenant Heinrich: and the arrival of the Americans at Dachau, 677–8
Skoplje (Yugoslavia): and a deception plan, 492–3; German pull-back planned, 575; Yugoslav forces enter, 612
Skorzeny, Captain Otto: seizes Mussolini, 461; seizes Horthy, 603; infiltrates American lines, in the Ardennes, 618, 621, 622
Skrodow (Poland): Soviet prisoners-of-war murdered at, 482
'Skunk': an Enigma key, broken, 334
Slapton Sands (southern England): an invasion exercise attacked off, 520; a second invasion exercise held off, 521
Slavin (a Soviet partisan): and an anti-partisan sweep, 358
Slavs: Hitler's contempt for, 155–6, 458; a grim future for, 354; their 'age-long struggle' ended, 692
Slim, General William: in Burma, 694; at Singapore for the Japanese surrender, 723
Slochy (Poland): inhabitants of, murdered, 199–200
Slonim (Poland): a counter-attack at, 206; anti-partisan actions at, 355, 395
Slovakia: Poles captured while trying to escape to, 95; forced labourers taken from, 129, 427; joins Tripartite Pact, 143; Jews of, 232, 310, 335, 365, 507, 582; news of Auschwitz reaches, 546; a Soviet partisan unit reaches, 561; uprising in, 580, 583, 604; an Allied escape line from, by air, 593–4, 599; a 'Free Slovakia' proclaimed in, 604; revolt in, crushed, 608; Red Army approaches, 615
Slovenia (Yugoslavia): traffic through, to be disrupted, 521
Slovenski Gradec (northern Yugoslavia): final German surrender in, 694
Slovik, Eddie E.: shot for desertion, 636
Slutsk (near Leningrad): liberation of, 490
Slutsk (western Russia): a signals centre, 192; executions in, 246; a protest about executions in, 250–1; Soviet partisans near, 398

Smith, General Bedell: and the German surrender, 689
Smith, General Holland M.: and a 'piece of folly', 353
Smith, Reg: his warning, 576
Smithfield Market (London): a rocket bomb falls on, 648
Smolensk (Russia): and Polish prisoners-of-war, 53; a signals centre, 192; on a defence line, 201; and Enigma, 210, 237; encircled, 212, 217; actions against partisans near, 244; partisan activity continuing near, 246; Soviet prisoners-of-war near, 247; rumours concerning, 324; supplies through, threatened by partisans, 358, 363; a German Army plan to kill Hitler at, 412; German orders reach, and are also read in Britain, 420; a German anti-partisan sweep near, 441; imminent German loss of, 462; Germans withdraw from, 464
Smukala (Poland): torture and death at, 14
Sneland I (Norwegian merchant ship): sunk, 689
Snow: in the mountains of Yugoslavia, 172; first flurries of, on Russian front, 232; first flurries at, at Rastenburg, 242; first fall of, in Leningrad, 242; and Germany's 'wildest dreams', 245; falls on the Moscow front (25 October 1941) 251; stays on the ground, at Rastenburg (1 November 1941), 253
'Snow': a double agent, 15–16
Soames, Captain Christopher: helps rescue prisoners-of-war, 460
Sobibor (Poland): a death camp at, 292, 310, 317, 322, 326, 331, 335, 351, 370, 376, 395, 439; a revolt in, 467
Sochaczew (Poland): a punishment publicized in, 127
Sochaux-Montbéliard (France): sabotage at, 498
Sochi (Black Sea): 193; a German objective, 363
Socotra (Indian Ocean): a listening post, 429
Soest (Germany): bombed, 649
Sofia (Bulgaria): railway yards at, bombed, 170; an anti-German government formed in, 589; and Churchill's fear of Soviet control in, 686; in the 'Soviet sphere', 728
Soissons (France): Hitler at, 542
Sokal (Poland): on the eve of war, 196
Sokolka (Poland): villagers shot in, 466–7
Sokolovo (southern Russia): battle at, 410
Sokoly (Poland): Jews murdered in, by Poles, 646
Soldau (East Prussia): a concentration camp at, 14; German mental patients killed at, 70
Solec (Warsaw): holds out, 585
Sollum (Egypt): occupied by Italy, 125, 145; occupied by Rommel, 178; the Barham sunk off, 262
Solnechnogorsk (near Moscow): Germans reach, 262
Solomon Islands (Pacific Ocean): plans for liberation of, 341; the Kako sunk in, 352; American advances in, 355, 391, 444; continuing battles in, 449, 466, 495

Solta Island (Yugoslavia): raid on, 509
Soluch (Cyrenaica): an ill-fated flight from, 417
*Somali* (British destroyer): sunk, 359
Somaliland: British advance in, 153
Sommer, Margarete: her courageous protest, 250
Somme River (France): Germans reach, 69, 70; French hold, 81; Hitler's anxiety concerning, 82, 83; battle on, 86; and the Normandy deception plan, 546, 552
Somogyi (a Hungarian Jew): dies at Auschwitz, 634
Sompolno (Poland): Jews of, murdered, 298
Sonnenstein (near Dresden): medical experiments at, 228
'Sonya': receives, and passes on, atomic secrets, 241
Soputa-Sonananda Track (New Guinea): Japanese hold, 384
Sorge, Richard: his espionage work, 45, 142, 147–8, 159, 161, 168, 179, 183, 206, 224, 245; arrested, 246; executed, 611
*Soryu* (Japanese aircraft carrier): sunk, 330
Sosnkowska, Jadwiga: and the bombing of Warsaw (1939), 13; and the fall of Warsaw (1939), 18
Sosnowiec (East Upper Silesia): labour camp at, 525
Sospel (France): executions in, 568
Souk el-Arba (Tunisia): American parachute landing at, 378
Sousley, Private Franklin R.: and an Iwo Jima photograph, 643
Sousse (Tunisia): overrun, 419
South Africa: declares war on Finland, Hungary and Roumania, 267; troops from, in the Western Desert, 338, 358, 371; pilots from, fly over Auschwitz, 513–4; a pilot from, wounds Rommel, 556; a pilot from, finds safety in Poland, 570; pilots from, aid Warsaw, 596; pilots from, bomb German-held railways, 611 war dead of, 514; a pilot from, wins the Victoria Cross, 644; troops of, in Italy, 660; Air Force deaths of, 746
South America: Hitler denies designs on, 92; and a cruel deception, 469, 520
Southgate (London): a rocket bomb hits, 594
Southampton (England): troops reach, from France, 96; Polish Government-in-Exile reaches, 101; bravery above, 119; bombed, 123, 143
*Southampton* (British cruiser): crippled, 149
Southern Rhodesia: volunteers from, 115; Askari war dead from, 746
South Tyrol (Italy): future of, 341
South Wales: bombed, 109, 504
Southwark (London): eighteen people killed at, 136
Souvée, Henri: crosses into Germany, 590
Soviet Far East: troops brought from (May 1941), 177, 183; further troops brought from (October 1941), 245
Soviet–Japanese Neutrality Pact: signed (April 1941), 173
Soviet Union: and the German–Soviet Pact, 1–2, 9, 15, 20, 36, 44; and the Baltic, 23, 141, 159; and Finland, 31,

33, 34, 36, 38–9, 40–2, 44, 47; and Japan, 45, 478, 602, 705, 708, 710, 711, 715, 735; and Lithuania, 94; and Roumania, 104, 141; and atomic secrets, 107–8, 348, 595; and the German commerce raider *Komet*, 109; German plans against, 111, 113, 114, 117, 120, 123, 124, 135, 137, 141, 142, 144, 155, 158–9, 160, 188; German invasion of, 198–9, 200–11; British aid to, 207, 314, 359; and American aid to, 468, 658; British Intelligence help to, 208, 341, 366; signs a mutual assistance pact with Britain, 210; and Iran (Persia), 226, 296; decoy British air raids on behalf of, 315–6; continuing Allied aid to (1943–5), 396; receives statistics of British war dead, 426; and Hitler's anti-Bolshevik Legion, 430; and Berlin, 455; and the Jet aircraft, 488; and the Normandy Landings deception plan, 506; receives aerial reconnaissance photographs, 519; and Poland's post-war frontiers, 559, 679–80; and the Warsaw uprising, 564, 567, 572, 580–1, 590, 592, 593; and Bulgaria, 589; and Roumania, 590; and Yugoslavia, 596, 661, 680; and the future of post-war Europe, 679–80, 686–7; to have a post-war veto, 574, 701; signs a Treaty with Czechoslovakia, 701; acquires Ruthenia, 701; acquires part of East Prussia, 711; acquires Vilna and Lvov, 711; declares war on Japan, 715, 717, 720; forcible repatriation to, 728; and the 'iron curtain', 728–9; and the Warsaw Pact, 729; and the Marshall Plan, 732; German prisoners-of-war to be returned from, 738; to receive reparations, 739; wartime death toll of, 746;
*see also index entries for* Stalin, Stalingrad, Leningrad, Moscow, Prisoners-of-war
Sowacoad (Amboina Island): fate of prisoners-of-war on, 297
Spaatz, General Carl: and German fuel oil targets, 535; witnesses the final German instrument of surrender, 690; and the choice of Hiroshima as an atomic bomb target, 710
Spain: 103, 134; Hitler's pressure on, 134, 143, 145–6; Hitler's plan for, 189; a British commando finds no refuge in, 360; and an Allied deception, 423; an airman finds safety in, 455; soldiers from, fight on the Eastern Front, 465; and an Allied deception plan, 494; war dead of, on the Eastern Front, 746
Spanish Morocco: German designs on, 141
*Spartan* (British destroyer): sunk, 495
'Special Himmler Troops': carry out reprisals, 622
Special Operations Executive (SOE): established, 106; operations by, in German-occupied Europe, 162, 180, 189, 236, 319, 334, 338–9, 370, 378, 440, 461, 475, 482, 484, 504, 515, 519, 538, 543, 551; a disaster for, in Holland, 334; agents of, hanged, 578, 651, 654–5; operations of, in the Far East, 694, 702, 722
Special Task Forces (of the SS): in preparation, 169; in action, 188, 207, 213, 218–9, 220, 221, 223, 232, 239,

241, 243, 246, 247, 250, 267, 280
'Special Unit': kills mental patients (in 1940), 70
Speer, Albert: and Hitler's 'dreams', 102; and the new Berlin, 174, 225, 235, 250; and Hitler's plans for Trondheim, 196; and Dr Todt, 282; succeeds Dr Todt, 299; and forced labour, 299; and the bombing of Cologne, 329; and the German rocket bomb, 333, 416, 434, 455, 473–4; and German submarine pens, 348; and the 'Atlantic Wall', 352, 358; armaments, and Allied bombing policy, 427, 448; increased authority for, 457; and the Jet aircraft, 488
*Spence* (US destroyer): losses on, 618
Speyer (Germany): French cross Rhine at, 655
Sphakia (Crete): evacuation from, 185
Spicheren (France): Hitler in, 35
Spitzbergen (Arctic Ocean): a commando raid on, 226
Split (Yugoslavia): Germans seize, 463; and a deception plan, 492–3; German units at, attacked, 509
Spooner, Rear Admiral E. J.: dies, 307
Sports Palace (Berlin): Hitler speaks in, 296
Springfield (Illinois): and 'a frenzy of suspicion', 618
Square of the People: to be built in Berlin, 248
Srebnik, Shimon: survives his would-be execution, 630
Stadtilm (Germany): American forces enter, 663
Stalin, Joseph: and the German–Soviet Boundary and Friendship Treaty, 16; his sixtieth birthday, 35; and the German–Soviet commercial treaty, 44; receives Intelligence reports from his spy in Tokyo, 45, 142, 147–8, 159, 161, 168, 179, 183, 206, 224, 245; and Japan, 45, 173, 245, 468; and the Baltic States, 111; to be deceived, 115, 181; and German preparations against Russia, 142, 149–50, 168; General Pavlov's warning to, 157; caution of, 164, 179; and Yugoslavia, 169, 395, 596; and Russian military preparations (before June 1941), 168, 170–1, 173–4, 174, 177, 179–80; becomes Soviet Premier, 180; British help for, 190–1, 202 and the imminence of war, 190–1, 192, 194, 196; and the coming of war, 198, 201, 206–7, 214; receives Intelligence from Britain, 202, 208, 210, 217, 239, 366, 372, 381; and American aid, 218; and Hitler's 'greatest weakness', 219; Volga Germans deported by, 231; and the defence of Kiev, 232, 236; and the siege of Leningrad, 233; and the continuing aid from Britain and the United States, 239–40, 241, 251–2, 353 and the atomic bomb, 241, 478; and the battle for Moscow, 246, 264; and 'a war of extermination', 253; and 'holy Russia', 254; and the defence of Stalingrad, 341, 346, 358–9, 367; and the Second Front, 352; and Churchill, 347, 352, 357, 366, 367, 385, 415, 417, 489, 536, 600, 610, 679–80; his partisan order, 407; his hopes (March 1943), 415; at Teheran (November 1943), 478–9; and the political future of

Stalin, Joseph—*contd.*
Poland (1944–5), 488, 497, 554, 627, 638, 679–80; and the bombing of Berlin, 489; and the liberation of Sevastopol, 522; not to be offended, 530; and 'a source of joy' to, 536; and the renewed Soviet offensive (summer 1944), 536, 548–9; and the Warsaw uprising, 564, 567, 572, 580–1, 586, 590, 593, 594, 596 discusses post-war Europe with Churchill, 600; and Japan, 602, 640, 705 and Greece, 623; and the Allied balance of forces (in February 1945), 639; and German reparations, 640; and Berlin, 657; and Himmler's offer to surrender to the Western Allies, 670; and the 'age-long struggle of the Slav nations', 692; at Potsdam, 705, 705–7; and Austria, 705–6; and Poland's post-war frontiers, 706–7; and the atomic bomb test, 708; a rehabilitation, after the death of, 739

Stalingrad (Russia): a German objective, 144, 312, 325, 345; German assault on, 341, 347, 352, 353, 355, 358, 358–9, 360–1, 361, 363, 365, 367, 369; final battles in, 370, 374, 377, 378; diversion of transport aircraft from, 376–7; gives hope to captive peoples, 380; Soviet counter-offensive near, 380, 385; Intelligence concerning, sent to Stalin, 385; Soviet successes at, 387, 390, 395, 397, 398; Goebbels declares 'victory' at, 398; von Paulus surrenders at, 398; two days of mourning over, in Berlin, 399

'Stalingrad Action': in the Kovno ghetto, 399

Stalino (Russia): Germans reach, 245; Germans evacuate, 459

Stanislawow (Poland): and Soviet partisans, 202; Jews deported to the deaths from, 310; Red Army enters, 562

Star of David: to be 'a message to go all over the world', 576

Stara Gradiska (Yugoslavia): Jews murdered at, 390

Staraya Russa (Russia): Germans cut off near, 303; Germans finally driven from, 499

Staraya Sinyava (Russia): Jews murdered in, 235

Stark, Hans: 'I believed in the Führer', 740

Stark, Admiral Harold R.: and Japanese intentions, 263; and a 'warning', 264

Starokonstantinov (Russia): a Soviet defence line at, 205

Starr, George ('Hilaire'): sabotage by, 484, 543

Stary Ciepielow (Poland): Poles killed in, 384

Stary Oksyol (south Russia): Germans driven from, 399

Stauffenberg, Lieutenant Claus von: gravely wounded in Tunisia, 419; and the growing opposition to Hitler, 544, 551, 553–4, 555, 556; and the Bomb Plot, 557–8; a cousin of, hanged, 566; the man who arrested him, hanged, 650

Stavanger (Norway): and the German invasion of Norway, 42, 45, 48, 52, 53; an execution at, 379

Stavelot (Belgium): civilians murdered at, 620

Stavropol (Caucasus): Germans reach, 347

Stawiski (Poland): Germans shoot Jews in, 223

Steckelsdorf (near Berlin): Jews deported from, 326

*Steel Seafarer* (US merchant ship): sunk, 230

Steenbergen (Holland): airmen shot down over, 595

Stehla (Elbe): American and Soviet soldiers meet at, 673

Stein, Edith: her fate, 350–1; sanctified, 351

Stein am Rhein (Switzerland): bombed in error, 644

Steiner, SS General Felix: Hitler's orders to, 669–70; Hitler disappointed by, 670

Stellbrink, Karl Friedrich: executed, 315

Stenda, Robert: a volunteer, 224; killed, 225

Stepinac, Archbishop: protests from, 306, 409, 424

Stepney (London): rocket bomb deaths in, 653

Sternbeck (Czechoslovakia): Red Army enters, 690

Stettin (Germany): Jews deported from, 49; German troops embark at, 52; an escape through, 510; Hitler demands the holding of the railway line to, 643; acquired by Poland, 711; and the 'iron curtain', 728

Stettinius, Edward R.: and Molotov, 686

Stevens, Major R. H.: kidnapped, 27; his kidnapper's promotion, 94–5

Steyr (Austria): bombed, 501

Stieff, Major-General Helmuth: and the Hitler bomb plot, 551

Stilwell, General Joseph ('Vinegar Joe'): withdraws from China to India, 321

Stimson, Henry L.: and the atomic bomb, 673–4, 696, 704–5, 707, 708

Stip (Greece): partisan activity near, 601

Stirling Island (Solomons): New Zealanders land on, 471

Stockholm (Sweden): 464; and a British deception, 522; a V2 rocket examined in, 539

Stojka, Stanislaw: shot, 435

Stok, Flight Lieutenant van der: escapes, 510

Stolbtsy (White Russia): Germans driven back to, 544

Straelen (Germany): Churchill flies from, to view the battle, 652

Stralsund (Germany): victims from, 32

Strank, Sergeant Michael: and an Iwo Jima photograph, 643

Strasbourg (France): Germans advance to, 97–8; medical experiments in, 299; skeleton collection at, to be destroyed, 608; Allies enter, 613–4; a war crimes trial at, 730

*Strasbourg* (French battle cruiser): escapes, 107

Strassburg (Volga): deportations from, 232

'Stratford': to land in Norway, 42; and Finland, 46

Straubing (Bavaria): a death, after liberation, in, 693

Strausberg (near Berlin): Red Army at, 672

Streicher, Julius: hanged, 731

Stresa (Italy): a clandestine mission to, 597

Strippel, SS Lieutenant Arnold: found guilty, and awarded compensation, 741

Strong, Brigadier-General George V.: reaches London, 120

*Stronghold* (British destroyer): sunk, 304

Stroop, SS Brigadier Jürgen: and the Warsaw ghetto revolt, 428; executed, 735

Strumen River (Greece): reprisal actions near, 243

Stuart, Captain William F.: in Yugoslavia, 430; killed, 436

Stuckart, Wilhelm: and the 'Final Solution', 292

Student, General Kurt: in Holland, 61, 66; on Crete, 182; in the Ruhr, 657, 659

Studland Bay (southern England): a practice invasion at, 468

Stuelpnagel, General Karl von: and the July Bomb Plot, 558; hanged, 583

Stuelpnagel, Otto von: orders reprisals, 175; commits suicide, 733

'Suicide Group': a German pilot proposes, 371

Stumme, General: dies of a heart attack, 371

Stümpff, General Hans-Jurgen: signs the instrument of surrender, 690

*Sturdy* (British submarine): sinks a Japanese cargo ship, with its passengers, 614

*Stureholm* (Swedish merchant ship): and an act of rescue, 138

Stuttgart (Germany): bombed, 504; French forces enter, 669

Stutthof (Danzig): a concentration camp at, 14; Poles murdered at, 32; Jews murdered at, 57; mass evacuation from, 633; evacuees from, killed by Allied bombs, 675; evacuees from, at Lübeck, 683–4

Subic Bay (Philippines): Japanese troops sent from, 295

Suchozebry (Poland): fate of Soviet prisoners-of-war in, 373

Suchumi (Black Sea): a German objective, 363

Suda Bay (Crete): Italian naval action in, 165

Sudan: a survivor reaches England through, 77

Sudetenland: and Hitler's 'mission', 11; expulsions from, 699–700

Suez Canal (Egypt): 90, 136, 145; danger to, 157; Rommel's plans for capture of, 177; urgent need for defence of, 187; British to be driven from, 189; Rommel's final thrust towards, 357

Suffolk, 20th Earl of: in France, 95; killed, 183

'Sugar Loaf' (Okinawa): battle for, 694–5

Sukhiniki (Russia): Russians retake, 296

Sukosan (Yugoslavia): bombed, 505

Sulejow (Poland): bombed, 4

Suluks: revolt of, 469

Sumatra (Dutch East Indies): death of,

307; oil installations on, bombarded, 708; a Japanese surrender on, 725

Sumy (Ukraine): Russians recapture, 406

'Sunday': helps escapees, 288

Sunday Express (London): its headline, as Red Army advances, 486

Sunday Times (London): reports whereabouts of an ss officer, 742–3

Sundberg, Dolores: dies, 31

Sundowner (private yacht): at Dunkirk, 82

Suner, Serano: meets Hitler, 143

Suomussalmi (Finland): battle at, 34, 36

'Super Fortress': bombs Japan, 540

Surcouf (French submarine): a sailor killed on, 107

Surplus Property Act (of 1944): amended, 730

Susloparov, General Ivan: and the German surrender, 689

Süssman, Lieutenant-General: killed, 184

Sutlej (British merchant ship): torpedoed, 500

Suttill, Francis: hanged, 651

Sutton Coldfield (England): a secret disclosed at, 526

Suvorov, General: an Order named after, 346–7

Suwalki (Poland): Poles killed in, 512

Suzuki, Admiral Kantaro: rejects Potsdam Declaration, 709; votes for surrender, 716

Suzuki, General: commits suicide, 667

Sverdlovsk (Urals): evacuations to, 199, 214, 230

Svoboda, Colonel Ludwig: and the battle for Kiev, 473; and the battle for the Carpathians, 604

Swales, Captain E.: his courage, 644

Swansea (Wales): bombed, 125

Swastika: flies on Mount Elbruz (Caucasus), 354; flies in Stalingrad, 365

Sweden: negotiations through, 19; fate of a merchant ship from, 29; and German iron ore, 37, 42, 46, 51, 55, 78 and Finland, 39, 40, 42, 46; 'playing at soldiers', 225; granite from, Hitler's plans for, 235; Hitler's forecast for the Jews of, 295; and Germany's euthanasia killings, 302; a secret meeting in, 328; a crash landing in, 359; a Norwegian parachutist finds safety in, 404; a Danish patriot smuggled into, 453; Danish Jews find safety in, 464; and an Allied deception plan, 494; Allied escapees reach safety in, 510; a V2 rocket examined in, 539; a diplomat from, protects Jews, 550; Danish resistance fighters escape to, 651; inmates from Ravensbrück evacuated to, 669; and the surrender of Japan, 716

Swedish Embassy (Berlin): bombed, 510

Swedish Stock Exchange (Stockholm): and a British deception plan, 522

Sweeney, Major Charles W.: flies to Kokura, then on to Nagasaki, 715

Swiecie (Poland): murders at, 19

Swiety Krzyz (Poland): Soviet prisoners-of-war murdered at, 482

Swinemünde (Germany): to become Polish, 706

Switzerland: an escape to, 7; 'playing at

soldiers', 225; Hitler's forecast for the Jews in, 295; to allow Jews in, 357; a secret design smuggled through, 463–4; Jews smuggled to, 512; news of Auschwitz reaches, 546; negotiations through, and an execution, 601; bombs fall on, in error, 644, 645; an ss General negotiates with the Allies in, 648; and the surrender of Japan, 716

'Sword' Beach (Normandy): landing at, 534

Sword of Honour: awarded (to Stalingrad), 406

Swords (to Knight's Cross): awarded, 86, 688–9

Sydney (Australia): Japanese submarine attack on, 329–30

Sydney (Nova Scotia): convoys from, 132, 232, 244

Sydney (Australian cruiser): in action, 205; sunk, 259

Sylt (Germany): bombed, 49

Sym, Igo: shot, 161

Syracuse (Sicily): British forces enter, 442

Syria: plans for, 137; arms from, 168; battle for, 188–9

Szabo, Violette: captured, 538; executed, 634

Szalasi, Major: sets up government in Budapest, 603

Szarkowszczyzna (eastern Poland): Jews killed at, 345

Szczgiel, and his son: shot, 36

Szczurowa (southern Poland): Gypsies murdered at, 339

Szeged (Hungary): Red Army reaches, 601

Szekesfehervar (Hungary): a German counter-attack at, 634; German defences at, broken, 651

Szenes, Hannah: her parachute mission, 508–9; executed, 611

Sztojay, Dome: comes to power in Hungary, 509

'T.4': and Germany's euthanasia programme, 11, 103, 147, 228

T-34 (Russian tank): in action, 236, 243, 244, 259, 271, 275, 443

TGD.: an unbroken German communications link, 353

TNT (trinitrotuluol): Britain acquires, 81

Tabarka (Tunisia): British forces occupy, 378

Tabau, Jerzy: an eye-witness at Auschwitz, 470

Tacloban (Philippines): a landing near, 604

Taelveg (Norway): resistance and reprisals in, 321

Taganrog (Russia): Germans reach, 245; Germans evacuate, 265; Russians re-enter, 456; an eye-witness to mass murder in, 480

Tahitians: at Bir Hakeim, 187

Taiho (Japanese aircraft carrier): sunk, 543

Taiwan: see index entry for Formosa

Takao (Formosa): a ship bombed in, 618

Takao (Japanese cruiser): disabled, 710

Takrouna (Tunisia): battle at, 422

'Tallboy' (12,000 pound bomb): used against the Tirpitz, 612

Tallinn (Estonia): evacuation of, 227; murders in, 514; Red Army enters, 596

Tamandu (Burma): Japanese driven from, 646

Tamils: 'die like flies', 422

Tamu (India-Burma border): a mission crosses, 404

Tanaka, Colonel: no prisoners to be taken by, 280

Tanambogo (Solomons): landing on, 350

Tangmere (southern England): missions to France from, 468, 475

Tank Annihilation Squads: on the Eastern Front, 238

Tankan Bay (Kurile Islands): and Pearl Harbour, 261

Tannenberg (East Prussia): German troops evacuate, 632

Tarakan Island (Dutch Borneo): Japanese land on, 288; Japanese complete conquest of, 290; Australian troops land on, 683

Tarana (British naval vessel): rescues prisoners-of-war, 360

Taranto (Italy): naval battle off, 140; Allies seize, 460

Terauchi, Field Marshal: laid low, 723

Tarawa Atoll (Gilbert Islands): Japanese land at, 276; Americans land on, 476

Target for Tonight (film): 216

Tarnopol (Eastern Galicia): 201; a partisan group at, 202; Jews murdered in, 209; Jews deported to their deaths from, 309; Red Army captures, 516

Tarnow (Poland): Poles sent to Auschwitz from, 95

Tarsao Camp (Burma-Thailand): deaths in, 477

Tartu (Estonia): Germans reach, 208; Jews murdered in, 235; Soviet forces enter, 580

Tarusa (Russia): occupied, 246

Tass (Soviet News Agency): and Finland, 31

Tassafaronga (Solomon Islands): battle off, 384

'Tate': a double-agent, 126

Tébessa (Tunisia): Rommel halted at, 402

Tedder, Air Chief Marshal Sir Arthur: and 'an awful load of hatred', 529; witnesses the final instrument of surrender, 690

Teheran (Persia): Churchill, Stalin and Roosevelt meet at, 478–9

Teleki, Count Pal: commits suicide, 169

Temple, Captain Neville: killed, 613

Tempelhof airport (Berlin): British bombs fall near, 121; Russians seize, 674

Tench, Colonel Charles: lands on Japanese soil, 723

Tenedos (British destroyer): sunk, 314

Teniers: paintings by, looted, 162

Tenna River (Italy): a rescue mission to, 527

Tennant, Captain: at Dunkirk, 83

Tenneville (Ardennes): Germans driven from, 626

Terboven, Josef: in Norway, 56, 128, 161; and the Jews, 205; proclaims a state of emergency, 232; commits suicide, 693

Terek Region (Caucasus): counter-attack in, 383

Terioki (Finland): Finns enter, 228

Termoli (Italy): a rescue mission from, 527

Tessy (Normandy): a Panzer Division reaches, 543

Thadden, Elizabeth von: betrayed, and arrested, 460; hanged, 589

Thaelmann, Ernst: shot, 582

Thailand (Siam): Japanese invade, 276; and the 'Railway of Death', 336, 345, 701; end of the war in, 721; and a route of pilgrimage, 738–9

Thames Estuary (England): and convoys, 7; and the magnetic mine, 29

Thanbyuzayat (Burma): and the 'Railway of Death', 336

Thasos (Greece): Germans occupy, 176

Thaton (Burma): Japanese in, surrender, 725

The Eternal Jew (film): anti-Semitic, 144, 151

'The Golden Gate in Forty-Eight': An American soldiers' slogan, 655

The Times (London): and a Jewish pledge, 6; and 'Mass Butchery in Poland', 332; and an act of sabotage-deception, 453; and a protest about Hirohito's funeral, 745

Theresienstadt (north of Prague): a concentration camp ghetto established at, 266; Jews deported from, to their deaths, 332, 348, 351, 372, 395, 461, 465, 507, 595, 598, 608; Jews from, at Maly Trostenets, 548; Jews being deported to, as the war ends, 691

Thermopylae (Greece): Allied defence of, 175; Allied troops forced to withdraw from, 176

Thessaly (Greece): resistance in, 465, 539

Theune (Walcheren Island): a bombing disaster in, 598

Thiel, Dr: killed, 453

Thielbeck (German refugee ship): at Lübeck, 683–4; sunk, 684

Thielt (Belgium): a gap near, 76

Thierack, Otto: and the fate of 'asocials', 361; commits suicide, 731

Thijssen, Jan: shot, 646

Thionville (France): bombed, 522

Third World War, the: the 'first casualty' in, 720

Thirty Years' War: cited as a precedent for mass murder, 735

Thomas, General Wilhelm Ritter von: and the German rocket bomb, 416

Thomas, Sergeant Ernest T.: raises the flag, 642

Tomas F. Nickel (US destroyer): sunk, 717

Thomsen, Hans: and 'Magic', 178

Thor (German commerce raider): its success, 169

Thousand Year Reich, the: at an end, 681; recalled, 729

Thrace (a province of Greece): to be annexed by Bulgaria, 176; deportation of Jews from, 414

Thümmel, Paul: a vital source, 25, 120

Thuringia (Germany): and Dr Karl Brandt's dismissal, 666

Thursby, Flight Sergeant Reginald:

shot down (1944), 566–7; his remains found, and buried (1985), 742

Thyssen, Fritz: his protest, 36

Tibbets, Colonel Paul: and the atomic bomb, 595

Tientsin (China): Japanese action at, 275

Tiergarten (Berlin): fighting in, 676

Tiesenhausen, Lieutenant von: sinks the Barham, 262

Tiger Tanks: in action at Kursk, 443

Tigris (British submarine): in North Russia, 223

Tikhvin (near Leningrad): Germans approach, 253; Germans occupy, 254; Russians attack, 274; Russians gain, 275, 283

Tilsit (Germany): Jews murdered near, 213

Time magazine (New York): a report in, from Saipan Island, 541

Time and Tide (London): a protest to, 48

Time Square (New York): dancing in, 673

Timor (Duch East Indies): struggle on, 297

Timoshenko, General Semyon Konstantinovich: and Finland, 41; and the German danger, 158, 168, 191; final preparations by, 193; and the eve of war, 194, 196; and the coming of war, 199; and the Soviet withdrawal from Kiev, 236; and the defence of Stalingrad, 341

Tinian Island (Marianas): battle on, 541, 559; mass suicide on, 563–4; American bombers from, attack Tokyo, 648; the atomic bomb brought to, 709; two atomic bombs flown from, 712, 715

Tinnsjo, Lake (Norway): heavy water goest to bottom of, 500

Tipperary (Eire): a hero from, 138

Tippoo Sultan: his descendant a Resistance heroine, 438

Tirpitz (German battleship): in preparation, 114; in the Arctic, 308; its dry dock, attacked, 312; in northern Norway, 340; a plan of attack against, 372; disabled, 463; bombed, 513; sunk, 612

Tisza River (Hungary): Soviet forces cross, 601, 608

Titanic (ocean liner): 5, 82

Titian: paintings by, evacuated, 206

Tito (Josip Broz): leads Communist partisan forces in Yugoslavia, 182, 207–8, 236; a British emissary reaches, 236; attacked by Mihailovic, 255; an anti-partisan sweep against, 392, 431, 436–7; British air supplies for, 440; an Allied mission at, 462; continued efforts of, 472; forced to move his headquarters yet again, 489; an offensive by, 521; a German attempt to capture, 527; fights side by side with Red Army, 587; flies to Moscow, 596; signs a treaty with the Soviet Union, 661

Tiulenev, General: and the imminence of war, 194

Tjebia Island (off Sumatra): deaths on, 307

Tjilatjap (Java): an abortive mission to, 304

Tlumacz (Eastern Galicia): Jews

deported to their deaths from, 315

Tobruk (Libya): 104, 109, 148, 149; the Italians driven from, 153; Australian troops besieged in, 172, 175, 205; to be 'eliminated', 189; a ship sunk off, 262; German siege of, broken, 265; Rommel withdraws west of, 279; Rommel advances towards, 293; Rommel attacks, 316; Rommel takes, 335; an unsuccessful attack on, 360; Rommel's fuel ships sunk at, 371; Rommel forced to abandon, 378

Todt, Dr Fritz: and the labour camp system, 46, 50; and Hitler's musings, 245; his warnings, 266, 283; killed, 299; his funeral, 301

Todt Organization: see index entry for Organization Todt

To Hell and Back (film): a soldier's story, 634

Togo, Shigenori: and a Japanese message about a negotiated peace, 701; votes for surrender, 716

Tojo, General Hideki: comes to power in Tokyo, 245; executed, 733

Tokyo (Japan): a new Government in (July 1940), 111; Intelligence reports reach Stalin from, 45, 143, 147, 162, 168, 183, 206, 224, 245; information required by, about Pearl Harbour, 164; a practice black out in, 249; and the order to attack Pearl Harbour, 253; reinforcements sent for, from, 295; bombed, 317, 321, 324, 645, 648, 696; and Guadalcanal, 392; and the death of Yamamoto, 420; a message to, about Hitler's strategy, read in London and Washington, 492; a message to, about no imminent cross-Channel landing, read in London, 522 and the Normandy Landings deception, 555; and Resistance in Italy, 587; and the German oil shortage, 591, 616; a Soviet spy executed in, 611; and the atomic bomb, 675, 694; and the resolve to fight on 'to the bitter end', 697; and the sinking of the Indianapolis, 709; a final bombing raid on, 718; MacArthur moves to, 723; war crimes trials to be held in, 728

Tokyo Bay (Japan): and the surrender of Japan, 721–2

Tokyo War Crimes Trials: evidence at, 302, 639

Tolbukhin, Marshal Fedor Ivanovich: and the liberation of the Crimea, 515, 522

Tolmezzo (Italy): Italian partisans killed near, 600

Toner, Second Lieutenant Robert F.: dies in the desert, 418; his skeleton and his diary discovered, 739

Tonkiele (Poland): Soviet prisoners-of-war murdered at, 482

Tonkin, J. E.: parachuted behind German lines, 551

Tomb of the Unknown Soldier (Paris): wreaths laid at (1940), 140

Tone (Japanese heavy cruiser): sunk, 709

Toombs, Private Alfred: eye-witness to a massacre, 78–9

Topf, J. A. and Son: renew a crematorium patent, 737

Topham, Corporal F. G.: his courage, 652

Topola (Yugoslavia): and a reprisal action, 243

Torgau (Elbe): American and Soviet forces meet at, 673

Torigni (Normandy): a German Division reaches, 543

Torun (Poland): a concentration camp at, 14; encircled, 634

Tosno (near Leningrad): fighting at, 495

Total War Mobilization: Goering made Reich Commissar for, 559

Touff, Rabbi Elio: warned in time, 466

Toul (France): two German spies executed at, 612

Toulon (France): French warships reach, 107; German plans to control, 146, 383; Allied landing near, 568, 571; Allies enter, 582

Toulouse (France): an airman shot down over, reaches safety, 455; a German Division moves from, 543

Tournai (France): Germans advance to, 75

Tours (France): French Government at, 93; a British agent lands at, 338–9; sabotage near, 551

Tovey, Admiral Sir John: and the destruction of the *Bismarck*, 186

Tractor Factory (Stalingrad): holds out, 369

Trajkovic, Sloboda: murdered, 456

Transcaucasia (Soviet Union): to be used as a German base, 189

Transjordan Frontier Force: enters Iraq, 182

Transition Agreement: establishes West Germany as a State, 735–6

'Transportation': a plan to destroy German railway yards, 519, 530

Trans-Siberian Railway: and Soviet goods for Germany, 179

Transylvania: Red Army enters, 601

Trappes (France): bombed, 507, 530

Treaty of Dunkirk: signed, 732

Treaty of Versailles: and Poland, 19; and 'unconditional surrender', 711

Treblinka (Poland): a death camp at, 292, 310, 343–4, 347, 351, 354, 369, 370, 376, 391, 393, 520; revolt at, 446; discovery of evidence concerning, 734

Trencin (Slovakia): uprising in, 583

Trent, Leonard Henry: his leadership, 425

Trentino (Italy): Germans take control in, 463

Trento (Italian heavy cruiser): sunk, 333

Trepper, Leopold: one of Stalin's spies, 150, 159, 233

Treschkow, Major-General Henning von, 218; and the first and second German officers' plans to kill Hitler (March 1943), 412, 414; commits suicide (July 1944), 558

Treuenbrietzen (south of Berlin): Red Army enters, 671

Tributs, Admiral Vladimir Filipovich: and German plans, 193, 194; and the evacuation of Tallinn, 227

*Trident* (British submarine): in North Russia, 223; torpedoes the *Prinz Eugen*, 302–3

Tri Duby (Slovakia): and an escape line, 593–4

Trieste (Italy): German control in, 463; Jews deported to Auschwitz from,

466, 488, 514; a partisan from, shot, 593; and the 'iron curtain', 728

Trignano viaduct (Italy): attacked, 157

Trincomalee (Ceylon): naval losses at, 315

Trinidad: German submarines near, 301

*Trinidad* (British cruiser): crippled, 314; sunk, 325

Tripartite Pact (of Germany, Italy and Japan): 141; Roumania and Slovakia join, 143; Bulgaria refuses to join, 149; Bulgaria joins, 160; Yugoslavia joins, 165; denounced, 166

Tripoli (Libya): German reinforcements for, 153, 157; Hitler urges retention of, 156; petrol barges sunk near, 393; Germans and Italians driven from, 395

Tripolitania (Libya): 'must be held', 149

Triumphal Arch: to be built in Berlin, 248

Trobriand Islands (Pacific): Americans land on, 439

Tromsö (Norway): King Haakon embarks from, 88; Jews deported from, 205; submariners buried in, 463; *Tirpitz* sunk at, 612

Trondheim (Norway): Allied plans for, 42, 45, 48, 52, 53, 55, 56, 58; Hitler's plans for, 196, 291; Jews deported from, 205; and a deception plan, 347; and a torpedo mission, 372; executions in, 373; and an Allied deception plan, 494; a German bomber seeks sanctuary in Britain from, 683

Troppe, Alfred: warns Hitler, 666

Trotobas, Michael: parachuted into France, 378; his sabotage mission, 440; caught and killed, 477

Trott zu Solz, Adam von: hanged, 581

'Troy' (escape line): an organizer of, executed, 673

Truk Island (Carolines): Americans attack, 499; Americans attack again, 520; Japanese troops on, surrender, 722

Truman, Harry S.: succeeds Roosevelt, 662; and the death of Ernie Pyle, 668; and the atomic bomb, 673–4, 675–6, 696–7, 707, 708, 711, 716–7; and the American-Soviet demarcation line in Europe, 680; Churchill sets out his fears to, 686–7; at Potsdam, 706–7; and an offer of peace to Japan, 707–8, 708–9; and Japan's willingness to surrender, 716–7

Trus, Kirill: executed, 251

Truskolasy (Poland): Poles executed at, 4

Tsakiropolous (a member of the Foreign Legion): decapitated, 693

Tschurkin, Ivan: killed, 611

Tsimlyansky (southern Russia): Germans reach, 347

Tsymbal: Sergeant Andrei: a partisan, in action, 510

Tuapse (Black Sea): a German objective, 363

'Tube Alloys': atomic bomb research, 241, 319, 348; and German installations, 667

Tuchola (Poland): Hitler visits, 6

Tuguegarao (Philippines): Japanese capture, 278

Tula (Russia): evacuations from, 206; battle near, 268; parachutists trained at, 369

Tulagi (Solomon Islands): Japanese attack on, 322; landing on, 350; battle near, 419

Tulasne, Major Jean-Louis: in action at Kursk, 445

Tulle (France): reprisals in, 536; ambushes near, 543

Tulloch, Major: behind the line in Burma, 667–8

Tunis (Tunisia): to be held, 376, 383, 419; the Jews in, and the Italians, 386; to be 'the Verdun of the Mediterranean' (Hitler), 419; battle for, 419, 425; captured, 425; Pantelleria Island attacked from, 438

Tunisia: the struggle for, 376, 377, 378, 383, 384–5, 387, 389, 396, 402, 406, 410, 415–6; final phase of the battle in, 419, 422, 425; Axis surrender in, 426

'Tunisian Tip': Axis forces withdraw into, 426

Turciansky St. Martin: seized, 580

Turek (Poland): ill-treatment of Jews in, 24

Turin (Italy): bombed, 90, 450; a pilot killed over, 317; a strike in, 410; Italian partisans active near, 587; Italian partisans seize control of, 674–5; American troops enter, 680

Turkey: proclaims 'non-belligerency', 104; and Hitler's eastern plans, 137; maintains neutrality, 166; Jews find refuge in, 465; and an Allied deception plan, 494; and a British-organized escape line, 495–6; ends chrome shipments to Germany, 517; declares war on Germany, 645; Soviet pressure on, 728

Turku (Finland): attack on, repulsed, 34

Turnu Severin (Roumania, Danube): Red Army reaches, 584

Tuscany (Italy): and a parachute mission, 525

Tutcheva, Vera: her husband rehabilitated, 739

Tuttlingen (Upper Danube): a mass grave discovered at, 673

Twelfth British Army: and an Allied deception, 493–4

Two-Ocean Navy Expansion Act: signed, 111

Tyre (Lebanon): British troops enter, 189

Tyszelman, Szmul: executed, 222–3

U-29 (German submarine): and the *Courageous*, 10

U-30: and the *Athenia*, 4

U-32: forced to surface, 133

U-33: sunk, 45

U-47: sinks the *Royal Oak*, 21; sunk, 162

U-81: sinks the *Ark Royal*, 255

U-96: sunk, 655

U-110: captured, 180

U-156: sinks the *Laconia*, 360

U-176: destroyed, 422

U-192: sunk, 425

U-234: surrenders to the Americans (12 May 1945), 693

U-331: sinks the *Barham*, 262

U-559: sunk off the Nile Delta, 373–4

U-567: lost without trace, 281

U-630: sunk, 425

U-2336: sinks two Allied merchant ships (on 7 May 1945), 689

Ube (Japan): bombed, 712
Udet, Ernst: insulted, 115; commits
  suicide, 257
Uelzen (Germany): a German counter-
  attack near, 666
Ukraine, the: German designs on, 120;
  the evacuation of factories from, 199;
  Jews killed in, 218–9; battles in, 231;
  poor roads of, 283; Soviet partisans
  in, 383; discontent in, 458
Ulex, General: protests, 43
Uljan Island (Yugoslavia): Italians
  occupy, 173
Ullersdorf (Germany): slave labour at,
  525
Ulm (Germany): Rommel's State
  funeral in, 602
Ulster (Northern Island): American
  troops reach, 295
'Ultra': the combined 'Enigma',
  'Purple' and 'C38m' decrypts,
  brought into a standard form, 429;
  and the German withdrawal across
  the Straits of Messina, 451; and the
  Normany Landings deception plans,
  494; and General Guderian's itinerary,
  517; and German strength in north-
  western France, 519, 521, 528–9; and
  oil, 523; and a proposed German ruse,
  523; and the German assessment of
  Allied cross-Channel timing, 531; and
  the effect of Allied deception plans in
  Normandy, 533, 540, 552; and the
  Normandy battle, 536, 538–9, 540,
  543, 566, 567; and the 'Flying Bomb',
  551–2; and German fuel shortages,
  577; and Hitler's orders to hold the
  Scheldt, 585; and growing partisan
  activity in northern Italy, 587; and the
  pressure on German raiways, 610–11;
  and the arrest of German agents in
  America, 615; and the Allied bombing
  of the Saar road and rail network,
  624; and 'firestorms', 639; and
  German atomic energy research, 645;
  and the Granville raid (March 1945),
  648; and the crossing of the Rhine,
  652; and a counter-offensive in the
  Ruhr, 657; and a counter-attack
  towards Eisenach, 659; and a grave
  German food shortage, 674
          see also index entries for 'Enigma',
  'Magic', 'Purple', 'C38m'
Uman (Ukraine): Hitler and Mussolini
  visit, 225; mass murder of Jews at, 233
Umanskii, Constantine Alexandrovich:
  160; receives warnings of German
  intentions, 163
Umezu, General Yoshijiro: signs
  instrument of surrender, 722
Uncle Sam: not on Bataan, 294
Union Factory (Auschwitz): 525, 623;
  and a revolt at Auschwitz, 600
Union Jack: flies again, in Singapore,
  723
'United Nations': established, 286;
  committed to the 'destruction' of
  German and Japanese militarism, 302;
  and aid to Russia, 395; and the
  continuing war, 484; and the 'grand
  pacification' of Europe, 728–9
United Nations Charter: signed, 701;
  and the future of Europe, 728–9
United Nations Children's Emergency
  Fund (UNICEF): established, 732
United Nations Organization:
  estalished, 574

United Nations War Crimes
  Commission: estalished, 469
United States. the: and the Athenia, 4;
  and a peace mission, 48; 'powerful aid'
  from, 81, 91–2; and the fall of France,
  93, 94, 97; and the sinking of the
  Lancastria, 98; industrial resources of,
  and France, 99; and the future of
  Britain, 103; its tenacious neutrality,
  104; its continuing aid to Britain, 106,
  107, 113, 136, 139, 148, 156, 186; and
  Mers-el-Kebir, 107; and Japan (in
  1940), 108, 109; volunteers from,
  reach Britain, 115; senior officers
  from, reach Britain, 120; Intelligence
  sharing of, with Britain, 154; and a
  German spy, 155;and China (in 1940),
  129; the 'arsenal of democracy', 148;
  warns Russia of impending attack,
  160; and the Jews, 187; 386; 550; and
  Iceland, 190, 208; German and Italian
  assets in, frozen, 190; Churchill's
  broadcast to (June 1941), 192; and the
  atomic bomb, 212, 271, 363, 384, 399,
  420, 434, 505, 591, 594–5, 625, 628,
  673–4, 696–7, 704, 707, 708, 711; aid
  to Russia from, 218, 223, 239–40, 251–
  2, 296, 367, 658; and Japan (in 1941),
  216, 222, 226, 238, 245, 263, 268, 271;
  and Germany (in 1941), 230, 244–5,
  255; Roumania and Bulgaria declare
  war on, 280; Combined Chiefs of Staff
  set up in, 282; German submarine
  successes off, 290, 318, 330; and the
  Philippines, 216, 253, 262, 263, 271,
  275, 307, 391, 485, 592, 596, 601, 604–
  5, 606, 730; troops from, reach Britain,
  291, 295; troops from, surrender in
  Rangoon, 306; Signals Intelligence
  successes of, 330, 368, 415–6, 492, 701;
  and an Enigma success, 330; a
  Japanese submarine off the Pacific
  Coast of, 336; aid to British forces in
  Egypt from, 336, 337, 338; and the
  Dieppe raid, 354; Japanese bombs fall
  on, 359; an airman from, betrayed,
  436; 'we cannot reach', (Hitler), 473;
  protests against the deportation of
  Hungarian Jews, 550; and the Warsaw
  uprising, 568, 570, 572; to have a post-
  war veto, 574, 701; imposes a veto on
  news on kamikaze pilots, 617; war
  dead of (by January 1945), 629; and
  Hiroshima, 675–6, 694, 710, 712–4,
  715; and Nagasaki, 715–16; and
  Japan's suggestion for a negotiated
  peace, 701; a Signals Intelligence
  failure of, 709–10; German scientists
  reach, 724; and post-war atomic
  power, 729–30; war dead brought
  back to, 733; agreements of, with
  Japan, 735; and Nazi war criminals,
  742, 744; Jews from, revisit Germany,
  743; wartime death toll of, 746
          see also index entries for
  Roosevelt, Washington, 'Ultra',
  'Magic', 'Purple'
United States Army Air Force: and war
  supplies for Britain (1940), 66; and oil,
  523
United States Congress: and Japan, 108;
  and Lend Lease, 149; and the arming
  of American merchant ships, 255;
  Churchill's address to, 430
United States Eighth Air Force: an early
  target of, 378; strikes into Germany,
  397, 413; launches 'Blitz Week', 446

United States Treasury: and money for
  resistance in Poland, 412
Unknown Soldier of the Second World
  War: a memorial to, unveiled (1958),
  738
Unter den Linden (Berlin): and Dachau,
  678
Upham, Second Lieutenant Charles: his
  courage, 185
Upper Silesia: repression in, 4; mass
  evacuations from, 631; acquired by
  Poland, 711
Ural mountains: 181, 207, 212, 226; to
  be Russia's new frontier, 235;
  factories transferred to, 241, 245, 275
Ural Maru (Japanese transport ship):
  torpedoed, 597–8
Uranium: as a source of explosive
  power, 14, 167, 212, 384; and a
  German factory, to be bombed, 645;
  handed to a Soviet diplomat, 702
Uranus: and uranium, 167
Ursel (Belgium): a gap near, 76
Uruguay: and the Graf Spee, 34
Urville-Hague (Cherbourg Peninsula):
  an intercept station at, destroyed, 531
Ushachi (White Russia): Jews
  murdered at, 291
Ushijima, General: commits suicide, 700
Ushio (Japanese destroyer): put out of
  action, 612; survives the war, 709
Usmiani, Major Antonio: released, 648
Ustachi: mass murder by, 225, 247
'Utah' Beach (Normandy): an
  American landing on, 534; a German
  naval attack on, 538
Utrecht (Holland): 'Death Candidates'
  in, 646
Uzda (Russia): an anti-Partisan sweep
  near, 460
Uzice (Yugoslavia): Tito's partisans
  capture, 236

'V1': the German pilotless plane
  ('Flying Bomb'), in preparation, 434,
  457, 463–4, 474, 479, 497, 505;
  launched, 539, 542, 645; used against
  Antwerp, 601
'V2': the German rocket bomb, 333,
  434, 453, 474; the assembly factory
  for, bombed, 439; misfired, is
  examined in Sweden and in Britain,
  539; a warning concerning, 557; fails
  to explode, and smuggled into Britain,
  561; launched against Britain, 589,
  594, 614, 640, 641, 648; launched
  against Antwerp, 612, 614–5, 621;
  evacuated from Peenemünde, 643;
  launched from Holland, 649, 652;
  tested, by the British, 724
V.E. Day (Victory in Europe Day): 690
Vac (Hungary): Red Army crosses
  Danube at, 616
'Valentin' (Lieutenant Joly): killed, 554
Valetta Harbour (Malta): bombed, 150;
  a convoy enters, 382
Valiant (British battleship): reaches
  Egypt, 122; escorts troops to Crete,
  148; in action off Matapan, 166;
  damaged off Crete, 185; badly
  damaged at Alexandria, 280
'Valter': Tito's name in Moscow, 182
Vampire (British destroyer): sunk, 315
Van Dyk: paintings by, evacuated, 206
Vandegrift, Major-General Alexander
  A.: and Japanese soldiers in action,
  350

Vanhove, Joseph Jan: a German spy, hanged, 554

Vannes (France): occupied, 100; a clandestine operation at, 162

Vatican, the: warned, 59; warnings sent out from, 59; shelters Jews, 467

Vaulot, Eugene: wins the Knight's Cross, 676, 679

Vederso (Denmark): a funeral in, 488

Vedral, General: killed, 604

Veesenmayer, SS Brigadier-General Dr Edmund: and the deportation of Jews from Hungary, 527

Vegesack (Germany): bombed, 413

Velikiye Luki (Russia): battle at, 227; partisans near, 309; Germans driven from, 390

Velizh (Russia): partisans near, 309

Vella Lavella Island (Solomons): Americans land on, 451; Japanese hold out on, 466

Velletri (Italy): Americans enter, 527

Venev (near Moscow): Germans attacked at, 259; Germans drive Russians from, 262; battle near, 268

Venice (Italy): a report from, about Italian resistance, 587

Venlo (Holland): a kidnap at, 26

Ventotene Island (Bay of Naples): captured, 461

Vercors (France): an anti-Resistance sweep in, 557

Verdun (France): the 'hero' of, 81; captured by the Germans, 96, 97; Tunis to be 'the Verdun of the Mediterranean', 419; an attempted suicide (1944) on the battlefield of, 558

Verona (Italy): Jews deported to Auschwitz from, 564; Italian partisans in, betrayed, 593

Verkhne-Bakanskaya (Caucasus): reprisals at, 383

Vermork (Norway): to be attacked, 319; parachutists near, 376; a second parachute landing near, 404; a bombing raid on, 475

Vernon (France): British troops cross Seine at, 580; Allies advance beyond, 581

Verona (Italy): Italian troops leave for Russia from, 201; a trial, and executions in, 488; a parachutist, tortured in, 525; Jews deported to Auschwitz from, 546

Versailles (France): Germans to enter, 91

Vershovsky (Mayor of Kremenchug): shot, 239

Versis, Major: commits suicide, 175

Velasquez: paintings by, evacuated, 206

Velichko, Captain P. A.: parachuted into Slovakia, 561; seizes a Slovak town, 580

Vian, Captain Philip: rewarded, 42

Vianga (North Russia): British pilots in action near, 233

'Vic': an escape line, 475

Vichy France: Pétain's Government at, 106; and French Indo-China, 108, 111, 216; Hitler's demands on, 133, 134; possible British bombing of, 135; and Syria, 137, 168, 188–9, 194; loses Gabon, 141; Hitler's planned occupation of, 146; police force of, hand over a refugee, 151–2; and Madagascar, 323; and the Allied landings in North Africa, 344, 376;

and the Jews, 355–6; occupied by Germany, 377, 383

Victor Emmanuel, King of Italy: and the fall of Mussolini, 446, 448; soldiers loyal to, 461

Victoria, Queen: 58, 465

Victoria Cross: awarded 42, 119, 138, 184, 201, 280, 287, 312, 316, 317, 354, 425, 427, 463, 477, 512, 539, 540, 567, 594, 595, 644, 652, 670, 710; a winner of, killed five years later on a bombing mission, 682–3

Victoria Point (Burma): evacuated, 278

Victoria Station (London): a plane crashes on, 125; a 'Flying Bomb' hits, 548; a boat train leaves, for Paris, 630; Hirohito met at, 741

Victorious (British aircraft carrier): in action, 307

'Victory or Siberia': a slogan in Berlin, 637

Victory Day: in the Soviet Union (9 May 1945), 692; in Yugoslavia (15 May 1945), 694

Vienna (Austria): 7; and Hitler's mission, 11; Jews deported from, 23, 245, 263, 329, 504; and Napoleon's son, 102; Hitler in, 160, 165; Flak Towers to be built in, 365; Jews from, at Maly Trostenets, 548; executions in, 598; Red Army approaches, 646, 654, 657; fighting in suburbs of, 659, 660; Red Army master of, 666; future of, discussed at Potsdam, 705; in the 'Soviet sphere', 728

Vietinghoff, General von: refused permission to withdraw, 667; agrees to unconditional surrender, 676

Vigan (Philippines): Japanese land at, 276

Viipuri (Finland): attacked, 47

Vila (Kolombangara Island): skirmish off, 449

Villaines (France): two commandos killed at, 573

Villefranche (France): fighting at, 100

Vilna (Poland): Jews murdered near, 213, 217, 219, 228–30, 249, 250; Jews in ghetto of, 267; the fate of a Soviet prisoner-of-war and a Jewess in, 281; Jews mourn in, 286; Jews in, contemplate resistance, 293; sabotage and reprisals in, 331; a Jewish revolt near, 516; the Red Army enters, 554; acquired by Russia, 711

Vincennes (US heavy cruiser): sunk, 350

Vinnitsa (Ukraine): Germans advance towards, 206; Jews killed in, 219, 235; Hitler's 'Werewolf' headquarters in, 343, 352, 358, 359, 365, 367, 368; Red Army enters, 510

Vinogradov, General: in Finland, 34, 36

Vire (Normandy): Americans enter, 562

Vis Island (Adriatic Sea): Tito flies to Moscow from, 596

Visegrad (Yugoslavia): a German defence line at, 615

Vishinsky, Andrei: and the Warsaw uprising, 570

Vistel, Alban: his protest, 528

Vistula River (Poland): and the German-Soviet partition of Poland, 16; and the Red Army's advance, 562; and the Warsaw uprising, 566, 593, 594

Vistula Army Group: Himmler given command of, 634; in action, 640;

Himmler's successor at, dismissed, 676

Vitebsk (Russia): 201, 214; Soviet partisans near, 221, 309, 352; Jews murdered in, 243, 281; a defence line to be strengthened near, 462; Russians attack east of, 468; a tenacious German defence at, 472; an eye-witness to mass murder at, 480; battle for, 485; a partisan success at, 544; Red Army enters, 546; a German general captured near, paraded in Moscow, 556

Vittel (France): Jews sent to Auschwitz from, 520

Vivant, Louis: escapes, 499

Vizagapatam (India): bombed, 315

Vladivostok (Soviet Far East): and Japan, 312; an American bomber crashes near, 318

Vodice (Yugoslavia): bombed, 505

Vogelsang (East Prussia): fighting near, 689

Volga River (Russia): 147; Soviet troops move westward from, 181; children evacuated to, 204; deportations from, 231; factory evacuations to, 241, 245; Soviet Government evacuated to, 244; and Hitler's proposed 'East Wall', 312; German forces reach, 355; 358; a counter-attack on, 359; Siberian troops cross, 363; Soviet soldiers ferried to safety across, 369; battle on banks of, at Stalingrad, 377

Volkenrode (Germany): aviation experts brought to Britain from, 702–3

Völkischer Beobachter (Berlin): and the Russian soldier's 'contempt for death', 204; and the imminent arrival of the Allies on German soil, 587

Volkovysk (Poland): a signals centre, 192

Vologda (Russia): railway line to, cut, 253

Volokolamsk (Moscow region): Germans reach, 251; courage near, 259; Russians recapture, 278

Volos (Greece): ships sunk at, 161

Voltaire (British armed merchant cruiser): sunk, 169

Vomécourt, Pierre de: parachuted into France (1941), 180

Vonnegut, Kurt: and the aftermath of Dresden, 641–2

Vormann, General Nikolaus von: finds Hitler 'a tired, broken man', 597

Voronezh (Russia): a German objective, 312; captured, 340; a German defence line near, 341; Germans driven from, 397; battles west of, 398

Voroshilov, Marshal Klimenti: 42, 146, 199, 206

Voroshilovgrad (southern Russia): Germans lose, 402

'Vulture': a German cypher key, broken, 102, 237

Vyazma (Russia): Germans advance towards, 217; partisan activity to be carried out near, 217; a defence line near, 218; Russians driven back to, 242; Russians forced to abandon, 243; partisan activity near, 246, 327; Russian parachute troops reach, 291; Red Army liberates, 410; German retreat west of, 414

Vytegra (North Russia): reinforcements group at, 267

Wachtel, Colonel: and the 'Flying Bomb', 540
Waddell, Sub-Lieutenant Alexander: on a Japanese-held island, 471
Wadke Island (Pacific): battle on, 526
Waechtler, Fritz: executed, 668
Wageningen (Holland): German surrender signed in, 687
Wagner, General Eduard: and 'guerrilla war', 5; and Hitler's 'intention', 6; and the death sentence, 8; and the battle for Moscow, 242, 251
Wagner, Dr Herbert: surrenders to the Americans, 683
Wagner, Robert: hanged, 730
Wainwright, Lieutenant General Jonathan M.: on Corregidor, 316; surrenders, 323; returns from captivity, 721-2
Wake (US gunboat): surrenders, 275
Wakefield (British destroyer): sunk, 80
Wake Island (Pacific): to be re-inforced, 263, 737; bombed, 272; defended, 278; overrun, 282; attacked in retaliation, 302; fate of American prisoners-of-war on, 466; Japanese soldiers on, lay down their arms, 722; Japanese officers on, taken for trial, 725; a 1941 mission to, recalled, 737
Walcheren Island (Holland): to be held, 585; bombed, 598; seized, 610, 611
Waldau, General Hoffman von: and German successes in Russia, 218; and the 'real trial' to come, 232-3; 'our wildest dreams ... washed out', 245
Waldheim, Lieutenant Kurt: in Russia, 225; in Yugoslavia, 339; in Greece, 490, 527, 601; his medal, 669
Wales: German 'agents' in, 15
Walke (US destroyer): suicide attack on, 628
Walker, Able Seaman: and an Allied air raid on Germany, 624
Wallace, Henry: and Truman's reluctance to drop a third atomic bomb, 716-7
Wallenberg, Raoul: protects Jews, 550, 610, 623; imprisoned, 654
Wallis, Dr Barnes: and the 'bouncing bomb', 427
Walloon Legion: in action on the Eastern Front, 503
Walmer Castle (British merchant ship): sunk, 237
Walter, Helmuth: agrees to help Western Allies, 690; reaches Britain, 727
Wandsworth Prison (London): a spy, shot in, 325
Wannsee (Berlin): a discussion at, on the 'Final Solution', 292
Wansen (Silesia): a German counter-attack near, 687
Warburton-Lee, Captain: killed, 54
'War of the Rails' ('Rail War'): declared by the Soviet Supreme Command, 444; intensifies, 448, 468; succeeds, 544
'War crimes': to be punished, 290-1, 469, 715; trials for, 444, 480, 505, 613, 708, 724, 725, 725-6, 726, 727, 727-8, 729, 730, 730-1, 732, 733-4, 734-5, 735, 739-40, 740, 741
War Crimes Amendment Act (1989): passed into law, 744
War Labour Cross: awarded for

carrying out executions, 256
Ward (US destroyer transport): hit by a kamikaze pilot, 617
Warlimont, Colonel Walther: and the German plans against Russia, 113, 115, 145
War Merit Cross: awarded, 669
Warm Springs (Georgia): Roosevelt dies at, 662
Wartenburg, Count Peter Yorck von: opposes Nazism, 450; hanged, 566
'War victim': an executed war criminal acquires status of, 735
Warwick, Squadron Leader J. B.: shot down, 595
Warsaw (Poland): bombed, 2; battle for, 8, 9-11, 13-14, 15, 18; Hitler in, 19; labour camps near, 23; arrests in, 27, 127; beatings in, 28; executions in, 32, 161-2, 369, 479, 495, 498; the fate of the Jews in, 37, 47, 129, 130, 152, 298, 504, 505, 508; British leaflets dropped on, 49; forced labourers taken from, 129; Poles from, reported to have died, 147; Poles in, help Jews, 384; a warehouse in, with the eye-glasses of victims, 400; resistance in, 413; a dancer from, kills an SS man, 469; Jews in hiding in, found and killed, 481; a killing, and reprisals in, 496, 498; uprising in, 561, 562-3, 564-5, 567-8, 570, 572, 573-4, 580-1, 584, 585-6, 590, 592, 593, 595-6; last phase of uprising in, 596, 597; liberated, but in ruins, 630; in the 'Soviet sphere', 728; Jürgen Stroop executed in, 735
Warsaw Ghetto (Poland): established, 130; a Christian shot dead near, 144; Jews shot in, 145, 257, 279, 329, a deportation from, 152; starvation in, 179, 244, 261, 298; smiles in, 199; and Pearl Harbour, 276; optimistic rumours in, 324; a 'good mood' in, after the bombing of Cologne, 329; deportations from, to Treblinka, 343-4, 346, 351, 393, 428; resistance in, 393-4, 421; resistance in, crushed, 428, 435; survivors of, killed at Majdanek, 473; Jews and non-Jews killed in ruins of, 505; rubble to be cleared in, 525
Warsaw Pact: established, 729
Warspite (British battleship): in action, 109
Warthegau: Poles expelled from, 27, 37; a protest from, 29; statistics of the murder of Jews in, 414; Germanification of, 508; the ruler of, hanged, 729
Washington DC: 21; successes for Britain in, 65-6, 81, 113; a broadcast from, 90; senior Anglo-American officers meet in, 154; and Lend-Lease, 156; and German espionage, 159; and intercepted Japanese messages, 238, 249, 268, 271; and the atomic bomb, 271; Churchill in, when Tobruk falls, 335; Churchill in, when the Sicily deception plan succeeds, 423-4; and a decision on Allied strategy (May 1943), 426; and Allied bombing policy, 432-3; and American aid to Russia, 468; a boost to morale announced in, 540; news of Auschwitz reaches, 546; Roosevelt's last, undelivered, speech in, 663; and a magnanimous act, 730; those 'in authority in', condemned, 737-8

'Wasp': a German air corps key, broken, 287
Wasp (US aircraft carrier CV-7): takes planes towards Malta, 318; a second Mediterranean 'dash' by, 319; sunk, in the Pacific, 361
Wasp (US aircraft carrier CV-18): successor to CV-7, a suicide bomb attack on, 650
Waskiewicz, Pilot Officer Mieczyslaw: killed, 174
Waterhen (an Australian warship): sunk, 205
Waterman, Douglas: executed, 468-9
Waters, Private Harold: executed, 358
Watney, Lieutenant Cyril: his sabotage mission, 490
Watt, Harry: his film, 216
Watten (Channel Coast): 'Flying Bomb' launched from, 539, 540; bombed, 543
Wau (New Guinea): Japanese driven back from, 399
Wavell, General Sir Archibald: withdraws from Java, 303
Waverley (British converted paddle steamer): sunk, 79-80
Wawer (Poland): reprisals in, 36
Wealdstone (near London): bogus sabotage at, 255
'Weasel': a German cypher key, broken, 343
Weatherley, Major Robin: killed in Yugoslavia, 455
Webling (Bavaria): SS men killed at, 678
Webster, Sergeant: and a 'death march', 631
Weclas, Stanislaw: sentenced to death, 183
Wedemeyer, Major Alfred C.: and Russia's future, 232
Weichs, Field Marshal von: and the 'grim partisan situation', 472
Weidinger, Otto: awarded the Swords to his Knight's Cross, 689
Weidling, General Karl: and the last days of Berlin, 673, 676, 679, 682
Weidner, Gabrielle: killed, 512
Weidner, John: saves Jews, 512
Weilheim (Bavaria): Horthy imprisoned in, 603
Weimar (Germany): anti-Nazi leaflets distributed in, 408; Gestapo at, seek destruction of Buchenwald, 661
Weinryb, Menachem: and the murder of Jews at Gardelegen, 663
Weiss, Ernst: commits suicide, 95
Weissensee (Carinthia): an arrest, and suicide in, 696
Weizmann, Dr Chaim: offers services of the Jews, to the democracies, 6; appeals for Allied bombing of railway lines to Auschwitz, 546; seeks 'restitution' for the Jews, 723-4
Weizsäcker, Baron Ernst von: and Hitler's mood, 233, 235
Weizsäcker, Richard von: and Germany (1933-1945) 'led by criminals', 744
Wejherowo (Poland): Poles shot in, 27
Weliczker, Leon: an eye-witness, 438
Welles, Sumner: seeks a peace formula, 48; warns Russia of German intentions, 160, 164
Wellington Barracks (London): a 'Flying Bomb' at, 542
Wells, Lieutenant: and Operation XD, 67

Wells, Stan: 'God punish Germany', 633–4

Welshman (British minelayer): reaches Malta, 324

Wencel, Stanislaw: sentenced to death, 183

Wenck, General: in the Harz mountains, 661, 666; ordered to Berlin, 676; Hitler asks for, 679

Wende, Josef: executed, 612

Wendisch Even (northern Germany): the German surrender at, 685

Wenzel, Johann: a Soviet agent, captured, 334

'Werewolf': Hitler's Vinnitsa headquarters, 343, 352

Werra, Franz von: escapes, 154; visits Hitler, 172

Werth, Alexander: in Moscow, 214

Wesel (Rhine): Allies cross Rhine at, 652

'Weser-exercise': against Scandinavia, 46

Wessex (British destroyer): sunk, 73

West, Sergeant Horace T.: court-martialled, 445

West Berlin: elections in (1989) and a former ss officer, 745

West Germany: new leaders and new values in, 723; agrees to pay reparations, 735, 735–6, 736, 739; becomes a separate State, 735; her reparations debts (of 1914–18) resolved, 736; becomes an independent sovereign State (as the Federal German Republic), 738; troops of, train in Britain, 739

Westerbork (Holland): Jews deported to Auschwitz from, 310, 386, 398, 459; British forces draw near to, 585

Western Front (1914–18): Hitler revisits (1940), 104

Western Prince (British merchant ship): brings arms to Britain, 107

West Ham (London): rocket bomb deaths at, 641

Westminster College (Fulton, Missouri): Churchill's warning in, 728–9

Wetzel, Judge Alfred: and the use of gas vans to kill Jews, 249

Wetzel Eberhard: on Poles and Jews, 29

Weygand, General Maxime: his plan, 70, 74; his appeal, 86–7; wants to surrender, 90; and the fall of Paris, 92; calls for an armistice, 93

Weymouth (England): radar station at, bombed, 116

Wheless, Captain Hewitt T.: his courage, 278–9

Whelp (British destroyer): in Tokyo Bay, 722

White, Wing Commander John: killed, 476

Whitechapel (London): an unexploded bomb at (1989), 739

Whitehall (London): to be defended, 69; Intelligence reaches, 72

White House (Washington): two rescuers welcomed to, 449

'White Rose': a dissenting voice, 404–5

White Russians: murdered, 213; a protest about the murder of, 250–1

White Sands (New Mexico): German rocket equipment sent to, 695

Whitmarsh, Pilot Officer Reginald: killed, 46

'Why We Fight': a film series, 322

Wiart, General Carton de: unable to disembark, 55

Wickström, Rolf: executed, 232

Wiegand, Karl von: Hitler's interview with, 93

Wiener Neustadt (Austria): bombed, 451

Wieruszow (Poland): Jews murdered at, 4

Wierzbica (Poland): Poles killed in, 398

Wiesel, Elie: and the 'Kingdom of Night', 661

Wijsmuller, Geertruida: helps save children, 67

Wilhelm (the ex-Kaiser): in Holland, 62; his nephew dies of wounds received in action, 70; his war aim recalled, 85, 92; dies, 188; his former Private Secretary, and the Hitler Bomb Plot, 559

Wilhelm Gustloff (German transport ship): sunk, 635; alleged looting of, 743

'Wilhelm Hansen' (William Joyce): apprehended, 696

Wilhelm of Hohenzollern, Prince: dies of his wounds, 70

Wilhelmina, Queen: crosses the North Sea, 64

Wilhelmshaven (Germany): bombed, 5, 396, 428, 429

Williams, Brigadier Edgar: and the German aim to retake Antwerp, 616

Williams, Gwilym: a double agent, 15

Wilson, General Sir Maitland: and the Arab Legion, 182; and the Dalmatian Coast, 494

Winant, Gilbert: witnesses Blitz, 173

'Window' (a radar jamming device): and the bombing of Hamburg, 446

Wingate, Brigadier Orde: his sabotage columns, 404; his glider landings, 506

Wirmer, Joseph: hanged, 589

Wismar (Germany): battle near, 687

Wistedt (Germany): an act of courage in, 670

Witonska, Eleonora: murdered, 669

Witonska, Roman: murdered, 669

Wittenberge (Germany): American forces reach Elbe at, 661

Wittlich (Germany): and a possible armistice, 662

Wittman, ss Captain Michael: killed, 566

Witzleben, Field Marshal Erwin von: 'The Führer is dead', 558; hanged, 566

Wizernes (Channel Coast): a German rocket launching site at, 455

Wloclawek (Poland): a 'Jewish action' at, 12

Wlodawa (Poland): Jews sent to their deaths from, 424

Wola (Warsaw): bombed, 565; subjugated, 565

Wola Przybyslawska (Poland): Poles executed in, for helping Jews, 384

Woldenberg (Pomerania): Red Army reaches, 634

'Wolf's Lair' (East Prussia): Hitler's East Prussian headquarters, 199; Hitler leaves, for 'Werewolf', 343; Hitler returns to, 441; Hitler leaves for the last time, 613; overrun, 633; acquired by Poland, 711

Wolff, ss General Karl: and medical experiments, 32; an eye-witness to mass murder, 220; and the deportations of Jews from Warsaw to Treblinka, 351–2; negotiates a surrender, 648; brought to trial, 740

Wolomin (Poland): Soviet tanks at, 562

Wood, Master Sergeant John C.: hangs war criminals, 708, 731

Wood Green (London): rocket bomb deaths at, 641

Woodlark Island (Pacific Ocean): Americans land on, 439

World Aryan Order: a member of, a fictitious German agent, 537

World Organization: to be established, 658

Wormhout (France): massacre at, 78–9; and a former ss officer, living near Hamburg, 743

Worrall, Major Philip: parachuted into Greece, 461–2

Wotje (Marshall Islands): American air attacks on, 297

Woyrsch, ss General Udo von: 4, 12

Wroughton, Sergeant Walter: in Yugoslavia, 430

Wünsche, ss Major Max: captured, 566

Wuntho (Burma): and a sabotage mission, 404

Wuppertal (Germany): bombed, 434, 439

Wurm, Bishop: protests about murder of Jews, 481

Württemberg (Germany): French troops rech, 673; the right of Gypsies to compensation denied in, 734

Würzburg (Germany): a graduate of, and euthanasia, 11; Jews deported to their deaths from, 310, 436

Wüstegiersdorf (Germany): slave labour at, 525

Wykeham-Barnes, Group Captain: leads the Aarhus raid, 610

Xanten (Germany): Jews revisit (1988), 743

Yahagi (Japanese cruiser): sunk, 660

Yakhroma (near Moscow): Germans reach, 262; Germans driven from, 270

Yalta (Crimea): Germans enter, 254; Soviet forces enter, 517; the 'Big Three' meet at, 638; Soviet promises at, 'broken', 658, 679

Yamamoto, Admiral Isoroku: and Pearl Harbour, 140; shot down, 430

Yamato (Japanese battleship): a suicide mission by, 660

Yamashita, General Tomoyuki: hanged, 728

Yanina (Greece): Jews sent to Auschwitz from, 510; Greek hostages shot near, 527; Germans attacked near, 584

Yaroslavl (Russia): children evacuated to, 204

Yarra (Australian sloop): sunk, 304

Yawata (Japan): bombed, 540

Yefremov, Colonel: his last words, 318

Yeisk (southern Russia): Soviet forces reaches, 399

Yelets (near Moscow): battle at, 270

Yelnya (Russia): German victory at, 220; Soviet capture of, 230; partisans in region of, 296–7, 308; Soviets recapture, 456

Yeremenko, Colonel: drives westward, 553

Yevell, Colonel: his trophy, 674

Yokohama (Japan): bombed, 317, 648; a possible atomic bomb target, 694; MacArthur enters, 721

Yokoi, Sergeant Shoichi: emerges on Guam (1972), 740–1

Yokosuka (Japan): bombed, 317; an American Division lands at, 721

Yontan Airfield (Okinawa): a suicide mission against, 695

York (England): bombed, 319

York (British cruiser): damaged, 164

Yorkshire (England): and a deception plan, 523

Yorktown (US aircraft carrier): sunk, 330

Young, Doreen: her fiancé shot down, 566–7; his remains buried, 742

Young, Sir Mark: rejects surrender, 280

Ypres (Belgium): battle near, 73

Yugoslavia: refuses to join Axis, 157; joins Axis, 165; turns against Axis, 166; to be attacked, 166–7; invaded, 170; German conquest of, 170–3; German rule in, 173; formal surrender of, 174; Hitler visits northern region of, 178; Tito's partisans in, 207–8, 440; atrocities in, 247; resistance in, 284; anti-partisan sweeps in, 288, 298, 309, 323, 339, 386–7, 392, 395, 436; fate of the Jews in, 295, 390, 406; reprisals in, 450, 451; Allied help for partisans in, 504–5; and a planned Allied escape line, 508; a partisan offensive in, 521; partisans active in, 575, 601; Allies and partisans launch joint offensive in, 584; Jews in, rescued, 585; Red Army reaches, 587; reaches agreement with the Soviet Union, 596; its future, discussed in Moscow, 600; liberation of, 604; and the Dalmatian Coast towns and islands, 610; signs a treaty with the Soviet Union, 661, 680; German forces retreat through, 669, 672; slave labourers from, liberated, 674; to be 'police-governed', 686–7; breaks away from Soviet bloc, 723; receives reparations, 739; wartime death toll of, 746

Yurgin, Captain Pavel: reaches East Prussia, 571

Yuza Hill (Okinawa): attack on, 697

Yvoir (Belgium): Germans retreat through, 585; a parachute landing near, 587

Zabotin, Colonel: receives uranium, 702

Zagare (Lithuania): Jews killed at, 241

Zagorsk (Russia): reinforcements gather, 265

Zagreb (Yugoslavia): German troops enter, 172; Tito leaves, 182; synagogue demolished in, 286; protests in, 306, 409; the Chief Rabbi of, deported to Auschwitz, 424; further deportations to Auschwitz from, 432; German forces retreat through, 669, 672; Pavelic's final appearance in, 686

Zakrzewski, Professor: shot, 162

Zambrow (Poland): Soviet prisoners-of-war murdered at, 482

Zamkowy, Samuel: killed, 28

Zamosc (Poland): Jews sent to their deaths from, 317; Jewish boys murdered in, 406–7

Zaporozhe (Ukraine): dam destroyed at, 227; Hitler flies to, 459

Zara (Italy): Italians to march from, 170; bombed, 500–1; Yugoslav partisans enter, 610

Zarfatti, Roberto: deported, 514

Zasavica (Yugoslavia): Jews and Gypsies murdered at, 243

Zay, Jean: shot, 541

Zborow (Eastern Galicia): Jews killed in, 207

Zdzieciol (White Russia): Jews murdered in, 351

Zeebrugge (Belgium): attack on, 74

Zeeland (Holland): Dutch resist in, 64

Zehbe, Robert: bales out, 125

Zeitzler, General Franz: and the war in Russia, 363; urges a withdrawal, 389

Zelewski, General Erich von dem Bach: and mass murder, 221; and the Jews of Estonia, 252–3; and the Warsaw uprising, 564, 565, 597; and the abduction of Horthy, 603

Zell-am-See (Austria): bombed, 500–1

Zelzate (Belgium): Allied airmen sheltered in, 512

Zemun (Yugoslavia): a death march to, 295

Zgierz (Poland): an execution in, 309–10

Zharchinski, Lieutenant: killed, 671

Zhdanov, Andre: leaves for his holiday (19 June 1941), 193

Zhitomir (Russia): Jews killed in, 218, 219–20; Himmler's headquarters at, 343; Germans driven from, 474

Zhlobin (Russia): Germans driven from, 208

Zhukov, Marshal Georgi: victorious in the Far East, 2; and the German

danger, 158–9, 168; and Soviet preparations (May 1941), 177; tries to warn Stalin (May 1941), 191; and the imminence of war, 194, 196; and the coming of war (June 1941), 198, 201; and the siege of Leningrad, 233; and the battle for Moscow, 243, 264; and the battle for Stalingrad, 358–9; and the Soviet offensive into central Poland (January 1945), 629; and the surrender of Berlin, 682, 683; and the final German surrender, 690; receives British medals, 702

Ziffer, Adolf: deported to Auschwitz, 338

Zilina (Slovakia): uprising in, 583

Zinchenko, Colonel: in Berlin, 676

Zindels, Lieutenant Abram: his heroism, 468

Zirje Island (Yugoslavia): bombed, 505

Zlarin Island (Yugoslavia): bombed, 505

Zlatin, Miron: deported, and shot, 514

Zoliborz (Warsaw): holds out, 585; Soviet aircraft drop supplies to, 592; Polish resistance in, 596

Zolkiew (Eastern Galicia): murder of Jews at, 415

Zolochew (Eastern Galicia): Jews murdered in, 210

Zoppot (Danzig): Hitler in, 11

Zossen (Germany): plans laid at, 45; signals from, decrypted in Britain, 429; conspirators at, 597; overrun, 670; a counter-attack at, fails, 674

Zuckerman, Yitzhak: and Jewish resistance, 393

Zuider Zee (Holland): aircraft recovered from (1975), 741

Zulu (British destroyer): sunk, 360

Zurawski, Mordechai: survives his would-be execution, 630

Zurich (Switzerland): bombs fall on in error, 645; secret negotiations in, 648

Zvietkovo (near Moscow): battle at, 267

Zvolen (Slovakia): partisans seize areas near, 583; an escape line near, 593

Zwaluw (Belgian fishing vessel): at Dunkirk, 81

Zwarycz, Anna: sentenced to death, 505

Zweibrücken (Germany): action at, 6

Zychlin (Poland): Jews from, murdered, 304

'Zyklon B': and mass murder, 220

Zylberberg, Mordechai: leads resistance, 440